Sponsored by:

SIGCHI

special interest group computer human interaction

AF753701

November 16 - 19

Dresden, Germany

ITS 2014

Proceedings of the 2014 ACM International Conference on

Interactive Tabletops and Surfaces

Association for Computing Machinery

Advancing Computing as a Science & Profession

Association for
Computing Machinery

Advancing Computing as a Science & Profession

The Association for Computing Machinery
2 Penn Plaza, Suite 701
New York, New York 10121-0701

Notice to Past Authors of ACM-Published Articles

ACM intends to create a complete electronic archive of all articles and/or other material previously published by ACM. If you have written a work that has been previously published by ACM in any journal or conference proceedings prior to 1978, or any SIG Newsletter at any time, and you do NOT want this work to appear in the ACM Digital Library, please inform permissions@acm.org, stating the title of the work, the author(s), and where and when published.

ISBN: 978-1-4503-2587-5 (Digital)

ISBN: 978-1-4503-3388-7 (Print)

Additional copies may be ordered prepaid from:

ACM Order Department
PO Box 30777
New York, NY 10087-0777, USA

Phone: 1-800-342-6626 (USA and Canada)
+1-212-626-0500 (Global)
Fax: +1-212-944-1318
E-mail: acmhelp@acm.org
Hours of Operation: 8:30 am – 4:30 pm ET

Printed in the USA

Welcome to ACM ITS 2014

We are very happy to welcome you to the ninth *ACM International Conference on Interactive Tabletops and Surfaces*, held November 16-19, 2014 in Dresden, Germany. Since its inauguration as the Tabletop Workshop in 2006, the conference series has been devoted to an exploration of new approaches for the design, development and use of emerging tabletop and interactive surface technologies. The nine years over which the conference has been held have seen a tremendous evolution in technologies supporting surface-based interaction, leading this year's program to include a range of novel topics around the use of both horizontal and vertical surfaces, mobile surfaces in various sizes, mixed-surface interaction, and embodied interaction around the many displays that surround us.

The city of Dresden, also described as 'Florence on the river Elbe', serves as an appropriate location for the study of interactive surfaces. Dresden is a historic city of culture and beautiful architecture, hosting stunning art treasures and one of the world's finest symphony orchestras. This cultural and musical heritage represents the tradition of interacting with our world around us, while at the same time Dresden is a thriving modern city on the forefront of technological advances. It is the home of Europe's largest micro-electronics cluster, of the Technische Universität Dresden as one of Germany's elite universities and a city densely populated by numerous research institutions in key areas such as information and communication technology, new-generation materials and biotechnology. Therefore, held in a city of science and culture, ITS 2014 will focus on the *culture of interaction*, thereby reflecting that interactive surfaces have become part of our everyday life and culture.

Since its earliest days ITS has involved partnership between industry and academia, and this is as true as ever in 2014, which features a strong selection of papers devoted both to pure research and to concrete application of surface technologies. This year, the conference received 112 paper and note submissions from all over the world, of which 31 were selected, for an acceptance rate of 27.7%. The peer-review process was rigorous, with a remarkable team of 35 research and industry leaders ensuring that each submission was reviewed fairly and by the most appropriate reviewers. Papers submitted to ITS received this year a total of 435 reviews and meta-reviews. Acting on the community's feedback, we have kept the "review and resubmit" system for those papers which offered excellent contributions but needed some further work and feedback to get to the high quality and originality level expected of ITS work. The *application* review process has also matured; this process allows contributions that have a practical relevance for practitioners and have been explored in real settings to be fully represented.

A traditional highlight of ITS is its demonstration session, held on the first night of the main conference. The demo session serves to showcase novel technologies, an enormous range of inspiring ideas of the use of interactive surfaces, and provides lively opportunity for exchange of ideas, techniques and experience. This year's session includes 14 demonstrations from academic presenters plus several industrial exhibits.

In addition, the ITS poster session will allow early access to work in progress, with 23 posters presented. Six students are presenting their work in the Doctoral Symposium. We are especially grateful to Sheelagh Carpendale, James D. Hollan and Andy Wilson, who will give invaluable advice to the students in the panel of experts. A collection of studios, tutorials and workshops allow focused work on cutting-edge topics such as personal fabrication, collaboration or tactile interaction prior to the main conference.

We welcome two distinguished keynotes. The opening plenary will be presented by Professor Jun Rekimoto of the University of Tokyo and Sony Computer Science Laboratories, on "A New You: From Augmented Reality to the Augmented Human". The closing keynote will be delivered by Professor Joachim Sauter of the University of the Arts in Berlin and co-founder of ART+COM, on "Sensitive Skins in Media Art and Design".

We are highly grateful to our sponsor ACM SIGCHI and the corporate supporters, without whom the conference would not have been possible. The Deutsche Forschungsgemeinschaft (German Research Foundation) provided a highly-generous platinum level of sponsorship. Our lead industrial partners are Multitouch at the Gold level, SMART Technologies and WACOM at the Silver level, Microsoft and SurfNet at the Bronze level, and GRAND Network of Centres of Excellence as a Friend of ITS.

Finally, conferences such as ACM ITS are organized completely by volunteers who selflessly perform a tremendous amount of work. We list on the following pages the many people who contributed to organization and to the peer-review process underlying an academic conference. To all of you, we offer our most sincere and grateful thanks.

Raimund Dachselt
ITS'14 General Chair
Interactive Media Lab,
Technische Universität Dresden

Nicholas Graham
ITS'14 General Chair
School of Computing,
Queen's University

Kasper Hornbæk
ITS'14 Program Chair
Department of Computer Science, DIKU,
University of Copenhagen

Miguel Nacenta
ITS'14 Program Chair
SACHI Research Group,
University of St Andrews

Table of Contents

Session 4: Multi-Surface

Session 5: Children and Learning

Session 6: Space, Activities and Workplace

Session 7: Touch, Pressure and Reality

Session 8: In the World

Session 9: Tangibles

Posters

Demonstrations

Doctoral Symposium

Tutorials, Workshops and Studios

ITS 2014 Conference Organization

General Chairs: Raimund Dachselt *(Technische Universität Dresden, Germany)*
Nicholas Graham *(Queen's University, Canada)*

Program Chairs: Kasper Hornbæk *(University of Copenhagen, Denmark)*
Miguel Nacenta *(University of St. Andrews, UK)*

Posters Chairs: Petra Isenberg *(INRIA, France)*
Johannes Schöning *(University of Hasselt, Belgium)*

Demos Chairs: Christophe Bortolaso *(Queen's University, Canada)*
Ulrich von Zadow *(Technische Universität Dresden, Germany)*

Doctoral Symposium Chairs: Mark Hancock *(University of Waterloo, Canada)*
Jürgen Steimle *(MPI Saarbrücken, Germany)*

Tutorials, Workshops and Studios Chairs: Kentaro Fukuchi *(Meiji University, Japan)*
Nicolai Marquardt *(University College London, UK)*

Proceedings Chair: Fabrice Matulic *(Technische Universität Dresden, Germany)*

Local Arrangements Chairs: Ramona Behling *(Technische Universität Dresden, Germany)*
Ricardo Langner *(Technische Universität Dresden, Germany)*

Student Volunteers Chairs: Y.-L. Betty Chang *(University of Waterloo, Canada)*
Ulrike Kister *(Technische Universität Dresden, Germany)*

Sponsor Chair: Stacey Scott *(University of Waterloo, Canada)*

Industry Chairs: David Smith *(Clemson University, USA)*
Edward Tse *(SMART Technologies, Canada)*

Web Chairs: Annett Mitschick *(Technische Universität Dresden, Germany)*
André Viergutz *(Technische Universität Dresden, Germany)*

Publicity Chair: Aaron Genest *(Solido Design Automation, Canada)*

Madness Chair: Roman Rädle *(University of Konstanz, Germany)*

Mobile Chairs: Eiji Hayashi *(Carnegie Mellon University, USA)*
Stephen Oney *(Carnegie Mellon University, USA)*
Jason Wiese *(Carnegie Mellon University, USA)*

Steering Committee: *Chair:* Chia Shen *(Harvard University, USA)*
Sheelagh Carpendale *(University of Calgary, Canada)*
Shahram Izadi *(Microsoft Research, UK)*
Gerald Morrison *(SMART Technologies, Canada)*
Miguel Nacenta *(University of St. Andrews, UK)*
Siram Subramanian *(Bristol University, USA)*
Andy Wilson *(Microsoft Research, USA)*

Program Committee: Jason Alexander *(University of Lancaster, UK)*
François Berard *(Grenoble Institute of Technology, France)*
Gilles Bailly *(TELECOM ParisTech, France)*
Andy Crabtree *(University of Nottingham, UK)*
Florian Echtler *(University of Regensburg, Germany)*
Carl Gutwin *(University of Saskatchewan, Canada)*
Mark Hancock *(University of Waterloo, Canada)*
Ken Hinckley *(Microsoft Research, USA)*
Uta Hinrichs *(University of St Andrews, UK)*
Eve Hoggan *(HIIT, Aalto University, Finland)*
Jonathan Hook *(University of Newcastle, UK)*
Tommi Ilmonen *(Multitouch, Finland)*
Petra Isenberg *(INRIA, France)*
Yuichi Itoh *(University of Osaka, Japan)*
Giulio Jacucci *(University of Helsinki, Finland)*
Mikkel Jakobsen *(University of Copenhagen, Denmark)*
Yvonne Jansen *(INRIA, France)*
Ian Joscelyne *(Promethean, UK)*
Nicolai Marquardt *(University College London, UK)*
Paul Marshall *(University College London, UK)*
Frank Maurer *(University of Calgary, Canada)*
Emma Mercier *(University of Illinois, USA)*
Mathieu Nancel *(University of Canterbury, New Zealand)*
Esben W. Pedersen *(University of Copenhagen, Denmark)*
Johannes Schöning *(Hasselt University, Belgium)*
Stacey Scott *(University of Waterloo, Canada)*
David Smith *(Clemson University, USA)*
Jürgen Steimle *(Saarland University, Germany)*
Bruce Thomas *(University of South Australia, Australia)*
Melanie Tory *(University of Victoria, Canada)*
Edward Tse *(SMART Technologies, Canada)*
Andy Wilson *(Microsoft Research, USA)*
Frederic Vernier *(Université Paris Sud, France)*
Katrin Wolf *(T-Mobile Labs Berlin, Germany)*
Shengdong Zhao *(Singapore National University, Singapore)*

Additional reviewers:

Alexander Adams
Dzmitry Aliakseyeu
Florian Alt
Michelle Annett
Craig Anslow
Ahmed Arif
Maryam Azh
Saskia Bakker
Till Ballendat
Tom Bartindale
Lyn Bartram
Scott Bateman
Olivier Bau
Andrea Bellucci
Peter Bennett
Guillaume Besacier
Anastasia Bezerianos
Sourav Bhattacharya
Jon Bird
Renaud Blanch
Sebastian Boring
Stan Borkowski
Christophe Bortolaso
Michael Boyle
Anke Brock
John Brosz
Alan Chamberlain
Y.-L. Betty Chang
Olivier Chapuis
Xiang Anthony Chen
Aurélie Cohé
Christopher Collins
Florian Daiber
Chi Tai Dang
Andreea Danielescu
Tanja Döring
Andre Doucette
Pierre Dragicevic
James Eagan
Yasmine El-Glaly
Niklas Elmqvist
Rebecca Fiebrink
Danyel Fisher
Morten Fjeld
Clifton Forlines
Dustin Freeman
Mathias Frisch
Sven Gehring
Christian Geiger
Saul Greenberg
Jan Gugenheimer
Jonna Häkkilä
Michael Haller
Ian Hargreaves
Chris Harrison
Tomi Heimonen
Florian Heller
Niels Henze
Juan David Hincapié-Ramos
Nicolas Holliman
David Holman
Kasper Hornbæk
Lode Hoste
Steven Houben
Yingdan Huang
Jochen Huber
Shah Rukh Humayoun
Alexandra Ion
Pourang Irani
Tobias Isenberg
Jacek Jankowski
Hans-Christian Jetter
Ricardo Jota
Andrew Joyce-Gibbons
Sasa Junuzovic
Martin Kaltenbrunner
Abhijit Karnik
Mohammadreza Khalilbeigi
Ahmed Kharrufa
Jeeeun Kim
David Kirk
Søren Knudsen
Vassilis Kostakos
Per Ola Kristensson
Marcel Lancelle
Tobia Langlotz
Yann Laurillau
Bongshin Lee

Additional reviewers (continued):

Daniel Leithinger
Samantha LeVan
Robert Lindeman
Lars Lischke
Li Liu
Markus Löchtefeld
Pedro Lopes
Michelle Lui
Kris Luyten
Zhihan lv
Kent Lyons
Xiaojuan Ma
Sylvain Malacria
Anders Markussen
Michael Marner
Roberto Martinez Maldonado
Fabrice Matulic
James McNaughton
Nemanja Memarovic
Karyn Moffatt
Meredith Morris
Gerald Morrison
Ann Morrison
Jörg Müller
Miguel Nacenta
Kosuke Nakajima
Takuya Nojima
Diana Nowacka
Halla Olafsdottir
Antti Oulasvirta
Volker Paelke
Michel Pahud
David Pallant
Sharoda Paul
Thomas Pederson
Simon Perrault
Florian Perteneder
Joshua Peschel
Martin Pielot
Emmanuel Pietriga
Krzysztof Pietroszek
Thomas Pietrzak
Anne Marie Piper
Roman Rädle
Stuart Reeves
Stefan Rennick-Egglestone
Patrick Reuter
Jochen Rick
Mark Robinson
Michael Rohs
Anne Roudaut
Jaime Ruiz
Daisuke Sakamoto
Pablo Sauras-Perez
Martin Schmitz
Holger Schnädelbach
Marcos Serrano
Teddy Seyed
Orit Shaer
Chia Shen
Buntarou Shizuki
Sowmya Somanath
Martin Spindler
Sophie Stellmach
Wolfgang Stuerzlinger
Maki Sugimoto
Jingjing Sun
Aurélien Tabard
Nick Taylor
Paul Tennent
Alice Thudt
Peter Tolmie
Martin Tomitsch
Theophanis Tsandilas
Jayson Turner
Dimitar Valkov
Deltcho Valtchanov
Davy Vanacken
Andrew Vande Moere
Radu-Daniel Vatavu
Jo Vermeulen
Simon Voelker
Daniel Vogel
Ulrich von Zadow

Additional reviewers (continued):

Chat Wacharamanotham
Julie Wagner
James Wallace
Robert Walter
Peter Wardrip
Nadir Weibel
Stephen Wheatley
Wesley Willett
Julie Williamson
Raphael Wimmer
Lonce Wyse
Robert Xiao
Min Xin
Koji Yatani
Haimo Zhang

ITS 2014 Sponsor & Supporters

ITS 2014 gratefully acknowledges our sponsoring SIG and the support of the following organizations:

Sponsor: SIGCHI

Academic Supporter: DFG

Gold Supporter: MULTI TOUCH

Silver Supporters: wacom · SMART™

Bronze Supporters: Microsoft · SurfNet

Friends of ITS: Graphisme, animation et nouveaux médias grand Graphics, Animation and New Media

Additional Supporter: IML INTERACTIVE MEDIA LAB DRESDEN

Keynote

A New You: From Augmented Reality to Augmented Human

Jun Rekimoto
The University of Tokyo
Sony Computer Science Laboratories, Tokyo
rekimoto@acm.org

ABSTRACT

Traditionally, the field of Human Computer Interaction (HCI) was primarily concerned with designing and investigating interfaces between humans and machines. The primary concern of Surface Computing is also still about designing better interfaces to information. However, with recent technological advances, the concept of "enhancing", "augmenting" or even "re-designing" humans themselves is becoming a very feasible and serious topic of scientific research as well as engineering development. "Augmented Human" is a term that I use to refer to this overall research direction. Augmented Human introduces a fundamental paradigm shift in HCI: from human-computer-interaction to human-computer-integration. In this talk, I will discuss rich possibilities and distinct challenges in enhancing human abilities. I will introduce recent projects conducted by our group including design and applications of wearable eye sensing for augmenting our perception and memory abilities, design of flying cameras as our external eyes, a home appliance that can increase your happiness, an organic physical wall/window that dynamically mediates the environment, and an immersive human-human communication called "JackIn".

ACM Classification Keywords

H.5.1 Information Interfaces and Presentation: *Artificial, augmented, and virtual realities*

BIOGRAPHY

Jun Rekimoto received his B.A.Sc., M.Sc., and Ph.D. in Information Science from Tokyo Institute of Technology in 1984, 1986, and 1996, respectively. From 1986 to 1994, he worked for the Software Laboratory of NEC. During 1992-1993, he worked in the Computer Graphics Laboratory at the University of Alberta, Canada, as a visiting scientist. Since 1994 he has worked for Sony Computer Science Laboratories (Sony CSL). In 1999 he formed, and has since directed, the Interaction Laboratory within Sony CSL.

ITS 2014, November 16–19, 2014, Dresden, Germany.
ACM 978-1-4503-2587-5/14/11.
http://dx.doi.org/10.1145/2669485.2670531

At Sony CSL, Rekimoto initiated and has led the "Real-World User Interfaces" project since 1994. This project produced several notable research accomplishments, including NaviCam (a situationally-aware mobile assistant), Pick-and-Drop (a direct-manipulation technique for inter-appliance computing), Multiple-Device Digital Whiteboard, Augmented Surfaces, and TimeScape (a time-machine user interface environment). Some of these are being commercialized in Sony's VAIO personal computer series.

Rekimoto's research interests include computer augmented environments, mobile/wearable computing, virtual reality, and information visualization. He has authored dozens of refereed publications in the area of human-computer interactions, including ACM, CHI, and UIST. One of his publications was recognized with the 30th commemorative papers award from the Information Processing Society Japan (IPSJ) in 1992. He also received the Multi-Media Grand Prix Technology Award from the Multi-Media Contents Association Japan in 1998, the Yamashita Memorial Research Award from IPSJ in 1999, and the Japan Inter-Design Award in 2003. In 2007, He elected to ACM SIGCHI Academy.

Keynote

Sensitive Skins in Media Art and Design

Joachim Sauter
University of the Arts, Berlin
ART+COM, Berlin
js@artcom.de

ABSTRACT
After the spread of personal computers in the mid 1980ies, media art and design focussed primarily on the screen as an interface for nearly two decades. In order to overcome the limitation of the screen as a small rectangular, flat, single-user device, ART+COM developed touch-sensitive surfaces applicable to objects of almost any size and form in the early years of the new century. When encountering these new interfaces in exhibitions and in the museum, the audience accepted them emphatically. Instead of being faced with some wall projection with a classic single-user input interface as usual, visitors were enabled to explore content together and interact with each other. The first touch-sensitive tables Behind The Lines (2003) and floating.numbers (2004) for the Jewish Museum in Berlin turned users into interactive participants who could jointly explore the data surface and discuss what they had discovered. The installations' implicit form of a table encouraged users to interact with each other - after all, tables have served as places of communication and exchange throughout human history. Driven by the success of this multi-user, face-to-face experience ART+COM developed dozens of content and context specific installations ranging from large, rectangular tables to amorphous touch-sensitive sculptures.

The talk will discuss the history of installations and spaces using dynamic sensitive surfaces including sensitive tables, sculptures, floors, costumes and architecture and spanning from ART+COMs pre- to post-sensitive-surface era.

ACM Classification Keywords
H.5.2 User Interfaces: *Interaction styles*

BIOGRAPHY
After graduating from the academy of fine arts in Berlin, Joachim Sauter studied at the 'German Academy for Film and Television', Berlin. Since the early 1980s, he has been working as a media artist and designer. From the beginning, Joachim Sauter has focussed on digital technologies and is experimenting how they can be used to express content, form and narration. Fuelled by this interest, he founded ART+COM in 1988 together with other artists, designers, scientists and technologists. Their goal was to practically research this new up-and-coming medium in the realm of art and design. Until now, he is leading this interdisciplinary group.

In the course of his work he was invited to participate on many exhibitions. Beside others he showed his work at 'Centre Pompidou' Paris, 'Stejdilik Museum' Amsterdam, 'Museum for Contemporary Art' Sidney, 'Deichtorhallen Hamburg', Kunsthalle Wien, 'Venice Biennial','ICC' Tokyo, 'Getty Center' Los Angeles, MAXXI Rom. He received several awards like the 'Golden Lion, Cannes', the 'D&AD Black Pencil', the 'Ars Electronica Interactive Award', the 'British Academy for Film and Television Interactive Award', ADC New York and ADC Germany Gold, the 'Grand Clio', the 'Red Dot Grand Prix', the 'Design award of the Federal Republic of Gemany' and many other national and international awards'.

Since 1991 he is full professor for "New Media Art and Design" at the 'University of the Arts' Berlin and since 2001 adjunct professor at UCLA, Los Angeles.

ITS 2014, November 16–19, 2014, Dresden, Germany.
ACM 978-1-4503-2587-5/14/11.
http://dx.doi.org/10.1145/2669485.2670530

Exploring Narrative Gestures on Digital Surfaces

Mehrnaz Mostafapour, Mark Hancock
Department of Management Sciences
University of Waterloo, Canada
first.last@uwaterloo.ca

ABSTRACT
A significant amount of research on digital tables has traditionally investigated the use of hands and fingers to control 2D and 3D artifacts, has even investigated people's expectations when interacting with these devices. However, people often use their hands and body to communicate and express ideas to others. In this work, we explore narrative gestures on a digital table for the purpose of telling stories. We present the results of an observational study of people illustrating stories on a digital table with virtual figurines, and in both a physical sandbox and water with physical figurines. Our results show that the narrative gestures people use to tell stories with objects are highly varied and, in some cases, fundamentally different from the gestures designers and researchers have suggested for controlling digital content. In contrast to smooth, pre-determined drags for movement and rotation, people use jiggling, repeated lifting, and bimanual actions to express rich, simultaneous, and independent actions by multiple characters in a story. Based on these results, we suggest that future storytelling designs consider the importance of touch actions for narration, in-place manipulations, the (possibly non-linear) path of a drag, allowing expression through manipulations, and two-handed simultaneous manipulation of multiple objects.

INTRODUCTION
Storytelling is an expressive form of art that can empower the expression of thoughts, beliefs, and emotions through narrative. The idea of storytelling often evokes thoughts of common media such as books, movies, and video games, but people tell anecdotes to one another every day around dinner tables, campfires, and water coolers. When narrating a story, people often make gestures with their hands, arms, and body to enhance the story, to build suspense, to exaggerate emotion, or to simply better engage the audience.

Digital tables [4,9,16] are a promising medium through which these anecdotes could be told, as the audience and storyteller can gather around the table, much like they would at a dinner table or campfire, and they support the ability to perform gestures that are immediately observable to the audience. The digital surface can then be used as a supportive medium that the storyteller can adopt to further enhance the storytelling experience; that is, their storytelling gestures could be made to have a greater impact on their story. A narrator can use on-screen objects to set the scene of a story, to draw paths or elements relevant to the plot of the story, or to improve a description of a story's characters.

While there has been a significant amount of research exploring the use of gestures on digital tables [23,24,36,37], and the use of one's fingers and hands to move and rotate artifacts [10,21,30], the understanding of a "gesture" in the literature has largely focussed on the control of on-screen content. Nonetheless, this research attempts to develop an understanding of people's behaviour [30] and simple gestures that people expect to use on digital surfaces [23,36]. Hinrichs and Carpendale [15] have highlighted the need to support the expressive power of gestures; however, much is still not known about the use of digital tables to support the creative processes involved in storytelling. What kinds of gestures do people perform to convey meaning in a story? Do gestures used to control on-screen artifacts interfere with storytelling gestures? How does the digital medium differ from the physical in its storytelling potential?

Some research already explores the use of digital tables for storytelling [10,13,39]. These prototypes allow a person to create a story by manipulating on-screen 3D artifacts [10]. These designs show promise for the support of this creative process, and integrate natural gestures and physical interaction techniques to improve the storytelling experience. However, this research has not yet explored whether and how these prototypes are used to tell stories and the gestures people use to convey these narratives.

In this paper, we present an observational study of people creating a story on a digital table, in a physical sandbox, and in water. We focussed our observations on the physical gestures used to tell a story as people narrate, create dialogue, and move characters. Our findings suggest that narrative gestures are inherently different than regular gestures; people use them to convey meaning to the audience. Beyond simple movement and rotations, storytellers animate characters in a variety of ways to convey meaning, and combine these narrative gestures with two hands in ways typically not expected from traditional movement and rotation interaction techniques. Moreover, the way people combine movements from multiple hands has meaning that may interfere with the common use of multiple hands and fingers to move and rotate digital artifacts in 3D.

ITS'14, November 16–19, 2014, Dresden, Germany.

ACM 978-1-4503-2587-5/14/11…$15.00
http://dx.doi.org/10.1145/2669485.2669510

RELATED WORK

In this section we first review the-state-of-the-art surface-based storytelling prototypes. We then review previous research on non-object mediated narrative gestures and the research on exploring hand gestures used to navigate on a digital surface. We then review the research comparing the interaction between physical and digital objects.

Storytelling on Multi-touch Surfaces

Storytelling is a powerful means of communication that empowers people to express their thoughts, beliefs, and emotions through narrative [19,35]. Given the importance of storytelling, many research prototypes already support storytelling on digital surfaces [1,10,13,29,39]. These prototypes support a variety of storytelling features, such as the ability to move and rotate photos [1,13,39] or 3D toys [10], to draw on the background [2,6,29], to record the story being told [30], and the ability to add one's own content, for example images from an existing photo collection [39] or captured from the surrounding physical environment [1]. These storytelling prototypes and applications have enabled collaboration [1,13,39], and supported therapy for children [10] or persons with aphasia [39]. While the purpose of these applications is to enable users to create a story, there is little research on how narrators manipulate objects to enact character actions and story events. In this paper, we study the way people benefit from hand gestures to manipulate on-screen objects to illustrate story events, with the intent of informing the design of such applications.

Narrative Gestures

Narrative gestures are usually used in conjunction with speech to illustrate an event or to communicate meaning [20,22]. Using hand gestures not only helps to engage the audience, but also serves as a tool for narrators to better focus and think [6,7]. These gestures are categorized as: *iconics*, *metaphorics*, *deictics*, *beats*, and *butterworths* [1,20,22]. Iconics are used to resemble and illustrate a concrete object or event, for instance, a gesture that depicts the act of hitting may be synchronous with the utterance, "she hit him on the shoulder". Metaphorics are similar to iconics except that they are used to depict abstract concepts, such as an upward hand gesture accompanied by the utterance "his IQ is very high". Deictics are hand movements used to point to a particular element, for instance, a pointing gesture to a door while speaking about that door. Beats are used to punctuate and give emphasis to discourse, for instance, a very quick and steady hand movement accompanying the utterance "that's it". Butterworths correspond to speech failure [1,22], for example, hand movements while trying to recall something. While narrative gestures have been studied in the context of open-handed non-object mediated communicative gestures that accompany speech [1,22], our work extends this literature by investigating storytelling that involves manipulating objects (e.g., story characters), in particular when illustrating story events through manipulating tangible and on-screen objects.

Gestures on Multi-Touch Surfaces

Many studies have investigated gestures on multi-touch surfaces to understand and develop natural [23,24,36], ergonomic [25,26], or novel interaction techniques [10,32,37]. This research primarily focuses on understanding and designing interaction techniques for digital surfaces to perform common tasks (e.g., movement, scaling, etc.); however, these studies have not considered the context of illustrating a story or describing an object. The focus of our work is not to design specific interaction techniques, such as the number and combination of fingers used to interact with the objects [11,25,38], nor to identify people's expectations about what command a gesture should invoke [5,24], nor to develop multi-user gestural interaction,23], but to study the nature of interactions and physical actions used to perform story events and character actions in the context of narration. We thus observe physical and digital interactions of the storytelling process, using an exploratory approach similar to Hinrichs and Carpendale's [15].

Physical vs. Digital Interactions

Comparing the method of interaction with objects in a digital 2D and physical 3D space helps to incorporate methods of physical interaction into the design of multi-touch devices [33]. For instance, Scott et al. [31] studied collaborative interactions in the physical world to provide their territoriality framework that can be applied in the design of collaborative applications on digital tables. Terrenghi et al. [33] studied the nature of interactions in 3D and 2D by asking participants to sort pictures and complete a puzzle in a physical environment and on a digital table. Using a similar method, North et al. [28] compared gestures used to "manipulate many small objects, in three different interaction paradigms: physical, multi-touch, and mouse interaction," [28, p. 5] to understand the similarities and differences between the interactions used in these environments. These examples used lab studies, where they asked participants to complete tasks in different environments. In our work, we use a similar approach that compares how people manipulate objects in physical environments and on the digital table in the context of narration and storytelling.

OBSERVING STORYTELLING GESTURES

To investigate the use of narrative gestures, we focused our attention on the act of *illustrating a story*—a specific instance of storytelling where the narrator enacts character movements and story events by manipulating figurines—as in this act, people frequently demonstrate a variety of emotion and draw the audience in in a variety of ways. We thus focused our attention on the following research questions:

- *How does a narrator make use of gestures to illustrate story events?*
- *How do these gestures differ when the story is told in a digital space, rather than a physical one?*
- *How do the digital or physical artifacts in the story affect the gestures performed?*

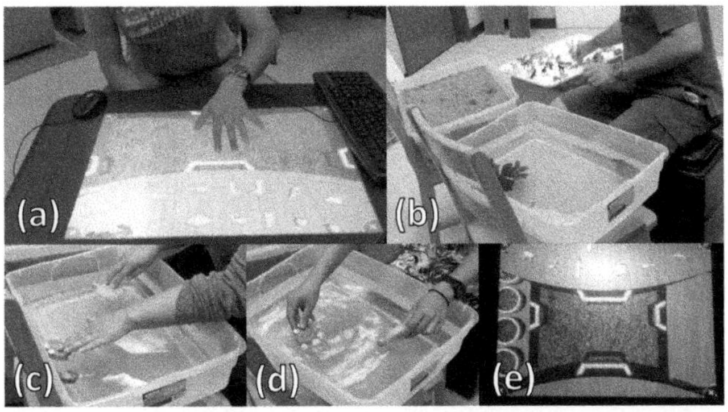

Figure 1. The setup of the study in (a) the digital condition, (b) the sand and water conditions. Participants would sometimes (c) touch objects or (d) grasp objects. A screenshot of the digital sandtray (e) had a figurine, paint, and resize drawer.

To provide a basis for developing interaction techniques in digital mediums, HCI researchers frequently study physical interactions [28,31,33,34]. Thus, to develop a better understanding of narrative gestures, we observed participants illustrating a story to the experimenter in one digital and two physical conditions. As a basis for the digital storytelling, we used an application designed to support storytelling—a digital sandtray [11,19]. We had participants tell a story in this digital medium, and the original physical setup of a sandbox. Because the digital medium only allows interaction in 2D, while physical sandboxes allow movement on and above the surface, we included another physical condition where interaction could occur in a 2D plane, water. Water allows for both forms of physical interaction; participants were able to either touch and push, or grasp and move objects to manipulate them (Figure 1c & 1d).

Participants

Twenty-nine university students aged 19 to 45 (*Mdn*=26) participated in our study (11 female). Six (21%) did not own and had never used a multi-touch device. Twenty-three (79%) owned a multi-touch device, such as a smartphone or tablet, twenty of whom (87%) for more than a year. Only two (7%) had worked with a digital table before.

Apparatus

Participants were asked to illustrate a story in one digital and two physical environments. In all conditions, we modelled the environment after sandtray therapy, a type of art therapy that provides clients with a tray of sand and a shelf full of figurines with which to tell a story. Clients use these figurines to create and tell a story to the therapist [19]. We chose this setting for several reasons: (1) this type of storytelling is already used in the practice of therapy, and so our results can directly inform this current practice, (2) an existing digital tabletop display application, was available and modelled directly after this physical practice [11], (3) this form of storytelling had already been refined by therapists to quickly engage the client in storytelling, and have the story take on personal meaning.

In the digital condition, participants created and told a story on a SMART Table, a rear-projected 92 cm × 74 cm multi-touch table with a resolution of 1024 × 768 pixels and a height of 64 cm. The software used for the study on the digital table was Hancock et al.'s [11] sandtray application (Figure 1a & 1e). This multi-touch sandtray application was built in Java and includes three drawers: a characters drawer that includes a set of figurines, a paint drawer that enables drawing on the background, and a resize drawer that allows resizing of figurines (Figure 1e).

This prototype supports the illustrating of a rich narrative by enabling narrators to move and rotate objects both in a 2D and 3D space. Narrators can move objects on the surface with one point of contact, and rotate them in a 2D space through two points of contact. These same two points can be used to lift or lower an object by spreading them apart or pinching them together. In order to rotate objects in a 3D space, narrators need to have two fixed points of contact and use a third touch to rotate the object in the space along any desired axis. For a more complete description of the these interaction technique, see [10,11].

In both sand and water, participants completed the story in two 90 cm×70 cm trays with a depth of 16 cm. The top edge of both trays was adjusted to be the height of the SMART Table. The seat was adjusted so participants could reach all available areas on the digital table and in the trays. A set of different toys was provided next to the trays (Figure 1b).

Note that a rabbit, a turtle, and a tree figurine were provided in all three environments, but the other physical and digital figurines were not similar. Two groups of toys were provided in the physical conditions, including a group of 6 decorative items and a group of 44 animal figurines. Some of the toys were specifically made for water (bath toys), so that they would float. Participants could choose any of the toys for both the water and sand conditions, regardless of whether they were bath toys (i.e., intended for use in water). Also 161 figurines were provided in the digital table from which 6 figurines were different types of tree and flower figurines. The figurines included some animals, some fictional characters (e.g., a Pegasus), some furniture figurines (e.g., a couch), and some transportation vehicles (e.g., an airplane).

Conditions

Our primary factor in the design of this study was the story telling *environment*, with three levels: *sand*, *water*, and *digital* table. We used a within-participants design where each participant was asked to tell a story in all three media. We included a secondary between-participants factor where half the participants were asked to stick to the script of the original story (fixed) and the other half were allowed to deviate in theme and plot (free-form); however, in practice, participants tended to ignore this request, with many in the fixed condition deviating frequently and many in the free-form condition sticking to the original plot. Thus, we did not consider this secondary factor in our analysis.

Task & Data Collection

All of the participants were given a short summary of the famous children's story "The Tortoise and the Hare" to read. In the given story, the rabbit was a boastful character that was challenged by the tortoise to a race. The rabbit lost the race because he decided to sleep along the way. Additional setting information (e.g., place, time, etc.) was not described to participants. Each participant started by reading the story, and then proceeded to illustrate his/her story in all three environments. The experimenter played the role of an audience member as each participant told his/her story, with the experimenter sitting in front of him/her and actively listening (i.e., displaying emotional responses, such as smiling/laughing at funny moments, making eye contact, and otherwise responding to the narrative), without physically interfering with the surface and objects. Note that all reactions were genuine, and no script or acting was used. While we recognize these reactions may have influenced participant behaviour, we believe it created a more realistic setting, and the absence of these reactions would have been more detrimental to our results (e.g., not laughing at a joke).

Each session was videotaped and participants completed a post-study questionnaire, which included demographic questions and asked participants to explain their comfort level while manipulating objects in different environments.

Data Elimination

Note that the results from five participants were eliminated from the data and all the presented analysis is done based on the data gathered from the 24 remaining participants. Four participants were eliminated because they only narrated stories in two environments, as they did not have enough time to complete the whole study in the allotted hour. The results of a fifth participant were eliminated because she was not easily able to work with the digital table, so the experimenter had to interfere. After elimination, the order of presentation of the storytelling environment was still balanced (4 participants per order), with the exceptions of the order sand, digital, water (5) and water, sand, digital (3).

GESTURE CLASSIFICATION

Character actions and story events are different from story to story; one story might be about characters who are climbing mountains while another story might be about characters who are sitting in a room and talking to each other. Therefore, in order to analyze how participants exploit possible actions (e.g., lifting, rotation, and dragging) to manipulate objects and enact character actions, we selected a set of story events and character actions that were common among all the stories told. We thus followed a two-pass video analysis strategy suggested by Jacucci et al. [18].

Video Analysis and Gesture Classification

In the first pass, we watched all the study sessions and identified the actions commonly used by all participants:

Dialogue: In all stories, there was always at least one conversation between two or more characters in which a story character was talking. For instance, when a narrator said, "The turtle said, 'Let's see who wins.'"

Narration: In all stories, there was always at least one point at which the narrator was explaining what was going on. In these moments, the narrator usually described a scene, a story event, or a character's thoughts, feelings, etc. For instance, when a narrator said, "The animals decided to come and watch the race," or, "The rabbit was very angry."

Character movements: In all stories, there was at least one character who moved from one location to another.

Throughout this section, we use the term "narrate" to describe verbal utterances and "illustrate" to describe any narrative act that involves visual cues or physical action (e.g., object movement).

In the second pass, we used a grounded theory approach to elucidate and identify different categories of narrative gestures. However, our method of coding was similar to McNeill's [22]. We looked at the utterance and simultaneous hand gesture to see when a particular gesture was used. Throughout this section, we discuss when our gestures could be categorized using McNeil's terminology (iconics, metaphorics, deictics, beats, and butterworths [22]), but chose a grounded theory approach, since these gestures were not intended for gestures with objects, specifically.

Gestures for Dialogue and Narration

We observed that while participants were illustrating *dialogue* or *narration* they performed the following gestures:

Touch/Hold: Participants sometimes touched a character on the digital table, or touched/held a character in their hand in the physical conditions. This included any touches more than 2 seconds. We found that people sometimes touch/hold an object when talking about it. These types of gestures can be considered as deictic gestures that are used to point to an element. However, in this case narrators actually touched the object instead of just pointing to it. We also observed that participants touched or held objects when they were thinking about what to say or when they wanted to come up with a creative storyline to tell. In this case narrators usually touched an object even if that object was not related to what they were talking about. This could be due to the reason that touching/holding an object could help narrators to focus on what they were saying. This type of touch/hold gesture could be considered as butterworths that are used as an effort to recall a word or a sentence.

Jiggle: Participants sometimes touched/held an object while doing small up-down or right-left motions (Figure 3). These events were coded as jiggle actions, and not as touch/hold actions. Jiggling was mostly used to resemble talking, dancing, or emotions such as anger, happiness, etc. For instance, a participant jiggled the rabbit and accompanied it with the utterance "The rabbit said no way!" In these cases, jiggling

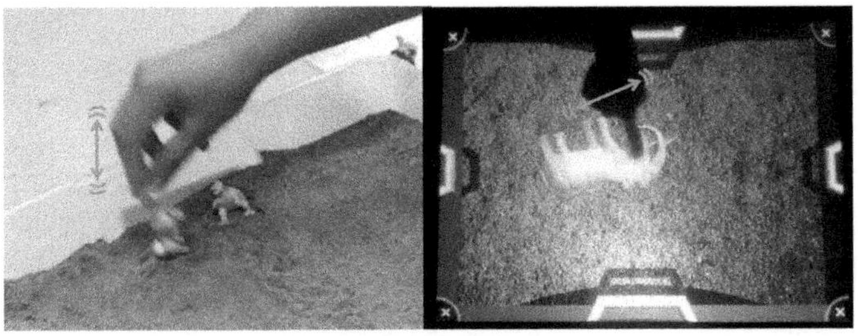

Figure 2. Jiggling

could be considered an iconic gesture through which narrators want to represent a particular meaning or event. However, jiggling could also be considered as a beat gesture, since it is used to emphasize a particular concept. Meaning that by jiggling, participants not only represented talking, but also emphasized *how* a character talks, (e.g., when the character was angry they jiggled faster).

Tap: Participants sometimes touched/held an object for less than 2 seconds. As our smallest unit to measure the time was a second, any touch gesture up to two seconds was considered as a tap. Tap could be considered a deictic gesture, since it was mostly used to point to particular elements of the scene (e.g. a scenic element or a story character).

Above surface hand gestures: Participants sometimes narrated the story while performing hand gestures above the surface (i.e. digital table, sand or water). These gestures include all five of McNeil's gestures [22].

As an example of how we coded dialogue one participant stated, "the rabbit said, 'I am much better at running,'" as she jiggled the rabbit to enact talking. We classified this gesture as a *jiggle* in the *dialogue* category. We followed the same method for coding narration.

Gestures for Character Movements

We also observed that *character movements* were performed through four types of gestures which could be considered iconic or beat gestures [1,20,22]:

Dragging: Moving an object while always in contact with the surface. This gesture could be considered iconic, as the narrator only wants to illustrate movement.

Dragging while jiggling: Moving an object forward while jiggling it. This gesture could be considered as either iconic or as a beat gesture, as the narrator not only illustrates that a character is moving but also emphasizes how it moves.

Lift and drag: In the physical conditions, participants sometimes picked an object up and moved it to another location. The same action could be performed on the digital table through lifting and dragging an object. This type of gesture could again be considered as an iconic gesture, as it only depicts that a character moves from one location to another without any visual information about how it moves.

Repeated lift and drag: Participants moved an object through several small/repeated lift and drags (e.g., to show that the rabbit is jumping to get to the finish line). Repeated lift and drag could effectively illustrate "hopping". Similar to dragging while jiggling, this gesture could also be considered as both iconic and as a beat gesture.

As an example of how we coded character movements, one participant said "the turtle went slowly but surely" and did slow, deliberate, left and right motions while moving the turtle, which we classified as: *dragging while jiggling* in the *character movement* category.

Two-Handed Interactions

In addition to coding gestures used for dialogue, narration, and character movements, we noticed that many participants performed interesting combinations of gestures with both hands (Figure 3). While we observed asymmetric bimanual actions [8] (e.g., the bimanual interaction required to rotate objects in the digital sandtray), of particular note were the two-handed gestures driven by the narrative being told, such as simultaneous drags to represent two characters racing. We thus coded examples of simultaneous gestures on two figurines. To simplify this analysis, we considered all touch, jiggle, tap, and rotate gestures as *in-place* actions and all character movements, including drag, drag and jiggle, repeated lift and drag, and lift and drag, as *move* actions. Therefore, three simultaneous bimanual actions were observed: *move+move*, *in-place+move*, *in-place+in-place*. Note that these gestures cannot easily be classified using the common HCI terminology of "symmetric" and "asymmetric" [8], since actions were sometimes half-way between (e.g., characters running at different speeds, or one character interrupting the dialogue of another).

We counted the number of instances that each gesture occurred for each action (dialogue, narration, or character movement). Sustained gestures were counted in 10 second intervals: a drag gesture held for 23 seconds would be counted as 3 drags (two 10 second and one 3 second drag).

RESULTS

We separate our analyses according to the codes identified in the first pass of analysis. Specifically, we separately con-

Figure 3. Two-Handed combination

sider gestures used to perform *dialogue and narration*, *character movements*, and *two-handed interaction*.

While the sample size in our tests is 24 and the data may not be normally distributed, parametric tests have been shown to be robust to violations of these assumptions [27], hence we used Repeated Measures Analyses of Variance (RM-ANOVAs) with storytelling environment and gesture as primary factors. We also included action (dialogue vs. narration) as a factor when analyzing these data, as the gestures used to perform these actions were often similar. We note the exact test used in each subsection.

Our dependent measure was the number of instances of each gesture, either as a raw count or normalized by condition. Normalized results appear as percentages (%), and were calculated using the number of instances of all gestures within that condition (e.g., water, sand, or digital) as the denominator. When this denominator was zero (i.e., no gestures were performed in that condition), we represented this as 0%. The decision to normalize had the effect of focusing the analysis on the differences in frequency of gesture within each condition (e.g., which gestures were used to illustrate), rather than on the number of instances across conditions (e.g., how many gestures were performed in sand vs. water vs. digital). We chose normalized analysis when investigating story-centred actions (dialogue, narration, and character movements) and raw counts when investigating interaction-centred actions (two-handed interaction). Note that mean differences between storytelling environments or any factor other than gesture are nonsensical for normalized data, since the conditions add up to 100%. We thus consider only main effects and interactions involving gesture in our normalized analyses.

Gestures for Dialogue and Narration

We analyzed dialogue and narration with a 3 environment (digital, water, sand) × 2 action (dialogue vs. narration) × 4 gesture (jiggle, touch, tap, above-surface) RM-ANOVA.

There was a significant main effect of gesture ($F_{3,69}$=15.97, p<.001), shown in Figure 4, green. Pairwise comparisons revealed that tapping was used significantly less than every other type of narrative action (p<.001) and that above-surface gestures were used significantly less than touching (p=.01), and less than jiggling, but this difference was not significant (p=.06). There was no significant difference between touching and jiggling (p=1.00). Thus, while some dialogue and narrative actions were represented using above the surface gestures, participants tended to prefer contact with the objects (i.e., touch/jiggle). It may be that contact with the story objects helps the narrator focus on the story being told. However, the effect of gesture can be further explained by the interactions.

Two-Way Interaction: Environment and Gesture

We found a significant interaction between environment and gesture ($F_{6,138}$=5.3, p<.001, Figure 4, blue). We performed post-hoc pairwise comparisons grouped by gesture.

Jiggling: We found jiggling to be used significantly more in sand than in water (p=.02). There was no significant difference between water and the digital table in terms of jiggling (p=1.00). This finding may suggest that participants had difficulty accomplishing jiggling on the digital table and in water, or that sand lends itself better to this action.

Touching/Holding: We also found that touching was used significantly more in water than sand (p=.02). However there was no significant difference between water and digital (p=.47), nor between sand and digital (p=1.00). We suspect that participants felt the need to hold objects in place in the water condition to prevent them from floating away.

Tapping: There were no significant differences between all the environments in terms of tapping (p=1.00); participants did not tend to tap much in any environment, as per the main effect. This may suggest that participants preferred to touch objects for longer than 2 seconds while narrating.

Above-surface: Participants used more above-surface hand gestures in digital than both sand (p=.01) and water (p<.01). This finding indicates a possible hesitation by participants when using the digital table vs. physical media; they felt a need to indicate dialogue or narration, but resisted using another gesture (jiggle, touch, or tap). This may be due to the Midas Touch phenomenon [12,14]. Interestingly, this phenomenon may have partially extended to (gritty)

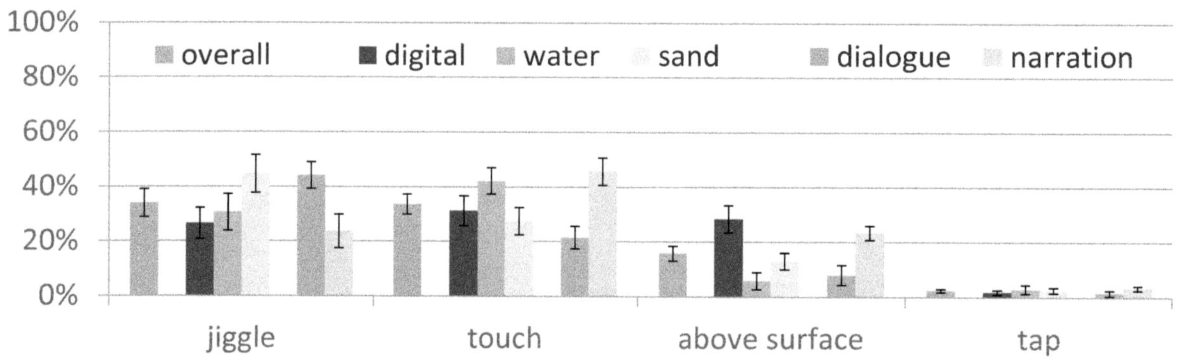

Figure 4. Main effect of gestures used for dialogue and narration (left, green), interaction between environment and gesture (middle, blue), and interaction between gesture and action (right, orange). Means are normalized (%), and show error bars (SE).

sand, though this difference may also be due to participants' apparent need to "hold" objects in water.

Two-Way Interaction: Action and Gesture
We also found a significant interaction between action and gesture ($F_{3,69}$=24.9, p<.001, Figure 4, orange). Above-surface and touch gestures were used significantly more (p<.001) when participants were narrating than when they were enacting dialogue. Conversely, participants jiggled objects significantly more to enact dialogue than when they were narrating a part of the story (p<.001). There was no significant difference between dialogue and narration in terms of tapping (p=.18). This finding suggests that participants used the more animated jiggling action to indicate dialogue, and preferred more touching and above surface actions when narrating a part of the story.

Three-Way Interaction: Environment, Action, Gesture
There was also a significant three-way interaction between environment, gesture, and action ($F_{6,138}$=4.4, p<.001), but we did not explore this interaction further.

Gestures for Character Movement
We analyzed character movement with a 3 condition (digital, water, sand) × 4 gesture (drag, drag & jiggle, repeated lift & drag, lift & drag) RM-ANOVA.

There was a significant main effect of gesture ($F_{3,69}$=36.31, p<.001, Figure 5, green). We found that lift and drag was used significantly less than both dragging and dragging while jiggling (p<.001). This result may suggest that participants preferred to "perform" object movement. That is, the journey from one location to another was as important as the start and end locations. Similarly, repeated lift and drag was used significantly less than dragging and dragging while jiggling (p<.001); however, this may be partially explained by the interaction between environment and gesture (see below), as this gesture was not easy to perform on the digital table. There was no significant difference between dragging and dragging while jiggling (p=1.00) nor between lift and drag and repeated lift and drag (p=.38).

Two-Way Interaction: Environment and Gesture
We also found a significant interaction between environment and gesture ($F_{6,138}$=23.32, p<.001, Figure 5, blue). Post-hoc pairwise comparisons were grouped by gesture.

Dragging: Dragging was used significantly more in digital than each of water (p<.002) and sand (p<.001). Dragging in water was also used significantly more than sand (p<.002). As participants could easily move objects on the surface of water, but not in sand. This finding also suggests that dragging was the most used action to move the object around the digital table. That is, participants tended to mostly drag objects to move them around the digital table.

Dragging while jiggling: This action was used significantly more in sand than on the digital table (p<.001), and water

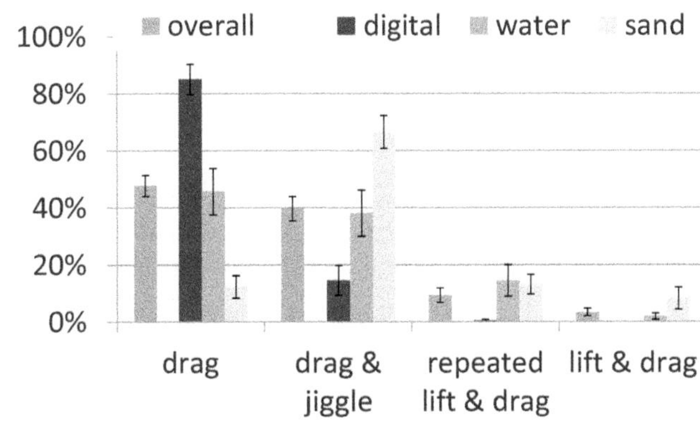

Figure 5. Main effect of gesture (left, green) and gesture × environment interaction (right, blue) for character movement.

(p<.02). It was also used significantly more in water than on the digital table (p<.05). Participants could move objects without jiggling them to show that they are moving; however, they jiggled objects (i.e. animated movements) while moving them. And this happened significantly more in the physical conditions than on the digital table.

Repeated lift and drag: This action was used significantly less on the digital table than in the sand (p<.003) and in the water (p<.05). There was no significant difference between sand and water (p=1).

Lift and drag: There were no significant differences between the environments in terms of this type of movement, and it was not used much overall. This finding might suggest that participants preferred to be in contact with the objects and enact how they move while moving them from one point to another point, instead of just picking them up and putting them down in another location.

Two-Handed Interactions
Participants used two-handed manipulation while either manipulating one object or two objects at a time.

Manipulation of one object: Manipulation of one object, was always performed using only one hand in physical conditions; however, participants sometimes used two hands to rotate or move one object on the digital table. In order to perform 2D and 3D rotations in the sandtray application, participants were required to have respectively two or three points of contact with the surface [10]. Therefore we observed a variety of bimanual interactions to rotate an object on the digital table. We also sometimes observed that participants moved (i.e. drag, drag while jiggling, lift and drag) an object on the digital table using two hands (usually one finger from each hand)

Manipulation of two objects: While in some instances, participants used bimanual actions to interact with one object, we observed that sometimes they used two-handed coordination to simultaneously interact with two different on-screen objects. To the best of our knowledge little work has been done on studying two-handed coordination while simultaneously manipulating more than one object, we focused on investigating these types of actions to first understand what types of two-handed coordination are generally used while working with two different objects and second to explore how frequently narrators tend to use these two-handed manipulations in the different environments.

We ran a 3 environment (digital, water, and sand) × 3 combination (in-place+in-place, in-place+move, and move+move) RM-ANOVA on the number of times that participants used any combination. There was a significant main effect of environment ($F_{2,46}$=28.08, p<.001). The number of times that participants used two-handed coordination in water (M=2.3, SE=0.3) was significantly more than each of sand (M=0.9, SE=0.2) and digital (M=0.3, SE=0.1, p<.001). This result could be due to the fact that participants often hesitated to leave objects on the water to float, and instead kept them in their hands. The number of times participants used two-handed coordination in the sand was also significantly more than the digital condition (p<.009). These results suggest that participants used significantly more two-handed interaction in the physical environments than on the digital table. This may be because certain interactions on the digital table (e.g., rotation) required two or three points of contact with the object, and consequently participants were not able to manipulate other objects at the same time.

While bimanual interaction techniques are a common approach for manipulation of objects on a digital surface [11,21,30], this finding might suggest that there are some down sides, as they could constrain the animated manipulation of more than one object at a time. We recommend a more in-depth study to understand both the benefits and drawbacks that bimanual interaction might cause in different contexts. In both the physical conditions of our study, we observed that participants were able to rotate the rabbit and move the turtle figurine at the same time to show two simultaneous events in the story. However, this representation could not be easily performed in the digital condition as the participants needed to use three points of contact to rotate the rabbit, so they used two fingers of one hand and one finger from the other to rotate it. Consequently, they could not manipulate any other object at the same time.

We also found a significant main effect of two-handed combination ($F_{2,46}$= 10.616, p<0.001, Figure 6, green). We found that *in-place+in-place* were used together significantly more than both *in-place+move* (p=.005) and *move+move* (p=.013). However, there was no significant difference between *in-place-move* and *move+move* (p=.243). The increase in *in-place+in-place* is best explained through the interaction between environment and combination, as this effect was likely dominated by the water condition.

Two-Way Interaction: Combination and Environment

There was a significant interaction between environment and combination ($F_{8,184}$=7.35, p<.001, Figure 6, blue). Post-hoc pairwise comparisons were grouped by combination.

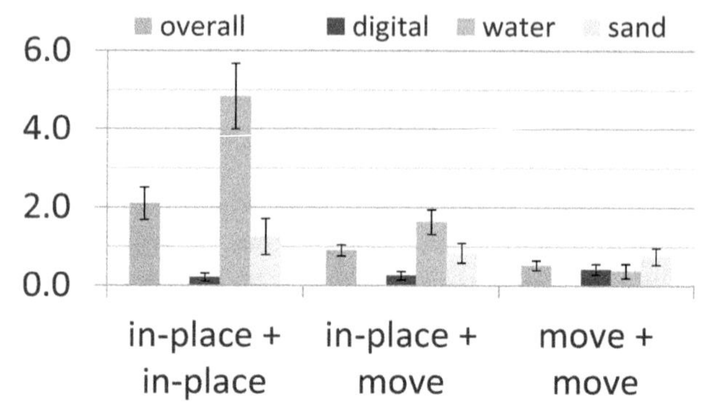

Figure 6. Mean counts and standard error (SE) of simultaneous two-handed actions, showing a main effect (left, green) and environment × combination interaction (right, blue).

In-place+in-place: This combination was used significantly more in water than both sand and digital (p<.001). The difference between sand and digital was not significant (p=.06). Note that this combination was used far more in water (M=4.8, SE=0.8) than in any other combination and environment (M < 1.7). This may be because participants did not appreciate figures "floating away", and so performed many in-place actions in the water with two hands where they just held the characters.

In-place+move: This combination was used significantly less in the digital condition than both sand (p=.05) and water (p=.001). This may again be because participants wanted to keep at least one character "still" in the water. There was no significant difference between sand and water (p=.243).

Move+move: There was no significant difference between environments in *move+move* combination (p>.40).

Crossed Hands

We observed eight incidents on the digital table in which participants crossed their hands while moving two objects simultaneously (Figure 7), three times in water and never in the sand. When characters would cross paths in the sand, participants would exchange figures between hands; however, they hesitated to change hands in the other environments. In the water, changing hands could have resulted in objects floating on the water for few seconds and that could have been undesirable in the story. On the digital table, participants may have been concerned that the objects would "drop" or lose their orientation once they let go.

Limitations

The focus of our study was to find out what types of narrative gestures are used on a digital surface and how they are different from the gestures used in physical environments. While this study had some limitations, we believe they do not alter the main contributions of the paper. This study was done one on one, as opposed to with a larger audience. However, our findings still show differences from traditional gestures, even with only one audience member. Nonetheless, future work could analyze larger audiences. Even

Figure 7. Participants crossed their hands on eight separate occasions while telling their stories.

though some digital interactions, such as repeated lift and drag, were sometimes hard to perform, which may be seen as a study limitation, participants still demonstrated similar gestures in physical environments that we feel indicate a need for new 3D object interaction techniques.

DISCUSSION

Our results show that the object-mediated narrative gestures in our study had some similarities to open-handed narrative gestures [1,20,22] and were mostly used to convey meaning by, for instance, touching a character to show that it is being described or by jiggling while moving to enact how characters move. We also observed that, most of the time, participants preferred to touch and hold or to manipulate objects while telling a story, instead of only pointing to them from above the surface. This observation might suggest that participants preferred to be in contact with objects and be engaged with the process physically. We suggest the following design considerations based on our observations:

Consider touch to narrate actions. In most digital surface applications, input is often handled through directly touching the screen. In a similar vein to others who have noted a potential Midas Touch problem [12,14,17,40], our study shows that narrators sometimes touch the screen to mention an object or to focus on what they are saying, and may not consider the act a command. Considering these unique touches is important in designing narrative applications.

Consider in-place manipulations of on-screen objects. Designers should also be aware of narrative in-place actions while designing interactive applications. For instance, in Microsoft Windows (7 and 8), when a person jiggles a window, other windows on the desktop minimize. This type of interaction may interfere with the narrative.

Consider the path to get there. While in some circumstances, it may be more desirable to consider more efficient and automatic interaction techniques (e.g., to avoid fatigue), we found that designing assistive or automatic interaction may not be always a good design decision, as narrators may prefer to be engaged with the narration process and movements related to story events. For instance, designing voice commands for movements or a move interaction that involves tapping an object and then tapping its target destination may seem more optimal, but may not be desirable for a narrative application, as narrators may prefer to move the objects around with their hands to engage in the process.

Support expressive and animated actions through manipulation techniques. We also observed that, while participants tended to animate character actions and story events, animated movements were employed more in physical environments than on the digital table. This finding might suggest that manipulating objects on the digital table was not as easy as it was in the physical conditions. Therefore, designers should exploit new technology to enable narrators to be more expressive and animated in their movements.

Consider two-handed, simultaneous manipulation of multiple on-screen objects. We also found that two-handed interactions were often used to simultaneously manipulate two objects. These types of actions were used significantly more in physical environments than on the digital table. This could be due to the fact that certain actions (2D and 3D rotation) were mostly performed by participants while using two hands and that could prevent them from manipulating any other object at the same time. However, this constraint did not exist in physical environments. Therefore, while a bimanual interaction technique could be suitable for movement and rotation in many circumstances, it might not always be suitable for narrative or expressive applications.

CONCLUSION

In this paper, we reported on a large and detailed observational study to explore how people make use of gestures to tell a story on a digital surface, a physical sandbox, and in water. We showed that these expressive gestures are fundamentally different than the movement and rotation gestures common on a digital table, and that people use two hands to richly and creatively express meaning in a story.

ACKNOWLEDGEMENTS

We thank the Natural Sciences and Engineering Council of Canada (NSERC), NSERC's Digital Surface Software Application Network (Surfnet), and the Graphics Animation & New Media (GRAND) NCE for funding.

REFERENCES

1. Cassell, J., 2001, Nudge Nudge Wink Wink: Elements of Face-to-Face Conversation for Embodied Conversational Agents. In Embodied conversational agents. MIT Press, Cambridge, MA, USA, 1-27
2. Daeman, E., Dadlani, P., Du, J., Li, Y., Erik-Paker, P., Martens, J., & De Ruyter, B. (2007). Designing a free style, indirect, and interactive storytelling application for people with aphasia. *INTERACT'07*, 221–234.
3. Decortis, F. and Rizzo, A. (2002). New Active Tools for Supporting Narrative Structures. *Personal and Ubiquitous Computing*, Vol. 6, 416-429
4. Dietz, P., & Leigh, D. (2001). DiamondTouch: a multi-user touch technology. In *Proc. UIST*, 219-226.
5. Epps, J., Lichman, S. and Wu, M. (2006). A study of hand shape use in tabletop gesture interaction. In *Ext. Abstracts CHI*, 748-753.

6. Goldin-Meadow, S. (1999). The role of gesture in communication and thinking.*Trends in cognitive sciences*, *3*(11), 419-429.
7. Goldin-Meadow, S. (2005). *Hearing gesture: How our hands help us think*. Harvard University Press.
8. Guiard. Y. (1987). Asymmetric divisoin of labor in human-skilled bimanual action: the kinematic chain as a model. *J. Motor Behavior*, 485–517.
9. Han, J. Y. (2005). Low-cost multi-touch sensing through frustrated total internal reflection. In *Proc UIST*, 115-118.
10. Hancock, M., Carpendale, S., and Cockburn, A. (2007). Shallow-depth 3D interaction: Design and evaluation of one-, two- and three-touch techniques. In *Proc. CHI*, 1147–1156.
11. Hancock M, Cate T, Carpendale S, Isenberg T. (2010). Supporting sandtray therapy on an interactive tabletop. In *Proc. CHI*, 2133–2142.
12. Hansen, J.P., Tørning, K., Johansen, A.S., Itoh, K., and Aoki, H. Gaze typing compared with input by head and hand. In Proc. *ETRA*, ACM Press (2004), 131–138.
13. Helmes, J., Cao, X., Lindley, S.E., and Sellen, A. (2009). Developing the story: designing an interactive storytelling application. In *Proc. Tabletop*, 49-52.
14. Hinckley, K., Yatani, K., Pahud, M., Coddington, N., Rodenhouse, J., Wilson, A., Benko, H., and Buxton, B. (2010). Pen + touch = new tools. In *Proc. UIST*, 27-36.
15. Hinrichs, U., and Carpendale, S. (2011). Gestures in the wild: studying multi-touch gesture sequences on interactive tabletop exhibits. In *Proc. CHI*, 3023–3032.
16. Hodges, S., Izadi, S., Butler, A., Rrustemi, A., & Buxton, B. (2007). ThinSight: versatile multi-touch sensing for thin form-factor displays. In *Proc. UIST*, 259-268.
17. Jacob, R.J.K. (1993). Eye movement-based human-computer interaction techniques: Toward non-command interfaces. *Advances in human-computer interaction* 4, 151-190.
18. Jacucci, G., Morrison, A., Richard, G. T., Kleimola, J., peltonen, P., Parisi, L., and Laitinen, T. (2010). Worlds of information: designing for engagement at a public multi-touch display. In *Proc. CHI*, 2267–2276.
19. Kalff, D. M. (2003). *Sandplay: A psychotherapeutic approach to the psyche*.
20. Kendon A. (2004). Gesture: Visible action as utterance. Cambridge U Press.
21. Martinet, A., Casiez, G., and Grisoni, L. (2012). Integrality and separability of multitouch interaction techniques in 3D manipulation tasks. *Trans. Vis. & CG* 18(3), 369–380.
22. McNeill, D. (1992). Hand and mind: What gestures reveal about thought. University of Chicago Press.
23. Morris, M.R., Huang, A., Paepcke, A. and Winograd, T. (2006). Cooperative gestures: Multi-user gestural interactions for co-located groupware. In *Proc. CHI*, 1201-1210.
24. Morris, M.R., Wobbrock, J.O., and Wilson, A.D. (2010). Understanding users' preferences for surface gestures. In *Proc. GI*, 261–268.
25. Moscovich, T. (2007). *Principles and Applications of Multi-touch Interaction*. Brown University.
26. Nielsen. M, Storring. M, Moeslund. T, and Granum, E. (2004). A procedure for developing intuitive and ergonomic gesture interfaces for HCI. *LNCS*, 2915, 409-420.
27. Norman, G. (2010). Likert scales, levels of measurement and the "laws" of statistics. Advances in health sciences education, 15(5), 625-632.
28. North. C, Dwyer. T, Lee. B, Fisher. D, Isenberg. P, Robertson. G, and Inkpen-Quinn. K. (2009). Understanding multi-touch manipulation for surface computing. In *Proc. HCI Int.*, 236–249.
29. Polkinghorne, D. (1988). *Narrative knowing and the human sciences*. Suny Press.
30. Reisman, J. L., Davidson, P. L., and Han, J. Y. (2009). A screen-space formulation for 2D and 3D direct manipulation. In *Proc. UIST*, 69–78.
31. Scott, S.D., Carpendale, M.S.T., and Inkpen, K. (2004). Territoriality in Collaborative Tabletop Workspaces. In *Proc. CSCW*, 294-303.
32. Shen, C., Ryall, K., Forlines, C., Esenther, A., Vernier, F., Everitt, K., Wu, M., Wigdor, D., Morris, M.R., Hancock, M., Tse, E. (2006). Informing the design of direct-touch tabletops. *IEEE CG&A*, 26(5), 36-46.
33. Terrenghi, L., Kirk, D., Sellen, A., Izadi, S. (2007). Affordances for Manipulation of Physical versus Digital Media on Interactive Surfaces.In *Proc. CHI*, 1157-1166.
34. Underkoffler, J., and Ishii, H. (1999). Urp: A luminous-tangible workbench for urban planning and design. In *Proc. CHI*, 386-393.
35. White, M., & Epston, D. (1990). *Narrative means to therapeutic ends*. WW Norton & Company.
36. Wobbrock, J.O., Morris, M.R. and Wilson, A.D. (2009). User-defined gestures for surface computing. In *Proc. CHI*, 1083-1092.
37. Wu, M. and Balakrishnan, R. (2003). Multi-finger and whole hand gestural interaction techniques for multi-user tabletop displays. In *Proc. UIST*, 193-202.
38. Wu, M., Shen, C., Ryall, K., Forlines, C. and Balakrishnan, R. (2006). Gesture registration, relaxation, and reuse for multi-point direct-touch surfaces. In *Proc. Tabletop*, 185-192.
39. Zancanaro, M., Cappelletti, A., & Stock, O. (2003). StoryTable: Computer supported collaborative storytelling. In *Proc. UIST Extended Abstracts*.
40. Zhai, S., Morimoto, C., and Ihde, S. (1999). Manual and gaze input cascaded (MAGIC) pointing. In *Proc CHI*, 246-253.

Web on the Wall Reloaded: Implementation, Replication and Refinement of User-Defined Interaction Sets

Michael Nebeling, Alexander Huber, David Ott and Moira C. Norrie
Department of Computer Science, ETH Zurich
{ nebeling, norrie }@inf.ethz.ch

ABSTRACT
System design using novel forms of interaction is commonly argued to be best driven by user-driven elicitation studies. This paper describes the challenges faced, and the lessons learned, in replicating Morris's Web on the Wall guessability study [6] which used Wizard of Oz to elicit multimodal interactions around Kinect. Our replication involved three steps. First, based on Morris's study, we developed a system, *Kinect Browser*, that supports 10 common browser functions using popular gestures and speech commands. Second, we developed custom experiment software for recording and analysing multimodal interactions using Kinect. Third, we conducted a study based on Morris's design. However, after first using Wizard of Oz, Kinect Browser was used in a second elicitation task, allowing us to analyse and compare the differences between the two methods. Our study demonstrates the effects of using mixed-initiative elicitation with significant differences to user-driven elicitation without system dialogue. Given the recent proliferation of guessability studies, our work extends the methodology to obtain reproducible and implementable user-defined interaction sets.

Author Keywords
guessability studies; mixed-initiative design; user-defined multimodal interaction sets.

ACM Classification Keywords
H.5.2. User Interfaces: Input devices and strategies

INTRODUCTION
Within the larger HCI community, there is currently a lot of interest in user-defined gesture, speech and multimodal interaction sets and how they may inform the design of new systems. Given the recent proliferation of guessability studies, this paper raises two important issues. First, most studies thoroughly adopt Wobbrock et al.'s [14] methodology in order to obtain a user-defined interaction set, but without considering implementation issues or involving experts. Rather, it is common to completely remove system dialogue to focus on users and their interaction preferences. The majority of studies end with reporting a suitable interaction set based on computed agreement scores and consensus thresholds. However, important aspects for system design, such as conflicts and consistency of suggested interactions, as well as the design implications of supporting alternative interactions, are often not even considered. The second important issue we address is replication. Revisiting, replicating and reproducing HCI findings is increasingly valued within our community. Still, there are many issues that make it a challenge for our discipline [2]. In particular for guessability studies, there is a lack of guidelines and tools to support replication.

This paper describes our investigation around *Kinect Browser*—a new multimodal web browser that we designed to support 10 common browser functions using Kinect. Kinect Browser was developed based on Morris's Web on the Wall study [6] that focused on eliciting multimodal interactions by potential end-users using Wizard of Oz. However, her guessability study alone was not sufficient to design our system. Despite her thorough investigation, we as system designers struggled to identify a conflict-free and consistent interaction set from her findings that would be feasible to implement. In addition, there were other fundamental questions concerning the implementation using Kinect that her study did not address. We therefore decided to replicate and extend Morris's Web on the Wall study. In addition to user-driven elicitation using Wizard of Oz, we investigate the impact of using a system both for recognition of suggested interactions and execution of associated functions. Compared to Morris's study, ours produced similar results, but also revealed potential issues of the methodology, demonstrating that it is vital to include system dialogue even in the early stages of design.

This paper is mainly about the design process of Kinect Browser. Being a functional prototype of a Kinect-based web browser, it differs from previous research such as [4] that targeted developers with the goal of providing a JavaScript library for processing Kinect's data streams within the browser. While our system in itself offers a valuable contribution, we see three primary contributions in our work. First, we add to the growing body of knowledge surrounding the optimal methodology for user-driven elicitation studies, such as those popularised by Wobbrock et al. [14]. Our elicitation study is the first to pay attention to what the system can do while asking users what they would like to do. Second, our paper also provides data about popular gestures and speech commands for a living room TV setting. The data was collected using new tools specifically developed for recording and post-hoc analysis of Kinect's depth, video and audio streams. We

ITS 2014, November 16–19, 2014, Dresden, Germany.

http://dx.doi.org/10.1145/2669485.2669497

Source	Methods (Size)	Focus; Main Findings/Contributions
Wobbrock et al. [14]	Think-aloud + Video + Logs ($N = 20$)	**user-defined gestures;** 27 referents with author-rated complexity scores; user agreement scores; taxonomy of surface gestures
Nacenta et al. [9]	Custom experiment software ($N_1 = 6$, $N_2 = 9$, $N_3 = 12$)	**gesture memorability;** user-defined better than pre-designed or random gestures; differences due to association errors rather than gesture form errors
Oh et al. [11]	Think-aloud + Video + Logs + \$N recogniser ($N = 20$)	**personal gestures;** focus on familiar rather than novel gestures; constrained by gesture recognition issues; proposal for mixed-initiative gesture definition
Morris [6]	Wizard of Oz ($N = 25$; 11 pairs, 1 triad)	**multimodal interactions;** 15 referents; mostly speech, rarely multimodal—instead gesture synonyms; max-consensus and consensus-distinct ratio

Table 1. Previous user-driven elicitation studies that influenced the design of the one presented in this paper.

share both the code and the data with the community. We consider this generally useful to those developing Kinect-based systems. Finally, the paper offers a contribution in the form of replication of prior work from our research community, namely Morris's Web on the Wall study [6]. Understanding which aspects of her findings did and did not replicate in our study is interesting for generalisability. In particular, we discuss using Wizard of Oz for user-driven elicitation, focusing on issues of reproducibility and implications for design.

RELATED WORK

One of the most important design challenges for Kinect Browser is the rich design space when it comes to gesture, speech and multimodal interaction sets using Kinect. In building Kinect Browser, we felt that there is currently still a lack of guidelines and tools to address this issue in a way that is both reproducible and technically sound. Table 1 gives an overview of the studies that formed the basis of our own investigation, summarising their methods and main findings.

Wobbrock et al. [14] were the first to suggest a study design that focuses on the user by excluding the system dialogue from the investigation. Their elicitation task was based on showing the *effect* of a gesture, and then prompting users for the *cause* by asking them to perform suitable one or two-hand gestures. As the suggestions were quite diverse, they provide a first agreement metric and user scores together with a taxonomy of surface gestures. The other studies are based on this methodology for elicitation tasks. With the exception of Morris's [6], most studies are focused on gestural interaction and commonly use the think-aloud protocol and video analysis in combination with user logs. Also our study adopts a similar design, but additionally uses Kinect for both data collection and analysis. While our intention is to support reproducibility and help build a corpus of multimodal interactions using Kinect by sharing our data with the community, it is often not clearly described for previous studies whether and how they made use of any collected data, even when touch surfaces [8], mobile phone accelerometers [12], or Kinect sensors [3] were used as additional recording tools.

Previous studies have shown several advantages of user-defined gesture sets. For example, Nacenta et al. [9] conducted three experiments on gesture memorability, showing higher rates for user-defined gestures compared to pre-designed and stock gesture sets. Interestingly, the relatively high differences in recall rates were due to association errors rather than gesture form errors. In their study, user-defined gesture sets were also preferred and found easier to learn and remember. Although not formally assessed, memorability also played a role in our study, as users had to remember and repeatedly perform custom multimodal interactions.

The study by Oh et al. [11] focused on gesture customisation. Even though participants were encouraged to iteratively personalise gestures, they generally focused on the familiar rather than creating novel gestures. Post-hoc analysis showed relatively high recognition rates for a multistroke extension of \$1 recogniser [15], but users' design choices were sometimes biased by misconceptions about the recogniser's abilities. To improve the gesture creation process, the authors suggest a mixed-initiative approach in which the process is monitored and, once an ambiguous gesture has been recognised, users would be prompted for, or automatically suggested, modifications to improve the gesture. In our investigation on Kinect Browser, we implemented such a mixed-initiative approach by adding a task in which users defined, tested and *refined* their multimodal interactions while using Kinect.

Our design decisions for Kinect Browser were based on the observations made by Morris [6]. She adopted the study design proposed by Wobbrock et al. [14] for eliciting speech commands and multimodal interactions in addition to gestures for web browsing on a living room TV. Along the scenario of planning a shared weekend activity, Wizard of Oz was employed to demonstrate 15 common web browser functions, showing the effect of each function and asking users to define an interaction that may have caused it. A key aspect addressed in her paper is how to measure consensus among participants, which becomes an issue due to the many degrees of freedom in which multimodal interactions can be defined. Specifically, the paper provides two new agreement metrics: *max-consensus* and the *consensus-distinct ratio.* The first results in the percentage of participants that suggested the most popular interaction, while the latter represents the number of interactions that achieved a consensus threshold of two in proportion to the total number of proposed interactions.

In her study, both gesture and speech seemed effective. Speech was most commonly suggested, followed by gesture, while multimodal suggestions composed of gesture *and* speech were rare. Rather, one of the key observations was that the same function was triggered by multiple independent interactions of the same user, instead suggesting *multimodal synonyms* using either gesture *or* speech to invoke the same action. This was explained by shortcomings of both modalities. First, gesture input had perceived drawbacks related to

Figure 1. Kinect Browser was implemented as a "browser-in-browser" interface, but always operated in fullscreen so that the actual host browser, Firefox, was not visible to participants.

ergonomics and exertion. But also speech interaction was often regarded as potentially disturbing to other members of the household, while ambient noise and conversations might impact speech recognition.

Most of her participants assumed that their hands would be tracked similar to using a computer mouse, and basic interactions such as clicking links, scrolling or zooming were based on mouse and touch interaction paradigms. In addition to typical click and press gestures for confirming selections, also holding positions for a certain amount of time, i.e. dwell, was frequently suggested. We considered all these proposals to be suitable for Kinect Browser. While her participants were free to sit, stand, or otherwise move about, all of them remained seated for the elicitation. Likewise, Kinect Browser is currently optimised for seated mode, and so are the gestures which are currently limited to the upper body.

However, for several reasons, it was not straightforward to build on Morris's study and learn from her suggested design implications. First, her study did not actually involve the use of Kinect and consider essential browser functions such as scrolling and zooming. Second, not all results were conclusive. For example, the elicited interaction set is not conflict-free and still requires adjustments to individual user preferences. Third, some of her design decisions may have biased some of the results. For example, users were influenced by their previous experience with the existing desktop browser that was used for the Wizard of Oz parts. Finally, users were recruited in pairs and worked as a team to propose interactions, which may impact the study protocol and ultimately exclude individual use scenarios. These issues together motivated us to conduct a study of our own.

KINECT BROWSER

Although specifically designed for our elicitation study, Kinect Browser is a functional prototype that can be used for browsing most existing sites on the web without any modifications. The core of Kinect Browser consists of three components: a *browser-in-browser interface* supporting common browser functions (Figure 1), a *gesture and speech recogniser* based on Kinect, and a *multimodal configuration* mapping gestures and/or speech commands to browser functions.

The interface of Kinect Browser is shown in Figure 1. Similar to existing browsers, Kinect Browser leaves most of the screen real estate to the web site, but adds a special function area on top. Our function area consists of a set of icon buttons that can be associated with browser functions, e.g. for going back and forward in the history or to the previous and next tab. The remainder of the function area is filled with tabs. The area in the top-right corner gives feedback about the connection status, and can also be used to connect to, or disconnect from, Kinect. Therefore, Kinect Browser's design is kept rather simple and does not resemble any specific web browser in order to reduce bias.

Our current implementation supports 10 browser functions: Click Link, Scroll, Zoom In/Out, Go Back/Forward, Select Tab, Next/Previous Tab, and Reload Page. This means that most of the 15 referents proposed in [6] are covered by our implementation. In addition, we also included support for scrolling and zooming as essential browser functions, and explicitly distinguished selecting a specific tab and switching to the next or previous tab. In further distinguishing Morris's Switch Tab referent, we wanted to raise potential conflicts with gestures and speech commands for going back and forward in the navigation history, and study whether and how users would aim to resolve any conflicts. At the same time, we ignored advanced referents such as Open Link in Separate Tab, Select Region, Bookmark Page, Close Tab and others requiring text input. Text input using Kinect, as required for the Search Engine Query or Enter URL referents, is an important research issue of its own out of scope of this paper. In a first step, we aimed to support all essential browser functions required for navigating within and between pages to assess the basic browsing experience based on multimodal interactions.

Kinect Browser tracks both hands independently, showing two cursors for the left and right hand on the screen. Hand positions within a 50x50cm interaction window centred on the Kinect origin are mapped to screen coordinates. This setting may require calibration with regards to different screen and user characteristics (size, position, distance, etc.). Based on an iterative design process and inspired from Morris [6], we added support for 25 interactions: 9 gestures (dwell/grip/press, drag up/down, flick hand left/right, two-hand pinch open/close) and 16 speech commands ("scroll up/down", "zoom [in/out]", "[go] back/forward", "tab #", "next/previous tab", "refresh/reload [page]"). We complemented our recogniser with $1 [15] to support unistroke gestures, e.g. circle hand. This required a mapping from 3D space to 2D, which we currently achieve by only mapping the x and y-axes. Note that we did not add explicit recognition support for interactions comprising both gesture *and* speech, as these were rarely proposed in Morris's study.

To adapt to users' multimodal interaction preferences, Kinect Browser currently builds on a simple configuration tool in which variables can be toggled and set to the desired values.

STUDY DESIGN

Morris [6] used a three-part study based on *interviews* concerning possible scenarios for web browsing on a living room TV using Kinect, an *elicitation task*, and a *post-study questionnaire*. Our study was composed of five parts with two elicitation tasks followed by a task in which Kinect Browser was used individually and tested in its anticipated setting.

Questionnaires and Tasks

We used a *pre-study questionnaire* in the beginning of the study asking participants to rate likeliness of the scenarios and importance of browser interactions proposed by Morris, as well as collecting background information such as prior influences in terms of operating systems and browsers, knowledge of Kinect, participants' handedness, age and gender.

The actual elicitation was conducted in two parts. *Task 1* was based on the elicitation task of Morris using Wizard of Oz to collect interactions proposed by participants for the 10 browser functions supported in Kinect Browser. Like Morris, we told, and always reminded, participants that they could use any combination of gesture, speech or combined input, and that they should not worry about the capabilities of Kinect, as the experimenter would act as the Wizard of Oz and ensure that the system "reacted" properly to their interactions. As in previous user-driven elicitation studies, for each function, the experimenter stated the function name and demonstrated

Figure 2. Study setup consisting of a Kinect and a large screen for Kinect Browser, as well as a camera for video recording.

the *effect*, then asked the participant to suggest interactions as a *cause* of this function to be executed. We used Kinect for recording and tracking in the background, but similar to Wobbrock et al. [14], no feedback was provided and no interactions were triggered by the system. When participants demonstrated an interaction, the experimenter used the mouse and/or keyboard to produce the result of the browser function. As this task was partly designed to replicate Morris's study, we will use it later to compare and correlate the findings.

Task 2 followed a similar design, but the goal was now to produce a personal configuration for Kinect Browser. In this task, Kinect Browser replaced the Wizard part and was step-wise adapted to react to preferred interactions. Again, participants elicited interactions for each browser function. When participants suggested multiple interactions or interactions that Kinect Browser was not able to recognise, the experimenter suggested modifications to the suggested interaction, or the closest interaction implemented by Kinect Browser. Participants were then asked whether they would still prefer the interaction they suggested initially, or would like to switch to the one available in the system. As participants suggested interactions for each browser function, the experimenter supplied the necessary settings to Kinect Browser, and asked participants to demonstrate the interaction and test whether the system reacted as expected.

The common scenario for both tasks was to plan a (shared) weekend activity, in our example a trip to the Rhine Falls, where participants were asked to look up facts on the Rhine Falls web site[1] as well as Wikipedia. All suggested interactions were scored according to preferences. Each task concluded with a *post-task qustionnaire* based on Morris's post-study questionnaire [6], collecting subjective feedback on both elicitation tasks, allowing us to check for differences.

Technical Setup

The setup used for the study is illustrated in Figure 2. A dual-monitor setup was used to show Kinect Browser on the participant's screen and all interactions as they were tracked by Kinect on the experimenter's screen. The participant's screen was a ca. 63" projection surface with 1024x768 resolution. The Kinect was set to seated mode and placed 3.5 metres

[1] http://www.rheinfall.ch/home

away in front of the couch where participants were seated at 5 metres distance to the screen. Morris's original study was conducted using a 63" TV at 1600x1200 pixels at 3.5 metres distance. We used the same distance between Kinect and participants in our study, but the distance to the screen was increased to counterbalance the lower resolution.

In addition to creating video recordings of participants' interactions, we used custom experiment software specifically developed for our multimodal elicitation study to be able to record skeletal tracking information from Kinect together with audio and video. We also added logging to Kinect Browser, allowing simultaneous recording of browser interactions and Kinect data. Log files can be loaded into the experiment software for visualising all tracked events on a timeline. After the study, we used the data to produce skeletal tracking statistics and correlated it to user feedback.

Participants

Like Morris, we recruited 25 participants in order to enable comparison in terms of the max-consensus and consensus-distinct metrics. The median age of our sample was 26.5 years; 6 were female, and all participants right handed. Rather than doing the study in pairs, we conducted individual, 1-hour sessions with all participants, but allowed for discussions of interaction proposals. While this carries the potential of altering the results, it was necessary for Task 2 where otherwise specific skeleton selection strategies and a co-browsing interface [7] would have been required.

Also in contrast to Morris's study, our participants had little to no experience with Kinect. The idea here was to reduce potential bias towards certain interactions based on conventions emerging in the gaming community, which was noted by Morris. The majority of participants stated that they use Chrome or Firefox on Windows or Mac, followed by Android, iOS and Linux with their respective web browsers, which we collected as other potential influences. Again as in Morris's study, our pre-study questionnaire indicated that most participants could identify with the scenario of choosing a movie to see, followed by finding and viewing photos online, and looking up trivia and facts (all on average above 3 on a 5-point Likert scale). Other scenarios proposed by Morris, such as using social media applications and research for work or school projects, scored much lower for our participants, which may indicate further differences between the two samples. Additional scenarios frequently suggested by our participants included trip planning, which was the scenario used for the remainder of the study, as well as watching videos on Youtube, or checking news web sites. The most important browser functions, as rated by participants, included going back and forward in the history (median 7 on a 7-point Likert scale), tabbed browsing, bookmarks, and search (all median 6). Other functions explored by Morris, but that we did not include, such as finding or selecting content within the page, seemed less important (median 5).

RESULTS

This section presents the results of our investigation. We start with our participants' preferred interactions. This is directly followed by feedback and observations from our two elicitation tasks as well as user feedback on Kinect Browser. Special emphasis will then be given to the post-task ratings in our study and how they compare to Morris's post-study ratings.

Referent	Interaction	# Web on the Wall	# Kinect Browser Task 1	# Kinect Browser Task 2
Click Link	hand-as-mouse + click/grip	7	11	18
	hand-as-mouse + dwell	6	0	0
	hand-as-mouse + push/press	N/A	5	1
Scroll Page	arm out and move same	(0-2)	11	2
	arm out and move opposite		7	0
	grip and drag opposite	N/A	5	17
	grip and drag same		1	6
Zoom In	two-hand pinch	(1-2)	18	12
	"zoom"	1	0	0
	"zoom in"	0	3	9
Zoom Out	two-hand pinch	(1-2)	17	11
	"zoom out"	0	4	9
Go Back	"back"	7	3	5
	flick hand (arrow)	7	5	4
	flick hand (book)	4	10	9
	"go back"	N/A	4	7
Go Forward	"forward"	6	3	6
	flick hand (arrow)	5	5	4
	flick hand (book)	5	9	9
	"go forward"	N/A	5	6
Select Tab	click tab	7	14	13
	"tab <number>"	3	3	6
	"tab <title>"	N/A	6	2
Next Tab	"next tab"	4	2	8
	flick hand (book)	3	4	2
	select tab	N/A	10	12
Previous Tab	"previous tab"	N/A	2	7
	flick hand (book)		4	2
	select tab		9	10
Reload Page	"refresh", "refresh page"	9	4	5
	"reload", "reload page"	N/A	6	10
	move hand in spiral motion	3	8	9

Figure 3. Preferred mapping of browser functions to gesture/speech interactions with number of occurrences according to Morris's and our own study. For both studies, the highest-scoring referent(s) for each metric are indicated with grey shading (consensus threshold 3).

Preferred Browser Control Techniques

Figure 3 shows popular mappings based on Morris's consensus metrics. As in Morris's study, participants suggested a range of gesture-based and speech-based interactions, and there was no uniform interaction set. Prior to the study, also the authors scored their preferences based on their experience of designing the system. Some of their choices matched several popular mappings. Yet, none of our 25 participants, and also none of the authors, proposed the same configuration. Also nobody suggested the one that would result from associating only the most popular interaction with every browser function. Nevertheless, there is good correlation of our results with Morris's in terms of the most popular interactions.

With a total of 449 interactions in Task 1 and 458 interactions in Task 2, participants proposed an almost equal number of interactions in both tasks independent of the Wizard of

Referent	Task 1 (Gesture)	Task 1 (Speech)	Task 1 (Multi...)	Task 2 (Gesture)	Task 2 (Speech)	Task 2 (Multi...)
Click Link	60%	16%	24%	82%	9%	9%
Scroll Page	80%	20%	0%	79%	21%	0%
Zoom In	66%	34%	0%	50%	50%	0%
Zoom Out	67%	33%	0%	55%	45%	0%
Zoom In/Out	67%	33%	0%	52%	48%	0%
Go Back	62%	38%	0%	56%	44%	0%
Go Forward	63%	37%	0%	57%	43%	0%
Select Tab	60%	40%	0%	59%	41%	0%
Next Tab	69%	26%	5%	54%	46%	0%
Previous Tab	71%	23%	6%	54%	46%	0%
Switch Tab	66%	30%	3%	56%	44%	0%
Reload Page	56%	44%	0%	45%	55%	0%
Total	65.26%	30.73%	4.01%	59.61%	39.30%	1.09%

Figure 4. Proportions of 449 proposed interactions in Task 1 and 458 in Task 2 showing the overall preference for gesture for both tasks and a gradual transition to speech when actually using the Kinect in Task 2.

Oz or mixed-initiative elicitation method. Despite the large amount of proposed interactions, our current implementation of Kinect Browser already covered 691 (76%) of them. This means that more than 3/4 of the interaction proposals by users were fully supported and could already be tested. Not covered were the small amount of multimodal interactions and some, usually distinct, gestures and speech commands.

Interestingly, in Task 2, participants tended to refine their interactions or made slightly different proposals compared to Task 1. The majority of participants only learned in Task 2 about the capabilities and limitations of the Kinect sensor and many argued that this prompted them to adjust their interactions. However, the preferred interactions typically stayed the same. As we will discuss later, the main difference between the proposals in Task 1 and Task 2 is in the Scroll Page referent were participants commonly switched from the arm-out-and-move to the grip-and-drag interaction using their hands.

In terms of modality, the preferred interactions in Morris's study were composed of 56% speech, 41% gesture, and 3% multimodal commands. As shown in Figure 4, our participants most commonly suggested gesture (Task 1: 65%, Task2: 60%), then speech (Task 1: 31%, Task 2: 39%), and also rarely multimodal (Task 1: 4%, Task 2: 1%). Similar to Morris's study, participants noted several drawbacks for both modalities. In particular in view of scenarios such as listening to music, talking to a colleague on the phone, having friends over, etc., speech was considered inferior (P9: *"This has to work with gestures, or it's not gonna work at all for me"*).

Overall, there was the trend of using gesture for more frequent functions. One exception was P10 who advocated the assignment of voice commands for more frequent functions, and gesture for less frequently used functions, since speech input seemed "surprinsingly" robust. As in Morris's study, participants commonly defined *multimodal synonyms*, stating that the preferred interaction depends on the situation, and that they would like to have both gesture commands and speech commands available. Still, P21 noted, *"there should be the possibility to have an only gesture/speech-based set of actions"*, which is in fact a possible configuration.

Figure 4 also shows the use of interaction modalities on a per-function basis. For within-page functions such as clicking, scrolling and zooming, gesture was predominant, while between-page functions such as going back and forward or switching tabs were often almost equally controlled with speech. The Click Link and Switch Tab referents were the only ones that were associated with multimodal interactions. For Click Link, this involved pointing with the hands and then clicking by saying "click", "select" or "open", while for Switch Tab, some participants suggested to say "tab" before flicking the hand left or right to navigate through tabs.

Post-Task Ratings

Figure 5 shows the average ratings of Morris's and our participants for Morris's post-study questionnaire [6]. We will first compare her results with our Task 1, before discussing differences between Tasks 1 and 2, and our observations.

In Task 1, we obtained similarly positive ratings for questions on whether participants would enjoy operating the browser in this manner, whether they had fun, whether gesture commands seemed effective, and whether the interactions felt natural. The other ratings, most notably the one that concerned the effectiveness of speech commands, were considerably lower. We could not test for statistical differences since not all ratings were reported in [6].

We also critically note that several participants first hesitated in answering some of the questions in Task 1 (e.g. P9: *"I did not operate the browser in this task."*). P10 commented: *"I just said what I want in this task so that would be how agreed or disagreed I was in above questions"*. The questions on whether they felt tired and physically uncomfortable were even deemed inappropriate by four participants (e.g. P3: *"Only proposing gestures and showing them once is not enough to feel tired or uncomfortable (at least for me)"*). These critical remarks relate to the Wizard of Oz method, specifically, the fact that there was no system dialogue.

In Task 1, participants frequently indicated a preference for gesture rather than speech. Many explained that it would be difficult to say which gesture would be better, as it was not "really possible" to see whether the gesture could actually be recognised. P25 added that *"Kinect will need to be clever"*. Then, after testing the gesture recogniser in Task 2, there was often a shift towards speech commands (P9: *"I am starting to like speech more now since it works"*). P5 commented: *"Some of the gestures felt physically uncomfortable; speech commands seemed to perform better, but I think I lack practice using gestures."* P20 criticised the lack of system dialogue especially in Task 2: *"Give more visual feedback!"*

A Friedman test to evaluate differences in the post-task ratings of Task 1 and Task 2 was significant ($p < .001$). Follow-up pairwise comparisons using Wilcoxon tests confirmed that operating the browser in this manner was significantly less enjoyable in Task 2 ($p < .03$). Also gesture commands seemed significantly less effective in Task 2 ($p < .001$). Although there were similar differences for speech commands, they were not significant. Notable is the increase in the tired and physically uncomfortable ratings in Task 2, where the former differences were significant ($p < .01$).

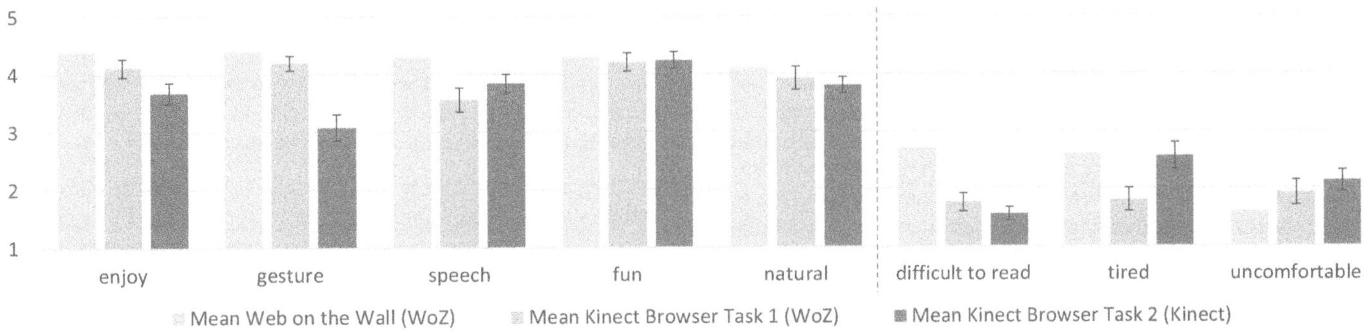

Figure 5. Mean post-study/task ratings for Morris's and our study on 5-point Likert scale (error bars show standard error)

Finally, although users were repeatedly asked to suggest gesture, speech, or multimodal interactions independent of whether the Wizard or Kinect were responsible for recognition, multimodal suggestions were more frequent in Task 1.

We note that the fixed order starting with Task 1 was required to make sure we properly replicate Morris's study. Participants were asked to fill in questionnaires and offered a break between tasks. Although unlikely, there might be some bias regarding the method and some ratings.

Feedback and Observations during Elicitation

Our detailed observations relate to pointing and clicking, use of gesture and speech, and roles of hands.

Pointing and Clicking

All participants except for one suggested using their hands for directly pointing at the screen, i.e. in x/y direction; P15 instead suggested pointing on a horizontal surface along the x/z-axes. The preferences for activating targets were less clear. Most participants felt that the click/grip gestures were most efficient and less tiring, but the many false-positives for KinectInteractions' Grip gesture caused frustration. The dwell and push gestures were generally considered problematic, as they seemed more difficult to control, more time consuming, and often accidentally clicked links. In particular, dwell caused confusion when one hand was actively used to target, while the other was already hovering a link. While the Wizard was able to distinguish which hand was actively used for pointing, our system considered both hands if they were inside the interaction window. The majority of participants expressed that it was generally difficult to select a particular target independent of which gesture was used. To avoid cursor movement during selection, multimodal interactions hand-as-mouse + "click/select/open" were preferred by 14 participants in Task 1 and 5 in Task 2.

Use of Gesture

Prior influences from touch were evident in almost all proposed gestures. Participants commonly tried to adapt touch gestures using finger movements to hand gestures using arm movements. At the same time, they frequently paid attention to potential conflicts in the suggested interaction set. For example, similar to Morris's study, some participants initially suggested to extend an arm out to the side or in front of their body and moving it up and down for the Scroll Page referent. However, they soon realised the potential for conflicts as they suggested similar interactions for the Click Link and Go Back/Forward referents. The majority then commonly suggested the grip + drag up/down gesture also implemented in Kinect Browser. Scrolling in the opposite direction to the hand movement was generally preferred and considered most similar to touch scrolling on smartphones.

Another common theme was to define mirror gestures for function pairs Scroll Up/Down, Zoom In/Out, Go Back/Forward, and Next/Previous Tab with essentially the same gesture being suggested, but then performed in opposite direction. On the other hand, this sometimes also made gesture recall more difficult and even caused conflicts. For example, similar to Morris's study, participants typically argued for either the *book* or *arrow* metaphor when suggesting flick hand gestures for going back and forward in the history or for switching tabs. Yet, when asked to demonstrate the gestures repeatedly, the metaphors were sometimes confused and participants first had to remind themselves of how flick scrolling was actually in common touch interfaces.

Roles of Hands

Most participants suggested symmetric use of hands so that they could flexibly switch between hands. Participants commonly started using the dominant hand for pointing. But they frequently switched hands, in particular, when they had to select targets on the other half of the screen. Some participants assigned opposing roles to hands. For example, P4 defined Next/Previous Tab by pointing with the right hand to the right-top corner and with the left to the left-top corner, respectively. Flick gestures were typically preferred for the Go Back/Forward rather than the Next/Previous Tab referents due to seemingly higher frequency of use. Tabs were instead frequently just clicked or controlled using speech. Still, four participants in Task 1 and 2 in Task 2 wanted to use the flick gestures for both referent pairs. To resolve conflicts, they assigned different roles to hands or used bimanual interaction. To give an example for the first case, P13 and P20 used the left hand for tabs and the right hand for history navigation. Alternatively, P3 defined flick gestures with one hand for Go Back/Forward and two hands for Next/Previous Tab.

Use of Speech

Similar to Morris's study, participants commonly used signifiers such as "go", "history" or "tab" to trigger the function pairs Go Back/Forward and Next/Previous Tab. While this was considered a natural command for the former, it felt less natural to say "tab next/previous" vs. "next/previous tab", but still more consistent in terms of the overall command set. Yet, also speech recognition had drawbacks as it was frequently considered *"too slow"* and not all functions could equally be triggered using speech. For example, using hands for scrolling and zooming allowed for continuous scroll and zoom, while the "scroll up/down" and "zoom in/out" commands scrolled page-wise and zoomed in steps. P20 considered selecting tabs or links difficult for non-English titles.

Discussion

Overall, the feedback on Kinect Browser was quite positive. All participants could identify with using Kinect for web browsing in the studied setting, and most commonly considered it for lean-back, but also purposeful, use [5], as in our trip planning scenario. Generally, the supported interactions seemed a good fit, but not all were equally easy to perform or felt as effective. Participants particularly appreciated that Kinect Browser was ready to support most of the interactions they suggested and therefore able to adapt to their personal multimodal configurations for common browser functions.

All aspects of our system were implemented using Kinect's SDK and the KinectInteraction toolkit. Therefore, the issues noted by participants should not be attributed to poor implementation. Since our study was conducted with state-of-the-art input sensing techniques, the issues we faced and were able to study thanks to our system are likely to be faced by others. The majority of issues related to accuracy of skeletal tracking, false positives in gesture recognition (e.g. grip), and minor issues with speech recognition. As a common effect, we observed frequent switches to speech modality. P9: *"Gestures did not really work and caused a lot of frustration. I feel like I would need to concentrate more on the gestures than actually browsing."* P3: *"To perform the given tasks, I used more voice commands than previously anticipated, since they seemed to work better for me than gestures. This is also due to issues with Kinect tracking my hands (jumping dots, jittering)."* Participants attributed the issues to the Kinect sensor, our recogniser, or both (e.g. P13: *"As soon as Kinect accuracy gets better, this will be a really fun tool. Currently, the tool sadly confuses several interactions."*), but also felt that training might be required (P13: *"Like with any new system, it takes some time and exercise to get the gestures right."*).

To follow this up, we used our experiment software to produce accuracy statistics and correlated them with Kinect Browser's gesture/speech logs and our video analysis. On average, only 84% percent of processed joints were successfully tracked, and this varied by 19% between participants. Although it seemed during the study that participants frequently resorted to speech commands when skeletal tracking and gesture recognition were poor, based on the collected data, there was no such correlation. The fact that gesture was still predominant despite the gradual transition to speech was due to the fact that frequent browser functions such as Click Link required gestures and because participants often started out using gesture and, only after some time, switched to speech.

Nonetheless, pointing and clicking might be improved by adding common smoothing and filtering techniques that we have not implemented yet. For example, gesture recognition rates may be improved using more advanced relaxation techniques [16]. Other techniques from perspective-based [10], finger-based [13] and proxemic interaction [1] may also be adopted to improve the tracking based on Kinect.

While Kinect Browser can already be used with many web sites, not all requirements are fully supported. For example, text input remains an open issue, as our study was mostly concerned with within-page and between-page navigation. At this stage, bookmarks can be loaded from the host browser. In the future, our implementation could be extended with speech commands, or a specific text input interface, to enter URLs and other data in the browser or current web page, e.g. for login. We refrained from defining speech commands for all links and tabs, although this was often assumed by participants, and is also technically possible. We could automatically generate Kinect grammar once a page has been loaded, but this might drastically increase the potential for conflicts with other speech commands. It is also no general solution, as not all interactive elements are always properly labelled.

REFLECTION

We have presented our investigation around Kinect Browser, a new multimodal web browser using Kinect developed based on Morris's Web on the Wall [6] and our own study. We will use this section to reflect on our investigation. We will start with the contribution and issues of generalisability, applicability and limitations. We will then elaborate on the lessons learned. After highlighting again the main findings of our work, we will conclude with a set of guidelines and concrete recommendations for future elicitation studies.

Contribution and Limitations

There are three important parts to this research that distinguish it from prior work. First, a key aspect of our work was to develop an actual system based on Morris's guessability study as an example. While we found her study very valuable and were also successful in developing Kinect Browser, going through the process and trying to apply her findings during development was not straightforward and posed several challenges that we had not previously anticipated. Second, we wanted to investigate reproducibility by modelling Task 1 on top of Morris's study. Our community struggles with replication [2] and our work allows result comparison across papers, something that is rarely possible to this extent. Third, by deviating from the common protocol and involving an actual system in Task 2, we wanted to explore the effects of using a mixed-initiative elicitation method. Our hope with this was to first obtain an unframed interaction set, but then also expose participants to the technology for which the study was conducted and see how they would act on recognition issues and aim to resolve any conflicts concerning their proposals.

While focusing on a first example of system inclusion in the elicitation process, we believe that many of the effects we observed would generalise to other domains, other types of systems and systems with varying levels of implementation.

First, our system was designed for multimodal web browsing using Kinect. However, many of the proposed interactions are not specific to web browsing as they concern basic tasks, such as clicking, scrolling and zooming, as well as going back and forward in the history or tabs, which are common to most applications (undo/redo, window management, etc.).

Moreover, many of the participants' proposals seemed to favour gesture-based interaction and were inspired by their previous use of touch interfaces. Similar to Morris, we would argue that, by opening our investigation to multimodal interaction using Kinect rather than limiting ourselves to touch surfaces as in previous studies [8, 14], we in turn opened the design space for a more general interaction set. Further, we showed that most proposals can be implemented using Kinect, but this is just one example of a low-cost input tracking system that we used for demonstration.

Finally, our investigation benefited from Morris's prior work since we anticipated most interaction proposals thanks to her findings. While important for the replication aspect of our paper, it might be mistaken as a limitation given that elicitation studies are usually conducted as a first step where there are no prior results. We critically note that Morris's study was not a prerequisite and that it is in our methodology that a useful basis for implementing the system is formed (cf. Task 1).

Lessons Learned

Apart from the accepted issues of elicitation studies discussed by Wobbrock et al. [14] and Morris [6], we believe that our study revealed two important issues. First, similar to Morris, Task 1 of our study was based on Wizard of Oz, relying on the experimenter rather than the system. Second, as suggested by Wobbrock et al. and commonly done by others, system dialogue was removed, but the lack of feedback was noted as an issue. We elaborate on both issues in more detail below.

Wizard of Oz was necessary to simulate parts of the system that were not implemented yet due to the lack of technical support, e.g. finger tracking using Kinect, or insufficient design knowledge, e.g. popular gesture or speech commands. However, we felt during the study that many potential sources of bias may lie in the nature of the method itself. For example, when scrolling or zooming were shown as continuous actions using the mouse wheel, participants were more likely to suggest gestures. After showing them as discrete actions using Page Up/Down and +/- keys, participants tended to suggest speech commands. Likewise, when asked for speech commands for the Reload referent, participants were likely to just repeat "reload", making it a popular suggestion. Moreover, in Task 1, participants commonly paid less attention to gesture form and potential errors, as they relied on the Wizard to react properly to their interactions. Although participants often suggested the same gestures in both tasks, our recogniser, which we had always running in the background, showed generally lower recognition rates in Task 1.

The use of Wizard of Oz for the purpose of eliciting multimodal interactions therefore also incurs a certain cost for system design as it may not be suitable to obtain accurate interaction proposals. One interesting new idea is to use a second study participant as the Wizard instead of the experimenter. Lee et al. [3] elicited freehand gestural interaction for navigating Google Earth maps using pairs of users where one would function as the *performer* and the other as the *recogniser*. Although this introduces another variable to the study design, they generally observed a good interplay of performer and recogniser. Interestingly, even human intelligence of the recogniser was not always sufficient to correctly interpret the interactions intended by the performer. This led to strong effects such as slower and larger gestures for some pairs.

The most important aspect of our investigation is the idea of dividing the elicitation process into two parts, first using a human recogniser and then a system-based recogniser. This mixed-initiative design allowed participants to first think without any technological constraints, but then also get a feel for the technology and perhaps reconsider their interaction proposals to make them feasible for implementation. To our knowledge, our study is the first to embed a system in the elicitation task. This is in contrast to Wobbrock et al. [14] and many follow-up studies that commonly argued for excluding system dialogue from the investigation in order to observe users' unrevised behaviour, and then drive system design to accommodate it. Yet, by including a system such as Kinect Browser, we were able to see interesting effects that we consider equally important and crucial to drive system design. Our lessons learned mainly manifest at three levels.

First, previous elicitation studies commonly sought consensus among participants in terms of proposed interaction sets. For referents where consensus was low, the suggested way out was to use on-screen widgets [14] or multimodal synonyms [6]. However, this is not always possible, especially not for all functions. Therefore, as also argued by others, we designed the system in a way that it can easily be adapted to support multiple alternative interactions per referent.

Second, awareness of users' *revised* behaviour, and being able to observe how they may try to work around issues, may be crucial. For example, most participants initially argued for gesture as the primary interaction modality, but gradually shifted towards speech. This demonstrated a plausible escape strategy that was only possible since we considered multimodal synonyms right from the beginning. This also echoed in significant differences between Tasks 1 and 2 in terms of whether gestures felt effective for controlling the system. It was not clear whether this change in behaviour was mostly due to poor recognition or lack of training. We then developed statistics based on our experiment software and video analysis to distinguish issues related to Kinect and our implementation. As we found no strong correlation, we might agree with those participants that felt more need for training.

Third, using the system rather than just relying on the Wizard raised the issue of designing appropriate feedback for users. Similar to Wobbrock et al. [14], our system provided no feedback to users other than showing the *effect* of their interaction as soon as it was successfully recognised. This was the same in both conditions not to increase bias towards one or the other elicitation method. Yet, this had the consequence that, in contrast to when the Wizard was responsible for recognition, there was only little feedback on Kinect's tracking accuracy. This was noted as an issue (P22: *"It would be great to have an indicator that shows how 'good' the Kinect sees me.*"). In the future, our accuracy statistics could provide live feedback on uncertainties in the tracking, allowing users to learn how they may be overcome by adjusting their pose.

Guidelines and Recommendations

Based on our experience with mixed-initiative elicitation, we offer the following guidelines and recommendations.

Draft the system: First, we find it necessary to involve a system in elicitation studies even though the key idea of obtaining a user-defined interaction set remains the same. Elicitation exercises should attempt to cover all referents required for a system to work, including basic ones such as pointing, clicking, scrolling and zooming. Clearly, the quality and accuracy of results achievable with mixed-initiative elicitation depend on the state of the implementation. While current software and hardware limitations may have a negative effect, it was particularly interesting to see how participants coped with recognition issues and explored alternative interactions.

Make it adaptable: We developed Kinect Browser in a way that it clearly separates the system's behaviour from the recognition code that triggers it. Specifically, we implemented 10 common browser functions and 25 separate interactions. This enabled us to configure the same function for different gestures and speech commands that may or may not be combined. Per configuration, Kinect Browser supports 1,585 possible mappings of interactions to browser functions so that every function is associated with at least one interaction. In principle, the recognition code can be shared, or varied, between implementations and even completely replaced to experiment with other technologies than Kinect.

Share code and data: Finally, elicitation studies should be recorded and the data shared with the community. Our review of the literature showed that this is rarely the case. But it would make results more practical and reproducible. With our custom experiment software, we developed a first set of tools for recording Kinect data and analysing user-defined interaction sets. These tools prove not only useful for our study, but could in the future also be used by others for studying and sharing their user-defined interaction sets. This may soon allow us to extract some sort of natural user interface design patterns, which our community is still relatively short of.

CODE AND DATA

To enable replication and extension of our results, our study material including the Kinect Browser source code, the multimodal interaction sets and our analysis are available at: `https://github.com/globis-ethz/kinectbrowser`.

REFERENCES

1. Ballendat, T., Marquardt, N., and Greenberg, S. Proxemic Interaction: Designing for a Proximity and Orientation-Aware Environment. In *Proc. ITS* (2010).
2. Hornbæk, K., Sander, S. S., Bargas-Avila, J. A., and Simonsen, J. G. Is Once Enough? On the Extent and Content of Replications in Human-Computer Interaction. In *Proc. CHI* (2014).
3. Lee, S.-S., Chae, J., Kim, H., Lim, Y.-K., and Lee, K.-P. Towards more Natural Digital Content Manipulation via User Freehand Gestural Interaction in a Living Room. In *Proc. UbiComp* (2013).
4. Liebling, D. J., and Morris, M. R. Kinected Browser: Depth Camera Interaction for the Web. In *Proc. ITS* (2012).
5. Lindley, S. E., Meek, S., Sellen, A., and Harper, R. H. R. Its Simply Integral to What I do: Enquiries into how the Web is Weaved into Everyday Life. In *Proc. WWW* (2012).
6. Morris, M. R. Web on the Wall: Insights from a Multimodal Interaction Elicitation Study. In *Proc. ITS* (2012).
7. Morris, M. R., and Horvitz, E. SearchTogether: An Interface for Collaborative Web Search. In *Proc. UIST* (2007).
8. Morris, M. R., Wobbrock, J. O., and Wilson, A. D. Understanding Users Preferences for Surface Gestures. In *Proc. GI* (2010).
9. Nacenta, M. A., Kamber, Y., Qiang, Y., and Kristensson, P. O. Memorability of Pre-designed and User-defined Gesture Sets. In *Proc. CHI* (2013).
10. Nacenta, M. A., Sallam, S., Champoux, B., Subramanian, S., and Gutwin, C. Perspective Cursor: Perspective-Based Interaction for Multi-Display Environments. In *Proc. CHI* (2006).
11. Oh, U., and Findlater, L. The Challenges and Potential of End-User Gesture Customization. In *Proc. CHI* (2013).
12. Ruiz, J., Li, Y., and Lank, E. User-Defined Motion Gestures for Mobile Interaction. In *Proc. CHI* (2011).
13. Vogel, D., and Balakrishnan, R. Distant Freehand Pointing and Clicking on Very Large, High Resolution Displays. In *Proc. UIST* (2005).
14. Wobbrock, J. O., Morris, M. R., and Wilson, A. D. User-Defined Gestures for Surface Computing. In *Proc. CHI* (2009).
15. Wobbrock, J. O., Wilson, A. D., and Li, Y. Gestures without Libraries, Toolkits or Training: A $1 Recognizer for User Interface Prototypes. In *Proc. UIST* (2007).
16. Wu, M., Shen, C., Ryall, K., Forlines, C., and Balakrishnan, R. Gesture Registration, Relaxation, and Reuse for Multi-Point Direct-Touch Surfaces. In *Proc. Tabletop* (2006).

User-defined Interface Gestures: Dataset and Analysis

Daniela Grijincu
School of Computer Science
University of St Andrews
dg76@st-andrews.ac.uk

Miguel A. Nacenta
School of Computer Science
University of St Andrews
mans@st-andrews.ac.uk

Per Ola Kristensson
Department of Engineering
University of Cambridge
pok21@cam.ac.uk

ABSTRACT
We present a video-based gesture dataset and a methodology for annotating video-based gesture datasets. Our dataset consists of user-defined gestures generated by 18 participants from a previous investigation of gesture memorability. We design and use a crowd-sourced classification task to annotate the videos. The results are made available through a web-based visualization that allows researchers and designers to explore the dataset. Finally, we perform an additional descriptive analysis and quantitative modeling exercise that provide additional insights into the results of the original study. To facilitate the use of the presented methodology by other researchers we share the data, the source of the human intelligence tasks for crowdsourcing, a new taxonomy that integrates previous work, and the source code of the visualization tool.

Author Keywords
Gesture design; user-defined gestures; gesture elicitation; gesture analysis methodology; gesture annotation; gesture memorability; gesture datasets.

ACM Classification Keywords
H.5.2. Information Interfaces and Presentation: User Interfaces—*Input devices and strategies*

INTRODUCTION
Gesture-based interfaces are already common in a variety of devices such as game consoles, mobile phones, TVs and public displays and the study of gesture interfaces is a growing area of research in human-computer interaction. Gesture interface research often requires studies with human participants who perform or invent gestures that are later analyzed by researchers. The data can for instance be used to recommend better gesture sets for control of specific systems, or to allow designers to make better decisions about the gestures that they integrate (e.g., [7, 44]).

Gestures collected in experiments are often video recorded, but most of the time the rich data that was collected (for example, the videos of gestures) are only analyzed once and with the specific focus of the paper that motivated the study. Data reuse represents a lost opportunity in research—other researchers can potentially extract new insights from video, and the accumulation of data from different sources can potentially open up new types of analysis, such as quantitative modeling (which typically demands large amounts of data) and meta-analyses. However, sharing high-quality datasets requires significant amounts of work to annotate it for analysis purposes, and to ensure it is easily accessible to other researchers.

In this work we set out to contribute an example of sharing and annotating gesture data and creating a tool that facilitates explorations and further analyses. We acquired the data from our recently published study on gesture memorability [26]. We then designed and developed a crowdsourcing task to annotate the data. The annotated data is made available through an on-line visualization and exploration tool and further analyzed using machine learning techniques.

The main contributions of this paper are:

- a dataset of user-defined gestures;
- a crowdsourced gesture-annotation procedure;
- an integrative taxonomy for hands-and-arms gesture classification;
- an interactive visualization tool to access the annotated dataset;
- a complementary analysis, using machine learning techniques, of the annotated gesture dataset.

We put special emphasis on sharing the annotated videos, the source files that enable the crowdsourcing of the categorization task, and the exploration web application source in order to reduce the effort required of other researchers to share their data and to enable further analysis and research of existing and future gesture datasets.

RELATED WORK
Gesture-based interfaces were first adopted in 2D input devices (see [46] for a recent review) for a number of applications such as issuing commands (e.g., [4, 5, 18]), and writing text (e.g., [3, 10, 17, 27]). The popularisation of 3D sensors and accelerometers has also spurred extensive research on 3D gestures (e.g., [16, 35, 38, 39]) and commercial applications that are controlled via in-air gestures are now commonplace. Three areas of related research bear direct relevance to our work: (1) how gestures are designed or selected for specific

ACM 978-1-4503-2587-5/14/11 ...$15.00.
http://dx.doi.org/10.1145/2669485.2669511

applications, (2) gesture memorability, and (3) existing gesture sets, taxonomies and classifications.

Gesture Design Process

The variety of distinct gestures that could be recognized by a gesture-based system is very large, even in gesture-based interfaces that only depend on 2D input. A suitable gesture subset must then be defined and selected, for which several research groups have provided tools (e.g. [15, 19, 20, 45]). These tools allow interface designers and implementers to easily create gesture sets that are recognizable by the system, but they do not address the question of how to choose gestures that are appropriate for end-users.

Based on the concept of user elicitation [28], Wobbrock et al. [44] proposed to define gesture sets for a multitouch interface via a systematic process in which a representative sample of the intended end-users are asked to create gestures for specific actions. The final gesture set is the set with maximum user agreement in the sample of the intended end-users. The motivation behind gesture elicitation is that it results in gesture sets that are better related to the actual needs and expectations of the intended users of the system [25]. Gesture elicitation has often been used for on-air gestures [37], multi-touch gestures [7, 8, 22, 28, 44], unistroke gestures [43], pen-gestures [9], foot gestures [1] and mobile motion gestures [35]. For a discussion on the advantages and possible biases of the technique see also [24].

In addition to gesture sets chosen *a priori* by designers (e.g. [23]), or defined *a priori* by a group of participants in a gesture elicitation exercise, gestures can also be defined by users themselves. This approach has several advantages, including better accessibility for people with impairments [2, 26], better memorability [26], familiarity for the access of information [30], and might also offer added expressivity in artistic interfaces [21] (limitations of this approach are discussed in [26] and [29]). This paper focuses on a dataset of gestures that were user-defined and meant to be remembered (a subset of the gestures in [26]).

Gesture Memorability

Researchers studying gesture-based interfaces have focused on the study of several desirable characteristics of gesture sets, including learnability, discoverability, immediate usability [19], and memorability [26].

This paper presents data focused on gesture memorability, which is a critical characteristic of gesture sets. Prior work on gesture memorability includes Cockburn et al. [6], who in the context of single-stroke gestures studied the effect of inducing effort on overall gesture memorability. Their experiments showed that an effort-inducing interface improved recall rates but it was also considered less enjoyable due to the additional effort. A study by Appert and Zhai [4] analyzed how users learn and remember keyboard shortcuts compared to gestures, reporting that the latter category was more memorable. More recently, Jansen [14] investigated how well users can remember interaction gestures for controlling a TV set, based on different teaching methods. Jansen [14] reports that the gestures perceived as most intuitive by the participants were associated with objects from the TV interface or with the gestures task description. Jansen [14] states that users can correctly remember 61-71% of ten (for them unfamiliar) user-elicited gestures depending on the teaching method used to train them. However, there is no information on the specific features that characterize the most memorable gestures.

In this paper we continue Nacenta et al.'s [26] gesture memorability work, which investigated how participants remember three free-form gesture sets designed for three different applications: a word processor, an image editor and a web browser. For each application, the authors chose 22 different actions for which to design the gestures that are currently still representative for most existing activities available on software systems. Nacenta et al.'s [26] study distinguishes between pre-designed gestures (created by designers), stock gestures that are system generic (i.e. not designed for an specific action), and user-defined gestures that are created by the users themselves. A gesture was considered correctly recalled (or memorable) if it was reproduced with the same hands, fingers and overall path and timing. If the gesture was recalled with small articulation differences (e.g. different finger) but maintaining most of the characteristics of the original gesture, then it would be judged as *close*. Otherwise, if too few similarities were found between the original and the reproduced gesture, it would be considered as incorrectly recalled by the participant. The experiments conducted in the study revealed that self-defined gestures were more memorable (up to 44% more gestures recalled than with the pre-designed gestures) and preferred by users. Although these results are important, they offer little guidance regarding the specific characteristics that make gestures memorable. This work focuses on enabling further analysis of memorability through the annotation, sharing and descriptive analysis of the set of gestures that were generated by participants in [26].

Taxonomies and classifications

The first step to understand why some gestures are better than others is to define criteria (dimensions) that separate those gestures into relevant categories. Multiple such categorizations exist. Quek [33] provides a well-cited classification scheme that differentiates acts (where the gesture's shape and movement is directly related to the intended action) from symbols (where the gesture is arbitrary, but linked to its referent by a language agreed-upon in advance). Pavlovic [31] expands on this work by adding manipulative gestures and putting Quek's [33] categorization within the broader context of human movements. Focusing on the quality and morphology of gestures, Laban [41] created a notation system to describe dance performances that can be applied to description of human gestures. Dimensions derived from Laban's include distinctions of speed, continuity and effort of gestures. Vatavu and Pentiuk [40] and Ruiz et al. [35] describe categorizations that distinguish between information contained in posture and movement.

A more recent taxonomy is the one created by Wobbrock et al. [44] for their seminal elicitation study of multi-touch gestures. They manually classified the gestures obtained into different dimensions such as form, nature, binding and flow, which allowed them to point out that participants of their study preferred single hand gestures to two-hand gestures and that their gestures are influenced by desktop idioms. Simpler categorizations are implicit in the work of Epps et al. [7], who distinguished among common hand shapes and pointing behaviors (e.g. L-shape, C-shape, fist), and Jansen [14], who identified a set of features relevant for interactive TVs.

Available Gesture Sets

In addition to the final gesture set elicited by Wobbrock et al. [44], others have shared proposed gesture sets for specific applications (e.g. multi-touch graph manipulation [36], interaction with omni-directional video [34]), and also stock sets for use in any application [11]. These are generally described through sequences of illustrations, and only occasionally through video. To our knowledge, we are the first to share a full data set of videos as created by participants for specific actions. Moreover, we also provide the labeling (categorization) of each gesture according to a new classification scheme that summarizes existing taxonomies, enabling further research and analysis of the gesture set.

GESTURE CLASSIFICATION METHOD

The starting point of our work is a gesture corpus. We use the self-defined subset of Nacenta et al.'s third study in [26], which consists of 396 user-defined, video recorded 3D gestures performed by 18 participants for 66 different actions (22 actions each). The gestures were created by the participants so that, on request, they could trigger a set of 66 different actions that were selected from common features out of three applications: a web browser, a word processor and an image editor. Each participant only created gestures for one of the three applications. Participants knew that they would be asked to remember the gestures at the time of gesture creation. As a result of the experiment, each gesture was annotated with a label that indicates whether the gesture was remembered in a subsequent test. This memorability label has three possible values: memorable (the gesture was remembered), not-memorable (the gesture was not remembered) or close (the gesture was only partially remembered). Additionally, due to the structure of the experiment, each gesture is annotated with a label that indicates whether or not the gesture was reinforced. Reinforced gestures comprised half of the gesture set that a participant would have to create (11 gestures), but instead of being tested only on the next day, reinforced gestures were also tested (with correctness feedback) immediately after all gestures were created. See their original experiment paper [26] for details.

In most previous studies that classify user-defined gestures the authors themselves classified the gesture sets [44, 14]. This approach does not scale well as the number of gestures go up and is also subject to a possible strong author bias. In this paper we propose an alternative method suitable for annotating large sets of gestures by using a crowdsourcing service to obtain the classifications.

Gesture Taxonomy

The purpose of the categorization (enabling further research) and the chosen methodology imposes a number of constraints that no existing gesture categorization covers completely. This forced us to create a new taxonomy of gestures. Specifically, the new taxonomy has to:

- be descriptive of the type of gestures that people actually perform;
- describe the morphological aspects of the gesture (e.g. number of fingers);
- describe semantic aspects of the gesture (how it relates to the action);
- capture differences in gesture complexity;
- summarize the state of the art (other taxonomies);
- be unambiguous and easy to classify even by non-experts; and
- be succinct.

To achieve these goals we started by compiling a classification schema based on previous gesture taxonomies, with an eye on aspects that could have an impact on gesture memorability. To make sure that the taxonomy was as descriptive as possible of the gestures' features, we manually classified a random sample consisting of 10% of the corpus and used the distribution of the gestures' features to reduce redundancy and ambiguity in the final classification. For example, we noticed from the videos that it was very difficult to discriminate different speeds of movement (aspect proposed by Laban [41]), and as a result, most gestures appeared to have the same, normal (slow) speed. Therefore we decided to omit this dimension from our schema in order to avoid confusing the crowd workers. The final taxonomy, which is displayed in Table 1, is also the result of further modifications after initial piloting of the crowdsourcing process, which is described in the next subsection. Notice that some dimensions are contingent on the category selected in another dimension.

Crowdsourcing

We chose the CrowdFlower platform to classify this corpus because of its large and varied worker base, its sound quality control service, the availability of an infrastructure to train workers using test questions and control their reliability, and the ability to receive feedback from workers on the difficulty and ambiguity of the tasks.

We programmed a web-based application that implemented a gesture classification task based on our taxonomy. The design of the Human Intelligence Task (HIT) interface is critical: if the task unnecessarily hard or confusing it would directly affect the quality of the collected data. Further, a poor HIT design can disincentivize workers to participate [13]. Therefore, we invested a significant amount of effort in designing the interface (see Figure 1). For example, the application was designed to minimize scrolling so that crowd workers could play the gesture in a video any number of times while deciding on each of the classification sub-tasks. Since there are more classification sub-tasks than what can fit on a typical computer screen, these were scrolled horizontally on a button-activated content slider that showed one dimension at

Dimension	Features	Provenience	Choice Type
1. Localization	in air, on surface, mixed	new	single
2. Number of hands	unimanual, bimanual symmetric, bimanual asymmetric	W. et al. [44], P. et al. [32]	single
3. Hand form (HF)	spread, flat, mixed, other	Jansen [14], E. et al. [7]	single
3.1. Hand orientation (if 3 is spread, flat or mixed)	horizontal, vertical, mixed	Jansen [14]	single
4. Additional hand forms	single index finger, single other finger, multiple fingers, fist, grab-release sequence, C-shape, L-shape, other	E. et al. [7]	multiple
5. Hand form and path	same hand form, multiple hand forms, same hand form and path, multiple hand forms and path, mixed	W. et al. [44], V. et al. [40]	single
6. Gesture path	straight, flexible, n/a (no path)	Laban [41]	single
6.1. Gesture path flow (if 6 is straight or flexible)	continuous, segmented	Laban [41]	single
6.2. Gesture path shape (if 6 is flexible)	open, closed, mixed	new	single
7. Relation to gesture action DR - directly related or NR - not related	alphabet letter or number DR, shape of an object DR, arbitrary NR	W. et al. [44], Q. [33], R. et al. [35]	single
8. Relation to gesture workspace	object dependent, workspace dependent, independent	W. et al. [44], R. et al. [35]	single
9. Gesture meaning	metaphorical, symbolical, abstract	W. et al. [44], R. et al. [35]	single

Table 1. Proposed Gesture Taxonomy. 'same hand form' in (5) corresponds to Wobbrock et al.'s static hand pose, but the original formulation proved difficult to understand for crowd workers. 'multiple hand forms' correspond therefore to dynamic hand poses.

a time. Because some of the dimensions involve movement (e.g. additional hand forms, hand form and path in Table 1), we included simple animations that exemplified certain gesture features. The interface forced an answer for all classification subtasks, but tasks that were contingent on other responses only appeared when appropriate (e.g. the hand orientation dimension is shown only if the hand form is spread, flat or mixed).

Some categorizations require semantic judgments of the relationship between the action and the gesture. For this the interface provides, next to the video, the name of the target action and snapshots of the state of the application before the action is executed, and after the action is triggered. This is analogous to how the videos were presented in the original study when the gestures were created.

Test questions are the most important quality control mechanism on the CrowdFlower platform and the best way to ensure that high quality data is acquired. We randomly transformed 30 of the total number of recorded videos into test questions, using CrowdFlower's interface for creating test questions. For each test question, we selected the acceptable answers, which crowd workers would have to answer correctly while working on the task. Special care was taken to ensure an even distribution of test question answers, and also to skip over gesture dimensions which would be too difficult or subjective. CrowdFlower also offers a method called Quiz Mode that ensures that only contributors who understand the task are able to contribute to the task output. By default, and if Quiz Mode is enabled in the settings, CrowdFlower requests that workers complete four test questions before their trust score can be evaluated and their judgements can be incorporated into the task output. For our task on CrowdFlower, the trust threshold was set to 70%. Contributors that were not able to pass the Quiz Mode were permanently disqualified from working on the task. However, even workers that passed the Quiz Mode were still continuously tested as they worked in the task through the method called Work Mode, which keeps the workers trust scores updated and ensures a sustained quality of their answers.

The crowd workers classified five videos per block (for a US$.80 payment), with at least three crowd workers classifying each video. When multiple workers disagreed on the categorization, the chosen answer was the majority vote weighted by the trust scores of the workers.

The task was first piloted on local students, and then piloted again on a small set of crowd workers. This led to final adjustments of the interface and the taxonomy.

DATASET EXPLORATION TOOL

In the spirit of open data and replication in HCI [42], one of the main goals of our work is to enable further analysis of the annotated dataset that we are sharing. Although sharing experimental data is beginning to become an accepted (and encouraged) practice, we find that shared data often requires too much initial work to even consider using it. To ameliorate this problem and reduce the access threshold, we have cre-

(a)

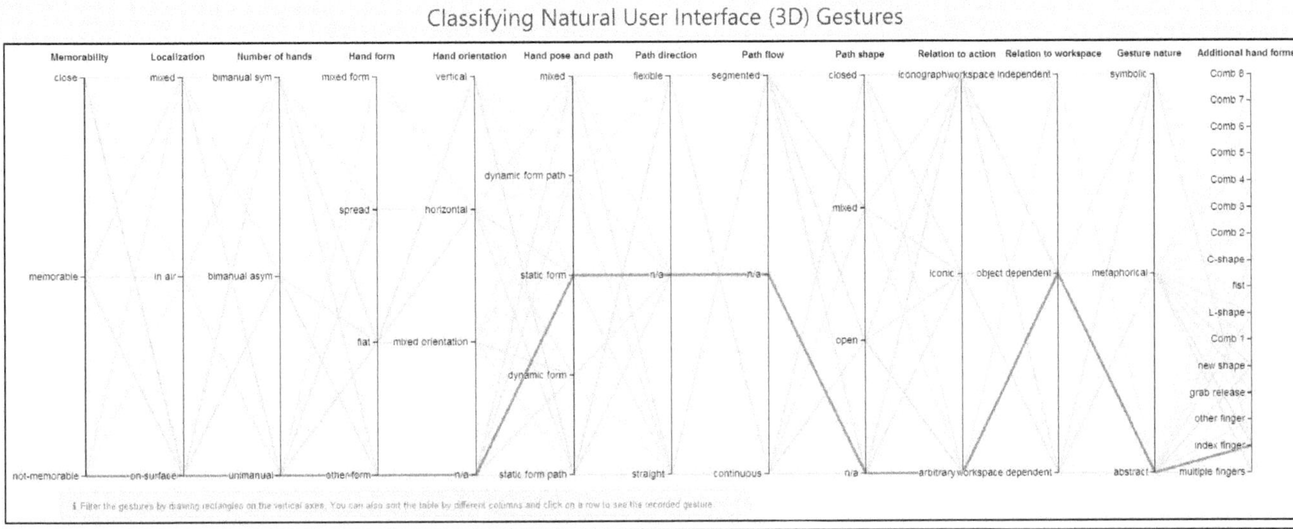

(b)

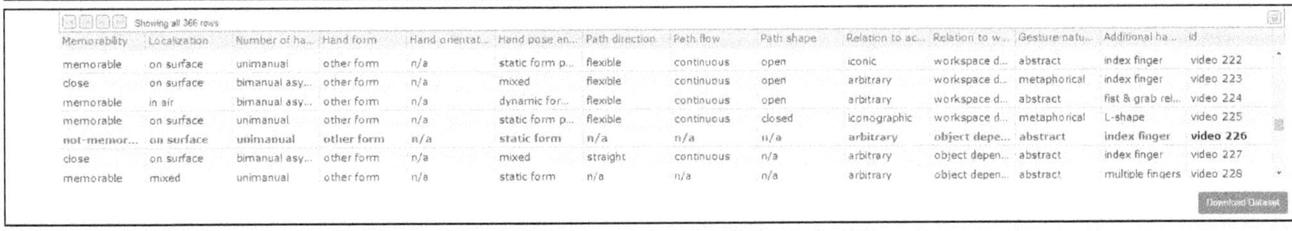

Memorability	Localization	Number of ha...	Hand form	Hand orientat...	Hand pose an...	Path direction	Path flow	Path shape	Relation to ac...	Relation to w...	Gesture natu...	Additional ha...	id
memorable	on surface	unimanual	other form	n/a	static form p...	flexible	continuous	open	iconic	workspace d...	abstract	index finger	video 222
close	on surface	bimanual asy...	other form	n/a	mixed	flexible	continuous	open	arbitrary	workspace d...	metaphorical	index finger	video 223
memorable	in air	bimanual asy...	other form	n/a	dynamic for...	flexible	continuous	open	arbitrary	workspace d...	abstract	fist & grab rel...	video 224
memorable	on surface	unimanual	other form	n/a	static form p...	flexible	continuous	closed	iconographic	workspace d...	metaphorical	L-shape	video 225
not-memor...	on surface	unimanual	other form	n/a	static form	n/a	n/a	n/a	arbitrary	object depe...	abstract	index finger	**video 226**
close	on surface	bimanual asy...	other form	n/a	mixed	straight	continuous	n/a	arbitrary	object depen...	abstract	index finger	video 227
memorable	mixed	unimanual	other form	n/a	static form	n/a	n/a	n/a	arbitrary	object depen...	abstract	multiple fingers	video 228

Figure 2. Data exploration tool. (a) presents the parallel coordinates visualization of different gesture dimensions and features; and (b) shows a table containing information about the annotations of the gestures, allowing filtering interaction

ated a web application that provides access to all the videos, represents the classification data, and allows interactive exploration of the dataset.

The tool, which can be accessed online at **`http://udigesturesdataset.cs.st-andrews.ac.uk/`**, has three main connected components: a parallel coordinates panel, an interactive spreadsheet, and a gesture page. The parallel coordinates visualization [12] represents each gesture as a line that crosses each of the 13 vertical axes at a different height depending on the classification of the gesture (see Figure 2.a). The first axis represents the memorability value (whether the gesture was ultimately remembered or not) and each of the remaining axes represents one of the 12 dimensions of our taxonomy. This visualization is implemented with D3[1] and Parcoords[2]. Gestures can be selected by filtering in one or more dimensions, and dimensions can be reordered via pick-and-drop. Filtering and picking is interactively connected to the spreadsheet section, so that only filtered gestures will appear in the spreadsheet panel.

The spreadsheet (Figure 2.b) allows direct access to the data. Each row represents a gesture and each column corresponds to a dimension. Hovering over a row will highlight the corresponding gesture in the parallel coordinates area above. The spreadsheet widget is implemented using SlickGrid[3]. Clicking on a row opens a gesture page (Figure 3), in which the video of the gesture can be played and all the information about the gesture also appears (classifications, memorability, intended action, and application). Finally, the application contains a button that triggers the download of the raw data.

[1]http://d3js.org/

[2]http://syntagmatic.github.io/parallel-coordinates/

[3]https://github.com/mleibman/SlickGrid/wiki/

DESCRIPTIVE ANALYSIS

For all 396 recorded videos from the corpus we received a total of 1783 judgments, of which 1270 were considered trusted and 513 untrusted (this count does not include judgments on test questions). This results on an average of 9.63 crowd workers classifying each gesture. Because all gestures were judged by several workers, we also obtained a measure of inter-rater reliability (IRR) for each of the different dimensions (see the IRR scores in Table 2). These values represent the average across all gestures of the percentage of workers that agreed with the algorithmic classification described at the end of the *Crowdsourcing* subsection above.

Our IRR is a measure of the trustworthiness of the overall classification. Moreover, the independent IRR measures can serve as a proxy measure of how ambiguous/difficult the different dimensions are to categorize. As expected, dimensions that required semantic judgments (8 and 9 from Table 1) had more modest agreement rates. Additionally, dimension 6.1 (whether a gesture's path is open, closed, or contains the two types) was also particularly difficult. Nevertheless, all IRR values are above 70%.

In total, 185 crowd workers completed the task and 60 of them sent us feedback. Feedback from crowd workers indicated

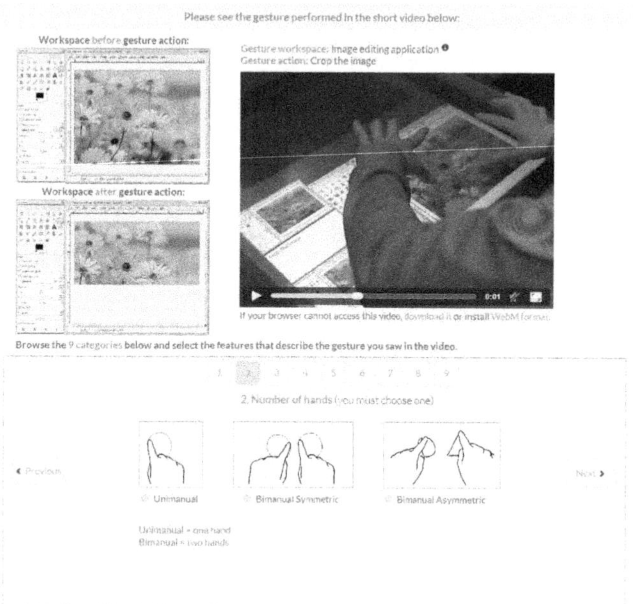

Figure 1. Gesture classification task implemented on CrowdFlower

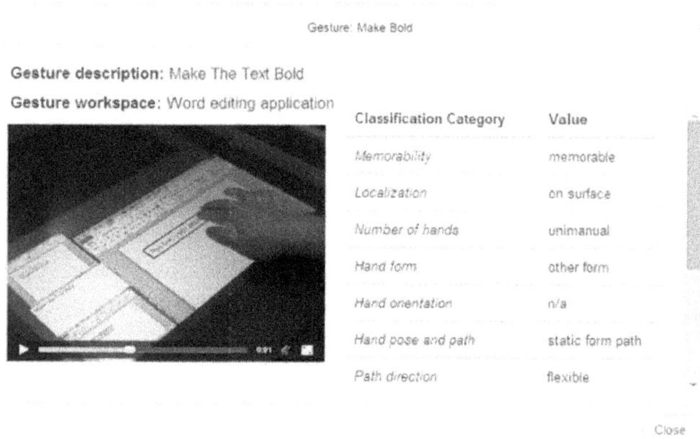

Figure 3. Data exploration tool showing the gesture performed

that they considered the payment fair (4.2 out of 5), that the instructions were clear (3.8 out of 5), that the test questions were fair (3.5 out of 5), and that the task was difficult (2.8 score out of 5 for the ease of the task). The final average worker trust score (computed by CrowdFlower based on their performance on test questions and work in the task) was 0.892.

Gesture Categorization Results

The gestures classified in each dimension for all features are displayed in Table 2. The results indicate that some dimensions are heavily biased towards a particular type of gesture (e.g., most gestures use only the index finger, one hand, or continuous path flows), whereas other dimensions are more balanced (e.g., similar number of gestures are object and workspace dependent, metaphorical and abstract).

Some of these results support previous findings [7, 44, 39]. It is remarkable that even after more than five years since Wobbrock et al's [44] study, with multi-touch interfaces being now pervasive, there is still such a strong bias towards single finger, single hand gestures.

STATISTICAL MODELING

The labeling procedure described above and the discrete nature of the outcome variable of the gestures (memorable, not-memorable, and close) make the dataset amenable to classification algorithms that might be able to provide additional insight into the factors that affect memorability. The starting point is the 43-dimensional feature vector for each gesture, where each value is binary and represents each of the possible gesture classifications of the taxonomy (Table 1). The dependent variable (memorability) has three possible values: memorable, non-memorable, and close, which were heavily imbalanced (312, 39, and 45 cases respectively).

Feature Selection

As some of the features could potentially introduce noise, we decided to pre-select the most relevant subset of features for describing the dataset. We tested combinations of the nine gesture classification dimensions (Table 1), generating 510 possible subsets (the empty and the complete set were excluded). Each generated subset was evaluated based on a 10-fold cross-validation accuracy obtained with Support Vector Machines (SVMs) trained with the Radial Basis Function kernel and parameters C and γ obtained via a grid search. The best results were obtained with a selection of 28 features corresponding to dimensions 2, 4, 6, 6.1, 6.2, 7, 8 and 9 from the classification schema described in Table 1. We generated the feature vectors with the new selection of features and updated the initial training set.

Modeling Approaches

We attempted to predict the memorability label of gestures using different supervised machine learning techniques suitable for a 3-class problem and training using binary feature vectors. We first experimented with Logistic Regression using the Weka[4] open source software for data mining and measured the 10-fold cross-validation results. We report the weighted average scores between the three classes of gestures obtained for different measurements in Table 3. Table 3 reveals that the results for predicting gesture memorability using logistic regression were not satisfactory as the learned model was highly biased towards predicting only memorable gestures, which represented over 70% of the training samples and for which the false positive rate was very high (over 70%).

Decision tree classifiers were another suitable technique for our problem, having the additional benefit of being relatively easy to visualize and interpret. We experimented with a range of different types of decision trees available in Weka such as Best-First Tree, ID3, J48 and also random trees and random forests. The best results were obtained with the ID3 algorithm, which achieved a modest F-score of 0.64. This is only a small improvement with respect to the 10-fold cross-validation scores obtained with logistic regression.

[4]http://www.cs.waikato.ac.nz/ml/weka/

Finally, we tried Support Vector Machines (SVM) in their `libSVM` implementation[5]. The best results were obtained with a Radial Basis Function kernel and with C and γ parameters obtained via grid search (we also tried multiple kernel functions such as linear, polynomial, string based and sigmoid). Table 3 reveals that SVMs performed slightly better, the F-score was 0.68, and overall accuracy was 70%.

DISCUSSION

We set out to achieve a better understanding of the data obtained in [26] through an analysis and categorization of the dataset. To achieve this, we chose to take advantage of crowdsourcing as a tool for the categorization of videos. We believe that this approach has many advantages and the potential to significantly further HCI research on gestures if more researchers analysed (and shared) the obtained gestures in this manner.

The approach is more scalable than expert classification and much faster—once the HIT was prepared it only took 13 hours for the full task to be completed. We were initially concerned that crowd workers might not be able to achieve acceptable consensus about certain dimensions. Specifically, we were concerned about the dimensions that involved semantic judgements. However, the results indicate that the classifications are of a high quality (all IRR >70%). We suspect that this is due to the careful setup of the HIT and the simplified taxonomy. It is conceivable that groups of gesture experts can perform categorizations with higher agreement, but this kind of expertise is not easy to identify and recruit, and we conjecture that the results would be largely the same and orders of magnitude more expensive.

We have included our templates in this paper's complementary materials so that other researchers can take advantage of our work and annotate and share their gestures at a lower cost and effort.

Taxonomy

The taxonomy is a critical element of both the research and methodological parts of this work. We designed it to balance generalizability and detail from previous work with the simplicity and conciseness required for a viable human intelligence task. The measures of agreement from the crowd worker judgements show that the taxonomy enables consistent categorizations, although some of the dimensions imply harder distinctions. Specifically, the two dimensions that imply semantic judgements (8, 9) or gesture path shape (6.2) were between 70% and 80% agreement.

Although we created this taxonomy to learn more about memorability and gestures, we believe it captures most of the morphological and semantic characteristics of arm and hand gestures. Therefore we believe that this taxonomy can be useful to researchers in this area as an alternative that is: a) very expressive, b) concise, and c) validated for classification through crowdsourcing. For explicit purposes beyond what the current version can describe and classify, the taxonomy can be extended with new dimensions.

[5]http://www.csie.ntu.edu.tw/ cjlin/libsvm/

Types of gestures

The distributions of gestures that we obtained offer an interesting view of current user expectations regarding gestures on and above surfaces. First, the preference for single hand, single finger gestures suggests that the conceptualization of "finger as cursor" is still strong and common actions would probably benefit from this kind of gesture. Second, in presence of a display surface, people still prefer to design gestures that come in contact with the surface, even when they were explicitly told that this was not a constraint (see [26]). Third, although in-air dynamic gestures can be extremely rich in form, which might be perceived as useful for memorability, the chosen gestures were heavily biased towards simple hand postures that tended to be unchanging (gesture changes are uncommon) and with the hands describing simple paths (i.e. non-segmented and open).

We believe this rich gesture data can support gesture interface designers. For instance, using our exploration tool a designer can get an idea of how naturally users propose certain gestures, or get inspired when creating advanced gestures by exploring the less common gestures created by the participants.

Modeling and its Challenges

The annotation of the data made possible to explore the data using statistical modeling techniques. Our intention was to identify models that would be able to predict memorability based on the characteristics of a gesture. This approach was only partially successful in that, although there is some information in the annotation that allows the best algorithm (SVMs) to classify with performance above chance, the predictions are not sufficiently accurate. Their performance is relatively close to assuming that all gestures will be memorable.

There are several factors that explain why the prediction ability of the models is low. First, although our dataset is substantial in size for this kind of study, it is not large compared to the typical dataset sizes required for accurate statistical modeling. Second, the data is heavily biased towards memorable gestures, which makes modeling difficult. Third, memorability is inherently difficult to predict, with many possible intervening sources of noise, including individual differences and personal experience.

Nevertheless, a detailed look at the more interpretable models (specifically, decision trees), and the results of the feature selection stage (discussed in the *Modeling* Section) suggest that some dimensions contain more information than others towards explaining memorability. Specifically, we suspect that three gesture dimensions deserve particular attention: gesture meaning, gesture path, and gesture flow.

Summary of insights

The following points summarize the main insights obtained from the annotation process and analyses presented in this paper:

- Crowdsourcing is a fast and reliable tool for gesture categorization.

Dimension	Features	#	%
1. Localization (IRR 89%)	on surface	353	89
	in air	22	6
	mixed	21	5
2. Number of hands (IRR 98%)	unimanual	285	72
	bimanual symmetric	56	14
	bimanual asymmetric	55	14
3. Hand form (IRR 89%)	flat	98	25
	spread	25	6
	mixed	6	2
	other	267	67
3.1 Hand orientation (IRR 85%)	horizontal	76	19
	vertical	30	8
	mixed	23	6
4. Additional hand forms (IRR 89%)	single index finger	205	52
	single other finger	3	1
	multiple finger	48	12
	grab-release	12	3
	c-shape	8	2
	l-shape	19	5
	fist	5	1
	other	100	25
5. Hand form and path (IRR 82%)	same HF	41	10
	multiple HF	26	7
	same HF and path	289	73
	multiple HF and path	12	3
	mixed	28	7
6. Gesture path (IRR 87%)	straight	204	52
	flexible	107	27
	n/a	85	21
6.1 Gesture path flow (IRR 88%)	continuous	228	56
	segmented	83	21
6.2 Gesture path shape (IRR 74%)	open	74	19
	closed	17	4
	mixed	16	4
7. Relation to gesture action (IRR 81%)	alph. letter or nr DR	51	13
	shape DR	64	16
	arbitrary NR	281	71
8. Relation to gesture workspace (IRR 78%)	object depend.	173	44
	workspace depend.	219	55
	independ.	4	1
9. Gesture meaning (IRR 72%)	metaphorical	171	43
	symbolical	15	4
	abstract	210	53

Table 2. Distributions of the gesture annotations obtained from CrowdFlower

Method	TP	FP	Prec	Rec	F1	ROC	Acc %
Logistic Regression	0.65	0.61	0.62	0.65	0.63	0.54	65
ID3	0.67	0.6	0.61	0.67	0.64	0.56	68
SVMs	0.70	0.58	0.67	0.70	0.68	0.59	70

Table 3. Performance measures obtained using the best classifiers. From left to right: true positives, false positives, precision, recall, F-score, receiver operating characteristic and accuarcy.

- Crowdsourcing categorization results are reasonably reliable.
- Users still predominantly define single-point and single-hand gestures.
- Users tend to create gestures where the hand form does not change.
- Gesture meaning, path and flow are promising characteristics in the further study of memorability of gestures.

Limitations and Future Work

The work that we present is based on data obtained through a memorability study. Participants created gestures with the specific goal of remembering them afterwards. Although we tried to create a process and taxonomy that generalizes to other desirable features beyond memorability, such as discoverability and performance, some of the findings are inevitably biased by the memorability focus of the experiment that generated the original data. Future annotations of user-defined gestures, including those from elicitation studies, can help build up a consistent knowledge base on the types of gestures that people naturally propose.

Although we provide materials in the additional files that should simplify categorization of other gesture datasets through crowdsourcing, the setup require additional work. Videos and existing data still need to be linked to the new HIT and the interface tested, even if no modifications to the classification task are required. In the future it would be useful to develop a platform that simplifies the classification and storage of gesture collections of several types.

CONCLUSION

Gesture research can benefit from more researchers sharing and annotating their datasets. In this work we show an example of how an existing video gesture dataset can be annotated using crowdsourcing tools and then made available for exploration through a visualization tool. In addition to the methodological contributions, which include a revised integrative taxonomy of arm and hand gestures, we show how further analysis of the annotated data can lead to a better understanding of gestures that go beyond the analysis offered in the original paper. Our dataset can be accessed here: `http://udigesturesdataset.cs.st-andrews.ac.uk/`.

REFERENCES

1. Alexander, J., Han, T., Judd, W., Irani, P., and Subramanian, S. Putting your best foot forward: Investigating real-world mappings for foot-based gestures. In *Proceedings of the 30th International Conference on Human Factors in Computing Systems*, CHI '12 (2012).
2. Anthony, L., Kim, Y., and Findlater, L. Analyzing user-generated youtube videos to understand touchscreen use by people with motor impairments. In *Proceedings of the SIGCHI Conference on Human Factors in Computing Systems*, CHI '13, ACM (New York, NY, USA, 2013), 1223–1232.

3. Anthony, L., and Wobbrock, J. O. $n-protractor: A fast and accurate multistroke recognizer. In *Proceedings of Graphics Interface 2012*, GI '12, Canadian Information Processing Society (Toronto, Ont., Canada, Canada, 2012), 117–120.
4. Appert, C., and Zhai, S. Using strokes as command shortcuts: Cognitive benefits and toolkit support. In *Proceedings of the SIGCHI Conference on Human Factors in Computing Systems*, CHI '09, ACM (New York, NY, USA, 2009), 2289–2298.
5. Bau, O., and Mackay, W. E. Octopocus: A dynamic guide for learning gesture-based command sets. In *Proceedings of the 21st Annual ACM Symposium on User Interface Software and Technology*, UIST '08, ACM (New York, NY, USA, 2008), 37–46.
6. Cockburn, A., Kristensson, P. O., Alexander, J., and Zhai, S. Hard lessons: Effort-inducing interfaces benefit spatial learning. In *Proceedings of the SIGCHI Conference on Human Factors in Computing Systems*, CHI '07, ACM (New York, NY, USA, 2007), 1571–1580.
7. Epps, J., Lichman, S., and Wu, M. A study of hand shape use in tabletop gesture interaction. In *CHI '06 Extended Abstracts on Human Factors in Computing Systems*, CHI EA '06, ACM (New York, NY, USA, 2006), 748–753.
8. Findlater, L., Lee, B., and Wobbrock, J. Beyond QWERTY: Augmenting touch screen keyboards with multi-touch gestures for non-alphanumeric input. In *Proceedings of the SIGCHI Conference on Human Factors in Computing Systems*, CHI '12, ACM (New York, NY, USA, 2012), 2679–2682.
9. Frisch, M., Heydekorn, J., and Dachselt, R. Investigating multi-touch and pen gestures for diagram editing on interactive surfaces. In *Proceedings of the ACM International Conference on Interactive Tabletops and Surfaces*, ITS '09, ACM (New York, NY, USA, 2009), 149–156.
10. Goldberg, D., and Richardson, C. Touch-typing with a stylus. In *Proceedings of the INTERACT '93 and CHI '93 Conference on Human Factors in Computing Systems*, CHI '93, ACM (1993), 80–87.
11. Hotelling, S., Strickon, J., Huppi, B., Chaudhri, I., Christie, G., Ording, B., Kerr, D., and Ive, J. Gestures for touch sensitive input devices, July 2 2013. US Patent 8,479,122.
12. Inselberg, A. Multidimensional detective. In *Proceedings of the 1997 IEEE Symposium on Information Visualization (InfoVis '97)*, INFOVIS '97, IEEE Computer Society (Washington, DC, USA, 1997).
13. Jacques, J. J., and Kristensson, P. O. Crowdsourcing a hit: measuring workers' pre-task interactions on microtask markets. In *Proceedings of the 1st AAAI Conference on Human Computation and Crowdsourcing*, HCOMP '13, AAAI Press (Menlo Park, CA, USA, 2013), 86–93.
14. Jansen, E. Teaching users how to interact with gesture-based interfaces; a comparison of teaching-methods. diploma thesis, University of Technology Eindhoven, 2013.
15. Kin, K., Hartmann, B., DeRose, T., and Agrawala, M. Proton: Multitouch gestures as regular expressions. In *Proceedings of the SIGCHI Conference on Human Factors in Computing Systems*, CHI '12, ACM (New York, NY, USA, 2012), 2885–2894.
16. Kristensson, P. O., Nicholson, T., and Quigley, A. Continuous recognition of one-handed and two-handed gestures using 3D full-body motion tracking sensors. In *Proceedings of the 2012 ACM International Conference on Intelligent User Interfaces*, IUI '12, ACM (New York, NY, USA, 2012), 89–92.
17. Kristensson, P. O., and Zhai, S. SHARK^2: A large vocabulary shorthand writing system for pen-based computers. In *Proceedings of the 17th Annual ACM Symposium on User Interface Software and Technology*, UIST '04, ACM (2004), 43–52.
18. Kristensson, P. O., and Zhai, S. Command strokes with and without preview: Using pen gestures on keyboard for command selection. In *Proceedings of the SIGCHI Conference on Human Factors in Computing Systems*, CHI '07, ACM (New York, NY, USA, 2007), 1137–1146.
19. Long, Jr., A. C., Landay, J. A., and Rowe, L. A. Implications for a gesture design tool. In *Proceedings of the SIGCHI Conference on Human Factors in Computing Systems*, CHI '99, ACM (New York, NY, USA, 1999), 40–47.
20. Lü, H., and Li, Y. Gesture coder: A tool for programming multi-touch gestures by demonstration. In *Proceedings of the SIGCHI Conference on Human Factors in Computing Systems*, CHI '12, ACM (New York, NY, USA, 2012), 2875–2884.
21. Merrill, D. J., and Paradiso, J. A. Personalization, expressivity, and learnability of an implicit mapping strategy for physical interfaces. In *In the Extended Abstracts of the Conference on Human Factors in Computing Systems (CHI05* (2005), 2152–2161.
22. Micire, M., Desai, M., Courtemanche, A., Tsui, K. M., and Yanco, H. A. Analysis of natural gestures for controlling robot teams on multi-touch tabletop surfaces. In *Proceedings of the ACM International Conference on Interactive Tabletops and Surfaces*, ITS '09, ACM (New York, NY, USA, 2009), 41–48.
23. Microsoft, Inc. Using gestures. `http://bit.ly/OXOvT4`, June 2014.
24. Morris, M. R., Danielescu, A., Drucker, S., Fisher, D., Lee, B., schraefel, m. c., and Wobbrock, J. O. Reducing legacy bias in gesture elicitation studies. *interactions 21*, 3 (May 2014), 40–45.

25. Morris, M. R., Wobbrock, J. O., and Wilson, A. D. Understanding users' preferences for surface gestures. In *Proceedings of Graphics Interface 2010*, GI '10, Canadian Information Processing Society (Toronto, Ont., Canada, Canada, 2010), 261–268.

26. Nacenta, M. A., Kamber, Y., Qiang, Y., and Kristensson, P. O. Memorability of pre-designed and userdefined gesture sets. In *Proceedings of the SIGCHI Conference on Human Factors in Computing Systems*, CHI '13, ACM (New York, NY, USA, 2013), 1099–1108.

27. Ni, T., Bowman, D., and North, C. Airstroke: Bringing unistroke text entry to freehand gesture interfaces. In *Proceedings of the SIGCHI Conference on Human Factors in Computing Systems*, CHI '11, ACM (New York, NY, USA, 2011), 2473–2476.

28. Nielsen, M., Störring, M., Moeslund, B., and Granum, E. A procedure for developing intuitive and ergonomic gesture interfaces for hci. In *Gesture-Based Communication in Human-Computer Interaction*, vol. 2915 of *Lecture Notes in Computer Science*. Springer Berlin Heidelberg, 2004, 409–420.

29. Oh, U., and Findlater, L. The challenges and potential of end-user gesture customization. In *Proceedings of the SIGCHI Conference on Human Factors in Computing Systems*, CHI '13, ACM (New York, NY, USA, 2013), 1129–1138.

30. Ouyang, T., and Li, Y. Bootstrapping personal gesture shortcuts with the wisdom of the crowd and handwriting recognition. In *Proceedings of the SIGCHI Conference on Human Factors in Computing Systems*, CHI '12, ACM (New York, NY, USA, 2012), 2895–2904.

31. Pavlovic, V. I., Sharma, R., and Huang, T. S. Visual interpretation of hand gestures for human-computer interaction: A review. *IEEE Transactions on Pattern Analysis and Machine Intelligence 19*, 7 (July 1997), 677–695.

32. Piumsomboon, T., Clark, A., Billinghurst, M., and Cockburn, A. User-defined gestures for augmented reality. In *CHI '13 Extended Abstracts on Human Factors in Computing Systems*, CHI EA '13, ACM (New York, NY, USA, 2013), 955–960.

33. Quek, F. K. H. Toward a vision-based hand gesture interface. In *Proceedings of the Conference on Virtual Reality Software and Technology*, VRST '94, World Scientific Publishing Co., Inc. (River Edge, NJ, USA, 1994), 17–31.

34. Rovelo Ruiz, G. A., Vanacken, D., Luyten, K., Abad, F., and Camahort, E. Multi-viewer gesture-based interaction for omni-directional video. In *Proceedings of the 32Nd Annual ACM Conference on Human Factors in Computing Systems*, CHI '14, ACM (New York, NY, USA, 2014), 4077–4086.

35. Ruiz, J., Li, Y., and Lank, E. User-defined motion gestures for mobile interaction. In *Proceedings of the SIGCHI Conference on Human Factors in Computing Systems*, CHI '11, ACM (New York, NY, USA, 2011), 197–206.

36. Schmidt, S., Nacenta, M. A., Dachselt, R., and Carpendale, S. A set of multi-touch graph interaction techniques. In *ACM International Conference on Interactive Tabletops and Surfaces*, ACM (2010), 113–116.

37. Seyed, T., Burns, C., Costa Sousa, M., Maurer, F., and Tang, A. Eliciting usable gestures for multi-display environments. In *Proceedings of the 2012 ACM International Conference on Interactive Tabletops and Surfaces*, ITS '12, ACM (New York, NY, USA, 2012), 41–50.

38. Sodhi, R., Benko, H., and Wilson, A. Lightguide: Projected visualizations for hand movement guidance. In *Proceedings of the SIGCHI Conference on Human Factors in Computing Systems*, CHI '12, ACM (New York, NY, USA, 2012), 179–188.

39. Vatavu, R.-D. User-defined gestures for free-hand tv control. In *Proceedings of the 10th European Conference on Interactive Tv and Video*, EuroiTV '12, ACM (2012), 45–48.

40. Vatavu, R. D., and Pentiuc, S. G. Multi-level representation of gesture as command for human computer interaction. *Computing and Informatics 27*, 6 (2008), 837–851.

41. von Laban, R. *The mastery of movement*. Dance Books, Binsted, Hampshire, UK, 2011.

42. Wilson, M., Mackay, W., Chi, E., Bernstein, M., and Nichols, J. Replichi sig: From a panel to a new submission venue for replication. In *CHI '12 Extended Abstracts on Human Factors in Computing Systems*, CHI EA '12, ACM (New York, NY, USA, 2012), 1185–1188.

43. Wobbrock, J. O., Aung, H. H., Rothrock, B., and Myers, B. A. Maximizing the guessability of symbolic input. In *CHI '05 Extended Abstracts on Human Factors in Computing Systems*, CHI EA '05, ACM (New York, NY, USA, 2005), 1869–1872.

44. Wobbrock, J. O., Morris, M. R., and Wilson, A. D. User-defined gestures for surface computing. In *Proceedings of the SIGCHI Conference on Human Factors in Computing Systems*, CHI '09, ACM (New York, NY, USA, 2009), 1083–1092.

45. Wobbrock, J. O., Wilson, A. D., and Li, Y. Gestures without libraries, toolkits or training: A $1 recognizer for user interface prototypes. In *Proceedings of the 20th Annual ACM Symposium on User Interface Software and Technology*, UIST '07, ACM (2007), 159–168.

46. Zhai, S., Kristensson, P. O., Appert, C., Andersen, T. H., and Cao, X. Foundational issues in touch-surface stroke gesture design—an integrative review. *Foundations and Trends in Human-Computer Interaction 5*, 2 (2012), 97–205.

A Survey on Multi-touch Gesture Recognition and Multi-touch Frameworks

Maurico Cirelli
mauricio.cirelli@usp.br

Ricardo Nakamura
ricardo.nakamura@poli.usp.br

Escola Politécnica da Universidade de São Paulo
Av. Prof. Luciano Gualberto, travessa 3, 380, São Paulo, SP, Brazil

ABSTRACT
The multi-touch gesture recognition problem has drawn great attention from the human-computer interaction (HCI) community, mainly since multi-touch surfaces and other touch-capable devices reached the mainstream market. In the past decade, several multi-touch gesture recognition techniques and multi-touch frameworks were proposed. When we started our research on touch-based gestures recognition, we identified some surveys focused on computer vision or accelerometers. However, in several multi-touch surface devices, the multi-touch sensor is the only input method available. We here present a survey on touch-based gestures recognition techniques and frameworks, and propose an extended set of requirements such techniques and frameworks should meet in order to provide better support to multi-touch surface applications.

Author Keywords
Multi-touch; gesture; recognition; frameworks; multi-touch surface; interactive table

ACM Classification Keywords
H.1.2. User/Machine Systems: Human factors; H.5.2. User Interfaces: Input devices and strategies (e.g., mouse, touch-screen); H.5.2. User Interfaces: Interaction styles (e.g., commands, menus, forms, direct manipulation)

General Terms
Human Factors; Algorithms; Design.

INTRODUCTION
Gestures are the most fundamental way in which users interact with multi-touch tables. Back to 1986, Rhyne and Wolf defined gestures as hand markings, entered with a stylus or a mouse, that indicate scope and commands [36]. We may recast this definition to our context: gestures are movements users perform with their hands on the touch surface in order to activate an application function.

ITS 2014, November 16–19, 2014, Dresden, Germany.

http://dx.doi.org/10.1145/2669485.2669509

In the context of interactive tables, gestures may also be classified as *on the surface* or *above the surface*, with no physical contact, gathering information about one or more hands and their projections to the touch surface. For instance, Strothoff et al. [42] use the projection of users' hands to control a triangle in a three dimensional virtual space.

According to their semantics, gestures may be classified into two categories: *symbolic* and *direct manipulation* gestures [44]. The former category contains gestures defined by their trajectory and they mimic a context-dependent action or sign. The same gestures may have no meaning if performed in other contexts. The latter contains the most common gestures for direct manipulation of interface objects, such as moving or rotating an image in a picture viewer application [32] or sharing ideas in a brainstorming activity [5]. Such gestures are used in many different applications and are thus weakly dependent on the application context.

Nygärd proposed a set of criteria to classify gestures according to their shape and trajectory [34]. Accordingly to his classification, gestures may belong to three groups: *open trajectories*, *closed trajectories* and *crossing trajectories*. Examples of such gestures are given in Figure 1.

Figure 1: Examples of gestures accordingly to Nygärd

In large multi-touch tables, several users usually interacting with each other through gestures performed on the surface. In this context, gestures may be *collaborative* or *individual*. When gestures are collaborative, we have two or more different users combining gestures in order to execute a single action in the application [32].

With respect to the space in which the gestures are performed, we may classify them into two categories: two-dimensional (gestures performed on the touch surface) and three-dimensional (hand gestures performed freely in the air) [3, 46]. 3D gestures are often recognized by vision or accelerometer based techniques, as described in other surveys [31, 28, 4]. In our research, we focus on multi-touch, 2D gestures in the context of interactive tables (also known as multi-touch surfaces).

Although we have found several ways to group gestures into different categories and several different criteria, we missed a classification which considers time-related information about gestures. Thus, we would like to propose two new categories: *sequential* and *atomic* gestures.

Atomic gestures are single movements which a single user performs with his or her hands in order to activate a single function in the application. Several examples fall into this category, such as dragging an image around the screen, tapping a button or activating a character's skill in a game.

Sequential gestures are well-defined sequences of atomic gestures with time-constrained intervals between each of them, which a single user must perform with his or her hands, in order to activate a different application function. As an example of use of this kind of gesture, we may describe the use of a special character's skill in a game (also known as *combos*). In traditional devices, such as controller-based videogames and computer games, users must perform a sequence of commands in order to activate a character's special action. Games such as those from the *Mortal Kombat* and *Harry Potter* trademarks make intense use of this kind of interaction. In gesture-based devices, such as *Nintendo Wii*, we also have games, such as *Dragon Ball Budokai Tenkaichi 3*, which uses several accelerometer-based gestures in a well-defined sequence in order to execute a special action.

The idea behind sequential gestures is that each movement from the sequence is a valid atomic gesture and triggers its respective action, but the execution of all of them in the correct sequence triggers an additional event to the application. The canonical example of sequential gesture is *double tap*, because it is composed of two valid atomic gestures (*tap*) in a well-defined sequence with a time-constrained interval between them. Also, the combination of the two atomic gestures generates a different event to the application layer.

Finally, Table 1 summarizes the characteristics of multi-touch gestures which will guide our discussion on the strengths and weaknesses of each of the multi-touch gestures recognition techniques and frameworks we review in the following sections.

Table 1: Gestures classes by properties

Properties	Classes
Degrees of Freedom	2D or 3D
Spatial	On the surface or above the surface
Semantics	Symbolic or direct manipulation
Trajectory Complexity	Open, closed or crossing gestures
Number of Users	Individual or collaborative
Number of Fingers	Single-touch or Multi-touch
Timing	Atomic or sequential

In this paper we review the state of art techniques for multi-touch gesture recognition and frameworks for multi-touch applications. Our goals are to summarize the concepts of each technique, discussing their strengths and weaknesses and to point out directions for future multi-touch researches.

In the next section, we describe the multi-touch gesture recognition problem. Then, we review the state of the art multi-touch gesture recognizers and frameworks. Finally, we propose an extended set of requirements for multi-touch frameworks and recognizers, based on the characteristics of multi-touch gestures and multi-touch surface applications.

THE RECOGNITION PROBLEM

We here use Rubine's definition for *gestures recognizers*: a piece of software that is responsible for interpreting the touch input provided by the sensors and for generating a gesture event to the application whenever a valid gesture is performed by users [37].

Hinrichs and Carpendale experimentally showed that gestures depend on interaction and social contexts and that many different gestures could be performed in order to activate the same action [12]. This shows that the application gestures set may be larger than its actions set. Their study provides two major requirements for gestures recognizers: to be very fast, in order to not harm the interaction; and to be very flexible and accurate, in order to allow a large gesture set to be correctly processed by the applications.

Some modern operating systems, such as Windows 8, Android and iOS, come with a gesture recognition engine built-in[1], which usually supports only a small set of most common direct manipulation gestures. When an application needs a custom gesture, developers are required to implement their own algorithms to match them from low-level touch events (raw input events from the sensors device drivers). Several authors agree that this is tedious, complicated, error-prone task, which usually delivers a confused and hard to maintain source code [25, 38, 45]. This has been the core motivation for developing extensible and flexible gestures recognizers and multi-touch frameworks.

The gesture characteristics from Table 1 influence gesture recognizers in different ways. For instance, gestures made *above the surface* usually require an additional segmentation step before the classification itself. Symbolic gestures require the recognition process to be conducted after the gesture is performed, while direct manipulation gestures require an *online* recognition process to provide continuous feedback to applications. The gesture shape and trajectory may influence the pattern recognition algorithm, due to the need of scale, translation and orientation invariances in multi-touch surfaces. In multi-user applications, both individual and collaborative gestures require the recognizer capability of identifying to which user each moving finger belongs. Multi-touch gestures require addressing the *finger permutation problem*: there should not be a fixed order to place fingers onto the screen. Finally, each gesture from a sequence must be tracked and buffered in order to identify sequential gestures.

We conducted an ad-hoc literature review, starting by searching at proceedings from important HCI conferences in three databases (ACM, IEEE and Google Scholar). We used general keywords, such as *multi-touch*, *gesture* and *recognition*. We collected recent results that do not deal with computer vision, accelerometers and 3D gestures, reviewed them and their related-work references in order to expand our view of

[1]For further information about gestures recognition in Android and iOS systems, we direct readers to [27] and [25] respectively.

this field and to find results which inspired recent researches. In order to get a better understanding of the techniques discussed here, we studied their implementation and searched for evolution or applications based on them.

We found two main approaches to build gestures recognizers: by defining multi-touch gestures formally and, then, trying to identify them according to that formal model; or by specifying the application gestures by examples and using a pattern recognition technique to identify them among other possible gestures.

FORMAL GESTURE DEFINITIONS

In this section, we discuss different models for multi-touch gestures and how a recognizer would match the raw input data received from the multi-touch sensor to a meaningful gesture accordingly to the proposed model.

Despite the differences between these models and their respective interpreters, they share a common characteristic: the developers must describe each gesture using the same formal model. These models vary from simple object description languages, such as eXtended Markup Language (XML), to formal grammars and logical rules.

Gesture Definition Markup Language

Back in 2009, the Natural User Interface (NUI) Group proposed the Gesture Definition Markup Language (GDML), a XML dialect to formally describe single-touch gestures [33]. Although this project seems to be discontinued, it gives us a simple example of how a gesture can be formally described.

In this language, a gesture is represented by an object structure with five attributes: *Gesture*, *Sequence*, *Acquisition*, *Update*, and *Loss*. Together, they describe the sequence of events, data format, time and geometric constraints that define a gesture.

The GDML authors also extended this language to support multi-touch gestures and the composition of simpler gestures into more complex ones. For instance, it is possible to describe a *double tap* gesture as two *tap* gestures within a maximum interval of time, while the *zoom* gesture is the same as two *drag* gestures towards or away from each other. However, due to its simplicity, GDML has three important limitations:

- It is almost impossible to describe trajectories using this model: it lacks structures to describe directions and, even if it had them, the sequence of *update* structures would get bloated very quickly.
- It imposes severe time and space constraints.
- The events are generated only when the finger is removed from the screen, reducing the feedback rate needed by applications. This is specially harmful for interactions based on direct manipulation gestures.

Gestures by semiotics

Towards the formalization of multi-touch gestures, we describe the GeForMT (Gesture Formalization for Multi-Touch) language [22]. This approach is rooted on semiotics and aims to define a formal, yet simple and readable, grammar to describe gestures, without those syntactic overhead added by XML. The main idea behind GeForMT is to describe gestures by *atomic* movements. Such movements are not gestures themselves, but part of an atomic gesture. GeForMT has the following elements:

Pose Function Describes how the hand is posed during the gesture.

Atomic Gestures A gesture description consists of a sequence of atomic movements: Move, Point, Depoint, Hold, Line, Circle, Semicircle.

Composition Operators Allows the composition of different simpler movements to define more complex gestures.

Focus Defines which interface element is being manipulated by the gesture.

Area Constraints Defines the space constraints of each movement which composes a gesture.

With GeForMT it is easier to describe gestures than by using GDML. For instance, a *rotate* gesture is the composition of a one-finger hold and another finger semi-circle, focusing an object:

```
1F(HOLD(o)) + 1F(SEMICIRCLE(o))
```

GeForMT supports directions, which are helpful to describe (*simple*) trajectories. It does not enforce scaling constraints, such as maximum ranges or diameters and supports multi-touch gestures. Also, it supports composition of atomic movements sequentially or asynchronously. However, this technique also has some limitations and some implementation issues, which must be addressed:

- Directions are dependent on the orientation, which is not specified by the language. If we assume that the orientation is relative to the multi-touch surface itself, the gestures will not be orientation invariant. An alternative is to set these directions relatively to the focused object, which is not a trivial feature to implement
- The language does not support constraints relative to speed, acceleration or more complex geometric shapes
- The language does not support fluid trajectories, because it has quite a few possible directions. To address this issue, an extension to GeForMT, which incorporates the $1 recognizer [45], was proposed in 2012 [20].
- The language does not support a temporal time-out between two movements (useful for sequential gestures)
- The language supports multi-touch, but is restricted to single-user applications without concurrent actions (two or more gestures being performed at the same time)

As any formal language, the recognition process is, actually, the process of matching if a given string of symbols is accepted by the language definition. The GeForMT authors have implemented a recognizer based on the described model, but they do not discuss how the raw input stream is converted into a string of symbols from the proposed language before being interpreted.

The Gesture Definition Language

The Gesture Description Language (GDL) is a domain specific language for describing multi-touch gestures proposed by Khandkar and Maurer in 2010 [23]. A gesture code in GDL has three sections:

Name The name of the gesture. Must be unique within the same application, but at runtime, developers may override existing gestures.

Validate One or more *validate* blocks defines the set of primitive rules which defines a gesture. Each *validate* block defines a step in a sequential gesture. If it is an atomic gesture, then only one *validate* block is needed.

Return Describes which information will be returned in the generated gesture event.

The language comes with a set of 15 built-in primitive rules to describe geometric, timing and fingers properties from the gestures. A great feature of GDL is that it is extendible: it is possible to create your own primitive rules and your own return types.

GDL has brought some capabilities we have not seen in previously discussed techniques: it allows developers to customize the language accordingly to their needs, by defining their own rules and return types. However, GDL still does not support collaborative gestures (multi-user applications in general) and it is not clear how the language and its recognition engine deal with ambiguities between gestures definitions. For instance, if a user performs a *double tap* gesture, how the system distinguishes it from two different *tap* gestures? Which events would be generated?

Defining gestures using regular expressions

Proton [25], and its evolution Proton++ [24], are gestures recognizers based on the formalism of regular expressions. Regular expressions are easy to interpret using finite automata and many modern languages, such as C# and Java, comes with built-in tools to process them, without the need of a specific compiler.

The idea behind Proton is that a gesture is a sequence of touch events. If we represent each touch event (and its properties) by a symbol, then a gesture can be described by a string of symbols from the given language.

Proton defines each gesture event as a symbol composed of three properties: the action (*touch down*, *touch move* or *touch up*), the touch identification (*id*) and the object touched (*shape*, *background* or *anything*). The object touched is obtained from a function that developers must implement and attach to the lower level stream generator, because it is very application dependent.

As an example, a *drag* gesture on a *shape* might be defined accordingly to Proton's notation as: $D_1^s M_1^{s*} U_1^s$, which means that finger 1 touched down a shape followed by any sequence of touch moves on the same shape, ending with a touch up over the same shape. The Proton's stream generator captures the raw input data from the sensors and generates a string of symbols accordingly to this notation. Then, the recognition process tries to match this string of symbols against each of the gestures regular expressions.

Proton also handles possible ambiguities between different gestures. For instance, the *tap* gesture may be defined as $D_1^s U_1^s$, which would also be matched by the above *drag* regular expression. Although it is possible rewrite the *drag* gesture in order to solve this ambiguity, modifying it to $D_1^s M_1^{s+} U_1^s$, this might be impossible in the general case. In order to solve ambiguities, the system allows developers to define a score function, which estimates the confidence degree of a decision.

Proton also has two other important features: it comes with a gestures editor inspired by music tablatures, called *gestures tablature*, and the possibility to generate events when any part of the regular expression is matched, which is necessary to handle direct manipulation gestures.

Despite its unique features, Proton only supports those three properties in each symbol. Proton++ overcomes this problem and allows developers to define their own properties in each symbol with a custom stream processor. However, the stream generator still assumes that only one gesture is being performed at that time, which makes the system unsuitable for multi-user applications, but very powerful for single-user ones (without concurrent gestures).

However, their main limitation is related to the nature of regular expressions, which are, by definition, a sequence of a fixed set of symbols (the language alphabet). This implies hard constraints, the same issue we discussed previously for the original GeForMT and GDL: it is hard to describe the complex trajectories found in many symbolic gestures. To illustrate that, suppose that we have added four direction properties to the set of symbols: N, S, E and W. We would have problems if we meant to create a gesture that moves towards the NE. Although we could add NE, SE, NW and SW directions, we would fall into the same problem if the trajectory is somewhere between N and NE, for example.

Finally, the recognizer does not handle the finger permutation problem by itself, making the description of multi-touch gestures harder and more error-prone.

Recognizing Gestures using Logical Inference

Midas [38] is a multi-touch gesture engine which describes gestures as a set of logical rules. These logical rules are processed by a logical inference engine against a set of facts, deciding which gesture has been performed. The main motivation of Midas is to allow gestures re-usability and extensibility. As gestures are described by a logical rule, they can be used to build new gestures.

The fact base consists of all current input detected, called cursor (the moving finger). Each cursor has the following properties: position (x and y coordinates), speed (x and y coordinates), time and id. The rules base consists of the gestures definitions. A set of built-in operators (predicates) is provided:

Temporal Operators Provide predicates to verify the temporal relationship between facts.

Spatial Operators Provide predicates to verify the spatial relationship between facts.

List Operator Provide predicates to group facts into a list of common facts. The list will contain all facts that follow the given constraints, such as time period and id.

Movement Operators Provide predicates to obtain the direction of the movement (*up*, *down*, *left* and *right*).

Midas addresses the ambiguity problem by allowing developers to define *priorities* for each gesture. When two or more gestures are possible to be deduced from the facts base, Midas will chose the one with highest priority. As fingers are logical variables, Midas has implicitly solved the *finger permutation problem*.

Although Midas supports time and space interval constraints, it still imposes hard constraints. Valid gestures could fall out of such intervals, but very close to them. Midas could address this issue using *fuzzy operators*, defining *vague* rules, such as *a small time interval*.

To help developers create custom gestures based on complex trajectories, Hoste et al. have included a *gesture spotting* algorithm before running the Midas recognition process. Their algorithm extracts a set of control points from the unknown gesture based on a previously added gesture sample. This gives developers the ability to create logical rules based on the shape of such gestures [14]. It would also be possible to define a logical rule based on the result of a template matching algorithm and to deny gestures when they become invalid or if they have been poorly matched.

Midas has also been incorporated to the Mudra multimodal fusion engine, supporting multi-user environments and collaborative gestures [15]. Finally, Midas declarative approach has been exploited in parallel events processing techniques, providing soft real-time gesture recognition [35].

In this section we discussed most of the approaches towards the formalization of multi-touch gestures published recently in depth. Some techniques [13, 8, 10, 41] were not discussed because they are similar to the ones we described.

DEFINING GESTURES BY EXAMPLES

In this section, we discuss a different approach to recognize gestures, which can be seen as the *dual* of the *formalism*-based one: while in the formalism approach users must reproduce the gesture model, the *learning*-based approach lets users define the gestures they want to use. Most of these techniques are developed on top of machine learning concepts.

This technique is also known as *user-defined gestures* [44] and has drawn great attention from the tabletop community, since the $1 recognizer was published in 2007 [45]. However, recognizing gestures from examples is an old idea: in 1991, Rubine proposed GRANDMA: a model to recognize single-touch gestures from a set of examples [37].

The GRANDMA Recognizer

GRANDMA (Gestures Recognizers Automated in a Novel Direct Manipulation Architecture) algorithm models a single-touch gesture by its timed-trajectory in the two dimensional plane, which means that each gesture is a single sequence of (x, y, t) points, ignoring points which are less than 3 pixels away from the previous one. Then, it extracts a set of 13 *features* (properties) from a given gesture and matches them against each gesture class using the classic *Linear Discriminant Analysis* (LDA).

A Nearest Neighbour Approach

The $-Family of touch gesture recognizers has been developed since the release of the $1 recognizer for single-touch gestures in 2007 [45]. These algorithms are based on the *K-Nearest Neighbours* (KNN) technique, which defines a *distance* measure between the unknown gesture and those which have been previously added to the system during the *training* step.

$1 calculates the *Average Euclidean Distance* between a gesture $\mathbf{g}$ in the gesture base and the unknown gesture $\mathbf{t}$, which is converted to a similarity measure and is used to estimate the similarity between an unknown gesture and each gesture in the gesture base.

Different sensors may sample touch-inputs at different rates, generating a different number of touch-points per trajectory. In order to get sampling rate invariance, $1 introduces a new pre-processing phase: it re-samples each trajectory in order to have a set of N equidistant touch points per sequence of (x, y) coordinates. Then, in order to make gestures invariant to translation and scale, $1 re-scales all gestures to fit the $[-1, 1]$ square interval and translates the transformed gesture center of mass to $(0, 0)$. This process is performed for each *sample gesture* during the *training phase* and repeated for each *unknown gesture* during the *classification phase*.

In order to achieve orientation invariance, $1 rotates each gesture by its *indicative angle* (the angle between its centroid and the first point) and applies the *Golden-Section Search* method, which consists in rotating each candidate gesture by an angle $\theta \in (0, 2\pi)$, step-by-step, while the similarity between the unknown gesture and the rotated candidate gesture grows. This is a brute force method, which demands a large amount of computation, slowing down the recognition process.

Almost at the same time, in 2010, two extensions of the $1 recognizer were published: the *Protractor* [29] and $N [1] recognizers. The former presented a closed-form solution to the rotation invariance and the aspect-ratio problems of $1, using the *Inverse Cosine Distance* and significantly improving the time spent to classify an unknown gesture. The latter presented an extension of $1 for multi-touch gestures.

After its pre-processing phase, $1 models each gesture $\mathbf{g}$ as a sequence of (x, y) coordinates, defining a $(N * 2)$-dimensional vector, where N is the number of touch points per gesture. $N extends this model to multi-touch gestures by considering each finger trajectory as a $(N * 2)$-dimensional vector and concatenating each finger vector into a new $(N * F * 2)$-dimensional vector, where F is the number of fingers used to perform the gesture. This new model works the best if we compare an unknown gesture only to candidates with the same number of fingers.

In 2012, Protractor and $N solutions were merged into a new recognizer: $N-Protractor [2]. However, as any previously discussed solution, $N-Protractor also has its limitations[2]:

Fingers Permutations When users perform multi-touch gestures, fingers can be placed on the screen in any order. For instance, a two-finger gesture (F1 and F2) would generate two different vectors: [F1, F2] and [F2, F1], which would be classified differently. In order to avoid this issue, $N-Protractor automatically adds all possible finger permutations to the gestures base. This combinatoric increases the number of candidates, slowing down the classification process and making it much more error-prone. This issue was addressed by the $P recognizer [43] at the cost of losing the gesture trajectory information.

Large Gestures Base $N-Protractor is good for prototyping because the KNN technique does not require a real *training* process, as opposed to GRANDMA. However, this is also a drawback, because the classification routine must compare the unknown gestures to all gestures (and their finger permutations) on the base. In real applications, when tens of different gestures (and different numbers of fingers) are available, the classification process suffers a significant loss of speed and, sometimes, precision.

Timing-based gestures $N-Protractor does not use timing information to define gestures, therefore, it is impossible to distinguish gestures that differ only in duration or speed, such as *tap* and *press and hold*.

Free-Form Gestures $N-Protractor is not capable of recognizing free-form gestures such as *drag* and *lasso* because their trajectories are not well-defined.

Continuous Feedback As GRANDMA, $N-Protractor assumes that the sequence of gestures is provided by another part of the system and the recognition process must be triggered manually, making it difficult to provide continuous feedback to applications.

Learning Automata for Gesture Recognition

Gesture Coder [27] is a multi-touch gesture recognizer which has been proposed to address the problem of continuous feedback from previous *user-defined gestures recognizers* without dealing with the complexity of manually building finite automata to describe them.

The idea behind *Gesture Coder* is to *learn* different automata for each gesture defined by users, using a complex learning algorithm. To support this idea instead of a trajectory-based recognizer, authors claim that the number of fingers involved in a gesture and the spatial relationship among them are often more important than their absolute trajectories.

Gesture Coder learns the finite automata state transitions and generates events to the application in all these transitions, giving an opportunity to developers to add a specific code to handle these events and to provide continuous feedback to applications if necessary.

Gesture Coder addresses the ambiguity problem by detecting in each state if an event may generate two or more possible gestures transitions. In such states, a *Binary Decision Tree* is trained in order to output the probability of each gesture in these states from the finger motion. After the training phase, *Gesture Coder* generates the finite state machine code (in Java), which must be plugged into the main application and can be customized by developers.

FORMALISM VERSUS LEARNING

In this section, we summarize a discussion between the *user-defined gestures* and the *formal gestures* approaches, exploring their strengths and weaknesses, which shall be useful for future researches on the topic.

Formalization of multi-touch gestures still lacks an efficient way to deal with complex trajectories. The use of gesture spotting algorithms to extract a set of control points from an unknown gesture has been used with the Midas recognizer and has given it the ability to recognize complex trajectories, but the proposed solution is not rotation invariant, which is an important factor for multi-user interactive tables.

On the other hand, requirements such as modularization and composition of gestures have been successfully addressed. Continuous feedback have been partially addressed, since segmentation is not fully-implemented in the most advanced recognizers and there is no way to predict future events in order to cancel a gesture that has became untrue (such as the Gesture Coder's *cancelled state*).

The *learning* approach has some advantages over the *formalism*-based one, which must be highlighted:

- Defining gestures by examples does not require designing each gesture according to a given model
- Retraining the recognizer allows developers to easily add or remove gestures from the data set
- It is easy to design complex trajectories as one just need to reproduce them during the training process

The *learning* approach also has some drawbacks: it still cannot handle free-form gestures and it is more difficult to provide continuous feedback to applications. Also, only GRANDMA recognizer considers temporal gestures data (duration) and is able to negate poorly classified gestures, but handles only single-touch gestures. Temporal relationship between gestures, temporal data for multi-touch gestures and the denial of poorly classified multi-touch gestures have not been covered by the proposed learning-based techniques so far.

[2]$N limitations: `http://depts.washington.edu/aimgroup/proj/dollar/limits/` - accessed at 22nd, April, 2014

We understand that the most promising results are based on mixed solutions, such as Gesture Coder [27] and Midas with Gesture Spotting [14]: using both learning algorithms to match complex trajectories and formalisms to generate continuous events, recognizing *free-form* gestures and denying poorly classified or cancelled gestures.

Analysing the current state of the art recognizers from the gestures properties presented in Table 1, we understand that Midas with Gesture Spotting is the most capable recognizer, supporting:

- 2D gestures *on the surface*
- Both symbolic and direct manipulation gestures
- Complex trajectories, without spatial invariance
- Individual and collaborative gestures in multimodal environments
- Both atomic and sequential gestures

MULTI-TOUCH GESTURES FRAMEWORKS

In this section we describe the state of the art multi-touch frameworks. A framework is a set of abstractions, interfaces and standards developed to solve a class of problems in a flexible and extensible manner [11]. In our context, a framework abstracts multi-touch gestures concepts, allowing developers to create custom gestures and handle their respective events in their applications.

Several multi-touch frameworks were proposed in the past few years, each trying to address different developers needs. Although their implementation varies, their most high-level architecture remains almost unchanged, because their base goal is still the same: to link different input hardware and different graphical toolkits (application level) [9].

The link between these two parts of the system is built on top of a layered architecture, which looses coupling between each part of the system and allows great extensibility and customization. The Hardware Abstraction Layer (HAL) abstracts the sensors hardware and device drivers, defining a common interface for receiving raw touch events. The TUIO protocol has become the *de facto* standard to provide such integration [19].

On top of HAL, Echtler and Klinker define a *transformation layer*, which is responsible for converting input data from the sensors to screen coordinates. The *interpretation layer* does the actual *gestures recognition*, embedding gesture *features* into an *event* object, transmitted to the *widgets layer*, which represents the Graphical User Interface (GUI) components (polygonal *regions* where gestures are performed).

The *gesture recognizer*, is only part of this more complex architecture, which abstracts the gestures handling and their integration to interface objects, allowing developers to easily build new applications on top of it.

Currently there are several frameworks with the most recurring multi-touch gestures such as *tap* or *drag* built-in, such as MT4j [16], Surface SDK, Multitouch Vista, Breeze Multitouch [30] and Miria [6], ranging between proprietary and open source. Usually, when a vendor releases a new multi-touch surface, it also provides a custom multi-touch framework, such as the *DiamondSpin Framework* [40] for the *DiamondTouch Table* [7] or the reacTIVision [18] for the reacTable [17].

Kammer et al. studied several frameworks and compared them against a set of criteria (Table 2), in order to help developers to find the most suitable for a given application [21].

Table 2: Kammer et al. Criteria

Classes	Criteria
Features	Visualization Support Gesture Extensibility Standard Gestures
Scope	Gesture Parameters Tangible Objects Touch
Architecture	Event System Hardware Independence Platform Independence

According to the authors, some of the mentioned frameworks are platform independent (MT4j, Miria and Splash-UI) and others are not (Surface SDK). There are also frameworks which focus on tangible objects (Surface SDK) or on touch (MT4j, Sparsh-UI and Breeze Multitouch). Some frameworks also provides a presentation layer, which contains some widget controls specially developed for multi-touch applications (MT4j, Surface SDK and Breeze Multitouch), implementing the full stack proposed by Echtler and Klinker.

Their criteria are mostly focused on the developers needs, by evaluating how a framework would answer to questions such as:

- How to create new gestures?
- How to port my application to different platforms?
- Does it handle touch input or tangible objects?
- Is it integrated to custom GUI components?

As discussed previously, different *gesture recognizers* have their own limitations, which affects users interaction in different ways. Problems such as *orientation invariance*, *recognition performance* and *continuous feedback* are ignored by their set of criteria. To address this problem, we propose an extended set of requirements that a gestures recognition framework should meet to provide better support to interactive table applications:

1. **Be Flexible and Extensible** This is the major motivation for all the researches reviewed here: to allow developers to create their custom gestures without needing to handle low-level input data.

2. **Be Fast** Gestures recognition algorithms must be fast in order to not harm the users interaction due to recognition latency.

3. **Be Accurate** Misidentification of gestures may cause several issues to the interaction, as users may lose their current work or may waste time undoing unwanted actions triggered by an incorrect recognition.

4. **Support Multi-Touch and 5. Multi-Users** Multi-touch surfaces are most often used to support collaborative applications. Thus, handling multi-touch gestures from several users simultaneously is a requirement for recognition systems. Multi-touch gestures may cause the *fingers permutation problem*, while multi-user environments require identifying which fingers belong to each gesture each user is performing.

6. **Support Spatial Invariance** Most multi-touch surface applications must not enforce a fixed orientation and participants may interact from any position around the table [26]. Also, gestures may be performed at any place around the screen and at different scales. Thus scale, translation and rotation invariances are also important requirements for interactive table applications.

7. **Provide Continuous Feedback** Applications must be continuously notified about gesture events when these gestures are being used to manipulate objects on the screen, such as rotating, moving or resizing them. Such gestures should be cancelled when they become untrue.

8. **Allow Easy Prototyping** During the prototyping phase of any multi-touch surface application, developers and interaction designers work together in order to run several user experiments to identify which gestures will be used in their applications. This is an iterative process which requires making it easy to modify the gestures set and handle their respective events at the application level.

9. **Support Symbolic Gestures** Symbolic gestures are often used to execute single-shot actions in tabletop applications, playing the role of command's *shortcuts* or *hotkeys*, which are common in other platforms. These gestures are defined by their trajectory, both in spatial and time coordinates.

10. **Allow Time-Constrained Gestures** Most applications uses *tap* or *press and hold* gestures in order to manipulate objects on the screen. These gestures are examples of spatially identical gestures, but very different from the timing perspective.

11. **Support Territories** Users perform different actions in different multi-touch surface territories [39]. Therefore, a gesture framework must allow developers to define which gestures are allowed in each territory, avoiding delegating this decision to the application level.

12. **Recognize Free-form Gestures** Gestures such as *drag* and *lasso* can not be described by their trajectories. Therefore, recognizers must also handle such kind of free-form gestures.

13. **Support Sequential Gestures** A well-defined sequence of multi-touch gestures can trigger a new action at the application level (*combos of gestures*). A gestures framework must allow developers to specify these sequences and their time constraints and must notify the application whenever these sequences are detected.

14. **Support Cooperative Gestures** As multi-touch surfaces are often used to support collaborative applications, frameworks should support cooperative gestures.

Table 3 evaluates some of the multi-touch gestures frameworks and recognizers discussed in this paper according to the proposed criteria (•: supported; ○: unsupported; –: not enough data). Unfortunately, from Kammer et al. review on multi-touch frameworks and our review on multi-touch gesture recognizers, none of these solutions meets all of the proposed criteria.

Table 3: Frameworks and Recognizers Analysis

Criteria	Midas	Proton++	$N-Protractor	MT4J
1	•	•	•	•
2	•	–	•	–
3	–	–	•	–
4	•	•	•	•
5	•	○	○	○
6	○	○	•	○
7	•	•	○	•
8	○	•	•	○
9	•	○	•	○
10	•	•	○	•
11	•	○	○	•
12	•	•	○	•
13	•	•	○	○
14	•	○	○	○

CONCLUSION

We reviewed the state of art techniques and frameworks for defining and recognizing multi-touch gestures for multi-touch surface applications. We discussed their strengths and weaknesses, which we understand are important for both people who are starting on this field and people who are interested in addressing discussed issues in future researches.

Finally, from the concepts from the multi-touch surfaces interaction field, such as territoriality, orientation and collaboration, and the limitations of the current state of the art gestures recognition systems, we proposed an extension to Kammer et al. set of criteria that a framework should meet to provide better support to multi-touch surface interaction.

Unfortunately, none of the state of the art techniques or frameworks discussed in this paper meets all the proposed requirements. We would like to point out that although some new sensors, such as Kinect and Leap Motion have been released and have gained great attention from the tabletop community recently, interaction with multi-touch gestures is still not fully supported and is an important and challenging area for future researches.

REFERENCES

1. Anthony, L., and Wobbrock, J. O. A lightweight multistroke recognizer for user interface prototypes. In *Proceedings of Graphics Interface 2010*, GI '10, Canadian Information Processing Society (Toronto, Ont., Canada, Canada, 2010), 245–252.
2. Anthony, L., and Wobbrock, J. O. $n-protractor: a fast and accurate multistroke recognizer. In *Proceedings of Graphics Interface 2012*, GI '12, Canadian Information Processing Society (Toronto, Ont., Canada, Canada, 2012), 117–120.
3. Chen, F.-S., Fu, C.-M., and Huang, C.-L. Hand gesture recognition using a real-time tracking method and hidden markov models. *Image and Vision Computing 21*, 8 (2003), 745–758.
4. Chen, L., Wang, F., Deng, H., and Ji, K. A survey on hand gesture recognition. In *Proceedings of the 2013 International Conference on Computer Sciences and Applications*, CSA '13, IEEE Computer Society (Washington, DC, USA, 2013), 313–316.
5. Clayphan, A., Collins, A., Ackad, C., Kummerfeld, B., and Kay, J. Firestorm: a brainstorming application for collaborative group work at tabletops. ITS '11, ACM (New York, NY, USA, 2011), 162–171.
6. Codeplex. MIRIA SDK, 2011.
7. Dietz, P., and Leigh, D. DiamondTouch: a multi-user touch technology. In *Proceedings of the 14th annual ACM symposium on User interface software and technology*, UIST '01, ACM (New York, NY, USA, 2001), 219–226.
8. Echtler, F., and Butz, A. GISpL: gestures made easy. In *Proceedings of the Sixth International Conference on Tangible, Embedded and Embodied Interaction*, TEI '12, ACM (New York, NY, USA, 2012), 233–240.
9. Echtler, F., and Klinker, G. A multitouch software architecture. In *Proceedings of the 5th Nordic conference on Human-computer interaction: building bridges*, NordiCHI '08, ACM (New York, NY, USA, 2008), 463–466.
10. Echtler, F., Klinker, G., and Butz, A. Towards a unified gesture description language. In *Proceedings of the 13th International Conference on Humans and Computers*, HC '10, University of Aizu Press (Fukushima-ken, Japan, Japan, 2010), 177–182.
11. Govoni, D. *Java Application Frameworks*, 1 ed. Wiley, June 1999.
12. Hinrichs, U., and Carpendale, S. Gestures in the wild: studying multi-touch gesture sequences on interactive tabletop exhibits. In *Proceedings of the 2011 annual conference on Human factors in computing systems*, CHI '11, ACM (New York, NY, USA, 2011), 3023–3032.
13. Hoste, L. Software engineering abstractions for the multi-touch revolution. In *2010 ACM/IEEE 32nd International Conference on Software Engineering*, vol. 2, IEEE (May 2010), 509–510.
14. Hoste, L., De Rooms, B., and Signer, B. Declarative gesture spotting using inferred and refined control points. In *Proceedings of the 2nd International Conference on Pattern Recognition Applications and Methods (ICPRAM 2013)* (Barcelona, Spain, 2013), 1–6.
15. Hoste, L., Dumas, B., and Signer, B. Mudra: A unified multimodal interaction framework. In *Proceedings of the 13th International Conference on Multimodal Interfaces*, ICMI '11, ACM (New York, NY, USA, 2011), 97–104.
16. Institute, F. MT4j - multitouch for java, 2011.
17. Jord, S., Geiger, G., Alonso, M., and Kaltenbrunner, M. The reacTable: exploring the synergy between live music performance and tabletop tangible interfaces. In *Proceedings of the 1st international conference on Tangible and embedded interaction*, TEI '07, ACM (New York, NY, USA, 2007), 139–146.
18. Kaltenbrunner, M. reacTIVision and TUIO: a tangible tabletop toolkit. In *Proceedings of the ACM International Conference on Interactive Tabletops and Surfaces*, ITS '09, ACM (New York, NY, USA, 2009), 9–16.
19. Kaltenbrunner, M., Bovermann, T., Bencina, R., and Costanza, E. TUIO: A protocol for table-top tangible user interfaces. In *6th International Gesture Workshop* (2005).
20. Kammer, D., Henkens, D., and Groh, R. GeForMTjs: A javascript library based on a domain specific language for multi-touch gestures. In *Proceedings of the 12th International Conference on Web Engineering*, ICWE'12, Springer-Verlag (Berlin, Heidelberg, 2012), 444–447.
21. Kammer, D., Keck, M., Freitag, G., and Wacker, M. Taxonomy and overview of multi-touch frameworks: Architecture, scope and features. In *Workshop on Engineering Patterns for Multitouch Interfaces* (2010).
22. Kammer, D., Wojdziak, J., Keck, M., Groh, R., and Taranko, S. Towards a formalization of multi-touch gestures. ITS '10, ACM (New York, NY, USA, 2010), 49–58.
23. Khandkar, S. H., and Maurer, F. A domain specific language to define gestures for multi-touch applications. In *Proceedings of the 10th Workshop on Domain-Specific Modeling*, DSM '10, ACM (New York, NY, USA, 2010), 2:1–2:6.
24. Kin, K., Hartmann, B., DeRose, T., and Agrawala, M. Proton++: a customizable declarative multitouch framework. In *Proceedings of the 25th annual ACM symposium on User interface software and technology*, UIST '12, ACM (New York, NY, USA, 2012), 477–486.
25. Kin, K., Hartmann, B., DeRose, T., and Agrawala, M. Proton: multitouch gestures as regular expressions. In *Proceedings of the 2012 ACM annual conference on Human Factors in Computing Systems*, CHI '12, ACM (New York, NY, USA, 2012), 2885–2894.

26. Kruger, R., Carpendale, S., Scott, S. D., and Greenberg, S. How people use orientation on tables: comprehension, coordination and communication. In *Proceedings of the 2003 international ACM SIGGROUP conference on Supporting group work*, GROUP '03, ACM (New York, NY, USA, 2003), 369–378.

27. L, H., and Li, Y. Gesture coder: a tool for programming multi-touch gestures by demonstration. In *Proceedings of the 2012 ACM annual conference on Human Factors in Computing Systems*, CHI '12, ACM (New York, NY, USA, 2012), 2875–2884.

28. LaViola, Jr., J. J. A survey of hand posture and gesture recognition techniques and technology. Tech. rep., Brown University, Providence, RI, USA, 1999.

29. Li, Y. Protractor: a fast and accurate gesture recognizer. In *Proceedings of the SIGCHI Conference on Human Factors in Computing Systems*, CHI '10, ACM (New York, NY, USA, 2010), 2169–2172.

30. Mindstorm. Breezemultitouch, 2010.

31. Mitra, S., and Acharya, T. Gesture recognition: A survey. *Trans. Sys. Man Cyber Part C 37*, 3 (May 2007), 311–324.

32. Morris, M. R., Huang, A., Paepcke, A., and Winograd, T. Cooperative gestures: multi-user gestural interactions for co-located groupware. In *Proceedings of the SIGCHI conference on Human Factors in computing systems*, CHI '06, ACM (New York, NY, USA, 2006), 1201–1210.

33. NUIGroup, T. Gesture definition markup language (GDML), 2009.

34. Nygard, E. S., and Thomassen, A. *Multi-touch Interaction with Gesture Recognition*. PhD thesis, 2010.

35. Renaux, T., Hoste, L., Marr, S., and De Meuter, W. Parallel gesture recognition with soft real-time guarantees. In *Proceedings of the 2Nd Edition on Programming Systems, Languages and Applications Based on Actors, Agents, and Decentralized Control Abstractions*, AGERE! '12, ACM (New York, NY, USA, 2012), 35–46.

36. Rhyne, J. R., and Wolf, C. G. Gestural interfaces for information processing applications. Tech. Rep. RC12179, IBM Corporation, Yorktown Heights, NY, 1986.

37. Rubine, D. Specifying gestures by example. *SIGGRAPH Comput. Graph. 25*, 4 (July 1991), 329–337.

38. Scholliers, C., Hoste, L., Signer, B., and De Meuter, W. Midas: a declarative multi-touch interaction framework. In *Proceedings of the fifth international conference on Tangible, embedded, and embodied interaction*, TEI '11, ACM (New York, NY, USA, 2011), 49–56.

39. Scott, S. D., Sheelagh, M., Carpendale, T., and Inkpen, K. M. Territoriality in collaborative tabletop workspaces. In *Proceedings of the 2004 ACM conference on Computer supported cooperative work*, CSCW '04, ACM (New York, NY, USA, 2004), 294–303.

40. Shen, C., Vernier, F. D., Forlines, C., and Ringel, M. DiamondSpin: an extensible toolkit for around-the-table interaction. In *Proceedings of the SIGCHI conference on Human factors in computing systems*, CHI '04, ACM (New York, NY, USA, 2004), 167–174.

41. Spano, L. D., Cisternino, A., and Patern, F. A compositional model for gesture definition. In *Proceedings of the 4th International Conference on Human-Centered Software Engineering*, HCSE'12, Springer-Verlag (Berlin, Heidelberg, 2012), 34–52.

42. Strothoff, S., Valkov, D., and Hinrichs, K. Triangle cursor: interactions with objects above the tabletop. ITS '11, ACM (New York, NY, USA, 2011), 111–119.

43. Vatavu, R.-D., Anthony, L., and Wobbrock, J. O. Gestures as point clouds: a $p recognizer for user interface prototypes. In *Proceedings of the 14th ACM international conference on Multimodal interaction*, ICMI '12, ACM (New York, NY, USA, 2012), 273–280.

44. Wobbrock, J. O., Morris, M. R., and Wilson, A. D. User-defined gestures for surface computing. In *Proceedings of the SIGCHI Conference on Human Factors in Computing Systems*, CHI '09, ACM (New York, NY, USA, 2009), 1083–1092.

45. Wobbrock, J. O., Wilson, A. D., and Li, Y. Gestures without libraries, toolkits or training: a $1 recognizer for user interface prototypes. In *Proceedings of the 20th annual ACM symposium on User interface software and technology*, UIST '07, ACM (New York, NY, USA, 2007), 159–168.

46. Yoon, H.-S., Soh, J., Bae, Y. J., and Seung Yang, H. Hand gesture recognition using combined features of location, angle and velocity. *Pattern Recognition 34*, 7 (2001), 1491–1501.

HuddleLamp: Spatially-Aware Mobile Displays for Ad-hoc Around-the-Table Collaboration

Roman Rädle[1], Hans-Christian Jetter[2], Nicolai Marquardt[3], Harald Reiterer[1], Yvonne Rogers[3]
[1] HCI Group, University of Konstanz, {roman.raedle,harald.reiterer}@uni-konstanz.de
[2] Intel ICRI Cities, University College London, h.jetter@ucl.ac.uk
[3] UCL Interaction Centre, University College London, {y.rogers,n.marquardt}@ucl.ac.uk

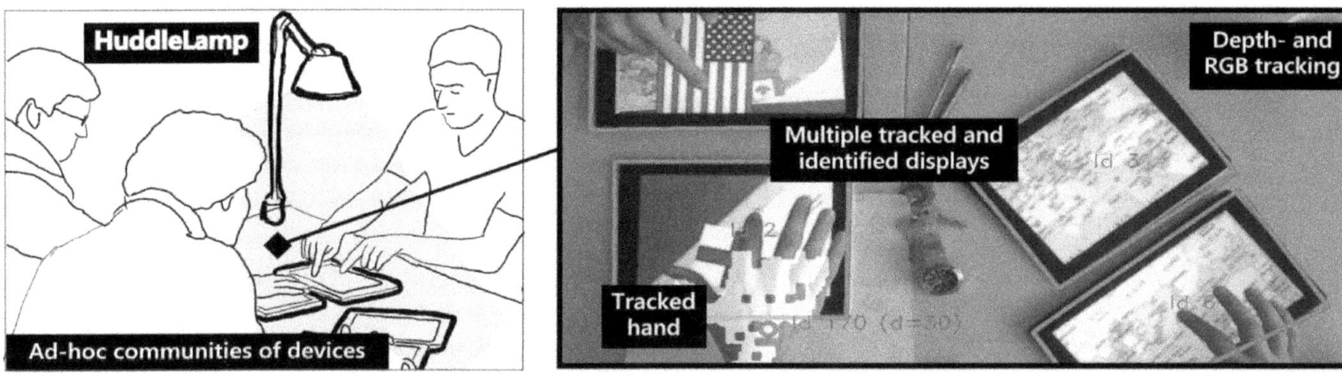

Figure 1. The HuddleLamp detects and tracks mobile devices and users' hands for ad-hoc multi-device collaboration on desks.

ABSTRACT

We present HuddleLamp, a desk lamp with an integrated RGB-D camera that precisely tracks the movements and positions of mobile displays and hands on a table. This enables a new breed of spatially-aware multi-user and multi-device applications for around-the-table collaboration *without* an interactive tabletop. At any time, users can add or remove displays and reconfigure them in space in an ad-hoc manner without the need of installing any software or attaching markers. Additionally, hands are tracked to detect interactions above and between displays, enabling fluent cross-device interactions. We contribute a novel hybrid sensing approach that uses RGB and depth data to increase tracking quality and a technical evaluation of its capabilities and limitations. For enabling installation-free ad-hoc collaboration, we also introduce a web-based architecture and JavaScript API for future HuddleLamp applications. Finally, we demonstrate the resulting design space using five examples of cross-device interaction techniques.

Author Keywords

Mobile devices; cross-device interactions; depth camera; ad hoc collaboration; society of devices; ubicomp ecologies.

ACM Classification Keywords

H.5.2 [Information Interfaces and Presentation]: Input

ITS 2014, November 16–19, 2014, Dresden, Germany.
ACM 978-1-4503-2587-5/14/11.
http://dx.doi.org/10.1145/2669485.2669500

INTRODUCTION

We are witnessing an explosive growth of the number and density of powerful mobile devices around us. However, their great majority are still blind to the presence of other devices and performing tasks among them is usually tedious [6] and lacks recognizable guiding principles [25]. We envision a future where mobile devices can contribute their interaction resources (e.g., their multi-touch displays) to a community of devices in their proximity that then serves as one seamless multi-device user interface (UI). At any time, users can dynamically compose and reconfigure this UI according to their current needs and the task at hand.

In this vision, users can seamlessly add or remove devices from the community in an ad-hoc fashion without explicit setup or pairing. Instead, this happens implicitly as a by-product of natural use in space, for example, by bringing multiple devices to the same room, placing them side-by-side on a table or desk, and moving them around as needed. Ideally, users will experience these co-located cooperating devices and reconfigurable displays as one seamless and natural UI for ad-hoc co-located collaboration.

As a first incarnation of this vision, we present *HuddleLamp*, a desk lamp with an integrated low-cost RGB-D camera that detects and identifies mobile displays (e.g., smartphones or tablets) on tables and tracks their positions and orientations with sub-centimetre precision. Users can add or remove off-the-shelf, web-enabled devices in an ad-hoc fashion *without* prior installation of custom hardware (e.g., radio modules, IR markers) or software. Because of HuddleLamp's web-based pairing, adding a new device is simply done by opening a URL on the device and putting it on the table so that it is visible to the camera.

HuddleLamp also tracks users' hands to enable interactions between and above devices, such as 'pick, drag, and drop'.

This enables a new kind of computer-supported around-the-table collaboration *without* interactive tabletops. Users can still sit around ordinary tables that can remain cluttered with non-digital objects (e.g., printouts, maps, notebooks) while their digital collaborations happen using spatially-aware mobile screens that blend into existing spatial and social practices. Unlike traditional interactive tabletops, HuddleLamp needs only few *low-cost* and *off-the-shelf* hardware components, so it can be used in improvised settings or where the costs for hardware and administration typically prohibit the use of large interactive tabletops, e.g., public libraries, schools, community centres.

In the remainder of this paper, we focus on our following contributions:

- As our primary contribution, we introduce our *novel hybrid sensing approach* for HuddleLamp. This approach combines RGB *and* depth input for detecting and tracking movements of multiple mobile screens with sub-centimetre precision by exploiting their optical characteristics in both the RGB and IR range. We evaluate the tracking quality of our approach in terms of *accuracy*, *precision*, and *reliability* with a controlled experiment and discuss capabilities and limitations.
- As secondary contributions:
  - we introduce our web-based architecture and JavaScript API for enabling truly ad-hoc, walk-up-and-use applications with no need for installing any native mobile apps or instrumenting devices with any markers or hardware before collaborating.
  - we validate our architecture and API with five example interaction techniques that used to be possible only in instrumented rooms or on and above large tabletops. They demonstrate the future design space for spatially-aware multi-device around-the-table collaboration with HuddleLamp.

RELATED WORK

HuddleLamp relates to four different strains of previous research that we sample and discuss below.

Spatial Interaction in Instrumented Environments. The use of space and spatial configurations plays a key role in human cognition [11] and natural social interactions [6]. To leverage our spatial skills for interaction, one approach is to create instrumented rooms that capture the spatial interactions and configurations of users and objects as system input. For example, LightSpace uses multiple depth cameras and projectors to provide interactivity on and between physical surfaces [37]. The steerable Beamatron [36] projects directly into the environment, and the LuminAR actuated desktop lamp design allows touch detection and projection onto desks [17]. As a mobile solution, SurfacePhone [38] uses a similar approach to facilitate single or multi-user around-the-phone interactions through projected interfaces. The OmniTouch [8] wearable device introduces a high flexibility of where and when such interfaces are displayed. We focus on enabling ad-hoc device assemblages and interaction around tables with the mobile devices people already carry, such as phones and tablets. Conductor [7] recently introduced techniques for orchestrating such cross-device interactions, which HuddleLamp facilitates by automatically tracking spatial relationships between devices, allowing for fluent transfer and sharing.

Greenberg argued that we can enhance the interaction with ubicomp technology by designing systems that consider fine-grained inter-entity relationships, such as the distance or orientation between people and devices [6]. As proxemic interactions this has been applied in various contexts, such as the interaction with a large surface media player [1], games [6], or interactive advertisements [35]. Later, the GroupTogether system considers people's spatial F-formations [14] during small group collaboration to initiate cross-device interactions [21]. The majority of these systems rely on high-end motion capturing systems [20] that are ideal for prototyping interaction techniques but are difficult to deploy in environments out of the lab. To enable lightweight, ad-hoc scenarios of use, our system keeps the effort for instrumentation minimal, only uses a single RGB-D camera for tracking, and does not require any additional augmentations of devices.

Presence, Pairing, and Position of Co-located Mobile Devices. To enable cross-device interactions [19], the system first needs knowledge about the presence and position of other devices around it. Various techniques establish such connections: synchronous gestures [27] that pair devices when stitching stroke across the screens [10]; other approaches include shaking devices simultaneously [12], bumping [27], or performing pinching gestures [24]. Another approach is to use custom sensing hardware, for example infrared-, hall-, or radio-based position sensing. Siftables use infrared emitters and transceivers for detecting nearby cubes [23]. Likewise, mobile devices with magnets and hall sensors can sense presence [13], or instrumented phones can utilize custom-built radio tracking for positioning [18] – though often with relatively coarse-grained spatial resolution (~1m). Similarly, GroupTogether requires custom-built radio-based position trilateration for device positions [21]. As explained shortly, our novel sensor fusion approach brings this tracking to a new level by not requiring any radio-based trilateration hardware and allowing precise sub-centimetre tracking.

Alternatively, built-in cameras can infer device location information. Back facing phone cameras can infer relative positions from extracted features in the downward-facing camera images (e.g., legs, feet) [3]. Similarly, Schmitz et al. [29] and Li et al. [16] use the front facing camera of devices to detect fiducial markers on the ceiling. Improving this tracking for reliably handling different environmental conditions remains an on-going research challenge. Alternatively, cameras positioned above a table can track the spatial layout of devices placed on the table below. Rekimoto's tracked devices' location by attaching fiduciary markers [28], an approach later also applied to track multiple devices for DynamicDuo [26]. Kray et al. later used a related approach to determine the position of phones in one of three discrete spatial zones that trigger sharing actions between the phones [15]. Taking these approaches further, we consider both depth- and RGB-tracking data to improve tracking quality for devices placed on a table.

Reconfigurable Tiled Displays. A special case of co-located mobile devices are (re)configurable tiled displays. ConnecTables [34] allow dynamically reconfigurable display assemblages when devices are in proximity. At a larger scale, Phone as a Pixel [30] creates ad-hoc large-scale displays composed of smaller devices, each serving as a pixel of a large virtual display. The position of each pixel/device is calculated by decoding a sequence of colour transitions that encodes the ID of that device with a camera [30]. Similarly, the web-based Junkyard Jumbotron system stitches together devices' screens to a single large virtual display [2]. Even though it is not built for real-time tracking, it allows a manual process where users take pictures of fiduciary markers shown on the screens and send it to a server for calibration processing. One approach towards allowing the display of *dynamic* digital content are Schmitz' [29] and Li's [16] ad-hoc multi-displays for mobile interactive applications, though their tracking performance or accuracy is not yet tested.

Above and around the surface interactions. For more expressive interactions, the interaction space with surfaces can be extended to include the space above and around the surface. Recent work explored this continuous interaction space with lenses above [32] or around tabletops [22], with techniques for picking up and manipulating content on an interactive touch surface [9]. TangibleLenses [31] and FlexPad [33] enable handheld interactions with rigid or flexible surfaces, and LightSpace allows bi-manual gestures to transfer content between multiple surfaces [37]. One important design goal of the HuddleLamp system is to enable similar cross-device interactions (including tracking people's gestures), around the ad-hoc assemblages of phones and tablets on a table.

HUDDLELAMP'S TECHNICAL SETUP

In the following, we describe HuddleLamp's technical setup, and its architecture and algorithms. To facilitate replication outside our lab, we used only off-the-shelf hardware and free or open source software components. We provide the source code as open source[1].

Hardware Components

HuddleLamp uses a low-cost *short range time-of-flight* (TOF) depth camera which delivers a 1280×720 RGB colour image and a 320×240 depth image at 25 or 30 fps. It shares its technical specifications with a Creative Senz3D or SoftKinetic DepthSense 325. The camera is fixed to an Artemide Tolomeo Tavolo desk lamp (Figure 2) in which it replaces the light bulb (top right corner of Figure 2). Using the lamp, users can conveniently move the camera into its downward-facing operating position that lies 0.8m above the horizontal surface to track. This results in a rectangular tracking region of approximately 1.0×0.6m from which the camera receives sufficient RGB and depth information to track mobile devices, their spatial configurations, and users' hands and to distinguish them from non-interactive objects.

The camera was chosen for its small size (110×30×25mm) and low-noise depth data. A further advantage of this particular camera and its Perceptual SDK by Intel is that its RGB and depth images can be aligned without calibration. Therefore it is easy to retrieve RGB values for depth pixels and vice versa. This facilitates the processing of data in our hybrid sensing approach. However, in principle, hybrid sensing should also work with other TOF cameras (e.g. Kinect v2) and a higher resolution and larger field of view.

For vision processing and for communicating with the mobile devices via a web socket server, we use a Windows PC or laptop (Figure 2, left). For better portability, we have considered integrating a single-board PC (e.g. Raspberry Pi) directly into the lamp. However, at this stage, the vision processing is still too computationally expensive to achieve our targeted tracking rate of 25-30 fps with ARM CPUs.

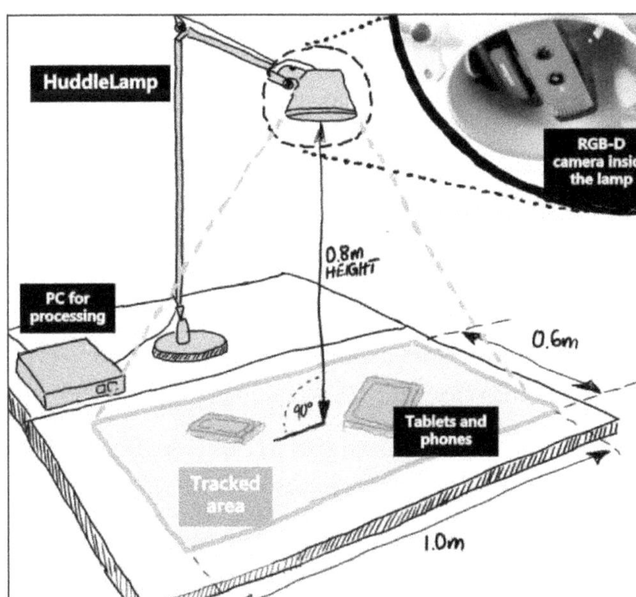

Figure 2. Technical setup of HuddleLamp with an integrated RGB-D camera (Tracking region: 1.0×0.6m).

Software Components & System Architecture

The computer vision application for processing the RGB and depth data was implemented in C# for WPF/.NET 4.5.1 and Emgu CV (OpenCV bridge for C#). For finding and decoding fiducial markers in the RGB stream we use the

[1] http://www.huddlelamp.org

glyph decoder of the AForge.NET library[2]. While the vision application is active, the incoming camera data is processed and all the identified device and hand positions, device orientations, and device occlusion states are streamed as JSON to connected mobile devices via a web socket server.

Client applications on the mobile devices access this stream using HuddleLamp's JavaScript API for browsers such as Safari (Mobile), Chrome, and Internet Explorer. If desired, the API also provides a shared virtual workspace that is spatially-situated in the physical tracking region and can be accessed with the devices. It uses a shared object storage implemented on top of the Meteor web framework[3] to distribute rendering and interaction across devices.

HUDDLELAMP'S HYBRID-SENSING

HuddleLamp's main purpose is to identify and track mobile screens of different sizes with sub-centimetre precision and to distinguish them from other objects or hands. To this end, we combine RGB and depth information and verify our results with virtual fiducial markers. This 'hybrid sensing' compensates for the limitations of sensing RGB, depth, IR, or fiducials alone and, unlike [16,18,20,21,23, 28], works without instrumenting devices or rooms with custom radio-hardware, markers, or tags.

Detection of Mobile Screens Using Low IR Reflectance

The first step of hybrid sensing is detecting the regions that possibly contain mobile screens. For this we use two optical characteristics that all mobile screens we worked with have in common. First, they are obviously rectangular and thus can be easily recognized as rectangles in a camera image. Our second characteristic, however, is not visible to the eye and we only learned about it during own experimentation:

We found that mobile screens generally have a very low reflectance for the modulated IR signal that is emitted by TOF cameras. Therefore, whenever a screen enters the view, the screen and its bezel absorb rather than reflect the IR signal. The reflected signal becomes so weak that the camera cannot reliably measure depth and returns 'low confidence' for most pixels inside of screens. However, depth values are available for pixels outside of screens, e.g., from the table's surface. Figure 3 shows this in side-by-side comparisons of RGB images (left) and depth confidence images (right). The right images are created simply by drawing all pixels that have a depth value in black and all 'low confidence' pixels in red ('low confidence' means signal intensity is < 87; intensity ranges from 1 to 32,767). The top row of Figure 3 shows low IR reflectance for devices of very different size, generation, screen type, screen brightness, and screen content (1. Samsung/Google Nexus 10; 2. LG/Google Nexus 5; 3. Nokia Lumia 620; 4. Apple iPad Air; 5. Lenovo ThinkPad Yoga; 6. Microsoft Surface 2 Pro; 7. Apple iPad 3; 8. Apple iPod Touch; 9. Samsung Galaxy S2; 10. Apple iPhone 4; 11. Nokia 106).

[2] http://www.aforgenet.com/

[3] https://www.meteor.com/

Figure 3. Low IR reflectance of mobile screens and objects.

The second row illustrates that low IR reflectance (here that of an Apple iPad Air) cannot only be observed when devices are perpendicular to the camera, but also for other angles (from bottom to top: 45°, 31°, 22.1°, 18.6°).

The third row shows that many everyday objects (from left to right: sheet of paper, notepad, watch, cup, back of Apple iPad, book) have normal to high IR reflectance and their depth is measured correctly. They therefore disappear among the other black pixels in the depth confidence image. The other objects (from left to right: Microsoft Surface tablet under notepad, Microsoft Surface keyboard, Apple logo on back of Apple iPad, Apple iPhone on book) have low IR reflectance and thus show in the right image as red shapes. Generally speaking, apart from screens, black or dark grey objects with a matte non-glossy finish are likely to have a low IR reflectance. However, as we explain below, such false positives can be easily identified as non-screen objects at a later stage.

The novelty of our screen tracking approach lies in not discarding but using these regions of low IR reflectance with missing depth values. The only other approach that we are aware of that uses IR reflectance (in that case structured light from a Kinect v1) to distinguish materials (e.g. skin from paper) is [33]. We can achieve a similar segmentation of screens from non-screens 'for free', by using a TOF camera and a threshold for signal strength without additional computation. Unlike Dippon et al. [4], we can therefore avoid the need for object detection and segmentation algorithms that use actual depth data.

In Figure 4, the RGB image R1 and the depth confidence image D1 show the example of eight mobile screens on a table under realistic lighting conditions. Thereby D1 is almost completely unaffected by ambient light, screen content, screen backlighting, or even the bright reflections from overhead light sources in R1. Since IR tracking works with its own light sources, D1 would also look very similar in a room that appears completely dark to the human eye. In general, IR reflectance tracking is very reliable with regard to all kinds of other light sources and it is very easy to extract the positions and orientations of screens from an image like D1 just by using low-pass filtering, Canny edge detection, and finding contours and convex hulls. The result of this process is shown in image D2 and contains 7 out of 8 screens.

Sauron's Eye

Only using the depth confidence image would however have limitations. One limitation lies in D1's centre region, which we informally refer to as 'Sauron's eye' (Figure 4). Here the IR signal from the camera hits the screen surface with almost 90°. The IR signal is directly reflected back into the depth sensor with great intensity and saturates a small region of pixels in the centre. This results in a small red ellipse in the centre of D1 that is the 'pupil' of Sauron's eye (like low confidence pixels, saturated pixels in D1 are red). Around this inner ellipse, the reflectance remains high, but not high enough to saturate. Therefore there is another elliptical region around the saturated pixels, for which the depth values can be read. They show as a black 'iris' region around the pupil that only gradually turns into red pixels when moving further away from the centre. Finally, Sauron's eye is contained by the device bezels that typically have a lower IR reflectance than screens.

Hybrid Sensing: Fusing RGB and IR Detection

While the depth confidence image enables reliable tracking without strong interference from other light sources, Sauron's eye negatively affects the tracking quality in its centre. The closer screens get to it, the less visible they are in D1. For example, one smartphone from R1 becomes almost invisible in D1 with only parts of its bezels still visible. Another disadvantage of D1 is its low resolution of 320×240 or less compared to R1 with 1280×720. This reduces the accuracy of tracking positions and orientations. To compensate for these disadvantages, we employ a hybrid sensing approach that complements the results from depth confidence tracking with those of RGB tracking in R1. This RGB tracking method uses standard processing steps such as binary thresholding, low-pass filtering, Canny edge detection, and finding contours and convex hulls. R2 in Figure 4 shows the result with five of eight possible screens from the example RGB image R1.

It is important to notice the limitations of this simple RGB tracking: While it does not have a blind spot in the centre and has higher accuracy because of the higher resolution, the reflections from overhead light sources can easily deform device contours or cut through them, so that they are not recognized as screens anymore. Also, the devices' bezels must always have a colour that is clearly distinguishable from the table's surface. In summary, the RGB tracking is less reliable but more accurate and thus can serve to improve tracking whenever it can provide more accurate positions and orientations or the depth confidence tracking fails. Therefore RGB and depth tracking mutually complement each other. Consequentially, the merged result in H1 (Figure 4) contains all eight screens.

Identification of Displays, Display Size, and Orientation

After having determined the positions of rectangles that potentially are screens in the current frame, the vision processing associates them with the history of tracked rectangles from previous frames. This association is done by smoothing all previous positions of each rectangle using a Kalman filter and pairing these predicted points with the closest rectangle in the current frame. This enables the vision system to track the rectangles' movements over time, assign them with an internal ID, and look into their past.

However, the detected rectangles in Figure 4 are not necessarily actual screens. At this stage of the processing, the result contains regions that are only likely candidates for being a screen, but can also be false positives, e.g., the afore-mentioned dark non-glossy objects with low IR reflectance and a rectangular shape, e.g., tablet covers or protective pouches made from felt. To identify such false positives, we ask the screens to display fiducial markers and by this verify that they are actually interactive displays. To this end, the vision system broadcasts an identification request to all connected, but so far unidentified, devices. They react by displaying a fiducial marker containing a unique ID

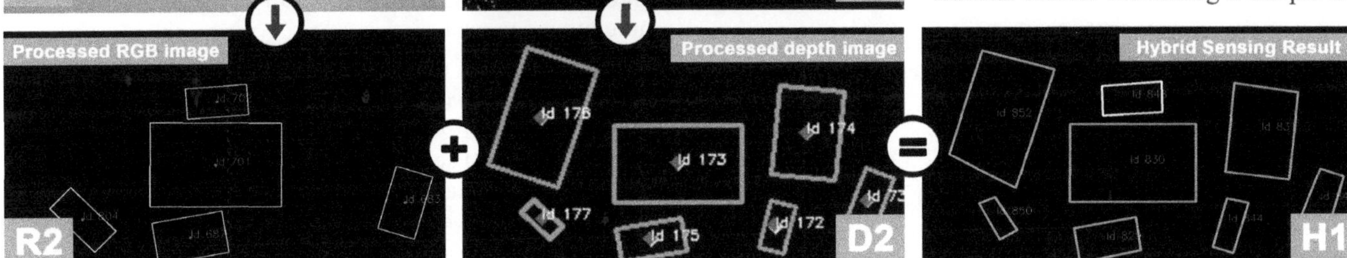

Figure 4. Hybrid Sensing. R1: RGB camera input. D1: Depth confidence image containing 'Sauron's eye' (dashed ellipse). R2: Mobile screens detected in R1. D2: Mobile screens detected in D1. H1: Merged result of hybrid sensing from R2 and D2.

on a white background that covers their screen (Figure 5). The vision system then looks for the presence of such a marker in the RGB image and decodes their value to verify that a new device has joined the huddle (and not a false positive) and to associate the corresponding region with the device ID. This process or pairing procedure usually takes only 1-2 seconds, and the fiducial markers disappear immediately once a device has been identified.

This identification process in the RGB image also enables us to determine the orientation and size of the screen in camera coordinates. The initial orientation is that of the found marker and the screen size is determined by the size of the white background surrounding it. This data is later used by the vision system to track the current orientation and also by our JavaScript API to compensate for different screen sizes, orientations, and resolutions (see below).

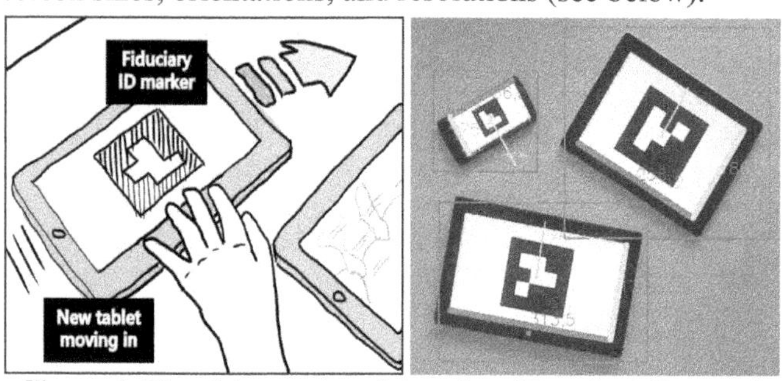

Figure 5. The vision system determines ID, orientation, and screen size using fiducial markers on a white background.

Hand Detection and Tracking

HuddleLamp's hand detection and tracking happens entirely in the depth image. Using background subtraction, depth thresholding, and flood fill segmentation, we identify contours in the depth image that could contain an arm and hand, based on the assumption that users always reach into the camera from outside (Figure 6). The hand position can then be approximated by the centroid of the hand's depth minima. Like for the screens, these positions are tracked over time by using a Kalman filter and a distance threshold.

Figure 6. Segmentation of hands and arms (white overlays) and estimated location and height of hands (red circles).

Our hand tracking is not intended for providing a detailed representation of finger positions or detecting hand gestures, but to provide light-weight low-precision information about hands' locations and depths for cross-device or above-the-table interaction techniques. For more precise manipulations of on-screen objects, users can continue to use the low-latency and high-precision multi-touch detection of their capacitive touchscreens. For example, in the interaction techniques described below, we only used our hand tracking for low-precision tasks, such as using the hand position to determine the destination device for a cross-device 'pick, drag, and drop' gesture. The exact on-screen position for dropping the object is determined using the device's touchscreen and not the hand tracking.

Technical Evaluation of Hybrid Sensing

We conducted a controlled experiment to evaluate precision, accuracy, and reliability of hybrid sensing and RGB-only tracking. They are defined as follows: 1.) *precision* is the standard deviation of the tracked position and orientation of a fixed tablet over time and thus measures noise and jittering (units: mm or degree); 2.) *accuracy* is the spatial accuracy of a tablet's position compared to a ground truth (unit: mm); 3.) *reliability* is the percentage of frames in which a present tablet was tracked (its tracking state is 'true') during measurement (unit: %).

As apparatus we used a setup like in Figure 2 with a tracking region of 1020mm×570mm and a camera height of 780mm. The effective usable resolution for the RGB image was 1280×720 pixels and for the depth image 283×159 pixels. We used a black Apple iPad 2 as mobile device.

For the experiment, we studied seven different conditions divided into three categories: *Lighting*, *Occlusion*, and *RGB-only*. The *Lighting* and *Occlusion* conditions used hybrid sensing. In *RGB-only* hybrid sensing was turned off.

The *Lighting* conditions had different levels of illumination: 20 lux, 1600 lux, 2200 lux. For comparison: 400 lux is the recommended illumination for offices and classrooms and 1000 lux for hospital examination and treatment or for difficult industrial assembly. In the 2200 lux condition we simulated strong ambient light using two R7 halogen lamps (400W) with a peak emission in IR (approx. 800nm).

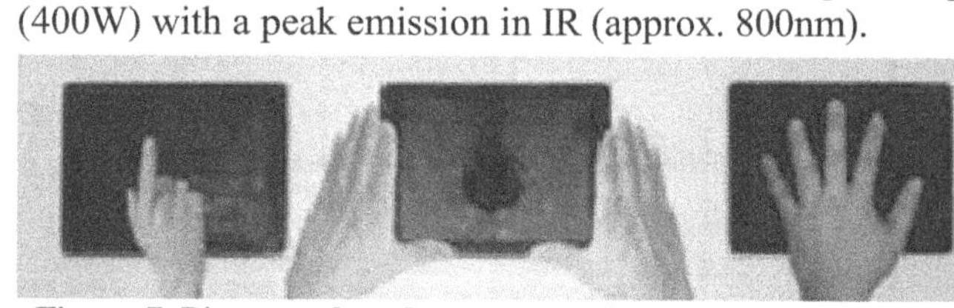

Figure 7. Picture taken from camera input stream shows the three levels of occlusion: *1 finger*, *2 hands*, and *1 hand*.

The illumination for the three *Occlusion* conditions was held constant at 1600 lux. The conditions simulated occlusion with *1 finger*, *1 hand*, and *2 hands* (Figure 7). The *RGB-only* condition was also at 1600 lux but without simulating any occlusion.

In each condition, a tablet was systematically moved to 21 different positions on a table where it was fixed for a frame-by-frame measurement of tracking state, position, and orientation for 10 seconds. The positions were defined by a 3x7 grid on the table that had a grid distance of exactly 100mm and was centred in the camera image. The grid distance served as ground truth for accuracy measurement.

Results

The results show sub-centimetre precision and accuracy for all conditions (Table 1). As expected, the best precision and accuracy was achieved for *RGB-only* due to the higher resolution of the RGB image but with a low reliability of only 89.5% due to the reflections of ceiling and ambient light sources. Under the same conditions, switching to hybrid sensing increased the reliability to 100% with only a small decline in precision and accuracy due to increased dependence from the lower resolution depth image when RGB tracking failed. Still, accuracy remained below 2.3mm and thus well inside the sub-centimetre range.

For the *1 hand* and *2 hands* occlusion, the reliability of hybrid sensing decreased to 89.8% since it sometimes failed to track occluded tablets close to Sauron's eye. In contrast, 20 lux or 2200 lux did not negatively affect the 100% reliability of hybrid sensing, but its accuracy and precision. Nonetheless, the worst accuracy was still below 3.5 mm and well inside the sub-centimetre range. As we discuss below, there is however an upper limit for ambient light.

Condition	Precision [in mm or degree]			Reliab. [in %]	Accuracy [in mm]			
	Mean (of all SD points)			SD	Mean		SD	
Lighting	X	Y	Angle		X	Y	X	Y
20 lux	1.22	1.26	.32	100.0	3.34	3.40	2.16	1.48
1600 lux	.78	1.05	.29	100.0	2.10	2.24	1.47	1.67
2200 lux	1.25	1.24	.37	100.0	3.29	2.80	2.25	1.41
Occlusion								
1 finger	.95	.74	.17	100.0	2.33	2.68	1.65	1.92
1 hand	1.08	1.02	.32	99.9	2.27	2.43	1.97	1.71
2 hands	1.36	1.81	.44	89.8	3.61	3.49	2.88	2.25
RGB-only								
1600 lux	.60	.63	.14	89.5	1.78	1.13	1.24	.70

Table 1. Precision and accuracy of HuddleLamp's hybrid sensing and RGB-only tracking.

Challenges and Limitations of Hybrid Sensing

The natural segmentation of mobile devices using their low IR reflectance worked robustly for different lighting conditions and we achieved to process the hybrid RGB and depth input at the maximum frame rate of the camera (30 fps) with an Intel Core i7 laptop. As we discuss below, there is still a perceptible latency on the UI, but it is not originating from hybrid sensing, but from web sockets and rendering on mobile devices which are slower than on PCs.

Since we use an overhead camera, users' arms and hands can sometimes occlude devices and deform device contours during touching or moving mobile screens. As the experiment shows, this can decrease reliability to 89.8%, so that devices and their ID are sometimes lost and a fiducial marker must be flashed again for device identification. This can interrupt the users' flow of interaction, especially when reflections of overhead light sources inhibit marker recognition and make it necessary to move the device in a reflection-free area. We could potentially improve this by using alternative means of optical device identification, e.g., flashing full screen colour sequences as in [30].

Finally, there is an unavoidable upper limit of ambient light for all consumer TOF cameras with an integrating CMOS detector. They stop working as soon as the IR light that is reflected into the detector from the sun or other light sources becomes many times stronger than the modulated camera signal. Therefore HuddleLamp's depth confidence tracking does not work outdoors on bright days or if sunlight shines directly on an indoor table. However, this upper limit was not reached even in our 2200 lux condition.

HUDDLELAMP'S JAVASCRIPT API

For enabling truly ad-hoc multi-device collaboration, it is necessary to provide an API that lets devices of all operating systems easily join the devices on the table without prior installation of native apps or applications. HuddleLamp achieves this by providing an API for writing collaborative applications with HTML5, CSS3, and JavaScript, so that the application becomes simply a web page that can be opened in every device's browser. As soon as this web page is loaded, users can put their device on the table into the camera's view and by doing so add that device to the huddle. For the users' convenience, a QR code with that URL can be attached to the lamp or desk. After joining a huddle, the web-based application can access the JavaScript API to make optional use of three key features:

1) It provides a web socket connection from the application to the vision server that returns a JSON data stream with device and hand positions, device orientations, and device occlusion states. This data is also provided as events using the JavaScript observer pattern (Listing 1).

```
var huddle = Huddle.client()
  .on("devicefound", function() {
    console.log("devicefound");
  })
  .on("devicelost", function() {
    console.log("devicelost");
  })
  .on("proximity", function(data) {
    console.log(data);
  })
  .connect(host, port);
```

Listing 1. HuddleLamp's JavaScript API to access the data stream from the vision server.

2) The API provides a shared virtual workspace that can be accessed from all mobile devices. This workspace contains objects that can be arranged in space using the well-known multi-touch user manipulations from tabletops, e.g., drag, pinch-to-zoom-and-rotate, flick. However, in contrast to tabletop SDKs (e.g. the ScatterView control of the Microsoft Surface SDK), it is synchronized for all connected devices via a server. We implemented a shared object storage on top of the Meteor web framework, so that all manipulations on one device become instantly visible on all other devices to enable collaborative cross-device work.

3) The API enables a homogeneous rendering of the workspace across different devices with respect to their different locations, screen sizes, and resolutions. Each device can become part of a multi-device display that renders the virtual workspace on the individual screens as if the workspace was physically situated in the tracked region

on the table. Only that part of a workspace (e.g. a map) and its objects (e.g. images, videos) is rendered that lies underneath the device, correctly preserving absolute positions and orientations. The API achieves this by translating, rotating, and scaling the local rendering of the workspace based on the devices' individual screen size, position, orientation, and aspect ratio that were determined by hybrid sensing. There is no need to create a database of devices with their screen sizes. The API thus enables a fully interactive and reconfigurable Junkyard Jumbotron [2].

Validation of API with Example Interaction Techniques

To validate the design of our API, we implemented five examples of existing and novel cross-device gestures and interaction techniques that used to be possible only in instrumented rooms, as part of fixed installations or exhibits, or above instrumented surfaces. These examples serve as validation, but they also demonstrate the possible design space for future HuddleLamp applications.

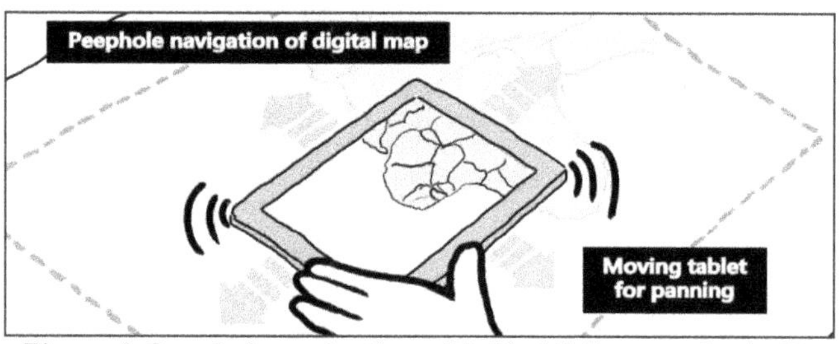

Figure 8. Peephole navigation with HuddleLamp: physically navigating a large virtual map with a tablet.

1.) Peephole Navigation

Peephole navigation is a classic technique for navigating large information spaces such as maps using spatially-aware displays. A mobile device acts as a lens [32] or peephole [5] to physically navigate virtual information as if it was situated in physical space, e.g. by moving or rotating a device to control what is shown on the screen. HuddleLamp's API with a spatially-situated workspace enables peephole navigation with one or more mobile displays of different sizes. For example, we built a demonstrator in which users can move one or more tablets to physically navigate in a virtual world map (Figure 8).

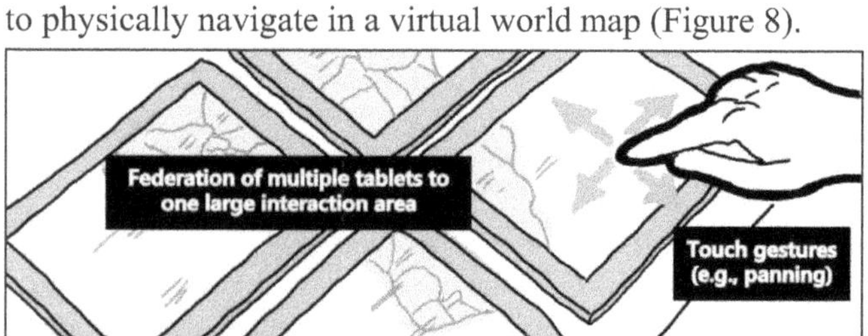

Figure 9. An illustration of synchronous huddle navigation.

2.) Huddle Navigation

We extended peephole navigation to the novel technique of 'huddle navigation'. It enables users to create large multi-device displays that are similar to interactive tabletops simply by moving multiple tablets or smartphones side-by-side (Figure 9). By this, users let devices join into a 'huddle'. Users can zoom, rotate, and pan all screens in the huddle synchronously with multi-touch. They can also create two or more huddles based on device proximity. Each huddle then zooms, rotates, and pans independently to support collaboration of multiple users or user groups.

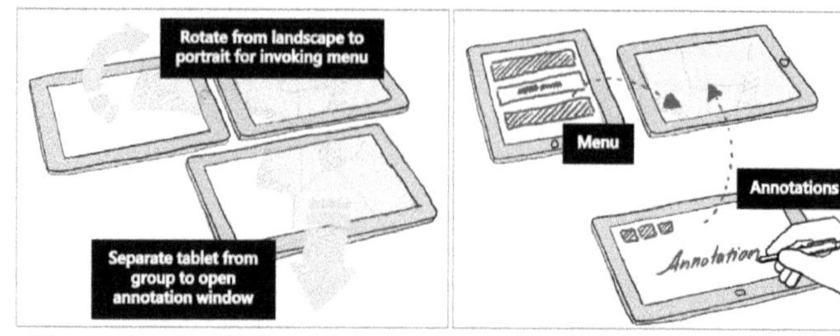

Figure 10. Spatially-aware menus and modes change the role of devices based on their orientation or distance.

3.) Spatially-Aware Menus and Modes

In the previous example, a tablet that was moved close to a map huddle automatically turned into an extension of the map. But we also used proximity and orientations for more complex behaviour such as 'spatially-aware menus and modes'. For example, when a user rotates a tablet in a huddle from landscape to portrait orientation, this reveals a tool palette or menu where display parameters for the entire huddle can be altered, e.g., visible layers or data points of a map. When moving the tablet away from the huddle and closer to the user, the tablet automatically switches into notetaking mode and users can use a stylus to take personal notes or for annotating content (Figure 10). With a good mapping of spatial relations to switching menus or modes, a HuddleLamp application can achieve a seemingly intelligent spatially-aware behaviour that proactively supports the users during collaboration. This also enables smooth transitions between tightly-coupled collaboration (tablet is shared in the huddle) and loosely-coupled parallel work (tablet is picked up and used as personal display).

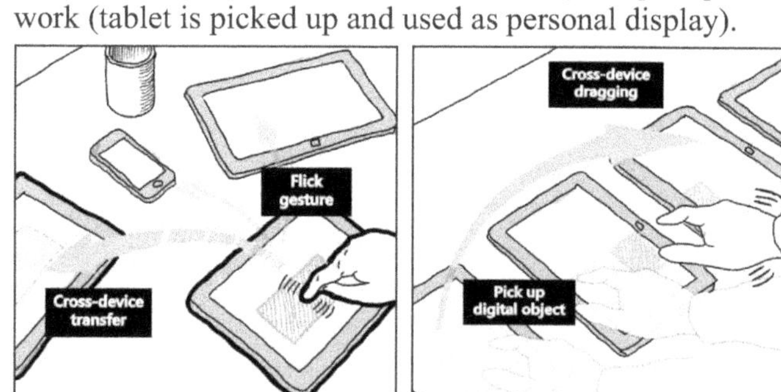

Figure 11. Cross-device flicking and Touch&Flick Browsing.

4.) Cross-Device Flicking and Touch&Flick Browsing

Cross-device flicking is an interaction technique to enable users to flick objects with their fingers (Figure 11 left). A simple physics simulation makes objects accelerate and stop at new locations in the workspace. Objects can stop on the same screen, but also fly to the screen of another device.

A variation of cross-device flicking is 'touch-and-flick browsing'. We implemented this technique for web browsing with multiple tablets or smartphones. Content items from a web page such as a link, video, or image can be opened on another screen simply by touching and flicking them towards a neighbouring device. The content is then shown on the destination device using the entire available screen space, similar to how links can be opened in new tabs or new windows in desktop browsers.

5.) Pick, Drag, and Drop

A different way of moving objects between devices is the 'pick, drag, and drop' hand gesture. An example of such an above-the-table object manipulation technique that uses 3D graphics and physics simulations has been discussed in [9]. It has inspired us to implement our own 'above-the-tablets' technique, but with using a simpler 2D implementation. The gesture is initiated by tapping an object on a source mobile screen to pick it up and then lifting the hand and moving it above the desk to drag it to another destination device (Figure 11 right). During 'pick, drag, and drop', HuddleLamp continuously tracks the hand position and the picked object travels with the hand over the surface and across the screens lying beneath it. To drop the object, users move their hand above the destination device and then tap its touchscreen at the destination location. Inspired by Hilliges et al. [9], the current height of the hand above the surface is also used to increase the rendered size of the object to create a simple illusion of 3D movement in space.

Challenges and Limitations of the HuddleLamp API

During implementation of the examples, we identified two limitations of the API that we will address in future:

First, there is a small but noticeable delay between the physical movement of a screen and the corresponding reaction of the UI. While the vision processing works at the maximum frame rate of the camera (30 fps), the web socket connection, the synchronization of devices with Meteor, and particularly the different rendering performances of browsers and devices induce a noticeable latency. Best results were achieved using Safari Mobile on Apple iPad 2/3/Air, Apple iPhone 4/5S, and Microsoft Surface 2 Pro with Chrome. Less successful were tests with mobile devices of older generations (e.g. Apple iPad 1, Apple iPhone 3G) and surprisingly with Google Nexus 5&10.

Second, the recognition of multi-touch gestures such as pinch-to-zoom is limited when they span device boundaries. Currently, gestures are only recognized if all fingers are on a single device. They cannot be performed by putting one finger on one device and other fingers on a different device. Nonetheless, for each individual device they are correctly recognized and processed and their results are immediately synchronized with all other devices.

DISCUSSION AND FUTURE WORK

There are also more higher-level questions raised by HuddleLamp which lead us to directions for future work:

A clear limitation of HuddleLamp compared to traditional tabletops is the absence of a large screen that also displays touch-enabled interactive content around the mobile screens on a table. Does this inhibit its usefulness in real-world scenarios? This disadvantage has to be weighed against HuddleLamp's advantages in terms of low-cost portability, ad-hoc interaction, and distributed rendering. Furthermore, it supports high-resolution output and responsive input on a capacitive multi-touch screen, sometimes with a pressure-sensitive stylus (e.g. on a MS Surface tablet). This is often not the case for large tabletops with optical touch detection.

Furthermore, although we already realized a series of spatially-aware cross-device interaction techniques, we have only scratched the surface of what can be done in future with ad-hoc communities of spatially-aware and reconfigurable displays and devices. We consider HuddleLamp only as the first step towards realising this greater vision. One of the great advantages that we see in HuddleLamp or similar approaches is that they make digital tools for co-located collaboration available to the masses. They can be used where motion-capturing tracking systems and large tabletops or surfaces are too expensive to buy, setup, and maintain. Consequentially, we are now working on applications for engaging a great variety of users, e.g., playful exploration of urban data in public libraries or community centres, collaborative search tools for schools, or novel kinds of informational games in museums.

CONCLUSION

We have described HuddleLamp, a sensing system in the form of a desk lamp with an integrated RGB-D camera that tracks the movements of multiple mobile displays on a table for around-the-table collaboration. We described our implementation and our approach of hybrid sensing, i.e., detecting mobile screens by exploiting their optical properties in the IR range and additionally using RGB images and fiducial markers to better track screens and to distinguish them from other objects or users' hands. After a technical evaluation of our hybrid sensing approach, we also introduced HuddleLamp's web-based architecture and JavaScript API for ad-hoc collaboration that enables users to add or remove displays and reconfigure them in space at any time without installing any software. We discussed how this can be used to create large multi-device tiled displays for multi-user and multi-touch interaction. Beyond our five demonstrated examples of different interaction techniques, we believe that HuddleLamp's setup and hybrid sensing tracking will allow the rapid exploration of future cross-device interactions supporting group collaborations.

ACKNOWLEDGMENTS

This work was conceived of at Dagstuhl Seminar 13452. We would like to thank Katherine Isbister (and others of the Game Innovation Lab at NYU) and Ashley Karr for their valuable comments. We also thank Mario Schreiner for his JavaScript implementation of Touch&Flick Browsing and Oscar Robinson and Jonny Manfield for parts of the Huddle JavaScript API. Finally, we thank Francesco de Gioia for his thoughts and work on our tracking algorithms.

REFERENCES

1. Ballendat, T., Marquardt, N., and Greenberg, S. Proxemic Interaction: Designing for a Proximity and Orientation-Aware Environment. Proc. of ITS '10, ACM (2010).
2. Borovoy, R. and Knep, B. Junkyard Jumbotron, http://jumbotron.media.mit.edu. 2011.
3. Dearman, D., Guy, R., and Truong, K. Determining the Orientation of Proximate Mobile Devices Using Their Back Facing Camera. Proc. of CHI '12, ACM (2012), 2231–2234.
4. Dippon, A., Wiedermann, N., and Klinker, G. Seamless Integration of Mobile Devices into Interactive Surface Environments. Proc. of ITS '12, ACM (2012), 331–334.
5. Fitzmaurice, G.W. Situated information spaces and spatially aware palmtop computers. Comm. of ACM 36, 7 (1993).
6. Greenberg, S., Marquardt, N., Ballendat, T., Diaz-Marino, R., and Wang, M. Proxemic Interactions: The New Ubicomp? ACM Interactions 18, 1 (2011), 42–50.
7. Hamilton, P. and Wigdor, D.J. Conductor: Enabling and Understanding Cross-device Interaction. Proc. of CHI '14, ACM (2014), 2773–2782.
8. Harrison, C., Benko, H., and Wilson, A.D. OmniTouch: wearable multitouch interaction everywhere. Proc. of UIST '11, ACM (2011), 441–450.
9. Hilliges, O., et al. Interactions in the air: adding further depth to interactive tabletops. Proc. of UIST '09, ACM (2009).
10. Hinckley, K., Ramos, G., Guimbretiere, F., Baudisch, P., and Smith, M. Stitching: pen gestures that span multiple displays. Proc. of AVI '04, ACM (2004), 23–31.
11. Hollan, J., Hutchins, E., and Kirsh, D. Distributed Cognition: Toward a New Foundation for Human-computer Interaction Research. ACM Trans. Comput.-Hum. Interact. 7, 2 (2000).
12. Holmquist, L., et al. Smart-Its Friends: A Technique for Users to Easily Establish Connections between Smart Artefacts. Proc. of UbiComp, Springer (2001), 116.
13. Huang, D.-Y., Lin, C.-P., Hung, Y.-P., et al. MagMobile: Enhancing Social Interactions with Rapid View-stitching Games of Mobile Devices. Proc. of MUM '12, ACM (2012).
14. Kendon, A. Conducting Interaction: Patterns of Behavior in Focused Encounters. Cambridge Press, Cambridge, 1990.
15. Kray, C., et al. Group Coordination and Negotiation through Spatial Proximity Regions around Mobile Devices on Augmented Tabletops. Proc. of TABLETOP, IEEE (2008).
16. Li, M. and Kobbelt, L. Dynamic Tiling Display: Building an Interactive Display Surface Using Multiple Mobile Devices. Proc. of MUM '12, ACM (2012), 24:1–24:4.
17. Linder, N. and Maes, P. The Design Evolution of LuminAR: A Compact and Kinetic Projected Augmented Reality Interface. CHI '12 Ext. Abs., ACM (2012), 1435–1436.
18. Lucero, A., Holopainen, J., and Jokela, T. Pass-them-around: Collaborative Use of Mobile Phones for Photo Sharing. Proc. of CHI '11, ACM (2011), 1787–1796.
19. Lucero, A., et al. Mobile Collocated Interactions: Taking an Offline Break Together. interactions 20, 2 (2013), 26–32.
20. Marquardt, N., et al. The Proximity Toolkit: Prototyping Proxemic Interactions in Ubiquitous Computing Ecologies. Proc. of UIST '11, ACM (2011).
21. Marquardt, N., Hinckley, K., and Greenberg, S. Cross-Device Interaction via Micro-mobility and F-formations. Proc. of UIST '12, ACM (2012), 13–22.
22. Marquardt, N., Jota, R., Greenberg, S., and Jorge, J.A. The continuous interaction space: interaction techniques unifying touch and gesture on and above a digital surface. Proc. of INTERACT, Springer (2011), 461–476.
23. Merrill, D., Kalanithi, J., and Maes, P. Siftables: towards sensor network user interfaces. Proc. of TEI, ACM (2007).
24. Ohta, T. and Tanaka, J. Pinch: An Interface That Relates Applications on Multiple Touch-screen by Pinching Gesture. Proc. of ACE '12, Springer-Verlag (2012), 320–335.
25. Oulasvirta, A. When Users "Do" the Ubicomp. interactions 15, 2 (2008), 6–9.
26. Piazza, T., et al. Dynamic Duo: Exploring Phone-Tablet, Combinations for Mobile Usage. WIP, TEI '13, ACM (2013).
27. Ramos, G., et al. Synchronous Gestures in Multi-Display Environments. Human-Computer Interaction 24, 1 (2009).
28. Rekimoto, J. and Saitoh, M. Augmented surfaces: a spatially continuous work space for hybrid computing environments. Proc. of CHI '99, ACM (1999), 378–385.
29. Schmitz, A., Li, M., Schönefeld, V., and Kobbelt, L. Ad-Hoc Multi-Displays for Mobile Interactive Applications. The Eurographics Association (2010), 45–52.
30. Schwarz, J., et al. Phone As a Pixel: Enabling Ad-hoc, Large-scale Displays Using Mobile Devices. Proc. of CHI '12, ACM (2012).
31. Spindler, M., et al. Tangible Displays for the Masses: Spatial Interaction with Handheld Displays by Using Consumer Depth Cameras. Personal Ubiquitous Comput. 18, 5 (2014).
32. Spindler, M., Stellmach, S., and Dachselt, R. PaperLens: advanced magic lens interaction above the tabletop. Proc. of ITS '09, ACM (2009), 69–76.
33. Steimle, J., Jordt, A., and Maes, P. Flexpad: Highly Flexible Bending Interactions for Projected Handheld Displays. Proc. of CHI '13, ACM (2013), 237–246.
34. Tandler, P., et al. Connectables: Dynamic Coupling of Displays for the Flexible Creation of Shared Workspaces. Proc. of UIST '01, ACM (2001), 11–20.
35. Wang, M., Boring, S., and Greenberg, S. A Public Advertising Display that Captures and Preserves the Attention of a Passerby. Proc. of PerDis '12, ACM (2012).
36. Wilson, A., et al. Steerable Augmented Reality with the Beamatron. Proc. of UIST '12, ACM (2012), 413–422.
37. Wilson, A.D. and Benko, H. Combining multiple depth cameras and projectors for interactions on, above and between surfaces. Proc. of UIST '10, ACM (2010), 273–282.
38. Winkler, C., et al. SurfacePhone: A Mobile Projection Device for Single- and Multiuser Everywhere Tabletop Interaction. Proc. of CHI '14, ACM (2014), 3513–3522.

Uminari: Freeform Interactive Loudspeakers

Yoshio Ishiguro *
Disney Research Pittsburgh,
4720 Forbes Avenue,
ishiy@acm.org

Ali Israr
Disney Research Pittsburgh,
4720 Forbes Avenue,

Alex Rothera
Disney Research Pittsburgh,
4720 Forbes Avenue,

Eric Brockmeyer
Disney Research Pittsburgh,
4720 Forbes Avenue,

{israr, alex.rothera, eric.brockmeyer}@disneyresearch.com

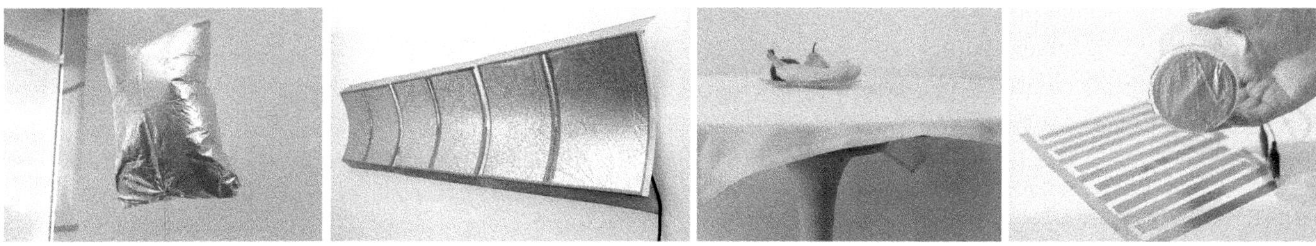

Figure 1. Freeform Interactive Loudspeakers are flexible, lightweight and used in interactions with everyday objects. (a) The lightweight electrostatic loudspeakers are integrated in a *balloon*. (b) The electrostatic loudspeakers can be made into *large curved wall* surfaces. (c) Our *speaker table* accepts touches and weight on it. (d) *Tangible objects* are made speaker by equipping them with passive layer of conductive paper.

ABSTRACT

We present freeform interactive loudspeakers for creating spatial sound experiences from a variety of surfaces. Surround sound systems are widely used and consist of multiple electromagnetic speakers that create point sound sources within a space. Our proposed system creates directional sound and can be easily embedded into architecture, furniture and many everyday objects. We use *electrostatic loudspeaker* technology made from thin, flexible, lightweight and low cost materials and can be of different size and shape. In this paper we propose various configurations such as single speaker, speaker array tangible speaker and microphone configurations for creating playful and exciting interactions with spatial sounds. Our research of freeform speakers can create new possibilities for the design of various interactive surfaces.

Author Keywords

Interactive architecture; furniture design; interactions; electrostatic loudspeakers; freeform speakers

ACM Classification Keywords

H.5.2. Information interfaces and presentation (e.g., HCI): User Interfaces - Auditory feedback.

* Currently at Nagoya University.

ACM 978-1-4503-2587-5/14/11…$15.00
http://dx.doi.org/10.1145/2669485.2669521

INTRODUCTION

Sound and visuals are important ingredients for creating interactive systems that produces an engaging and believable user experience. Traditionally, these systems utilize a high definition visual display alongside multidimensional surround sound systems to render precise spatial sounds collocated with the animated visuals. Current display technologies, however, pose limitations in the overall user experience due to their structural and functional limitations, as well as due to the high cost and power demands associated with acquiring and using such technologies. Our research is inspired by such limitations and we explore technologies that are cost effective, scalable and multi-functional. Overcoming functional limitations in everyday objects is an emerging conceptual framework in the current HCI community [6,7,25].

In recent years, research concepts like *Programmable Matter* [7], *Programmable Physical Architectures* [26], *Programmable Reality* [5] and *Organic User Interfaces* [11] have been introduced that, at least conceptually, extends the flexibility and functionality in real physical objects and morph them into forms that are more suitable for natural and seamless user interactions. For example, display technology has progressed into more flexible, scalable and freeform configurations by use of organic electroluminescent, electrophoretic ink, liquid crystal, LED and beam-steering technologies [11]. These technologies are frequently used in highly immersive virtual reality environments.

On the other hand, freeform and organic functionality in sound reproduction systems has been limited and traditionally large and bulky electromagnetic surround sound speakers are used for 3D sound reproduction (such as

[12]). These surround sound systems are not applicable in interactive and transformable spaces due to the following restrictions:

- Sound localization area is limited
- A large number of speakers are required
- The speakers are placed throughout the environment
- An extensive calibration process is required for a given space configuration

Recently, Ishiguro and Poupyrev presented 3D speakers that utilized 3D printing technology and electrostatic loudspeaker technology to fabricate small objects with loudspeaker function [13]. Due to the layered feature of the electrostatic speaker technology, these objects, such as toys, emit sound all around its external surface.

In this paper, we introduce *freeform electrostatic loudspeakers* (ESL) that can be easily integrated in structures, furniture and everyday objects. A simple ESL [9, 18] consists of two layers of conductive material separated by an insulator medium. An alternating potential difference between the two conductors creates electrostatic coupling between them and moves the air around the layer to produce sound. The ESLs are lightweight, flexible, scalable, cost and power efficient and can be made into almost any shape and size. They have high durability and ideal for use in spatially restrictive and kinetic spaces and structures. Unlike [13], where the focus was to manufacture small toys and objects, the present work utilizes the ESL technology for large-scale objects, such as architecture and furniture. Moreover, we extend the practical use of ESL and introduced programmable and interactive audio environments. We call this system *Uminari*. In Japanese literature, *Uminari* means 'rumbling in the sea'.

The organization of the paper is as follows: In the next section we discuss relevant background related to freeform ESLs. This is followed by the design and evaluation of a series of ESLs made in our facility. A pair of preliminary user evaluation studies follows this. We then explore the application space for these loudspeakers where we have integrated them into architecture, furniture and everyday objects. The paper concludes with a discussion and remarks.

BACKGROUND

Freeform structures, hardware and interactions have become increasingly common, in recent years, which has allowed researchers, designers and engineers to expand their designs with no boundaries [7,14,19,20,22,27]. Furthermore, with advances in rapid prototyping techniques, 3D printing, open source software and novel material research, freeform culture has progressed in to making everyday objects, increasing their functionality and accessibility [4,7]. The challenge, however, is to incorporate functionality beyond the conventional modality of structures; for example, it is not trivial to develop a large erected wall that can be folded to a form that is portable and easily deployed. We are inspired by the physical limitations of objects and structures and equip them with functionality that expands user interactions with such objects and structures.

User interactions on surfaces have been the focus of many studies in HCI where functional capabilities of surfaces were enhanced [2,3,6,8,15]. Incorporating modal functionality not only increases user interactions in these environments but also prompt "surprise" elements in controlled settings, such as in amusement parks, interactive installations, educational classrooms, museum exhibits [2,10, 24].

We utilize electrostatic speaker technology to enhance structures and everyday objects with sound reproduction capabilities. The technology is well explored and published [9,18,21] and has been applied to commercial speaker systems. Recently, Ishiguro and Poupyrev [13] combined these techniques with 3D rapid printing technology to fabricate the loudspeakers as small and complex shaped objects. This research showed high flexibility and scalability of electrostatic loudspeakers embedded in toys, ornaments, and small decorative pieces.

The traditional method for enhancing the functional capabilities of objects with a sound source is to embed a traditional speaker in the object, such as in *Acoustable* [1]. In this case, large cavities are designed inside the object to place the speaker and power system, and shape of the object is designed to optimize the sound quality. The entire object resonates and produces sound as if it were coming from the object. However, the shape and size of the speaker highly depend on the size, shape, form and functionality of the object. Moreover, sound localization is limited and sound quality is greatly affected when the system is used with other objects.

Another way to add sound reproduction capabilities to objects is to utilize the parametric speaker technology [16,28]. This technology utilizes ultrasound to modulate with the sound signal, producing highly directional sound at the source. This modulated sound is aimed towards objects equipped with a layer of special reflective material, which absorb the ultrasound carrier and reflects the sound as if it was reproduced at the object instead of at the source.

Other alternatives for freeform speaker technology include the use of piezoelectric elements and electro active polymers in the speakers [23]. These materials are lightweight and can be fabricated into any shape and size. However, the raw material and fabrication techniques are quite expensive, and in the case of for large size speaker application, not practical.

DESIGN OF FREEFORM LOUDSPEAKER

Principles of ESL Technology

The basic principles of electrostatic sound reproduction are simple and were explained in detail in [9, 13]. In a simple construction, an ESL consists of a thin conductive diaphragm and an electrode plate, separated by an insulation layer as shown in Figure 2. When the high alternating voltage difference is applied between the diaphragm and the electrode, then the electrostatic attraction forces are generated between these conductive layers and produce relative motion between them. The thin diaphragm pulls towards the electrode plate and displaces the air along its motion. If the high voltage is replaced by amplified audio signal, then the displaced air would create an audible signal and the diaphragm actuated with electrostatic force would become a speaker.

It has been demonstrated that ESLs allow for high quality sound reproduction, outperforming traditional electro-magnetic speakers in both high and medium sound frequency ranges [18,21].

Configurations of ESL

In this section we describe practical configurations of ESLs. These configurations will be used in applications described in the next section.

Single-Side Configuration

The single-side configuration is the simplest form of ESL and consists of two layers (a diaphragm and an electrode) separated by an insulator (Figure 2). In the ESL speakers reported here we connect the ground to the diaphragm and the audio signal to the electrode (Figure 3b). To create different potential between two conductive materials (diaphragm and body), they both had different potentials from the ground as shown in figure 3a. However, this is dangerous for the human body which normally has potential same as ground. It is important that interactive speakers embedded in objects are safe and can be touched by users. Therefore, the grounded electrode is placed on top and protects the user touching the speaker from the high-voltage audio source, making it safe to handle and manipulate the object with embedded speakers. This becomes particularly important in the interactive applications. This configuration can be used as surface of tabletops, walls, toys, floating objects, hanging center pieces, and many more. In this configuration, either the diaphragm or the electrode of both could be free to move and the high voltage audio signal can be either applied to the diaphragm or to the electrode, allowing ESLs to be utilized in variety of situations. Moreover, the ESL can be used as a microphone by replacing the voltage driver with a pre-amp circuitry.

Array Configuration

An extension of the *single-side* is the *array* configuration as shown in Figure 3c. The array allows ESLs to be placed spatially, where each loudspeaker is controlled independently. Multiple sound patterns can be channeled through individual loudspeakers creating a moving, expressive and dynamic sound system. All loudspeakers in the array can have a common ground plane. Therefore, a single diaphragm surface could be used with multiple loudspeaker electrodes.

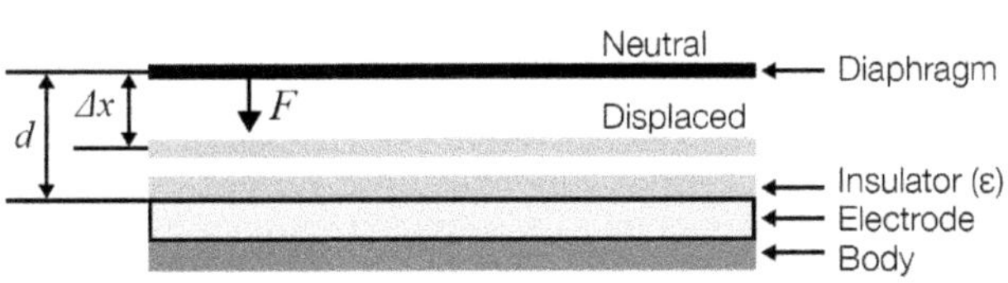

Figure 2. Construction of an electrostatic loudspeaker

Passive Loudspeaker Configuration

Figure 3d shows the *passive loudspeaker configuration*. In this configuration, high voltage electrodes and the ground electrodes are arranged on the same surface, and an object with passive diaphragm (conductive sheet) is placed on the surface. The surface itself cannot produce sound, however, the conductive surface of the object creates potential difference between the diaphragm and the high voltage electrode as well as between the diaphragm and the ground electrode. Changing the potential difference changes the electrostatic potential of the diaphragm. Therefore, the passive object behaves as a switch for sound reproduction.

Advantages of Electrostatic Loudspeaker

Ease of construction

One of the most important features of the ESL is ease of its construction. Instead of winding coils in a specific manner around a magnet for electromagnetic speakers and complicated fabrication methods for piezoelectric speakers [17], the ESL can be made in the nominal laboratory and/or workshop settings using everyday components.

Size and shape

Due to the ease of construction and cost, the ESLs can be made in different sizes using the same construction procedure. Unlike piezoelectric and electromagnetic speakers, where the cost of magnet, coils and piezoelectric material increases exponentially with size, the cost is linearly related to the size of the loudspeaker. Moreover, the same electronic driver is used for small and large loudspeakers. There is no added cost or power requirements for the driver, which is not the case with other speaker technologies. And the ESLs can be made in different shapes, such as curved, spiral, circular, cylindrical, etc.

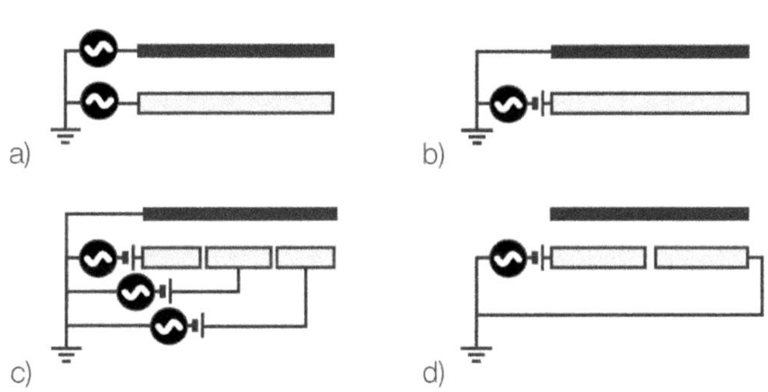

Figure 3. Four configurations of ELSs.
(a) Conventional speakers, (b) single-sided, (c) arrayed, and (d) passive electrostatic loudspeakers.

Weight

ESLs are inherently light and could be made with conductive paper and sheets, such as Mylar and Indium tin oxide (ITO) coated polyethylene terephthalate (PET). Other conductive materials such as Graphene and Carbon nanotube (CNT) structure can also be used for the construction of transparent ESLs. Due to its lightweight characteristics, ESLs are ideal for floating and hanging objects, such as balloons, lampshades, and for pages of storybooks.

Power requirement

The overall loudness depends on the potential difference across the two surfaces, and not the current. Therefore, very minute current is required to generate sound (~ 1.5 mA). In electromagnetic speakers, current is a basis factor to generate torque to move the mass in order to generate sound, which could require higher amperage especially in large size speakers.

Cost

The minimal construction of an ESL requires two sheets of thin conductive material, wires, tape and electronic driver. These items are quite cheap and easily available in a typical general or hardware store.

SONIC PERFORMANCE OF FREEFORM ESL

The performance of ESL depends on many factors, mainly shape and size of the speaker surface. In this section, we measure the performance of freeform ESLs for their reliability and use in a variety of interactive applications. Specifically, we are interested in measuring the detailed frequency response, effect of size on uniformity and directivity of sound, and effect of loading placed on the diaphragm of the ESL. We also measure the performance of ESL microphone in a normal setting. These measurements are necessary for understanding the behavior of ESL with a variety of sound and interactions, and serve as a reference for designers extending the freeform nature of ESL.

Two test speakers are assembled by stretching a thin aluminized mylar sheet on top of a perforated stainless steel sheet. The dimensions of the smaller loudspeaker are 15 cm long by 15 cm wide and that of the larger are 35 cm long by 19 cm wide. These speakers are housed in an acrylic frame as shown in Figure 6. All measurements are taken in a quiet room with background noise level below 45 dB SPL. For testing ESL microphone, a small panel equipped with a simple microphone pre-amp circuitry is also produced and sound recordings are evaluated.

The audio signal is generated through a pc output through an audio interface and passed through a transistor based custom driver, which amplifies the input signal from ~1V_{p-p} to ~1000 V_{p-p}. The positive terminal of the output is connected to the fixed metallic mesh (electrode) and the ground terminal is connected to the aluminized mylar. The sound is measured with a digital sound pressure level (SPL) meter (Extech Instruments Corp., model 407730, Nashua, USA) place 15 cm away from the surface of the speaker.

Sound Quality

The sound quality is measured by taking the frequency response of the larger speaker. Instead of running a typical frequency sweep, we use single frequency sinusoids to measure gain, distortion, harmonics and residual background noise levels. Figure 4 shows the Fast Fourier Transform (FFT) spectrum of the measured sound signal at 0.5 kHz, 1 kHz, 2 kHz and 4 kHz. The magnitude of the FFT is normalized by number of samples. Similar to the measurements made in previous literature (such as [21]) distortion and harmonics of 500 Hz sinusoids were significant and could be sensed by a normal ear. At frequencies 1000 kHz and higher, signal distortion were low and very low harmonic overtone.

Sound Uniformity and Sound Directivity

One important feature of the electrostatic loudspeaker technology is that the sound radiates uniformly throughout the surface of the speaker, which is not possible with point sound source of electromagnet speakers. Figure 5 shows the measurements taken from the SPL meter at seven locations (-200mm, -100mm, -50mm, 0mm, 50mm, 100mm and 200mm) along the surface of the two electrostatic loudspeakers. The plotted data is normalized at 0 SPL of 0 mm measurements.

For the smaller loudspeaker, the maximum sound level was recorded at the center of the speaker and the sound intensity is maintained along most of the width, before it steeply

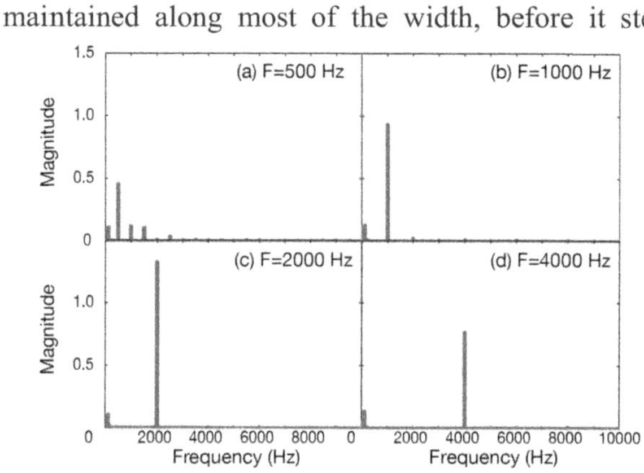

Figure 4. FFT spectrum of electrostatic loudspeakers at (a) 500 Hz, (b) 1000 Hz, (c) 2000 Hz and (d) 4000 Hz.

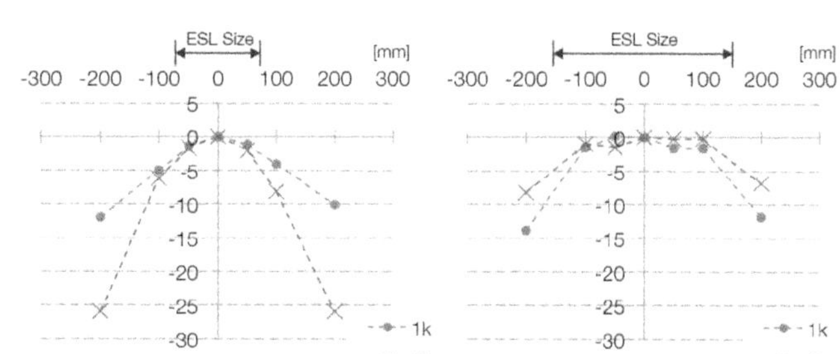

Figure 5. Measurement of Sound Pressure Levels along the surface of a 150 mm wide loudspeaker (*left*) and 350 mm wide loudspeaker (*right*).

reduced towards the edges. Similarly, the sound intensity of the larger loudspeaker was not changed across the width of the loudspeaker and the sound intensity significantly decreased beyond its width. This shows that the electrostatic loudspeakers radiate sound uniformly along its surface and therefore are a good candidate for maintaining sound directivity.

Effect of Loads

A normal electromagnetic speaker generates sound by moving a coil and diaphragm. Any load or obstruction placed on the diaphragm hinders the motion and as a consequence the sound intensity is significantly compromised. The ESL has minimal effect of loading placed on its diaphragm. Figure 6 shows the effect of loading on the diaphragm of the larger electrostatic loudspeaker. The overall shape of the frequency spectrum was maintained, however the intensity level was reduced by ~5 dB when a load of 500 g was placed on the loudspeaker.

Measurements of ESL Microphone

The performance of ESL microphone is assessed by comparing the frequency response of the sound recorded by an ESL microphone and by a conventional microphone (*Electro-Voice*, model 635N/D-B). Figure 7 shows the frequency response of both microphones when a white noise (top) and a whistle (bottom) are played on a conventional electromagnetic speaker placed in between the two microphones, 20 cm from each microphone. The level of white noise is 77 dB and that of whistle is 95 dB measured with the SPL meter 20 cm away from the speaker. The gain of the microphones is adjusted to record comparable levels.

Figure 7 shows that the spectrum of two microphones matches in the mid-frequency range; however, the low-frequency sound (<1000 Hz) is dampen by the ESL microphone. Moreover, the ESL recording has a uniform noise across the spectrum. The sound quality of ESL microphone can be improved by software sound processing and modified electronics.

PRELIMINARY INTERACTION USER STUDIES

The sonic performance of the freeform ESL used in various applications is described in the previous section. In this section, we evaluate the performance of electrostatic loudspeaker and microphone in two user studies. Both studies are designed to evaluate functional reliability of ESL while a human user interacts with them. In the first preliminary study, we compare the performance of ESL with conve ntional stereo speakers in sound localization. In the second study, we evaluate the performance electrostatic microphone in understanding speech.

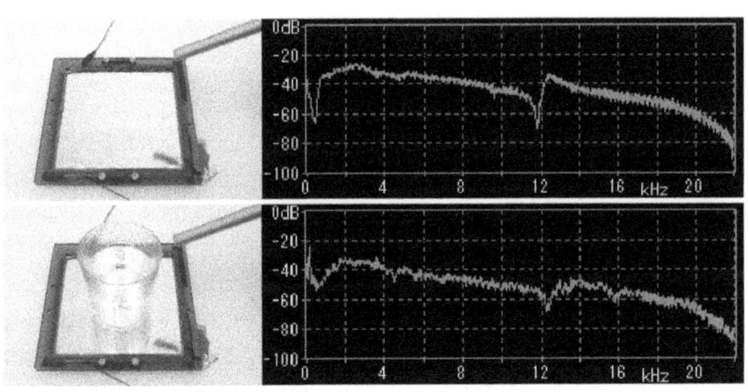

Figure 6. Frequency response measurements of an electrostatic loudspeaker in the free unloaded state (*top*) and in the loaded state (*bottom*)

Study 1: Evaluation of Electrostatic Loudspeaker

A typical application of ESL is to embed them in large walls with projected imagery. Any non-collation of imagery and sound will deteriorate the user experience and absorption with the content. Therefore, in the first study we measure the localization performance of an ESL and compare it with conventional stereo speakers.

Procedures

We mount an ESL (102 cm wide by 45 cm high) on a wall and attach conventional speakers (*Bose*, model Computer MusicMonitor speakers) on the two extreme sides of the ESL. Participants stand in front of the center of the ESL and listen to the sound from ESL and stereo speakers. In a trial, a sound is produced either through the ESL or through stereo speakers and participants indicate if the "perceived sound source is directly in front of them". They are asked to stare straight at the center of the ESL and respond by saying 'yes', if they feel that the sound source is on the surface they are looking at, or by 'no', if otherwise. A 3.7 second animated sound is used throughout the experiment. The stereo speakers are balanced equally to simulate the sound source at the midline between the two conventional speakers. Three participant locations are tested. These locations are 30, 152 and 274 cm in front of the ESL along the midline of the ESL.

Ten participants (5 males, 19 to 56 years old) take part in the study. None of the participant report auditory impairments. They are recruited from our research facility and are not paid for their participation. Each participant is tested for 60 trials (3 distances x 2 sound sources x 10 repetitions) that lasts ~10 minutes. Participants also try a few training trials before starting the experiment.

Results

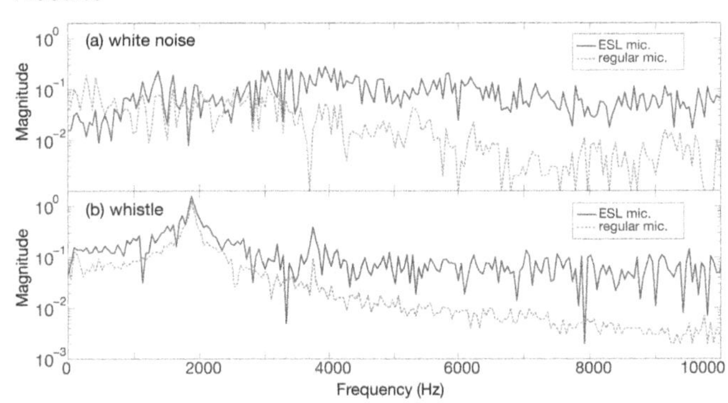

Figure 7. Spectrum of (a) white noise and (b) whistle recoded with ESL and standard microphones.

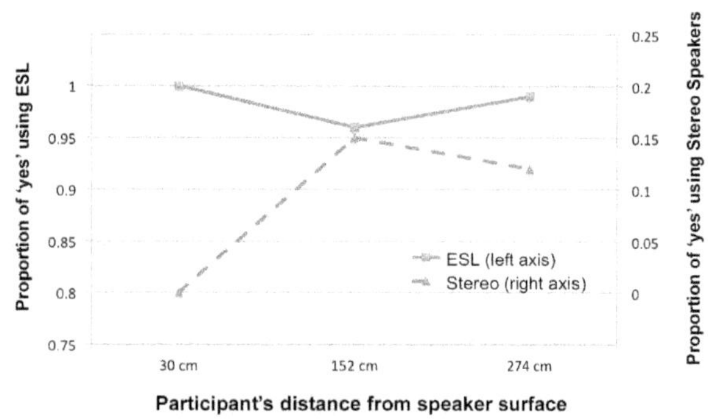

Figure 8. Sound source localization performance of ESL and conventional stereo speaker

Figure 8 shows proportion of 'yes' (p('yes')) when the sound was produced by ESL and by conventional stereo speakers as a function of the location of participants. At 30 cm separation (very close to the speaker), participants always responded 'yes' to ESL and never to the stereo speakers, indicating that the ESL provides the best collocation performance of projected imagery at close proximities. At distances 152 cm and 274 cm, the rating of ESL was high (>95% of the time); however p('yes') using stereo speakers also started to improve. Pairwise T-tests showed that the localization performance was significantly different between 30 cm and 152 cm ($p=0.04$) and 30 cm and 274 cm ($p=0.03$), however it was not different between 152 cm and 274 cm ($p=0.4$). In conclusion, the ESL is better than the stereo speakers in localizing the sound source on the surface, and therefore enhances the interactions with the projected content on the surface.

Study 2: Evaluation of Electrostatic Microphone

An application of the electrostatic microphone is to capture the sound from the environment and use it for sensing or communication purposes. In this preliminary study, we evaluate the microphone configuration of the ESL for speech communication.

Procedures

Two non-native (one male and one female) speakers utter five non-sense consonant-vowel (CV) syllables and are recorded using the ESL based microphone. These syllables are /ba/, /pa/, /be/, /ve/ and /he/. The first two syllables differ in *voicing* and other three syllables differ in *place* and *manner* of articulation. This speech corpus is used to evaluate how well the phonetics can be recorded through the microphone.

Twelve participants (8 males, ages 22 to 38 years old) listen to each of the ten syllables. Half of the participants are asked to guess the syllable (unprompted) and the other half are given possible five responses (prompted). The order of test syllables is randomized for each participant. The mono-channel microphone recording is saved as stereo signal and played only once though a headphone worn by participants.

		Response				
		/ba/	*/pa/*	*/be/*	*/ve/*	*/he/*
Stimulus	*/ba/*	1.00	0.00	0.00	0.00	0.00
	/pa/	0.50	0.50	0.00	0.00	0.00
	/be/	0.00	0.00	0.92	0.08	0.00
	/ve/	0.00	0.00	0.00	1.00	0.00
	/he/	0.00	0.00	0.00	0.00	1.00

Table 1. Stimulus-response confusion matrix of prompted speech identification using ESL microphone

Results

Participants correctly identified unprompted syllables 43 out of 60 times. In many cases, /ve/ was identified as /we/ and /pa/ uttered by the male speaker was always responded as /ba/. For prompted syllables, participants correctly identified the syllable 88% of time. The stimulus-response matrix is shown in Table 1. All /pa/'s uttered by the male speaker were identified as /ba/, and participants made only one error response (/be/ identified as /ve/). In general, the ESL microphone transmits sound and speech signal reliably with the exception of /b/ from /p/ that could be due to the distortion in low-frequency signal by the ESL microphone.

DESIGN SPACE AND APPLICATIONS

In previous sections, we describe the design freedom and characteristics of freeform ESLs, which allows them to be used in wide range of applications. Due to the shape, size and flexibility in these ESLs, we focus the applications to architecture, furniture and everyday objects that have been made and installed for in-house testing and evaluation. In each subsection below, we also highlight design and interactions associated with each application.

Architectures

Large Curved Walls

The freeform ESLs are very good candidate to embed in large and complex shaped walls because it has high flexibility of shape and it is scalable. We integrated the ESLs into a wall setting as shown in Figure 9. The requirements for the installations were: (i) An immersive multisensory experience, (ii) on a large high definition curved display, and (iii) spatial media to make animations feel real and collocate the sound with moving visuals.

We fabricated an array of six ESL panels and mounted them on a curved frame on the wall. The array was covered with a single sheet of white paper, which was used as a surface for projected graphics. A high definition projector was mounted on the ceiling that projected animated video sequences on the wall as shown in Figure 9. Instead of replicating our electronic driver for six channels, we designed a multi-channel ESL driver, which consist of multiple high voltage amplifiers using a single high voltage power supply. A single 1000 V (1.25mA) high voltage supply (EMCO, model QH10) was mounted on the motherboard that provided the high voltage reference to up to eight channels. The sound experience was designed in max/msp that channeled six outputs through a MOTU USB audio interface (model UltraLite-mk3 Hybrid). We divided the display into six sections and used sound fading techniques to create seamless sound movements related to the motion of animated objects.

We demonstrated the installation to technical staff and guests visiting the facility to gather feedback. All guests agreed that the installation was immersive as the sound was collocated with the projected imagery and moved with the animated imagery along the wall. They were also intrigued by the flexibility of the ESL in limited space. Guests frequently moved close to the display and touched it. In order to avoid passing high voltages (current was limited to less than 1.25 mA) to guests, the ground potential electrode (metal mesh panels) was placed on the outside and the diaphragms connected to the high voltage audio signal were placed in between the wall and ground potential electrode. Therefore guests could not touch the diaphragm.

Morphing Structures

Our freeform ESLs are light and generate directional and uniform sound along the surface of diaphragm. We used these speakers for transforming room environments as shown in the creative concept in Figure 10. In addition to the features of ESLs described above, we also used them to work as a microphone with modifications to the driver. In this case, the same ESL unit was used as a sound reproduction as well as the sound recoding device. The requirements of the installation were: (i) A room transforms into different configurations, (ii) each panel has a speaker and a microphone, (iii) sound is directional and targets specific guest from the audience, and (iv) transforming panels must be lightweight.

Figure 10 shows the moving speaker structure. The loudspeaker panels were suspended by thin strings, whose lengths were controlled by a series of servomotors. By varying the length of strings, the artist could vary the height and alignment of each panel. A user whispered to the ESL and the sound was played back through the speaker array. The recorded sound was processed in a max/msp patch and passed through the speaker array to create animated sound experience with dynamically morphing structures. The installation was used for internal testing and measurements.

Furniture

Interactive Tabletops

In this installment, we integrated an array of nine freeform ESLs on the top surface of a wooden table and enhanced tabletop activity between users. Eight speakers are placed radially across the table and the ninth circular speaker is embedded in the center as shown in Figure 11. The centerpiece was also mounted with a subwoofer to produce low-frequency sound. The setup was similar to that used in the large curved wall installation above. A projector was mounted on the ceiling to project animated images on the table. The resulting installation was used in an interactive dinning situation where dynamic sounds were produced while users had a dinner served on the table.

Six highly skilled concept designers and media artists, who evaluated the performance of ESL and provided recommendations. The main feedback was that the installation had a surprise element and could not be achieved only with normal loudspeakers. The sound localization was effective but sound levels were low and distorted. We modified the amplifier driver noting that the amperage would be lost in transistor circuitry. The larger amperage (10 mA) improved both the quality and perceived loudness of the sound. Due to the minimal effect of loading on ESL, the food served on the table did not affect the sound quality. Guests also spilled water on the table that did not affect the sound and safety quality.

Figure 9. Freeform ESLs are arranged to form a curved projection surface. The sound and animated graphics are collocated using the arrayed configuration.

Figure 10. A user interacts with moving ceiling panels that can record users' sound and play them at different locations in the room.

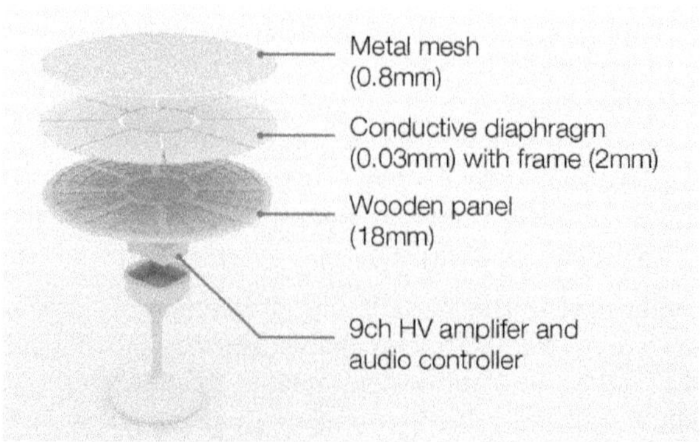

Figure 11. The surface of a large round table is embedded with an array of freeform electrostatic loudspeakers.

Cushions

By using soft conductive cloth - cushions, pillows, mattresses and similar soft materials can also reproduce sound. Figure 12 shows an ESL pillow. The pillow is made by wrapping two layers of conductive cloth around a pillow. Each conductive layer acts like a diaphragm. A normal non-conductive fabric covers the, thus isolating conductive diaphragm from direct user contact. Low sound levels were reproduced by the soft pillow speaker because the distance between the two diaphragms was not close enough to reproduce enough audible sound pressure level. However, when a user put the head on the pillow, then the diaphragms are pressed against each other and produce light perceivable sound. This sound level was sufficient to utilize the pillow, because the head (and consequently the ears) would be directly placed on the pillow.

Other Everyday Objects

Toys and Tangibles

In all previous cases, we implemented the active mode of the freeform ESL, that is, the entire speaker configuration was integrated onto the surface, for example, on the wall surface or on the table surface. In some situations, interactions were desired with passive tangible objects. Here an object equipped with a passive diaphragm layer is placed on a fixed electrode pattern embedded on a surface. Figure 13 shows a table with a grid pattern made from conductive tape and the tangible object. The tangible object only creates sound when placed on the table and can be used as toys for playful user experience.

Floating Speakers

The lightweight nature of ESL allows them to be a candidate for floating lightweight objects, such as balloons, as shown in Figure 1. In this case, the high voltage electrode was placed inside the balloon and the outer diaphragm layer was grounded. The quality of sound reproduced with these floating loudspeakers depends on the pressure of air inside the balloon. An inflated balloon would generate louder sound than a half inflated balloon.

DISCUSSION AND CONCLUDING REMARKS

In this paper, we have explored programmable matter to reproduce sound for everyday interactions, by integrating loudspeakers into surrounding architectures, furniture, tangible objects, soft materials, floating and many other everyday objects. We have modified the current electrostatic speaker technology and configured them to produce durable, safe and interactive environments. The resulting freeform electrostatic loudspeakers are flexible, lightweight, scalable and inexpensive.

In a series of experimental measurements, we determined that ESL has following characteristics:

- Low frequency sounds are distorted higher than the high frequency sounds.
- The sound radiates out of the entire surface of the diaphragm.
- The sound is highly directional
- The effect of loading on the diaphragm is minimal.

The construction of freeform ESL is simple and requires components that are easily available in a typical workshop setting. These components are selected on the basis of applications they were used in; for example, lightweight and paper-like Aluminized Mylar sheet was used in balloon and a solid metallic mesh was used in the wall. Other materials such as copper plates, conductive ink and transparent ITO could also be utilized.

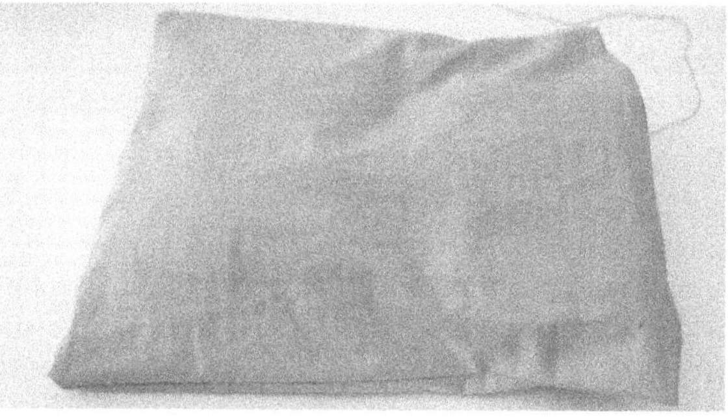

Figure 12. The freeform electrostatic loudspeakers are flexible and used in a soft cushion.

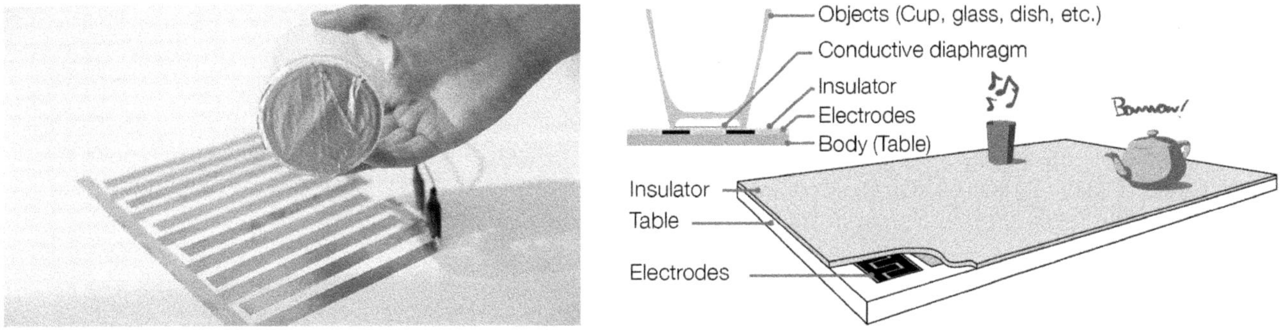

Figure 13. Tangible and everyday objects become interactive speakers by placing them on an electrode grid.

Another advantage of the freeform ESL is that it can be configured to many possible configurations with slight modification in the structure. Because of the electrostatic coupling generated between the two conductive surfaces and the relative motion between these surfaces produces sound, any one of the surface could be used as a diaphragm and any surface could be grounded while the other is connected to the high voltage. The quality of sound does not vary with changing the polarity of the speaker.

One important feature of the freeform ESL is that the entire diaphragm surface vibrates and reproduces sound. This is different than the conventional electromagnetic speakers, in which the coils around the magnet vibrates and the motion is translated to the diaphragm. This provides two advantages in favor of ESL.

1) The loading on the loudspeaker diaphragm only hinders the movement of the surface directly under the loading. Other parts of the speaker will still vibrate and generate sound. Unlike conventional speaker where the loading affects the entire sound generation process, the sound quality in electrostatic loudspeakers is slightly depreciated with the loading.
2) The sound emits uniformly and a user walking along a wall equipped with an ESL would feel that the sound source is moving along him/her. This is not possible with conventional speakers as the perceived sound intensity decreases as the user move away from the speaker and vice versa. Therefore, electrostatic loudspeakers also enhance the sound listening experience.

Safety Issues

In practice, we have used a low-power, high-voltage direct current power supply to amplify the sound signal up to 1000 V. The output current, however, is limited to 1.25 mA. Therefore, when a user touches the high voltage diaphragm only, they do not feel an electrical shock. But if the user touches both the high voltage diaphragm and the ground electrode, it can be painful and dangerous.

One way to prevent direct user contact with the high voltage source is to isolate the electrodes by placing them inside the objects and structures that are not accessible during interactions. In all configurations proposed in this paper, (except for tangible passive loudspeakers) we have placed the high voltage electrode inside the structure and covered it by the ground electrode. Moreover, these electrodes were insulated to reduce any mishap due to accidental contact between the skin and electrode. The resulting ESL are safe but care must be taken during fabrication, testing and installation of ESLs.

In future we will add isolation breakdown detection circuits for ensuring that these speakers are more safe and interactive.

Limitations

Current freeform ESLs are handmade and there are variations in between the speakers. These variations are mainly due to not maintaining uniform tension along the surfaces and maintaining uniform distance between the two electrode surfaces. This results in poor sound quality and inconsistent sound production throughout the surface. However, these procedural variations can be reduced in a calibrated production process.

The freeform ESLs could produce sound levels up to 80 dB. Replacing the high voltage source to higher voltage can produce higher sound levels. However, this will also increase the safety concern and increase the thickness of the insulation protective layer, and ultimately the size and weight of each speaker.

The inherent nature of the freeform ESL is that it distorts low frequency content of the incoming sound. Therefore, low frequency sound should be filtered out in the pre-processing stage to eliminate distortions and artifacts. The ESL can be combined with a low frequency subwoofer to play the entire spectrum of sound signal. It should be noted that high frequency sound is more important in sound localization, therefore augmenting the low frequency subwoofer would only complement the sound perception and the main interaction could be still done with the ESL.

The ESL structure can be used as a microphone by replacing the high-voltage driving amplifier with a pre-conditioning amplifier. In addition to the sound input, the ESL microphone could also be used to detect locations and interactions of users in front of the ESL. Moreover, ESL can also be used for haptic feedback by optimizing the low-frequency (< 500 Hz) response. These functionalities of ESL require further exploration and will be investigated in future.

In spite of limitations in the current freeform ESL, we have integrated them in to a large variety of user interaction scenarios. We believe that these loudspeakers will expand in to new modality for programmable matter and interactive surfaces.

REFERENCES

1. http://www.acoustable.com
2. Bau, O., Poupyrev, I., Israr, A., & Harrison, C. (2010). TeslaTouch: electrovibration for touch surfaces. In Proc. UIST'10 (pp. 283-292). ACM.
3. Benko, H., Wilson, A. D., & Balakrishnan, R. (2008). Sphere: multi-touch interactions on a spherical display. In Proc. UIST'08 (pp. 77-86). ACM.
4. Chua, C. K., Leong, K. F., & Lim, C. S. (2010). *Rapid prototyping: principles and applications*. World Scientific.
5. Coelho, M., Poupyrev, I., Sadi, S., Vertegaal, R., Berzowska, J., Buechley, L., Maes, P., & Oxman, N. (2009). Programming reality: from transitive materials to organic user interfaces. In CHI'09 Extended Abstracts (pp. 4759-4762). ACM.
6. Follmer, S., Leithinger, D., Olwal, A., Hogge, A., & Ishii, H. (2013). inFORM: dynamic physical affordances and constraints through shape and object actuation. In Proc. UIST'13 (pp. 417-426). ACM
7. Goldstein, S. C., Campbell, J. D., & Mowry, T. C. (2005). Programmable matter. *Computer*, *38*(6), 99-101.
8. Han, J. Y. (2005). Low-cost multi-touch sensing through frustrated total internal reflection. In Proc. UIST'05 (pp. 115-118). ACM.
9. Hanna, C.R. Theory of the electrostatic loud speaker. The Journal of the Acoustical Society of America 2(2) (1930), 143–149.
10. Harrison, C., & Hudson, S. E. (2008). Scratch input: creating large, inexpensive, unpowered and mobile finger input surfaces. In Proc. UIST'08 (pp. 205-208). ACM.
11. Holman, D., & Vertegaal, R. (2008). Organic user interfaces: designing computers in any way, shape, or form. *Communications of the ACM, 51*(6), 48-55.
12. IOSONO GmbH, www.iosono-sound.com.
13. Ishiguro, Y., & Poupyrev, I. (2014). 3D printed interactive speakers. In Proc. of ACM conference on Human factors in computing systems (pp. 1733-1742)..
14. Ishii, H., Wisneski, C., Orbanes, J., Chun, B., & Paradiso, J. (1999). PingPongPlus: design of an athletic-tangible interface for computer-supported cooperative play. In Proc. of the SIGCHI conference on Human Factors in Computing Systems (pp. 394-401). ACM.
15. Kim, S. C., Israr, A., & Poupyrev, I. (2013). Tactile rendering of 3D features on touch surfaces. In Proc. UIST'13 (pp. 531-538). ACM.
16. Kurihara, K., & Tsukada, K. (2012). SpeechJammer: A System Utilizing Artificial Speech Disturbance with Delayed Auditory Feedback. arXiv preprint arXiv:1202.6106.
17. Lee, C. S., Kim, J. Y., Lee, D. E., Joo, J., Wagh, B. G., Han, S., ... & Koh, S. K. (2003). Flexible and transparent organic film speaker by using highly conducting PEDOT/PSS as electrode. Synthetic metals, 139(2), 457-461.
18. Lloyd, B., Goldman, R.B., and Roop, R.W. Design and Performance of a High-Frequency Electrostatic Speaker. The Journal of the Acoustical Society of America 27(6) (1955), 1128–1133.
19. Malone, E. and Lipson, H. Freeform fabrication of ionomeric polymer-metal composite actuators. Rapid Prototyping Journal 12, 5 (2006), 244–253.
20. Malone, E. and Lipson, H. Multi-material freeform fabrication of active systems (2008). ESDA'08, ASME, pp. 1–9.
21. Medley, A. P., Billson, D. R., Hutchins, D. A., & Davis, L. A. J. (2006). Properties of an electrostatic transducer. The Journal of the Acoustical Society of America, 120(5), 2658-2667.
22. Palette Kits, http://www.palettegear.com/
23. Paradiso, J. A. (1996). The interactive balloon: Sensing, actuation and behavior in a common object. IBM Systems Journal, 35(3.4), 473-487.
24. Poupyrev, I., Schoessler, P., Loh, J., & Sato, M. (2012). Botanicus Interacticus: interactive plants technology. In ACM SIGGRAPH 2012 Emerging Technologies (p. 4). ACM.
25. Rekimoto, J., & Saitoh, M. (1999). Augmented surfaces: a spatially continuous work space for hybrid computing environments. In Proc. CHI' 99 (pp. 378-385). ACM.
26. Rekimoto, J. (2012). Squama: modular visibility control of walls and windows for programmable physical architectures. In *Proc. of the International Working Conference on Advanced Visual Interfaces* (pp. 168-171). ACM.
27. Scott, P. J., & Jiang, X. (2014). Freeform surface characterisation: theory and practice. In Journal of Physics: Conference Series (Vol. 483, No. 1, p. 012005). IOP Publishing.
28. Sugibayashi, Y., Kurimoto, S., Ikefuji, D., Morise, M., & Nishiura, T. (2012). Three-dimensional acoustic sound field reproduction based on hybrid combination of multiple parametric loudspeakers and electrodynamic subwoofer. Applied Acoustics, 73(12), 1282-1288.

Multi-push Display using 6-axis Motion Platform

Takashi Nagamatsu
Technical University of Munich
Arcisstrasse 21,
80333 Munich, Germany
Kobe University
5-1-1, Fukae-minami, Higashi-nada, Kobe 658-0022, Japan
nagamatu@kobe-u.ac.jp

Masahiro Nakane
Kobe University
5-1-1, Fukae-minami, Higashi-nada, Kobe 658-0022, Japan
131w109w@stu.kobe-u.ac.jp

Haruka Tashiro
Kobe University
5-1-1, Fukae-minami, Higashi-nada, Kobe 658-0022, Japan

Teruhiko Akazawa
Kobe University
5-1-1, Fukae-minami, Higashi-nada, Kobe 658-0022, Japan
akazawa@maritime.kobe-u.ac.jp

ABSTRACT
This study designed and developed a novel tactile display that provides a multi-push sensation by using a 6-axis motion platform. The display mechanically controls the position and orientation of a surface panel. A user touching an on-screen button with one finger can push the button vertically. When the user subsequently touches the display with a second finger, the surface panel declines and the position of the first finger remains unchanged. Thus, the user can push at two positions on the surface panel. We also developed a prototype system with six servomotors and a touch panel based on the principle of frustrated total internal reflection.

Author Keywords
Touch panel; tactile feedback; 6-axis motion platform

ACM Classification Keywords
H5.2 [Information interfaces and presentation]: User Interfaces. - Haptic I/O.

INTRODUCTION
Touch panel technology is widely used in applications such as mobile phones, ATMs, ticket-vending machines, and car navigation systems. Conventional touch panels provide audio and visual feedback to the user in order to clarify the system's status and responses. Although some forms of tactile feedback, such as vibration, are used in certain touch panels, the sensation of operation of such touch panels is different from that when depressing conventional push-buttons. Previous studies have aimed to incorporate the push-button sensation into touch panels [6, 9]. However, these touch panels do not offer multi-position tactile feedback. In this study, we develop a novel technique that incorporates a multi-push sensation into a touch panel.

ITS 2014, November 16–19, 2014, Dresden, Germany.

ACM 978-1-4503-2587-5/14/11...$15.00
http://dx.doi.org/10.1145/2669485.2669512

RELATED WORKS
Several techniques have been developed that provide tactile feedback on a touch panel. For example, Active Click [3] provides tactile feedback in the form of vibration; this technique is currently used extensively in applications such as mobile phones and car navigation systems. However, vibration is different from natural tactile feedback. TeslaTouch [1] technology is based on electrovibration, which does not make use of any moving parts. It provides a wide range of tactile feedback sensations to fingers moving across a touch surface but does not provide a push sensation.

Some previous studies constructed a moveable display panel. For example, TouchMover [11] is a visual+haptic device that combines 3D stereo visualizations, multi-touchscreen interactions, force sensing, and 1D haptic actuation perpendicular to the display panel. Further, Gesture output [10] is a technique that actuates the user's finger in two dimensions by using a transparent foil overlaid on the touchscreen. Finally, WobblySurface [9] controls the rigidity of a surface panel such that when a user touches an on-screen button, the normally rigid surface becomes wobbly and is able to be pushed mechanically like a button; it uses three degrees of freedom. Thus, the maximum number of degree of freedom achieved thus far is three.

Other studies developed systems for realizing localized tactile sensation. For example, MudPad [7] realizes multi-position tactile feedback; however, it has a soft contact surface. Harrison et al. [6] and Tactus [12] developed techniques that provide dynamically changeable physical buttons on a visual display; however, the tactile features in these displays are statically arranged. inFORM [2] provides localized tactile sensation by using numerous pins.

Thus, a technique that provides a multi-push sensation through a flat hard contact surface has yet to be developed.

PRINCIPLE FOR REALIZATION OF MULTI-PUSH SENSATION
We developed a novel technique that allows users to push at multiple positions on a surface panel. This technique is based on the principle of declining the surface panel, as shown in Figure 1. When the user touches the surface panel

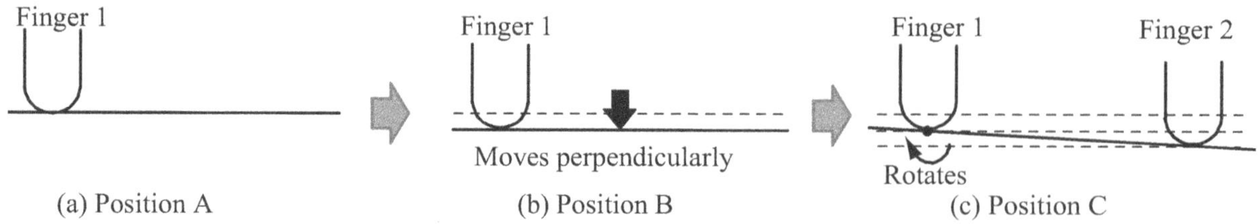

Figure 1. Principle for realizing multi-push sensation.

with Finger 1 (Figure 1 a), the panel moves along the normal vector of the plane formed by the surface panel and comes to rest at the position shown in Figure 1 b. Next, when the user pushes the surface panel with Finger 2, the panel rotates around the point of contact of Finger 1.

We define the positions of the surface panel shown in Figures 1 a–c as Positions A, B, and C, respectively.

DESIGN

To realize the concept of a multi-push display, we designed the system as shown in Figure 2.

The surface panel is supported by six rods connected to six servomotors. One end of each rod connects to the surface panel and the other end connects to the arm of a servomotor via ball joints. This mechanism is the so-called Stewart platform.

In our system, a finger touch is detected by the frustrated total internal reflection (FTIR) technique [4]. Infrared light-emitting diode (IR LED) arrays are installed on two opposite sides of the surface panel, and the positions of the fingers are detected by an IR camera.

An image is back-projected by a projector onto the screen located under the surface panel. A notable characteristic of our system is that the screen and touch panel are isolated from each other. Since the surface panel is transparent, the image on the screen is static. Thus, the image of only the button area can be changed when the on-screen button is pushed.

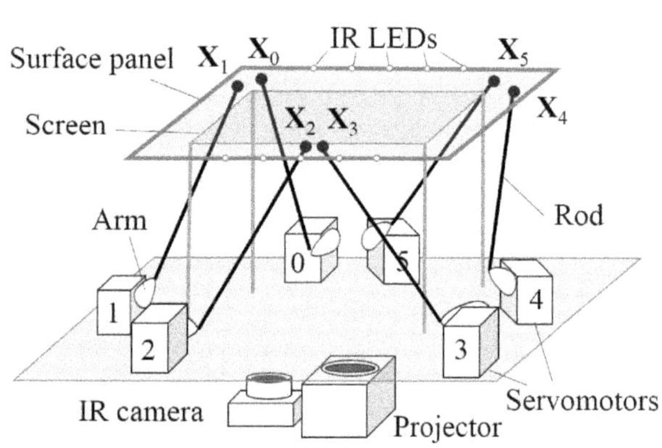

Figure 2. Design of multi-push display.

$\mathbf{X}_0$, $\mathbf{X}_1$, $\mathbf{X}_2$, $\mathbf{X}_3$, $\mathbf{X}_4$, and $\mathbf{X}_5$ correspond to the position vectors of the connection points of the rods from servomotors 0–5, respectively.

CONTROL OF SURFACE PANEL

Estimation of Finger Position in the World Coordinate System

We estimate the position of finger touch in three dimensions by means of the IR camera. We detect the corresponding 2D position on the surface panel by using three fiducial markers attached to the panel. The position vectors of the fiducial markers in three dimensions are denoted as **A**, **B**, and **O**. In our system, **A**, **B**, and **O** change in response to the movement of the surface panel; nevertheless, the system is constantly aware of them at any point in time.

Let ${}^c\mathbf{A}$, ${}^c\mathbf{B}$, and ${}^c\mathbf{O}$ denote the positions of the fiducial markers on the surface panel, as captured by the camera, in the 2D camera image coordinate system, and let ${}^c\mathbf{F}$ denote the finger position in the 2D camera image coordinate system. Then, these positions are related as follows:

$$({}^c\mathbf{F} - {}^c\mathbf{O}) = a({}^c\mathbf{A} - {}^c\mathbf{O}) + b({}^c\mathbf{B} - {}^c\mathbf{O})$$

Here, a and b are coefficients that can be calculated since there are two equations. Thus, the position **F** is expressed in the 3D world coordinate system as follows:

$$\mathbf{F} = a(\mathbf{A} - \mathbf{O}) + b(\mathbf{B} - \mathbf{O}) + \mathbf{O}$$

Determination of New Position of Surface Panel

When the first finger touches the surface panel, the position of the surface panel, i.e., $\mathbf{X}_0$, $\mathbf{X}_1$, $\mathbf{X}_2$, $\mathbf{X}_3$, $\mathbf{X}_4$, and $\mathbf{X}_5$, is easily determined by moving the surface panel vertically. In our study, the push depth is set to 2 mm on the basis of the study of Nakane et al. [8], who examined the depth of the pushed distance of a surface panel of a pushable display.

When the second finger touches the surface panel, the system causes the surface panel to decline. The vector of the rotation axis, **l**, shown in Figure 3, is defined as

$$\mathbf{l} = (\mathbf{F}_2 - \mathbf{F}_1) \times \mathbf{n}$$

where $\mathbf{F}_1$ and $\mathbf{F}_2$ are the touch positions of the first and second fingers, respectively, and **n** is the normal vector of the surface panel. The rotation angle α is calculated from the push depth as follows:

$$\alpha = \arcsin\left(\frac{depth}{d}\right),$$

where *depth* is the depth pushed by the user and d is the distance between the touch positions of the two fingers on the surface panel. Thus, the angle through which the system rotates the surface panel is determined. The new positions of $\mathbf{X}_0$, $\mathbf{X}_1$, $\mathbf{X}_2$, $\mathbf{X}_3$, $\mathbf{X}_4$, and $\mathbf{X}_5$ are determined by rotating the surface panel by angle α along the axis $\mathbf{l}$.

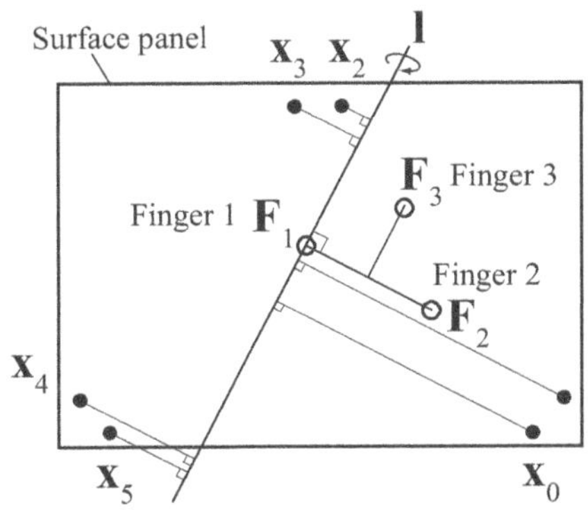

Figure 3. Rotation axis, touch positions of fingers, and connecting points of rods on the surface panel.

Determination of Rotation Angle of Servomotors

In order to move the surface panel, we must determine the rotation angle of each servomotor. The position $\mathbf{X}$ in the world coordinate system is transformed to the position ${}^i\mathbf{X}$ in the coordinate system of the servo motor i as follows:

$${}^i\mathbf{X} = {}^i\mathrm{R}_w\left(\mathbf{X} - {}^i\mathbf{T}_w\right)$$

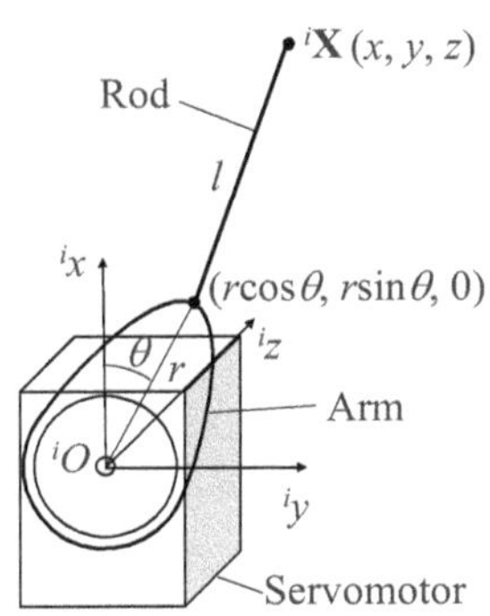

Figure 4. Coordinate system of servo motor *i*.

where ${}^i\mathrm{R}_w$ and ${}^i\mathbf{T}_w$ are, respectively, the rotation matrix and the translation vector from the world coordinate system to the coordinate system of servo motor i. These are determined by measuring the direction and position of the servomotors.

Figure 4 shows a servomotor, an arm, and a rod in the coordinate system of servo motor i; here, l is the length of the rod connecting the panel to the servo arm, r is the arm length, and θ is the angle of rotation of the servomotor.

θ must be determined such that the end of the rod passes through the position ${}^i\mathbf{X} = (x, y, z)$. Therefore, the relation satisfies the following equation:

$$l^2 = (r\cos\theta - x)^2 + (r\sin\theta - y)^2 + (0 - z)^2$$

Then, we have

$$\sin(\theta + \beta) = \left(x^2 + y^2 + z^2 + r^2 - l^2\right) \Big/ \left(2r\sqrt{x^2 + y^2}\right),$$

where β satisfies $\sin\beta = x\big/\sqrt{x^2 + y^2}$ and $\cos\beta = y\big/\sqrt{x^2 + y^2}$.

Therefore,

$$\theta = \arcsin\left(\frac{x^2 + y^2 + z^2 + r^2 - l^2}{2r\sqrt{x^2 + y^2}}\right) - \beta \quad \text{or} \quad \theta = \pi - \arcsin\left(\frac{x^2 + y^2 + z^2 + r^2 - l^2}{2r\sqrt{x^2 + y^2}}\right) - \beta.$$

We select an appropriate θ value according to the direction of the servomotor.

IMPLEMENTATION

A prototype system was implemented, as shown in Figure 5. The system consists mainly of a surface panel, six servomotors (Kondo Kagaku Co., Ltd., KRS 4033HV), a screen, an IR camera, IR LEDs (Vishay Intertechnology, Inc., VSMG2700), a PC, and a projector.

Figure 5. Implemented system.

Before operation of the system, the focus of the projector was adjusted on the screen and projection area was adjusted at the time when the surface panel took the Position A.

Figure 6 shows the system in operation, where it was implemented with one half of a keyboard.

Figure 6. System in operation.

In this stage of implementation, the surface panel immediately moves downward when a touch is detected.

EXPERIMENT

We conducted an experiment to verify the fundamental function that the position of the first finger remains unchanged when the second finger pushes the surface panel.

Paper tapes (Tapes 1 and 2) were used as contact faces to represent finger contact. The positions of Tapes 1 and 2 among Positions A, B, and C on the surface panel were compared.

During this experiment, we paused the operation of the system and measured the distances of Tapes 1 and 2 from the floor by using a laser distance meter, as shown in Figure 7.

We performed 10 sets of measurements by changing the positions of Tapes 1 and 2.

The experiment yielded an average distance of 0.2 mm for Tape 1 between Positions A and B, and an average distance of 2.0 mm for Tape 2 between Positions B and C. From these values, we concluded that the developed system was effective.

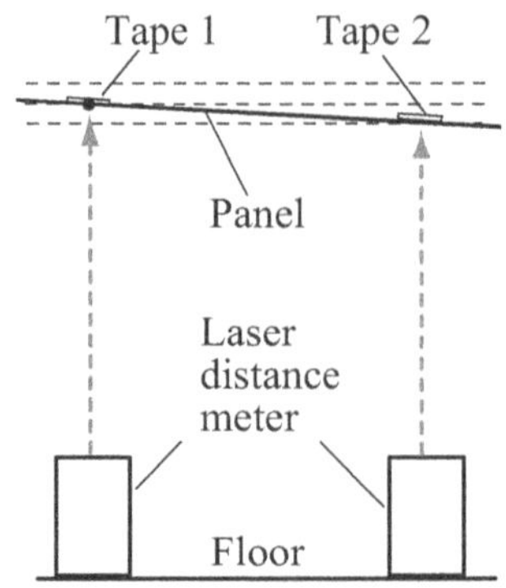

Figure 7. Measurement of distances

DISCUSSION

We have proposed a novel technique that provides a multi-push sensation through a flat hard contact surface.

We implemented the prototype system to allow a user to push at only two positions. However, this design of the system additionally allows a third position to be pushed. Figure 3 shows the third finger position $\mathbf{F}_3$ (which is not on the line connecting $\mathbf{F}_1$ with $\mathbf{F}_2$). If the system rotates the surface panel along the axis formed by the line connecting $\mathbf{F}_1$ and $\mathbf{F}_2$, pushing at the third position can be achieved. In future work, we intend to focus on this operation.

If the two fingers used for pushing are in close proximity, the panel should have a larger angle of decline; however, such a large angle induces an unnatural movement of the panel and is sometimes impossible to realize owing to hardware issues. Therefore, the system needs special consideration regarding the interface design, e.g., sufficient distance between two buttons (at least 20 mm in our implementation).

A motion platform has the limitation of travel. Therefore, in the next version of this system, we intend to add the functions of washout and wash back, similar to those of a flight simulator.

Compared to multi-pin systems such as inFORM [2], our system has a higher resolution and a simpler structure, although the maximum number of positions at which the user can push is three. Compared to small setup systems such as Active Click [3] and Tactus [12], our current implementation realizing multi-push sensation is bulky, so it is unsuitable to apply it to mobile systems. Downsizing is necessary in the future work.

Our system has the potential to provide not only push sensation but also other kinds of sensations. Future work in this direction includes the development of a different sensation for each push point, e.g., by giving them different elasticities.

CONCLUSION

This paper proposed the design and development of a novel tactile system that provides a multi-push function by using a 6-axis motion platform. The system is based on the principle of declining the surface panel. A user touching an on-screen button with one finger can push the button vertically. When the user subsequently touches the display with a second finger, the surface panel declines and the position of the first finger remains unchanged. Thus, the user can push at two positions on the surface panel. The effectiveness of the system was verified by constructing a prototype system.

REFERENCES

1. Bau, O., Poupyrev, I., Israr, A., and Harrison, C. TeslaTouch: Electrovibration for touch surfaces. In *Proc. UIST 2010*, ACM Press (2010), 283-292.
2. Follmer, S., Leithinger, D., Olwal, A., Hogge, A., and Ishii, H. inFORM: Dynamic physical affordances and constraints through shape and object actuation. In *Proc. UIST 2013*, ACM Press (2013), 417-426.
3. Fukumoto, M. and Sugimura, T. Active Click: Tactile feedback for touch panels. *Ext. Abstracts CHI 2001*, ACM Press (2001), 121-122.
4. Han, J.Y. Low-cost multi-touch sensing through frustrated total internal reflection. In *Proc. UIST 2005*, ACM Press (2005), 115-118.
5. Harrison, C. and Hudson, S.E. Providing dynamically changeable physical buttons on a visual display. In *Proc. CHI 2009*, ACM Press (2009), 299-308.
6. Hoshino, T., Tsukada, Y., and Minimoto, T. Tactile Driver: A touch panel system that can emulate actual tactile movement. In *Proc. Workshop on Interactive System and Software 2002*, (2002).
7. Jansen, Y., Karrer, T., and Borcher, J. MudPad: Tactile feedback and haptic texture overlay for touch surfaces. In *Proc. ITS 2010*, ACM Press (2010), 11-14.
8. Nakane, M., Echizen, S., Kamahara, J., and Nagamatsu, T. A study on tactile feedback for pushable touch display, In *Proc. 75th National Convention of IPSJ*, IPSJ (2013), 4-69 - 4-70.
9. Nagamatsu, T., Echizen, S., Akazawa, T., and Kamahara, J. WobblySurface: Tactile feedback by holding/releasing a surface panel. In *Demo ITS 2011*, ACM Press (2011).
10. Roudaut, A., Rau, A., Sterz, C., Plauth, M., Lopes, P., and Baudisch, P. Gesture output: Eyes-free output using a force feedback touch surface. In *Proc. CHI 2013*, ACM Press (2013), 2546-2556.
11. Sinclair, M., Pahud, M., and Benko, H. TouchMover: Actuated 3D touchscreen with haptic feedback. In *Proc. ITS 2013*, ACM Press (2013), 287-296.
12. Tactus. http://tactustechnology.com/technology

Multi-Surface Interactions with Geospatial Data: A Systematic Review

Zahra Shakeri Hossein Abad, Craig Anslow, Frank Maurer
Department of Computer Science, University of Calgary
{zshakeri,craig.anslow,frank.maurer}@ucalgary.ca

ABSTRACT
Even though Multi Surface Environments (MSE) and how to perform interactions in these environments have received much attention during recent years, interaction with geospatial data in these environments is still limited, and there are many design and interaction issues that need to be addressed. Alongside the rapid rise in the use of Geographic Information Systems (GIS) in group-based decision making, interaction with geospatial data has become highly important. In order to summarize the earlier research in this area, this paper presents a systematic review of MSE interactions with geospatial data. The review analyzes existing papers on MSE interaction techniques, discusses issues related to interaction with geospatial data in MSEs, and provides a comparison between common GIS tasks and existing interaction techniques in MSEs. Our results indicate that a substantial number of GIS tasks have not been investigated in MSEs.

Author Keywords
Geospatial data; Interaction techniques; Multi-surface environments; Systematic review

ACM Classification Keywords
H.5.2. Information Interfaces and Presentation (HCI): Miscellaneous

INTRODUCTION
Recently, there has been an increased research interest in designing and developing applications in Multi Surface Environments (MSE). By MSE we mean *"a system where interaction is divided over several displays, such as digital tabletops, wall displays and personal devices like tablets or mobile phones"* [19] (See Figure 1). The diversity of devices in these environments, ranging from smartphones to high-resolution wall displays, with different capabilities, provides a collaborative environment that enables multiple users to easily and seamlessly create, share, and manipulate data. While considerable studies into MSEs have looked at how users interact with MSEs and how different configurations affect collaborations and interactions, there is limited research on what interaction techniques with geospatial data are most effective in these environments. Interacting with geospatial data when group-based decision-making is required can be challenging. For example a number of domains including emergency operation centres, traffic control rooms, and military command and control centres utilize geospatial data. These domains are increasingly transitioning towards MSEs and require the design of appropriate gestures to interact with geospatial data across multiple devices.

ITS 2014, November 16–19, 2014, Dresden, Germany.
Copyright © 2014 ACM 978-1-4503-2587-5/14/11 ...$15.00.
http://dx.doi.org/10.1145/2669485.2669505

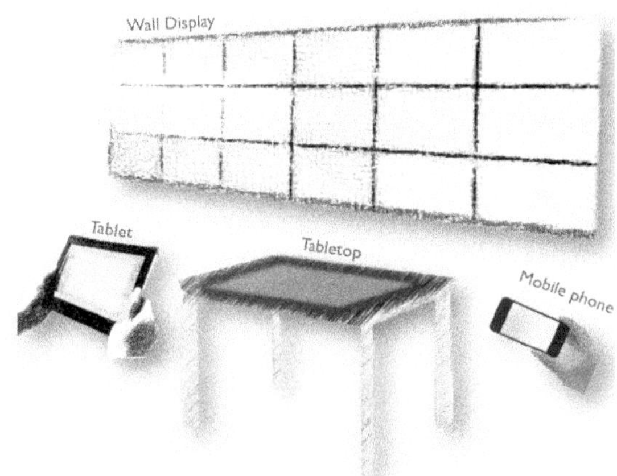

Figure 1: An example of a Multi Surface Environment consists of Wall display, Tablet, Tabletop and Mobile phone.

To summarize the research on multi-surface interactions with geospatial data we conducted a system literature review. This review seeks to analyze, classify, and present the common tasks and interaction techniques in MSEs. Moreover, it provides a comparison between these tasks and common geospatial tasks and activities that users can perform during their work with digital maps. We address the following questions:

RQ1: What interaction techniques can users perform in MSEs?

RQ2: What interaction techniques can users perform for geospatial tasks/activities in MSEs?

The paper is structured as follows: we review the existing literature discussing common geospatial tasks/activities and bring an overview of these tasks from system and cartography perspective. We then describe the review method that we used to select and analyze the papers for our review and describe the selected methodology for analyzing each of the included papers. We discuss the results and findings of the review based on our research questions. Finally, we conclude the review with some recommendations for future research.

COMMON TASKS TO WORK WITH DIGITAL MAPS

User interactions with geospatial data (i.e. digital maps) can be highly complex with lots of tasks and analysis that cannot be done easily with ordinary paper maps [7]. In this section, we present actual tasks that GIS analysts perform and classify these tasks into two categories, which are provided by Davies [6]:

- System perspective tasks (e.g. interactions with the commands and menus)
- Cartography perspective tasks (e.g. interaction with the data inside a map)

System Perspective Tasks

Davies [6, 7] has conducted two studies (survey and observation) to explore the common tasks from a system perspective that analysts perform during their interaction with digital maps. In the first study, respondents were asked to write free-text answers to a question "What tasks do you currently do with your GIS?" In the second study, 21 GIS users were asked to determine how often they perform the tasks from a predefined checklist of 48 common GIS activities/tasks. The results of these two studies indicate that zooming, panning, map presenting/plotting, digitizing objects, and adding information to them, and searching for specific information are basic system tasks which the majority of GIS analysts perform during their interaction with digital maps.

Cartography Perspective Tasks

McCann [18], Calkins and Obermeyer [5], and Knapp [16] each have provided a category of tasks that users perform during their interaction with digital maps. These categories have been extracted from the information perspective rather than the system. Considering that the tasks provided by McCann [18] include tasks which have been presented by Obermeyer and Knapp [5, 16], in this section we only focus on McCann's tasks:

1. Symbol detection: determination of the presence/absence of a symbol at a certain point on a map.
2. Symbol interpretation: association of a detected symbol with a concept stored in the user's memory.
3. Pattern detection and interpretation: identifying patterns to code map information such as lakes and vegetation.
4. Determine the attributes of map features: interpretation of symbol characteristics, which code attributes of the map feature such as determining a town population.
5. Calculate, count, measure, estimate, interpolate: these tasks are often introduced by a question like; *'How many?'*, *'How far?'*, and *'How long?'*
6. Comparison of symbols/patterns: determining whether two symbols/patterns show the same/different map features.
7. Annotation, updating, highlighting: user interaction with the map display to change the data on it.
8. Communication: passing information among map users to discuss features of the environment, make plans or solve problems.
9. Map memorization: processing map information combined with other knowledge about the environment, which together provide a deeper understanding of the environment.
10. Determine absolute location of a map feature: searching for the nearest reference markers related to the feature.
11. Determine relative location of a map feature: this task usually is introduced by a question such as *'Where is town X relative to town Y?'* and requires that the user process information about both distance and direction.
12. Search for a map feature: selecting a set of map features from criteria that may include type, attributes and spatial locations. (e.g., find all Italian restaurants within 3 minutes drive to downtown).
13. Integrate discrete map information: this task is characterized by questions such as 'what is the extent of the flooding?' and user should characterize map features that satisfy the criteria.
14. Determine spatial and temporal changes: comparing the distributions of features which occur in different regions, or occur in the same region, but over a period of time.
15. Inferring unportrayed features: forming hypothesis about the unportrayed features on the map based on information available from the map or other non-map data.
16. Orientation: matching a map feature with a geographical location.
17. Visualization: a user imagines what features and their relationships will look like when viewed in the environment.
18. Where am I?: locating map users in the environment.

It is important to note that the main focus of these cartographic tasks is on users' goal, whereas the *system perspective* tasks focus on what users have to do with the system to achieve these goals [6, 7].

REVIEW METHOD

This study follows the systematic review methodology described by Biolchini et al., Gough et al., and Kitchenman et al. [4, 11, 15] and consists of the following distinct steps: inclusion and exclusion criteria, paper selection and search strategy, quality assessment, data extraction, results, and discussion.

Step1: Inclusion and Exclusion Criteria

Papers were considered for inclusion in this review if they presented interaction tasks and techniques in MSEs. Inclusion of papers was not limited to empirical studies. In this review we considered both application and experience papers. We excluded papers that were not related to MSEs tasks and techniques. As an example of exclusion, we found several papers that mentioned only "interaction in MSE" in their future work section and were outside the scope of this systematic review. We did not include papers that only focused on one device. Editorials, position papers and keynotes were excluded in this step.

Step2: Paper Selection

Identifying unbiased and comprehensive papers is the primary goal of a systematic review [11]. Comprehensiveness (recall) should be balanced with relevance (precision); high recall of a search reduces its precision and may return more irrelevant papers. For this reason, information retrieval plays a crucial role in the systematic review process and is a key

Iterations	# of Papers at each iteration	BWS	FWS	Expert Knowledge
1	36	6	3	0
2	45	5	1	0
3	51	0	12	1
4	64	1	0	0
5	65	0	0	0

Table 1: Iterations of information retrieval. BWS= Backward Snowballing, FWS= Forward Snowballing

Multi-Surface Keywords	Geospatial Keywords	HCI Keywords
Tabletop	Geospatial	Interaction
Big Display	Geographic	Gesture
Wall display	Map	Collaboration
Multi-Surface	GIS	Communication
Multi-Display	Location	CSCW
Digital Surface		Groupware

Table 2: Search Keywords

factor that distinguishes a systematic review from other forms of literature reviews [11].

Search Strategy

Development of appropriate search terms is an iterative process, and consists of modifying the search terms based on the papers that have already been retrieved [17]. At the first step, we started with 378 papers and used the following steps iteratively to retrieve the relevant papers. We continued modifying the search terms until we were unable to find any additional papers that we considered relevant. The result of each iteration is given in Table 1.

Google Scholar (GS): GS provides a simple and quick way to perform a search for scholarly literature across many disciplines and sources [1]. At the first stage of information retrieval, we queried GS using the search terms listed in Table 2 and found 378 papers at this step. Dean et al. [9] recently performed an experiment to evaluate if GS is sufficient to be used alone for systematic reviews and concluded that GS does not meet the required search standards for systematic reviews, and is not able to identify all known and relevant papers in a specific area. For this reason, at the next step we searched electronic databases to find more relevant papers.

Electronic Databases: At this step, we searched the following electronic databases by using search terms that are listed in Table 2:

- ACM Digital Library, ScienceDirect, Elsevier, SpringerLink, IEEE Xplore, Scopus, ISI Web of Science, Wiley InterScience Journal, and Kluwer Online.

Furthermore, we manually searched HCI and GIS journals and conference proceedings:

- HCI: *IJMMS, TOCHI, ACM sigchi Bulletin, ITS, CHI, CSCW, ECpapersSCW, DIS, GROUP, ICMI, IWAI (workshop)*
- GIS: *COSIT, ACM SIGSPATIAL, GIS, IGRSM, JOSIS, RSETE, IGARSS, Geoinformatica*

Snowballing: In some cases, it was not possible to find all of the relevant papers by searching databases. Snowballing, which is *"a powerful technique for identifying high quality sources in obscure locations"*, can be used as a supplement for the search process [13]. Before applying this technique, we reviewed all of the retrieved papers from the previous steps and judged their relevance based on title, keywords and abstract. In a few cases that *inclusion* decision was not possible based only on these criteria, we reviewed the outline, conclusion and references of the papers.

After creating a base list of 36 relevant papers, we then used snowballing by scanning the reference list (backward snowballing [13]) of identified papers in the previous step. Furthermore, there were papers that have been published after the selected papers, so we performed citation tracking (forward snowballing [13]) to identify relevant papers citing the papers in the previous step.

Expert Knowledge: Some relevant papers that have unrelated titles or use different wording in their text, might be ignored in searching databases or snowballing [11, 13]. In this step we found one more paper by asking academic colleagues.

Step3: Quality Assessment

Evaluating the quality and relevance of individual papers included in a review plays a key role in the review process and has a direct impact on the quality and reliability of the review [11]. By quality we mean the extent that each paper contributes to answering our review questions [10]. To this end, the quality assessment was performed for each of the 65 selected papers after the information retrieval step. Three main issues should be considered when evaluating the quality of research papers [2]:

- *Rigour*: Has a thorough and appropriate approach been applied to key research methods in the study?
- *Relevance*: How useful are the findings to the software industry and research community?
- *Credibility*: Are the findings well presented and meaningful?

Table 3 gives the summary of the quality assessment criteria related to each of these issues. These criteria are provided by the Critical Appraisal Skills Programme (CASP) [2]. In addition to these criteria, we added some more criteria based on existing issues in HCI research [12, 14].

While novelty is highly valued in HCI papers, evaluating the results and generality of previous papers, which can be achieved by replication, is a key challenge in HCI research [14]. As the majority of HCI research are conducted without an underlying theory, replication is not possible unless the exact experiment is performed. Greenberg and Thimbleby [12] presented the following factors that contribute to difficulties in replicating HCI experiments:

- Lack of enough information and data in HCI papers due to page limitations and difficulties to describe interactive systems in words.
- Using very specific and context-dependent platforms to perform the experiments. For example software packages

Screening Questions
1. Does the paper present information on *task based* interactions in MSE? 2. Is there a clear statement of the aim of the research? 3. Is there an adequate description of the context in which the research was carried out?
Rigorous
4. Have the researchers justified the research design? (e.g. have they decided which method to use?) 5. Have the researchers explained how the participants or cases were identified and selected? 6. Have the researchers justified the method that were chosen? 7. Has sufficient data been presented to support the findings and claims?
Relevance
8. Does the researcher discuss the contribution the paper makes to existing knowledge or understanding?
Credibility
9. Is there a clear statement of findings? - Have the researchers discussed the credibility of their findings? - Are the conclusions justified with the results? - Are the findings discussed in relation to the original research question?
Replicability
10. Was there enough information to allow replication? - Are experimental artifacts and circumstances accessible to community? - Are stable and widely used hardware and software platforms used to perform the study? - Are descriptions of interactive systems critical to the experiment available?

Table 3: Quality criteria [2, 12, 14]

with a very short life-span, using some unavailable prototype systems that were developed by the researcher, or running the experiment on a specific version of an operating system.

- Presenting a summary of the collected data, which makes it difficult to regenerate the data through replication.

Criteria related to *replicability* issues are listed in Table 3. Each of the 10 criteria was rated on a scale of 0-1 (0=No, 1= Yes) and we included or excluded papers based on the value of criterion 1. At this stage, after reading the full text, from 65 papers evaluated for quality, 37 papers were excluded from further analysis, for not providing information on task-based interactions in MSEs. Most of these papers, with a few exceptions, have focused on design and infrastructure of MSEs, especially spatial awareness and smooth transition between different devices (n=32). Five other papers only provided details about information sharing in MSEs. At the end of the *quality assessment* step, we selected 28 papers for data extraction and analysis (See Section Systematic Literature Review Papers for the papers in this review). A summary of the quality assessment results for these papers is presented in the results section.

Step4: Data Extraction

During this step, we applied a revised version of the grounded theory methodology to extract data from each of the 28 primary papers included in this review [23]. During the paper selection process, we categorized papers into two different groups: papers related to MSE interactions with geospatial data, and papers related to interaction techniques in MSEs.

In grounded theory we analyze all of the included papers line by line to extract concepts, which involves with high volumes of qualitative data. To help with this process, we used *Saturate* [21], which is a web-based open coding tool to enable traceability between codes and data. We started analyzing each set of papers as follows.

Of the 9 papers in the first group of papers, we selected a random paper and read and coded each data point of the text that was relevant to the scope of our review. With the same procedure, we highlighted all of the selected papers in this group. At the next step, we re-read all of the highlighted words, sentences and expressions and categorized them base on their common properties and similarities. This process of "generating higher-abstraction level type categories from a set of concepts/variables" [23] is called open coding. After building a clear structure of concepts during the open coding stage, we made an initial axial coding to find the relationship and links between categories and their subcategories (see Table 4).

We read the remaining papers (n=19) one by one and performed both of the analytical coding steps (open coding and axial coding) iteratively, moving between papers, concepts, categories and sub-categories until 'theoretical saturation' was achieved. Theoretical saturation occurs when no new information, concept or relationship emerges from the data and analytical coding process [22, 23]. Table 4, gives an overview of the results of applying grounded theory on all of the papers included in this review.

RESULTS

In this review, we analyzed 28 papers and categorized them into two main categories: (1) papers on MSE interactions with geospatial data [P1-P9], and (2) papers on MSE interaction tasks and techniques [P10-P28]. Before going into the main results of this review, first, we provide an overview of the primary papers included in this review according to the concepts they cover and briefly describe their methodological quality based on the quality criteria that has been addressed in the *Quality Assessment* section.

Overview of Papers

With regard to the concepts and open codes that have been extracted during the 'Data Extraction' step, we can see from Table 4 that the *Interaction Devices* code were addressed in all of the included papers in this review and more specifically combination of 'Tabletop+Wall Display' and 'Tablet+Tabletop+Wall Display' have been used more than other combinations of devices. The majority of papers focused on interaction techniques and relationships between different entities in MSEs. Papers that have addressed *Hand Gestures* to perform geospatial tasks, *Spatial Relationship* between devices, and *Orientation* issues in MSEs come next, with them being 14 (50%), 10 (35%), and 9 (32%) of papers respectively. *Scalability Issues* and *Privacy* in MSE, were addressed in 8 (29%) papers each. *Communication* between

Category	Open Code	Concepts
Relationships Between Entities (47)	**Spatial Relationship (11)** [P4, P7, P10, P12, P16, P20-22, P25-26] [# of papers: 10]	Spatial relationship between walls and table (1), Distance independent interaction (1), Different point of views for different displays (1), Spatial relationship between different devices (6), Slide-under as a spatial relationship (1), Seamless interaction (1)
	Orientation (19) [P1-2, P4, P7-8, P12, P16, P23, P26] [# of papers: 9]	Optical tracking technologies (1),Device orientation and location (3), Tracking objects with optical markers (3), Using markers to determine location and orientation (1), Synchronizing and coordinating different views (1), Measuring device to determine position and orientation (2), Tracking objects position (1), Flexible work division (1), Sensor-enabled phones (1), Perspective correction (2), Rotate wall's point-of view (POV) and tilt from tabletop (2)
	Communication (4) [P2, P4, P8, P9], [# of papers: 4]	Wireless communications (3), Interface components are visible on mobile device (1)
	Scaleability Issues (13) [P1-3, P6-7, P9, P20, S24] [# of papers: 8]	Maps with different scales (3), Quality of navigation (2), Increase resolution of map with tablet (3), Providing detail view (2), Overlay interface to improve resolution (1), Automatic image processing algorithm (1), Scalability of user interface (1)
Interaction Tasks and Techniques (45)	**Hand Gestures (36)** [P1, P4, P7-8, P10-11, P13, P17 ,P21-23, P25, P27-28] [# of papers: 14]	Flicking (3), Pinching (1), Zooming (5), Mouse Click (1), Pouring (1), Bi-manual operations (2), Sliding (2), Dragging (4), Panning (2), Throwing (3), Swiping (1), Five finger touch (1), Rotation (1), Pointing (4), Chucking (1), Bumping (1), Position up (2), Camera gesture (5)
	Add Annotations (7) [P4-5, P9], [# of papers: 3]	Drawing (3), Pre-defined graphics (2), Tagging (2)
	3D Interaction (2) [P8], [# of papers: 1]	3D interaction (2)
Workspace (58)	**Conflict Management (12)** [P4-5, P8, P27] [# of papers: 4]	First to touch technique (1), Same map on different surfaces (1), Same view with same latitude and longitude (1), Control changes of views from table (1), Shared view across distributed surfaces (2), Table as primary input device (2), Conflicting views on a shared device (1), Asynchronous collocated collaboration (1), Different roles (1), Separating action and reflection (1)
	Privacy (18) [P1-2, P4-7, P9, P28] [# of papers: 8]	Immediate visibility of content on shared wall display (1), Value of data differs among different members (1), Different views displayed on multiple machines (1), Working together and working separately (1), Access to details and annotation capabilities by smaller devices (2), Private domain data (iPad) (1), Visibility of objects on wall is locally (1), Tablet as private workspace (2), General views and local tasks (1), Open access vs dynamic interaction (1), Authorized reviewers (1), Shared and private working areas (1), Private working area (3), Large display as shared environment (1)
	Interaction Devices (28) [P1-28] [# of papers: 28]	Tabletop + Wall display (5) Tablet + Tabletop + Wall display (5) Table + Wall + PC/Laptop (3) Laptop + Wall display (2) Tablet + Tabletop (2) Mobile phones+ Tablet (2) Mobile phone + Wall display (2) Mobile phone + Tablet + Wall display (1) Tabletop + Three Wall Displays + Tablet (1) Tablet + Tabletop + Stereoscopic display (1) Tabletop + Large display + Fovea-Tabletts (1) Tabletop + Wall display + Mobile phone + Laptop (1) Tabletop + Wall display + Mobile phone + Motion tracking system (1)

Table 4: Overview of concepts extracted from the papers included in this review. Numbers in parentheses show the number of occurrences of each code in the included papers

different devices, *Conflict Management* approaches, *Add Annotation*, and *3D Interaction* as interaction techniques, were addressed in only 4, 4, 3, and 1 papers respectively.

Regarding the quality of publications, as mentioned in the *Quality Assessment* section, we evaluated each of the primary papers according to the 10 quality criteria on the CASP [2] and by principles of good HCI research [12] (see Table 3). After evaluating papers based on their quality, we found that: most of the papers did not have a clear and sound description of their methods and issues of replicability and validity were not addressed properly. The data collection and analysis methods were not explained clearly and not enough details were provided. The rest of this section is structured based on the research questions of this review.

RQ1- Interaction Tasks and Techniques in MSEs

In order to answer RQ1 of this review, we use the output of the grounded theory process that has been presented in Table 4. This table represents three levels of the grounded theory approach: concepts, open codes, and axial codes (categories of open codes). In this section we discuss each of these categories combined with their related codes and concepts in more detail.

(1) Relationship Between Entities

This category includes concepts related to the spatial relationship between different devices in MSEs, device orientation techniques, scalability issues as well as technologies, and different ways that devices in MSEs can communicate with each other.

- *Spatial relationship:* This code refers to the position of each device in MSE relative to other devices in the environment. Out of 23 papers in the *relationships between devices* category, 10 papers addressed spatial relationship. For example, Piazza et al. [P12] proposed the *side-under* technique using a magic lens and Toolglass [3] to control the relative position of devices during their interactions. In this technique, one device can be inserted underneath another device and their spatial relationship is controlled by using the distance between the centre-point of the devices. The other papers in this category only addressed concepts related to the spatial relationship between devices.

- *Orientation:* By orientation we mean the relative positions or directions between different devices and users in MSE. In the context of performing collaborative tasks in MSEs, different entities inside the environment need to determine their position and orientation with regard to other entities. Among included papers in this review, [P1, P2, P4, P7, P8, P12, P16, P23, P26] have addressed orientation technologies or techniques in MSEs. For example, Yao et al. [P8] presented a collaborative workspace which includes advanced display systems and optical tracking technologies and is used to track the orientation and position of entities inside a room.

-*Communication:* Four papers [P2, P4, P8, P9] addressed communication between devices in MSEs. All of them use wireless networks to connect each device with other devices in a room. Other included papers in this review did not address communication.

- *Scalability issues:* With respect to scalability issues in MSEs, Peinsip-Byma et al. [P6] uses an automatic image processing algorithm that offers users a detailed view of shared information on a tabletop or wall display on their personal device. Satyanarayan et al. [P24] provides an overlay technique which enables collaborative interaction on wall displays in different scales. [P1, P6, P9] use another device (i.e., Tablet, mobile phone) to provide a personalized view with high resolution. Other papers in this category only address scalability issues in MSEs.

(2) Interaction Tasks and Techniques

Hand gesture, Adding annotation, and 3D interaction are interaction techniques that have been discussed in several papers. In this section, we briefly describe each of these techniques.

- *Hand Gestures:* Flicking [P7, P11, P13], Pinching [P7], Zooming [P1, P7, P22, P25, P28], Mouse Click [P4], Pouring [P7], Bi-manual Operations [P4, P8], Sliding [P7, P11, P21], Dragging [P10, P17, (P27-28)], Panning [P22, P25], Throwing [P11, P13, P23], Swiping [P11], Five figure touch [P11], Rotation [P11], Pointing [P11, P16, P19, P22], Chucking [P11], Bumping [P11], Camera gesture [P2, P7, P11] and Position up [P11] are hand gestures used for interaction and collaboration among users in MSEs. Each of these gestures along with their description are presented in Figure 3.

- *Add Annotation:* This technique consists of Drawing [P5], Pre-defined graphics [P9] and Tagging [P5]. These interaction techniques enable users to highlight particular information and improve the attention of participants during their interactions.

- *3D Interaction:* 2D and 3D displays in this technique [P8] provide a seamless touch interaction with 3D objects in MSEs.

(3) Work Space

In this category, conflict management, privacy control, and interaction devices are the main concepts that have been addressed in the papers of this review.

- *Conflict Management:* In the last few decades, empirical studies have shown that in collaborative and interactive workspaces, conflict is inevitable [8]. Among four papers of this review that have addressed *conflict management*, study by Forlines et al [P4], used *first to touch technique* to manage the conflict between user interactions and [P27] manage this conflict by defining tabletop as the primary input device. Two other papers (P[5], P[8]), only mentioned this conflict as an issue in MSEs without providing any solution for it.

- *Privacy:* While smooth transfer of information among team members is a requirement in collaborative activities, users should be able to have control of their individual workspace. Of all the papers in this review, seven papers [P(1-2), P(4-7), P9, P28] highlighted concepts related to privacy in MSEs. Defining a large display as the shared environment and own devices as private environments is the main approach that have been used in these papers.

Bump: Make temporary physical contact between two devices for contact transfer [19]
Flick: Quickly brush surface with fingertip, [24]
Drag: Move fingertip over surface without losing contact [24]
Pinch: Touch surface with two fingers/hands and bring them closer together [24]
Zoom: Touch surface with two fingers/hands and move them apart without lifting them from the screen [24]
Rotate: Touch surface with two fingers and move them in a clockwise or counterclockwise direction [24]
Camera: Capture shared information on a personal devices (e.g., Tablet, Mobile phone) and view and manipulate the data with higher resolution
Swipe: Drag objects on the surface, but faster than dragging
Pour: Send objects from tablet to a tabletop, in close proximity [20]
Chuck (Throw): Throwing or passing objects to another device [19]

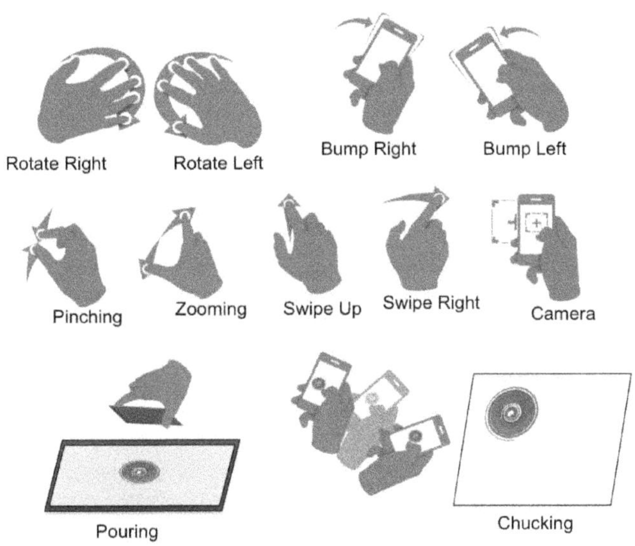

Figure 2: MSEs' hand gestures that have been addressed in the included papers

- *Interaction Devices:* Regarding the interaction devices, tablets, tabletops, wall displays, mobile phones and PC/laptops are the most frequently used devices in the included papers in this review. Stereoscopic display [P8], motion tracking system [P22] and Fovea-Tablett [P2] are other devices that were used in only one paper each. Stereoscopic display provides an accurate and detailed 3D presentation of data and allows users to interact in 3D mode. A motion tracking system enables tracking devices and people in MSE with high accuracy and minimal delay. Fovea-Tablett is a small portable display unit with high pixel density which enables users to have access to a small portion of shared information with high resolution.

GIS System Tasks	MSE Tasks and Techniques
Pointing	Mouse Click [P4], Pointing [P(13-14), P19, P22]
Search attributes	Mouse Click [P4], Pointing [P(13-14), P19, P22], Bi-manual operations [P4, P6]
Associate	Mouse Click [P4], Drawing annotation[P(4-5), P9]
Zooming	Zooming [P1, P7, P22, P25, P28]
Panning	Panning [P22, P25]
Printing report	Mouse Click [P6]
Digitizing features	Drawing annotation[P(4-5), P9], Pre-defined graphics[P9], Tagging[P6]
Map presenting	Mouse Click [P6]
Data Conversion	Mouse Click [P6], Dragging [P10, P17, P(27-28)]
Map creation from coordinates	Mouse Click [P6], Drawing annotation[P(4-5), P9]
Measurements	Mouse Click [P6], Pointing [P(13-14), P19, P22]
Editing features	Mouse Click [P6], Pointing [P(13-14), P19, P22]

Table 5: Mapping between GIS system tasks/activities and MSE tasks/techniques

RQ2- Interaction with Geospatial Data in MSEs

In order to answer RQ2, first we need to answer the following questions:

- RQ2-1: What interaction techniques are proposed in MSEs to perform geospatial tasks from a *system* perspective in MSEs?
- RQ2-2: What interaction techniques are proposed in MSEs to perform geospatial tasks from a *cartographic* perspective in MSEs?

GIS System Perspective Tasks in MSE (RQ2-1)

In order to answer RQ2-1, about the relation between common GIS tasks from a system perspective and existing MSE tasks and techniques, we draw a mapping between these two categories. In Table 5, for each of the GIS system, there is at least one corresponding task in MSEs. For example, in order to perform the *editing features* task from the left column, we can use *mouse click* or *pointing* tasks from the right column to select the feature on the map and then edit it.

GIS Cartographic Perspective Tasks in MSE (RQ2-2)

Earlier in the paper, we presented the common tasks that users can perform during interaction with digital maps from a cartography perspective. Aiming to answer the RQ2-2, we com-

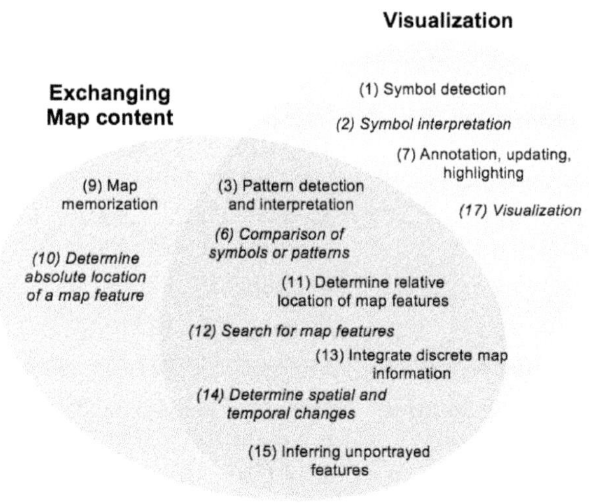

Figure 3: Classification of common cartographic GIS tasks

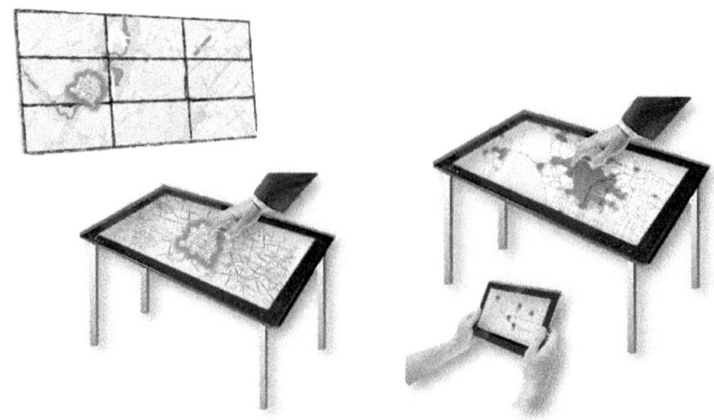

(a) Pattern detection and interpretation (b) Symbol interpretation

Figure 4: Examples of cartographic GIS tasks in MSEs

pared these tasks with interaction techniques and tasks that are provided by papers included in this review (Table 4). In this case, we found that there is little discussion on cartographic GIS tasks in MSEs and most of these tasks are not discussed or supported by the MSE literature. While most of the prerequisites for performing cartographic GIS tasks in MSEs, such as *defining relationships* among different entities inside the environment, core *interaction tasks and techniques* and addressing issues related to *workspace* are addressed by papers in this review, there are still some specific issues related to visualization and exchanging geospatial data that need to be addressed. In the next section, we discuss these issues in more detail.

DISCUSSION

Our review is the first systematic review that provided a mapping between GIS tasks and existing tasks and techniques in MSEs. Related work and papers in this area, only addressed a limited number of papers related to their research goal. We found papers in this review by using an iterative search strategy and defining explicit inclusion and exclusion criteria.

Our systematic review has a number of implications for future research. The results of the review illustrate the need for more research on the useful interaction techniques to perform cartographic GIS tasks. As in recent years geospatial data has become a key component in group-based decision making and is widely accessible and used by users, we believe that interaction with geospatial data in collaborative environments needs more attention by researchers in industry and academia.

As the uniqueness and complexity of geospatial data [6, 7], exchanging map content is a major challenge during performing GIS tasks in collaborative environments. Moreover, "Using colour effectively can and will enhance the ability of users to identify features, objects, and patterns" on the map [6]. Considering these two issues, we classified cartographic GIS tasks into two categories; (1) Visualization and (2) Exchanging map content, (see Figure 3).

In order to make this classification more clear and understandable, Figure 4 gives an example of each of these two categories. In Figure 4(a), a tabletop user has detected a specific pattern in an area while performing a *pattern detection and interpretation* task, which might be of interest to some members of the team. This user should be able to share this pattern on a public device without interrupting other members if they are working with the shared device. In Figure 4(b), a tablet user is displaying some symbols to represent real world objects on the map. At the same time, a tabletop user has detected some patterns on the map which are highlighted with red colour. In this situation, as red symbols are not properly readable on a red background, sharing symbol between these two devices requires some visualization techniques. More research on *visualization* and *exchanging* geospatial content are the other research implications of this review.

CONCLUSION

This systematic review has addressed the following research questions: (1) What are the proposed tasks/techniques that users can perform during their interaction in MSEs? (2) What useful interaction techniques are proposed in MSE to perform geospatial tasks/activities? In order to answer these questions, we initially identified 378 papers by searching the literature. 28 papers were selected as primary papers of this review, while the others were not relevant to address the research questions. To answer the first research question, we analyzed all of the identified papers by using a revised version of grounded theory method and extracted concepts related to interactions in MSEs. For the second research question, we compared the results of the first question with common GIS tasks and techniques from the system and cartographic perspectives. Our main finding from conducting this systematic review is although MSEs have received much attention during recent years and several platforms and applications have been developed in these environments, but there is still a need for specific interaction techniques to perform GIS tasks in MSEs.

REFERENCES

1. Google scholar. `http://scholar.google.com/intl/en/scholar/about.html`.
2. CASP checklists. `http://www.casp-uk.net/#!casp-tools-checklists/c18f8`, 2013.
3. Bier, E. A., Stone, M. C., Pier, K., Buxton, W., and DeRose, T. D. Toolglass and magic lenses: the see-through interface. In *Proc. of the ACM Conference on Computer Graphics and Interactive Techniques (SIGGRAPH)*, ACM (1993), 73–80.
4. Biolchini, J., Mian, P. G., Natali, A. C. C., and Travassos, G. H. Systematic review in software engineering. *System Engineering and Computer Science Department COPPE/UFRJ, Technical Report ES 679*, 05 (2005), 45.
5. Calkins, H. W., and Obermeyer, N. J. Taxonomy for surveying the use and value of geographical information! *International Journal of Geographical Information System 5*, 3 (1991), 341–351.
6. Davies, C. Tasks and task descriptions for gis. In *Cognitive Aspects of Human-Computer Interaction for Geographic Information Systems*. Springer, 1995, 327–341.
7. Davies, C. *Cognitive aspects of work with digital maps*. PhD thesis, Loughborough University, 1999.
8. Easterbrook, S. M., Beck, E. E., Goodlet, J. S., Plowman, L., Sharples, M., and Wood, C. C. *CSCW: Cooperation or Conflict?* Springer, 1993, ch. A survey of empirical studies of conflict, 1–68.
9. Giustini, D., and Boulos, M. N. K. Google scholar is not enough to be used alone for systematic reviews. *Online journal of public health informatics 5*, 2 (2013), 214.
10. Gough, D. Weight of evidence: a framework for the appraisal of the quality and relevance of evidence. *Research papers in education 22*, 2 (2007), 213–228.
11. Gough, D., Oliver, S., and Thomas, J. *An introduction to systematic reviews*. Sage Publications, 2012.
12. Greenberg, S., and Thimbleby, H. The weak science of human-computer interaction. In *Proc. of the ACM International Conference on Human Factors in Computing Systems (CHI)*, ACM (1992).
13. Greenhalgh, T., and Peacock, R. Effectiveness and efficiency of search methods in systematic reviews of complex evidence: audit of primary sources. *Bmj 331*, 7524 (2005), 1064–1065.
14. Greiffenhagen, C., and Reeves, S. Is replication important for HCI? In *Proc. of the CHI Workshop on the Replication of HCI Research*, ACM (2013).
15. Kitchenham, B. A., Pfleeger, S. L., Pickard, L. M., Jones, P. W., Hoaglin, D. C., El Emam, K., and Rosenberg, J. Preliminary guidelines for empirical research in software engineering. *IEEE Transactions on Software Engineering 28*, 8 (2002), 721–734.
16. Knapp, L. *A task analysis approach to the visualization of geographic data*. Springer, 1995.
17. Lefebvre, C., Manheimer, E., and Glanville, J. Searching for studies. *Cochrane handbook for systematic reviews of interventions. New York: Wiley* (2008), 95–150.
18. McCann, C. *Classification of Map-reading Tasks*. Defence and Civil Institute of Environmental Medicine, Department of National Defence, Canada, 1982.
19. Seyed, T., Burns, C., Costa Sousa, M., Maurer, F., and Tang, A. Eliciting usable gestures for multi-display environments. In *Proc. of the ACM International Conference on Interactive Tabletops and Surfaces (ITS)*, ACM (2012), 41–50.
20. Seyed, T., Costa Sousa, M., Maurer, F., and Tang, A. Skyhunter: a multi-surface environment for supporting oil and gas exploration. In *Proc. of the ACM International Conference on Interactive Tabletops and Surfaces (ITS)*, ACM (2013), 15–22.
21. Sillito, J. Tool Support for Collaborative Qualitative Analysis. `http://www.saturateapp.com`.
22. Strauss, A., and Corbin, J. M. *Grounded theory in practice*. Sage, 1997.
23. Wolfswinkel, J. F., Furtmueller, E., and Wilderom, C. P. Using grounded theory as a method for rigorously reviewing literature. *European Journal of Information Systems 22*, 1 (2013), 45–55.
24. Wroblewski, L. Touch Gesture Reference Guide. `http://www.lukew.com/ff/entry.asp?1071`, 2010.

SYSTEMATIC LITERATURE REVIEW PAPERS

[P1] Peinsipp-Byma, E., Geisler, J., and Bader, T. Digital map and situation surface: a team-oriented multidisplay workspace for network enabled situation analysis. In SPIE Defense, Security, and Sensing, International Society for Optics and Photonics (2009), 732703–732703.

[P2] Meissner, A., and Eck, R. Extending the fire dispatch system into the mobile domain. In Mobile Response. Springer, 2007, 143–152.

[P3] Yoshimoto, Y., Dang, T. H., Kimura, A., Shibata, F., and Tamura, H. Interaction design of 2D/3D map navigation on wall and tabletop displays. In Proc. of ITS. ACM (2011), 254–255.

[P4] Forlines, C., Esenther, A., Shen, C., Wigdor, D., and Ryall, K. Multi-user, multi-display interaction with a single-user, single-display geospatial application. In Proceedings of the 19th annual ACM symposium on User interface software and technology, ACM (2006), 273–276.

[P5] Dez, D., Tena, S., RomeroGomez, R., Daz, P., and Aedo, I. Sharing your view: A distributed user interface approach for reviewing emergency plans. International Journal of Human-Computer Studies 72, 1 (2014), 126–139.

[P6] Peinsipp-Byma, E., Eck, R., Rehfeld, N., and Geisler, J. Situation analysis at a digital situation table with fovea-tablett. In Electronic Imaging 2007, International Society for Optics and Photonics (2007), 64950E–64950E.

[P7] Seyed, T., Costa Sousa, M., Maurer, F., and Tang, A. Skyhunter: a multi-surface environment for supporting oil and gas exploration. In Proceedings of the 2013 ACM international conference on Interactive tabletops and surfaces, ACM (2013), 15–22.

[P8] Yao, J., Fernando, T., Tawfik, H., Armitage, R., and Billing, I. Towards a collaborative urban planning environment. In Computer Supported Cooperative Work in Design II. Springer, 2006, 554–562.

[P9] Sanneblad, J., and Holmquist, L. E. Ubiquitous graphics: combining hand-held and wall-size displays to interact with large images. In Proceedings of the working conference on Advanced visual interfaces, ACM (2006), 373–377.

[P10] Rekimoto, J., and Saitoh, M. Augmented surfaces: a spatially continuous work space for hybrid computing environments. In Proceedings of the SIGCHI conference on Human Factors in Computing Systems, ACM (1999), 378–385.

[P11] Seyed, T., Burns, C., Costa Sousa, M., Maurer, F., and Tang, A. Eliciting usable gestures for multi-display environments. In Proceedings of the 2012 ACM international conference on Interactive tabletops and surfaces, ACM (2012), 41–50.

[P12] Sakurai, S., Itoh, Y., Kitamura, Y., Nacenta, M. A., Yamaguchi, T., Subramanian, S., and Kishino, F. A middleware for seamless use of multiple displays. In Interactive Systems. Design, Specification, and Verification. Springer, 2008, 252–266.

[P13] Nacenta, M. A., Aliakseyeu, D., Subramanian, S., and Gutwin, C. A comparison of techniques for multi-display reaching. In Proceedings of the SIGCHI conference on Human factors in computing systems. 2005, 371–380.

[P14] Forlines, C., and Lilien, R. Adapting a single-user, single-display molecular visualization application for use in a multi-user, multi-display environment. In Proceedings of the working conference on Advanced visual interfaces, ACM (2008), 367–371.

[P15] McGrath, W., Bowman, B., McCallum, D., Hincapie?-Ramos, J. D., Elmqvist, N., and Irani, P. Branch-explore-merge: facilitating real-time revision control in collaborative visual exploration. In Proceedings of ITS 2012, ACM (2012), 235–244.

[P16] Nacenta, M. A., Sakurai, S., Yamaguchi, T., Miki, Y., Itoh, Y., Kitamura, Y., Subramanian, S., and Gutwin, C. E-conic: a perspective-aware interface for multi-display environments. In Proceedings of the 20th annual ACM symposium on User interface software and technology, ACM (2007), 279–288.

[P17] Collomb, M., and Hascoe?t, M. Extending drag-and-drop to new interactive environments: A multi-display, multi-instrument and multi-user approach. Interacting with Computers 20, 6 (2008), 562–573.

[P18] Lee, J., Lee, J., Kim, H., and Kim, J.-I. Gesture-based interactions on multiple large displays with a tabletop interface. In Universal Access in Human-Computer Interaction. Ambient Interaction. Springer, 2007, 936–942.

[P19] Lee, H., Jeong, H., Lee, J., Yeom, K.-W., and Park, J.-H. Gesture-based interface for connection and control of multi-device in a tabletop display environment. In Human-Computer Interaction. Novel Interaction Methods and Techniques. Springer, 2009, 216–225.

[P20] van de Camp, F., and Stiefelhagen, R. Gluetk: a framework for multi-modal, multi-display human-machine-interaction. In Proceedings of the 2013 international conference on Intelligent user interfaces, ACM (2013), 329–338.

[P21] Piazza, T., Fjeld, M., Ramos, G., Yantac, A., and Zhao, S. Holy smartphones and tablets, batman!: mobile interactions dynamic duo. In Proceedings of the 11th Asia Pacific Conference on Computer Human Interaction, ACM (2013), 63–72.

[P22] Beaudouin-Lafon, M. Lessons learned from the wild room, a multisurface interactive environment. In 23rd French Speaking Conference on Human-Computer Interaction, ACM (2011), 18.

[P23] Dachselt, R., and Buchholz, R. Natural throw and tilt interaction between mobile phones and distant displays. In Proc. of CHI Extended Abstracts, ACM (2009), 3253–3258.

[P24] Satyanarayan, A., Weibel, N., and Hollan, J. Using overlays to support collaborative interaction with display walls. In Proceedings of the 2012 ACM international conference on Intelligent User Interfaces, ACM (2012), 105–108.

[P25] Baur, D., Boring, S., and Feiner, S. Virtual projection: exploring optical projection as a metaphor for multi-device interaction. In Proceedings of the SIGCHI Conference on Human Factors in Computing Systems, ACM (2012), 1693-1702.

[P26] Chung, H., North, C., Self, J. Z., Chu, S., and Quek, F. Visporter: facilitating information sharing for collaborative sensemaking on multiple displays. Personal and Ubiquitous Computing 18, 5 (2014), 1169–1186.

[P27] Schneider, B., Tobiasz, M., Willis, C., and Shen, C. Walden: multi-surface multi-touch simulation of climate change and species loss in thoreaus woods. In Proceedings of the 2012 ACM international conference on Interactive tabletops and surfaces, ACM (2012), 387–390.

[P28] Wigdor, D., Jiang, H., Forlines, C., Borkin, M., and Shen, C. Wespace: the design development and deployment of a walk-up and share multi-surface visual collaboration system. In Proceedings of the SIGCHI Conference on Human Factors in Computing Systems, ACM (2009), 1237–1246.

The Effect of View Techniques on Collaboration and Awareness in Tabletop Map-Based Tasks

Christophe Bortolaso[1], Matthew Oskamp[1], Greg Phillips[2], Carl Gutwin[3], T.C. Nicholas Graham[1]

[1] School of Computing
Queen's University
{christophe.bortolaso, 7mao, nicholas.graham}@queensu.ca

[2] Department of Electrical and Computer Engineering
Royal Military College of Canada
greg.phillips@rmc.ca

[3] Department of Computer Science
University of Saskatchewan
gutwin@cs.usask.ca

ABSTRACT

Digital tabletops have become a natural medium for collaborative planning activities involving maps. Such activities are typically mixed-focus, where users switch between high-level and detailed views of the map and between individual and collaborative work. A wide range of view-sharing techniques such as lenses, zooming and radar views provide both shared and individual access to the same workspace. However, it is not yet sufficiently clear how the choice of view techniques affects collaboration in mixed-focus scenarios. In this paper, we explore the effect of different view techniques on collaborative map-based tasks around tables. We report on two studies in the context of military planning, one in a controlled environment and one in an open-ended scenario carried out by domain experts. Our findings show how the success of different techniques is sensitive to the form of collaboration and to the proximity of work on the table.

Author Keywords

Digital tabletops; mixed-focus collaboration; digital maps.

ACM Classification Keywords

H.5.3 **[Information Interfaces and Presentation (e.g. HCI)]**: Collaborative Computing.

INTRODUCTION

Tables provide many benefits for co-located collaboration. One of their main strengths is their flexibility in supporting many different configurations of shared activity – they naturally allow people to maintain a strong group focus, to carry out individual tasks in different areas of the table, or to switch between these configurations simply and easily. Collaboration that involves these shifts between individual and group focus is called "mixed-focus collaboration" [10].

ITS 2014, November 16–19, 2014, Dresden, Germany.

ACM 978-1-4503-2587-5/14/11…$15.00
http://dx.doi.org/10.1145/2669485.2669504

However, a problem arises for mixed-focus collaboration when people work with a single large artifact that takes up the entire table, such as a map. This is a common occurrence in tabletop work and maps are used in many digital-table applications such as emergency response [17], utility grid management [23], geological exploration [4] and command and control [3, 22].

In situations where the table is used for a single large artifact, it becomes much more difficult for people to carry out individual tasks, because they cannot always re-configure their tabletop work area to provide a view that is appropriate for their work. For example, two people might need to carry out different tasks in the same area of a map, but only one person can have their hands and arms in the space at a time. Similarly, people may need different map zoom levels for their individual tasks, but only one level can be used.

Some digital surfaces attempt to solve this problem with augmented view mechanisms that provide multiple representations of the workspace (e.g. [8, 13, 25]). This can allow different people to have different views of the table, and can provide alternate external representations (such as overviews) that stay constant regardless of the zoom level or scroll location of the main table view. Where a traditional table would require that people accommodate the physical restrictions of artifact size, orientation, and layout, digital tables can create different views for different purposes – for example, allowing one person to zoom into a map while another person views their area at a high level.

Having different views on the same table can be very useful for individual work, since each person's view can be customized to the needs of the individual task. However, there is little understanding about whether having multiple views changes the ways in which people engage in mixed-focus collaboration. For example, we know little about whether individualized views can improve group performance, whether individual views compromise the shared focus that is possible on physical tabletops, and whether people are able to easily change their views to match the requirements of the mixed-focus collaboration. Without this knowledge, it is difficult for designers to know whether their tabletop systems will in fact support the collaboration styles and changes that will occur in real use.

We carried out two studies of augmented-view tabletop systems that provide new information on these issues. The first controlled study showed that group performance improves when the view configuration matches the spatial arrangement of the group's tasks. The second study showed that in a realistic task, people do not always choose the view configuration that best matches the demands of their current tasks. These results reveal potential contradictions and tradeoffs in the design of multiple-view tabletop systems.

Our work makes three main contributions. First, we quantify the performance benefits that can arise from choosing a view configuration that matches the spatial organization of a group task. Second, we show that despite these performance advantages, people often use a non-optimal configuration – suggesting that the overhead in managing views can reduce the benefits. Third, we provide new insights into why people use (or don't use) different views in different situations. Our results show that the use of flexible view configurations for tabletop systems is more complex than previously thought, and provide new design opportunities and research questions for future work.

BACKGROUND: MIXED-FOCUS MAP-BASED PLANNING

Digital tabletops have shown great promise for supporting collocated tasks. Wallace et al. [26] compared collaboration using a shared tabletop to the use of individual tablets, finding that the tabletop enhanced group performance. But mixed-focus collaboration requires more than simply the ability to view a shared artifact on a table. For example, Isenberg et al. have demonstrated the need to support different coupling styles in visual analytics tasks [14].

Planning around maps serves as an excellent example of why space-sharing mechanisms are required. Groups often need to work on different parts of the map at different levels of detail. Tang et al. were the first to analyze and compare the use of different space sharing techniques (filters, lenses and shadowboxes) for collaborative route planning tasks on maps [25]. They identified six different coupling styles and found these styles to be related to variables such as the preferred view technique, physical arrangement around the table, and the incidence and handling of interference.

Recently Jakobsen and Hornbaek [15] studied the use of a high resolution multitouch wall display for exploring a document collection. Their findings confirmed the validity of Isenberg's and Tang's previous work for vertical displays, showing that users had no difficulty in switching between coupling styles and that proximity and tight collaboration were correlated.

The research presented in this paper builds on this previous work with a focus on collaboration around a single, large shared artifact, such as a map. Collaborative work around large maps strongly differs from collaboration around multiple documents. The mechanisms used to manage the space and deal with interference raise several issues that need to be further explored, specifically the impact of space-sharing mechanisms on performance and collaboration. We seek to extend the work of Tang et al. by deeply examining the impact of choice of view sharing technique on task performance, and on how expert users choose to work when provided with a range of view sharing interaction techniques. As we discuss below, these aspects are particularly crucial in domains where there is time pressure on the collaboration.

We have explored space-sharing techniques in the domain of military map-based planning [3]. Typical tasks include deploying units in a defensive position, coordinating an attack using units under different peoples' control, and planning safe movement through a hostile area. Traditionally, military planners use a "bird table": a large physical table covered in a map. A small group of people can discuss the movement and disposition of units by pointing at the map, and drawing with markers on acetate sheets overlaying the map.

In map-based planning, people change focus in two dimensions: *Collaboration Coupling* and *Level of Detail*. In the *Coupling* dimension, planners move between *group work* (e.g. planning objectives, observing progress of others, and coordinating actions) and *individual work* (e.g. detailed planning for the units for which they are responsible). Planners may engage in **tightly-coupled coordination** (moving units at the same time while attending to others' work), **loosely-coupled coordination** (moving units at the same time, but not attending to others' work), and **turn-taking**, where one person moves units while others observe, possibly commenting on progress. Additionally, planners need to shift focus between different *Levels of Detail*. When developing a high-level course of action, planners may wish to see a map of the entire battlefield; when they are planning a detailed route or deployment, they may need to zoom the map to a scale where terrain details are available.

Digital maps can support movement within these two dimensions, but there are tensions to resolve. For example, if two people want to perform loosely-coupled unit movement requiring zooming at different points in the map, they may compete over which part of the map to zoom.

ORMIS: DIGITAL TABLETOP FOR MILITARY PLANNING

In order to investigate mixed-focus collaboration ranging over these two dimensions of coupling and level of detail, we enhanced the OrMiS tool for military planning [3] to provide representative view sharing techniques.

OrMiS shows a map on a 55" tabletop display. Military units are shown on the map using standard NATO symbols: a rectangle with an oval represents an armoured unit while a rectangle with a cross represents infantry. As with a traditional military bird table, OrMiS supports tightly-coupled discussion through the shared map, which planners can observe and reference via pointing and gesturing. The tabletop also provides group awareness during individually-focused work, as it is possible to see what others are doing on other parts of the table.

In OrMiS, plans can be enacted by the creation of routes. Routes are drawn using a touch-based polyline interaction technique (see Figure 1.3). To create a route, a user drags a finger from a unit to a destination. When their finger is lifted off the table a waypoint is created. The user then touches and drags from the waypoint symbol to create the next step in the route. The route can be edited by dragging or deleting waypoints.

In order to support detailed work, we added representative view sharing techniques to OrMiS. These provide *zooming* through table-level pinch and panning gestures, *overview+detail* through bi-focal lenses, and *focus+context* through radar views. These allow planners to work at and move between different forms of coordination and different levels of zoom. We now discuss these view sharing techniques in detail.

Global Zoom/Pan

Zooming is a common technique for providing more detail about a visual artifact such as a map. More precisely, zooming changes the user viewport magnification level [6, 27]. Zooming is typically combined with panning. OrMiS's *global zoom* is a traditional pinch-to-zoom technique as seen in most touch-based map applications.

We hypothesize that global zoom best supports discussion and tightly-coupled coordination around a focused area of the map. However, global zoom poorly supports collaboration around detailed views of non-proximate parts of the map. A zoom or pan operation by one user changes all other users' views, perhaps even removing from the display the part of the map others are working with. This can be a problem for users working separately on detailed views of different parts of the map.

Focus+Context

An alternative to global zooming is lenses, which provide *detailed focus* on one part of the map, while retaining *global context.* Lenses often rely on distortion of the visual space (e.g., "fisheye" lenses) to maintain visual continuity between different foci [9, 19, 20]. However, distortion can cause problems of interpretation [5] and focus targeting [9]. In contrast, magnification-only lenses [1, 2] are not subject to distortion issues but occlude the space adjacent to the magnified area. Despite these problems, lenses help users acquire a rapid overview of the data space through their peripheral vision while focusing visual attention on a specific area. Lenses have been proposed for supporting mutual awareness in interactive tabletop interfaces [8, 21].

We added a focus+context facility to OrMiS via bi-focal lenses (Figure 1.1) [1]. Users can place a lens on the table, and can zoom within the lens using a traditional pinch-to-zoom gesture. Lenses can be dragged to change the part of the map being magnified. Lenses support collaboration by allowing one user to focus on part of the map without disturbing the view of other users. Since the lens is visible on the main map, users can still view what others are working on, helping to maintain group awareness. Lenses may occlude part of the map, and if two users wish to zoom nearby parts of the map, their lenses may overlap. Originally, we used fisheye lenses [19] to maintain visual continuity. However, pilot testing revealed that distortion of the map interfered unacceptably with planning tasks. We hypothesize that bi-focal lenses are appropriate when users are performing loosely-coupled work at different levels of detail on non-proximate parts of the map.

Overview+Detail

Both global zoom and bi-focal lenses have the potential to hinder awareness of the broader context of work. Global zoom focuses on just part of the map, meaning that events on the other parts are no longer visible. Bi-focal lenses occlude parts of the underlying map, and when zoomed, can make it difficult for others to understand what part of the underlying map is being viewed.

Prior research suggests that this awareness problem can be addressed via an overview+detail interface, such as a radar view [6]. This approach provides two views: one that shows the entire workspace in miniature, and one that shows a zoomed-in view of a portion of the space. This approach is found in well-known interfaces such as Google Maps' mini view or StarCraft's mini map. Recent variants of overview+detail interfaces have added off-view

Figure 1. 1) The OrMiS tabletop interface showing lenses and the battlefield; 2) the OrMiS radar view; 3) Route planning

visualization techniques [13] and hierarchical links between overview and detail [16]. Overview+detail techniques are known to require additional mental and motor effort when the views' output spaces are physically separated [12]. Despite this, radar views have been shown to support awareness in collaborative situations [11].

As a representative implementation of an overview+detail technique, we added secondary displays to OrMiS (see Figure 1.2). These separate radar views display the entire map with all visible units and routes. A blue rectangle shows the area of the map currently visible on the table. Two concentric rings represent the lenses. The outer circle represents the size of the lens on the screen and the inner circle shows the lens's current focus. The filled orange area depicts the part of the map occluded by the lens. We hypothesized that these radar views would help planners to retain spatial context, and to view parts of the map occluded by a colleague's lens.

Route Planning as Mixed-Focus Collaboration

In order to evaluate how mixed-focus collaboration can be supported over a single large artifact, we focused on the problem of planning routes for military units. This task involves work at different levels of coupling. Different planners are typically responsible for different sets of units, but the movement of all the units must be coordinated, e.g., to ensure that units arrive at a location at the same time, or that traffic jams do not develop when units share a road.

Typically planners collaboratively develop high-level plans based on **discussion** using **high-level views**. Planners then work on routes for their own units, while maintaining awareness of the other planners' activities; this involves **loosely-coupled coordination** using **detailed views**. Some specific tasks may require **tightly-coupled** unit movement using **detailed views**, such as coordinating the shared use of a bridge. If problems arise, the group may return to discussion around a high-level view. Military route-planning therefore involves several points on the two axes of collaboration and level of detail, and thus serves as a strong example of mixed-focus collaboration over a large shared object.

We performed two studies, described in the next two sections, to examine how people worked in performing route planning tasks. The first study directly addresses the efficacy of the three basic techniques of global zooming/panning, bi-focal lenses, and radar views in supporting mixed-focus tasks. The second study presents domain experts with a realistic task, to see how well the techniques worked in combination, and to better understand peoples' choices around which technique to use under what circumstances.

STUDY 1: PERFORMANCE OF VIEW TECHNIQUES

Our first study sought to find out whether there is a difference in performance between view techniques in a mixed-focus task. The task involved both individual work at a detailed level of zoom and coordination between pairs of participants. Two variants of the task involved working at distant and proximate parts of the map.

System and Task

Participants were asked to collaboratively solve a maze on a digital tabletop using the global zoom, bifocal lens and radar view techniques described in the last section. Figure 2 shows an example of a maze. The goal for both participants was to draw a route for their unit through the green wall to the goal area, following one of a set of available paths. Two types of maze were used: Figure 2.1 shows two mazes at distant parts of the table, and Figure 2.2 shows two mazes located close together. Within the maze, participants needed to choose which route to take at a sequence of three forks. Each road exiting a fork was labeled with a blob shape. One of the two blobs appeared in both participants' paths; the participants needed to identify the common blob and ensure that they both followed the path labeled with that blob. All paths had the same length and the same number of forks. To avoid learning effects, blobs were randomly distributed. Blobs were designed to be abstract enough so users could not easily describe them verbally, thus requiring them to look at their partner's workspace. The task was completed when both units reached their goal.

Participants specified routes using the polyline technique shown in Figure 1.3. The map was covered in black at the beginning of each trial so users could not determine the path prior to drawing the route. The map was revealed as

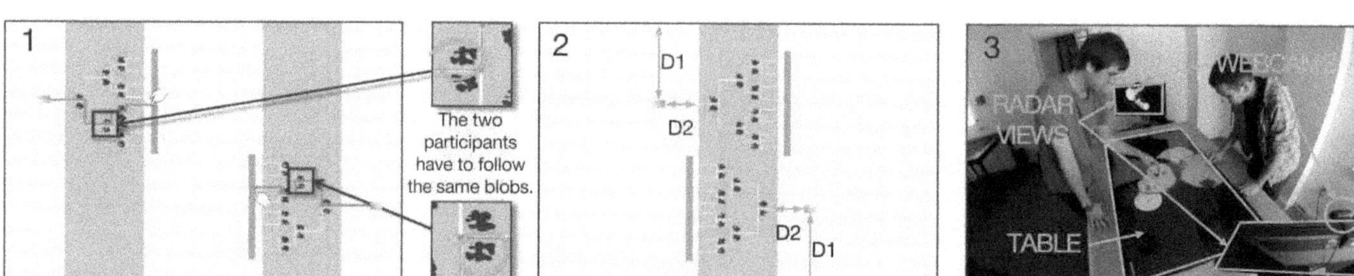

Figure 2. 1) Setting of the path on different regions. An example of the two paths following the same blobs on a turn is highlighted. 2) Setting the paths on the same region. The distances D1 and D2 are highlighted. 3) The study setup.

users drew a route. The intention of the task was to require participants to draw routes using a detailed view, and to coordinate their actions as they reached the fork points.

Procedure

20 participants (12 male, 8 female) were recruited from a local university. Since the task was abstract, it was not necessary to recruit military experts. All participants knew each other prior to the study, were between 19 and 30 years old and were daily users of touch-based devices. The experiment followed a 2×2×2 within-participant design:

	10	pairs of participants
×	2	**interaction techniques** {*Lens, Global Zoom*}
×	2	**radar conditions** {*Displayed, Not Displayed*}
×	2	**spatial arrangement** {*same region, different region*}
×	2	trials
	160	Total trials (16 per participant)

The trials were balanced for order using a Latin square. Participants performed each condition three times, with the first trial used for training. Sessions ended with a custom questionnaire and a semi-structured interview.

Apparatus and Measures

We used a 55" digital tabletop based on a PQ Labs G4S frame. As shown in Figure 2.3, two 1080p 23" screens were positioned on either side of the table to display radar views. The radar views were oriented consistently with the point of view of the participant. From pilot studies, we determined that paths should be 8 pixels wide, small enough to make it impossible to draw a route without zooming. The lenses were 14.5" in diameter, large enough for comfortable interaction and small enough to fit on the table.

We digitally logged all touches and associated positions, and video-taped the session. As shown in Figure 2.3, three cameras were used: a main camera focused on the tabletop surface while two webcams on the radar view screens showed when the participants looked at the radar views.

Hypotheses

This study tested the following assumptions about the suitability of view-techniques for different situations:

H1 *When participants are working on different regions of the map, lenses will be faster than global zoom*

H2 *When participants are working on the same region of the map, global zoom will be faster than lenses*

H3 *Conditions providing the radar view will be faster than equivalent conditions not providing it*

Results

We first report on performance for the different conditions, and then discuss the effectiveness of radar views.

Performance

Figure 3 shows the completion time of trials for each condition. We removed outlier trials where completion times were two standard deviations from the average. An RM-ANOVA identified a significant main effect of technique on completion time ($F_{1,7}$=3.847, p=.002, η^2=.355). Post-hoc t-tests with a Bonferroni adjustment revealed that the difference between *lens* and *global zoom* was significant both when working on different regions ($F_{1,8}$=17.307, p=.001, η^2=.477) and on the same region ($F_{1,8}$=16.074, p=.001, η^2=.486).

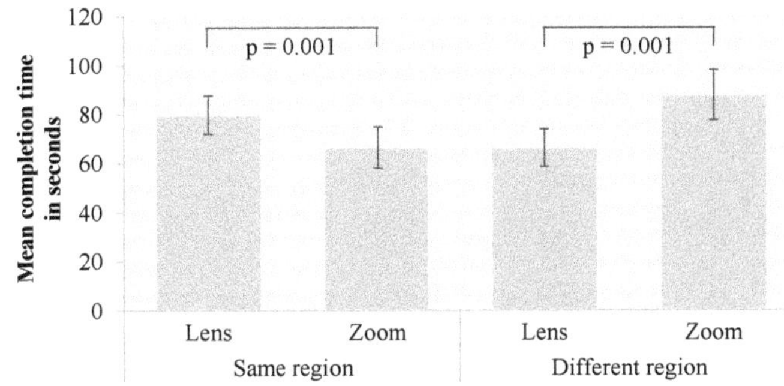

Figure 3. Mean Completion time per condition in seconds

As shown in Figure 3, users were faster with *lens* (M=66.28, SD=15.16) than *zoom* (M=87.65, SD=20.36) when working on different regions. Thus, hypothesis **H1** is supported by our data. Similarly, users were faster with *zoom* (M=66.43, SD=16.93) than with *lens* (M=79.72, SD=15.62) when working on the same region. Thus, hypothesis **H2** is supported by our data.

A post-hoc t-test revealed that the presence of radar had no significant impact on users performance ($F_{1,8}$=.615, p=.438, η^2=.016). The presence of an overview did not have an effect on group performance. Thus, **H3** is not supported.

Following the experiment, participants completed a questionnaire asking which interaction technique they preferred when they were working on the same or different regions. 19 of 20 participants preferred the lenses in the different region condition. However, surprisingly, only 11 of 20 participants preferred the global zoom in the same-region condition.

Role of Radar Views

We used the webcam video streams to count how many times participants looked at the radar view in each trial. Figure 4 illustrates this data. An RM-ANOVA revealed a significant main effect of condition on the number of times users looked at the radar view ($F_{1,9}$=4.023, p=.017, η^2=.309). Post-hoc t-tests with a Bonferroni adjustment revealed that on the condition *lens+radar*, the number of looks at the radar view between working on the same or different region was significant ($F_{1,9}$=10.321, p=.011, η^2=.534). Similarly, on the condition *zoom+radar* displayed the number of looks at the radar view between working on the same or different region was significant ($F_{1,9}$=8.800, p=.016, η^2=.494).

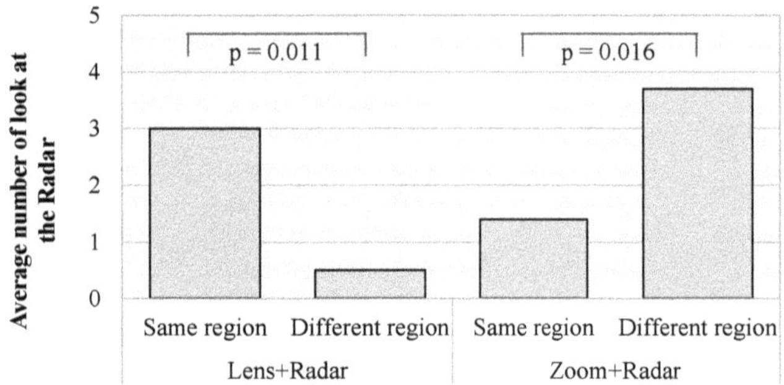

Figure 4. Average number of occurrences of looking at the radar view per trial

As shown in Figure 4, the radar was used significantly more in situations where the view technique performs poorly. We used an open coding process [24] to identify why participants looked at the radar view in these situations. This revealed that in the majority of cases, participants consulted the radar view while attempting to match blobs which were occluded by a lens or were off-screen (i.e., 76% of the time using *lens* in the *same region* condition and 58% of the time using *zoom* in the *different region* condition).

Discussion of Study 1

The first study confirms that there is a performance benefit to using particular view techniques for work on distant versus close regions of a map. Lenses were faster when users' actions took place in different regions of the map. We believe that this is because users could work separately and at a zoom level that was appropriate for moving their units. In contrast, the use of lenses on a proximate region of the map can lead to overlapping of lenses, making it difficult for users to work at the same time.

Conversely, the global zoom proved faster when users' actions took place on proximate regions of the map. The global zoom allowed users to share the same region without creating occlusion problems that could force turn-taking. However, when working on distant areas of the map, it was not possible for both users to zoom at the same time, effectively forcing the users to take turns.

Our radar views had no impact on user performance. This is inconsistent with previous studies of single user applications [12]. Our video analysis showed that the radar view is more watched in high-interference conditions – when using lenses proximately, or global zoom for non-proximate work. While the radar view does not increase performance, it may improve mutual awareness. As reported by one participant "*I think the easiest was when we were using the radar, and then one person could look in their thing, and then the other person would look ahead and then be like 'Okay, now go up, or down.'*"

Overall, these results suggest that people should use different view techniques depending on the proximity of their work areas on the map. This motivated our second study, which looked at whether people choose to use the most efficient technique in order to get those performance benefits in an open-ended and realistic scenario.

STUDY 2: REALISTIC MILITARY PLANNING TASK

Our second study looked at how people choose to configure and re-configure their view environment when working on a realistic mixed-focus task – and in particular, whether people choose the views that perform best for their current work focus. We asked officer candidates from a military university to perform a realistic planning scenario using OrMiS. Unlike the first study, participants were permitted to use any of the view sharing techniques.

System and Task Description

We used the version of OrMiS presented above, including all view techniques (*global zoom, lens,* and *radar view*). Lenses could be created on demand through a long-press menu; the global zoom was always active on the main table display, and the two radar views were always available.

Participants were asked to perform a simple but realistic planning scenario, shown in Figure 5. Each participant controlled different military units; one controlled armored units and the other infantry units. The scenario had two steps which the participants performed sequentially:

Part 1: Move units from A_1 and A_2 to rendezvous at B.

Part 2: Move units through hostile territory from B to the goal position at C. We instructed participants to use a standard military strategy in which armour drives slowly along the road while the infantry walks in the woods beside the road to flush out any ambushing enemies.

Procedure

Twelve male participants (18-30 years old) were recruited from a military university. All participants held the Basic Military Officer Qualification–Land (BMOQ-L), qualifying them as experts in topographical standards used in military maps and strategies used to deploy troops on land. Participants knew each other prior to the study. Participants were first trained with the system, and were given approximately 20 minutes to become familiar with the application and the interaction techniques. Participants were then asked to perform the scenario described above. There was no time limit to perform the task; on average, groups took just over nine minutes (*M*=9:12, *SD*=2:00). The

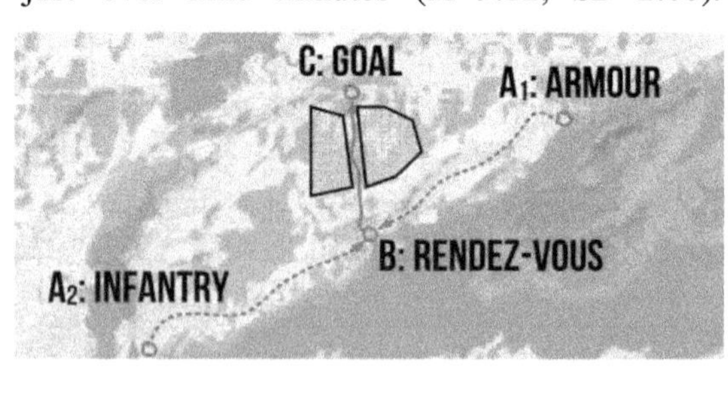

Figure 5. Scenario used in the second study.

exercise was followed by a semi-structured interview.

We used the same equipment as for the first study: a 55" tabletop and two 24" screens to display the radar views. As in the first study, and as shown in Figure 2.3, a main camera recorded the tabletop surface while two webcams recorded looks at the radar views.

Analysis

We used an open coding process [24] to identify behaviors and events of interest during the sessions. The videos for all 12 sessions were analyzed by two coders. All three points of view (i.e. the main camera and two web cams) were combined in one stream and analyzed simultaneously.

Fifty-five minutes of video were analyzed. Six specific situations were coded, either related to one user in particular (e.g., looking at the radar view) or related to the two users working collaboratively. Codes indicated which views and interaction techniques participants were using:

Lens:	Period of time interacting inside a lens
Zoom:	Period of time interacting on the zoomed map
Radar:	Occurrence of a participant looking at the radar view
Single:	Only one participant interacting on the table
Neither:	Neither participant interacting on the table
Both:	Participants interacting simultaneously on the table

Based on our observations during the first study, we assumed that lenses would be used when users needed to work on distant parts of the map (i.e., in part 1) and that global zoom would be used when participants needed to work closely together (i.e., part 2 of the task). We assumed that the radar view would support awareness overall.

Results

A summary of the coding results is shown in Table 1. In the next paragraphs, we use the coding data to answer our main research questions about the use of different views and the way the group coordinated their work.

Use of Views during the Parts of the Scenario

Groups had free choice of view sharing techniques at all times. In part 1 of the task, all six pairs created and used individual lenses to direct their units (see Figure 6.1). Coding data showed that participants interacted with lenses 56.5% of the time in the first part of the task (see Table 1).

	% of Duration		Occurrence	
	Part 1	Part 2	Part 1	Part 2
Lens	56.5%	19.1%	51	11
Zoom	19.6%	48.4%	32	29
Radar	-	-	14	38
Single	20.9%	46.9%	10	45
Both	21.5%	5.9%	47	146
Neither	2.3%	15.3%	78	49

Table 1. Summary of coding results

Participants also used the main table view in part 1 (20% of the time), which included time for setting up the lenses (since the global zoom view was the default view on the table). Participants did not zoom or pan the global view at all during this phase. The remaining 20% of time for part one of the task was taken up in simply waiting for the units to move to the rendezvous point after planning the routes.

At the rendezvous point, all six groups stopped to talk about what strategy to adopt for the second part of the scenario. However, contrary to our expectations, not all of the groups chose to use the global zoom for part two of the task. Four groups chose to use the global zoom, but two groups decided to continue using lenses – even though the group was now working in the same part of the map, and a single global view could show both participants' work areas.

In part two of the task, coding data showed that interaction with the zoom view accounted for 48.4% of the time, and interaction with lenses accounted for 19.1% of the time. However, these amounts reflect the fact that four groups only used the zoom view, and two only used the lenses.

Unexpected Use of Lenses in Part 2 of the Task

Two groups of the six decided to not use the main zoom in the second part of the task but instead shared a lens, thus forcing them to interact (sometimes awkwardly) inside a very small space (see Figure 6.4). These two groups, upon reaching the rendezvous point, destroyed their respective lenses and then created a new one to be shared. One group also shared a lens with one participant in charge of planning his units' route while the other was responsible for dragging the lens (see Figure 6.4). This led to awkward physical proximity in which participants had to move their bodies close together and cross their arms.

There are several reasons why participants may have chosen lenses in the second part of the task – for example,

Figure 6. The sequential use of interaction techniques across the scenario: 1) In the part 1 of the scenario, participants worked with two lenses; 2) close to the rendezvous point, participants worked close together, but continued to use lenses; 3) In the part 2, participants had zoomed the map and started taking turns; 4) Participants shared a lens in the part 2 of the scenario.

interface inertia, reluctance to work in the same area, or interest in the novelty of the lens technique – and we discuss these further below. Regardless of the reason, however, our results show that a third of the groups decided to use the lens technique, rather than switching to the technique (i.e., zoom) that Study 1 showed to be significantly more efficient when working close together.

Coordination between Users with Global Zoom

In the second part of the scenario, planners needed to move their units in tightly-coordinated fashion from the rendezvous (point B in Figure 5) to the final objective (point C in Figure 5). Four of the six groups used the global zoom for this part of the task (see Figure 6.3).

Video coding revealed that participants interacted simultaneously only 5.9% of the time during the part 2 of the task. In Table 1, 146 occurrences of *Both* on Part 2 are reported. This corresponds to the very short periods of time where the switch form a user to another was performed. A qualitative analysis on the videos revealed that all four groups adopted a turn-taking strategy when using global zoom. The participant in charge of controlling the armored units always initiated the turn taking. This may have been because the scenario directed the armour to follow the road, and the infantry to flank the armour. Two strategies were used for turn-taking on the global zoom: 1) Two groups took long turns, each drawing the entire route from point B to C, one after the other; 2) two groups took short turns, drawing small parts of the route (usually one or two waypoints) and then permitting the other to continue.

As we discuss further below, these results suggest that global zoom views are not always used in parallel, even when there is room for both participants to operate.

The Role of the Radar View in Maintaining Awareness

Previous work suggests that radar views are extremely useful for maintaining overall awareness of a space [11]. We counted the number of times that participants looked at the radar view, shown in Figure 7. An ANOVA showed an overall effect of the number of people interacting with the table on the use of the radar view ($F_{1,2}$=12.428, p=.002, η^2=.699). Post-hoc tests revealed that when a single person is using the table, use of the radar is significantly higher than when both are interacting ($F_{1,2}$=12.428, p=.017, η^2=.713). Single-person use was also higher than when

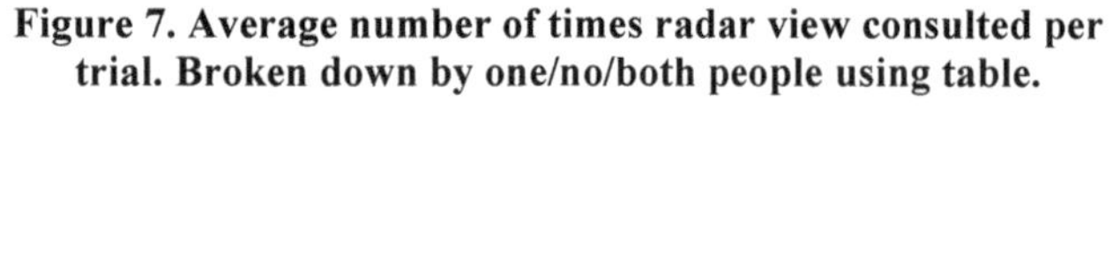

Figure 7. Average number of times radar view consulted per trial. Broken down by one/no/both people using table.

nobody was interacting – but this is not surprising since at the end of the task, both participants simply watched the units follow the planned route.

The radar view was mainly used in the second part of the scenario. 73% of radar view events occurred in the second part of the scenario (see Table 1: 38/(38+14) = 73%); 56% occurred while participants were working directly on a globally zoomed map, while only 36% of the radar view events occurred when participants were working with lenses. Video analysis showed that participants used the radar for awareness to monitor units while they moved along routes, thus providing a sense of the remaining time required to reach the destination point.

These results indicate that the radar was mostly used when people were waiting for their turn in the second part of the scenario. We further discuss the use of the radar view and its role in the task in the following sections.

DISCUSSION AND IMPLICATIONS FOR DESIGN

In the following sections, we discuss some of the surprising results uncovered by the study, propose explanations for these events, and highlight their underlying implications for the design of tabletop systems.

Users Don't Necessarily Pick the Performant Technique

Our first study showed that group performance significantly improves when the view configuration matches the spatial arrangement of the group's tasks. We were consequently expecting that planners in study 2 would choose the view configuration that best matched their current tasks.

However, observations showed that in practice users do not necessarily pick the most efficient technique. We observed that some planners continued to use lenses as they were getting closer together, even though switching to zoom would have led to more efficient work and better awareness. We do not believe that participants forgot the global zoom technique, since participants were trained with the techniques for about 20 minutes before the study. We can therefore assume that they were aware of the existence of both techniques.

The change of view technique (i.e., to zoom) typically happened only when users found a quiet moment in the task to communicate. Two groups of the six seemed to never find this quiet moment, and shared a lens until in the end of the task. We report this phenomenon as an *interface inertia* effect. Several reasons explain this behavior:

Politeness. Our observations suggest that switching from lens to global zoom requires verbal communication to negotiate a common agreement about which technique to use. In practice, participants do not necessarily pause to communicate, even if it is in their interests in terms of performance. The group may have difficulties in finding the right time to break the flow of the task to change the view technique, which may have led to inertia.

Task Structure. The structure of the task determined how participants used the techniques (rather than comfort or effectiveness). Participants were aware that the task was composed of two parts. They may have preferred to not interfere with the other person before the first part ended, anticipating that they would have to communicate and coordinate before starting the second part.

Overall our observations led us to reconsider and to extend previous findings. While Tang et al.'s work recommended providing "fluid transitions between coupling styles" [25] and Isenberg's et al. to "design for transient behavior" [14], we observed that transitions between techniques can be difficult to accomplish in practice. Social conventions may prevent users from choosing the most effective technique for a defined situation. It is therefore important that further work investigate the details of settings where switching occurs (e.g., in our case from loosely coupled to tightly coupled and vice-versa). In addition, although inertia has been observed in single-user settings, we are the first to look at it in collaborative settings where factors such as not wanting to interrupt the partner's task flow or politeness could increase the inertia.

Social Conventions May Override Space Constraints

Our first study showed that global zoom out-performed lens when participants worked on the same region of the map. Consistent with the observations of Tang et al. [25], most groups preferred the global zoom when the task required tightly-coupled coordination. However, we observed that in practice users chose to take turns for tightly-coupled tasks even when they had enough space to work simultaneously when using the zoom. This is a surprising result. Users had been working in parallel up to this point in the task and had ample room to work together without colliding.

Reluctance to Interfere. With our system, one participant could inadvertently pan the map and move the area where the other user person was working. In practice users were very cautious when touching the map and showed fear of panning the map while the other person was working. As one participant stated: *If you touch the map while the other is doing his thing, it moves!*" (Group1). Similarly, a participants Group 3 was explaining that they "*had to create a seniority of who was allowed and who was in control of the board, because at some points I would go touch something and it would screw him up*".

Touch Avoidance. Participants may have also opted for the strategy that would minimize physical contact. Previous research highlights peoples' tendency to avoid physical contact around a shared space [7]. In our study, turn-taking clearly minimized the risk of contact even at the cost of efficiency. For instance, one participant clearly stated that he would have preferred splitting the space rather than having to work simultaneously on the same map: "*When there are two people playing with it, we can zoom and I can do my waypoints so we can do both but I imagine that in a real scenario if there is two people touching* [...] *I think we could crop one part of the map* [...] *but not the rest of the map* [...] *and something to lock it so it can't get zoomed in with a little icon on the side, because we tried to move our stuff and our fingers got close.*" (Group 2)

Overall, these findings suggest that social conventions about turn-taking when working on the same artifact may override mechanical constraints such as available space. This has not been reported before in the tabletop literature. It strongly underlines the limitations of tabletops for working simultaneously around a shared artifact. This also emphasizes the need to make observations in realistic situations. Indeed, this result is quite counter-intuitive – the strategies that groups use in controlled studies may not carry over to realistic tasks.

Inactive Users Rely on Contextual Views

Our first study showed that while the radar view did not increase performance, it improved mutual awareness when parts of the map were not visible. We observed in our second study that users rely on the radar view when they are not interacting with the table during the second part of the scenario (i.e. the most tightly coupled part of the task). We wondered why users preferred to look at the vertical screen rather than the horizontal table when they are not interacting. Several reasons may explain this behavior:

Stable perception frame. When users are not interacting with the map, they may not understand which part of the map is currently visible on the table. Looking at the radar view provides a stable frame where the entire context can be seen. User comments suggest that this was useful to assess overall progress on the mission: "*I found [the radar] useful especially for the last part, I had an idea approximately where he was but just by looking at the map I don't know if it would have been possible... overall it is not very useful to add [the radar] but it gives an overall of the map*" (Group 1).

Comfort. Two participants reported ergonomic and orientation issues: "*The table should be higher or angled... there is clearly one side that's better*". One participant complained about pain in his neck at the end of the study, indicating the importance of making the height of the table comfortable for extended touch interaction. In fact, vertical surfaces are known to be more comfortable [18] than horizontal surfaces. This may explain users' preference for the radar view while waiting for the other planner.

These findings provided insight about the role of external overviews for mixed-focus collaborative tasks. We showed in study 1 that while the presence of overview displays does not significantly impact users' performance, it can improve awareness. Our second study emphasized the importance of an external overview to maintain awareness in a comfortable manner.

CONCLUSION

In this paper, we studied the combination of multiple view techniques to support collaborative map-based tasks on digital tabletops. We performed two studies to evaluate the performance and use of these techniques. Our results revealed that 1) view techniques do affect performance and awareness, 2) users do not necessarily pick the right technique, 3) social conventions may override space constraints, and 4) inactive users rely on contextual views.

These results show that there are several subtleties in the ways that view and collaboration interact. These subtleties have not been observed in previous work and can lead to new insights in the design of tabletop applications. Our observations in a realistic context provide new information about designing tabletop interfaces for collaborative activities.

Of course, future work is required to further investigate transitions in mixed-focus tabletop work, particularly in complex and realistic task settings and including complementary support to a digital tabletop for sharing space such as individual windows, personal devices (e.g. computers, tablets), and high resolution displays.

REFERENCES

1. Apperley, M.D., Tzavaras, I. and Spence, R. 1982. A bifocal display technique for data presentation. *EUROGRAPHICS'82*, 27–43.
2. Appert, C., Chapuis, O. and Pietriga, E. 2010. High-precision magnification lenses. *CHI '10*, 273–282.
3. Bortolaso, C., Oskamp, M., Graham, T.C.N. and Brown, D. 2013. OrMiS: A Tabletop Interface for Simulation-Based Training. *ITS '13*, 145–154.
4. Burns, C., Seyed, T., Bradley, K., Duncan, R., Balasch, A., Maurer, F. and Sousa, M.C. 2012. Multi-Surface Visualization of Fused Hydrocarbon Microseep and Reservoir Data. *GeoConvention*, 2–5.
5. Carpendale, S., Ligh, J., Pattison, E. and Light, J. 2004. Achieving higher magnification in context. *UIST '04*, 71–80.
6. Cockburn, A., Karlson, A. and Bederson, B.B. 2008. A review of overview+detail, zooming, and focus+context interfaces. *ACM Computing Surveys*. 41, 1, 1–31.
7. Doucette, A., Gutwin, C., Mandryk, R.L., Nacenta, M. and Sharma, S. 2013. Sometimes when we touch: how arm embodiments change reaching and collaboration on digital tables. *CSCW '13*, 193-202.
8. Forlines, C. and Shen, C. 2005. DTLens: multi-user tabletop spatial data exploration. *UIST '05*, 119–122.
9. Gutwin, C. 2002. Improving focus targeting in interactive fisheye views. *CHI '02*, 267–274.
10. Gutwin, C. and Greenberg, S. 1998. Design for individuals, design for groups. *CSCW '98*, 207–216.
11. Gutwin, C., Greenberg, S. and Roseman, M. 1996. Workspace awareness support with radar views. *CHI '96*, 210–211.
12. Hornbæk, K., Bederson, B.B. and Plaisant, C. 2002. Navigation patterns and usability of zoomable user interfaces with and without an overview. *TOCHI* 9, 4, 362–389.
13. Ion, A., Chang, Y.-L.B., Haller, M., Hancock, M., Scott, S.D. and Chang, B. 2013. Canyon: Providing Location Awareness of Multiple Moving Objects in a Detail View on Large Displays. *CHI 2013*, 3149–3158.
14. Isenberg, P., Fisher, D., Morris, M.R., Inkpen, K. and Czerwinski, M. 2010. An exploratory study of co-located collaborative visual analytics around a tabletop display. *IEEE VAST*, 179–186.
15. Jakobsen, M.R. and Hornbæk, K. 2014. Up close and personal: Collaborative work on a high-resolution multitouch wall display. *TOCHI. 21*, 2, 1–34.
16. Javed, W., Ghani, S., Elmqvist, N. and Lafayette, W. 2012. Polyzoom. *CHI '12*, 287–296.
17. Kobayashi, K., Narita, A., Hirano, M., Kase, I., Tsuchida, S., Omi, T., Kakizaki, T. and Hosokawa, T. 2006. Collaborative simulation interface for planning disaster measures. *CHI EA '06*, 977–982.
18. Pedersen, E.W. and Hornbæk, K. 2012. An experimental comparison of touch interaction on vertical and horizontal surfaces. *NordiCHI '12*, 370-379.
19. Pietriga, E. and Appert, C. 2008. Sigma lenses: focus-context transitions combining space, time and translucence. *CHI '08*, 1343–1352.
20. Pindat, C., Pietriga, E., Chapuis, O. and Puech, C. 2012. JellyLens. *UIST '12*, 261–270.
21. Schmidt, D., Chong, M.K. and Gellersen, H. 2010. IdLenses: dynamic personal areas on shared surfaces. *ITS '10*, 131–134.
22. Scott, S.D., Allavena, A., Cerar, K., Franck, G., Hazen, M., Shuter and T., Colliver, C. 2010. Investigating Tabletop Interfaces to Support Collaborative Decision-Making in Maritime Operations. *ICCRTS 2010*.
23. Selim, E. and Maurer, F. 2010. EGrid: supporting the control room operation of a utility company with multi-touch tables. *ITS '10*, 289-290.
24. Strauss, A. and Corbin, J.M. 1998. *Basics of Qualitative Research: Techniques and Procedures for Developing Grounded Theory*. SAGE.
25. Tang, A., Tory, M., Po, B., Neumann, P. and Carpendale, S. 2006. Collaborative coupling over tabletop displays. *CHI '06*, 1181–1190.
26. Wallace, J.R., Scott, S.D. and MacGregor, C.G. 2013. Collaborative sensemaking on a digital tabletop and personal tablets. *CHI '13*, 3345.
27. Van Wijk, J.J. and Nuij, W.A.A. 2003. Smooth and efficient zooming and panning. *INFOVIS'03*, 15–22.

Spatial Querying of Geographical Data with Pen-Input Scopes

Fabrice Matulic, David Caspar, Moira C. Norrie
ETH Zurich, Institute of Information Systems
8092 Zurich, Switzerland
{matulic|norrie}@inf.ethz.ch, dcaspar@student.ethz.ch

ABSTRACT
Querying geographical data on map applications running on touch devices is mainly performed by typing queries using virtual keyboards. Some of those devices are additionally equipped with styli to facilitate freehand sketching and annotating. As shown by prior work, such hand-drawn sketches can also be used for intuitive and effective spatial querying of geographical data. Building on that groundwork, we present a set of pen-based techniques to selectively convert map annotations into spatial queries with implicitly or explicitly specified scopes. We show how those techniques can be used for trip-planning tasks involving route-finding and searching of points of interest. In a controlled user study comparing the usability and efficiency of the techniques for different querying patterns, we establish participants' general preference for explicit input scopes and obtain indications that, provided handwriting is correctly recognised, input times are comparable to that of a standard (soft) keyboard-based interface. Based on those results and participant feedback, we propose a number of enhancements and extensions to inform the design of future pen-based map applications.

Author Keywords
Maps; GIS interfaces; geospatial querying; pen and touch interaction

ACM Classification Keywords
H.5.2.

General Terms
Human Factors; Design.

INTRODUCTION
The high popularity of map applications and services on mobile devices is well established. According to GlobalWebIndex, a market research firm, Google Maps is the n°1 application on smartphones with approximately half of the global smartphone population using it [1]. Because the vast majority of current mobile devices are operated by touch, the user interfaces of map applications have naturally been optimised for that particular type of input, although they still borrow much from their desktop counterparts. Perhaps one of the most evident carryovers from desktop map applications is the search interface, which, even on touchscreens, relies on a dedicated query field and (virtual) keyboard input. With the recent resurgence of the stylus as a supplementary input instrument on some of the latest smartphone and tablet models, it is worth exploring and studying UI designs for map applications that may be more adapted to those new devices and interaction paradigms.

In this paper, we consider the popular map task of geospatial querying, specifically, searching for points of interest (POI) within user-defined areas, on pen and touch-enabled tablets, e.g. finding restaurants in or near a city, searching for hotels along a specified path etc. With those types of scenarios in mind, we investigate the feasibility and usability of techniques, where the pen is used both as a regular marking tool to annotate maps and as an instrument to enter spatial queries and their scopes.

While there are examples of stylus usage for area-constrained map queries in prior work, most of the relevant approaches considered the stylus in combination with speech, as part of multimodal dialogues [4, 6, 14-18, 21]. In those systems, the pen's role is mainly to specify the spatial context of the search query, which is formulated through speech. While speech can be a useful input mode for spatial queries, depending on the context, vocal commands might not always be possible (because of environmental noise, user accents etc.) or the feature might not be available altogether. Besides, recent observations show that for short and simple user-computer dialogues such as those involved in POI searching, users tend to not interact multimodally in the first place [7]. Hence, we surmise an approach focused on pen (and touch) input potentially applies to more widespread interaction patterns on modern tablets and digital surfaces at large, especially in stationary conditions.

The contributions we make in this paper are the following:

- We create a set of pen-based techniques that allow users to annotate interactive maps and to selectively use those annotations to perform localised spatial queries. Those queries allow explicit and implicit specification of search regions as well as different temporal precedence between

http://dx.doi.org/10.1145/2669485.2669513

scope definition and query term input. We tackle both area- and path-based queries, where the latter may follow a route-finding action for which we also provide pen gestures. We also include support for chained queries with re-use of ink data.

- We conduct a controlled user study, in which we evaluate the usability of our techniques and compare their input performance to that of a virtual keyboard-based interface modelled after popular map applications on tablets. We report quantitative and qualitative results, based on measured task metrics and user feedback. Our analysis includes a critical assessment of our current designs as well as suggestions for extensions, with a view to inspire future work on pen-based map applications.

RELATED WORK

There is a sizeable body of work in the literature dealing with various kinds of stylus-based UIs for geographic information systems (GIS) and map-related applications. For instance, taking advantage of people's intuitive ability to draw with pens, researchers developed sketch-based systems to retrieve topological data [2, 8] and to input geospatial content [5, 9, 24]. Less reliant on complex sketch-recognition algorithms, [22] shows an example of how simple pen strokes can be used to perform spatio-temporal queries to retrieve geotagged multimedia content.

With regard to location-constrained POI and route searching (and therefore closer in intent to our work), a popular approach to tackle the problem has been to combine stylus input with speech in multimodal interfaces [4, 6, 14-18, 21]. The rationale is that while the object of the query can be efficiently conveyed through speech, the pen is more convenient to specify the spatial scope or context in which the query should apply. Most of the work in that area understandably concentrates on the intricacies of integrating the two modalities to correctly and effectively interpret the user's commands rather than studying the individual input modes in depth. Among those cited systems, only MATCH [16], [4] and [21] include the possibility to also enter text queries solely with the stylus via handwriting. However, the publications do not contain much detail about the design of those pen-only interactions and empirical results beyond general handwriting recognition accuracy are not provided. In particular, there is no data showing how successfully the recognition algorithms are able to differentiate selection strokes from handwritten text. Furthermore, in those systems all pen input is interpreted as locative or query data (with limited query structures and vocabulary) and there is no support for regular inking on the maps. As a result, there is no need for a switching mechanism to distinguish between annotations and commands, which makes the design of stylus interactions more straightforward. CoMPASS [6] is a multimodal system with explicit support for annotations, but those are entered via dictation and the pen is only used to correct misrecognised input.

As pointed out in the introduction, multimodal input with speech has its limitations and we feel the pen-only case has been under-investigated, especially in modern contexts. The latest crop of touchscreen devices and currently dominating interaction paradigms indeed suggest another kind of multimodal input tandem, albeit with a very different role distribution: pen and touch. As demonstrated by extensive prior work on the subject, the combination of those two types of input enable rapid and fluid transitions between coarse touch-based navigational gestures and finer-grained pen interactions to enter content and commands [3, 10, 12, 19]. We consider those properties to be of particular relevance to map-related tasks, with a division of labour consisting of multitouch for panning and scaling the map, while the stylus is used for annotations and commands.

Finally, a particular issue that we investigate is the temporal precedence of scope vs. term specification for directly inputting spatial queries, i.e. which part typically comes first and under what circumstances. In [21], Oviatt et al. report that in multimodal query patterns, the pen, which typically sets the locative context, is much more likely to precede speech, which is mainly used to formulate the action to be taken. The authors interpret this behaviour as being the result of inherent properties of the two modes, with the permanence of the ink possibly enabling people to visualise a frame of reference for subsequent vocally articulated queries. The alternative explanation that the observed sequence of actions might not be mode-dependent but driven by their type is not considered and the authors do not provide any in-depth analysis of temporal precedence for unimodal pen input that would shed some light on that issue. We think this is an interesting question that merits further empirical study, all the more because it also applies to map-searching UIs where the pen is only used for query input.

APPROACH

When planning trips and itineraries using paper maps, it is not uncommon to annotate and sketch those maps in order to help the cognitive process and record or emphasise important information. For instance, a person might want to circle a specific area to indicate a location where to stop and, within that area, mark particular places of interests. Because those notes are produced by freehand drawings and handwriting, they also carry a personal dimension, which becomes lost in map applications based on print text input via the keyboard. While naturally not equivalent to paper maps in terms of affordances, we believe tablets and interactive surfaces equipped with styli give us the chance to take advantage of many of those properties, in addition to providing the digital tools and services of interactive maps to which people have become accustomed. We envision travel-planning scenarios, where, in a preparatory phase, users make freehand notes on maps and search for geographic content, find routes etc. before printing out the results to obtain a personal paper map with all the necessary details for the trip.

We therefore approach the problem with the aim of blending natural pen interaction and traditional features of digital maps in the designs so that users can smoothly and efficiently transition between annotating and command input. In particular, we wish to investigate how annotations can be converted to commands to support use cases where handwritten notes or symbols may also denote search tasks to be performed. This ability to use the interactive map as a "smart" note canvas further suggests the adoption of a clean interface design in which the map area is maximised and space-consuming widgets used as sparingly as possible.

ANNOTATING

As per the division of labour principle [12], the pen's main role is to ink, i.e. to input regular annotations on the map as if it were a virtual sheet of paper. Users therefore use the stylus to input ink on the screen and delete strokes using the rubber end of the pen. Individual annotations are determined through logical ink clusters based on spatio-temporal proximity, i.e. strokes that are close to each other are grouped together to form single annotation entities. Such annotations can be selected via finger taps (see spatial querying below) and moved to other locations on the map through dragging actions. As the notes are essentially virtual ink on a stretchable (zoomable) map, they scale along with it through pinch/spread gestures. As a result, the annotations may become less readable at extreme zoom levels. To address that issue, we include a gesture allowing annotations to be transferred as is between zoom levels. The gesture is performed by holding the ink with a finger while performing the scale operation and releasing the finger to paste the annotation back on the map at the new zoom level.

Partially as an alternative solution to the above problem but also to provide a tool that users of popular map applications will be familiar with, we additionally support collapsible annotations attached to pushpins. Pushpins are created with a single-stroke 'ρ' gesture, starting from the bottom end to differentiate it from the letter 'p' (which, if adhering to handwriting standards, is normally started from the top). The pushpin can then be tapped to display a canvas on which notes can be written. Because the size of pushpins is independent of the map zoom level, users can always access attached annotations, whose sizes also remain constant.

SPATIAL QUERYING

The first set of commands that we consider is querying for POIs in or around a particular location. Common map services such as Google Maps, whether for desktop or mobile devices, do not allow users to specify custom regions to restrict the scope of queries. To execute a local search for POIs, a user may enter the query with the desired location (e.g. "hotels in London") or proceed in two steps by first moving to the target location (either by manually navigating to it or by entering the place as a query) and then performing the POI search. In either case, the results, a collection of small pushpins representing the POIs on the map, will not be limited to the target location but will cover the entire visible area of the map. If the map is zoomed out, the search area is correspondingly expanded and new results fill the screen. What is more, issuing a second query for a different type of POI will either cause the new results to replace or appear along with the previous ones. In other words, it is not possible to execute a sequence of different POI queries, each of which having its own spatial scope, and view all the results together on the map. This not only increases clutter and user confusion, but can also be a serious impediment when several queries need to be input in different locations, as when planning a trip.

As argued above, styli offer interesting potential to quickly and intuitively specify the spatial context of queries and thus address the aforementioned limitations. That user-defined context can take the form of closed or open shapes indicating respectively whether the search query should be executed within an area or along a path. Furthermore, scopes can be easily combined and dynamically assigned to different queries, which provides additional flexibility. Here, differentiated pen and touch input comes as a particularly useful asset, as it enables unambiguous role assignments for sketching (pen) and selection (touch). We explore this potential and how it can be translated into different querying techniques based on new or existing annotations and following different conversion patterns.

From Annotations to Queries

To allow the user to assign a semantic role to desired ink data so that they can issue queries and specify their scopes, adequate mechanisms need to be devised. An obvious solution would be to select markings (with touch) and press a button or summon an in-place menu with command options [13]. Our design philosophy outlined above, however, advocates a minimal use of widgets, which, in addition to taking valuable screen space, we think introduce disruptions into the "flow" of pen interaction sequences. A possible alternative to trigger the annotation-query conversion with the stylus only would be through a recognisable delimiter [11] or gesture. This is an option that we find more appealing for a pen-driven interface, provided the gestures are sufficiently easy to execute. For our techniques, we chose the question mark as the main trigger symbol, as it conveys the notion of a query and is also directly detected by the handwriting recogniser, which already interprets the handwritten search terms. The drawback, of course, is that question marks cannot be used in plain annotations.

A spatial query basically consists of a scope element and an expression articulating the query object. The scope, defining a particular map context (region or path) within which the query will be executed, is often not precisely determined, as users generally search for POIs in a rough area or in the approximate vicinity of a location. Therefore, that context may be explicitly specified via a drawn circle or a path, but it could also possibly be implicit and, for instance, inferred from the handwritten content itself.

With those issues in mind we create three querying techniques, one implicit and two explicit, described hereafter.

Figure 1: The QUERY? technique with implicit scope. When the question mark is appended to the query text, the results appear in the largest city close to the user ink.

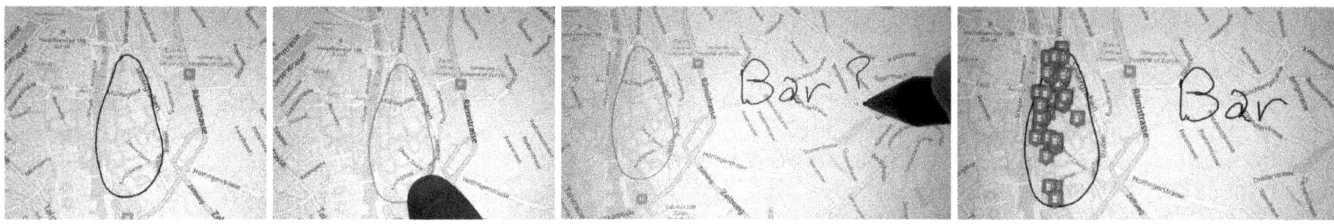

Figure 2: The *SCOPE→QUERY?* technique. First, one or more inked elements representing scopes are selected (here, a region), then the query object is input. The query is launched upon adding the question mark.

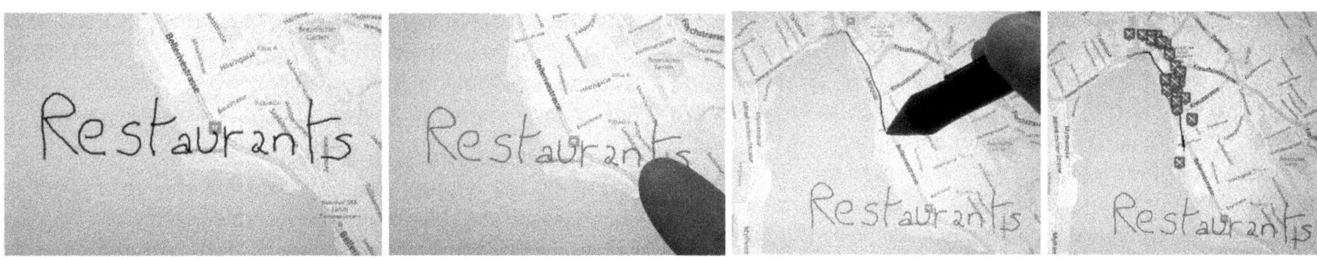

Figure 3: The *QUERY→SCOPE* technique. First one or more annotations to be used as query objects are selected, then the scope is input (here, a path). The query is launched upon release of the pen.

Querying around Text – Implicit Scope

Our technique with implicit scope considers the ink of the query text itself to determine the target search area. The intended use of this technique is for general POI searches within major cities, for which there is no need to specify an explicit region with the pen. To execute such a query, the user writes a question mark at the end of an annotation (newly input or existing) to trigger the request (Figure 1). When the handwriting recogniser detects the question mark, the latter is removed (since it is considered a gesture) and the POI search executed in the largest city located within a particular radius from the centroid of the ink data. In our current implementation, the radius is an eighth of the real distance between the two lateral edges of the map view. The value is therefore independent of the ink size but dependent on the zoom level, which allows users to execute more or less local queries.

We hereafter refer to this query technique as *QUERY?*.

Querying with Explicit Scopes

For spatial queries, where the scope is not self-evident from geographical features (such as the boundaries of a city) or when users know more or less precisely the target area of their search request, the pen offers a convenient possibility to explicitly specify that context using freeform sketches, as shown in prior work. In our application we only distinguish between two types of interpreted ink data: text and scope. To differentiate between the two categories, we use a simple model based on the number of strokes of an ink cluster: when converted, a single-stroke element denotes a scope (for open shapes, a path and for closed shapes, a region), whereas multi-stroke clusters are construed as handwriting.

As with the previous technique, appropriate selecting and trigger mechanisms are required to respectively designate the ink to use for the query and to launch it. Because the query here is composed of at least two elements (one or more scopes + one or more query terms), which are not necessarily located close to each other, an appended question mark alone does not suffice. We therefore introduce a selection step, where users tap the ink clusters (with a finger) they would like to include in the query. Thus, the query input sequence consists of tapping existing markings that should be part of the query and/or inserting new ink + issuing the trigger.

The case of a single spatial query, where the user directly enters both parameters is particularly interesting as it raises the question of temporal precedence, i.e. which part of the query is input first. We create two query techniques tailored to each pattern: the first, which we call *SCOPE→QUERY?*, considers the scope as the first argument, followed by the term(s) and the question mark trigger. Hence, the query input sequence for this technique is: scope selection → query term input → appending the question mark to the term to launch the query (Figure 2). Step 2 can be omitted if existing annotations should be used for the query. In that case, the user need only append the question mark to the desired annotation to indicate that it should form the query object (similar to *QUERY?*).

The second technique reverses the scope-term order, i.e. it requires first the term(s) and then the scope. In the latter case, however, because scopes are single-stroke non-text elements, we can also use them as triggers. Specifically, when users select a text annotation to activate it as a query term, the next stroke automatically designates the scope and at the same time launches the query. This shortcut slightly speeds up query input, but it also requires users to pay attention whether there is any selected text when they would like to insert further annotations.

The input sequence is therefore: query term selection → scope input = query trigger (Figure 3). We refer to this query technique as *QUERY→SCOPE* (without the question mark).

While for direct query input the choice of entering first the search terms or the scope is predominantly a matter of personal preference, cases where the necessary ink is already present will likely incite users to opt for one technique over the other. For instance, if there is already an annotation with the desired query term and only the scope is missing, *QUERY→SCOPE* will most likely be more appropriate. Thus, the two techniques are not mutually exclusive and can be used alternatively, depending on the situation.

Awareness Support

Since the conversion of text annotations to machine-understandable search terms is based on handwriting recognition, we provide means for users to obtain feedback from the result of the conversion in order for them to be able to check the correct interpretation of their handwritten text.

This feedback, which appears in the form of a small tooltip box, is activated when the user holds their finger on the annotation. Additionally, to maintain user awareness about currently selected elements and the successful launch of their queries we include a notification bar displaying that information at the bottom of the screen.

Displaying and Interacting with the Results

The results of search queries are displayed in a manner similar to popular map applications, that is, using pushpins with symbols representing the found POIs. Those pushpins can be tapped to show information about the associated location. By default, a new query does not cause existing pushpins to be removed, since one of the purposes of the interface is to be able to easily combine different spatial queries to support multi-stage trip-planning. As mentioned previously, contrary to traditional map applications, query results do not fill the entire screen, but are neatly confined to their respective scopes, which limits clutter and hence allows us to adopt that strategy. However, this means users have to explicitly delete pushpins when needed. We provide two methods to do so: to remove individual pushpins, users can simply rub them off using the rubber end of the stylus. For a group of pushpins associated with a particular query, users can toggle their visibility by tapping the handwritten text of the query. Erasing the latter with the digital rubber removes the results permanently.

ROUTE PLANNING

One of the most widely used features of map applications is route planning, which allows people to search for itineraries between two or more locations using a variety of means of transport. Beyond just obtaining directions, there is often also a need to be able to search for POIs along those routes, for instance to find service stations on a long motorway stretch. While a number of navigation tools and trip-planning sites support such kinds of needs (e.g. bestroadtripplanner.com, mapquest.com), most of them have rather rigid widget-based UIs that do not lend themselves to pen interaction. Moreover, they also suffer from the above-described problem of limited blending capabilities when executing several POI search requests with different scopes.

Routes can be considered as special paths that are computed rather than directly input by the user. Hence, if the pen-enabled map application already handles (user-drawn) path-based queries, it is only one step away from supporting POI-searching along routes. We integrate that functionality through a pen gesture consisting of tracing lines between pushpins marking the start and end points of the route to calculate on the map. Thus, when the user starts to drag the pen from a pushpin, a straight line to the pen tip is drawn indicating that the gesture has been initiated. The user can then release the pen on a second pushpin to complete the action and issue the route-finding request. In the physical world, this gesture is akin to stretching a string between (real) pushpins to connect marked locations on a paper map.

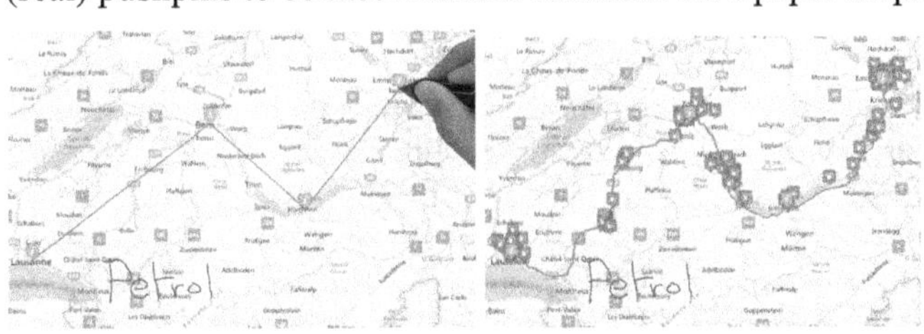

Figure 4: With a query term selected, a user connects pushpins (left). When the stylus is released, the route is calculated and the corresponding query launched along its path (right).

Computed routes appear as path strokes and are treated similarly, that is, they can be selected for path-based spatial queries as well as deleted with the digital rubber. Additionally, users can chunk a route-finding operation with a path-based query using the *QUERY→SCOPE* technique. In that combination, the hand-drawn stroke of the second step is replaced by the pushpin-connecting action described above. Upon release of the stylus, the route is calculated and the selected query executed along that route (Figure 4).

Regarding the type of routes that we support, our prototype currently only considers car travel, but other types of transport supported by route-planning APIs could conceivably be added in the future.

ENABLING TECHNOLOGIES

Our prototype is implemented in C# and deployed on a pen and touch-capable Wacom Cintiq Companion[1], which has a 13.3″ screen with a full HD resolution (1920 × 1080). Wacom provides an SDK with support for simultaneous use of the two modalities, which allows us to bypass the limitations imposed by the operating system (Windows 8), where only one input type can be active at a time. We use that capability to implement a less absolute palm rejection scheme based on a touch-blocking area below the pen-holding hand similar to [23]. This more flexible approach improves the fluidity of transitions between pen and touch interactions, especially when the stylus is in range.

Further software components and libraries that we rely on are a customised Bing Maps WPF control for the main map interface and MyScript 6.1[2] for handwriting recognition. As for map services, we use the Google Places API[3] for spatial queries and the Bing Maps REST Services[4] for routing.

EVALUATION

Protocol

Design

To evaluate and compare our techniques we conducted a user study, with a focus on the three spatial querying techniques to keep the experiments tractable in terms of time and complexity (we aimed for maximum 1.5-hour sessions). These experiments were also to be restricted to direct querying, where all annotations were to be used for searches, since the goal was not to evaluate our rudimentary ink segmenting algorithm.

Even though traditional map applications do not support freeform region-constrained queries, we were interested in estimating the potential costs and benefits of our techniques in terms of input efficiency compared to regular touch-based query entry on a soft keyboard. Hence, we decided to include a fourth keyboard-based baseline technique modelled after Google Maps (note that we could not use Google's mobile map application itself because flexible usage of custom maps was not possible).

Faced with the choice of devising an open experiment in which users were free to use the techniques according to their preferences or closed trials, where each query method was studied in turn individually, we opted for the latter design, as we wanted to make sure to collect enough data for each technique in order to make fine-grained comparisons.

Likewise, we adopted a within-subjects design for our study so that our participants could compare and provide feedback on their experiences with all of our techniques.

As one of the main scenarios we aimed to support is POI searching as part of a travel plan, we created a set of tasks around that activity consisting of sequences of POI queries to be executed one after the other. Each of those series was meant to symbolise short imaginary trips (but without any route-planning) within the country of Switzerland, with the "trips" composed of several stages in which particular kinds of POIs such as hotels, bars, banks etc. had to be searched.

In real contexts, a POI search rarely stops after issuing the query, as users typically check the results they obtained by tapping pushpins on the map to view details about the locations. To be closer to such real-world situations while still remaining in the conditions of a controlled experiment, we added a selection step after the query so that a stage was deemed completed after two result pushpins inside a designated area (a rectangle frame) had been tapped. We opted for marked regions rather than specific location names because we could not assume all of our participants were familiar with the geography of Switzerland. Furthermore, since we were using external map APIs, we had no control over the returned results and so we could not rely on fixed, expected correct answers in our protocol.

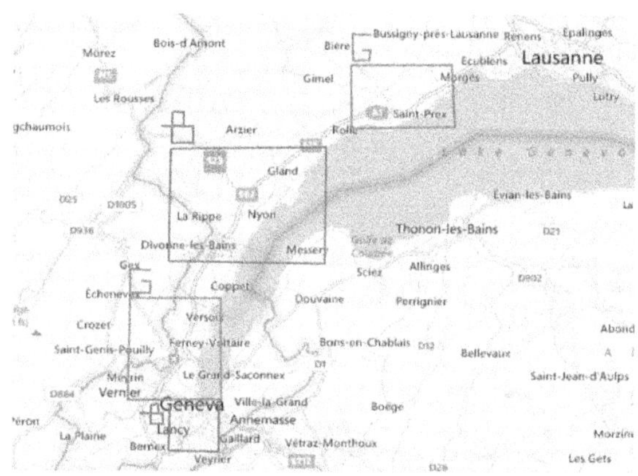

Figure 5: Example of a sequence with the query pattern ABAB. The type of POI to search for is denoted by the border colour and the adjacent letter (here 'G' for "Garage" and 'B' for "Bank")

The steps for a study participant to complete a given stage were: navigate to the target area (using classic multitouch gestures), perform a spatial query (with the pen or the virtual keyboard) and tap two pushpins located inside the area (with touch). To achieve a good balance between map navigation and querying interactions, while at the same time keeping the chain of operations clear and straightforward for participants, we included 4 such stages per sequence. Furthermore, as annotation re-use was a key feature of our techniques that we wanted to investigate, we constructed those sequences following different query repetition patterns, where the type of the POI to be searched was varied. Our three patterns were: 1) no repetition, that is, a different

[1] http://cintiqcompanion.wacom.com/CintiqCompanion/en
[2] http://www.myscript.com
[3] https://developers.google.com/places
[4] http://msdn.microsoft.com/en-us/library/ff701713.aspx

type of POI for each query (pattern ABCD), 2) 2 alternating types (pattern ABAB) and 3) a single type reused throughout the sequence (pattern AAAA). Figure 5 shows an example of the alternating query pattern ABAB. We produced 3 sequences for each pattern type, which means a full trial for a given technique consisted of 3 patterns × 3 sequences/pattern × 4 queries/sequence = 36 queries in total. At the beginning of each sequence, the map view was reset so that the whole of Switzerland was visible with the 4 different frames of the stages. The interface remained frozen until a button was pressed to initiate the start of the subtask. The sequence ended upon selection of the second pushpin of the 4th stage.

As per the within-subjects design, our participants carried out the tasks using our 3 querying techniques as well as with our keyboard-based control environment. The keyboard used for that condition was the standard Windows 8 virtual keyboard and the UI was as similar as possible to the regular Google Maps tablet application. In particular, it also integrated the query auto-complete feature to potentially save typing time when matching suggestions appear.

Participants

For our study we recruited 16 volunteers, 11 males and 5 females aged between 20 and 38 years old, among the students and staff of our university. The pre-study questionnaires asking people about their personal experiences with map applications and tablets revealed that save for one person, who used a local provider, all participants were regular users of Google Maps. The distribution among device type was fairly even, as 12 people reported they used map services on desktop PCs and 13 on mobile devices. Regarding familiarity with digital styli, 6 participants mentioned they had never used one before, 9 were occasional users and 1 was a regular user.

Participants performed the tasks in the 4 conditions successively. To mitigate biases, the order in which the techniques were used was rotated among participants following a Latin square. People were given ample time to train on mock tasks using each technique prior to engaging with the real trials. Regarding the speed at which participants were supposed to carry out the tasks, they were instructed to execute them at a pace that felt natural and comfortable, as if they were using a map application for real searching tasks. After a set of tasks with a given technique was completed, participants were briefly interviewed and asked for feedback about the technique they had just tested. At the end of a full session, a more extensive interview was conducted, where participants were given the chance to provide comparative criticism. They were also handed a post-study questionnaire to rate various aspects of the techniques on Likert scales. For quantitative analysis, we logged all low-level input events with their time stamps as well as entered characters and issued queries. In total, therefore, we recorded data for 16 participants × 4 conditions × 36 queries/condition = 2304 queries.

Environment

Our study environment consisted of the Wacom tablet placed horizontally on a table with participant and experimenter sitting on opposite sides. We opted for this setting, because we thought it was the most likely configuration in which a tablet would be used for a pen-based planning task of moderate duration. A second intention was to remain close to fixed tabletop conditions so that to a certain extent our results could be extrapolated to those devices.

Results

Task Completion Times

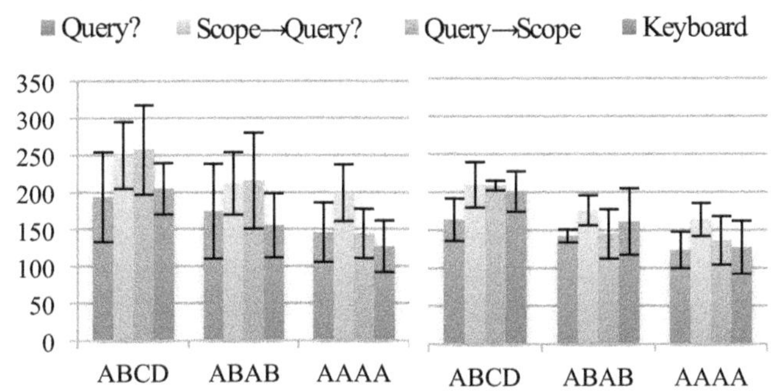

Figure 6: Average task completion times in sec. for all participants (left) and for participants with the fewest mistakes (right). Error bars indicate standard deviation.

We consider first the task completion times for each of the three querying patterns. Those results are shown in Figure 6 (left). As we can see, participants generally seem to have taken more time, on average, with the techniques requiring explicit scope input, which makes sense, as additional pen actions were required. This observation is true for all techniques and querying patterns, except for one case, namely AAAA with *QUERY→SCOPE*, which appears to have performed equally well as *QUERY?*. As for the keyboard condition, it seems to be mostly on a par with *QUERY?*. The large standard deviations, however, hint at considerable disparities among participants and so statistical analysis is necessary to determine which differences are significant.

One-way repeated ANOVAs performed on the data for the 3 patterns all exhibited significant effects at the $p < 0.05$ level ([$F_{ABCD}(3, 45) = 5.994$, $p = 0.006$], [$F_{ABAB}(3, 45) = 5.390$, $p = 0.003$] and [$F_{AAAA}(3, 45) = 14.881$, $p < 0.001$]), hence we carried out post-hoc tests with Bonferroni corrections to find out the significantly different pairs.

The results confirm those assumptions. For AAAA, *SCOPE→QUERY?* was significantly slower than the 3 other techniques ($p < 0.001$ in all cases), which is due to users having to locate the query text to reuse and append a question mark to it after having input the scope stroke. *QUERY→SCOPE* here was much more convenient and efficient, as only one query text input and selection action at the beginning sufficed to issue successive search requests for all subsequently entered scopes. This shows the advantage of combining scope input with command triggering in sequences of queries of the same type. However, this becomes a disadvantage with non-repeating patterns as users have to explicitly deselect text they do not want to reuse. Consequently, for ABCD and ABAB, the two spatial querying techniques with explicit scopes perform similarly and are both significantly or almost significantly worse than the virtual keyboard (for ABAB $p < 0.02$ and for ABCD $p \approx 0.05$ for both techniques). As for *QUERY?*, apart from AAAA, we obtain main effects with ABCD and *SCOPE→QUERY?* ($p < 0.048$), which we mainly attribute to the standard deviation obtained for that technique that happens to be low enough to pass the 0.05 threshold.

As stated above, the variations between those completion times are relatively large. From our observations of participants executing the tasks during the study, we surmised that this heterogeneity could be due to errors and the resultant corrections they had to make, especially when the handwritten text was not properly recognised. A look at the logs confirmed that presumption: despite training, a number of people had more trouble achieving the required handwriting quality for correct interpretation by the recogniser.

To explore how far mistakes might have had an impact, we decided to extract and compare the completion times of participants who made no or only very few errors for each query pattern. Thus, we culled the results of people who deleted at most 3 strokes for the pen techniques and 2 characters with the keyboard. We ended up with 4 or 5 data points for the pen techniques and 10 or more for the keyboard (people made more errors with the former than the latter). We present the updated chart in Figure 6 (right) but we refrain from making any statistical comparisons, since we have unequal numbers of data points corresponding to different participants. Nevertheless, we can see from the chart that the pen techniques seem to have improved performances and that the spread among participants is reduced compared to the keyboard. In numbers, the pen techniques show a 20% improvement on average, whereas completion times for the keyboard remain the same. For the standard deviation, the reductions are between 40% and 56%, i.e. even greater. For *QUERY?* with the ABCD pattern, the performance increase is such that the technique appears to be more efficient than the keyboard.

While not very rigorous, these indicators suggest that the room for improvement with the pen techniques is greater than with the onscreen keyboard. This is not surprising, considering people are used to keyboards, physical or virtual, compared to handwriting queries. Even though we provided training time to our participants to become acquainted with our pen-based querying techniques, it was evidently not sufficient.

We would also like to emphasise again at this point that the pen techniques come with the additional benefit of allowing users to specify scopes for their queries, something which is not possible with the keyboard-based interface. In essence, therefore, there is some evidence that our pen techniques can be at least as efficient as the keyboard, while also providing relevant added value to the user, not to mention the ability to freely annotate maps.

Subjective Suitability of the Query Techniques

We finally turn our attention to the subjective evaluation of the suitability of our querying techniques for each task pattern as perceived by our participants. Their ratings are shown in Figure 7.

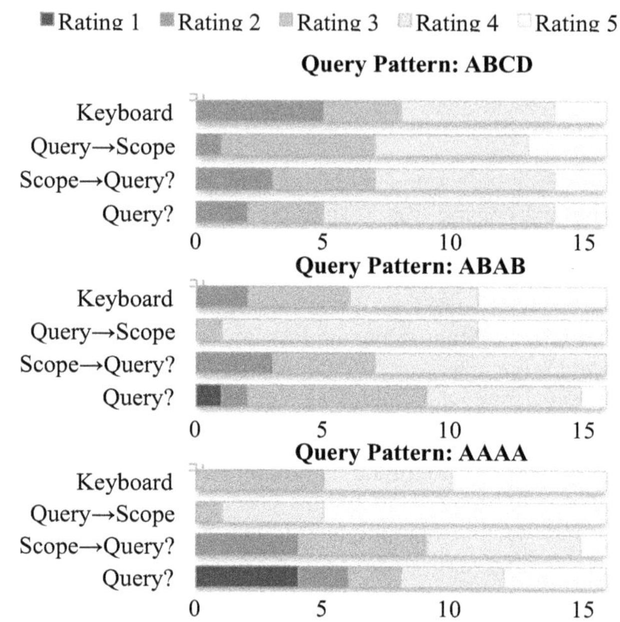

Figure 7: Ratings by the 16 participants of the suitability of the querying technique for each task pattern from 1 = completely unsuitable to 5 = perfectly suitable.

Whereas for distinct queries (ABCD), all techniques seem to be relatively equivalent in terms of suitability, when query repetitions are involved, *QUERY?* and to a lesser extent *SCOPE→QUERY?* were considered less adequate, even though for *QUERY* with AAAA, the opinions are very diverse. Those tendencies are statistically confirmed by Friedman and post-hoc Wilcoxon signed-rank tests, where we found statistically significant differences for ABAB ($\chi^2(3) = 10.748$, $p = 0.013$) and AAAA ($\chi^2(3) = 11.844$, $p = 0.008$) but none for ABCD ($\chi^2(3) = 1.524$, $p = 0.677$). In the first two cases, *QUERY?* and *SCOPE→QUERY?* were judged significantly less suitable than *QUERY→ SCOPE* ($p < 0.01$ in all cases).

With respect to the keyboard, the p-values for the two techniques in AAAA are above the Bonferroni-corrected threshold of 0.0125 (respectively $p = 0.080$ and $p = 0.03$). Interestingly, for the keyboard vs. *QUERY→ SCOPE* we obtain $p = 0.038$, which is, again, above the modified threshold. Bonferroni is a relatively conservative correction, however, and there might be a significant difference in those cases as well. This assumption is also supported by the feedback given by participants, who expressed that they generally preferred the keyboard and *QUERY→ SCOPE* over the two other pen techniques for repeated queries. This is not all too surprising, as for our repeated query tasks, the re-used element was the query text and so the pen technique allowing that parameter to be fixed at the beginning was understandably judged to be more convenient. For *SCOPE→QUERY?* and *QUERY?* on the other hand, participants had to locate the handwritten query text in order to append the query-triggering question mark, often after dragging the ink to a desirable position on the map.

Overall, the most favoured spatial querying technique with the pen was *QUERY→ SCOPE*, especially for searches where the query text was re-used for several regions. It is interesting to note that it is not necessarily the most efficient pen technique, especially in non-repeated query patterns where *QUERY?* is quicker. The latter technique was in fact the least liked among our participants, which overwhelmingly expressed they preferred to be able to explicitly specify regions and paths and thus be in control of both query parameters.

Beside misinterpreted handwriting, the main criticism voiced by users regarding *QUERY→ SCOPE* is that they had to remember to deselect annotations if they did not want to re-use them in subsequent queries. This is a general design issue when dealing with mode switching, where a decision has to be made whether a switch should apply only to the next action or be maintained until explicitly cancelled by the user [11]. Depending on what the typical target usage pattern of such a technique is, annotations can remain continuously active for successive commands after selection or be automatically deselected after a scope stroke has been input. Our intention here was to favour repeated re-use and so our design adopted the former behaviour.

A further general limitation of our pen techniques pointed out by our participants is the necessity to find inked query terms on the map to be able to re-use them. This especially caused extra effort when a single annotation was re-used for repeated queries in several different regions, as in patterns ABAB and AAAA. Our participants dealt with this problem in two ways: the majority (12 people) inked the query terms in a strategic location that was close enough to all target regions. Those participants mainly operated at a low zoom level to be able to view the whole area of interest and thus minimise the need to navigate the map. The other 4 participants adopted the alternative strategy of writing query terms in the direct proximity of generally magnified target regions and moving the ink between the different zones. In those cases, users had a better visibility of each stage area, but more navigation effort was required. To alleviate this problem, two participants suggested that the application should include a proxy widget such as a button to facilitate query term re-use. We initially considered integrating such a feature, but we eventually decided against it because we deemed that annotations pertaining to particular locations would be entered in their vicinity so that a need to re-use terms for places that are far apart would not arise. This is similar to how people would annotate paper maps, where an annotation would most likely be re-written if it is relevant to two distant areas. Another reason for not integrating buttons is that it would go against the philosophy of a plain widget-less and mostly ink-based interface.

With regard to the matter of temporal precedence of query text vs. scope input, we did not record any strong preference for one or the other order from our participants, when the situation did not dictate that one type of parameter should be entered first. The suitability ratings for the ABCD pattern do not point to a clear winner, nor did participants express any particular partiality when explicitly asked about that matter during the interviews. Thus, we presume that the parameter order is mostly driven by context or associated mode [21] rather than cognitive predispositions.

ENHANCEMENTS AND FUTURE WORK

Following our study, we identified several avenues to improve and extend our techniques, based on our observations and the feedback obtained from our participants. We present some of those ideas here, one of which has already been realised.

Our application currently only supports direct pointer-based input for pushpins, which means users need to know exactly where to place their markers. This behaviour is again modelled on physical paper map interaction. The ability to enter unknown addresses or geocodes is however a very compelling feature of standard map services and we think addresses could also be handwritten with the stylus. Should such an inked address be inserted directly on the map, the system would need to transfer the text to the correct location upon detection. Automatic note transfer or duplication could also be a solution to the ink positioning re-use problem mentioned above. On the other hand, such schemes would also introduce a loss of control for users as they would no longer always directly input or manipulate their ink.

Our techniques were mainly designed to address three query input situations: direct entry, re-use of existing scope(s) with a new query term and the re-use of existing query term(s) with new scope. The case, where several existing scopes and terms are included in the query parameters is not supported. Thus, to handle this condition, we created a fourth technique *(SCOPE|QUERY)+→?* which enables users to select any number of annotations of any type and then trigger the query by writing a question mark anywhere on the map. When the mark is entered, all selected terms are aggregated and the compound queries executed in each of the selected scopes, thereby allowing multiple annotations to be flexibly re-used in arbitrary combinations.

The conversion of annotations could be further enhanced by introducing some level of natural language processing (NLP) to understand notes. Currently, recognised text is sent as is to the map service API, which forces users to write queries directly in their annotations. To allow more natural and casual annotating as when people plan trips on paper maps, the system could attempt to interpret annotations and automatically derive appropriate queries, e.g. a note saying "stop here for lunch" would trigger a search for restaurants etc. Some of the multimodal systems described in the literature integrate NLP-based functionality with varying breadths of supported vocabulary and interpretation power. Those NLP engines are often built on top of specialised or closed GIS, which limits their capabilities. We think it would be interesting to design an NLP layer that hooks into widespread consumer map APIs such as Google Places or Bing Maps, which, incidentally already include some level of support for queries entered in natural language.

As acknowledged above, there is much improvement potential for our ink type segmentation and classification. The focus of this work was not on shape or gesture recognition and so we opted for an easy method to differentiate between strokes defining scopes, text and gestures, i.e. using spatial-temporal proximity of ink clusters and other simple metrics. Our participants were instructed on how to make sure their strokes were properly classified and recognised. A more robust implementation based on smarter segmentation algorithms would alleviate those constraints and might also possibly further reduce query input times.

Finally, while we mostly tested our techniques on a 13.3″ Wacom tablet, we believe they are also applicable to larger interactive surfaces such as digital tabletops. With their greater screen real estate, even, we think some of the problems identified in our study (specifically the issue of scattered notes that need to be located) would be mitigated and therefore we think those devices would make interesting platforms for future deployments and experiments. As for future studies, further and perhaps more open trials that more closely follow real planning scenarios on maps will be needed to substantiate the advantages of scope-constrained spatial querying.

CONCLUSION

In this paper we tackled the problem of spatial querying geographical data on pen and touch devices. We proposed a set of techniques to selectively re-use annotations inked on an interactive map to issue queries constrained by explicitly or implicitly set scopes. We showed how our techniques could be utilised in trip-planning scenarios, in which users search for points of interests within custom regions or along paths (hand-drawn or based on computed routes). The controlled user study revealed the potential of our stylus-driven techniques and we hope our results, along with our suggestions to take this work further, will encourage and inspire future endeavours on pen-driven geographical systems.

REFERENCES

1. GlobalWebIndex Device Report Q2 2014.
2. Blaser, A. D. and Egenhofer, M. J. A visual tool for querying geographic databases. In *Proc. AVI '00*, 211-216.
3. Brandl, P., Forlines, C., Wigdor, D., Haller, M. and Shen, C. Combining and measuring the benefits of bimanual pen and direct-touch interaction on horizontal interfaces. In *Proc. AVI 2008*, 154-161.
4. Cheyer, A. and Julia, L. Multimodal maps: An agent-based approach. In *Multimodal Human-Computer Communication*, 1374, (1998), 111-121.
5. Cohen, P. R., Johnston, M., McGee, D., Oviatt, S., Pittman, J., Smith, I., Chen, L. and Clow, J. QuickSet: multimodal interaction for distributed applications. In *Proc. MULTIMEDIA '97*, 31-40.
6. Doyle, J., Bertolotto, M. and Wilson, D. A Survey of Multimodal Interfaces for Mobile Mapping Applications. In *Map-based Mobile Services*, (2008), 146-167.
7. Ehlen, P. and Johnston, M. Multimodal interaction patterns in mobile local search. In *Proc. IUI '12*, 21-24.
8. Ferri, F., Grifoni, P. and Rafanelli, M. Querying by Sketch Geographical Databases and Ambiguities. In *Database and Expert Systems Applications*, 3588, (2005), 524-533.
9. Forbus, K. D., Usher, J. and Chapman, V. Qualitative spatial reasoning about sketch maps. *AI magazine*, 25, 3 (2004), 61-72.
10. Hamilton, W., Kerne, A. and Robbins, T. High-performance pen + touch modality interactions: a real-time strategy game eSports context. In *Proc. UIST 2012*, 309-318.
11. Hinckley, K., Baudisch, P., Ramos, G. and Guimbretiere, F. Design and analysis of delimiters for selection-action pen gesture phrases in scriboli. In *Proc. CHI '05*, 451-460.
12. Hinckley, K., Yatani, K., Pahud, M., Coddington, N., Rodenhouse, J., Wilson, A., Benko, H. and Buxton, B. Pen + touch = new tools. In *Proc. UIST 2010*, 27-36.
13. Hinckley, K., Zhao, S., Sarin, R., Baudisch, P., Cutrell, E., Shilman, M. and Tan, D. InkSeine: In Situ search for active note taking. In *Proc. CHI 2007*, 251-260.
14. Hui, P.-Y. and Meng, H. M. Joint interpretation of input speech and pen gestures for multimodal human-computer interaction. In *Proc. INTERSPEECH 2006*, 1197-1200.
15. Hurtig, T. A mobile multimodal dialogue system for public transportation navigation evaluated. In *Proc. MobileHCI '06*, 251-254.
16. Johnston, M., Bangalore, S., Vasireddy, G., Stent, A., Ehlen, P., Walker, M., Whittaker, S. and Maloor, P. MATCH: an architecture for multimodal dialogue systems. In *Proc. ACL '02*, 376-383.
17. Jokinen, K. User Interaction in Mobile Navigation Applications. In *Map-based Mobile Services*, (2008), 168-197.
18. Krüger, A., Butz, A., Müller, C., Stahl, C., Wasinger, R., Steinberg, K.-E. and Dirschl, A. The connected user interface: realizing a personal situated navigation service. In *Proc. IUI '04*, 161-168.
19. Matulic, F. and Norrie, M. Pen and Touch Gestural Environment for Document Editing on Interactive Tabletops. In *Proc. ITS 2013*, 41-50.
20. Oviatt, S., DeAngeli, A. and Kuhn, K. Integration and synchronization of input modes during multimodal human-computer interaction. In *Proc. CHI '97*, 415-422.
21. Silva, G. C. d. and Aizawa, K. Retrieving multimedia travel stories using location data and spatial queries. In *Proc. MM '09*, 785-788.
22. Vogel, D., Cudmore, M., Casiez, G., Balakrishnan, R. and Keliher, L. Hand occlusion with tablet-sized direct pen input. In *Proc. CHI '09*, 557-566.
23. Willems, D. J. and Vuurpijl, L. G. Pen gestures in online map and photograph annotation tasks. In *Proc. IWFHR 2006*, 297-402.

Surface Ghosts: Promoting Awareness of Transferred Objects during Pick-and-Drop Transfer in Multi-Surface Environments

Stacey D. Scott[1,2], Guillaume Besacier[1,2,3], Julie Tournet[1,2,4], Nippun Goyal[1], Michael Haller[5]
[1]Systems Design Engineering and [2]Games Institute, University of Waterloo, Waterloo, Ontario, Canada;
[3]CITU Paragraphe (EA349), Université Paris 8, Saint-Denis, France; [4]Télécom Bretagne, Brest, France;
[5]Media Interaction Lab, University of Applied Sciences Upper Austria, Hagenberg Austria.
{stacey.scott|guillaume.besacier|julie.tournet|nippun.goyal}@uwaterloo.ca, michael.haller@fh-hagenberg.at

Figure 1. Pick-and-Drop transfer on a multi-surface environment with no visual feedback (left), with Surface Ghosts visual feedback with implicit ownership (middle), and with Surface Ghost visual feedback with explicit ownership (right).

ABSTRACT
Rekimoto's *Pick-and-Drop* (P&D) transfer technique is commonly used to support multi-surface object transfer (e.g., between a shared tabletop and tablet) due to its easily understood metaphor of emulating object movement in the physical world. Current multi-surface implementations of P&D provide little to no feedback during transfer, causing confusion for the person performing the action as well as others in the environment. To address this issue, we investigated the use of virtual embodiments to improve awareness of transferred objects, in the context of a real-world group task that relied heavily on cross-device transfer. An iterative design process led to the design of *Surface Ghosts* virtual embodiments, which take the form of semi-transparent "ghosts" of the transferred objects displayed under the "owner's" hand on the tabletop during transfer. A user study that compared two Surface Ghosts designs—varied by how explicitly the "owner" was indicated—showed that both designs improved awareness of transferred objects when compared to a no-feedback control condition, especially for *tabletop-to-tablet* transfers.

ITS '14, November 16–19, 2014, Dresden, Germany.

ACM 978-1-4503-2587-5/14/11...$15.00
http://dx.doi.org/10.1145/2669485.2669508

Author Keywords
Cross device transfer; digital tabletops; tablets; multi-surface interaction; shared and personal surfaces

INTRODUCTION
Multi-surface environments require efficient mechanisms to move digital content across surfaces. For instance, a person may wish to share a sketch by moving it from a personal tablet to a shared tabletop. Cross-device transfer techniques exist that enable transfer across multiple displays [1, 23]. Rekimoto's [27] Pick-and-Drop (P&D) technique, which enables a user to "pick" up a virtual object from one device and "drop" it onto another device, is used by many large- and multi-surface researchers due to its easily understood metaphor that emulates familiar object movement in the physical world [14, 26, 28]. P&D's point-to-point design provides highly efficient transfers and enables context-dependent automated state changes of dropped objects. For instance, a dropped playing card can be automatically rotated or placed face-up or face-down depending on the drop location. This minimizes adjustments the user must make after transfer, allowing them to focus on the task.

A shortcoming of P&D is that transferred objects are often *invisible* during the transfer process [14, 27, 28]. In previous work [28], we compared P&D with other transfer techniques in a multi-user, multi-surface environment. We found this lack of visual feedback caused confusion during P&D transfer, both for the person performing the transfer (the "owning" user) and for others in the environment. Our previous experiences using P&D for transfer on a pen-based interactive wall [15], have shown some users expect similar behaviour to the common *drag-and-drop* technique and, thus, become confused when objects disappear during P&D

transfer. They then retry the action, thereby dropping the object in its initial location. This causes the objects to "flicker" on the surface, further confusing the user.

To address these usability issues of P&D, we explored the use of virtual embodiments [5, 12, 32, 34] to increase awareness of transferred objects. To improve ecological validity of our research, we situated our investigations in the context of a real-world group task that relied heavily on object transfer between shared and personal spaces, namely a commercial competitive strategic card game. Within this context, it became apparent that existing virtual embodiment approaches for representing transferred objects, such as casting a shadow from the transferred object [27] or displaying only its shadow [16, 18], were either too subtle or lacked distinguishing details of different application content to provide sufficient awareness information during P&D transfer.

These insights, along with inspiration from existing approaches [9, 12, 16, 25, 34], led to the design of the *Surface Ghosts* virtual embodiments, which take the form of "ghosted" semi-transparent representations of transferred objects displayed on the tabletop during P&D transfer. Surface Ghosts provide prominent and information-rich visual feedback specifically designed to improve awareness of transferred objects in multi-user, multi-surface settings.

The main contributions of this work include:

- the first in-depth study of P&D in a multi-user, multi-surface setting and in the context of a real-world task that depends on frequent cross-device transfer,
- the Surface Ghosts design, which improves on existing approaches for representing transferred objects in subtle, yet important, ways for the studied context, and
- empirical evidence that two evaluated Surface Ghosts design alternatives, which provided either implicit or explicit feedback of the "owning" user, both improved awareness of transferred objects during P&D transfer.

RELATED WORK

Object Transfer across Large Surfaces

A variety of drag-and-drop-style extensions have been developed for transfer across large surfaces, including techniques that drop an object onto a distant folder or location [3, 6-8, 15]. Other techniques leverage the direct-touch nature of large surfaces, such as flick or toss gestures that move objects across a display surface [37, 38]. Pick-and-Drop [27] has also been used for transfer on digital pen-based wall and tabletop surfaces [14], and was found to be more efficient than drag-and-drop in these contexts [26]. Another approach is to move objects from one surface location to another by using virtual "portals," where objects placed on a portal in one location then appears on a corresponding portal in another location [4, 35].

Object Transfer across Multiple Devices

Existing cross-device transfer techniques generally fall into three main categories. *Contiguous virtual workspace* techniques utilize the physical configuration of adjacent displays to facilitate transfer. Dragging, flicking, or pouring an object off the edge of one display moves it onto the (physically and virtually) adjacent display [2, 17, 18, 21, 24, 30]. The *virtual portals* technique mentioned above can also be used to transfer objects across devices when portals are located on different devices [1, 11, 18 28]. Finally, *physical proxy* techniques enable more dynamic device mapping by virtually binding the transferred object to a physical object (proxy), which can then be moved to any destination device [30]. P&D uses this approach, where the transferred object is bound/unbound to a digital pen.

P&D in Touch-based, Multi-Surface Environments

Touch-based multi-surface environments present several challenges for implementing P&D. No digital pen is available to serve as the proxy. Our existing *Adapted Pick-and-Drop* (A-P&D) technique [28] addressed this issue by, metaphorically, using the user's hand as the physical proxy between a shared tabletop and personal tablet surfaces. Dedicated personal areas were provided on the tabletop surface for each user, where any pick or drop would be associated to the "owning" user, enabling simultaneous, multi-user transfers. In a study comparing A-P&D to a virtual portals technique, we found A-P&D to be more efficient, but that its lack of visual feedback of transferred objects introduced confusion and errors.

This work uses a similar multi-touch P&D technique (i.e. the user's hand serves as the proxy for transferred content). However in this work, P&D can be initiated anywhere on the tabletop via above-the-surface sensing capabilities that differentiates between users. We also extend our earlier work by introducing visual feedback, in the form of the Surface Ghosts virtual embodiments, during P&D transfer.

Virtual Embodiment Techniques

Virtual embodiments are visual representations of users' presence, location, and actions in a shared workspace [13, 22, 29]. Virtual embodiments have typically been used to promote workspace awareness [13] during remote collaboration, for example, providing a telepointer to represent a remote collaborator's cursor in a shared whiteboard application or showing a virtual avatar for a remote teammate in a virtual world game. Recently, they have been used in co-located tabletop environments, for instance, to promote awareness of indirect interactions in a tabletop workspace [9, 25] and interactions above a 3-dimensional tabletop [16]. Two specific types of embodiments are most relevant to this work: embodiments that represent virtual objects being held "above" or "outside of" an interactive surface (object embodiments), and embodiments that represent users' physical actions above an interactive surface (user embodiments).

Object embodiments

Rekimoto's original P&D technique displayed a temporary virtual embodiment of a transferred object when the digital pen hovered (within millimeters) of the target display. The

(a) (b) (c)

Figure 2. Object embodiment techniques: (a) shadow casting, (b) silhouette shadow, and (c) Surface Ghost embodiment.

embodiment showed the transferred object casting a grey shadow on the display (Figure 2a) to indicate the object was still "above the display". Hinckley et al. [18] utilized a "shadow" object embodiment to represent objects being remotely copied between adjacent tablet displays using their Stitching technique. This shadow embodiment displayed a plain, filled silhouette (Figure 2b) of the remote object on the target display before the copy operation was confirmed. Hilliges et al. [16] utilized a similar silhouette-based shadow to represent virtual objects that have been "lifted" off of a 3-dimensional tabletop workspace.

As illustrated in Figure 2a, Rekimoto's shadow casting embodiment provides very subtle feedback of the object's state. As tabletops commonly use dark backgrounds this feedback could be overlooked. Similarly, a "natural" (i.e. dark) silhouette shadow could also be easily missed. Also, this approach provides little distinguishing information about the transferred object when most or all application content is the same size and shape, such as in a digital card game. As discussed below, our Surface Ghosts embodiment (Figure 2c) builds on these existing designs by providing the content details provided by the shadow casting approach but in a more obvious non-active, "above-the-display" visual representation, like the silhouette shadow.

User embodiments

Virtual embodiments have also been used extensively in distributed surface environments to represent remote collaborators' above-the-surface interactions, especially their gestures above the surface [5, 10, 12, 34]. These embodiments commonly take the form of a filled or empty silhouette shadow of the remote user's body [10] or arms [34]. Tang et al.'s VideoArms technique [33] projected raw video feed of remote users' arms on top of silhouette arm shadow embodiments to help distinguish between multiple remote collaborators.

Various forms of virtual arm embodiments, from silhouette shadows to minimal stylized versions, have been explored to promote awareness of co-located collaborators' indirect interactions on a shared tabletop [9, 25]. Doucette et al.'s [9] study of virtual arm embodiments in this context found that more obtrusive (i.e. opaque, large, or permanent) arm embodiments provided more awareness of others' actions, but also restricted cross-table interactions. One version of the Surface Ghosts design uses silhouette shadow arm embodiments attached to the Surface Ghost object embodiment to clearly indicate the "owning" user.

USABILITY PROBLEMS AND DESIGN REQUIREMENTS

As aforementioned, P&D has been previously shown [15, 28] to have usability problems, especially for multi-user, multi-surface contexts. To help articulate these problems, Figure 3 illustrates the three phases of the P&D process—Pick, Transfer, and Drop—in the context of a shared tabletop and multiple personal tablets, the particular multi-surface configuration of interest in our work. Providing highly usable and effective P&D interaction requires careful design at each stage.

Our earlier work [28] found that P&D without visual feedback was cognitively demanding for users, as they were required to keep track of objects "in the aether", as described by their study participants. Thus, we focused primarily on improving the Transfer Phase (and somewhat on the transitions between the Transfer Phase and the Pick and Drop Phases to create a smooth user experience).

With this focus in mind, we identified the following design requirements for the Transfer Phase:

R1. Provide *persistent* feedback of transferred objects,
R2. Clearly indicate the type of transferred objects, and
R3. Clearly indicate the number of transferred objects.
R4. Clearly indicate who is transferring the object(s).

When multiple people are utilizing personal tablets at a shared tabletop, especially when seated, they tend to position their tablets directly along the edge of the tabletop for ready access and ergonomic comfort. This configuration results in the Transfer Phase occurring largely over the tabletop, whether transfer originates from the tabletop or from the tablet, as indicated in Figure 3. Thus, providing visual feedback of the transferred object on the tabletop during transfer satisfies our requirement to provide persistent feedback (R1). We initially explored various forms of virtual embodiment techniques described above, including silhouette shadow approaches. Through an iterative design process, however, we found that these approaches did not adequately satisfy our design requirements. Initial tests re-

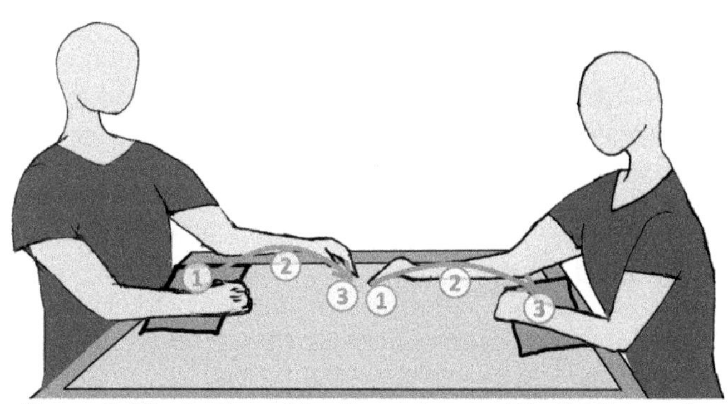

Figure 3. Illustration of the three phases of the P&D transfer process: (1) Pick, (2) Transfer, and (3) Drop, for tabletop to tablet (left) and tablet to tabletop (right) P&D transfers.

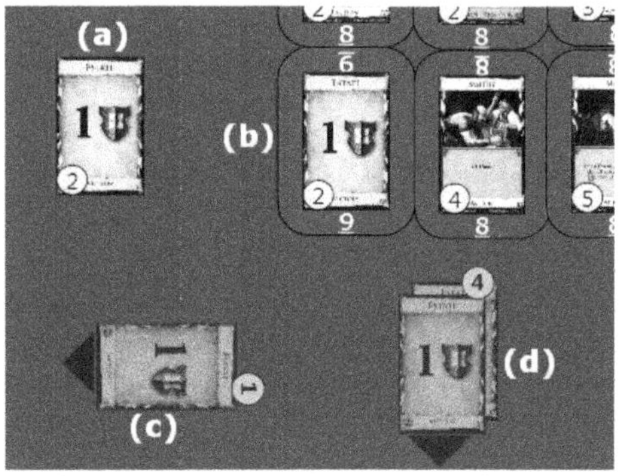

Figure 4. Surface Ghosts in the context of a tabletop card game: (a) a normal card, (b) a deck of cards (c) a Surface Ghost (with Implicit Ownership feedback) of one card being transferred by the Left Player, and (d) a Surface Ghost of multiple cards being transferred by the Bottom Player.

vealed that realistic representations of an arm shadow (i.e. semi-transparent black) were overlooked, mistaken as actual shadows rather than computer-generated information. Hence, they did not convey the intended awareness information of who was performing the transfer (R4). Similarly, in the card gaming task used in our study, representing transferred objects as silhouette shadows would not convey the necessary information about what type of object (e.g. resource card, treasure card, etc.) is being transferred (R2), since all cards are the same size and shape.

Instead, we determined that the visual feedback needed to be less subtle and more informative. This insight, and further design iterations, led to the development of *Surface Ghosts* object embodiments, described below. This object embodiment is displayed in the tabletop interface directly below the "owner's" hand, to indicate who is performing the transfer (R4). Given the potential for distraction in a multi-user environment, we were not certain that this behavior would be sufficient to strongly satisfy R4. Thus, we developed two versions of Surface Ghosts, which vary in how explicitly they indicate the "owning" user.

SURFACE GHOSTS VISUAL DESIGN

The Surface Ghost object embodiment is displayed as a semi-transparent (transparency level 50%), greyscale version of the transferred object. When multiple objects are being transferred at once, they are stacked together and a counter displays the total number of transferred objects. Figure 4 illustrates the Surface Ghost object embodiment designs for single-object (4c) and multi-object (4d) transfers in a digital card game. During our iterative design process, we explored several visual representations for the multi-card Surface Ghost object embodiment, such as displaying all cards as a fanned out "hand of cards". Ultimately, we found the stack representation better suited to a multi-user setting, as it utilizes a known, minimal, amount of space. Moreover, users in our task context found the number of cards to be the essential information.

Implicit and Explicit Ownership Feedback

In a group task that allows concurrent, multi-user transfers, it becomes important to clearly indicate who is performing each transfer. The Surface Ghost virtual embodiment provides several implicit indications of who "owns" the transferred object: the embodiment is oriented toward its owner, and is displayed beneath the owner's hand, which it follows as they move their hand above the tabletop.

We added one further, yet still subtle, visual indication of ownership in the first Surface Ghosts design alternative we tested, called the Implicit Ownership design. In this version, ownership is further indicated with a large dark arrow attached to the bottom of the Surface Ghost embodiment, which "points" to the owning user (Figure 4(c and d)). The arrow color matches text contained in the Surface Ghost.

In a second version, called the Explicit Ownership design, the black arrow is replaced by a full arm embodiment in the form of a semi-transparent (transparency level 50%) white silhouette of the owner's arm, with the Surface Ghost embodiment displayed in the arm embodiment's hand (Figure 5). The arm embodiment color matches the Surface Ghost's white background color, since, as aforementioned, a dark embodiment often went unnoticed, mistaken for a real shadow by the users. Including the arm embodiment conveys more explicitly who is transferring the object (more strongly satisfying R4), but also requires more elaborate above-the-surface tracking.

Surface Ghosts Dynamics

The Surface Ghosts embodiments, and their associated ownership feedback, are only visible during transfer. To provide a smooth visual transition to and from the Transfer Phase, a fading animation is used during "picks" and "drops", and a brief animation moves (and rotates if necessary) the object from its original position to the center of the user's hand. To realize the Surface Ghosts feedback, persistent tracking of the user's hand position (and arm in the case of Explicit Ownership) above the tabletop is needed. To accomplish this, we use Genest et al.'s [12] KinectArms toolkit that enables tracking of multiple users' hand

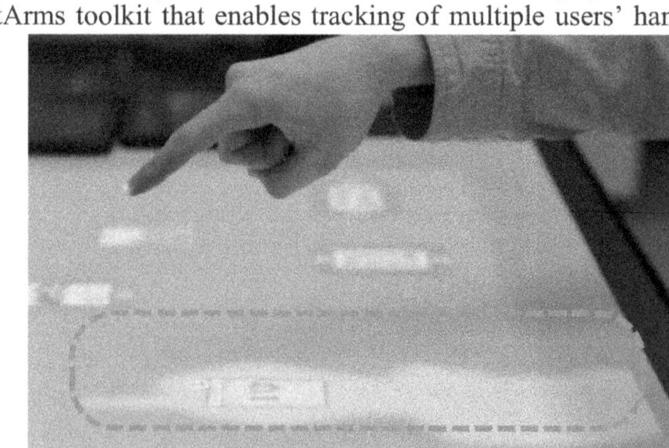

Figure 5. Surface Ghosts with Explicit Ownership in a tabletop card game context.

and arm interactions above a table via a Microsoft Kinect[1] depth sensor mounted above a table. We customized this toolkit to identify the user associated with each detected arm, based on the user's known location[2] at the table. Realizing the Surface Ghosts feedback and relies on the user identification and above-the-table tracking information in order to correctly bind transferred objects to the correct user's hand and to provide persistent feedback of the transferred object during simultaneous P&D transfers. In addition, the Explicit Ownership design uses the KinectArm's arm tracking data to project the arm embodiment on the tabletop during transfer.

USER STUDY

To evaluate the effect of Surface Ghosts on awareness of transferred objects during P&D transfers, we conducted a within-subjects user study in which groups played a digital implementation of the commercial card game *Dominion*[3].

Participants

Twenty-one participants (17 male, 4 female, ages 20-38) were recruited from a local university. Participants performed the study in groups of three. To promote natural group behaviour, participants signed-up with their friends as a group, with the additional requirement that each person had prior experience playing the *Dominion* game.

Equipment and Setting

The study took place in a university laboratory, which contained a digital tabletop, described below, surrounded by three adjustable chairs. Three laptops were set-up on nearby desks for administration of study questionnaires.

The digital tabletop was a custom-built laser light plane (LLP) table that provided a surface area of 130x90cm with a 1200x800 rear-projected display. The open-source toolkit Community Core Vision (CCV)[4] was used to process touch input on the table. User identification of tabletop touches and of above-the-table arm movements was obtained using a Microsoft Kinect mounted 1.5m above the digital table and an adapted version of the KinectArm toolkit [12]. Participants used 7-inch Samsung Galaxy Tab tablets as their private displays. Communication between the tabletop and tablets occurred via a local Wi-Fi network.

Participants tabletop and tablet interactions were video- and audio-taped. The software recorded detailed interaction logs as well as a continuous screen capture. Finally, researchers observed the sessions from the back of the room.

Experimental task: Dominion card game

Participants played the *Dominion* card game, which is a strategic, competitive card game that uses specialized decks of cards and requires players to employ elaborate strategies to expand their respective "kingdoms" and win the game. *Dominion* was selected as a task for studying P&D transfer because it requires a significant amount of card movement between shared decks (located on a table) and each player's private "hand of cards". Also, *Dominion* is a popular card game, which facilitates recruitment of expert users. Finally, similar strategic gaming contexts have been shown to elicit a high level of task engagement [28, 36]. The latter two points are important for the ecological validity of laboratory-based studies of interaction techniques, as expert users who become highly engaged in an activity are more likely to exhibit realistic, externally valid, behaviour.

Game play in *Dominion* typically occurs on a turn-by-turn basis, though players can take some actions during other players' turn. In a typical turn, a player draws a minimum of five cards from shared decks, and then makes several card-based actions (e.g. revealing one or more cards to "buy" resources, or discarding unused cards).

In our digital implementation of the *Dominion* game, the shared decks are located on the tabletop, while players' private hands of cards are on their personal tablets (Figure 6). P&D picks are triggered via a contextual menu on the tabletop or an upward swipe gesture (to the top edge of the display) on the tablet. Drops are triggered by a touch gesture on the tabletop or a downward swipe gesture (from the top of the display) on the tablet. Cards dropped on a deck on the table are automatically added on top of the deck, which can be merged or moved as the players see fit.

Participant groups each played *Dominion* in three feedback conditions: a no feedback (NF) control condition, used in our previous work [28]; Surface Ghosts with Implicit Ownership (implicitSG); and Surface Ghosts with Explicit Ownership (explicitSG). The NF condition is also representative of other existing proxy-based P&D techniques, e.g. a "puck" [20] or a set of keys [31], that offered no digital feedback mechanism during transfer.

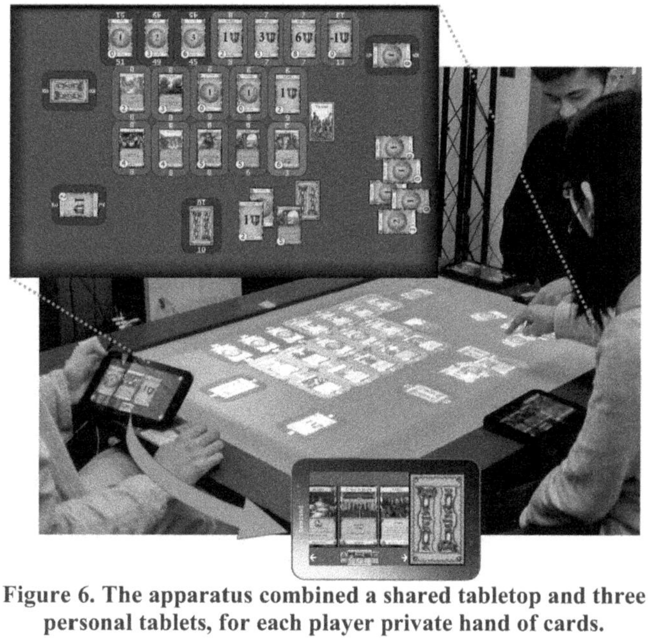

Figure 6. The apparatus combined a shared tabletop and three personal tablets, for each player private hand of cards.

[1] http://www.microsoft.com/en-us/kinectforwindows/
[2] User identification is currently limited to four users, one per table side.
[3] Published by Rio Grande, used with permission.
[4] http://ccv.nuigroup.com/

Procedure

Participants first completed an informed consent form and a background questionnaire. Groups were then given instructions on the digital tabletop and tablet hardware systems, as well as the Dominion gaming interface. Next, they played three sessions of the Dominion game, one with each type of feedback, with the order of presentation of feedback conditions counter-balanced across groups. Each game session lasted between 28-45 minutes, depending on the strategies used by the players. After each game, they completed a post-condition questionnaire eliciting feedback on the design they just experienced. After the final session, participants completed a post-experiment questionnaire gathering comparative feedback on all three conditions, and were thanked and paid for their participation. The study was approved by the university's ethics review board.

Data Analysis

The post-condition questionnaires contained 7-point Likert-scale questions and freeform questions that focused on awareness, effort, and enjoyment. The post-experiment questionnaire gathered ranking information on the three conditions, as well as additional comments from players. Likert-scale questions were analyzed using Friedman tests. Interaction data from the computer logs were analyzed using Repeated-Measures Analysis of Variance (RM-ANOVA). An alpha of α=.05 was used in all tests. One group experienced significant technical errors, and we excluded their data from analyses. The remaining 6 groups (18 participants) still represented a full counter-balance.

Analysis of the video and other qualitative data collected from the study was based on the Interaction Analysis approach [19], where the group of researchers met over several weeks to iteratively review the data and determine emergent themes of interaction behaviour to be further analyzed through coding and basic transcription. Group discussions were used to organize and synthesize the data into the themes presented in this paper.

RESULTS

The data analysis revealed that participants made extensive use of P&D transfer to move cards around during the study. A total of 4455 P&D transfers were performed across all game sessions, with 1541 of these transfers occurring from ***tabletop-to-tablet***, 2344 from ***tablet-to-tabletop***, and 570 between ***two tabletop locations***. The latter transfer type was unexpected and will be discussed further below. The greater number of transfers from tablet to the tabletop was expected due to game mechanics. The study results also revealed that both versions of Surface Ghosts facilitated P&D transfer. The specific impact of these feedback techniques on awareness and system interaction is described below. The study also provided an opportunity to examine the overall P&D process, beyond the feedback mechanisms provided during transfer. This examination revealed that participants adapted and appropriated the provided interaction techniques in unexpected ways to facilitate their system interactions. We expand on these behaviours below.

Impact of Surface Ghosts Visual Feedback

Analysis of the post-experiment questionnaires revealed that 12 out of 18 participants preferred to play the game with Surface Ghosts feedback, while 6 out of 18 preferred the control (NF) condition. Those who preferred Surface Ghosts feedback were evenly split across the implicitSG and explicitSG conditions.

Perceived Awareness of Transferred objects

The post-condition questionnaires included several awareness-related questions to determine how well each feedback design conveyed information about the transferred object. These questions also distinguished between the direction of transfer (tabletop-to-tablet or vice versa). Table 1 summarizes participants' responses.

We first examine participant responses for ***tabletop-to-tablet*** transfers. The analysis revealed a significant difference across conditions of participants' reported awareness of *when they had a card in their hand* during these transfers

Table 1. Perceived awareness of transferred objects during Pick-and-Drop (P&D) transfers between devices.

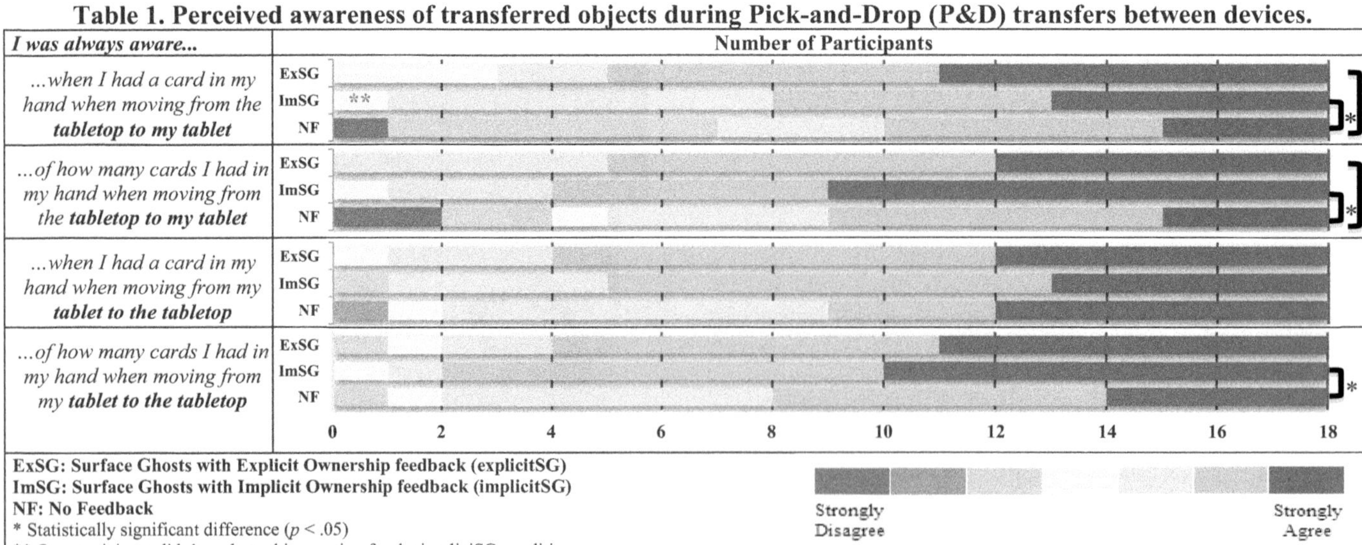

Figure 7. A player using the Surface Ghost counter to keep track of how many cards they have currently picked up.

($\chi^2(2)$=7.127, p=.028). Post-hoc comparisons revealed significant differences between the NF condition and both the implicitSG (p=.028) and explicitSG (p=.014) conditions, with both feedback conditions rating higher (i.e. providing more awareness) than the NF condition. No difference was found between implicitSG and explicitSG (p=.712).

The analysis revealed similar results for participants' reported awareness of *how many cards they had in their hand* during these transfers, with a significant difference across conditions ($\chi^2(2)$=11.160, p=.004), and NF being rated significantly lower than either implicitSG (p=.003) or explicitSG (p=0.022). Again, no significant difference was found between implicitSG and explicitSG (p=.714).

Examination of participants' responses for ***tablet-to-tabletop*** transfers revealed less impact of implicitSG and explicitSG feedback on awareness. No significant differences were found for the first question (*awareness of when they had a card in their hand*), and fewer differences were found for the second question (*how many questions they had in their hand*). For this question, a significant difference was found across conditions ($\chi^2(2)$= 9.63, p=.008), but post-hoc comparisons only revealed a difference between NF and implicitSG (p=.003), with implicitSG being rated higher. No differences were found between NF and explicitSG (p=.131) or implicitSG and explicitSG (p=.160).

Overall these results show that both Surface Ghosts designs were perceived as more effective at promoting awareness of transferred objects during ***tabletop-to-tablet*** transfers than during transfers in the opposite direction (***tablet-to-tabletop***). Examining the video data and participants' free-form questionnaire responses elucidated this inconsistent impact of Surface Ghosts by revealing *how* participants used this visual feedback.

Main Uses of Surface Ghosts Visual Feedback

Our qualitative data analysis revealed that participants primarily used Surface Ghosts to support three aspects of P&D transfer: confirming that a pick or drop worked, keeping track of how many cards were picked up (for themselves and for their opponents), and confirming that picked up cards went to the right player. Most players positioned their tablets along the edge of the tabletop, outside its active surface. Hence, the Surface Ghosts feedback was typically unavailable during picks and drops on the tablet, which likely contributed to the reduced effectiveness of both Surface Ghosts designs for promoting awareness during ***tablet-to-tabletop*** transfers. Next we detail how Surface Ghosts were used to support the aforementioned aspects of P&D transfer.

Confirming "picks" and "drops". A main use of the Surface Ghosts feedback was to confirm that a pick or a drop action worked (primarily on the tabletop). The data revealed that the local animation of the Surface Ghost embodiment "flying" from the card's original location (at the user's fingertip) to under their palm (more robustly tracked) was often used to confirm picks. Also, players commonly shifted their hand and wrist positions during pick actions to facilitate viewing the Surface Ghost embodiment (primarily) or arm embodiment (occasionally) during this pick confirmation process. Similarly, players often double-checked that the Surface Ghosts feedback disappeared after a drop operation. In the control (NF) condition, the lack of feedback often resulted in participants having to redo a whole sequence of actions. When unsuccessful actions occurred in the Surface Ghosts conditions, participants would quickly diagnose the issues, immediately correct it, and then continue with the transfer.

Counting "picks". Players made extensive use of the counter provided on the multi-object Surface Ghost embodiment to keep track of how many cards they had picked up during multi-card transfers, as illustrated in Figure 7 and by the following comment, *"The count showing how many cards have been picked up from the table was useful"* (P14, G5).

In the control (NF) condition, players relied on counters attached to each deck to determine how many cards they had picked up, by tracking how much the number decremented after each pick up. This method was cognitively demanding: counts must be kept in memory, and players must recall the original deck count if distracted during pickups. In contrast, the Surface Ghost counter could be interpreted directly, without mental calculation, and was available if players missed the original pickup actions.

Some players also used the multi-object ghost counter to police opponent player's actions, by monitoring how many cards they were transferring, as illustrated by the comment, *"... without [the Surface Ghost counter] I had a hard time remembering how many cards I had drawn which led me to get distracted. Also difficult to tell [in NF condition] if others are lying/cheating because can't see the number of cards"* (P18, G7).

Confirming ownership of a picked card. Surface Ghosts were also used to confirm that cards on the tabletop were picked up by the right person. Due to technical limitations of above-the-table tracking, user identification was occasionally incorrect when players were interacting in close proximity. When this occurred during pickup, the card(s) would be associated with the wrong user. As part of the pick confirmation behaviour described earlier, players commonly relied on the local animation of the Surface Ghost embodiment to confirm the correct association. Figure 8 illustrates an example where the local object ghost animation helped participants to detect an incorrect association, during simultaneous proximal interactions.

If this animation was missed, the persistent feedback provided by Surface Ghosts embodiments was useful. The Explicit Ownership arm embodiment was particularly useful in diagnosing inaccurate user identification, as evidenced by the comment, *"the ghost hand was occasionally helpful when the software accidentally thought the wrong person picked up a card"* (P5, G1).

System Interactions

To investigate the impact of Surface Ghosts on overall transfer performance, transfer times were calculated using an averaged time that accounted for multi-card transfer situations (where a player picks up multiple cards and then does a single drop for those cards), calculated as follows for an *n*-card transfer:

$$time = \frac{(t_d - t_{p1}) + (t_d - t_{p2}) + \cdots + (t_d - t_{pn})}{n},$$

where t_{p1} represents the time of pick 1, t_{pn} represents the time of pick *n*, t_d, represents the time of the drop.

Analysis of ***tabletop-to-tablet*** transfer times revealed a significant difference across conditions ($F_{2,10}$=5.578, p=.024). Post-hoc comparisons revealed that transfers with explicitSG were significantly slower than with implicitSG (p=.035), by an average of 640 ms. No significant differences were found between explicitSG and NF (p=.196) or between implicitSG and NF (p=1.0). No significant differences were found for ***tablet-to-tabletop*** transfer times ($F_{2,10}$=.793; p=.479) or ***tabletop-to-tabletop*** transfers times ($F_{2,10}$=.214; p=.811).

The delays in tabletop-to-tablet transfers that occurred during the Explicit Ownership condition may have resulted from our approach to displaying the arm embodiment. Since Kinect depth sensor data are low resolution and noisy, we averaged ten image frames (empirically determined to provide a smooth, stable image while still maintaining responsiveness), which introduced a lag of up to 150 ms. This caused the arm embodiment to lag behind a user's physical arm if moved quickly across the table. Thus, players may have waited for their arm ghost "catch up" with their physical arm during transfer. The same averaging approach is used to determine the position of the Surface Ghost embodiment beneath the user's hand, introducing similar repositioning lags, yet the results indicate users were less concerned with the Surface Ghost embodiment maintaining pace with their physical arm position.

Appropriation of P&D for Within-Device Transfers

Analysis of the video and interaction log data also revealed participants unexpectedly appropriated the P&D technique for transferring cards between different tabletop locations, rather than using drag-and-drop transfer. All participants in all conditions exhibited this behaviour. Between 7% (with implicitSG and NF) and 11% (with explicitSG) of all P&D transfers occurred from one tabletop location to another. Participants discovered the use of P&D for within-tabletop transfers spontaneously, often accidentally, during game play. The interaction logs revealed that distance was not a main factor in players' decision to employ P&D transfer for within-tabletop transfers. Players could be seen using drag-and-drop to transfer cards over long distances (including locations beyond their arms' reach), while using P&D to transfer cards over short distances (centimeters away).

DISCUSSION

The results confirmed that both Surface Ghosts design alternatives satisfied our design requirements to promote awareness of the *type and number of objects in transit* (R2 and R3), and of *which user is transferring the objects* (R4) during P&D transfer. They also revealed that Surfaces Ghosts were significantly more effective during P&D transfers originating on the tabletop, compared to those originating on the tablet. Examination of *how* participants used the Surface Ghosts feedback revealed that this asymmetric effect resulted because both Surface Ghosts design inadequately satisfied R1 (*provide persistent feedback during transfer*), as discussed further below. Also, the study revealed that the arm embodiment feedback provided in the Explicit Ownership provided positive error recovery benefits, but negatively impacted transfer times. The implications of these findings are discussed below.

Asymmetric Awareness Benefits

As aforementioned, P&D transfer consists of three phases: *Pick*, *Transfer*, and *Drop*. Surface Ghosts were designed to provide *persistent* user feedback during the Transfer Phase, with the assumption that this phase was where the feedback

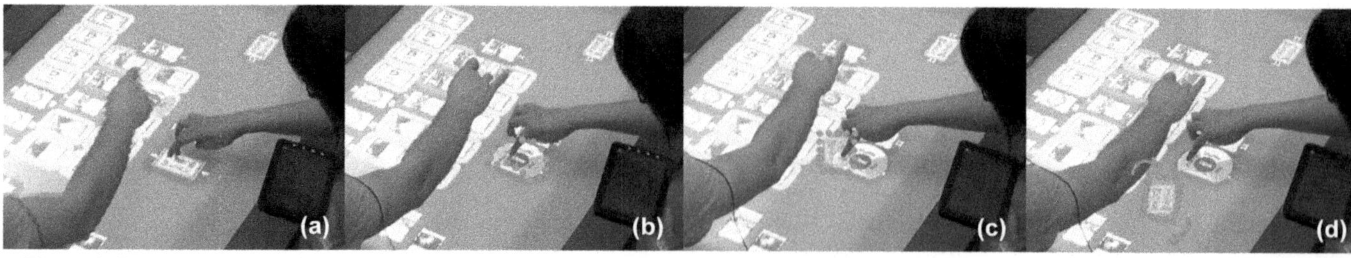

Figure 8. Players using the Surface Ghost animation to recognize that a picked card went to the wrong player: a) Left Player waits to interact near Right Player's hand b) Right Player's *contextual menu* (highlight) is color-coded for, and oriented toward Left Player due to inaccurate user identification, yet Right Player does not appear to notice, c) Right Player picks up a card, and d) the *Surface Ghost* (highlight) flies toward Left Player's hand, and Right Player says, "I am under the impression that you might have my cards".

would be most useful in our particular multi-surface context. Since we expected users to position their tablets directly adjacent to the tabletop surface (confirmed by the study), Surface Ghosts were expected to be visible for the majority of the Transfer Phase (also confirmed by the study). Yet, the study revealed that participants utilized Surface Ghosts extensively during the Pick Phase, especially during multi-object transfers, where Surface Ghosts helped them keep track of how many objects they had picked up. When picking multiple cards from the tablet,, the user's hand remains positioned outside of the active tabletop surface area. Consequentially, Surface Ghosts were found to be more effective during ***tabletop-to-tablet*** transfers, than during ***tablet-to-tabletop*** transfers.

The choice of study task may have influenced the observed importance of the Pick Phase during P&D transfer, as the frequently required multi-card transfers in the Dominion game involved longer, more complex pick interactions compared to single-card transfers. Nonetheless, providing a feedback design that supports all three P&D phases, in either transfer direction, would be ideal. The results suggest that providing similar visual feedback on the tablets would better support the overall P&D process. However, the lack of hover detection on the tablet[1] and its reduced screen real estate suggests a more simplified approach may be needed, rather than simply extending Surface Ghosts feedback onto the tablet. Further work is needed to determine the most effective visual feedback to provide on the tablet to better support the entire P&D process.

Implicit vs. Explicit Ownership Feedback

Both Surface Ghosts designs promoted awareness during P&D transfers, particularly for transfers originating on the tabletop. The Explicit Ownership design, however, offered more persistent user-specific feedback that also facilitated identifying and adapting to system errors. This support came at the cost of slower transfer performance. The data suggest participants may have waited for the laggy arm embodiment to "catch up" to their physical arm during transfer. Higher fidelity above-the-surface sensing capabilities may address this issue.

Notwithstanding the potential to provide arm embodiment feedback without delays, offering this type of visual feedback requires sophisticated sensors that can distinguish between multiple users and detect and track, in real-time, a user's whole hand and arm above the tabletop surface. Since the more minimalist Implicit Ownership design was as effective in most circumstances for promoting awareness during P&D transfer, this Surface Ghosts design would generalize well to less elaborate technical setups. For example, if only point-based user identification was available, via special rings or wristbands worn by users, it would still be possible to provide Surface Ghosts with Implicit Ownership, as described in this paper. If above-the-table tracking was available without user identification, a modified version of this design could be offered that did not orient the Surface Ghost embodiment as it moved across the table, and that delayed the user-binding of the virtual object until the tracked point crossed a specific tabletop edge, where each side of the table (or portion of the table edge) could be associated to a specific user.

[1] The ability to hold the tablets at oblique angles creates difficulties for using the same above-the-table tracking approach for providing Surface Ghosts feedback on the tablets.

CONCLUSION AND FUTURE WORK

The study revealed that providing *Surface Ghosts* virtual embodiments significantly improved awareness during P&D transfers from the ***tabletop to the tablet***, as compared to a no feedback control condition. However, Surface Ghosts provided fewer awareness benefits during ***tablet-to-tabletop*** transfers. This asymmetric benefit was due to the fact that the Surface Ghosts feedback was primarily used during the Pick phase of P&D. Since the tablets were typically positioned adjacent to the tabletop, the Surface Ghosts feedback was unavailable during picks on the tablet. In ongoing work, we are investigating the use of local feedback on the tablet during picks (and drops) to better support the entire P&D process.

The study also revealed that Surface Ghosts with Explicit Ownership helped users cope with common technical issues encountered on multi-touch surfaces, minimizing frustration and improving the overall user experience. However, this feedback also introduced delays in transfer times, likely due to participants waiting for their arm embodiment to "catch" up to their physical arm during transfer. Further work is needed to refine the Explicit Ownership design to maintain its awareness benefits while minimizing its negative impact on transfer performance.

ACKNOWLEDGEMENTS

This project was funded in part by NSERC SurfNet Research Network, SSHRC IMMERSe Research Network, and the LEIF Canada-EU Exchange Program. Thanks to the Surface Research Group at the University of Waterloo for invaluable project feedback. We graciously thank Phil McClelland for early work and concepts on this project.

REFERENCES

1. Bachl, S., Tomitsch, M., Kappel, K., Grechenig, T. (2011). The effects of personal displays and transfer techniques on collaboration strategies in multi-touch based multi-display environments. *Proc. Interact'11*, 373-390.
2. Baudisch, P., Cutrell, E., Hinckley, K., Gruen, R. (2004). Mouse ether: accelerating the acquisition of targets across multi-monitor displays. *Ext. Abs. CHI'09*, 1379-1382.
3. Baudisch, P., Cutrell, E., Robbins, D., Czerwinski, M., Tandler, P., Bederson, B., Zierlinger, A. (2003). Drag-and-pop and drag-and-pick: Techniques for accessing remote screen content on touch-and pen-operated systems. *Proc. Interact'03*, 57-64.
4. Besacier, G., Rey, G., Najm, M., Buisine, S., Vernier, F. (2007).Paper metaphor for tabletop interaction design. *Proc. HCI'07*, 758-767.

5. Coldefy, F. & Louis-dit-Picard, S. (2007). DigiTable: an interactive multiuser table for collocated and remote collaboration enabling remote gesture visualization. *Proc. CVPR'07*, 1-8.
6. Collomb, M. & Hascoët, M. (2008). Extending drag-and-drop to new interactive environments: A multi-display, multi-instrument and multi-user approach. *Interacting with Computers*, 20 (6). 562-573.
7. Collomb, M., Hascoët, M., Baudisch, P., Lee, B. (2005). Improving drag-and-drop on wall-size displays. *Proc. Graphics interface '05,* 25-32.
8. Doeweling, S. & Glaubitt, U. (2010). Drop-and-drag: easier drag & drop on large touchscreen displays. *Proc. NordiCHI'10*, 158-167.
9. Doucette, A., Gutwin, C., Mandryk, R.L., Nacenta, M., Sharma, S. (2003). Sometimes when we touch: how arm embodiments change reaching and collaboration on digital tables. *Proc. CSCW'13* , 193-202.
10. Everitt, K.M., Klemmer, S.R., Lee, R., Landay, J.A. (2003). Two worlds apart: bridging the gap between physical and virtual media for distributed design collaboration. *Proc. CHI'03*, 553-560.
11. Fei, S., Webb, A.M., Kerne, A., Qu, Y. , Jain, A. (2013). Peripheral array of tangible NFC tags: positioning portals for embodied trans-surface interaction. *Proc. ITS'13*, 33-36.
12. Genest, A.M., Gutwin, C., Tang, A., Kalyn, M., Ivkovic, Z. (2013). KinectArms: a toolkit for capturing and displaying arm embodiments in distributed tabletop groupware. *Proc. CSCW'13*, 157-166.
13. Gutwin, C. & Greenberg, S. (2002). A descriptive framework of workspace awareness for real-time groupware. *J. CSCW*, 11 (3-4), 411-445.
14. Haller, M., Leitner, J., Seifried, T., Wallace, J.R., Scott, S.D., Richter, C., Brandl, P., Gokcezade, A., Hunter, S. (2010). The NiCE discussion room: Integrating paper and digital media to support co-located group meetings. *Proc. CHI'10*, 609-618.
15. Hascoët, M. (2003). Throwing models for large displays. *Proc. HCI'03*, 73-77.
16. Hilliges, O., Izadi, S., Wilson, A.D., Hodges, S., Garcia-Mendoza, A., Butz, A. (2009). Interactions in the air: adding further depth to interactive tabletops. *Proc. UIST'09*, 139-148.
17. Hinckley, K. (2003). Synchronous gestures for multiple persons and computers. *Proc. UIST'03*, 149-158.
18. Hinckley, K., Ramos, G., Guimbretiere, F., Baudisch, P., Smith, M. (2004). Stitching: pen gestures that span multiple displays. *Proc. AVI'04*, 23-31.
19. Jordan, B. & Henderson, A. (1995). Interaction analysis: Foundations and practice. *J. Learn. Sci.*, 4(1), 39-103.
20. Kobayashi, K., Narita, A., Hirano, M., Tanaka, K., Katada, T., Kuwasawa, N. (2008). DIGTable: A Tabletop Simulation System for Disaster Education. Proc. Pervasive2008, 57–60.
21. Marquardt, N., Hinckley, K., Greenberg, S. (2012). Cross-device interaction via micro-mobility and f-formations. *Proc. UIST'12*, 13-22.
22. Moore, R.J., Gathman, E.C.H., Ducheneaut, N., Nickell, E. (2007). Coordinating joint activity in avatar-mediated interaction. *Proc. CHI'07*, 21-30.
23. Nacenta, M.A., Gutwin, C., Aliakseyeu, D., Subramanian, S. (2009) There and back again: cross-display object movement in multi-display environments. *Human-Computer Interaction*, 24 (1-2). 170-229.
24. Olsen Jr, D.R., Clement, J., Pace, A. (2007). Spilling: Expanding hand held interaction to touch table displays. *IEEE Tabletop'07*, 163-170.
25. Pinelle, D., Gutwin, C., Nacenta, M.A. (2008). The effects of co-present embodiments on awareness and collaboration in tabletop groupware. *Proc. Graphics Interface*, 1-8.
26. Rekimoto, J. (1998). A multiple device approach for supporting whiteboard-based interactions. *Proc. CHI'98*, 344-351.
27. Rekimoto, J. (1997). Pick-and-drop: a direct manipulation technique for multiple computer environments. *Proc. UIST'97*, 31-39.
28. Scott, S.D., Besacier, G., McClelland, P. (2014). Cross-device transfer in a collaborative multi-surface environment without user identification. *Proc. CTS 2014*, 219-226.
29. Stach, T., Gutwin, C., Pinelle, D., Irani, P. (2007). Improving recognition and characterization in groupware with rich embodiments. *Proc. CHI'07*, 11-20.
30. Streitz, N.A., Tandler, P., Müller-Tomfelde, C., Konomi, S. (2001). Roomware: Towards the next generation of human-computer: interaction based on an integrated design of real and virtual worlds. In Carroll, J. (ed.) *Human-Computer Interaction in the New Millennium*, Addison Wesley, 551-576.
31. Streitz, N.A., Jörg G., Holmer, T., Konomi, S., Müller-Tomfelde, C., Reischl, W., Rexroth, P., Seitz, P., Steinmetz, R. (1999). i-LAND: an interactive landscape for creativity and innovation. Proc. CHI'99 120-127.
32. Tang, A., Boyle, M., Greenberg, S. (2004). Display and presence disparity in mixed presence groupware. *Proc. OzCHI'04*, 73-82.
33. Tang, A., Neustaedter, C., Greenberg, S. (2007). VideoArms: Embodiments for mixed presence groupware. In Bryan-Kinns, N., Blanford, A., Curzon, P., Nigay, L. (eds). *People and Computers XX - Engage*, Springer London, 85-102.
34. Tuddenham, P. & Robinson, P. (2009). Territorial coordination and workspace awareness in remote tabletop collaboration. *Proc. CHI'09*, 2139-2148.
35. Voelker, S., Weiss, M., Wacharamanotham, C., Borchers, J. (2011). Dynamic portals: a lightweight metaphor for fast object transfer on interactive surfaces. *Proc. ITS'11*, 158-161.
36. Wallace, J.R., Pape, J., Chang, Y.-L.B., McClelland, P.J., Graham, T.C.N., Scott, S.D., Hancock, M. (2012). Exploring automation in digital tabletop board game. *Ext. Abs. CSCW'12*, 231-234.
37. Weber, S., Ghanam, Y., Wang, X., Maurer, F. (2008). APDT: An agile planning tool for digital tabletops. In P. Abrahamsson et al. (eds.) *Agile Processes in Software Engineering and Extreme Programming*, Springer, 202-203.
38. Wilson, A.D., Izadi, S., Hilliges, O., Garcia-Mendoza, A., Kirk, D. (2008). Bringing physics to the surface. *Proc. ITS'08*, 67-76.

PolyChrome: A Cross-Device Framework for Collaborative Web Visualization

Sriram Karthik Badam[1] and Niklas Elmqvist[2]
[1]Department of Computer Science and [2]College of Information Studies
University of Maryland, College Park, MD, USA
{sbadam, elm}@umd.edu

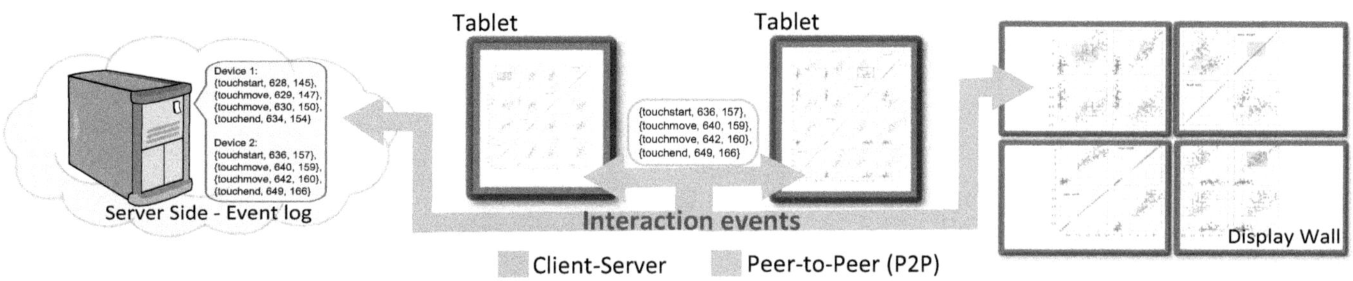

Figure 1. A web-based collaborative visualization of a scatterplot matrix of Anderson's *Iris* dataset with brush and link interaction enabled. Using PolyChrome, the brushes created on the tablets are represented on the display wall through operation distribution, and are also stored on a server.

ABSTRACT

We present PolyChrome, an application framework for creating web-based collaborative visualizations that can span multiple devices. The framework supports (1) co-browsing new web applications as well as legacy websites with no migration costs (i.e., a distributed web browser); (2) an API to develop new web applications that can synchronize the UI state on multiple devices to support synchronous and asynchronous collaboration; and (3) maintenance of state and input events on a server to handle common issues with distributed applications such as consistency management, conflict resolution, and undo operations. We describe PolyChrome's general design, architecture, and implementation followed by application examples showcasing collaborative web visualizations created using the framework. Finally, we present performance results that suggest that PolyChrome adds minimal overhead compared to single-device applications.

ACM Classification Keywords

H.5.2 Information Interfaces and Presentation: User Interfaces—*Interaction styles*; I.3.6 Computer Graphics: Methodology and Techniques—*Interaction techniques*

Author Keywords

Co-browsing; cross-device interaction; multi-display environments; distributed visualization;

http://dx.doi.org/10.1145/2669485.2669518

INTRODUCTION

Given today's relentless advancements in display technology, mobile devices, and wireless connectivity, the concept of *collaborative visualization* on multiple devices such as large displays, tabletops, tablets, and smartphones is becoming increasingly prominent [23]. In parallel development, the web is quickly turning into a prime platform for managing and analyzing large amounts of data using visualization [7] and visual analytics [33]. Collaborative web browsing [9, 14] (co-browsing), where browsers on multiple different devices are connected, is one paradigm that allow us to combine both of these trends to enable *cross-device interaction* [42]. So far mostly restricted to applications within human-computer interaction, co-browsing synchronizes browsers by sharing both current browser state and interaction events, including navigation through scrolling, selection through mouse clicks, and input from keyboard and touch displays. Applying this idea to visualization and visual analytics would turn the web browser into an environment for cross-device visualization.

The concept of harnessing multiple networked devices for deep data analytics anywhere and anytime is called *ubiquitous analytics* (ubilytics) [12], and draws upon a significant body of existing work that supports synchronous and co-located collaboration using distributed user interfaces [30], distributed visualization [18], and post-WIMP interaction models [16]. Ubiquitous analytics is inspired from Mark Weiser's vision (ubiquitous computing [42]) of seamless interaction with everyday objects and activities for information processing. Utilizing the web as a medium for collaboration can easily be the most platform-independent way to make further progress towards these common visions of ubiquitous computing and analytics. However, to build ubilytics environments using multi-device ecosystems over the web, we need a unified framework to replicate shared state and manage the shared visual space of multiple devices.

In this paper, we address this need by presenting POLYCHROME, a web application framework for exploring the design choices in sharing and synchronizing web applications in collaborative settings. Because the framework is built entirely in JavaScript, participating devices need no special software beyond a modern web browser. Interaction sharing and synchronization among devices using PolyChrome is performed through a secure peer-to-peer (P2P) network, while persistent data such as login details, display configuration preferences, shared state, and consistency management is managed by a dedicated server. PolyChrome provides three contributions to the visualization on interactive surfaces community:

- *Augmented legacy websites:* Augmenting standard web browsers to distribute legacy websites and visualizations across multiple devices and synchronize interaction between them. We target both dynamic websites for visualization created using toolkits such as D3 [7], as well as static websites such as Wikipedia.
- *Collaborative web visualizations:* Providing the interaction and display space distribution mechanisms to create new collaborative web visualizations that utilize multiple devices. This is widely useful in all types of collaboration, including the four combinations of synchronous vs. asynchronous and co-located vs. distributed collaboration [3].
- *Consistency and synchronization management:* Providing framework modules to store the user interaction (represented as operations). Combined with the initial state of a website, the interaction logs are useful for synchronizing devices within the collaborative environment, consistency management, and interaction replay [27].

The remainder of this paper is structured as follows: we first review existing research on web-based visualizations, collaborative visualizations, collaborative web browsing, and operation transformation algorithms for groupware. We then derive and motivate design considerations for our framework. We present the PolyChrome architecture and give several application examples of using PolyChrome for both new and legacy web-based visualization. We close the paper by discussing advantages and disadvantages of PolyChrome along with a preliminary evaluation.

BACKGROUND

In this section, we review existing research in the related areas in visualization, cross-device interaction, and operation transformation for groupware.

Web-based and Collaborative Visualizations

Rohrer and Swing [35] more than a decade ago discussed the possiblity of utilizing the web as a visualization platform, citing its inherent device and platform independence as well as its pervasiveness, but it is only recently that the web became both the source of information as well as the underlying delivery mechanism for interactive visualization. Many Eyes [41] was among the first to allow a visualization of arbitrary datasets over the web. By doing so, they opened up a new opportunity for social analysis and enhanced collaboration in analytics by acting as a space to share visualizations, opinions, and conjectures.

In the past decade, toolkits designed for supporting web visualization such as Protovis [6], JavaScript InfoVis toolkit [5], and D3 [7] have come into prominent use. Protovis [6] aimed at making visualizations more accessible to the web and interaction designers by using a declarative specification of visualization as consisting of graphical primitivates called "marks", such as bars (for bar charts), lines (for line charts), and labels. In contrast, D3 [7], created by Bostock et al., supports web visualization through direct manipulation of the document object model (DOM) of a webpage without any intermediate representations. D3 uses the document as the scene graph and performs at least twice as fast as Protovis [6]. While these toolkits are oriented towards building visualizations over the web, they have not yet attempted to support features for collaboration between multiple users.

Collaboration in the analytics process has been shown to increase sensemaking performance: Mark et al. [28] showed significant benefits in using collaborative visualizations in both distributed and co-located settings, and Balakrishnan et al. [4] found better performance for analysts using shared visualization compared to single-user ones. Drawing on this body of work, Isenberg et al. [23] define the research area of collaborative visualization and derive its unique challenges. Collaborative visualizations in co-located settings often utilize large wall displays, floor displays, tabletops and tablets. Accordingly, several visualizations have been adapted to such settings [22, 25, 40]. Some approaches exist to facilitate the collaborative sensemaking itself; for example, Branch-Explore-Merge [29] supports the whole spectrum of coupled and decoupled collaboration when analyzing datasets.

Collaborative Browsing and Cross-Device Interaction

Collaborative web browsing [9, 14] involves multiple users viewing a single webpage collaboratively using their individual devices through synchronous or asynchronous coupling of their browser interfaces. Traditionally, this is accomplished either by replicating the content of one browser over the connected browsers in distributed collaboration or by allowing virtual avatars to operate on a single web browser in case of co-located collaboration. GroupWeb [15, 17] presents one of the earliest groupware adaptations of a web browser. It allows (1) document slaving for synchronized pages by making sure that the browsers display the same webpage, (2) relaxed "what you see is what I see" by keeping the visuals similar across devices, (3) view slaving for synchronous scrolling, gestures through telepointers, and (4) group annotations.

Another way to look at co-browsing is to see it as a medium for *cross-device interaction* [42]: interaction that spans two or more devices. Accordingly, over the past decade and half, collaborative browsing has evolved from simplistic methods to chain multiple displays into full multi-device environments. Websplitter [20] targets web-based presentations involving multiple displays and hand-held devices. Instead of mirroring webpages across devices, they provide the ability to orchestrate a composite presentation, including audio and video, across multiple devices according to their capabilities. PlayByPlay [43] supports synchronous and asynchronous collaborative browsing and allows the user to toggle options for receiving actions of other users, sending their own actions, and resyncing with a previously synchronized user. Synchronite [39] works with more dynamic webpages by capturing the mousing events and replicates them among connected devices, thus creating low latency collaboration and reduced data traffic.

Hydrascope [21], a framework for adapting existing web applications (legacy) to multi-surface environments, faces issues with its approach for reverse-engineering these applications, and they counter this by providing some general design guidelines for web applications. Calderon et al. [8] mention the general requirements for going beyond common browser interactions and coupling mobile displays as lessons learned while developing the RED framework for multi-display applications. More recently, Panelrama [44] allows development of web-based collaborative applications through custom panels, but this work does not fully support legacy applications or dynamic web visualizations. Other research work in development of cross-device web interfaces includes XDStudio [31]. In contrast to these frameworks, PolyChrome utilizes existing HTML elements, supports legacy applications while providing a developer API for designing cross-device applications, couples any two devices with a web broswer, and synchronizes using interaction events.

Operation Transformation

Real-time collaborative applications often require management of consistency and conflicts inherently caused by simultaneous collaborative use. In the quest to allow concurrent use in distributed environments, *operation transformation* (OT) has become an established method compared to the alternatives such as turn-taking, locking, and serialization [10, 11].

The early approaches GROVE [10] and REDUCE [37, 38] both adopt fully distributed architectures and maintain a buffer of executed operations on each device. In particular, the REDUCE approach promises intention preservation—the final state on all devices being what the user intended—along with convergence and causality preservation. REDUCE introduces two kinds of operation transformations: inclusion transformations (IT) that transforms an operation O_a against operation O_b such that the impact of O_b is included, and exclusion transformation (ET) that transforms an operation O_a against operation O_b such that the impact of O_b is excluded.

The JUPITER approach [32] serves as an inspiration for recent OT algorithms used in Google Docs. Kumawat and Khunteta [26] review OT algorithms along with the challenges faced in the field and recent achievements. Current frameworks designed with built-in mechanisms for consistency management include Apache Wave [1] and ShareJS [2] that work with a centralized server, linear history buffer, and operation transformation for managing the global state. In PolyChrome, we draw upon this work to achieve consistency in collaborative visualizations by utilizing operation transformation algorithms through a framework that sees user interaction on the web as a series of native browser-level operations.

DESIGN: CROSS-DEVICE VISUALIZATION TOOLKITS

Multi-device ecosystems are becoming increasingly popular in office and academic settings [13, 34]. The presence of large screens, tabletops, and tablets not only increases the screen space but also the interaction space to utilize the various unique abilities of each device. Many existing platforms utilize the idea of connecting the devices in the ecosystem with a client-server or a peer-to-peer architecture [25, 29], to allow for ubiquitous analytics [12]. With the increasing use of the web as a platform for visualization and visual analytics, we believe that it is time to augment toolkits for web visualizations with the ability to allow collaboration at a device level. Here we describe the design choices involved in building ubiquitous visual analytics applications over the web and how these choices can be supported through a software framework for binding web browsers on separate devices together.

Operation Distribution

At a software level, interaction events or operations, a common term in Operation Transformation, form the building blocks for any interaction with a visualization. For example, brush-and-link coordination is one of the common interaction techniques used in multi-view visualizations, and it is performed through one or more selection operations. In multi-device ecosystems for ubiquitous analytics, these operations need to be captured and shared with other devices to propagate the effects of an interaction on the display space. While a simple model for operation distribution would involve sending every operation to all the devices in the network, this may not turn out to be useful in some collaborative scenarios. We have identified various styles (design patterns) of operation distribution or replication (Figure 2).

P1 **Explicit Sharing:** Here the visualization user explicitly decides when the operation sharing should happen, which operations to share and whom to share them with. This is helpful in building private and public workspaces that can allow for branch and merge style collaboration [29]. While an operation that happens on the private workspace is not shared with others, the operation that happens on a public space is passed on to all the devices with user intervention.

P2 **Implicit Sharing:** Here the operations are automatically shared with the connected devices without the need for additional application logic. This creates a fully-aware environment where each device knows the interaction happening on others. This method requires additional application logic for consistency management since interaction can happen at the same time on multiple devices. Typical usage scenarios include distributed user collaboration scenarios that provide the visual feedback of a user interaction to all the other users.

The explicit and implicit sharing models form the two extremes of a hypothetical operation sharing scale (Figure 2). In a typical collaboration, some of the devices may use explicit sharing through user intervention, while others may prefer implicit sharing. Another sharing model on this hypothetical scale, is the **unilateral sharing** model where one device (leader) always shares its operations automatically, while the other devices (lagger) only listen to the operations shared by

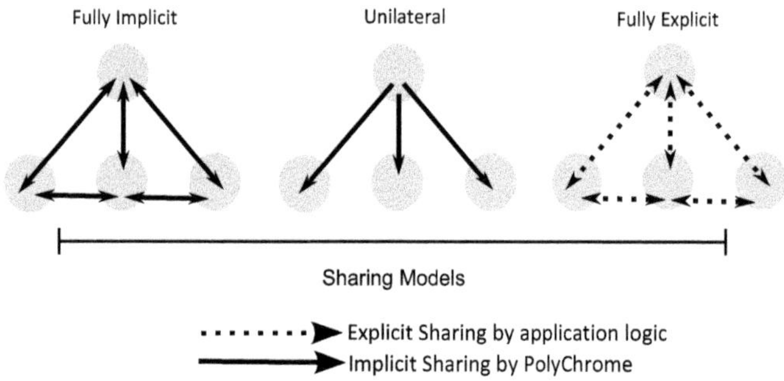

Figure 2. A hypothetical sharing scale ranging from fully implicit to fully explicit sharing. During implicit sharing, the operations are automatically shared with all connected devices. On the other end, explicit sharing allows the developer of the collaborative visualization to define explicit application logic for sharing interaction. Unilateral sharing model is a real-world example that can be applied during presentations.

the leader. This model is useful during presentations and many other guided collaboration scenarios.

To achieve the various design choices in operation distribution especially in concurrent use, transformation of these operations (OT) to the context also needs to be taken into account. Previous research in OT mostly deals with collaborative text editors and document editors where the operations are clearly defined (for example, insert and delete) and the applications allow undo/redo by default. In contrast, typical web visualizations directly deal with the document object model (DOM), thus providing different ways to realize operations. The definition of operation guides the operation transformation algorithms [26, 37, 38] for concurrent use of web applications. Some example operation definitions include,

P3 **Data-centric operation:** Here an operation can be defined on the data structures guiding the visualizations. Any interaction performed in this approach needs to be translated into a change in the data variables (operation) that is shared with other devices in the network.

P4 **Interaction-centric operation:** Here an operation can be defined as an interaction event that is handled by the web browser. This includes different types of browser-level events such as scroll, mouse events such as mouse click, move and mouse up, touch events such as touch start, touch move, and touch end, and key presses. These events/operations can be captured, shared, and then performed on the DOM of the webpage on each device.

As most OT algorithms dictate, collaborative visualizations also require a way to save operations on a server (i.e., an interaction log) to maintain the global state and resynchronize devices that are out-of-sync using context-specific algorithms.

Display Space Management

Multi-device environments often consist of devices of different resolutions, aspect ratios, and screen sizes. This causes a distribution of the unified display space, i.e., the rendering of the web visualization in the browser between multiple devices in the ecosystem. The distribution of the display space leads to different renderings on the devices that may cover whole or part of the global display space, or the unified display space covering all the devices. Figure 3 shows several local display configurations for a two-display environment. Considering these aspects, one of the design considerations here is to support the following patterns for distributing the display space between multiple devices (inspired by Javed and Elmqvist [24]).

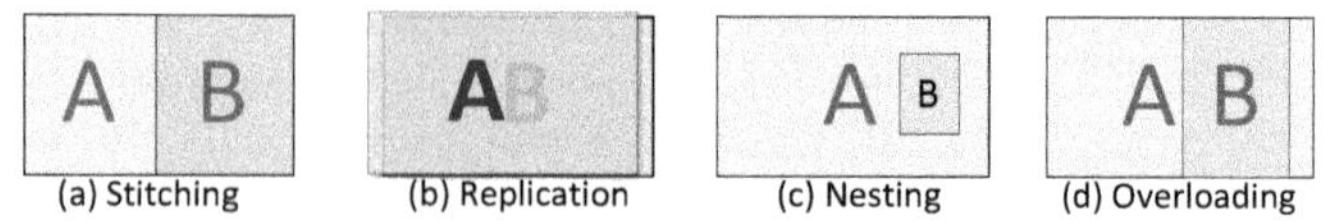

Figure 3. Various display space configurations for a two-device environment. (a) Splitting the display space between the two devices is useful for multi-screen displays, (b) replicating (mirroring) the display space among the two devices is useful during distributed collaboration, and (c, d) nesting and overloading are useful for small-screen mobile devices.

P5 **Replicating:** This strategy shows the exact same view on all devices. The global display space of the ecosystem is, therefore, a *superimposition* of the individual screens. This pattern typically occurs during webpage mirroring in co-browsing, and is widely useful in distributed collaboration where the users work from different locations.

Usage scenarios: Public presentations where the view of the presentor can be mirrored on the displays held by the audience, or distributed collaboration between multiple users to perform document analysis through tools such as Jigsaw [36] that require building synchronized views.

P6 **Stitching:** Here the entire display space is split between devices, with no two devices sharing any part of the display. The global display space is now formed by *juxtaposing*, or stitching, the individual displays.

Usage scenarios: Multi-display visual analytics.

P7 **Nesting:** Here one or more devices hold the entire display space, while others show bits and pieces of the display space relevant to the device or the user.

Usage scenarios: Co-located settings with mobile devices alongside large displays and desktop computers.

Javed et al. [24] also discuss *overloading*, where a view utilizes the space allocated for another view, and this is covered by nesting in the context of web visualizations. Figure 3 shows the design patterns in display space configuration.

Supporting Legacy Applications

While supporting development of new web-based collaborative visualizations, it is equally important to provide as much backward compatibility to the numerous existing web-based visualizations. For example, there are web visualizations built using D3, Protovis, and the JavaScript InfoVis Toolkit. These generally depend on the native browser events for the event handling, and SVG, CSS, and HTML5 for graphical rendering. To support these legacy applications, we propose to use a proxy module that augments a standard web visualization or web application with additional support for event sharing and display configuration between the involved devices.

Additional Design Considerations

The intended user of this design treatment for cross-device visualization toolkits is an application programmer (i.e., an "end-user" programmer), who is building ubiquitous web visualizations. Thus, we must consider the above design choices for operation management, display space configuration, conflict resolution, consistency management, and synchronization among devices. In addition to these, we must also support multiple device modalities for both input and output including tabletops, multi-screen displays, desktop computers, and mobile devices. Finally, a software framework for this should also accommodate future technologies and allow third parties to contribute new functionality.

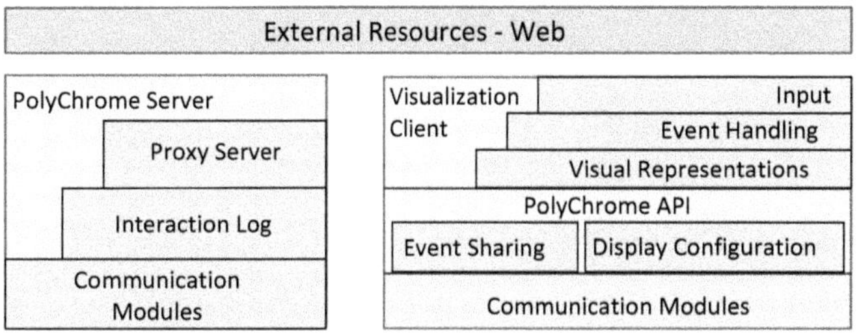

Figure 4. Architecture: The visualization client is connected to the PolyChrome API modules for event sharing and display configuration. The PolyChrome API automatically connects all the devices over a peer-to-peer network for event sharing. Every client is also connected to the PolyChrome server to store the interaction. This framework also provides proxy server modules for using legacy applications collaboratively.

THE POLYCHROME FRAMEWORK

PolyChrome is a generic software framework for building web-based cross-device visualizations. It is implemented using HTML, JavaScript, and CSS. Due to this strict reliance on standard web technology, it is entirely cross-platform and works on any device with a modern web browser. PolyChrome consists of both client and server-side modules. The server modules of PolyChrome have been built using Node.js, as the event-driven nature and non-blocking I/O of Node.js helps in efficiently managing interaction logs of multiple users over time. The client-side modules of PolyChrome contain the PolyChrome API that supports operation distribution and display space configuration. Figure 4 depicts the PolyChrome architecture, including the proxy server that converts legacy web applications into collaborative applications, operation distribution, input, and rendering (visual representation) layers. The framework interacts directly with the *document object model* (DOM) structure within the browser for display space configuration and also capturing browser events as operations (design pattern P4). PolyChrome framework uses PeerJS[1] for P2P communication (using WebRTC[2]) between the devices such as tabletops, tablets, and multi-screen displays, and communication via sockets from a client to server.

PolyChrome consists of four modules: (1) operation (event) sharing; (2) display space configuration; (3) conflict, concurrency, and synchronization management; and (4) a proxy server for serving legacy applications. The design philosophy of PolyChrome is to treat the view of a web visualization at any time instance as a state that changes with user interaction (as in Figure 5). In essence, browser-level DOM events are the operations in PolyChrome applications. By capturing the user operations at the most atomic level on the browser in the form of DOM events, we can reconstruct the state of the visualization from the original rendering. For this reason, the communication between clients of PolyChrome only happens in the form of event sharing, thus leaving the job of rendering to the clients (a philosophy inspired by Synchronite [39]). Browser-level events can be recreated using the event details such as event type, coordinates with respect to the page and client, and the target element in the DOM, but interaction over time with continuous movement of the mouse can lead to conflicts and consistency issues when concurrently performed on multiple devices. For example, in a two-device environment, if the mouse movement is attached to an event handler, sharing the mouse movement with other devices can lead to conflicts in terms of both events and order of the events, and this can propagate into a consistency issue if the handling sequence and context are different. In fact, the effects can be fatal if the application logic for handling such scenarios through OT logic is not encoded into the system.

The PolyChrome clients are connected over a peer-to-peer channel for event sharing, and they can also choose to connect to the server to store their interaction logs. This counters the major setback of using client-level web technologies, i.e., the lack of proper persistent storage of the interaction of a user when the webpage is closed. For example, when a client drops out of the network, the interaction made on the client is lost if it is not stored on some other host. Unless there is a common global state maintained by all devices, this leads to data loss and consistency issues. To counter this, PolyChrome maintains the state of all devices on a server in the form of an event log that contains the information and order of all events generated on all connected devices in a session over time.

The PolyChrome framework currently allows space configuration, i.e., the choice of rendering part or whole of the web application based on the design pattens (P5 to P7) in the Design section by assuming the global space to be the default state of a webpage rendered in a normal browser. The global space configuration is therefore device and webpage independent, and is encoded into each PolyChrome client to facilitate seemless conversion from the local to the global configurations. Every PolyChrome client transforms events to the global space configuration, and these events are interpreted accordingly on other clients by an inverse transformation.

The concurrency and synchronization modules of PolyChrome can be used for handling (1) newly joined clients that require the previous user interactions to work in collaboration or interaction replay, (2) multiple collaboration scenarios including co-located collaboration on a display wall involving multiple mobile devices, and unilateral collaboration during presentations involving a presentor and audience with their own personal devices, and (3) synchronization of clients that are out-of-sync with interaction on other devices. This

[1] `http://peerjs.com/`

[2] `http://www.w3.org/TR/webrtc/`

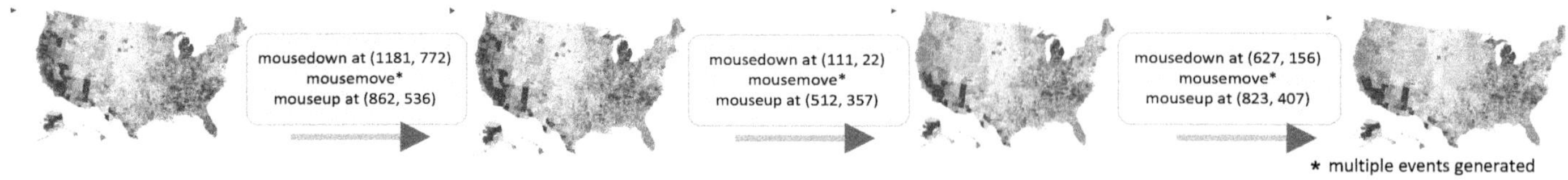

Figure 5. An example interaction with a Choropleth map of unemployment rates in U.S from 2008, created using D3. Upon user interaction (by drawing a rectangular shape on the map), the counties within a selected region are highlighted. PolyChrome provides API-level support for capturing and sharing the browser events that are triggered during this interaction with other connected devices, thus supporting collaborative visualization.

happens when the users work on their private space without sharing or receiving interaction events [29]. The PolyChrome server modules also provide the ability to load collaborative versions of legacy applications with the help of a proxy server that attaches PolyChrome client software to the web source of legacy websites. In the next few subsections we will elaborate on PolyChrome's modules in more detail.

Event Sharing Modules

The event sharing modules provide the basic network-level communication support to share and synchronize the user operations on different devices. PolyChrome achieves this by capturing browser events, communicating these events in a serialized form through a shared peer-to-peer channel created using PeerJS, and then triggering DOM events encapsulated in a PolyChrome Event class on each client. PolyChrome allows two types of event capture mechanisms:

1. **Explicit capture:** An application developer using PolyChrome API can choose to handle event sharing explicitly. By verifying whether an event is generated PolyChrome (encapsulated in a PolyChrome event class) or otherwise, the users can recycle native DOM events, which involves sharing the event with all devices in the P2P network (design pattern P1). The recycled DOM event is then triggered by PolyChrome. The event is at the same time shared with the server by the PolyChrome client (on which the event was created). The events are stored on the server asynchronously on an interaction/operation log in the filesystem with details such as the client identifier, timestamp, event type, spatial co-ordinates and target DOM element details.
2. **Implicit capture:** PolyChrome also allows the users to choose an implicit capture style in which all the events generated on a client are automatically captured at the document level irrespective of their targets. The events captured are analyzed to find their actual targets and are automatically shared with other clients without explicit application logic (design pattern P2). The events are then handled by the original client (on which they were created) through the application logic created for handling the respective event.

These methods for event capture allow for different styles of collaboration as discussed in the Design section. These capture methods can also be applied to settings such as collaborative search, team analytics [25], and general brainstorming processes involving divergence and convergence [19], where the users enjoy the private space on their tablets and merge their ideas with the common displays after a significant breakthrough. PolyChrome can also be used to emulate a unilateral sharing model, as defined previously in the Design section, during presentations (for example) where the presentor performs the interaction which is shared with the audience, with no communication in the opposite direction.

Display Space Configuration Modules

Webpage rendering on a standard browser is defined through the HTML for the static elements, JavaScript for the dynamic structure, and CSS for the style elements for managing alignment, colors, transforms, and effects such as shadows. For PolyChrome, the rendering of a webpage or a dynamic visualization depends on the device type on which it is rendered. For example, rendering on a multi-screen display requires splitting and stitching the webpage across the multiple screens. PolyChrome allows individual devices to manage the local configuration while keeping them informed of the global space. The global space configuration is the DOM rendering of the webpage on a standard web browser. Events generated on each device are scaled to this global space, and then sent to other devices by the PolyChrome API, where they are transformed to the corresponding local configuration. For example, in a multiple monitor setup, the webpage rendering is split and stitched from multiple parts, and PolyChrome maintains the local transforms of each monitor to convert the spatial coordinates of an event into the local space using an affine 2D transform that can take the local translation, scaling, and rotation of each display into account. Events generated on a device can accordingly be converted to the global space using the inverse transform.

This method applies to any screen configuration through CSS-level element transformations that are graphics accelerated on modern browsers, such as Google Chrome. An alternative mechanism would require device-dependent display states that are prone to complex operation distribution logic.

Persistence, Consistency, and Synchronization

Persistence in PolyChrome is achieved by clients sharing their events with a server, which stores the timestamped events in an interaction log. Since the Node.js server is asynchronous in nature, the clients can continue their workflow once the events are sent to the server. This event log can act as an history buffer that is typically used in some modern OT algorithms [26, 32] for consistency management. Furthermore, the PolyChrome framework creates an opportunity to fully allow collaborative use of web visualizations by embedding a concurrency management model. This event log on the server can also be used to update newly joined devices with past interaction events, and also opens up the design space for event caching and chunking on the server to distinguish the semantic importance of various events. For example, in a visual exploration scenario, while all the events are recorded, only a few might be responsible for the detection of a trend or an anomaly during the sensemaking process. Tagging and caching these events can help during (for e.g.) report generation when these events can be replayed to recreate the process by which the corresponding trend or the anomaly was found.

Proxy Server

To support legacy applications currently available on the web, PolyChrome also contains a proxy server built using Node.js that automatically injects the PolyChrome client modules into legacy websites and web applications. PolyChrome uses an invisible HTML *div* element spanning the entire webpage to capture an event and then identify the target behind this invisible element. The events captured are automatically synchronized, thus allowing collaborative use of legacy applications. This automatic sharing approach for legacy applications can face issues in the presence of custom application-specific events (such as D3's brush events). Although these modules are currently experimental, they allow for running a wide range of sample visualizations created with D3[3] in a multi-device environment.

IMPLEMENTATION

We have implemented PolyChrome as a heterogeneous JavaScript framework that uses PeerJS for peer-to-peer event sharing and a Node.js server application with modules for proxy server, interaction log management, and server-based consistency and synchronization. The basic PolyChrome client consists of approximately 1,500 lines of JavaScript code and works with the most popular D3 visualization toolkit for both computers and mobile devices.

To avoid dependency problems of asynchronous updates, PolyChrome events maintain the ID of the target element in the DOM. Based on the target ID, the corresponding element in the DOM becomes the target on the connected devices. Since one cannot be sure whether every element in the DOM has an ID, the deterministic structure of a DOM tree is utilized to assign an ID to each element during PolyChrome initialization. Newly created DOM elements are also assigned with an ID by the PolyChrome API when needed, thus accounting for the dynamic nature of modern websites. PolyChrome also provides modules to generate pseudo-random values to achieve similar DOM trees even for webpages with random alignment. This mechanism can also be used to distribute identical random numbers across the lightly-connected components in the network. For example, since a force-directed layout starts with random spatial positions, distributing them on multiple devices can lead to inconsistencies.

The PolyChrome framework contains modules for a control panel that is automatically attached to each client. This panel is opened through a toggle button and provides additional controls for event sharing and display configuration to the user, including shortcut methods for some display configurations. It also shows a list of connected devices along with the events generated by each device. Users can also use the control panel to toggle event sharing for specific event types.

[3]`https://github.com/mbostock/d3/wiki/Gallery`

APPLICATION EXAMPLES

We describe two collaborative visual applications for interactive surfaces built using PolyChrome as well as one example of a legacy visualization. The PolyChrome source, along with several examples, are publicly available on GitHub.[4]

Scatterplot Matrix Exploration

Scatterplot matrices (SPLOMs) allow exploration of the relationship between groups of every two variables in a multivariate dataset, and expands in size for every new dimension added to the dataset. For example, Anderson's *Iris* dataset consists of four variables: sepal width, sepal length, petal width, and petal lengths of three species of flowers. The SPLOM in Figure 6 contains sixteen scatterplots. With increasing dataset size, screen space becomes an increasingly valuable commodity for visual exploration. To facilitate collaborative analysis of SPLOMs, we have created a web application using PolyChrome and D3 that visualizes a given multivariate dataset. Brush-and-link interaction is enabled on the visualization to allow the user to see patterns of data points selected on one scatterplot (using brushing) on other scatterplots in the tabular view (linking) through highlighting. Using the PolyChrome API, a device-specific interaction handling is embedded within the code by identifying mobile devices. The brushes created on the mobile devices are shared with a display wall and are highlighed as rectangles on the display wall. The event sharing in this example only happens from mobile devices to the display wall (unilateral sharing model), thus creating an interaction overview on the shared space.

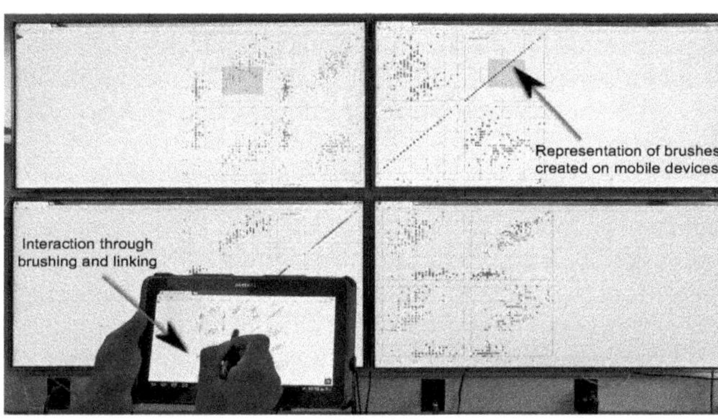

Figure 6. A collaborative web for exploring a scatterplot matrix using brush-and-link interaction on multiple devices.

The application allows users to work on their tablets using brush and link interaction to explore the dataset, while visualizing the brushes on an overview visualization on the display wall. The visualizations and the interaction are created using D3, and the entire application is written using HTML, JavaScriptS, and CSS with less than 30 lines of code to initiate PolyChrome, configure the display, and share events. This example is currently available with the PolyChrome source.

Geographical Map Exploration

The second example uses Google Maps for map exploration using pan and zooming on a web-based multi-display environment (Figure 7). Instead of using the native mouse

[4]`https://github.com/karthikbadam/PolyChrome`

movement events to share the pan interactions, we detect the change in the center of the Google Map (supported by Google Maps API) and share this visual event as a PolyChrome custom application-specific event. These type of events are more meaningful as they represent a visual change, and therefore, they can be semantically tagged for consistency management and synchronization.

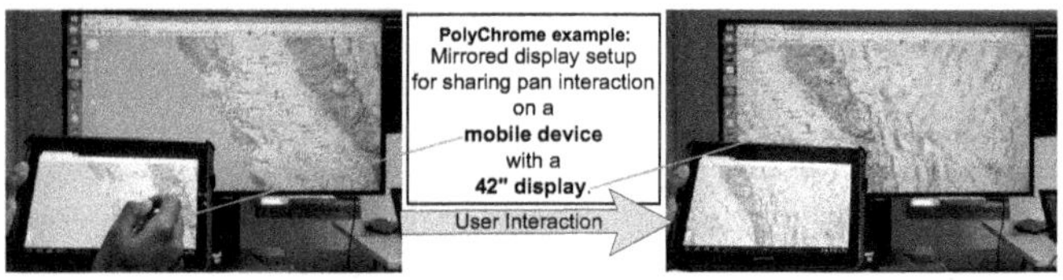

Figure 7. Cross-device Google Maps example where PolyChrome custom event modules are triggered when the map is panned on a device.

This example was created using HTML, JavaScript, and CSS using the Google Maps JavaScript API for the map view, and D3 to show some targets on the map to guide exploration. This example uses less than 20 lines of code using the PolyChrome client API modules, which includes creating an event handler, capturing, and sharing navigation events.

Legacy Application

PolyChrome supports legacy visualizations built using visualization toolkits such as D3. Figure 8 shows an example of a web-based ScatterDice tool applied to box office data.[5] PolyChrome fetches the legacy application using the proxy server and attaches the PolyChrome client modules to it, thus allowing for collaborative exploration of the movie data. The interaction events that happen on one device are shared implicitly with others by the PolyChrome client. This includes the click events, mouse events for drawing shapes, and selection events supported by the legacy application.

PolyChrome also works with the examples provided as part of the D3 toolkit, as well as other toolkits that enable exploration of SVG visualizations, such as VisDock.[6] However, running some of these legacy applications depends on the security configuration, event handling mechanisms in the source webpage, and the capabilities of the proxy server.

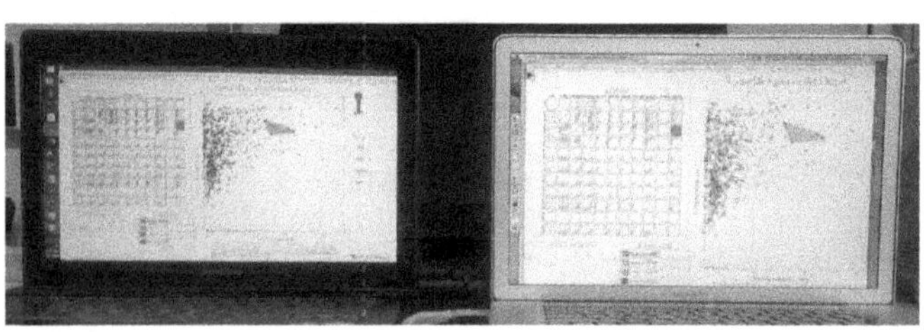

Figure 8. ScatterDice project attached with PolyChrome client modules to synchronize interaction among the devices.

EVALUATION

We performed a preliminary analysis to see the impact of the number of clients using PolyChrome on the time delay between the creation of an event and the execution of the event

[5] `http://tiny.cc/scatterdice`

[6] `https://github.com/VisDockHub/NewVisDock`

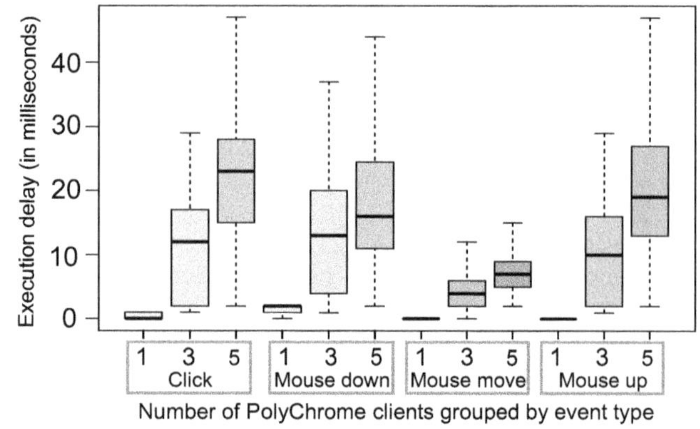

Figure 9. A preliminary performance evaluation of PolyChrome: Three different setups were tested for delays caused by the PolyChrome client in executing various events.

on all connected devices (execution delay) during the implicit sharing model (used in legacy applications). We used a basic drawing application as a surrogate for the legacy visualizations with options to add strokes and also perform mouse clicks. Ten strokes spanning a diagonal of the displays were drawn ($>$ 100 *mousemove* events per stroke) and ten mouse clicks were performed on each client for one, three, and five PolyChrome client setups. These interactions were handled through *click*, *mousedown*, *mousemove*, and *mouseup* events. When the execution delays were analyzed, we found that for the three setups (one, three, and five clients), execution delays increased as the number of clients increased, but they were still in the order of milliseconds (Figure 9). Furthermore, we also found out that the operation of identifying the target element is the root cause of the these delays as it requires a traversal of the DOM tree. The delay was minimal for *mousemove* events, because when this event follows a *mousedown* the targets of both are the same and therefore, PolyChrome skips the target identification step in this case. This analysis helped us identify the potential aspects for further analysis, and also the median increase in delay ($<$ 10 ms from three to five clients) with more clients in the environment.

This suggests that we should strive to achieve better target identification with lower delays. Furthermore, it guides our future evaluation efforts for PolyChrome in terms of the overall performance by profiling event distribution process, developer adoption, and even the mechanics of multi-device visualization and display space configuration strategies.

IMPLICATIONS

The definition of operation as discussed in the design patterns P3 and P4 opens a new space in the field of collaborative visualization for Operation Transformation. This leads to the concurrent use of collaborative web visualization without the need for locking and turn-taking methods to restrict concurrency. The operations in PolyChrome are browser events, and this design choice may lack support for "undo" in some cases. On the other hand, using a data-centric operation that essentially works with the data variables guiding the visualization lacks the ability to support legacy applications and custom data structures. Further evaluation of this is needed.

The choice of hybrid communication modules with peer-to-peer (P2P) and client/server for operation distribution and interaction log respectively leads to fault tolerant yet real-time system. The hybrid system has the ability to surpass the liabilities of both communication types. P2P-based distributed systems face consistency issues in regards to display synchronization and event sharing, while client-server systems face scalability, robustness, security, and trust issues. By combining both and using client/server only for operation/interaction log (for conflict management) the PolyChrome framework gains the advantages of both communication methods.

In the end, no single toolkit works for all situations, and PolyChrome is just the first offering of many potential toolkits for cross-device visualization. We look forward to seeing other toolkits that take different design approaches than us.

CONCLUSION AND FUTURE WORK

We have presented the PolyChrome framework for building web-based collaborative visualizations for multi-surface environments. Beyond the basic functionality to utilize implicit, explicit sharing models, and display space configuration through transformation to the global shared space, PolyChrome comes with a proxy server that supports collaborative use of legacy websites. Due to the presence of a server, operations on various devices can be stored, utilized, and analyzed for many purposes. These interaction logs can be used to serve newly joined devices with previous interaction, replay events during asynchronous collaboration, and maintain synchronization among devices. We validated PolyChrome using several applications built using the framework as well as with some informal performance testing.

In the future, we plan on extending the framework to provide ways to support standard collaboration styles out of the box, embed operation transformation strategies into the framework, allow interpretion through tagging event logs on the devices, adapt the framework to additional hardware and software platforms, and perform an in-depth evaluation.

ACKNOWLEDGMENTS

This work was partially supported by U.S. National Science Foundation award IIS-1253863. Any opinions, findings, and conclusions or recommendations expressed in this article are those of the authors and do not necessarily reflect the views of the funding agency.

REFERENCES

1. Apache Wave. `http://incubator.apache.org/wave/`, accessed June 2014.
2. ShareJS. `http://sharejs.org/`, accessed June 2014.
3. Baecker, R. M. *Readings in Groupware and Computer-Supported Cooperative Work.* Morgan Kaufmann Publishers, San Francisco, 1993.
4. Balakrishnan, A. D., Fussell, S. R., and Kiesler, S. Do visualizations improve synchronous remote collaboration? In *Proceedings of the ACM Conference on Human Factors in Computing Systems* (2008), 1227–1236.
5. Belmonte, N. G. The JavaScript InfoVis Toolkit. `http://philogb.github.io/jit/`, accessed March 2014.
6. Bostock, M., and Heer, J. Protovis: A graphical toolkit for visualization. *IEEE Transactions on Visualization and Computer Graphics 15*, 6 (2009), 1121–1128.
7. Bostock, M., Ogievetsky, V., and Heer, J. D^3: Data-driven documents. *IEEE Transactions on Visualization and Computer Graphics 17*, 12 (2011), 2301–2309.
8. Calderon, R., Blackstock, M., Lea, R., Fels, S., de Oliveira Bueno, A., and Anacleto, J. Red: a framework for prototyping multi-display applications using web technologies. In *Proceedings of the ACM International Symposium on Pervasive Displays* (2014).
9. Domingue, J., Dzbor, M., and Motta, E. Collaborative semantic web browsing with magpie. In *The Semantic Web: Research and Applications*. 2004, 388–401.
10. Ellis, C. A., and Gibbs, S. J. Concurrency control in groupware systems. In *Proceedings of the ACM SIGMOD Record* (1989), 399–407.
11. Ellis, C. A., Gibbs, S. J., and Rein, G. Groupware: some issues and experiences. *Communications of the ACM 34*, 1 (1991), 39–58.
12. Elmqvist, N., and Irani, P. Ubiquitous analytics: Interacting with big data anywhere, anytime. *IEEE Computer 46*, 4 (2013), 86–89.
13. Endert, A., Bradel, L., Zeitz, J., Andrews, C., and North, C. Designing large high-resolution display workspaces. In *Proceedings of the ACM Conference on Advanced Visual Interfaces* (2012), 58–65.
14. Esenther, A. W. Instant co-browsing: Lightweight real-time collaborative web browsing. In *Proceedings of the World Wide Web Conference* (2002), 107–114.
15. Greenberg, S. Collaborative interfaces for the Web. In *Human Factors and Web Development* (1997), 241–254.
16. Greenberg, S., Marquardt, N., Ballendat, T., Diaz-Marino, R., and Wang, M. Proxemic interactions: the new ubicomp? *Interactions 18*, 1 (2011), 42–50.
17. Greenberg, S., and Roseman, M. GroupWeb: A WWW browser as real time groupware. In *Extended Abstracts of the ACM Conference on Human Factors in Computing Systems*, ACM (1996), 271–272.
18. Grimstead, I. J., Walker, D. W., and Avis, N. J. Collaborative visualization: A review and taxonomy. In *Proceedings of the Symposium on Distributed Simulation and Real-Time Applications* (2005), 61–69.
19. Hailpern, J., Hinterbichler, E., Leppert, C., Cook, D., and Bailey, B. P. TEAM STORM: demonstrating an interaction model for working with multiple ideas during creative group work. In *Proceedings of the ACM Conference on Creativity & Cognition* (2007), 193–202.

20. Han, R., Perret, V., and Naghshineh, M. WebSplitter: a unified XML framework for multi-device collaborative web browsing. In *Proc. ACM Conference on Computer Supported Cooperative Work* (2000), 221–230.

21. Hartmann, B., Beaudouin-Lafon, M., and Mackay, W. E. Hydrascope: creating multi-surface meta-applications through view synchronization and input multiplexing. In *Proceedings of the ACM International Symposium on Pervasive Displays* (2013), 43–48.

22. Isenberg, P., and Carpendale, S. Interactive tree comparison for co-located collaborative information visualization. *IEEE Transactions on Visualization and Computer Graphics 13*, 6 (2007), 1232–1239.

23. Isenberg, P., Elmqvist, N., Scholtz, J., Cernea, D., Ma, K.-L., and Hagen, H. Collaborative visualization: definition, challenges, and research agenda. *Information Visualization 10*, 4 (2011), 310–326.

24. Javed, W., and Elmqvist, N. Exploring the design space of composite visualization. In *Proceedings of the IEEE Pacific Symposium on Visualization* (2012), 1–8.

25. Kim, K., Javed, W., Williams, C., Elmqvist, N., and Irani, P. Hugin: A framework for awareness and coordination in mixed-presence collaborative information visualization. In *Proceedings of the ACM Conference on Interactive Tabletops and Surfaces* (2010), 231–240.

26. Kumawat, S., and Khunteta, A. A survey on operational transformation algorithms: Challenges, issues and achievements. *International Journal of Computer Applications 3*, 12 (2010), 3038.

27. Manohar, N. R., and Prakash, A. The session capture and replay paradigm for asynchronous collaboration. In *Proceedings of the European Conference on Computer-Supported Cooperative Work* (1995), 149–164.

28. Mark, G., Kobsa, A., and Gonzalez, V. Do four eyes see better than two? collaborative versus individual discovery in data visualization systems. In *Proceedings of the International Conference on Information Visualisation* (2002), 249–255.

29. McGrath, W., Bowman, B., McCallum, D., Hincapie-Ramos, J.-D., Elmqvist, N., and Irani, P. Branch-explore-merge: Facilitating real-time revision control in collaborative visual exploration. In *Proceedings of the ACM Conference on Interactive Tabletops and Surfaces* (2012), 235–244.

30. Modahl, M., Bagrak, I., Wolenetz, M., Hutto, P., and Ramachandran, U. Mediabroker: An architecture for pervasive computing. In *Proceedings of the IEEE Conference on Pervasive Computing and Communications* (2004), 253–262.

31. Nebeling, M., Mintsi, T., Husmann, M., and Norrie, M. Interactive development of cross-device user interfaces. In *Proceedings of the ACM Conference on Human Factors in Computing Systems* (2014).

32. Nichols, D. A., Curtis, P., Dixon, M., and Lamping, J. High-latency, low-bandwidth windowing in the jupiter collaboration system. In *Proceedings of the ACM Symposium on User Interface and Software Technology* (1995), 111–120.

33. Payne, J., Solomon, J., Sankar, R., and McGrew, B. Grand challenge award: Interactive visual analytics palantir: The future of analysis. In *Proceedings of the IEEE Symposium on Visual Analytics Science and Technology* (2008), 201–202.

34. Raskar, R., Welch, G., Cutts, M., Lake, A., Stesin, L., and Fuchs, H. The office of the future: A unified approach to image-based modeling and spatially immersive displays. *Computer Graphics 32* (1998), 179–188.

35. Rohrer, R. M., and Swing, E. Web-based information visualization. *IEEE Computer Graphics & Applications 17*, 4 (1997), 52–59.

36. Stasko, J., Görg, C., and Liu, Z. Jigsaw: Supporting investigative analysis through interactive visualization. *Information visualization 7*, 2 (2008), 118–132.

37. Sun, C., and Ellis, C. Operational transformation in real-time group editors: issues, algorithms, and achievements. In *Proceedings of the ACM conference on Computer supported cooperative work* (1998), 59–68.

38. Sun, C., Jia, X., Zhang, Y., Yang, Y., and Chen, D. Achieving convergence, causality preservation, and intention preservation in real-time cooperative editing systems. *ACM Transactions on Computer-Human Interaction 5*, 1 (1998), 63–108.

39. Thum, C., and Schwind, M. Synchronite – a service for real-time lightweight collaboration. In *Proceedings of the International Conference on P2P, Parallel, Grid, Cloud and Internet Computing* (2010), 215–221.

40. Tobiasz, M., Isenberg, P., and Carpendale, S. Lark: Coordinating co-located collaboration with information visualization. *IEEE Transactions on Visualization and Computer Graphics 15*, 6 (2009), 1065–1072.

41. Viégas, F. B., Wattenberg, M., Van Ham, F., Kriss, J., and McKeon, M. ManyEyes: A site for visualization at internet scale. *IEEE Transactions on Visualization and Computer Graphics 13*, 6 (2007), 1121–1128.

42. Weiser, M. The computer for the 21st Century. *Scientific American 265*, 3 (1991), 94–104.

43. Wiltse, H., and Nichols, J. PlayByPlay: collaborative web browsing for desktop and mobile devices. In *Proceedings of the ACM Conference on Human Factors in Computing Systems* (2009), 1781–1790.

44. Yang, J., and Wigdor, D. Panelrama: enabling easy specification of cross-device web applications. In *Proceedings of the ACM conference on Human factors in computing systems* (2014), 2783–2792.

ActivitySpace: Managing Device Ecologies in an Activity-Centric Configuration Space

Steven Houben, Paolo Tell, Jakob E. Bardram
The Pervasive Interaction Technology Laboratory
IT University of Copenhagen, Rued Langgaardsvej 7, DK-2300 Copenhagen, DK
{shou,pate,bardram}@itu.dk

Figure 1. The configuration space is activated by placing the master device in the space (A). All other devices that are added to the space become part of the same activity space (B). The space visualizes the resource attached to each device (B). Resources can be moved between devices or stored in the space (C). Devices can be pinned to the space, to maintain the distributed configuration while allowing for device mobility (D).

ABSTRACT
Mobile devices have become an intrinsic part of people's everyday life. They are multifunctional devices providing ubiquitous access to many different sources of information. Together with traditional personal computers, these devices form a device ecology that provides access to an overlapping information space. Previous studies have shown that users encounter a number of fundamental problems when interacting with these device ecologies, such as lack of transparency, control, intelligibility and context. To mitigate these problems, we introduce *ActivitySpace*: an activity-centric configuration space that enables the user to integrate and work across several devices by utilizing the space between the devices. This paper presents the conceptual background and design of *ActivitySpace* and reports on a study with nine participants. Our study shows that *ActivitySpace* helps users to easily manage devices and their allocated resources while also exposing a number of usage patterns.

Author Keywords
Activity-Centric Computing; Configuration Work; Configuration Space; Activity Configuration

ACM Classification Keywords
H.5.2. **[Information Interfaces and Presentation]**: User Interfaces

INTRODUCTION
Mobile devices, such as smart phones and tablets, have become an intrinsic part of people's everyday life. These devices provide ubiquitous access to many different sources of information and allow users to consume as well as to produce information by selectively choosing the appropriate modality, input and output bandwidth, and interaction techniques. Together with laptops and desktop computers, these devices have become part of a device ecology in which each device acts as a specialized portal into users' personal or shared information space. The user-device mapping is quickly changing from being a one-to-one to a one-to-many or even to a many-to-many relation. In this setup, complex device ecologies are constructed and maintained by users to access collaborative distributed information spaces.

Although file sharing systems such as DropBox work across several devices, they are mostly designed according to a traditional single device paradigm, providing little or no support for more complex workflows that engage multiple devices simultaneously in the interaction. Previous studies [14, 31, 36] have highlighted numerous problems when using these tools, including lack of transparency, control, intelligibility, and context. In response to these issues, a large body of prior work has explored interaction techniques used to move information visually from one device to another (e.g., [12, 18, 34]). However, these approaches neither consider the users' ongoing activity nor how users construct these cross-device configurations. Therefore, these attempts are oblivious to the set of resources relevant to the user's activity, the ecology of devices used to manipulate those resources, and the role that such resources have within the activity. In essence, employing multiple devices to execute a particular task requires users to put a significant effort in what we call *configuration work*, the effort required to *setup*, *manage*, *understand* and *use* information, applications and services, which are distributed across several devices.

To mitigate this distributed configuration problem, we introduce *ActivitySpace*, a distributed activity-centric information management system that visualizes the active work setup of the user across all connected devices using the surrounding

ITS 2014, November 16–19, 2014, Dresden, Germany.

ACM 978-1-4503-2587-5/14/11 ...$15.00.
http://dx.doi.org/10.1145/2669485.2669493

space between the active devices. As illustrated in Figure 1, *ActivitySpace* provides a configuration space that works as a mediating interface between the user interfaces of all connected devices. A configuration space allows users to (i) manage and aggregate all devices that are part of the same device ecology, (ii) visualize all resources that are part of the ongoing activity across all devices, and (iii) configure devices by manipulating resources through interaction or by the physical properties of the configuration space.

In this paper, we first present the conceptual background of activity-centric configuration spaces. We continue by discussing the design, interaction techniques and technical implementation of the *ActivitySpace* system. Finally, we present a scenario-based user study and conclude the paper by discussing the lessons learned from the implementation and evaluation of the system.

RELATED WORK

ActivitySpace draws upon different fields of related work: (i) smart spaces and distributed user interfaces, (ii) interactive tabletops, and (iii) activity-centric computing.

The seminal work by Weiser [43] has originated a large body of research into smart spaces and distributed user interfaces (DUI). Early systems such as iLand [41] and iRoom [23] provided the first information spaces spanning across multiple screens. Aris [6] focused on supporting legacy application relocation through an interactive space window manager. Impromptu [7] supports the sharing and distribution of legacy application across different devices. Shared Substances [17] proposed to explicitly decouple data from functionality to increase support for multi-device environments. These multi-device environments have opened up a design space for cross-device interactions ranging from basic techniques such as Pick and Drop techniques [34], Touch and Interact [18], and Touch and Point combinations [10] to more advanced coupling of devices such as Deepshot [11], which uses a camera to move applications between devices.

Augmented Surfaces [35] is one of the earliest attempts of using projectors to augment a table for creating a seamless workspace and cross-device interaction techniques. The DiamondTouch system [15] is a multi-user touch system supporting collaborative work. Similarly, UbiTable [38] used the DiamondSpin toolkit [39] to support quick and seamless collaboration using shared and private zones on the table. DeskJockey [45] moved away from the explicit interaction on the table and explored its use for passive extension of the workspace. Bluetable [44] introduced a technique based on computer vision and Bluetooth to pair mobile devices to a surface. The FourBySix [19] system extends the tabletop with a flexible mouse and keyboard input system. PhoneTouch [37] allows users to touch the surface with their phones to support a range of interaction techniques. Tide [40] is a lightweight device composition system that allows users to access their smartphone applications on a tabletop using a VNC protocol. Finally, MagicDesk [5] augments the physical desk to bridge the gap between multi-touch interfaces and traditional WIMP interfaces. Despite the success of tabletops in a range of scenarios and domains, supporting complex device ecologies around tabletops remains an open issue [4]. The main difference to prior work is that the primary role of the desk in *ActivitySpace* is to mediate the interconnections between different devices that are in use. Although the desk can be used to interact with resources, it is primarily a visualizer of cross-device information exchange.

Task- or activity-centric computing has been proposed as a computing paradigm that supports users' activities rather than the resources and tools used to perform such activity. Activities are computational representations of work that encapsulate all resources and tools relevant for a specific work setting. Much of the prior work focused on the re-framing of the desktop interface [29, 16, 3, 42, 21], but a number of systems have also explored the sharing of activities across different heterogenous devices [1, 2, 26]. These systems primarily focus on simply replicating the activity model on other devices. However, in a multi-device setting this approach has severe limitations as it lacks support for distributing parts of the activity over all devices used by the same user.

PROBLEMS IN MULTI-DEVICE MANAGEMENT

On average, users own about three to six computing devices [14, 21, 36], including desktop computers, laptops, smartphones, tablets, game systems and e-readers. With the inclusion of additional devices, such as cameras, music players and smart watches, this number can increase up to 10 devices per user [24]. Although a number of tools provide support for cross-device management, studies (e.g., [14, 31, 36]) show that users encounter several challenges when doing so. These challenges can be categorized as problems associated with (i) managing one coherent work activity across several devices; (ii) aggregating and pairing devices; (iii) getting a clear model of what role a device plays in a multi-device setup; and (iv) managing resources across multiple devices.

Activity Management

One of the core problems in multi-device management is that devices are designed with a focus on applications and files, not on the activities people are using them for [14, 21]. Often users' tasks are not confined within a single device, but span these devices in different configurations based on the work condition. In highly mobile situations, people might prefer to use information on one mobile device, but once they are in an office, they might want to change that configuration. In essence, we need to move away from viewing devices as a single source of information to considering them as portals into an information space [28]. Supporting users to seamlessly move or partition parts of their task in the form of resources or UI controls across devices, allows them to better appropriate the interactive capabilities of the different devices used for working on the task (activity) they are performing.

Using and pairing devices

Device multiplicity allows users to choose the appropriate form factor, input bandwidth and interaction techniques for a particular resource. However, although using multiple devices has become common practice, devices are designed and optimized for a single-user/single-device user experience. This implies that devices are not aware of each other or their capabilities, unless they are equipped with special sensors. Basic operations such as moving files, redirecting input or quickly changing tasks are therefore cumbersome, as they require multiple steps and interactions with all devices in use [14]. Additionally, incorporating and pairing new devices in ongoing work creates a device setup overhead, which influences and determines whether a device is used at all [31]. To allow multiple devices to form one seamless distributed workspace, devices would benefit from mutual awareness about the information they contain, including their location and proximity, sensors and input capabilities [27]. This would also allow for more advanced interaction techniques such as cross-device drag and drop or push and pull information between devices [12, 18, 34].

Device role

Users frequently consider their devices as being either the *primary or master device* or being a *secondary or slave device* [24]. Most applications running on these devices, however, do not represent or incorporate this notion of *device role*. Specially, in the recent shift of mobile devices from supporting specific tasks to becoming full information accessors, the changing role of these devices can play an important part in cross-device interaction. If devices can be aware of their role and use pattern, they would facilitate cross-device application and resource management [14]. One example of such role-based functionality, is the ability of a laptop (used as primary device) to send SMS's from a desktop interface over a connected smartphone (attached as secondary device) [31].

Resource management

Many modern tools such as Dropbox or iCloud provide useful functionality such as automatic synchronization, but often lack visibility and control. Although they are a valuable technical distribution mechanism for file sharing, they neither immediately communicate which other users have access to the shared data nor whether the device can actually meaningfully consume the data [36]. Additionally, users do not always trust automatic file sharing. They often find it difficult to understand what actions are applied to their information and how they can reverse or undo these actions [14], pointing at a lack of intelligibility about the functioning of the data synchronization. There is a clear need for an additional control layer on top of these technical infrastructures that makes these underlying processes more visible to the end-user. Managing and accessing information across devices still poses significant configuration problems [14].

CONFIGURATION SPACE

As a conceptual background for describing the challenges and solutions for multi-device management, we introduce the three core concepts of *configuration work*, *activity configuration*, and *configuration space*.

Configuration work is defined as *the meta work required to find and set up all necessary resources needed to perform a specific task.* It is the overhead required to *setup*, *manage*, *understand* and *use* information, applications and services that are part of the ongoing interaction. Next, we define *activity configuration* as *a description of a work context (including files, applications and other meta information, coordination and communication tools) that is a reflection of the real ongoing activity.* This concept inherits from activity-based

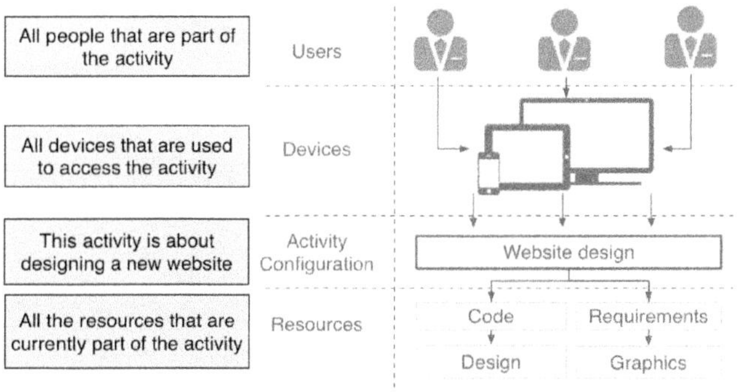

Figure 3. Activity configurations allow multiple users to access the encapsulated resources and services using multiple devices.

computing [2] and as illustrated in Figure 3, an activity configuration specifies which participants are part of the activity, what resources are used, and what devices are used as part of the activity. Compared to the traditional activity-based computing model [2] we introduce a new device layer. In addition to sharing or distributing an activity configuration between users, activities can be also *fragmented* across devices. Thus, a single activity configuration and its resources can span across several devices, and changes to its state are propagated and visualized on these attached devices. By explicitly using activities as fundamental first-class computational structures, such activity configurations can be (i) constructed, (ii) shared, and (iii) restored across devices. Thus, the notion of activity configuration is designed to reduce the amount of configuration work.

A *configuration space* is designed to support activity configurations and reduce configuration work across multiple devices and activities. A *configuration space* is defined as a *digitally augmented physical action space [33] that visualizes the activity of the user across all connected devices, using the surrounding space between the active devices.* Figure 1 illustrates a configuration space. The space is created using a specialized device (such as a projector, interactive surface, or a body worn projector) that mediates the interaction between other devices and their user interfaces. A configuration space can be either public or private and has three fundamental functions:

Device management – Dynamically and visually create and manage device ecologies by coupling or decoupling devices. Based on the changing focus of the users, the space allows users to automatically or manually change the role of the device.

Activity management – Create, copy, move, share, distribute, and fragment activity configurations across all devices in the ecology. The space allows for auto-configuration of devices using the configuration of previous activity states or other similar devices.

Interaction – Configure devices by manipulating resources through interaction or by the physical properties of the configuration space. By leveraging the physical dimensions of the space or interaction techniques, users can pair devices, move resources between devices and re-configure activity configurations.

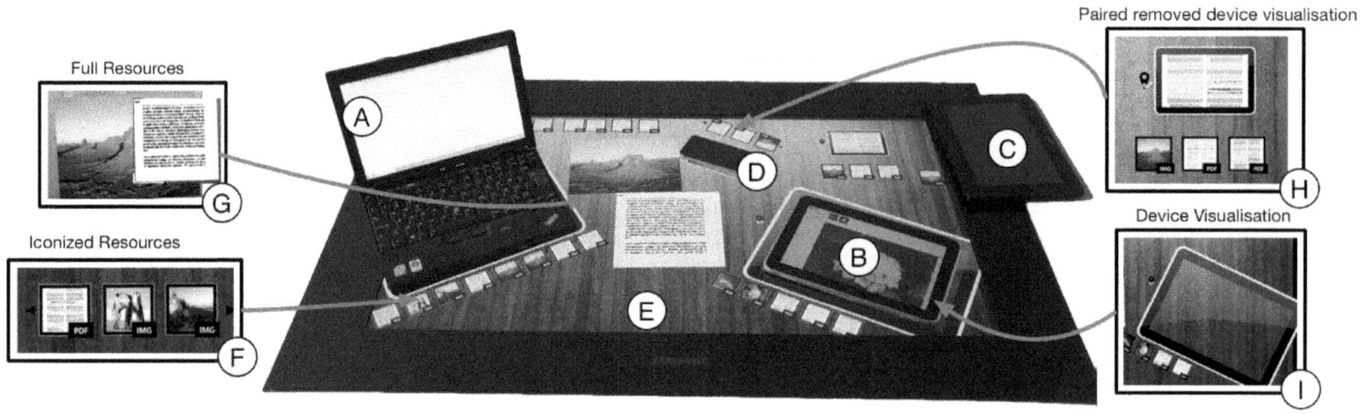

Figure 2. ***ActivitySpace*** **supports activity-centric resource management spanning across (A) laptops, (B-C) tablets and (D) phones using an (E) interactive desk as mediating configuration space. The configuration space visualizes all devices (H-I) and their allocated resources (F-G), that are part of the current activity. Additional devices can be added by placing them in the configuration space. Moving resources to a device is done by drag and drop. When the user suspends an activity, the entire space configuration on all linked devices is persisted. When the activity is resumed, the entire configuration is reestablished.**

ACTIVITYSPACE

ActivitySpace is an implementation of the *configuration space* concept. It is a distributed activity-centric information management system that allows users to create, manage and distribute applications, resources and services across several devices. Figure 2 shows *ActivitySpace*, which uses an interactive surface (e.g., a desk or meeting table) (Figure 2E) as a configuration space that allows users to interconnect and move information between devices on top of it. *ActivitySpace* consists of three parts: (i) a configuration space application that mediates the linkage to other clients; (ii) a number of platform specific clients for laptop, tablet, and phone devices; and (iii) a distributed activity-centric infrastructure that is used both for distribution of activities and resources, as well for discovery and pairing of devices.

Configuration Space

ActivitySpace is built around a personal interactive surface that works as the *configuration spaces* (Figure 2E). This space allows users to (i) easily add or remove devices to the ongoing work context, (ii) fragment resources across available devices, and (iii) save and restore such cross-device configurations when resuming and suspending activities.

Device Management

Activity-centric devices can run in three modes: (i) isolated, (ii) master, and (iii) slave. When set to *isolated*, devices shield all activities to become a single device activity system that does not allow any external connection to access the local set of activities. Whereas, if set to either of the remaining modes, devices participate in a distributed activity system. In *master* mode, a device allows attached devices to access its activity system making it distributed, which results in all activities part of the system being visualized on the devices. In *slave* mode, the device is attached to the activity system of a master device, which implies that the device has only access to resources assigned by the master device. When a new device is placed on the interactive space, the surface detects the device and adds a new visualization to indicate that it was added. If no other device is associated with the space, the newly detected device is marked as master device, meaning it has active control over other devices added to the space. If the device is not the first detected device on the space, it will similarly add a visualization to the space, but by default connect the device as a slave to the master device. Removing slave devices from the space will disconnect them from the master and cause their visualization in the space to be removed. If the master device is removed while there are connected slave devices, the first attached slave device will become the master. If no slave devices are connected, the space terminates the session. The device visualization includes a frame surrounding the physical device and two icons (Figure 2I). The first icon, visible only in case of connection failure, indicates whether the device is successfully connected to the activity system. The second one, located on the side of the device, is used to *pin* the device to the surface. Pinning a device allows users to physically remove the device from the space to allow for local mobility; in this condition, the frame surrounding the physical device becomes the placeholder representing the linked device. Finally, when multiple devices are added to the space, the resources connected to each specific device are visualized (Figure 2F). This mechanism supports both individual workflows in which all devices are owned by the same user, but also collaborative workflows where devices of other users are added to the activity system, thus providing them with access to the shared resources and activities.

Resource Management

Each time the configuration space is refreshed by linking a device as master or by switching activity from a master device already linked, the entire configuration space layout is saved and updated to the correct one. This allows users to create and switch between cross-device spatially organized activity configurations. Switching an activity on the master device causes all attached devices to change accordingly, thus, updating the attached resources visualized on the space. Creating a new activity clears all resources and provides users with a blank canvas, similar to a virtual desktop. By default each resource is shown in a iconized state. Users can use touch input to interact with the resources. The configuration spaces do not provide any occlusion handling when resources are in full scale mode. However, when iconized, resources can never be occluded by devices as they will automatically snap to either the device or dock on the side closest to the loca-

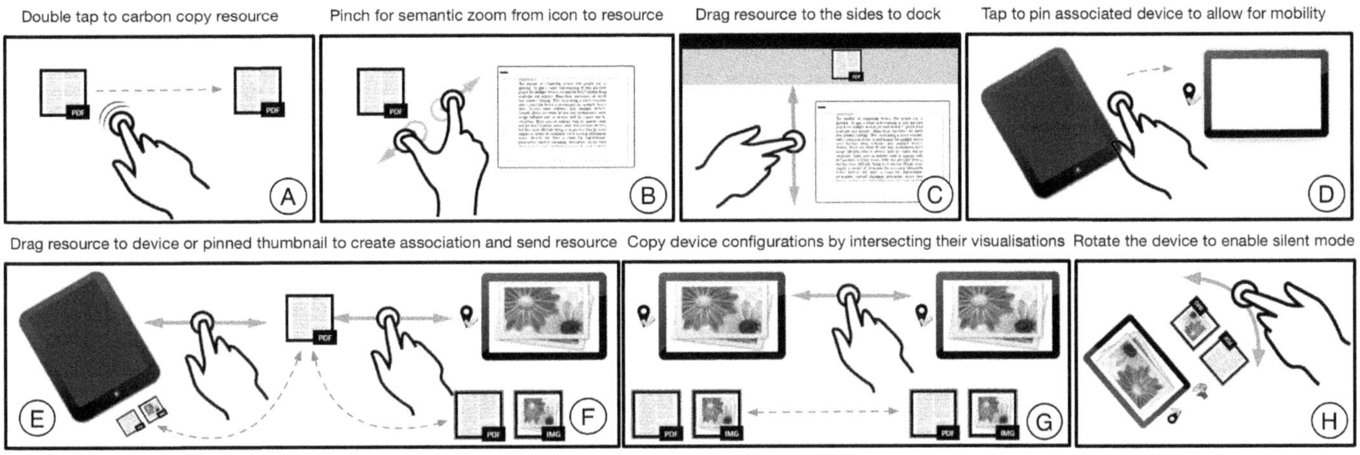

Figure 4. The configuration space provides a number of basic techniques to interact with resources and devices. User can copy (A), scale (B) or dock (C) resources on the space or drag them to another device (E). The space also allows users to pin their device (D), copy entire device configurations (G) and use spatial orientation to configure device properties (H).

tion of the resource (similar to [25]). This ensures that icons can be managed efficiently without moving the configuration problem to the physical space.

User Interaction

Figure 4 provides an overview of the interaction techniques supported in ActivitySpace, designed to facilitate visual and physical management of resources and devices on the space:

A : Copying – To support the copying of resources (e.g., to share with another user), users can *double tap* the icon, causing the space to create a carbon copy of the resource. If the copied resource is in the space and not assigned to another device, it will be connected to the original icon with a visual line to indicate the relation between the nodes. This connection is removed either when one of the nodes is attached to a device by dragging it to the visualization, or by double tapping one of the icons to delete the copy.

B : Viewing – By using the *pinch* gesture, users can semantically scale the resource from the iconized view to a full representation in a window (see Figure 2G). This window can be moved, rotated and scaled. Users can iconize a window by using the pinch gesture to scale down the touch window to less than 150 pixels, by using the minimize button or by double tapping the resource.

C : Docking – Users can organize the space, by docking resources to the edges of the space. Dragging the resource (iconized or in a window) to the edge of the space will cause the space to render the resource as an icon and fix it to the side of the space. By dragging the docked icon back into the space, the previous state is restored.

D : Pinning – Users can pin the device to the space by tapping the icon next to the visualization. A pinned device can be removed from the space without losing connection to the space.

E : Moving – Icons can be dragged onto the space itself, thus detaching them from the devices. This allows users to utilize the entire configuration space to manage, compare or simply store resources.

F : Sending – Icons can be dragged and dropped onto the visualizations of other devices. This will cause the underlying activity system to send the resource to that device, which in turn will show the full resource on the screen. The visualizations of the devices are updated to reflect the changes in the device configuration. To avoid accidentally sending the resource to a device on the space, they can only be sent to another device while in icon mode.

G : Reconfiguration – To support fast and easy device reconfiguration, entire device configurations can be copied by bumping either the real devices or their visualizations together. The configuration is copied from the device that is moved first to the second device. This allows multiple users to quickly and easily copy an entire working context without manually dragging all resources to the space, simply to move them to another device.

H : Availability – Devices (e.g., phones) can be put in *silent mode* by simply rotating them to a specific angle. The visualization updates accordingly and shows an icon that communicates the state of the phone. This approach allows users to very quickly reconfigure their availability without actually having to interact with the phone UI.

Activity-Centric Devices

Figure 5 shows the *activity-centric desktop interface* used on the laptop devices. This design leverages prior work in activity-centric computing for personal computers [3, 21] and provides users with an activity workspace supporting ad hoc configurations of windows, applications, and files. Ongoing activities are visualized on an activity bar, which mimics the normal Windows Taskbar and can be docked on any side of the screen. Clicking the buttons on the activity bar will cause the activity node to repopulate the desktop workspace with the windows and files associated with that activity. The bar is also used to create new activity workspaces and to modify activities. Files can be added to an activity by dragging and dropping them on the activity buttons in the activity bar.

Figure 6 shows the *mobile interface* used on tablets and phones that provides users with an activity-aware resource viewer and reading tool. The interface presents an overview of all resources related to an activity and allows users to annotate and modify the resources. Users can either switch activi-

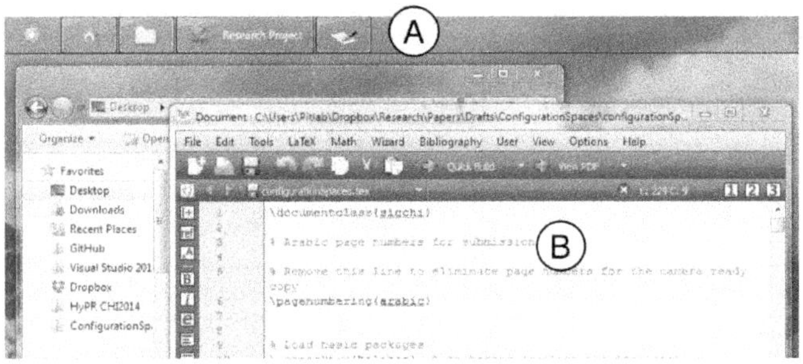

Figure 5. The activity-centric desktop application runs an activity manager allowing users to organize files and applications into an activity workspace (B). Activities are accessed and managed using the activity bar (A). Clicking an activity button on the bar will load the workspace of the associated activity.

ties using the activity sidebar on the tablet (master or isolated mode) or connect the tablet to the activity node running on the configuration space (slave mode).

Activity-centric Infrastructure

ActivitySpace is built using NooSphere [22], which is a distributed activity-centric infrastructure for management of activities, resources, devices, and users. It provides a set of basic technical services related to distributed activity configurations. The services provided range from distributed event management (using web sockets) to file and resource synchronization, from ad hoc broadcast and discovery (using Zeroconf) to a distributed context processor. The infrastructure allows the persistence of entities in the form of activities, resources linked to activities, users, and device data models. Additionally, the system supports the distribution, sharing, and fragmenting of activities across different connected devices.

Each device in *ActivitySpace* runs a specialized activity node, which is composed of an activity manager and an activity client. When running in master mode, the activity manager (AM) is used as a proxy to activities that are stored locally or in the cloud. The AM allows the device to share and distribute activities with other devices through a REST interface and web sockets. To allow other devices to connect to the AM, it runs a discovery and broadcast service (using Zeroconf). The activity client (AC) is used in slave mode and simply connects to another AM that is currently running. Using a similar discovery service, it searches for nearby AMs. Each device is augmented with a fiducial marker that uniquely identifies the device. The value encoded in the marker matches the identifier that is part of the information broadcasted by the device.

The interactive surface application runs a specialized activity node that is composed of several activity clients. When the surface applications detects a fiducial marker, it launches a discovery service to search for a device with a matching AM identifier. If no other devices are connected to the space, it loads all the activities of the AM of the detected device, and visualizes them on the space. If the AM of an other device is already connected to the space, the surface application commands the device into slave mode, and attaches the AC of that device to the AM of the previously detected master device. When the slave device is removed from the interactive space, the surface application disconnects the device from the

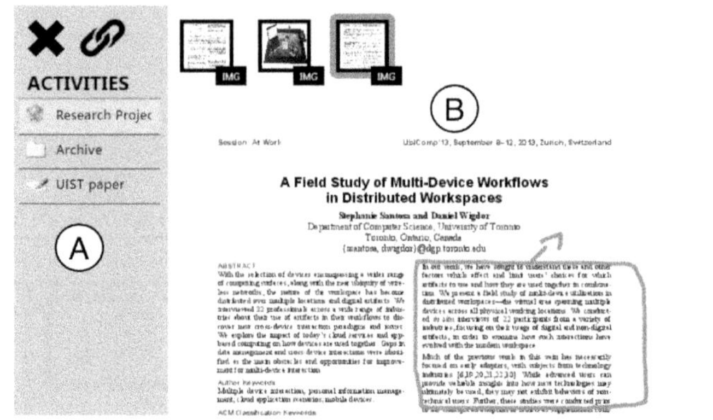

Figure 6. Mobile devices (tablets and smartphones) run an activity-aware resource visualizer and active reading tool (B). The activity bar (A) lists available activities and tools.

AM of the master device and resets the disconnected device back to its original mode. The surface application thus actively mediates the ad hoc peer to peer configuration between attached master and slave devices.

When multiple devices are connected through the interactive space, they are essentially all connected to the AM of the master devices. This means that the activities of that AM are shared and fragmented on the interactive space and slave devices. All devices (including the surface) use an event mechanism to send and receive information on (i) which devices are located on the space, (ii) which activity is currently selected in the AM of the master device and (iii) what resources are assigned to each device. All interactions with the interactive space are tunneled to the AM of the master device and propagated to all slave devices using the event system. The different cross-device activity configuration states (including location of devices, allocated resources, and spatial layout on the interactive space) are stored in the AM of the master device. The surface application can access these configurations to visualize and update them when users explicitly interact with the space or attached devices.

STUDY

To verify the usefulness of the configuration spaces concept and collect user feedback on the design of the *ActivitySpace* system, we conducted a scenario-based user evaluation [13]. The goals of this study were to (i) observe how participants would use the system for cross-device tasks, and (ii) elicit user input on the perceived usefulness of using mediating spaces for cross-device configuration work.

Study Setup

Nine users (two female and seven male, mean age = 30, σ = 4,85) from different backgrounds (such as clinical work, software development, business, and research) participated in the study. Participants rated themselves as generally experienced computer users ($\tilde{x}$= 4; *iqr*= 2 on 5-point Likert scale) and reported to be highly experienced with using multiple devices (average amount of devices = 6, σ = 1,74 including laptops, desktop computers, tablets, phone, and smart-TVs). The study was conducted in a controlled lab environment in which an interactive desk was deployed. The desk consisted of a Microsoft PixelSense built into a normal adjustable office desk. The other devices used in the experiment were a standard

Lenovo X100 laptop running Windows 7, two HP Elitepads running Windows 8, and an iPhone. All interactions with devices where logged and the experiment was videotaped.

Method

The study consisted of three phases. First, users were introduced to the general concept and functionality of the system. They were then asked to conduct a scenario using the think aloud method. The scenario focused on six key features of the system: (i) device coupling and decoupling, (ii) cross-device resource allocation, (iii) activity switching, (iv) multi-user interaction, (v) interruption management, and (vi) mobility. Participants were asked to complete both individual tasks, covering more basic functionality of the system, and collaborative tasks, focusing on the sharing of resources and activities. In the scenario, participants collected, compared and shared a number of example websites, logos and other data needed to build a new website for a company using available devices. After they successfully organized the required information in activities, they prepared a tablet with the information needed to give a presentation. After returning from the presentation, they continued to work on finding information across different activities, until interrupted by their boss who asked if the user could provide him with website designs and logos thus starting a collaborative session on the desk. Finally, after completing the scenario, participants were asked to complete a short survey, which was used as the basis for a semi-structured interview in which they were asked (i) to provide feedback on the usefulness of *ActivitySpace* and (ii) to explore potential use cases for configuration spaces.

Results

User Feedback

Figure 7 presents an overview of the results of the questionnaire on the usefulness of the different aspects of the system. Participants argued that *activities* provided them with a stable cross-device information management concept ($Q1$: $\tilde{x}$= 4; *iqr*= 1). During the scenarios, we observed how participants quickly became accustomed to using activities and even reasoned in activities. Switching between activities on all devices was considered easy ($Q2$: $\tilde{x}$= 4; *iqr*= 1) and most participants used both the tablets and the laptop computer to control the currently selected activity. They simply used the device that was most convenient. The consistent and persistent spatial configuration of devices and resources helped users to quickly switch between different work context without loosing overview:

> – *"When you organize all files into activities, you avoid having too many files and clutter on the desk. You only have what you need or what you are working on." – P4*

We also observed different activity creation patterns. Some users would create a new activity for each specific sub-task right before they initiated the sub task, while others would create a number of empty activities up front. Participants also used a wide range of names and icons for the activities, as it helped them reflect better on the content of the activities. During the scenarios, some users would also update the name or icon to *"make it better reflect the work they were doing"* – P1. Because the activity structure is essentially an open ended configuration tool, participants used activities and switched between them in very different ways. As one user argued: *"flexibility is super important as not everyone thinks the same." – P8* Although the configuration space itself would actively display the name of the ongoing activity, very few users noticed this, as the spatial organization as well as the views on the devices were enough information to recall the activity. In general, most participants felt comfortable using activities across devices since they already achieved this to a certain degree in their usual device ecology using workarounds:

> – *"I guess that organizing information in activities is something everyone already tries to do, but with a lot of effort and workarounds." – P3*

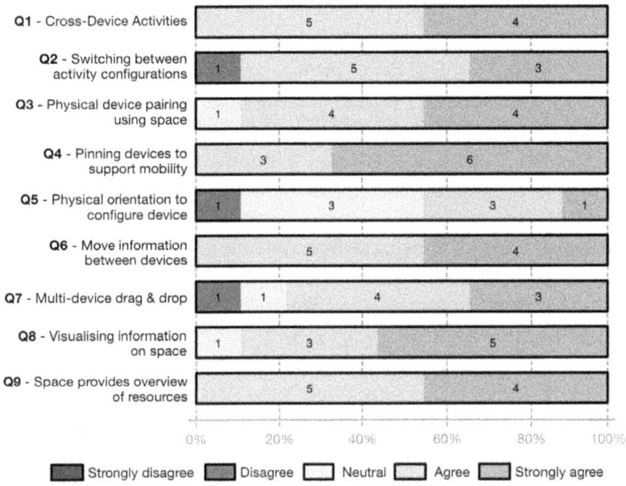

Figure 7. The results of the a 5-point Likert-scale questionnaire on the usefulness of the different parts of the system. The numbers in the bar represent the amount of participants.

Utilizing the configuration space to connect different devices to the same activity was considered very useful ($Q3$: $\tilde{x}$= 4; *iqr*= 1). Many users mentioned in the interviews that connecting devices to exchange one piece of information is often a tedious process that involves cloud storage or multiple interactions with devices. Using a physical connection between the mobile device and the space to add the device to the ongoing activity session was considered to be very useful and intuitive. Pinning the devices to the desk to allow for local mobility was also considered as a very useful feature ($Q4$: $\tilde{x}$= 5; *iqr*= 1). Participants generally mentioned during interviews that the device thumbnails helped in creating consistency between situations where the device was placed on the desk or when it was used in mid-air. Using the physical orientation to configure properties of the device was considered less important ($Q5$: $\tilde{x}$= 3; *iqr*= 1). Most participants considered this a *"nice feature"* – P2, but not really relevant to maintaining cross-device information overview.

Moving resources between different connected devices was perceived as very easy and useful ($Q6$: $\tilde{x}$= 4; *iqr*= 1). Participants appreciated the simplicity of dragging information across the space from one device to another ($Q7$: $\tilde{x}$= 4; *iqr*= 1). The externalization of resources on the space was considered as the best feature of the system. Because each of the devices visualized the associated resources in an iconized state, participants had a good overview on (i) which resources were part of the activity, and (ii) on which device the resources were allocated (*Q*8: $\tilde{x}$= 5; *iqr*= 1). This allowed them to efficiently *fragment* resources contained in an activity across different devices in use. Participants easily switched between the different resource viewing modes using the pinch gestures demonstrating the effectiveness of the modal interaction supported through semantic zooming. All participants agreed that that use of a configuration space provided them with a clear overview of all their activities, devices, and contained resources (*Q*9: $\tilde{x}$= 4; *iqr*= 1). The idea of using a physical space to make the connection between devices more visible was considered as very useful:

> – *"I really like the idea of using the empty space between devices to show what's on them. Most of my devices are currently already on or around my desk, so why not use this space."* – *P4*

Even during the relatively short scenarios, we observed how participants quickly took ownership over the desk. Conceptually, the configuration space is a public mediating infrastructure that requires a master device from a user to actually access that user's information. Participants liked this idea of a public space that can be used to *"do multi-device work"* – P2 and mentioned that, similar to normal tables and desks, most of them are public until one person claims ownership over it. In that case, they argued that the configuration space should be able to store local session information. The desk could for instance be used as a master log-in device that provides automatic authentication for all applications across devices. The configuration space concept was considered to be useful for both individual and collaborative work as users argued that the fundamental problem in both cases lies in providing easy and quick task and information exchange capabilities. However, the highly social character of the multi-user sharing model was received with mixed feelings. Since sharing essentially happens by one user allowing another user to place their device in their configuration space, some users argued that this might have some privacy implications related to what activities or what resources the visiting user can access.

Observations

While using devices and resources on the configuration space, we observed a number of distinct patterns of use, that occurred with most participants:

Pull and push devices – When working with information that was on both the device and on the desk, participants often moved devices around the configuration space to make more room for interacting with resources that were located on the space. Participants would consistently push devices to the back when they were no longer being used, and pull them back to the front of the space when needed.

Device on the edge – When some secondary devices (such as a mobile phone or tablet) were not in active use, participants would pin them to the desk, and place them on the edge of the configuration space outside of the tracked zone. Although the devices were not in use, participants generally kept them connected to the configuration space, "just in case".

Figure 8. Touch interaction data of 9 users plotted on the desk space. The data shows circular movements of resources around visualisations (orange color). Other colors represent the touch input of participants which is primarily focussed in the front middle of the desk.

Implicit zones – During the multi-user scenarios, users would implicitly create zones in which each of the devices of the different users were located. The structure of these zones differed between users, but participants generally organized their devices in physical proximity to each other. The proximity of the devices as well as their spatial position were thus a helpful tool for users to distinguish between devices but also to get an overview of all the resources on the desk.

Maneuvering around devices – When moving resources or devices around in the space, users would often carefully maneuver them around other devices that were located on the space (orange plot in Figure 8), to avoid that a resource was accidentally associated with a wrong device.

Interaction zone – As seen in Figure 8, most interactions with resources and devices were done on the front middle of the desk, within the private zone of users. Users would move resources and devices into a focused interaction zone and essentially use the rest of space as a permanent peripheral display for configuration work or storage [20].

Devices as folders – Some users would drag and drop a number of resources to a specific device that was pinned to the space but not actively in use. This was done not to actually use them on the device, but to simply bundle them inside one physical device. Therefore, they used devices as a *physical folder* to organize a number of related resources into one manageable structure that can be moved around in the physical space.

Cross-device drag and drop – Because iconized resources can never be occluded by a device as they automatically snap to the overlaying device, we observed that long drag and drop operations across the configuration space would often result in several discrete drag and drop operations between intermediate devices. So rather than occluding the resource, the device would simply "absorb" and "pop up" the iconized resource at the bottom of the device.

DISCUSSION

The central goal of *ActivitySpace* is to provide users with a transparent platform for creating, maintaining, and sharing ad hoc device ecologies in which devices are visually connected on a *configuration space* using *activity* as a central computational concept.

As devices are increasingly becoming portals into a shared and collaborative ubiquitous information space, it has become apparent that devices can no longer be considered separate entities, but rather part of larger artifact ecology [24]. As one user concluded:

– *"None of the things that we are currently using [in our company] is really working. We need to rethink how devices are connected and used." – P1*

Users essentially do not act *with* computing devices, but rather *through* computing devices. Bødker and Klokmose [8] therefore proposed to relate the notion of artifact ecologies [24] to human activities because *"the artifact ecology of an individual is highly dynamic"* [9] as it is constructed by the user through their activities. We build on this concept as we describe users' device ecologies as *ad hoc and dynamic interrelations between interconnected devices which are part of the same motive-oriented activity or task.* By connecting the activity of users explicitly to their devices, users are presented with a cross-device representation that moves away from the predominant application and document-centric paradigm.

ActivitySpace employs the concept of a configuration space to embrace this notion of *activity-centric device ecologies.* It supports visual and direct feedback on the connection of devices and the distribution of resources that are part of the same ongoing activity. By providing users with a physical space that has clear affordances and boundaries, users were able to easily manage multiple tasks containing multiple resources across different devices. The explicitness of placing devices in the configuration space provided users with a *stable concept* that helped them better understand and manage which of their devices are currently being used as part of their *active device ecology.* This point of view allowed users to appropriate individual devices as physical proxies for digital information [35] that could be included or excluded from their active device ecology.

ActivitySpace currently allows users to select one activity to be visualized on the configuration space and on the connected devices. Although individual devices can be decoupled from this shared activity view, the space can only visualize one activity: the one it is mediating. Participants however discussed that this could be greatly expanded by, e.g., using the space to compare a number of different activities at the same time. During the interviews, many participants essentially argued for moving more management or configuration tools to the desk, and step away from the use of the notebook as master device. One user proposed to have a cross-device task bar on the desk that could be used to switch tasks on different devices, but also give access to the sound and display properties of the device and even have a centralized notification mechanism. Participants also argued that visual feedback on the actual sending process of resources between devices, could be made even more explicit by using animations or other patterns that visualize the transition between devices in a more gradual way as described in the Gradual Engagement Pattern [27].

Sharing activities or specific resources is done using a social sharing model, in which users physically allow each other to place devices into their configuration space. Including the sharing of activity configuration into the fundamental concept improves some of the technical issues related to finding and agreeing on which tool or platform to use. However, it also creates a continuous public-private tension that is intrinsic to any interconnected artifact [32]. Allowing another user to enter one's private space is an explicit act of breaking the boundary between the self and other users [32] and is part of a continuous negotiation of intent [30]. A confirmation of this negotiation process observed during the evaluation is that each participant explicitly allowed the second user to access the configuration space, but only in a zone that was implicitly created through the spatial configuration of the devices of the owner. Although this highly social and spatial sharing model provides a stable concept for sharing information, it also opens discussion on what happens when the owner of the configuration space is not physically there. This privacy tension also explains why participants were so explicit about the purpose of configuration spaces as either public spaces—usable by anyone—or private spaces—clearly owned by one user.

ActivitySpace currently uses augmented tables and desks, using build-in interactive surfaces. This concept can however be expanded to other approaches using for instance top-mounted projectors to cover even larger spaces or support tracking of devices above and around the configuration space. Furthermore, mobile devices such as augmented reality glasses or body-worn projectors can support mobile configuration spaces. Finally, future work could explore in more depth how task management across devices can be unified in one centralized access point.

CONCLUSION

This paper introduced *ActivitySpace*, which is a distributed activity-centric information management system that allows users to create, manage and distribute applications, resources and services across different devices that are part of the same activity. *ActivitySpace* uses interactive surfaces as mediating configuration spaces that visualize the active device ecology of users. The scenario-based study demonstrated the usefulness of activity as a central concept for distributed interaction, and how the configuration space provided users with a stable concept for managing their device ecology. Finally, the study highlighted a number of usage patterns on how users appropriated the space for multi-device work.

ACKNOWLEDGMENTS

This work was supported by the EU Marie Curie Network iCareNet under grant number 264738. Thanks to Steven Jeuris and Aurelien Tabard for comments, suggestions, and feedback on an early version of this work.

REFERENCES

1. Bardram, J., Gueddana, S., Houben, S., and Nielsen, S. Reticularspaces: Activity-based computing support for physically distributed and collaborative smart spaces. In *Proc. of CHI'12*, ACM (2012), 2845–2854.
2. Bardram, J. E. Activity-based computing for medical work in hospitals. *TOCHI 16*, 2 (2009), 10.
3. Bardram, J. E., Bunde-Pedersen, J., and Soegaard, M. Support for activity-based computing in a personal computing operating system. In *Proc. of CHI'06*, ACM (2006), 211–220.

4. Bellucci, A., Malizia, A., and Aedo, I. Light on horizontal interactive surfaces: Input space for tabletop computing. *ACM Computing Surveys (CSUR) 46*, 3 (2014), 32.
5. Bi, X., Grossman, T., Matejka, J., and Fitzmaurice, G. Magic desk: bringing multi-touch surfaces into desktop work. In *Proc. of CHI'11*, ACM (2011), 2511–2520.
6. Biehl, J. T., and Bailey, B. P. Aris: an interface for application relocation in an interactive space. In *Proc. of GI'04*, Canadian Human-Computer Communications Society (2004), 107–116.
7. Biehl, J. T., Baker, W. T., Bailey, B. P., Tan, D. S., Inkpen, K. M., and Czerwinski, M. Impromptu: a new interaction framework for supporting collaboration in multiple display environments and its field evaluation for co-located software development. In *Proc. of CHI'08*, ACM (2008), 939–948.
8. Bødker, S., and Klokmose, C. N. The human–artifact model: An activity theoretical approach to artifact ecologies. *Human–Computer Interaction 26*, 4 (2011), 315–371.
9. Bødker, S., and Klokmose, C. N. Dynamics in artifact ecologies. In *Proc. of NordiCHI'12*, ACM (2012), 448–457.
10. Bragdon, A., DeLine, R., Hinckley, K., and Morris, M. R. Code space: touch+ air gesture hybrid interactions for supporting developer meetings. In *Proc. of ITS'11*, ACM (2011), 212–221.
11. Chang, T.-H., and Li, Y. Deep shot: a framework for migrating tasks across devices using mobile phone cameras. In *Proc. of CHI'11*, ACM (2011), 2163–2172.
12. Chen, N., Guimbretiere, F., and Sellen, A. Designing a multi-slate reading environment to support active reading activities. *TOCHI 19*, 3 (2012), 18.
13. Convertino, G., Neale, D. C., Hobby, L., Carroll, J. M., and Rosson, M. B. A laboratory method for studying activity awareness. In *Proc. of NordiCHI'04*, ACM (2004), 313–322.
14. Dearman, D., and Pierce, J. S. It's on my other computer!: computing with multiple devices. In *Proc. of CHI'08*, ACM (2008), 767–776.
15. Dietz, P., and Leigh, D. Diamondtouch: a multi-user touch technology. In *Proc. of UIST'01*, ACM (2001), 219–226.
16. Dragunov, A. N., Dietterich, T. G., Johnsrude, K., McLaughlin, M., Li, L., and Herlocker, J. L. Tasktracer: a desktop environment to support multi-tasking knowledge workers. In *Proc. of IUI'05*, ACM (2005), 75–82.
17. Gjerlufsen, T., Klokmose, C. N., Eagan, J., Pillias, C., and Beaudouin-Lafon, M. Shared substance: developing flexible multi-surface applications. In *Proc. of CHI'11*, ACM (2011), 3383–3392.
18. Hardy, R., and Rukzio, E. Touch & interact: touch-based interaction of mobile phones with displays. In *Proc. of MobileHCI'08*, ACM (2008), 245–254.
19. Hartmann, B., Morris, M. R., Benko, H., and Wilson, A. D. Augmenting interactive tables with mice & keyboards. In *Proc. of UIST'09*, ACM (2009), 149–152.
20. Houben, S., and Bardram, J. E. Activitydesk: multi-device configuration work using an interactive desk. In *In CHI'13 EA Abstracts*, ACM (2013), 721–726.
21. Houben, S., Bardram, J. E., Vermeulen, J., Luyten, K., and Coninx, K. Activity-centric support for ad hoc knowledge work: a case study of co-activity manager. In *Proc. of CHI'13*, ACM (2013), 2263–2272.
22. Houben, S., Nielsen, S., Esbensen, M., and Bardram, J. Noosphere: An activity-centric infrastructure for distributed interaction. In *Proc. of MUM '13*, ACM (2013).
23. Johanson, B., Hutchins, G., Winograd, T., and Stone, M. Pointright: experience with flexible input redirection in interactive workspaces. In *Proc. of UIST'02*, ACM (2002), 227–234.
24. Jung, H., Stolterman, E., Ryan, W., Thompson, T., and Siegel, M. Toward a framework for ecologies of artifacts: how are digital artifacts interconnected within a personal life? In *Proc. of NordiCHI'08*, ACM (2008), 201–210.
25. Khalilbeigi, M., Steimle, J., Riemann, J., Dezfuli, N., Mühlhäuser, M., and Hollan, J. D. Objectop: occlusion awareness of physical objects on interactive tabletops. In *Proc. of ITS'13*, ACM (2013), 255–264.
26. MacIntyre, B., Mynatt, E. D., Voida, S., Hansen, K. M., Tullio, J., and Corso, G. M. Support for multitasking and background awareness using interactive peripheral displays. In *Proc. of UIST'01*, ACM (2001), 41–50.
27. Marquardt, N., Ballendat, T., Boring, S., Greenberg, S., and Hinckley, K. Gradual engagement: facilitating information exchange between digital devices as a function of proximity. In *Proc. of ITS'12*, ACM (2012), 31–40.
28. Moran, T. P., and Zhai, S. *Beyond the desktop in seven dimensions*. The MIT Press, 2007, ch. 11, 335–354.
29. Muller, M. J., Geyer, W., Brownholtz, B., Wilcox, E., and Millen, D. R. One-hundred days in an activity-centric collaboration environment based on shared objects. In *Proc. of CHI'04*, ACM (2004), 375–382.
30. O'Hara, K. Interactivity and non-interactivity on tabletops. In *Proc. of CHI'10*, ACM (2010), 2611–2614.
31. Oulasvirta, A., and Sumari, L. Mobile kits and laptop trays: managing multiple devices in mobile information work. In *Proc. of CHI'07*, ACM (2007), 1127–1136.
32. Palen, L., and Dourish, P. Unpacking privacy for a networked world. In *Proc. of CHI'03*, ACM (2003), 129–136.
33. Pederson, T., Janlert, L.-E., and Surie, D. a situative space model for mobile mixed-reality computing. *Pervasive Computing, IEEE 10*, 4 (2011), 73–83.
34. Rekimoto, J. Pick-and-drop: a direct manipulation technique for multiple computer environments. In *Proc. of UIST'97*, ACM (1997), 31–39.
35. Rekimoto, J., and Saitoh, M. Augmented surfaces: a spatially continuous work space for hybrid computing environments. In *Proc. of CHI'99*, ACM (1999), 378–385.
36. Santosa, S., and Wigdor, D. A field study of multi-device workflows in distributed workspaces. In *Proc. of UbiComp'13*, ACM (2013), 63–72.
37. Schmidt, D., Chehimi, F., Rukzio, E., and Gellersen, H. Phonetouch: a technique for direct phone interaction on surfaces. In *Proc. of UIST'10*, ACM (2010), 13–16.
38. Shen, C., Everitt, K., and Ryall, K. Ubitable: Impromptu face-to-face collaboration on horizontal interactive surfaces. In *Proc. of UbiComp'03*, Springer (2003), 281–288.
39. Shen, C., Vernier, F. D., Forlines, C., and Ringel, M. Diamondspin: an extensible toolkit for around-the-table interaction. In *Proc. of CHI'04*, ACM (2004), 167–174.
40. Sicard, L., Tabard, A., Hincapié-Ramos, J. D., and Bardram, J. E. Tide: Lightweight device composition for enhancing tabletop environments with smartphone applications. In *Human-Computer Interaction–INTERACT 2013*. Springer, 2013, 177–194.
41. Streitz, N. A., Geißler, J., Holmer, T., Konomi, S., Müller-Tomfelde, C., Reischl, W., Rexroth, P., Seitz, P., and Steinmetz, R. i-land: an interactive landscape for creativity and innovation. In *Proc. of CHI'97*, ACM (1999), 120–127.
42. Voida, S., and Mynatt, E. D. It feels better than filing: everyday work experiences in an activity-based computing system. In *Proc. of CHI'09*, ACM (2009), 259–268.
43. Weiser, M. The computer for the 21st century. *Scientific american 265*, 3 (1991), 94–104.
44. Wilson, A. D., and Sarin, R. Bluetable: connecting wireless mobile devices on interactive surfaces using vision-based handshaking. In *Proc. of GI'07*, ACM (2007), 119–125.
45. Ziola, R., Kellar, M., and Inkpen, K. Deskjockey: exploiting passive surfaces to display peripheral information. In *Proc. of INTERACT 2007*. Springer, 2007, 447–460.

SleeD: Using a Sleeve Display to Interact with Touch-sensitive Display Walls

Ulrich von Zadow, Wolfgang Büschel, Ricardo Langner, Raimund Dachselt
Interactive Media Lab, Technische Universität Dresden
Dresden, Germany
uzadow,bueschel,langner,dachselt@acm.org

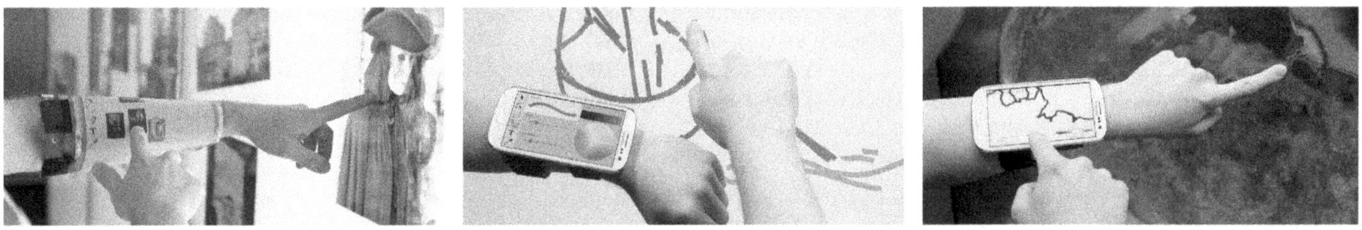

Figure 1. SleeD prototypes: e-Ink mockup (left), smartphone-based prototype showing tool palette (center) and interactive personal view (right)

ABSTRACT
We present SleeD, a touch-sensitive Sleeve Display that facilitates interaction with multi-touch display walls. Large vertical displays allow multiple users to interact effectively with complex data but are inherently public. Also, they generally cannot present an interface adapted to the individual user. The combination with an arm-mounted, interactive display allows complex personalized interactions. In contrast to hand-held devices, both hands remain free for interacting with the wall. We discuss different levels of coupling between wearable and wall and propose novel user interface techniques that support user-specific interfaces, data transfer, and arbitrary personal views. In an iterative development process, we built a mock-up using a bendable e-Ink display and a fully functional prototype based on an arm-mounted smartphone. In addition, we developed several applications that showcase the techniques presented. An observational study we conducted demonstrates the high potential of our concepts.

Author Keywords
multi-touch; display wall; wearable display; multi-user; collaboration; information visualization; arm display

ACM Classification Keywords
H.5.2. Information interfaces and presentation: User Interfaces - Graphical user interfaces.

INTRODUCTION
Wall-sized interactive displays are becoming more common and have been shown to provide numerous benefits [2]. Their potentially very high resolution means that they are usable from a distance as well as in reach of the hands, making them suitable for the exploration of large amounts of data. Collaboration is well-supported and physical navigation – moving around to access data – becomes possible, exploiting human spatial awareness [5]. At the same time, they have inherent limitations. Data shown is generally visible by all collaborators and thus public. It is hard to identify the user and provide a user-specific interface. In addition, it is unclear where user interface elements such as tool palettes should be placed on a very large display [2].

In contrast, the most widespread type of computing device – the smartphone – is an inherently personal device that connects users with their digital ID, providing easy access to private data in everyday situations. Due to their small size, smartphones have limited ability to show large amounts of data; also, sharing views with other people is hard at best. Furthermore, hand-held devices cannot be used in situations where both hands must be free, leading to devices such as the Motorola WT4000 arm-worn terminal used by warehouse workers [30]. The recent trend towards smart watches (such as the Sony SmartWatch 3 or the Apple Watch) points in the same direction and showcases a second benefit: quick, effortless activation of the device.

Numerous researchers have combined smartphones and other hand-held devices with shared displays in the past (e.g., [20, 24, 26, 27, 29]). This makes it possible to use the modalities – display output, touch input, sound and haptic feedback – available on the personal device to extend interaction with the large display. It also allows personalized interaction and access to private data when using the large display.

We propose combining large display walls with a touch-enabled sleeve display – the *SleeD*. Using an arm-mounted device in combination with a wall-sized display is novel and provides unique additional benefits. First, touch interaction with a wall is one of the situations in which having both hands

ITS 2014, November 16–19, 2014, Dresden, Germany.

ACM 978-1-4503-2587-5/14/11 ...$15.00.
http://dx.doi.org/10.1145/2669485.2669507

free is advantageous, because it allows bimanual interaction. Second, interaction becomes seamless and facilitates a quality of *flow*: When the user touches the wall, the hand assumes the role of conduit between personal data on the SleeD and public data on the vertical display (see Figure 1). Third, arm-worn devices support *effortless activation* [3]: While the SleeD is available at the flick of a wrist, hand-held devices must be retrieved from pockets or other storage, making it much easier to integrate the device into other activities.

Our individual contributions in this paper are:

- The SleeD Concept: This includes physical considerations such as placement and properties of the display as well as an analysis of different levels of coupling between SleeD and wall. We also present a range of novel user interface techniques that support modal interfaces and provide personal storage as well as personalized views.
- Prototypes: We present two wearable hardware prototypes. The first one is non-interactive and based on a bendable e-Ink display. The second is realized using a conventional smartphone attached to the arm. In addition, we present several software applications based on the second prototype that showcase the concepts and techniques described.
- User Study: We report on an observational user study that shows the high potential of the concepts and techniques.

In the following, we present the proposed SleeD device and two scenarios illustrating typical usage, followed by reviewing related work. Underlying concepts are described in the subsequent section, followed by a description of the prototype hardware and software. We then describe the conducted user study and conclude with an outlook to future work.

SleeD

We envision a wearable arm display covering most of the forearm in length and circumference (see Figure 2). The device is an unobtrusive, lightweight system with a touch-sensitive high-resolution color display. It otherwise has the input and output capabilities of today's smartphones, including accelerometers and vibro-tactile feedback as well as audio in- and output. SleeD is not significantly more cumbersome than normal clothing, allowing everyday use. We see it fulfilling several roles.

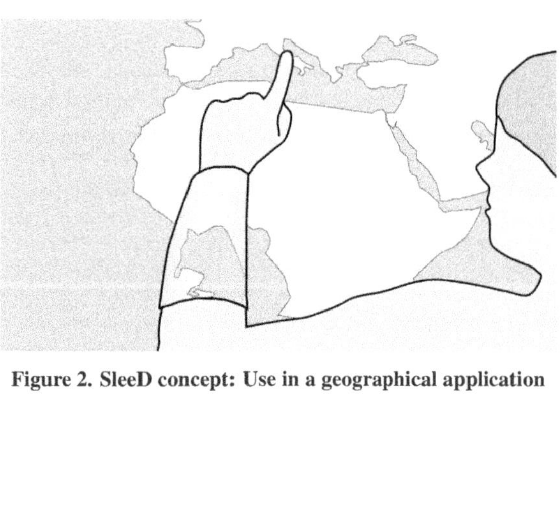

Figure 2. SleeD concept: Use in a geographical application

First, SleeD is a *personal device* that provides arbitrary applications and allows access to personal data, similar to today's smartphones. Following Martin [18], the development of smartphones could well mimic wristwatch development: Once the weight of the device is reduced sufficiently, the benefits of effortless activation and hands-free usage come to the fore. A second role – again, hinted at by the development of the wristwatch [18] – is that of a *fashion accessory*. In addition, we foresee a third role: The SleeD can greatly *enhance interaction with other devices*, among them large interactive displays. It serves as a conduit between personal and public data. Furthermore, it can provide a personal clipboard and user-specific tool palettes as well as show contextual information – all while allowing bimanual interaction on the large display. In this paper, we concentrate on the third role.

While the envisioned device cannot be built entirely using current technology, ongoing research in the area of flexible displays and circuitry will likely provide the means for such a device in the near future [10].

Walkthrough

In the following, we present two scenarios of typical uses of our envisioned system to illustrate our concept.

I. Jane works in the field of geoinformatics, often analyzing large geographical datasets. She stands in front of a wall-sized interactive display that shows a map. A SleeD is attached to her left forearm, showing an overview of the entire map. By touching the map on the SleeD, Jane selects the part of the map to be shown on the vertical display. Thus, she can quickly zoom in on an area of interest, benefiting from the high-resolution wall display.

She then approaches the wall to see more details. When she touches it, the wearable switches to a detail view of the area touched (see Figure 2), leveraging the higher pixel density of the SleeD. Probing is also supported. In this mode, the arm display shows additional data on the current touch point and thus avoids clutter on the vertical display. These personal views are especially useful when John, a colleague of hers, arrives and they work on the dataset in collaboration: By zooming and filtering their personal views, they avoid disrupting the view on the wall. When Jane is ready to share insights, she transfers her personal view to the wall and they discuss the results together.

II. Mark and Jennifer work for a media company. They use SleeDs in combination with a display wall for selecting and annotating photos. When Mark finds interesting pictures, he touches them with his SleeD hand and uses the other hand to quickly drag them to his personal display. To copy the photos to a different location in the shared workspace, he simply flicks them from the wearable back to the wall. Since the SleeD is mounted on his arm and not a hand-held device, he can seamlessly switch to working with paper artifacts such as printed magazines and photos.

His colleague Jennifer can quickly change between different editing modes, such as annotating or image manipulation using a tool palette on the SleeD. Still, her hands remain free for bi-manual work on the larger display. Tool palettes and other context- and mode-sensitive user interface elements are displayed on the SleeD, staying with her as she moves along the wall. Just as importantly, the tool configurations are her personal configurations: When she switches to a tool for color correction, she doesn't interrupt Mark's ongoing work.

These scenarios showcase several important aspects of the proposed system integrated in an end-user context: effortless activation; quick, lightweight, user-specific mode switches; personal display and storage spaces as well as clipboards; overview-and-detail support; and hands-free interaction on the wall. In comparison to hand-held mobile devices, changing the focus between vertical display and personal device is less cumbersome, because the SleeD does not have to be put away when not actively in use.

RELATED WORK

Our work builds on research in a number of different areas, including large wall-sized displays, wearable computing and interaction of mobile devices with large displays.

Interactive Wall-Sized Displays

Distant interaction with wall-sized displays has been investigated at least since Krueger's Videoplace [15]. More recently, when wall-sized displays reached resolutions in the tens and hundreds of megapixels, they again became a research focus, most prominently in the areas of information visualization and analysis. For an overview we refer to Andrews et al. [2], who describe the state of research. Among others, they identify precise selection at multiple scales and placement of control panels as research issues, suggesting hand-held devices as one possible solution. They stress that interaction effects should be "localized based on the user's position and focus."

Wearable Computing

The commercial trend towards miniaturization discussed in the introduction also finds itself in scientific work on wearable forearm devices. Closest to us is Olberding et al.'s work on display-enhanced forearms [22]: they suggest a display on the upper side of the forearm and explore the interaction space, using the user's sleeve to control visibility of display portions to the public. With Facet, Lyons et al. [17] present a multi-display system circling the wrist. Tarun et al. [31] proposed using flexible display devices that could be used both hand-held or as a wristband, adapting its user interface to the current configuration. These papers did not consider multi-device interaction, something that we focus heavily on in combining the SleeD with an interactive wall-sized display. Recently, Chen et al. [8] used a smart watch in conjunction with a smartphone. While our approach consists of a very different setup, some of their techniques could potentially also be included in our system.

An early precursor to our body-centric approach to interaction with the SleeD is found in Pierce et al.'s work on Toolspaces [23], where tools in a virtual world are placed in fixed positions relative to the user's body. More recently, Harrison et al. [12] used the skin of the arm as a touch input device, combining it with a pico-projector to project a user interface. Again, multi-device interaction is not considered.

Mobile Devices and Large Displays

Interaction between hand-held devices and large displays has been studied numerous times, mostly with a focus on individual interaction techniques. Early work was presented by Rekimoto [25] who used hand-held computers as personal devices for collaborative work on digital whiteboards, supporting private clipboards and tool palettes.

More recently, significant work by Schmidt et al. [26, 27] examined cross-device interaction between phones and interactive surfaces. They proposed a collection of interaction techniques in areas such as data transfer, personalization, or localized feedback. This research is expanded upon by Seifert et al. [28], who investigate UI mechanisms for moving data from a mobile phone to a table. One of the issues they identified is that "only one hand is available for interacting with the table" while holding the phone. In contrast, our approach keeps the user's hands free, allowing bimanual interaction on the display wall. Using a mobile device to personalize interfaces was also investigated by Spindler et al. [29], who offload user interface palettes onto secondary hand-held displays and thereby free the associated display space. Similarly, Adachi et al. [1] proposed a forearm menu in combination with a tabletop. However, both approaches are projection-based and thus limit the interaction space and display fidelity in comparison to our work. The idea of using mobile personal palettes is also found in Haller et al.'s work on the NiCE Discussion Room [11], who use pen interaction with static, palm-sized printed menus to interface with a large interactive whiteboard.

A different variant of personalized interfaces is presented by Voida et al. [33]. They combine a tabletop and a hand-held device for focus-context interaction, using the hand-held to display a focus lens. Beaudouin-Lafon et al. [6] present a similar setup using a tablet and a wall. Daiber et al. [9] combine a cell phone attached to the back of the user's hand with a tabletop display to enhance a map viewer, displaying map contents on the phone. In contrast, our approach uses a wearable display and supports additional interaction techniques for personal clipboards and tool palettes.

Summarizing the above section, we build upon a rich set of techniques that have been explored in the context of interaction with mobile phones, contributing the first work that uses a wearable device in combination with a wall-sized display.

CONCEPTS

In this section, we delineate the proposed SleeD concepts in more detail. We identify basic physical considerations and analyze the levels of coupling available when combining the two devices. Furthermore, we propose a number of novel UI techniques that support multiple users, personal storage and the ability to display additional personal views.

Physical Considerations

In general, we assume that SleeD will be worn on the non-dominant arm, allowing the dominant hand (DH or non-SleeD hand) to interact with it. Both hands are free to interact with the wall; in particular, touches with the non-dominant hand (NDH or SleeD hand) can be used as a frame of reference for interactions on the SleeD. Possible configurations are devices that are worn below, above, or as part of the clothing.

We find Wagner's distinction of interaction into the categories *relative to the body* and *fixed in the world* [34] to be useful in describing multi-device interactions. Accordingly, we use a *body-centric* reference frame to describe positions on the arm-mounted display, with the proximodistal dimension along the arm and the axial dimension around it (see Figure 3) and propose using a separate *wall-centric* reference frame that is fixed in the vertical display. We suggest using the arm's proximodistal dimension to signify connectedness with the wall: The distal region (near the hand) shows data or widgets with a strong relationship to the wall, while the proximal region can show SleeD-specific items such as personal data or general menus. Additionally, it may be advantageous to offer a user interface that allows users to rotate its contents in the axial direction. This is particularly interesting for vertical menus, where the curvature of the arm provides a natural focus and items on the top and bottom serve as context.

Also, in contrast to conventional displays, only parts of the SleeD are visible to the user at any point in time. In particular, the anterior region (inner side of the arm) will generally be inaccessible when the SleeD hand is touching the wall. There are other differences between the posterior (outer side of the arm) and anterior regions as well: The anterior region is less visible to others; also, more physical effort is required to view and interact with its contents. This should be taken into account when designing interactions.

An important consideration in multi-device interaction with large displays is minimizing the number of gaze shifts [24], and the trade-off between placing UI elements on the wall or the SleeD should be carefully considered. Since the SleeD's position on the user's arm is fixed, we can leverage proprioception (the perception of the position of one's own body parts) to enable eyes-free interaction on the SleeD. For absolute positioning, we can exploit the fact that users are able to reliably discriminate and touch up to six different points on their forearm [16]. Precise relative positioning is possible without restrictions [32].

Multi-device interaction also needs to allow for differences in the capabilities of the displays. Most importantly, resolution differences need to be taken into account. In our case, this means that the SleeD will be able to display a comparatively large amount of data despite its small display size. An additional consideration is color reproduction: Displays often have very different color fidelity, making it hard to compare two views on different devices.

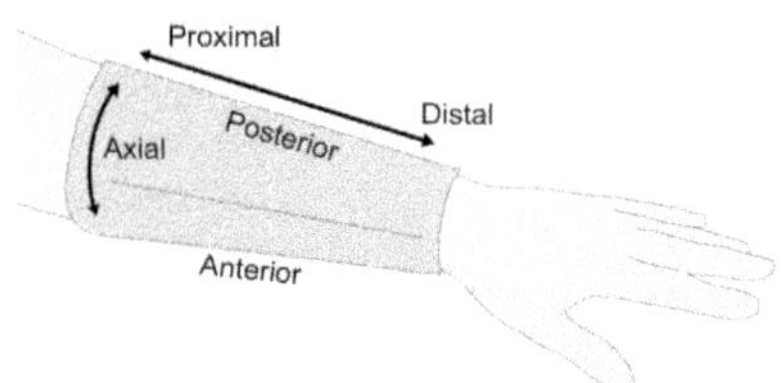

Figure 3. Body-centric view of the SleeD

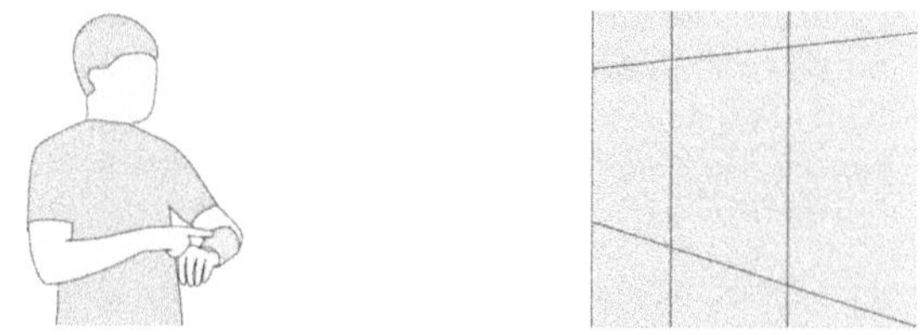

Figure 4. Logical Coupling: Interaction from a distance

Coupling Modes Between SleeD and Wall

Focusing again on the combination of a wearable display with a large display wall, we identify different levels of coupling between these devices. They are characterized firstly by the physical and logical distance between wall and SleeD. Second, it matters whether touch interaction with the vertical display uses the SleeD hand or the other. We propose distinguishing between *decoupled*, where the SleeD is used independently of other devices; *logical coupling*, signifying wall interaction from a distance; *loose physical coupling*, where only the non-SleeD hand interacts with the wall; and *close physical coupling*, meaning that the SleeD hand touches the wall as well. Of these, close physical coupling is the most interesting to us, because it brings forth many of the unique advantages of the envisioned device combination.

Decoupled

In the most basic setup, the SleeD is used in a stand-alone fashion. As described earlier, it replaces or augments today's smartphones and offers much of the same features in this usage scenario with the additional benefits of hands-free operation and near-instantaneous activation as well as being usable as a fashion accessory when not in use.

Logical coupling

When the user approaches a wall-sized display withing viewing range, it becomes possible to use the SleeD to interact with it (see Figure 4). At this point, the SleeD is used in a fashion that is similar to a remote control (with the difference that both hands are free when not directly interacting). Among others, interaction techniques like the distant pointing investigated by Jota et al. [14] and Nancel et al. [20], as well as Nancel et al.'s pan-and-zoom [21] and Seifert's PointerPhone [28] become available. Body-centric and wall-centric reference frames are not fixed with respect to one another, since the user's mobility is unrestricted. Logical coupling is also where frequent gaze shifts between devices were found to impair interaction [24], making eyes-free interaction important.

This level of coupling is likely a transitional state – after all, much of the wall's resolution remains unused because the human eye is unable to perceive the individual pixels from afar. Still, it allows, e.g., general setup of a visualization or the opportunity to step back and get an overview.

Loose physical coupling

In this and the following state, the user is able to physically touch the wall (see Figure 5). While the user cannot see the complete wall, she can perceive all information in her field of view. In loose coupling, the DH interacts with the vertical display, while the NDH with the SleeD does not. This allows the user to rotate her arm, providing access to all parts of the display and maximizing available screen space. Body-centric and wall-centric reference frames are less independent of one another than in the logical coupling state, since the user's movement is restricted with respect to the wall to a certain degree.

Close physical coupling

In this state, the user is touching the wall with the SleeD arm. Body-centric and wall-relative reference frames are fixed in relation to each other; the wearable is easily positioned in relation to the screen. This creates a classic kinematic chain [4] in that the SleeD hand serves as a frame of reference for the non-SleeD hand. For closely coupled touch interaction on the wall, the user's arm rotation is largely given by human anatomy, limiting access to the anterior region of the device.

In contrast to interaction with a hand-held mobile device touching the wall, the display contents remain easily visible in close physical coupling, and direct interaction with the SleeD remains possible (see Figure 5, right). This provides an inherent *quality of pointing*: The SleeD's distal end points at the wall, and the hand can be seen as an extension of the device. Additionally, movement along the proximodistal axis produces a *flow* towards or away from the wall. This can be used in user interface design, for instance by using swipe gestures to move items to and from the wall. We also support this by placing interface elements that are semantically closely related to the wall (e.g., clipboards to transfer data) spatially near the wall as well, in the distal region of the SleeD.

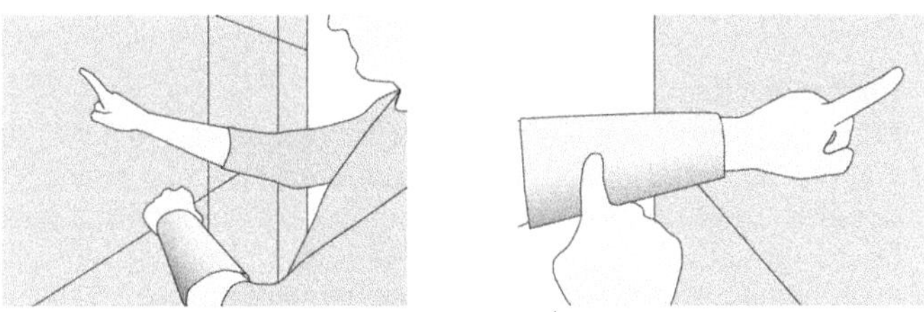

Figure 5. Loose (left) and close (right) physical coupling

User Interface Techniques

Based on the preceding considerations on physical aspects and modes of coupling, we propose a number of specific user interface techniques that leverage the advantages of both devices. These span a number of use cases, among them personal storage and data transfer, user-specific interfaces and personal views and coexist easily in applications. Many of the use cases have been explored before in the context of cross-device interaction between hand-helds and large displays (e.g., Schmidt et al. [27]); we contribute specific, novel interface techniques. Many of them exploit the fact that the SleeD is easily visible in close coupling scenarios to enable a natural flow of interaction.

Local Storage: SleeDTransfer

Since data visible on a SleeD is implicitly personal, we can use it as an interface to personal data collections. In this context, we contribute *SleeDTransfer*, a technique for data transfer between the devices that uses a *drop zone* at the distal end of the SleeD (see Figure 6). Following flow principles, users can drag an item to the drop zone in close coupling to transfer it from the SleeD to the wall. Conversely, touching an item on the wall causes a proxy to appear in the drop zone; dragging the proxy from the drop zone transfers the item. Additionally, in loose coupling, items can be dragged to the drop zone to preselect them for transfer. The actual transfer is then initiated with a touch on the wall. Both move and copy operations can be realized and distinguished, e.g., by using a two-finger drag to signify a copy operation.

The same interaction technique can be used to enable user-specific multi-item clipboards, in effect making it possible to efficiently move items from one position on the wall to another – even when other users are blocking the path. Additionally, the preselection technique allows for a number of items to be made public efficiently with one touch; it also preserves privacy, since the selection happens on the personal device and not on the public display.

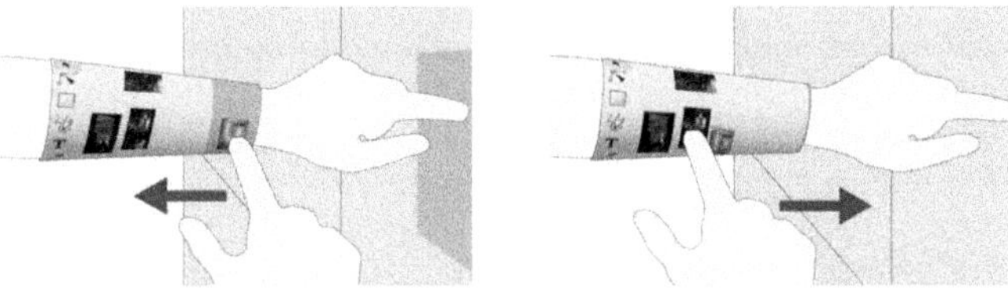

Figure 6. Transfering data between wall and SleeD using *SleeDTransfer*.

User-specific Interfaces: SleeDPalettes and SleeDMenu

A SleeD can be used to present tool palettes (see Figure 7) or other arbitrary interfaces that control the application on the wall. These *SleeDPalettes* have several advantages: They free shared screen space and minimize visual clutter. They can also take a user-specific application state into account, be personalized for their users and show information that should not be visible to others (e.g., PIN code input). Furthermore, they allow user-specific modes. Unlike most palettes on hand-held mobile devices (and, incidentally, traditional painter's palettes), *SleeDPalettes* are always reachable and still allow the user to interact bimanually with the large display, making fast and seamless mode changes an important advantage of wearable interfaces. Similar to the tool palettes, the SleeD can also show a context-sensitive menu – the *SleeDMenu* – when the wall is touched. It activates on the SleeD, its content depending on the touch position's underlying data.

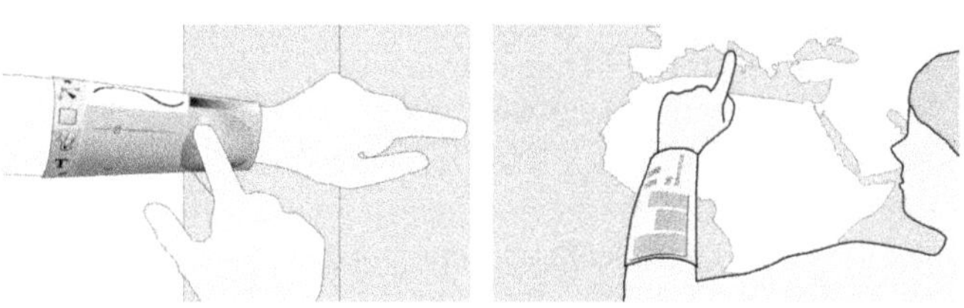

Figure 7. *SleeDPalette* (left) and *SleeDProbe* (right)

Personal Views: SleeDDetail, SleeDLens and SleeDProbe

The wearable provides the user with an additional screen that generally remains visible when the SleeD hand is touching the wall in a close coupling scenario. This enables a range of techniques that particularly benefit collaborative information visualization applications. In particular, we can show arbitrary personal views that change based on the current touch point. In this context, we propose several novel techniques.

With *SleeDDetail*, we contribute an adaptation of Overview and Detail techniques (see Figure 2). While the wall shows an overview of an area (e.g., in a map), the SleeD shows an enlarged view of the area around the touch point. *SleeDLens* generalizes this: We propose showing an arbitrary modified view of the area around the current touch position on the arm display. A touch-based UI on the SleeD allows the user to adjust view parameters. This is novel in that it moves Bier's Magic Lenses [7] to a separate display while still retaining the immediate connection between lens and context through close coupling. In addition, we propose using the personal display for probing in *SleeDProbe*. While exploring a visualization at close range, additional data can be shown specifically for the current touch position (e.g., a country's demographic data, see Figure 7, right), and corresponding audio or haptic feedback is possible as well. Snapshots of this data can be saved to compare different positions.

All the personal view techniques have in common that they avoid cluttering the shared view and allow multiple users to work on the wall without interfering with each other. Working with private data is also possible.

Remote Control: SleeDOverview

In loose coupling, SleeD can be used as remote control. We contribute *SleeDOverview* in this context: While the SleeD shows an overview of available data, the wall shows a detail view. Interaction on the wearable changes the view on the wall. This gives users a powerful way of quickly selecting the data window they would like to work with. This technique also combines very well with the inverse scenario described above: A user can select a detail view from afar, approach the wall to work on this detail view and then show an even smaller part of the data on the SleeD for close inspection.

Precision Input: SleeDCursor

A variation of the *SleeDDetail* technique above provides us with a natural workaround for the well-known fat finger problem: We propose *SleeDCursor*, where the wearable shows an unoccluded view of the area touched on the wall in close coupling. Even the effects of minimal changes in touch position are clearly visible on the arm display, allowing precise positioning in an intuitive way. Moreover, since both hands are free to interact, touch precision can be improved drastically by using the wall touch for a coarse preselection and the SleeD for the actual selection task.

IMPLEMENTATION

We developed the SleeD concept and the associated software in an iterative fashion. Initially, we built several cardboard mockups of arm-mounted displays and solicited comments from in-house HCI experts. Many of the initial concepts and ideas for UI techniques stem from these discussions. We followed up on this by building two hardware prototypes and several small applications in order to further refine the SleeD concept and to verify it. As a large display, we used a wall consisting of twelve 55" multi-touch displays with a total dimension of 5x2 meters and 24 megapixels total resolution. We do not track user IDs in the prototype setup, making it single-user-only at the moment.

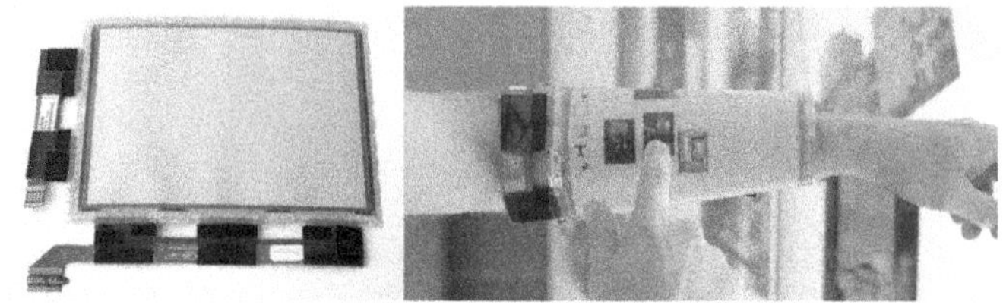

Figure 8. Prototype I (Wizard-of-Oz) using a Plastic Logic e-Ink display.

Prototype I

In the early stages of our work, we built a prototype based on a 10.7" bendable display – a Plastic Logic organic e-Ink display[1] – with at 4:3 display ratio (see Figure 8). With a size of 216x163mm and a specified bend radius of 1.5cm, it fits comfortably on an adult forearm when bent around its longer side. The display is lightweight enough to be carried for extended amounts of time. However, the update speed of current e-Ink displays (> 300ms in our case) severely limits possible interactions and touch functionality is not readily available.

Still, since the display's dimensions are very close to the envisioned form factor, the prototype allowed us to conduct initial experiments concerning functionality and placement of UI elements using Wizard-of-Oz-type mockups that heavily influenced the concepts described above. One interesting result of the tests was that, similar to a watch, the SleeD needs to be at least semi-fixed near the wrist for the zone underneath the arm to be usable. The reason lies in human anatomy: Since the forearm's bones twist around each other, a device fixed only at the proximal end of the forearm will not move when the forearm is turned around its axis.

Prototype II

For *Prototype II*, we used a 4.8" 16:9 cellphone – a Samsung Galaxy S3 – and added a forearm mount (see Figure 9). We decided upon this form factor after experiments with a cardboard model of a 6.1" phone: The larger phone is too wide to be used comfortably when attached to the arm. The cell phone hardware, while being smaller and heavier than the envisioned display, allowed us to quickly develop actually usable high-fidelity software prototypes, although we could not test the specifics of a curved display.

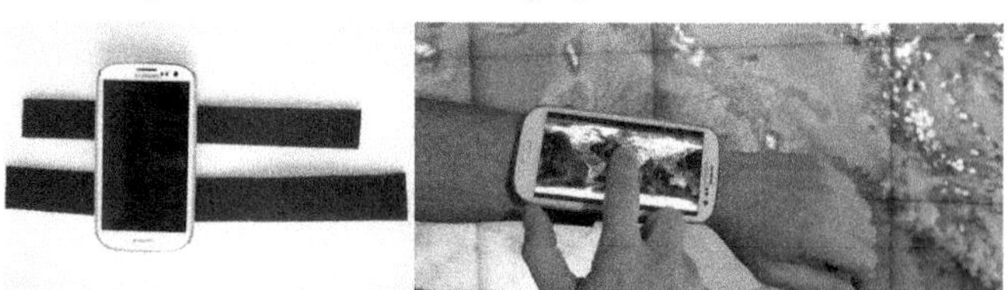

Figure 9. Prototype II based on a Samsung Galaxy S3 phone (left). The map viewer, using the second prototype to show an overview (right).

Applications

We built three applications to verify the user interface concepts. The first is a showcase graphics editor/picture viewer; the others are two map viewers that implement the personal view techniques described above. All software runs on Prototype II, and all applications were built to support left- and right-handed usage. Some of the interface concepts needed

[1] http://www.plasticlogic.com/

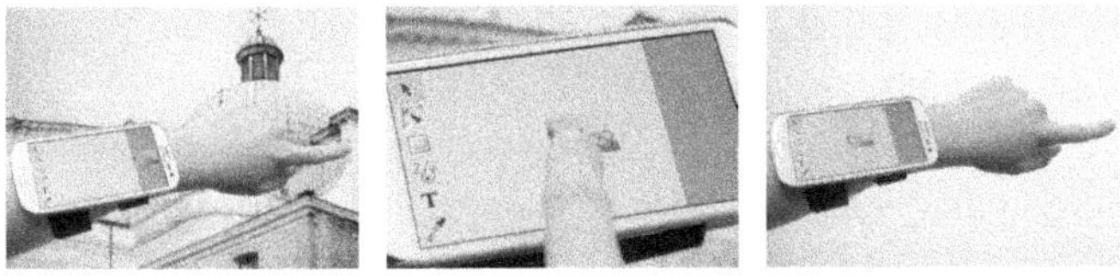

Figure 10. Using the drop zone to move an image to the SleeD.

to be adapted to the smartphone form factor: The display is smaller and planar, providing less room for output and exacerbating the fat finger problem. However, it still allowed us to test most of our concepts with today's hardware.

Graphics Editor/Picture Viewer

The first application integrates two distinct modes and explicitly supports the quality of *flow*, mentioned earlier. In the first mode, it acts like a typical multi-touch picture viewer with additional private multi-item clipboard support on the SleeD. *SleeDTransfer* is fully implemented: Transfer to and from the wall using the drop zone at the *distal* end of the device as well as preselection functionality are available (see Figure 10).

Figure 11. Fingerpaint mode (left) and its tool palette (right).

The second mode allows fingerpainting, implementing a tool palette on the SleeD (*SleeDPalette*, see Figure 11). In this mode, users can paint by touching the wall. They can select colors using an HSL-based color chooser and select the line width using a slider. A vertical menu at the *proximal* end of the SleeD allows switching between the two modes.

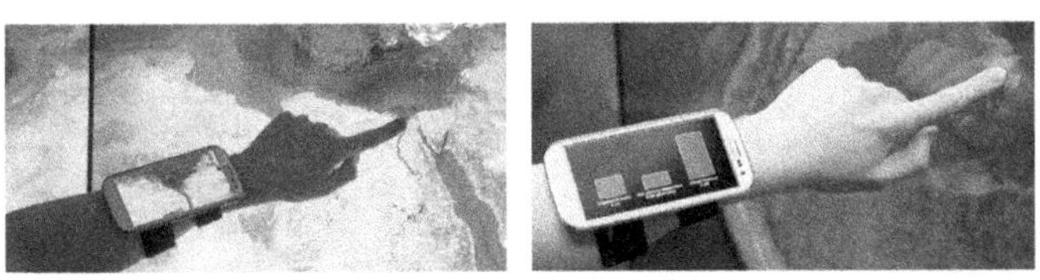

Figure 12. Map viewer showing a detail view (left) and probing (right).

Map Viewers

In the two SleeD map viewers, we implement the Personal View techniques presented above. We used gigapixel-sized NASA Blue Marble images[2] for the maps; additional data came from NASA Earth Observatory[3] images.

The first map viewer shows a world map on the SleeD and a detail view on the wall (see Figure 9, right). It is designed to be used in *logical coupling mode*, at a distance from the wall.

The second one shows the world map on the wall and implements *SleeDDetail*, *SleeDLens* and *SleeDProbe* functionality in three separate modes. In all of them, the data displayed on the SleeD changes based on the geographical location touched on the wall. In *SleeDDetail* mode (see Figure 12, left), the SleeD displays a detail view of the world map. In *SleeDLens* mode (see Figure 1, right), it displays a map with global temperature data localized on the touch point. Using a slider, users can select which year of temperature data to display. Finally, in *SleeDProbe* mode (see Figure 12, right), the SleeD displays a bar chart with data (cloud fraction, vegetation and vegetation CO_2 intake) for the current touch point.

[2]http://visibleearth.nasa.gov

[3]http://earthobservatory.nasa.gov

Realization

All applications were implemented using the libavg framework[4] and all application-level code was written in Python. The application runs on a single dual-processor Xeon workstation that drives the twelve wall displays. SleeD display contents are generated on this machine as well using off-screen rendering. A custom libavg plugin encodes them using jpeg compression and streams them to the SleeD, where they are decompressed by a small java app and displayed. Conversely, touches on the SleeD are streamed to the workstation and fed into the libavg input framework. Since the plugin runs in a separate thread, application performance is not impacted.

To show the gigapixel images, we built a second libavg plugin that handles image pyramids. It loads the tiles needed on-demand using a thread pool of jpeg loaders and uses an LRU cache to avoid reloading when possible.

USER STUDY

To verify the SleeD concept, we ran an observational study in a laboratory setting using the phone-based prototype and our display wall. The study was designed to investigate a broad range of user interface techniques and concepts, thus providing maximum insight into their usefulness and acceptance. At this stage in development, we were mainly interested in qualitative feedback. Seven unpaid participants (male, aged 23-40) volunteered for the study. Two of them had minor experience with an interactive display wall and one had used a smart watch. No others had used wearable computers before.

Study Procedure

The study consisted of individual sessions of about 45 minutes per participant. We videotaped the study and took notes. After obtaining informed consent, we gave each participant a short introduction to the SleeD concept and let them fill out an initial questionnaire about their background. The interaction with the prototype itself consisted of a diverse selection of the most important tasks, with a short explanation of the available functionality and usage given before each task:

- *SleeDTransfer*: Participants were asked to sort around 20 photos on two axes using the clipboard functionality. Sort criteria were lightness for the horizontal axis and the amount of water displayed in the image for the vertical axis. Since we wanted to focus solely on the new functionality, we asked the participants not to drag the images on the wall directly.
- *SleeDPalette, SleeDMenu*: We asked users to switch to drawing mode, trace an image displayed on the wall using the arm display to change colors, switch back and move the image away.

[4]http://www.libavg.de

- *SleeDOverview*: Using an overview map on the SleeD and a detail image on the wall, participants had to navigate to three self-chosen places.
- *SleedDetail, SleeDCursor*: Participants were asked to follow the river Nile from its mouth to Lake Victoria using the second map viewer (overview on the wall). They had to repeat this task four times in counterbalanced order, once for each combination of possible SleeD arm and active hand.

After each task, we solicited comments and initiated a discussion about the tested functionality. Finally, we asked each participant to fill out a second questionnaire containing 16 five-point likert scale questions and free-form comment fields on: NASA TLX-based task load, the concepts, and the realization of the prototype. In the comment fields, participants were asked to list positive and negative aspects of both concept and prototype.

Results

In general, the feedback we received was very encouraging (see Figure 13). The quantitative questions on the concept all had an average rating of better than 2 (1=very good, 5=very bad). In particular, participants thought the concepts were very useful (1.29). Physical demands were rated at 1.86 on average (1=very low, 5=very high). The answers on prototypes ranged on average from 1.9 to 2.7 (1=very good and 5=very bad). These quantitative results were very promising but should not be over-interpreted due to the small sample size. More importantly, we collected rich qualitative feedback by evaluating the videos, the questionnaires and the notes taken during the sessions.

With very few exceptions, interfaces were usable on the first try after a short explanation without live demonstration. Three participants made explicit positive comments on the smoothness of the prototype interface (Participant S3: The prototype *"felt real and natural, very smooth interaction"*). S6 noted that the *"interaction techniques were very well designed"* and S4 spoke of a *"very cool concept"* in general.

Photo Sorting

In the photo sorting tasks, *SleeDTransfer*, the natural flow and the concept of the drop zone were commented on favorably (e.g., S5 spoke of a *"seamless transition between personal space and wall"*). Private storage was used extensively, with many participants picking up a number of similar images and dropping them sequentially in the destination area. S6 remarked that preselection *"made it really easy to move a lot of objects at once, especially if I had to place them far away."*

S2 and S3 found sorting on the SleeD to be hard because of the small display, pointing to the advantages that an arm-sized device would have. S6 would have liked the ability to pre-sort items on the SleeD, then drop the finished layout on the wall.

Map Viewer

In the *SleeDDetail* task (Nile tracing), preferences for the different configurations were not very strong: Three subjects preferred loose coupling with the dominant hand touching. The other three combinations of touching hand and coupling were each preferred by one participant, and one participant was undecided. S2 commented that it was easier to hold the arm display steady in loose coupling configurations.

Regarding *SleeDCursor*, S5 commented that showing detail on the SleeD solves the occlusion problem. Also, two participants were surprised by the ease with which precise positioning was possible by rolling the finger, while three participants that did not discover this technique commented on imprecise positioning, and one participant changed his mind mid-task. Hence, it seems probable that the technique is very effective but has a small learning curve.

Issues of Perceptual Transition

In the drawing task, participants found it difficult to choose the right brush parameters on the SleeD, since the displays had differing sizes, resolutions and color reproduction. Thus, the typical emerging workflow involved trying out different settings. One possible solution for this would be placing the preview on the wall.

For both map tasks, gaze direction became important: S1 and S2 commented that gaze switches were an issue for the *SleeDDetail* task, and this was easily visible in the videos as well. In the *SleeDOverview* task, participants needed to look at the SleeD to set the initial touch point, then switch their gaze to the wall to fine-tune the touch location to get optimal performance. Instead, several participants continued looking at the SleeD for some time.

Hence, we concur with Rashid et al. [24] that issues of perceptual transition need to be considered: Different sizes, pixel densities and color reproduction of the displays, gaze shifts and the changing orientation of the SleeD with respect to the wall all need to be accounted for when designing user interfaces for this combination of devices. This is clearly an area that warrants further investigation.

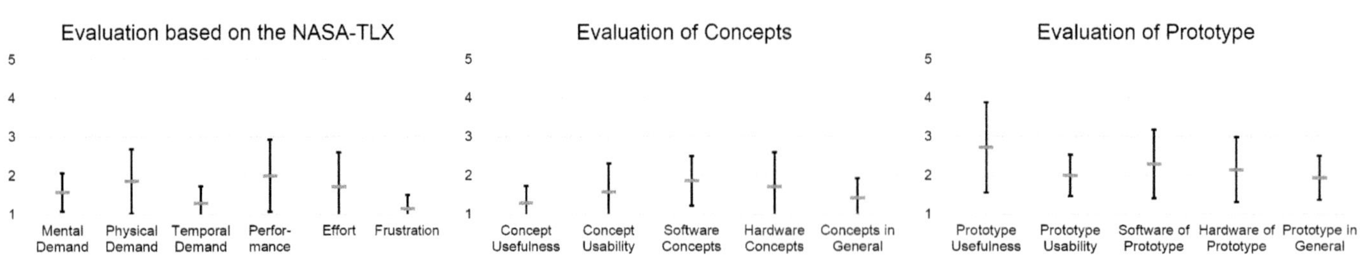

Figure 13. Results of the questionnaire. The plots show the average value per question, with whiskers showing the standard deviation. Possible answers ranged from 1 ("very good" or "very low" in case of workload) to 5 ("very bad" or "very high" in case of workload).

Physical Considerations

In spite of the positive quantitative rating for physical demands, fatigue due to the prototype's weight was mentioned several times as a potential problem in case of prolonged usage. This was most noticeable in the *SleeDDetail* tasks when the SleeD was mounted on the arm touching the wall (close coupling) and may have been a consequence of the high weight (133 g) of the cellphone-based prototype.

S4 and S5 mentioned that the SleeD is hard to use for very high or low wall positions, because the display orientation changes with the arm position. However, the participants were picking up and releasing photos over the complete height of the wall (from 40 cm to 250 cm) and we believe that wall interaction in general should be restricted to more accommodating heights. Furthermore, a SleeD that actually encircles the arm has more visible regions and thus will support more arm positions.

DISCUSSION

The study strongly suggests that the concepts used are sound. We investigated a diverse selection of interaction techniques and application areas, showing that the general idea is versatile and widely applicable. Importantly, nearly all study participants asked for more features, e.g., pinch to zoom in the map application, erasers and an eye dropper to choose color in the drawing application. We believe this is a very positive sign, since it shows that the concepts were clear to them and they were envisioning actual usage. Furthermore, it points to the possibility of creating complete coherent application user interfaces using this hardware combination.

Unfortunately, the current state of hardware development prevents a study with the envisioned hardware. Accordingly, we could not test features that depend on a larger, curved display, among them rotating menus and interaction on the posterior of the arm. However, we could test most concepts individually and in combination in our study. Furthermore, the study results point to several shortcomings of the current prototype that a full SleeD will likely solve. Among these are the weight of the device (leading to fatigue) as well as the smaller, flat display that impedes interaction on the device itself and is only visible in certain arm positions.

Concerning practical realization, the emergence of flexible OLED display prototypes makes it likely that the hardware restrictions of the current prototypes will be lifted in the foreseeable future. OLEDs need no backlight; the corresponding lower weight should alleviate the issues with physical fatigue. In addition, user ID recognition for multi-device systems has been demonstrated in numerous varieties. Of the proposed techniques, the IdWristbands [19] promise to be the easiest to integrate into our setup: The SleeD just needs to be able to pulse an infrared LED in the direction of the wall. Fiberio [13] points to a solution that can become commercially viable in the long term.

SleeD also has multiple benefits in comparison to concepts based on hand-held devices. Many of our techniques leverage the fact that the mobile device's display is visible and can be interacted with in close coupling situations. This applies to context-sensitive menus, seamless interaction including the drop zone and the flow concept, personal views, precision input and probing. We believe that combined with effortless switching to bimanual interaction with the wall (or with other objects such as pen and paper), this points towards powerful and truly seamless interaction using both devices.

CONCLUSION

In this paper we presented SleeD, a novel approach that combines arm-mounted touch devices with large interactive display walls. We contributed the SleeD concept, including physical considerations, an analysis of the forms of coupling between the wearable and the wall, and a diverse range of user interface techniques. Our iterative design process also yielded two hardware prototypes based on a bendable e-Ink display and a conventional smartphone. The presented sample applications further illustrate our concepts and underline the envisioned usage of this type of future devices.

Finally, we also reported on an observational user study that covers a broad range of the envisioned interaction. The valuable feedback that we received shows the high potential and broad applicability of our proposed concepts – as well as pointing towards future work in the area. This includes quantitative studies on individual techniques and a study of multi-user interaction. Furthermore, a true curved, high-performance SleeD prototype is an important piece of future work when the hardware reaches maturity.

ACKNOWLEDGEMENTS

This work was funded in part by the German Research Foundation (DFG) through the project IPAR (DA 1319/2-1). We would like to thank Plastic Logic for supporting the development of Prototype I and André Viergutz for his support.

REFERENCES

1. Adachi, T., Koura, S., Shibata, F., and Kimura, A. Forearm menu: Using forearm as menu widget on tabletop system. In *Proc. ITS*, ACM (2013), 333–336.
2. Andrews, C., Endert, A., Yost, B., and North, C. Information visualization on large, high-resolution displays: Issues, challenges, and opportunities. *Information Visualization 10*, 4 (2011), 341–355.
3. Ashbrook, D. L., Clawson, J. R., Lyons, K., Starner, T. E., and Patel, N. Quickdraw: The impact of mobility and on-body placement on device access time. In *Proc. CHI*, ACM (2008), 219–222.
4. Balakrishnan, R., and Hinckley, K. The role of kinesthetic reference frames in two-handed input performance. In *Proc. UIST*, ACM (1999), 171–178.
5. Ball, R., North, C., and Bowman, D. A. Move to improve: promoting physical navigation to increase user performance with large displays. In *Proc. CHI*, ACM (2007), 191–200.
6. Beaudouin-Lafon, M., Huot, S., Nancel, M., Mackay, W., Pietriga, E., Primet, R., Wagner, J., Chapuis, O., Pillias, C., Eagan, J., Gjerlufsen, T., and Klokmose, C.

Multisurface interaction in the wild room. *Computer 45*, 4 (Apr. 2012), 48–56.

7. Bier, E. A., Stone, M. C., Pier, K., Buxton, W., and DeRose, T. D. Toolglass and magic lenses: the see-through interface. In *Proc.*, SIGGRAPH, ACM (1993), 73–80.
8. Chen, X. A., Grossman, T., Wigdor, D. J., and Fitzmaurice, G. Duet: Exploring joint interactions on a smart phone and a smart watch. In *Proc. CHI*, ACM (2014), 159–168.
9. Daiber, F., Gehring, S., Löchtefeld, M., and Krüger, A. TouchPosing: multi-modal interaction with geospatial data. In *Proc. MUM*, ACM (2012), 8:1–8:4.
10. Geller, T. The promise of flexible displays. *Commun. ACM 54*, 6 (June 2011), 16–18.
11. Haller, M., Leitner, J., Seifried, T., Wallace, J. R., Scott, S. D., Richter, C., Brandl, P., Gokcezade, A., and Hunter, S. The NiCE discussion room: Integrating paper and digital media to support co-located group meetings. In *Proc. CHI*, ACM (2010), 609–618.
12. Harrison, C., Tan, D., and Morris, D. Skinput: appropriating the body as an input surface. In *Proc. CHI*, ACM (2010), 453–462.
13. Holz, C., and Baudisch, P. Fiberio: A touchscreen that senses fingerprints. In *Proc. UIST*, ACM (2013), 41–50.
14. Jota, R., Nacenta, M. A., Jorge, J. A., Carpendale, S., and Greenberg, S. A comparison of ray pointing techniques for very large displays. In *Proc. Graphics Interface*, CIPS (2010), 269–276.
15. Krueger, M. W., Gionfriddo, T., and Hinrichsen, K. Videoplace — an artificial reality. In *Proc. CHI*, ACM (1985), 35–40.
16. Lin, S.-Y., Su, C.-H., Cheng, K.-Y., Liang, R.-H., Kuo, T.-H., and Chen, B.-Y. Pub - point upon body: exploring eyes-free interaction and methods on an arm. In *Proc. UIST*, ACM (2011), 481–488.
17. Lyons, K., Nguyen, D., Ashbrook, D., and White, S. Facet: a multi-segment wrist worn system. In *Proc. UIST*, ACM (2012), 123–130.
18. Martin, T. L. Time and time again: Parallels in the development of the watch and the wearable computer. In *Proc. ISWC* (2002), 5–14.
19. Meyer, T., and Schmidt, D. IdWristbands: IR-based user identification on multi-touch surfaces. In *Proc. ITS*, ACM (2010), 277–278.
20. Nancel, M., Chapuis, O., Pietriga, E., Yang, X.-D., Irani, P. P., and Beaudouin-Lafon, M. High-precision pointing on large wall displays using small handheld devices. In *Proc. CHI*, ACM (2013), 831–840.
21. Nancel, M., Wagner, J., Pietriga, E., Chapuis, O., and Mackay, W. Mid-air pan-and-zoom on wall-sized displays. In *Proc. CHI*, ACM (2011), 177–186.
22. Olberding, S., Yeo, K. P., Nanayakkara, S., and Steimle, J. AugmentedForearm: exploring the design space of a display-enhanced forearm. In *Proc. Augmented Human*, ACM (2013), 9–12.
23. Pierce, J. S., Conway, M., van Dantzich, M., and Robertson, G. Toolspaces and glances: storing, accessing, and retrieving objects in 3d desktop applications. In *Proc. I3D*, ACM (1999), 163–168.
24. Rashid, U., Nacenta, M. A., and Quigley, A. The cost of display switching: a comparison of mobile, large display and hybrid ui configurations. In *Proc. AVI*, ACM (2012), 99–106.
25. Rekimoto, J. A multiple device approach for supporting whiteboard-based interactions. In *Proc. CHI*, ACM (1998), 344–351.
26. Schmidt, D., Sas, C., and Gellersen, H. Personal clipboards for individual copy-and-paste on shared multi-user surfaces. In *Proc. CHI*, ACM (2013), 3335–3344.
27. Schmidt, D., Seifert, J., Rukzio, E., and Gellersen, H. A cross-device interaction style for mobiles and surfaces. In *Proc. DIS*, ACM (2012), 318–327.
28. Seifert, J., Bayer, A., and Rukzio, E. PointerPhone: Using mobile phones for direct pointing interactions with remote displays. In *Human-Computer Interaction–INTERACT 2013*. Springer, 2013, 18–35.
29. Spindler, M., Cheung, V., and Dachselt, R. Dynamic tangible user interface palettes. In *Human-Computer Interaction–INTERACT 2013*. Springer, 2013, 159–176.
30. Stein, R., Ferrero, S., Hetfield, M., Quinn, A., and Krichever, M. Development of a commercially successful wearable data collection system. In *Proc. ISWC* (1998), 18–24.
31. Tarun, A. P., Lahey, B., Girouard, A., Burleson, W., and Vertegaal, R. Snaplet: Using body shape to inform function in mobile flexible display devices. In *Proc. CHI Extended Abstracts*, ACM (2011), 329–334.
32. Thomas, B., Grimmer, K., Zucco, J., and Milanese, S. Where does the mouse go? An investigation into the placement of a body-attached touchpad mouse for wearable computers. *Personal Ubiquitous Comput. 6*, 2 (Jan. 2002), 97–112.
33. Voida, S., Tobiasz, M., Stromer, J., Isenberg, P., and Carpendale, S. Getting practical with interactive tabletop displays: designing for dense data, "fat fingers," diverse interactions, and face-to-face collaboration. In *Proc. ITS*, ACM (2009), 109–116.
34. Wagner, J., Nancel, M., Gustafson, S. G., Huot, S., and Mackay, W. E. Body-centric design space for multi-surface interaction. In *Proc. CHI*, ACM (2013), 1299–1308.

Structure Editing of Handwritten Mathematics

Improving the Computer Support for the Calculational Method

Alexandra Mendes
Computer Science Department
York St John University, UK
a.mendes@yorksj.ac.uk

Roland Backhouse
School of Computer Science
University of Nottingham, UK
roland.backhouse@nottingham.ac.uk

João F. Ferreira
School of Computing
Teesside University, UK
HASLab/INESC TEC
Universidade do Minho, Portugal
joao@joaoff.com

ABSTRACT
We present a structure editor that aims to facilitate the presentation and manipulation of handwritten mathematical expressions. The editor is oriented to the calculational mathematics involved in algorithmic problem solving and it provides features that allow reliable structure manipulation of mathematical formulae, as well as flexible and interactive presentations. We describe some of its most important features, including the use of gestures to manipulate algebraic formulae, the structured selection of expressions, definition and redefinition of operators in runtime, gesture's editor, and handwritten templates. The editor is made available in the form of a C# class library which can be easily used to extend existing tools. For example, we have extended Classroom Presenter, a tool for ink-based teaching presentations and classroom interaction. We have tested and evaluated the editor with target users. The results obtained seem to indicate that the software is usable, suitable for its purpose and a valuable contribution to teaching and learning algorithmic problem solving.

Author Keywords
handwritten mathematics; structure editor; Tablet PCs; computer science education; mathematics education; calculational method; C# class library; gestures

ACM Classification Keywords
H.5.2. Information Interfaces and Presentation (e.g. HCI): User Interfaces

General Terms
Algorithms; Design; Mathematics; Reliability; Human Factors

INTRODUCTION
Students, scientists, and engineers have the need to effectively communicate and present mathematical results. For that, computers are often used, but writing and presenting mathematical content using a computer is hard. The difficulty in writing is mainly due to the input devices commonly used: the keyboard does not support all mathematical symbols and the use of the mouse to click in buttons to input the symbols is time-consuming. For presentations, the blackboard, transparencies, and electronic slides are commonly used, but these media have some limitations. For instance, although the use of the blackboard allows interaction with the audience, it requires the presenter to write everything during the presentation, which is time-consuming and can lead to errors. Ordinary transparencies and electronic slides can be prepared in advance, avoiding errors and saving time. However, they work more like a guideline than as a medium for discussion and interaction since it is difficult to adjust them during the presentation. This does not encourage interactivity and, in presentations involving mathematical content, there is often the need to provide examples and details according to queries and responses from the audience. Moreover, electronic slides are usually created using the mouse and the keyboard as input devices, and these make it hard and laborious to write documents containing mathematics.

An easier way to write and present mathematical content is to use pen-based devices like Tablet PCs and handwrite the desired mathematical content [8, 12, 19]. We currently use a Tablet PC to teach algorithmic problem solving to first-year undergraduate students and we find that it simplifies the writ-

Figure 1. MST editor in action on a Tablet PC. Selecting well-formed sub-expressions is necessary to manipulate mathematical expressions.

ACM 978-1-4503-2587-5/14/11 ...$15.00.
http://dx.doi.org/10.1145/2669485.2669495

ing of mathematical content. Moreover, the feedback from the students shows that they enjoy the interactivity that comes with the use of the Tablet PC. However, because teaching algorithmic problem solving involves a large number of syntactic manipulations, we feel the need for a structure editor able to reliably manipulate the non-standard mathematics that we use.

In an attempt to combine the benefits of Tablet PCs with the advantages of using the computer's capabilities to manipulate structured information reliably, we have developed a structure editor[1] named Math/pad Tablet (MST). This editor aims to facilitate the presentation and manipulation of mathematical content by providing a way to input and manipulate structured handwritten mathematics, and by providing features that contribute to flexible and interactive presentations. Figure 1 shows the editor in action. As pictured, the tool allows the use of a stylus pen to handwrite and manipulate mathematical content (like algorithms). The main audience of the system are teachers presenting mathematical content in the calculational style that is used, for example, in algorithmic problem solving [2, 3, 10, 14, 22], but it can also be used in other contexts.

The novelty of the MST editor and what distinguishes it from existing related tools is that:

- it is the first structure editor for handwritten mathematics oriented to the calculational mathematics involved in algorithmic problem solving;
- it allows definition and redefinition of mathematical operators in runtime;
- it supports the definition of handwritten templates;
- it is developed as a C# library, which can be easily used to extend and combine existing tools.

It is important to note that the focus of this work is on structure editing and not on handwriting recognition. In this paper, we describe the context, goals, and design of the MST editor. We discuss the integration of the editor with an existing tool, Classroom Presenter [1], and we show how it can be used to do and teach mathematics. We show the results of an evaluation performed with target users/audience and we conclude with a discussion on the current issues of the system and how we plan to develop it further.

RELATED WORK

There exist several tools and packages that are capable of dealing with handwritten mathematics. For example, the *Freehand Formula Entry System* (FFES) [20] allows the freehand entry and editing of formulae using a pen and a tablet. FFES also allows the generation of LaTeX from its input. Another existing tool is the *Infty Editor* [21]. This editor supports online recognition of handwritten mathematical expressions and as soon as a character is written, it is automatically rewritten as neat strokes in an appropriate position and size. This editor provides output in several different formats, including LaTeX and MathML. These tools act mainly as mathematics input systems, while our tool aims to provide an editor for complete mathematical documents and presentations with the ability to manipulate the mathematical structure of the handwritten expressions.

More advanced tools are able to provide mathematical sketching, which is a pen-based approach for mathematical problem solving. Users write mathematics and supporting diagrams to create graphical animations that can be manipulated and can verify the correctness of the mathematics. The concept of mathematical sketching was first developed in the seminal work of *MathPad*^{2} [17]. Another example is *MathBrush* [16], which allows the handwritten input and recognition of mathematical expressions. It allows the use of gestures to manipulate expressions and is able to evaluate them by passing them to a computer algebra system. *MathPaper* [25] is another tool that recognizes handwritten mathematics. It allows free-form handwritten entry of multiple mathematical expressions to provide symbolic and numerical computational assistance. It uses real-time recognition and supports gestural and widget-based interactive editing. This tool also explores novel approaches to entering and manipulating matrices and allows handwritten entry of mathematical algorithms. *AlgoSketch* [18] was created in the context of the MathPaper project and it is a pen-based algorithm sketching prototype with supporting interactive computation. It allows writing and editing of 2D handwritten mathematical expressions in the form of pseudocode-like descriptions to support the algorithm design and development process. *MathJournal* [24] is an interactive tool for the Tablet PC that provides a natural and intuitive environment for mathematical and engineering problem solving. The software recognizes, interprets and provides solutions for handwritten or hand-drawn mathematical and engineering constructions. This tool recognizes a great number of mathematical symbols. It evaluates several kinds of mathematical expressions and, given an expression, plots the corresponding graph. Our work overlaps with the works described above in that it also supports handwritten input, manipulation of mathematical expressions, and the use of gestures. Some of the gestures available in the MST editor are similar to the gestures available in these tools (e.g. like in *MathPad*^{2}, the scratch-out gesture is used to erase content). However, the default actions that we associate with gestures are defined based on our teaching experience and on what we usually do on the blackboard (e.g. the semi-circle is used to apply distributivity). These associations can be changed by the user at any time using the gesture editor provided. It is important to note that our tool also differs from these works on the emphasis and domain of application: while these tools emphasize the recognition and evaluation of expressions, our focus is on syntactic manipulation of mathematical expressions and composition of mathematical structures, particularly applied to the calculational method supporting algorithmic problem solving.

Recent mathematical sketching tools that emphasize diagrammatic reasoning are *VectorPad* [5], which allows users to write down vector mathematics and present animations

[1]We use the terms *editor* and *library* interchangeably to refer to the work presented in this paper. Even though the work is available in the form of a library, its features form a structure editor.

illustrating different vector operations; *SetPad* [7], which allows users to write down set expressions and presents Venn diagrams associated with them; and *SketchSet* [23], a sketch tool for Euler diagrams whose curves can be arbitrary shapes. Finally, Hands-On Math [26] is a multi-touch and pen-based system (running on a Microsoft Surface) which allows freeform sketching and visualization of simple algebraic expressions. Similar to *SetPad* and *Hands-on Math*, we support the selection of sub-expressions and non-trivial manipulation rules like distributivity; however, a difference is that in our tool all the results of manipulations remain handwritten, i.e., there is no conversion to typeset. Also, to the best of our knowledge, none of the tools described in this section support user-definition of new mathematical operators in runtime nor the definition of handwritten templates.

In terms of mathematical structure editors designed to be used with keyboard and mouse, the closest work is Math∫pad [4]. In fact, the Math∫pad system has inspired the project presented in this paper. Its focus is on calculational mathematics and its ultimate goal was to provide a system that could eliminate the use of pen and paper for the calculations of the intended users of the system. However, that did not happen and Math∫pad's creators believe the main problem lies with the interaction limitations of computers (see page 15 of [4]). One of the goals of the MST editor is to overcome these limitations.

CONTEXT AND GOALS

The MST editor was developed in the context of teaching and research on correct-by-construction program design. More than two decades of research in this area have created a new discipline of algorithmic problem solving and shed light on the underlying mathematical structures, modeling, and reasoning principles. Starting with the pioneering work of Dijkstra and Gries [10, 14], a *calculational method* emerged, emphasizing the use of systematic mathematical calculation in the design of algorithms. Exponents of the calculational method prefer to work with uninterpreted formulae and manipulate them according to their symbols and associated rules (the motto is: "*let the symbols do the work*").

An example of a representative calculational proof is Van Gasteren's proof [9] of the theorem

(1) $$(m\times p)\nabla n = m\nabla n \;\Leftarrow\; p\nabla n = 1 \quad ,$$

where ∇ represents the greatest common divisor. The proof is as follows:

$$\begin{array}{ll} & m\nabla n \\ = & \{ \quad p\nabla n = 1 \text{ and } 1 \text{ is the unit of multiplication } \} \\ & m\times(p\nabla n)\ \nabla\ n \\ = & \{ \quad \text{distributivity and associativity } \} \\ & (m\times p)\ \nabla\ (m\times n)\ \nabla\ n \\ = & \{ \quad (m\times n)\nabla n = n \quad \} \\ & (m\times p)\nabla n \ . \end{array}$$

$$\begin{array}{lcll} m & \nabla & n & \text{(initial expression)} \\ \boxed{m\times p} & \nabla & n & \\ m\times\boxed{(p\nabla n)} & \nabla & n & \text{(final expression)} \end{array}$$

Figure 2. Transformation of $m\nabla n$ into $m\times(p\nabla n)\nabla n$. The red sub-expressions are replaced by the boxed expressions.

Note how each step of a calculational proof is usually accompanied by a hint justifying the validity of that step. Some relevant advantages of this format are that the hints reduce the search space, there are no repeated intermediate expressions, and we can immediately conclude that $m\nabla n = (m\times p)\nabla n$, just by looking at the first and last expressions and at the relations connecting them. The equality holds if the properties used in the hints are valid, meaning that $p\nabla n = 1$ is a sufficient condition. This calculational format is used in several research communities (e.g. by researchers on functional programming) and in teaching at many universities (e.g. a study suggests that discrete maths students prefer and understand calculational proofs better [11]).

Handwritten presentations of calculational proofs

The motivation for the creation of the MST editor is the need for a software tool supporting the teaching of algorithmic problem solving, in particular, using the calculational style. Teaching algorithmic problem solving involves a great deal of syntactic manipulations of uninterpreted and unconventional mathematical formulae that existing tools do not support. Working with uninterpreted formulae and manipulating them in a syntactic way requires a great deal of copy and substitution of expressions. For instance, in a handwritten presentation of the proof shown above, we would have to handwrite the expression $p\nabla n$ three times (once in the theorem statement, once in the first hint, and once in the result of the first step). In general, expressions can be arbitrarily large, meaning that copying and substituting them by hand can easily result in errors. The emphasis on substitution of equals for equals leads to proofs where each step only changes part of an expression. For example, in the first step of the proof above, only the first operand of ∇ is changed; in the third step, only the second operand of the first ∇ is changed. Moreover, syntactic manipulations like those on the distributivity step require a substantial mental effort from the writer as they have to perform in their mind a sequence of steps and write down the final result — which again, can easily result in errors.

To improve the user interaction with handwritten calculational proofs, there is the need for a structure editor providing straightforward, flexible and reliable manipulation of mathematical handwritten formulae. The editor should assist with the process of doing mathematics and ensure that human errors are less likely to be introduced. For example, a reliable way to obtain the result of the first step of the proof above is to copy the expression $m\nabla n$, replace the first operand by the expression $m\times p$, and finally, replace the p in the newly introduced sub-expression by $p\nabla n$. Figure 2 illustrates the three steps involved in this transformation.

The MST editor supports the type of manipulations described above, but it also considers other aspects relevant to mathematical structure editors. For example, above we have chosen the symbol ∇ to represent the greatest common divisor, because we wanted to demonstrate a common need when doing mathematics: we often need to define and conjecture new operators that satisfy certain algebraic rules. This is supported in the MST editor because users can add and redefine operators as they wish. When using the MST editor, everything remains handwritten even after manipulations are performed, as it is likely that the user will further add handwritten text, handwritten mathematical expressions, and possibly unstructured handwritten blocks (like sketches and diagrams) to the document. It is undesirable to mix different writing and font styles, as doing so, can make presentations confusing. Furthermore, certain actions can be triggered by the use of gestures, helping to make writing mathematics a continuous process, without interruption from having to select options from menus.

In summary, the MST editor was created to overcome some common obstacles when using a calculational style to teach algorithmic problem solving: i) difficulty writing mathematics in a digital format; ii) errors introduced during presentations, e.g. whilst writing calculations; iii) demonstrate the dynamics of algorithmic problem solving — that is, work with uninterpreted formulae and manipulate them according to their symbols and associated rules; iv) keep the audience engaged. To the best of our knowledge, there is no other tool that supports calculational mathematics in an handwritten form with the facilities needed in a research and teaching environment.

The focus of this work is on structure editing and not on recognition of handwriting. As such, we do not discuss problems related with handwriting recognition. The editor is built assuming that the correct recognition result is obtained and it works independently of the recognition engine. As it is not realistic to assume that a recognizer will always return the correct result, the library includes a simple editor for the recognition results. This editor allows the user to correct any errors in the recognition results. The library can be used even without a recognizer: if the user handwrites an expression and manually inputs the correct recognition result, the expressions will have the correct structure. This means that all the features still work, since they only depend on the existing structure.

THE MST EDITOR

The MST editor assists in the presentation of the dynamics of algorithmic problem solving [2, 3, 22], by allowing straightforward, flexible and reliable manipulation of non-standard mathematical expressions [13, 14]. All the relevant features of the editor are implemented in the form of a class library that we call *MST library*. The central feature of the library is the definition of structure for handwritten mathematical expressions. This allows syntactic manipulation of the expressions, making it possible to accurately select, copy and apply algebraic rules, while avoiding the introduction of errors. To facilitate structured manipulation, we introduce gestures to apply manipulation rules. By default, and where applicable, the gestures used for each rule match the visual idea that is usually associated with its application: for instance, for distributivity we use a semi-circle starting at the operator that will be distributed and ending over the operator through which it will be distributed — this matches our visual idea that one operator will be propagated over the other. All default gestures were chosen based on our teaching experience and on what we usually do on the blackboard. However, the association between gestures and rules can be customized at anytime to suit the user's needs. As each user is different, fixed gestures may not be suitable for everyone.

In the context of teaching, applying an algebraic rule and obtaining the result instantaneously, may not be good enough. With this in mind, the library supports the animation of certain structure manipulations. The purpose of these animations is to show, step-by-step, how a rule is applied to an expression. We believe that this can help students understand how the rule works.

Other features of this library include an operator editor that allows the definition (in runtime) of operators, redefinition of their precedences and kinds (infix, prefix, etc.), user-defined handwritten representations of characters, handwritten templates and automatic space adjustment of some mathematical structures.

Our class library is implemented in C# (using Microsoft's Tablet PC API) and it was created in a way that makes it easy to be used and extended by other programmers[2]. In particular, it can evolve with new technological developments: for instance, it is possible to change the handwritten mathematics recognizer being used[3] — which is important, because the area of handwritten recognition is still evolving.

In the following sections we provide more details about the main features of the class library.

Mathematical Structure

Mathematical structure is very important for writing calculations. Without knowing the formulae's structure, we can not manipulate it. Selecting well-formed sub-expressions is necessary to enable manipulations. For that reason, we provide a reliable and simple way of selecting expressions and sub-expressions.

Using the MST library, one can click[4] in separate elements of an expression to obtain a selection according to its structure. To illustrate how this works, consider the expression $a + b{\times}c + d + e$. A single click in any of the symbols that form the expression, selects the symbol itself. A double-click, however, has a different effect. If one double-clicks in one of the variables (a, b, c or d) the selection obtained is still

[2]The library is organized in modules, each one supporting a main feature of the system. It also follows certain design patterns, for example the Strategy pattern for choosing the recognizer to be used.

[3]Currently, the system is based on a proprietary mathematical symbol recognizer from MapleSoft.

[4]We use the term *click* to denote the action of pressing down, and possibly releasing a button, on a pointing device. When using a Tablet PC and a pen, we can also use the term *tap*.

the character that was clicked — no other selection can be obtained by clicking on a variable. However, if a double-click is performed on an operation symbol, the selection expands. In Figure 3, the result of a double-click on the last addition operator is shown. Because the structure of the addition operator is known, it selects, together with the operation symbol, the two arguments of the operator (d and e).

Figure 3. Double-click on the last addition operator.

Figures 4 and 5 show that a double-click on the first and on the second addition operators, respectively, selects again the addition operator together with its two arguments — but now, one of the arguments contains more than just a variable. As the multiplication has higher precedence than the addition, it is selected as one of the arguments of the addition. For the first addition symbol, if the selection was only $a + b$ it would not replicate the semantics of the original expression.

Figure 4. Double-click on the first addition operator.

Figure 5. Double-click on the second addition operator.

It is possible to extend the selection by continuously clicking in one of the operators. For instance, if, with $a + b{\times}c$ selected (as in Figure 4), one does another double-click on the first addition, the selection is extended to $a + b{\times}c + d$. Double-clicking on the first addition again selects the whole expression — that is, the selection is extended to contain $+e$.

One action that benefits heavily from this selection feature, is the copy of expressions and sub-expressions. One way to copy expressions using our library is to select the expression that one wants to copy and then, while holding the side button of the pen, touch with the tip of the pen in the area of the screen where the copy should be placed and release the button. Alternatively, a gesture can be used. Another action that depends on the accurate selection feature is the algebraic manipulation of expressions. In the next section, we give more details about this feature.

Structure Manipulation

One of the main goals of the library is to provide the means to perform syntactic manipulation of mathematical formulae. The idea is to apply rules to expressions automatically — automatically in the sense that the user does not have to determine the result of applying the rule. The main motivation behind the automatic use of rules is the motto: "*let the symbols do the work*". This feature allows working with uninterpreted formulae and manipulate them according to their symbols and associated rules. Also, it shows the dynamics of the symbols, avoids the introduction of syntactic errors, and requires less effort from the user.

As an example, consider the boolean expression $a{\vee}(b{\wedge}c)$. As $\vee$ distributes over $\wedge$, it can be useful to apply the distributivity rule automatically to obtain $(a \vee b) \wedge (a \vee c)$. Our library supports this type of manipulation.

Following the principles of the calculational method, our library has the general knowledge of how to apply rules but does not know if applying a certain rule is semantically correct. Checking the validity of applying a rule is the user's responsibility. We want the user to be in control and not the tool.

The main actions supported by the library are distributivity and factorization, associativity, symmetry, group and ungroup[5], and substitution of equals for equals. This ensures some of the reliability and flexibility that we want to provide. The rules supported consist purely of syntactic manipulation since the aim of the library is to support the calculational method.

One novel feature of the library is that everything on the screen remains handwritten, i.e., there is no conversion of the handwriting to typeset. Even the results of manipulations are handwritten. Tools like *MathPaper* [25] have the option of leaving the original input handwritten; however, the result of manipulating that input is presented in typeset. Our editor differs from that by keeping the original input and all the results of manipulations in their handwritten form. To show handwritten results, manipulation rules use the ink of the formulae being manipulated and rearrange it as needed. If a manipulation action needs a character that is not present in the formulae being manipulated, it will retrieve its handwritten representation from a database of characters defined by the user.

For most manipulation rules, gestures are used to trigger them. In the next section, we give more details on this.

Use of gestures

Gestures are a straightforward way of triggering actions. Using a gesture instead of a menu option is quicker and less interruptive. One of our main goals is to provide mechanisms that interfere as little as possible with the user's thought. For that reason, gestures are used to perform editing tasks and to manipulate algebraic formulae. For each action we provide default gestures that, in our view, are intuitive for that particular task. We also provide a gesture editor that allows the user to change the association between gestures and actions.

Examples of gestures that we have defined for editing tasks are the *circle* gesture, which is used to select the content inside the circle, and *right-down* and *right-up* gestures, which are used to add and remove vertical space (see Figure 6).

[5]The actions of grouping and ungrouping can be used to change the precedence of operators. For example, if given $a{\times}b + c{\times}d$ we ungroup the sub-expression $a{\times}b$, the first $\times$ and the $+$ will have the same precedence. To return to the original expression, we can group the sub-expression $a{\times}b$.

(a) Circle. (b) Right-down. (c) Right-up.

Figure 6. Gestures for editing tasks.

To apply mathematical rules to expressions, gestures are also used. Examples of two gestures that we use to apply the distributivity rule are depicted in Figures 7.a and 7.b. In this case, the distributivity of boolean disjunction through conjunction is used $(a \vee (b \wedge c) = (a \vee b) \wedge (a \vee c))$. In Figure 7.a, the *semi-circle* gesture (drawn from left to right) is used to indicate that the disjunction is to be distributed over conjunction. The result presented in Figure 8 is then automatically obtained. Similarly, in Figure 7.b, the symbol $\vee$ is selected, dragged, and then dropped over the $\wedge$ symbol so that the first distributes over the second. Again, the result (Figure 8) of applying the rule is automatically obtained.

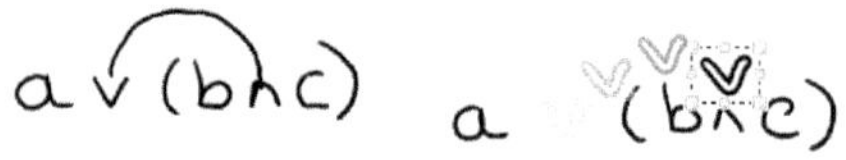

(a) Semi-circle (b) Drag-and-drop

Figure 7. Gestures for mathematical rules.

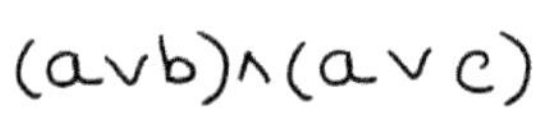

Figure 8. Result of applying the distributivity rule.

Some other commonly used rules, like symmetry, have gestures associated with them. We believe that the use of gestures is a good way to illustrate the dynamics of the symbols and to help the user writing calculations.

Animations of certain algebraic rules

Applying algebraic rules automatically and obtaining immediately a final result is helpful while solving mathematical problems. However, in a teaching environment, showing the final result of applying a rule may not be enough. When one sees a rule in action for the first time, one might need to see how the rule works in more detail in order to understand what it does. For that reason, we provide an option of animating the application of rules. Animations consist in moving slowly the several elements that form the formulae until they reach their position in the final result. As suggested in [6] and [15], animation and visualization techniques can improve student learning. This confirms our belief that animations can help the students keep track of the steps involved in the calculations.

Automatic layout adjustment

Often, while writing a document, the user has to adapt the layout of what is already written to allow more space to keep writing. This type of action interrupts the user's thought. Our library supports automatic space adjustment when the user needs it (the current version only supports quantifiers written in the Eindhoven notation [10]). For example, if the user is editing the summation quantifier shown in Figure 9, the characters marked in red are adjusted automatically as the user writes inside the quantifier expression.

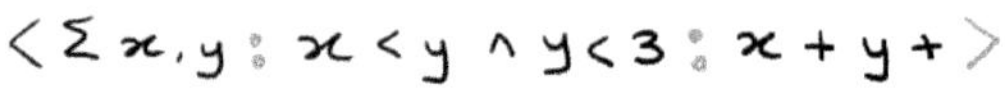

Figure 9. Summation quantifier.

If the user is writing near one of these characters, the expression extends automatically, relieving the user from the work of having to adjust it manually. In the example of Figure 9, the expression $x+y+$ is unfinished, so if one starts to write the rest of the expression, the '$\rangle$' symbol will move to the right, allowing space to finish it.

Handwritten templates

The MST library contains a mechanism for handwritten templates. Users are able to store expressions with structure and use them whenever they want. These can be seen as templates and, using substitution of equals for equals, can be composed to obtain more complex expressions. For example, the user may define templates for the GCL language [10] that can be reused later, avoiding the burden of having to recognize it again. Figure 10 shows two handwritten templates. The expressions denoted by *e* in the figure are placeholders that can be replaced by other expressions. The idea is that templates can be composed to write complex expressions/algorithms.

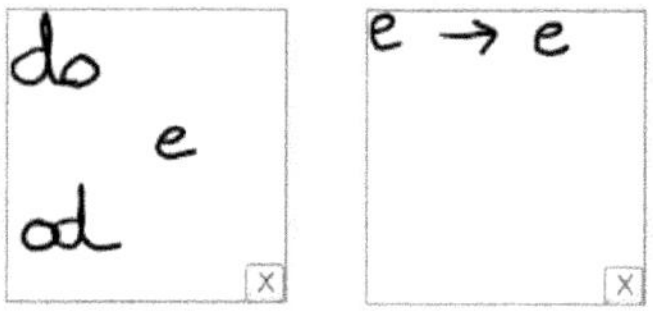

(a) do .. od (b) Guard

Figure 10. Two handwritten templates for the GCL language.

INTEGRATION WITH OTHER TOOLS

The MST library was designed to be easily added to other tools. For example, we have extended Classroom Presenter [1] (CP), an award-winning Tablet PC tool for ink-based teaching presentations and classroom interaction. Although we had no documentation about *CP*, we were able to use our library and its features within this tool.We only had to import the library and extend the user interface to allow the use of the imported features. Thus, we believe that, given appropriate documentation, other programmers can easily extend existing tools to make use of our library's features.

Using the Extended Classroom Presenter

In this section, the proof of theorem (1) shown previously is presented to demonstrate how the features available can be used to do mathematics. The gestures defined by default are used. Recall that the theorem to prove is:

$$(m \times p) \nabla n = m \nabla n \quad \Leftarrow \quad p \nabla n = 1 \quad .$$

The full proof starts with the expression $m \nabla n$ and, assuming the right-hand side of the implication, transforms it into

$(m\times p)\nabla n$. To prove it using the tool, the user starts by writing the theorem and recognizing it. The next step is to copy $m\nabla n$. For that, the user selects it (double-clicking on the second ∇):

$$(m\times p)\nabla n = m\nabla n \Leftarrow p\nabla n = 1$$

and copies it using the gesture *Check*:

$$(m\times p)\nabla n = m\nabla n \Leftarrow p\nabla n = 1$$

The result is:

$$(m\times p)\nabla n = m\nabla n \Leftarrow p\nabla n = 1$$
$$m\nabla n$$

In this example, the *Check* gesture is overloaded. It is used for copy and for substitution of equals for equals (also called *Leibniz* rule). Next, the hint for the step is written. For that, the user can select the expression $p\nabla n = 1$:

$$(m\times p)\nabla n = m\nabla n \Leftarrow p\nabla n = 1$$
$$m\nabla n$$
$$= \{$$

and use the *Check* gesture, once again, to copy:

$$(m\times p)\nabla n = m\nabla n \Leftarrow p\nabla n = 1$$
$$m\nabla n$$
$$= \{$$

The user can extend the hint with handwritten text. Next, the initial expression $m\nabla n$ is selected:

$$(m\times p)\nabla n = m\nabla n \Leftarrow p\nabla n = 1$$
$$m\nabla n$$
$$= \{\, p\nabla n = 1 \text{ and } 1 \text{ is the unit of multiplication} \,\}$$

and copied:

$$m\nabla n$$
$$= \{\, p\nabla n = 1 \text{ and } 1 \text{ is the unit of multiplication} \,\}$$

The new copy is manipulated as shown in Figure 2. The user starts by replacing m by $m\times p$. So, $m\times p$ is selected:

$$(m\times p)\nabla n = m\nabla n \Leftarrow p\nabla n = 1$$
$$m\nabla n$$
$$= \{\, p\nabla n = 1 \text{ and } 1 \text{ is the unit of multiplication} \,\}$$
$$m\nabla n$$

and *Leibniz* is applied to m:

$$m\nabla n$$
$$= \{\, p\nabla n = 1 \text{ and } 1 \text{ is the unit of multiplication} \,\}$$
$$m\nabla n$$

The result is:

$$m\nabla n$$
$$= \{\, p\nabla n = 1 \text{ and } 1 \text{ is the unit of multiplication} \,\}$$
$$m\times p\nabla n$$

After a number of steps to replace p by $p\nabla n$ and add brackets (omitted), we reach a point where distributivity is applied (using the semi-circle gesture):

$$(m\times(p\nabla n))\nabla n$$
$$= \{\, \text{distributivity} \,\}$$
$$(m\times(p\nabla n))\nabla n$$

The result is the following:

$$(m\times(p\nabla n))\nabla n$$
$$= \{\, \text{distributivity} \,\}$$
$$(((m\times p)\nabla(m\times n)))\nabla n$$

The editor allows the user to remove the brackets surrounding the expression $(m\times p)\nabla(m\times n)$ (steps omitted). After removing the two sets of brackets, it is not possible to select the sub-expression $(m\times n)\nabla n$, because the expression $(m\times p)\nabla(m\times n)$ remains grouped. To proceed with the calculation, the user has to ungroup it. That is done by selecting the expression:

$$(m\times p)\nabla(m\times n)\nabla n$$

and using the ungroup option from the menu:

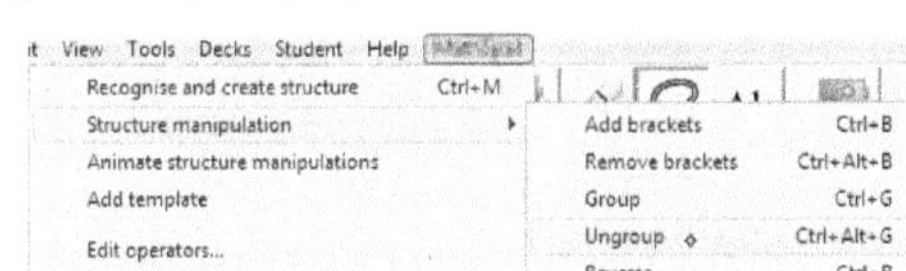

Now, the following step consists of replacing $(m\times n)\nabla n$ by n. Omitting the steps used to write the hint, the next step is to select the expression that was obtained in the previous step of the calculation:

$$(m\times p)\nabla(m\times n)\nabla n$$
$$= \{\, (m\times n)\nabla n = n \,\}$$

and then, copy it:

$$
\begin{aligned}
& (m \times p) \nabla (m \times n) \nabla n \\
= \ & \{ (m \times n) \nabla n = n \}
\end{aligned}
$$

Finally, the hint is used to replace $(m{\times}n)\nabla n$ by n. First, select n:

$$
\begin{aligned}
& (m \times p) \nabla (m \times n) \nabla n \\
= \ & \{ (m \times n) \nabla n = n \} \\
& (m \times p) \nabla (m \times n) \nabla n
\end{aligned}
$$

and then using *Leibniz*:

$$
\begin{aligned}
& (m \times p) \nabla (m \times n) \nabla n \\
= \ & \{ (m \times n) \nabla n = n \} \\
& (m \times p) \nabla (m \times n) \nabla n
\end{aligned}
$$

The final result is obtained and the proof is concluded. The complete proof is as follows:

$$
\begin{aligned}
& m \nabla n \\
= \ & \{ p \nabla n = 1 \text{ and } 1 \text{ is the unit of multiplication} \} \\
& (m \times (p \nabla n)) \nabla n \\
= \ & \{ \text{distributivity} \} \\
& (m \times p) \nabla (m \times n) \nabla n \\
= \ & \{ (m \times n) \nabla n = n \} \\
& (m \times p) \nabla n
\end{aligned}
$$

We believe that this proof illustrates well the advantages of having a structure editor of handwritten mathematics for presentations. Not only the steps are made easier, but also the user can be sure that manipulation errors will be avoided, since the tool will perform the manipulations for them. Another advantage that is relevant in a teaching context is that the use of rules is explicit. For example, to select the subexpression $(m{\times}n)\nabla n$, the user is forced to ungroup the expression $(m{\times}p)\nabla(m{\times}n)$; this corresponds to the use of associativity, which is often missed by students.

EVALUATION AND USER FEEDBACK

To gain feedback about the concept and functionality of the MST editor, we invited computer science teachers/researchers and students to trial the software. One of the main goals was to check if the features provided were regarded as helpful in the context of teaching using the calculational style. The extended version of *CP* was used for the evaluation. The tests were designed so that teachers would experiment with the software as a presenting tool and the students would experience it as a learning tool. Students did not use the software. The idea was to emulate the situation that occurs more often in practice: the teacher delivers some mathematical content and students observe and take notes. Although the editor can be used by students to assist them in the learning process, it was created with the teaching process as a main concern, i.e. with teachers as its main target *users* and students as *observers*.

In the teachers group there were 8 (eight) testers. These were teachers/researchers and PhD students who have previously been exposed to the calculational method. This group was given a guide detailing some steps that they had to follow in order to write a proof using the system (the one shown in the previous section). A questionnaire was given to record their opinion and they were observed by a monitor.

In the students group there were 74 (seventy four) second-year undergraduate students. All students had already been exposed to the calculational method. The test consisted of a 20-minute presentation followed by an anonymous questionnaire. The presentation started with an introduction to the system and an overview of its features. The system was then used to present the calculational proof shown in the previous section as it would be done in a lecture.

The results obtained in both tests seem to indicate that the software is both usable and suitable for its purpose. They also indicate that the features are not immediately easy to use but become easy with little practice.

Of particular interest is the task given to the teachers, where, for each step, they were asked to record the level of difficulty in using each feature involved. The results obtained clearly indicate that the level of difficulty decreased as the users got familiar with the software. The level of difficulty reported by most users at the first use of each feature decreased with further uses. The monitor noticed that during the first minutes of the test, most users struggled to perform the tasks[6]. However, they soon got used to the software/pen and performed the remainder of the test without problems.

In Table 1 the average results reported for the features used during the task are presented[7]. For features that had multiple uses, the results for the first and last use are reported. For the remainder, the results for the first use are shown. The level of difficulty was expressed using a scale from zero (Very easy) to four (Very difficult).

Feature	First use	Last use
Selection	2.00	0.75
Copy	1.38	0.50
Leibniz	0.50	0.63
Add brackets	0.38	n/a
Distributivity	1.00	n/a
Remove brackets	0.50	n/a
Ungroup	1.00	n/a

Table 1. Level difficulty reported (0 - Very easy; 4 - Very difficult)

For the *Selection* and *Copy* features it is clear that the difficulty decreased. For *Leibniz*, although only slightly, the level of difficulty increased. However, it is still reported as easy to perform. This increase can possibly be linked to the respective steps of the proof: *Leibniz* is triggered by drawing a

[6]Most problems were due to the users being unfamiliar with the use of Tablet PCs.

[7]The average results are rounded to two decimal places.

check over a symbol; the first point of the hand-drawn check symbol is used to determine which symbol should be substituted; in the last use of *Leibniz* the symbol to be substituted is much smaller than in the first use making it more difficult to target it. All the other features were regarded as *easy* or *very easy* to use at the first attempt.

When asked how easy it was to complete the task using the software, the average result was 0.88 meaning that, on average, the users found it easy to use the software.

The results also show that teachers find the software useful for teaching and students find it useful for learning. For instance, teachers were asked to give their opinion about the statement "The features provided by this software can help with teaching mathematics". Clearly they found it useful as 5 (62.5%) of them do agree and 3 (37.5%) do strongly agree. One of the students' tasks was to comment on the statement "Did the software help you understanding the manipulations involved?"; 63 (85%) answered Yes whilst only 8 (11%) answered No; 3 (4%) students did not answer. This shows that, for this proof, the software has definitely helped them understanding the steps involved. Thus, the editor seems to be regarded as a helpful contribution to teaching mathematics in a calculational style. The use of gestures to trigger actions was well received by both teachers and students. When asked to comment the statement "Gestures are a good way to trigger actions", only one student disagreed, three students were neutral, and the remainder of the students and all the teachers agreed. We believe this result is due to the kinesthetic nature of gestures, which helps students visualize syntactic manipulations. When students were asked if they would use the software for other purposes, 38 (51%) answered Yes, 28 (38%) answered No, and 8 (11%) did not provide an answer. Some of their suggestions for other uses include verification of proofs, mathematics in general, and physics.

Both groups were asked for suggestions for improving the software. The suggestions included displaying the syntax trees of expressions, linking gestures to a sequence of actions, manipulating brackets by using gestures, connecting with theorem provers, adding replay feature for sessions, suggesting applicable rules, and further developing the system so that students can receive support from the teacher when away (including chat/video calls).

DISCUSSION AND CONCLUSION

The use of Tablet PCs for teaching and presentations brings many advantages. We currently use a Tablet PC to teach algorithmic problem solving to first-year undergraduate students and, according to their feedback, they enjoy the interactivity that comes with the use of the Tablet PC. Based on the evaluation of the system, we believe that our library will further improve this interactivity.

The benefits of presenting the mathematics involved in algorithmic problem solving with the features provided can be enormous. It is possible to demonstrate the dynamics of problem-solving in a manner that improves on blackboard-style of teaching by exploiting the reliability of computer software in copying and manipulating structured information. It is possible to show in real-time the steps of a calculation and to see how the expressions are transformed from one step to the other.

From our experience, using a Tablet PC only as a device to write on does not exploit its full potential. The Tablet PC's computational capabilities can be a valuable help to write calculations and to show the dynamics of the symbols (that the calculational method stresses so much). Even if the presenter does not want to emphasize syntactic manipulations, having, for example, a feature that allows reliable copy of expressions is a huge improvement.

All the features presented in this paper contribute, in our view, to the flexibility and reliability that we want to provide and, more importantly, they help in doing mathematics without interfering with the user's thought. Although this library was created with presentations in mind, it can also support students and researchers in solving mathematical problems.

The evaluation of the library with teachers and students has confirmed that the features available are usable, suitable for their purpose, and useful for teaching and learning. However, it has also shown that familiarity with the use of Tablet PCs and with the features of the tool are important usability factors. In the future we expect to carry out an experiment where students use the tool to handwrite and manipulate mathematical content (we also plan to use large surfaces, such as walls and tables).

It is important to note that our library is just a prototype. There are still many challenges ahead, the most important being the improvement of recognition of handwritten mathematics. Even though recognition of handwritten mathematics is outside the scope of this work, having a recognizer oriented to the mathematical structures used in teaching algorithmic problem solving in a calculational style would make the editor more usable. Moreover, the current functionalities can still benefit from more improvements and testing. After a more stable library is achieved, our next step will be to look into connecting it with a theorem prover so that the system can produce automated proofs and support the user in writing a proof by suggesting valid steps. Another avenue that we may pursue is the support for algorithm animation. It would also be interesting to investigate how the features described in this paper could be integrated into systems that support more advanced interactions (like Hands-On Math [26]).

Even though this is not a professional tool, it can still be used for presentations and it is a starting point for what can become a very useful tool.

ACKNOWLEDGMENTS

We thank the anonymous reviewers for the helpful comments. The work presented in this paper was supported by FCT (Portuguese Foundation for Science and Technology) with grant SFRH/BD/29553/2006.

REFERENCES

1. Anderson, R., Anderson, R., Chung, O., Davis, K. M., Davis, P., Prince, C., Razmov, V., and Simon, B.

Classroom presenter - a classroom interaction system for active and collaborative learning. In *WIPTE* (2006).

2. Backhouse, R. *Program Construction*. John Wiley & Sons, 2003.
3. Backhouse, R. *Algorithmic Problem Solving*. John Wiley & Sons, 2011.
4. Backhouse, R., and Verhoeven, R. Mathspad: A system for on-line preparation of mathematical documents. *Software - Concepts and Tools 18* (1997), 80–89.
5. Bott, J. N., and LaViola Jr., J. J. A pen-based tool for visualizing vector mathematics. In *SBM*, M. Alexa and E. Y.-L. Do, Eds., Eurographics Association (2010), 103–110.
6. Catrambone, R., and Seay, A. F. Using animation to help students learn computer algorithms. *Human Factors: The Journal of the Human Factors and Ergonomics Society 44*, 3 (2002), 495–511.
7. Cossairt, T. J., and LaViola Jr., J. J. Setpad: A sketch-based tool for exploring discrete math set problems. In *SBM*, K. Singh and L. B. Kara, Eds., Eurographics Association (2012), 47–56.
8. Cromack, J. Technology and learning-centered education: Research-based support for how the Tablet PC embodies the seven principles of good practice in undergraduate education. In *38th ASEE/IEEE Frontiers in Education Conference*, IEEE (2008).
9. Dijkstra, E. W. Indirect equality enriched (and a proof by Netty). Available from `http://www.cs.utexas.edu/users/EWD/ewd13xx/EWD1315.PDF` [Last accessed: 29 June 2014], December 2001.
10. Dijkstra, E. W., and Scholten, C. S. *Predicate Calculus and Program Semantics*. Springer Verlag, NY, 1990.
11. Ferreira, J. F., and Mendes, A. Student's feedback on teaching mathematics through the calculational method. In *39th ASEE/IEEE Frontiers in Education Conference*, IEEE (2009).
12. Fitzgerald, T. J. The Tablet PC takes its place in the classroom. The New York Times, 9 September 2004. Available from `http://www.nytimes.com/2004/09/09/technology/circuits/09jott.html` [Last accessed: 29 June 2014].
13. Graham, R. L., Knuth, D. E., and Patashnik, O. *Concrete Mathematics: A Foundation for Computer Science*. Addison-Wesley, 1994.
14. Gries, D., and Schneider, F. *A Logical Approach to Discrete Mathematics*. Springer Verlag, NY, 1993.
15. Grissom, S., McNally, M. F., and Naps, T. Algorithm visualization in CS education: Comparing levels of student engagement. In *Proceedings of the 2003 ACM Symposium on Software Visualization*, SoftVis '03, ACM (New York, NY, USA, 2003), 87–94.
16. Labahn, G., Lank, E., MacLean, S., Marzouk, M. S., and Tausky, D. Mathbrush: A system for doing math on pen-based devices. In *Document Analysis Systems*, K. Kise and H. Sako, Eds., IEEE Computer Society (2008), 599–606.
17. LaViola Jr., J. J., and Zeleznik, R. C. Mathpad^2: a system for the creation and exploration of mathematical sketches. *ACM Trans. Graph. 23*, 3 (2004), 432–440.
18. Li, C., Miller, T. S., Zeleznik, R. C., and LaViola Jr., J. J. Algosketch: Algorithm sketching and interactive computation. In *SBM*, C. Alvarado and M.-P. Cani, Eds., Eurographics Association (2008), 175–182.
19. Simon, B., Anderson, R., Hoyer, C., and Su, J. Preliminary experiences with a Tablet PC based system to support active learning in computer science courses. In *ITiCSE '04: Proceedings of the 9th annual SIGCSE conference on Innovation and technology in computer science education*, ACM (New York, NY, USA, 2004), 213–217.
20. Smithies, S., Novins, K., and Arvo, J. Equation entry and editing via handwriting and gesture recognition. *Behaviour & IT 20*, 1 (2001), 53–67.
21. Suzuki, M., Tamari, F., Fukuda, R., Uchida, S., and Kanahori, T. INFTY: an integrated OCR system for mathematical documents. In *ACM Symposium on Document Engineering*, ACM (2003), 95–104.
22. Verhoeven, R., and Backhouse, R. Towards tool support for program verification and construction. In *FM'99 - Int. Formal Methods Symposium*, J. W. Jeanette Wing and J. Davies, Eds., Springer Lect. Notes Comp. Sci. (1709) (1999), 1128–1146.
23. Wang, M., Plimmer, B., Schmieder, P., Stapleton, G., Rodgers, P., and Delaney, A. SketchSet: Creating Euler diagrams using pen or mouse. In *VL/HCC*, G. Costagliola, A. J. Ko, A. Cypher, J. Nichols, C. Scaffidi, C. Kelleher, and B. A. Myers, Eds., IEEE (2011), 75–82.
24. Wenzel, L., and Dillner, H. MathJournal - an interactive tool for the Tablet PC. Available from `http://www.xthink.com/downloads/MathJournal_2003.pdf` [Last accessed: 29 June 2014].
25. Zeleznik, R., Miller, T., Li, C., and Laviola, Jr., J. J. Mathpaper: Mathematical sketching with fluid support for interactive computation. In *SG '08: Proceedings of the 9th international symposium on Smart Graphics*, Springer-Verlag (Berlin, Heidelberg, 2008), 20–32.
26. Zeleznik, R. C., Bragdon, A., Adeputra, F., and Ko, H.-S. Hands-On Math: a page-based multi-touch and pen desktop for technical work and problem solving. In *UIST*, K. Perlin, M. Czerwinski, and R. Miller, Eds., ACM (2010), 17–26.

P.I.A.N.O.: Faster Piano Learning with Interactive Projection

Katja Rogers[1], Amrei Röhlig[1], Matthias Weing[1], Jan Gugenheimer[1], Bastian Könings[1],
Melina Klepsch[2], Florian Schaub[3], Enrico Rukzio[1], Tina Seufert[2], Michael Weber[1]
[1]Institute of Media Informatics, [2]Institute of Psychology and Education
Ulm University, Germany, [firstname.lastname]@uni-ulm.de
[3]School of Computer Science, Carnegie Mellon University, Pittsburgh, fschaub@cs.cmu.edu

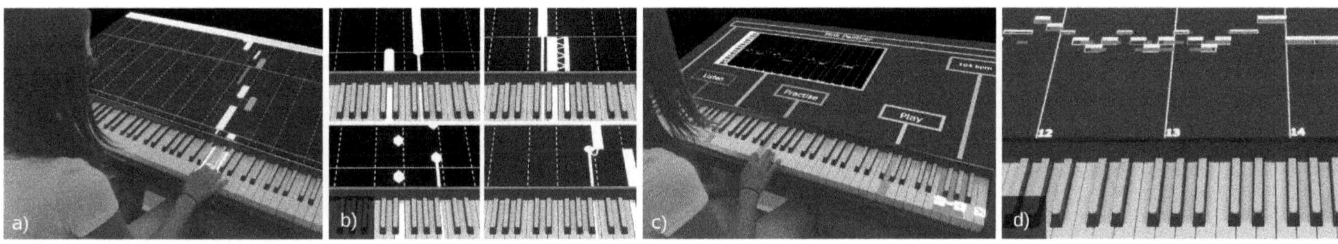

Figure 1. In P.I.A.N.O., (a) music notation is projected onto the piano to facilitate direct mapping of notes to respective piano keys. Correct fingering is supported with color highlights. (b) The basic piano roll notation is extended to support articulations (legato, staccato) and note ornaments (trill, grace notes). (c) The learning process is supported by three learning modes (*listen, practice, play*). (d) After *practicing* a song, the *play* mode provides detailed feedback on the achieved skill level.

ABSTRACT

Learning to play the piano is a prolonged challenge for novices. It requires them to learn sheet music notation and its mapping to respective piano keys, together with articulation details. Smooth playing further requires correct finger postures. The result is a slow learning progress, often causing frustration and strain. To overcome these issues, we propose P.I.A.N.O., a piano learning system with interactive projection that facilitates a fast learning process. Note information in form of an enhanced piano roll notation is directly projected onto the instrument and allows mapping of notes to piano keys without prior sight-reading skills. Three learning modes support the natural learning process with live feedback and performance evaluation. We report the results of two user studies, which show that P.I.A.N.O. supports faster learning, requires significantly less cognitive load, provides better user experience, and increases perceived musical quality compared to sheet music notation and non-projected piano roll notation.

Author Keywords

Piano; music; instrument learning; interactive projection; piano roll notation; muscial expression; CAMIT.

ACM Classification Keywords

H.5.5 Information Interfaces and Presentation: Sound and Music Computing; K.3.1 Computers and Education: Computer Uses in Education—*Computer-assisted instruction*.

http://dx.doi.org/10.1145/2669485.2669514

INTRODUCTION

Hallam [13] has shown that children and young people benefit from the positive effects of music-making on personal and social development. Learning to play piano as an adult is often motivated by self-actualization and enjoyment [18]. Active music-making has also been found to enhance the health and well-being of elderly people, and can even contribute to recovery from depression [5]. However, those positive effects will only occur when playing is enjoyable and rewarded [13].

For novices, learning to play piano is a prolonged challenge. One reason for this is that conventional sheet music notation (e.g., the western notation based on a five-line staff) does not support the mapping of notes to piano keys very well [32, 23]. First, reading sheet music, called *sight-reading*, requires a vertical to horizontal mapping of notes' pitch information to the respective piano keys. Second, it requires learners to map complex note symbols and articulation marks to the notes' duration and their individual expression. While trained pianists process this mapping automatically, it is a burdensome challenge for novices [28]. Furthermore, in order to play accurately, correct *fingering* is required, i.e., which fingers to use for specific notes and note sequences [27]. These burdens often result in frustration and high dropout rates from piano courses [11], which could be lowered by supporting motivation and faster learning progress [36].

In this paper, we present P.I.A.N.O. to effectively support learning to play piano with interactive projection. In order to avoid the need for sight-reading and to reduce a learner's cognitive load, we developed an enhanced note visualization based on *piano roll notation* (see Fig. 1a). The notation originates from paper rolls used in the late 19th century, on which position and length of holes indicated notes' pitch and duration [7]. Using this approach in a graphical visualization allows the direct inference of the duration of notes (represented as vertical bars). Furthermore, by projecting notes onto the piano, a note's pitch information (a bar's horizontal position) can be mapped directly to the respective piano key. Different colors of notes support correct fingering. We extended the basic piano roll notation with support for legato and staccato articulations, as well as trill and grace note ornaments (see Fig. 1b) as a first step towards fully visualizing sheet music.

P.I.A.N.O. provides three different modes to support the learning process (see Fig. 1c). In the *listen* mode, learners can listen to a song and follow its note visualization to become familiar with its rhythm and melody. The *practice* mode waits for correct key presses before advancing the note visualization. Learners are further supported by live feedback in finding correct keys. To evaluate the learning progress, the *play* mode measures the accuracy and errors of a performance. A detailed feedback screen facilitates identification of parts requiring further practice (see Fig. 1d).

We conducted two user studies to evaluate learning progress, required cognitive load, and user experience of learners when learning a song with P.I.A.N.O. compared to sheet music notation and basic piano roll notation without projection. The results of our within-subjects study (n_1=56) show that P.I.A.N.O. reduces the initial hurdle of starting to play piano by facilitating faster learning with less cognitive load. Results of a week-long between-subjects study with the three systems (n_2=18) show that P.I.A.N.O. facilitates playing with less errors and offers a steeper learning curve for novices practicing a song for one week (please note that the metaphor "steep learning curve" refers to a quick progress in learning throughout the paper). A qualitative rating of the final performances from the second study by 6 piano experts shows that P.I.A.N.O. also increases perceived quality and overall impression of the played music.

Contributions

The main contributions of our work are (1) results showing a significant reduction of cognitive load when learning piano playing with a projection-augmented piano that supports direct mapping of music notation to piano keys. (2) An enhanced piano roll notation conveying rich note information that does not require sight-reading and demonstrates the feasibility of visualizing complex sheet music notation. (3) Three learning modes (*listen*, *practice*, and *play*) that provide song preview, live feedback, and performance evaluation optimized for roll notation that effectively support the learning process. (4) Validation of the effectiveness of the aspects above with quantitative and qualitative evaluation in two user studies, and rating of perceived quality by piano experts.

We first summarize related work before describing the P.I.A.N.O. system in detail, followed by a presentation of its comparative evaluation. We conclude with a discussion of advantages, limitations, and potential extensions of our approach.

RELATED WORK

Music Games

Rhythm games, like *Guitar Hero* [1], reconcile a novice's desire to make music with speed of progress. In such games, colored notes scroll down the screen to a line of markers, which must be mapped to colored buttons on instrument-shaped controllers, and pressed in time to score points. Piano games use basic piano roll notation in a similar fashion. For instance, in the Android app *Pianist HD* [2], vertical bars of different length scroll towards a visual touch keyboard. The arcade game *Keyboardmania* [34] indicates pitch information by showing dots instead of bars on a display above a small keyboard similar to a real piano. The biggest drawback of those games is the use of controllers instead of real instruments and simulated music making, which provides entertainment to players but does not support learning to play real instruments. However, such games can nevertheless contribute to the development of some musical skills, such as visual tracking and rhythmic performance [12, 25].

Synthesia [30] merges rhythm games with actual piano learning on real instruments. A digital piano can be connected via a MIDI interface to a PC, which displays a basic piano roll notation of notes flowing towards a virtual keyboard. Scoring is calculated by correct pitch and duration of each note and can be shared online with other players. The high activity of the scoreboard[1] and the large number of tutorials for specific songs on Youtube[2] show that Synthesia is a widely adopted method for self-educated piano playing. However, players still need to map visual note representations to the instrument. P.I.A.N.O. projects notes directly onto the piano instead. Furthermore, Synthesia's basic piano roll notation provides no information about articulations or note ornaments.

Augmented Pianos

Basic approaches for augmenting a piano keyboard are *Disney's Piano Sound Book* [6] and the *Laugh & Learn Baby Grand Piano* [10] for preschool children. Here, light-up keys ease the mapping of a simplified sheet music notation to the keys of the toy piano. Casio also offers real digital pianos with light-up keys [4].

The main drawbacks of such approaches are that they only indicate the very next keys to play and that they rely only on sheet music notation, which does not support direct mapping of notes to keys [32, 23]. This direct mapping is supported in P.I.A.N.O. by projecting an enhanced piano roll notation directly onto the piano and its keys.

Direct Mapping of Notes to Keys

Toshio Iwai [17] artistically combined projection with direct note mapping to piano keys. Similar to the piano roll notation, light dots could be drawn as notes on a projected surface with a trackball. The light dots then moved towards the piano and were played automatically. While the projection method is similar to our approach, users could only draw dots and not directly play the piano. Yang and Essl [38] augmented a digital piano with a projection setup similar to P.I.A.N.O. They implemented different visualization methods, including a basic piano roll notation, to discuss their influence on the design space of an augmented piano. However, their visualization provided neither any information about articulation or fingering, nor performance feedback. P.I.A.N.O. significantly extends the projection approach by supporting these features and the learning process with interactive learning modes.

In contrast to our goal of supporting piano playing without sight-reading knowledge, Takegawa et al. [31] propose a projection-augmented piano to support learning of sheet music notation. Notes of the sheet notation are visually connected to piano keys

[1] `http://www.synthesiagame.com/scoreboard.aspx`

[2] 1,440,000 search results for "Synthesia" as of September 2014

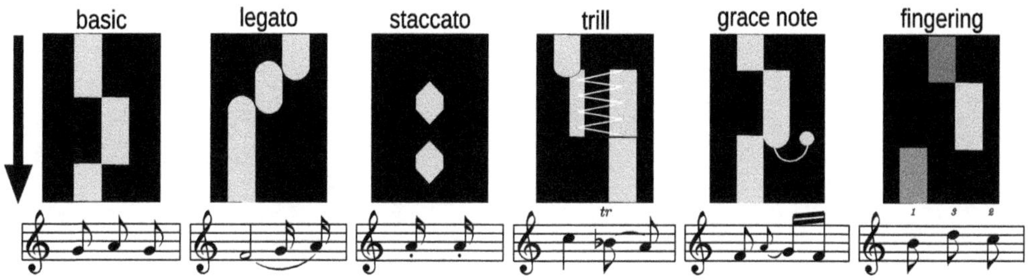

Figure 2. Different note and fingering representation in P.I.A.N.O. (*top*) compared to five-staff notation (*bottom*).

in order to support note to key mapping. The results of a between-subjects study (n=9) suggest that the method efficiently supports sheet music learning. However, the evidence is preliminary with only three learners per method and a short practice session of 30 minutes. Recently Raymaekers et al. [24] presented "The Augmented Piano" (TAP), with a setup similar to P.I.A.N.O.The system also provides a gamified alternative, wherein instead of note visualization the user shoots spaceships with the keys. However, no evaluation of their system was provided.

To the best of our knowledge, our work is the first to provide an extensive evaluation of an enhanced projected roll notation in a short-term study (n_1=56) and a one-week longitudinal study (n_2=18) to compare performance development between different learning systems. Furthermore, we do not aim to teach sight reading, but rather piano playing with a combination of our enhanced note visualization (with articulation marks and ornaments as a first step towards fully visualizing sheet music), correct fingering, and the three tightly coupled integrated learning modes optimized for roll notation.

Fingering Support

The *Concert Hands* [26] are finger sleeves worn during play, which signal correct fingering. Hands are also autonomously guided to the right position by a wrist pilot on a rail mounted in front of the piano. Huang et al. [15] propose a similar glove to passively learn correct fingering by indicated vibrations.

In Synthesia [30], correct fingering is supported by a color for each hand, and numbers (1–5) displayed with notes indicating which finger to use. However, numbers have to be assigned to notes manually beforehand, which requires learners to know which fingering approach is best suited for a song.

Xiao et al. [37] propose a remote piano tutoring system based on projected hands and autonomously moving keys of a player piano. Both student and teacher place a camera on top of the keyboard to capture hand positions and another one in front of the pianist to capture body language. Captured video is projected on to each others' piano. This way, piano teachers can remotely guide accurate fingering and body language.

P.I.A.N.O. uses different note colors to indicate correct fingering, similar to the *Glow Piano Lessons* app for iOS devices [16]. However, in contrast to the iOS app, only notes for important finger switches are colored, in order to draw attention to them without overstraining learners. While this approach requires a short learning phase of color-to-finger mapping, it facilitates fast fingering decisions during play.

THE P.I.A.N.O. SYSTEM

Rather than relying on sheet music, P.I.A.N.O. projects music notation directly onto the instrument. Notes are represented in piano roll notation, i.e., upcoming notes move towards the keyboard, which allows direct mapping of notes to the respective piano keys without any sight-reading knowledge. The current keys to play are illuminated to further ease this mapping. In contrast to basic roll notations common in music video games, our note visualization supports not only pitch and duration of notes, but also additional articulation marks, and recommended fingering, in order to provide similar information as conventional sheet music notation. The learning process itself is supported with different interactive modes following social learning theory [3].

Note Visualization

A major goal in the design of our note representation was to ease the learning process by shifting cognitive capacity from notation mapping to music playing. Traditional sheet music uses a static, symbolic notation, which is hard to match to the analogous actions required in playing the piano [32, 23]. McLachlan et al. [23] also found that spatial, graphical notations lead to improved performance in novices. Therefore, we represent notes with pictorial analogies to reduce extraneous cognitive load for the learner. We refined our note representation in an iterative process with many discussions within our research team (including two piano players and two band members with an average experience of 15 years in playing different instruments), as well as multiple practice sessions and semi-structured interviews with four participants [33].

In our system, upcoming notes are projected on the extended surface behind the keyboard to provide a preview (see Fig. 1a). On the keyboard itself, the current keys are highlighted to signal to the learner what to play. In our pre-study, many participants looked predominantly at the piano keys. Although this visual scope increased upwards with longer practice, we found a preview of upcoming notes on the keys to be very helpful as it indicates where hands have to move next. Therefore, upcoming notes are highlighted with thin extension lines, as shown in Figure 1 a) and b).

Figure 2 shows the main elements of our note visualization. The horizontal and vertical position of notes indicate what key to press (pitch) and when; their vertical length indicates the note's duration, i.e., how long the key has to be pressed. Shape and color of notes provide additional information. Our current visualization supports the articulations *legato* and *staccato*. Legato notes overlap and are extended by a half circle to indicate smooth playing without pause. In contrast, we encoded staccato with triangular ends to evoke "pointier" notes, which should be played

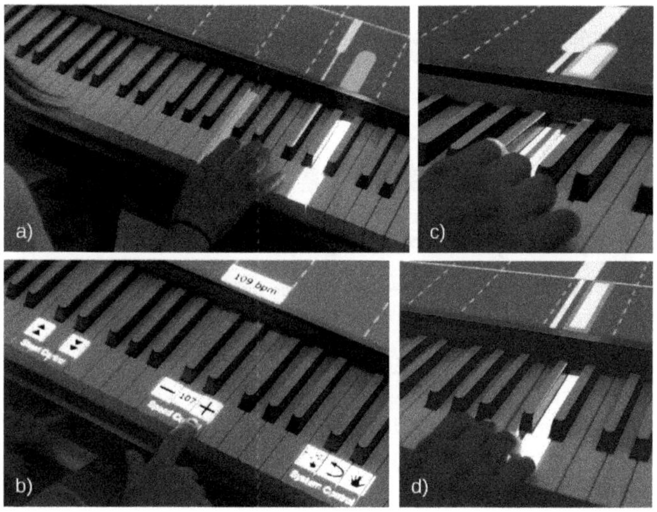

Figure 3. (a) In practice mode, an incorrectly played note is highlighted in red, the correct key in white. (b) The pedal-activated menu allows control of mode-specific settings, e.g., adapting the speed or scrolling through the visualization. (c) Live feedback in play mode highlights correctly played notes with green and (d) errors with red borders.

short and disjointedly. Common ornaments in sheet music are *trill* and *grace notes*. Trills are visualized with interconnecting lines between two notes to indicate fast repeated switching between them. A grace note is a short note played directly before the next one; it is indicated by a connected dot.

Fingering is indicated through colored notes with one color for each finger of the right hand. We chose the colors for their contrast between each other in order to prevent mistakes due to chromatic similarity. Our pre-study showed that fingering information for every note overwhelms learners. Therefore, similarly to sheet music, P.I.A.N.O. highlights only important finger switches. Notes without fingering information are gray and can be played with any suitable finger.

Learning Modes

Social learning theory [3] distinguishes four steps of learning. The first is *attention*; learners observe a process. In the *retention* step, learners try to remember what they observed. With *reproduction*, learners perform the observed behavior themselves. Further practice leads to improvement and skill advancement. *Motivation* consists of reinforcement and punishment to ensure that learners continue practice; this is essential for observational learning to be successful. P.I.A.N.O. supports social learning theory by offering three learning modes: *listen*, *practice*, and *play* (accessible from the main menu, see Fig. 1c). System and navigation controls are available by pushing down any of the piano's foot pedals. Mode-specific controls, e.g., adjusting speed, are then projected onto the keys and can be activated via keypress (see Fig. 3b).

Listen mode (attention)

In the *listen* mode, learners can listen to the song and follow its note visualization (*attention*). Thus, learners become acquainted with the characteristics of different song parts. This auditory learning aspect was revealed as highly important in conversations with experts (i.e., a professional piano teacher and a professor of psychology). Following social learning theory [3], the

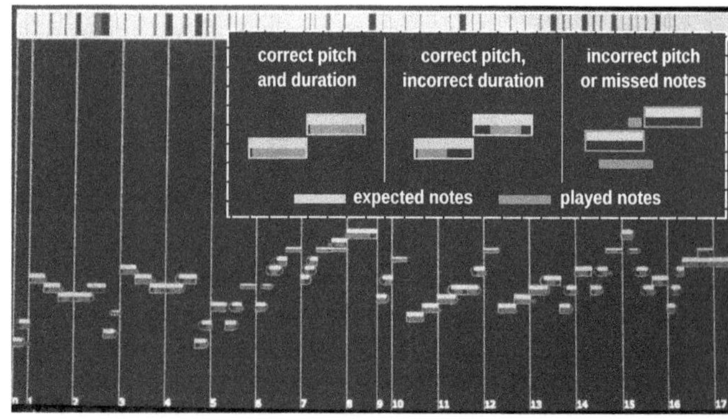

Figure 4. The play mode shows a detailed feedback screen. It shows notes played by the user (*blue bars*), notes played with correct pitch and duration (*green border*), correct pitch but incorrect duration (*yellow border*), and incorrect or missed notes (*red border*). The progress bar at the top provides a respective overview, with missed song parts in *black*.

synchronized playback of auditory and visual information should increase learners' attention.

Practice mode (retention)

The *practice* mode provides learners with an environment to practice accurate playing in order to support retention. The system encourages correct playing without haste by waiting for correct key presses and duration before continuing in the song. When a wrong note is played, the system brightly highlights the correct key and marks the wrongly-pressed key in red (see Fig. 3a). The pedal-operated context menu allows leaners to jump back and forth in the current song, change the speed or song part, or return to the main menu (see Fig. 3b).

Play mode (reproduction and motivation)

After practice, learners can assess their performance in the *play* mode by playing the song in one piece, hereby reproducing the previously observed and memorized behavior (*reproduction*). The speed of the song is adjustable to allow evaluation at various speeds. While playing, the learner receives with live feedback as part of the note visualization. A green border around the currently played note indicates a correctly played note; a red border indicates an incorrectly played note (see Fig. 3c & d). A progress bar at the top provides a summarized overview of correct (green), incorrect (red), and missed song parts (black). The progress bar is also shown in the final feedback screen (see Fig. 4), which provides detailed information of played notes (blue), and expected notes (grey). A colored border indicates correctly played notes (green), incorrectly played or missed notes (red), and notes played with correct pitch but incorrect duration (yellow). This feedback allows learners to identify which parts were played well and which require further practice, thus, it provides *motivation*.

Technical Aspects

We use a standard digital piano (Thomann DP-25), which supports MIDI communication. It is connected to a desktop computer (Intel Core i5-3470, 4 GB RAM, Intel HD Graphics 2500) via a MIDI/USB interface (Roland UM-One). The projection on the piano is created by a short-throw projector (BenQ MW516) displaying the computer's video output. It is mounted above the piano using a tripod. A smooth projection

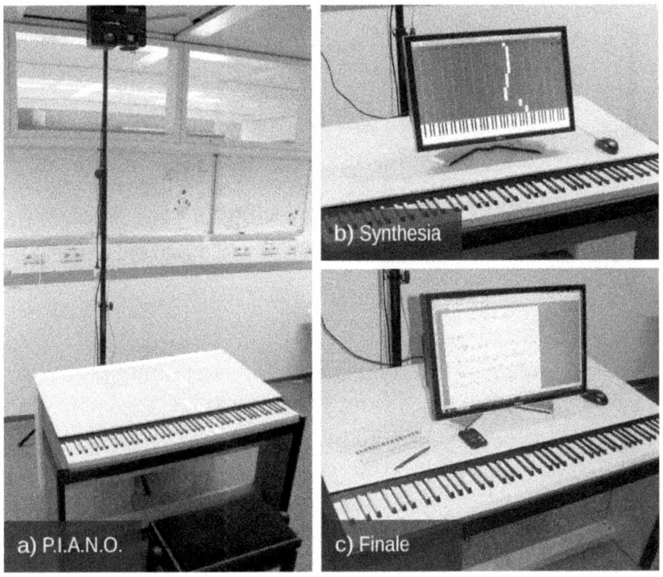

Figure 5. Setup of the compared systems in the user studies: (a) P.I.A.N.O. (interactive projection), (b) Synthesia (piano roll notation), and (c) Finale (sheet music notation).

surface is provided by a wooden plate attached to the piano, covering its top and extending towards the back (see Fig. 5a).

The MIDI protocol identifies key presses and their duration: each key press and release generates an event message , including a corresponding timestamp. This allows us to compare the system's representation of a song's expected notes with notes played on the piano in order to provide live feedback. The internal representation of a song, used for evaluation as well as visualization, is generated by parsing song files in MusicXML format [22]. Thus, any song available in this format can be played with P.I.A.N.O.

In listen mode, the computer generates MIDI messages to control piano playback. In practice mode, played notes are evaluated to generate the colored hints indicating correctly or incorrectly pressed keys (see Fig. 3c & d). In play mode, live feedback is generated based on real-time information of pressed keys. In addition, all key presses and key releases are logged throughout a learner's performance. This log is then compared to the ideal performance generated by the system to yield the result screen displayed at the end (see Fig. 4).

EVALUATION

In order to examine P.I.A.N.O.'s impact on the learning performance of novices, we conducted two experimental studies. We evaluated the learning performance with the interactive projection of P.I.A.N.O. in comparison to a more game-orientated *roll notation* and the traditional way of learning the piano with *sheet music*. As specific comparison systems, we selected commercially available software: *Synthesia* [30], a popular educational piano game, and *Finale* [21], a music software with traditional sheet music notation. Using software for all three systems enabled us to evaluate performance with a consistent quantitative measurement approach.

The first study (n_1=56) employed a within-subjects design to compare initial performance, experienced cognitive load, and perceived user experience of the three systems. A between-subjects study followed (n_2=18) to assess learners' performance over one week. We were further interested in the systems' impact on perceived quality and overall impression of performances. Thus, final recordings of the second study were blindly and independently rated by 6 piano experts.

System Setup

As the three systems were identical for both studies, we first outline their setup and the employed quantitative measurement approach, before discussing the specifics of the studies. Figure 5 shows the experimental setup of each system. The P.I.A.N.O. system was set up as described above (see Fig. 5a). For Synthesia and Finale, we used a 24"-display which was placed in front of the learners (see Fig. 5b & c). Sound settings were consistent for all systems and sound output was directly generated by the piano's built-in speakers.

Synthesia [30] was chosen due to its popularity with self-tutoring piano learners. Synthesia visualizes notes in a basic piano roll notation. It offers a *melody practice* feature, similar to our practice mode, as well as a *song recital* feature that demands a defined speed similar to our play mode. Fingering information is limited in both its availability and visualization, and there is no visualization of articulation techniques. When connected to a piano via MIDI, Synthesia can assess a learner's performance from piano key presses.

Finale [21] is a software for composing and displaying sheet music. To achieve comparable conditions to our play mode between all systems, it was essential that the dynamic indication of the current position within a song was supported. Finale displays a dynamic marker that runs through the depicted sheet music at a defined speed. In addition, learners were offered a metronome to support keeping a song's rhythm. In contrast to P.I.A.N.O. and Synthesia, sheet music requires learners to perform sight-reading. Thus, learners were given additional help in form of a notation guide and an image mapping each note in staff notation to the keyboard. The piano's middle C note was marked with a colored sticker.

In order to obtain consistent quantitative performance results of all systems, we implemented a measurement tool that recorded the piano's MIDI output, i.e., actually pressed keys, in synchronization with the evaluated system. Similar to Drake and Palmer [8], recorded session logs were analyzed against expected correct notes: We differentiated between *missed notes*, *incorrectly pressed notes* (pitch errors) and *correctly pressed notes* (correct pitch). Incorrectly pressed notes were counted independently from the number of expected notes, i.e., pressing a wrong key twice during the duration of one expected note resulted in two incorrectly pressed notes. This allowed for a more precise distinction of incorrect performances. Correctly pressed notes were further sub-classified regarding their duration, i.e., *correct* and *incorrect duration notes*. Duration was evaluated based on absolute length comparison and relative timestamp matching.

User Study 1: Initial Performance and User Experience

In a within-subjects study with the three systems, we evaluated the performance of novices with no previous piano experience in learning to play the right-hand part of a song in 15 minutes. We expected that *learning with P.I.A.N.O. would result in higher learning performance* (more correctly pressed notes, less incorrectly pressed and missed notes) (H_1) than Synthesia and Finale, due to the direct mapping of notes onto keys. For the same reason, we expected that *P.I.A.N.O. would create less intrinsic, less extraneous, and higher germane cognitive load* (H_2). *Intrinsic cognitive load* (ICL) results from the learning material itself, its element interactivity, and prior knowledge of the learner [29]. *Extraneous cognitive load* (ECL) occurs due to the design of the learning environment, whereas *germane cognitive load* (GCL) arises from the learner's intrinsic motivation and concentration on understanding the learning material. Hence, a system should strive for low ICL and ECL, but high GCL [29]. Finally, we expected that *P.I.A.N.O.'s user experience would be rated higher* (H_3) than those of the other systems.

Method and Material

With the help of two experienced pianists and a professional piano teacher, we selected three songs of similar difficulty and length (16 bars, 26 seconds) that have a dominant melody played with the right hand. The songs were chosen from a grade 1 syllabus of exam pieces from the Associated Board of the Royal Schools of Music [20]: "*Das Ballett*" by D. G. Türk, "*Minuet in G*" by W. A. Mozart, and "*Moderato*" by A. F. Gedike. To verify that the songs were of similar difficulty, we performed a treatment check based on learning performance with sheet music notation. We could not find a significant difference regarding correctly pressed notes. (song 1 vs. 2: *MD*=1.91, *SE*=4.40, n.s.; song 1 vs. 3: *MD*=3.62, *SE*=4.34, n.s.; song 2 vs. 3: *MD*=5.53, *SE*: 4.34, n.s.).

At the beginning of the session, participants completed a questionnaire regarding their demographic information, and musical background (i.e., experience with other instruments, and sight-reading skills). We further used a subtest of "the kit of factor-referenced cognitive tests" [9] to assess learners' spatial ability. Each participant interacted with all three systems and learned a different song with each. The order of systems and songs was counter-balanced (Latin square). For each system, participants were first given a written introduction to the specific system, and encouraged to try out the described features. Participants then listened to the assigned song three times (P.I.A.N.O.'s *listen* mode, Synthesia's *watch and listen only*, and Finale's *playback* mode). This was the only time when listening to the song was allowed. Playing performance was measured at four times: after listening to the song *without practice* (T_1), *after practicing the first half of the song (5 min.)* (T_2), *after practicing the second half of the song (5 min.)* (T_3), and a final measurement *after practicing the whole song (5 min.)* (T_4). However, each measurement corresponds to the learning performance for the whole song as measured in the system-specific play-through mode (P.I.A.N.O.'s *play* mode, Synthesia's *song recital*, and Finale's *dynamic-marker* mode).

After each system session, participants completed an 8-item survey [19], designed to differentiate between the three parts of cognitive load. Each item posed a statement to be rated on a 7-point Likert scale. Perceived user experience of each system was assessed with the AttrakDiff survey [14], which consists of 28 bipolar verbal anchors rated on a 7-point scale. AttrakDiff results in four scales: *perceived pragmatic quality (PQ)* measuring the support for achieving a goal, *hedonic quality – stimulation (HQ-S)* measuring perceived novelty and potential to grab users' attention,

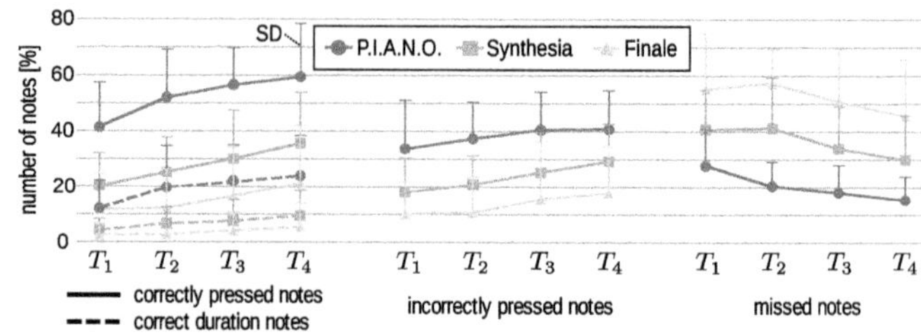

Figure 6. Learning performance for P.I.A.N.O., Synthesia, and Finale in first study for measurements T_1–T_4.

hedonic quality – identification (HQ-I) measuring potential of identification with the system, and *perceived attractiveness (ATT)*.

Sessions lasted about two hours on average, with 20-30 min. per system. Due to the long duration, participants were offered snacks and drinks, and afterwards allowed to choose from a variety of larger sweet collections as compensation.

Participants

A total of 56 right-handed learners participated in the study, all of them novices in playing piano. The average age of participants was 23 years (*SD*=3.92); they were fairly balanced in gender (32 female, 24 male), and most were students. Some participants had a basic level of ability to read sheet music; on average, participants achieved 6.98 out of 15 points in the test of sight-reading skills (*SD*=4.59).

Learning Performance

Figure 6 shows the results of the quantitative analysis of the learners' short-term learning performances. For all measurements (T_1–T_4), P.I.A.N.O. learners achieved a higher percentage of correct notes and also performed better regarding duration accuracy. An analysis of variance with repeated measures (rANOVA) revealed a significant difference in the number of *correctly pressed notes* ($F(2,88)=121.64$, $p<.001$, $\eta^2=0.73$) and *correct duration notes* ($F(1.37,61.85)=85.31$, $p<.001$, $\eta^2=0.66$) for all three systems. An analysis of contrasts showed that P.I.A.N.O. learners hit significantly more correct notes than Synthesia ($F(1,44)=120.42$, $p<.001$, $\eta^2=0.73$) and Finale learners ($F(1,44)=173.31$, $p<.001$, $\eta^2=0.80$), and also played more *correct duration notes* compared to Synthesia ($F(1,45)=78.04$, $p<.001$, $\eta^2=0.63$) and Finale ($F(1,45)=108.83$, $p<.001$, $\eta^2=0.71$).

With respect to *incorrectly pressed notes*, Figure 6 shows that P.I.A.N.O. learners also pressed more incorrect notes on average than learners of the other systems. An rANOVA revealed significant differences between all systems ($F(1.75,76.92)=60.11$, $p<.001$, $\eta^2=0.58$). The contrasts show that learning with P.I.A.N.O. results in more incorrectly pressed notes than learning with Synthesia ($F(1,44)=60.62$, $p<.001$, $\eta^2=0.58$) or Finale ($F(1,44)=85.70$, $p<.001$, $\eta^2=0.66$). However, on average, P.I.A.N.O. learners also tried to play more notes, which is reflected in the lower number of *missed notes*. Missed notes significantly differ between all systems (rANOVA: $F(1.73,77.79)=89.83$, $p<.001$, $\eta^2=0.67$) and P.I.A.N.O. learners missed significantly less notes than Synthesia learners ($F(1,45)=72.30$, $p<.001$, $\eta^2=0.62$) and Finale learners ($F(1,45)=165.04$, $p<.001$, $\eta^2=0.79$). In summary, with the exception of incorrectly pressed notes, the

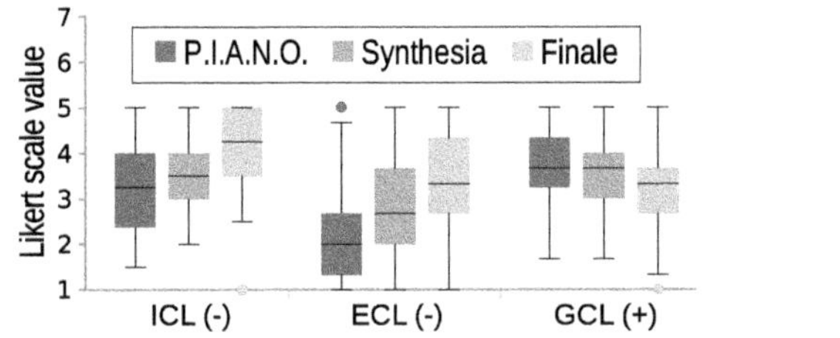

Figure 7. Intrinsic, extrinsic, and germane (positive) cognitive load of P.I.A.N.O., Synthesia, and Finale in study 1.

combined results confirm our hypothesis that P.I.A.N.O. improves initial learning performance (H_1).

Cognitive load

Figure 7 shows the cognitive load results. Internal consistency (Cronbach's α) of items was confirmed for intrinsic cognitive load (ICL) (P.I.A.N.O.: α=.81; Synthesia: α=.79; Finale: α=.70), extrinsic cognitive load (ECL) (P.I.A.N.O.: α=.81; Synthesia: α=.86; Finale: α=.87), and germane cognitive load (GCL) (P.I.A.N.O.: α=.62; Synthesia: α=.53; Finale: α=.58).

According to an rANOVA, significant differences existed for ICL ($F(2,108)=18.39$, $p<.001$, $\eta^2=0.25$), ECL ($F(2,108)=16.88$, $p<.001$, $\eta^2=0.24$), and GCL ($F(2,108)=10.02$, $p<.001$, $\eta^2=0.16$). P.I.A.N.O. induces significantly lower ICL than both Synthesia ($F(1,54)=5.02$, $p<.05$, $\eta^2=0.09$), and Finale ($F(1,54)=38.00$, $p<.001$, $\eta^2=0.41$), indicating that the complexity of the note notation is reduced by P.I.A.N.O.'s projected roll notation compared to Synthesia or Finale. ECL was also rated significantly lower with P.I.A.N.O. than with Synthesia ($F(1,54)=9.64$, $p<.01$, $\eta^2=0.15$) or Finale ($F(1,54)=28.71$, $p<.001$, $\eta^2=0.35$). This suggests that P.I.A.N.O. reduces split attention: In Synthesia, attention is split between the keyboard and the display. The metronome may further split attention in Finale. P.I.A.N.O. learners only needed to follow the projected notation which is seamlessly integrated with the keyboard.

Furthermore, P.I.A.N.O. induces significantly more positive GCL than Finale ($F(1,54)=18.59$, $p<.001$, $\eta^2=0.26$). We could not find a significant difference between P.I.A.N.O. and Synthesia ($F(1,54)=2.88$, n.s.); presumably their roll notations promote similar motivation. Thus, H_2 can be accepted, as P.I.A.N.O. induces lower intrinsic and extrinsic load than Synthesia and Finale, and higher germane load than Finale.

User experience

The per-item ratings of the three systems on the AttrakDiff scales are shown in Figure 8. P.I.A.N.O. was ranked highest in almost all cases, with Finale consistently ranked lowest. Significant differences exist for perceived pragmatic quality (PQ) ($F(2,108)=19.97$, $p<.001$, $\eta^2=0.25$), stimulation (HQ-S) ($F(2,108)=117.76$, $p<.001$, $\eta^2=0.69$), and attractiveness (ATT) ($F(2,108)=24.75$, $p<.001$, $\eta^2=0.31$). Differences were not significant for the identification scale (HQ-I). More specifically, for all scales P.I.A.N.O. was rated significantly higher than Synthesia (PQ: $F(1,54)=8.64$, $p<.01$, $\eta^2=0.15$; HQ-S: $F(1,54)=46.78$, $p<.001$, $\eta^2=0.46$; ATT: $F(1,54)=11.85$, $p<.001$, $\eta^2=0.18$), and Finale (PQ: $F(1,54)=28.26$, $p<.001$, $\eta^2=0.34$; HQ-S: $F(1,54)=225.33$, $p<.001$, $\eta^2=0.81$; ATT: $F(1,54)=39.50$, $p<.001$, $\eta^2=0.42$). As a result, H_3 can also be accepted.

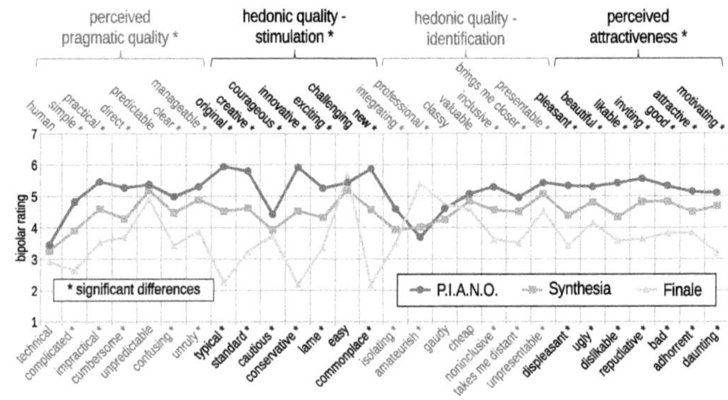

Figure 8. User experience results rated with AttrakDiff's 28 bipolar verbal anchors.

User Study 2: One-week Performance

In the first study, P.I.A.N.O. and its interactive projection outperformed classic piano roll notation (Synthesia) and sheet music notation (Finale) for most of the quantitative performance metrics, cognitive load, and user experience. These results suggest that projecting an enhanced note visualization onto the piano significantly eases piano learning for novices. In order to validate P.I.A.N.O.'s superiority regarding performance (correct, incorrect, and missed notes), we conducted a second study with the primary goal of evaluating learner performance over a longer period of time. We recruited a new group of participants (n_2=18) that practiced with one of the systems each day for one week. We opted for a between-subjects design to avoid performance interference from multiple systems. Our hypothesis was that *P.I.A.N.O. would retain a steeper learning curve over one week than Synthesia or Finale*, based on measured performance (H_4).

Method and Material

In order to avoid a ceiling effect, the song for Study 2 was chosen through a preliminary study with 3 participants in order to select a song of which the right-hand part was neither too easy nor too hard to learn. Based on the results, we chose a slightly simplified version of Schumann's *Träumerei* (16 bars, 116 notes), wherein the difficulty consisted mostly of legato articulation and several two- and three-note chords. Three groups, each consisting of six participants were monitored while they practiced with one system (P.I.A.N.O., Synthesia, or Finale) for a total of 5 consecutive days. Each daily session consisted of a brief questionnaire regarding their pre-session physical condition, followed by listening to the song one time, a 15-minute practice session, and a daily play-mode measurement (D_1–D_5).

Participants

A total of 18 learners participated in this study; mainly students, 26 years old on average (SD=4.45), and balanced in gender (9 female, 9 male), which were evenly distributed across the three groups. The preliminary sight-reading test revealed no differences in the average sight-reading skills among learners of P.I.A.N.O. (M=8.8, SD=5.42), Synthesia (M=9, SD=4.69), and Finale (M=8.3, SD=4.32).

Learning Performance

The participants' learning curves for the three systems are depicted in Figure 9. For all measurements, P.I.A.N.O. learners achieved a higher percentage of correct notes, with better duration

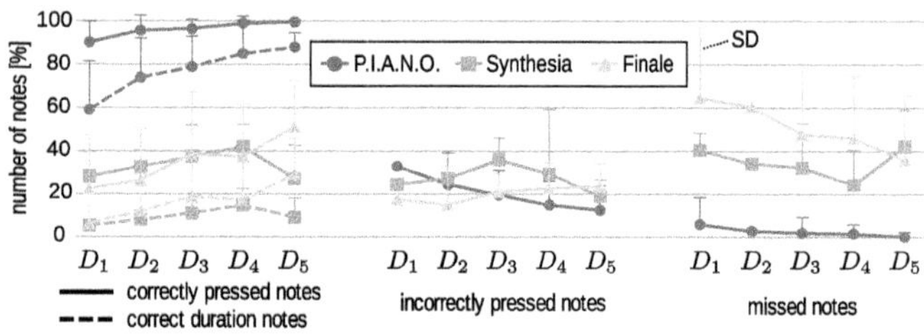

Figure 9. Development of learning performance in second study for 5 consecutive days (D_1–D_5).

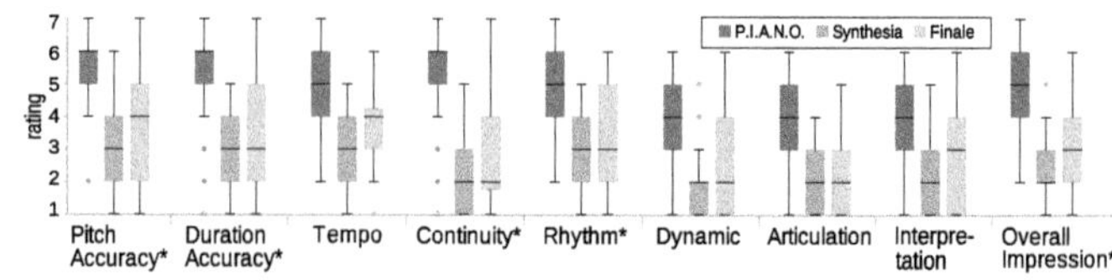

Figure 10. Expert ratings of perceived quality for 12 recordings (6 practice, 6 play) of each system.

accuracy (on average 88% *correct duration notes* on the last day) and lower percentage of *incorrectly played* and *missed notes* (12% and 0.3% on last day). An rANOVA revealed significant differences in the learning performance regarding *correctly pressed notes* ($F(2,15)=34.26, p<.001, \eta^2=0.82$), *correct duration notes* ($F(2,15)=51.43, p<.001, \eta^2=0.87$), and *missed notes* ($F(2,15)=12.41, p<.01, \eta^2=0.62$) at all five measurements. A significant interaction of system and measurement point was found, showing a steeper learning curve of P.I.A.N.O. learners regarding *correctly pressed notes* ($F(3.62,3)=5.15, p<.01, \eta^2=0.41$), *correct duration notes* ($F(4.81,3)=4.24, p<.01, \eta^2=0.36$), and *missed notes* ($F(3.50,3)=3.59, p<.05, \eta^2=0.32$) compared to those of Synthesia and Finale learners. For *incorrectly pressed notes*, an rANOVA showed no significant differences between systems ($F<1$, n.s.) or measurements ($F(2.00,13)=1.88$, n.s.). However, a difference in interaction was found ($F(4.00,3)=3.69, p<.05, \eta^2=0.33$); *incorrectly pressed notes* decreased over time for P.I.A.N.O. learners, were unstable for Synthesia learners, and increased for Finale learners. Together the results for *correctly/incorrectly pressed notes*, *correct duration notes*, and *missed notes* confirm our hypothesis that P.I.A.N.O. leads to an improvement in learning performance over time (H_4).

Expert Evaluation: Perceived Quality

6 piano experts were recruited (4 piano teachers, 2 professional players) with 28 years of experience on average, in order to gain qualitative performance ratings. We expected that *experts would rate recordings of P.I.A.N.O. learners higher than those of Synthesia and Finale learners in terms of perceived quality and overall impression* (H_5).

Method and Material

On the final day of study 2, we recorded one *practice* and one *play* session of each participant, resulting in 36 recordings (12 for each system). *Play* sessions were used for the expert evaluation because they provided consistent tempo, which is necessary for a realistic and comparable scenario. However, in some cases the play mode resulted in incomplete recordings when learners were unable to recover from playing mistakes. *Practice* sessions, therefore, allowed us to provide experts with more complete recordings for their ratings.

Each expert listened to all 36 recordings and filled out a survey for each. Recordings were anonymized regarding the system and playing mode. The three evaluated systems were presented to the experts in randomized order to avoid fatigue and assimilation effects. The rating criteria in the survey were a subset from a music performance adjudication set created by Wrigley et al. [35], and consisted of *pitch accuracy*, *duration accuracy*, *tempo*, *rhythm*, *continuity*, *dynamic*, *articulation*, *interpretation*, and *overall impression*. Each criterion had to be rated on a 7-point Likert scale (from *very poor* to *very good*). Furthermore, experts could comment on positive and negative aspects about the session in a text field. As a reward, each expert received a 10-Euro shopping coupon.

Results

The ratings for associated play and practice sessions were combined by calculating their means. Calculated inter-rater reliability (Krippendorff's α) showed reliable ratings for 5 of the 9 scales: *pitch accuracy* (α=0.68), *duration accuracy* (α=0.66), *rhythm* (α=0.69), *continuity* (α=0.61), and *overall impression* (α=0.70). P.I.A.N.O. recordings were rated higher for all scales compared to recordings of Synthesia and Finale (see Fig. 10). For the reliable scales, ANOVAs revealed significant differences in pitch accuracy ($F(2,15)=24.30, p<.001, \eta^2=0.76$), duration accuracy ($F(2,15)=11.92, p<.01, \eta^2=0.61$), continuity ($F(2,15)=15.61, p<.001, \eta^2=0.68$), rhythm ($F(2,15)=14.47, p<.001, \eta^2=0.66$), and the overall impression ($F(2,15)=13.67, p<.001, \eta^2=0.65$). Thus, we can confirm our hypothesis H_5 for these scales.

DISCUSSION

Both user studies revealed significant differences in multiple variables between the three systems. P.I.A.N.O. learners were able to play more correct notes upon first play, and improved their performance more notably regarding duration accuracy, incorrectly pressed notes (pitch errors), and missed notes. The group of piano experts further confirmed that performances of P.I.A.N.O. learners achieved higher overall impression and perceived quality after one week of practice. Additionally, learning with P.I.A.N.O. resulted in less negative intrinsic and extrinsic cognitive load, more positive germane cognitive load, and provided a better user experience.

These results confirm the effectiveness of our projected piano roll notation, which allows direct mapping of notes onto the keys and does not require sight reading skills. Learners are able to concentrate on playing respective keys correctly (in terms of duration and basic articulation), rather than having to translate sheet music notation and find the correct keys. While trained pianists process mapping of sheet music notation automatically, it is a burdensome challenge for novices [28] and often leads to frustration [11, 36] – as also indicated by the lower average germane load measured for Finale. As one Finale learner commented: *"Without sight-reading skills, this task is very complex and absolutely frustrating."* P.I.A.N.O. eliminates this hurdle and allows song playing instantly. Most P.I.A.N.O. learners commented that time went by very quickly and that they had fun: *"Great when you want to learn playing piano in 5 minutes"*; *"very innovative and intuitive system which is fun to use."* In summary, learning piano with interactive projection appears to be easier and more fun than learning with sheet music notation or piano roll notation without direct mapping.

Limitations and Future Work

The study participants were drawn mainly from the current and former student population, and thus provide a fairly consistent age and educational background. Further studies are needed to investigate different populations, e.g., children or older adults. The second user study took place over the course of one week. While the measured learning curves proved highly promising for P.I.A.N.O., their further development over several weeks, months or even years is also of interest and might provide further valuable insights.

P.I.A.N.O. currently supports only right-hand song parts to target an early stage of learning. In order to provide support for more advanced learners and learning progression, we plan to extend our system to accommodate left-hand parts, as well as advanced features of conventional sheet music (e.g., crescendo or fermata). These visualization features could dynamically appear based on learners' performance. The system should also support fingering recognition, i.e., determining whether the learner pressed the key with the correct finger. We are currently integrating fingering recognition into our system, and plan to evaluate its influence on learning performance in a longitudinal study over several weeks.

Some learners were concerned about being too dependent on the system, and the lack of sheet music notation: *"Without the system I would not be able to play the song."* and *"You do not learn sight-reading."* While it was not our goal to support sight-reading skills, roll notation is unlikely to efficiently support the development of such skills. However, most learners in our studies were not interested in learning sheet music.

A common concern of consulted piano teachers was that the projected roll notation may lead to too much focus on correctness ("stiff playing"), thus hindering the development of richer musical expression. However, the results of our expert evaluation seem to refute those concerns. Although some qualitative scales (e.g., articulation and interpretation) did not provide significant differences, they do show higher tendencies. Some experts were initially concerned about rating novices who practiced for only one week, but were positively surprised (without knowing the used system) by recordings performed by P.I.A.N.O. players. This is also reflected in the significantly higher ratings on the overall impression scale. Although P.I.A.N.O. does not directly teach advanced musical expression, it could support learners in focusing on musical expression rather than on mapping notes to keys, by avoiding the burden of sight-reading. We plan to conduct extended longitudinal studies to examine whether these assumptions hold for practice spanning several weeks or months.

Developing musical expression is a prolonged process and playing correct notes is essential before proceeding to advanced skills. Our studies show that our approach supports quick success in terms of correctness at the first stage of piano playing. This success is essential for beginners when learning an instrument, as it motivates learners, could lower dropout rates and could even encourage people to start playing piano. While P.I.A.N.O. does not intend to replace individualized advice by expert piano teachers, it provides a significant improvement over current self-tutoring approaches. Piano teachers should further guide players with detailed advice, e.g., on fingering techniques and musical expression. This valuable advice remains irreplaceable by a system, although systems like MirrorFugue [37] try to support giving such advice remotely. In contrast, our aim was to support novices without sight-reading knowledge in faster learning and playing, focusing on developing basic playing skills and articulation. Our results show that this goal has been achieved, highlighting the validity of our chosen approach.

CONCLUSION

In this paper, we introduced P.I.A.N.O. as a novel approach to learning piano without sight-reading skills. Our enhanced piano roll notation is capable of depicting a note's pitch and duration, as well as a variety of articulation techniques (legato, staccato, grace notes, and trill notes). The projected notation allows a direct mapping of notes to respective keys, while three different modes further support the learning process. We conducted two user studies to compare the learning performance of P.I.A.N.O. to Synthesia and Finale, which use a basic piano roll notation without direct mapping and traditional sheet music, respectively. The results show that P.I.A.N.O. induces less cognitive load, better supports initial learning performance and faster progress over one week of practice, provides better user experience and leads to better perceived quality than Synthesia and Finale. Based on our results, we argue that the projected roll notation is a viable alternative to sheet music notation for beginners looking for a rewarding approach towards learning to play the piano.

ACKNOWLEDGMENTS

The authors would like to thank all study participants, the anonymous reviewers for their valuable feedback. This work was partially supported by the Transregional Collaborative Research Centre SFB/TRR 62 "Companion-Technology of Cognitive Technical Systems" funded by the German Research Foundation (DFG).

REFERENCES

1. Activision Publishing, Inc. Guitar Hero, accessed: Jun. 2014. `http://guitarhero.com/`.
2. Android appliaction. Pianist HD, accessed: Jun. 2014. `https://play.google.com/store/apps/details?id=com.rubycell.pianisthd`.
3. Bandura, A., and McClelland, D. C. Social learning theory. *General Learning Press* (1977).
4. Casio. Lighted keys keyboard LK-280, accessed: Jun. 2014. `http://www.casio.com/products/Digital_Pianos_&_Keyboards/Lighted_Keys/LK-280/`.
5. Creech, A., Hallam, S., McQueen, H., and Varvarigou, M. The power of music in the lives of older adults. *Research Studies in Music Education 35*, 1 (2013).
6. Disney. *Mickey Mouse Clubhouse Piano Sound Book: Mickey's Piano Party*. Publications International, 2009.
7. Dolan, B. *Inventing entertainment: the player piano and the origins of an American musical industry*. Rowman & Littlefield Publishers, Lanham, Md., 2009.
8. Drake, C., and Palmer, C. Skill acquisition in music performance: Relations between planning and temporal control. *Cognition 74*, 1 (2000), 1–32.
9. Ekstrom, R. B., French, J. W., and Harman, H. H. *Manual for kit of factor-referenced cognitive tests*. Educational Testing Service, Princeton N.J., 1976.

10. Fisher Price. Laugh & Learn Baby Grand Piano, accessed: Jun. 2014. http://www.fisher-price.com/en_AU/brands/babytoys/products/40014.

11. Giomi, E. C. "I do not want to study piano": early predictors of student dropout behavior. *Bulletin of the Council for Research in Music Education*, 161 (2004).

12. Gower, L., and McDowall, J. Interactive music video games and children's musical development. *British Journal of Music Education 29*, 1 (2012), 91–105.

13. Hallam, S. The power of music: Its impact on the intellectual, social and personal development of children and young people. *International Journal of Music Education 28*, 3 (2010), 269–289.

14. Hassenzahl, M., Burmester, D. M., and Koller, F. AttrakDiff: a questionnaire to measure perceived hedonic and pragmatic quality. In *Mensch & Computer*, Springer (2003).

15. Huang, K., Starner, T., Do, E., Weiberg, G., Kohlsdorf, D., Ahlrichs, C., and Leibrandt, R. Mobile music touch: mobile tactile stimulation for passive learning. In *Proc. CHI '10*, ACM (2010).

16. iOS application. Glow Piano Lessons, accessed: Jun. 2014. https://itunes.apple.com/us/app/glow-piano-lessons/id441970188.

17. Iwai, T. Piano–as image media. *Leonardo 34*, 3 (2001).

18. Jutras, P. J. The benefits of adult piano study as self-reported by selected adult piano students. *Journal of Research in Music Education 54*, 2 (July 2006), 97–110.

19. Klepsch, M., and Seufert, T. Subjective Differentiated Measurement of Cognitive Load. In *Proc. 5th Intl. Cognitive Load Theory Conf.* (2012).

20. London-Based Examinations Board. Associated Board of the Royal Schools of Music (ABRSM), accessed: Jun. 2014. http://de.abrsm.org/en/home.

21. MakeMusic, Inc. Finale - music notation software, accessed: Jun. 2014. http://www.finalemusic.com/.

22. MakeMusic, Inc. MusicXML, accessed: Jun. 2014. http://www.musicxml.com/.

23. McLachlan, N. M., Greco, L. J., Toner, E. C., and Wilson, S. J. Using spatial manipulation to examine interactions between visual and auditory encoding of pitch and time. *Frontiers in Psychology 1* (2010).

24. Raymaekers, L., Vermeulen, J., Luyten, K., and Coninx, K. Game of tones: Learning to play songs on a piano using projected instructions and games. In *Proc. CHI EA '14*, ACM (2014), 411–414.

25. Richardson, P., and Kim, Y. Beyond fun and games: A framework for quantifying music skill developments from video game play. *Journal of New Music Research 40*, 4 (2011), 277–291.

26. Rubato productions. Concert Hands, accessed: Jun. 2014. http://www.concerthands.com/products.html.

27. Sloboda, J. A., Clarke, E. F., Parncutt, R., and Raekallio, M. Determinants of finger choice in piano sight-reading. *Journal of Experimental Psychology: Human Perception and Performance 24*, 1 (1998), 185–203.

28. Stewart, L., Walsh, V., and Frith, U. Reading music modifies spatial mapping in pianists. *Perception & psychophysics 66*, 2 (2004), 183–195.

29. Sweller, J., Van Merrienboer, J. J., and Paas, F. G. Cognitive architecture and instructional design. *Educational Psychology Review 10*, 3 (1998), 251–296.

30. Synthesia LLC. Synthesia - piano game, 2013. http://www.synthesiagame.com/.

31. Takegawa, T., Terada, T., and Tsukamoto, M. A piano learning support system considering rhythm. In *Proc. ICMC '12*, Michigan Publishing (2012).

32. Tan, S.-L., Wakefield, E. M., and Jeffries, P. W. Musically untrained college students' interpretations of musical notation: sound, silence, loudness, duration, and temporal order. *Psychology of Music 37*, 1 (2009), 5–24.

33. Weing, M., Röhlig, A., Rogers, K., Gugenheimer, J., Schaub, F., Könings, B., Rukzio, E., and Weber, M. P.I.A.N.O.: Enhancing Instrument Learning via Interactive Projected Augmentation (demo). In *UbiCom '13 Adjunct Proceedings* (2013).

34. Wikipedia. Keyboardmania. version ID: 542589199, 2013. http://wikipedia.org/wiki/Keyboardmania.

35. Wrigley, W. J., and Emmerson, S. B. Ecological development and validation of a music performance rating scale for five instrument families. *Psychology of Music 41*, 1 (2013), 97–118.

36. Wristen, B. Demographics and motivation of adult group piano students. *Music Education Research 8*, 3 (2006), 387–406.

37. Xiao, X., Pereira, A., and Ishii, H. MirrorFugue III: conjuring the recorded pianist. In *Proc. NIME'13* (2013).

38. Yang, Q., and Essl, G. Visual associations in augmented keyboard performance. In *Proc. NIME '13* (2013).

Exploring Visual Cues for Intuitive Communicability of Touch Gestures to Pre-Kindergarten Children

Vicente Nacher, Javier Jaen, Alejandro Catala
ISSI Group, Dpto. Sistemas Informáticos y Computación, Universitat Politècnica de València.
{vnacher, fjaen, acatala}@dsic.upv.es

ABSTRACT
Pre-kindergarten children are becoming frequent users of multi-touch technology and, according to previous studies they are able to perform several multi-touch gestures successfully. However, they do not use these devices supervised at all times. Consequently, interactive applications for pre-kindergarteners need to convey their underlying design intent and interactive principles with respect to touch interaction. In this paper, we present and evaluate two approaches to communicate three different touch gestures (tap, drag and scale up) to pre-kindergarten users. Our results show, firstly, that it is possible to effectively communicate them using visual cues and, secondly, that an animated semiotic approach is better than an iconic one.

Author Keywords
Touch interaction; Communicability; pre-kindergarten

ACM Classification Keywords
H.5.2. [Information interfaces and presentation]: User Interfaces - Evaluation/methodology, Interaction Styles

INTRODUCTION
Recent studies [10] have revealed that very young children are frequent users of multi-touch devices. In fact, children encounter touch technology often before they can even speak, they do not use these devices supervised at all times and they often want to do things on their own, instead of having their parents show them. Moreover, recent work [7] has also revealed that children between the ages of two and four are able to perform a wider set of touch gestures than those typically used in commercial learning applications (tap and drag). In this context, a key challenge to address is the efficient and effective communication of the gestures that are expected at a given moment from these very young users, i.e., languages need to be designed for applications to convey their underlying design intent and interactive principles [9] with respect to touch interaction. These languages would allow the autonomous interaction of very young children with direct touch applications without the continuous intervention and guidance of adults.

ITS 2014, November 16–19, 2014, Dresden, Germany.
Copyright © 2014 ACM 978-1-4503-2587-5/14/11...$15.00.
http://dx.doi.org/10.1145/2669485.2669523

In this paper we perform a communicability evaluation to appreciate how well pre-kindergarten users understand the messages that communicate a given expected touch gesture using two different semiotic systems. The semiotic systems under consideration in this work are of graphical nature because, although it has already been tested that including instructions in the form of short text pieces is adequate for primary school children [3, 8], pre-kindergarten users do not have the required abilities to understand text messages.

The obtained results suggest that it is possible to design visual languages for communicating touch gestures for pre-kindergarten children. The animated approach that is proposed in this work is more effective to communicate dynamic gestures, i.e. gestures that follow trajectories on the screen, in terms of both intuitiveness and potential learnability.

RELATED WORK
The problem of communicability has received recently a great deal of attention in the context of applications for adults [2, 11]. Moreover, several works have studied the way in which instructions are given in applications for children. The work in [3] explored different ways to provide instructions in applications targeted at 5-6 year old children in desktop computers. This study resulted in some design recommendations such as giving visual cues to trigger attention to find new content, providing help in the form of text adapted to such target users, and providing separate video instructions so that children can focus on the explanation given. This work also found that audio help could overcome some limitations of written instructions like in [8].

Another previous work [1] has proposed a character-based language to communicate multi-touch gestures in a learning application with 5-6 year old children. Researchers associated each gesture to a specific virtual character in the learning application that appeared when a gesture was requested. The characters were chosen in such a way that the gesture was "recallable": a jumping grasshopper for a double tap, a walking ladybug for a drag gesture, a hovering butterfly for a tilting gesture and so on.

McKnight and Fitton [6] performed an initial test of common touch-screen terminology with native English children aged between 6 and 7. Children had little or no trouble in understanding the majority of the instructions provided in both textual and audio form as they completed the task easily.

These previous works have attempted several semiotic systems consisting of text, audio and/or visual elements for very young children aged 5-7. However, there is no study that explores the more challenging pre-kindergarten age range. Therefore, in this work we explore the communicability of two languages for pre-kindergarten users so that interactive applications can effectively communicate touch gestures.

LANGUAGES OVERVIEW

In order to adequately select the candidate languages that would be evaluated, a number of workshops took place with pre-kindergarten educators. A summary of the design rationale is described here for the two languages that were selected after this design process with pedagogy experts:

-*Animated Hand language*: this language uses the metaphor of a hand with one extended finger to simulate by means of an animation the required gesture. The rationale behind this language is that the object to be manipulated with a multi-touch interaction is accompanied by an animated virtual hand that provides visual cues about the gesture that should be carried out. We considered several options to visualize the form of a hand in our preliminary designs, and discussed with educators about the suitability of displaying either an isolated finger or an entire hand. Having an isolated finger was discarded and a Mickey Mouse's hand was selected by the educators for the evaluation phase (see Figure 2). For the tap gesture the hand appears and disappears once. For the remaining gestures, the hand(s) follow(s) the expected trajectory that the user's hand(s) should follow when performing the expected gesture (see Figure 1 for animated sequences).

-*Iconic language*: in this case the semiotic language selected by the educators consists in a static image or icon of a hand with accompanying symbolic arrows describing the expected gesture (see Figure 2). The icons used are extracted from a commercial icon set created to aid in the design, development, implementation and promotion of multi-touch interfaces [4], designed by a professional interactive designer and developer. This iconic language can also be found in Leap Motion applications. It was decided to maintain a naturalistic hand representation to evaluate this widely used commercial icon set in its original form to consider its suitability for pre-K children.

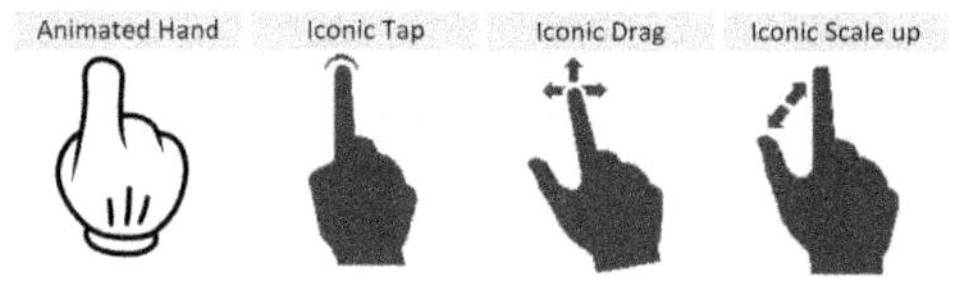

Figure 2. Evaluated semiotic elements.

EXPERIMENTAL STUDY

The goal of this study is to obtain preliminary results about the effectiveness of two semiotic systems, one based on animations and another based on icon features, to communicate touch gestures to prekindergarten children. In this respect we have considered three categories of gestures: one-hand dynamic interactions, which require movements describing a clear trajectory; bi-manual dynamic interactions, with both hands describing trajectories; or in-place interactions, in which one hand does not actually describe a trajectory but tap at a very specific pace or in a specific way. In each category a representative gesture was selected to perform this first evaluation study: *Drag*, *Scale Up* and *Tap* respectively.

Therefore, the main research questions of this work are formulated as follows:

RQ1: Is any of the considered languages effective in communicating intuitively each of the considered touch gestures to pre-kindergarten children?

RQ2: Is the effectiveness of the communication process improved after a short training process?

RQ3: Is the inherent complexity of tracking several animated hands manageable?

RQ4: Is the effectiveness of the communication process affected by gender?

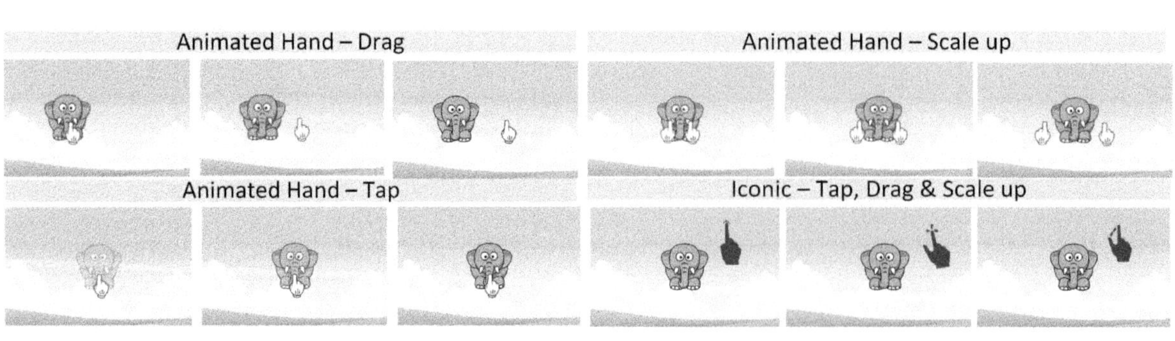

Figure 1. Description of animated visual cues and icons used in the considered gesture subset by language.

Participants

Parental authorization was obtained before carrying out the study. Twenty four children aged between twenty-five and thirty-eight months took part in the experiment (Mean (M) = 31.67, Standard Deviation (SD) = 4.02). The minimum age limit was chosen because children are in a pre-operational stage from 2 years old onwards. They begin to think in terms of images and symbols, and develop symbolic play with imaginary objects, which means they could be candidates for multi-touch technology at this early age as discussed in [6]. Fourteen participants were female. One group by language was defined.

Apparatus

The interaction framework for the experiment was implemented in Java using JMonkeyEngine SDK v.3.0beta. The devices used for the experiment were a Motorola MZ601 and a Samsung Galaxy Note 10.1 tablet with Android 3.2 both with capacitive multi-touch screens.

Procedure

Initially, the experimenter showed each gesture without using any language (i.e. without visual stimuli associated to the gesture) and asked the children to interact to ensure that they were able to perform each gesture. This ensures that the evaluated children had the developmental cognitive and physical abilities to perform the proposed gestures.

After this activity, the participant performed an evaluation test consisting of 2x3=6 randomized trials (two repetitions of each gesture Tap, Drag and Scale up). In each test trial an image of an animal appeared on the screen (see Figure 2) and a visual stimulus describing the required gesture was displayed. The visual stimulus belonged to the language previously assigned to each subject (see Design). Once it was shown, the system awaited the user interaction without any external adult guidance. If the gesture was successfully completed, the platform gave a positive audiovisual feedback in the form of animated stars and applauses. If the experimenter observed that the participant did not carry out the gesture in less than 10 seconds, it was marked as undone and the child went on to the next trial. The system recorded the number of correct interactions. The goal of this first evaluation phase (Intuitive Phase) was to evaluate the capacity of the language to communicate a gesture without any previous language exposure.

Next, the participants carried out a specific language training activity. This training activity was designed to teach children which gestures are expected to be performed given the visual stimuli provided by the language. It was carried out under the supervision of the experimenter who explained the visual instructions to them and the associated gestures.

Finally, an evaluation test was carried out without delay (Immediate Recall phase). In this way, this phase evaluates the impact on the overall performance of a short training session with the visual languages, i.e., to know whether the inclusion of a short guided tutorial with the proposed visual languages makes children more effective in the subsequent unsupervised interaction.

Design

Each child was only exposed to one language, which was assigned randomly at the beginning of the session. The *success rate (successful interactions/total interactions)* by gesture and session in a given language expressed as a percentage was obtained for each participant. This was the dependent variable used in the analysis when searching for differences between the intuitive and immediate recall phases. As data did not meet normality assumptions and given the need to handle repeated measures, the analysis was be carried out by applying the Aligned Rank Transform in order to report using ANOVA with three factors: *gender*, *phase* (Intuitive vs. Immediate Recall) and *language* (Animated Hand vs. Iconic).

RESULTS

Table 1 shows the mean success rate for each gesture by *language, gender* and *phase*.

	Language				Gender			
	Animated		Iconic		F		M	
	P1	P2	P1	P2	P1	P2	P1	P2
Tap	54.2	62.5	45.8	54.2	57.1	64.3	40	50
Total	58.3		50		60.7		45	
Drag	100	100	70.8	70.8	89.3	89.3	80	80
Total	100		70.8		89.3		80	
Scale	70.83	100	12.5	4.2	25	42.9	65	65
Total	85.4		8.3		33.9		65	

Table 1. Success by language, gender by phase for each task. (P1= Intuitive Phase, P2=Immediate Recall Phase)

The ANOVA revealed significant main effects of the *language* factor for the drag [$F(1,48) = 21.754$, $p < .001$] and the scale up tasks [$F(1,48) = 120.048$, $p < .001$]. No significant main effects were revealed for the tap task [$F(1,48) = 1.594$, $p = .214$]. This suggests that using animated hands in dynamic gestures (i.e. those requiring trajectories) is significantly more effective than using a static iconic alternative.

The analysis revealed significant main effects of the *phase* factor for the scale up task [$F(1,48) = 6.407$, $p = .015$], but not for the tap [$F(1,48) = 0.861$, $p = .360$] or drag tasks [$F(1,48) = 0.246$, $p = .360$]. This means that a short training session has only a significant effect on the success rates of the scale up task. Moreover, for this gesture the interaction *language*phase* was found significant [$F(1,48) = 15.386$ $p < 001$], what accounts for how the performance dropped using the Iconic language, in contrast to what happened with the Animated language, which was fully learned by all the participants after only one training session.

The analysis shows significant main effects of the *gender* factor for scale up [$F(1,48) = 22.074$, $p < .001$], with males performing more successfully (65% vs. 33.9%). No differences were found for the tap [$F(1,48) = 2.648$, $p = .112$] and the drag gestures [$F(1,48) = 3.791$, $p = .059$].

DISCUSSION AND FUTURE WORK

In response to RQ1, the results show that the Animated Hand language has a better performance to communicate touch gestures that involve movement of contact points on the surface. This is a valuable result because developmental psychologists such as Levine and Piaget suggested that kids develop spatial reasoning during middle childhood [5]. However, our study suggests that basic reasoning related to the interpretation of moving elements on a surface can be effectively performed during early childhood. On the other hand, differences between languages for the in-place gesture (i.e. tap) were not significant. In fact both languages resulted in equally poor performance because they were unable to convey in an intuitive way the tap operation. In our opinion, this type of reasoning is more complex because it involves a process of classification and association of a visual stimulus to a gesture whose nature cannot be interpreted in terms of spatial analogy with the stimulus. This type of reasoning, as pointed out by Piaget is developed by children at a later stage.

The results obtained after a single training session found that the success improved in general, especially for dynamic gestures, although this improvement was only statistically significant for the scale up operation. Hence, the answer to RQ2 is that a single training session is not enough to learn all the considered gestures being particularly problematic the gestures that do not involve movements on the surface.

Moreover, results showed that tracking several animated hands seems manageable, what responses affirmatively to our RQ3. The scale up task has a 70.83% success percentage without any previous explanation and reaches 100% after the learning phase.

In response to our RQ4, about whether gender would make a difference, results showed that the success was only significantly different for the gesture requiring two contact points (i.e. scale up), for which male pre-kindergarten children seem to be more effective than female ones in understanding the required gesture. This is consistent with existing preschool literature on gender differences in visual-spatial cognition reviewed by Levine, and colleagues [5]. They found that, on average, preschool boys are more accurate than girls on spatial tasks.

The previous results suggest that designers of direct touch applications for pre-K children should include animated elements to communicate touch gestures that require moving contact points on the surface if children need extra information to proceed. However it remains to be studied more effective mechanisms to communicate static gestures such as tap, double tap and long-pressed. Although these results are promising, there are clear limitations to our work. The experiments involved only one interactive element at a time in the user interface and it remains to be evaluated the effectiveness of animated languages when the interaction area is cluttered with many touchable elements or with elements that may be manipulated with several different gestures. It also remains to be verified whether the inclusion of additional gestures with their corresponding semiotic elements will have an impact on the overall performance because pre-kindergarten children are not able to recall such a variety of different elements.

ACKNOWLEDGMENTS

Work supported by the MINECO (grant TIN2010-20488) and GVA VALi+d program (grant APOSTD/2013/013).

REFERENCES

1. Baloian, N., Pino, J. A., and Vargas, R. Tablet gestures as a motivating factor for learning. *In Proc. ChileCHI'13*, (2013), 98–103.
2. Hofmeester, K., and Wolfe, J. Self-revealing gestures: teaching new touch interactions in windows 8. In ACM CHI EA '12 (2012), 815–828
3. Kähkönen, M. and Ovaska, S. Initial observations on children and online instructions. *In Proc. IDC '06*, (2006), 93.
4. Lee, R. Gestures. http://gesturecons.com/.
5. Levine, S.C., Huttenlocher, J., Taylor, A., and Langrock, A. Early sex differences in spatial skill. Developmental Psychology, 35, (1999) 940-949.
6. McKnight, L. and Fitton, D. Touch-screen technology for children: Giving the Right Instructions and Getting the Right Responses. *In Proc. IDC '10*, ACM Press (2010), 238.
7. Nacher, V., Jaen, J., Navarro, E., Catala, A., and González, P. Multi-touch gestures for pre-kindergarten children. International Journal of Human-Computer Studies 73 (2015), 37-51. http://dx.doi.org/10.1016/j.ijhcs.2014.08.004
8. Niemi, H. and Ovaska, S. Designing spoken instructions with preschool children. *In Proc. IDC '07*, (2007), 133.
9. Prates, R.O., de Souza, C.S., and Barbosa, S.D.J. Methods and tools: a method for evaluating the communicability of user interfaces. *Interactions 7*, 1 (2000), 31–38.
10. Rideout, V. *Zero to Eight: Children's Media Use in America*. Common Sense Media, 2011.
11. Walter, R., Bailly, G. and Müller, J. StrikeAPose: Revealing Mid-Air Gestures on Public Displays. *In Proc.* ACM CHI'13 (2013), 841-850.

Improving Pre-Kindergarten Touch Performance

Vicente Nacher[1], Javier Jaen[1], Alejandro Catala[1], Elena Navarro[2], Pascual Gonzalez[2]
[1]ISSI Group, Dpto. Sistemas Informáticos y Computación, Universitat Politècnica de València
[2]LoUISE Research Group, Computing Systems Department, University of Castilla-La Mancha
{vnacher, fjaen, acatala}@dsic.upv.es; {elena.navarro, pascual.gonzalez}@uclm.es

ABSTRACT
Multi-touch technology provides users with a more intuitive way of interaction. However, pre-kindergarten children, a growing group of potential users, have problems with some basic gestures according to previous studies. This is particularly the case of the double tap and long pressed gestures, which have some issues related to spurious entry events and time-constrained interactions, respectively. In this paper, we empirically test specific strategies to deal with these issues by evaluating off-the-shelf implementations of these gestures against alternative implementations that follow these guidelines. The study shows that the implementation of these design guidelines has a positive effect on success rates of these two gestures, being feasible their inclusion in future multi-touch applications targeted at pre-kindergarten children.

Author Keywords
Multi-touch interaction; gestures; usability evaluation; pre-kindergarten; guidelines

ACM Classification Keywords
H.5.2. [Information interfaces and presentation]: User Interfaces - Evaluation/methodology, Interaction Styles.

INTRODUCTION
Multi-touch technology provides users with a more intuitive way of interaction [8] and, nowadays, it is widespread accepted. This fact has boosted a new approach to developing applications for children. As pointed out in [7], children between zero and eight years old are frequent users of digital media in the USA.

Recent work in [6] presented an empirical evaluation of a set of multi-touch gestures and their suitability for children between two and three years. This work pointed out that some basic interactions (e.g. tap, drag, scale up, scale down and one finger rotation) can be performed effectively and could, therefore, be included in educational applications for pre-kindergarten children. However, it also revealed some issues with the long pressed and double tap gestures because fine motor skills are still under development at this early age and because of the cognitive complexity of some interactions. Firstly, in the long pressed gesture, the spurious initial or entry dragging events produced by the lack of precision of pre-kindergarteners prevent the system from detecting the gesture. Secondly, in the double tap gesture the standard time required between taps is much shorter than the actual pace at which pre-kindergarteners are able to perform. Authors of this previous work stated a set of design guidelines to deal with, among others, these specific issues. Regarding the spurious entry events in the case of the long pressed gesture, we consider in this work a filtering process to ignore these initial dragging events. On the other hand, we can adjust the required speed for the double tap interaction to the actual ability of the target user. This paper addresses the evaluation of these two assisted strategies for pre-kindergarteners to validate empirically their effectiveness.

ITS 2014, November 16–19, 2014, Dresden, Germany.
Copyright 2014 ACM 978-1-4503-2587-5/14/11...$15.00
http://dx.doi.org/10.1145/2669485.2669498

RELATED WORK
There are some interesting studies targeted at children that focus on the direct manipulation interaction style and direct touch. For instance, the works in [1] and [9] involved subjects aged between 3 and 6, and between 9 and 11, respectively, in testing the use of the stylus for learning purposes. They concluded that the stylus interaction had a shorter learning period and other advantages over the traditional mouse and keyboard alternatives.

The differences between single-touch and multi-touch interaction were analyzed in [2] for 7 to 10 year-old children's groups. Results pointed out that although touch did not have an effect in the interaction in terms of frequency or equity, it did influence the communication of subjects and encouraged them to talk to each other about their collaborative actions.

There are several studies that have addressed the different issues affecting multi-touch interaction with adult users[3,4,5]. However, these users under normal conditions are not affected by entry precision problems or cognitive-motor issues as pre-kindergarteners are.

EXPERIMENTAL STUDY
The overall goal of our experimental study is to identify whether the proposed assisted strategies, filtering initial spurious dragging events and adjusting the required speed between taps, for the long pressed and double tap gestures actually contribute to overcome the problems identified in

[6]. More specifically, the present study research questions are formulated as follows:

- Do the implemented assisted strategies for the gestures under study (i.e. long pressed and double tap) have a positive effect on pre-kindergarteners´ performance?
- In the specific case of the gestures following the design guidelines, is there a significant relationship between gesture performance and gender or age group?

In order to answer these questions we need to contrast the implemented gestures following the design guidelines against their baseline implementations without guidelines, i.e., applied as provided by current OS runtimes (e.g. Android). To this purpose, we took the existing dataset from [6], which already evaluated both the success rate and the completion time for the baseline implementation, and then we carried out an experiment that follows the same procedure to collect the data observations with the implementation of the assisted gestures.

Participants

Thirty-two children aged between twenty-two and forty-six months took part in the experiment of the two gestures with design guidelines (Mean (M) = 31.31, Standard Deviation (SD) = 6.25). The genders of the children were balanced. Parental authorization was obtained before carrying out the study. The children were divided, as in the previous study [6], into two age groups: 22 to 30 months and 31 to 46 months, with 8 males and 8 females per group.

Apparatus

The interaction framework for the experiment was implemented in Java using JMonkeyEngine SDK v.3.0beta. The devices used for the experiment were a Motorola MZ601 and a Samsung Galaxy Note 10.1 tablet with Android 3.2 both with capacitive multi-touch screens.

Tasks

Long Pressed

A static image of an animal appears in a random position on the screen (see Figure 1). Participants are requested to carry out a long pressed gesture on the target image until the target disappears. The task will succeed when the participants put their finger in the target image and hold it at least 500 milliseconds. The implemented design guideline consists of a filtering process for ignoring the spurious undesired interaction events that may occur at the beginning of the gesture. The filtering ignores any short drag gesture (less than 1 cm) around the first initial contact point.

Double Tap

A static image of an animal appears in a random position on the screen (see Figure 1). Participants are requested to double tap on the target image with one finger in order to pass the test.

Figure 1. Example of long pressed and double tap task

The default allowed interval for the double tap gesture in Android devices is 300 milliseconds. Therefore, we have considered as a design guideline higher time intervals up to 2000 milliseconds to study their impact on the success rate for this gesture.

Procedure

For each task, the children participated in a 5-minute learning session with an instructor. Then, the experimental platform asked them to perform the task with no external adult intervention. They had to perform three repetitions of each gesture as described in the Tasks section. When the gesture was successfully completed, the platform gave a positive audiovisual feedback. If the instructor observed that the participant did not carry out the task in a given time, it was marked as undone and the child went on to the next one.

For each interaction, the system recorded the start time (seconds needed to go into action after the visual stimulus was shown), completion time (milliseconds until the gesture was completed), success (performed correctly or incorrectly), and in the case of the double tap gesture, the time elapsed between taps. Additional notes were taken by an external observer during the experimental sessions to register any incidental information that could be worth discussing later.

RESULTS

Assisted vs non-Assisted Interaction

In the following, we will refer to the technique in which the design guidelines were implemented as "assisted" interaction. We will contrast these data against the dataset provided by the authors of [6], to which we will refer as "non-assisted" interaction.

Success Rate

In order to aggregate the success variable over the three repetitions, if a participant performed successfully either zero or one tests in a specific task, they were considered incapable of performing it. On the other hand, if they successfully performed two or three tests in a specific task, they were considered capable of doing it because they actually showed their ability to consistently reproduce the gesture several times.

Task	Technique	Mean	SD
Long Pressed	non-Assisted	0.5000	0.5080
	Assisted	0.9062	0.2961
Double Tap (1200 ms)	non-Assisted	0.6250	0.4919
	Assisted	0.8438	0.3689

Table 1. Success rate by task and technique

According to this codification, the success rate in the long pressed task can be expressed as a percentage, as shown in Table 1 for each task and technique. Additionally, to enable a fine-grained analysis of this variable when considering the double tap gesture, we have studied how the success rate would be for different maximum allowed times between consecutive taps as shown in Figure 2.

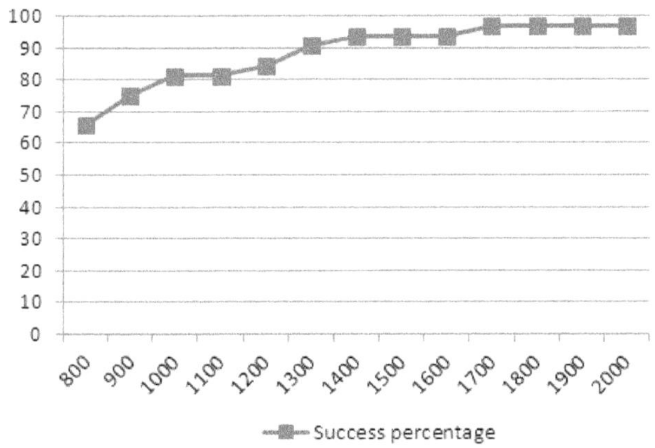

Figure 2. Success rate by maximum allowed time between taps in milliseconds

As hypothetized, the implementation of assisted techniques following the suggested guidelines increases the success rate for both gestures. A Pearson's chi-squeare test showed that there is a significant strong relationship between the carried out *technique* and the *success rate* for the long pressed task (Pearson $\chi2$ (1, N = 64) =12.650, p<0.001). Regarding the double tap task, the minimum time interval between taps for which we found significant differences in the variable *success rate* between techniques was 1200 milliseconds ($\chi2$ (1, *N* = 64) =3.925, p=.048). If lower intervals are considered, the success rates obtained are not significantly different from the ones obtained with the Android standard 300ms interval. Higher intervals do not provide significantly better success rates.

Completion Time

The average of each subject's successful tasks is used to obtain the average completion time (see Table 2) value per task and technique. If the test is not performed successfully it is not included in the completion time analysis.

Task	Technique	Mean (s.)	SD
Long Pressed	non-Assisted	9307.78	5817.10
	Assisted	8053.77	6070.38
Double Tap	non-Assisted	4480.38	2800.65
	Assisted	3332.16	2292.82

Table 2. Completion time (msec.) by task and technique

The assisted techniques took less time to complete with respect to the baseline implementation, although differences were not found statisically significant. In this regard one-way between-subject ANOVAs with the independent variable *technique* and the dependent variable *completion time* demonstrated that there is not a significant main effect of the *technique* for neither the long pressed (F(1, 54) = .584, p = .448) nor the double tap task (F(1, 52) = 3.393, p = .071).

Age and Gender Influence

As it was previously stated, we are also interested in knowing whether the implemented design guidelines have a different effect in the response variables (*success rate* and *completion time*) with respect to age or gender. This is interesting given that a prior study [6] found that only age has an effect on completion time for the double tap with no assisted implementation, and that there are no significant differences on the success rate by age or gender.

Success Rate

No significant differences on the sucess rate for both tasks were found by either age or gender. This is comfirmed by the Pearson's chi-square tests on the long pressed success rate by the *gender* factor ($\chi2$ (1, N = 32) =0.368, p=.544) or by the *age group* factor ($\chi2$ (1, N = 32) =3.310, p=.069); as well as on the double tap success rate by *gender* ($\chi2$ (1, N = 32) =0.237, p=.626) and *age group* factor ($\chi2$ (1, N = 32) =2.133, p=.144).

Completion Time

In this respect, older children performed significantly faster only with the long pressed gesture. No other effects were found significant for any gesture and factor. Specifically, a two-way between-subjects ANOVA on the *completion time* for the long pressed task revealed a significantly main effect of the *age group* factor (F(1, 31) = 8.751, p = .006). Completion time doubled for the youngest group on average (M_{young}=11.1s and M_{old}=5.2s). There was no significant main effect of the *gender* factor (F(1, 31) = 0.559, p = .461).

The corresponding analogous statistical analysis for the double tap task did not revealed significant main effects of *age group* (F(1, 28) = 0.135, p = .717) or *gender* (F(1, 28) = 0.017, p = .897).

DISCUSION AND CONCLUSIONS

The design guideline implemented for the long pressed gesture comprises a filtering process to ignore initial dragging events that are produced as a consequence of a motor precision problem which was identified in previous experiments. The results show a statistically significant better success rate (90.62%) when the filtering is applied than the one observed in previous experiments without filtering (50%). The improved success rate when the filtering is applied is not affected by age and gender. Moreover, the average completion time when the filtering is applied is not significantly different from the completion time obtained without filtering. However, as it was the case when no filtering was present, younger children need a significantly higher time to complete the task than older ones. This is because younger children are less precise and perform significantly more undesired dragging events that are larger than 1cm in size. These were not removed by the implemented filter, forcing users to restart the interaction. These very young users would need a filtering process coping with larger undesired dragging events. Nevertheless, this may result problematic for interactive objects that may accept both long pressed and dragging events because dragging operations would not start until the size threshold of the filter would be surpassed.

The design guideline for the double tap gesture proposes the implementation of an extended time interval between consecutive taps. The results show that, if the default time interval between taps for Android devices (300ms) is increased to 1200ms, we obtain significantly better success rates (62% success @300ms versus 84.38% success @1200ms on average). Smaller time intervals do not provide significantly better success rates when compared to the default Android time interval. The improved success rate, when the new 1200ms time interval is used, is independent of age and gender. In addition, the results show that the completion time for this task has no significant main effects of age or gender. However, it is worth mentioning that we have carried out additional trials considering external stimuli to motivate children to interact quicker (i.e. encouraging them to go beyond their natural pace). These preliminary tests suggest that it is possible to obtain faster successful double tap interactions (a success rate of 91.67% with a 600ms gap) in the presence of adults motivating pre-kindergarteners. This will be the subject of a future experimental design considering factors such as age, gender, source (human or computer) type and intensity of the stimuli. It must also be taken into account that these stimuli may have some counter effects that have already been observed such as subjects performing more than two taps in the presence of stimuli or increased stress levels when children are continuously encouraged to perform faster than their natural pace.

To sum up, the obtained results demonstrate that the inclusion of the proposed design guidelines make these two gestures more feasible for pre-kindergarten children. These two gestures (double tap and long pressed) complete now the previous set [6] of feasible gestures (tap, drag, scale-up, scale-down and one-finger rotation) that may be effectively performed in this early age range, what contributes to the continuous enhancement of assisted techniques for this challenging target user group of very young children.

ACKNOWLEDGMENTS

This work received financial support from the Spanish Ministry of Education under the National Strategic Program of Research and Projects TIN2010-20488 (CREATEWORLD) and TIN2012-34003 (insPIre). This work is also supported by a postdoctoral fellowship within the VALi+d program from Conselleria d'Educació, Cultura i Esport (Generalitat Valenciana) to A. Catalá (APOSTD/2013/013).

REFERENCES

1. Couse, L.J. and Chen, D.W. A Tablet Computer for Young Children? Exploring Its Viability for Early Childhood Education. Journal of Research on Technology in Education 43, 1 (2010), 75–98.
2. Harris, A., Rick, J., Bonnett, V., et al. Around the table: are multiple-touch surfaces better than single-touch for children's collaborative interactions? In Proc. CSCL'09, 335–344.
3. Hoggan, E., Nacenta, M., Kristensson, P.O., Williamson, J., Oulasvirta, A., and Lehtiö, A. Multi-Touch Pinch Gestures : Performance and Ergonomics. In Proc. ITS'13, 219–222.
4. Hoggan, E., Williamson, J., Oulasvirta, A., Nacenta, M., Kristensson, P.O., and Lehtiö, A. Multi-Touch Rotation Gestures : Performance and Ergonomics. In Proc. CHI'13, 3–6.
5. Nacenta, M.A., Baudisch, P., Benko, H., and Wilson, A. Separability of Spatial Manipulations in Multi-touch Interfaces. In Proc. GI'09, 175–182.
6. Nacher, V., Jaen, J., Navarro, E., Catala, A., and González, P. Multi-touch gestures for pre-kindergarten children. International Journal of Human-Computer Studies 73 (2015), 37-51. Available online http://dx.doi.org/10.1016/j.ijhcs.2014.08.004
7. Rideout, V. Zero to Eight: Children's Media Use in America. Common Sense Media, 2011.
8. Smith, S.P., Burd, E., and Rick, J. Developing, evaluating and deploying multi-touch systems. International Journal of Human-Computer Studies 70, 10 (2012), 653–656.
9. Terra, D., Brinkman, W.P., and Heynderickx, I. Ease-of-Use and Enjoyment of Traditional vs. Stylus Input for Children in a Brazilian Primary School. LatinDisplay, (2009), 151–155.

DT-DT: Top-down Human Activity Analysis for Interactive Surface Applications

Gang Hu Derek Reilly Mohammed Alnusayri Ben Swinden Qigang Gao
Faculty of Computer Science, Dalhousie University
Halifax, Nova Scotia, Canada
{ghu, reilly, alnusayr, swinden, qggao@cs.dal.ca}

ABSTRACT
As environmental and multi-display configurations become more common, HCI research is becoming increasingly concerned with actions around these displays. Tracking human activity is challenging, and there is currently no single solution that reliably handles all scenarios without excessive instrumentation. In this paper we present a novel tracking and analysis approach using a top-down 3D camera. Our hierarchical tracking approach models local and global affinities, scene constraints and motion patterns to find and track people in space, and a novel salience occupancy pattern (SOP) is used for action recognition. We present experiences applying our approach to build a proxemics-aware tabletop display prototype, and to create an exhibit combining a large vertical display with an interactive floor-projection.

Author Keywords
Human body detection; whole body interaction; top-down tracking; saliency map; proxemics; Kinect

ACM Classification Keywords
H.5.m. Information Interfaces and Presentation (e.g. HCI): Miscellaneous

INTRODUCTION
Reliable tracking of multiple people in arbitrary environments has been a goal of broad interest in computer vision, and finding robust solutions is at the foundation of a wide range of demanding human activity analysis systems, in areas such as human-computer interaction, surveillance, and health care.

In particular, being able to track the location, orientation and action of individuals relative to displays and other people permits application designs that extend surface-based computing. For example, we might interpret gestures above a table surface [33], offer different interactive possibilities based on one's distance from a display [31], or change the nature of an interactive surface depending on the presence of onlookers [6]. Such applications can involve multiple mobile and/or stationary displays (or display ecologies [28, 33]), or single large interactive displays, including public vertical displays [6, 31], tabletops [2, 20], and floor displays. To date, most interactive systems of this type have required significant environmental infrastructure [33] on-body markers or instrumentation [28, 33], and/or custom, specialized hardware [2, 20], limiting the feasibility of such applications in present-day systems. Although much progress has been made in recent years [1, 5, 8, 9, 16, 35, 37], tracking human activity remains a very challenging problem due to numerous performance-related factors such as articulated body structure, illumination variation, occlusion and background clutter, and there exists no single tracking approach that can successfully handle all scenarios. With the development of the low-cost Kinect camera and advancements in human skeleton joint detection techniques [29], good performance of human body detection has been achieved in a controlled environment. However, occlusion still occurs when the camera is placed horizontally, and this cannot be handled by state-of-the-art skeleton-based human detection methods without applying several operational constraints (a clear and wide open area, a front facing camera position, enough spatial distance between users, limited number of concurrent tracking targets).

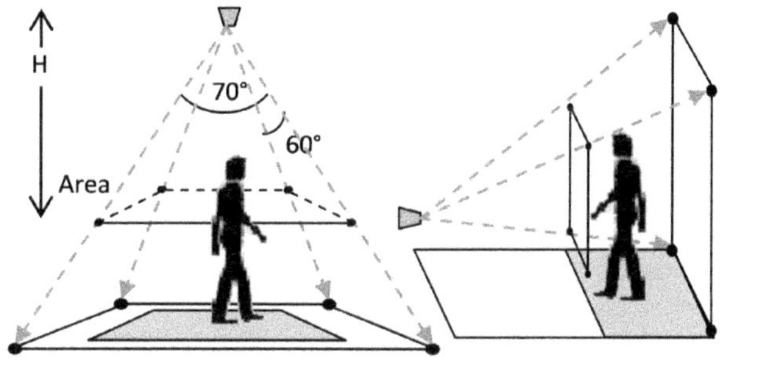

Figure 1. Tracking space comparison of top and front view. Tracking area of top view is determined by the height H, $Area = 4H^2 \cdot \frac{tan35 \cdot tan30}{cos30 \cdot cos35}$, where 35° and 30° are the half of the horizontal and vertical view angles. Green areas are the effective tracking zones in both settings. Top-view tracking better utilizes the room space, and provides a flexible tracking zone.

Occlusion disappears in many cases if we have a bird's-eye view on the world. Despite losing facial appearance and frontal body shape, many human movements and actions are still distinguishable from the top-down, and some even more so. For instance, broad limb movements (punch, throw, push, kick, etc.) can be well-perceived, as can a person's movement trajectory. Given the camera's field of view and optimal depth sensing range between 1-3 meters [19], a front view

ITS 2014, November 16–19, 2014, Dresden, Germany.

http://dx.doi.org/10.1145/2669485.2669501

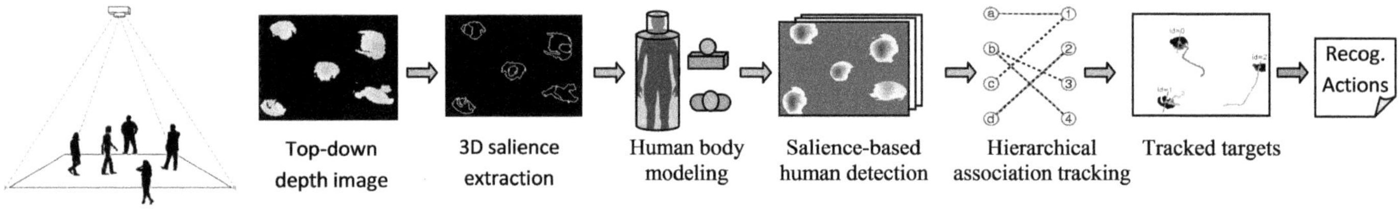

Figure 2. Example system environment (leftmost) and processing pipeline.

squeezes the effective tracking area into a rectangular region on one side of the space (see Figure 1). In contrast, top-down tracking gives an approximately square tracking region, with the maximum area determined as a function of the sensor's height and its optimal depth tracking range. Human motion detection methods using top-down views have been explored in prior research [15, 17, 23, 24, 32] and applied in some HCI research [4, 21, 22, 25, 27, 30]. However, due to the limitations of 2D images, a top-down human body was usually represented as a generic blob, and could not be distinguished from other objects, raising the probability of false positives. In this work, we present a complete solution to human detection, tracking and action recognition via a single top-down 3D camera. It is comprised of a saliency-based human body detection model, a hierarchical tracking framework, and a 4D spatiotemporal human action classifier. In addition, a configuration and management tool allows for quick setup and control, and a socket-based communication package is adopted for integration with distributed interactive applications. We also define key extension points in the software, allowing the system to evolve to suit different application requirements.

Our implementation was developed incrementally in response to the requirements of 2 interactive applications: one involves tracking individuals around a tabletop display, and the other is an interactive exhibit with vertical and floor-projected displays. In this paper we describe both applications and discuss evaluation results derived from this work, to illustrate the performance of our system and to document the process of using it in development.

Our work therefore makes two main contributions. First, we introduce a robust method for top-down tracking of human position, orientation, and action using a low-cost, commodity sensing device (the Kinect). Second, we validate the tracker from both performance and system design/development perspectives using two very different interactive surface applications.

RELATED WORK

There is a long history of approaches to human detection and tracking in the field of computer vision. Many techniques have been successful in outdoor scenarios for tracking pedestrians [1, 5, 8, 9, 16, 35, 37] and in indoor scenarios with strict constraints [29], such as a clear and wide open area, a front facing camera position, enough spatial distance between users, and a limited number of concurrent tracking targets. Tracking people indoors is challenging as people are engaged in a wide range of activities (and so found in different poses). Lighting and occlusion due to objects in the scene can also pose problems. Earlier solutions [26] required that users wear Lycra suits and optical or magnetic markers, to track targets or specific body parts. Other approaches fuse camera data with worn sensors (gyroscopes, accelerometers and magnetometers) [3, 36] to increase robustness and precision. Tracking approaches based on worn devices or markers are intrusive, can require significant setup and can be expensive.

With the development of visual sensor devices, pure vision-based tracking systems are able to provide reasonable performance at low cost. In [7], cues from the upper body, facial features, 3D shape, skin color, and motion detector data are fused for human detection, and a MCMC(Markov chain Monte Carlo)-based framework is applied to provide tracking results. Multi-view solutions can address occlusion, allowing multiple people to be tracked in cluttered environments, at the cost of increased system complexity and setup. For example, in [38] multiple cameras detect and track targets and a multi-camera fusion module combines local tracks of a person into a global view. Scene constraints can further help to reduce ambiguities and improve tracking accuracy. For example, foreground likelihood from all views can be combined into a reference view, and a planar homography constraint applied to track the feet of the people in the scene [18]. In [12], the tracking hypotheses based on pedestrian detection windows and local optical flow trajectories [11] are combined to get more robust overall tracking. Various additional approaches have been proposed to handle occlusion. They often require additional information, such as stereo disparity [10] or a 3D scene context [34].

Human motion detection methods using top-down ("top-view") cameras have been explored in prior research because occlusion disappears in many cases with an undistorted bird's-eye view. [23] uses a ceiling camera to trigger/terminate target detection and tracking, but uses other camera views for feature extraction and modeling. In [15], a ceiling-mounted camera and a laser range finder are used to detect people in the scene. A human detection method in [17] uses real-time depth images and applies Haar-like filtering based on a human model to extract the convex shape of shoulder-head-shoulder, but it neither maintains the human identities nor tracks the movements.

One of the earliest top-down human activity analysis systems is KidsRoom [4], an interactive, responsive play-space simulating a children's bedroom where kids are guided through an adventure story. KidsRoom is able to track up to four children at a time. The lighting, sound effects, performance of the score, and illustrations projected on the two walls of the room respond to actions performed in the room. Three ceiling-mounted cameras were used, one in the center tracking the positions of all children, and two in corner regions dedicated to capturing specific actions recognized in these spots. Human actions were modeled by the global motion representations Motion Energy Images (MEIs) and Motion History Images (MHIs), and were recognized only if well-performed. In [21], a multiplayer game is presented using one top-view camera placed above the playing area. The tracker maps each player's 2D movements to avatar movements in the game. This work was later extended to support tracking the global position and shape that the players form as a group [22].

All of the top-down tracking work discussed so far uses background subtraction to locate individuals, and extracts global motion representations for posture recognition. This global-based approach does not keep temporal ordering properties, and is not suitable for detecting activities that extend beyond a few frames. Immersive Cinema [30], uses a ceiling-mounted camera to detect and track a visitor by segmenting color/texture patterns from the top-down view. This solution cannot handle arbitrary target-floor patterns. A system presented in [25] uses a ceiling-mounted infrared video camera to track a single person in a VR environment. Bystander [27], an immersive, interactive system, uses a ceiling-mounted infrared camera to coarsely track human position and motion in groups. The tracked group motion data is exploited to reveal "flocking behavior" when browsing collections in museums and galleries.

Our proposed DT-DT system differs from the approaches mentioned above. It takes advantage of the top-down camera setting to yield both a less occlusive space and a simple yet expressive shape view for human activity tracking and analysis. Our solution utilizes shape features, a hierarchical framework, and 4D spatiotemporal motion representation to detect, track and recognize human activities in real-time.

SYSTEM IMPLEMENTATION

In this section we detail the implementation of the "Dal Top-Down Tracker" (DT-DT) system. DT-DT is both low-cost and portable, requiring only a Kinect sensor and a computer. Using a v2 Kinect with angular FOV of 70° horizontally and 60° vertically, we can track adults of average height (1.5m∼1.9m) in an approximately $2 \times 2.5m^2$ area if mounted at 3m (a common ceiling height). DT-DT was developed for Windows in C++. We extract depth images using the OpenNI drivers and preprocess them using the OpenCV library. All shape feature extraction, human detection, tracking and action recognition algorithms were custom implemented and tested on an Intel Core 2 Duo CPU (2.8GHz). Figure 2 shows a flowchart of our tracking and analysis approach; we describe each phase below.

(a) 8 GET types (b) CPP types

Figure 3. Bottom-up GET and CPP features.

Human Body Detection in 3D Top-down View

Some conventional features of human bodies, e.g. color, facial patterns, body structures, etc., are not available with a top-down view. However, contour features exploit object boundary information and are able to provide shapes in arbitrary view settings. Thus, in our approach, each object is represented as a group of generic edge tokens (GETs) and Curve Partitioning Points (CPPs) (Figure 3) defined as PCPG model in [13, 14]. GETs and CPPs are perceptual shape features that are extracted from edge contours. 8 types of segmented edge tokens, GETs, are connected at points (CPPs) along the edge curves [14]. Since each edge pixel from depth images has XYZ values, 3D GETs/CPPs can be derived accordingly. 3D GETs/CPPs can be further clustered into several groups according to their spatial distribution. Each clustered group contains the bottom-up saliency features representing a target object (human body), and is assigned a salience weight indicating the shape significance. From a bird's-eye view, standing or mobile human bodies have less variance. To distinguish human bodies from other objects, we apply prior knowledge to evaluate the likelihoods of a human body target, as follows:

Shoulder-Head-shoulder shape

the convex shape of shoulder-head-shoulder is a reliable human body feature in a 3D top-down view that we exploit. We divide each clustered GET/CPP group into 2 regions (top and bottom) according to their depth distribution. Heuristically the top region should be the head, and the bottom includes the shoulders and possibly lower body parts, if the object is the human body. The depth changes between 2 parts of the body are obvious, as you can see in Figure 2 where significant grayscale difference is presented in a depth image. As a result, a ratio of overall depth values of edge pixels from the top and bottom regions above a threshold can be taken as reliable evidence for shoulder-head-shoulder detection.

Head-shoulder size difference

In some cases, when a person is far from the central region of the top-down FOV, the head-shoulder depth ratio fails because of a lack of depth disparity. Fortunately, the size difference between the bottom and top regions of the target is still a stable discriminative property. We expect the size of the top region to be around one third of the bottom part.

Relative position of head and shoulder

The human head is set in between the shoulders. The position relationship between the top and bottom parts of the tracked object is also discriminative for detecting human bodies.

Applying these three priors on the bottom-up saliency entities gives us the weighted candidate objects (clustered GET groups). Human body detection is determined by the output of the saliency map, i.e. the object with a high enough probability score is deemed a person in the scene.

Hierarchical Association Tracking

Multi-person tracking is carried out within a hierarchical association tracking framework similar to [16], where the final global level association is refined based on the affinity measure from the local level. Figure 4 shows the overall tracking approach.

Local-level: Individual people detected in each frame have location information, height, and a salience score. At this local tracking stage, multiple short target traces (tracklets) are the result of tracking-by-detection, i.e. are extracted within a short time period (less than 0.2s), and used as intermediate tracking results according to the body detection responses (locations, heights and salience weights).

Global-level: Since local-level association will leave some targets unmatched, i.e. there might be several tracklets for a single player due to detection error or momentary absence, global-level tracking refinement is needed for reliable results. Two tracklets are believed to be the same target if their motions and spatiotemporal gap are highly coherent compared to others, i.e. the speeds and directions of 2 tracklets should be similar, and their spatial distance and temporal interval should not be significant within a connected time period. In order to support various application domains, scene constraints are also considered at the global stage. For example, in the basic setting, we impose entering and leaving constraints into the tracking system: the region surrounding the 4 edge lines of the FOV is defined as the EE-zone (entry/exit) of the system. We assume that people cannot enter/exit the tracking area without passing through the EE-zone. Likelihoods of enter/exit object events are determined using spatial and temporal factors:

- the direction and distance to the closest boundary edge,
- the direction and distance to the area center,
- the duration of its tracklet's head within the EE-zone.

If the head of a long trajectory stays in the EE-zone and gets closer to its closest edge, it is more likely to be a leaving target, and if the head of a tracklet in the EE-zone gets closer to the region center it is most likely to be an entering target. In general, the global level tracking process tries to form long-term stable movement trajectories for individuals, and is a MAP (maximum a posteriori probability) association problem with priors of scene constraints. It is adapted to other contexts by a process of associating rules with specified regions. For example, when tracking people around a tabletop, the boundary of the table can further constrain the tracking area. This approach offers a high degree of configurability, as discussed later.

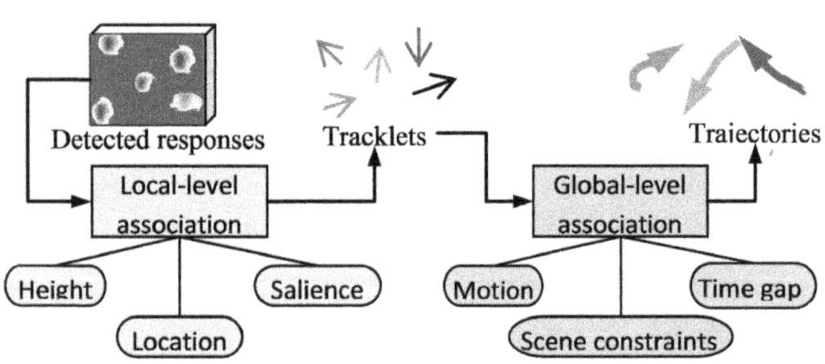

Figure 4. Online hierarchical association tracking.

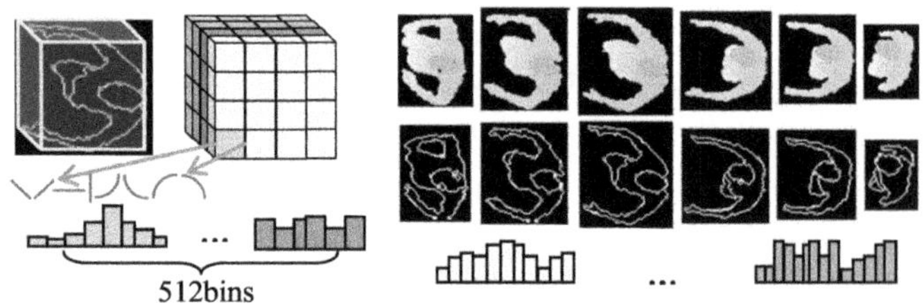

Figure 5. Salience Occupancy Patterns for action representation. Each tracked 3D target from a frame is represented as a 512-bin vector, while a gesture or action is represented as a longer vector which concatenates multiple 512-bins from a sequence of frames.

Salience Occupancy Pattern for Action Recognition

Given the tracked results, we often want to recognize gestures or actions of the tracked targets. To do this we have built a novel human action model for top-down 3D views, characterized by 4D spatiotemporal Salience Occupancy Patterns (SOP). In each frame, a SOP feature computes the occupancy information according to the occurrence of 8 types of 3D GETs (for each tracked target), and the temporal occupancy patterns within a time window are used to discriminate different actions. Specifically, a given target's 3D space is divided into $w \times h \times z$ $(4 \times 4 \times 4)$ spatial cells, each of which has 8 GET type bins (see Figure 5) giving 512 bins for a tracked target per frame. The size of a certain GET type voxel that falls into each bin is counted, and the L2-norm is computed within each cell. We currently use a 10-frame window to detect gestures/actions, which empirically gives good performance in the current setting, tested using several gestures/actions involving wide limb movements. The final human action descriptor with 5120 bins is a concatenation of the SOPs obtained from all cells, which is the input to an SVM classifier for recognition.

Adaptability and Reuse

Besides the tracking and recognition components, the system has been designed to promote reuse, via a configuration UI, a flexible communication protocol, and extensible APIs. In this section we discuss the current design (see Figure 6a) and implementation of these utilities and highlight relevant ongoing work.

Configuration UI

A built-in configuration UI (Figure 6b)provides access to the following settings:

- *Device configuration*: set up the camera view, verify the height, and depth threshold.
- *Scene constraints customization*: different applications have different scene boundary shapes. It is also not unusual that static objects in the scene have similar shape appearances to human bodies. In order to reduce the search space and minimize the false positive rate, this UI allows users pick and mark boundaries in the scene where the tracking process will be restricted. This feature is being expanded to allow different rules to be applied to different regions. For example, specific actions might be recognized

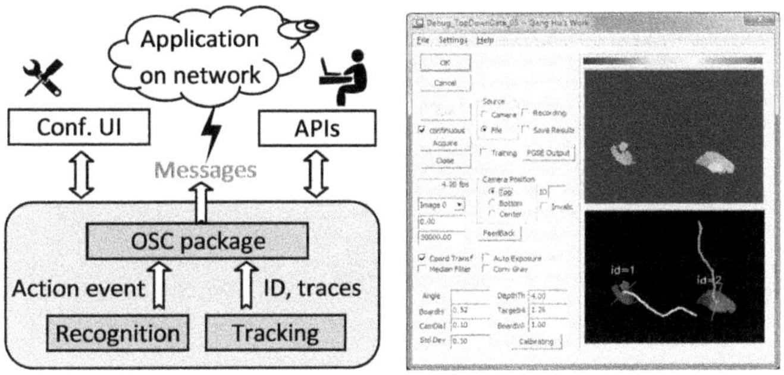

(a) System components (b) Configuration UI

Figure 6. Toolkit components and Configuration UI.

in a "hot spot", or the depth threshold for tracking might be increased in a seated area.

- *Action/Gesture modeling*: allows users to add/define new actions to recognize. This tool currently collects a training dataset, and builds an action model based on this. Support for interactive, real-time capture and labeling of training datasets is being implemented.
- *Testing*: collects test data, and provides a video stream for comparing system results with ground truth. In future, this will support comparison of different detection, tracking, and activity recognition approaches.

Communication Protocol

To facilitate the integration of DT-DT into a wide range of applications, Open Sound Control (OSC) is adopted as the communication protocol for exchanging data (e.g. tracking data and control messages). OSC is supported by many platforms and languages, provides a lightweight, flexible messaging format, facilitates distributed application models, and is increasingly used for interactive spaces including exhibits and large display kiosks. In addition to sending tracking and action recognition data, DT-DT's operating parameters can be adjusted at runtime via commands sent over OSC.

Extensible APIs

DT-DT currently uses open APIs (OpenNI and OpenCV) for preliminary processing. Developers can take advantage of these packages to support their use of DT-DT (for example, to record tracking data, training results, or recognition output in different formats).

Building support for configuration and implementing the prototypes discussed below has allowed us to isolate key extension points in each workflow phase (detection, tracking, and action recognition). For example, developers may want to add detection for groupings of people, define new scene constraint rules for tracking, add additional action recognition procedures (for finer-grained actions, for example), or they may wish to replace entire workflow phases with different approaches. Doing so requires adapting the configuration UI as well as adding new behavior.

EVALUATION

We have used DT-DT in two interactive applications. One is an interactive multi-display application supporting interaction based on body position, orientation, and gestures, created as part of an exhibit called My Mother's Kitchen. The other is Proximity Table, a context-aware proximity-based interactive tabletop system designed to support walk-up-and-use shared surface scenarios in settings like museums. We discuss each here to demonstrate the flexibility of our approach, to report evaluation results, and to highlight challenges posed by these applications that have informed DT-DT's design.

My Mother's Kitchen

My Mother's Kitchen is an interactive exhibit that explores changes in the design and use of kitchens throughout the 20th century. The exhibit contains three re-creations of historical kitchens as well as the future kitchen. The future kitchen is a multi-display application including an interactive floor projection showing a stylized floor plan of a kitchen.

Usage

Visitors of the future kitchen exhibit walk onto the floor plan, reorganizing elements in the plan (e.g. appliances) by performing an in-air "pick up" and "holding" gestures over the item, walking to the desired location and performing a corresponding "drop" gesture. A large vertical display is positioned in one corner of the exhibit; when visitors walk into a zone in front of the display, they can select from a number of modern, exotic and futuristic items to add to the kitchen (e.g., herb garden, hibachi) using a point and dwell gesture. By using a swiping gesture the selected items are dropped onto the floor plan.

Application Setup

A projector and a Kinect camera are suspended above the exhibition space. The menu and floor plan application is implemented using Unity3D in C#. It receives coordinate data and gesture events as well as person IDs from DT-DT via OSC, and then updates the position of an avatar, and relocates the virtual kitchen elements as visitors interact with them. It communicates events via OSC to an independent sound application written in Max/MSP, which triggers environmental sound effects. Figure 7 shows screenshots of this application, where a yellow box follows the visitor whose movement is tracked by DT-DT.

An additional requirement for DT-DT emerged as we considered support for gestural control of the "menu" component of the application. The result was to support partitioning the tracking region into functional subspaces, each with different rules regarding what is detected and communicated by DT-DT. In front of the menu we are not interested in tracking visitor positions, only specific gestures. Because the gestures are different from the floor-plan area, the possibility of confusion is reduced. Using OSC it is straightforward to add additional action-related data (position of an outstretched arm, for example).

(a) Projected kitchen floor plan (b) Virtual kitchen (c) Vertical display

Figure 7. Future Kitchen Project.

Technical Evaluation

The evaluation has three parts: 1) detection and tracking performance, 2) action recognition performance on recorded videos, and 3) field study during the exhibition in May 2014.

We evaluated detection and tracking performance on recorded datasets consisting of 40-minute depth videos with 320×240 resolution taken in the exhibition space. Placed 5m high, the first generation Kinect sensor gives a total tracking area of approximately 2×2.5 meters. 6 users including professional dancers randomly walked in the area and performed 4 actions including pick-up (PU), put-down (PD), holding(HD), and raise an arm (RA).

We use the detection rate (recall) to evaluate detection performance and compare it with other methods for top-down human detection. We compared detection rates of three detection methods: conventional mean-shift method, Haar-like Filtering method [17], and the proposed method on our dataset. Our detection method has a detection rate of 95.5%, vs. 88.3% and 86.5% for Mean-shift and Haar-like filtering respectively (Table 1). We adopted common metrics to evaluate the tracking performance:

- **GT**: The number of trajectories in ground truth;
- **MT**: Mostly Tracked trajectories ($\geq 80\%$);
- **ML**: Mostly Lost trajectories ($< 20\%$);
- **PT**: Partially tracked trajectories (btw 20% and 80%);
- **FRAG**: Fragmentation, interrupted ground true;
- **IDS**: ID Switches, two trajectories switch their IDs.

We compared the performance of our low-level tracking method with the hierarchical tracking approach. This

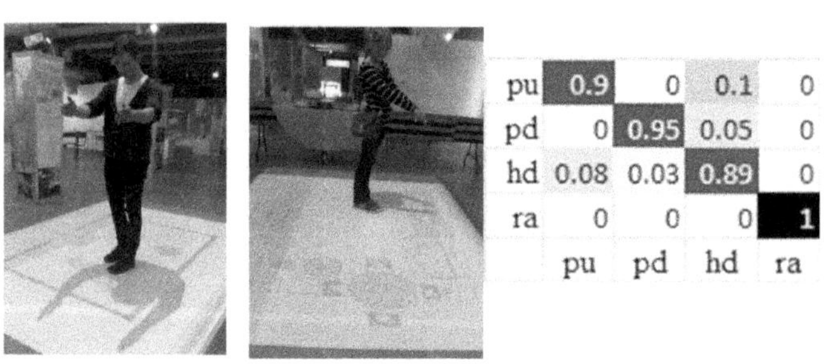

(a) Perform gestures (b) Confusion matrix

Figure 8. Gesture Recognition.

Method	Detection rate
Mean-shift	88.3%
Haar-like filtering	86.5%
Our approach	95.5%

Table 1. Detection accuracies on our dataset.

Method	GT	MT	ML	PT	FRAG	IDS
Local tracking	52	40	7	5	11	5
Global tracking	52	45	4	3	8	4

Table 2. Results of local and global level tacking.

comparison data demonstrates the progressive improvement achieved by the global-level tracking association (Table 2).

For action recognition, we trained SVM classifiers for SOP-based action representation with a χ^2-RBF-kernel using Leave-One-Out (LOO) cross validation, and a one-against-rest approach was applied to select the class with the highest score as the recognized one. Figure 8b shows the confusion matrix for the classification. A strong majority (89% to 100%) of gestures are well-classified. The "holding" gesture requires that both hands are raised up in front of the body, and kept steady, while in "pick-up" both hands are raised from the sides, ending in the "holding" position. The matrix shows some confusion between these gestures, and between "holding" and "put down".

We completed the "My Mother's Kitchen" field study in May, where DT-DT ran continuously during the 10 day period of the exhibit. 88 attendees used the Future Kitchen. Observers noted when participants entered the tracked region and when they attempted gestures. The comparison of DT-DT's system logs and observation notes shows that DT-DT's body detection accuracy is around 98% across attendees of varying ages, builds (heights and weights) and of both genders. The gesture detection precision was approximately 85%. Considering that all attendees were new to the system, it is an encouraging result.

Proximity Table

We are also using DT-DT in a proximity-based interactive tabletop system. Proximity Table supports collaborative and independent use of a shared, walk-up-and-use tabletop display (this includes forming subgroups, breaking away, swapping locations, watching from behind, and shifting from bystander to participant).

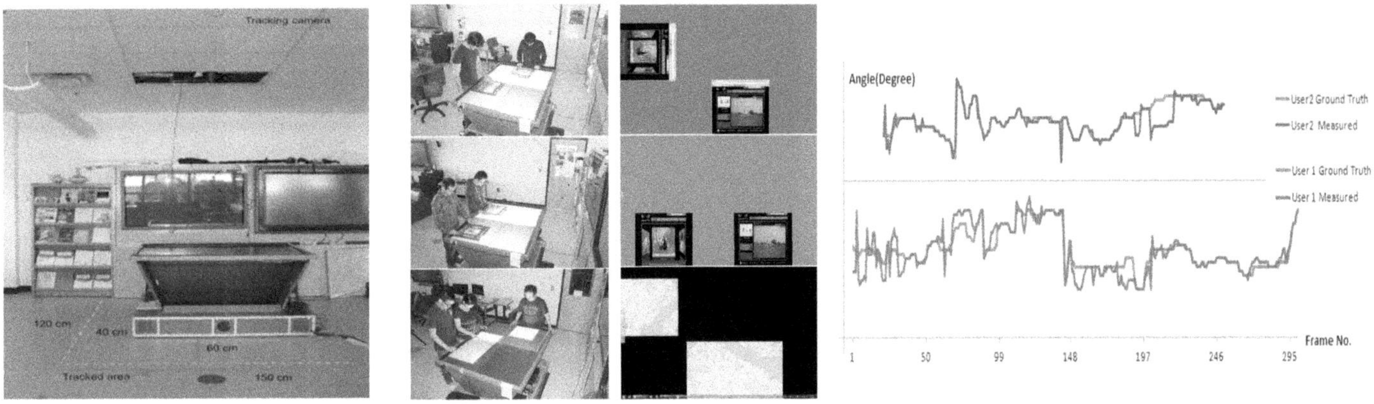

(a) Camera setting (b) Individual users/group with their documents on the table (c) Orientation comparison

Figure 9. Tabletop Prototype.

Application Requirements

To capture user activities, a Kinect camera is placed on the ceiling of our lab and captures a 1m perimeter around 2 sides of a 70" horizontal display (Figure 9a). Other tabletop prototypes that track users around the table include Klinkhammer et al.'s work [20], and Medusa [2], which uses a multitude of proximity electric field sensors to locate users around a tabletop computer and associates touches with them. These approaches cannot track individuals who are behind people interacting with the table, which we explore here with DT-DT.

This configuration introduced new requirements for DT-DT. First, as the central region is not traversable (the table is there), heuristics regarding entering and leaving targets needed to become more configurable. Our approach is to model the table edge as an additional scene constraint: it is the destination of the entering target, and also a good reference for the leaving target. Second, groups may crowd quite closely together when interacting with tabletop displays (children, for example). This suggests a need for a 3D group appearance model to detect and track group-level activities, e.g., mingling and dispersing.

Interaction Techniques (Scenarios)

- *Creating / Remove Areas*: When a new user reaches the table they will be recognized by the tracking system and the tabletop application will create new interaction area for that user. When a user leaves the table the tracking system sends their ID to the table in order to remove the area.
- *Moving Areas*: Each interaction area has a toggle button to activate/deactivate a following feature. When activated, the work area follows its user as he/she moves around the table. If a user passes behind another user, the system will manipulate Z-order so the moving area passes under the stationary one in order to not disturb others. This is an advantage of top-down tracking over the use of sensors around the table. When deactivated, a user can leave their work area to look at and discuss the work of other users.
- *Increase and Decrease Area Size*: When a user U1 comes within a defined threshold of another user U2 the system will wait for 5 seconds and if in that time U1 does not touch the "place workspace" button, the system will store U1's work area and will increase the size of U2's work area, to support collaboration. When U1 leaves the group the system will wait for 5 seconds before decreasing the size of U2's work area and restoring the work area for U1.
- *User Orientation*: Orientation data of a user provides a useful cue for tabletop collaboration. To better utilize the orientation obtained from DT-DT, novel orientation logic with heuristics involving expected facing angle relative to the table are used.

Technical Evaluation

The development of Proximity Table is ongoing. We provide an initial qualitative assessment of the interaction techniques here, and an evaluation of the orientation tracking logic.

By taking advantage of DT-DT's global level customized scene constraints, Proximity Table is able to accurately detect when individuals are approaching and departing from the table boundaries, and to create and remove corresponding window areas.

Proximity Table is able to detect and track the users' movements and relocate their window areas smoothly as they move. At the same time, DT-DT is able to track individuals who are located behind people interacting with the table. Proximity Table accurately rearranges the window orders of the users according to the spatial location and distance to the tracking boundaries (tabletop edges). Group activity analysis is another DT-DT feature that plays a critical role in Proximity Table, which is able to increase and decrease area size as users form groups and break away. Figure 9b shows that a group is allocated a larger size window than a single user.

The orientation of the tracked users may also provide useful information about group behavior; for example, if one person rotates toward the work area of the person beside them, Proximity Table may provide the option to increase or merge work areas. We present evaluation results of target orientation data against ground truth here. In Figure 9c, 2 users' measured orientation vs. ground truth is presented (in degrees, over time). The red lines represent ground truth. We can see that the measured data are almost consistent with ground truth.

Fluctuations in frames 1-50 for user 1 are due to him walking around the perimeter of the tracking region.

DISCUSSION

Summary of System Features

Our original motivation for developing DT-DT was to avoid occlusion and exploit a simple human detection model. Through our work we have identified and implemented several other key features that facilitate the development of a wide range of multi-person interactive applications. Leveraging domain knowledge: prior knowledge about the domain, environment and motion patterns is valuable for object tracking. DT-DT models these high-level semantics as constraints to narrow down the searching space.

Minimally invasive for HCI studies: HCI study results are impacted by excessive instrumentation, as this affects user experience. DT-DT does not require worn tags, sensors or other devices, while addressing some limitations of front-facing camera approaches.

Readily integrated with other systems: OSC and DT-DT's configuration UI facilitates use in a wide range of interactive kiosks, exhibits, and other applications. It is also simple to use the tracking results alone, widening usage towards remote monitoring.

Real-time tracking performance: the speed of our tracking system is up to 15fps for human detection, tracking, and communication using our test hardware, which is sufficient for many real-time HCI applications.

Privacy preserving: deployment of vision technology is sometimes met with skepticism by the public at large. DT-DT only maintains weak identities of individuals when in tracking range, and tracks from the top-down (rather than face-forward), which can ease such concerns.

To date, we have identified two major target application domains. One is to track user positions and recognize/analyze actions involving wide limb movements (punch, throw, push, kick etc) in multi-display applications, as with future kitchen. The other application area is for group activity analysis and support around shared displays. A top-down view provides a global picture of the behaviors of groups, as with the Proximity Table.

Limitations and Future Work

There are several limitations and potential improvements to our system that we will explore in future work. In our experiments, fast motion would cause image blur and generate false negatives. We would like to find solutions to increase robustness, such as increasing processing speed, improving the top-down shape appearance model, and providing a better motion prediction model for targets.

The tracking area of the current system is limited by the capacity of a single camera (in our case, a first-generation Kinect), which is a roadblock for system deployment. Specifically, the FOV of the Kinect camera requires that it be placed higher than the average ceiling (3m) in order to achieve a tracked region larger than $2m^2$. The camera cannot also be placed arbitrarily high as it needs to compute a depth image, and with high enough resolution for our system. While advances in hardware can alleviate some of these constraints (as does the wider FOV of the v2 Kinect), chaining sensors would provide a wider tracking area, and broaden the application domain.

Modeling scene scenarios and user patterns is application-dependent, and it should occur in the high-level tracking stage. Currently, only boundary constraints are used in our system. Our current applications have unique scene scenario and user motion patterns. For example, in the Proximity Table application, the effective tracking area is bounded near the table edge. To date our work has addressed the unique requirements of our applications in an ad hoc manner. Providing a generic framework that supports different scene scenarios and user patterns would be beneficial for HCI researchers, and we hope that our ongoing work in this area will contribute to this goal.

Strong identities of individuals may be necessary for some tracking applications. In nature, top-down tracking lacks several user identity features, and requires space between each user for disambiguation (i.e. if 2 users are very close to each other, DT-DT currently would see a single user or class the data as an invalid target). Potential improvements of DT-DT in this area involve applying physical models of grouping behaviour for recognition, attempting to identify users based on the top-down body model, or using data from other sensors to fill the gaps.

CONCLUSION

Tracking multiple people in arbitrary environments is a challenging problem. Here we tackle human detection, tracking and action recognition for around-display interactions while avoiding occlusion by using a top-down 3D camera. A saliency map-based 3D model integrates both bottom-up salience and higher-level priors to provide selective visual features for human detection. The tracking task is handled in a hierarchical association framework, where local and global affinities, motion patterns and scene constraints are modeled to obtain optimal trajectories of multiple targets. Based on the tracking results, a novel salience occupancy pattern (SOP) descriptor is computed as the representation for action recognition. This human tracking and action recognition system, DT-DT, has been applied in two very different interactive surface application contexts, uncovering features and approaches that increase its generality, including a flexible communications protocol, a configuration UI, and key points for extension or modification. DT-DT has been used so far to track large gestures in a multi-display exhibit, and to build a tabletop UI that responds to group behaviour at and around the table.

ACKNOWLEDGMENTS

This work is supported by the grants from Boeing Company, MITACS and GRAND.

REFERENCES

1. Andriyenko, A., Schindler, K., and Roth, S. Discrete-continuous optimization for multi-target

tracking. In *Computer Vision and Pattern Recognition (CVPR), 2012 IEEE Conference on*, IEEE (2012), 1926–1933.

2. Annett, M., Grossman, T., Wigdor, D., and Fitzmaurice, G. Medusa: a proximity-aware multi-touch tabletop. In *Proceedings of the 24th annual ACM symposium on User interface software and technology*, ACM (2011), 337–346.
3. Bleser, G., and Stricker, D. Advanced tracking through efficient image processing and visual–inertial sensor fusion. *Computers & Graphics 33*, 1 (2009), 59–72.
4. Bobick, A. F., Intille, S. S., Davis, J. W., Baird, F., Pinhanez, C. S., Campbell, L. W., Ivanov, Y. A., Schütte, A., and Wilson, A. The kidsroom: A perceptually-based interactive and immersive story environment. *Presence: Teleoperators and Virtual Environments 8*, 4 (1999), 369–393.
5. Breitenstein, M. D., Reichlin, F., Leibe, B., Koller-Meier, E., and Van Gool, L. Robust tracking-by-detection using a detector confidence particle filter. In *Computer Vision, 2009 IEEE 12th International Conference on*, IEEE (2009), 1515–1522.
6. Brudy, F., Ledo, D., Greenberg, S., and Butz, A. Is anyone looking? mitigating shoulder surfing on public displays through awareness and protection. In *Proceedings of The 3rd International Symposium on Pervasive Displays*, PerDis (2014), 1–6.
7. Choi, W., Pantofaru, C., and Savarese, S. Detecting and tracking people using an rgb-d camera via multiple detector fusion. In *Computer Vision Workshops (ICCV Workshops), 2011 IEEE International Conference on*, IEEE (2011), 1076–1083.
8. Collins, R. T. Multitarget data association with higher-order motion models. In *Computer Vision and Pattern Recognition (CVPR), 2012 IEEE Conference on*, IEEE (2012), 1744–1751.
9. Dalal, N., and Triggs, B. Histograms of oriented gradients for human detection. In *Computer Vision and Pattern Recognition, 2005. CVPR 2005. IEEE Computer Society Conference on*, vol. 1, IEEE (2005), 886–893.
10. Enzweiler, M., Eigenstetter, A., Schiele, B., and Gavrila, D. M. Multi-cue pedestrian classification with partial occlusion handling. In *Computer vision and pattern recognition (CVPR), 2010 IEEE Conference on*, IEEE (2010), 990–997.
11. Fragkiadaki, K., and Shi, J. Detection free tracking: Exploiting motion and topology for segmenting and tracking under entanglement. In *Computer Vision and Pattern Recognition (CVPR), 2011 IEEE Conference on*, IEEE (2011), 2073–2080.
12. Fragkiadaki, K., Zhang, W., Zhang, G., and Shi, J. Two-granularity tracking: Mediating trajectory and detection graphs for tracking under occlusions. In *Computer Vision–ECCV 2012*. Springer, 2012, 552–565.
13. Gao, Q., and Wong, A. Curve detection based on perceptual organization. *Pattern Recognition 26*, 7 (1993), 1039–1046.
14. Hu, G., and Gao, Q. A non-parametric statistics based method for generic curve partition and classification. In *Image Processing (ICIP), 2010 17th IEEE International Conference on*, IEEE (2010), 3041–3044.
15. Hu, N., Englebienne, G., and Kröse, B. J. Bayesian fusion of ceiling mounted camera and laser range finder on a mobile robot for people detection and localization. In *Human Behavior Understanding*. Springer, 2012, 41–51.
16. Huang, C., Wu, B., and Nevatia, R. Robust object tracking by hierarchical association of detection responses. In *Computer Vision–ECCV 2008*. Springer, 2008, 788–801.
17. Ikemura, S., and Fujiyoshi, H. Human detection by haar-like filtering using depth information. In *Pattern Recognition (ICPR), 2012 21st International Conference on*, IEEE (2012), 813–816.
18. Khan, S. M., and Shah, M. A multiview approach to tracking people in crowded scenes using a planar homography constraint. In *Computer Vision–ECCV 2006*. Springer, 2006, 133–146.
19. Khoshelham, K., and Elberink, S. O. Accuracy and resolution of kinect depth data for indoor mapping applications. *Sensors 12*, 2 (2012), 1437–1454.
20. Klinkhammer, D., Nitsche, M., Specht, M., and Reiterer, H. Adaptive personal territories for co-located tabletop interaction in a museum setting. In *Proceedings of the ACM International Conference on Interactive Tabletops and Surfaces*, ACM (2011), 107–110.
21. Laakso, S., and Laakso, M. Design of a body-driven multiplayer game system. *Computers in Entertainment (CIE) 4*, 4 (2006), 7.
22. Laakso, S., and Ruikka, P. Mofun circus–iterative process in creating pervasive body-driven multiplayer game (2007).
23. Lanz, O., Chippendale, P., and Brunelli, R. An appearance-based particle filter for visual tracking in smart rooms. In *Multimodal Technologies for Perception of Humans*. Springer, 2008, 57–69.
24. Lin, Q., Zhou, C., Wang, S., and Xu, X. Human behavior understanding via top-view vision. *AASRI Procedia 3* (2012), 184–190.
25. Pietroni, E., and Antinucci, F. the approval of the franciscan rule: virtual experience among the characters of giotto's work. In *Proceedings of the 11th International conference on Virtual Reality, Archaeology and Cultural Heritage*, Eurographics Association (2010), 171–178.

26. Qian, G., Chellappa, R., and Zheng, Q. Bayesian structure from motion using inertial information. In *Image Processing. 2002. Proceedings. 2002 International Conference on*, vol. 3, IEEE (2002), III–425.

27. Robertson, T., Mansfield, T., and Loke, L. Designing an immersive environment for public use. In *Proceedings of the ninth conference on Participatory design: Expanding boundaries in design-Volume 1*, ACM (2006), 31–40.

28. Seyed, T., Burns, C., Costa Sousa, M., Maurer, F., and Tang, A. Eliciting usable gestures for multi-display environments. In *Proceedings of the 2012 ACM international conference on Interactive tabletops and surfaces*, ACM (2012), 41–50.

29. Shotton, J., Sharp, T., Kipman, A., Fitzgibbon, A., Finocchio, M., Blake, A., Cook, M., and Moore, R. Real-time human pose recognition in parts from single depth images. *Communications of the ACM 56*, 1 (2013), 116–124.

30. Sparacino, F. Scenographies of the past and museums of the future: from the wunderkammer to body-driven interactive narrative spaces. In *Proceedings of the 12th annual ACM international conference on Multimedia*, ACM (2004), 72–79.

31. Vogel, D., and Balakrishnan, R. Interactive public ambient displays: transitioning from implicit to explicit, public to personal, interaction with multiple users. In *Proceedings of the 17th annual ACM symposium on User interface software and technology*, ACM (2004), 137–146.

32. Weerachai, S., and Mizukawa, M. Human behavior recognition via top-view vision for intelligent space. In *Control Automation and Systems (ICCAS), 2010 International Conference on*, IEEE (2010), 1687–1690.

33. Wilson, A. D., and Benko, H. Combining multiple depth cameras and projectors for interactions on, above and between surfaces. In *Proceedings of the 23nd annual ACM symposium on User interface software and technology*, ACM (2010), 273–282.

34. Wojek, C., Walk, S., Roth, S., and Schiele, B. Monocular 3d scene understanding with explicit occlusion reasoning. In *Computer Vision and Pattern Recognition (CVPR), 2011 IEEE Conference on*, IEEE (2011), 1993–2000.

35. Yang, B., and Nevatia, R. Online learned discriminative part-based appearance models for multi-human tracking. In *Computer Vision–ECCV 2012*. Springer, 2012, 484–498.

36. You, S., and Neumann, U. Fusion of vision and gyro tracking for robust augmented reality registration. In *Virtual Reality, 2001. Proceedings. IEEE*, IEEE (2001), 71–78.

37. Zhang, L., Li, Y., and Nevatia, R. Global data association for multi-object tracking using network flows. In *Computer Vision and Pattern Recognition, 2008. CVPR 2008. IEEE Conference on*, IEEE (2008), 1–8.

38. Zhao, T., Aggarwal, M., Kumar, R., and Sawhney, H. Real-time wide area multi-camera stereo tracking. In *Computer Vision and Pattern Recognition, 2005. CVPR 2005. IEEE Computer Society Conference on*, vol. 1, IEEE (2005), 976–983.

NetBoards: Investigating a Collection of Personal Noticeboard Displays in the Workplace

Erroll Wood **Peter Robinson**
Computer Laboratory
University of Cambridge, UK
{erroll.wood, peter.robinson}@cl.cam.ac.uk

ABSTRACT
NetBoards are situated displays designed to fulfil and augment the role of non-digital personal noticeboards in the workplace. Traditionally, these are small corkboards or whiteboards situated outside offices belonging to individuals or small groups of people. By replacing these with large, networked, high-fidelity touch-enabled displays, we attempt to replicate the existing physical systems' flexibility and ease-of-use, while enabling more expressive content creation techniques and remote connectivity. We have developed an understanding of the deployment environment and every-day noticeboard practices using an ethnographic study which guided system design. Users can write messages or sketch drawings on their NetBoard, as well as post images and other web-based media. NetBoards can be accessed over the internet, allowing remote viewing and modification. Initial observations of 9 deployed units demonstrate the system's flexibility, showing it being used for maintaining group awareness, workplace personalization, playful communication, and showcasing research.

Author Keywords
Ubiquitous Computing / Smart Environments; Multi-display environments; Human-centered design

ACM Classification Keywords
H.4.3. Communications Applications: Bulletin boards

INTRODUCTION
Personal non-digital information displays are ubiquitous in the workplace and play an important role in communicating group awareness, social grooming, and workplace personalization [2, 14]. Though past research has struggled with the practicalities of deploying large collections of displays, technology has steadily improved over the past years, becoming cheaper, larger, higher-resolution, and more power-efficient. As a result, we have developed and deployed NetBoards – digital equivalents of traditional personal noticeboards that aim to capture the ease of use and flexibility of the existing system, while using technology to offer enhanced expressiveness, interactivity, and connectivity.

ACM 978-1-4503-2587-5/14/11...$15.00.
http://dx.doi.org/10.1145/2669485.2669499

Figure 1: NetBoards are interactive personal noticeboards situated outside offices. They are used to maintain group awareness and build a sense of community in the workplace.

Although existing noticeboard practices are effective, several issues are apparent. As it is generally the office occupant's responsibility to maintain displayed information, postings can become out-of-date (or *stale*) when their owner forgets to remove them. In some cases, the effort of modifying one's noticeboard can seem too high, causing it to become neglected. Situations also arise where office-owners wish to post information about their whereabouts to their colleagues, but are unable to do so precisely because they are absent. While contacting someone at the office and instructing them to edit the noticeboard on their behalf is an option, this is disruptive and far from ideal.

The success of a situated display system depends on choosing the right types of content, and this requires an understanding of the social nature of its deployment environment. We therefore used a long-term ethnographic study to determine what is appropriate to display outside offices, and investigate typical interaction methods afforded by non-digital noticeboards. These obersvations guided our development of a framework optimized for what people are familiar with, while attempting to improve upon their flexibility and ease of use.

Following a survey of related work, we present our study on how existing non-digital noticeboards are used in our workplace, describing our observations and consequential design choices. We briefly discuss a prototype deployment, and then describe in detail the current system's features, installation, and operation. We finally share our initial experiences and discuss the system's reception in the workplace. The source code is available under an open source license for the benefit of the research community and anyone who wishes to deploy the system themselves [15].

RELATED WORK

Situated displays outside offices

Though it has become easier and cheaper to deploy collections of displays, there are only a few previous works specifically concerning displays situated outside individual offices. McCarthy et al's *OutCast* system is the earliest such example – they embedded a touch-screen into the wall of a cubicle-office, enabling the occupant to display information to passers-by [11]. OutCast allows users to either passively cycle through content chosen by the office owner, or interactively explore content or leave text messages. Though they aimed to study a wide deployment of their systems, they only report a single installation of OutCast being deployed.

Cheverst et al. present a range of in-depth works describing the design, development, management, and longitudinal evaluation of two interactive office door display systems in an academic laboratory environment [1]. *Hermes 1* consists of 10 wall-mounted pen-enabled PDAs that allow office visitors to hand-write messages, and office-owners to create and display multi-media content including text and images [5]. Office-owners were also able to remotely create text-messages using email, and view the contents of their display through a web-portal. They later implemented *Hermes 2* consisting of 40 more advanced units equipped with larger screens, cameras, and microphones, enabling further message-types to be sent and displayed. Content from multiple users can also be displayed on a single device, important for shared offices. They also deployed a *Hermes Photo Display* – a larger display in a communual area where researchers and students could post photos for general viewing.

Nguyen at al. developed *Dynamic Door Displays* – door-mounted interactive displays that allowed visitors to check an office-owner's calendar or location [13]. However, work on this project halted before a significant deployment or evaluation was carried out.

Situated displays in the workplace

There is a rich body of literature exploring how workplace situated displays can improve awareness, promote collaboration, and enlighten community. We present a brief review of some milestone works with relevant findings.

Alongside OutCast, McCarthy et al. present *GroupCast* – a TV-based situated display that invokes spontaneous conversation between passers-by [11]. It does this by choosing content it knows to be of interest to passing users, hoping to generate serendipitous discussion. The *Notification Collage* system allows distributed and co-located colleagues to post assorted media messages including live video, photo slideshows and text messages onto a large public screen [6]. They found it was often used like a bulletin board, with posted items generating discussions. *MessyBoard* is a large projected shared bulletin board that can be collaboratively decorated by shared office occupants [3]. Its creators found that usage patterns differ widely between user-groups, with one group focussing on work, while another preferred posting humorous pictures and playing games. By facilitating playful behaviour, they claim to make communication more enjoyable, reducing the boredom of work-related communication [4].

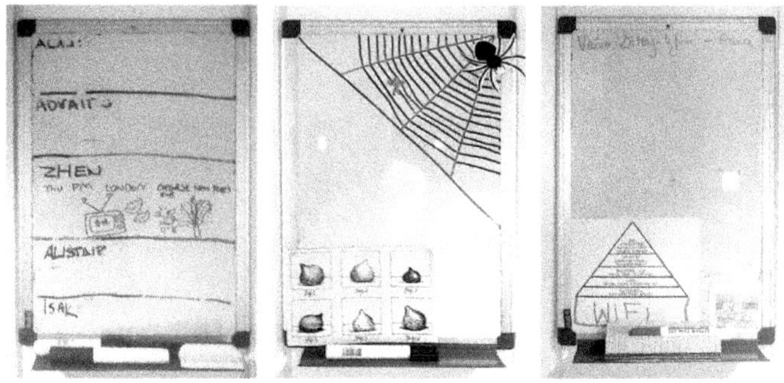

(a) A notice of absence outside a shared office (b) A playful sketch and printed humourous item. (c) A notice of absence with humorous images

Figure 2: Sample photos from our non-digital noticeboard survey, showing typical use patterns.

SURVEY OF EXISTING NOTICEBOARD USE

For a situated system to become accepted by users in their daily routines, it must be carefully designed to minimize the disruption of existing every-day practices. If it does not fit in with the existing behavioural expectations and associations of its deployed location, successful user adoption is unlikely.

We therefore conducted a pre-deployment study to provide an understanding of how the existing non-digital noticeboards are used. If we explore how people use existing technology, we can develop an experience optimized for what they want and are familiar with. Over the course of six months we recorded the content of existing office noticeboards by periodically taking photographs of them whenever they were modified. This resulted in a comprehensive corpus of 47 photos exhibiting both the *methods* used to create and modify content, and the *categories* of content left or put on display.

Environmental context

NetBoards is deployed throughout the Graphics & Interaction Group space at the University of Cambridge Computer Laboratory. The research group consists of 22 members, most of whom are PhD students, and is situated along a single corridor with 13 offices. Most offices are therefore multi-occupancy, generally shared between two people. This is a different workplace environment from previous peripheral display research conducted in large, shared offices [3] or cubicle environments [11], and comes with different behavioural expectations. Each office has a small non-digital whiteboard situated outside its doorway – these semi-personal noticeboards inspired the development of the NetBoards project. The group has several shared spaces with larger noticeboards – a meeting room, experimental laboratory, and a kitchen.

Non-digital methods for creating content

We found that noticeboard content is created and modified using two methods only: *inking* – people use coloured whiteboard markers to write messages and sketch small pictures;

and *printing and sticking* – people print out text and images, and affix them to a noticeboard with sticky-tape. The whiteboard medium primarily affords inking, thus making it the most used method of content creation and modification. While printed items are popular and attract attention, printed content has a longer average lifetime, often being left for months without modification or removal. On discussing this with users, they revealed that they dont't want to frequently replace printed items as they are wary of wasting paper, and put off by the effort involved.

As many noticeboards are shared, users follow simple protocols to reduce author ambiguitiy when necessary. Messages are often preceeded by the author's name (Figure 2c), or noticeboards are separated with horizontal lines into multiple panes – one for each office occupant (Figure 2a).

Typical categories of content

Despite the wide range of possible message-types that could be posted using inking or printing, we discovered that most fit into three broad categories:

Notice of absence – brief messages announcing someone's current or forthcoming absence, either long or short-term.

Humour – jokes or printed content (e.g. comics, images), sometimes posted in reaction to a previous message.

Play – written, sketched, or printed items of a playful nature.

We discuss the nature of each message-category in turn:

Notices of absence

The most frequently left type of message concerned office absences. In a large research group, someone is always away on vacation or at a conference. Even when not actually abroad, group members are often away on university-related business in town, or conducting off-site experiments. It may seem archaic to rely on non-digital noticeboards for announcing these absences, especially considering the ubiquitous use of online calendars and internet messaging. However, it can be undesirable to message an entire research group or department – this would be seen as spam to those not interested. Also, even if someone lets their colleagues know about an upcoming absence, it is easy to forget such matters.

Displaying an office absence outside an office has natural benefits: people looking for the occupant immediately have an idea of when they'll be back or how to appropriately contact them, and colleagues passively learn about each other's activities, assisting group coordination. These messages are always inked, and are removed when the occupant returns.

Humorous images and jokes

Humor is pervasive and provides many benefits in the workplace, including stress relief, team unification, motivation, and idea generation [10]. *Photocopylore* is a typical office phenomenon enabled by technology, where folklore-style humor is printed[1] out and displayed or passed between individuals [7]. Workers use it to exercise creativity and it can be a part of social processes such as boundary crossing and community-forming [7]. We found that workers display a range of such material on their noticeboards, including both work-related humor (e.g. jokes about programming) and more generic humor (e.g. popular comic strips). Some occupants also *elaborated* on photocopylore – inking onto it their own additions (Figure 2c). Once put up, these printed items have long life-times, and eventually become a form of permanent decoration. Jokes are also sometimes handwritten, but this is less common.

Playful content

Playful content differs from humor in that it is not necessarily designed to make someone laugh, but rather provide light-hearted amusement and distraction in what can sometimes be a serious environment. These often involve inked sketches, and can sometimes accompany messages of a different category, e.g. drawings of Chinese New Year festivities accompanying a notice of absence (Figure 2a). These represent semi-permanent personalizations of the workplace. Workers personalize their environment to express their identity and individuality, and make the workplace more pleasing to inhabit. Research has shown that personalization is significantly associated with work environment satisfaction [14].

Non-noticeboard displayed content

A small plate that displays occupant names is embedded in each office door. Some office occupants also decorated this with pictures of themselves or other sentimental material. We discovered the larger shared whiteboards in the group exhibited two further types of content: advertisments promoting work related to a group member, and work-related content, e.g. maths and sketches used to explain a geometric concept.

Resulting design choices

The flexibility of non-digital noticeboards enables them to support a variety of uses. Rather than implement a set of rigid and disjoint noticeboard applications, we should rather attempt to replicate and extend this flexibility. Inking gives users freedom in the level of expression and abstraction they use in their messages – rather than have an application display the detailed contents of someone's online calendar, people can instead leave more discreet messages to control personal information.

It is also apparent that group members value the creativity and aesthetics of what they choose to display. Though some messages could be simply posted as text, they instead choose more expressive approaches including sketches and drawings. This can also be seen in the printed photocopylore they put on display, especially for items left up for long periods of time. We should therefore aim to improve the expressivenes of inking, without making it overly complex, and make it easier for people to post images.

Notices of absence were the most frequently left type of message. Allowing some form of remote access is therefore important since it can sometimes be inconvenient or even impossible to post a notice of absence in person.

[1] Before printers became commonplace, photocopiers were used.

(a) A group member inking a message using a system prototype. (b) Prototypes were driven by rear-mounted Raspberry Pi computers.

Figure 3: We conducted a prototype system deployment to gague interest and assess user-acceptance.

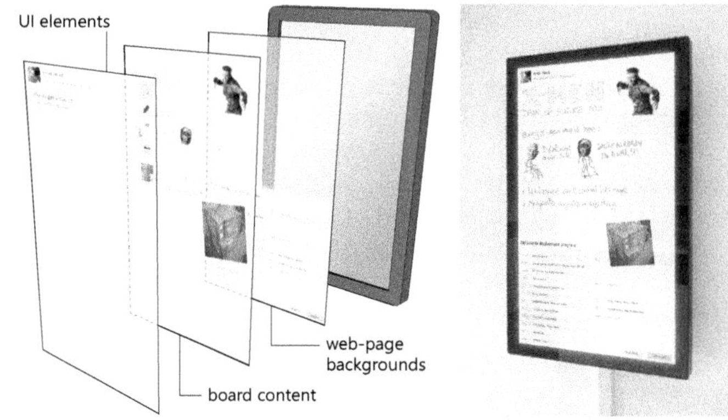

Figure 4: NetBoards display layers: UI elements (controls and office occupant details), board content (inked items and raster images), and optional web-page backgrounds.

PROTOTYPE DEPLOYMENT

When experimenting with large collections of expensive hardware, iterative cycles of design, development, deployment, and observation are critical in ensuring the system fulfils its goals and ends up being well-received.

We deployed five prototypes to gauge the acceptance of digital noticeboards and determine their typical use patterns. We chose a representative demographic of PhD students, post-docs, and a professor to see how different group members would use their display. Each board consisted of a 22-inch touchscreen powered by a Raspberry Pi (700MHz processor, 512MB RAM)[2]. Users could ink messages and sketches using their hands, add pictures using a web-interface, and set up web-pages to appear as a background. Following observations of prototype use, we re-implemented the system with improved software and superior hardware.

Prototype observations

The large displays lining the corridor caught the attention of passers-by frequently, and often piqued their curiosity enough for them to spontaneously interact with the screens and enter discussion with their owners. By generating excitement, the system overcomes major thresholds that can cause situated display system to fall into disuse [12]. However, various issues detracted from the prototype deployment.

We found that two important factors governed the acceptance and uptake of NetBoards prototypes: *dependability* – users will only bother to use a new digital system if they expect it to work; and *ease-of-use* – system adoption is unlikely if it is hard to use or requires much learning.

The prototype touchscreens were old models and operated using surface-acoustic-wave (SAW) technology. This meant users had to press harder on panels than they expected, and could not interact with the system accurately using their fingers. This lack of touch-accuracy influenced interface design choices that further affected ease-of-use – users had to switch between interface modes where they first wrote in large letters, and then shrunk messages down. This mode-switching became confusing and tedious, discouraging the types of spontaneous interaction we'd hoped for. These SAW panels cannot register multiple touch-points, so we could not support typical multi-touch interaction techniques and gestures that users are used to, e.g. pinch to scale and translate. We therefore decided to use superior capacitive multi-touch panels for the current installation.

While the Raspberry Pi's low price and power requirements make it ideal for large scale deployments, we found its limited computational resources were insufficient for a responsive and feature-rich inking interface, making them frustrating to use. We also experienced intermittent hardware failure following long periods of uptime. A robust hardware and software framework is critical for a system to be deemed dependable enough for daily use. We therefore decided to upgrade to more powerful and reliable PC systems.

THE NETBOARDS SYSTEM

Each NetBoard is a 22-inch portrait-oriented wall-mounted touchscreen (capacitive multi-touch, 1080×1920 px.) driven by a PC (Windows 8.1, 3.40 GHz processor, 4Gb RAM). Each PC drives two NetBoards. There are currently nine NetBoards deployed over the corridor, shared between seventeen people. As shown in Figure 4, each display consists of three layers: *UI elements* with interface widgets and details of office occupants; a *board content* layer contains inked messages, sketches, and raster images; and optional *web-page backgrounds* that can display any web-page chosen by the user. NetBoards can also be viewed and edited using web-apps, so can be accessed remotely or by desktop computers.

NetBoard displays are split up vertically between separate occupants in shared offices, showing a profile picture, name, and description for each individual. This approach was influenced by existing practices (Figure 2a), and resolves potential author ambiguity issues.

Creating content

Inking is the primary method of *board content* creation – users can write or draw on NetBoards using their hands (finger painting) or a passive stylus. As is typical for inking applications, users can choose between a range of different colours

[2]Raspberry Pi – **www.raspberrypi.org** (accessed 27/06/14)

Figure 5: Remote inking may be inconvenient, so users can write a short text *status* to share contextual information.

and pen thicknesses. Inked strokes are stored as vector paths which are optimized and simplified to reduce memory usage and speed up rendering. When editing remotely, users can ink with a mouse or active stylus. When editing from a desktop machine, users can also drag and drop images from their PC or a web browser into their NetBoard– this fulfils the role of printing and sticking.

Modifying content

One of our aims is to improve upon the flexibility of non-digital noticeboards, and let users express themselves in better ways. Non-digital noticeboards allow few methods for modification once content has been created. Non-digital inked content cannot be moved, and only be erased. Printed items may be moved and re-stuck elsewhere (this was never observed in practice), but cannot be resized.

Instead we allow greater freedom of expression by implementing a range of typical content modification techniques. These include content re-ordering and multi-touch gestures for translation, rotation, and resizing. Users can easily reorganize and decorate their board using these familiar interaction techniques. While before their content was limited by how small they could write, users can now selectively adjust the saliency of items based on age and importance. The web-apps also support typical mouse-based editing techniques.

Secondary features

As well as implementing digital equivalents of non-digital interaction techniques, we included additional features to make editing easier and extend system flexibility. Instead of inking handwritten messages, users can set up a short text message *status* for display using web-apps, e.g. "Out for a haircut 11am". They can also set a *duration* for each status, after which the status will be removed. This avoids confusion arising from stale messages. Inking a notice of absence remotely on a small device might be challenging, so users can type short status messages instead (Figure 5).

Some previous works have implemented numerous disjoint applications or modules for peripheral situated workplace displays [8, 11]. Instead we let users choose a web-page for display behind their board content. This decision was made considering the technical nature of the group – most members have the skills to write their own scripts and web-pages for

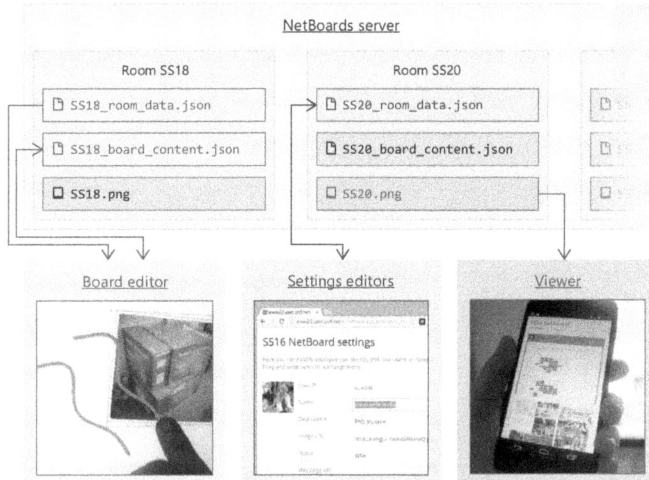

Figure 6: Our client-server architecture. *Board editors* load room data, and update content data following changes. *Settings editors* update room data, e.g. user details. Lightweight *viewer* clients download an image only.

custom content. This allows users finer grained control over what they choose to display, though it requires additional effort on their part.

Underlying architecture

We chose to implement NetBoards using web-based technologies. Mobile phones and tablet computers have become ubiquitous, and it is important to let users access the system regardless of their chosen device. Web-apps allow instant and remote interaction without the hassles of installation or software updates, and function across a range of devices.

Each wall-mounted NetBoards installation runs a web-browser in *kiosk-mode* – a full-screen mode that prevents users from tampering with the machines. Scripts and a custom written browser plugin are configured to load and initialize NetBoards on PC startup. Users create and modify content using a web-app editor. Inked content and pictures are processed by *Paper.js*[3], a vector graphics scripting framework for the HTML5 Canvas element.

Data storage and synchronization

NetBoards allows users to view and edit content remotely, so data must be synchronized across distributed devices. When a user modifies NetBoard content, the inked vector paths and raster images are exported to JSON and uploaded to our server. This file can then be parsed by Paper.js for display in most web-browsers. We use Lamport timestamps with file version numbers to determine a partial order of content updates with minimal overhead [9]. While this cannot handle multi-user real-time editing, it was deemed sufficient considering the asynchronous nature of communication.

Portable devices generally have lower computation resources than NetBoards installations and desktop machines, so it may

[3]PaperJs – **http://paperjs.org/** (accessed 27/06/14)

(a) A NetBoard movie review. Collaborative comments made by visitors are highlighted (yellow).

(b) A weekly schedule showing office occupant availability, and photos from a recent vacation.

(c) Notices of absence and playful sketches on a NetBoard shared by four occupants.

(d) Showcased research (green). A visitor jokes that the equipment resembles a "nose-picker" (yellow).

Figure 7: Screen captures from several NetBoards installations. Items of note, e.g. NetBoard visitor comments, are highlighted.

not be desirable to load Javascript libraries and render complex vector paths on-the-go. We therefore periodically render each NetBoard as a raster image server-side using PhantomJS – a WebKit layout and rendering engine[4]. These can be displayed natively on mobile devices. Each office's NetBoard also has associated *room data*. This includes occupant names, descriptions, profile pictures, and statuses. These are modified using simple web forms.

USER EXPERIENCES

NetBoards has been in use, though under continuous development, for a number of months. We have collected qualitative data about its use via informal feedback and interviews, and recorded snapshot data from the NetBoards themselves whenever changes were made. We summarize our observations in the following section.

NetBoards attract attention

NetBoards captures the attention of existing department members and visitors alike as they pass by, and they often enter discussion with group members about the system itself. Office occupants notice when passers-by pay attention to their NetBoard, particularly if they stop to examine it. This encourages them to decorate their board further, e.g. if an office occupant notices a passer-by enjoying a funny image they have put on display, they feel encouraged to share more humuorous content in the future.

NetBoards support awareness

Users frequently need to notify their colleagues about absences and often use their NetBoard to do so, either by inking messages (Figure 7c) or by setting a text status. They value being able to do this remotely and independently – without having to contact someone in the corridor to write a message for them. In this way NetBoards provides an improved mechanism for supporting group awareness and sharing knowledge of people's contexts and activities.

As well as simple notices of absence, one user written their own background webpage to display a weekly "diary" showing when they are busy or free (Figure 7b). To maintain privacy, they do not disclose the nature of appointments, just their own availability. Being one of group's senior members, they are often sought by students for discussion, so this displayed schedule information assists group members in scheduling communication and collaboration.

Images and pictures are popular decorations

Personalization and self-expression are psychologically important mechanisms that make places more pleasing to inhabit, help workers cope with stress by relaxing and inspiring them, and convey individuality [14]. As expected, images have become popular NetBoards decorations, ranging from funny comics (Figure 7d) to vacation photos (Figure 7b). When a pair of PhD students went abroad for a conference, they remotely updated their NetBoard almost daily with photo updates of research, culture, and social events. While printed items eventually became stale, NetBoard images experience frequent turn-over. Users sometimes annotate images, or ink elaborations onto them (Figure 7a).

People collaboratively decorate NetBoards

In the past people generally only wrote or sketched on their own non-digital noticeboards. However, group members and visitors now often edit or decorate each-others noticeboards in a playful manner. As shown in Figure 7a, one user put

[4]PhantomJS – `http://phantomjs.org/` (accessed 27/06/14)

together a review of a recent movie using a collage of pictures and inked bullet points – lists of "pros" and "cons". Other group members then added further bullet points to share their own opinions.

NetBoards are used to showcase work

Our research group frequently has visitors, and the NetBoards system often captures their attention as they tour offices in the corridor. One group member embedded a looped video of his current research as his NetBoard's background-webpage, as well as images of his custom-built research hardware (Figure 7d). NetBoards provides an ideal platform to passively and subtly introduce research to passers-by, potentially leading to resulting discussion.

FUTURE WORK

Though our early experiences with the system suggest it is valuable to group members, we are planning a longitudinal study to track the system's use and reception over time. A logging system will record how often people remotely view and modify NetBoard instances – this will give us a better idea of how well the system supports and enhances group awareness. We will also record data about individual changes to board content, revealing how people use inking and images for communication and decoration. Quantitative data can suggest courses of qualitative investigation, so we plan to conduct a series of further interviews and questionnaires.

We will continue to improve dependability and ease-of-use. Like all distributed systems, NetBoards will always be prone to network and hardware failures. The current course of action involves manual intervention so a more autonomous solution is preferred. Though choosing web-based technologies has many benefits, it leads to several challenges. One user wants to show off their research with webcam-based computer vision demos on their NetBoard, so we are looking for a way to support traditional PC applications in the system.

We are also keen to expand NetBoards's deployment elsewhere, and have had many requests to do so. Research has shown that different research groups use ubiquitous technologies in very different ways [4], and we would like to explore how use patterns change depending on the nature of co-located groups' projects and collaboration.

CONCLUSIONS

We have described the motivation, design, and early observations of NetBoards, showing how its flexibility enables a range of uses from communicating group awareness to workplace personalization and decoration. The system is still evolving with constant user feedback and feature requests, so we plan to continue our cycle of iterative re-design, deployment, and observation. We hope that others can learn from our experiences, and be inspired to deploy NetBoards or experiment with their own similar systems in different contexts.

REFERENCES

1. Cheverst, K., Taher, F., Fisher, M., Fitton, D., and Taylor, N. The design, deployment and evaluation of situated display-based systems to support coordination and community. In *Ubiquitous Display Environments*. Springer, 2012, 105–124.
2. Churchill, E. F., Nelson, L., Denoue, L., Helfman, J., and Murphy, P. Sharing multimedia content with interactive public displays: a case study. In *Proc. 5th conf. on Designing interactive systems*, ACM (2004).
3. Fass, A., Forlizzi, J., and Pausch, R. Messydesk and messyboard: two designs inspired by the goal of improving human memory. In *Proc. 4th conference on Designing interactive systems: processes, practices, methods, and techniques*, ACM (2002).
4. Fass, A. M. Messyboard: Lowering the cost of communication and making it more enjoyable. Tech. rep., DTIC Document, 2005.
5. Fitton, D., and Cheverst, K. Experiences managing and maintaining a collection of interactive office door displays. In *Ambient Intelligence*. Springer, 2003.
6. Greenberg, S., and Rounding, M. The notification collage: posting information to public and personal displays. In *Proc. SIGCHI conference on Human factors in computing systems*, ACM (2001).
7. Hatch, M. J., and Jones, M. O. Photocopylore at work: Aesthetics, collective creativity and the social construction of organizations. *Studies in Cultures, Organizations and Societies 3*, 2 (1997), 263–287.
8. Huang, E. M., and Mynatt, E. D. Semi-public displays for small, co-located groups. In *Proceedings of the SIGCHI conference on Human factors in computing systems*, ACM (2003), 49–56.
9. Lamport, L. Time, clocks, and the ordering of events in a distributed system. *Communications of the ACM 21*, 7 (1978), 558–565.
10. Lyttle, J. The judicious use and management of humor in the workplace. *Business Horizons 50*, 3 (2007).
11. McCarthy, J. F., Costa, T. J., and Liongosari, E. S. Unicast, outcast & groupcast: Three steps toward ubiquitous, peripheral displays. In *Ubicomp 2001: Ubiquitous Computing*, Springer (2001), 332–345.
12. Müller, J., Alt, F., Michelis, D., and Schmidt, A. Requirements and design space for interactive public displays. In *Proceedings of the international conference on Multimedia*, ACM (2010), 1285–1294.
13. Nguyen, D. H., Tullio, J., Drewes, T., and Mynatt, E. D. Dynamic door displays.
14. Wells, M. M. Office clutter or meaningful personal displays: The role of office personalization in employee and organizational well-being. *Journal of Environmental Psychology 20*, 3 (2000), 239–255.
15. Wood, E. Netboards. `http://www.cl.cam.ac.uk/research/rainbow/projects/netboards/`, 2014.

Supporting Situation Awareness in Collaborative Tabletop Systems with Automation

Y.-L. Betty Chang[1,3], Stacey D. Scott[1,3], Mark Hancock[2,3]
[1]Systems Design Engineering, [2]Department of Management Sciences, [3]Games Institute
University of Waterloo, Waterloo, Ontario, Canada
{betty.chang|stacey.scott|mark.hancock}@uwaterloo.ca

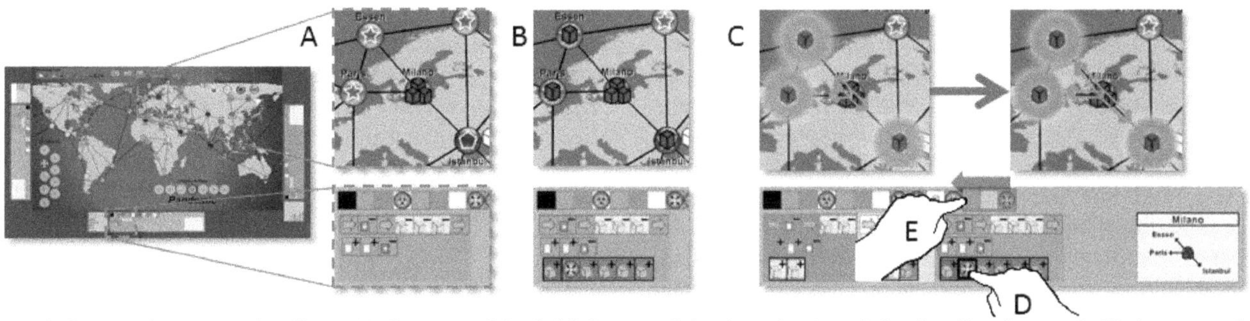

Figure 1: Interactive event timelines. A) Cut-out of the initial state of the data (top) and the timeline (bottom). B) Automated system changes appear (top) and are reflected in the timeline (bottom). C) & D) Touching the timeline invokes a replay of the changes (top, left to right) and details at the right of the specific event. E) A slider can be used to navigate through all past events (bottom).

ABSTRACT
Human operators collaborating to complete complex tasks, such as a team of emergency response operators, need to maintain a high level of situation awareness to appropriately and quickly respond to critical changes. Even though automation can help manage complex tasks and rapidly update information, it may create confusion that negatively impacts operators' situation awareness, and result in sub-optimal decisions. To improve situation awareness in co-located environments on digital tabletop computers, we developed an interactive event timeline that enables exploration of historical system events, using a collaborative digital board game as a case study. We conducted a user study to examine two factors, placement of timelines for multiple users and location of awareness feedback, to understand their impact on situation awareness. The study revealed that interaction with the timeline was correlated with improved situation awareness, and that displaying feedback both on the game board and timeline was the most preferred.

Author Keywords
Digital tabletop; gaming; automation; situation awareness; interaction design; collaboration

ACM Classification Keywords
H.5.2. User Interfaces.

ACM 978-1-4503-2587-5/14/11...$15.00.
http://dx.doi.org/10.1145/2669485.2669496

INTRODUCTION
There is growing interest in using digital tabletops to support co-located group activities that involve complex, often dynamically changing data. Tabletop interfaces have been proposed for crisis and disaster management [7,29], military simulation [2], and military and commercial maritime operations [6,36]. In these complex domains, decision-makers need to maintain a high level of awareness of changing system data to respond quickly, with appropriate strategies. However, when changes occur in these environments, human operators may become confused by the system state, leaving them "out-of-the-loop" [9] and unable to respond appropriately when necessary. As digital tabletop applications begin to leverage automation to manage complex data inherent to many real-world application domains, keeping users "in-the-loop" will become essential.

To address automatic changes and provide awareness of the current system state, we explored using interactive event timelines (Figure 1) to enable interactive exploration of system event history. We used a popular collaborative tabletop board game, *Pandemic*[1] (Figure 2, left), as a case

Figure 2: (Left) The physical Pandemic board game; and (Right) The digital Pandemic board game.

[1] Pandemic was published by Z-Man Games, used with permission. We implemented the digital tabletop game.

study to rapidly prototype design concepts, and to enable lab-based studies with a complex task for which "experts" could be easily recruited. Moreover, Pandemic has been shown to elicit the out-of-the-loop automation problem [42].

In this paper, we describe our interactive event timeline design, and a laboratory-based study to investigate design factors we hypothesized would impact the amount of timeline interaction and, consequently, impact participants' situation awareness. These two factors were timeline placement (i.e. one shared timeline per group or replicated timelines per individual) and feedback location (i.e. display feedback next to the timeline, in the shared area, or both locations). The study revealed that at the individual level, more interaction with the timeline correlated with higher situation awareness, and that individual replicated controls led to more interaction than shared controls. At the group level, aggregate situation awareness measures taken were consistently high across groups, despite more interaction by the "driver" when timelines were shared. This consistently high group situation awareness also suggests the success of our interactive timeline design.

We first present the related work, and discuss challenges in designing for digital tabletop systems with automation. We then present our conceptual design and our design factors, timeline placement and feedback location. Next, we introduce the Pandemic game case study and the design of the interactive timeline. We then present the study method and results. Finally, we discuss the implications of our findings.

RELATED WORK

There has been substantial research done in awareness [23], and our work specifically aims to improve the users' *situation awareness* and *workspace awareness* in a collaborative system with automation. Our work also relates to the specific area of *automation on digital tabletops*. This section provides an overview of and situates our work within the literature in these three areas.

Situation Awareness

Situation awareness describes operators' awareness of the environment, and has been applied to many domains, including air traffic control [38] and nuclear plant operation [3]. Endsley [12] defined situation awareness as the perception of changes in the system state (level 1), the comprehension of changes (level 2), and the prediction of future states (level 3). The second level of situation awareness requires the operators to connect multiple pieces of knowledge (level 1) to infer their meaning and form an understanding of the perceived changes, and the third level describes the ability to predict the future state of the system.

This automation literature has widely identified the phenomenon of *change blindness* as a key cause of deficient situation awareness in automated systems [8]. Change blindness refers to a person's inability to recognize changes in the environment after interruption or deviation in attention [32]. This phenomenon can be mitigated by the use of animation to guide users' attention to changes [4] and to help understand these changes [1]. However, users in collaborative tabletop systems may miss the animation completely due to interruption from a collaborator or the large size of the tabletop display.

The interruption recovery literature has explored the use of persistent, interactive information displays to mitigate change blindness and to rapidly improve situation awareness following an interruption. Interactive visual representations of historical event data have been found to help mitigate change blindness after interruptions, for example, using interactive event logs in tabular format [37] and interactive graphical event timelines [34].

Sasangohar et al. [34] found that interactive event timelines that allowed operators to highlight historical events on the main task display (a map) via event bookmarks displayed on a graphical timeline reduced recovery time and improved decision accuracy after interruptions. They argued that the interactive event timelines provided a "simplified representation of important events [that] facilitated the quick encoding of perceptual information and minimized the visual search" (p. 1155). On a large digital tabletop interface, promoting situation awareness while minimizing visual searches across the entire interface would be ideal. Thus, our work applies this interactive event timeline concept to digital tabletops with automation.

Workspace Awareness

Extensive research has shown the collaborative value and the information richness provided by the objects, people, and environment in co-located collaborative settings [17,19,31]. While situation awareness focuses on a person's knowledge of a system or environment state, the concept of workspace awareness describes a person's knowledge of their collaborators and their actions within a shared (physical or virtual) workspace [31].

In distributed settings, workspace awareness has been supported through techniques such as virtual embodiment (telepointers, virtual arms, avatars) [14,26,40]. Although a significant amount of workspace awareness information can be gained "for free" in a co-located tabletop setting, explicitly indicating others' actions in the shared workspace can also be beneficial, especially during complex tasks. For example, the Cambiera [20] collaborative document analysis system explicitly indicates when a teammate performs similar searches or opens the same documents.

The Cambiera design supports feedthrough, which refers to the information gathered from observing artifacts in the shared workspace [31]. With automation, the feedback for collaborators' actions can happen in an instant, and can prevent users from observing the changes. Our interactive event timelines were also designed to support feedthrough to facilitate workspace awareness.

Automation on Digital Tabletop Systems

There has been substantial tabletop research on interaction techniques for digital object manipulation, menu invocation, information sharing, and tangible interaction (e.g., [22,39,41,43]). In the collaborative tabletop space, significant work has been done on information visualization, coordination and collaboration styles, and the use of control widgets (e.g., [20,21,27]).As more sophisticated tabletop applications are developed for complex domains [2,6,7], situation awareness for automation becomes increasingly important. Yet, little previous work has studied dynamically changing data with historic events. Existing tabletop systems that incorporate dynamic data in a tabletop application provide little to no provision for viewing historical system data and focus on novel interfaces for sharing or collaborating with the current, real-time view of the system state [2,5,25,35].

DESIGNING TABLETOP SYSTEMS WITH AUTOMATION

Automation in traditional manufacturing settings refers to reducing manual workload with machines, or changing physical materials from one state to another [30]. Nowadays, automation is also used to reduce mental workload, and may involve the changing state of virtual objects. For example, a computer can sort an inventory list and present it in different views to support different task goals. Computer applications with automation can reduce mundane work and improve efficiency by delegating work based on the respective strengths of computers and humans. However, as described above, automation can negatively impact situation awareness, often due to change blindness or state changes not even being displayed to the human operator.

As illustrated in Figure 3A and Figure 3B, collaborators at a digital table can be unaware of a change occurring in the system interface due to a variety of distractions inherent to this environment, including other people or changes occurring across the large display. Moreover, even when a change occurs within a person's field of view they may still miss the change due to limited attentional capacity.

Conceptual Design

To address these issues introduced by the use of automation in a digital tabletop system, we explored the use of interactive event timelines, which provide persistent information about historical system events and fit into a person's field of view, despite the large size of the table. To update their awareness of the current system state, a person can examine and explore the timeline, which provides a high level overview of the system state (Figure 3C). To get more in-depth information, they can invoke further feedback on the shared display and their personal area (Figure 3D). We considered two key design factors in the design of these timelines:

Control Placement. With multiple people at the digital table, there are many choices about who and how the timeline can be controlled. Morris et al. [27] examined individual replicated versus shared centralized controls in a collaborative photo tagging application on digital tabletops. They found that while individual controls were more preferable, shared controls resulted in a higher level of collaboration. The event timeline is a control for invoking feedback, but is also a visualization of historical events. Thus, it was unclear how shared versus individual timelines would impact collaboration and situation awareness. Providing replicated timelines would ensure each person could view and manipulate the timeline. On the other hand, a shared timeline may contribute to improved collective situation awareness.

Feedback Location. When interacting with the timeline, detailed information about the events being explored can be displayed locally (on the timeline) or in the shared space. These alternatives may better facilitate either individual control or group function, respectively [15]. Displaying feedback on the timeline provides a consistent location to look for the information, and it fits into a person's field of view. Feedback in the shared space provides more contextual information to the individual and is also visible to the group. The latter approach may better facilitate feedthrough by using animation in the shared space to help individuals stay aware of group activities [31]. However, the size of the display may still necessitate searching for the feedback, and it may also distract others.

We investigated the impact of interactive event timelines, and of these two design factors, through a case study on improving situation awareness in a cooperative board game.

Figure 3: Problem of automation and conceptual design of the interactive event timeline. A) Some users are paying attention to each other and some to the tabletop display. Red arrows represent attention directed to. B) Data in the center changed and users are searching for the change. C) User explores the event timeline and D) interacts with the event timeline to locate changes.

CASE STUDY: TIMELINE DESIGN FOR PANDEMIC

We chose to situate our investigations in the context of the cooperative board game, *Pandemic*, for several reasons. Games allow for a more rapid, human-centred prototyping process, since it is easy to recruit subject matter experts of popular games and we can easily manipulate parameters, such as degree of difficulty. Previous work has shown that digital versions of the Pandemic game can elicit situation awareness deficiencies due to automation [42].Pandemic requires 3 to 4 players to engage in intense discussion on strategies and resource management (Figure 2, left). Players work as a team to save the world from epidemics and outbreaks of diseases. Players win by curing all the diseases, and lose if they run out of time (not having enough cards to draw from) or if the game state is out of control (too many outbreaks or diseases). Every turn, players carry out their strategies to manage the disease spread while making progress on cures. Then, players act as the game board (opponent) and draw cards to spread diseases.

Special events, called epidemics, happen repeatedly at random intervals to make the game more challenging. Outbreaks of diseases may also happen if the game state is out of control. It is important for players to stay aware of these critical events so they can effectively strategize.

Our custom-built digital tabletop version of Pandemic (Figure 2, right) provides automation to reduce manual workload and enforce rules. For example, the game automates opponent (the game board) actions by placing disease cubes based on cards drawn and resolving epidemic events. This involves several steps of drawing cards, shuffling a deck of cards, and placing disease cubes.

Interactive Event Timeline

We designed the interactive event timeline (Figure 4) to improve player awareness of the game's automated actions, and based our design on task analysis for experienced to expert players. It allows players to explore previous game events, including both player and computer actions. The timeline fits into a player's personal workspace and persists on the game board for players to interact with at any time.

The timeline consists of two main components: an *overview* (Figure 4C) and a *detail* view (Figure 4G). The overview provides a high level view of the game progression, and the detail view provides information for all the game actions that occurred during the selected turns.

The overview shows each player's turn in chronological order, colour-coded by the in-game player colour (orange, yellow, and white). Symbols on the overview denote special events (epidemic and outbreak) that happened during the particular turns. Players can drag the viewport (Figure 4F) or tap on a given player turn on the overview to navigate through the game history and reveal details of the turn of interest in the detail view. Dragging the viewport on the overview updates the detail view in real-time (Figure 1E).

The detail view contains the player turns currently selected (Figure 4G). Each turn consists of three rows corresponding

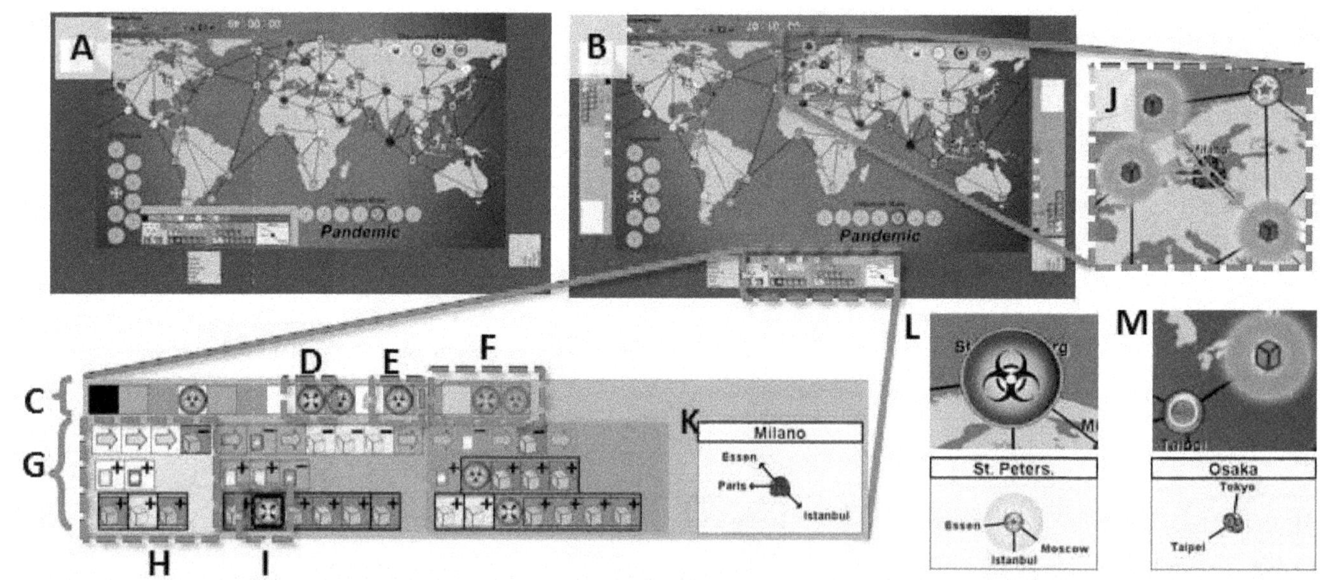

Figure 4: The interactive event timeline design. A) Shared timeline with both feedback locations. B) Individual timeline with both feedback locations. C) Overview showing the players' turns so far with symbols denoting important game events, such as D) outbreak and E) epidemic. F) Viewport for navigating through the game history. G) Detail view showing game events from the selected turns. H) A player's turn in the game, consisting of three rows. A row represents one phase in a player's turn, and an event block represents an action carried out by either the player or the game, black bounding boxes showing related game events (symbols denoting the type of the event e.g., arrow for moving to different cities, bottle for discovering a cure, and +/- for adding or removing game pieces). I) Selected event will have a black bounding box and J) animation in the center and K) information near timeline will be shown. Different events have different feedback, J) and K) for an outbreak event, L) for an epidemic event, and M) for an infection event (plus cube symbol on timeline).

to the three phases in the game (Figure 4H). The first row represents player actions. The second and third rows represent two types of automated actions: cards drawn for players and cities infected. Each block represents one game event (Figure 4I) with a symbol denoting the type of event. Related blocks are grouped by a black bounding box. The colour of each block is derived from the colour coding scheme used in the Pandemic board game. The timeline provides a compact summary for game events. The game event blocks are also interactive. When a game event block is selected, additional information is displayed on the shared game board and/or next to the timeline.

We designed these timelines to study our research question of interest: how do the placement of the timeline control (individual or shared) and the location of the feedback it provides (on the game board or next to the timeline) affect each player's, and the group's, situation awareness?

STUDY

We conducted a laboratory-based study to examine the feedback location and control placement factors. Participants played different implementations of the Pandemic game and answered questions on their knowledge of the board game state to test their situation awareness.

Participants

Participants were recruited from the local community, specifically targeting experienced Pandemic players. Players had to sign up in groups of three. Thirty-six paid participants (23 male, 13 female, ages 22 to 36) were recruited, with all team members having previous experience playing Pandemic prior to the study. The gender ratio likely reflected the population of local Pandemic players.

Design

We used a 2 control placement (between) × 3 feedback location (within) mixed design. The order of the three feedback locations (next-to-timeline, on-board, and both) was counterbalanced, with half using a single shared control and half using replicated individual controls.

Equipment & Setting

Each group of participants was seated in the lab around a 95 × 148 cm (3840 × 2160 pixel) digital table with an embedded PQ Labs frame to detect touches. Two participants sat at the short edge, and one participant at the long edge, to avoid the situation of one participant seeing the game board upside down (Figure 2, right). The computer was running 64-bit Windows 7 using on Intel® Xeon® CPU E5-1603 @ 2.80 GHz with 4 GB of RAM. Two digital camcorders were placed at different angles to capture the game sessions.

Questionnaires

We measured the players' situation awareness, gaming experience, workload, and general preference in each condition. There were two types of questionnaires. The first was a gameplay questionnaire, which consisted of PENS [33] for player experience, NASA-TLX [16] for workload, and questions on their awareness and teamwork.

The second was a situation awareness (SA) questionnaire. To develop SA questions, we followed the steps outlined in the SAGAT methodology [10,13] by first defining the goal of the game (i.e., win by discovering four cures). Then we identified the sub-goals (e.g., keep diseases under control to allow time for collecting cards) and decisions to be made to achieve them (e.g., determining the top priority cities to treat next turn). Knowledge needed to make these decisions was then defined (e.g., disease distribution and infections coming up). We created an initial set of 22 SA questions.

Three researchers then independently classified the SA questions into three levels of situation awareness (SA1–SA3) as defined by Endsley [11]. The three raters agreed on thirteen questions (inter-rater reliability (Fleiss' Kappa) = .54, $p<.001$), and the remaining questions were discussed to determine their classification and iterated until consensus was reached. Through this process, additional three questions were derived, and we have a total of 25 questions (13 SA1, 7 SA2, and 5 SA3). Because 6 unique questions were required for each SA level (3 sets of 2 questions per SA level), two researchers devised one final SA3 question. Questions were in the form: "name one city/colour/player that...", or "estimate the number of turns away from...". For example, "Name one city that was just infected last turn." (SA1), "Name one set of cities (if any) that may create a chained outbreak." (SA2), and "Which colour is at the top priority for the current game state?" (SA3).

We conducted four pilot studies. The pilot participants confirmed that the questionnaires required intense thinking but that the questions were clear.

Procedure

The study sessions lasted approximately 2.5 to 3 hours. Participants first completed consent forms and background questionnaires. There were three parts to the study: training, Pandemic challenges, and a playthrough of a full game.

Training

After the researcher explained the interface, participants played with no timeline for 10 minutes and completed the gameplay questionnaire. Then, with the same procedure, participants practiced on the same version they would see in the first condition given in the Pandemic challenge phase.

Pandemic Challenges

For each condition, participants started in the middle of a Pandemic game and played for 2 rounds (2 turns for each player). We constructed 3 initial game states (scenarios) from real gameplay with some controlled parameters, such as the number of critical events that happened and the number of cures discovered. The order of the initial game states was randomly chosen.

Players individually completed post-condition questionnaires, which consisted of both the gameplay and the situation awareness (SA) questionnaires. The order of the three SA questionnaires (discussed above) was randomly selected. The same set of initial game states and SA questions were used across all groups. Participants completed a preference questionnaire at the end of this phase.

Full Game

In this final phase, participants played a full game with a configurable version, in which players could freely open up to three timelines that could be moved anywhere on the tabletop. They could minimize and reopen these timelines at any time. Each timeline allowed players to indicate where the feedback generated by that specific timeline was displayed (next-to-timeline, on-board, or both) via toggle widgets at the top of the timeline. All groups had the same game setup. Participants completed the gameplay questionnaire with a free form area for comments after playing.

Finally, the researcher debriefed the participants with the goal and details of the study, and conducted an unstructured interview to receive any additional feedback.

Data Collection & Analysis

During gameplay, we collected various data, including video recordings from two different angles, screen recordings, computer logs, audio recordings, and questionnaires. From the computer logs, we extracted player interactions with timelines. Two types of touch events were captured: *navigation*, when participants explored different turns by dragging the viewport or tapping the overview (Figure 4C), and *invocation of detail*, when participants tapped or brushed game cubes in the detail view (Figure 4G). The situation awareness questionnaire results were scored as optimal (1), sub-optimal (0.5), and incorrect (0) for each question.

Following the experiment, one SA question was reclassified from SA2 to SA3, since participants uniformly interpreted the question differently than intended. Specifically, participants were asked to name the colour that requires the most attention now, which we intended to be the colour with the fewest remaining cubes, (i.e., comprehension of changes, SA2), but participants interpreted this as the colour that would likely be depleted in the upcoming few turns (i.e., forecasting, SA3). Two other questions were also dropped completely due to potential misinterpretation. One question asked players to estimate the number of turns until the next epidemic game event, but none of the participants received the "optimal" score and 32 players (88.9%) were incorrect. This likely occurred due to observed distrust of the automation: comments during the study and on questionnaires indicated a belief that the computer was intentionally making the game more difficult when shuffling and triggering epidemic game events, resulting in an unrealistically pessimistic outlook of the situation. The second dropped question contained an error, which referred to the wrong game phase, and it was unclear how the participants may have interpreted it. The questionnaire in our final analysis nonetheless had an even spread of questions across SA levels (6 in SA1, 5 in SA2, and 5 in SA3).

We analyzed the situation awareness questionnaires using a 2 (control placement) × 3 (feedback location) repeated measures analysis of variance (RM-ANOVA). Since the SA score is computed by the average of each questionnaire, this measure is interval data, which is most appropriately analyzed by a parametric test, such as ANOVA [28]. An intraclass correlation analysis showed that situation awareness scores of the participants in the same group correlate ($ICC_{2,3}$=.66, p=.02), so we have included group as a covariate when the data is analyzed at the individual participant level. A first-order partial correlation controlling for group effects was used to test the relationship between situation awareness scores and interaction count. When relevant, scenario order and SA questionnaire order were included as between-participants covariates to mitigate order effects.

RESULTS

Our analysis revealed that participants used the timeline to understand the automation results and, in general, found the timeline beneficial. In terms of control placement, we found that the amount of player interaction with the timeline positively correlated with situation awareness score. In terms of feedback location, players preferred when feedback was in both places. Groups did well overall and there was no difference in cross-group situation awareness scores (all high). We detail these results for the *purpose of interaction*, *control placement*, *feedback location*, and *group interaction*.

Purpose of Interaction

Players interacted with the timeline to discover the results of automation and to review other players' actions. Figure 5 shows traces of interaction for all participant trials with *individual* controls and feedback in *both* locations. Most interaction occurred at the bottom-left corner, where the latest automation results were displayed (since the timeline auto-scrolls to the new turn). This shows that players frequently used the timeline to understand automated computer actions, as confirmed by the comment, *"I mainly used*

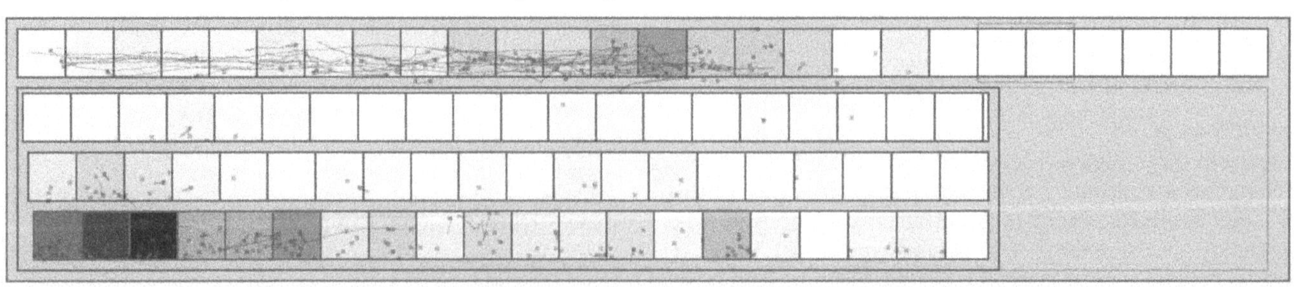

Figure 5: Aggregate traces of player interaction (points=touch down, lines=touch move) for individual control placement and feedback on both. Cells (game event cubes) are shaded by interaction count (darker = higher).

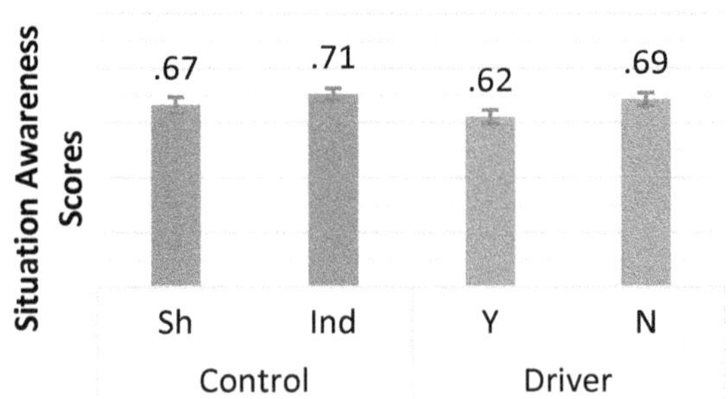

Figure 6: Mean situation awareness scores for shared and individual controls (left) and drivers vs. non-drivers in the shared condition (right).

the game log to identify the individual cities that were infected when I missed the on-board animations" (P35).

Overall, players found the timeline beneficial for reviewing previous turns and strategy formation, as evidenced by the comments, *"It was really fun to move it and show people what I was talking about while feeling like I was in the Matrix." (P25)*, and *"It allowed us to look back at the previous moves to determine the best move." (P26).*

Control Placement

We examined the differences across control placement to see its impact on situation awareness.

Situation Awareness and Interaction Count

The RM-ANOVA on the awareness score revealed a main effect of control placement ($F_{1,28} = 4.7$, $p = .04$, Figure 6, left). On average, players with *shared* controls had lower situation awareness scores than players with *individual* controls. This result suggests that players with individual timelines have better situation awareness. The RM-ANOVA on timeline interaction also revealed a significant main effect of control placement ($F_{1,10} = 6.2$, $p = .03$, Figure 7, left), where participants with *shared* controls used the timeline significantly less, suggesting that individual timelines encouraged greater interaction.

A partial correlation analysis on timeline interaction and SA score (control for group) revealed a positive correlation ($r_{105} = .20$, $p = .04$). This result matched our expectation that more interaction with the timeline would lead to higher situation awareness. This result also confirms that the timeline may be beneficial for improving situation awareness.

Feedback Location

The RM-ANOVAs on awareness score and interaction count revealed no significant main effects or interactions involving feedback location. However, we observed differences in participants' usage and reported preferences.

When feedback was located *next-to-timeline*, it allowed close proximity between their fingers and the feedback, which provided quick and easy navigation across multiple game events (commented by six players). This was confirmed by the comments, *"having the information close to where I placed my finger was most convenient," (P22)*, and

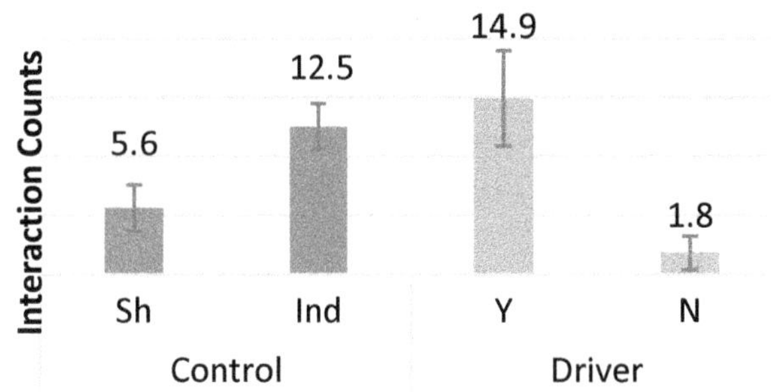

Figure 7: Mean interaction counts for shared and individual controls (left), and drivers vs. non-drivers in the shared condition (right).

"I was able to quickly flip through them [game events] without having to take my eyes off the game log box [with the next-to-timeline feedback]." (P4) Yet, seven participants identified the main drawback being the lack of context and disconnection between the timeline and the game, as evidenced by the comment, *"having information only in the log (timeline) lacks the direct feedback of having information available on the board." (P8).*

When feedback was *on-board*, six players commented that it provided greater awareness of surrounding cities and gave more contexts to a particular game event. However, 58% of the participants ranked it as their least favourite condition, likely because of the large surface (3 players) and the difficulty in visually searching for the feedback (8 players). This trade-off was summarized by the comment, *"the highlights gave geographic context while taking longer to locate." (P3).* Moreover, there was confusion over who triggered the animation (commented by 6 players), as indicated in the comments, *"on the game board makes things clearer, where people are in relation to the site in question, etc, but gets distracting when three different people are querying." (P33)*, and, *"When displaying information on the game board it was occasionally confusing if it was someone triggering log information or a game action taking place." (P8).* This confusion impacted the players' decisions about where the feedback should appear when playing the configurable version, as illustrated in an excerpt from one group's configurable game play session:

```
P14 (Middle): [Touched timeline, and Bogota
    was highlighted]
P15 (Left): Hey Bogota just outbroke! [Real-
    ized that it was P14] Oh no, you are
    just smashing things. I hate you! I hate
    the board thing! Turn your board off,
    please!
P14 (Middle): Alright [laughed and turned off
    the on-board feedback].
P15 (Left): Inform us when you are going to
    turn it on; otherwise, I go, 'oh no Bo-
    gota just outbroke!'
P13 (Right): It's kinda funny, but I also
    found it distracting when people do it.
P15 (Left): It's okay as long as you tell
    people you are doing it.
```

Feedback in *both* places was ranked as the favorite setup for 81% of the players. This provided the best of both worlds, with duplicate information, with both quick navigation and geographical context, as confirmed by the comments:

> *"The combination of the two allowed for both immediately accessible feedback as well as more information if needed." (P3)*,

> *"Information displayed on both the board and near the log was the most useful, since I could see information quickly while still seeing what area of the board was being affected." (P32)*, and

> *"Seeing the log [the information] in both the game log and the board makes it easier to see where future potential outbreaks could happen." (P23).*

We also ran an RM-ANOVA on the time spent per turn, calculated as the time between when the system finished automating events and played the animation to the time the next player made the first move, which revealed a significant main effect of feedback ($F_{2,20}=4.2$, $p=.03$). Post-hoc pairwise comparisons showed that players spent more time between each turn with *on-board* feedback than with feedback in *both* locations (p = .03). It appears that players spent more time searching and understanding the automation result with only on-board feedback.

Group Interaction

Observations during the study revealed that, as a group, situation awareness seemed to be very high, despite individuals having low situation awareness scores. We thus further investigated this phenomenon by analysing a group SA score. We also further investigated differences in SA scores and interaction counts between drivers and non-drivers when groups used a *shared* timeline versus *individuals* (all drivers) when each player had their own timeline.

Combined Situation Awareness

In addition to individual SA scores, we calculated a group SA score based on the maximum score from players in the same group for each question. We ran RM-ANOVA on this data, and found that the main effect of control placement was not significant ($F_{1,10}<0.1$, $p=.94$) nor was feedback location ($F_{2,20}=1.2$, $p=.33$). All groups scored high in situation awareness ($M=.87$, $SD=.06$).

Shared Interaction with the Timeline

When the control placement was *shared*, players interacted with the timeline as a group. Our observations revealed that one player was typically responsible for interacting with the timeline (*driver*), while the entire group was watching, narrating, and understanding the game together. Since drivers are the primary people interacting, they had a higher interaction count than the non-drivers. Figure 7 (right) illustrates interaction counts for drivers in *shared*, non-drivers in *shared*, and players in *individual*. Note that the drivers in *shared* have similar interaction count as the players in *individual* (Figure 7, left, Ind). The following excerpt illustrates how players narrate together while trying to understand the automation results with a *shared* timeline:

```
[After seeing an epidemic animation, players
    were discussing strategy]
P18 (Left): Is an epidemic due?
P17 (Middle): [Touched timeline on epidemic
    city] It's there [Epidemic animation
    played on the board @ Miami]
P18 (Left): Yeah
P17 (Middle): Then 3 more black [cubes].
    [Continued to touch the timeline]. Al-
    giers
All players: Karachi and Istanbul.
```

We performed a 3 feedback location × 2 player type RM-ANOVA on SA score, and the main effect of player type was not significant ($F_{1,5}=2.93$, $p=.15$), nor was the feedback location ($F_{2,10}=.15$, $p=.86$). This extends our earlier correlation between SA and interaction count, suggesting that interactions of drivers still led to higher awareness in non-drivers, and we thus believe that all group members were actively engaged in the process.

With *individual* timelines, participants tended to explore the results simultaneously or work together to understand the game state. The following excerpt illustrates players working together to understand automation results with *individual* timelines:

```
P22 (Right): Did Ho Chi Minh get hit as well?
    [Tapped on the Ho Chi Minh game event on
    P22's timeline] and what was the yellow
    one?
P23 (Middle): [Tapped on the yellow game
    event next to Ho Chi Minh on P23's time-
    line] Lima.
```

Figure 6 (right) illustrates the situation awareness for different categories of players. In terms of situation awareness, the drivers and non-drivers in the *shared* are not significantly different. However, players in *individual* have higher situation awareness than players in *shared*.

DISCUSSION

Our results showed that more interaction with event timelines can improve situation awareness, and suggests that we should design to promote this interaction. Although providing *shared* controls results in a process more similar to the physical game when resolving game events, *individual* controls allowed more and simultaneous interaction and resulted in higher situation awareness. The individual timelines allowed for a higher level of situation awareness without requiring the same amount of manual work needed on the physical board. This result suggests that we do not have to mimic real-world processes, but through interaction with timelines, we can improve situation awareness without requiring the same level of work.

Players' interactions with the timeline can be easily observed by their hand postures. When feedback is provided on the board, the results of interaction facilitated feedthrough. The results showed that the players sometimes were confused about whether an animation was initiated by the computer system or the collaborators, and they had to search for the feedback. While the feedback next to the timeline fits into a player's field of view, participants commented on the disconnection between the timeline and the game board. These results suggest that the timeline should more extensively incorporate the concept of feedthrough by making results clearer for both the individual and the group.

Overall, groups had a high level of situation awareness, in contrast to results from a previous study of a digital version of Pandemic [42] and from our training condition, both of which offered no mechanism for players to explore past events. This finding suggests that the timelines were effective in providing relevant historical game information. For both *shared* and *individual* control placements, players did not always interact with the timeline after each automation animation, and instead relied on other players interacting with the timeline and narrating game events. These results suggest that players can also benefit from other players' interactions with the timeline, providing evidence that players work together to achieve higher performance.

Study Limitations and Generalizability

As with any lab-based study, there are some limitations to the results. While our study has high precision, and we used a commercial board game to achieve higher realism, these decisions come at the cost of some generalizability [24]. Nonetheless, we think our findings are a useful addition to research into awareness in complex collaborative scenarios that involve automation, such as emergency response. Specifically, we chose Pandemic as the experimental task, both because it is representative of a highly popular commercial game genre, cooperative games, and because it emulates some key aspects of non-gaming tasks. Keeping track of and responding to the evolving game state places high cognitive demand on players, and success in the game depends on successful teamwork that utilizes the capabilities of different roles, as well as effective forecasting of future events and planning for future game moves. The game challenges players in their coordination, advanced planning, decision making, and resource management skills. Including only experienced Pandemic players also provided a realistic play scenario, which allows us to collect results that reflect the benefits and future improvements of timelines for expert use, without the need for extensive training.

CONCLUSION & FUTURE WORK

We presented an interactive event timeline that provided visualization of historical game events and allowed interaction to explore this history. We conducted a study to examine two factors, control placement and feedback location, to understand their impact on situation awareness. The results showed that having individual timelines for each player encouraged interaction with the timeline and improved situation awareness. Overall, groups had high situation awareness, which suggest that the timeline was useful.

In the future, we would like to explore ways to enhance the players' workspace awareness, to facilitate collaborative exploration of historical game events, and to support decision planning and making processes. Specifically, we want to improve the link between players' interactions with the timeline to the feedback on the game board so that players can easily understand the results of their interaction and collaborators can distinguish between events triggered by the system versus by other players. Another area for further study is the use of visualization algorithms [18] to simplify the generation of the event timeline for more generalizable use in other board game or non-gaming applications.

ACKNOWLEDGEMENT

The project was funded by Games Institute, GRAND, Leif exchange program, NSERC, NSERC SurfNet, and SSHRC IMMERSe. We thank Matt Leacock, Z-Man Games, Todor Doychev (digital game artwork adapted and modified for this research), and Mylène Mengual (animated highlights).

REFERENCES

1. Baudisch, P., Tan, D., Collomb, M., et al. Phosphor: explaining transitions in the user interface using afterglow effects. *UIST'06*, 169–178.
2. Bortolaso, C., Oskamp, M., Graham, T.C.N., et al. OrMiS: a tabletop interface for simulation-based training. *ITS '13*, 145–154.
3. Carvalho, P.V.R., dos Santos, I.L., and Vidal, M.C.R. Safety implications of cultural and cognitive issues in nuclear power plant operation. *Applied Ergonomics 37*, 2 (2006), 211–23.
4. Chang, B.-W. and Ungar, D. Animation: from cartoons to the user interface. *UIST '93*, 45–55.
5. Conversy, S., Gaspard-Boulinc, H., Chatty, S., et al. Supporting air traffic control collaboration with a tabletop system. *CSCW'11*, 425–434.
6. Domova, V., Vartiainen, E., Azhar, S., et al. An interactive surface solution to support collaborative work onboard ships. *ITS '13*, 265–272.
7. Döweling, S., Tahiri, T., Sowinski, P., et al. Support for collaborative situation analysis and planning in crisis management teams using interactive tabletops. *ITS '13*, 273–282.
8. Durlach, P.J. Change blindness and its implications for complex monitoring and control systems design and operator training. *HCI 19*, 4 (2009), 423–451.
9. Endsley, M.R. and Kiris, E.O. The out-of-the-loop performance problem and level of control in automation. *J. HFES 37*, 2 (1995), 381–394.
10. Endsley, M.R. Situation awareness global assessment technique (SAGAT). *IEEE National Aerospace and Electronics Conference*, (1988), 789–795.
11. Endsley, M.R. Design and evaluation for situation awareness enhancement. *HFES 32*, 2 (1988), 97–101.
12. Endsley, M.R. Toward a theory of situation awareness in dynamic systems. *J. HFES 37*, 1 (1995), 32–64.

13. Endsley, M.R. Direct Measurement of situation awareness : validity and use of SAGAT. In M.R. Endsley and D.J. Garland, eds., *Situation Awareness Analysis and Measurement*. Lawrence Erlbaum, Mahwah, NJ, 2000, 131–157.
14. Gutwin, C., Greenberg, S., and Roseman, M. Workspace awareness in real-time distributed groupware : framework , widgets , and evaluation. *Proc. HCI on People and Computers XI*, (1996), 281–298.
15. Gutwin, C. and Greenberg, S. Design for individuals , design for groups : tradeoffs between power and workspace awareness. *CSCW '98*, 207–216.
16. Hart, S.G. and Staveland, L.E. Development of NASA-TLX (Task Load Index): results of empirical and theoretical research. In P. Hancock and N. Meshkati, eds., *Human Mental Workload*. Amsterdam, North Holland, 1988, 139–183.
17. Heath, C. and Luff, P. Collaboration and control: crisis management and multimedia technology in London underground line control rooms. *CSCW 1*, 1-2 (1992), 69–94.
18. Humphrey, C.M. and Adams, J.A. General visualization abstraction algorithm for directable interfaces: component performance and learning effects. *IEEE Trans. on Sys. Man and Cybernetics -Part A: Systems and Humans 40*, 6 (2010), 1156–1167.
19. Hutchins, E. The technology of team navigation. In J. Galegher, R.E. Kraut and C. Egido, eds., *Intellectual Teamwork*. Lawrence Erlbaum, NJ, 1990, 191–220.
20. Isenberg, P. and Fisher, D. Collaborative brushing and linking for co-located visual analytics of document collections. *Computer Graphics Forum 28*, 3 (2009), 1031–1038.
21. Isenberg, P., Hinrichs, U., Hancock, M., et al. Digital tables for collaborative information exploration. In C. Müller-Tomfelde, ed., *Tabletops-Horizontal Interactive Displays*. Springer-Verlag, London, 2010, 387–405.
22. Kruger, R., Carpendale, S., Scott, S.D., et al. Fluid integration of rotation and translation. *CHI '05*, 601–610.
23. Markopoulos, P., Ruyter, B. de, and Mackay, W., eds. *Awareness Systems: Advances in Theory, Methodology and Design*. Springer-Verlag, London, 2009.
24. McGrath, J.E. *Groups: Interaction and Performance*. Prentice-Hall, Inc., Englewood Cliffs, NJ, 1984.
25. Micire, M., Desai, M., Courtemanche, A., et al. Analysis of natural gestures for controlling robot teams on multi-touch tabletop surfaces. *ITS '09*, 41–48.
26. Moore, R.J., Gathman, E.C.H., Ducheneaut, N., and Nickell, E. Coordinating joint activity in avatar-mediated interaction. *CHI '07*, 21–30.
27. Morris, M.R., Paepcke, A., Winograd, T.,et al. TeamTag: exploring centralized versus replicated controls for co-located tabletop groupware. *CHI '06*, 1273–1282.
28. Norman, G. Likert scales, levels of measurement and the "laws" of statistics. *Advances in Health Sciences Education 15*, 5 (2010), 625–632.
29. Paelke, V., Nebe, K., Geiger, C., et al. Designing multi-modal map-based interfaces for disaster management. *ACHI'12*, 95–100.
30. Parasuraman, R., Sheridan, T.B., and Wickens, C.D. A Model for types and levels of human interaction with automation. *IEEE Trans. on Sys. Man and Cybernetics - Part A: Systems and Humans 30*, 3 (2000), 286–297.
31. Pinelle, D., Gutwin, C., and Greenberg, S. Task analysis for groupware usability evaluation: modeling shared-workspace tasks with the mechanics of collaboration. *ACM Trans. on CHI 10*, 4 (2003), 281–311.
32. Rensink, R.A. Change blindness. In *McGraw-Hill Yearbook of Science & Technology*. McGraw-Hill, New York, 2005, 44–46.
33. Ryan, R.M., Rigby, C.S., and Przybylski, A. The motivational pull of video games: a self-determination theory approach. *Motivation and Emotion 30*, 4 (2006), 344–360.
34. Sasangohar, F., Scott, S.D., and Cummings, M.L. Supervisory-level interruption recovery in time-critical control tasks. *Applied Ergonomics 45*, 4 (2014), 1148–56.
35. Scott, S., Allavena, A., Cerar, K., et al. Investigating tabletop interfaces to support collaborative decision - making in maritime operations. *Int. Command and Control Research and Technology Symposium*, (2010).
36. Scott, S.D., Mercier, S., Cummings, M.L., et al. Assisting interruption recovery in supervisory control of multiple UAVs. *Proc.HFES* (2006), 699–703.
37. Smallman, H.S. and John, M. St. CHEX (Change History Explicit): new hci concepts for change awareness. *Proc. HFES* (2003), 528–532.
38. Smith, K. and Hancock, P.A. Situation awareness is adaptive, externally directed consciousness. *Human Factors 37*, 1 (1995), 137–148.
39. Spindler, M., Tominski, C., Schumann, H., et al. Tangible views for information visualization. *ITS '10*, 157–166.
40. Tuddenham, P. and Robinson, P. Territorial coordination and workspace awareness in remote tabletop collaboration. *CHI '09*, 2139–2148.
41. Voelker, S., Weiss, M., Wacharamanotham, C., and et al. Dynamic portals : a lightweight metaphor for fast object transfer on interactive surfaces. *ITS '11*, 158–161.
42. Wallace, J.R., Pape, J., Chang, Y.-L.B., et al. Exploring automation in digital tabletop board games. *CSCW Companion*, (2012), 231–234.
43. Yoshikawa, T., Shizuki, B., and Tanaka, J. Handywidgets : local widgets pulled-out from hands. *ITS '12*, 197–200.

An Empirical Characterization of Touch-Gesture Input-Force on Mobile Devices

Faisal Taher Jason Alexander John Hardy Eduardo Velloso
School of Computing and Communications, Lancaster University
Infolab21, Lancaster LA1 4WA
{f.taher, j.alexander, jhardy, e.velloso} @lancaster.ac.uk

ABSTRACT
Designers of force-sensitive user interfaces lack a ground-truth characterization of input force while performing common touch gestures (zooming, panning, tapping, and rotating). This paper provides such a characterization firstly by deriving baseline force profiles in a tightly-controlled user study; then by examining how these profiles vary in different conditions such as form factor (mobile phone and tablet), interaction position (walking and sitting) and urgency (timed tasks and untimed tasks). We conducted two user studies with 14 and 24 participants respectively and report: (1) force profile graphs that depict the force variations of common touch gestures, (2) the effect of the different conditions on force exerted and gesture completion time, (3) the most common forces that users apply, and the time taken to complete the gestures. This characterization is intended to aid the design of interactive devices that integrate force-input with common touch gestures in different conditions.

Author Keywords
Force sensing; characterization; touch screen gestures; mobile devices; force profiles.

ACM Classification Keywords
H.5.2. User Interfaces: Evaluation / Methodology.

General Terms
Human Factors; Design; Experimentation.

INTRODUCTION
Force plays an important role in our interactions with the surrounding environment, e.g. from carefully holding a newborn child, to vigorously opening the lid of an uncooperative food container. Force is also prevalent in artistic expression: pianists use force to amplify specific notes, and artists vary brush-stroke force to emphasize features in a painting. This routine application of varying force in everyday life has implications for the design of interactive systems. Interactive force sensitive devices already exist in gaming (e.g. PlayStation 3 controller), design (Wacom tablets), and music (e.g. electronic keyboards). Numerous research prototypes employ force sensors to augment existing devices such as mobile phones (e.g. [1, 11, 28]), keyboards and mice (e.g. [3, 5]), and develop novel techniques (e.g. Zliding [18]). For example, force input can be used to replace larger hand motions (e.g. flicking [11] on a touch screen device) with more subtle motions [25] such as pressing harder or softer on a button.

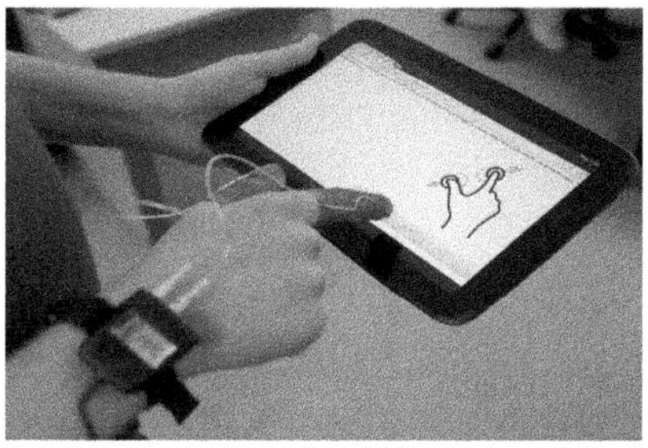

Figure 1: A study participant wearing the FingerTPS equipment performing a zooming-in task on a Nexus 10 tablet.

Despite the wide presence of numerous commercial and research-based force sensitive devices, we still lack a thorough understanding of the behavioral and quantifiable characteristics of force that users exert when carrying out common touch gestures (e.g. zooming into an image using a pinch gesture). This paper provides such a characterization for interactive mobile surfaces by: (1) presenting force profile graphs that illustrate high-level behaviours of touch gestures, (2) describing the effect of different conditions on force and time, and (3) providing the most common forces applied, and the time taken to complete the gestures.

This characterization benefits designers of interactive devices to integrate force as an input modality with standard touch gestures such as zooming, rotating, panning, tapping, and typing (as discussed in [13, 21]). Furthermore, our characterization informs the design of such systems in different conditions (or contexts of use). We believe that the prevalent use of touch gestures and the additional interaction dimension provided by force-input (e.g. [15]) can lead to novel and useful interaction techniques.

To develop this characterization, we conducted two lab-based user studies with 14 (8 male, 6 female) and 24 participants (12 male, 12 female) respectively. In both studies, participants wore the FingerTPS force sensing

ITS 2014, November 16–19, 2014, Dresden, Germany.

http://dx.doi.org/10.1145/2669485.2669515

finger gloves[1] (Figure 1) and completed a series of touch gestures (pinching, panning, tapping, typing, and rotating) on standard touch screen devices. The force sensors were included in the wearable equipment rather than integrating sensors into the devices in order to enable the findings to be generalizable across similar devices. The first study involved a single condition (i.e. seated, tablet and without time-pressure) with multiple repetitions of each gesture in order to derive baseline interaction force profiles. In the second study, participants completed the gestures under varying conditions (seated, walking, phone, tablet, urgent, non-urgent) in order to examine how these conditions affected the baseline force profiles.

RELATED WORK

Force input has been widely researched in the context of input/interaction techniques, ways of sensing force, and its application on interactive mobile surfaces. Force input, for instance, removes restrictions on screen real-estate by providing fine-grained control for interactions such as menu traversal [28]. Heo and Lee [9] suggest that using force is more natural compared to traditional touch screen interactions (e.g. multi-touch to flick a page of an e-book). Hwang et al. [11] state that force input can free users from repetitive movements (e.g. flicking) as well as free up the non-dominant hand [10, 26].

Force Input with Mobile Devices

Common force input tasks on mobile devices include menu-selection [27, 28], and text-entry [1, 4, 15]. Wilson et al. [28] experimented with menu-selection techniques such as *Dwell* (selecting an item by remaining at the target) and *Quick Release* [19]. Brewster and Hughes [1] designed a mobile keyboard which mapped soft and hard presses to lower and uppercase letters (removing the need for a shift-key). McCallum et al. [15] augmented the standard 12-button mobile keyboard to include force sensing up to four levels (soft press invokes first character, harder press second character, etc.). An evaluation of the prototype suggested that users would require more training (due to errors). In addition to text-entry, Clarkson et al. [4] also explored mapping force levels to scrolling and the navigation of 3D objects. Stewart et al. [25] investigate force interaction using one and two-sided mobile devices. The authors explore an iPhone Sandwich device [6] and found that force interaction in a mobile setting is preferable using the two-sided interaction paradigm (i.e. grasping the device with force sensors on the front and back).

Scott et al. [24] suggested more complex force interactions such as stretching, squeezing, bending, and twisting. With full screen deformations, such as those in the Gummi concept [23], not yet technologically possible, they explored minor deformations suitable for current LCD-displays. Their user study showed promising results for the twist and bend interactions with improved proficiency in task completion (e.g. map navigation, text entry) over time.

Holman and Hollatz [10] and Wilson et al. [26] experiment with using the edges of mobile devices to apply force input. Wilson et al. [26] carried out a comparative user study with normal touch screen gestures, and found that workload ratings remained the same, whilst force input was slightly faster for carrying out tasks such as zooming and rotation. Similarly, Holman and Hollatz's Unifone [10] prototype showed better performance when comparing force-based input with touch-input for tasks such as map navigation.

Combining Force with Touch Gestures

The use of standard touch gestures is becoming prevalent in Smartphones and tablet devices and therefore provides a useful opportunity for combining force with such gestures. Rendl et al. [20] conducted a study and found that users were able to effectively carry out multi-touch gestures (pinch, swipe and stretch) with a small number of force levels. Heo and Lee [9] explored the usability of force sensitive tapping, pivoting, pressing, sliding and dragging (derived from a general tap and a slide) and found higher degrees of force levels can be problematic for users. Lee et al. [14] found that touch gestures that involve up and down movements are preferred with force input. Harrison and Hudson [8] describe the applications of *shear* gesture interaction (force and directionality sensing), e.g. applying a clockwise motion with a finger to increase media volume.

Approaches for Measuring Force Input

To measure force input, both software and hardware based approaches have been utilized. One common example involves Force Sensing Resistors (FSRs), which consists of flat polymer-based sheets fitted with semi-conductors and electrodes [29]. Several research prototypes [6, 9, 24, 26, 28] have produced accurate force readings, while the challenges were concerned with integrating the external FSRs into existing devices (i.e. selecting appropriate locations), achieving optimal sensitivity (e.g. the iPhone Sandwich [6]) for accurate force readings, and handling interference from device deformations [24].

Other approaches have utilized existing mobile device technology. VibPress [11] uses mobile phone hardware such as the accelerometer and the built-in vibration motor to measure force, which resulted in relatively high accuracy during a user study. Goel et al. [10] use a mobile phone's gyroscope and vibration motor to detect light, medium and heavy force input. Hwang and Wohn [12] utilize the built-in microphone of a mobile device and map sound amplitude to force-input levels. A user study showed high accuracy at lower levels (95%), and slightly lower accuracy at higher levels (71.3%). A similar approach is used by Pedersen and Hornbaek [16] involving a method that detects the amplitude in the sound waves generated by a finger tap.

[1] http://www.forceprofile.com/products-fingertps (last accessed 13th of June 2014).

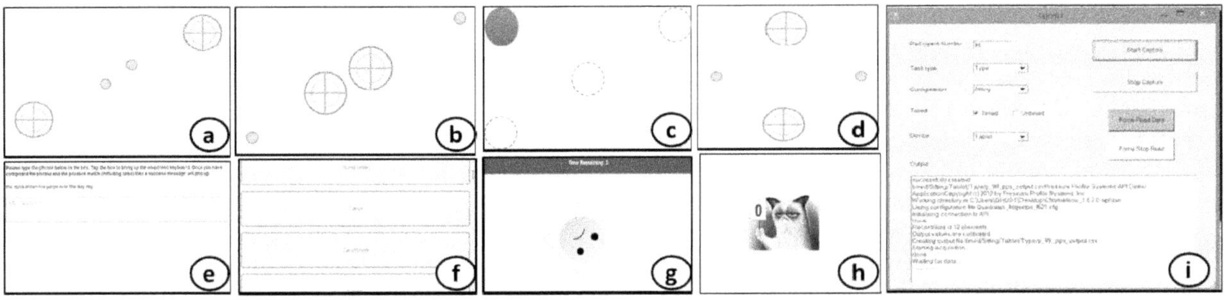

Figure 2: Touch gesture application - (a) zoom-out task, (b) zoom-in task, (c) tapping task (dotted circles show where next circles appear), (d) rotate task, (e) typing task, (f) panning task, (g) study 2 rotate task, (h) study 2 zooming task, (i) capture application

The authors note the importance of device surface acoustics (the material and how it amplifies sound), coupled with microphone positioning to achieve optimal force detection. Another interesting technique is proposed by Boring et al. [2], which uses contact size of a thumb (i.e. *Fat Thumb*) rather than force sensors to measure force. This approach also enables users to change contact size without actually applying more force, and thus avoiding friction (e.g. the interactions proposed by Roudaut et al. [22]).

INVESTIGATING FORCE PROFILES

To characterize force input patterns when carrying out touch gestures on mobile devices, we conducted a controlled laboratory user study. The study provided baseline force profiles that were used in study 2 to examine the impact of different conditions.

Selecting Gestures

There are four common, low-level touch gestures that form the basis for the majority of interaction: tapping, panning, zooming, and rotating. We used the de-facto standard actions for these gestures (single finger tap, single finger pan, pinch-to-zoom, two-finger rotate) in the user studies by asking participants to perform a number of tasks (described in the next sections).

Experimental Setup

We used the following hardware and software to prompt user tasks and record input forces: A web-based application (JQuery/PHP) was developed to include tasks based on the gesture interactions described above. A Samsung Nexus 10 inch tablet was used to display the web-application. Study participants wore the FingerTPS force sensing system, which included wearables on fingers equipped with force sensors, and a Bluetooth module that wirelessly captured sensor data (see Figure 1). Finally, a C# application controlled data capture and saved sensor data including timestamps in milliseconds and force values in grams, as CSV files (Figure 2i), which can be found online[2].

Web-Based Touch Gesture Application

The following tasks were supported by the web application:

Zooming: Users must pinch two circles on the screen, which served as start locations for the index finger and thumb, to target locations shown as traditional crosshair targets. This was split into two tasks, i.e. zooming in (Figure 2a) and zooming out (Figure 2b).

Tapping: Users tapped on blue circles that appeared on the screen every 3 seconds with their index finger as target selection (see Figure 2c). The circles appeared on the four corners and the center of the display. Once a circle was pressed, it disappeared to confirm selection and to prompt the next circle.

Rotating: Users were asked to rotate two circles 90 degrees anti-clockwise using their thumb and index finger towards target locations shown as two crosshair targets (Figure 2d).

Typing: Users typed a phrase ("The quick brown fox jumps over the lazy dog") using their index finger, and without auto-complete or other methods such as Swipe (Figure 2e). The task is completed once users have correctly typed the given phrase. While typing is simply a series of tapping actions, users are typically well practiced in rapid entry.

Panning: Users must carry out the panning action on a list (Figure 2f) to simulate a "browsing" action (i.e. scroll down a list using their index finger).

FingerTPS Configuration

The FingerTPS system consists of a set of force sensitive finger gloves that wirelessly send real-time sensor readings via Bluetooth to a USB receiver. Once the sensors are calibrated, the force data was recorded in units such as grams. The C# control application (Figure 2i) enabled us to avoid capturing unusable data when participants were idle. Given the nature of the gestures used in the study, only two finger sensors were required (thumb and index finger). The sensors were capacitive, which enabled participants to normally carry out touch screen interactions.

Method

Participants were required to carry out each of the touch gesture tasks on the tablet. All tasks, except the typing task (which involved typing out a phrase, i.e. 43 repetitions), involved 5 repetitions each.

[2] http://www.scc.lancs.ac.uk/interactivesystems/projects-/TouchForceCharacterisation/

Participants

Fourteen participants (6 female, 8 male) with an average age of 30.43 years took part in the study. Each participant took approximately 20 minutes to carry out the study and was provided with refreshments. Individual tasks took between 2 to 5 minutes to complete. All 14 participants were highly experienced with touchscreen devices and 5/14 participants indicated that the force sensing equipment may have changed the way in which they would normally carry out the touch gestures. Two participants were left-handed and they carried out the rotation task clockwise. Further, the force-sensing finger gloves could be worn on either hand.

Procedure

Participants were asked to wear the force sensing equipment, which was then calibrated in order to address individual differences in finger size and in the exertion of the baseline calibration force (i.e. 464 grams). Following this, they were provided instructions for carrying out the gestures, which began with a trial interaction to ensure they understood the task. Once the tasks were completed, a short demographic questionnaire was provided.

Results

Data Analysis

We employed a systematic process, which is described next, that enabled us to generate profile curves of input gestures (e.g. pinching, tapping, etc.).

Preprocessing and Thresholding: As the sensor noise (when participants were not applying force) contained minor peaks above 0 grams, we applied a threshold above the sensor baseline. This was set each time the sensor was calibrated and removed noise from the analysis, whilst also making it easier to extract the peaks. For each participant, the threshold was examined visually to ensure valid data was transferred into the analysis. This also accounted for calibration drift across interaction repetitions.

Normalization and Interpolation: The time taken to complete a task was different for each participant and therefore the time values of all gestures were normalized with a scale of 1. We then derived 100 sample points from the gesture repetitions by using linear interpolation with the known force values. Interpolation was used in order to derive equal numbers of sample points such that the gesture repetitions could be directly compared and clustered.

Clustering and Averaging: The k-means clustering algorithm was used to classify similar repetition curves which enabled us to, for instance, differentiate between users who may initially press harder compared to others. To achieve this, the data was organized such that all repetitions were time-normalized and applied into an $N \times M$ matrix where N is the repetition and M is 100 interpolated time index values. This enabled direct comparison between the individual repetitions for clustering. We then searched for the lowest value of K that classified all the observed data; starting with a high value of K ($K=N$) and iteratively reducing it until all visually similar shapes were placed in the same cluster. Clusters that represented less than 10% of the repetitions were disregarded as outliers. To ensure the resulting clusters made sense in context, the results were inspected visually to ensure that the clusters accurately represented different observed force-profile graph shape-characteristics described later. After the gesture repetitions were partitioned, the force values were averaged and force-normalized to produce representative profiles for the gestures. These are discussed in the next sections.

Force Profiles

The force profiles are presented as force and time-normalized curves to depict the shape profile of force for each input gesture. Therefore, the actual force and time values were omitted as we were interested in the shape of the curves, which provide high-level descriptions of how users apply force over time. In cases where more than one curve is described we calculated the difference of all points between the normalized curves and report this as a percentage for comparison purposes. In addition, repetitions with incorrect sensor readings were removed from the analysis. The expected number of total repetitions for each gesture was 602 for typing, and 70 repetitions each for tapping, panning, rotating and zooming. The repetitions below the expected number were caused by unusable sensor data where participants did not press down on the force sensor attached to the finger gloves. The repetitions above the expected number were caused by the occasional unresponsiveness of the gesture application, leading participants to press twice.

Typing: The force profile for typing (Figure 3) shows a short press as illustrated by the sharp increase in curve slope, followed by a short decrease in curve slope until the peak is reached. This is followed by the sensor drop-off. Typing typically consists of short interactions similar to how we type with physical keyboards (common touch screen keyboards also yield different characters with a long press, however this was not required in our study). In total, 422 repetitions (i.e. key presses) were analyzed.

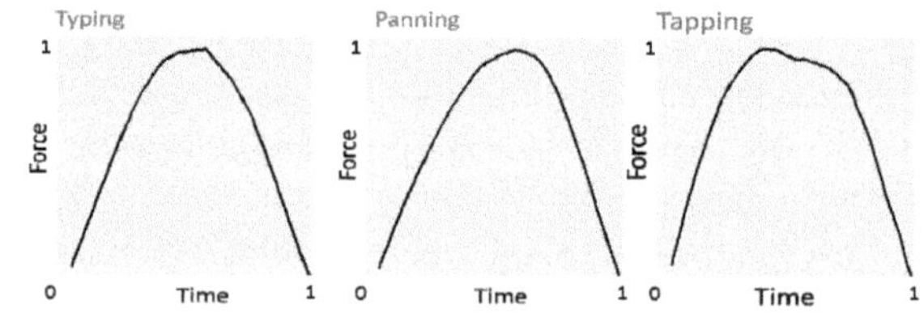

Figure 3: Force profiles for (left) the typing touch gesture, (middle) the panning gesture, (right) the tapping gesture.

Panning: The panning profile curve (Figure 3) illustrates an initial sharp increase followed by a decrease in curve slope, until peak force is reached. The short press indicates a "flicking" action to browse through a list. In total, 67 repetitions were analyzed.

Tapping: The tapping profile (Figure 3) has a larger plateau around the peak indicating a longer press (e.g.

compared to typing and panning). The plateau after the peak is reached indicates that the press is held down longer compared to the previous two gestures. A tap interaction is typically ensued by expecting feedback that the button has been pressed, thus causing a plateau in the peak region of the interaction. The tapping task analysis consisted of 78 repetitions in total.

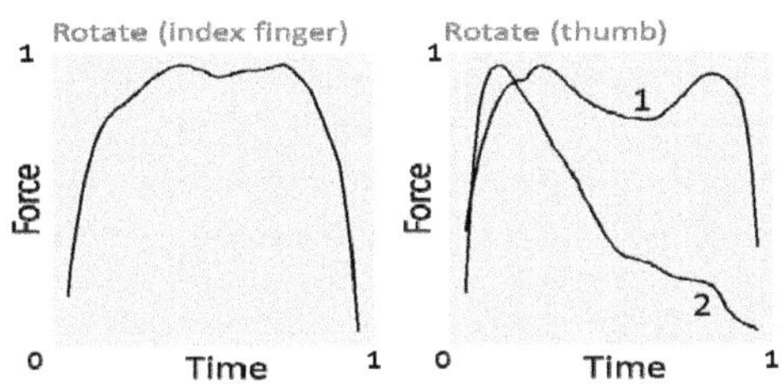

Figure 4: Force profiles for (left) the index finger during the rotate gesture, and (right) the thumb.

Rotating: The force values for the index finger and thumb were analyzed for the rotating touch gesture (Figure 4), revealing a single profile graph for the index finger and two distinct profiles for the thumb. The index finger curve shows a rapid increase to the peak force, followed by force variations (caused by the continuity of a rotate interaction) and the sensor drop off. The thumb analysis revealed two profile curves: curve 1, which resembles the shape of the index finger profile albeit with a larger decline in force applied mid-interaction. In contrast curve 2 shows a gradual decrease in force immediately after peak force is reached (i.e. participants initially pressed hard on the screen, followed by gradually reducing force). The difference between curves 1 and 2 is 35.82%. It was evident that the index finger had more consistent coordination (in terms of force) in comparison to the thumb. The analysis involved 68 index finger repetitions and 43 thumb repetitions.

Zooming: The zoom-out gesture (Figure 5a and 5b) consists of a single profile curve for the index finger (70 repetitions) and two profile curves for the thumb (65 total repetitions). The index finger curve shows an initial hard press and then easing-off towards the end of the gesture. Curve 2 for the thumb is consistent in shape with the index finger. However, curve 1 shows more variation in force once peak force is reached, indicating a harder press throughout the interaction. The difference between the two thumb profile curves is 12.43%.

The index finger and thumb during the zoom-in gesture (Figure 5) indicate a less forceful initial press, followed by increasing force as the task continued, till the sensor drop off at the end. In total, 63 repetitions were analyzed for the index finger, and 28 repetitions for the thumb. Both zoom-in and zoom-out gestures show that the shape of the index finger profile and at least one corresponding thumb profile are consistent with each other. This indicates that both the thumb and index finger move together during a zoom gesture. The curves also illustrate that participants applied more force when their fingers were further apart (at the start of the zoom-out task, and towards the end of the zoom-in task) compared to when they are closer together.

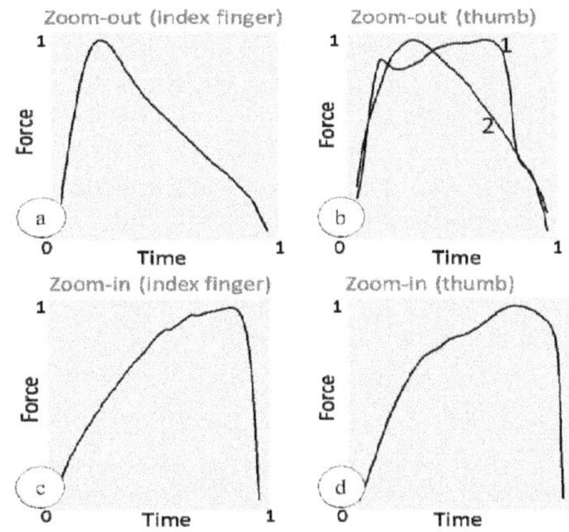

Figure 5: Profiles for (a) zoom-out using the index finger and (b) thumb, (c) zoom-in using index finger, and (d) thumb.

Summary

The study revealed consistent curves across all participants, which we were able to cluster together and develop high-level profiles that illustrate the characteristics of each touch gesture. Furthermore, the study confirmed our approach of analyzing touch input gestures and enabled us to carry out the next user study under different conditions.

INVESTIGATING FORCE AND CONTEXT

The second study aimed to investigate whether different conditions (or contexts of use) affect the force profiles developed in the first study, which involved a single and tightly-controlled condition. This enables us to make generalizable statements about the way in which users apply force whist carrying out touch gestures. It was anticipated that the shape of the profile curves would appear similar, however the different conditions are likely to cause variations in force and gesture completion times.

Selecting Conditions

Users perform touch-based gestures in a multitude of applications, devices, environments, and contexts. We chose a set of representative situations to form the characterization by situating each of these gestures into a series of generalizable conditions. These conditions are:

- Form factor (mobile phone vs. tablet): We hypothesized the trade-off between increased screen size vs. increased weight and awkwardness of device grasping will lead to study participants applying more force on the tablet.
- Interaction position (sitting vs. walking): The inherent nature of phones and tablets mean they are deployed in a range of static and moving contexts. We predict that input force would increase in non-static conditions as users compensate for the device vibrations associated with non-static interaction.
- Urgency (timed vs. untimed): Many game applications, as well as external environmental factors mean users

sometimes feel a sense of urgency to interact. We induce urgency by limiting task completion time and predict that study participants will apply more force in urgent conditions compared to non-urgent.

Experimental Setup

The web-based touch gesture application used in the first study underwent the following modifications: Firstly, the rotating task involved rotating an image to a specific orientation (replacing the targets – Figure 2g). Second, the zooming tasks involved resizing an image, rather than dragging two points to target locations (Figure 2h). Third, in the panning task users continued to pan until they found a specified keyword (Figure 2f). Finally, in addition to the Nexus 10 tablet, participants were supplied with a Nexus S mobile phone with a screen size of 4 inches.

In addition, we captured the six gestures under conditions where users feel a sense of urgency (e.g. whilst playing games). These tasks all included a timed and an untimed version. In the timed version, users are required to complete the tasks before a counter (displayed at the top of the application interface), which was intentionally kept to a low number to create a sense of urgency, reaches zero. The timed tasks were limited to: 20 seconds for typing, 5 seconds for zooming, 10 seconds for panning, 8 seconds for rotating, and 15 seconds for tapping.

Method

The user study consisted of a 2x2x2 factor design, which involved the form factor, interaction position, and urgency (see Table 1). The six gesture tasks were repeated in each condition. A within-subjects approach was used where each participant was exposed to the eight conditions. The conditions were counterbalanced using a Latin square and the order in which participants carried out the tasks was randomized. A different number of gesture repetitions were used by the participants to complete the tasks.

Table 1: Conditions explored in the 2nd study (C=Condition)

C1: tablet, walking, timed	C2: tablet, walking, untimed
C3: tablet, sitting, untimed	C4: tablet, sitting, timed
C5: phone, walking, untimed	C6: phone, walking, untimed
C7: phone, sitting, untimed	C8: phone, sitting, timed

Participants

We recruited 24 participants (12m, 12f), with an average age of 29.5 years. Each participant was rewarded with 8 GBP for each session, which lasted between 45 and 60 minutes. In general, all 24 participants were experienced with Smartphones and tablet devices. Only 7/24 participants were experienced with force sensing devices such as game controllers and Wacom tablets. Only one participant was left handed. Three participants stated that they believed the force sensing finger gloves reduced the responsiveness of touch events on the gesture application.

Procedure

Each participant was briefed on the study objectives and procedure, and asked to sign a consent form. Each trial involved a calibration phase, familiarization phase, and the experimental conditions. These are described below.

Calibration and Familiarization: Participants were asked to wear the force sensing equipment, which was calibrated in order to address individual differences in finger size and in the exertion of the baseline calibration force value (i.e. 464 grams). Once the sensors were calibrated, they carried out the six tasks on the web-application in a "test-mode" to become familiar with the application. Following this, participants completed each task once, in the untimed mode on the tablet and sitting down. Whilst participants were carrying out the tasks, the force readings were observed on the FingerTPS application to validate correct calibration.

Experimental conditions: Following the familiarization phase, participants were instructed to repeat the tasks under different the conditions described in the Experimental Setup. During the walking condition, participants walked in a figure 8 inside the room (approximately 8x4 meters). Once the experimental conditions were completed, participants were asked to fill in a short questionnaire to collect demographic data.

Results

Analysis of Force Profiles

The focus of this study is twofold; firstly we compare the profiles constructed in the first study with the second study as a means of validating and revising our models. We then examine the variations in force levels and time taken to complete the gestures in the different conditions. We also report the average forces exerted and the average gesture completion times for all conditions, including density plots that illustrate common ranges of these forces and times. We adopted the same procedure in processing the data for each gesture task as described in the first study (i.e. preprocessing, thresholding, normalization, interpolation, clustering, and averaging).

Typing: It was clear from the analysis that the force profile for typing (Figure 6a) indicated a more rapid increase to the peak force, followed by the sensor drop-off. Thus, participants in study 2 were pressing for shorter periods of time. The difference between the typing profile from study 1 and the profiles for each condition in study 2 ranged from 9.78% to a maximum of 17.79%. As these differences are relatively significant, a revised profile curve (with a steeper slope to the peak force) for the typing gesture is proposed (Figure 6d). In total, 5939 repetitions were analyzed in study 2 and we found that the curves across all the conditions were highly similar in shape.

Panning: The panning gesture profiles that emerged from the second study revealed relatively high differences compared to the profile from study 1(ranging from 14.73%

to 18.49%). Figure 6b shows, for instance, that the sensor drop-off occurs further away from the peak, thus indicating a dragging action. A revised panning profile is therefore provided (Figure 6e) which shows a plateau around the peak force region. In study 2, participants were looking for a specific keyword, therefore it was expected that participants would combine a flicking action with a dragging action to verify that they have found the keyword. The panning gesture consisted of 2657 repetitions in total across the 8 conditions and there was little difference of profile curves in between the conditions.

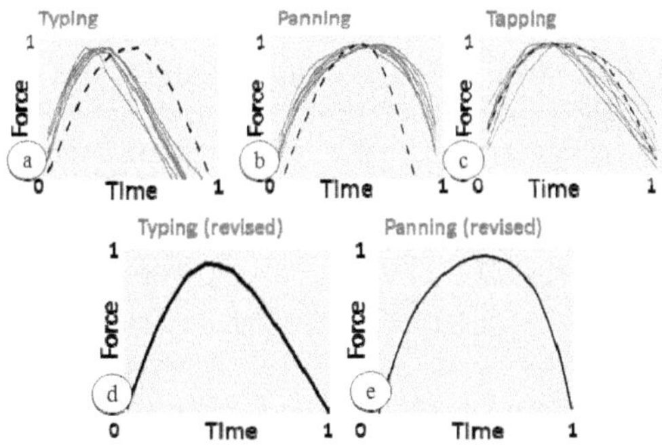

Figure 6: Dotted lines represent study 1 curves. Each solid line represents a condition in study 2: (a) typing, (b) panning, (c) tapping, (d) revised typing profile, (e) revised panning profile.

Tapping: The tapping gesture profile from study 1 provides a suitable representation of study 2 results, with differences ranging from 2.33% to 8.66%. The tapping curves from study 2 (Figure 6c) indicated a quick press with a small delay once peak force was reached (i.e. users typically waited for feedback before releasing a tap interaction). A total number of 1661 repetitions were analyzed.

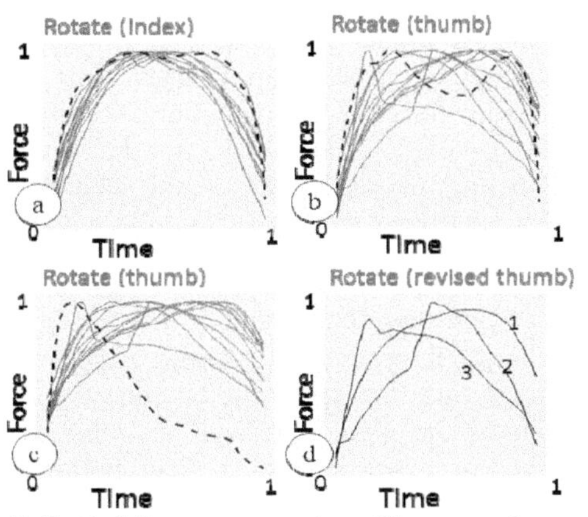

Figure 7: Dotted lines represent profile curves from study 1. Rotate profile curves (solid) from study 2 for (a) index finger, (b) and (c) thumb and (d) revised thumb profiles for rotate.

Rotating: Figure 7a illustrates that the index finger profile from study 1 closely fits the curves generated in study 2 (with differences ranging from 5.4% to 14.27%). The profile indicates a sharp increase to peak force (Figure 7a), the continuation of the gesture with slight variations in force and followed by the sensor drop-off. A total of 1377 repetitions were analyzed for the index finger. All curves across the 8 conditions were also highly similar. In contrast, the thumb produced higher variation (Figure 7b and 7c) across the 8 conditions (ranging from 11.2% to 42.12%). Therefore, the two profile curves from study 1 do not adequately represent the thumb in a rotate interaction. As a result, a set of three profile curves are proposed (Figure 7d). The maximum difference between the three revised curves is 13.21%. Although the differences are not significantly high, it is clear that the shapes are distinct. Curve 1 consists of a smoother interaction where participants press on the device in a highly controlled manner. Curve 2 involves a rapid increase in force (i.e. a hard press) followed by gradually lifting off from the device. Finally, curve 3 begins with a softer press until peak force is reached, followed by a relatively steep decrease in force. In total, 1191 repetitions of the thumb were analyzed.

Zooming-In: The index finger curves across the 8 conditions (Figure 8) were highly similar in shape to the corresponding profile from study 1 (differences ranging from 5.2% to 12.95%).

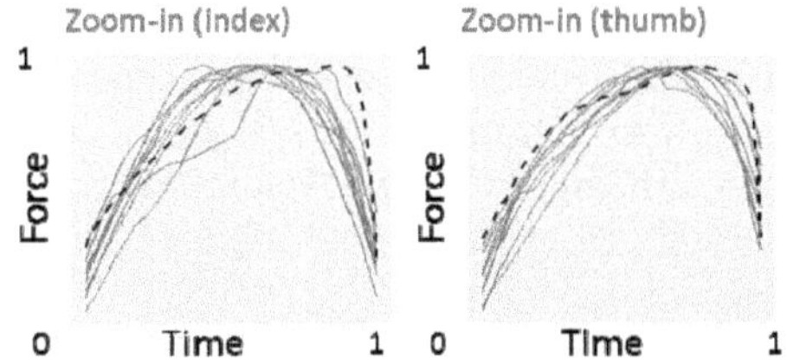

Figure 8: Dotted lines represent profile curves from study 1. Zoom-in profile (solid) curves from study 2 for (left) index finger, and (right) thumb profile.

It shows a gradual increase to peak force and to the end of the gesture, followed by the sensor drop-off. Similarly, the thumb analysis revealed a low level of variation compared to the thumb profile curve from study 1 (ranging from 2.94% to 12.13%). The thumb profile is also consistent with the index finger, with a gradual increase in force over time. A total of 1192 repetitions were analyzed for the index finger, and 983 for the thumb.

Zooming-Out: The profile curves for the index finger zoom-out gesture derived from the 8 conditions in study 2 (Figure 9a) were highly distinct to the profile curve presented in study 1 (differences ranging from 18.33% to 29.14%). The profile from study 1 shows an initial hard press, followed by gradually decreasing force. However, study 2 curves show a hard press which plateaus around the peak force region, indicating that participants pressed and held for longer. Therefore, a revised profile curve for the index finger is proposed (Figure 9d). The analysis for the thumb showed relatively high variation in comparison to curve 1 from study 1 (ranging from 9.12% to 23.15%) and a higher variation compared to curve 2 from study 1 (9.82% to 30.06%). As a result of these differences, two revised profile curves are proposed. Curve 1 shows a rapid increase in force to the peak force, and curve 2 shows a slower increase in force. In total, 1061 index finger repetitions and 911 repetitions for the thumb were analyzed.

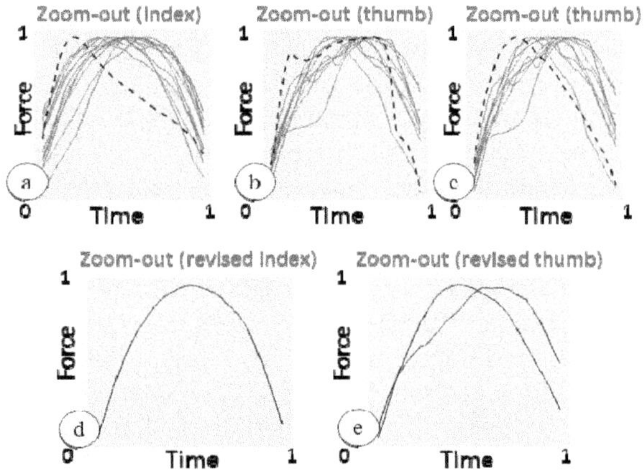

Figure 9: Dotted lines are profiles from study 1. Zoom-out profiles from study 2 for (a) index finger, (b) and (c) thumb and revised profile curves for (d) index finger and (e) thumb.

Effect of Conditions on Force and Time

To investigate whether the different conditions had an effect on time and force, we carried out multiple factor regression analysis on each of the gestures to determine which factors had significant effects. Each condition had three factors, which were form factor (mobile vs. tablet), position (sittings vs. walking) and urgency (timed task vs. untimed task).

Typing: Participants typically applied more force on a tablet ($F_{1,6537}=178$, $p<0.001$) or under urgency-induced tasks ($F_{1,6537}=21.9$, $p<0.001$). In terms of interaction length, participants typically pressed for longer durations on the mobile phone ($F_{1,6537}=6.98$, $p<0.01$).

Panning: Participants exerted more force on the tablet ($F_{1,2655}=19$, $p<0.001$), and whilst they were walking ($F_{1,2655}=22$, $p<0.001$). Panning repetitions were also longer in duration on the mobile phone ($F_{1,2655}=92.2$, $p<0.001$).

Tapping: Force variations for tapping were caused by position ($F_{1,1659}=3.93$, $p<0.05$), where less force was generally exerted whilst participants were sitting down.

Rotate: Participants applied less force whilst sitting (thumb: $F_{1,1189}=5.91$, $p<0.05$; index finger: $F_{1,1374}=11.8$, $p<0.001$) and also less force on the phone (thumb $F_{1,1189}=3.11$, $p=0.078$; index finger: $F_{1,1374}=16.1$, $p<0.001$).

Zoom-out: For zoom-out, participants pressed harder on the phone with their thumb ($F_{1,909}=27.3$, $p<0.001$) and harder with their index finger whilst walking ($F_{1,1059}=22.4$, $p<0.001$). Participants spent longer zooming-out on the mobile phone with their thumb ($F_{1,909}=4.02$, $p<0.05$).

Zoom-in: Participants exerted more force with their thumb on the phone ($F_{1,997}=16.7$, $p<0.001$) but with less force using their index finger ($F_{1,1190}=8.62$, $p<0.01$). Participants also applied less force with their index finger whilst sitting ($F_{1,1190}=13.4$, $p<0.001$). Participants spent longer with their thumb on the phone ($F_{1,997}=3.6$, $p<0.05$).

Distribution of Force and Time

To provide a general understanding of gesture force and time, Table 2 displays the averages for all gestures, and Figure 10 (on the next page) displays density plots showing the distributions of peak forces and gesture completion times. The force and time values in this case were not normalized. We found that the distribution of peak forces and completion times were highly skewed to the right (see Figure 10, next page), therefore we report the interquartile (i.e. between 25% and 75% of the distribution) mean as a measure of central tendency, and the interquartile range (IQR) as a measure of spread. These are shown in Table 2.

Table 2: IQR Mean force and time for gestures and conditions with range in brackets Mean=$\bar{x}$, T=thumb, I=index finger

Gesture	Force (grams)	Time (milliseconds)
Typing	$\bar{x}$: 41.53 (20.37, 73.09)	$\bar{x}$: 119.66 (100, 150)
Tapping	$\bar{x}$: 69.05 (22.72, 163.9)	$\bar{x}$: 188.69 (125, 300)
Panning	$\bar{x}$: 55.16 (26.17, 96.16)	$\bar{x}$: 233.65 (150, 350)
Rotate	T: $\bar{x}$:15.74 (3.86, 40.2) I: $\bar{x}$: 32.46 (9.81, 72.8)	T: $\bar{x}$: 300 (150, 450) I: $\bar{x}$: 288.12 (150,450)
Zoom-In	T: $\bar{x}$: 33.81 (2.73, 69.6) I: $\bar{x}$: 54.96 (11.37, 103.78)	T: $\bar{x}$: 292.38 (150, 450) I: $\bar{x}$: 274.64 (150, 425)
Zoom-Out	T: $\bar{x}$: 28.03 (4.49, 98.97) I: $\bar{x}$: 45.56 (13.36, 131.99)	T: $\bar{x}$: 294.44 (150, 450) I: $\bar{x}$: 274.64 (150, 425)

In general, rapid entry tasks like typing show that the mean force and gesture completion time were much lower compared to other gestures. Tapping and panning show higher force and time values indicating slower presses caused by awaiting confirmation of a tap or searching for a keyword in a list. It is likely that the higher mean force in tapping was caused by the occasional unresponsiveness of the gesture where participants would press harder if an initial tap was unregistered by the gesture application. For two-finger gestures such as rotating and zooming, the mean forces exerted were generally low whilst the mean times were higher than typing, tapping and panning. The index finger exerted more force than the thumb gestures, which denotes its dominance during two-finger gestures.

For illustrative purposes, the density distributions (Figure 10) show 95% of all force and time values for each gesture, including dotted lines that show the interquartile range. The upper section of the plots show the distribution of force values and the lower section show the distribution of gesture completion times. The plots indicate that although there is variation between the conditions for each gesture, there are commonalities in the general range of force exerted, and the general time taken to complete the gestures. Thus, forces and completion times outside this range are uncommon, e.g. the forces for typing vary across conditions, but fall within a range of 0 to 150 grams.

DISCUSSION

The two user studies described in this paper presented a number of insights that characterize touch gesture input force on mobile devices. It was evident from the gesture profiles of both studies that typing and tapping gestures consisted of quick presses. The panning gesture illustrated a plateau in the peak force region, indicating a dragging action and continuous (as well as consistent) application of force. In contrast, continuous gestures such as rotating and zooming produced more variable forces over time. The index finger profiles for rotate, zoom-in, and zoom-out showed consistency across all the conditions in contrast to the thumb profiles, which produced more variation. There was a higher degree of control with the index finger in the gesture interactions compared to the thumb. This is also reflected in the force variation analysis where we found that participants applied more force with their index finger for the rotation and zooming gestures.

Force variations were mainly affected by the form factor and interaction position, which contrasted our prediction that urgency would cause the most variation (i.e. participants would press harder under time pressure). Participants generally pressed harder on the tablet whilst typing, panning, rotating, and with their index finger for zooming. We believe that participants compensated for the weight of the tablet and exerted more force. Participants also took longer to complete typing, panning, and zooming gestures on the mobile phone. It is likely that the smaller screen size of the phone caused participants to be more precise in carrying out gestures. For instance, pressing the right letters on a touch keyboard requires more precision on a smaller screen. Similarly, participants were likely to press-and-hold for longer during panning tasks to ensure the searched keyword was in view. The interaction position affected tapping, panning, rotating, and zooming gestures, with participants applying more force whilst walking. This matched our prediction where participants press harder to compensate for device vibrations caused by movement. Urgency only affected the typing gesture, i.e. more force was applied under urgency-induced conditions. The density plots (Figure 10) provide general ranges that the design of force-sensitive devices which integrate standard touch gestures can adopt. We found that forces and completion times above these ranges, for instance, were uncommon.

Implications and Usage

The results in this paper can aid designers of touch screen, flexible display, and force-sensitive surfaces by enabling them to differentiate between gesture inputs (tapping, pinching, zooming, rotating) and force inputs (e.g. tapping harder to achieve a different result than a key-press). For instance, the density plots (Figure 10) shows that it is uncommon to apply forces above 150 grams for the typing gesture. Our findings can also help calibrate such devices such that the gestures adhere to the force and time ranges shown in Figure 10. The differences found between forces applied on mobile and tablet devices can also inform designers that a higher force tolerance must be included for larger devices (tablets) for standard touch gestures. The force profiles of the studied gestures can be used to aid gesture recognition in force-sensitive surfaces (e.g. a force sensitive surface that indirectly controls content through touch gestures). Our studies showed that, for instance, whilst a typing gesture is a simple increase and decrease in force values, a rotation gesture consists of varying forces.

Limitations

The findings of our user studies are based on a specific set of devices (i.e. Nexus S phone and Galaxy 10 tablet) and a specific application (i.e. the touch gesture application). However as Smartphones and tablet devices with capacitive touch screens are commonplace, we believe that our results are generalizable to similar devices. The gesture application was designed for standard gesture tasks; however the FingerTPS equipment was somewhat restrictive in that participants were only able to use their fingers that were attached with the force sensors (e.g. users might choose to type with multiple fingers). Furthermore, the data capture rate of the FingerTPS equipment was relatively low (40 Hertz), thus limiting the sample points in each repetition. A higher data capture rate, for instance, would have enabled higher granularity when plotting the curves (i.e. better indications of where force variations might occur). Furthermore, there are numerous avenues for future characterizations including tests for the influence of device lag, different contents and contexts, typing with various fingers, and using clock-wise rotations.

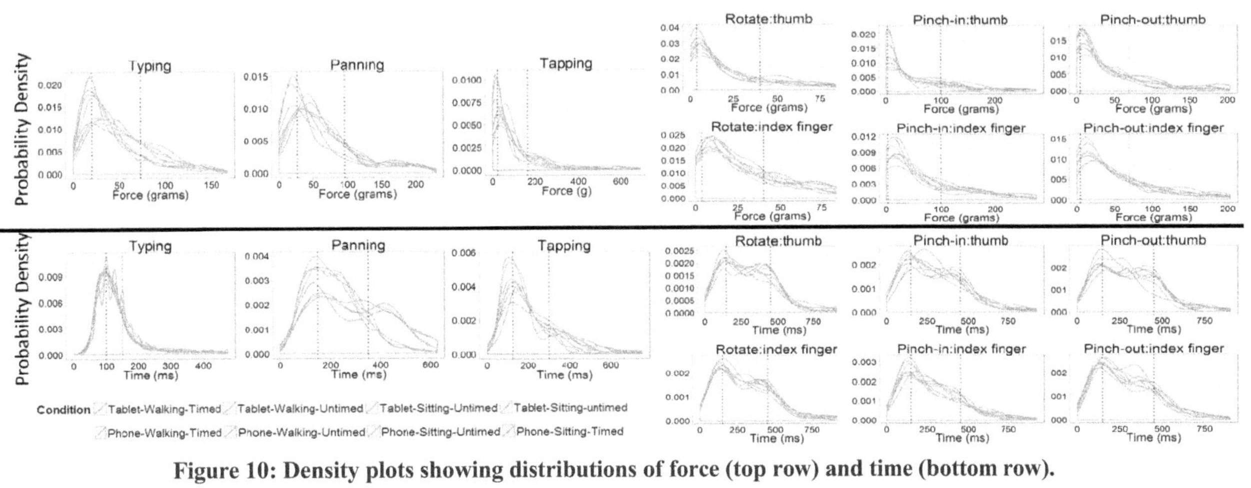

Figure 10: Density plots showing distributions of force (top row) and time (bottom row).

CONCLUSION

In this paper we presented a characterization of force input for standard touch gestures on mobile devices by carrying out two user studies. The studies investigated: (1) force profiles that depict typing, panning, tapping, zooming, and rotating gestures, (2) the effect of different conditions on force exerted and time spent completing these gestures, and (3) common force and gesture completion time ranges. Our contributions included profiles of each gesture which indicate that typing and tapping gestures were consistently short presses whilst panning involved a dragging action. Two-finger gestures such as zooming and rotating revealed higher consistency and control for the index finger, and high variability in force over time for the thumb. It was also evident that force and gesture completion time was mainly affected by form factor and interaction position. The gestures were longer on the phone, more force was applied on the tablet, and more force was applied whilst participants were walking. Further, despite the variations between conditions, participants applied force and completed tasks within specific force/time ranges. This characterization aims to enable designers of interactive mobile devices to integrate force and standard touch gestures to augment interactivity, as well as design for different conditions.

ACKNOWLEDGEMENTS

This work forms part of GHOST, a project funded by the European Commission's 7th Framework Programme, FET-Open scheme (grant #309191).

REFERENCES

1. Brewster, S. A., & Hughes, M. (2009). Force-based text entry for mobile devices. In *Proc. MobileHCI '09*, 9.
2. Boring, S., Ledo, D., Chen, X., Marquardt, N., Tang, A., & Greenber, S. (2012). The fat thumb: using the thumb's contact size for single-handed mobile interaction. In *Proc. MobileHCI'12*, 39–48.
3. Cechanowicz, J., Irani, P., & Subramanian, S. (2007). Augmenting the mouse with force sensitive input. In *Proc. CHI '07*, 1385–1394.
4. Clarkson, E., Patel, S., Pierce, J., & Abowd, G. (2006). Exploring continuous force input for mobile phones. *GVU Tech. Report.*
5. Dietz, P., & Eidelson, B. (2009). A practical force sensitive computer keyboard. In *Proc. UIST'09*, 55–58.
6. Essl, G., Rohs, M., & Kratz, S. (2009). Squeezing the sandwich: A mobile force-sensitive two-sided multi-touch prototype. In *Proc. UIST '09.*
7. Goel, M., Wobbrock, J., & Patel, S. (2012). GripSense: using built-in sensors to detect hand posture and force on commodity mobile phones. In *Proc. UIST'12*,545-554.
8. Harrison, C., & Hudson, S. (2012). Using shear as a supplemental two-dimensional input channel for rich touchscreen interaction. In *Proc. CHI'12*, 3149–3152.
9. Heo, S., & Lee, G. (2011). Force gestures: augmenting touch screen gestures with normal and tangential forces. In *Proc. UIST'11*, 621–626.
10. Holman, D., & Hollatz, A. (2013). Unifone: Designing for auxiliary finger input in one-handed mobile interactions. In *Proc. TEI'13*, 177–184.
11. Hwang, S., Bianchi, A., & Wohn, K. (2013). VibPress: estimating force input using vibration absorption on mobile devices. In *Proc. MobileHCI'13*, 31–34.
12. Hwang, S., & Wohn, K. (2012). PseudoButton: enabling force-sensitive interaction by repurposing microphone on mobile device. *CHI'12 EA,* 1565–1570.
13. Kammer, D., Wojdziak, J., Keck, M., Groh, R., & Taranko, S. (2010). Towards a formalization of multi-touch gestures. In *Proc. ITS '10*, 49–58.
14. Lee, B., Lee, H., Lim, S.-C., Lee, H., Han, S., & Park, J. (2012). Evaluation of human tangential force input performance. In *Proc. CHI '12*, 3121–3130.
15. McCallum, D., Mak, E., Pourang, I., & Subramanian, S. (2009). ForceText: force input for mobile phone text entry. *CHI'09 EA*, 4519–4524.
16. Pedersen, E. W., & Hornbæk, K. (2014). Expressive Touch : Studying Tapping Force on Tabletops. In *Proc. CHI'14,* 421-430.
17. Quinn, P., & Cockburn, A. (2009). Zoofing!: faster list selections with force-zoom-flick-scrolling. In *Proc. OzCHI'09,* 185–192.
18. Ramos, G., & Balakrishnan, R. (2005). Zliding: fluid zooming and sliding for high precision parameter manipulation. In *Proc. UIST'05*, 143–152.
19. Ramos, G., Boulos, M., & Balakrishnan, R. (2004). Force widgets. In *Proc. CHI '04*, 487–494.
20. Rendl, C., Greindl, P., Probst, K., Behrens, M., & Haller, M. (2014). Presstures: exploring force-sensitive multi-touch gestures on trackpads. *CHI'14*, 431–434.
21. Richardson, T., Burd, L., & Smith, S. (2013). Guidelines for supporting real-time multi-touch applications. *Software: Practice and Experience.*
22. Roudaut, A., Lecolinet, E., & Guiard, Y. (2009). MicroRolls: expanding touch-screen input vocabulary by distinguishing rolls vs. slides of the thumb. In *Proc. CHI'09*, 927–936.
23. Schwesig, C., Poupyrev, I., & Mori, E. (2004). Gummi: a bendable computer. In *Proc. CHI'04*, 263–270.
24. Scott, J., Brown, L., & Molloy, M. (2009). Mobile device interaction with force sensing. In *Proc. Pervasive Computing'09,* 133–150.
25. Stewart, C., Rohs, M., Kratz, S., & Essl, G. (2010). Characteristics of force-based input for mobile devices. In *Proc. CHI'10*, 801–810.
26. Wilson, G., Brewster, S., & Halvey, M. (2013). Towards utilising one-handed multi-digit force input. *CHI '13 EA*, 1317–1322.
27. Wilson, G., Brewster, S., & Halvey, M. (2011). The effects of walking, feedback and control method on force-based interaction. *MobileHCI'11*, 147–156.
28. Wilson, G., Stewart, C., & Brewster, S. A. (2010). Force-based menu selection for mobile devices. In *Proc. MobileHCI '10*, 181–190.
29. Yaniger, S. (1991). Force sensing resistors: A review of the technology. *Electro International'91*, 666–668.

Characterising the Physicality of Everyday Buttons

Jason Alexander
Lancaster University, UK
j.alexander@lancaster.ac.uk

John Hardy
Lancaster University, UK
john@highwire-dtc.com

Stephen Wattam
Lancaster University, UK
s.wattam@lancaster.ac.uk

ABSTRACT
A significant milestone in the development of physically-dynamic surfaces is the ability for buttons to protrude outwards from any location on a touch-screen. As a first step toward developing interaction requirements for this technology we conducted a survey of 1515 electronic push buttons in everyday home environments. We report a characterisation that describes the features of the data set and discusses important button properties that we expect will inform the design of future physically-dynamic devices and surfaces.

Author Keywords
Buttons; Physicality; Input force;

ACM Classification Keywords
H.5.2. Information Interfaces and Presentation (e.g. HCI): User Interfaces – Input Devices and Strategies

INTRODUCTION
Physically-dynamic surfaces—those that can self-modify their geometry—have the potential to revolutionise the touch display industry. One of the key milestones in the development of this technology is the ability to present the user with physical buttons that dynamically appear on the display surface at *any position* and of *any size*. To help inform interaction requires and the exploration of accompanying material and engineering challenges, this paper surveys, characterises, and discusses the physical properties of existing everyday push-buttons.

Physical push buttons are pervasive. The properties of these buttons—size, shape, trigger, force, travel distance, audible feedback, etc.—all contribute to the understanding that certain buttons operate in certain ways, despite their diverse functionality and aesthetic properties. These properties allow distinct groups of buttons to feel similar across devices. For instance, the keys on a computer keyboard are easy to distinguish from those on a washing machine. When absent, this tactile familiarity can lead to an uneasy experience, such as when adopting touch-screens for text input [4].

Interactive systems often emulate the properties of existing objects to build user understanding. To transfer the familiarity and affordances of physical buttons to shape-changing surfaces, it is first important to understand the properties of the buttons already in the physical world. To that end, the contributions of this paper are: (1) A detailed survey of over 1500 physical electronic push buttons from 11 different household rooms. Each button is annotated with 20 unique properties, including 5 force profile samples. (2) A characterisation that describes the features of the data set, discusses important button properties, and the relationships between them. The paper concludes with a reflection on the limitations of the collected data and implications for future physically-dynamic surfaces.

ITS 2014, November 16–19, 2014, Dresden, Germany.

http://dx.doi.org/10.1145/2669485.2669519

RELATED WORK

Physical Buttons
Previous physical button investigations have focussed on *mechanical* push buttons, establishing just-noticeable force differences and user preferences [6], force-displacement transitions [12], keyboard design factors [11], and methodologies for modelling their feel [5]. Our examination adds to work in this area by characterising *electronic control* buttons that typically have a far shorter input stroke and a greater emphasis on aesthetic design.

Touch-Screen Buttons
The lack of kinesthetic feedback on touch enabled surfaces has long posed a challenge for interaction designers [4]. The addition of tactile [2] and audio [10] feedback to touchscreen buttons can improve input performance and, along with principles of affective design [15], users' subjective opinion. Tashiro et al. [16] identified buckling and restitution as important tactile characteristics for reproducing the 'click' sensations, with Park et al. [13] using the vibration magnitudes to guide haptically-augmented soft button design.

Buttons on Physically-Dynamic Display Surfaces
Researchers have produced dynamically available buttons using electromagnetic actuation, pneumatics, and Shape Memory Alloys (SMAs). Early work used linear actuators to displace rods [9] and SMAs [14] to actuate light tubes. Tilt Displays [1] actuate small OLED screens, with the authors postulating that buttons could extrude from the touch-screen. Dynamically adjustable resistance using electromagnetic solenoids can help to prevent typing errors [8].

To create crisp shapes with multiple states and continuous input, Harrison and Hudson [7] used air-filled chambers to make shapes (e.g. buttons) protrude, lie flat, or sink into a display. Rear projection cast an image on pre-defined cutouts, while pressure-sensing was used for continuously variable parameters. Tactus[1] uses a conceptually similar model, where an overlay on the touch-screen is inflated with liquid.

[1] `http://www.tactustechnology.com/`

CHARACTERISING BUTTONS IN THE PHYSICAL WORLD

Survey Method

Everyday environments are full of devices that utilise simple push-button interfaces. We surveyed the physical buttons for electronic controls in 11 typical household rooms, cataloguing a total of 1515 individual buttons. In total we collected 20 measurements for each button, presented here in approximate groupings for clarity:

- **Button:** Width, height, shape, curvature, texture, material, protrusion above surface, toggability;
- **Action:** Distance travelled when pressed, force profile required to activate, is the trigger action audible;
- **Context:** House, room, appliance, function on appliance, number of co-located identical buttons, functions performed by identical buttons, device type (handheld or free standing), degree of sustained use (i.e. a computer keyboard compared to a microwave), similarity of construction material to surroundings.

Button activation force was collected using a FingerTPS[2] force sensing glove. Each button was pressed five times while recording the forces imparted by the finger. The peak of the activation force and overall profile were extracted. For consistency, a single researcher pressed all buttons, using the index finger on their dominant hand. We achieved an inter-button variance of approximately $100g$ using this method. Button dimensions were measured using a vernier caliper.

Dataset Summary

The survey profiled 1515 individual buttons from 112 appliances, of which 344 had non-identical characteristics (line 1, Table 1). The most common type of button is rectangular (line 3), flat (line 6), in landscape orientation (line 4), and constructed from plastic (line 7). The vast majority (99%, line 10) are single state buttons (return to their starting position once triggered) and make an audible noise when pressed (89%). The mean force required to trigger a button was $326g$ (line 11) although this varied widely across the sample.

Button Characteristics

We now present a deeper analysis of our sample in order to identify meaningful relationships and interaction between button properties.

Button travel distance is small: The average distance a button travels when pressed is $1.48mm$ (σ : $1.04mm$). Typically, buttons that travel less than $1.00mm$ have a greater peak force applied (μ : $494.9g$, σ : $534g$) than those which move farther (μ : $242.7g$, σ : $370g$). This difference was confirmed statistically significant beyond the 1% level using a t-test ($t_{749.3} = -9.53, p \leq 0.001$). There were no significant sample-wide correlations between button dimensions and distance travelled.

Buttons are seated level with or above the plane: Table 2 details properties of buttons according to their relationship with the surrounding plane. There are a small number (<1%)

[2]`http://www.pressureprofile.com/products-fingertps`

	Characteristic	Value
1	Buttons surveyed	Total: 1515, unique: 344
2	Appliances surveyed	112
3	Button shapes	Rectangular: 71.8%, circular: 15.9%, elliptical: 9.5%, other: 2.8%
4	Button orientation	Landscape: 62.8%, equal dimensions: 24.1%, portrait: 13.1%
5	Pressable surface area	$\mu : 171.7mm^2, \sigma : 316.8mm^2$
6	Curvature	Flat: 74.7%, concave: 15.2%, convex: 10.2%
7	Construction material	Plastic: 73.0%, Rubber: 26.4%, Metal: 0.6%
8	Appearance	Differs from surrounds: 59.7%, Identical to surrounds: 40.3%
9	Audible trigger	Yes: 89.1%, no: 10.9%
10	Togglability	Full return: 99.3%, toggle: 0.7%
11	Input Force	$\mu : 326.4g, \sigma : 447.2g$

Table 1. Summary of the push-button dataset

	Count	Surface Area (mm^2)	Seating Depth (mm)
Below	12 (<1%)	$\mu : 143, \sigma : 199.6$	$\mu : 1.65, \sigma : 1.13$
Level	297 (19.6%)	$\mu : 291, \sigma : 576.6$	NA
Above	1206 (79.5%)	$\mu : 125, \sigma : 93.5$	$\mu : 0.89, \sigma : 0.85$

Table 2. Properties of buttons seated above, level, and below the plane

of buttons seated below the plane (line 1), that have, on average, smaller surface areas than those level with (line 2) or above (line 3) the plane. Buttons are on average seated $0.89mm$ below the plane or $1.65mm$ above the plane. Of the 12 buttons below the plane six (50%) were to control power to an appliance.

Buttons below the plane are harder to press: Figure 1 shows the peak force distribution of buttons according to their relationship with the surrounding plane. An ANOVA ($df_{2,\,1512} = 3.385, p \leq 0.05$) shows that buttons seated below the plane require greater peak input force (μ : $625.4g$, σ : $420.9g$) than those seated in line (μ : $337.0g$, σ : $601.1g$) or above it (μ : $320.57g$, σ : $399.7g$). This result is in part due to the 'wasted' force a user applies to the surrounding plane when attempting to activate the button.

Button shapes are distributed around a finger's width: Figure 2 provides a frequency-density plot showing that buttons of all shapes tend to be between half a finger and a finger in width [3] (the left peak). A second peak to its right shows a large number of rectangular buttons around widths of $18mm$—these resemble computer keyboard buttons, which often occur in large numbers. Although the sample contains few buttons with irregular shapes, the distribution indicates that they often have larger and more varied widths than the other types of button. We believe this is due to irregular buttons often forming part of the casing for an appliance.

Landscape orientation is more common than portrait: Viewing buttons in their natural orientation, 62.8% were landscape, symmetric buttons accounted for 24.1%, and those in portrait orientation just 13.1%. This stems from various design factors including textual button labels and physical selection abilities. In the majority of languages, text is written horizontally (either within the button or below it) requiring more horizontal than vertical space.

On devices with a high-concentration of co-located buttons, landscape orientation can reduce the chance of a press unintentionally triggering multiple buttons as our fingertips have

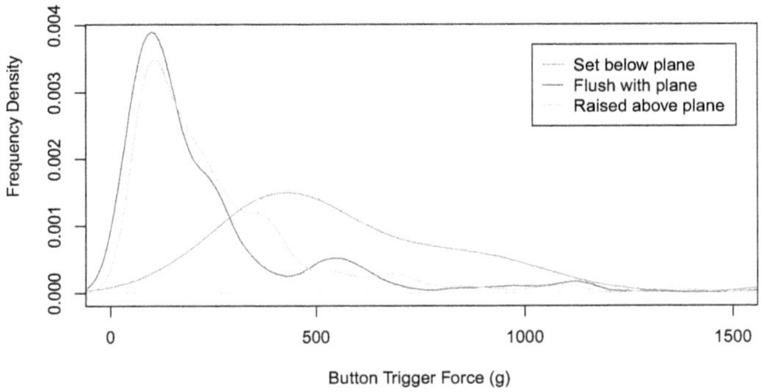

Figure 1. Peak force required to trigger buttons, based on relationship to surrounding plane

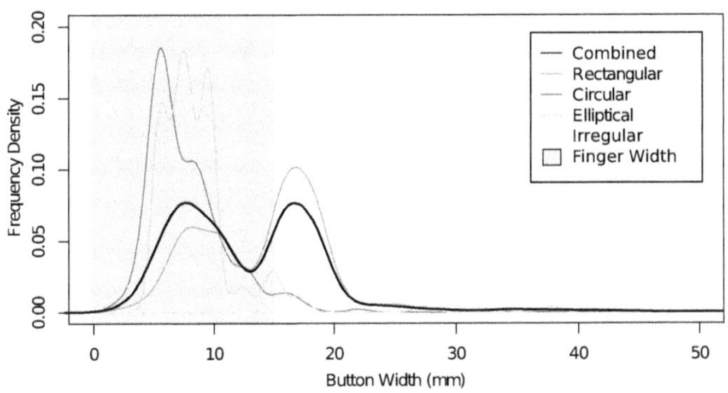

Figure 2. Button width distribution by shape, overlaid with width of a typical adult index finger

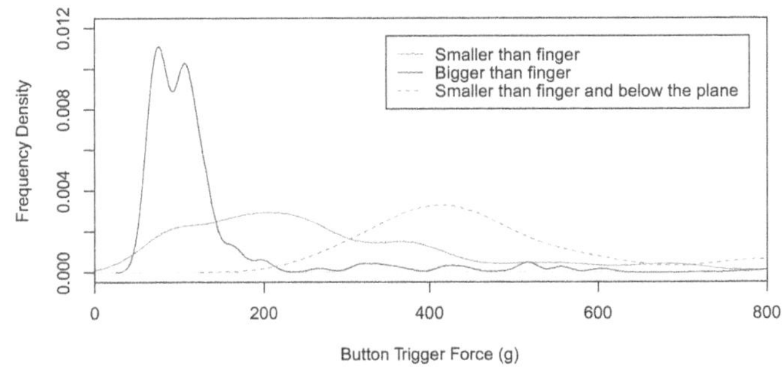

Figure 3. Peak force required to trigger buttons relative to the width of a typical adult index finger

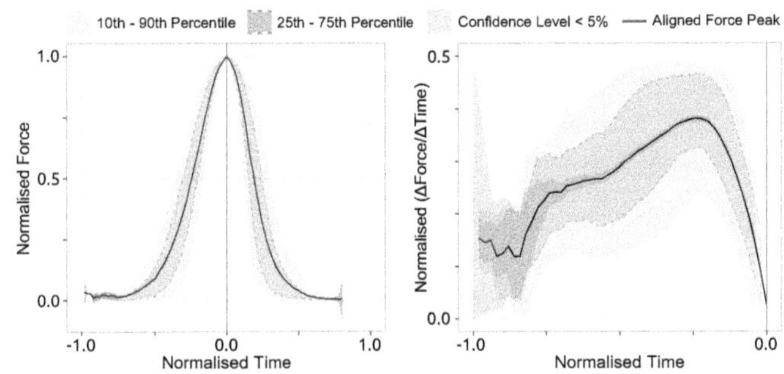

Figure 4. Force and time profile (left) and rate of force increase (right). These are computed by normalising and maxima-aligning all samples

a landscape profile. Portrait style buttons requiring fingertip interaction generally result in poor ergonomic design.

Bigger buttons are pressed with less force: Figure 3 shows that most buttons larger than a typical adult index finger ($15.82mm \pm 2.26mm$) [3] are pressed with less force ($\approx 100g$) than those which are smaller. The smaller buttons are subjected to a much wider range of forces. Although a heteroscedastic t-test indicates that the two groups are significantly different ($t_{876.6} = 2.564, p \leq 0.05$), we suspect that the higher variance on smaller buttons can be explained by the blunt nature of the finger 'wasting' force on the surroundings. This is supported by the higher force recorded when examining buttons smaller than a finger which are also seated below the surrounding plane.

Longer presses correlate with higher peak force: There is a positive correlation between the interaction time for each press (μ : $0.56s$, σ : $0.30s$) and the peak force reached ($r_{1494} = 0.73, p<.001$). Figure 4 (left) shows a 'typical' press profile. This is differentiated in Figure 4 (right) to reveal the rate at which the force applied increases.

Buttons with audible feedback require less input force: The majority of buttons (89.1%) incorporated audible feedback into the trigger mechanism. Buttons with audible feedback require less input force (μ : $287.9g$, σ : $376.3g$) than those without audio feedback (μ : $641.8g$, σ : $754.2g$). A t-test indicates significant differences between the two groups ($t_{1513} = 9.89, p \leq 0.001$), although examination of the distributions indicates additional data would be beneficial. Of the silent buttons, 77.5% were rubber.

Button input on hand-held devices requires greater force: We classified each appliance as either *hand-held* or *free-standing*. Hand-held devices are those which are designed to be held when pressing buttons; Free-standing devices do not require holding under normal operation. During force testing, handheld devices were placed on solid surfaces, to alleviate human variance. People tend to press buttons on hand-held devices with more force, requiring on average $357.5g$ (σ : $363.5g$) to trigger, while freestanding devices received $298.1g$ (σ : $510.2g$) of force. A heteroscedastic t-test shows this difference to be significant ($t_{1432.25} = 2.625, p \leq 0.01$).

Buttons used in short bursts are smaller: We classified devices based on two degrees of typical user interaction duration: *sustained* (e.g. games console controllers) and *short burst* (e.g. a router reset button). Cross-referencing this data with button dimensions revealed two significant groups ($t_{1512.8} = -14.5, p \leq 0.001$) where smaller buttons (μ : $10.1mm$, σ : $8.1mm$) are often used in short bursts, and larger buttons (μ : $16.5mm$, σ : $9.2mm$) are used over longer periods of time.

Toggle buttons are rare: We observed only 11 toggle buttons (those that remain depressed once engaged). In the virtual world toggle buttons are commonly used to indicate mode (e.g. when *bold* is selected in a word processor). In the physical world this mode-indication is often addressed by LED indicators or a physical state change within the appliance. Five of the observed toggle buttons were for power control, the remainder were for function selection.

DISCUSSION

Generalisably

This characterisation has presented a range of features of typical household buttons. The dataset is localised to houses in the United Kingdom with occupants of medium–high socio-economic standing, meaning a large concentration of modern, electronically controlled devices were present. We observed remarkable consistency across many different types of appliance, acquired for wildly varying tasks (such as washing clothes, drilling holes, or reading ebooks), and see no reason for our findings not to generalise within this group.

The effect a designer has on the properties we measured remains unclear: while some appliances will have undergone much 'button-related' design (such as game controllers and keyboards), others are likely to be influenced by more indirect factors such as cost, manufacturing restrictions, available space, and aesthetics. An inspection of the design and manufacturing process would be required to extract the source of button-design decisions.

Towards Buttons for Physically-Dynamic Displays

The collected data shows how the physicality of buttons can provide implicit information to the user (e.g. reset buttons are harder to press) and can reflect the needs of the interaction (e.g. lightly tapping keys or pressing small buttons harder ensure activation). Dynamic adjustment of button size and offset relative to the surrounding plane could lead to novel interaction mechanics. E.g., using physical conditions to make actions harder to invoke ('delete friend' or 'power-off').

One of the most important properties for recreating button input in physically-dynamic displays is the ability to reproduce appropriate force profiles based on users' physical world experiences. Short travel distances and the physical sizes of buttons have immediate implications for the resolution and actuation design of materials. Similarly, the observed force-profiles indicate the required operational range to recreate the experience/familiarity of physical buttons. Physically-dynamic displays can extend this feature to measure the user's input force on-the-fly in order to detect complex input signals, distinguish between intentional and unintentional activation, or detect 'error' conditions where users exert more force than normal in an attempt to reinforce control.

CONCLUSION

This paper has presented a survey of 1515 physical buttons in household environments. Through our characterisation of these buttons we have extracted a number properties that can guide researchers in the positive transfer of real-world knowledge to physically-dynamic surfaces. We believe the ergonomics ingrained in this data set will continue to be relevant in a generation of physically-dynamic surfaces.

ACKNOWLEDGEMENTS

This work forms part of GHOST, a project funded by the European Commission's 7th Framework Programme, FET-Open scheme (grant #309191).

REFERENCES

1. Alexander, J., Lucero, A., and Subramanian, S. Tilt Displays: Designing Display Surfaces with Multi-axis Tilting and Actuation. MobileHCI '12, ACM (2012).
2. Brewster, S., Chohan, F., and Brown, L. Tactile Feedback for Mobile Interactions. CHI '07, ACM (2007), 159–162.
3. Buryanov, A., and Kotiuk, V. Proportions of Hand Segments. *International Journal of Morphology 28* (09 2010), 755 – 758.
4. Buxton, W., Hill, R., and Rowley, P. Issues and Techniques in Touch-sensitive Tablet Input. SIGGRAPH '85, ACM (1985), 215–224.
5. Colton, M. B., and Hollerbach, J. M. Reality-based Haptic Force Models of Buttons and Switches. In *Robotics and Automation '07*, IEEE (2007), 497–502.
6. Doerrer, C., and Werthschuetzky, R. Simulating Push-buttons using a Haptic Display: Requirements on Force Resolution and Force-Displacement Curve. EuroHaptics '02 (2002).
7. Harrison, C., and Hudson, S. E. Providing Dynamically Changeable Physical Buttons on a Visual Display. CHI '09, ACM (2009), 299–308.
8. Hoffmann, A., Spelmezan, D., and Borchers, J. TypeRight: A Keyboard with Tactile Error Prevention. CHI '09, ACM (2009), 2265–2268.
9. Iwata, H., Yano, H., Nakaizumi, F., and Kawamura, R. Project FEELEX: Adding Haptic Surface to Graphics. SIGGRAPH '01, ACM (2001), 469–476.
10. Lee, S., and Zhai, S. The Performance of Touch Screen Soft Buttons. CHI '09, ACM (2009), 309–318.
11. Lewis, J., Potosnak, K., and Magyar, R. Keys and keyboards. *Handbook of human-computer interaction* (1997), 1285–1315.
12. Miller, T., and Zeleznik, R. The design of 3D haptic widgets. In *Symposium on Interactive 3D Graphics*, ACM (1999), 97–102.
13. Park, G., Choi, S., Hwang, K., Kim, S., Sa, J., and Joung, M. Tactile Effect Design and Evaluation for Virtual Buttons on a Mobile Device Touchscreen. MobileHCI '11, ACM (2011), 11–20.
14. Poupyrev, I., Nashida, T., Maruyama, S., Rekimoto, J., and Yamaji, Y. Lumen: Interactive Visual and Shape Display for Calm Computing. SIGGRAPH '04, ACM (2004).
15. Swindells, C., MacLean, K. E., Booth, K. S., and Meitner, M. J. Exploring Affective Design for Physical Controls. CHI '07, ACM (2007), 933–942.
16. Tashiro, K., Shiokawa, Y., Aono, T., and Maeno, T. A Virtual Button with Tactile Feedback Using Ultrasonic Vibration. In *Virtual and Mixed Reality*, R. Shumaker, Ed., vol. 5622 of *LNCS*. 2009, 385–393.

Towards Habitable Bits: Digitizing the Built Environment

Yuichiro Takeuchi
Sony Computer Science Laboratories Inc.
3-14-13 Higashigotanda
Shinagawa-ku, Tokyo 141-0022 Japan
yutak@acm.org

ABSTRACT
Recently, there has been a growing number of research efforts aimed at the *digitization of architectural space*. Whereas conventional attempts at integrating digital technology into architectural space have typically viewed architecture as an inflexible backdrop onto which layers of digital devices/services/information can be *overlaid*, the newly emerging efforts instead strive to *inject architecture itself* with the distinct plasticity of digital bits. In this paper, we will first provide a review of this nascent body of work, weaving together the disparate streaks of technical development into a consilient research trajectory that can be interpreted as a modern-day extension to Weiser's original vision of Ubiquitous Computing. Next we turn to the two decades' worth of criticisms raised against the UbiComp ideal, to expose what perspectives are missing from the fledgling efforts, and to identify the roles the HCI community can play in shaping the future of this promising line of work.

Author Keywords
Habitable bits; habitable user interfaces (HUIs); synthetic space; ubiquitous computing; responsive architecture; augmented architecture; printable architecture.

ACM Classification Keywords
H.5.m. Information Interfaces and Presentation (e.g. HCI): Miscellaneous.

INTRODUCTION
Despite its publication in a popular magazine as opposed to a scholarly journal, "The Computer for the 21st Century"—the famed essay by Mark Weiser [61] in which he introduced his vision of Ubiquitous Computing—has firmly emerged as one of the most impactful writings in computer science of the past several decades. The level of accuracy with which Weiser had anticipated future technical advances is uncanny; the popular notion of an ongoing shift towards a *post-PC era* is all but an exact facsimile of Weiser's words, with only small differences in terminology (Weiser used *tabs*, *pads* and *boards* instead of *smartphones*, *tablets* and *interactive surfaces*). The degree to which Weiser's influence can be felt both in and outside academia is a testament to the power of academic writing to generate profound societal impact.

ITS 2014, November 16–19, 2014, Dresden, Germany.

http://dx.doi.org/10.1145/2669485.2669506

Whereas many of the commentaries on Weiser's writings [51] have focused on his idea of "invisible computing" (the notion that interaction with computers should be as seamless and undemanding as writing on paper), here we would like to instead bring attention to "embodied virtuality"—another of the varied (but interconnected) themes touched on in his epochal essay—i.e., the idea that the distinctive properties of digital bits should cease to be accessible only within the PC, and instead be made to permeate across the full extent of the physical environment. The concept is eloquently expressed in the following short sentence from Weiser's essay (note the unique usage of the term *virtuality* here):

> The "virtuality" of computer-readable data—all the different ways in which it can be altered, processed and analyzed—is brought into the physical world.

A prescient statement, that more or less summarizes the myriad HCI innovations over the past 23 years. Indeed, the various research concepts/initiatives—e.g., mobile computing, tangible user interfaces, ambient displays, augmented reality, surface/tabletop computing, to name a few—have all contributed to the steady injection of "virtuality" into the physical world. At a quick glance, it appears that we have already turned embodied virtuality into an indisputable reality.

However, on close inspection we find that instead of virtuality fully permeating throughout the physical world, these intense developments have culminated to form multiple auxiliary layers of digital devices/services/information atop a primarily inert background of *static architecture*, i.e., the traditional built environment composed of ceilings, walls, floors and windows (Figure 1). Digital plasticity flourishes, but only on the auxiliary layers; it seldom (if ever) invades the architectural layer, which is largely assumed as invariant. This attitude is implicit but prevalent. A typical *augmented reality* city guide app for smartphones merely overlays panels and bubbles onto an otherwise unaltered city scenery, and a typical *interactive wall* in corporate offices only permits digital interaction with the 2D graphical contents displayed on its limited, stationary surface. For the most part, the pursuit of embodied virtuality so far has stayed one step short of *digitizing the built environment*.

The Achilles' heel of this attitude is that architecture is by no means a neutral, uninvolved background layer. Studies in environmental psychology [12, 55] have shown that our actions, thoughts and even emotional states are strongly influenced by

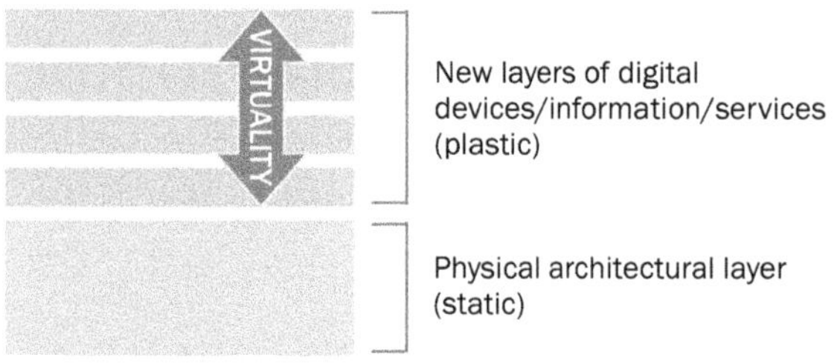

Figure 1. "Virtuality" only spreads within the new, auxiliary layers.

the design of the environment, both indoors and outdoors. To use an example rooted in our day-to-day lives as researchers, we will struggle to write papers, even if provided with a (hypothetical) perfect word processing software on a perfect laptop/tablet, if the environment is not conducive to such activities. (This manuscript was mostly written at a greatly conducive café in Berlin; trying to write at the local Thai joint never yielded quite as good results.) Architecture, far from being an impartial bystander, acts in fact as an active and potent manipulator of myriad human behavior—including our interactions with digital technologies [18].

What we are now witnessing is the spread of virtuality strictly under the reins of architecture. For us to truly infuse the benefits of virtuality throughout the physical world, architectural space itself will need to be digitized, i.e., imbued with the distinctive properties of digital bits (plasticity, interactivity, ease of modification/duplication/distribution, etc.).

As we will illustrate in this paper, there are emerging, but still largely isolated, efforts targeting precisely that goal. Though so far the HCI community has generally been reluctant to deal directly with the design of architectural space, we believe that this nascent group of efforts can act as harbingers of an exciting research direction, that offers the community an opportunity to further extend Weiser's vision for the coming decades. While the complete digitization of the built environment (Figure 2) will likely elude us even in the distant future, the range of technical approaches, with further development, may bring us ever closer to this seemingly improbable goal.

The paper will begin with an in-depth review of the emerging efforts (which exist primarily in HCI/CS research but also in diverse fields including Architecture and the Arts), categorizing them into the following three key approaches: *responsive architecture*, *augmented architecture* and *printable architecture*. Next, we turn to the wealth of commentaries on Weiser's ideas and their aftereffects that have arisen in the past 23 years both within and outside of the HCI community, using them to reveal missing perspectives in the future vision (*proximate future* [11]) underlying the newly emerging efforts. Finally, we will conclude by discussing what roles HCI research can play in steering and further developing this line of work.

The paper's primary contributions are: (1) weaving together a wide range of disparate, emerging technical efforts into a coherent narrative that extends Weiser's vision, offering a common framework/language within which relevant works can be couched, and (2) formulating a critique of said narrative that

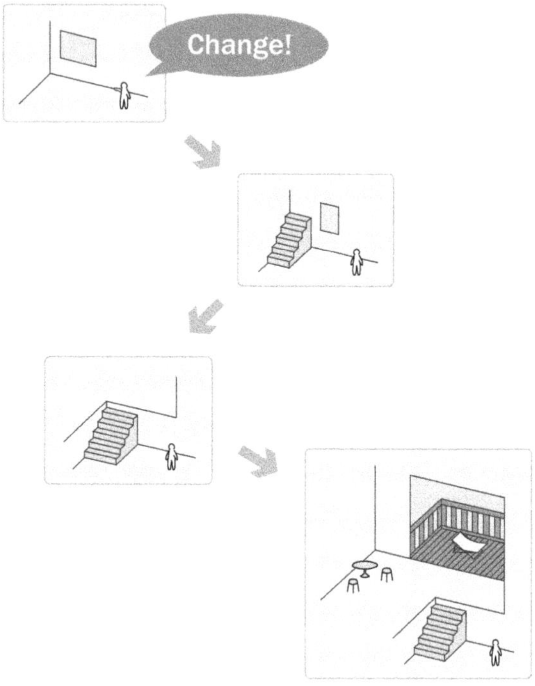

Figure 2. In a hypothetical, "fully-digitized" architectural space, transforming the environment will be as easy as changing the desktop wallpaper on a modern-day PC.

draws on criticisms raised against the UbiComp ideal, deriving from which a list of possible future contributions the HCI community can make in this domain. While the paper's scope may on surface appear to be overly broad and eclectic, discussions are held together by a consistent interest in the closer integration of digital technology and the physical world—a topic of central relevance to the HCI community.

HABITABLE BITS, SYNTHETIC SPACE

To be fair, humans already possess a number of technologies that manipulate space, which we use on a daily basis. Calling someone on the phone can instantly *compress space*, portable MP3 players effectively surround us with *auditory walls*, and airbnb enables us to freely convert our homes into hotels, etc. Combine this with the wealth of published research on tangible user interfaces, smart homes, urban informatics, etc., and we can easily see that the entire scope of *space-altering* technologies is practically infinite, and has been growing long before the arrival of the nascent efforts that are the central topic of this paper. The new efforts, however, possess the following traits that set them apart from their precedents:

- Builds upon a clear awareness of the power of architecture to influence human behavior and psychology
- Demonstrates an intention to explicitly *curb, control or enhance* the said power of architecture
- Accomplishes the above via digital manipulation of one or more of the physical properties of architectural space

The range of technologies that possess these traits is diverse. As should become clear later in this section as we list related

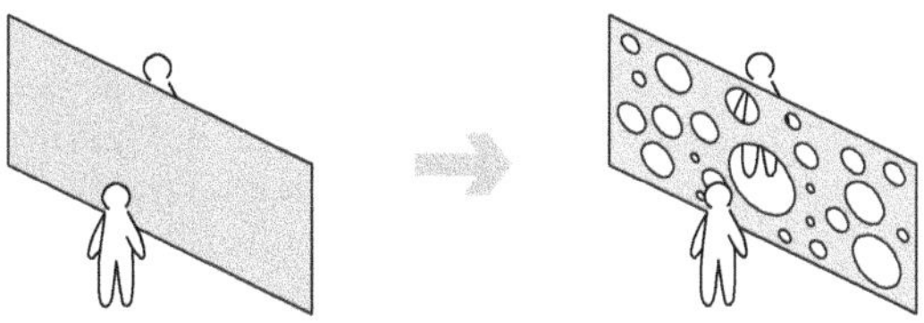

Figure 3. Responsive architecture. In this relatively small-scale example, the responsive wall's color changes to green and apertures appear on its surface, allowing passersby to see through to the other side.

work, we are not anticipating an imminent birth of some kind of a hyper-futuristic wonderland, where entire buildings/cities are made out of ceaselessly shapeshifting programmable matter. Rather, what we are observing is a steady pace of innovations occurring in heterogeneous technical domains, that will in time collectively chip away at the longstanding stability of the architectural environment. Ultimately, the ever-increasing latitude with which we can alter our surroundings will lead to the experience that we are living within a world built of "habitable" bits—or, to use a term introduced in a previous publication, living within "synthetic" space [57].

Within prior work, we have identified three key technical approaches—*responsive*, *augmented* and *printable architecture*, respectably—which we predict to serve as the main drivers of the coming digitization of architectural space. Below, we will provide a review of notable efforts belonging to each of these technical approaches.

Responsive Architecture

Responsive architecture refers to a class of architectural structures/environments, which can dynamically alter their shapes and/or appearances using kinetic transformation mechanisms, RGB displays, etc. The terminology is still not entirely fixed, and alternative names denoting similar concepts exist such as *interactive architecture* [23] and *kinetic architecture* [67] (although the latter may more appropriately be considered a subcategory due to its exclusive focus on kinetic transformation). In both academia and architectural practice, the label does not apply to input-only systems (for example wide deployment of sensors, surveillance cameras, etc.) and requires the existence of some form of digital output capability, often involving dynamic adaptation to input (Figure 3).

Responsive architecture as a research category has only begun to receive a serious look in the last few years in the academic HCI community [17, 26]. Hence the list of precedents is still short, and mostly comprises sporadic works presented outside the main tracks of top conferences [33]. The concept has long been of interest to architects, however, and there already exist examples of commercially successful applications such as revolving restaurants, retractable stadium roofs, *media facades* [63], etc. Although due to the immense cost (especially when involving mechanical transformations; fantastical visions like Archigram's *Walking City* [16] will likely remain fantasies for the foreseeable future) such constructions are seldom seen in residential or low-budget commercial projects, innovations in digital design/prototyping tools (e.g., *Grasshopper*) are rapidly dismantling many of the traditional hurdles associated with this domain. Hence it may not be irrational to expect growing usage of various responsive architecture in everyday environments, albeit at scales smaller than entire buildings—e.g., kinetic facades [34], adaptive furniture [36, 60], etc. This may be aided by the recent fascination within HCI with shapeshifting user interfaces [48], which can potentially yield new technologies applicable to the design of such structures.

Despite not making much inroads into responsive architecture *per se*, the HCI community has neither been oblivious nor indifferent to the capacity of architectural space to steer human behavior and provide overarching context to interactions [18]. Early works on media spaces [13] and ambient interfaces [66] are clearly built on a recognition of the power of architecture, for example. However, as has been the case with most efforts in HCI research, they have primarily been concerned with designing systems to be installed *atop* the architectural environment, instead of attempting to *actuate architecture itself.* Out of the mainstream topics pursued in HCI research, *interactive surfaces* may perhaps have the most to share (in both concept and technology) with responsive architecture. Interactive surfaces—i.e., architectural surfaces with digital I/O capabilities—have long been a staple in HCI research, having their roots in Weisers *boards*, and highlighted by Ishii [29] as one of the key components of *Tangible Bits*.

Seeing how research on interactive surfaces has evolved in recent years, we can identify three ways in which this area has progressively turned "architectural" in its concerns.

The first is the expansion in scale. From Augmented Surfaces [50] to Multitoe [7] and LightSpace [65], interactive surfaces have steadily increased their area of coverage to entire rooms, making the whiteboard-sized *boards* look minuscule in comparison. The quantitative growth in scale has brought forth a qualitative change in topology; interactive surfaces no longer coexist with users *as equal entities* inside the same room, but instead *enclose* users, in the same manner as architecture. The second is the diversification of context. While early works on interactive surfaces installed and studied them mainly in laboratory settings, many recent works investigate their use in everyday environments, such as homes [37] and streets [21, 47] This indicates how the technology has matured from its initial status as a novelty for research labs to a potentially commonplace constituent of the future built environment. The third is the evolution of interaction techniques. Humble touchscreens have since been joined by gesture input [42] and *proxemic interaction* [10]—a driving force behind this development is the recognition that as interactive surfaces begin to *enclose* users, we could no longer assume that users will adopt a fixed pose/position/distance when engaging with these surfaces.

The three developments all point to a future where interactive surfaces no longer are confined within perceivable boundaries and begin to permeate across the environment; we will not interact with them in the traditional sense, but will instead start to *inhabit* them. Put another way, research on interactive surfaces is proceeding along a path that an eventual collision and intermixing with responsive architecture seems inevitable.

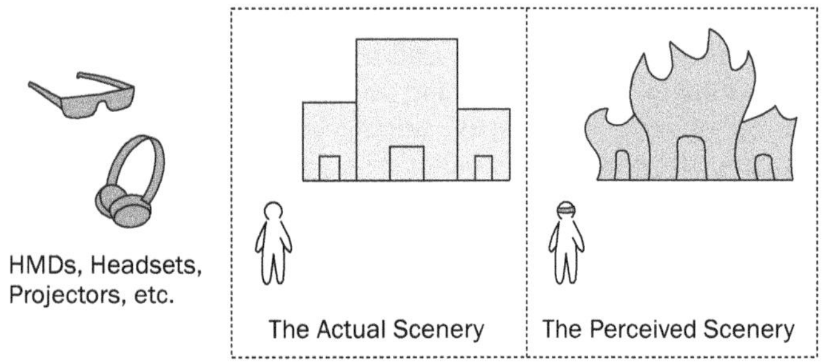

Figure 4. Augmented architecture. Augmented reality technology is used to filter the user's perception of space, offering the experience of a "digitized" architectural environment. Since the effects are illusory transformations need not follow real-world constraints, e.g., the laws of physics.

Augmented Architecture

Augmented architecture does not involve actual technical interventions to architecture itself; rather, the label represents a class of technologies that employ *augmented reality* to "filter" users' perceptions of the surrounding built environment, producing *equivalent* experiences of digitized architectural space (Figure 4). While one may rightfully argue that such technologies (that exert no power over architecture per se) should be discounted by definition when considering attempts at digitizing architectural space, in light of the possibly wide adoption of augmented reality technologies and the key roles they may come to play in shaping our future spatial experiences, we instead deem it myopic not to include them in our discussions. (However, we do exclude *virtual reality* from our discussions, keeping in line with Weiser's positioning of the technology as being diametrically opposed in principle to UbiComp.)

It may be possible to say that the entire premise of augmented reality involves the digitization of the environment. However, within prior work in this field we observe a curious reluctance towards actively manipulating architecture using this technology. (We gave an example earlier in this paper; a typical augmented reality app for mobile devices merely overlays panels/bubbles over an otherwise unaltered city landscape.) This reluctance has historical roots. Early works on augmented reality [20, 49], owing to technical limitations at the times, could only display simple (by today's standards) graphics on top of an unaltered live video feed. The metaphor has stuck, and today many augmented reality systems adhere to it despite the fact that technical advances have made real-time image processing feasible, even on mobile devices. Recently we are beginning to see a shift, however. Using techniques from diminished reality [43], ClayVision [59] has demonstrated how the field can move beyond mere overlays of virtual signage, presenting users with the capacity to grow, transform and remove buildings with ease. With fast, robust computer vision libraries for mobile platforms becoming more widely available, we expect similar efforts (that effectively inject *virtuality* into the architectural layer, although the transformations are illusory) to increase in number in the next several years. Future developments may lead to less cumbersome hardware (lightweight glasses, etc.), and higher fidelity that will further blur the line between external reality and the illusory effects.

Bachelard [9] argues that our experience of space is a holistic one that involves multiple sensory channels. If so, augmented architecture must cater to a wide range of modalities not limited to vision—otherwise the experience offered would not be felt as anything more than a superficial veneer. Although still sporadic, in HCI we can see a growing number of works that address this concern. For example, Weightless Wall [58] uses custom headsets to simulate sound-blocking walls that can be erected anywhere in a room, which is proposed as a key component of a new office design where workers can freely erect, delete or modify walls to suit their tasks at hand. Haptic augmentation is being studied as well; CabBoots [24] and Gilded Gait [56] are both footwear-shaped devices that can mechanically alter sensations of ground shape/texture. However, even with such promising developments, it must be noted that it is highly unlikely that augmented architecture will ever be able to cater to the full range of human sensation, which is a fundamental limitation of the approach. (We will later list and compare the respective advantages and drawbacks of the three key technical approaches.)

Projection-based (or *spatial*) augmented reality represents another important variation of augmented architecture technology. While the use of projection has a long history in HCI (being used to render interactive surfaces for example), the growing availability of low-cost depth sensors has made projection onto large, complex (non-planar) environments easier, which is evident in works such as IllumiRoom [30] where the living room is turned into an extension of the TV screen. The use of mobile/wearable projectors for spatial augmentation has been investigated as well [52, 45]—which may yield another viable approach to augmented architecture, provided that power outputs of compact projectors see sufficient increases.

While the most cutting-edge technical efforts in this area are still found predominantly in HCI/CS research, augmented reality has also attracted much attention in the fields of architecture and the arts, leading to large-scale implementations rarely seen in laboratory research. One example is the *N Building* [4] in Tokyo, whose front facade constitutes a giant QR code (fiducial marker) that allows pedestrians to see virtual animations by looking at the building through smartphone cameras. Spatial augmented reality has been widely adopted as well, in the form of *projection mapping* onto buildings which has become a popular attraction throughout the world.

Printable Architecture

Printable architecture (Figure 5) refers to a class of technologies that can automatically "print out" full-scale architectural structures from digital files, using techniques such as additive manufacturing (i.e., *3D printing*). Compared to responsive or augmented architecture, these technologies operate at considerably slower time scales—thus they do not support instantaneous transformations of environments like that illustrated in Figure 2. (More precisely, they do not actually support transformations at all; structures can merely be replaced with newly printed ones.) Even with such limitations, however, we believe the advent of printable architecture to be a key development towards the digitization of architectural space, due to its potential to bring the high degree and ease of consumer-level

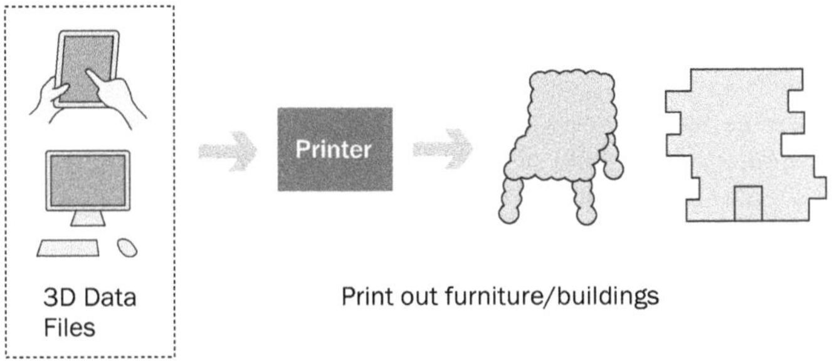

Figure 5. Printable architecture. Furniture/buildings are digitally fabricated from 3D data files, that can be newly created by users, downloaded from online repositories, etc.

customization—a characteristic property of digital media—to the design of architectural space.

Since the area is in an even earlier phase of development than responsive or augmented architecture, precedents are still few in number and also highly experimental in nature. So far there have been no notable efforts within HCI research that deal directly with printable architecture, and most technical developments are seen instead in the fields of architectural design and civil/environmental engineering. Printing out entire *habitable* buildings, which may well be the holy grail of printable architecture, is being attempted but existing efforts (e.g., D-Shape [2], Contour Crafting [35]) have not reached a level where we can expect practical usage in any short-term future. An alternative approach is to digitally fabricate smaller components, that are later assembled manually to produce the final design; this is the method adopted in 3D Print Canal House [1] and in some artistic installations [3]. At the furniture scale, 3D printing is already fully feasible, and one can find many products on the market fabricated using this technology, as well as directions/files to print one's own on websites (such as *Instructables*) for DIY hobbyists with access to digital fabrication facilities. Other, seemingly far-fetched approaches for automatic construction are also being investigated, for example *flight assembled architecture* [25] which relies on an army of quadcopter drones to construct brick buildings.

Overall, though printing out entire residential houses or apartments still seems to fall into the realm of science fiction—and appears to stay that way, in dense city centers at least—printing out smaller-scale structures (e.g., room interior, furniture) is quickly becoming viable. Perhaps a sensible prediction for the role of printable architecture in the short-term future may be that it will *complement*, and not *replace*, existing construction technologies, that still hold substantial leads in areas such as structural integrity, material choices, etc.

In HCI, while attention towards printing technology itself has surged in the last few years, the main concern has been developing techniques for printing *functional* objects such as optics [64] and electronics [31]—which likely are not directly applicable to printable architecture (unless we are printing responsive architecture, which may happen in the future). However, there is a respectable line of work on digital design tools, and a wide range of techniques have been developed [28, 54] over the years aimed at making 3D design more accessible and intuitive for non-professional users. While such works may not count as contributions to printing technology itself, they nevertheless will constitute an indispensable part of the printable architecture *ecosystem*.

Adherence to Architectural Conventions

Besides relying on straightforward technical classifications as above, another way to categorize and make sense of the range of technologies contributing to the digitization of the built environment is to look at their different attitudes toward our preconceived notions of architectural space—i.e., the timeworn, largely pan-cultural (in industrialized regions at least) image of rationally delineated space, composed of floors, walls, ceilings and windows.

We use the term *conservative* to refer to technologies that inject digital properties into architectural space, while still generally conforming to traditional ideas about the makeup of the built environment. Depending on the degree to which they adhere to traditional ideas, we further classify them into *literally conservative* and *metaphorically conservative* technologies.

Literally conservative technologies take a strictly traditionalist stance, faithfully retaining the "classic" experiential qualities of traditional architectural space. Responsive architecture that rely solely on kinetic transformation usually falls into this category; one good example is *Maison à Bordeaux*, designed by Rem Koolhaas [38], in which an embedded elevator moves the floor up and down within the house. Although each move of the elevator renews the spatial logic of the building, within each static state—i.e., when the elevator is standing still—the spatial experience is precisely that of a conventional architectural environment. A visitor may quite possibly not notice the dynamic capabilities of the building, until a transformation is actually observed or experienced. Printable architecture typically belongs to this category as well.

Such technologies are in contrast to those that are *metaphorically conservative*, i.e., technologies that introduce markedly foreign elements into the makeup of the environment, but are nevertheless designed to operate along traditional architectural metaphors. Many augmented architecture technologies belong to this category, as they are likely (even with future technical advances) incapable of offering *literal* experiences that operate on the entire spectrum of human sensation. For example, the sound-blocking virtual walls of Weightless Wall [58] are distinctly foreign elements not part of a conventional built environment, but the technology is still designed to have *metaphorical* similarity to real, physical walls.

In time, we can expect technologies to appear that act largely independent of conventional metaphors. We use the term *progressive* to refer to these yet hypothetical future technologies. In his essay, Weiser predicted a gradual adoption of UbiComp technologies, considering the adoptions of *tabs* and *pads* to be necessary conditions for the later adoption of *boards*. We expect a similarly stepwise process for the digitization of architectural space; *conservative* technologies will first provide the initial scaffolding, for the belated emergence of the more radical, *progressive* technologies.

	Responsive Architecture	Augmented Architecture	Printable Architecture
Offers Literal Experience	Yes	No	Yes
Range of Transformation	Moderate	Very High	High
Time Scale of Transformation	Instantaneous	Instantaneous	Slow
Cost	High	Low	High

Table 1. Comparison of the three key technical approaches.

Comparison of Technical Approaches
Table 1 shows the respective advantages and drawbacks of the three technical approaches we have discussed thus far.

Responsive and printable architecture both have the potential to offer *literal* (as defined earlier) experiences of architectural space. The capacity will likely be absent from the majority of augmented architecture systems, whose effects will predominantly operate on the user's sense of vision; while augmented reality glasses can make a smooth wall *look* bumpy, if the effect is merely visual it will still feel smooth when touched by hand. (In contrast, a responsive surface that can mechanically alter its texture [41] can be made to both look and feel rough.) Also, effects of (non-spatial) augmented architecture are only perceptible to those wearing the supported devices.

On the other hand, augmented architecture allows both immediate and wide-ranging modifications of environments; buildings can be made to wildly swing around as if they were made out of jelly [59]. Transformations of environments via printable architecture will not be as instantaneous, and those via responsive architecture will lack the high degree of freedom.

In terms of cost, augmented architecture will probably be the most reasonable, owing to its reliance on wearable or portable electronic devices. Costs of printable and responsive architecture will typically be higher, and will also be highly divergent depending on scale, choice of material, etc.

It is important to note that the three key technical approaches we have discussed had been identified based on existing work, and we do not rule out the possibility that other types of technologies will emerge that end up making larger contributions to the digitization of the built environment. In fact, we regard such scenarios as being entirely plausible—our opinion is that HCI and other related CS subfields have generally been hesitant to explore ideas that cross over with architectural design, which has thus far limited the types of technical contributions that could be made within this space.

THE IMPLIED FUTURE
We have now described the range of technical approaches that we expect to play primary, but not necessarily exclusive, roles in the coming digitization of the built environment. However, descriptions of individual technologies by themselves fail to give a holistic sense of what life could actually be like in such a future. Here, as Weiser had done in his original essay (albeit with a word of caution about the inevitably quixotic nature of such efforts), we would like to extrapolate from today's rudimentary fragments of *habitable bits* to provide a hypothetical scenario of everyday life, in a world where embodied virtuality has fully run its course.

In a tiny studio apartment in a dense city center, Sal awakens. She smells coffee—the array of sensors laid out under her 3D printed bed had detected her awakening, and promptly started the coffee machine. With mug in hand Sal glances at the wall, which flickers as if to say good morning, and begins to display various information such as news headlines, weather forecast, and her health status measured by the bed during her sleep.

Sal starts to prepare for work. She had recently moved to this town; as is typical here the apartment is old and cramped, but her newly printed interiors (complete with a small indoor garden) are optimized to make the most efficient use of space.

The office is roughly a 15-minute walk from Sal's apartment. From her bag Sal takes out her *glasses* and puts them on. Not that she has any problems with eyesight, but the glasses allow her (in addition to seeing her friends' status updates at the periphery of her vision) to customize the urban landscape to her liking. Several cafés on the street immediately begin glowing in different colors, indicating their levels of crowdedness. Sal enters the least crowded one, and soon comes out with a muffin in her hand.

Sal walks across a plaza, at the heart of which there is a large public monument emitting light in various bright colors. This is not an illusory effect created by the glasses—the light is actually being emitted, and its colors reflect the current mood of the city obtained by performing sentiment analysis on the citizens' public status updates. Looking at the bright colors, Sal surmises that many people are excited about the soccer match scheduled to take place later in the day.

Buildings around intersections appear translucent through the glasses. This lets Sal easily be aware of any cars/bicycles that may be heading in her direction when crossing streets. Multiple RGB/depth cameras (whose images are anonymized at the hardware level) are installed throughout intersections to make this possible. This is one of a range of technologies that have made streets—now busier than ever, due to diversified means of transportation—much safer for pedestrians/cyclists.

On the edge of the sidewalk, Sal notices a line of glowing tiles on the ground. She halts her walk and pays attention to them; suddenly lush trees emerge from the tiles' surfaces. The trees are not real, but are visualizations of the city's plans for lining its streets with trees. In this way, by using the glasses citizens can see and comment on their cities' design proposals. While this hasn't changed the messy nature of planning politics, the technology has given citizens an ever wider array of channels through which they can affect and take part in the process.

After passing by an interactive mural and a series of buildings adorned with 3D printed gardens, Sal arrives at the office. The floor is crowded—although telepresence systems are in place that now allow remote workers to communicate seamlessly as if they are working in the same room, the relative advantages of face-to-face communication have still not eroded, and thus many of Sal's colleagues make the conscious choice to physically commute to work. The office is of an open-plan design, largely devoid of walls other than those structurally necessary and several others made of *switchable glass*. Sal picks up her *headset* from her desk and puts them on; this, working together with her glasses, lets her create translucent, sound-blocking walls (whose effects are shared by all employees wearing the headsets) anywhere in this congested office. Feeling the need to concentrate as she reads through a technical document, Sal encircles herself with walls to temporarily isolate herself from the surrounding noise.

Sal hears someone knock on the virtual wall—it is Jon, a colleague with whom Sal has been working together on a project. After chatting briefly inside the wall, they decide to get some coffee and Sal deletes the wall. At the coffee machine the two bump into several other colleagues, and they all share updates on their respective projects. Above their heads, shapeshifting chandeliers offer enjoyment emitting soft, relaxing light.

Having finished her job for the day, Sal walks toward the station to meet her friend Mary; they had promised to go to dinner together. On her way is a park, where she can see children playing games on a brightly illuminated landscape—a projector system is installed in the park capable of rendering various games tailored to the number and ages of children on site. Sal sees children frantically jumping across what looks like stone platforms floating on a lava field.

Sal finds Mary; they hadn't yet decided on what or where they would like to eat. The two sync their glasses, so that they both see a similarly transformed city. Sal utters "*find restaurants*", and promptly all non-restaurant buildings turn into short, featureless gray blocks. Mary says "*I feel like Thai tonight*", and again a group of buildings promptly turn flat and nondescript. The respective heights of the remaining buildings reflect their average ratings on a restaurant review website. Sal adds "*I'm a bit short on money lately, I need to keep it under 30 dollars*", which leads to yet another batch of flat, gray blocks. The two head for the tallest remaining building in sight—i.e., the highest rated Thai restaurant within their budget—and enjoy their meal. The wholly 3D printed interiors of the restaurant makes them feel as if they are dining in an ancient Thai temple.

Having parted from Mary, Sal again walks across the plaza as she heads home. The monument is glowing in a sad, blue color, and has visibly shrunk in size compared to the morning—Sal guesses that their team has lost the soccer match.

Sal arrives home, takes a shower and then goes to sleep; when morning comes, the wall beside her bed will glow in a warm, orange light to gently wake her up.

Although the above scenario is mere speculation, the short vignette illustrates how simple extrapolation of emerging technologies hint at an impending drastic shift in our relationships with architectural space. The optimistic (one may say *techno-utopian*) tone is a reflection of the fact that these technologies are still in phases of early development, and their descriptions in literature tend to focus on elucidating seductive future possibilities in bold, graphic terms, rather than offering cautious reflections on their real-world feasibility or implications. For example, consider the following excerpt from [30]:

> When the game starts, the room magically transforms to look like a cartoon, matching the shading in the video game. The colors of the room become super-saturated and cartoon edges appear on your bookshelves. You come across an enemy in the game, and suddenly a streaking bullet flies towards your character and then out of the television.

Or this passage from [57], that gives off an even more techno-utopian ring:

> The "synthetic" office of the future may consist of rooms with variable sizes and forms, that constantly shrink or expand according to what activity is taking place inside. A room with many workers having a lively discussion could be increased in size, at the expense of unused or scarcely occupied rooms.

The future vision implied in these emerging works is one of a world where individuals have the capacity to freely transform or customize the surrounding built environment, new aesthetic styles flourish, city streets boast impeccable safety/accessibility for all, and citizens play increased roles in the planning and construction of their city landscapes. Contrary to past visions about future cities laid out in urban informatics [22, 46], what is plastic here is not only the transparent layers of digital information overlaid *atop* the city, but also the physical built environment made of glass, concrete and steel. What appears to be missing, however, are sober assessments of whether this vision has any chance of materializing (as UbiComp successfully has) in the real world, and if it does, what kinds of ramifications that will entail for society at large.

CRITICAL REFLECTION

We have shown how varied efforts are now emerging that aim at digitizing architectural space, but also how they are still in phases of early development, where optimism and fascination take center stage instead of critical assessments of their feasibility and implications. While Weiser's original vision was at least as (if not far more) technically optimistic and ambitious, the vision has been variously shepherded, fleshed out and reshaped over the past 23 years as ideals dovetailed with reality. The real-world manifestation of UbiComp now unfolding before our eyes may be *messier* [11] than what Weiser (and the early pioneers of the field) had anticipated, but what has been lost in theoretical purity has been replaced by practical efficacy to benefit our lives. Likewise, efforts at digitizing the built environment will also need to be tempered, and steered away from their present juvenile states. Ideally, this should happen *right now*, as opposed to later. As Lanier notes [40], in digital technology early design decisions (regardless of whether they had been made based on sound logic) tend to become fixed in place as *de facto standards*, that are too entrenched to replace later with better-designed alternatives.

As the digitization of the built environment can be interpreted as a logical extension to UbiComp, many of the criticisms and reflections on Weiser's vision made over the past two decades should be applicable here as well. Below, we will list some of the most notable commentaries on the UbiComp ideal raised within the academic community, and examine their relevance to the nascent attempts at realizing habitable bits.

The Illusion of Universality

Weiser's vision (or at least its representation in his essay) has been called out as being inherently paternalistic [19], built on an implicit assumption that his lab in Silicon Valley can serve as some modern equivalent of a colonialist capital, where the most important technical breakthroughs exclusively originate and from which they subsequently "trickle down" towards the rest of the world. Reality has proven this model to be wrong. Technical innovation is carried out by a multipolar network of individuals and groups that cannot be pinned down based on either geography (*Silicon Valley*) or institution type (*research laboratory*), and the same technology is often adopted in entirely separate ways by groups operating under different economic, cultural or social contexts [32]. The real-world manifestation of UbiComp is a global achievement, and its product is anything but a homogeneous, universal entity.

The same criticism wholly applies to the digitization of architectural space. Although in the scenario presented earlier, Sal now lives in a dense city center as opposed to suburbia (which is to some extent our deliberate decision to reflect the societal changes that have occurred during the past 23 years, but more importantly is an acknowledgment of the fact that an increasing number of HCI/CS research now targets urban settings), but to think that such an environment can serve as a universal prototype for the entire future world is just as naive as assuming that Xerox PARC could fit the bill two decades ago.

From Vision to Messy Reality

Weiser's Sal inhabited a world where the hundreds/thousands of computing devices spread across the environment all work together seamlessly and faultlessly. This has not yet been materialized, and we have no good reason to think it will ever be. Weiser had predicted that mobile devices (*tabs and pads*) will not be personal, but exist in large numbers scattered across the environment like post-it notes. Clearly this did not come true; one convincing explanation for this [5] is that Weiser failed to anticipate how passing around data between devices will continue to be so cumbersome and unreliable after so many years. Devices will not only have trouble communicating with each other, but will also often fail [15] due to numerous unpredictable reasons including software bugs, power outages, etc. Finally, humans (*users*) add another potential point of failure to the entire system [44], with our limited mental/physical capabilities and propensity to make mistakes. Far from the clockwork precision imagined by Weiser, the real-life UbiComp is a messy, imperfect system with limited built-in robustness.

The digitization of the built environment, if realized, will also take on a messy, imperfect form. The claim that in the future, transforming the architectural environment will be as easy as changing the wallpaper image on a present-day PC [57] takes for granted the smooth functioning of myriad, heterogeneous technical components that will be required in such a scenario, as well as glancing over the fact that switching the wallpaper image on a PC may not necessarily be an easy task for *everyone*. Also, if we were to turn into reality the idea (touched on in the scenario) of using digitized architecture for bottom-up/DIY urban design, the most likely pitfall will not be technical, but will instead be what is perhaps the *messiest* aspect of human society—i.e., politics.

Social/Ethical/Political Implications

Weiser did not necessarily shy away from discussing the possible risks of his vision, as evidenced by his assertion that we investigate how to better deal with privacy. However, privacy is but one of a wide range of negative consequences argued to be brought about by UbiComp [8, 14]. Will UbiComp make our lives richer through automation, or will it make them even more stressful by blurring the line between work and leisure? When society increasingly relies on UbiComp infrastructure, what will be the costs (economic, social, etc.) of its malfunctions and failures? How much environmental damage will result from manufacturing all these new digital devices, that use rare materials and are largely non-recyclable? These are only a few of the many potential issues raised within the academic community, that have actually turned out to be grave concerns over the past two decades. Such concerns are not only carried over to the digitization of the built environment, but are often exacerbated, owing to the increased scale.

THE ROLES OF HCI RESEARCH

Despite being accused of numerous oversights and shortcomings, UbiComp as a concept has been remarkably successful, providing theoretical foundations for a wide range of technological wonders that we now take for granted. (So successful, that Abowd [5] has declared it to have all but "disappeared"—i.e., the concept is now so widely accepted that it is no longer possible to define any work as being *uniquely UbiComp*.) The HCI community has made a range of contributions instrumental to this process, exhibiting a distinct set of assets that make it well-equipped to take on similarly pivotal roles in the eventual realization of habitable bits. Below, we will list three different ways in which the community can contribute in further exploring this research trajectory, steering the efforts we have discussed so far toward more constructive directions.

As a Home for Vision-Oriented Discussions

One distinguishing attribute of the HCI community is its penchant for placing sweeping visions regarding the evolution of computing at the forefront of discussions, as opposed to being concerned narrowly with particular technical domains. While HCI may not be the community best suited for bringing about the most fundamental technical innovations either for responsive, augmented or printable architecture, its proven record in nurturing and promoting a concept makes it the most suitable community for rigorous discussions regarding the overall narrative to take place—e.g., whether the digitization of architectural space is a real, ongoing phenomenon or a mere illusion, whether it is a worthy extension to UbiComp or a trivial subfield, how can the vision be directed and fleshed out, what repercussions will arise for which domains, etc.

Though such discussions may rightfully take place outside of HCI, one would be hard-pressed to name another community with as respectable a tradition of accepting vision-oriented research (e.g., Ishii and Ullmer [29]) as first-rate academic contributions; within HCI, discourse on habitable bits can potentially take center stage, not relegated to the fringes.

As a Birthplace of New Design Methodologies/Toolkits

Perhaps unsurprisingly given its long favorable stance toward application-driven research, HCI has been the birthplace of a number of design methodologies [27, 39], prototyping techniques [6], toolkits [53], etc., that have subsequently been widely adopted in both research and practice. Many of these techniques are aimed at assisting designers effectively collect and utilize information about target users/contexts, allowing them to iteratively create applications tailored to the *messy* and *heterogeneous* realities that had not been accounted for with sufficient depth in Weiser's original vision.

As with UbiComp, applications will again be *the whole point* [62] of habitable bits, and hence the community's concern for methodologies/toolkits should be of benefit if it can be guided into contributing to this direction. Established HCI methdologies will likely fail in the face of architecture-scale system design—we do not know how to iteratively develop systems for which creating a series of full-scale prototypes is not feasible, and we also do not know if existing methodologies are applicable to the design of systems whose life spans are measured in decades not months or years. A new set of techniques/tools will need to be devised, taking cues from multiple disciplines including conventional HCI and architectural design.

As a Multidisciplinary Hub

HCI has always maintained an unabashedly multidisciplinary scope, which is reflected in the makeup of its community that now enlists members with backgrounds in computer science, engineering, industrial design, psychology and philosophy to name a few. While alternative communities exist that already are rigorously exploring the intersection between digital technology and architecture / urban design (e.g., civil engineering, smart city research, computer-aided design), their focus is not as all-inclusive, and none of them has quite as rich a tradition of interdisciplinary collaboration as HCI.

This fact makes HCI a highly promising community to tackle questions that escape disciplinary silos; for example, how can we reconcile the notion of augmented architecture (that practically enables people to live in their own *solipsistic* fantasies) with the notion of shared, public space? No existing community can adequately respond to such questions, but HCI seems to have the best chances of *evolving* into one that can.

CONCLUSION

In this paper, we have described how technologies are emerging that aim at an eventual *digitization of architectural space*. We have reviewed relevant prior work, and exposed the optimistic future vision implied within these technical efforts. We have then offered a critique of this vision, by drawing on past criticisms raised against the original UbiComp ideal. Finally, we have described several ways in which the HCI community can make use of its unique set of strengths, in shaping the future of this nascent direction of research.

HCI has long been obsessed with injecting digital technology into the physical environment, and recent innovations such as shapeshifting UIs and physical prototyping toolkits are giving us ever greater capacities to customize and transform our surrounding physical environments. Nonetheless, as we have argued in this paper, HCI has generally treated architectural design as being *off limits* of sorts. The emerging efforts we have described in this paper signal a bold departure from that longstanding indifference, an attitude we hope will be adopted by the broader HCI community. We believe that the time is ripe for HCI to evolve into a field that studies and designs the environment of the future *in its totality*, not only its niche subset we have been preoccupied for so long. GUIs, TUIs, etc. have been thoroughly studied; the new frontier for HCI now lies in the study and design of *HUIs—Habitable User Interfaces*.

REFERENCES

1. 3D Print Canal House (http://3dprintcanalhouse.com/). Retrieved Sep. 16, 2014.
2. D-Shape (http://www.d-shape.com). Retrieved Sep. 16, 2014.
3. Digital Grotesque (http://www.digital-grotesque.com). Retrieved Sep. 16, 2014.
4. N Building (http://www.teradadesign.com/works/architecture/n-building.html). Retrieved Sep. 16, 2014.
5. Abowd, G.D. What Next, Ubicomp? Celebrating an Intellectual Disappearing Act. Proc. UbiComp 2012. pp.31-40.
6. Abowd, G.D., Hayes, G.R., Iachello, G., Kientz, J.A. Prototypes and Paratypes: Designing Mobile and Ubiquitous Computing Applications. Pervasive Computing, 4 (4). pp.67-73. 2005.
7. Augsten, T., Kaefer, K., Meusel, R., Fetzer, C., Kanitz, D., Stoff, T., Becker, T., Holz, C., Baudisch, P. Multitoe: High-Precision Interaction with Back-Projected Floors Based on High-Resolution Multi-Touch Input. Proc. UIST 2010. pp.209-218.
8. Questioning Ubiquitous Computing. Proc. CSC 1995. pp.230-237.
9. Bachelard, G. The Poetics of Space. Beacon Press. 1994.
10. Ballendat, T., Marquardt, N., Greenberg, S. Proxemic Interaction: Designing for a Proximity and Orientation-Aware Environment. Proc. ITS 2010. pp.121-130.
11. Bell, G., Dourish, P. Yesterday's Tomorrows: Notes on Ubiquitous Computing's Dominant Vision. Personal and Ubiquitous Computing, 11 (2). pp.133-143. 2007.
12. Bell, P.A., Greene, T.C., Fisher, J.D., Baum, A. Environmental Psychology (Fifth Edition). Lawrence Erlbaum Associates. 2001.
13. Bly, S.A., Harrison, S.R., Irwin, S. Media Spaces: Bringing People Together in a Video, Audio, and Computing Environment. Comm. of the ACM, 36 (1). pp.28-46. 1993.
14. Bohn, J., Coroama, V., Langheinrich, M., Mattern, F., Rohs, M. Social, Economic, and Ethical Implications of Ambient Intelligence and Ubiquitous Computing. Ambient Intelligence. pp.5-29. 2005.
15. Chetan, S., Ranganathan, A., Campbell, R. Towards Fault Tolerant Pervasive Computing. Technology and Society Magazine, 24 (1). pp.38-44. 2005.
16. Cook, P. Archigram. Princeton Architectural Press. 1999.
17. Dalton, N., Green, K., Marshall, P., Dalton, R., Hoelscher, C., Mathew, A., Kortuem, G., Varoudis, T. Ar-CHI-Tecture: Architecture and Interaction. Ext. Abst. CHI 2012. pp.2743-2746.

18. Dourish, P. Where the Action Is: The Foundations of Embodied Interaction. MIT Press. 2004.
19. Dourish, P., Mainwaring, S.D. Ubicomp's Colonial Impulse. Proc. UbiComp 2012. pp.133-142.
20. Feiner, S., MacIntyre, B., Haupt, M., Solomon, E. Windows on the World: 2D Windows for 3D Augmented Reality. Proc. UIST 1993. pp.145-155.
21. Fischer, P.T., Hornecker, E. Urban HCI. Spatial Aspects in the Design of Shared Encounters for Media Facades. Proc. CHI 2012. pp.307-316.
22. Foth, M. Handbook of Research on Urban Informatics: The Practice and Promise of the Real-Time City. Information Science Reference. 2008.
23. Fox, M., Kemp, M. Interactive Architecture. Princeton Architectural Press. 2009.
24. Frey, M. CabBoots: Shoes with Integrated Guiding System. Proc. TEI 2007. pp.245-246.
25. Gramazio, F., Kohler, M., D'Andrea, R. Flight Assembled Architecture. Editions HYX. 2012.
26. Gross, M.D., Architectural Robotics, Inevitably. Interactions, 19 (1). pp.28-33. 2012.
27. Hutchinson, H., Mackay, W., Westerlund, B., Bederson, B.B., Druin, A., Plaisant, C., Beaudouin-Lafon, M., Conversy, S., Evans, H., Hansen, H., Roussel, N., Eiderback, B. Technology Probes: Inspiring Design for and with Families. Proc. CHI 2003. pp.17-24.
28. Igarashi, T., Matsuoka, S., Tanaka, H. Teddy: A Sketching Interface for 3D Freeform Design. Proc. SIGGRAPH 1999. pp.409-416.
29. Ishii, H., Ullmer, B. Tangible Bits: Towards Seamless Interfaces between People, Bits and Atoms. Proc. CHI 1997. pp.234-241.
30. Jones, B.R., Benko, H., Ofek, E., Wilson, A.D. IllumiRoom: Peripheral Projected Illusions for Interactive Experiences. Proc. CHI 2013. pp.869-878.
31. Kawahara, Y., Hodges, S., Cook, B.S., Zhang, C., Abowd, G.D. Instant Inkjet Circuits: Lab-Based Inkjet Printing to Support Rapid Prototyping of Ubicomp Devices. Proc. UbiComp 2013. pp.363-372.
32. Kayan, S., Fussell, S.R., Setlock, L.D. Cultural Differences in the Use of Instant Messaging in Asia and North America. Proc. CSCW 2006. pp.525-528.
33. Khan, O. Open Columns: A Carbon Dioxide (CO2) Responsive Architecture. Ext. Abst. CHI 2010. pp.4789-4792.
34. Khoo, C.K., Salim, F.D. Lumina: A Soft Kinetic Material for Morphing Architectural Skins and Organic User Interfaces. Proc. UbiComp 2013. pp.53-62.
35. Khoshnevis, B. Automated Construction by Contour Crafting—Related Robotics and Information Technologies. Automation in Construction, 13 (1). pp.5-19. 2004.
36. Kinch, S., Gronvall, E., Petersen, M.G., Rasmussen, M.K. Encounters on a Shape-Changing Bench: Exploring Atmospheres and Social Behavior in Situ. Proc. TEI 2014. pp.233-240.
37. Kirk, D., Izadi, S., Hilliges, O., Banks, R., Taylor, S., Sellen, A. At Home with Surface Computing? Proc. CHI 2012. pp.159-168.
38. Koolhaas, R. Living, Vivre, Leben. Birkhauser. 1999.
39. Landay, J.A., Borriello, G. Design Patterns for Ubiquitous Computing. Computer, 36 (8). pp.93-95. 2003.
40. Lanier. J. You are Not a Gadget: A Manifesto. Alfred A. Knopf. 2010.
41. Leithinger, D. Lakatos, D., DeVincenzi, A., Blackshaw, M., Ishii, H. Direct and Gestural Interaction with Relief: A 2.5D Shape Display. Proc. UIST 2011. pp.541-548.
42. Malik, S., Ranjan, A., Balakrishnan, R. Interacting with Large Displays from a Distance with Vision-Tracked Multi-Finger Gestural Input. Proc. UIST 2005. pp.43-52.
43. Mann, S., Fung, J. EyeTap Devices for Augmented, Deliberately Diminished, or Otherwise Altered Visual Perception of Rigid Planar Patches of Real-World Scenes. Presence, 11 (2). pp.158-175. 2002.
44. Maxion, R.A., Reeder, R.W. Improving User-Interface Dependability through Mitigation of Human Error. Intl. Journal of Human-Computer Studies, 63 (1-2). pp.25-50. 2005.
45. Mistry, P., Maes, P. SixthSense: A Wearable Gestural Interface. SIGGRAPH Asia 2009 Sketches. no.11.
46. Mitchell, W.J. City of Bits: Space, Place, and the Infobahn. MIT Press. 1996.
47. Muller, J., Walter, R., Bailly, G., Nischt, M., Alt, F. Looking Glass: A Field Study on Noticing Interactivity of a Shop Window. Proc. CHI 2012. pp.297-306.
48. Rasmussen, M.K., Pedersen, E.W., Petersen, M.G., Hornbk, K. Shape-Changing Interfaces: A Review of the Design Space and Open Research Questions. Proc. CHI 2012. pp. 735-744.
49. Rekimoto, J., Nagao, K. The World through the Computer. Proc. UIST 1995. pp.29-36.
50. Rekimoto, J., Saitoh, M. Augmented Surfaces: A Spatially Continuous Work Space for Hybrid Computing Environments. Proc. CHI 1999. pp.378-385.
51. Rogers, Y. Moving on from Weiser's Vision of Calm Computing: Engaging UbiComp Experiences. Proc. UbiComp 2006. pp.404-421.
52. Rukzio, E., Holleis, P., Gellersen, H. Personal Projectors for Pervasive Computing. IEEE Pervasive Computing, 11 (2). pp.30-37. 2012.
53. Salber, D., Dey, A.K., Abowd, G.D. The Context Toolkit: Aiding the Development of Context-Enabled Applications. Proc. CHI 1999. pp.434-441.
54. Saul, G., Lau, M., Mitani, J., Igarashi, T. SketchChair: An All-in-One Chair Design System for End Users. Proc. TEI 2011. pp.73-80.
55. Sundstrom, E., Sundstrom, M.G. Work Places: The Psychology of the Physical Environment in Offices and Factories. Cambridge University Press. 1986.
56. Takeuchi, Y. Gilded Gait: Reshaping the Urban Experience with Augmented Footsteps. Proc. UIST 2010. pp.185-188.
57. Takeuchi, Y. Synthetic Space: Inhabiting Binaries. Ext. Abst. (alt.chi) CHI 2012. pp.251-260.
58. Takeuchi, Y. Weightless Walls and the Future Office. Proc. CHI 2010. pp.619-628.
59. Takeuchi, Y., Perlin, K. ClayVision: The (Elastic) Image of the City. Proc. CHI 2012. pp.2411-2420.
60. Takeuchi, Y., You, J. Whirlstools: Kinetic Furniture with Adaptive Affordance. Ext. Abst. CHI 2014. pp.1885-1890.
61. Weiser, M. The Computer for the 21st Century. Scientific American, 264 (3). pp.94-104. 1991.
62. Weiser, M. Some Computer Science Issues in Ubiquitous Computing. Comm. of the ACM, 36 (7). pp.75-84. 1993.
63. Wiethoff, A., Gehring, S. Designing Interaction with Media Facades: A Case Study. Proc. DIS 2012. pp.308-317.
64. Willis, K., Brockmeyer, E., Hudson, S., Poupyrev, I. Printed Optics: 3D Printing of Embedded Optical Elements for Interactive Devices. Proc. UIST 2012. pp.589-598.
65. Wilson, A.D., Benko, H. Combining Multiple Depth Cameras and Projectors for Interactions On, Above, and Between Surfaces. Proc. UIST 2010. pp.273-282.
66. Wisneski, C., Ishii, H., Dahley, A., Gorbet, M., Brave, S., Ullmer, B., Yarin, P. Ambient Displays: Turning Architectural Space into an Interface between People and Digital Information. Proc. CoBuild 1998. pp.22-32.
67. Zuk, W., Clark, R.H. Kinetic Architecture. Von Nostrand Reinhold Company. 1970.

ePlan Multi-Surface: A Multi-Surface Environment for Emergency Response Planning Exercises

Apoorve Chokshi, Teddy Seyed, Francisco Marinho Rodrigues, Frank Maurer
University of Calgary, Department of Computer Science
2500 University Drive NW, Calgary, Alberta, T2N 1N4
{apoorve.chokshi, teddy.seyed, fm.rodrigues, frank.maurer}@ucalgary.ca

ABSTRACT
Emergency response planning is a process that involves many different stakeholders who may communicate concurrently with different channels and exchange different information artefacts. The planning typically occurs in an emergency operations centre (EOC) and involves personnel both in the room and also in the field. The EOC provides an interesting context for examining the use of tablets, tabletops and large wall displays, and their role in facilitating information and communication exchange in an emergency response planning scenario. In collaboration with a military and emergency response simulation software company in Calgary, Alberta, Canada, we developed *ePlan Multi-Surface*, a multi-surface environment for communication and collaboration for emergency response planning exercises. In this paper, we describe the domain, how it informed our prototype, and insights on collaboration, interaction and information dissemination in multi-surface environments for EOCs.

Author Keywords
crisis management; cross-device interactions; emergency management; emergency operations; emergency; gestures; mobile devices; multi-surface environments; peripheral interactions; risk communication; tabletops;

ACM Classification Keywords
H.5.2 [User Interfaces]: Graphical user interfaces (GUI), Input Devices and Strategies, Interaction Styles. H.5.3 [Groups & Organization Interfaces]: Collaborative computing, computer-supported cooperative work

INTRODUCTION
Large scale emergencies and disasters highlight the vulnerability of modern society to collapses of infrastructure that is crucial to daily life (e.g. roads, phone service, and electricity). A significant challenge with emergencies also arises from the different types that can occur, from

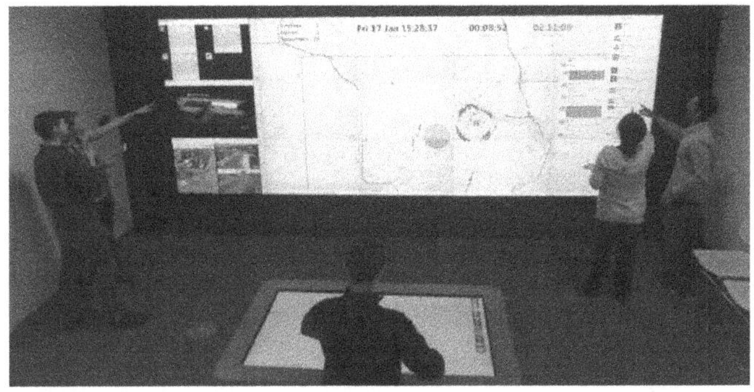

Figure 1 – Users collaborating in the ePlan Multi-Surface environment

unplanned events like natural disasters, train derailments, and chemical spills, to planned large-scale events like the Olympics and the World Cup.

Events such as the 2013 floods in Southern Alberta, as well as other recent major events and natural disasters have resulted in significant efforts by authorities worldwide to investigate how information and communication technologies (ICT) can both facilitate and improve upon existing emergency planning and response capabilities. These technologies are primarily found in emergency operations centre (EOC), where trained personnel need to make informed decisions in situations that can be both stressful and highly volatile while information is uncertain and incomplete.

For EOC personnel, a primary challenge is the number of information sources and amount of data that needs to be analyzed and continually monitored during an emergency. These sources include personnel in the field (e.g. firefighters, police, emergency medical services (EMS) or military) or third party sources (e.g. newspapers, television channels or citizens). As Van de Walle noted, "accurate and timely information is as crucial as is rapid and coherent coordination among the responding organizations. [23]"

For each information source, there are different protocols before information can be exchanged effectively in the EOC and between personnel. The source of information determines how it can enter the EOC (i.e. via video, audio, or text). A traffic or incident camera could live-stream into the EOC, tweets could arrive via text, and information from ground-personnel may arrive via text messages, by phone or

ITS 2014, November 16–19, 2014, Dresden, Germany.
Copyright 2014 ACM 978-1-4503-2587-5/14/11...$15.00
http://dx.doi.org/10.1145/2669485.2669520

radio. EOC personnel need to ascertain the importance, authenticity, and accuracy of the information. Emergency personnel report through their chain-of-command, reporters (print, web, television and radio) may have their information fact-checked before broadcast, while citizens may live-tweet, post updates, or send emails as an emergency unfolds. When the EOC receives information updates from their personnel, reporters, or citizens, they may also need to monitor developing traffic congestion, incident cameras, and operational decisions that are continually made.

Multi-surface environments (MSE), are environments that contain multiple heterogeneous devices (e.g. tablets, wall displays, tabletops) that are spatially aware of each other, as well as the users in the environment [18]. This provides an environment amenable to emergency response planning in multiple ways.

First, by providing different areas for information triage (Figure 1), an MSE allows for different information sources to be viewed on different devices. Tablets can be used for personal, private workspaces from which personnel can privately communicate with colleagues. Tabletops serve as a semi-public collaboration and cooperation area, and large wall displays serve as information radiators that publicly aggregate information from multiple sources.

Secondly, because MSEs are spatially aware (devices and people are tracked), it can support the sharing of information between these public and private devices through spatial interactions. For example, flicking or pouring information can occur such that it is context aware. A flick directed towards a wall without the wall display will not send information whereas a flick towards the wall display will render information on the device.

As Seyed *et al.* [19] highlight, "significant research has been done into different types of interactions, as well as collaboration for multi-display environments; however, very little work has gone into exploring multi-surface environments with real industrial partners." As part of the effort to validate these interactions in commercial environments, we explored collaboration and communication for multi-surface environments in the context of emergency response planning, the domain of our industry partner.

In this paper, we present *ePlan Multi-Surface*, a prototype for an EOC of the future that harnesses a multi-surface environment to enable tablets, tabletops, and a large wall display to interact with one another to create a connected communication environment. We also discuss the space of multi-surface environments and interactions in the context of EOCs and challenges presented during implementation.

BACKGROUND & RELATED WORK

Emergency Response Planning

Emergency operations centres (EOCs) are central environments that allow for people from multiple organizations to gather for emergency planning exercises, during emergency events, or during the recovery phase after an emergency event. An EOC can be found in both public and private enterprises who need to conduct planning exercises on an on-going basis to ensure preparedness in emergency situations [15]. In these emergency-planning exercises (Figure 2), multidisciplinary teams of experts collaborate to define how they should prepare or respond to various scenarios [22].

When emergency responders are training for the different scenarios, they conduct one of two general types of exercises: tabletop exercises and live exercises.

Tabletop Exercises

Tabletop exercises are based on the simulation of a realistic scenario and are either real-time or on an accelerated time. They can be run in a single room, or in a series of linked rooms that could simulate the division between responders who need to communicate and be co-ordinated. People involved in these exercises are expected to know the plan and they are invited to test how the plan works as the scenario unfolds. This type of exercise is particularly useful for validation purposes, particularly for exploring weaknesses in procedures [9].

Live Exercises

Live exercises are a live rehearsal for implementing a plan, and can be particularly useful for testing logistics, communications, and physical capabilities. They are a useful training tool to help build experiential learning by having

Figure 2 – Images from tabletop emergency response planning exercises from A) FEMA Operations Supervisor in planning session (Image courtesy FEMA/George Armstrong), B.) FEMA cross-border tabletop exercise (Image courtesy FEMA/Eilis Maynard) C.) US Navy command and control center afloat (Image courtesy US Navy/ Bobby Northnagle)

participants develop confidence in their skills and by providing experience on how it would be to use the plan's procedures in a real event [9].

Personnel & Artefacts

In both real and simulated emergency situations, the EOC provides a key liaison role between municipal officials, external resources and policy makers. To help EOC staff coordinate emergency response with other key stakeholders and personnel, clearly defined principles are used, typically called the Incident Command System [8].

Paper-based maps and documents are commonly used in both exercises (Figure 2) where they are referenced and annotated. Depending upon the situation, responders (e.g. police, EMS, and hazardous materials (HAZMAT)) communicate with people both inside and outside the room. It is vital that people inside the room have the most current information to form a common operating picture (COP) – a *"continuously updated overview of an incident compiled throughout an incident's life cycle from data shared between integrated systems for communication, information management, and intelligence and information sharing."*[1] A COP helps to support decision-making, and to also to ensure that personnel in the field are working with current information.

Tabletops and Surfaces

Emergency response planning is comprised of many important tasks, from detecting and monitoring the emergency to the deployment of resources and communication management [3] [10]. Emergency response planning is also inherently a peripheral process [2]; critical information about an emergency can arrive from numerous sources (e.g. first responders, reporters, or online sources) and information processing and analysis are typically done in parallel with the primary emergency response-planning activity [2] frequently with interruptions [7].

In the HCI research literature, emergency response planning is a well-explored area, with several different technologies (e.g. tabletops [3]) being used to assist in these tasks, as well as information management, collaboration, and efficiency [10]. However, common rules on interactions to improve collaboration are scarce as the interactions and interfaces are heavily impacted by the domain and the system's purpose. As highlighted by Bortolaso *et al.* [3], co-locating people around a device does not mean that the collaboration will be improved: the trade-off between simplicity and functionality must be evaluated multiple times during the system's development.

uEmergency is a forest fire simulation system running on a very large-scale interactive tabletop [16]. This tabletop's dimensions (381 x 203cm) allow several users to collaborate using the system concurrently while considering personal space (local and private workspace) and a global space (shared among all users and synchronized through a button). Users can interact with the system using a digital pen or touch gestures. It is possible to translate and resize a map using gestures with one and two fingers, respectively; to perform annotations dragging and dropping markers from a menu into the map; and changing the simulation's time point through a slider available on each personal workspace. Since all users are sharing on a physically large tabletop, collaboration is improved through visual cues from each user's actions.

Besides digital pen and touch gestures, physical tokens are also used in disaster planning systems on tabletops [12]. They act as input, changing simulation parameters according to their physical position above the tabletop, and provide feedback through images projected on them. The manipulation of physical tokens to interact with emergency systems has reduced the learning curve of these systems.

While many of these systems utilize single tabletops or other devices and show a benefit in emergency response situations [3], they do not consider peripheral interaction scenarios where multiple users interact with each other on tablets, tabletops, and wall displays. Concurrently, these users are also analyzing and receiving different sources of information while conducting their emergency response planning exercises.

This provides an opportunity for the exploration in using multi-surface environments that contain multiple heterogeneous devices (e.g. tablets, wall displays, tabletops) and which permit a variety of different tasks and interactions (e.g. "flicking" to different screens) [18]. This may be due to interface design, physical constraints such as orientation or screen size, or device constraints. The research space of multi-surface environments is well explored and significant research has been done in examining different ways in which interactions can take place [6][17][18].

The collaborative nature of emergency response planning and the presence of multiple and heterogeneous devices in a room provides an opportunity for the study and experimentation of different types of gesture-based and peripheral interactions in the emergency response domain, described in this work by ePlan Multi-Surface.

EPLAN MULTISURFACE

We developed *ePlan Multi-Surface*, in collaboration with a military and emergency response simulation software company, C4i Consultants Inc.[2] (C4i), located in Calgary, Alberta, Canada. Not only did C4i provide feedback and ideas on features for the prototype, but they also provided the

[1] FEMA- https://www.fema.gov/pdf/emergency/nrf/nrf-glossary.pdf

[2] C4i - http://www.c4ic.com/

company's desktop simulation engine, ePlan, which we integrated with the prototype.

This section summarizes the design considerations for the prototype and its features.

Design Considerations

While working with C4i, we continually discussed and iterated on features that supported three main design elements. These features were inspired by features requested by C4i, or were features that we were looking to test in another domain outside of oil and gas [19].

Privacy Levels in a Shared Environment

We endeavoured to create spaces where personnel in the room from the police, EMS, and HAZMAT could make notes and control how and when they shared information with colleagues from the other services in the room. For example, we wanted the support the ability of the police to discuss and share information internally, make necessary revisions, and then share information with EMS and HAZMAT teams. Taken together, the needs of the personnel and the affordances of the devices, we looked to support the user's ability to keep information private on the devices before publicly disclosing it.

Information Integration

There are multiple sources of information coming into an EOC from sources like the news media, Twitter[3], traffic cameras, incident cameras, personnel from the field, and from personnel in the room. In addition, through the simulation software, we had entities (buildings, people, and vehicles) that we were tracking on a large map to ensure we knew what was happening to the common operating picture (COP).

To reduce the information burden on personnel in the room, we sought a way to consolidate information from these sources so that users could focus on decision-making while knowing that the COP was updating in real-time. As we describe later, the large wall display acted as an information radiator where people could turn when seeking an update to the overall situation. This feature is in stark contrast to the tablets which displayed the local situation for each role independently.

Inter-Device Communication

Earlier we mentioned that communication was an important part of emergency response planning scenarios as there are multiple people in the room representing different organizations. When building this prototype, we were concerned with not only permitting the creation and dissemination of information between people in the same organization, but also people from different organizations.

Through the use of the MSE-API[4], we can support the sharing of information between the devices in the room through gestures (flick and pour) to reduce the users' burden in determining how to share information from their devices. Instead, users could focus on collaborating after they were able to establish a COP.

Usage Scenario

Throughout our iterative development process with C4i, we also grounded our development efforts with a mock incident created and validated by C4i with emergency response personnel. This incident is a train derailment in downtown Calgary, releasing a hazardous material.

Step 1: Emergency Alert Issued

At first, the head of the EOC (the 'chief'), the chief of the fire department in the case of the city of Calgary receives information in different mediums (text, email, and phone) from various sources (police, EMS, and HAZMAT) about an emergency event – the train derailment in the city's downtown. The chief then determines the type of emergency that is occurring and issues a local state of emergency alert to the city. While the chief is making his determinations, other EOC personal in the room are often interrupted with new information or are performing tasks simultaneously due to the evolving nature of the emergency.

Step 2: Response Representatives Assemble

After the alert has been issued, the relevant response personnel assemble in the EOC, and depending upon the severity of the event, these representatives may include members of the fire department, EMS, police, power companies, or the public works departments.

Step 3: Emergency Response Plan Execution

During the emergency response plan execution step, which lasts until the end of the emergency, numerous types of interactions occur. This session is the most critical component of an emergency response, as significant coordination and planning are done. This is where the chief would get the current status of the train derailment, set the evacuation radius for the spill, set roadblocks. Then, by triaging information from personnel in the room, the chief would share the updated COP with city officials and members of the public.

This step would be where, in the tabletop exercises mentioned earlier, the people involved in the exercise would be expected to know the plan to test how the plan works as the scenario unfolds. In the case of a live exercise, the personnel may test logistics, communications, and physical capabilities of the personnel. Executing the plan numerous times would help build experiential learning by having participants develop confidence in their skills. At the end of this step, a report is typically generated that summarizes the emergency and the contributions of the personnel involved.

[3] Twitter – http://www.twitter.com

[4] MSE-API - https://github.com/ase-lab/MSEAPI

Figure 3 - An overview of ePlan MultiSurface. (a) Highlighting the ePlan Multi-Surface environment, with different roles collaborating in an emergency scenario (green represents EMS, red represents fire, blue represents police and orange represents HAZMAT). (b) The wall display application and it's different components. (c) The tabletop application. (d) An iPad running in the EMS mode.

THE PROTOTYPE

To fulfill *privacy levels*, we created applications that catered to the privacy affordances of the three devices. The iPad, as a handheld device, was the most private, the tabletop application, as it has a limited amount of space around its surface and orientation, operated semi-privately where users can only see the screen if they were around it, while the wall display was a fully public space visible to all participants in the room.

We constructed three iPad applications to support roles for the police, EMS, and HAZMAT whereby they could make notes and share information with other personnel in the same role. This enabled the police, for example, to make and share information with other police members, alter those plans, and then finally share the plans with people from EMS, HAZMAT, and the rest of the room.

To support *inter-device communication* (communication between the room's iPads, tabletop, and wall display), we sought an API that would provide tracking of both people and devices. Furthermore, the API had to use low-cost sensors that could cover a sizable room [1] so that we could satisfy a requirement from our industry partner when showcasing the prototype to emergency management agencies in the area. We decided to use the MSE-API in its iteration that permitted the integration of multiple Kinects to cover a larger surface area as it provides gesture-initiated inter-device communication to track both people and devices in the room.

We supported *information integration* differently in all three applications:

The *iPads* are used for individual planning activities, and since we worked with both iPads and iPad minis, we built an application suitable for both dimensions[5]. The iPad applications integrated annotations and the entities from the ePlan simulation, and was able to send information to either the tabletop or wall display (Figure 3d).

The *tabletop* is used to integrate the role-specific (police, EMS, HAZMAT) plans into a comprehensive whole. Its information integration was based on its size, orientation, and location at the centre of the room. It was constructed to display ePlan's desktop simulation entities, and support the annotation on all three of the police, EMS, or HAZMAT layer. It was also able to receive information from the iPads, and send information to the wall display (Figure 3c).

The *wall display* is used to share factual information about the situation as well as the agreed upon plan. With both the largest screen and the most public device, the wall display showed different information sources simultaneously (Figure 3b). This figure shows how Twitter, ePlan's desktop simulation entities, live traffic cameras, news feeds, annotations, and messages were integrated. In addition, since it was not touch-enabled, it was a receiver of information from both the tabletop and iPads.

As mentioned above, not only did the devices afford different privacy levels, but their screen sizes also afforded different information integration requirements.

Infrastructure

As shown in Figure 3, *ePlan* is a multi-surface environment comprised of a number of components: A large, high-resolution wall display (Figure 3b); digital tabletop (Figure 3c); multiple Microsoft Kinects[6], multiple iPads; and, a laptop with the ePlan desktop simulation software.

The MSE-API framework provides device location and orientation that results in a spatially aware environment, and it was used to provide inter-device communication and multi-surface interactions with the aid of multiple Microsoft Kinects. Custom applications were created for the iPads, tabletop, and high-resolution wall display.

C4i's ePlan simulation software, which is used during training exercises, stores information about entities (e.g. people, vehicles, and buildings), their location, and their routing information on a backend ArcGIS[7] server, allowing the tabletop, tablet, and wall display to receive the same information as the desktop software updates the simulation. In addition to the simulation information stored on an ArcGIS server, the police, EMS, and HAZMAT planning layers for the iPads, tabletop, and wall display were also stored on separate ESRI's ArcGIS layers.

Tabletop

We built the tabletop application with the idea that it is a collaborative space where one or more users gather to discuss information before an action is taken and shared with the room. Users can create annotations on one of the police, EMS, or HAZMAT layers before relaying that information to the field. At the same time, the tabletop merges these three layers onto one map so that the chief can see a future COP before sharing that information with the entire room through a touch-enabled gesture to send the information to the wall display.

iPad

The iPad applications were created to support three different roles – police, EMS, and HAZMAT. These three roles are operated by independent chains-of-command, and thus we created three independent layers on which annotations are created to support the collaboration amongst personnel from that organization. By separating these tools in role-specific user interfaces, we expect to reduce the cognitive burden for the people using the iPads so that they can focus on their own

[5] iPad dimensions - https://www.apple.com/ipad/compare/

[6] Microsoft Kinect - www.xbox.com/en-CA/Kinect

[7] ESRI ArcGIS - http://www.esri.com/software/arcgis

job and are not be burdened with filtering away UI options that are not relevant for them. Reducing the tool set can be important to reduce errors in high-stress situations (like emergencies). All three application provide some common functionality that permits the user to change the emergency response planning scenario update frequency, annotate shapes and lines, as well as toggling between a street or map view. Each iPad application operates on an independent, private ArcGIS layer so that police annotations and entities are not merged with either the HAZMAT or EMS layers.

Wall Display

This application consolidates information from eight different sources onto a 9600 x 3600 high-resolution wall display as seen in Figure 3b:

(1) Shows the areas under review by the three iPad application;
(2) Represents a camera showing a live-feed from the incident zone;
(3) Represents the area where traffic cameras are live-streaming into the EOC;
(4) A ticker showing news headlines from the area;
(5) The map overview showing the entities (people, buildings, vehicles, etc.) from C4i's software along with annotations and other information shared from the tabletop and/or iPad applications;
(6) Lists the messages that have been received by the EOC;
(7) Live Twitter feed from people or organizations are being followed by the software; and,
(8) More detailed information about news items that are scrolling through in (4).

Overall, the wall display is used as an information radiator to share factual information about the situation as well as an agreed upon plan.

Multi-Surface Interactions

Earlier we described the general steps that people working in an EOC might take when executing the train derailment emergency response plan. Next, we highlight interactions in our multi-surface prototype for that same usage scenario:

Step 1: Emergency Alert Issued

In the first stage, the chief is stationed by the tabletop and receives updates from personnel in the room through a one-finger flick (or pour gesture) that transfer information from their iPads to the tabletop where the chief can triage the information. Simultaneously, the wall display updates with information from local traffic cameras, news feeds, and Twitter.

Step 2: Response Representatives Assemble

Personnel from the police, EMS, and HAZMAT gather in the room with private iPads containing information about their people and vehicles in the field, possible routing information for ground personnel, and preliminary plans for their people. These EOC representatives may then share relevant information using flick or pour gestures at their discretion or use the information from other representatives in their own assessment for allocating their resources during the emergency.

Step 3: Emergency Response Plan Execution

In ePlan multi-surface, emergency response personnel are collaborating and consuming new information rapidly using iPads, while also simultaneously trying to keep track and manage the emergency through the wall display and digital tabletop. Representatives can share information from their iPads to the tabletop – where it can be triaged with the chief and other representatives – using a one-finger flick (or pour gesture).

If the same person wanted to share the information with the entire room, they could use a two-finger flick to share that piece of data with the large wall display. The wall display allows everyone in the room to see the information; the tabletop is used to assist in collaborative emergency response planning; or other iPads are used to facilitate communication between different representatives. While personnel are sharing information with others via multi-surface interactions, information from other sources (news feed, traffic cameras, and Twitter) are updating the wall display to ground on-the-floor discussions.

PROTOTYPE CRITIQUE AND DISCUSSION

Getting feedback from users in the emergency management planning domain is extremely critical. As we worked closely with domain experts from C4i Consultants Inc., we asked them to continually provide feedback through the various stages of our collaboration, including the prototype that is presented in this work. The goal of this feedback is to discuss the potential of multi-surface environments and applications to their domain as well as to brainstorm future research. The feedback received is presented below in general themes.

Interactions and Gestures

As with other applications that have been developed by our group in the oil and gas domain [19], we started from the gestures and interactions defined in prior work [14]. Our group of users from C4i, however, gave mixed reviews to the gestures – point & flick, pour, and pull – that we implemented in the prototype. Point & flick along with pull gestures received positive reviews as *"natural gestures"*, however the pour gesture whereby the user takes the iPad and rotates the screen so that the iPad screen faces the tabletop was thought to be cumbersome and *"not natural"*.

Our users repeatedly referenced *"natural gestures"*, focusing on the ease of use and learnability of the interactions. During emergency response, there are users who regularly work in the EOC, and there are others who will come to work there during the emergency [8]. As described during one of the interviews *"On a typical day, the EOC houses 25 staff. At the height of the recent Calgary flooding, Burrell (city of Calgary fire chief) estimated nearly 200 people were working in and around the ops room [13]."* In the case of the city of Calgary, irregular EOC personnel come from "the city's business units, along with agencies like Enmax (the local power company), ATCO (a local natural gas provider), Alberta Health Services, and industry groups" [13]. Our interviewees also mentioned that the gestures needed to be easy enough to learn simply by a user *"peeking over a colleague's shoulder"* and that during these highly-intensive events, users may not be able to remember the difference between a *"three-finger and four-finger swipe"*.

During our interviews, our C4i collaborators also repeatedly acted out gestures that incorporated both the surface of the tabletop and iPad, followed by an in-air movement. This combination of on-device gesture plus in-air gesture felt more natural when they wanted to share content from their device to other devices in the room.

Information Overload

In the city of Calgary, our collaborators noted that police collect video from cameras placed both in the police cruiser along with cameras on the officer's uniform [4][5][20], and with this, and social media sources of information (e.g. Twitter, Facebook, Instagram, Pinterest, Tumblr) that were not available a decade ago, the amount of information could become overwhelming. With this quantity of data, C4i mentioned that maintaining situational awareness is critical in environments like EOCs. Furthermore, they mentioned the need, with the quantity of information at their disposal to "*see [both] the forest and the trees*".

Our interviewees also described how multi-surface environments and interactions could aid in information sharing where a user could swipe a picture, text, or video from their iPad or tabletop and have that information shared with a wider audience, especially when they compared this to the current situation where users "*go back to my desk to email that information to you"*. One subject remarked that the ease with which information sharing can take place using gestures should also reduce both the number of silos and the amount of information contained in those silos.

Technology Reliability

Throughout our interview sessions, a common concern was the Kinect tracking technology. When working, the three Kinects allowed for the coverage of the room, however, the tracking system would occasionally lose track of users and devices.

Our collaborators at C4i commented that a better system would allow for an AirDrop[8]-like or an *"AirDrop on steroids"* where the user can focus less on whether they are connected, and more on sharing content. Just like cellphones just work (with roaming charges) when people travel internationally, the tracking technology should be pervasive and reliable. They saw no issues in the possible privacy concerns with their suggestion to use on-board cameras on tablets, phones and computers to help track people and devices in the room.

Areas to explore

During our on-going collaboration with C4i, we kept track of items that we were able to implement for our current prototype, and those which could be explored during our continued collaboration. With that in mind, we generalized their feedback into four further themes:

Rate of Data Growth

We are seeing a tremendous growth in the amount of information available to users [21] and this growth is not likely to stop with the increased pervasiveness of cheap sensors that can provide directions to people while navigating New York City [11]. Our collaborators reaffirm this notion, seeing the increased use of metadata in military applications, and are sure that its use will follow into the civilian realm whereby emergency responders would be able to get historical and real-time information on cities, neighbourhoods, and buildings.

This additional information builds a more complete picture of the environment in which personnel in the field are entering. Furthermore, the people in the EOC will be able to simultaneously live-stream cameras from officers [5] and data on their location, foot speed, wind conditions, and fatigue level [11]. C4i indicated that our prototype would need to incorporate this information into information radiators or other applications without increasing the cognitive load on EOC operators.

Using Multiple Senses

In this prototype, we explored a small set of surface-related gestures (swipe, pull, pour, and flick), however our collaborators see the opportunity to augment the prototype with voice-based commands and haptic feedback. One interviewer commented how Siri[9] can function in busy, noisy locations, and thus sees an opportunity to add voice-base commands to the gestures. Moreover, currently when a user attempts to send information to the wall display or tabletop, they get feedback on the screen indicating whether it succeeded or failed. Alternatively, C4i suggested that we provide haptic feedback indicating the success or failure of these gestures so that the user need not look at their screen as they move about.

Security

As with any technological system, security cannot be an afterthought, however, it was something that we did not explore due to time and complexity. C4i indicated that should we explore security, we must examine *information security*, *device security*, and *personal security*. C4i considered information security to be how we secure the information (picture, video, or text); device security was related to whether a phone, tablet, or computer was secure enough to be authorized to be on the network); and, personal

[8] AirDrop - http://support.apple.com/kb/HT4783

[9] Siri - https://www.apple.com/ca/ios/siri/

security was about whether the person should be in the room. Each of these areas would present an interesting path to explore in future work, particularly in the context of multi-surface environments.

"Newness" of technology

A final comment made during our interview related to the new EOC that was opened by the Calgary Emergency Management Agency (CEMA) in 2012 [13]. *"Though the city of Calgary's EOC was recently opened with new technology, the moment it opened the technology was actually old".* These are critical, highly stressful environments that require that systems work – failure is not an option. The technologies that we developed (and used) during the prototype do not fit the reliability criteria of an EOC yet, however it can be used to draw requirements and commentary from EOC users who are working with older technology.

CONCLUSION

In this paper, we presented our prototype, *ePlan Multi-Surface*, a multi-surface environment for emergency response planning exercises that was designed with domain experts from C4i Consultants Inc. We discussed challenges such as collaboration, interaction and information dissemination in multi-surface environments for EOCs. We also presented a preliminary prototype critique and discussion about its utility for the domain.

Our future work involves extending the prototype and continuing with a more complete evaluation of the system and its impact for emergency response planning exercises. We believe that the emergency response domain is an ideal candidate for further exploration of multi-surface interactions and technologies in real-life applications as this domain stresses systems differently than applications in other domains.

ACKNOWLEDGEMENTS

We would like to thank Bruce Gilkes, Amy Swedlo, and Darren Rempel, and Clive Morgan from C4i Consultants Inc. for their insights, support and collaboration. Many thanks to our colleagues from the Agile Surface Engineering (ASE) Lab at the University of Calgary in building the ePlan Multi-Surface environment. We also thank the anonymous reviewers for their careful and valuable comments and suggestions. This research was supported in part by NSERC and by the NSERC SurfNet Research Network.

REFERENCES

1. Azazi, A., Seyed, T., Botros, F., Sabourin, D., Chan, E., and Maurer, F. Using Multiple Kinects to Build Larger Multi-Surface Environments. In *Proc. Workshop on Collaboration Meets Interactive Surfaces, ITS 2013*, ACM Press (2013).
2. Bakker, S., van den Hoven, E., and Eggen, B. Design for the Periphery. In *Proc. Eurohaptics 2010 Symposium Haptic and Audio-Visual Stimuli: Enhancing Experiences and Interaction.* (2010), 71-80.
3. Bortolaso, C., Oskamp, Matthew, Graham, N., and Brown, D. OrMiS: a tabletop interface for simulation-based training. In *Proc. ITS 2013*, ACM Press (2013), 145-154.
4. Calgary police dash cams show crashes, arrests Calgary Sun. http://www.calgarysun.com/2013/08/20/calgary-police-dash-cams-show-crashes-arrests
5. Calgary police keeping cameras on uniforms CBC News, http://www.cbc.ca/news/canada/calgary/calgary-police-keeping-cameras-on-uniforms-1.1410148
6. Dachselt, R., and Buchholz, R. Natural throw and tilt interaction between mobile phones and distant displays. *Ext. Abstracts CHI 2009.* ACM Press (2009), 3253-3258.
7. Edge, D. and Blackwell, A.F. Peripheral tangible interaction by analytic design. In *Proc. TEI 2009*. ACM Press (2009), 69-76.
8. Emergency Operations Centre Videos. City of Edmonton. http://www.edmonton.ca/for_residents/emergency_services/emergency-operations-centre-videos.aspx
9. Emergency planning and preparedness: exercises and training. https://www.gov.uk/emergency-planning-and-preparedness-exercises-and-training
10. Hofstra, H., Scholten, H., Zlatanova, S., and Alessandra, S. Multi-user tangible interfaces for effective decision-making in disaster management. *Remote Sensing and GIS Technologies for Monitoring and Prediction of Disasters*, Springer (2008), 243-266.
11. Howarth, B. The pioneers of Internet of Things. CIO (2014), http://www.cio.com.au/article/548616/pioneers_internet_things
12. Kobayashi, K., Narita, A., Hirano, M., Kase, I., Tsuchida, S., Omi, T., Kakizaki, T., and Hosokawa, T. 2006. Collaborative simulation interface for planning disaster measures. *Ext. Abstracts CHI 2006.* ACM Press (2006), 977-982.
13. Krause, D. Emergency ops centre the decision-making hub during Calgary flood. Metro News. July 4, 2013. http://metronews.ca/news/calgary/727665/emergency-ops-centre-the-decision-making-hub-during-calgary-flood/
14. MSE-API. https://github.com/ase-lab/MSEAPI
15. Perry, R.W. and Lindell, M.K. Preparedness for Emergency Response: Guidelines for the Emergency Planning Process.

In *Disasters, 2003, 27, 4.* Blackwell Publishing (2003), 336-350.

16. Qin, Y., Liu, J., Wu, C., and Shi, Y. uEmergency: a collaborative system for emergency management on very large tabletop. In *Proc. ITS 2012*. ACM Press (2012), 399-402.

17. Rekimoto, J. Pick-and-drop: a direct manipulation technique for multiple computer environments. In *Proc. UIST 1997.* ACM Press (1997), 31-39.

18. Seyed, T., Burns, C., Costa Sousa, M., Maurer, F., and Tang, A. Eliciting usable gestures for multi-display environments. In *Proc. ITS 2012*, ACM Press (2012), 41-50.

19. Seyed, T., Costa Sousa, M., Maurer, F., and Tang, A. SkyHunter: A Multi-Surface Environment for Supporting Oil and Gas Exploration. In *Proc. ITS 2013*, ACM Press (2013), 15-22.

20. Shingler, B. Cops with cameras: Growing number of police armed with recording devices. Canadian Press (2014), http://o.canada.com/news/police-body-worn-cameras-canada

21. Silver, N. The Signal and the Noise: Why So Many Predictions Fail — but Some Don't. Penguin Group (2012).

22. Tena, S., Aedo, I., and Díaz, P. Achieving Shared Understanding in Face-to-Face 'Tabletop' Exercises In *Proc. BCS-HCI 2013*. British Computer Society (2013). Article 61, 2 pages.

23. Van de Walle, B. and Turoff, M. Emergency Response Information Systems: Emerging Trends and Technologies. March 2007/Vol. 50, No. 3 COMMUNICATIONS OF THE ACM, 29–31.

Designing a Remote Video Collaboration System for Industrial Settings

Veronika Domova, Elina Vartiainen, Marcus Englund
ABB Corporate Research
Forskargränd 7, 721 78, Västerås, Sweden
{veronika.domova, elina.vartiainen}@se.abb.com, mpenglund@gmail.com

ABSTRACT
In industry settings, it is essential to keep the production up and running at all times. In case of new machine installation or process failure, technical support from the equipment manufacturer often needs to be contacted. In these cases, local workers and remote experts need to collaborate to solve the occurred problem. Ideally, in order to cut costs and speed up the process, the situation should be handled remotely, without bringing the expert to the site. This paper describes the design and implementation of a remote video collaboration system, which enables effective communication between a field worker and a remote expert. The system includes a smartphone/tablet application used by the field worker to capture and stream video to a desktop application of the remote expert. Furthermore, the system enables instantly synchronized snapshots and annotations between both parties. A performed field study testing the design choices, potential and limitations by including target users showed that the system holds good potential given that some key issues are handled.

Author Keywords
Video streaming; remote collaboration; mobile devices; peer-to-peer streaming; augmented reality; annotation.

ACM Classification Keywords
H.5.m. Information Interfaces and Presentation (e.g. HCI): Miscellaneous

INTRODUCTION
In industry settings, a minor halt in production will cost large amounts of money. Therefore, maintenance is a crucial element in keeping the production up and running at all times. In a case of equipment failure, replacement or installation, it is sometimes necessary to consult external experts regarding advanced maintenance, since regular personnel may not have the expertise to handle the issue by themselves.

Unfortunately, it can take a long time to get hold of the correct expert and bring him in to the site for providing the desired technical support. In addition, flying in an external expert can be very expensive, since the destination can be in another part of the world. Furthermore, the most suitable expert might not always be available for traveling. An alternative option could be to collaborate over a telephone line between the local worker and the expert. However, when communicating via phone, the expert does not have a real-time view of the environment or machinery, which might hinder the expert from correctly instructing field workers.

For these situations, efficient remote collaboration tools are needed. These tools should support the communication between the local worker and the remote expert in a way that allows the expert to have a good overall view of the local worker's environment. Furthermore, the local worker should understand the guidance from the expert without risk of misinterpretation. In order to achieve this, both participants should be able to view the specific machinery or equipment in a similar way, explicitly point at its specific parts and make visual remarks. The interaction should be immediate, with minimized delays.

In order to meet these challenges, many wearable systems have been developed for remote collaboration in earlier research projects (for example, [22, 13]). These systems equip the local worker with needed tools to record the environment for the remote expert. However, even though the wearable systems have aimed to be unobtrusive and support user's work practices, the existing solutions are not widely adopted in industrial settings. In our visits to several industrial plants (including process industry, mining, marine, and oil and gas platforms), we have not seen any wearable systems in use.

On the contrary, mobile and tablet devices are becoming more and more commonplace, and also reasonably prevalent in industrial settings [37]. Field workers are easily able to carry such devices and also use them for remote collaboration. The mobile devices today offer extensive capabilities for ubiquitous connectivity, media sharing and a wide range of interaction techniques. In addition, augmented reality applications on mobile devices may fit many situations, where context dependent information needs to be visualized efficiently.

This paper presents a collaboration system that enables an expert to remotely guide a local worker during a technical support task. The expert is located in his office and uses a desktop application for communication, while the local field worker is mobile and communicating through an application installed

ITS 2014, November 16–19, 2014, Dresden, Germany.

http://dx.doi.org/10.1145/2669485.2669517

on his mobile device. The local worker streams live video from the site by using the mobile device camera, and the video is replayed in the expert's desktop application. In addition, both of them can take and share high-quality snapshots of the video stream. Both the expert and the local worker can make annotations, using a virtual pointer or making an overlaying drawing, which appear on top of the video stream or a snapshot.

The system was designed specifically for industrial settings, which introduced specific requirements for the software architecture and connectivity. For example, the connection establishment and the video session setup process should be fast and require a minimum manual interference due to the potential urgency of the issue. To validate the applicability of the system in a real industrial setting, we conducted a user study with operators and field workers that used the system in their working environment in a water treatment plant.

BACKGROUND

Standard audio and video conferencing tools available on the market could be used for remote technical assistance. However, these tools are typically designed for supporting face-to-face communication and do not, for example, provide tools for annotations (for example, Skype[1] and Google Hangouts[2]), whereas the purpose and goal of the task-space remote collaboration is tightly connected to a local worker's workspace [18]. In complex industrial maintenance tasks it is more important to see, what the user is trying to do, rather than show his face. Another possible obstacle to using third-party video conferencing tools is that the communication channel is not normally established as peer-to-peer, but through a third-party server. This could introduce potential confidentiality issues as the data can be accessed in a non-authorized way.

In any remote collaboration it is important to estimate how the communication will exactly be organized. As discussed in [20], a remote expert can more effectively communicate with local workers, if the remote expert has good situational awareness and conversational grounding regarding the task. Situation awareness involves the expert being aware when the worker requires help. For example, the local worker should not be distracted before he is ready to receive assistance. Conversational grounding is the shared understanding of the task between the worker and the expert. It requires that the expert not only gives the required assistance but that the worker understands the assistance that is being given.

The effect of gestures on conversational grounding has been examined in multiple research studies (see, for example, [6, 15, 31, 1, 2, 12, 9, 10, 30]). The goal has been to support the remote collaboration between participants. One of the key findings has been that adding a pointing only interface did not improve the speed of collaborative tasks over a video-only interface. However, it did make identifying references easier. Furthermore, the shared drawing interface significantly improved the speed of collaborative tasks as compared to a video-only interface.

[1]Skype, http://www.skype.com

[2]Google Hangouts, http://www.google.com/hangouts/

Previous research has shown that using a head mounted display with a camera attached can allow a remote expert to provide effective support to the local worker, especially if they can create AR annotations within the workers view [25, 23, 33, 34, 22, 32, 13]. However, such systems have typically been expensive and have seen limited industry adoption. A more serious problem is that it is difficult for the remote expert to clearly understand the workspace of the local user. If their viewpoint is confined to video or still images coming from a head-worn camera, the remote expert can have very limited situational awareness.

A previous study by Wither, DiVerdi and Hllerer [39] also showed that HMD's pose a minor, if any, advantage over a hand held mobile device if used as a "magic eye", i.e. freely movable, when it came to tasks such as tracking and object acquisition.

Earlier research work described in [7, 24, 13, 14] is similar to our work described in this paper. Gauglitz et al. [7] describe a framework and prototype implementation for mobile remote collaboration. Their system uses the augmented reality paradigm and visual tracking to visualize annotations. These annotations are tied to the world even in unknown environments. Also in [24], a system is introduced that enables remote user support in a priori unknown environments. As in [7], the system can be used without preparation due to a tracking algorithm. The remote support is realized by streaming a live video to the expert who can select regions in the image and choose from several possible types of annotations including text, images and drawings.

In [14], the researchers introduce a mobile video call system, where the remote expert can control the viewpoint of the remote scene and augment the live video with freehand drawing. To enable the viewpoint control with ordinary mobile devices, the system enables the remote expert to switch between the front and rear cameras. The drawings are world-stabilized by vision-gyroscope sensor fusion, and the users can draw even larger than the field-of-view by moving the device itself.

All the previously mentioned collaboration systems have introduced functionality that lets experts guide local workers remotely. Particular techniques and implementations differ, but these systems mostly only support one-way annotations, i. e. from the expert to the field worker and the only input from the local field side is the live video. However, in many maintenance and complex repair tasks both the local worker and remote expert need to interact with each other, which requires that the system also supports input from the local worker. In other words, the collaboration system should provide means for two-way annotation between the participants. There are systems appearing on the market that are already addressing this issue (e.g. Onsight Connect [3]). Therefore, there is a need for more research in the area of remote video collaboration to evaluate the key requirements for the developed systems.

Furthermore, the applicability of remote collaboration systems to the current industrial working environments and pro-

[3]http://www.librestream.com/products/onsight-connect.html

cesses should also be carefully tested. This has not been commonly conducted in the previous studies as getting an access to a industrial environment can be difficult. This has been a general concern with a large part of previous research dedicated to augmented and mix reality as well as mobile HCI as a whole: a large focus has been put on performing laboratory studies to study the prototypes, but few have employed field studies to achieve insight. It can also be added that a large part of the research done has had other focuses than evaluation of collaboration or usability, but rather focused on user performance and engineering aspects [5, 16, 17].

REQUIREMENTS FOR VIDEO COLLABORATION SYSTEM

In order to contribute to the previously introduced challenges, we developed a remote collaboration system prototype that could be evaluated in an industrial environment with real users. The goal for the system was to enable efficient remote collaboration between a remote expert and a local worker in a technical support task. The system was designed to support a scenario, where a local worker is conducting a maintenance task that requires assistance from a remote expert. Therefore, a requirement (*R1*) for the system was to support input from both the field worker and the remote expert, since challenging maintenance tasks require discussion and interaction between both parties. This issue has not been addressed by earlier systems for remote video collaboration that have instead more focused on the expert guidance.

Further requirements for our prototype were defined based on earlier research studies [21, 20]. According to them, video streaming can improve the situational awareness of the remote expert, when the following issues are addressed by the developed system:

- Provide users with a wide field of view (*R2*).
- Clarify, what is part of the shared visual space (*R3*).
- Provide mechanisms to allow people to track one another's focus of attention (*R4*).
- Provide support for gesturing within the shared visual space (*R5*).

We used these requirements as a basis for the interaction principles of our system, while still focusing more on the collaboration aspect of the communication.

Our next concern was related to the hardware of the system. The intention was to avoid developing a complex wearable system. Instead, we wanted focus to be on a lightweight solution based on existing mobile technology. This requirement was mostly based on the knowledge that wearable systems are not widely adopted in industrial markets, regardless of the extensive research in the area. Alternatively, off-the-shelf mobile devices and tablets are powerful enough to support effective video collaboration that incorporates augmented reality visualizations [11]. Thus, we formulated the hardware requirement (*R6*) of the prototype system to include the use of modern light-weight and off-the-shelf mobile devices.

Finally, our last goal was to make a solution, which could be adopted for use in a variety of industrial settings. This implied that the system should be straightforward to install. In addition, the solutions should ideally only consist of an expert-side application (installed on a PC) and the field worker application (installed on a mobile device), allowing direct communication between them without any third-party servers or advanced configurations. Another concern was related to network communications, since instant interaction and feedback in remote collaboration rely on efficient connectivity. As the network conditions and security measures may vary between industrial sites (including low bandwidth, packet filtering, and firewalls), we anticipated that the system should be easily testable in terms of network parameters and adjustable to a specific condition. These issues led to the formulation of the final requirement (*R7*), which stated that the system should work without introducing additional equipment or software on site.

SYSTEM OVERVIEW

The collaboration between the local worker and the remote expert was designed for a mobile device (carried by the local worker) and PC (accessed by the remote expert). Therefore, the developed prototype system consists of a mobile application and a respective desktop application. We decided to use an off-the-shelf tablet device (*R6*), since a field worker needs to have a device that is easily carried along on the site. Figure 1 presents the user interfaces of the applications in the middle of a collaboration session. Both applications have the same look-and-feel and similar functionality. The video stream is displayed in the center of the screen, while overlaying colorful lines represent annotations, which are synchronized between the two parties. Captured snapshots are stored in a list on the left side of the screen, whereas application controls and drawing tools are on the right side.

When both applications are launched, the field worker can initiate the video stream to the remote expert. The PC application replays the received video stream to a remote expert, so he or she can observe the environment of the field worker. The wide field of the view (*R2*) was achieved by letting the field worker freely stream the video from site by using the camera of the tablet device.

The system allows both users to take snapshots of the video stream (*R3*). When a snapshot is taken, the video stream is temporarily paused and the system switches from the video stream mode to the snapshot mode (see Figure 2). The shared visual space can only be in one mode at any point in time, i.e. either the live video or a snapshot, which is the same for both parties (*R4*). Therefore, the screens of both mobile and desktop applications are always kept synchronized, i.e. both users see the same scene on their screens at any point in time. For instance, if the field worker takes a snapshot, his application switches to the snapshot mode. At the same time, the PC application used by the remote expert also changes to the snapshot mode displaying the captured snapshot.

Furthermore, the system provides functionality for creating instant annotations of the video stream and snapshots for both the field worker and remote expert (*R1*). Annotations can be created in two ways: (1) using a pointer (*R4*), and (2) making an overlaying drawing (*R5*). The pointer mode allows a

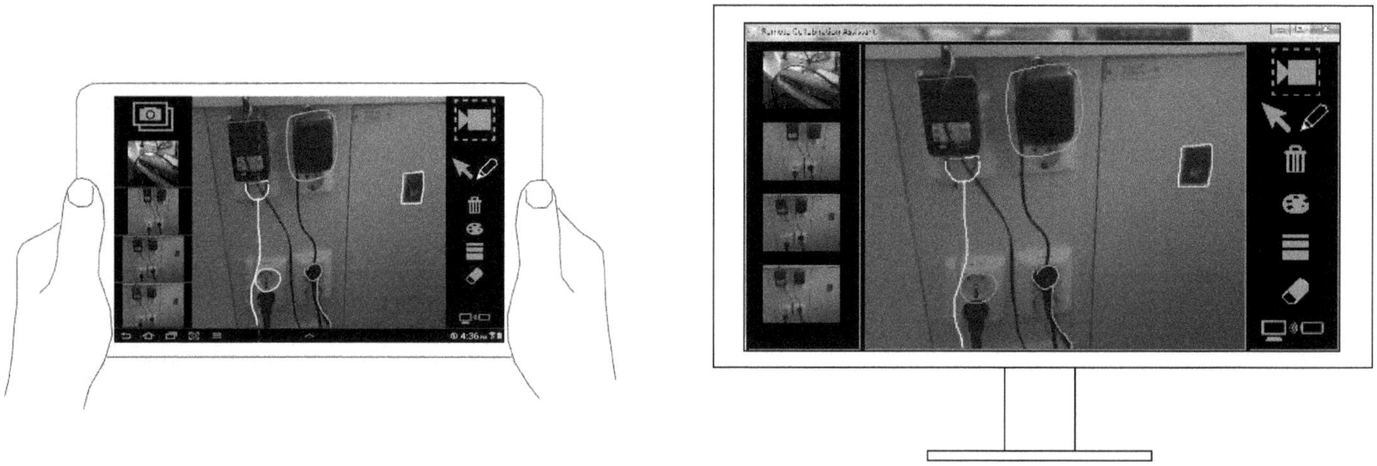

Figure 1. The snapshots showing the user interfaces of the mobile (left) and desktop (right) applications in the middle of a collaboration session.

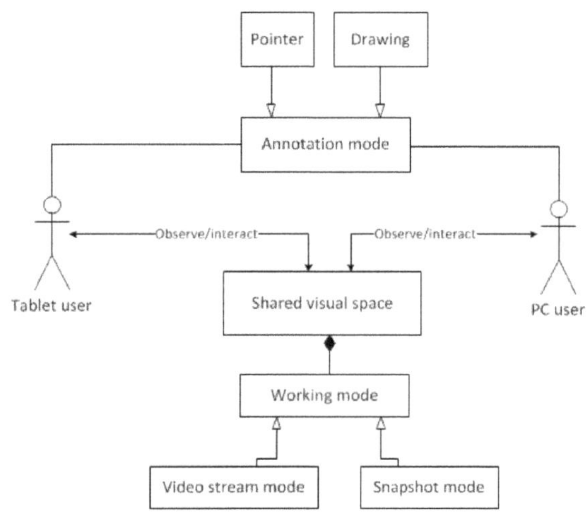

Figure 2. The interaction modes supported by the developed system.

user to annotate the video stream/snapshot with a movable pointer, which visually repeats the movements of a finger (in case of the mobile application) or a mouse (in case of the PC application). The drawing mode allows the user to draw on top of the snapshot/video stream. The user can also use additional tools related to the drawing process, such as selection of a color, line thickness, an eraser, or clearing the screen. All annotations are instantly synchronized between the applications. Therefore, whenever a user makes an annotation through the application interface, the annotation is instantly sent to the other user. Both users can annotate the media simultaneously, while each user can have his own annotation mode (i.e. the users can independently switch between the drawing and pointer modes) (as shown in Figure 2).

The system was designed to work within wireless networks. As seen in Figure 3, the system can be used in local area networks (e.g. secured intranets without access to the Internet) as well as through the Internet. The mobile and the PC applications communicate with each other directly, over a peer-to-peer connection (*R7*). The process of connection initialization is performed implicitly with a minimal user interference to enable a fast start-up of the system (*R7*). Yet, the system enables the user to configure the system (for example, connectivity ports or video parameters). The next section will explain the implementation of the system in detail.

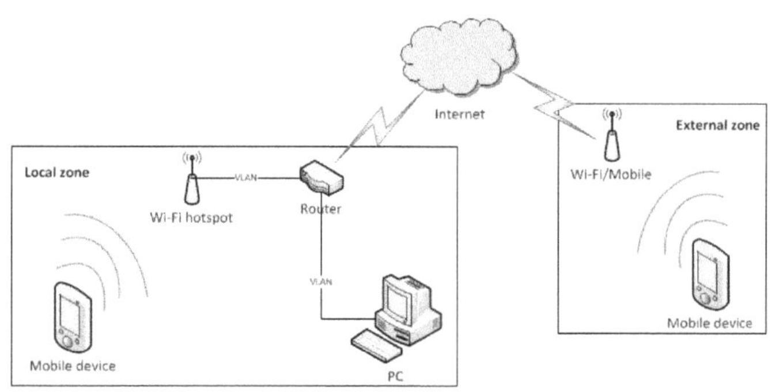

Figure 3. Overview of the connectivity of the developed system.

IMPLEMENTATION

As described earlier, the implemented prototype consists of two units: a mobile application and PC application. The mobile application was developed for Android OS (Honeycomb and later versions) and could be installed either on a mobile device or a tablet. The desktop application was developed for Windows OS using C#, .NET technology and designed for a stationary PC or a laptop. This section describes the implementation details of the system focusing on the architecture, communication details and data flow over the network.

Communication

The communication of our prototype system was based on the peer-to-peer networking model. The peer-to-peer architecture was partly chosen based on the fact that both communicating units keep their own model of the system and in general communicate as equal peers; also partly due to the networking requirement (*R7*) as discussed earlier. The peer-to-peer networking approach for video streaming solutions is nowadays relatively wide-spread and often considered as a promising technique due to cost-efficiency and the ease for deployment [26].

When the desktop application is launched, it opens a listening socket and waits for an incoming connection. After a mobile application connects, there are in total three communication channels established: a TCP channel for general background communication; a UDP channel for annotations of the video or snapshots; and an RTSP/UDP channel for live video streaming.

All the server sockets are open on the desktop application side, whereas a mobile application always opens the client sockets and requests for connections. The architecture was selected with respect to the overall purpose of the system: the desktop application (remote expert) provides the service to the requesting mobile applications, i.e. field workers, who are in a need of technical assistance. The service in this case is the guidance of the remote expert, i.e. the video stream and snapshots annotation. The video stream can be treated as the request data. The advantages of the selected approach are the following:

- A clear definition of the roles of the participants in the system.
- For establishing a video session, only mobile device applications should be aware of the remote expert application's listening address.
- The desktop application does not need to know anything about mobile applications before they connect.
- The desktop application is able to connect with multiple mobile applications simultaneously.

However, there are disadvantages as well. The approach becomes inefficient when establishing collaboration sessions between several remote experts. At the moment we do not support such a scenario, but it could be a potential extension of the system. Adjusting the system in its current form to support multiple destinations would require the mobile application to establish three new connections running in three new background threads per each new destination. This would significantly reduce the performance of the mobile application and increase its memory consumption.

Finally, in order to minimize the manual configuration, the mobile device application was designed to initially be aware of only the IP address and the main listening port of the remote expert application. Other necessary port numbers are sent through the network after the first communication channel has been established.

General background communication

The general background communication process includes the exchange of notifications between the two parties in order to synchronize the video session status. In addition, a user needs to be informed about interactions performed by the other party. These actions including establishing or ending communication, notifying about switching between snapshot and video stream modes, and changing the annotation mode are incorporated in the scope of the communication channel.

The general background communication was implemented by sending notifications through the TCP channel in a numeric form. Therefore, each activity within the system is represented with a one-byte integer code. In certain cases, there is additional accompanying numeric data. The decision was made in favor of TCP, as the system needs a confirmation that the other party has received the notification. The notifications are essential for the synchronization of applications' states, as there are no means to apply any restoring algorithms for lost packages. Furthermore, these notifications consist of not more than several bytes of information, and can be transmitted in one packet. As a consequence, the degradation of communication speed and additionally generated traffic will be minimal. We also experimented with reliable UDP with explicitly implemented acknowledgments mechanism, as described in [27], and with a simple Automatic Repeat Request (ARQ) protocol applied on top of UDP as in [8]. However, we did not see any significant improvements of performance when using these approaches. Instead, they somewhat complicated the communication logic of our system.

The general background communication process also takes care of agreeing on the basic video session details before starting the remote collaboration session. When the mobile application opens a connection with the desktop application, the mobile application is only aware of the IP address of the desktop application and its main listening port. However, as described earlier, a video session requires several communication channels, and also the needed video parameters. Therefore, certain configuration details exchanged between the mobile application and the remote PC application in the beginning. Firstly, the desktop application provides the port, in which it will listen for the incoming video stream. The port for annotations does not have to be negotiated, because the main listening port is re-used for this purpose. Secondly, the mobile application generates Session Description Protocol (SDP) data based on the camera settings and received video port number, and sends the information to the desktop application. The generated SDP data contains necessary information about the video stream session, which will be used by the desktop application in order to pre-configure the media player and re-play incoming video data.

The described approach reduces the amount of manual configurations needed for establishing communication. Therefore, we are able to minimize the amount of manual errors. Moreover, the approach allows to keep the solution flexible: the desktop application ports as well as mobile phone camera properties can be dynamically changed at the site.

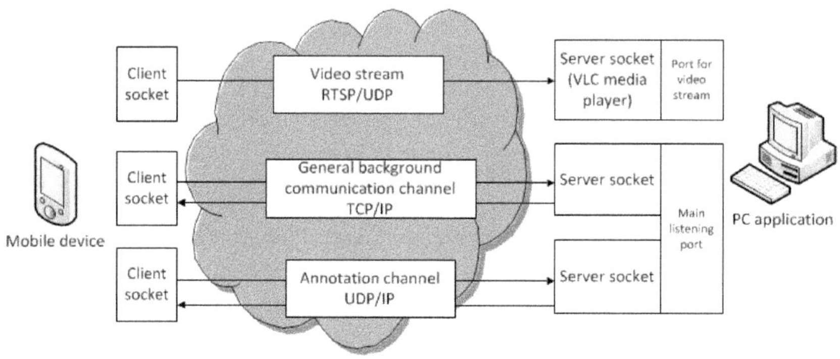

Figure 4. The connectivity of the developed system.

Video stream for collaboration

The video streaming process is initiated by the mobile application. The video data is captured from the mobile device camera, encoded using H.264 standard, packetized inside application logic, and sent over the network to the desktop application's listening port. The video streaming is based on the RTSP/UDP protocol in conjunction with SDP. Therefore, data packets are formed accordingly to the RTSP standard. The chosen standards are common technologies used in the domain of online video streaming, see, for example, [38, 29]. However, there are a number of other solutions, which can be more efficient in other specific cases. That is why they could be considered for future implementations, for example, those discussed and compared in [28, 3].

Snapshots taken from video stream

In the developed system, both parties are able to take snapshots of the video stream in order to concentrate on the particular details of the environment of the local worker. Snapshots can also be saved for later use or a reference. On both applications, snapshots can be taken by a single click on a button. Snapshots can be taken at any point, while the system is in the streaming mode, and snapshots are stored in a gallery for future reference.

We experimented with several approaches for synchronizing snapshots between the applications over the network. The first option uses the snapshot taken by one of the parties in both applications. That is, whenever one participant makes a snapshot, it is simultaneously and implicitly sent to the other participant. In this case, it is ensured that the parties will both have exactly the same snapshot to work with. However, the recipient party has to wait for the incoming snapshot, which depending on the bandwidth can be up to several seconds. Furthermore, when the snapshot is captured by the remote expert, the image quality will be low as the snapshot is taken from the re-played video stream frame.

Another approach included both applications taking the snapshot on their side. That is, whenever a user takes a snapshot, the other application gets an appropriate notification through the general communication channel and is also forced to take a snapshot. This solution is faster than the first approach since no time is spent on transmitting a snapshot over a network. However, it forces the PC application to always settle for a low quality image. Also, there is a minimal chance that snapshots do not capture the same scene due to a possible notification delay.

Finally, the third option, which we have currently implemented, always uses the mobile application to capture a snapshot as the mobile device is able to produce top-quality snapshots by using the built-in camera. In this case, whenever a PC application user wants to make a snapshot, the appropriate notification is sent to the mobile application requesting it to capture a snapshot and send it back. This approach introduces a delay, but the advantage is that the remote expert will always get the best quality snapshots to work with. To compensate for the delay, we have combined this approach with the first one by first showing on the desktop side the low-quality snapshot and updating that with the high-quality one, when it is received from the mobile application.

Annotation of the video stream and snapshots

The implemented prototype system enables users to make annotations on top of the video stream or snapshots in two ways: using a virtual pointer or making an overlaying drawing. Whenever the user interacts with the screen (using a mouse or a finger) and annotates the media, the mobile and desktop applications record a set of points where clicks, taps or drawings were performed. For example, whenever the user moves his mouse/finger on the screen by using the pointer mode, a virtual pointer will appear following his finger/mouse motion. At the same time, the recorded coordinates are transmitted over the network to the other party. The receiving application gets the coordinates, adjusts them to its screen resolution and visualizes the pointer movement.

Coordinates are transmitted over the annotation channel. The communication is based on the UDP/IP protocol, as a loss of packages in this case is not critical, but the performance is essential: the annotation depiction should be perceived as real-time by the participants. Otherwise, an annotation might lose its meaning if it is not seen simultaneously by both parties. A loss of packages can be tolerated, as in the worst case the remote party will get a more angular drawing instead of smooth lines. Also, the pointer might occasionally jump to a more outlying point than visually expected. However, this behavior is low priority compared to the immediacy of the synchronization.

The annotation synchronization is connected with the necessity to adjust the annotation point coordinates to the resolution of the receiving screen. The problem occurs because of the difference between the screen sizes: the mobile device screen is significantly smaller than the screen of a PC. In order to overcome this problem the coordinates of annotation points have to be scaled. Scaling is done by normalizing the coordinates. When the coordinates are received by another party, de-normalization is applied, i.e. the coordinates are multiplied with destination-screen dimensions. Both parties should have the areas for depicting video shaped with the same ratio of sizes (in our case the width to height relation is 4:3 in both applications). Currently, the communicating devices are not aware of each other's screen sizes, thus normalization/de-normalization is applied every time an annotation occurs. Another option would be to share the information of the screen sizes between the parties while the communication is being established.

USER STUDY

To evaluate the developed remote video collaboration system, we conducted a field study with target users. The purpose of the study was to gain initial feedback on how the design decisions are received, as well what the interest is for a collaboration tool as the one we propose.

Six participants all working as technicians (5) or control room operators (1) at a waste water treatment plant in Sweden took part in the study (Figure 5). The participants' experience working with their current tasks varied between 3 and 23 years. This combined with their age (32-55) was seen to offer a good basis for the study due to varied experience and age factors. The participants were recruited through a contact at the plant and based on interest.

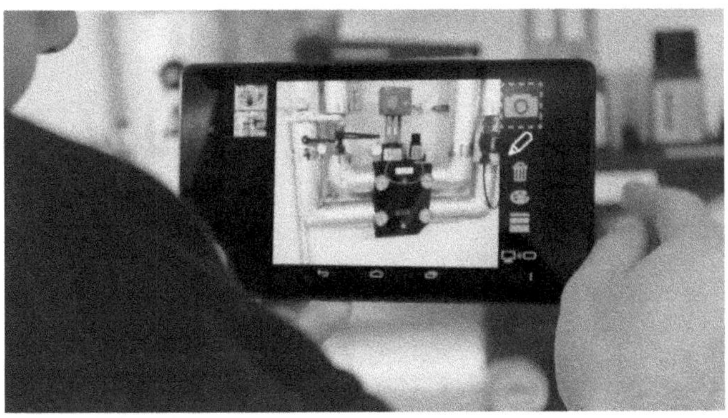

Figure 5. The system was evaluated with users working at waste water treatment plan.

The test session started with the participants having an individual introduction to how both the PC and mobile applications functioned. They also were able to familiarize themselves with the one they were to use (either PC or mobile). The participants chose the application they would in the study based on their actual work role. This lead to four taking on the role of technician (using the tablet application) and two acting as the expert (using the PC application) for the others.

The study was comprised of a simulated maintenance task that each participant pair identified as a situation in which they have had to cooperate. This task was performed on site using the system described. Due to the unpredictability of field studies (i.e. they being accentuated by being reliant on external actors, cooperation and interest), the performed studies had an ad-hoc quality to them. The evaluation sessions were all done following the same general procedure as presented but individual tasks performed depended on location (availability of testing environments and equipment) as well on the current participants (their area of expertise).

Data was collected by observing the technicians in the field as well as recording the session on a handheld video camera. The expert was also recorded using a stationary video camera. After the task was completed the participants took part in individual interviews aimed at gaining information about usability aspects such as the interface, features and general interaction.

Results

The results of the user study indicates that there was a general acceptance of the system. The participants perceived the prototype as having good potential for making daily tasks easier and faster to solve. However, it was also made clear that the limitations of the prototype would have to be rectified before the participants would be willing to accept it as a real working tool.

As mentioned, the overall opinion held by the participants was that this type of a system would be highly interesting and beneficial to them in their daily work. The main reasons were that it was perceived as a much more efficient means of conveying spatial information as compared to e.g. only using a cell phone. The participants also mentioned that it felt like the system made communication easier in general due to a better ability to share common reference points through the video, which has been observed in related studies [19, 36]. The ability to indicate points of interest through the annotation functionality was also appreciated. All these aspects led, according to them, to a general decreased risk of miscommunication which also had the potential to lower frustration and promote better cooperation. Some participants also expressed the tool could be used as a teaching tool for new or inexperienced co-workers that were in need of guidance. This would in turn remove the need for an experienced co-worker to have to go along with them to perform maintenance tasks.

Some issues did, however, appear. The lack of any form of voice communication within the application posed a serious problem for the participants. Their ability to efficiently communicate more complex task descriptions or procedures was hindered due to such functionality being omitted. In our study they participants ended up using their cell phones to assist their communication with each other. Voice communication would also be a requirement for any such product or service to be used by them. The downsides of voice communication were also mentioned (i.e. the difficulty of hearing verbal instructions in noisy environments), suggesting the addition of text input to act as a supplement to it. The reason was that the free hand drawing was not seen as good enough of a tool to be used for text communication. Furthermore, during the observations it was noted that requiring written or drawn communication via the device would decrease the efficiency, due to a legibility issues coming as a result of handwriting not being translated well onto the screen. This, though, is not to say that the drawing function was not appreciated. All participants expressed an appreciation for it as it simplified indicating what object or detail that was discussed, but stating that it could be further streamlined by adding common shapes (e.g. circles, rectangles) to its functionality. In regards to the drawing tool some comments also surfaced that indicated some superfluous functions, namely being able to change the width of the line drawn. The eraser tool was also often passed over and the clear screen function being used instead.

During the study the limitations of only utilizing a wireless network were experienced, which lead to the suggestion that the application should support communication over the cellular network as well. This also turned out to be a requirement due to the lack of wireless network coverage in all the areas of the plant as well as decreasing the need for the plant to invest in their own infrastructure and instead utilize existing one. Implementing communication over the cellular network would also lead to the possibility of moving security from the device to the VPN, which is the way such issues were handled at the study location. It should be noted though that although it would have been desirable to test the system over such a network it was not possible due to a lack of access to it. Another issue that was observed as a result of the connection problems was that the participants had difficulty in understanding the other participant's connection status as well as communication their own in regards to if the system was working well or was having issues such as a freeze.

A result of the, at times, weak connection the snapshot function was highly used, even when no annotations where desired or made. The reason for this was simply that the snapshot displayed in a much higher quality than the stream video. A participant also mentioned that from his point of view the video streaming was not as important as being able to share a snapshot. Such a solution, making the streaming optional, could lead to the system as a whole becoming more reliable, especially when dealing with a weaker connection. In addition, the participants suggested improvements to the snapshot feature: there should be a zoom function included as it was not always possible to get close enough to the objects to get a big enough picture of them. Adding some form of light control was also requested as it would ease video streaming and picture taking when in low-light environments and would not force them to hold a flashlight in one had, preventing them from interacting with the system.

In between observations and after interviews the participants pointed out other uses for the tool that had previously not been considered. Such an example would be to be able to use it to document potential safety hazards in an easier way by directly recording it via a picture or video clip and on the spot make a notification of it rather than having to jot down information and remember to make an official notification ones back at a work station. Linked to this is the expressed desire for a document sharing function so that e.g. blueprints could be shown further removing the need for transporting oneself to gain the needed information. Another potential function would be to introduce mobile to mobile communication as one might want to get into contact with the person who e.g. previously had similar problems or has expertise with a certain process but does not frequent the control room.

When asked about potential risks linked to the system the main concern was the tablet's fragility and that if it were dropped it could break. Despite this none would have preferred a head-mounted system as they were perceived as too bulky and inconvenient.

CONCLUSIONS

In this paper, we described the implementation of a system for remote video collaboration between a field worker on site and a remote expert as well as an initial usability test purposed to gain insight into our design decisions. The developed prototype system consists of a mobile application and a respective PC application. The mobile application streams video to the PC application by using its camera. The PC application replays the received video stream to the remote expert so they can observe the environment of the remotely located user.

The system was specifically designed for collaboration of the two parties, namely for the interaction between the field worker and the remote expert. Traditionally, the research systems designed for remote collaboration have focused on expert guidance rather than collaborative problem solving. In the developed system, both parties can capture snapshots by using their applications. The snapshots are always taken separately on both application to ensure the fast synchronization and interaction between the participants. In addition, the system allows users to annotate the media using virtual pointers and overlaying drawings. Also, the annotations are transferred in an optimal and fast way between the applications to ensure the real-time communication.

Furthermore, the resulted system introduced architectural solutions for remote video collaboration. For instance, the system setup was simplified significantly to ease the video streaming initialization. In addition, the real-time video and annotations were transferred between a mobile device and a PC without the need for a separate third-party server. Such peer-to-peer implementation is an effective solution for technical support in industrial settings since we cannot expect a connection to the Internet. We also paid a special attention to the testability of the system and made the connectivity implementation modular to adjust to different network contexts.

The results of our initial evaluation with users indicated that our overall design was well received and that most decisions regarding its design were well founded. The results did however also show that the system was missing some key features. Most serious among these were voice communication and cellular network integration. The ability to use voice communication proved to be a vital addition from the users points of view, while cellular network would be needed for the system to live up to the *R7* requirement previously identified. The problem with only relying on the wireless network also caused the participants to experience issues similar to some described by [4], mainly a problem in understanding if the collaborative partners view and actions are synchronous with what oneself is doing. The study thus gave us insight into what future work is needed to be performed as to assure the systems acceptance. In light of this further and extended usability testing will be needed at a later stage in the development to once again help validate or invalidate the next set or features and functions.

Findings of the study also seem to support earlier findings by [35] stating that chat functionality still has and will continue to have a place in media rich environments. The way our study supports this is that several of the participants expressed a desire for the inclusion of a text communication feature, not only to ease communication in noisy environments but also to aid in describing complex tasks offering a persistent list for both to refer to.

As a conclusion, we believe that mobile devices can significantly contribute to the area of remote collaboration in industrial environments in the near future. Mobile devices are cost-efficient, easily replaceable, well-suited for field workers' work practices and offer a powerful range of interaction and sensing technologies. Our system demonstrates the practical value that these devices are already able to offer today. The usability study further supports this through participants commenting that a tablet such as the one used (a Google Nexus 7) is a perfect size for such a device.

REFERENCES

1. Bauer, M., Kortuem, G., and Segall, Z. "where are you pointing at?" a study of remote collaboration in a wearable videoconference system. In *Proceedings of the 3rd IEEE International Symposium on Wearable Computers*, ISWC '99, IEEE Computer Society (Washington, DC, USA, 1999), 151–.
2. Chastine, J., Nagel, K., Zhu, Y., and Hudachek-Buswell, M. Studies on the effectiveness of virtual pointers in collaborative augmented reality. In *Proceedings of the 2008 IEEE Symposium on 3D User Interfaces*, 3DUI '08, IEEE Computer Society (Washington, DC, USA, 2008), 117–124.
3. Cheng, Y., Wang, Y., and Zheng, Z. Strategies research on selecting streaming media in network course development. In *Artificial Intelligence and Education (ICAIE), 2010 International Conference on* (2010), 457–460.
4. Dix, A. Cooperation without (reliable) communication: Interfaces for mobile applications. *Distributed Systems Engineering 171* (1995).
5. Dünser, A., Grasset, R., and Billinghurst, M. A survey of evaluation techniques used in augmented reality studies. Tech. Rep. September, Christchurch, NZ, 2008.
6. Fussell, S. R., Setlock, L. D., Yang, J., Ou, J., Mauer, E., and Kramer, A. D. I. Gestures over video streams to support remote collaboration on physical tasks. *Hum.-Comput. Interact. 19*, 3 (Sept. 2004), 273–309.
7. Gauglitz, S., Lee, C., Turk, M., and Höllerer, T. Integrating the physical environment into mobile remote collaboration. In *Proceedings of the 14th international conference on Human-computer interaction with mobile devices and services*, MobileHCI '12, ACM (New York, NY, USA, 2012), 241–250.
8. Gehlen, G., Aijaz, F., and Walke, B. Mobile web service communication over udp. In *Vehicular Technology Conference, 2006. VTC-2006 Fall. 2006 IEEE 64th* (2006), 1–5.
9. Gutwin, C., and Penner, R. Improving interpretation of remote gestures with telepointer traces. In *Proceedings of the 2002 ACM conference on Computer supported cooperative work*, CSCW '02, ACM (New York, NY, USA, 2002), 49–57.
10. Hayne, S., Pendergast, M., and Greenberg, S. Implementing gesturing with cursors in group support systems. *J. Manage. Inf. Syst. 10*, 3 (Dec. 1993), 43–61.
11. Henrysson, A., Billinghurst, M., and Ollila, M. Face to face collaborative ar on mobile phones. In *Mixed and Augmented Reality, 2005. Proceedings. Fourth IEEE and ACM International Symposium on* (2005), 80–89.
12. Hindmarsh, J., Fraser, M., Heath, C., Benford, S., and Greenhalgh, C. Fragmented interaction: establishing mutual orientation in virtual environments. In *Proceedings of the 1998 ACM conference on Computer supported cooperative work*, CSCW '98, ACM (New York, NY, USA, 1998), 217–226.
13. Huang, W., and Alem, L. Handsinair: a wearable system for remote collaboration on physical tasks. In *Proceedings of the 2013 conference on Computer supported cooperative work companion*, CSCW '13, ACM (New York, NY, USA, 2013), 153–156.
14. Jo, H., and Hwang, S. Chili: viewpoint control and on-video drawing for mobile video calls. In *CHI '13 Extended Abstracts on Human Factors in Computing Systems*, CHI EA '13, ACM (New York, NY, USA, 2013), 1425–1430.
15. Kirk, D., Rodden, T., and Fraser, D. S. Turn it this way: grounding collaborative action with remote gestures. In *Proceedings of the SIGCHI Conference on Human Factors in Computing Systems*, CHI '07, ACM (New York, NY, USA, 2007), 1039–1048.
16. Kjeldskov, J., and Graham, C. A review of mobile HCI research methods. In *Human-computer interaction with mobile devices and services*. Springer Berlin Heidelberg, 2003, 317–335.
17. Kjeldskov, J., and Paay, J. A Longitudinal Review of Mobile HCI Research Methods. In *Proceedings of the 14th international conference on Human-computer interaction with mobile devices and services*, ACM (2012), 69–78.

18. Klein, G., and Murray, D. Parallel tracking and mapping for small ar workspaces. In *Mixed and Augmented Reality, 2007. ISMAR 2007. 6th IEEE and ACM International Symposium on* (2007), 225–234.
19. Kraut, R., Fussell, S., and Siegel, J. Visual Information as a Conversational Resource in Collaborative Physical Tasks. *Human-Computer Interaction 18*, 1 (June 2003), 13–49.
20. Kraut, R. E., Fussell, S. R., and Siegel, J. Visual information as a conversational resource in collaborative physical tasks. *Hum.-Comput. Interact. 18*, 1 (June 2003), 13–49.
21. Kraut, R. E., Miller, M. D., and Siegel, J. Collaboration in performance of physical tasks: effects on outcomes and communication. In *Proceedings of the 1996 ACM conference on Computer supported cooperative work*, CSCW '96, ACM (New York, NY, USA, 1996), 57–66.
22. Kurata, T., Sakata, N., Kourogi, M., Kuzuoka, H., and Billinghurst, M. Remote collaboration using a shoulder-worn active camera/laser. In *Proceedings of the Eighth International Symposium on Wearable Computers*, ISWC '04, IEEE Computer Society (Washington, DC, USA, 2004), 62–69.
23. Kuzuoka, H., Kosuge, T., and Tanaka, M. Gesturecam: a video communication system for sympathetic remote collaboration. In *Proceedings of the 1994 ACM conference on Computer supported cooperative work*, CSCW '94, ACM (New York, NY, USA, 1994), 35–43.
24. Ladikos, E., Benhimane, S., and Navab, N. Model-free markerless tracking for remote support in unknown environments.
25. Lee, G. A., and Billinghurst, M. A user study on the snap-to-feature interaction method. In *Mixed and Augmented Reality (ISMAR), 2011 10th IEEE International Symposium on* (2011), 245–246.
26. Liu, J., Rao, S., Li, B., and Zhang, H. Opportunities and challenges of peer-to-peer internet video broadcast. *Proceedings of the IEEE 96*, 1 (2008), 11–24.
27. Malhotra, A., Sharma, V., Gandhi, P., and Purohit, N. Udp based chat application. In *Computer Engineering and Technology (ICCET), 2010 2nd International Conference on*, vol. 6 (2010), V6–374–V6–377.
28. Mandula, K., Meda, S., and Jain, D. Research and implementation of a mobile video streaming application for ubiquitous learning. In *Technology Enhanced Education (ICTEE), 2012 IEEE International Conference on* (2012), 1–6.
29. Massandy, D., and Munir, I. Secured video streaming development on smartphones with android platform. In *Telecommunication Systems, Services, and Applications (TSSA), 2012 7th International Conference on* (2012), 339–344.
30. Mortensen, J., Vinayagamoorthy, V., Slater, M., Steed, A., Lok, B., and Whitton, M. C. Collaboration in tele-immersive environments. In *Proceedings of the workshop on Virtual environments 2002*, EGVE '02, Eurographics Association (Aire-la-Ville, Switzerland, Switzerland, 2002), 93–101.
31. Ou, J., Chen, X., Fussell, S. R., and Yang, J. Dove: drawing over video environment. In *Proceedings of the eleventh ACM international conference on Multimedia*, MULTIMEDIA '03, ACM (New York, NY, USA, 2003), 100–101.
32. Poelman, R., Akman, O., Lukosch, S., and Jonker, P. As if being there: mediated reality for crime scene investigation. In *Proceedings of the ACM 2012 conference on Computer Supported Cooperative Work*, CSCW '12, ACM (New York, NY, USA, 2012), 1267–1276.
33. Rekimoto, J., and Nagao, K. The world through the computer: computer augmented interaction with real world environments. In *Proceedings of the 8th annual ACM symposium on User interface and software technology*, UIST '95, ACM (New York, NY, USA, 1995), 29–36.
34. Schmalstieg, D., Fuhrmann, A., and Hesina, G. Bridging multiple user interface dimensions with augmented reality. In *Augmented Reality, 2000. (ISAR 2000). Proceedings. IEEE and ACM International Symposium on* (2000), 20–29.
35. Scholl, J., McCarthy, J., and Harr, R. A comparison of chat and audio in media rich environments. In *Proceedings of the 2006 20th anniversary conference on Computer supported cooperative work - CSCW '06*, ACM Press (New York, New York, USA, 2006), 323.
36. Stevenson, D., Li, J., Smith, J., and Hutchins, M. A collaborative guidance case study. *Proceedings of the ninth conference on Australasian user interface 76*, January (2008), 33–42.
37. Vartiainen, E., Ralph, M., and Bjorndal, P. Challenges in using mobile devices in process industry. In *APCHI '13: Proceedings of the 11th Asia Pacific conference on Computer human interaction*, ACM (New York, NY, USA, 2013).
38. Vun, N., and Ansary, M. Implementation of an embedded h.264 live video streaming system. In *Consumer Electronics (ISCE), 2010 IEEE 14th International Symposium on* (2010), 1–4.
39. Wither, J., DiVerdi, S., and Hollerer, T. Evaluating display types for ar selection and annotation. In *Mixed and Augmented Reality, 2007. ISMAR 2007. 6th IEEE and ACM International Symposium on* (Nov 2007), 95–98.

The Usability of a Tabletop Application for Neuro-Rehabilitation from Therapists' Point of View

Mirjam Augstein
UAS Upper Austria
Softwarepark 11
4232 Hagenberg, Austria
mirjam.augstein@fh-hagenberg.at

Thomas Neumayr
UAS Upper Austria
Softwarepark 11
4232 Hagenberg, Austria
thomas.neumayr@fh-hagenberg.at

Irene Schacherl-Hofer
Occupational Therapist
Bachstraße 14
4492 Hofkirchen, Austria
ergotherapie@schacherl-hofer.at

ABSTRACT

The success of virtual environments in neuro-rehabilitation crucially relies on the acceptance of its users. Thus, in the development of virtual rehabilitation environments usually a user-centered design process is followed. Most approaches concentrate on the patient as end user, however, the target group might be two-fold. The fun.tast.tisch. project aims at the development of a tabletop-based software system for therapists and patients as supporting means in conventional neuro-rehabilitation. Both target groups are involved in the development process; different studies are conducted to ensure the therapeutic adequateness and the system's usability. The latter is especially important for therapists as they are responsible for navigating through the modules and configuring them for the patients individually. This paper describes two fun.tast.tisch. modules that have been evaluated regarding usability for therapists in a longer-term study in summer 2013 in a rehabilitation hospital, and presents the study's results.

Author Keywords

User-Centered Design, Usability, Multitouch, Tabletops, Neuro-Rehabilitation

ACM Classification Keywords

H.5.2 Input devices and strategies: User Interfaces; H.5.2 Interaction styles: User Interfaces; H.5.2 User-centered design: User Interfaces

General Terms

Human Factors

INTRODUCTION

Acquired brain injury, mostly caused by stroke or accidents, is often followed by a long process of (neuro-)rehabilitation. A relatively high number of patients (39 percent) incur cognitive impairment after acquired brain injury [24] which can also be accompanied by motor impairments. During the rehabilitation process, a patient is usually supported by a rehabilitation team including occupational therapists with individually selected exercises, training e.g., memory, attention, or visuo-spatial abilities [10]. Therapeutic intervention aims at restoring a person's independence, e.g., regarding everyday activities like eating, dressing, or housework, and generally encouraging social participation (that is often reduced after acquired brain injury, which negatively affects quality of life).

The fun.tast.tisch. project[1] (see [6, 7]) is an endeavor to develop a tabletop-based training software for neuro-rehabilitation, supporting both patients and therapists throughout the therapy process. The project team is highly interdisciplinary involving occupational therapists, software developers, interaction, graphic and object designers and assistive technology experts. A tabletop hardware (Samsung SUR40 with Microsoft PixelSense (SUR40)) was chosen for this purpose mainly for the following two reasons (also see [6, 28]). First, the table itself is a familiar object, thus patients and therapists do not have to overcome potential inhibitions regarding new technology and its handling. Conventional therapy sessions often take place around a common table, and several therapeutic exercises require a horizontal area in the size of a table to work on. Second, the horizontal surface allows for tangible objects to be placed on it which again facilitates including the use of objects (thus haptic experience) in the therapeutic exercises (due to its optical display, the table can recognize different objects in addition to touches). The latter is especially beneficial in cases where (fine) motor skills should be trained and also reduces the level of abstraction in some exercises and thus facilitates access. In fun.tast.tisch., we use two different kinds of objects: tagged ones that are recognized by the table based on a unique tag placed on the bottom of the object, and non-tagged ones that are recognized by the table based on their shape. The second kind was introduced because in some cases the objects need to be flipped over and used from their other side for therapeutic reasons, which rendered the use of tags inconvenient.

ITS '14, November 16 - 19 2014, Dresden, Germany

http://dx.doi.org/10.1145/2669485.2669516

[1]The project's name "fun.tast.tisch" originates in a wordplay in German language: "Tisch" is the German word for table, "tasten" is a German verb that can be translated with feeling by touch. Thus, the project's name suggests having fun with a touch-based interface on a table. Additionally, the name "fun.tast.tisch." sounds similar to the German word "fantastisch" which means "fantastic".

In addition to the main advantages described in the previous paragraph, the chosen tabletop multitouch technology allows for a high number of concurrent touches to be recognized, thus multiple users can interact with the table at the same time. The fun.tast.tisch. software includes several modules that can be used in a single and a multi-user (usually: one therapist and up to three patients) setting. Theoretically, the SUR40 is able to recognize more than 50 simultaneous inputs (either triggered by touch or by objects placed on the screen) [22]. However, in our project, numerous tests have shown that for performance reasons, the table could only (reliably) recognize and process about 15 tagged objects (using a tag set of 256 unique tags). We had to overcome this problem by introducing an own, simpler set of tags (with a lower number of unique tags) in order to make our multi-user modules applicable for the maximum-user setting.

The fun.tast.tisch. system by now includes over 10 training modules that have been tested and evaluated with the target group throughout the whole development process because we followed an iterative user-centered design approach. Additionally, the modules were (and will be) tested more exhaustively, i) in a longer-term study taking place in a rehabilitation hospital and ii) in a longer-term study with individual patients that receive periodic sessions in ambulant therapy. The fun.tast.tisch. modules aim at supporting the user in training different skills like memory, attention, motor skills, visual abilities such as visual exploration or visual-spatial skills.

For our studies we distinguish between and separately evaluate our software system for two target groups: therapists and patients. Regarding therapists, the usability aspect is of capital importance because therapists usually have to navigate through the menus of the overall system and of the individual modules to e.g., select the modules applicable for the individual patient, set the correct level of difficulty, switch between levels of difficulty, store a patient's results etc, while a patient usually only has to do the exercises. Regarding patients, we also aim at evaluating the therapeutic effects.

This paper discusses results of the first longer-term study that took place for several months in summer 2013 in a rehabilitation hospital in Upper Austria and aimed at the evaluation of the two fun.tast.tisch. modules. We focus on the usability and user experience from the therapists' point of view and provide an outlook on the next steps in the fun.tast.tisch. project.

RELATED WORK

This section provides an overview on related work in the area of virtual (neuro-)rehabilitation, not all of which, however, apply a tabletop technology.

A training environment applicable in neuro-rehabilitation should in general be stimulating in order to facilitate brain plasticity. Brain plasticity (i.e., other areas of the brain take over functions previously taken care of by the damaged ones) is the prerequisite for recovery after acquired brain injury and is influenced by environmental stimulation [19]. There is substantial evidence for the positive effect of using virtual environments or serious games in neuro-rehabilitation [16, 26, 8] e.g., regarding attention abilities [27, 32], memory [15] or spatial orientation [20]. Some fun.tast.tisch. modules also aim at supporting patients in (re-)training their memory, attention or spatial orientation skills. The module "shopping" as described in the next section, e.g., focuses on memory and related self-assessment.

In addition to training of cognitive skills, patients can also benefit from virtual rehabilitation environments regarding their motor skills. Sharlin et al. [29], e.g., discuss a rehabilitation approach where patients, with the help of tangible objects, have to reconstruct a 3D shape displayed on the screen, an activity that helps to train one's fine motor skills. In the fun.tast.tisch. project, we also include the use of tangible objects, e.g., in the Tangram (where objects do not only have to be used but also flipped over and placed on the surface with a certain rotation) or shopping (where physical coins have to be used to select digital objects on the screen) modules (see descriptions in the following section).

The application of tangible interfaces and use of real physical objects in cognitive therapy is also in the focus of de la Guía et al. [13]. They present the TraInAb (Train Intellectual Abilities) system, an interactive and collaborative set of games that facilitate the use of real physical objects like cards, coins or toys and can be used individually or by multiple users. The real objects are recognized by the system via NFC tags placed on them. The system consists of three components, a) the main component with main user interface that graphically displays game information, b) the mobile user interface, i.e., a user interface on a mobile device including the NFC reader needed to recognize the tagged objects which represent c) the tangible user interface. The two games described in [13] are close to everyday activities; users have to memorize objects and count money. The memory game is similar to the shopping module of fun.tas.tisch. described here regarding the general idea, however, the implementation differs significantly. In the memory game described in [13], a user has to memorize three cards that are first shown by the system and then disappear. Next, the system shows two of the cards again and the user has to memorize the third card. In our shopping module, the user him-/herself can decide how many items to memorize. Also, we aimed at keeping the game as close to an everyday setting as possible (e.g., the user can choose the kind of goods, can make use of a shopping list, etc.).

Martínez-Moreno et al. describe a tool that allows neuropsychologists to design interactive video therapeutic activities using graphic and natural language [21]. They state that successful rehabilitation should consider task reproducibility, accurate assessment and the possibility of monitoring the process and the patient's performance. The main focus of Martínez-Moreno et al. lies on letting therapists design rehabilitation tasks based on activities of daily living. Although their work differs from ours significantly (in the fun.tas.tisch. system, we do not aim at providing an authoring tool for rehabilitation exercises), we agree with them regarding the relevance of activities of daily living in the rehabilitation process. Both of the two modules described in the next section ultimately aim at improving patients' performance in daily living activities.

Colman presents an idea of using multi-player online video games for cognitive rehabilitation [11]. The approach is not yet sufficiently matured and in an early state of prototypic development still, however, the multi-player aspect in rehabilitation seems interesting to us as we included a multi-player setting in some of the modules in our system, too (see, e.g., the shopping module described in the next section).

Cruz et al. describe a rehabilitation tool designed for web-based cognitive training that can be used by patients at home under clinical prescription [12]. They argue that previous approaches did not meet all user needs because these e.g., followed a reductionist approach to rehabilitation, discouraged human relations in favor of self-executed exercises at home and increased the distance between patients and specialized health professionals. They further state that the acquisition of regular training routines and computer skills is not straightforward for people with cognitive problems. The rehabilitation tool described by Cruz et al. consists of two components, an online platform and a series of tools in the conventional exercise book format. The tool includes monitoring facilities coupled with biostatistics and long-term system analysis tools. Our approach also facilitates the interaction of patients and therapists. fun.tast.tisch. does not aim at replacing therapy sessions and being used by patients autonomously but at enhancing conventional therapy, e.g. by providing statistics that can give an overview on the patients' training history at a glance. We agree with the concern that people with cognitive disabilities might have problems acquiring the skills necessary for interacting with a computer system; thus, patients using fun.tast.tisch. do not have to interact with the system on their own but are supported by their therapist.

The user perspective is also in the focus of Annett et al. [3] who discuss a tabletop-based therapy system (also see [4], [2] or [1]) that has been applied in upper extremity motor rehabilitation and aims at supporting therapists and increasing patients' motivation. Both objectives coincide with ours basically. While the authors' previous work has widely focused on user movement, they specifically concentrate on user engagement and users' subjective impressions towards tabletop therapy in [3]. Annett et al. found out in their user evaluation that the benefit of technology lies not in technology itself but in its ability to provide responsive, dynamic content. These findings again correlate with ours, as the functionality of e.g., changing the level of difficulty on the fly, or of receiving immediate automated feedback has been mentioned as most relevant by our target groups also.

THE FUN.TAST.TISCH. MODULES

This section describes the two modules that were evaluated in a longer-term study in an Upper Austrian rehabilitation hospital in the summer of 2013. The description is based on the status of the modules that was used for the evaluation. The results of the study already led to improvements as described in Section Discussion.

Tangram Training

The Tangram module (also see the description in [6]) is based on conventional therapy with the dissection puzzle Tangram. It consists of seven geometric puzzle pieces called tans, which can be put together as a square (see Figure 1). In addition, these tans can be formed to countless variations of figures, geometric shapes and symbols. Although it was not originally developed for therapeutic treatment, Tangram is successfully used and recommended for cognitive therapy (e.g., after acquired brain injury) due to its specific demands on cognitive processing as reported by e.g., [23, 25, 17, 18, 5]. For therapeutic use Tangram can be modified, for example there is a need for templates with fewer parts and in original size (most Tangram puzzles available for purchase outside therapeutic context provide templates in a scaled-down version only). Essential information for the aim of Tangram training and practical experience regarding the specific effects in therapy can e.g., be found at [9], but there is still a demand for research to find more evidences for the effectiveness. This specific training is recommended to ultimately improve relevant functions of daily life with visual and constructive components, e.g., dressing and wheelchair navigation. The SUR40 technology offers completely new features for Tangram training. Digital types of feedback (e.g., light, sound) and object recognition (also see Section Introduction) can be used to create a motivating learning experience and promote the opportunity for self-control. The module offers means for effective adaptation of the level of difficulty. The appropriate level can be selected in a menu before starting the session, but it can also be varied by the therapist with the help of a simple control feature during training. A cylinder of acrylic glass (see Figures 1 and 2) can be placed on the surface to open a menu, and the chosen features influence the next templates (see Figure 2). The number of tans to be used can be chosen between 2 and 7, the templates can be displayed in original size or smaller and reference lines (marking the shapes of the individual tans) appear if desired (to make solving the puzzle easier).

Figure 1. The seven Tangram tiles and the cylinder that can be used to change the level of difficulty in the fun.tast.tisch. version of Tangram.

Summing up, the technology enables efficient training with rapid adjustment of difficulty and motivating feedback. The use of objects made of acrylic glass complies with the hygienic requirements of clinical practice. The shape of the individual tans can be recognized by our software (see Section Introduction). The parts of the Tangram puzzle developed for fun.tast.tisch. by object designers are translucent (see Figure 3) to enable special effects in the visual feedback. The documentation of the treatment is facilitated by digital statistics.

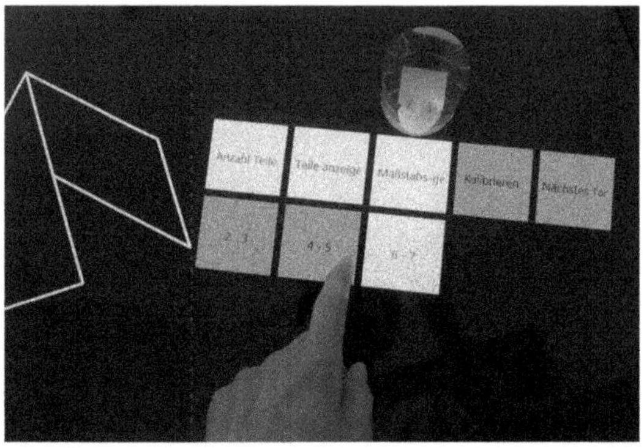

Figure 2. Changing the level of difficulty in the Tangram module (placing the cylindrical object on the screen brings up the menu).

Figure 3. Two (of seven) Tangram tiles forming a given shape.

The module Tangram has been created predominantly for adults with acquired brain injury. It was adapted for children in a separate module called "Tangram stories". Here, Tangram shapes are put together in the context of a story and realized with a design that is especially suitable for children (see Figure 4). One of the Tangram stories was also used for the study in summer 2013.

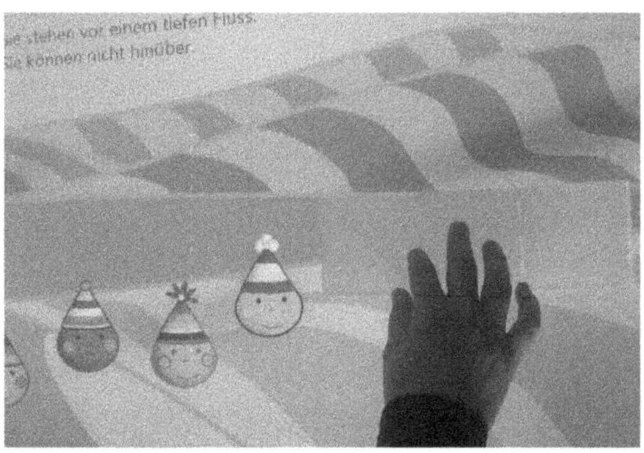

Figure 4. The children's version of Tangram (the green color highlighting the shape indicates that it has been solved successfully).

Shopping

The module "shopping" offers a virtual learning environment for cognitive memory functions. According to the recommendations of experts (e.g., [14, 25]) it is helpful to assess the own memory function in relation to the changed situation after brain injury and to learn strategies to enhance it. The aim is not primarily to remember as much as possible, but to assess one's ability adequately and apply compensations when needed. The module can be performed in individual and group settings with a maximum of 3 persons and a therapist. The group sharing can reduce the fear of failure and provides a protected environment for the use of external assistance. In addition, communication and visual perception is encouraged. The overall objective is to transfer the experience gained in this module to everyday life by using, for example, shopping lists or applying memory strategies.

Evidence-based recommendations as well as critical publications have influenced the development of the module. For example, Tam and Man [31] promote factors that enhance the acceptance of therapeutic computer programs: self-paced practice, performance feedback, appealing visual presentation, personalized workout contents. Evidence on the effectiveness of computer-based memory training can be found, e.g., at [15, 32].

The shopping module can be controlled by the user him-/herself, he/she can take as much time as needed and choose the appropriate level. The user decides how many goods to buy ($1 \leq n \leq 7$) and then receives a (digital) shopping list containing n randomly selected goods. These are offered as close-to-everyday-life photos. The user takes as much time as needed to remember the goods, and then presses the start button. Next, the screen displays a "shop" with 25 goods, among them are the articles of the participant's shopping list. Through placing of purchasing coins (tagged acrylic glass coins), items can be taken to the shopping cart. At any time help is available: by placing a "real" (i.e., tangible) shopping list made of transparent acrylic glass (see the tangible objects of the shopping module in Figure 6) on the surface, the original (digital) shopping list can be displayed. The use of a real object should facilitate the transfer to everyday life. Once the basket is filled with the right goods, feedback is provided on two sensory channels (visual and acoustic). In the next exercise, the degree of difficulty is not determined automatically, but must be selected again by individual self-assessment.

In the group setting, every user chooses the number of goods individually (thus, every user gets an individual shopping list to memorize), the goods are then presented in a shared shop (again containing 25 goods). The system distinguishes between the users based on a different set of tags for every user, i.e. every user has his/her own coins. The users themselves can identify their personal coins by a color code. In the multi-user setting, all users also have their individual physical shopping list (based on the same color code used for the coins). Figure 6 shows (one of) the shopping module's tangible object sets (with color code green). Figure 5 shows the shopping module in a group setting with three patients. The shopping coins on the picture are prototypes made of wood that have been replaced by the acrylic glass objects later.

STUDY

This section describes the study conducted in a rehabilitation hospital in Wilhering (Upper Austria) in summer 2013 from

Figure 5. The shopping module in a group setting with three patients and a therapist (not in the picture).

Figure 6. The tangible objects designed for the shopping module (coins and shopping list that can be placed on the screen).

beginning of June to end of October to evaluate the modules Tangram and shopping described in the previous section. During the whole time, the fun.tast.tisch. system was set up at the hospital and used by therapists and patients in the departments of neuro-psychology and occupational therapy.

Participants

The study considered two target groups: therapists and patients. In this paper we focus on the therapists' part and the usability, user experience and context of use aspects (see Section Categories). A total of 14 therapists participated in the study, 13 female and 1 male, 6 of them neuro-psychologists and 8 occupational therapists. The participants were between 31 and 51 years old. The therapists participated in the study voluntarily; the motivation was high due to the novelty of the technology in general and of its application in therapy settings in particular. 12 of the 14 therapists stated to have very high or high interest regarding the applicability of new technologies in therapy. 8 of the 14 therapists stated to have very high or high affinity for technology. The majority of the participating therapists were familiar with Tangram before the study; 11 of them stated to have already been using Tangram in conventional therapy (i.e., without the help of the tabletop) regularly or at least several times.

In total, 16 patients received training with the Tangram (two younger patients worked with the "Tangram stories" version) and shopping modules of fun.tast.tisch (5 male, 11 female). They were between 12 and 83 years old ($\overline{x} = 52.06$), 5 had severe, 4 slight motor impairments (6 of them had one clearly more impaired side, for 2 of them, both sides were affected). Patients were selected carefully for the study by the medical staff of the hospital because only patients with a diagnosis fitting exactly the training aims of the two available fun.tast.tisch. modules should participate.

Objectives

It was not aim of this study to evaluate the therapeutic effectiveness of the fun.tast.tisch. training (this will be done in a Randomized Controlled Trial in 2014 that will take place at the same hospital, see Section Subsequent Work). As already stated, the study focused on the evaluation of usability, user experience and context of use for therapists and patients separately, but with a general focus on the therapists. It was the main aim to find potential usability problems, e.g., in the therapist's navigation or the concepts of the modules. This study was the first of several longer-term studies and followed several smaller scale studies that were conducted before summer 2013 (see [6] for the results of one of them).

The premise of the study was that at least a part of the potential context of use, usability and user experience problems would become obvious only after a longer period of use and without a project team member available to help out. During the smaller scale studies conducted before, we already involved both target groups, but usually one of the project team members (mostly, one of the occupational therapists) supervised the training sessions. It was our aim to get therapists' feedback regarding the applicability of fun.tast.tisch. training in comparison to conventional therapy, its acceptance and details regarding the two presented modules.

General Setting

Training sessions with fun.tast.tisch. were integrated in the conventional therapy program and were repeated at least 5 times for every patient. Participating therapists received a detailed introduction to the use of fun.tast.tisch. in end of May 2013, before the study started.

The study included two paper-based questionnaires (A and B) for therapists, one to be answered after the first training session with a patient with fun.tast.tisch. (A), and one to be answered after the last training session with fun.tast.tisch. (B). The idea behind this process was to capture both, aspects that spontaneously pop up at the first use (i.e., a first impression), as well as aspects that become obvious only after a longer period of use. Working with only one questionnaire, we would probably have lost one of the two information levels.

The two questionnaires were not identical, however; we placed a majority of (e.g., the usability-related) questions in the first questionnaire only for the following reasons. Firstly, we assumed usability problems to be perceived more distinctly at the first notice. After having become used to them (i.e., after a longer period of using fun.tast.tisch.), the perception of the severity of a problem might change and the problem might become less significant in the eyes of the therapist. This might, however, secondly, have led to a misinterpretation on our side regarding the severity of usability problems. We thus chose very carefully the questions that should be asked twice and came up with a smaller subset (containing questions related to aspects we assumed to be identified better after a longer period of use). For the questions that were asked twice, in order to find out whether the results for the individual therapists differed among the two questionnaires, we conducted a transition analysis on the data we received (see Section Transition Analysis).

The questions in both questionnaires were categorized (see the following section for details) internally, i.e., the categories we used (e.g., usability) were not obvious to the probands. Part of the questions were single or multiple choice questions, the other part consisted of open questions (mainly, regarding problems that occurred during the training sessions or improvement suggestions). Not all therapists that participated in the study filled in the second questionnaire due to a lack of time. Thus, the results for the second questionnaire include the opinions of only 12 therapists (5 neuro-psychologists and 7 occupational therapists).

Categories

In order to obtain a view of the overall interaction we categorized the questions of our questionnaires along three main criteria: usability (US), user experience (UX) and the context of use (CU). General interpretations of US and UX as explained by Sharp et al. [30] guided our way in deciding which questions to ask.

UX-related questions, for instance, dealt with the perception of fun.tast.tisch.'s feedback (e.g., whether it was perceived as motivating, funny, distracting, etc.) or if individuals felt that cooperation between therapists and patients was generally working well. Furthermore, we wanted to find out how the changing of settings (e.g., level of difficulty) by the therapists on the fly (i.e., during an exercise) was perceived. According to the past experiences of the occupational therapists in the fun.tast.tisch. team with the use of Tangram in conventional therapy, this process can have a negative effect on the patient's motivation because i) it may take a while until a more adequate Tangram shape is found in the therapist's book, and ii) a patient can easily be demotivated if a therapist has to search for an easier shape to be solved by the patient. Because it was not possible to do an exhaustive questionnaire or interview with the patients due to ethical reasons, we included this aspect in our evaluation with the therapists [2]. In the fun.tast.tisch. Tangram module we aimed at providing an easy way to change the settings so a patient can hardly even notice the new level of difficulty. In total, questionnaire A contained 5, questionnaire B contained 2 questions related to UX.

US-related questions e.g., aimed at finding out if controls could be reached well or settings that have been made by the therapist had the expected effect on the behaviour of the system. Furthermore, they dealt with the general navigation through the system (e.g., whether the correct module was found and could be started without problems, whether it was possible to pause or stop the training or to log in to or log out from the system without problems). Regarding US, we generally aimed at receiving separate feedback regarding all control elements that the therapists needed to use in the given fun.tast.tisch. configuration. Thus, the number of US-related questions significantly exceeded the number of questions in the other categories. In total, questionnaire A contained 20 US-related questions, questionnaire B contained 7.

The motivation behind the evaluation of the CU aspect was on one hand to find out if the fun.tast.tisch. setting (involving also the ergonomic aspects regarding the table and the seating arrangement) is suitable for longer use. On the other hand, we wanted to obtain meta-data on the usage to be generally better able to interpret the answers to our questions. A CU-related question, for example, was used to find out what seating arrangement was used. The therapist can generally sit at the patient's more impaired side or at the other one, if there are any motor disabilities (there are therapeutic reasons that influence the sitting position). The seating arrangement can be of relevance, e.g., for other aspects in the US-category (e.g., whether a control element on the table could be reached well, etc.). Within the CU category, we, e.g., also found out whether a patient was sitting in a wheelchair or a normal chair. In total, questionnaire A contained 5 questions related to CU, questionnaire B contained 3.

Of course, a number of questions was not strictly classified to belong to only one of our three categories. In addition to the questions related to UX, US and CU, we collected some demographic information (e.g., age, gender, profession, etc.). Questionnaires A and B both contained 6 questions related to demographic information. Furthermore, we asked two general questions related to therapists' perception regarding advantages and disadvantages of fun.tast.tisch. training compared to conventional therapy.

RESULTS

This section provides an overview on the results of the study split up into the categories we introduced in the previous section (US, UX and CU). The results described in the following sections regarding US, UX and CU refer to questionnaire A. An additional section then deals with the significant differences between the results of questionnaires A and B.

User Experience

Concerning UX, the results predominantly show a positive picture. For example, no therapist complained about patients being distracted by the therapist adjusting settings, and according to the results, the overall cooperation between therapists and patients functioned well (stated by 14 out of 14). Moreover, the feedback was understood well (13 out of 14, 1 answer was missing) and predominantly described with positive adjectives (e.g. "funny", "motivating", "exciting", "adequate", "okay"). Figure 7 shows an additional overview on all questions we classified as UX-relevant that used a binary nominal scale ("yes" vs. "no"). In all cases, "yes" implies a positive perception, "no" a negative one. The figure does

[2] As mentioned before, the study in summer of 2013 included patients as well, however, we were only able to do a very short interview with the patients that could not cover the majority of the usability aspects in detail. The (usability) evaluation of the system from patients' point of view takes place mainly outside the hospital in support groups or in longer-term studies with individual patients.

not provide details related to the questions, it is intended to provide an overview on the perceived UX.

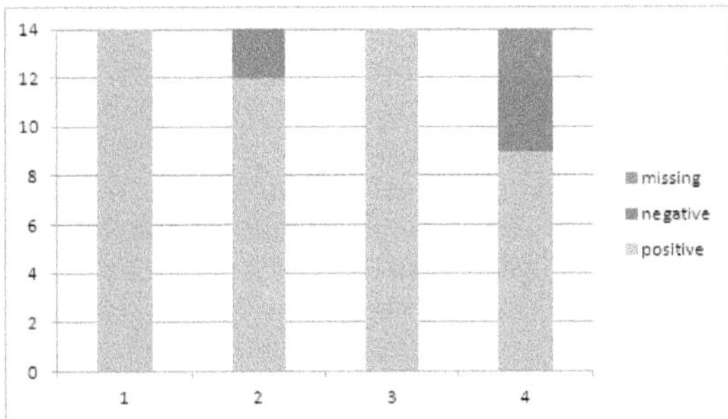

Figure 7. Overview on user experience as perceived by therapists.

Usability

As already mentioned, the number of US-related questions we asked (especially in questionnaire A) was relatively high. Generally, only few critical US issues were identified. Participants could mainly reach controls well (14), stating that (interactive) elements on the tabletop were placed "okay" (10) to "very well" (3). Most therapists stated that setting different levels of difficulty had the expected effect on the system (9 out of 12; 2 did not answer the related questions). Most users (11 of 14) knew how to pause the training and all of them (14) were able to exit it without problems. Controlling and selecting the next template in Tangram was understood well by the majority of the therapists (10 out of 13, 1 did not answer the question).

Figure 8 shows an overview on all questions we classified as US-relevant that used a binary nominal scale ("yes" vs. "no"). Again, the figure does not provide details related to the questions, it is intended to provide an overview on the perceived usability (in all cases, "yes" implies a positive perception, "no" a negative one). The question with the ID 11 in Figure 8 referred to whether the table recognized the correctly placed Tangram tiles as correct in all cases. This was the most severe US problem identified during the summer study, as the feedback did not always occur immediately after a correct shape was laid by the patient, in some cases the feedback was triggered too late, in other cases the shape (although correct) had to be manipulated again by the therapist before the table recognized it. This problem is related to the technology used by SUR40 which is extremely sensitive to light in general, and to changes in lighting in particular. This problem is however not only a technological one, it also massively influenced the perceived usability. The question with ID 4 in Figure 8 referred to whether it was obvious to the therapists that after using the interactive element labeled "start training" for the first time, the screen for initial setting of the level of difficulty would pop up before the training would actually be started. The question with ID 10 referred to whether it was obvious where the Tangram tiles should be placed (in the case of an original-size-shape, the tiles must be placed directly on it, in case of a scaled-down shape, the tiles can be placed anywhere on the screen). The question with ID 13 in Figure 8 referred to whether the changing of different dimensions of the level of difficulty had the expected effects.

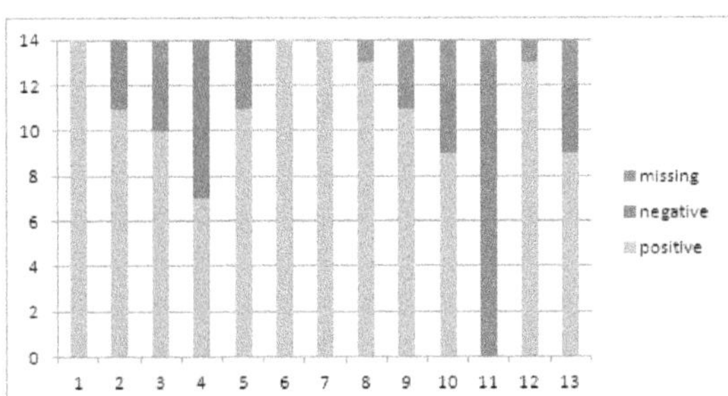

Figure 8. Overview on usability as perceived by therapists.

Context of Use

According to the therapists, no patient complained about the positioning of potentially paralyzed arms (a specific arm splint was used to keep the impaired arm in position). Generally, there have been very few complaints about sitting posture in questionnaire A (12 out of 14 therapists stated that the patient's sitting posture is suitable for a longer training). Yet, this perception slightly changed with increasing fun.tast.tisch. experience (see details in the following section).

Transition Analysis

As participants used the same unique anonymized code names for both questionnaires, it was possible to make comparisons between the participants' responses to questionnaires A and B and therefore find out differences over the time period of a number of training sessions. Regarding the US- and UX-related questions, we hardly could find significant differences comparing the results of questionnaires A and B. The most significant changes could be observed in the CU category, regarding the question if therapists thought that patients' sitting posture was suitable for (longer) training sessions. Four therapists who initially (i.e., in questionnaire A) had found the posture to be suitable changed their answer to "no" (see Figure 9) in questionnaire B. Furthermore, two therapists who saw no advantages of fun.tast.tisch. training compared to conventional therapy in the beginning, stated that there are advantages in questionnaire B. Also, two participants who initially saw no disadvantages of fun.tast.tisch. training compared to conventional therapy, changed their view over time. Finally, three participants who at first regarded the time-span between finishing a Tangram template and the appearance of feedback as "too long" changed their answer to "adequate" in the second questionnaire (this was the only considerable difference between the results of questionnaires A and B in the UX category) .

Comparison to Conventional Therapy

Most participants saw advantages in the usage of fun.tast.tisch. compared to conventional training. However, a narrow majority also identified disadvantages in questionnaire A (see Table 1). This differentiated view became even more distinctive in questionnaire B, where almost all participants saw advantages as well as disadvantages (see Table 2). This might have been caused by a better knowledge

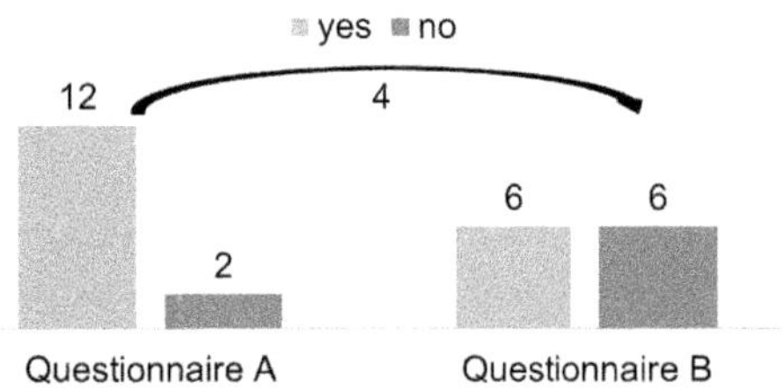

Figure 9. Transition analysis regarding the question whether the patient's sitting posture was suitable for a longer training from therapists' point of view (14 participants answered questionnaire A, 12 questionnaire B).

of the system, at the point in time when participants answered questionnaire B (at this point, they had already been guiding a higher number of training sessions).

	yes	no	missing
Do you see any advantages compared to conventional therapy?	10	2	2
Do you see any disadvantages compared to conventional therapy?	12	2	0

Table 1. Advantages and disadvantages of fun.tast.tisch. training in comparison with conventional therapy (questionnaire A)

	yes	no	missing
Do you see any advantages compared to conventional therapy?	9	1	4
Do you see any disadvantages compared to conventional therapy?	11	1	2

Table 2. Advantages and disadvantages of fun.tast.tisch. training in comparison with conventional therapy (questionnaire B)

Exemplarily, the therapists identified the following advantages compared to conventional therapy settings: the new technology facilitates patients' curiosity and motivation, the table's feedback is motivating, the table is perceived as "modern" and "trendy", the level of difficulty (in Tangram) can be easily set individually, and the modules can be used for both, adults and children (this is sometimes not the case in conventional settings, as many of the exercises are targeted towards children but used for all, according to the therapists).

Exemplarily, the therapists identified the following disadvantages compared to conventional therapy settings: the technology can cause problems (e.g., unexpected shutdown, user input not always interpreted correctly, the Tangram shapes were often not recognized correctly immediately), the table's height is not adjustable, the predefined levels of difficulty are not sufficient (especially, regarding the shopping module), the therapist does not have full control over the therapy setting, and the number of different training modules is limited.

DISCUSSION

The results of the study described in the previous section have shown that the problems identified by the therapists were mainly related to two aspects. First, there have been severe problems regarding the recognition of correctly solved Tangram shapes that are mainly related to technology (i.e., this is an optimization task for the software developers) that also lowered a bit the perceived overall usability of the system. Second, the therapists stated that especially regarding the shopping module (although it worked well during the whole study), the possibilities of varying the training were not sufficient (which makes it unsuitable for repeated use for the same patient). The latter aspect was also mentioned regarding the whole system; therapists stated that the selection of modules was limited and should be extended. However, the results have also shown that regarding the tested UX, US and also most CU aspects, the fun.tast.tisch. system was already in a quite matured state when it was tested at the hospital. Except for the technical issue related to correct recognition of solved Tangram shapes, no significant US and UX problems have been identified. We attribute these findings to the thorough involvement of therapists and patients in the user-centered design and development process.

The feedback of the therapists already led to several improvements and extensions of both modules, however, especially regarding the shopping module (as Tangram has already been tested more exhaustively before the study in small-scale user tests, see [6]). One concern mentioned by the therapists was that the training with the shopping module was not ideal for repeated application as it would be common in a rehabilitation hospital. There, it is necessary to be able to change the level of difficulty so that the training can be adjusted over time, which was not possible in the version that was applied in the study. Based on these points of criticism, the project team developed different ideas in cooperation with the therapists that participated in the study regarding the level of difficulty that have already been implemented.

For instance, the shop size can now be varied from 10 up to 25 goods in the single user setting (i.e., the level of difficulty can be adjusted). Additionally, the therapist can choose to apply distraction factors (e.g., noise or advertising signs). The introduction of distraction generally brings the scenario even closer to reality (shopping usually does not occur in a shielded, neutral space). For both kinds of distraction, noise (acoustic distraction) and advertisements (visual distraction), the level can be adjusted by the therapist. According to the selected level, the distraction appears more or less often. Furthermore, an additional kind of distraction was introduced in order to improve the user's individual memory span. If this kind of distraction is activated, a little game has to be played by the patient(s) between memorizing the goods and picking them from the shop. In this game, bills and coins that are moving around the screen have to be collected until a certain amount of money is reached. The duration of the game can be set by the therapist (the module offers four different stages).

Another adjustment that has already been made to the shopping module after the study involves the possibility to display the shopping list (that has to be memorized by the patient) in images or verbally (e.g., a picture of an apple versus the word "apple"). The version tested in the study contained only the image-based approach. Therapists suggested the introduction of the verbal version as another way of changing the level of difficulty. Additionally, patients can now choose between different shops, which is intended to increase motivation as the goods that have to be memorized are now interesting to the user with higher probability.

Regarding the Tangram module, a lot of further effort has been put in the optimization of recognition of the Tangram tiles, as this was one of the main points of criticism in the study (see Section Results). The module now offers an improved calibration component that facilitates therapists to change the table's calibration (optimized according to the current lighting situation) themselves. Recent test have proven a significant improvement compared to the version that was used during the study in summer 2013. In addition, several new templates have been implemented in order to give more variety for training sessions.

Regarding the therapists' concern that the choice of modules (i.e., different training exercises) was limited, we can already offer 14 different modules soon (most of them are already at the stage of extensive user tests in small-scale settings), two more are in the state of conceptualization at the moment. While the modules evaluated in the study concentrated on motor, visuo-constructive and memory skills, the full set of modules that will be offered by fun.tast.tisch. covers a much higher number of skills that are usually trained within the process of neuro-rehabilitation (e.g., attention, visual exploration, or visuo-spatial skills).

Regarding the potential problems in the CU area (e.g., due to the fixed height of the table), it could be a possible solution to use the table without the table legs included in the standard delivery but with individually constructed ones or a VESA-normed system. This is however not object to the fun.tast.tisch. project but should be an individual decision made by the rehabilitation institutions using it.

SUBSEQUENT WORK

There are subsequent endeavors along two dimensions. First, the fun.tast.tisch. project further aims at optimizing the system according to the needs of the two target groups. Thus, there will be another long term study that will include not only usability evaluation but also assessment of the training's effectiveness within the frame of a Randomized Controlled Trial in 2014. Additionally, there will be a single-patient long term study over a time frame of several months. Both of these studies will focus on the modules that have not been evaluated exhaustively before. Furthermore, there will be repeated small-scale user tests accompanying the further development of the system and its individual modules. A usability evaluation with a high number of non-target-group users will be conducted in addition to the target-group-centered studies in order to become aware of potential more general usability issues not related to the application domain. This evaluation will be conducted for seven fun.tast.tisch. modules. The Tangram module will not be included in the study any more as it has been evaluated more exhaustively already, the shopping module will be included in the improved version (see the previous section for improvements that have been made based on the results of the study described in this paper).

Second, the system itself will be under further development until late summer 2014. Additional modules are developed at the moment that primarily focus on motor skills. In one module, for example, a virtual taxi has to be controlled with a tagged object on the displayed roads to pick up passengers. Another module will be implemented to train more complex abilities as a combination of memory, attention, visual-spatial skills and language, also using tangible objects.

ACKNOWLEDGMENTS

The project fun.tast.tisch. acknowledges the financial support within the COIN – Cooperation and Innovation program, managed by the Austrian Research Promotion Agency and funded by the Federal Ministry for Transport, Innovation and Technology and by the Federal Ministry of Economy, Family and Youth. Project partners are LIFEtool - computer aided communication, ARTGROUP Advertising, University of Applied Sciences for Health Professions Upper Austria, University of Applied Sciences Upper Austria, Irene Schacherl-Hofer, softaware gmbh and TRANSPARENT DESIGN.

REFERENCES

1. Anderson, F., Annett, M., and Bischof, W. Tabletops in motion: the kinetics and kinematics of interactive surface physical therapy. In *CHI12 Extended Abstracts on Human Factors in Computing Systems* (2012), 2351–2356.
2. Annett, M., Anderson, F., and Bischof, W. F. Hands, tables, and groups make rehabilitation awesome! In *Proceedings of the 15th Annual CyberTherapy & CyberPsychology Conference* (2010), 3–8.
3. Annett, M., Anderson, F., and Bischof, W. F. User perspectives on tabletop therapy. In *Proc. of the 9th Intl. Conference on Disability, Virtual Reality & Associated Technologies* (Laval, France, 2012).
4. Annett, M., Anderson, F., Goertzen, D., Halton, J., Ranson, Q., Bischof, W. F., and Boulanger, P. Using a multi-touch tabletop for upper extremity motor rehabilitation. In *Proceedings of the 21st Annual Conference of the Australian Computer-Human Interaction Special Interest Group* (2009), 261–264.
5. Arbeitsgemeinschaft der Wissenschaftlichen Medizinischen Fachgesellschaften. Leitlinien für Diagnostik und Therapie in der Neurologie. Rehabilitation bei Störungen der Raumkognition, 2008.
6. Augstein, M., Neumayr, T., Ruckser-Scherb, R., Karlhuber, I., and Altmann, J. The fun.tast.tisch. project – a novel approach to neuro-rehabilitation using an interactive multiuser multitouch tabletop. In *Proceedings of the 2013 ACM International Conference on Interactive Tabletops and Surfaces* (St. Andrews, United Kingdom, 2013), 81–90.
7. Augstein, M., Neumayr, T., Schacherl-Hofer, I., and Öhlinger, S. Iterative user-centered design for interactive tabletop interfaces in neuro-rehabilitation. In *Mensch & Computer 2013: Interaktive Vielfalt, Interdisziplinäre Fachtagung* (Bremen, Germany, 2013), 309–312.

8. Broeren, J., Bellner, A.-L., Fogelberg, M., Göransson, O., Goude, D., Johansson, B., Larsson, P., Pettersson, K., and Rydmark, M. Exploration of computer games in rehabilitation for brain damage. In *Proceedings of the 7th International Conference on Disability, Virtual Reality and Associated Technologies* (2008), 75–80.
9. Bublak, P., and Kerkhoff, G. Praktische Erfahrungen mit Tangram in der Behandlung visuell-räumlicher und räumlich-konstruktiver Störungen bei Patienten mit Hirnschädigung. *Praxis Ergotherapie 8* (1995), 340–358.
10. Cicerone, K. D., Langenbahn, D. M., Braden, C., Malec, J. F., Kalmar, K., Fraas, M., Felicetti, T., Laatsch, L., Harley, J. P., Bergquist, T., Azulay, J., Cantor, J., and Ashman, T. Evidence-based cognitive rehabilitation: Updated review of the literature from 2003 through 2008. *Archives of Physical Medicine and Rehabilitation 92*, 4 (2011), 519–530.
11. Colman, J. E. Multi-player online video games for cognitive rehabilitation. In *CHI13 Extended Abstracts on Human Factors in Computing Systems* (2013), 1917–1920.
12. Cruz, V. T., Pais, J., Bento, V., Mateus, C., Colunas, M., Alves, I., Cautinho, P., and Rocha, N. P. A rehabilitation tool designed for intensive web-based cognitive training: Description and usability study. *Journal of Medical Internet Research 2*, 2 (2013).
13. de la Guiá, E., Lozana, M. D., and Penichet, V. M. Tangible user interfaces applied to cognitive therapies. In *Proceedings of IUI 2014 Workshop: Interacting with Smart Objects* (Haifa, Israel, 2014).
14. Der Vorstand der GNP, Der wissenschaftliche Beirat der GNP, Gauggel, S., and Sturm, W. Leitlinien der Gesellschaft für Neuropsychologie (GNP) für neuropsychologische Diagnostik und Therapie. *Zeitschrift für Neuropsychologie 16*, 4 (2005), 175–199.
15. Fernández, E., Bringas, M. L., Salazar, S., Rodríguez, D., García, M. E., and Torres, M. Clinical impact of rehacom software for cognitive rehabilitation of patients with acquired brain injury. *MEDICC Review: International Journal of Cuban Health & Medicine 14*, 4 (2012).
16. Habermann, C. Neuropsychologische Verfahren. In *Ergotherapie – Vom Behandeln zum Handeln*, C. Scheepers and U. Steding-Albrecht, Eds. Georg Thieme Verlag, 2007, 389–408.
17. Hartje, W., and Poeck, K. *Klinische Neuropsychologie*. Thieme, 2006.
18. Karnath, H.-O., Hartje, W., and Ziegler, W. *Kognitive Neurologie*. Thieme, 2006.
19. Kleim, J. A., and Jones, T. A. Principles of experience-dependent neural plasticity: Implications for rehabilitation after brain damage. *Journal of Speech, Language and Hearing Research 51* (2008), 225–239.
20. Kober, S. E., Wood, G., Hofer, D., Kreuzig, W., Liefer, M., and Neuper, C. Virtual reality in neurologic rehabilitation of spatial disorientation. *Journal of NeuroEngineering and Rehabilitation 10*, 17 (2013).
21. Martínez-Moreno, J., Sánchez-González, P., García, A., González, S., Cáceres, C., Sánchez-Carrión, R., Roig, T., Tormos, J., and Gómez, E. A graphical tool for designing interactive video cognitive rehabilitation therapies. In *Proceedings of the 13th Mediterranean Conference on Medical and Biological Engineering and Computing* (2014), 1803–1806.
22. Microsoft. Microsoft PixelSense, 2014. http://www.microsoft.com/en-us/pixelsense/whatissurface.aspx, last access: April 13th, 2014.
23. Niedeggen, M., and Jörgens, S. *Visuelle Wahrnehmungsstörungen*. Hogrefe, 2005.
24. Pantel, M., Coshall, C., Rudd, A. G., and Wolfe, C. D. Natural history of cognitive impairment after stroke and factors associated with its recovery. *Clinical Rehabilitation 17*, 2 (2003), 158–166.
25. Prosiegel, M., and Böttger, S. *Neuropsychologische Störungen und ihre Rehabilitation: Hirnläsionen, Syndrome, Diagnostik, Therapie*. Pflaum, 2007.
26. Rego, P. A., Moreira, P. M., and Reis, L. P. Architecture for serious games in health rehabilitation. In *New Perspectives in Information Systems and Technologies, Volume 2*, A. Rocha, A. M. Correia, F. B. Tan, and K. A. Stroetmann, Eds. Springer, 2014.
27. Röhrig, S., Kulke, H., Reulbach, U., Peetz, H., and Schupp, W. Effektivität eines neuropsychologischen Trainings von Aufmerksamkeitsfunktionen im teletherapeutischen Setting. *Neurologie & Rehabilitation 10*, 5 (2004), 239–246.
28. Schacherl, R. Microsoft Surface in der Therapie von Kindern mit Lernschwächen: Anwendungszenarien und deren Beurteilung. Master's thesis, University of Applied Sciences Upper Austria, Hagenberg, Austria, 2010.
29. Sharlin, E., Itoh, Y., Watson, B., Kitamura, Y., Sutphen, S., and Liu, L. Cognitive cubes: a tangible user interface for cognitive assessment. In *Proceedings of the SIGCHI Conference on Human Factors in Computing Systems (CHI02)* (Minneapolis, Minnesota, USA, 2002), 347–354.
30. Sharp, H., Rogers, Y., and Preece, J. *Interaction Design: Beyond Human-Computer Interaction*, 2nd ed. John Wiley & Sons, January 2007.
31. Tam, S.-F., and Man, W.-K. Evaluating computer-assisted memory retraining programmes for people with post-head injury amnesia. *Brain Injury 18*, 5 (2004), 461–470.
32. Westerberg, H., Jacobaeus, H., Hirvikiski, T., Clevberger, P., Östensson, M.-L., Bartfai, A., and Klingberg, T. Computerized working memory training after stroke – a pilot study. *Brain Injury 21*, 1 (2007), 21–29.

HyPR Device: Mobile Support for Hybrid Patient Records

Steven Houben, Mads Frost, Jakob E. Bardram
The Pervasive Interaction Technology Laboratory
IT University of Copenhagen, Rued Langgaardsvej 7, DK-2300 Copenhagen, DK
{shou, madsf, bardram}@itu.dk

ABSTRACT
The patient record is one of the central artifacts in medical work that is used to organize, communicate and coordinate important information related to patient care. In many hospitals a double record consisting of an electronic and paper part is maintained. This practice introduces a number of configuration problems related to finding, using and aligning the paper and electronic patient record. In this paper, we describe the exploration into the Hybrid Patient Record (HyPR) concept. Based on design requirements derived from a field study, followed by a design study using a technology probe, we introduce the *HyPR Device*, a device that merges the paper and electronic patient record into one system. We provide results from a clinical simulation with eight clinicians and discuss the functional, design and infrastructural requirements of such hybrid patient records. Our study suggests that the HyPR device decreases configuration work, supports mobility in clinical work and increases awareness on patient data.

Author Keywords
Hybrid Patient Record; Electronic Health Record; HyPR; EHR; Nomadic Work; Hospitals

ACM Classification Keywords
H.5.2 [**Information Interfaces and Presentation**]: User Interfaces; J.3 [**Computer Applications**]: Life and Medical Science.

INTRODUCTION
The patient record is one of the most important artifacts in medical work in hospitals as it is used as a central legal document to organize patient data, communicate relevant information with other clinicians and departments, and coordinate complex patient treatment procedures. In recent years, the Electronic Health Record (EHR) has been introduced in an effort to provide a higher level of quality in healthcare through a more efficient, safer and unified workflow. EHRs have a number of important advantages over traditional paper records, including a higher degree of security, simpler workflows, standardized documentation and more accurate and widely available access to patient data [26].

ITS 2014, November 16–19, 2014, Dresden, Germany.

ACM 978-1-4503-2587-5/14/11 ...$15.00.
http://dx.doi.org/10.1145/2669485.2669502

Figure 1. A Hybrid Patient Record (HyPR) device augments the paper patient record with color configuration and location tracking, while allowing clinicians to pair a tablet which shows the digital information associated with the paper record.

However, by attempting to replace paper records with an electronic counterpart, the affordances (such as handleability, manipulability and portability [15]) of paper-based interaction are removed. In many hospitals, the paper record is therefore still actively used as a central artifact for day to day work, despite the widespread deployment of EHR systems [25, 33]. These paper records are also frequently used for the storage of more informal documentation such as e.g., nursing notes or other working records, which again adds to their importance. Prior studies have even shown that paper helped some clinicians to be more efficient in their work [21]. Consequently, a typical setup in many hospitals is that the EHR system does not replace the paper-based record, but instead a *double record* consisting of both an electronic and paper part is maintained.

This double medical record introduces a number of configuration problems related to finding, using, and managing both the paper and electronic representation of the patient record. First, the usage of both electronic and paper records causes synchronization problems between both representations [27], forcing clinicians to deal with the paper and digital information simultaneous. Since digital information is often only available through desktop computers, it requires clinicians to sit at a desk when interacting with patient data. Second, since many hospitals require the use of a unique paper record, it is often transferred between different departments and wards as patients and clinicians move throughout the hospital. This causes paper records to be physically misplaced in the ward or even lost between departments resulting in clinical staff tracking down the record.

To mitigate these configuration problems, we introduce the Hybrid Patient Record (HyPR) device as shown in Figure 1.

The paper-based medical record can be augmented with the HyPR device, which supports notifications (color and sound), location tracking, and provides an easy way to link to the electronic patient record. This paper reports on the user-centered design and implementation of the HyPR device and presents four contributions: (i) we propose three design principles for hybrid patient records that are derived from a field study; (ii) we report on a design study, in which ten clinicians participated in a design walkthrough of a technology probe; (iii) we describe the design and technical implementation of a HyPR device and supporting infrastructure; and (iv) we analyze the preliminary results of a clinical simulation of the HyPR device.

RELATED WORK

A large body of research has explored the connection or linking of paper to digital data. One of the earliest approaches is DigitalDesk [29], an interactive desk that adds electronic features to physical paper and physical attributes to digital information using a top mounted camera and projector. Inspired by this work, the Paperlink [2] system attempted to scale this approach down by using a portable video pen. Based on this idea of a digitized pen (and commercial versions such as Anoto), other approaches such as the *Paper Augmented Digital Documents* (PADDs) [7], Paperproof [28] and PapierCraft [13] provide support for digital annotation of paper documents using pen gestures.

To increase support for mobility, several approaches proposed to use PDAs or phones as mediator between paper and digital information. Circa [9] proposes the "paper PDA" concept in which they use the *StickerLink* approach to link paper and digital information. A-book [16] overlays physical notes with a PDA and Pacer [14] uses a phone to link paper documents to digital versions based on visual features. Prism [24], S-Notebook [19], and ButterflyNet [31] further explored the design and impact of hybrid approaches in which paper notes and digital counterparts were linked together. Finally, a number of approaches explored the creation of broad hybrid workspaces, that included support for paper documents. Magictouch [18] is an early approach that uses RFID technology to detect the location of physical documents in a defined space. The Designers' Outpost [11] recognizes paper documents using a rear camera. IdeaVis [6] provides a hybrid brainstorm space by augmenting paper documents with interactive zones. Finally, Penbook [30] is a hybrid approach providing a touch screen together with a built-in projector integrated with a wireless pen to support handwriting for prescriptions or patient registration in hospitals.

A number of approaches have explored different ways to augment or enhance the medical record. Rodriguez et al. [20] demonstrated a location-aware information system for medical work, which estimates the clinicians' location to find available patient data and display it on a mobile device. Similarly, the MobileWard system [23] provides a context-aware mobile patient record system for hospital wards aimed at supporting autonomous adoption to the changing tasks or location of the nurses. A more radical approach to context-aware computing in hospitals is presented in the Activity-Based Computing project [3], which proposes a new paradigm for context-aware information access and collaboration in patient wards, using *activity* as a central construct. The augmented paper chart [32] augments a single paper chart with an Anoto interface, thus supporting seamless integration of traditional paper-based notes and digital storage. However, despite the fact that several studies point to the importance of the physical paper record, it has received remarkable little attention in the development of these new pervasive interactive patient record and information systems.

In general, prior work has primarily focused on ad hoc tracking and local linking of single paper documents to their electronic representation. But as pointed out by many studies of hospital work, medical workflow is highly nomadic and collaborative [3, 25]. The nomadic nature of clinical work puts forward a set of fundamental challenges in terms of locating and tracking artifacts, while the collaborative nature implies that support for exchanging and sharing artifacts, material, resources, and devices should be part of the system design. Compared to prior work, the core contribution of this paper is the physical/digital integration of the entire medical record in the nomadic and collaborative work setting of a hospital, thus complementing per-document approaches. The novelty of the HyPR device is thus its unique attempt to connect and align *the entire medical record* using a mediating sensor platform.

FIELD STUDY

To understand in depth how paper and electronic patient records are used, we conducted a field study. Over a period of two months, we studied five different medical departments, covering two patient bed wards, two surgical departments, and the emergency department. We performed task-centric, artifact-centric, and place-centric observations, contextual inquiries through shadowing of nurses, and post-hoc interviews.

The medical record

The hospital in this study uses one unique paper-based medical record for each admitted patient. It is a legal requirement that this patient record is present at the ward or department that is treating the patient. The paper record is made of a plastic binder with explicit color-coded sections for patient data, continuation (treatment history), nursing notes, various schemes and forms, observations, test results (e.g., blood tests and radiology examinations), and correspondence with other medical professionals. On the front, the binder has a label with the patient's name and ID written both in text as well as encoded in a bar code. On average the patient record is between 2 and 3 cm thick.

In parallel to the paper record, the hospital uses a number of specialized health information systems, such as radiology, medication, patient administration, and blood bank systems. Access to these systems have been collated in a portal, which is referred to as the electronic medical record. The paper and electronic medical records are used simultaneously in patient treatment and are equally important for medical work. Most information is duplicated in both records, whereas other information only exists in one or the other. This creates significant synchronization problems between the two versions of the records, which again leads to extraordinary work in manual updating, verification, and cross-referencing. For example, a lot of work is put into printing from the electronic medical record and storing print-outs in the paper records. This leads to significant problems of updating and replacing the printed documents in the paper record, when information changes in one of the electronic systems.

The different health information systems are primarily used to request or create new medical information, such as ordering blood tests at the hospital lab. The physical medical record, on the other hand, is primarily used to archive patient information. Because lab results e.g., need to be put into the paper-based record, the lab system is configured in such a way that when a lab result is ready, it is sent directly to the requesting ward's printer. In this way, the test results are physically presented and the printer becomes a coordinative artifact that signals when test results are ready. At a patient ward, there are typically up to 25 records of active patients. But since records from dismissed patients are stored at the ward, hundreds of archived records are at the department. Finding the right paper record is challenging as there is no visual differentiation between records; they are all stacked upon each other and scattered all over the ward in the nursing station, the secretary offices, and in the archiving room.

Patient Record in Nomadic Work

Medical work in hospitals is inherently nomadic [4], which implies that clinicians and the tools they use (including the patient record) move around inside wards, departments, and the entire hospital. The paper records are mostly used in offices, nursing stations, doctors' offices, and at the bedside of the patient. As mentioned earlier, it is a legal requirement that the record is present during medical treatment, which implies that the record always 'travels with the patient'. For example, when patients are send to other wards (e.g., for x-ray or surgery), the record is mounted in a special container on the side of the patient bed and travels with the patient to the receiving department. Moving the record around inside the hospital again causes it to get lost or misplaced both inside the ward and in other departments.

HYBRID PATIENT RECORD CONCEPT

Prior research on medical work (e.g., [5, 17]) and our field study have identified a range of challenges associated with handling medical records. At its core, these challenges are tied to clinicians' need to handle, align and coordinate physical and digital information simultaneously. One way of approaching this challenge is to digitize all information in medical work – a strategy that is being pursued in the creation of integrated electronic medical records (EMR) and hospital information systems (HIS). However, several studies (including [17, 25, 33]) show that despite the 'successfulness' of the deployment of EMRs, paper documentation, artifacts and records are still widely used in documentation as transitional artifact [5] or as redundant information source in medical work. As such, the findings from the medical domain back up findings from the office environment about the 'myth of the paperless office' [22]. Therefore, rather than designing for the 'paperless hospital', there is a need to design for the parallel management of both paper and electronic medical records, thereby creating a *hybrid* medical record. Inspired by our field study and prior work, we propose the following three principles for the design of patient records.

D1 Dual Use – Because the paper and electronic version of the record are almost always used simultaneously, setting up and removing the connection between the paper record and a device representing the electronic record should be instantly and easy. Both representations should be usable separately, without any changes to their original purpose or use. Since the paper record is used to identify the patient case, the hybrid record should use this patient context to load and visualize the correct data. To facilitate the usage of the double record, it should be integrated with existing practices, devices and technology.

D2 Recognizability – To support easy identification and recognition of a patient record (e.g., in a cluttered office space) the patient record should be able to relay and display various kinds of status and awareness information. Temporal visual and auditory cues (similar to the analogue affordance of e.g., sticky notes) should be supported to provide clinicians with an easy and fast configuration mechanism for self-reflection or coordination with other clinicians.

D3 Mobility – The patient record should support the nomadic workflow in hospitals, meaning that both the electronic and paper representation of patient data should be available in a portable and traceable form factor. To support clinicians in finding and managing the location of the record, the supporting infrastructure should support location tracking and remote access to the state of the paper record. Additionally, the location should be used to ease information retrieval.

To address and support dual use, recognizability and mobility in patient records, we propose the concept of a *Hybrid Patient Record* (HyPR). Conceptually, a HyPR setup consists of three parts: (i) the traditional paper patient record as used in hospitals today, (ii) the electronic record accessed from a tablet or phone, and (iii) a mediating platform that augments the paper record with a number of configurable properties and connects the paper record to the digital record on the tablet. The central purpose of this concept is to integrate the electronic patient record into the existing physical and mobile workflow of clinicians. By explicitly attaching digital information and notification systems to the existing paper record, the HyPR presents clinicians with a patient record that encapsulates existing practices but augments it with digital capabilities. In summary, the HyPR device allows for ad hoc integration of paper-based and digital information, authorized and fast access to digital information, customization of the record using the sensing platform, and traceability by location tracking.

DESIGN STUDY

To explore the feasibility of the HyPR device concept and to get a better understanding of the design and clinical implications of hybrid devices, we conducted a design study involving a group of clinicians from two different hospitals. The goal of this study was to get feedback on the design of a technology probe and use this as input for the design and implementation of the device. The study had two parts. First we introduced the concept of hybrid patient records to the clinicians in order to open up a discussion and brainstorm on the design dimensions and implications of the HyPR devices. Second, based on the use of a concrete prototype, we asked for detailed input on the perceived usefulness of the HyPR device in clinical work and the usefulness of its different features.

Technology Probe

Because it is often hard for clinicians to envision how they could benefit from technology, we performed a design walk-through on a fully working prototype. The technology probe was designed as an augmented hard-cover box with room for both the digital and physical paper version (Figure 2). To bridge the size mismatch between modern tablets and the paper record, the enclosure provides a dock for the tablet (Figure 2 B) and a slot for the paper record (Figure 2 C). The slot on the side allows for easy access and pushes the record together so it does not fall out while moving. The tablet dock is specifically designed so clinicians can securely mount their device, while still being able to use it. When interacting with both the paper and digital patient data, clinicians can simply remove the paper record from the slot and browse the paper and tablet data at the same time. The device is activated by inserting a patient record in the slot and mounting a tablet to the dock (Figure 2 A). The color and sound of the device can be controlled by using the application on the tablet. The enclosure thus creates a temporal connection between the paper record and tablet.

Study Setup

In total 10 clinicians (all female, mean age = 42, σ = 5,37) from two different wards participated in two separate design sessions. The first session included three clinicians from a surgical ward that the original field study discussed earlier, while the second session included 7 clinicians from the psychiatric ward of a different hospital that was not part of the prior field study. Participants included two doctors, a psychologist, a clinical specialist, a medical secretary and five nurses. All participants were highly experienced in day to day medical work in patient wards and rated themselves as average computer users ($\tilde{x}$= 3; *iqr*= 0). The design sessions were done *in situ* at the hospital ward of the participants.

Method

The design study consisted of three phases. First, participants were introduced to the concept of a hybrid patient record through a demonstration of the functionality of the technology probe. The introduction used a number of *scenarios* that were designed based on the field study discussed earlier and validated by the head nurse from the ward. After the introduction, a semi-structured interview and discussion session was initiated to allow the clinicians to provide feedback on the scenarios and the design of the technology probe. The data from the sessions were collected using audio and video recordings, note taking and pictures. After the semi-structured interviews, participants completed a 5-point Likert scale questionnaire, which was used to discuss the design and functionality of the technology probe.

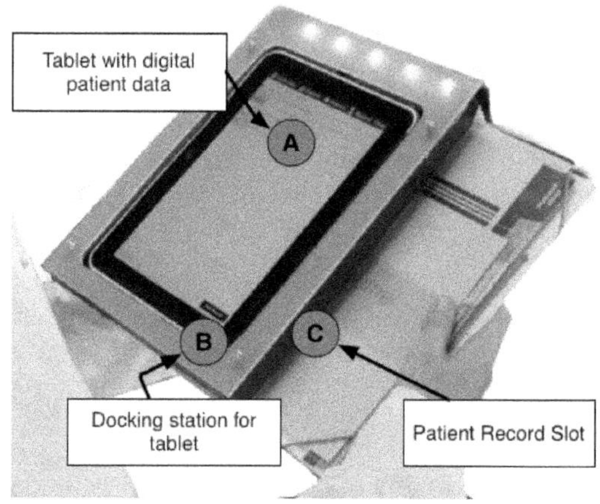

Figure 2. A fully working industrial prototype used as technology probe.

Results

In general, clinicians found that the HyPR device would be useful in clinical work. Although hospitals are trying to implement the vision of a 'paperless workflow', many clinicians realize that there are limitations to this vision, since much paper-based information does not exist in the digital world. This lack of one-to-one documentation between paper and digital information also greatly limits options to digitally augment individual records with e.g., Anoto technology. The basic functionality of being able to pair a paper-based and electronic record was considered as very useful. The contextualization of the visualized patient data, based on the paper record that was paired with the probe, was deemed as very important:

> – *"One of the key things of this device is the easiness of accessing patient data by getting rid of fixed computers and looking up patient data by simply placing the device on top of the paper record. That would save us a lot of time, and make the workflow a lot easier."* – *P3*

This instant and ad hoc pairing ability was especially valued for emergency cases in which patients are admitted with an acute problem:

> – *"Often when I have to treat acute patients – which I don't know in advance – this device would make it a lot easier to pair the paper record and the data in the electronic record. And I can do it anywhere and not only in front of my PC."* – *P8*

The ability to add color to the medical record was perceived as very useful. Clinicians mentioned that color is often used as a general coordination mechanism at the ward. For example, colored post-it notes are often used to indicate status information on patients. Tracking the device, thus locating the patient record was also considered very valuable. Clinicians responded that this would save them a lot of time and energy in finding the paper record, which can be stored anywhere, even *"under a pillow or in a drawer" (P1)*. As explained by one clinician:

> – *"Not only tracking the record in the system is useful, but also providing visible and audible feedback which makes the record easier to find when you know what*

room it is in – just like the key finder gadgets where you can whistle and it then makes a sound". – P2

Although the working area and input/output bandwidth is significantly lower than desktop computers, all clinicians preferred to use a tablet over a PC for all day to day medical work. In general, the inclusion of a portable tablet into the system setup was considered an improvement for clinical workflow.

However, there was a general consensus that the size of the system – in this case the docking station – should be designed to fit into the pocket of a standard white coat. Several clinicians argued that the mediating device (i.e the docking station for the tablet) should be much more closely integrated with the physical folder of the paper record, arguing that the current HyPR device should somehow be merged into the paper record:

– *"The idea of having a device that communicates with the paper journal, and using the journal to retrieve information on the device is super. However, I think the device as a separate object makes it laborious, and does not really fit the current work practice. If the clinician had his own tablet, which could interact with the patient record by simply placing it on top, would make it a lot more useful". – P5*

Finally, clinicians in general argued that since the patient record follows the patient throughout the hospital, the device should be usable in different types of wards and clinical conditions, such as in operating rooms or the x-ray department.

Summary

Clinicians first of all argued that most of the functionality provided by the mediating enclosure of the technology probe, such as *location tracking* and *visual cues*, would also be useful once the patient record is archived and thus no longer active at the ward. These requirements extend the concept of the HyPR device from an ad hoc temporal mediator for active patient cases to a permanent augmentation and deep physical integration with the paper record. Second, clinicians stressed the importance of the HyPR device's ability to cope with the medical environment. The device should e.g., be strong enough to survive being dropped; interaction with the device should be possible while wearing latex gloves; and clinicians should be able to sterilize the device. Furthermore, the device should be constructed from food-safe plastic. Finally, clinicians generally argued that having the tablet physically docked to the record would not support their work practices very well. The general consensus was that the HyPR device should be usable with different size tablets and even phones, and that pairing the tablet to the device should be faster.

HYBRID PATIENT RECORD DEVICE

Based on the design principles and the results from the design study, we constructed the *Hybrid Patient Record* (HyPR) device as shown in Figure 1, 3, and 4. The HyPR device and its underlying infrastructure (Figure 7) are designed to integrate paper-based and digital patient information into the nomadic workflow of clinicians. The HyPR device supports *dual use* by allowing for ad hoc pairing between the paper and digital information. And, it provides clinicians with a mechanism to dynamically change some of the physical properties (color and sound) associated with the record. Finally, the device is equipped with a location tracker to allow clinicians to easily find the paper record. The HyPR device works within a larger infrastructure that supports location tracking, device management, and access to the electronic medical systems.

Figure 3. Two clinicians interacting with a number of HyPR devices scattered in the patient ward.

Design

The HyPR (Figure 3) consists of three distinct parts: (i) a traditional paper record, (ii) a tablet used to access the electronic record and (iii) a HyPR device. The HyPR device is a rectangular plastic plate with the same width and height as the paper record. Compared to the technology probe, it does not have any layers as all the electronics are integrated in the plate. The paper record is attached to the plastic plate using metal clips to create a permanent connection to the device. In contrast to the technology probe in which an active patient record is loaded into the device by inserting it into the slot, this version of the HyPR device is a permanent augmentation of the record. This means that the HyPR device becomes an inherent and inseparable part of the paper record.

Functionality

The HyPR device provides three features: (i) *pairing* of the tablet and the paper record using proximity sensing, (ii) *light and sound* system that can be used to augment the record or notify other clinicians, and (iii) an integrated *location tracking* unit that allows clinicians to locate the record.

Clinicians can interact with the HyPR by placing a tablet on top of the paper record and HyPR device. By doing so, they pair the tablet to the record, causing the underlying infrastructure to fetch the digital patient information and push this to the active view of the tablet. Any changes made to the elec-

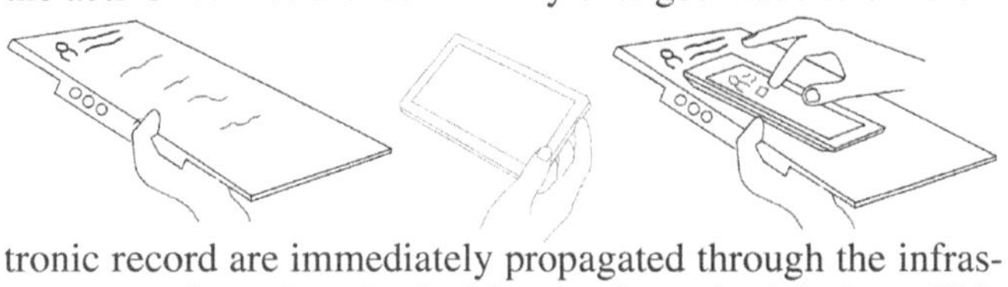

tronic record are immediately propagated through the infrastructure and synchronized with any other paired devices. This process essentially eliminates extra configuration work during e.g., ward rounds or during emergency situations in which manually fetching information would be too time consuming or inappropriate. The device is thus used as a proxy that provides clinicians access to the activity of the patient. Although the initial pairing process is done by proximity, both the tablet

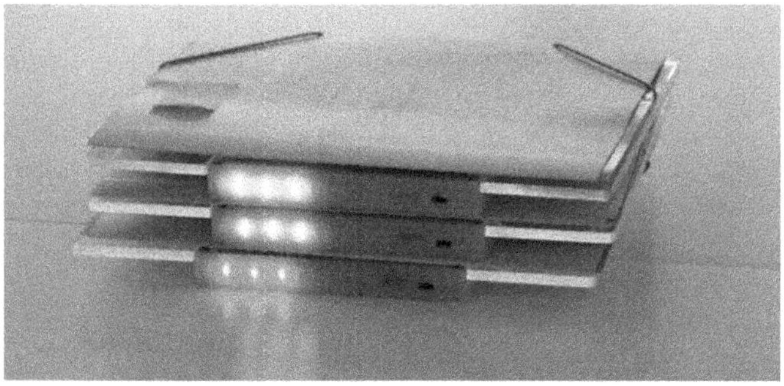

Figure 4. The color of the HyPR device can be configured to signal a wide range of things. For example, the colors can represent a specific nurse, patient status, or simply be used to highlight a patient record in an information dense environment.

and paper record can be used separately. When a user removes the tablet from the HyPR device, the data will remain coupled to the initial paper record until the user manually selects another patient, or pairs the tablet with another HyPR device. Furthermore, clinicians can also remotely connect to the record by selecting the patient case from the application. This allows multiple clinicians to work on the same patient case, while only having one physical journal. Only the paper record – not the tablet computer – is uniquely coupled to a HyPR device to ensure the infrastructure can correctly track and manage each record. (Supporting D1: Dual Use)

The HyPR device supports concurrent use and updates of both paper-based and digital information. For example, administration of medication in the medicine system can be done directly in the electronic medical record via the tablet computer. Similarly, ordering of lab tests can be done electronically by accessing the order-entry system. Simultaneously, paper-based information can be accessed from the paper-based record and ad hoc written notes can be added and stored temporarily in the physical folder. Moreover, electronic information – such as the lab results coming out of the printer – can be added in paper format to the folder. As such, the HyPR record supports blending paper-based and digital information in 'both directions'. (Supporting D1: Dual Use)

Once the device is paired, clinicians can change the physical properties of the HyPR record by changing its color scheme or identification sound. Figure 4 shows a number of different color configurations. These configurations can be used to relay status information. For example, a color can be associated with a specific nurse, thereby revealing who is the contact nurse for a specific patient. Or a color can represent a status change, by e.g., highlighting that there is a lab test result available for the patient. Moreover, sound and/or color can help locate records, which may be scattered all over the department. When the record is located in a cupboard or drawer, sound can be used to draw attention to the record. (Supporting D2: Recognizability)

The HyPR device supports nomadic medical work in several ways. First, in order to support location of medical records, the HyPR device is equipped with a location tag that broadcasts a unique value. This value is associated to a particular paper record, when the HyPR device registers the patient ID. Clinicians can look up the location of each patient record. Second, to minimize the burden of carrying both the augmented record and tablet, microsuction tape is attached to the front of the paper record to keep the tablet in place. Finally, the tracking capabilities of the HyPR device can be used to contextualize the patient's information. For example, if the HyPR device is taken to the patient's bed side (e.g., as part of a ward round), basic patient information and the latest entry in the record is shown, whereas the patient medicine treatment is shown if a nurse takes the HyPR record to the medicine room. (Supporting D3: Mobility)

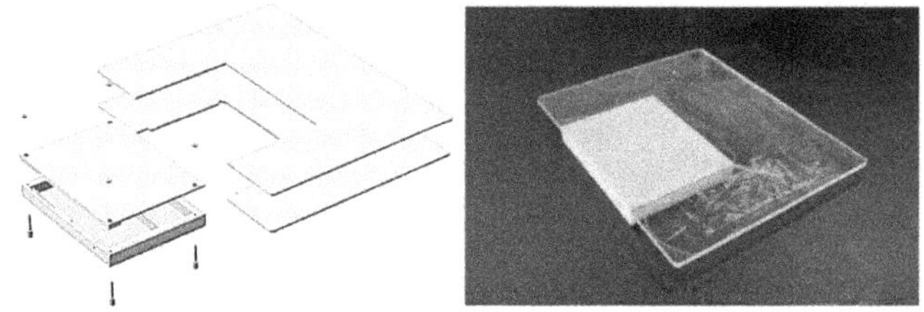

Figure 5. The physical parts of the HyPR device.

Technical Implementation

Figure 5 shows the design of the HyPR device. It consists of two different parts: (i) a rectangular plate of 2.5 mm food-safe transparent plastic, and (ii) an enclosure holding the electronics embedded into the side of the plate. Figure 6 shows the electronic architecture, which uses an Arduino ATmega168 chip 16 MHz crystal for basic processing; a RFID module with an antenna (125 kHz); a Texas Wifi CC 3000 module with antenna; an array of three high power RGB LEDs; a 2kHz range buzzer; an integrated rechargeable Volt battery pack with USB connector; a power switch; and a 35–45 kHz ultrasound tag with a dedicated 3V lithium battery.

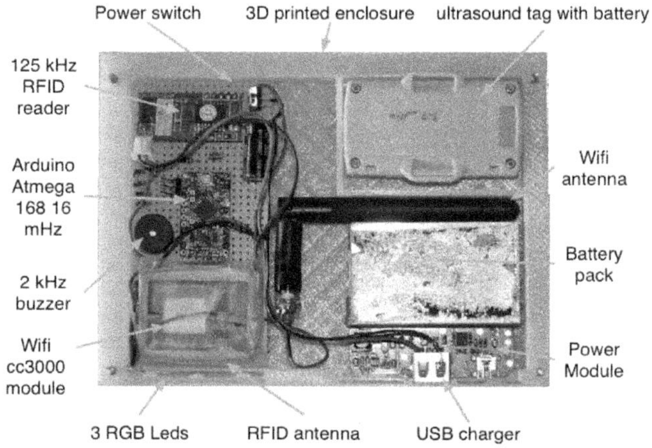

Figure 6. The electronics of the HyPR device.

To support two way communication between the tablet and the HyPR device, the firmware provides support for a custom protocol with a set of command messages. One set of messages allows the device to start a handshaking protocol when a tablet is paired and to send 'alive messages' that indicate that it is operating correctly. Other command messages allow the tablet to operate and configure the device's on-board buzzer and the RGB LED array based on e.g., user input or infrastructure changes. The RFID module continuously reads all nearby RFID tags and sends tag IDs to the Arduino board.

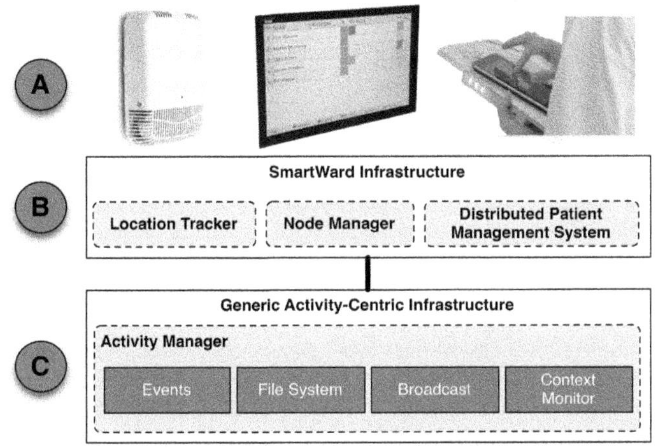

Figure 7. The *HyPR infrastructure* (B) is a distributed context-aware infrastructure designed to support multi-device location-aware collaborative workflows in patient wards. The infrastructure uses an ultrasound location tracker for location-aware services (A) and is built on top of a general purpose activity-centric infrastructure [10] (C).

When a new tag is detected, the device sends a message over Wifi to the infrastructure, which then pushes the data to the tablet. Similarly, any changes made on one of the paired tablets is send over Wifi to the HyPR device.

Infrastructure

Figure 7 shows the HyPR device infrastructure, which is an activity-aware patient management and information system designed to support multi-device location-aware collaborative workflows in patient wards. The infrastructure supports (i) large interactive screens for shared collaborative workspaces, (ii) tablet applications for mobile personalized tasks and detailed patient information, and (iii) desktop systems for integration with existing applications and services. The HyPR infrastructure is build on top of a generic distributed activity-centric infrastructure (detailed in [10]) that includes support for multi-device information management, context-awareness and ad hoc discovery and pairing of devices.

The infrastructure abstracts basic events, data, pairing, discovery and context services into a distributed *activity configuration*. These configurations connect all patient-related information resources, users and devices into one central reusable data model. This model is managed and distributed across all devices that are part of the same activity systems [10]. Devices such as tablets, pc computers, large displays are thus interconnected into one ad hoc distributed activity system, in which patient information is managed, synchronized and distributed as computational activity configurations. The hardware inside the HyPR device also connects to the infrastructure over Wifi and reports which tablet is detected. The infrastructure uses this information to push the right patient data to the paired tablet, or to update the properties of the HyPR device made through any of the connected devices.

Application

The HyPR application running on the tablet is a web-based stripped down electronic patient record that consists of a patient overview screen (Figure 8A) and a detailed patient record (Figure 8B). In the overview screen, all patients that are currently at the ward are listed with basic information including their name, medical procedure, assigned color and room number. Using this patient overview, clinicians can set to colored lights of a specific patient record to "blinking", thus asking for attention. Clinicians can also turn on the buzzing sound (which automatically stops after 15 seconds) of the record to quickly locate it when it is in a drawer or on a stack of other records.

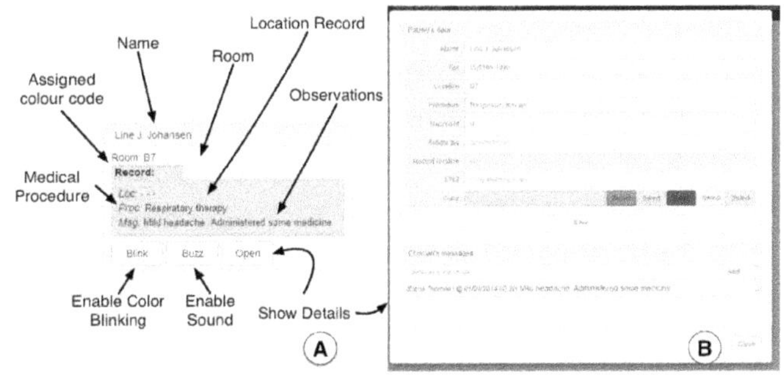

Figure 8. The details of the patient record.

The tablet is synchronized with the paper record through physical proximity. Placing the tablet on top of the paper record, automatically opens the detailed patient information of that patient to the tablet (Figure 8B). This view lists all detailed medical information and allows clinicians to add new medical data or messages. It can also be used to change the colored representation of the patient state. Changing this color in the details view updates the color on the HyPR device (Figure 4). When medical information is added remotely, through another tablet or computing device that is not physically paired to the paper record, the device's colored lights start blinking to signify an update. Once a clinician pairs the tablet, the new data is shown and the record stops blinking.

CLINICAL SIMULATION

To explore how clinicians would use the HyPR setup, we conducted a clinical simulation. Specifically, the study was set up to frame the use of the HyPR record within existing work practice as previously studied in the wards. In the medical domain, a clinical simulation is a frequently applied methodology used to train and educate clinicians in critical clinical scenarios, such as surgery, medicine prescription and administration, and emergency cases. It has proved very efficient and reliable for the initial phase of training and assessment of clinical staff [1]. Since the clinical simulation approach attempts to bring the dimension of clinical context into stronger focus, the method has lately been used also as a method for testing clinical systems with representative users doing representative tasks, in an ecological valid setting [12]. The goal of this simulation was to explore (i) the usefulness and usability of the HyPR device and (ii) the impact of HyPR devices on clinical work practices. Although a full description of the study is beyond the scope of this paper, we presents findings relevant to the system design of the HyPR device.

Study Setup

Over a period of 2 days, 8 clinicians (5 female + 3 male, mean age = 46, σ = 12,95) from three different wards (psychiatry, surgery, and emergency departments) participated in a clinical simulation. Participants included 5 doctors, 2 nurses and a psychologist. All clinicians were highly experienced in day to day medical work that involves managing and interacting with patient records, and rated themselves as experienced computer users ($\tilde{x}$= 4; *iqr*= 1). The clinical simulation was performed in a training–simulation ward that is identical to a full scale patient ward, and included both simulated patients (simulation dolls) as well as one human who was acting as a patient. The ward was organized and equipped as an oncology ward, but the scenarios were generic enough to be performed by clinicians with different clinical backgrounds. The study was conducted by two researchers, performing the roles of facilitator and observer.

Method

The study consisted of three phases. First, participants were introduced to the system and physical layout of the ward. After the introduction, participants were asked to complete three scenarios in pairs. The scenarios (that were based on observed situations from the field study) included (i) dual use, in which clinicians performed a ward round and calculated an early warning score (EWS) for four patients, (ii) recognizability and awareness, in which clinicians coordinated the arrival of a paper blood result, and (iii) mobility, in which clinicians searched for a lost record. Data from the scenario performances were captured by using video and audio recordings. Afterwards, participants completed a 5-point Likert scale questionnaire and an interview was conducted.

Results

Table 1 shows the results of the questionnaire on the usefulness of the final design and its specific features. The results of the questionnaire indicate that clinicians consider the final design of the HyPR device to be usable and useful in clinical work ($\tilde{x}$= 4,5; *iqr*= 1).

HyPR Usefulness (N=8)	*Min*	*Q1*	$\tilde{x}$	*Q3*	*Max*	*Iqr*
In general, the HyPR is useful	3	4	**4,5**	5	5	1
Pairing the PR and ER is useful	3	4	**4**	5	5	1
Color feature is useful	3	3,75	**4**	4,25	5	0,5
Tracking the PR is useful	4	4	**5**	5	5	1

Table 1. The results of the 5-point Likert scale questionnaire on the usefulness of the basic functions of a HyPR device. The table shows the minimum, maximum, median ($\tilde{x}$) and the inter quartile range (iqr) of the scores. PR:paper record; ER:electronic record.

Dual Use

The ability to simply place the tablet on top of the device to get instant access to digital data of a patient, was considered as very useful ($\tilde{x}$= 4; *iqr*= 1). During the ward round, almost all clinicians would immediately pair the device to the patient record, before actually checking the vital signs or talking to the patient. They thus preferred to configure and align both the electronic and paper record before commencing with assessing the patient. After this configuration, clinicians would often detach the tablet from the HyPR device. One clinician would typically hold the paper record to check the official early warning score (EWS) form, while the other clinician would check for messages on the tablet and add the EWS to the electronic record.

Although the feedback on the design of the HyPR device was more positive compared to the technology probe used during the design study, clinicians generally agreed that the device was still too heavy and too thick. In essence, they argued that for this device to be usable on a large scale, it has to be integrated in the paper record, thus being flat and flexible. There were also some issues with detecting the right HyPR device. When clinicians tried to pair the tablet with a HyPR device that was placed on a stack of other devices (e.g., Figure 4), the tablet would sometimes receive incorrect patient data. This opened discussion on security and privacy, as some clinicians mentioned that detailed access to patient data should be restricted to the assigned doctor and nurse. On the other hand, clinicians also saw the HyPR system as an opportunity to increase security. One suggestion was to actually physically lock the paper record to the HyPR enclosure until an authorized tablet is paired. This would ensure that only authorized browsing of the paper record would be possible.

Recognizability and Awareness

In general, most clinicians argued that using color was useful ($\tilde{x}$= 4; *iqr*=0,5) for coordination and communication between staff. During the scenarios, clinicians quickly adapted to using the color coding as part of the workflow. Although none of the clinicians felt that the color coding dictated a patient order for the ward round, most of them argued that having an extra layer of awareness on patient cases could improve coordination at the ward but also could help clinicians to reflect on their work. One doctor, for example, mentioned that the colors improved the structure of his round as they helped him prioritize patients. The blinking light feature when new critical messages were added to the electronic record received mixed responses. Some clinicians felt that using the colored lights on the record as a notification mechanism was very useful as they do not always carry a tablet when doing their work. Without the notification on the record, they felt that they might miss critical information. Other clinicians felt that the blinking colored lights were too distracting. Specially in cases where many records were in the same place, it could quickly escalate in a “Christmas tree”.

During the interviews, the clinicians suggested a number of use cases for the color coding. One theme of suggestions was based around coordination between clinicians. Examples such as triage, allocation of nurses and even to reflect the current state of the patient, were proposed as use cases for dynamic colors. A common argument was that one color did not provide enough granularity to communicate more complex information and communication streams. Most clinicians agreed that more colored light indicators could be added to support more applications. A second theme of suggestions was based around patient involvement. One example proposed by clinicians was to use the lights as a road map or guide for the patient, so they could keep track of the different steps in their procedure. However, some clinicians also argued that using these colored lights might worry or even frighten patients who might be unaware of the significance of the changing color. One clinician suggested that the device should include a ‘silent switch’, that would turn of the visual and auditory notifications.

Mobility

Tracking the patient record was considered as one of the most useful features of the system ($\tilde{x}$= 5; *iqr*=1). During the scenarios, most clinicians would follow a similar pattern in which they would first find the room of the patient and the location of the record. They would then proceed to the location of the record, and if the record was not immediately visible they would start the blinking light. If the record still could not be located, they would turn on sound. Most clinicians argued that this was an important feature as patient records get lost regularly. The color blinking feature was useful to find a record in stacks of other records, but clinicians would mostly use the sound to find the record inside a room. Although some of the records were inside the patient room, we observed that clinicians would still use the sound indicator, even if patients were sleeping in that room. Most clinicians agreed that finding the record was important enough to disturb a patient.

A main point of criticism on the current system was the sound of the buzzer. Some of the clinicians suggested that rather than using "another medical sounding sound", the HyPR device could use radically different sounds such as a singing bird, as this would sound less stressful or disturbing for patients. Clinicians also proposed to use the location tracking capabilities in a more integrated way. Rather than "simply" tracking the record, they suggested to set up more advanced functionality such as e.g., automatically check-in when the patient and record arrive at the ward.

DISCUSSION

Often, the term *paperless workspace* points to a vision of a completely digitized work environment in which paper is replaced by digital devices. However, an increasing body of evidence indicates that despite increased digitization, paper is still an important resource in accomplishing everyday work and collaboration. This is true for office environments [22] but also for medical work in hospitals [17, 25, 33]. The central focus of the HyPR device prototype is to explore the functional and clinical design of an augmented hybrid medical record bridging across both the physical and digital records. Our design study and preliminary evaluation show that clinicians generally agreed that such a hybrid record would significantly improve the existing workflow. As such, the HyPR device could be viewed as part of a solution to two long standing problems in nomadic clinical work [3]: configuration and mobility work.

The HyPR device provides clinicians with a tool to synchronize and merge the paper and contextual digital representation of patient data, which significantly reduces *configuration work*, i.e. the amount of work required to setup a working context for a specific patient. The augmented record becomes an entry point into the digital patient record. Many clinicians argued that automatically loading patient data on the tablet when placed on top of the HyPR device, would significantly reduce this configuration work. The location tracking features of the HyPR device provide clinicians with a spatial coordination tool designed to help reduce *mobility work*. Using the wall-based displays, clinicians can look up and track the physical location of the device throughout the ward and the hospital, and the interface of the tablet provides *location awareness* cues on the location of the patient record.

The HyPR device is designed to support the highly collaborative workflow in hospitals. It supports *user multiplicity* by allowing multiple tablets to be connected to the same HyPR device. This allows multiple clinicians to work simultaneously on the same patient case – some using the paper record and some using the digital counter-part. This feature mimics the way that paper-based records are often shared among clinicians in colocated collaboration (e.g., by the bed side or during a medical conference).

One of the central limitations of the current approach, however, is the deliberate absence of digital support for separate paper documents and forms. Although the current design does not exclude the integration of Anoto or similar pens to automatically digitize written notes and forms, this would require a substantial change of existing hospital work practices. The paper forms and electronic records simply do not align one to one, thus posing fundamental questions on how these tools can be integrated and how they would effect work practices. Furthermore, our study showed that support for paper documents should in particular also incorporate support for handling legacy documentation for both legal and practical reasons. The HyPR provides support to *align*, not to *integrate*, information from the paper and digital records into one system. As such, the HyPR concept allows for a fluent and gradual approach to digitizing the entire medical work.

The current HyPR design still places a large emphasis on the use of a physical paper record, which is augmented for easy connections to the digital workflow. The form factor of the HyPR device leverages the shape of the paper record. This implies that at the cost of the weight of the back plate and electronics, the HyPR provides affordances (such as *flexibility*, *markability*, *portability*, and *accessibility* [8]) that are very similar to those of the paper record by itself. This allows clinicians to manipulate and use the HyPR in the exact same way as the paper record, thus embracing a number of existing practices. As with many electronic devices, the battery life of the device often limits its full potential. The current design of the HyPR allows for up to 6 hours of continuous use but includes a standard USB connector for easy recharging. However, for real long term deployment, this would not be a workable solution. Although battery use can be greatly optimized, digitizing mobile patient records will require the careful design of charging strategies that are mobile and fit into the existing workflows of clinicians that use the record.

The notion of a Hybrid Patient Record opens up a number of interesting questions for future work. HyPR devices could be augmented to support complex multi-device interactions including interactive whiteboards or desktop computers. Additionally, the role and design of printers can be re-thought: a printer could e.g., only print patient results when the record is physically moved into the nurse's station. Finally, the physical design of the HyPR device could consider a smaller and more flexible form factor embedded into the patient record binder.

CONCLUSION

In this paper, we introduced the novel concept of a Hybrid Patient Record (HyPR). Based on a field and design study, we presented the design and implementation of a HyPR device that supports (i) dual use, by allowing the pairing of the paper and digital information, (ii) recognizability, by allowing for dynamic color and sound coding of the record, and (iii) mobility, by using a portable form factor and location tracking. We presented initial feedback from a clinical simulation indicating that the HyPR device decreases configuration work, supports mobility in clinical work, and increases awareness on patient data.

ACKNOWLEDGMENTS

This work was supported by the EU Marie Curie Network iCareNet under grant number 264738. Thanks to Mathias Schmidt, Thomas Snaidero, and Vaidas Sirtautas for helping with the implementation of the HyPR device. Thanks to Shahram Jalalinia for help on the technology probe and Sanne Jensen for helping conducting the medical simulation.

REFERENCES

1. K. Ahmed, M. Jawad, M. Abboudi, A. Gavazzi, A. Darzi, T. Athanasiou, J. Vale, M. S. Khan, and P. Dasgupta. Effectiveness of procedural simulation in urology: a systematic review. *The Journal of urology*, 186(1):26–34, 2011.
2. T. Arai, D. Aust, and S. E. Hudson. Paperlink: a technique for hyperlinking from real paper to electronic content. In *Proc. of CHI '97*, pages 327–334. ACM.
3. J. E. Bardram. Activity-based computing for medical work in hospitals. *ACM Transactions on Computer-Human Interaction (TOCHI)*, 16(2):10, 2009.
4. J. E. Bardram and C. Bossen. Mobility work: The spatial dimension of collaboration at a hospital. *Comput. Supported Coop. Work*, 14(2):131–160, Apr. 2005.
5. Y. Chen. Documenting transitional information in emr. In *Proc. of CHI '10*, pages 1787–1796. ACM.
6. F. Geyer, J. Budzinski, and H. Reiterer. Ideavis: a hybrid workspace and interactive visualization for paper-based collaborative sketching sessions. In *Proc. of NordiCHI '12*, pages 331–340. ACM.
7. F. Guimbretière. Paper augmented digital documents. In *Proc. of UIST '03*, pages 51–60. ACM.
8. R. H. Harper, K. P. O'Hara, A. J. Sellen, and D. J. Duthie. Toward the paperless hospital? *British Journal of Anaesthesia*, 78(6):762–767, 1997.
9. J. M. Heiner, S. E. Hudson, and K. Tanaka. Linking and messaging from real paper in the paper pda. In *Proc. of UIST '99*, pages 179–186. ACM.
10. S. Houben, S. Nielsen, M. Esbensen, and J. Bardram. Noosphere: An activity-centric infrastructure for distributed interaction. In *Proc. of MUM '13*, pages 100–110. ACM, 2013.
11. S. R. Klemmer, M. W. Newman, R. Farrell, M. Bilezikjian, and J. A. Landay. The designers' outpost: a tangible interface for collaborative web site. In *Proc. of UIST '01*, pages 1–10. ACM.
12. A. Kushniruk, C. Nohr, S. Jensen, and E. Borycki. From usability testing to clinical simulations: Bringing context into the design and evaluation of usable and safe health information technologies. *Yearb Med Inform*, 78:85, 2013.
13. C. Liao, F. Guimbretière, and K. Hinckley. Papiercraft: a command system for interactive paper. In *Proc. of UIST '05*, pages 241–244. ACM.
14. C. Liao, Q. Liu, B. Liew, and L. Wilcox. Pacer: fine-grained interactive paper via camera-touch hybrid gestures on a cell phone. In *Proc. of CHI '01*, pages 2441–2450. ACM.
15. P. Luff and C. Heath. Mobility in collaboration. In *Proc. of CSCW '98*, pages 305–314. ACM.
16. W. E. Mackay, G. Pothier, C. Letondal, K. Bøegh, and H. E. Sørensen. The missing link: augmenting biology laboratory notebooks. In *Proc. of UIST '02*, pages 41–50. ACM.
17. S. Y. Park and Y. Chen. Adaptation as design: Learning from an emr deployment study. In *Proc. of CHI '12*, pages 2097–2106. ACM.
18. T. Pederson. Magic touch: A simple object location tracking system enabling the development of physical-virtual artefacts in office environments. *Personal and Ubiquitous Computing*, 5(1):54–57, 2001.
19. T. Pietrzak, S. Malacria, and É. Lecolinet. S-notebook: augmenting mobile devices with interactive paper for data management. In *Proc. of AVI '12*, pages 733–736. ACM.
20. M. D. Rodriguez, J. Favela, E. A. Martínez, and M. A. Muñoz. Location-aware access to hospital information and services. *Information Technology in Biomedicine, IEEE Transactions on*, 8(4):448–455, 2004.
21. J. J. Saleem, A. L. Russ, C. F. Justice, H. Hagg, P. R. Ebright, P. A. Woodbridge, and B. N. Doebbeling. Exploring the persistence of paper with the electronic health record. *International journal of medical informatics*, 78(9):618–628, 2009.
22. A. J. Sellen and R. Harper. *The myth of the paperless office*. The MIT Press, 2003.
23. B. Skov and T. Høegh. Supporting information access in a hospital ward by a context-aware mobile electronic patient record. *Personal and Ubiquitous Computing*, 10(4):205–214, 2006.
24. A. Tabard, W. E. Mackay, and E. Eastmond. From individual to collaborative: the evolution of prism, a hybrid laboratory notebook. In *proc. of CSCW '08*, pages 569–578. ACM.
25. C. Tang and S. Carpendale. Evaluating the deployment of a mobile technology in a hospital ward. In *Proc. of CSCW '08*, pages 205–214. ACM.
26. P. C. Tang, J. S. Ash, D. W. Bates, J. M. Overhage, and D. Z. Sands. Personal health records: definitions, benefits, and strategies for overcoming barriers to adoption. *Journal of the American Medical Informatics Association*, 13(2):121–126, 2006.
27. R. H. Trigg, J. Blomberg, and L. Suchman. Moving document collections online: The evolution of a shared repository. In *Proc. of ECSCW '99*, pages 331–350. Springer.
28. N. Weibel, A. Ispas, B. Signer, and M. C. Norrie. Paperproof: a paper-digital proof-editing system. In *CHI'08 Extended Abstracts on Human Factors in Computing Systems*, pages 2349–2354. ACM, 2008.
29. P. Wellner. The digitaldesk calculator: tangible manipulation on a desk top display. In *Proc. of UIST '91*, pages 27–33. ACM.
30. C. Winkler, J. Seifert, C. Reinartz, P. Krahmer, and E. Rukzio. Penbook: Bringing pen+paper interaction to a tablet device to facilitate paper-based workflows in the hospital domain. In *Proc. of ITS '13*, pages 283–286. ACM, 2013.
31. R. Yeh, C. Liao, S. Klemmer, F. Guimbretière, B. Lee, B. Kakaradov, J. Stamberger, and A. Paepcke. Butterflynet: a mobile capture and access system for field biology research. In *Proc. of CHI '06*, pages 571–580. ACM.
32. M. S. Zamarripa, V. M. Gonzalez, and J. Favela. The augmented patient chart: seamless integration of physical and digital artifacts for hospital work. In *Universal Access in Human-Computer Interaction. Applications and Services*, pages 1006–1015. Springer, 2007.
33. X. Zhou, M. S. Ackerman, and K. Zheng. I just don't know why it's gone: maintaining informal information use in inpatient care. In *Proc. of CHI '09*, pages 2061–2070. ACM.

ACTO
A Modular Actuated Tangible User Interface Object

Emanuel Vonach Georg Gerstweiler Hannes Kaufmann
Interactive Media Systems Group, Vienna University of Technology
Favoritenstraße 9-11/188-2, 1040 Vienna, Austria
vonach@ims.tuwien.ac.at gerstweiler@ims.tuwien.ac.at kaufmann@ims.tuwien.ac.at

ABSTRACT
We introduce a customizable, reusable actuated tangible user interface object: ACTO. Its modular design allows quick adaptations for different scenarios and setups on tabletops, making otherwise integral parts like the actuation mechanism or the physical configuration interchangeable. Drawing on the resources of well-established maker communities makes prototyping especially quick and easy. This allows the exploration of new concepts without the need to redesign the whole system, which qualifies it as an ideal research and education platform for tangible user interfaces. We present a detailed description of the hardware and software architecture of our system. Several implemented example configurations and application scenarios demonstrate the capabilities of the platform.

Author Keywords
Tangible user interfaces; tabletop interaction; actuation; prototyping platform; widgets; haptics; physical control.

ACM Classification Keywords
H.5.2. Information interfaces and presentation: User Interfaces - Input devices and strategies / Haptic I/O.

INTRODUCTION
Despite convincing benefits of tangible user interfaces (TUIs) over other input modalities, like intuitive use, immediate feedback or minimal necessary visual attention (cf. [5, 10, 21]), they are hardly found outside research institutions. Especially the field of actuated tabletop TUIs, where tangible objects can be actively moved by the computer, still seems to be in its infancy [18]. Although a number of promising concepts and systems have been reported (as presented in the Related Work section), there are only few quantitative studies or applications beyond proof-of-concept.

ITS 2014, November 16–19, 2014, Dresden, Germany.

ACM 978-1-4503-2587-5/14/11...$15.00
http://dx.doi.org/10.1145/2669485.2669522

Figure 1: Modular actuated tangible objects: ACTOs.

This might be related to the fact that the construction of a custom-built actuated tabletop TUI is a prerequisite for research in this field. Previously proposed systems are limited to a specific range of applications and setup options, as explained in the following sections. In addition there is a high technical construction effort. Considerable expertise in fields like robotics and electronics is required. This poses a substantial impediment and a high threshold for scientists to be able to contribute to this exciting research area.

To address this situation we propose a modular design strategy for actuated tangible user interface objects (ACTOs) for tabletops as a research and prototyping platform (Figure 1). Because of the high grade of modularity, typically integral parts like actuation mechanism or physical configuration can be individually customized and interchanged, allowing reusability for different scenarios and setups. The ACTOs can be equipped with different I/O devices, ranging from simple buttons to complex sensors. The system is also very mobile and can be set up quickly anywhere. Multiple of our ACTOs can be employed on any flat surface. In order to lower the entry-threshold we build upon large open communities (Arduino and Android). These provide the convenience of countless tutorials, setup guides and code snippets, which is of considerable benefit for the TUI research community and also allows employment of the system for education in this area.

We present our design considerations, based upon extensive study of available literature, and elaborate on the developed hard- and software. We also report on several implemented example configurations and application scenarios to demonstrate the capabilities of the system. Even novices can quickly and efficiently extend our ACTOs, which is indicated by initial results from a feedback questionnaire.

It is our hope that our proposed system encourages and supports the exploration of various new concepts, application areas and quantitative studies, minimizing the time spent on the redesign of the system for different experiments.

MOTIVATION & CONTRIBUTION

Our motivation for this work originated from the idea to employ a tabletop TUI in a health related scenario. Existing published solutions in the area of actuated TUIs either report an actuation mechanism that is built into the surface with very high technological effort (e.g. [26]), and/or the tangibles lack flexibility in possible configurations (e.g. [20]). In any case the TUIs range of possible application scenarios is limited and in our opinion disproportionate to the high construction effort.

At present there are only few quantitative studies on tabletop TUIs and the same is true for general know-how on User Interface Design for TUIs. For comprehensive research studies a setup is needed that is useable for all kinds of scenarios, without having to spend weeks on redesign for every new experiment. It should be possible to investigate different input modalities and devices as well as various actuation mechanisms and tracking methods, without having to be an electronics expert. This would be beneficial for researchers and allow students to experiment with TUI concepts as well.

Addressing these premises, we propose a design strategy for ACTOs as a prototyping platform for research and education, which offers flexibility in almost any aspect. Our major contributions are:

- **Versatility:** The system is easily customizable in almost any way and the ACTOs can be equipped with a free choice of I/O devices like buttons, sensors and displays.
- **Reusability:** Our TUI is reusable for a wide range of scenarios, minimizing possible redesign times.
- **Actuation:** The actuation mechanism for movement is integrated in the ACTO, allowing the use on any flat surface. The integration of other actuation mechanisms like moving sliders is also possible.
- **Modularity:** Changing the physical configuration of an ACTO is a matter of minutes. Typically integral parts like actuation mechanism or tracking method can be interchanged.
- **Low entry threshold:** The integration of new hard- or software is alleviated through provided templates and the benefits of large open communities.
- **Mobility:** The system is self-sufficient and has no heavy or bulky components. It can be set up very quickly anywhere.
- **Extensibility:** Costs scale with the number of ACTOs, not the size of the working area.

RELATED WORK

Multi-touch surfaces became more and more common over the last years and a variety of new input and output devices are being announced day after day. Nevertheless well-known shortcomings like a lack of haptic feedback persist, one of many advantages of tabletop TUIs above other forms of input.

In this context the ActiveDesk by Fitzmaurice et al. [5] and the metaDESK by Ullmer and Ishii [23] have to be named, since their work laid the foundations for the field of tabletop TUI research. Both employ a rear projected display and electromagnetic tracking, but while the former introduces tangibles only as handles for digital objects, the latter directs more attention to the tangibles. They primarily use acrylic objects to minimize occlusion and introduce separate widgets like a passive scaling tool and a small active display on a supportive arm.

For their music interface reacTable Jordà et al. [11] employ simple passive tangibles tracked with fiducial markers. They provide their tracking framework reacTIVision and the TUIO protocol for tabletop TUIs openly [12]. Implementations are far spread in the open source community and include all major platforms.

For a general overview of the field we refer to the works of Shaer and Hornecker [22] or Karat and Vanderdonckt [13].

Actuation

In order to take advantage of the benefits of a tabletop TUI not only for input but also for output, the interface has to be bidirectional. Some form of actuation mechanism is required, so that not only the user but also the computer can actively move the tangibles. Brave et al. [2] demonstrated the first distributed actuated tabletop TUI with the PSyBench. Using two synchronized motorized chessboards, the system can position one object at a time with an electromagnet but does not control the rotation. With their Actuated Workbench Pangaro et al. [16] introduced the concept of actuated tangibles used for two-way communication with a computer system. They build an array of electromagnets under the surface of a table to position small pucks fitted with permanent magnets and an LED for optical tracking. However TUIs with an actuation mechanism built into the table involve high technological effort and are not very flexible in the size of the interaction volume or the mobility of the setup.

Rosenfeld et al. [20] use infrared controlled two-wheeled robots as a bidirectional TUI called Planar Manipulator Display. They are relatively big and slow, and aside from infrared LEDs for optical tracking, they do not provide any way to extend the available functionality. Kojima et al. [14] employ similar robots in an Augmented Reality game, the Augmented Coliseum. For tracking they integrate an arrangement of photo transistors into the robots to detect a fiducial on the display. They also propose extending them with additional features like pincers, but such a robot would have to be custom built [13].

Other inventive approaches include the Universal Planar Manipulator by Reznik and Canny [19] who propose actuating objects on a surface with vibration patterns. This is mechanically simpler than an array of electromagnets, but is relatively slow and has its limits for more complex movements. In a very recent publication by Follmer et al. [7], the authors describe actuating objects with their shape display inFORM. With a 30 x 30 array of motorized pins passive objects can be mechanically lifted and roll or slide to an intended location. The constructional effort for the system is immense.

Modularity & Widgets

Ishii [10] underlines the importance of tailored design of a tangible for a specific function to benefit from natural affordances, at the same time preserving a balance to a more general approach for the reason of reusability. There are several examples in related work how the functionality of a tangible can be customized.

Sensetable by Patten et al. [17] makes use of the capacitive sensing of two graphics tablets and electromagnetic tracking to localize a limited number of pucks. They provide a basic socket to attach very simple physical dials and modifiers. Weiss et al. [27] add tactile feedback to multi-touch tables by providing a number of passive widgets. These SLAP Widgets are made from acrylic to avoid occlusion of information. They include different knobs, sliders and even a keyboard, but basically represent overlays for touch input. None of these systems provide any form of actuation and with the exception of Weiss et al. they do not emphasize easy development of custom widgets for experimenting.

Weiss et al. [26] extend their acrylic widgets in more recent work with permanent magnets for actuation on a tabletop, calling them Madgets. The actuation is comparable to the Actuated Workbench [16], but the array of electromagnets is located under a TFT panel and in between the magnets there are fiber optic cables allowing optical tracking on the surface. The authors also use inducted current in the widgets, which allows the operation of very simple electronic components like a bell or an LED. Nevertheless more complex I/O devices like sensors would not be possible. Furthermore the system relies strongly on the electromagnets, which makes the setup relatively inflexible.

In the context of modularity and widgets, there are also a number of related projects beside tabletop TUIs. The ActiveCube by Watanabe et al. [25] is equipped with programmable microcontrollers. Several cubes fitted with sophisticated I/O devices like sensors, buzzers or lights form a network, providing the constellation and rotation of the structure. However to add new I/O devices, a complete cube has to be built. The individual cubes are relatively big and combining several ones results in a massive structure. A notable former Kickstarter project is Palette [4], a customizable physical computer interface. It is made up of a collection of individually combinable modules, each with a single input like a button, dial or slider. Various selections of ready-made modules can be ordered, but the design of custom modules is not possible.

There are some toolkits available intended for experimenting with hardware components for physical user interfaces, like Phidgets [8] or iStuff [1]. They aim at providing access to low-level components and I/O devices with a minimum of necessary electronics know-how. Nonetheless they are limited to a specific set of widgets and there are no similar examples for actuated TUIs.

DESIGN GUIDELINES

Investigating the related work in the field, a number of basic common requirements for a prototyping platform for tabletop TUI research and education become apparent. In order to be able to benefit from the natural affordances of a tangible and at the same time guarantee reusability for other applications, it has to be easily customizable to its specific function in any scenario (cf. Ishii [10]). In most cases tangibles are used in conjunction with a graphical display. Considering that display technologies for tabletops are manifold and in constant development, the tangibles we envision should be independent of the employed display and usable on any flat surface.

Furthermore it should be small to minimize possible occlusions of displayed data, as well as lightweight and wireless to avoid impediment or fatigue of the user. To be able to work with different tracking technologies, the integration of trackable components ranging from passive fiducial markers to active infrared LEDs should be possible.

Only active tangibles can provide the extent of flexibility we expect. Built-in inexpensive microprocessors should allow the integration of a wide range of components. They permit basic processing for the operation of a lot of active components at minimum costs. More complex calculations can be performed on a single more powerful host device. Although a mobile and self-sufficient setup would be desirable, it has to be kept in mind that in a lot of cases prototyping on a PC is advantageous, for example allowing access to existing libraries, separate I/O devices, multimedia, advanced computations, etc. Providing network integration would be important for different kinds of remote collaboration scenarios.

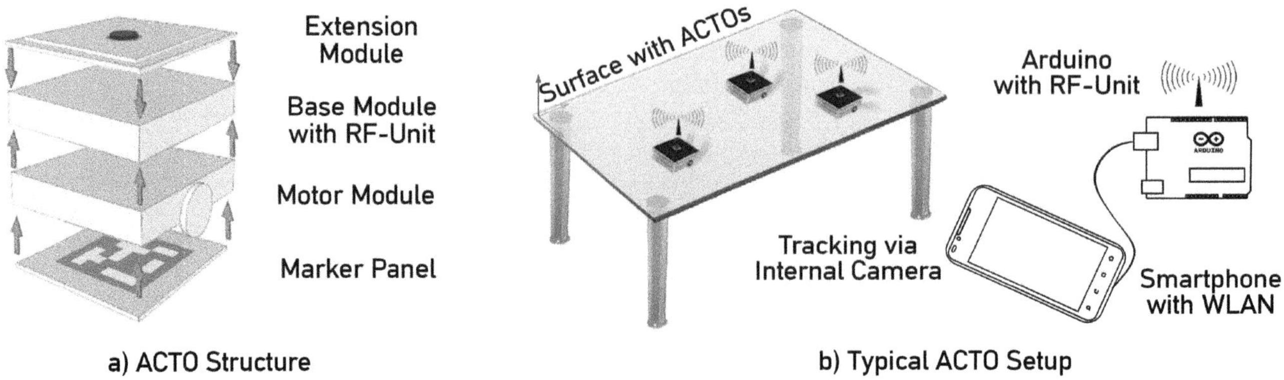

Figure 2: Overview of the ACTO concept.

For a flexible TUI, scalability and actuation are important factors. An actuation mechanism that is integrated into the table means extending the working volume or changing display technology would implicate an immense effort. Including the actuation mechanism into the tangibles allows costs to scale with the number of tangibles and almost unrelated to the size of the table. In fact it would be preferable, if the actuation mechanism would be interchangeable as well and no special surface would be required.

Finally as a prototyping platform it should be easy to learn and quick to modify, but not limited only to special hardware or available sensors for example for a specific toolkit.

HARDWARE ARCHITECTURE

In this chapter we present our approach to meet the previously established requirements for a tabletop TUI prototyping platform. The most important part of the system are the ACTOs, which were partly inspired by the easy-to-use concept of Arduino, an open-source electronics prototyping platform.

We successfully employed the Arduino platform in student-courses with electronics novices for years because it is versatile yet easy to learn. A well-established community providing tutorials, setup guides and code snippets lowers the entry threshold for novices considerably, but also experts and researchers benefit from the available resources. Most importantly the platform is not limited to a specific set of electronic components, which is why we adopted the concept for our system.

Our strategy for the hardware is based on a flexible and modular design (Figure 2a) to allow the construction of customized actuated widgets. An Arduino compatible "Base Module" with RF communication capabilities can be fitted with an optional "Motor Module" which incorporates the desired actuation mechanism for positioning and rotating the ACTOs. On top of the Base Module there is a socket for mounting a custom-made "Extension Module" which can be equipped with arbitrary I/O devices ranging from rotary knobs over vibration motors to graphical displays. The integration of an actuation mechanism in this module is also possible, for example for changing the physical state of a slider or dial. The design of the individual modules is described in detail in the following chapters.

All employed Base Modules communicate wirelessly to a "Server" Arduino which relays all data to an "ACTO Server App" on an Android smartphone (Figure 2b). This smartphone acts as the central processing unit running the control software for the system, handling coordination of the ACTOs, providing a GUI and the tracking. Since the setup requires no heavy or bulky components it can be set up very quickly anywhere. If desired, all necessary functionality can also be accessed via WLAN. This allows the development of an application not only directly for the Android device, but basically on any WLAN capable system.

Base Module

We designed our Base Module (see Figure 3) inspired by the Arduino Pro Mini reference design. In order to save space we discarded minor components like the reset button from the original design. We exchanged the microcontroller for the more powerful Atmel ATmega328P clocked at 16 MHz and powered via 5 V voltage regulator. Once the Arduino bootloader is installed, it can be programmed as comfortable as a conventional Arduino board over the Arduino IDE with an FTDI USB to serial board by Sparkfun.

Figure 3: Base Module in housing.

In contrast to most Arduino boards we enabled the analog pins A6 and A7, whereas we used A7 in a simple voltage divider configuration to provide low power shut off capability. For low power wireless communication we integrated the Nordic nRF24L01+ RF transceiver together with the necessary 3.3 V voltage regulator and a micro antenna. The transceiver is directly connected to the microcontroller via Serial Peripheral Interface (SPI).

On top of the Base Module, we devised a socket providing access to all available I/O pins supporting the easy attachment of custom Extension Modules. On the bottom a 4-pin socket and a power plug allow the connection of a Motor- and Tracking Module.

We put the Base Module into a casing that we produced out of acryl glass and nylon screw nuts. It also houses a 7.4 V LiPo battery with a capacity of 200 mAh. Openings for power plug and balancer connector of the battery as well as a power switch and a 3-pin socket for programming are cut into the housing.

Altogether there are 19 I/O pins, of which 4 provide PWM capability and 8 can be used as analog input pins. In addition 3.3 V, 5 V and 7.4 V are available as voltage source as well as 3 ground pins and 2 reset pins.

The size of the Base Module alone is 35 x 35 x 6 mm and it weighs 10 g. Including housing and battery it is 50 x 50 x 20 mm and 50 g. The hardware cost for one module is around 60 EUR.

Motor- and Tracking Module

In accordance with our modular design strategy, we devised an actuation mechanism which is completely packaged in a separate Motor Module and can be connected to the Base Module if desired. As a first example we decided to implement a two-wheel differential drive [9], since a comparable approach was already successfully employed in actuated TUIs ([14, 20]) and can be used on any flat surface. The simple mechanical structure and kinematic model are further advantages of this approach.

We used two metal gear motors with 1:50 reduction, rubber wheels and other small components for the mechanical part of the module (see Figure 4). The typically included passive caster wheel is not required, because the bottom of the module is less than 1 mm above ground.

The electrical layout of the module consists out of a 6 V voltage regulator and all the necessary components to build up two separate H-bridges. An H-bridge permits each motor to be operated independently from the other in both directions. In that way steering in any direction and turning on the spot are possible. The Motor Module is currently controlled over a connector to 4 I/O pins of the Base Module and powered directly over a separate plug to the battery.

Figure 4: Two-wheel drive Motor Module.

However based on our experience for a second generation of Motor Modules we would prefer commercially available H-bridge drivers operated over SPI, which would free up 4 more pins for custom usage and also facilitate more complex modules.

The lowermost module of the ACTO has to include possible components for a tracking system, if required. If actuation is desired, the Motor Module therefore has to incorporate these components. Otherwise it can also be replaced by an optional separate Tracking Module. In our case we fitted the circuit board of the Motor Module with a mounting for fiducial markers to be used with a camera based optical tracking system. Just as well it is possible to integrate LEDs, photo sensors or other means of tracking.

Extension Modules

The extension and customization of our ACTOs is a core functionality of our system and should be as easy as prototyping with Arduino. For the integration of custom Extension Modules we provide a 27-pin socket, allowing access to all available I/O and power pins. We designed a template of the socket layout for Fritzing - a simple open-source layout tool for printed circuit boards (PCB). This software is much like Arduino designed in an easy-to-use spirit and supports in particular the process to transfer a circuit from a breadboard directly to a functional PCB layout. This makes designing an Extension Board especially easy for students and novices.

An Extension Board for our ACTOs can incorporate any component that can also be operated via Arduino. This includes simple I/O devices like buttons, speakers or sensors, but also motors for other kinds of actuation than movement of the ACTOs. Though in order to avoid damage to hardware components an absolute maximum of 800 mA can be drawn from the 5 V pin respectively 150 mA from the 3.3 V pin.

For a variety of possible Extension Modules and application scenarios please refer to the Subjective Evaluation section.

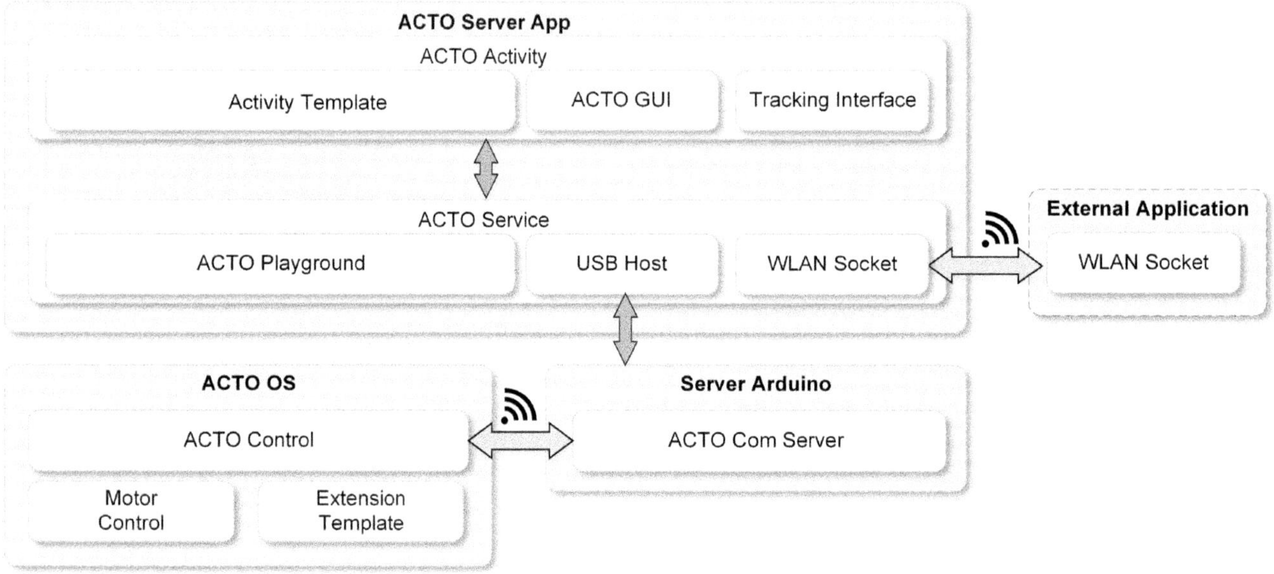

Figure 5: Overview of the ACTO framework.

SOFTWARE DESIGN

Several frameworks for TUIs are available, which are adequate and relatively easy to use, like reacTIVision [12]. However we require a system which is independent of the employed tracking technology and provides support for an extensive two-way communication protocol. Therefore we developed our own framework (see Figure 5).

Its key components are the ACTO Server App on the smartphone with an Activity Template for comfortable application development, the ACTO OS on the tangibles which includes a template for easy integration of new Extension Modules, and a communication protocol to interface all components and a possible WLAN client.

The ACTOs provide only minimal computational capabilities to reduce cost and power consumption. More complex processing and all application logic runs on an Android smartphone. This allows versatile application scenarios, since the system can be set up almost everywhere in a short period of time. An application can be developed on the platform of choice and it runs on most current USB-host capable Android smartphones. A developer just has to write an app based on the Activity Template in the ACTO Server App to be able to access all public functions of the framework. A simple ACTO GUI allows direct operation of the most important functions and provides visual feedback.

Furthermore the framework handles incoming tracking data from a separate thread. The application allows an easy integration of different tracking methods, as long as translation and rotation can be provided in the form of floating point values for each tracked ACTO within a tracking volume. For our test setup we integrated the Metaio SDK 5.3 [15], a free to use Augmented Reality development toolkit providing various optical tracking methods. We employ the front camera of the smartphone for tracking. This has the advantage, that the touch screen is still accessible when the device is placed on or under an interactive table. The drawback on most smartphones is a lower resolution and frame rate, which is why the back camera can be used as well if no GUI is required.

A separate ACTO Service manages most of the functionality of the ACTO Server, answers to commands from the ACTO Activity, reports I/O events on the ACTOs and implements a simple communication protocol. The ACTO Playground includes multiple algorithms for operation of a larger number of ACTOs. It generates and controls movement paths to intended destinations, handles collision avoidance and implements calibration algorithms for the interactive surface.

Since it is often beneficial to use a PC or other platform to run application logic, all public functions of the ACTO Server App are also accessible over WLAN. On the client side only the implementation of a WLAN socket and our communication protocol is required. The downside of the additionally introduced (visually not noticeable) delay is counterbalanced by the benefits of being able to use already available libraries or input devices and developing on the system and IDE of choice.

An Arduino board is connected via USB to the smartphone and is fitted with an nRF24L01+ transceiver module for communicating with the ACTOs. This Arduino acts as a communication server and just forwards any complete communication messages to the appropriate receiver or rejects incomplete messages. To be able to use an Arduino board in conjunction with an Android smartphone we integrated an USB host serial driver library [24] in our ACTO Server App.

The ACTO OS on the tangibles is implemented in Arduino-Code, which is basically a C/C++ variant. A developer can specify the pins used for the components of a custom Extension Module and their nature (input or output, analog, digital or PWM) in the Extension Template. If set up correctly, ACTO Control will automatically update all I/O events with the ACTO Server App. The ACTO OS also implements a protocol for motor control, which represents all possible steering maneuvers and speed settings with 2 bytes. The actual code for operation of the Motor Module is implemented in a separate Motor Control class, in that way the same protocol can be used for different possible actuation modules. We implemented the code for our two-wheel differential drive modules and included for example a feature to minimize slipping tires and to allow calibration in case the motors produce slightly different thrust. For wireless communication using the nRF24L01+ transceiver we integrated the Mirf library.

TEST SETUP & TECHNICAL EVALUATION

As a test setup we used an 84 x 64 cm glass table with a height of 104 cm as presented in Figure 6. The smartphone running the ACTO Server App was a Samsung Galaxy Nexus GT-I9250. It features Android 4.2, a 1.2 GHz dual-core CPU, 4.65" display, a 5 MP back-camera and a 1.3 MP front-camera. The Server Arduino was an Arduino UNO r3 with a Sparkfun nRF24L01+ transceiver module. For tracking with fiducial markers we employed the front camera with a reduced resolution of 320 x 240 pixels for minimum latency.

The smartphone was placed together with the Arduino onto an adjustable beam under the table. This allowed us to experiment with different tracking volumes by changing the distance of the smartphone camera to the glass surface. Marker tracking is always sensitive to constant and uniform illumination. With ideal lighting situation we can extend the tracking space to the full size of the glass table. For a good balance between tracking robustness and interactive volume we adjusted the distance to achieve an approximate working area of 48 x 35 cm. In this setup the resulting update rate of tracking data was 30 fps.

These values are only exemplary since they are highly dependent on factors such as the employed tracking SDK and camera, distance to the table surface, lighting conditions and many more.

The threads for I/O handling and motor control are decoupled from the tracking process. The average round-trip time of an input event on an ACTO, processed by the Server App and transmitted to another ACTO for output was measured with 24.8 ms. We also determined the actuation speed of our two-wheel drive Motor Modules with 39 cm/s and a rotational speed of 120 rpm. The total power consumption without Extension or Motor-Module is about 56 mA, which would mean a theoretical operating time of about 3.5 hours.

Figure 6: Exemplary setup with two ACTOs, a smartphone and an Arduino with RF-Module.

Both motors at full power draw a current of up to 100 mA, generally making up the biggest part of the overall power consumption of our ACTOs and thereby reducing the operating time considerably depending on motor usage. With our 3.5 Ah charger, an ACTO is recharged in under 5 minutes.

SUBJECTIVE EVALUATION

In order to evaluate the suitability of the ACTO system as a prototyping platform for researchers and students, we tested how easy it is to learn to use and extend the system.

For that purpose we offered the participation in the project as optional courses for computer science students at a Federal Higher Technical Institute as well as for computer science master students at our university. In order to allow a valid conclusion on researchers and students, all participants were in their final years of study and had no special experience with electronics or robotics.

We observed them during the process of applying our system for the first time. The estimated time spent on different parts of the process was interpreted as a measure for the effort of each step. A total of 10 students of the technical institute (age 17 - 19) and 4 master students (age 24 - 28), altogether 4 female and 10 male students, participated in our experiment over the last 2 years.

Their assignment was to sketch an application scenario for tabletop TUIs and design and to construct the appropriate Extension Modules for our system. We helped with pointing them to recommendable tutorials, with conceptual questions and provided the required equipment, but other than that the students were free to experiment with the topic on their own. On average they worked 30.9 hours with our system. At the end of each project we used a questionnaire to get subjective feedback on their experience. It included an introductory part with a consent form and standard questions about age, gender and prior experience.

Furthermore we asked about the estimated time spent for different parts of the construction process, a subjective estimation of the complexity of the Extension Module and the overall satisfaction with the result. The estimated times had to be answered in concrete numbers, for the other questions the participants could choose from a 5-point Likert scale with the highest rating at 5.

The questionnaire also included a Critical Incident Technique (CIT) [6] allowing the participants to elaborate on their three most positive and three most negative critical events to reveal any specific problems. Furthermore we asked the participants to score the 10 items of the System Usability Scale (SUS) [3] to rate usability of "developing an Extension Module for the system". The SUS generally provides a high-level subjective view of usability and is thus often used to compare usability between systems.

Use Case 1: Memory Extended

A group of three students of the technical institute called their project Memory Extended (Memex). They developed an audio memory game which works completely self-sufficient with two ACTOs. Their Extension Modules provide a differently colored 7-segment LED display including driver, a simple piezo-electric speaker and three differently colored LEDs (see Figure 7a). Later in the project they modified their original idea to a memory game for blind people which should allow them to learn conventional letters by following the movements of an ACTO with a finger. For that purpose the students replaced the display and the LEDs and constructed another Extension Module with a touch sensor and the piezo speaker for acoustic feedback. The students finished all Extension Modules and a simulation of the application, but did not perform user tests with actual blind people.

Use Case 2: Tangible Desktop Interaction

A completely different scenario was created by another five students of the technical institute. Under the caption Tangible Desktop Interaction (TDI) they devised an elaborate system for desktop interaction using two ACTOs in a Linux Ubuntu environment on a PC. Each Extension Module that they designed incorporates a vibration motor and two colored LEDs for direct visual and haptic feedback (see Figure 7b). In their scenario the ACTOs can represent icons or icon groups, windows or interface elements within an application. The current state is indicated by the LEDs on the tangibles and visual feedback on a traditional monitor. The ACTOs position themselves on the table according to their current function e.g. they move in and out of a designated taskbar region or take a position on the table relative to the currently represented item on the screen. The students implemented a number of tilt, rotate and move gestures to manipulate the icons and control a music player.

Figure 7: Selection of Extension Modules for the ACTO system: a) Memex. b) TDI. c) Rotary knob with RGB-LED. d) Breadboard-Extension. e) Alternative Motor Module.

They also conducted a small scale user study to evaluate their application, but due to lack of experience in interpreting and handling tracking data it did not perform as well as they had hoped and the results were inconclusive. However the construction of the ACTO Extension Modules as well as the incorporation of our system via WLAN on a PC proved to be unproblematic.

Other Extension Modules

In addition to the already presented modules the remaining five students also developed a number of Extension Modules. Two students of the technical institute constructed two Extension Modules, each comprising an RGB-LED built into a rotary knob with an integrated button for a music composition application (Figure 7c). Two master students devised two Extension Modules that form breadboard like boards for prototyping directly on the ACTO (Figure 7d). Another master student integrated different sensors for measuring physical properties ranging from light-intensity to air-pressure into Extension Modules for a medical examination scenario. Finally a master student developed an alternative Motor Module (Figure 7e) based on a "bristlebot" approach [28] to reduce power consumption, mechanical complexity and make sliding the ACTO sideways easier.

Beside the presented examples, two students of the technical institute conceptualized an idea for optimizing the route of ships: Water and wind currents are visualized on a projected map on a table, where an ACTO in form of a ship can move along a route. A sail or rudder can be adjusted as input and in addition actuated with a motor for output. The effects of different sail/rudder angles on speed, route, etc. are updated in real-time. Unfortunately these students did not finish their project.

Evaluation Feedback

Six students (3 female, 3 male, 1 representative per group) answered the voluntary final questionnaire, which provides us with subjective feedback.

The participants reported above average computer science experience (avg. 3.6) and low electronics know-how (avg. 2). They estimated an average of 10.5 hours for studying basic principles and tutorials. The electronic assembly of their Extension Modules took 17.6 hours in average. Finally another avg. 1.8 hours were invested into the construction of a casing and only 1 hour (avg.) to write the necessary Arduino code for operating the module. All participants rated the overall satisfaction with the resulting Extension Module very high (avg. 4.3)

From the employed CIT a lot of positive and only few negative incidents were reported concerning our system. The range of possibilities for modifying the features of an ACTO was pointed out positively. The already extensive basic functionality was valued highly as well. The negative comments concerned basic problems related to a lack of experience with soldering, understanding the nature of tracking data and bugs in the Fritzing software. However one very helpful comment by one of the master students showed up a basic flaw in the system that we fixed later. Some of the pins we used for operating the Motor Module conflicted with the use of the Inter-Integrated Circuit (I2C) bus. We also scored the SUS, although considering the low number of participants we are aware that the results reflect a notion at best. A SUS score of 68 is generally considered above average. We got an overall score of 72.9.

Possibilities & Limitations

The diversity of the realized Extension Modules and use cases demonstrates, that the ACTO platform offers unprecedented flexibility. The possibility to integrate almost any electrical component allows the investigation of new application scenarios, for example a control scenario to coordinate the operation of emergency service personnel. ACTOs could be actuated on a map to present an overview of the current situation to an operational commander, who can at the same time issue commands by manipulating position and input components on the tangibles. The creation of "serious toys" as rehabilitation tools could also be investigated. A game scenario could be highly customized to a patient, while data from different integrated sensors would allow the analysis of the rehabilitation progress. Highly interactive educational applications could make abstract topics like optics more tangible. A predefined scenario could be presented with real lasers and lenses on ACTOs to demonstrate certain phenomena, while learners could manipulate the setting and see an immediate effect.

Because of the high modularity of the ACTO system, changing the physical configuration of an ACTO is a matter of minutes. It permits the exploration of individual aspects like different forms of actuation, tracking technologies or input and output modalities independently from each other. The system can be implemented as a whole but also in part and can be employed without a PC or additional display.

The presented Motor Modules can be used on any flat surface. Our current tracking solution requires a transparent table. This setup is very flexible and mobile which allows quantitative studies on the employment of tabletop TUIs. Since size and form of the ACTOs can easily be changed, user interface design studies for TUIs can be realized.

There are limitations of the ACTO system. The size of the Base Module of 35 x 35 x 6 mm without battery is an absolute minimum form factor. Depending on the power requirements of the Extension Modules, especially if more elaborate actuated output modalities are desired, a suitable battery can enlarge this minimum form factor considerably. Our current Motor Modules do not support actuation of the ACTOs sideways. In order to drive to a destination the ACTO first has to turn towards it and turn back after arrival. This increases the time to actually reach an intended location. The working area and update rate are limited by our current tracking solution. Since we employ marker tracking, a large distance to the surface or a bad lighting situation can cause wrong or missing ACTO positions.

CONCLUSION & FUTURE WORK

We present a novel, general actuated tabletop TUI system which is customizable in almost any way and thus reusable for a wide range of application scenarios. Our initial evaluation indicates, that the system is suitable as a prototyping platform for TUI research. It can be successfully used and extended after a relatively short learning time and without special knowledge of electronics or robotics. It advances research of tabletop TUIs by minimizing the time spent on the redesign of the tangibles for different experiments, thereby stimulating the exploration of new application areas and facilitating quantitative studies. The participants reported high satisfaction with the resulting Extension Modules and generally enjoyed the course a lot. Therefore we conclude that the system is also well-suited for educational purposes to teach TUI concepts.

Due to the positive feedback we will keep offering the creation of Extension Modules in an optional course for master students. We will also employ the system for research to study new practical application areas e.g. for haptic feedback in Augmented Reality and as a medical examination tool for children. Although the platform proved to be adequate, we continuously improve the system. We want to explore solutions for different limitations of the system. For example our current Motor Modules are not well suited for tilted surfaces. Therefore we examine the technology used for toy cars that drive on walls and ceiling through suction. Finally we also want to integrate a more sophisticated tracking solution based on laser sensing and are continuously improving the ACTO Server App to make development of new applications as easy as possible.

In order to allow fellow researchers to benefit the most from our results, we provide all the templates, material lists and software on our project webpage https://www.ims.tuwien.ac.at/projects/acto.

ACKNOWLEDGMENTS

This work was funded by Sparkling Science, a research program of the Federal Ministry of Science, Research and Economy (BMWFW). We thank our partners HTBLVA Spengergasse and INNOC - Österreichische Gesellschaft für innovative Computerwissenschaften as well as Walter Hammerl and all the students who participated. Special thanks go to Michael Mehling, a former colleague who initiated the ACTO idea in our research group.

REFERENCES

1. Ballagas, R., Ringel, M., Stone, M., et al. iStuff: a physical user interface toolkit for ubiquitous computing environments. *Proc. of CHI '03*, ACM Press (2003), 537.
2. Brave, S., Ishii, H., and Dahley, A. Tangible interfaces for remote collaboration and communication. *Proc. of CSCW '98*, ACM Press (1998), 169–178.
3. Brooke, J. SUS: A quick and dirty usability scale. *Usability Evaluation in Industry*, (1996), 189–194.
4. Chu, C., Bidadi, A., Ting, F., et al. Palette. http://palettegear.com/.
5. Fitzmaurice, G.W., Ishii, H., and Buxton, W.A.S. Bricks: laying the foundations for graspable user interfaces. *Proc. of CHI '95*, ACM Press (1995), 442–449.
6. Flanagan, J.C. The critical incident technique. *Psychological Bulletin 51*, 4 (1954), 327–358.
7. Follmer, S., Leithinger, D., Olwal, A., et al. inFORM: Dynamic Physical Affordances and Constraints Through Shape and Object Actuation. *Proc. of UIST '13*, ACM Press (2013), 417–426.
8. Greenberg, S. and Fitchett, C. Phidgets: easy development of physical interfaces through physical widgets. *Proc. of UIST '01*, ACM Press (2001), 209.
9. Hannaford, B. and Okamura, A.M. *Springer Handbook of Robotics*. Springer Berlin Heidelberg, Berlin, Heidelberg, 2008.
10. Ishii, H. Tangible bits: beyond pixels. *Proc. of TEI '08*, ACM Press (2008), xv.
11. Jordà, S., Kaltenbrunner, M., Geiger, G., et al. The reacTable: a tangible tabletop musical instrument and collaborative workbench. *Sketches of SIGGRAPH '06*, ACM Press (2006), 91.
12. Kaltenbrunner, M. reacTIVision and TUIO : A Tangible Tabletop Toolkit. *Proc. of ITS '09*, ACM Press (2009), 9.
13. Karat, J. and Vanderdonckt, J. *Tabletops - Horizontal Interactive Displays*. Springer London, London, 2010.
14. Kojima, M., Sugimoto, M., Nakamura, A., et al. Augmented Coliseum: An Augmented Game Environment with Small Vehicles. *Proc. of TABLETOP '06*, IEEE (2006), 3–8.
15. Metaio GmbH. Metaio Augmented Reality SDK. 2014. http://www.metaio.com/products/sdk/.
16. Pangaro, G., Maynes-Aminzade, D., and Ishii, H. The Actuated Workbench: Computer-Controlled Actuation in Tabletop Tangible Interfaces. *Proc. of UIST '02*, ACM Press (2002), 181.
17. Patten, J., Ishii, H., Hines, J., et al. Sensetable: A Wireless Object Tracking Platform for Tangible User Interfaces. *Proc. of CHI '01*, ACM Press (2001), 253–260.
18. Poupyrev, I., Nashida, T., and Okabe, M. Actuation and Tangible User Interfaces: the Vaucanson Duck, Robots, and Shape Displays. *Proc. of TEI '07*, ACM Press (2007), 205.
19. Reznik, D.S. and Canny, J.F. C'mon part, do the local motion! *Proc. of ICRA '01*, IEEE (2001), 2235–2242.
20. Rosenfeld, D., Zawadzki, M., Sudol, J., et al. Physical objects as bidirectional user interface elements. *IEEE Computer Graphics and Applications 24*, 1 (2004), 44–49.
21. Schneider, B., Jermann, P., Zufferey, G., et al. Benefits of a Tangible Interface for Collaborative Learning and Interaction. *IEEE Transactions on Learning Technologies 4*, 3 (2011), 222–232.
22. Shaer, O. and Hornecker, E. Tangible User Interfaces: Past, Present, and Future Directions. *Foundations and Trends® in Human–Computer Interaction 3*, (2010), 1–137.
23. Ullmer, B. and Ishii, H. The metaDESK: models and prototypes for tangible user interfaces. *Proc. of UIST '97*, ACM Press (1997), 223–232.
24. Wakerly, M. usb-serial-for-android. 2012. https://github.com/mik3y/usb-serial-for-android.
25. Watanabe, R., Itoh, Y., Asai, M., et al. The soul of ActiveCube: implementing a flexible, multimodal, three-dimensional spatial tangible interface. *Computers in Entertainment 2*, 4 (2004), 15.
26. Weiss, M., Schwarz, F., Jakubowski, S., et al. Madgets : Actuating Widgets on Interactive Tabletops. *Proc. of UIST '10*, ACM Press (2010), 293.
27. Weiss, M., Wagner, J., Jansen, Y., et al. SLAP Widgets: Bridging the Gap Between Virtual and Physical Controls on Tabletops. *Proc. of CHI '09*, ACM Press (2009), 481.
28. Windell, O. Bristlebot: A tiny directional vibrobot. 2007. http://www.evilmadscientist.com/2007/bristlebot-a-tiny-directional-vibrobot/.

BullsEye: High-Precision Fiducial Tracking for Table-based Tangible Interaction

Clemens Nylandsted Klokmose[1,2] clemens@cs.au.dk
Janus Bager Kristensen[3] jbk@cavi.au.dk
Rolf Bagge[3] rolf@cavi.au.dk
Kim Halskov[2,3] halskov@cavi.au.dk

[1]Department of Computer Science, Aarhus University, DK-8200 Aarhus N, Denmark
[2]Center for Participatory IT, Aarhus University, DK-8200 Aarhus N, Denmark
[3]Center for Advanced Visualization and Interaction, Aarhus University, DK-8200 Aarhus N, Denmark

ABSTRACT

This paper proposes a series of techniques for improving the precision of optical fiducial tracking on tangible tabletops. The motivation is to enable convincing interactive projection mapping on tangibles on the table, which requires a high precision tracking of the location of tangibles. We propose a new fiducial design optimized for GPU based tracking, a technique for calibrating light that allows for computation on a greyscale image rather than a binarized black and white image, an automated technique for compensating for optical distortions in the camera lenses, and a tracking algorithm implemented primarily in shaders on the GPU. The techniques are realized in the BullsEye computer vision software. We demonstrate experimentally that BullsEye provides sub-pixel accuracy down to a tenth of a pixel, which is a significant improvement compared to the commonly used reacTIVision software.

Author Keywords

Fiducial tracking; Computer vision; Tangible tabletops; Tangible computing

ACM Classification Keywords

H.5.m. Information Interfaces and Presentation (e.g. HCI): Miscellaneous

INTRODUCTION

Over the last decade tabletop computing has gained significant interest in both academia and the industry. A popular technique for implementing tracking on an interactive table is to use computer vision, either by having one or more cameras mounted beneath a semi transparent surface, or by integrating optical sensors in a display surface[1]. Such optical tracking not only enables finger-based interaction, but also tracking of physical objects on the table, so-called tangibles. This is typically done by detecting shapes or unique fiducial markers attached to the bottom of the tangibles.

Figure 1: Interactive projection mapping on tangibles on an interactive tabletop.

A novel extension of tangible tabletops is to use interactive projection mapping on tangibles on the table [4], hereafter referred to as *tangible 3D tabletops*. This technique creates the illusion that the tangibles are display surfaces themselves (Figure 1). Although, in order to create and maintain a convincing illusion, the tracking of fiducials on the table must be extremely accurate.

ReacTIVision is one of the few freely available computer vision frameworks particularly designed for tabletop fiducial tracking[11][2]. To build custom tangible 3D tabletops, reacTIVision is currently the best candidate for fiducial tracking. However, we have found that the tracking technique applied in reacTIVision is too inaccurate for interactive projection mapping. Commercial alternatives to reacTIVision exist, such as Microsoft's PixelSense API or MultiTaction by MultiTouch Ltd but these frameworks are closed source and tightly coupled to specific hardware platforms.

In this paper we will present a computer vision framework, BullsEye[3], with a set of novel techniques for fiducial tracking to provide an accuracy high enough to convincingly enable interactive projection mapping on a tangible tabletop. While BullsEye is designed to enable tangible 3D tabletops it is also a framework for general tabletop fiducial tracking. Therefore, the presented improvements of fiducial tracking will benefit a regular tangible tabletop application based on optical tracking

[1]A technology used in Microsoft's PixelSense `http://www.microsoft.com/en-us/pixelsense`

[2]The fiducial tracking library *libfidtrack* from reacTIVision is also used in other frameworks such as in the Community Core Vision framework (`http://ccv.nuigroup.com`)

[3]BullsEye is available for download at `http://cavi.au.dk/bullseye`.

ITS 2014, November 16–19, 2014, Dresden, Germany.

ACM 978-1-4503-2587-5/14/11 ...$15.00.
http://dx.doi.org/10.1145/2669485.2669503

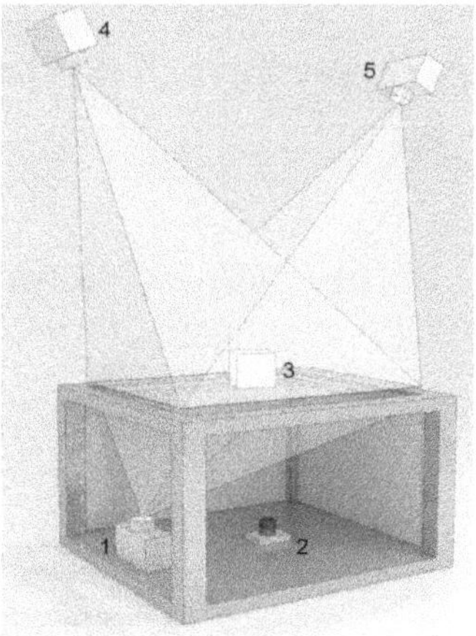

Figure 2: The main components of the tangible 3D tabletop. **1)** Bottom mounted projector for the surface of the table. **2)** Camera for tracking fingers and objects on the table. **3)** Objects on which the projection mapping is performed. The objects are equipped with fiducials and tracked by the bottom mounted camera. **4-5)** One or more top-mounted projectors for the projection mapping.

as well. The core advantage of BullsEye compared to reacTIVision is that BullsEye offers *subpixel precision* down to an average of one tenth of a pixel compared to the around one pixel precision we measure from reacTIVision. BullsEye furthermore facilitates significantly more precise and automated compensation for optical distortions in the optics of cameras. BullsEye does feature finger tracking, but in this paper we solely focus on the improved fiducial tracking to accommodate the precision required for interactive projection mapping.

In the next section we will present the requirements that spawned the need for a new tracking framework, followed by an overview of the central ideas employed in BullsEye and how they differ from those of reacTIVision. We will then present details on the implementation of BullsEye followed by an evaluation of its performance and compare it to reacTIVision.

Requirements

Interactive projection mapping on a tangible tabletop involves synchronizing fiducial tracking on the table with the rendering of a 3D scene displayed by one or more top-mounted projectors together with the image from the table projector or display (see Figure 2). To do this a virtual representation of an object must be mapped to the location and rotation of a physical object in real time. In figure 1 tangibles are used to navigate statistical data on a map by projecting the data relating to the position of the cubes on the map onto the cubes themselves.

In initial prototypes of tangible 3D tabletops we used reacTIVision for fiducial tracking. We experienced that the tracking accuracy was not high enough for this purpose. We have measured the error of reacTIVision to be between 0.5 and 1.5 pixels when detecting the position of a fiducial on a table with a 1280x1024 pixels camera input (See Experimental Evaluation). A one pixel error with a 1280x1024 camera input results in a metric precision of 0.78 mm when projecting on a 100 by 80 centimeter surface. This may seem as a high accuracy, and it is adequate for most tangible tabletop applications, but for the purpose of projection mapping the inaccuracy is easily discernible (as illustrated in figure 3). With BullsEye we aim for improving accuracy, and we demonstrate that a tenth of a pixel is a realistic aim. A tenth of a pixel offset is still discernible with the naked eye (as seen in figure 3 bottom middle) but a significant improvement over reacTIVision's accuracy.

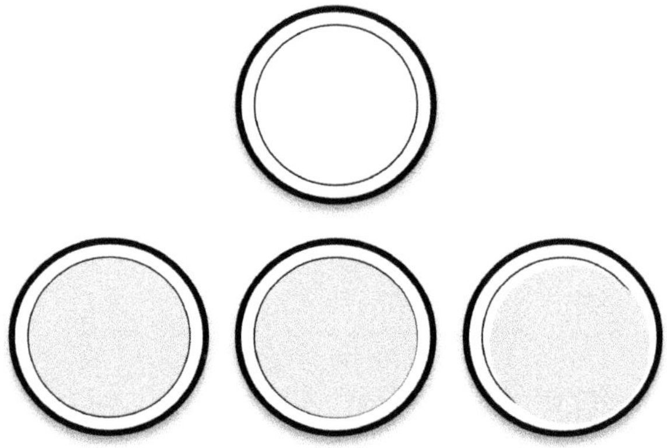

Figure 3: On a tangible similar in shape and size to a checker piece (top), a perfect projection of a green color is shown *bottom left*, *bottom right* shows how the projection with a worst case 1 pixel horizontal and vertical offset on a 100 cm long and 80 cm wide table and a camera with a resolution of 1280 by 1024 pixels. *Bottom middle* shows the worst case offset with the 1/10 pixel precision. On printed paper the offsets should approximately match what would be experienced on a physical table.

Optical distortion in the lens of the camera used for tracking can result in the tracked position being offset from the actual physical position of the object. The offset may differ across the area of the table. In order to provide a uniform precision across the surface of the table, any optical distortion must be compensated for through a calibration. To align the tracking and compensate for optical distortions reacTIVision applies a technique where a set of grid points are manually aligned to a calibration grid that is printed and placed on the table (Figure 6). Our experience is that the process of manually aligning the grid is laborious and error prone, and even if the alignment is done extremely meticulously the compensation is too coarse. With BullsEye we aim to automate this calibration, and make sure the distortion compensation is even across the surface of the tangible tabletop.

It is essential that the latency between the physical movement of a tangible and the update of the position of the projected virtual representation is kept as low as possible. Therefore, a requirement for any fiducial tracking software is that the tracking must be achieved within the time between frames coming from the camera.

With BullsEye we also want to support multiple cameras, which can enable us to construct large interactive table-tops (inspired by [18]), and we want to support multiple different types of cameras including PixelSense based cameras.

FIDUCIAL TRACKING IN BULLSEYE

In this section we present three central techniques applied in BullsEye: A fiducial design optimized for GPU tracking, an improved calibration of light to enable computation on grayscale values for increased precision, and an improved technique for compensating for optical distortions. The techniques will be compared to those of reacTIVision. At the end of the section we will go through the details of the shader steps involved in BullsEye's fiducial tracking algorithm.

Fiducial design

The tracking algorithm in BullsEye is primarily implemented in shaders on the GPU in contrast to reacTIVision's traditional CPU-based algorithm. A GPU implementation has some significant performance benefits compared to a CPU implementation as tracking can be parallelized if the fiducial design allows for it.

Tracking a fiducial involves three basic steps:

1. Find the center coordinates
2. Find the rotation angle
3. Extract the unique identifier

The reacTIVision tracking algorithm [2] is based on a topological fiducial recognition approach adopted and improved from d-touch [3]. The center of a reacTIVision fiducial (figure 4 right) is computed by the average centroid of black and white leafs in the topology of the fiducial (i.e. by the centroids of the fully black and fully white dots). The rotation is computed as a vector from the center of the fiducial to the average centroid of the black leafs. The unique identifier of a fiducial is extracted by constructing a region adjacency graph from the fiducial and computing a depth sequence string which uniquely identifies the fiducial. In other words; reacTIVision creates a tree-like structure representing how black regions contains white and vice versa, which can be serialized to a unique identifier (find more details in [2]). The reacTIVision fiducial tracking algorithm could possibly be implemented on the GPU; however, we decided to opt for a simpler fiducial design particularly designed for GPU based tracking.

The BullsEye fiducials (figure 4 left) are designed so that the three tracking steps can be easily implemented with shaders executed on the GPU. A BullsEye fiducial consists of a central white dot surrounded by a solid black ring and one or more data rings again surrounded by a solid white ring inside a black ring with three white studs. The data rings encode the fiducial id in binary form (white is 1 and black is 0). Figure 4 (left) has a seven bit data ring with the id 0100001 in binary or 66 in decimal. In the outer black ring there is a stud pointing up right, and two pointing down left. The studs indicate the rotation of the fiducial and should visually be interpreted as an arrow passing through the fiducial showing the orientation. Hence, both orientation and id are fairly easily human

Figure 4: A BullsEye fiducial (left) and a reacTIVision fiducial (right) (reprinted with permission)

readable. A ring-based shape was chosen as rings—given a center, radius and ring width—are easily identifiable on the GPU with relatively few texture lookups. This is advantageous since texture lookups are expensive operations. BullsEye fiducials are initially found by searching for white dots surrounded by a white ring with a fixed width at a fixed radius. By computing the center of the fiducial, the rotation can be computed by sampling for the position of the three white studs. Finally by knowing the rotation, the id can be read from the data rings in the fiducial.

Grayscale representation

One of the initial steps of the reacTIVision tracking algorithm is to perform binary thresholding on a grayscale version of the input image; given a threshold a grayscale pixel is either made black or white. We want to avoid binarization as it effectively means throwing away information and hereby loosing accuracy (as illustrated in figure 5).

To compute the center of the grayscale represented rectangle in figure 5(b), one can use a average of the center positions of the pixels weighted by their greyscale values, which in perfect conditions would give an accuracy proportional to the bit depth of the greyscale image. In the less than ideal conditions that we have when tracking fiducials on a real table, the grayscale image that we get from the camera image is noisy and influenced by background light and reflections. Noise resulting in a variation at a pixel of only a few grayscale values can through binarization result in a pixel changing from black to white; hereby offsetting the tracked center of a fiducial quite significantly. When computing the center from a weighted average of grayscale values, the same noise of a few grayscale values at a pixel will only have a minimal effect on the tracking. However, different lighting condition across the table can result in an erroneous position when based on a weighted average: If a fiducial is partially in a brighter lit area of a table, the position may be slightly offset towards the brighter lit area.

Similar to reacTIVision, BullsEye compensates for variations in lighting conditions across the table. ReacTIVision uses a snapshot of the background light on an empty table to compute a binarization threshold of the image segmented into 32 by 32 pixel tiles. In BullsEye we normalize the greyscale spectrum *per pixel* through calibration of light. The calibration involves continuously storing the brightest white and darkest black seen at a pixel in a texture and subsequently using that texture as input to a normalization of the grayscale values of the camera image during tracking. The darkest

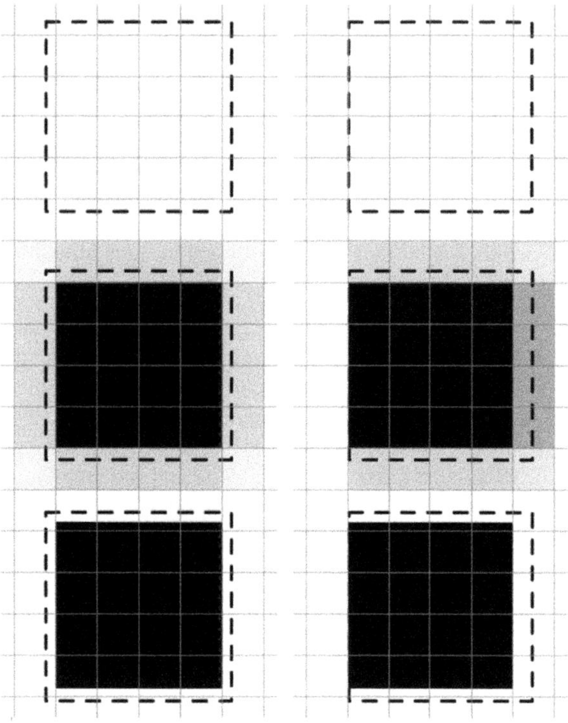

Figure 5: **Top**: The dotted rectangle illustrates how a physical rectangle on a table corresponds to the pixels of the camera image (the background grid). **Center**: Grayscale representation of the camera input. **Bottom**: Binary representation of the camera image. The rectangle has moved approx. a fifth of a pixel from **a** to **b**. Notice how the binary representation stays the same from a to b.

black is provided by an empty table, while the brightest white can be provided by moving a white object across the whole area of the table. The grayscale calibration texture for a table with two cameras can be seen in figure 9.

The result is that in BullsEye we can rely on computing weighted averages, hence achieving sub-pixel precision with a high noise tolerance.

Compensation for optical distortion

Similar to reacTIVision, BullsEye uses a printed calibration grid as input to the geometry calibration, but the alignment to the grid is automated rather than manual. The BullsEye calibration grid (Figure 7) consists of black dots in a uniform grid on a white background. By tracking the location of the black dots in the uniform grid on the printed sheet a position mapping texture can be produced that subsequently is used to correct the image from the camera.

The position mapping texture is computed in four steps implemented as a CPU algorithm: In the first step the user is prompted to click on a part of the input image showing the grid. We now perform a calibration of light where we search for the darkest and lightest spots on the image in a predefined area surrounding the user's click. This calibration is

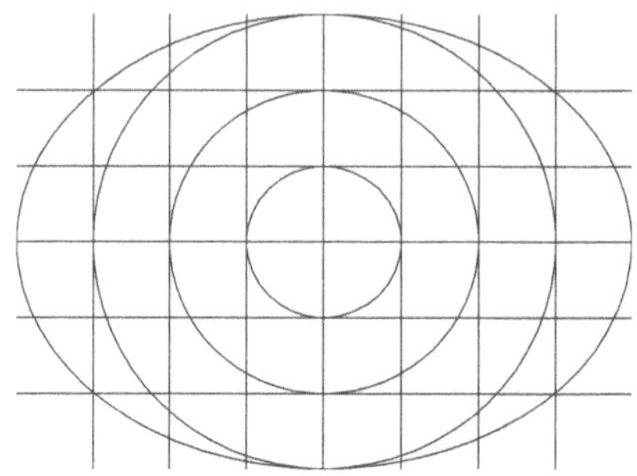

Figure 6: reacTIVision's geometry calibration grid

Figure 7: BullsEye's geometry calibration grid

used to compute a binarization threshold of the image to distinguish dots from the white background. In the second step we perform a blob extraction to track all the black dots on the printed grid. We apply a blob extraction algorithm inspired by connected-component labeling [6]. In step three we iterate through all the extracted blobs and for each blob we search for its immediate neighbor blobs to the left, right, top and bottom. We can now store the average distance between blobs and produce a data structure representing a uniform virtual grid of dots, where each dot stores its corresponding position in the original image. This grid may not cover the whole input image, or there may be holes in the grid. To compensate for this, the user can choose to automatically expand the grid. Through interpolating between the positions of neighboring blobs in the virtual grid we in step four generate a mapping texture. For each pixel corresponding to a pixel in a distortion corrected image, the mapping texture stores the position of where the pixel value should be looked up in the original camera input. The distortion corrected image can be combined from multiple camera inputs, hence the origin of the virtual grid is user configurable. The mapping texture is used as input to the shaders in the rendering pipeline as described below.

Tracking implementation

BullsEye does realtime image processing using shaders on the GPU to manipulate images in realtime. The core of the tracking algorithm in BullsEye is implemented as subsequent shaders in a rendering pipeline. BullsEye is implemented in Java and the OpenGL Shader Language [16].

Pixel shaders are pieces of code executed per pixel on an output texture. For each pixel the shader can sample in one or more input textures to produce the output color of the pixel.

Figure 8 illustrates the shader steps involved in the rendering pipeline of BullsEye. The input texture to the first shader

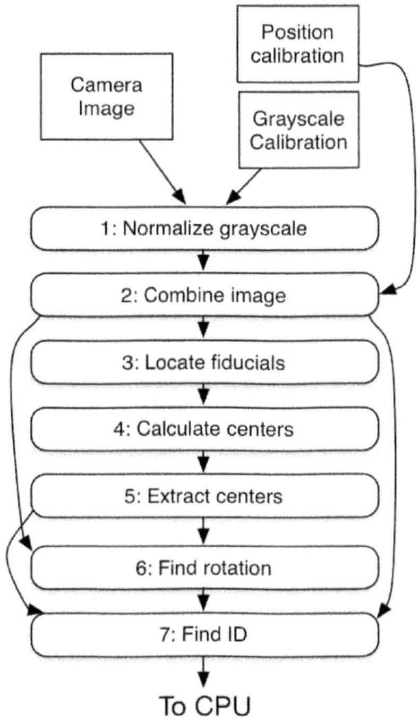

Figure 8: BullsEye's shader steps

Normalize Grayscale is the image from the camera converted to grayscale and the texture representing the grayscale calibration. Each pixel is normalized given the maximum and minimum light levels recorded in the calibration. Shader 2 combines the normalized images from one or more cameras into a combined image based on the per-camera distortion correction mapping texture which contains information about where a given pixel from the source image should be mapped to in the combined image. When combining camera inputs, overlap is handled by only using the input from one of the cameras in the overlapping area. The actual textures involved in the first two shader steps in a setup with a large table with two cameras is shown in figure 9.

To locate a BullsEye fiducial, shader 3 outputs the likelihood that a pixel contains the center of a fiducial. This is done by sampling at known distances in a circle around the given pixel and computing a color difference between what should be black and what should be white if the pixel contained the fiducial center; if we assume a pixel is the centre, we know the distance to the rings comprising the BullsEye fiducial and can compute and average difference between what should be black and what should be white. Listing 1 shows pseudocode for the BullsEye implementation of shader step 3. The output of this shader is a texture where the red color intensity represents the likelihood of the pixel being the center of a fiducial. The pixel with the highest red color intensity is assumed to contain the center of the fiducial. An input as shown in figure 10 (left) will produce an output as shown in figure 10 (right). The blue component represents the accumulated color difference in the outer white ring and inner black ring, and is used to filter off false positives.

Listing 1: Pseudo-code for locating fiducials (shader 3). *Input*: Combined and normalized image ($combinedTexture$) and the current texture coordinates ($textureCoords$). The constant $RADIUS$ is the radius to the outer edge of the outer white ring which is given through user configuration, and the constant $RING\_WIDTH$ is the width of a ring. *Output*: Likelihood of pixels containing the center of a fiducial

```
texColor = combinedTexture.colorAt(textureCoords)

if texColor.red < THRESHOLD:
  return BLACK
else:
  outsideSampleRadius = RADIUS + RING_WIDTH / 2
  outerSampleRingRadius = RADIUS - RING_WIDTH / 2
  innerSampleRingRadius = RING_WIDTH

  totalColor = totalCenterDifference = 0
  previousCenterColor = combinedTexture.colorAt(
      textureCoords + innerSampleRingRadius).red
  previousOutsideColor = combinedTexture.colorAt(
      textureCoords + RADIUS * RING_WIDTH * 1.5).red

  for i = 0; i<32; i++:
    radians = i * (2.0 * PI) / 32;
    dirVector = (cos(radians) * (1 / combinedTexture.size.
        x), sin(radians) * (1 / combinedTexture.size.y))

    outside = textureCoords + outsideSampleRadius *
        dirVector
    outerRing = textureCoords + outerSampleRingRadius *
        dirVector
    innerRing = textureCoords + innerSampleRingRadius *
        dirVector

    outSideColor = combinedTexture.colorAt(outside).red
    outermostColor = combinedTexture.colorAt(outerRing).
        red
    innermostColor = combinedTexture.colorAt(innerRing).
        red

    totalColor += min(outermostColor - outsideColor,
        texColor.red - innermostColor)
    totalCenterDifference += abs(innermostColor -
        previousCenterColor)+abs(outsideColor-
        previousOutsideColor)
    previousCenterColor = innermostColor
    previousOutsideColor = outsideColor
  totalColor /= 32
  totalCenterDifference /= 32

  return (max(totalColor, 0), 0, totalCenterDifference)
```

Shader 4 samples the center likelihood texture produced by shader 3 in an area around the given pixel coordinates and computes an average center position weighted by the likelihood value of the sampled pixels. If a sampled pixel has a higher center likelihood than the pixel at the given coordinates in the likelihood texture, the output pixel at those coordinates will be black. This way the output texture will contain only one pixel with color per tracked fiducial, where the color represents the center position of the fiducial[4]. Listing 2 shows the pseudocode for shader 4. The result of shader 4 is a primarily black texture. In the example of figure 9 shader 4 would produce a very large texture with just 8 pixels actually containing relevant information.

[4]In the unlikely situation that two pixels have the exact same floating point likelihood value, a filtering ensuring that no fiducials overlap will be applied on the CPU at a later stage.

Listing 2: Shader 4 pseudo-code. *Input*: Center likelihood texture ($likelihoodTexture$) and the current texture coordinates ($textureCoords$). Output: a texture with centers of fiducials in sub-pixel precision.

```
texColor = likelihoodTexture.colorAt(textureCoords)

circleLikeliness = texColor.red
edgeDiff = texColor.blue

if circleLikeliness <= CIRCLE_LIKELINESS_THRESHOLD ||
     edgeDiff >= FALSE_POSITIVE_FILTER_THRESHOLD:
       return BLACK
else
  pixelSize = 1 / likelihoodTexture.size
  position = vec2D(0.0,0.0)
  totalSum = 0

  for y = -SEARCH_AREA; y <= SEARCH_AREA; y++:
    for x = -SEARCH_AREA; x <= SEARCH_AREA; x++
      sampleCoord = textureCoord + vec2D(x , y) *
           pixelSize
      sampleColor = max(0, likelihoodTexture.colorAt(
           sampleCoord).red)

      if sampleColor > circleLikeliness:
        return BLACK

      position += samplePosition * sampleColor
      totalSum += sampleColor

  position /= totalSum
  totalSum /= pow(2.0 * SEARCH_AREA + 1.0, 2.0)

  return (position.x, position.y, totalSum);
```

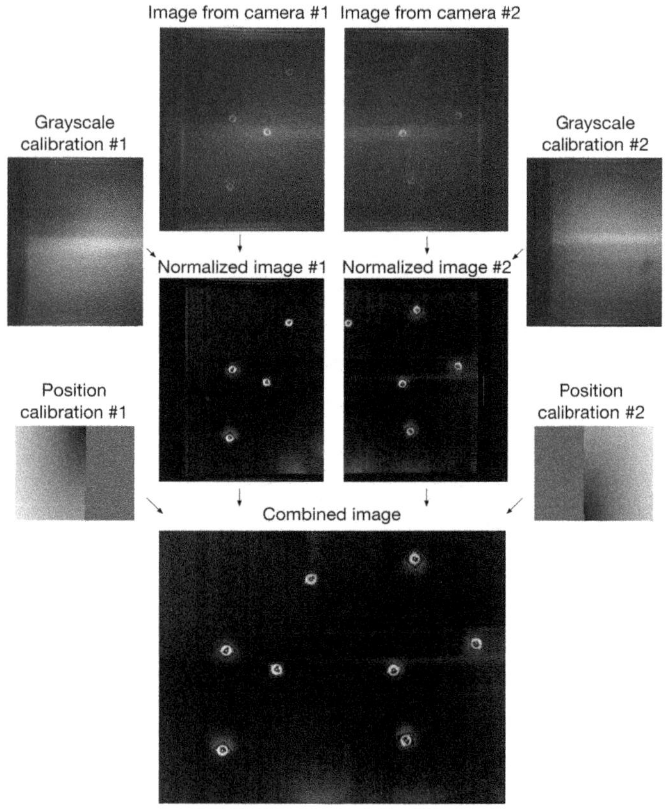

Figure 9: BullsEye's initial image processing

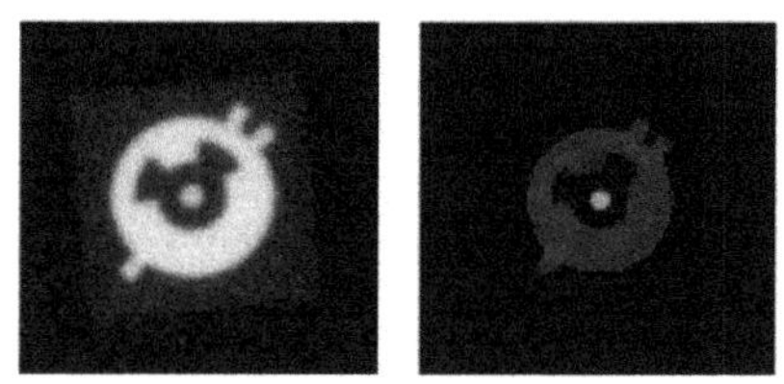

Figure 10: BullsEye's circletracking

As an optimization we apply a geometry shader in shader step 5 to compress the full sized texture produced by shader 4. The compressed output texture contains a block representation of the whole surface. Each row of pixels in the output texture represents a block of 64x64 pixels of the input texture and stores the position of up to eight fiducial centers contained in the block. Color values represent the coordinates of the fiducial centers. Therefore, for an input texture of 1024x768 pixels, the compressed texture will be 192x8 pixels, hence making the subsequent shader steps significantly faster. The maximum of eight centers per block is set to reflect the physical limitations of how many fiducials that can be placed within the area corresponding to 64x64 pixels in the camera image.

Given the centers from shader 5, the rotations are found by sampling the the block representation of the centers and the combined image from shader 2. The output of shader 6 is a block representation like that of shader 5 but containing orientations. This shader step is the most computationally intensive step, but the computations are only performed on pixels representing a fiducial. To compute the orientation a coarse estimate is found by iterating a full circle in 256 steps, and for each iteration computing a likelihood score for the given angle being the approximate orientation of the fiducial. The likelihood score is computed as the difference between the color where the white studs should be and the outer black ring. Given the coarse estimate a precise orientation is computed by iterating 20 degrees around the coarse estimate in 100 steps and computing an average weighted by the orientation likelihood at each step. Listing 3 shows the pseudocode for this shader step. The rotation could in principle be computed from a single stud, however, we opted for the fiducial design with multiple studs to increase accuracy and noise tolerance.

The final shader 7 can use the centers, rotations and the combined image to find the id of a fiducial and output a texture encoding positions, rotation and ids of fiducials.

The resulting texture is extracted to the CPU, where it is parsed and filtering and stabilization is performed. Finally the tracking data is translated to TUIO events [12] and emitted to a given application hostname and port.

BullsEye User Interface

BullsEye features a user interface that enables real-time tweaking of the parameters of the tracking (Figure 11). Furthermore the user interface allows for easy calibration of both light and geometry. Input from multiple cameras can be com-

Listing 3: Shader 7 pseudo-code. Input: Extracted centers and combined, normalized image. Output: Rotations of fiducials in sub-pixel precision.

```
center = texture.colorAt(textureCoords)

function getOrientationLikeliness(radians, center):
  /* Sample color in combined texture at front stud,
       besides front stud, at the two back studs and
       between the back studs relative to given radians
       and center */

  return min(frontStudColor - besidesFrontStudColor, (
       backStud1Color+backStud2Color)/2.0 -
       betweenBackStudsColor)

//Get a course orientation estimate
maxLikeliness = 0
bestRotation = 0
for int i = 0; i<256; i++:
  radians = i * (2.0 * PI) / 256
  likeliness = getOrientationLikeliness(radians, center)

  if currentValue > maxValue:
    maxLikeliness = likeliness
    bestRotation = rotation

//Find precise orientation
startRadians = bestRotation - 10 * (180/PI)
endRadians = bestRotation + 10 * (180/PI)

for float r = startRadians; r < endRadians; r+= (2.0 * PI)
     / 100:
  likeliness = getOrientationLikeliness(r, center)
  rotationWeightedSum += r * likeliness
  totalLikeliness += likeliness

weightedRotationAverage = rotationWeightedSum /
     totalLikeliness

return (weightedRotationAverage, 0, 0)
```

bined and their placement in relation to each other can be configured visually.

Limitations

BullsEye requires that the tag size is known, and it only operates with a single tag size at a time. ReacTIVision is agnostic towards tag size because of its topological fiducial recognition algorithm. It is possible to extend the BullsEye algorithm with support for multiple tag sizes. This would require the different supported tag sizes to be specified through configuration. Multiple tag sizes would have a drawback on performance since each tracking step using the tag size as input would have to be repeated per different tag size.

BullsEye employs a geometry shader for one of the shader steps, and only graphics cards supporting Open GL 3.2 or newer has support for geometry shaders. This leaves out running BullsEye on a credit-card computer such as the Raspberry Pi, but it will run on most popular integrated graphics cards such as the Intel HD Graphics series[5].

EXPERIMENTAL EVALUATION

In order to provide a ground truth for the positions and rotations of fiducials, we simulated a camera input where we could control the position of a fiducial. In order to compare the precision of BullsEye with reacTIVision we generated videos for both types of fiducials. Figure 12 shows a snapshot of the video with a BullsEye fiducial. These videos were fed to reacTIVision and BullsEye as were they input from a camera.

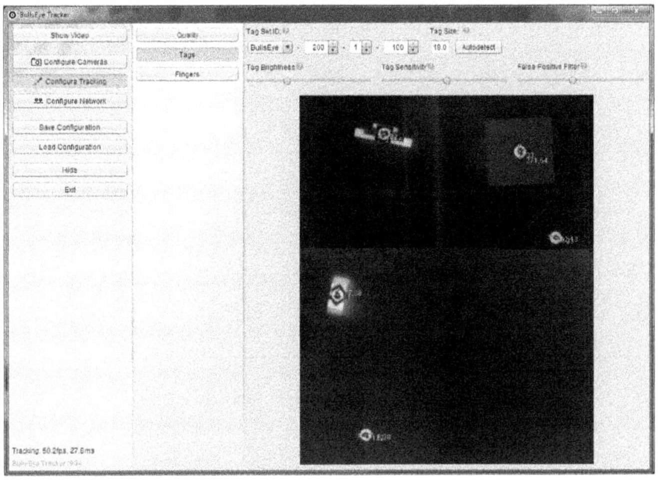

Figure 11: The user interface for BullsEye showing configuration options for fiducial tracking.

Figure 12: Snapshot from simulated camera input for BullsEye.

The videos were generated using Blender[6]. In Blender we modeled a 3D scene consisting of a camera placed below a flat surface together with two light sources. On the flat surface we placed a rectangle with a fiducial texture, and animated the fiducial diagonally across the table on a known path with a fixed rotation. The animation consisted of 600 frames over a period of 30 seconds (20 frames per second). The videos were generated with a resolution of 1280x1024 pixels.

We furthermore generated a video where the fiducial was shrunk over time, to provide data on how small a fiducial BullsEye and reacTIVision are capable of tracking[7].

To simulate an image from a real camera we added random noise and warped the geometry based on a lens profile from a

[5] `http://www.intel.com/support/graphics/sb/CS-033757.htm`

[6] `http://www.blender.org`

[7] For BullsEye we manually reconfigured the size of fiducials per frame.

Attribute	Mean	Standard deviation	Maximum
X	$0.37px$	$0.3px$	$1.28px$
Y	$1.35px$	$0.76px$	$2.9px$
Rotation	0.54°	0.31°	1.32°

Table 1: reacTIVision Absolute Error

Attribute	Mean	Standard deviation	Maximum
X	$0.08px$	$0.06px$	$0.29px$
Y	$0.07px$	$0.05px$	$0.27px$
Rotation	0.12°	0.09°	0.48°

Table 2: BullsEye Absolute Error

real camera[8]. When rendering the video from the 3D scene, the output was anti-aliased using a Mitchell-Netravali [14] filter.

To calibrate reacTIVision we used a simulated video input showing the reacTIVision calibration grid. The calibration of reacTIVision was done manually with our best possible efforts. To calibrate BullsEye we similarly used a simulated video input showing the BullsEye calibration grid, and let BullsEye calibrate automatically. The black calibration was performed with a simulated video showing an empty table, and for the white calibration a pure white rectangle was inserted on top of the table in the 3D scene.

In order to provide a fair comparison between the tracking of reacTIVision and BullsEye, we disabled a post-tracking stabilization step in the reacTIVision code that would filter out sub-pixel changes to a tracked fiducial position and rotation changes below three degrees.

Results

Figures 14, 13, and 15 show the error rates of reacTIVision and BullsEye for X-coordinates in pixels, Y-coordinates in pixels and rotation in degrees, respectively.

Table 1 shows statistics for the absolute error rates of reacTIVision, while table 2 show the statistics for BullsEye.

We see that BullsEye on average provides subpixel precision down to below a tenth of a pixel, and the maximum error rate measured were below a third of a pixel. The error rate of rotation is down to around a tenth of a degree in average with a maximum of half a degree.

Compared to reacTIVision, BullsEye is significantly more accurate with a 5 times more accurate average X-coordinate tracking, a 20 times more accurate average Y-coordinate tracking, and on average 4.5 times more accurate rotation tracking. Furthermore, the standard deviations in the error rates of BullsEye are significantly lower than those of reacTIVision.

[8]We used the lens profile from a Sony E-mount 18-200mm f/3.5-6.3 zoom lens.

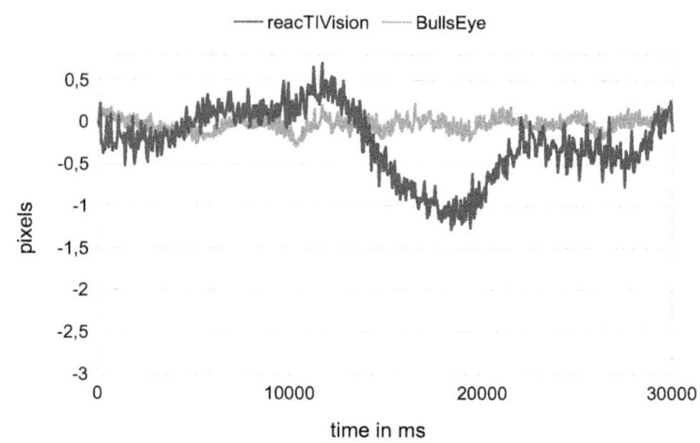

Figure 13: X-Coordinate error

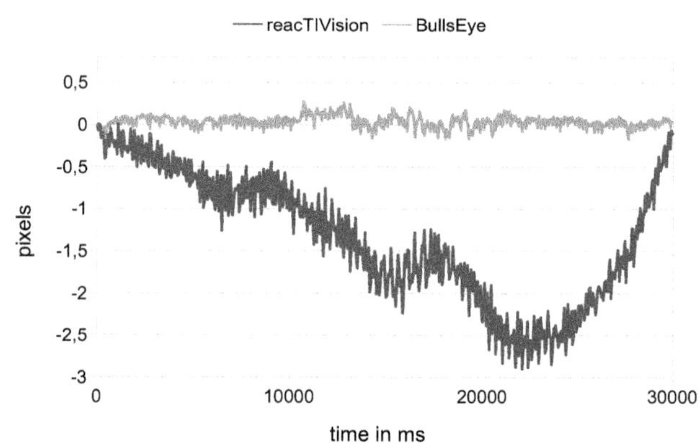

Figure 14: Y-Coordinate error

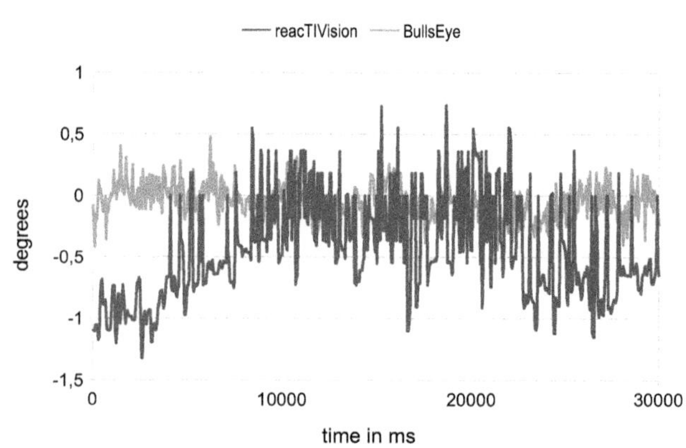

Figure 15: Rotation error

When tracking shrinking tags BullsEye lost tracking of a fiducial when the size of the fiducial (including padding) got below 29 pixels in diagonal size. This corresponds to 1.9% of the table diagonal or 2.4cm in diagonal on a 100 times 80 cm table. In comparison reacTIVision lost tracking of a fiducial when the size got below 57.3 pixels in diagonal which corresponds to 4.7 cm a similar sized table. It should be noted that reacTIVision in our initial measurements could track fiducial sizes equally as small as BullsEye. This, however, was a result of reacTIVision assuming that if it detects anything at the same location in consecutive frames it has the same id.

Discussion

In the generated video we used a standard 16:9 aspect ratio. This means that the resolution of Y-coordinates is almost half the resolution of X-coordinates. Our data therefore indicates that BullsEye is significantly more accurate on lower resolutions than reacTIVision. This may be attributed to a combination of a more inaccurate calibration of reacTIVision at lower resolutions, and that the effects of binarization are emphasized at lower resolutions.

The measurements of the X and Y coordinates are taken as the fiducials moved diagonally across the surfaces of the table. Curves in the coordinate plot therefore implies inadequate compensation for optical distortion. It is notable that the BullsEye plots of the X and Y coordinates do not curve like the reacTIVision plots do. The error rates of reacTIVision are products of the tracking algorithm combined with the less than optimal lens distortion calibration. An inaccurate calibration can explain the curves in the plots of the error rates for reacTIVision. Given a perfect geometric calibration of reacTIVision, which in theory should remove the curves in the error rates, the overall amplitude of the error rate in BullsEye would still be significantly lower than reacTIVision's.

The presented results are products of a simulated video input. We were not able to provide a ground truth for computing absolute error rates for tracking on a real video input. We have, however, observed similar improvements in relative tracking accuracy from reacTIVision to BullsEye by tracking on real video from one of our tabletops as those we see on our simulated input. Here a reacTIVision and BullsEye fiducial was placed side-by-side on a single tangible that was then moved across the tabletop.

EXPERIENCES AND PERFORMANCE

Besides being used in numerous research prototypes and student projects BullsEye has been used for two full scale tangible 3D tabletop installations deployed in the wild: Tangible Urban Planning demonstrates how tangible 3D tabletops can support collaborative activities in urban planning and development projects [5] (figure 16, top). Projected Play is a tangible 3D tabletop installation developed for LEGO World, a four-day in-door entertainment held in the city of Copenhagen and attracting more than 40.000 visitors in 2013 [9] (figure 16, bottom left). BullsEye has also been used for more traditional tangible tabletop applications such as the RADAR Table (figure 16, bottom right); a tangible music interface recently deployed at the 2011 SPOT music festival in Aarhus, Denmark, as well as been presented at numerous conventions and conferences [10].

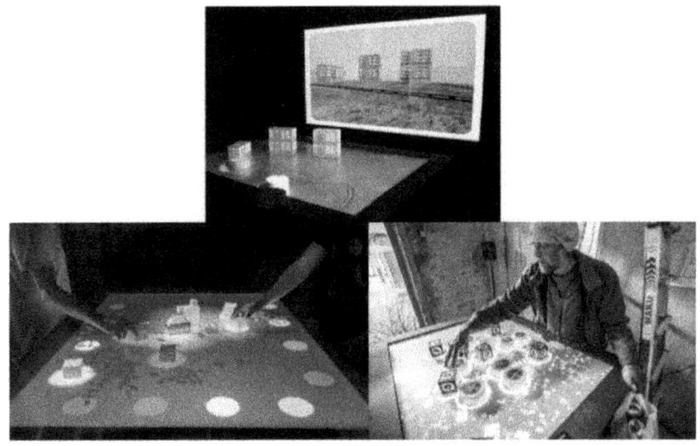

Figure 16: Examples of projects using BullsEye: Tangible Urban Planning (top), Projected Play (bottom left) and the RADAR table (bottom right).

We have used BullsEye for multiple different sized tabletops, both small with a single camera for tracking and larger with two cameras. We have implemented a PixelSense driver for BullsEye and installed BullsEye on our lab's Samsung SUR40 table. While we haven't been able to perform a similar comparison with the PixelSense tracking using simulated input as we did with reacTIVision, our experience is that the tracking on the SUR40 when using BullsEye is more accurate, and more robust to changing light conditions.

We have not performed a systematic evaluation of the performance of BullsEye. However, we have not experienced that BullsEye is a performance bottleneck in our tangible 3D tabletops. The largest interactive table of our lab uses two 50 frames per second input cameras with a combined resolution of 2560 by 1024 pixels. Running on a consumer grade PC[9], BullsEye can easily keep up with the input from the cameras (i.e. perform the tracking within 20 ms). We have had more than 100 fiducials placed simultaneously on this particular table without any significant decrease in tracking performance.

RELATED WORK

Improving the precision of fiducial tracking for interactive tabletops has not gained significant interest. However, some improvements of the original reacTIVision algorithm have been proposed. Topolo Surface [15] combines the topological approach of D-Touch [3] and reacTIVision [11] with an angle based encoding of fiducial IDs. The primary goal is to simplify the fiducial generation, allow for a wider ID range, and to encode checksums of IDs in the fiducials. The angle based encoding of fiducial IDs is similar to the one in BullsEye, and BullsEye could easily be extended with checksums on fiducial IDs. Topolo Surface is CPU based, and relies on a binarization step similar to that of reacTIVision. Unfortunately the paper does not evaluate the precision of the tracking, nor is the software available for comparison.

[9] Intel Core i7-3770 3.4GHz CPU, Nvidia GeForce GTX680 GPU and 4gb RAM

LightTracker [8] is a software framework for manipulating the image-processing pipeline at runtime particularly designed for touch, but can be extended for fiducial tracking as well (e.g. by integrating libfidtrack from reacTIVision). LightTracker provides a manual calibration with some attention to possible lens distortion. The light calibration technique of LightTracker is based on a similar idea to the one applied on BullsEye using an intensity map. The tracking in LightTracker is CPU based, although designed to exploit multiple threads to increase performance.

Fiducial tracking is not only used for tangible tabletops, but central in augmented reality [1] as well [13, 7]. For augmented reality, fiducials must be tracked in three dimensions with a movable camera, hence the tracking algorithm is quite different as for tabletop tracking and must compute distance to fiducials and their rotation in an extra dimension. Shibata and Yamamoto [17] demonstrate how to achieve subpixel precision in tracking fiducials for augmented reality using edge detection on the GPU. The paper benchmarks against the tracking in ARToolkit [13], and achieves similar improvements in precision as when we compare BullsEye to reacTIVision.

CONCLUSION

In this paper we have presented a series of techniques for improving the precision of optical fiducial tracking on tangible tabletops implemented as part of the BullsEye computer vision software. We have demonstrated that subpixel precision down to a tenth of a pixel can be achieved through a combination of a GPU based tracking algorithm, a fiducial design optimized for GPU tracking, a calibration of light allowing for computation on grayscale values and an automated technique for compensating for optical distortions in camera lenses.

ACKNOWLEDGEMENTS

We thank the staff at CAVI: Jonas Oxenbøll Petersen for work on the applications of BullsEye, and Peter Friis for his hardware expertise. We thank Henrik Korsgaard and Brian Bunch Christensen for comments and critique. This research has been supported by the interdisciplinary research center for Participatory IT at Aarhus University.

REFERENCES

1. Azuma, R. T., et al. A survey of augmented reality. *Presence 6*, 4 (1997), 355–385.
2. Bencina, R., Kaltenbrunner, M., and Jorda, S. Improved topological fiducial tracking in the reactivision system. In *Computer Vision and Pattern Recognition-Workshops, 2005. CVPR Workshops. IEEE Computer Society Conference on*, IEEE (2005), 99–99.
3. Costanza, E., Shelley, S. B., and Robinson, J. D-touch: A consumer-grade tangible interface module and musical applications. In *Proceedings of Conference on Human-Computer Interaction (HCI03)*, Springer (2003).
4. Dalsgaard, P., and Halskov, K. Tangible 3d tabletops: combining tangible tabletop interaction and 3d projection. In *Proceedings of the 7th Nordic Conference on Human-Computer Interaction: Making Sense Through Design*, ACM (2012), 109–118.
5. Dalsgaard, P., and Halskov, K. Tangible 3d tabletops. *interactions 21*, 5 (2014), 42–47.
6. Dillencourt, M. B., Samet, H., and Tamminen, M. A general approach to connected-component labeling for arbitrary image representations. *J. ACM 39*, 2 (Apr. 1992), 253–280.
7. Fiala, M. Artag, a fiducial marker system using digital techniques. In *Computer Vision and Pattern Recognition, 2005. CVPR 2005. IEEE Computer Society Conference on*, vol. 2, IEEE (2005), 590–596.
8. Gokcezade, A., Leitner, J., and Haller, M. Lighttracker: An open-source multitouch toolkit. *Computers in Entertainment (CIE) 8*, 3 (2010), 19.
9. Halskov, K., Dalsgaard, P., and Stolzes, L. Analysing engaging experiences with a tangible 3d tabletop. In *Proceedings of Advances in Computer Entertainment (ACE) 2014 (to appear)*, ACM (2014).
10. Hansen, N. B., and Halskov, K. Material interactions with tangible tabletops: a pragmatist perspective. In *Proceedings of the 8th Nordic Conference on Human-Computer Interaction (to appear)*, ACM (2014).
11. Kaltenbrunner, M., and Bencina, R. reactivision: a computer-vision framework for table-based tangible interaction. In *Proceedings of the 1st international conference on Tangible and embedded interaction*, ACM (2007), 69–74.
12. Kaltenbrunner, M., Bovermann, T., Bencina, R., and Costanza, E. Tuio: A protocol for table-top tangible user interfaces. In *Proc. of the The 6th Int'l Workshop on Gesture in Human-Computer Interaction and Simulation* (2005).
13. Kato, H., and Billinghurst, M. Marker tracking and hmd calibration for a video-based augmented reality conferencing system. In *Augmented Reality, 1999.(IWAR'99) Proceedings. 2nd IEEE and ACM International Workshop on*, IEEE (1999), 85–94.
14. Mitchell, D. P., and Netravali, A. N. Reconstruction filters in computer-graphics. In *ACM Siggraph Computer Graphics*, vol. 22, ACM (1988), 221–228.
15. Nishino, H. Topolo surface: A 2d fiducial tracking system based on topological region adjacency and angle information. *Journal of Information Processing 18* (February 2010), 16–25.
16. Rost, R. J. *OpenGL shading language*. Addison-Wesley Professional, 2004.
17. Shibata, N., and Yamamoto, S. Gpgpu-assisted subpixel tracking method for fiducial markers. *Journal of Information Processing 22*, 1 (2014), 19–28.
18. Wang, S., Bevans, A., and Antle, A. N. Stitchrv: multi-camera fiducial tracking. In *Proceedings of the fourth international conference on Tangible, embedded, and embodied interaction*, ACM (2010), 287–290.

An Interaction Model for Grasp-Aware Tangibles on Interactive Surfaces

Simon Voelker[1] Christian Corsten[1] Nur Al-huda Hamdan[1] Kjell Ivar Øvergård[2] Jan Borchers[1]
[1]RWTH Aachen University; Aachen, Germany; {voelker, corsten, hamdan, borchers}@cs.rwth-aachen.de
[2]Buskerud and Vestfold University College; Tønsberg, Norway; koe@hbv.no

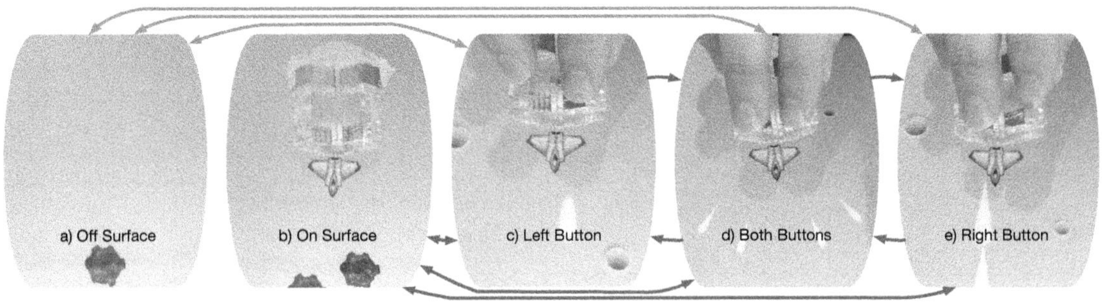

Figure 1. Interaction stages for a grasp-aware tangible space ship for an iPad game: The space ship is off surface (a) and not detected until the user places it on surface (b). When touching the left "button" (c) the ship shoots from the left, whereas adding the right finger fires from both sides (d). When releasing the left finger, only the right "button" is touched, thus shooting from the right. Releasing the finger results in (b) again.

ABSTRACT
Tangibles on interactive surfaces enable users to physically manipulate digital content by placing, manipulating, or removing a tangible object. However, the information *whether* and *how* a user grasps these objects has not been mapped out for tangibles on interactive surfaces so far. Based on Buxton's Three-State Model for graphical input, we present an interaction model that describes input on tangibles that are aware of the user's grasp. We present two examples showing how the user benefits from this extended interaction model. Furthermore, we show how the interaction with other existing tangibles for interactive tabletops can be modeled.

Author Keywords
Tangibles; Interaction Model; Interactive Surfaces

ACM Classification Keywords
H5.2 [Information interfaces and presentation]: User Interfaces. - Input Devices and Strategies.

INTRODUCTION
Tangibles on interactive surfaces [5] bring physical interaction to the user by addressing the haptic sense, exploiting physical affordances, and enabling eyes-free interaction [17]. They can serve as direct physical representations of digital objects [14], or as generic tools to physically manipulate any content [17]. When interacting with a tangible, the user necessarily grasps it—when placing the tangible object on the surface or right before and while manipulating it. Research on tangibles that are *not* used on interactive surfaces shows that the information whether and how a tangible is grasped can be used to enrich the expressiveness of tangible interaction: Touché [13], for example, augments a door knob with a grasp password by analyzing how the user grasps the knob, and HandSense [19] uses capacitive sensors to recognize whether an object is being held in the left or right hand. However, for tangibles on interactive surfaces, the design space for grasp has not been mapped out yet.

Our contribution is an extension of Buxton's interaction model [3] to characterize the state of grasp-aware tangibles on interactive surfaces. This model benefits designers to design, describe, and compare grasp-aware tangibles. We show how our model can be used to capture the interaction with existing tangibles and how grasp information can enrich the expressiveness of tangible interaction, e.g., as shown in Fig. 1.

ITS'14, November 16–19, 2014, Dresden, Germany.

http://dx.doi.org/10.1145/2669485.2669494

RELATED WORK
In [3], Buxton presents a Three-State Model for input devices, such as mouse, touch screen, and puck or stylus on a tablet. The model represents all possible interaction states of each device: an input device that has no effect on the system, such as a puck that is not in contact with the tablet surface yet, is considered in State 0 (*Out of Range*). The system starts detecting the puck in State 1 (*Tracking*) when the puck touches

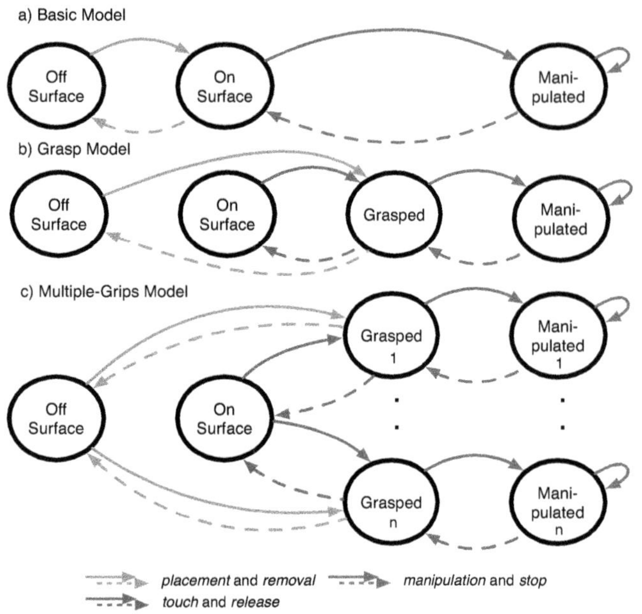

Figure 2. Consecutive tangible interaction models. (a) generalization of Buxton's Three-State Model to tangibles on interactive surfaces, (b) including *whether* and (c) *how* it is grasped and manipulated.

the tablet and is moved across the surface. When physical manipulation is involved, such as pushing a button on the puck, the device enters State 2 (*Dragging*).

This model enables designers to choose a suitable input device for an application or task, and to compare different input states. For example, Patten and Ishii [9] used Buxton's model to compare mouse input in a graphical user interface (GUI) with non-manipulable tangibles in a tangible user interface (TUI). Similarly, Bricks [5] and Urp [14] follow this model.

Buxton's model has been modified and extended to capture new strategies for touch input on interactive surfaces. Benko et al. [1] distinguished State 1 and 2 for finger input on touch screens by taking the size of a touch into consideration. Richter et al. [12] added a fourth state to Buxton's model to capture pressure input on pressure-sensitive touch screens.

INTERACTION MODEL

Fig. 2.a shows our basic model for tangibles on interactive surfaces, an adaptation of Buxton's Three-State Model for a puck on a tablet. When the tangible is *Off Surface*, it has no effect on the system until the user places it *On Surface*. As long as the tangible rests on the surface, the *On Surface* state is retained. When the user physically manipulates the tangible, it reaches the third state, *Manipulated*.

A manipulation can be translating the tangible [14], translating parts of the tangible [17], or transforming the tangible. Each of these manipulations is modeled as an individual *Manipulated* state. For example, the SLAP knob [17] has two *Manipulated* states, one for moving the tangible and one for rotating the knob. When manipulation stops, the tangible returns to the *On Surface* state until the user removes the tangible from the surface or manipulates it again.

However, before the user can manipulate a tangible, she needs to grasp it with her hands. Wimmer [19] has shown that such grasp information can be used as additional input for grasp-aware tangibles. Yet, this information has not been modeled for tangibles on interactive surfaces so far. By adding a separate *Grasped* state to our model, we will explain how grasp information can extend the interaction of tangibles on interactive surfaces. For simplicity and to avoid confusion, in this paper we refer to any direct contact between a user's fingers and a tangible as a grasp.

Grasping the Tangible

Using a basic model (Fig. 2.a) as a starting point for tangible interaction on interactive surfaces, we add a separate *Grasped* state that is reached when the user grasps the tangible—prior to placing, manipulating, or removing it from the surface. By adding this state, we derive two consecutive models which we refer to as *Grasp Model* and *Multi-Grip-Model*.

Grasp Model

The first extension is a single *Grasped* state that models whether the user is grasping a tangible or not (Fig. 2.b). This binary distinction can be used as a quasimode [10] or to trigger a transcendent action that stops as soon as the tangible is not grasped anymore. One example application that adheres to this model is to display additional tooltip information around a tangible while it is being grasped, as we show in our sample applications.

We include this *Grasped* state in the model based on the observation that each action in the basic model requires the user to grasp the tangible. While *placing* the tangible on the surface, the user stays in contact with it. Therefore, *placing* results in the *Grasped* state. When *releasing* the tangible, the state changes to *On Surface* until the user grasps the tangible, which necessarily involves *grasping* it, therefore leading back to the *Grasped* state. The tangible stays in this *Grasped* state until the user *manipulates* it. When manipulation stops, the user is still in contact with the tangible, therefore the *Grasped* state is re-entered. As *removing* the tangible from the surface is inverse to *placing* it, the *Off Surface* state is only reached via the preceding *Grasped* state.

In our model, any grasp interaction on the tangible's surface, such as tapping or sliding with a finger, is considered a sequence of grasps and therefore modeled by one or more *Grasped* states. Any physical manipulation on or with the tangible, such as exerting pressure or moving the object, however, is defined as manipulation, therefore, modeled by a *Manipulated* state(s).

However, some manipulations do not require the user to keep grasping the tangible to manipulate it, e.g., when flicking a tangible. If these manipulations stop without the user touching the tangible, it changes its state directly from *Manipulated* to *On Surface*. Furthermore, actuated tangibles such as Madgets [16] can be manipulated without the user touching them. These tangibles can transition from the *On Surface* state directly to the *Manipulated* state, that describes the actuated manipulation, and back. This can be achieved by simply adding the corresponding transitions.

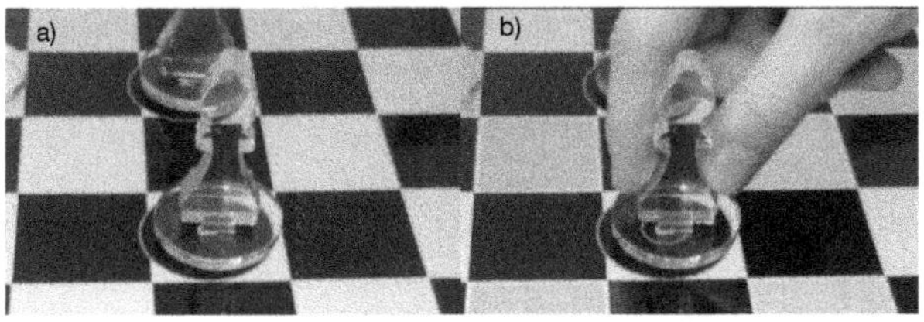

Figure 3. ***Grasp-Model*** **example:(a) A chess piece placed on a multi-touch surface. (b) By grasping a chess piece, the user is shown where he can move the playing piece (green squares) and where the piece can be hit by his opponent (red squares).**

Multi-Grip Model

So far, our model is limited to the binary information of *whether* a tangible is grasped or not. To include information about *how* the user is grasping the tangible, we extend the *Grasp* Model by expanding the *Grasped* state to several distinct states (Fig. 2.c).

Knowing how a tangible is grasped can be used to trigger different actions, such as shown in Fig. 1, where different grips are used to fire different projectiles. Leitner et al. [8] suggested that light pressure (acting as a simple grasp) on pressure sensitive tangible buttons, e.g. Geckos, could be reacted upon by showing a tooltip.

In our *Multi-Grip* Model, each different way of how a user could grasp a tangible is represented by its own $Grasped_i$ state (Fig. 2.c). For example, if the Touché [13] door knob can identify ten different grasps, the model would have ten different $Grasped_i$ states. As in the Grasp model, each $Grasped_i$ state is connected to the *Off Surface*, *On Surface*, and *Manipulated* states by the corresponding actions.

In addition, each $Grasped_i$ state can also directly influence the events that are triggered by the *manipulation* of the tangible. To combine the information of grasp and manipulation, each $Grasped_i$ state needs a *manipulation* transition to its own *Manipulated* state (Fig. 2.c). For example, the RGB color picker knob changes each color channel selectively depending on *where* the user grasps the knob while rotating (Video Figure).

In this model, transitions between the *Grasped* or *Manipulated* states are possible if the user is able to change *how* she grasps the tangible without releasing it. However, for visual simplicity, we omitted these transitions in Fig. 2.c.

APPLYING THE MODEL

In this section we explore the applicability of our model by providing three interaction design examples and an overview how other existing tangibles can be modeled. In both *Grasp Model* and (*Multi-Grip Model*) examples we used a combination of the PUCs marker setup by Voelker et al. [15] and a technique introduced by Rekimoto [11] to detect *whether* and *how* a tangible is touched on a capacitive touch display.

Grasp Model: Tutorial on Demand

In GUIs, tooltips provide help on demand without cluttering the screen. Using the new *Grasped* state, we can bring this principle to TUIs.

Tangible	Off-Surface	On-Surface	Grasped	Manipulated
SLAP Knob	1	1	–	2
Madgets Knob	1	1	–	4
CapWidgets	–	–	1	1
TUIC	–	–	1	1
Geckos	1	1	many	1
CapStones	–	–	1	1
Papillion	1	1	many	1

Table 1. Number of states of existing tangibles

Novice chess players are often unsure what moves a particular playing piece allows. To support the player, a tangible chess game on an interactive surface could offer a tutorial mode in which, whenever the player grasps a piece, all possible moves are highlighted on the board. This on-demand display reduces clutter and occlusion problems (Fig. 3.b).

In general, having the tangible react to being grasped can be exploited for quasimodes [10] that are activated prior to when the user manipulates a tangible. The user can safely explore the TUI before actually manipulating objects.

Multi-Grip model: Coarse-to-Fine Video Navigation

For demonstration purposes, we built a multi-granularity video navigation knob whose grasp zones semantically match different user grips (video Fig.). Turning the knob from the top with thumb and index finger (precision grip) results in fine motor adjustments and therefore could map to fine granularity, whereas grasping the tangible with the entire palm would map to coarser control.

This design does not require adding hinged mechanical parts to the tangible, and instead of using one tangible per granularity, it allows to select different granularities using just one physical controller. This simplifies tangible construction, saves space on the interactive surface, and allows the user to switch granularity levels without looking at the knob, e.g., by sliding the hand up and down along the grasp rings (Video Fig.).

Modeling Existing Tangibles

In this section we demonstrate the descriptive and comparative power of our interaction model (Table 1). For example, CapWidgets [7], TUIC [20], Geckos [8], CapStones [4], and Papillion [2] can detect the *Grasped* state, while SLAP [17] tangibles can only detect tangible manipulation. CapWidgets and CapStones cannot detect when a tangible is *On Surface* or *Off Surface* without user grasp and manipulation.

Hennecke et al. [6] designed pressure-sensitive tangibles (NoCs) with optical markers that behave differently when pressure, e.g., by a touch, is exerted or released. Using our model, each NoC marker can be modeled with a single *Grasped* state. When an NoC_i marker is grasped, the tangible enters a $Grasped_i$ state; when the grasp is released, the tangible goes back to the *On Surface* state. Multiple NoC markers on a single tangible can be modeled with an equivalent number of $Grasped_i$ states.

DISCUSSION AND FUTURE WORK

For tangibles whose surface can continuously detect *any* grasp, such as Geckos [8], our model would result in a large set of $Grasped_i$ states. However, many of those graps would be meaningless or are very similar to each other. For example, a knob that is rotated from the top with three fingers, the different angles between the fingers does not matter, all would be the same kind of rotating grasp. Hence, such grasps can be clustered into a single $Grasped_i$ state, therefore reducing the number of states for the corresponding model. This decision has to be made by the designer of the tangible.

As a next step, we could go beyond mere grasp-aware tangibles and expand our model to also include hover-aware tangibles, such as FlyEye [18], that exploit the proximity of a user's finger to the tangible as additional input. A chess piece, e.g., could already inform the user that no movement is possible before the user actually has to grasp it. This, by the way, would help the player follow the World Chess Federation rules, which require the player to move a chess piece once it is grasped.

CONCLUSION

Detecting whether tangibles on interactive surfaces are being grasped or not, and how they are being grasped, expands the design space of possible interactions with this class of user interfaces. We adapted and extended Buxton's well-established Three-State Model to represent these additional states, leading to our *Grasp* and *Multi-Grip* Models. Besides applying our model to existing tangibles for interactive tabletops, we implemented two sample applications to demonstrate the increased richness of interaction when applying our different models. We hope that our model facilitate future research and design in the new space of grasp-aware tangibles.

ACKNOWLEDGMENTS

This work was funded by the German B-IT Foundation, the Norwegian Research Council (project number 217788), and the German Research Foundation (DFG).

REFERENCES

1. Benko, H., Wilson, A. D., and Baudisch, P. Precise Selection Techniques for Multi-touch Screens. In *Proc. CHI '06*, 1263–1272.
2. Brockmeyer, E., Poupyrev, I., and Hudson, S. Papillon: designing curved display surfaces with printed optics. In *Proc. UIST '13*, 457–462.
3. Buxton, W. A Three-State Model of Graphical Input. In *Proc. INTERACT '90*, 449–456.
4. Chan, L., Müller, S., Roudaut, A., and Baudisch, P. CapStones and ZebraWidgets: Sensing Stacks of Building Blocks, Dials and Sliders on Capacitive Touch Screens. In *Proc. CHI '12*, 2189–2192.
5. Fitzmaurice, G. W., Ishii, H., and Buxton, W. A. S. Bricks: Laying the Foundations for Graspable User Interfaces. In *Proc. CHI '95*, 72–79.
6. Hennecke, F., Berwein, F., and Butz, A. Optical pressure sensing for tangible user interfaces. In *Proc. TEI '11*, 45–48.
7. Kratz, S., Westermann, T., Rohs, M., and Essl, G. CapWidgets: Tangible Widgets versus Multi-touch Controls on Mobile Devices. In *Proc. CHI EA '11*, 1351–1356.
8. Leitner, J., and Haller, M. Geckos: Combining Magnets and Pressure Images to Enable New Tangible-Object Design and Interaction. In *Proc. CHI '11*, 2985–2994.
9. Patten, J., and Ishii, H. A Comparison of Spatial Organization Strategies in Graphical and Tangible User Interfaces. In *Proc. DARE '00*, 41–50.
10. Raskin, J. *The Humane Interface: New Directions for Designing Interactive Systems*. Addison-Wesley Professional, 2000.
11. Rekimoto, J. SmartSkin: An Infrastructure for Freehand Manipulation on Interactive Surfaces. In *Proc. CHI '02*, 113–120.
12. Richter, H., Ecker, R., Deisler, C., and Butz, A. HapTouch and the 2+1 State Model: Potentials of Haptic Feedback on Touch Based In-vehicle Information Systems. In *Proc. AutomotiveUI '10*, 72–79.
13. Sato, M., Poupyrev, I., and Harrison, C. Touché: Enhancing Touch Interaction on Humans, Screens, Liquids, and Everyday Objects. In *Proc. CHI '12*, 483–492.
14. Underkoffler, J., and Ishii, H. Urp: a Luminous-Tangible Workbench for Urban Planning and Design. In *Proc. CHI '99*, 386–393.
15. Voelker, S., Nakajima, K., Thoresen, C., Itoh, Y., Øvergård, K. I., and Borchers, J. PUCs: Detecting Transparent, Passive Untouched Capacitive Widgets on Unmodified Multi-touch Displays. In *Proc. ITS '13*, 101–104.
16. Weiss, M., Schwarz, F., Jakubowski, S., and Borchers, J. Madgets: Actuating Widgets on Interactive Tabletops. In *Proc. UIST '10*, 293–302.
17. Weiss, M., Wagner, J., Jansen, Y., Jennings, R., Khoshabeh, R., Hollan, J. D., and Borchers, J. SLAP Widgets: Bridging the Gap Between Virtual and Physical Controls on Tabletops. In *Proc. CHI '09*, 481–490.
18. Wimmer, R. FlyEye: Grasp-Sensitive Surfaces using Optical Fiber. In *Proc. TEI '10*, 245–248.
19. Wimmer, R., and Boring, S. HandSense: Discriminating Different Ways of Grasping and Holding a Tangible User Interface. In *Proc. TEI '09*, 359–362.
20. Yu, N.-H., Chan, L.-W., Lau, S. Y., Tsai, S.-S., Hsiao, I.-C., Tsai, D.-J., Hsiao, F.-I., Cheng, L.-P., Chen, M., Huang, P., and Hung, Y.-P. TUIC: Enabling Tangible Interaction on Capacitive Multi-touch Display. In *Proc. CHI '11*, 2995–3004.

3D Tabletop User Interface Using Virtual Elastic Objects

Figure 1: 3D Interaction with a virtual elastic object

Hiroaki Tateyama
Graduate School of Science and Engineering, Saitama University
255 Shimo-Okubo, Sakura-ku, Saitama City, Japan,
hiroaki@is.ics.saitama-u.ac.jp

Takumi Kusano
Graduate School of Science and Engineering, Saitama University
255 Shimo-Okubo, Sakura-ku, Saitama City, Japan,
kusano@is.ics.saitama-u.ac.jp

Takashi Komuro
Graduate School of Science and Engineering, Saitama University
255 Shimo-Okubo, Sakura-ku, Saitama City, Japan,
komuro@mail.saitama-u.ac.jp

ITS '14, Nov 16-19 2014, Dresden, Germany
ACM 978-1-4503-2587-5/14/11.
http://dx.doi.org/10.1145/2669485.2669533

Abstract
In this paper, we propose a method to reduce the inconsistency between virtual and real spaces in manipulating a 3D virtual object with users' fingers. When a user tries to hold a virtual object, fingers do not stop on the surface of the object and thrust into the object since virtual objects cannot give reaction force. We therefore try to prevent fingers from thrusting into a virtual object by letting the object deform or glide through the fingers. A virtual object is deformed by using a spring-based model and solving the equation of equilibrium. Whether the object glides through the fingers or not is determined by calculating resultant force added to the object and resultant force of static friction when the fingers touch the object. Based on these methods, we constructed a 3D tabletop interface that enables interaction with virtual objects with a greater sense of reality.

Author Keywords
Virtual reality; 3D interaction; object manipulation; vision-based UI.

ACM Classification Keywords
H.5.2 [Information interfaces and presentation]: User Interface - *Interaction styles*

Introduction
With the progress of 3D displaying technology, research of interaction systems that allows users to manipulate

stereoscopic 3D virtual objects has been actively conducted.

For example, an interaction system that allows the users to move a 3D virtual object on an auto-stereoscopic display by putting their hand close to the table [1], but the users cannot manipulate the object directly. On the other hand, systems that enable direct interaction with a virtual object have also been developed. Yoshida et al. has developed a system that can present 42 different viewpoint images without glasses and that enables interaction with a sense of reality [2]. Interaction with a greater sense of reality in a virtual space has been realized by projecting proper 3D images according to the users' real-time viewpoint position and by moving virtual objects according to the users' motion following physical laws [3]. In another way, a high-speed stereo camera can be used to enhance a sense of reality in interaction with virtual objects. A system that detects users' fingers position with a high-speed stereo camera and that moves a virtual object linked to the position with little latency has been developed [4]. These systems enable interaction with virtual objects using users' hand, but interaction is limited to simple manipulations such as "pushing". On the other hand, there are systems that realize various manipulations such as "holding" and "lifting" [5, 6], which enables flexible and realistic interaction. However, there is a problem that virtual objects cannot give reaction force. When a user tries to hold a virtual object, for example, fingers do not stop on the surface of the object and thrust into the object. This causes inconsistency between the real space and the virtual space, and impairs the sense of reality. A solution for this problem has been proposed in the case of VR systems using a head-mounted display (HMD) [7, 8]. Users can control a virtual hand seen through the HMD with the movement of the users' real hand. The systems stop the virtual fingers on the surface of an object before the fingers thrust into the object. However, this method can be used when the users' real hand is invisible and only the virtual hand is visible to users.

In this paper, we elasticize the object and let it deform or glide through the fingers depending on the force added to the objects to prevent the fingers from thrusting into a virtual object. Thereby, we reduce the inconsistency between virtual and real spaces in manipulating a 3D virtual object with users' fingers. Also, we constructed a 3D tabletop interface based on the proposed method which enables interaction with virtual objects with a greater sense of reality.

Virtual Object Deformation

Virtual object deformation is a method to elasticize a virtual object and to let it deform along the shape of users' fingers. In this study, we use cylindrical objects and apply a spring-based model. We consider only the top-view shape of the objects and ignore the height of the objects. Figure 2(a) shows the spring-based model that is used to represent a virtual object. A certain number of control points are placed on the circumference uniformly and each control points are connected to the neighboring points and to the central point with a spring.

Since control points that compose a virtual object are closely-arranged when seen locally, they can be regarded as linearly connected points. Figure 2(b) shows approximated control points that are linearly connected.

There are two cases when control points move.

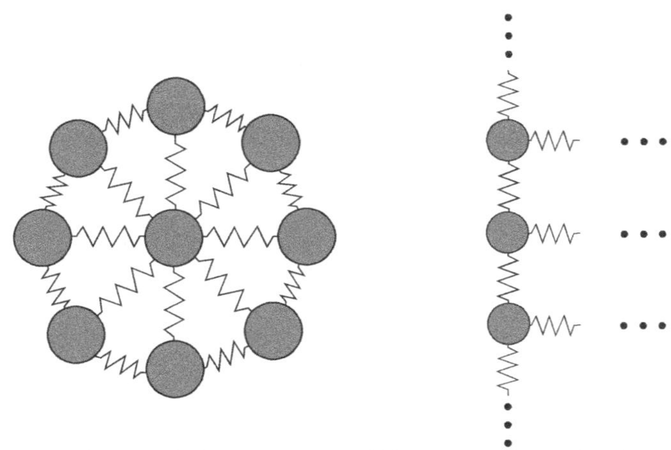

(a) **Cylindrical object** (b) **Linear approximation**

Figure 2: Spring-based model

- Control points are moved by a finger.
- Control points are moved by forces from neighboring springs.

Let x_i be the horizontal position of a control point i $(i = 1,2 \dots n)$. When a control point i is moved by a finger to the position a_i, x_i is determined by the following equation.

$$x_i = a_i \quad (1)$$

Figure 3 shows the equilibrium of forces when control points are moved by forces from neighboring springs.

Let L_0 be the natural length of vertical springs, L_i the length of a vertical spring after deformation, θ_i the angle of a vertical spring, and k_1, k_2 the spring constants of vertical and horizontal springs. The equation of the equilibrium of forces is written as follows.

$$k_1(L_i \sin\theta_i - L_{i-1} \sin\theta_{i-1}) + k_2 x_i = 0 \quad (2)$$

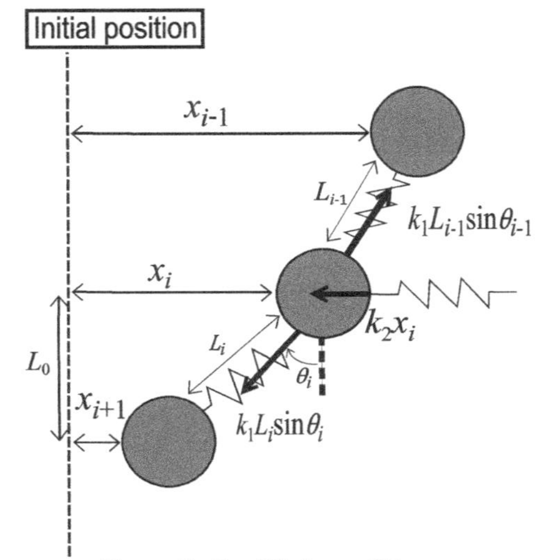

Figure 3: Equilibrium of forces

Using the following relations,

$$L_i \sin\theta_i = x_i - k_1 x_{i+1} \quad (3)$$
$$L_{i-1} \sin\theta_{i-1} = x_{i-1} - k_1 x_i \quad (4)$$

the equation can be transformed as follows.

$$(2k_1 + k_2)x_i - k_1 x_{i+1} - k_1 x_{i-1} = 0 \quad (5)$$

The positions of all control points can be calculated by solving a system of equations constructed from Eq. (1) and Eq. (5).

It is necessary to deform a virtual object along the shape of fingers. Figure 4 shows the flow of the object deformation algorithm.

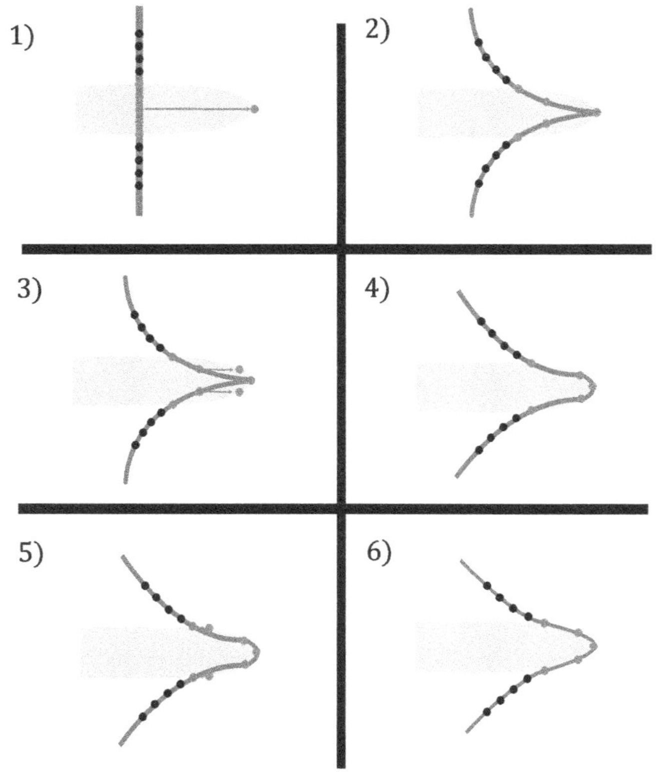

Figure 4: Object deformation algorithm

The details of the algorithm are as follows.

1) When the system detects that some fingers are inside a virtual object, the nearest control point to each fingertip is moved to the position of the fingertip.
2) Other control points are moved based on the equation of the equilibrium of forces.
3) If the destination of the control points is inside the finger, the points are fixed to the nearest contour of the finger.
4) Other control points are again moved based on the equation of the equilibrium of forces.
5) By repeating it until all the control points are outside fingers.
6) The result is presented to the user.

With this algorithm, users can manipulate virtual objects without the fingers' thrusting into the object.

Virtual Object Gliding

Virtual object gliding is a method to let a virtual object glides through the fingers when the object is deformed to some extent. This prevents the object from over-deforming even when fingers thrust into a virtual object deeply. Whether the object glides through the fingers or not is determined by calculating resultant force added to the object and resultant force of static friction when the fingers touch the object. Let n be the number of contact points between fingers and the object, N_i the force added to a contact point i, F the resultant force of N_i, θ_i the angle between N_i and F, and μ the friction coefficient. The condition to let the object glides through the fingers is as follows.

$$F > \sum_{i=1}^{n} \mu N_i \cos\theta_i \qquad (6)$$

Using this method, pushing manipulation and holding manipulation can be treated in a unified way. Figure 5 shows the forces applied to a virtual object when $n = 2$.

3D Tabletop Interface

Based on the proposed methods, we constructed a 3D tabletop interface system that enables interaction with virtual objects. We modified the system developed by

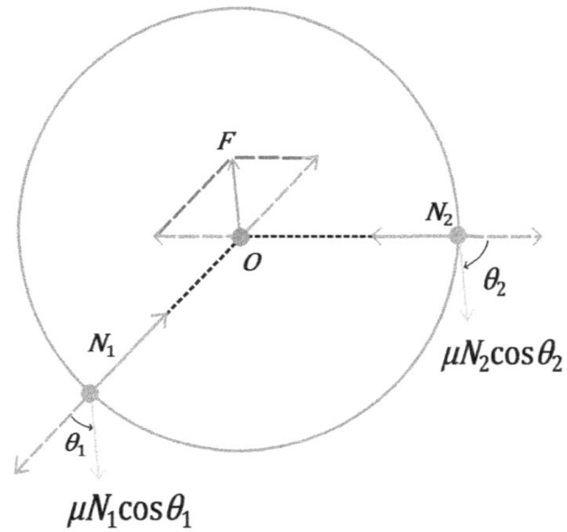

Figure 5: Forces applied to a virtual object

Kusano et al. [9] to construct our system. The system consists of an upwardly-placed multi-view auto-stereoscopic display and a camera installed above the display. The appearance of the system is shown in Figure 6. Users can interact with 3D virtual objects which are presented on the display. Hand regions are extracted from a camera image using color information and the system recognizes whether fingers are inside a virtual object.

We implemented virtual object deformation and gliding methods to the system. The result of deformation and gliding is illustrated in Figure 7. The processing time was short enough and the system ran at 60 fps in real time.

Conclusions

In this study, we proposed a method to reduce the inconsistency between virtual and real spaces in manipulating 3D virtual objects. By elasticizing a virtual object, the system prevents users' fingers from thrusting into the virtual object. Based on the approach, we constructed a 3D tabletop interface that enables interaction with virtual objects with a greater sense of reality.

Figure 6: 3D tabletop interface

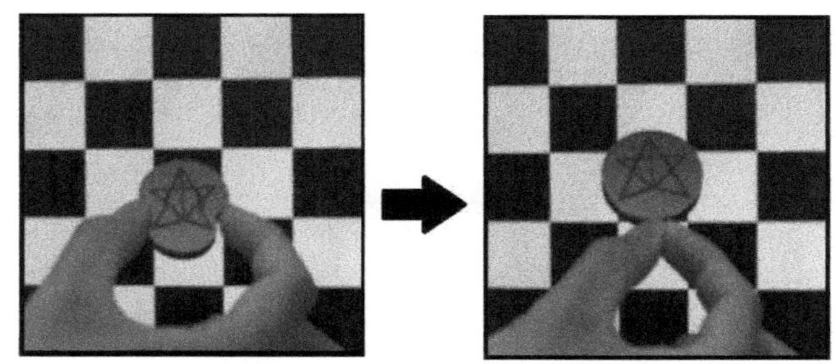
Figure 7: Object deformation and gliding

In future works, we will increase shapes of virtual objects such as "cube" and "triangular pyramid", realize more various operations such as "pushing" and "lifting", and construct practical application systems.

References

1. Kobayashi, K., Oikawa, M., Koike, T., Utsugi, K., Yamasaki, M., and Kitagawa, S. Character Interaction System with Autostereoscopic Display and Range Sensor. In *Proc. 3DUI 2007*, 95-98.
2. Yoshida, T., Kamuro, S., Minamizawa, K., Nii, H., and Tachi, S. RePro3D: Full-parallax 3D Display with Haptic Feedback using Retro-reflective Projection Technology. In *Proc. ISVRI 2011*, 49-54.
3. Benko, H., Jota, R., and Wilson, A. MirageTable: Freehand Interaction on a Projected Augmented Reality Tabletop. In *Proc. CHI 2012*, 199-208.
4. Niikura, T., and Komuro, T. 3D Touch Panel Interface Using an Autostereoscopic Display. In *Proc. ITS 2012*, 295-298.
5. Hilliges, O., Kim, D., Izadi, S., Weiss, M., and Wilson, A. HoloDesk: Direct 3D Interactions with a Situated See-Through Display. In *Proc. CHI 2012*, 2421-2430.
6. Lee, J., Olwal, A., Ishii, H., and Boulanger, C. SpaceTop: Integrating 2D and Spatial 3D Interactions in a See-through Desktop Environment. In *Proc. CHI 2013*, 189-192.
7. Prachyabured, M. and Borst, C.W. Dropping the ball: Releasing a virtual grasp. In *Proc. 3DUI 2011*, 59-66.
8. Burns, E., Razzaque, S., Panter, A.T., Whitton, M.C., McCallus, M.R. and Brooks Jr, F.P. The Hand is Slower than the Eye: A Quantitative Exploration of Visual Dominance over Proprioception. In *Proc. VR 2005*, 3-10.
9. Kusano, T., Niikura, T., and Komuro, T. A Virtually Tangible 3D Interaction System using an Autostereoscopic Display. In *Proc. SUI 2013*, 87.

Cyber Chamber: Multiuser Collaborative Assistance System for Online Shopping

Masafumi Muta
Rakuten Institute of Technology, Rakuten, Inc.
Shinagawa-ku, Tokyo, Japan
masafumi.muta@mail.rakuten.com

Kenji Mukai
University of Tsukuba
1-1-1 Tennodai,
Tsukuba-shi, Ibaraki, Japan
mukai.kenji@entcomp.esys.tsukuba.ac.jp

Ryoutarou Toumoto
University of Tsukuba
1-1-1 Tennodai,
Tsukuba-shi, Ibaraki, Japan
toumoto.ryoutarou@entcomp.esys.tsukuba.ac.jp

Motoi Okuzono
University of Tsukuba
1-1-1 Tennodai,
Tsukuba-shi, Ibaraki, Japan
motoi@entcomp.esys.tsukuba.ac.jp

Junichi Hoshino
University of Tsukuba
1-1-1 Tennodai,
Tsukuba-shi, Ibaraki, Japan
jhoshino@esys.tsukuba.ac.jp

Hiromi Hirano
Rakuten Institute of Technology, Rakuten, Inc.
Shinagawa-ku, Tokyo, Japan
hiromi.hirano@mail.rakuten.com

Soh Masuko
Rakuten Institute of Technology, Rakuten, Inc.
Shinagawa-ku, Tokyo, Japan
so.masuko@mail.rakuten.com

ITS '14, Nov 16-19 2014, Dresden, Germany.
ACM 978-1-4503-2587-5/14/11.
http://dx.doi.org/10.1145/2669485.2669534

Abstract
Recently, online shopping continues to thrive in modern societies, especially via tablets and smartphones; however, in current online shopping environments, there is insufficient support for shopping with several people, which is often what shoppers do together in the nonvirtual world. In this paper, we propose a novel system that provides a new online shopping experience for multiple users. Here, we developed Cyber Chamber, a system that enables users to interact with tablets and wall projection for each user to search items privately via their tablets and then share those publicly on the wall. To evaluate the effectiveness of our system, we performed experiments. From our results, we confirmed that our proposed system successfully supports the ease of discussion, information sharing, and ease with which multiple users can together consider combinations of goods.

Author Keywords
Online Shopping; E-Commerce; CSCW; Tablet; Projector

ACM Classification Keywords
H.5.2 [Information interfaces and presentation (e.g., HCI)]: User Interfaces—Interaction styles; H.5.3 [Information interfaces and presentation (e.g., HCI)]: Group and Organization Interfaces—Collaborative computing;

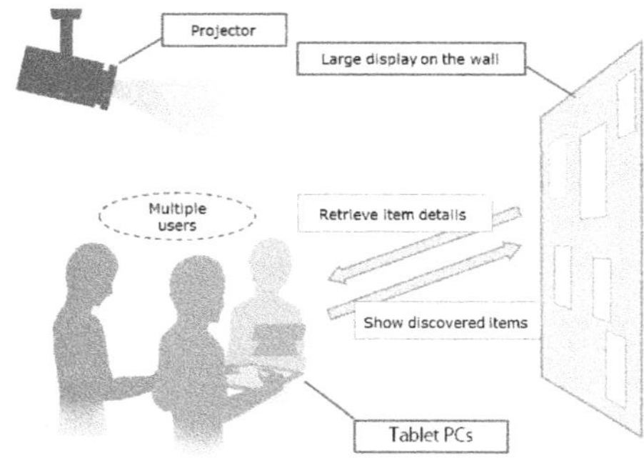

Figure 1: Conceptual Illustration

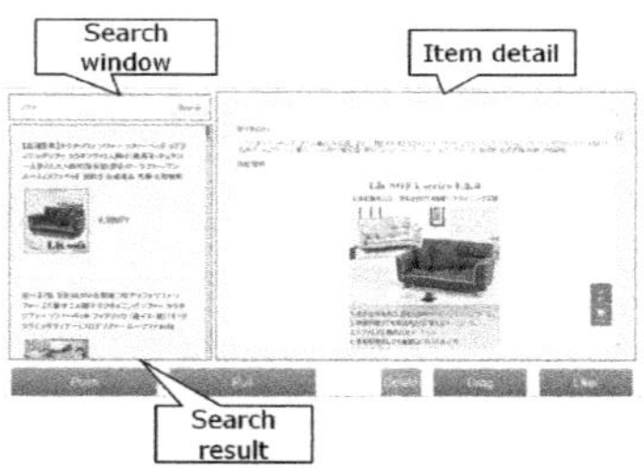

Figure 2: Cyber Chamber Client

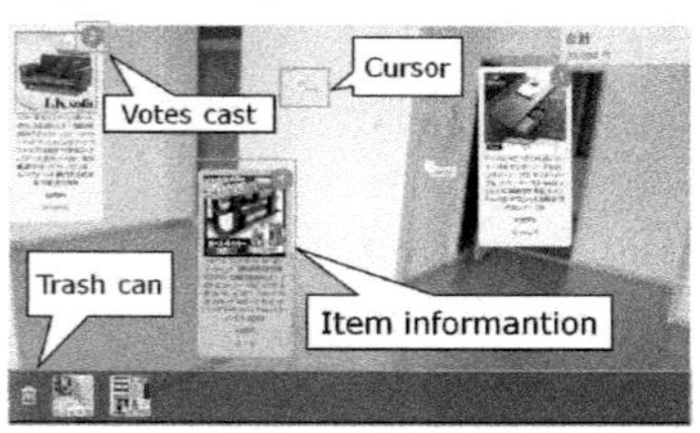

Figure 3: Cyber Chamber Board

Introduction

Recently, online shopping has become an integral part of our daily lives. Purchasing various products on a wide array of e-commerce websites is possible. According to a recent survey, 66% of Americans over the age of 18 purchased goods online in 2010 [1]. Further, the spread of wireless networks, smartphones, and tablets has expanded the number of opportunities for online shopping [2]. In most cases, online shopping is a solitary task. In contrast, shopping in the nonvirtual world often involves several people consulting one another while shopping, e.g., when shopping to buy home furnishings for a jointly used room. Online shopping, however, is difficult when several people are involved. A cause of this difficulty is that online shopping is performed on personal computers (PCs), tablets, and smartphones that are designed for one-on-one human–computer interaction, making it difficult to share products one wishes to buy with others. Further, people often want to consider the combination of various products together, e.g., to coordinate fashions or interior design ideas by viewing pictures side-by-side or sharing them with family or friends, tasks that cannot be performed easily by them via typical devices. To support an online shopping system in which several users consider product combinations, all participants must be able to search for products, easily share information with their co-shoppers, and line up all products on one shared screen. In this paper, we propose Cyber Chamber, a system that provides a forum for online shopping with several people, each using a tablet to search for products and share product information with one another. Such information is projected on a wall, as illustrated in Figure 1. Our system enables individual searches and facilitates consultation with co-shoppers by sharing product information and presenting product combinations. To verify the benefits and effectiveness of our system, we performed experiments in cooperation with a company that operates a major e-commerce website [3]. In our experiments, we asked a group of people to use our system to buy various home furnishings. Then we evaluated by questionnaires and conversation analysis. Results indicated that it is useful for the ease of discussion, information sharing, and considering combinations of multiple goods.

Related Work

In this paper, we propose a system that supports multiuser online shopping via tablets and large screen displays. Therefore, we investigated studies in the field of computer-supported cooperative work, as well as research focused on interactions with large screen displays. Amershi et al. [4] and Peak et al. [5] developed systems to share a display among multiple users, each user controlling a mouse and a mobile device. These studies are similar to our system in terms of a single shared display; however, the studies do not provide support to users who wish to consider purchasing together a combination of products because two or more products cannot be arranged and viewed on the shared display. WebSurface [6] and WeSearch [7] are systems that employ tabletop interfaces,

*"Projector" image is by Hakan Yalcin, from The Noun Project. (CC-BY). "Server" image is by aLf, from The Noun Project. (CC-BY)

Table 1: Features

Functions	Detail
Item search	search by entering a keyword in the search window
Item detail view	confirm detailed product information
Push	share information about products on the wall display
Pull	get product information from the wall display
Drag	move a product around within the wall display
Vote	vote for a product
Delete	delete a product from the wall display
Cursor	move cursor by tilting tablet up, down, left, or right
Item information	display product brand names, pictures, and prices
Trash can	deleted products are saved as history
Background image	set up a background picture that matches the purchase theme

enabling several people to simultaneously search and share information with one another. Special-purpose interfaces were constructed for these systems; however, in our study, we used tablets and a projector to avoid the need for such special interfaces, thus making our system accessible at home. SWINGNAGE [8] allows interaction between smartphones and large screen displays, targeting digital signage. A user downloads detailed advertisements from the display to the phone. Although SWINGNAGE has a configuration similar to that of our proposed system, it does not consider cooperative work by multiple users.

System Overview

Analysis of Requirements

In analyzing requirements for our proposed system, we found individual item search and item sharing as key needs for multiuser online shopping. Most e-commerce sites have massive amounts of products; thus, we should be able to search for items effectively. If we share only one device, people not operating the device cannot search items and can only make suggestions to the devices user. In such a situation, the device operator often leads the discussion, whereas others cannot easily have their opinion heard. We therefore decided that every user should have a tablet for him/her to perform individual searches. When shopping with others in nonvirtual environments, we can share items and hear opinions from one another; however, sharing items in a multitablet environment is difficult. When a person wishes to share information, he can show the display of his device or can suggest brand or product names for others to search for, but these approaches are inefficient, subject to error, and a nuisance to users. We therefore decided to provide a shared space via a projected display for users to recommend products from their own tablets as desired. Tablets should be able to download item information from the wall for users to further check the details on their own devices. We also found that voting on items presented on the wall and the ability to move them around (e.g., to be grouped, sorted, and so on) are very helpful to such a multitablet environment.

Implementation and Features

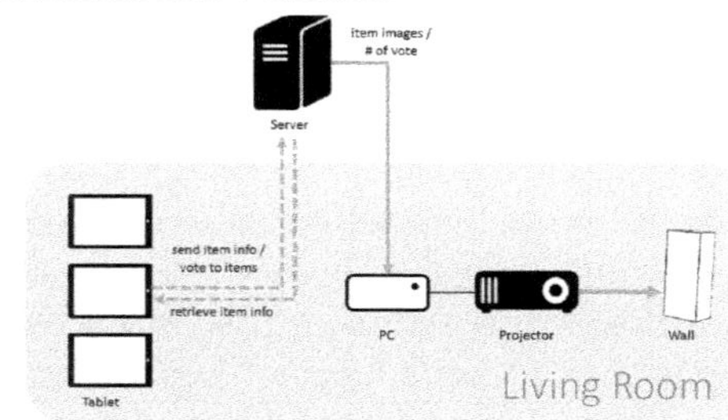

Figure 4: System Configuration*

Figure 4 shows our proposed system's configuration, consisting of a PC connected to a projector, tablets, and a central server. Each tablet display has the display shown in Figure 2, and Figure 3 is projected on the wall display. The PC (connected to the projector) and tablets are connected via a central server using the WebSocket protocol. The server is built on Node.js, and both applications for the PC and tablets are built as web applications. We call the PC application the Cyber Chamber Board and the tablet application the Cyber Chamber Client. Table 1 shows all features of the Cyber Chamber. Key features of our system include the "push" and "pull" functions. The push function implies sending an item from a tablet to the wall. More specifically, when a user finds an item that he/she wishes to share, he/she selects push on the tablet to share the brand name, picture, and price on the wall. Conversely, the pull function implies that details from the wall are downloaded to the tablet. A user can therefore check the detailed

Table 2: Interfaces used in the experiment

Interface D	Desktop PC
Interface T	Tablet Devices
Interface C	Cyber Chamber

Table 3: Budget

Budget Small	8 mats 100,000 yen
Budget Middle	10 mats 200,000 yen
Budget Large	12 mats 300,000 yen

Table 4: Experimental Order

Group1
D(Large)→T(Middle)→C(Small)
Group2
T(Small)→C(Large)→D(Middle)
Group3
C(Middle)→D(Small)→T(Large)

Table 5: Questionnaire

	Questionnaire
Q1	Were the products proposed by you considered by others?
Q2	Were you aware of the products that you did not notice without other people?
Q3	Could you pick up on the atmosphere of the entire room?
Q4	Could you imagine a room where the home furnishings you selected were going to be put?
Q5	Open-ended question

information of an item on his/her tablet by selecting pull on the device while his/her cursor is on the desired item. Note that when a user joins the system, he/she is assigned a cursor on the projected display, which he/she can then move by tilting his/her device.

Experiment

Experimental Setup

We performed experiments to validate our proposed system's usefulness. Participants were organized into three groups, each consisting of three men, for a total of nine men. The men were between 20 and 30 years old, each using his smartphone daily and shopping online at least once per month. The objective given to the participants was to prepare furnishings for a house that they would share with one another.† Each group was told to shop online via three different interfaces, as summarized in Table 2. To prevent the participants from reusing previous results with other interfaces, the monetary budget was changed for each experiment; Table 3 provides details regarding the three levels used. Note that when the budget was changed, the assumed room size was also changed accordingly. Each group's experiments were performed in a different order to prevent the sequences of interfaces used and budget sizes from influencing the participants behavior. Further, we identified the interface and budget combinations so as to not overlap; Table 4 shows the sequence of actual experiments. Before starting each experiment, we explained the purpose of the experiment to each participant and then described how to operate each interface, allowing each participant to practice with the interface. Next, we explained the purpose of shopping and got them started. We allotted 30 min to shop for each interface. At the end of the experiments, we asked each participant to answer a questionnaire, which is summarized in Table 5. As shown in the table, the questionnaire consisted of five questions, the first four of which the participants rated on a scale from 0 to 5. The fifth question was an open-ended question. We also performed video and audio recordings during each experiment.

Results

Figure 5 shows the results of the questionnaire performed after the experiments. From the figure, the vertical axis represents the average of the responses to each question. We performed multivariate testing ($p < 0.05$) using Steel's methodology between the Cyber Chamber (CC) and tablets groups, as well as between the CC and PC groups. Our results indicated that in Q1 and Q2, there was no significant difference observed between both the CC and tablets groups and the CC and PC groups. In Q3 and Q4, we observed significant differences between both the CC and tablets groups and the CC and PC groups. We also analyzed the conversation of the participants from the audio recorded during the experiments. When the CC was being used, the participants remarked about the convenience of showing product information on the wall and the ease of understanding recommended products when displayed side by side. In addition to these positive evaluations of our proposed system, the open-ended answers also contained positive evaluations of our system's usefulness. Comments included the comparison and consideration of the combinations of selected products, ease of information sharing among group members, and an appreciation of background pictures as auxiliary images.

Discussion

We defined Q3 and Q4 of the participant questionnaire to help determine whether CC facilitated a simpler multiuser shopping experience that involved the combinations of items. CC received significant positive results than the other approaches; thus, CC clearly makes it easier to shop with multiple people while considering the combinations of products. From Q1 and Q2, we attempted to determine whether CC serves as a good means of communication for sharing information and reaching consensus to be easy. From our results, although CC tends to have positive results, we cannot claim that it is statistically significantly more useful than the other approaches.

In addition to the questionnaire, some very interesting suggestions were obtained from the video and audio recordings of the experiments. First, people built consensus through different means, depending on whether they used desktop PCs or tablets (including CC). With desktop PCs, the participants tended to first build consensus around product attributes. For example, when buying a television, the first step was to reach consensus on the size and color. Next, they searched for specific products with those attributes. In contrast, people using tablets tended to reach consensus on specific products directly. We suggest that this is because they can propose a product after they know more about it. When searching items in parallel, users can check the details or make comparisons with other products to investigate specific products that they want; however, this is inefficient in an environment where the participants shared a PC, keeping others from searching until one of them learned about a specific item. Therefore, in a desktop PC environment, users will first consult one another about the desirable product attributes, and assuming they compromise, will then search for products that have the attributes they agree on. Next, during the product proposal process, more products were implicitly proposed while using CC. Rather than overt proposals, such as "What about this one?," we heard many proposals in the form of reports, such as "Look what I found" or "Here..." after one pushed the item to the wall. The intention to propose is expressed by the act of showing products on the wall, and those who noticed pushed items also noted that the proposal was made subjectively. When making a proposal, the user must temporarily block the work of others and draw attention, which is likely a psychological burden, particularly in a case when others are concentrating on their searches. We believe that this psychological burden is reduced when others voluntarily become aware of the proposal. Further, we observed that when a product was proposed while using CC, people often reacted by verbally indicating that the proposal was simply pending and not that it was accepted or rejected. When only desktop PCs or tablets were used and a proposal could not be decided on one way or another, the participants could not advance toward proposing another product; however, with CC, a product can be kept on the wall without being deleted while continuing on as the subject of consultations, while the group returns to searching for other products. We believe this feature encourages users not to rush to a conclusion but rather to check more items and make a final decision after having carefully considered many viable options and opinions of the group. In addition, when there is a general question that needs a positive or negative response, a person who responds will want to answer affirmatively and avoid a direct negative answer because the person has a general preference for agreement [9].

In this respect, CC is presumed to facilitate a smooth communication. When a participant does not want to accept a proposal, the system creates an escape route that avoids a direct negative answer, instead putting the proposal on hold while other solutions are searched for. The behavior analysis described above indicates that CC creates an environment in which products are easy to

†Scenario details: Your group has decided to share a house. Therefore, you need to buy home furnishings for a common-use living room. Please consult and collaborate with one another to decide what Western-style home furnishing products to buy. The room is 8, 10, or 12 mats in size. It has a window. And the budget is 100,000, 200,000, or 300,000 yen. Assume that air conditioning has already been installed. The house includes individual rooms in addition to the shared living space.

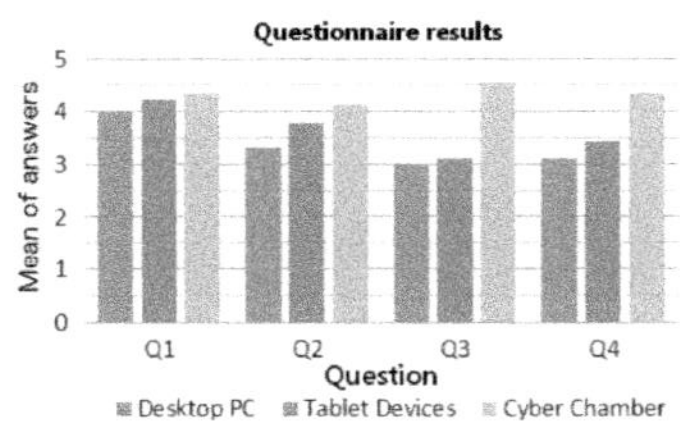

Figure 5: Experimental Result

propose and participants other than the proponent can easily concentrate on such proposals. For Q1 and Q2 of the questionnaire, as noted above, we cannot claim that CC is significantly useful than the other approaches; however, on the basis of a synthesis of the open-ended answers and the above analysis, we conclude that CC made it easy to propose products and provided opportunities to learn about products at the specific product level, not just the attributes proposed by others, thus facilitating information sharing and consultation among the participants. In this study, we had a limited number of participants. We therefore need to perform experiments with more participants. Further, all participants were men. We believe that the decision as to which a product is better than another might differ based on gender. How such differences affect the usability of our system will be an interesting topic for future study.

Conclusions and Future Work

In this paper, we proposed the Cyber Chamber system that provides a novel online shopping environment in which several people can shop together. We cooperated with a company that operates a leading e-commerce website to evaluate our system. We set up a purchase objective and compared three patterns, i.e., one PC, three tablets, and the Cyber Chamber system. From our results, we confirmed that our proposed system was significantly more useful than the other approaches in terms of the ease with which the combinations of goods could be considered. On the basis of our analysis of open-ended answers and the observed behavior of the participants, we conclude that our system is useful for the ease of discussion and information sharing. Henceforth, we need to further study the questionnaire answers in which no difference in usefulness was observed; for this purpose, we plan to perform the experiment with more participants.

Acknowledgments

We would like to thank Dr. Satomi Kuroshima for providing a constructive discussion and insightful comments on conversation analysis.

References

[1] The Pew Internet & American Life Project http://pewinternet.org/Reports/2010/Generations-2010.aspx.
[2] Soh Masuko, Yasuyuki Hayashi. KiTeMiROOM: a fashion-coordination system for mobile devices, CHI EA'13, New York (2013), 601-606.
[3] Rakuten, Inc. http://www.rakuten.com/.
[4] Saleema Amershi, Meredith Ringel Morris. CoSearch:A System for Co-located Collaborative Web Search. CHI'08, New York (2008), 1647-1656.
[5] Tim Paek, Maneesh Agrawala, Sumit Basu, Steve Drucker, Trausti Kristjansson, Ron Logan, Kentaro Toyama, Andy Wilson. Toward universal mobile interaction for shared displays. CSCWf04, New York (2004), 266-269.
[6] Philip Tuddenham, Ian Davies, Peter Robinson. WebSurface:an Interface for Co-located Collaborative Information Gathering. ITS'09, New York (2009).
[7] Meredith Ringel Morris, Jarrod Lombardo, Daniel Wigdor. WeSearch:Supporting Collaborative Search and Sensemaking on a Tabletop Display. CSCW'10, New York (2010), 401-410.
[8] Tokuo Yamaguchi, Hiroyuki Fukushima, Shigeru Tatsuzawa, Masato Nonoka, Kazuki Takashima, Yoshifumi Kitamura. SWINGNAGE: Gesture-based Mobile Interactions on Distant Public Displays. ITS'13, New York (2013), 329-332.
[9] Harvey Sacks. On the preferences for agreement and contiguity in sequences in conversation. Talk and social organisation (1987), 54-69.

Corona: Haptic Sensation Using Body-Carried Electrostatic Charge for Body Area Network Feedback Companion

Adiyan Mujibiya
Rakuten Institute of Technology,
Rakuten Inc.
4-13-9 Higashi-Shinagawa,
Shinagawa-Ku, Tokyo. Japan
adiyan@acm.org

ITS '14, Nov 16-19 2014, Dresden, Germany
ACM 978-1-4503-2587-5/14/11.
http://dx.doi.org/10.1145/2669485.2669535

Abstract
Improvements in Body Area Network (BAN) technical feasibility have encouraged research, which propose applications exploring data transferring touch interaction. In this work, we aim to provide tactile feedback for these applications to improve user experience. We propose *Corona*, a wearable tactile feedback device that uses electrostatic force to provide physical stimuli when a user touches objects that are electrically grounded, or of opposite polarity. Unlike previous approach, we neither physically actuate objects nor use any hand-worn tactile feedback devices. We introduce a mechanism to artificially build up electrostatic charge within the human body, and further leverage effects of electrostatic discharge to create novel physical stimuli. In this paper, we report underlying theory of operation as well as details of our prototype implementation. We illustrate our results using two applications: a) *SandStorm*: visualization of actuated force field using sand, and b) *CheckMate*: future vision of a touch-based transaction checkout system equipped with *Corona* to provide haptic sensation for more reassuring feedbacks.

Author Keywords
Haptic feedback device; physical stimuli; electrostatic charge and discharge; on-body sensor & actuator.

ACM Classification Keywords
H.5.m. Information interfaces and presentation: User Interfaces-Graphical user interfaces; Input devices & strategies.

Introduction
Intra-body and near-body communication technologies developed within Body Area Network (BAN) research such as NTT's RedTacton [5] and Ericsson's Connected Me project [1] provide promising solutions for more intuitive user experience by leveraging body contact (e.g. finger touches, handshakes, etc.) as a means of data transfer. These technologies unveil huge opportunities in consumer electronics applications such as user identification, contents transfer, mobile payment, and so on. Recent technical advancements in this domain have significantly improved state-of-the-art's practical feasibility, thus encourage Human-Computer Interaction (HCI) researchers to envision usage scenario and develop user interface. In this work, we focus on providing finger-touch feedback for BAN approaches, specifically when the designated action is registered by the system, or to notify user of certain events.

In our daily life, we rely on tactile sensations to provide necessary feedbacks that enable us to perform physical activities accurately and confidently. Previous work seeking to transfer this affordance into HCI often require instrumentation on either the objects-of-interest, or on the users' body (most effectively on hand or finger/s) using physical actuators or electrical stimuli.

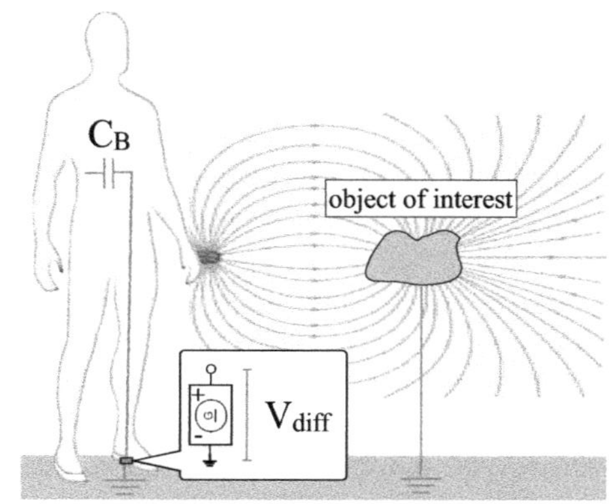

Figure 1. The human body acts as a capacitor (C_B) when coupled with *Corona*. The negative terminal of the unit is in contact with the earth, thus allows the body to build up a large voltage difference with respect to earth (V_{diff}).

Recently, researchers have explored body-channeled haptic mechanism (e.g. REVEL [3]). We aim to extend research in this domain by proposing much simpler analog circuitry and increasing feedback gain level that allows us to perform small-objects manipulation. Although not directly related to generating tactile feedback, an interesting approach using electrostatic force to evoke piloerection on the forearm has also been proposed [4].

We introduce *Corona*, a wearable device that allows a user to carry constant electrostatic charge on his/her body and therefore able to feel haptic sensations when s/he discharge it on objects that are grounded or of opposite polarity. We describe theory of operation in Figure 1. We aim to provide system controllable wide-gain haptic feedback that only requires minimal instrumentation to user or environment.

Implementation

Our body-coupled electrostatic charger prototype was configured from a Cockroft-Walton Ladder Network voltage multiplier, which consists of capacitors and diodes that converts AC or pulsing DC from a low voltage level to a higher DC voltage level. This is a fairly simple electronics that can also be found in off-the-shelf air ionizers. Unlike transformers, this method eliminates the requirement for the heavy core and the bulk of insulation/potting. Using only capacitors and diodes, these voltage multipliers can step up relatively low voltages to extremely high values, while at the same time being far lighter and cheaper than transformers. The small packaging allows us to embed the electrostatic charger unit into wearable objects, such as footwear. In our pilot experiment we found that the maximum voltage at the output of this circuit never reaches more than it's rated output due to voltage leakage through the component leads, known as corona discharge. Therefore, we need to make sure that the voltage multiplier gives us the intended voltage output thus gives enough thrust to initiate the tactile stimuli.

We use Arduino's analog output (5V DC with 40mA max current) as input to voltage multiplier, which outputs −4.5kV DC ±10%. Standard safety level for Electrical Muscle Stimulation (EMS) devices is regulated in [2]. Commercial EMS devices' maximum current is typically set at 100mA; our prototype is well under the safety guidelines.

Our proposed mechanism allows the human body to carry constant electrostatic charge by securing contact between the human body and positive-output of the voltage multiplier, while the negative-output is connected to ground. The static charge carries a very low DC current so that user won't perceive it. Static discharge events will occur when user touches anything grounded or of opposite polarity. Depending on the build-up charge intensity, these events will cause physical stimuli to the user and targeted object/s. We describe our prototype in Figure 2.

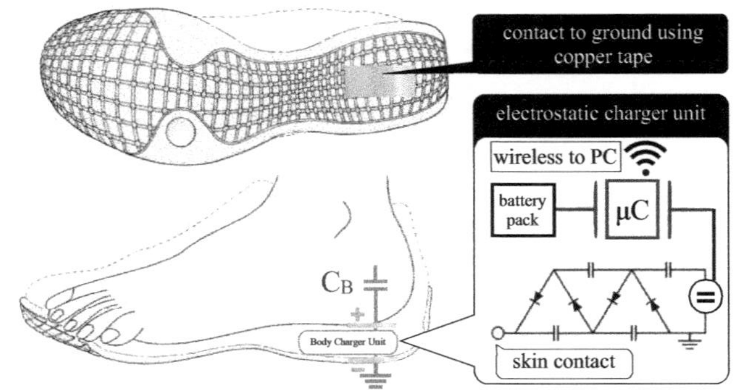

Figure 2. *Corona* device attached to the bottom of a shoe. We used battery-powered microcontroller (Arduino), which is connected wirelessly to a PC for signal control. We feed Arduino's analog out as an input to the voltage multiplier. Using this configuration, we achieved stable grounding and reduce wiring requirements.

Proof-of-Concept Applications

We describe our usage configuration in Figure 3. User will be required to wear a special footwear which has a *Corona* unit embedded in the bottom of the footwear (detailed in Figure 2). We developed two applications to demonstrate real-time interactive capabilities. First application, namely *SandStorm*, visualizes the physical force field generated by *Corona* using particles of sand. Continuous electrostatic discharge (corona discharge)

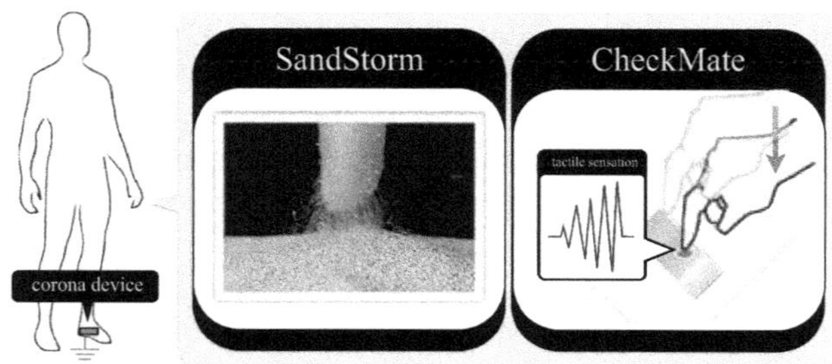

Figure 3. We developed two demo applications: *SandStorm*: interaction with small particles (sand), and *CheckMate*: a surface touch-based haptic feedback.

from user's body will create dramatic "storm" effects on sand particles. Second application, namely *CheckMate*, lets a user feel haptic feedback (small electric shock) when touching an object or surface (grounded electrode). The intensity of the electric shock is regulated by analog signal feed from a microcontroller.

Conclusion And Future Work

We described theory of operations, demonstrated technical feasibility, and highlighted interactivity of *Corona* by our proof-of-concept applications. For future iteration of this work, we plan to improve hardware design and explore other usages of body-charged electrostatics to provide haptic sensation for touch interactions. For example, extending near-body electric field communication technology with *Corona* as its tactile feedback channel. Using this setup, we can realize novel transaction method using finger/body touch (data transfer enabled by through- or near-body communication), and provide reassuring haptic feedbacks when user performs checkout actions. We believe that we can improve user experience in mobile transactions compared to traditional NFC/RFID based IC card approach. We illustrate our future work in Figure 4.

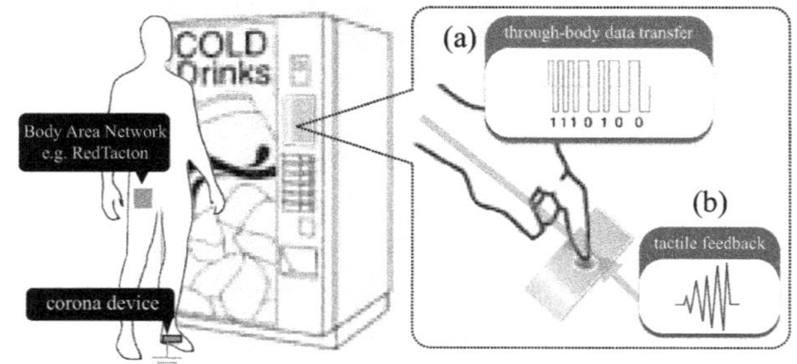

Figure 4. We envision applications using *Corona* as reassuring haptic feedback in short-but-critical touch-interactions, e.g. for vending machine checkout system using the body as data transmission channel (a), where user receives feedback when transaction has been registered (b).

References

[1] Connected Me project by Ericsson Inc. Available Online at: http://www.ericsson.com/thinkingahead/visionary-ideas/connected-me. Accessed at July 18th, 2014.

[2] Consumer Products: Electronic Muscle Stimulators. Available Online at: http://www.fda.gov/MedicalDevices/ProductsandMedicalProcedures/HomeHealthandConsumer/ConsumerProducts/ucm142478.htm. Accessed at June 30th, 2014.

[3] Olivier Bau and Ivan Poupyrev, "REVEL: tactile feedback technology for augmented reality," In *ACM Trans. Graph.* 31, 4, Article 89, 2012.

[4] Shogo Fukushima and Hiroyuki Kajimoto, "Facilitating a surprised feeling by artificial control of piloerection on the forearm," In *Proc. of AH '12*.

[5] Yuichi Kado and Mitsuru Shinagawa, "RedTacton: Near-body Electric-field Communications Technology and Its Applications," In *NTT Technical Review*. Vol. 8, No. 3, March 2010.

Evaluation of Visuo-haptic Feedback in a 3D Touch Panel Interface

Xu Zhao
Saitama University
255 Shimo-Okubo, Sakura-ku,
Saitama City, Japan
sheldonzhaox@is.ics.saitama-u.ac.jp

Takehiro Niikura
The University of Tokyo
Hongo 7-3-1, Bunkyo-ku,
Tokyo, Japan
takehiro_niikura@ipc.i.u-tokyo.ac.jp

Takashi Komuro
Saitama University
255 Shimo-Okubo, Sakura-ku,
Saitama City, Japan
komuro@mail.saitama-u.ac.jp

ITS 2014, November 16–19, 2014, Dresden, Germany.
ACM 978-1-4503-2587-5/14/11.
http://dx.doi.org/10.1145/2669485.2669536

Abstract
In this paper we evaluate the relation between visual and haptic feedback in a 3D touch panel interface and show the optimal latency for natural interaction. We developed a system that consists of an autostereoscopic display and a high-speed stereo camera. With this system, virtual objects are stereoscopically-presented, and the objects respond to the finger movement that is obtained using the stereo camera. We conducted an experiment to evaluate visual and haptic synchronization and the result showed that visual and haptic feedback was the most synchronized with latencies around 150 ms, while finger and button movements were more synchronized with smaller latencies. We also conducted a comparison experiment to explore which synchronization is more important and the result showed that the visual synchronization of finger and button movements is more important than visual and haptic synchronization.

Author Keywords
Stereoscopic display; Passive haptic feedback; Latency

ACM Classification Keywords
H.5.2 [Information interfaces and presentation]: User Interfaces – Input devices and strategies.

Introduction

Recently, touch panels are widely used in our living environment. Touch panels are not only easy to use, but also they can be used for general purposes since screen layout and UI components can be changed depending on the situation. However, we cannot feel much like we are touching objects directly since presentation and operation are restricted on a 2D surface. On the other hand, direct manipulation of virtual 3D objects that are stereoscopically or optically displayed in the air has been studied [1, 2, 3]. However, only visual and audio feedback is provided and users do not feel much haptic sense. Vibration devices can be used to provide tactile feedback [4], but users have to wear the devices. Non-contact tactile display using an ultrasound transmitter can also be used to provide haptic feedback [5], but it requires a large space.

In another way, the surface of the touch panel can be used to provide users with passive haptic feedback. In [6], users touch a 2D surface to select a 3D stereoscopic object and the relation between the 3D positions of rendered objects and the on-surface touch points was analyzed. In [7], users also touch a 2D surface to select a 3D stereoscopic object and depth perception of the users was evaluated. These studies show that 3D objects can be selected with passive haptic feedback by touching a 2D surface of the touch panel. However, the touched object does not move according to the finger movement and the users do not feel much like they are manipulating the object. In addition, when the depth of the rendered object is not around the display, the users feel unnatural since the depth of the finger and that of the object are different. A robotically actuated surface can solve this problem [8], but it requires mechanical hardware.

In this study, we use a system that consists of an autostereoscopic display and a high-speed stereo camera. With this system, virtual objects are stereoscopically-presented, and the objects respond to the finger movement that is obtained using the stereo camera. In this system, virtual buttons are floating a little in front of the display. First, a user's finger touches the surface of a button and the button moves backward according to the finger position. After that, the finger touches the surface of the display and gets passive haptic feedback from the surface. The timing of haptic feedback is inconsistent with that of visual feedback, which may cause a feeling of strangeness.

We can synchronize haptic feedback and visual feedback by adding a delay to the button movement. However, the delay also causes slow response, which impairs the sense of reality in object manipulation.

In this paper we evaluate the relation between visual and haptic feedback and show the optimal latency for natural interaction.

System Overview

For the experiment, we developed a system shown in Figure 1. The system consists of an autostereoscopic display and a high-speed stereo camera. The display was an 8.4″ parallax barrier autostereoscopic display from VMJ Inc., which shows relatively good 3D image quality. The minimum 3D viewing distance of the display is 0.65m, which is short enough for users to manipulate rendered 3D objects by hand. The stereo camera consists of two monochrome IEEE 1394 high-speed cameras Grasshopper from Point Grey Research Inc. with a lens having a focal length of 5 mm. We used the cameras at the frame rate of 120 fps (frame per second) with the image size of 640 × 480 pixels.

Figure 1. The experimental system

Since high-speed cameras have shorter latency than standard cameras, we can reduce the latency of the entire system and we can use a wide range of latencies (from short to long) for the experiment.

We created a 3D graphical user interface of a touch panel, in which users can push three buttons which are displayed stereoscopically.

Fingertip Recognition

The positional relationship of the cameras, the display and the finger, and the world coordinate system are shown in Figure 2.

First of all, the system binarizes the images from the cameras to obtain the finger region. We put a black board on the right side of the display, so that the system can extract the finger region easily and stably. Next, the system scans the binarized image line by line. When a line that has five or more white pixels is first found, the system regards it as a fingertip line.

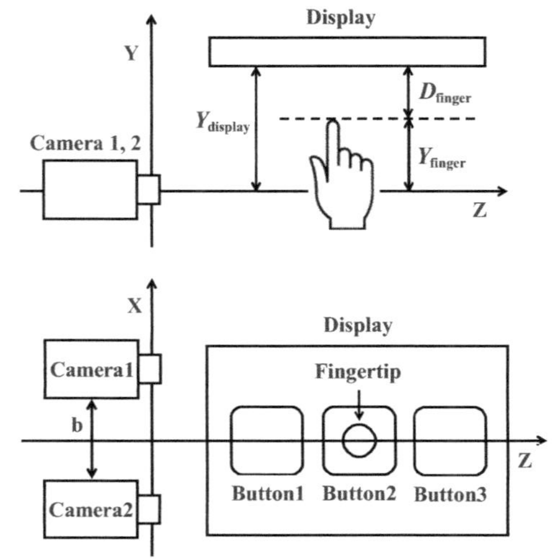

Figure 2. The layout of the system

By calculating the centroid of the white pixels in the fingertip line, the system obtains the coordinates of the fingertip in the image. After that, the system obtains the Y-coordinate of the fingertip in the three-dimensional space, which is used to calculate the distance of the finger from the display D_{finger}, on the following equation.

$$Y_{finger}[\mathrm{mm}] = \frac{y_L[\mathrm{pixel}] + y_R[\mathrm{pixel}]}{2(x_L[\mathrm{pixel}] - x_R[\mathrm{pixel}])} \cdot b[\mathrm{mm}] \quad (1)$$

(x_L, y_L), (x_R, y_R) are the positions of the fingertip in the left and right camera images. b is the baseline of the stereo camera. The Z-coordinate of the fingertip in the three-dimensional space, which is used to detect which button is pushed, is calculated on the following equation.

$$Z[\mathrm{mm}] = \frac{f[\mathrm{pixel}]}{x_L[\mathrm{pixel}] - x_R[\mathrm{pixel}]} \cdot b[\mathrm{mm}] \qquad (2)$$

where f is the focal length of the cameras.

Latency

Before conducting the experiment with different latencies, we measured the original latency of the system including camera input, image processing, CG rendering and display output. We created a program in which a button displayed on the screen moves vertically and horizontally according to the finger and took a video of both the finger and button movements using a high-speed camera at the frame rate of 300 fps. By counting the lag between the movements, we can obtain the latency of the system l_s. We measured the latency 10 times and the mean was just 100 ms and the standard deviation was 5.16 ms.

For the experiment, we added an artificial delay to the system. In order to add a delay without reducing the output frame rate, we stored the measured finger position data to a ring buffer. Let t be the current time and d_{add} be the added delay. The data at $t - d_{add}$ is read out from the buffer and is used to move the button. The total latency becomes $l = l_s + d_{add}$.

Visual Feedback

When D_{finger} is less than the distance of the button surface (17mm), the selected button moves back and forth according to D_{finger}. The button surface coincides with the display surface when the finger touches the display surface. Figure 3 shows the visual output of the system.

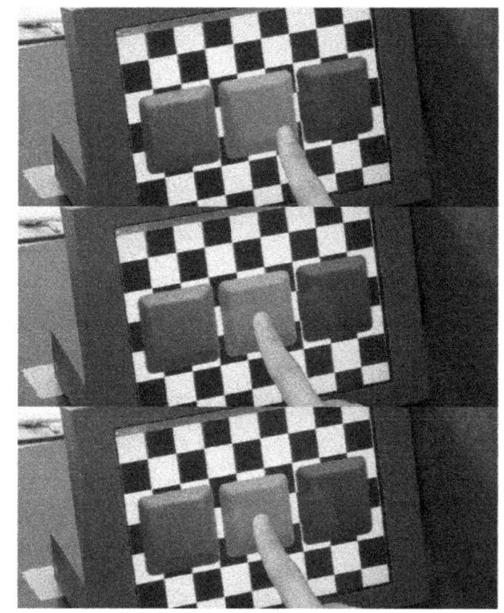

Figure 3. Visual output of the system

Evaluation of Visuo-haptic Feedback

In order to find the optimal latency for the 3D touch panel interface, we evaluated the visual and haptic senses with varying the latency of the system.

Experiment 1: Evaluation of visual and haptic synchronization

We selected 10 subjects (6 males and 4 females) aged 21-23 years old. We changed the latency to 100, 150, 200 and 250 ms (added delays were 0, 50, 100 and 150 ms respectively) in the randomized order. We asked the subjects to touch buttons 10 times for each latency. Then we asked the subjects the following questions.

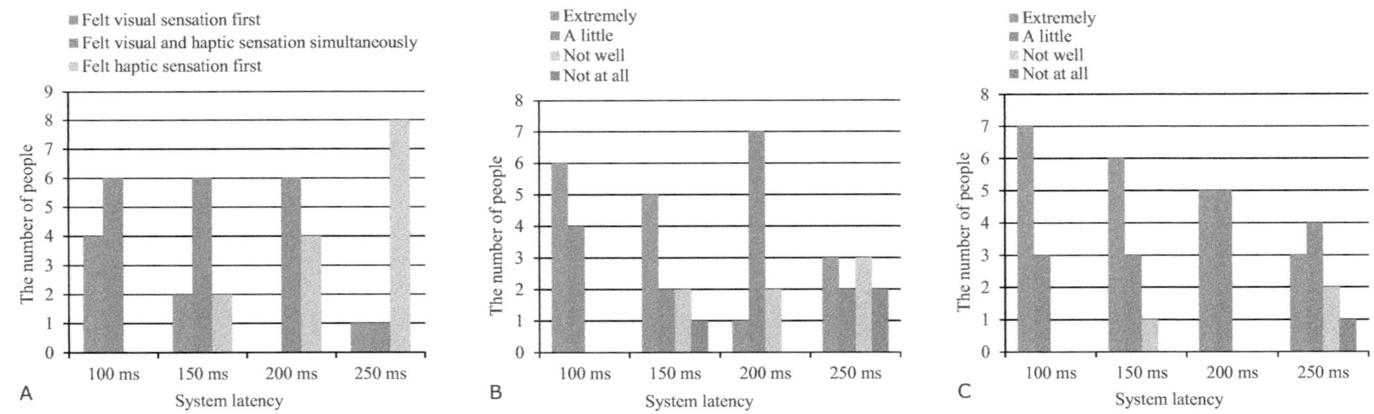

Figure 4. A: The order of touch feeling and object movement. B: Visual synchronization between finger and button movements while the finger was pushing the button. C: Visual synchronization between finger and button movements while the finger was leaving from the button.

- Did you feel the haptic sensation first or did the button move backward first?
- Did you feel that the button moves along with the finger movement while the finger was pushing the button?
- Did you feel that the button moves along with the finger movement while the finger was leaving from the button?

Figure 4A shows the result of the order of visual and haptic senses. When the latency was 100, 150 or 200 ms, more than half subjects answered that they felt visual and haptic sensation simultaneously. In contrast, when the latency was 250 ms, most subjects felt that the button starts to move after touching the screen. From the average scores, the best latency in terms of synchronization of visual and haptic feedback was around 150 ms.

Figure 4B and Figure 4C show the graphs of visual synchronization between finger and button movements while the finger was pushing the button and while the finger was leaving the finger from the button respectively.

From the graphs, we can see that the smaller the latency was, the more synchronized the subjects felt in both pushing and leaving cases.

Experiment 2: Evaluation of the sense of reality
From the experiment above, visual and haptic feedback was the most synchronized with the latencies around 150 ms, while finger and button movements were more synchronized with smaller latencies. We therefore conducted another experiment to explore which latency gives the greatest sense of reality to users. We chose 100, 150 and 200 ms latencies to compare. We selected 18 subjects (12 males and 6 females) aged

21-36 years old and asked the subjects to use a pair of systems with different latencies and asked them the following question.

- Which did you feel like pushing a real button more?

This was repeated for all the ordered pairs of latencies (6 pairs) in the randomized order. The data was analyzed by the Thurstone method and the result is shown in Figure 5. From the result, the best latency in terms of the sense of reality was 100 ms.

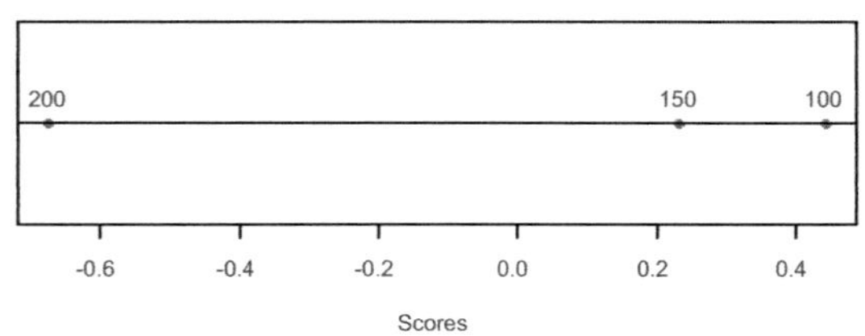

Finger 5. Evaluation of the sense of reality using the Thurstone method.

Conclusion

In this paper, we developed a system that consists of an autostereoscopic display and a high-speed stereo camera. The system allows users to push 3D virtual buttons that are floating in front of the display. When a user's finger touches the surface of a button, the button moves backward according to the finger position and then the finger touches the surface of the display and gets haptic feedback from the surface. The timing of haptic feedback is inconsistent with that of visual feedback, but we can synchronize haptic feedback and visual feedback by adding a delay to the button movement. We conducted an experiment to evaluate visual and haptic synchronization and the result showed that visual and haptic feedback was the most synchronized with the latencies around 150 ms, while finger and button movements were more synchronized with smaller latencies. We also conducted a comparison experiment to explore which synchronization is more important and the subjects felt the greatest sense of reality with the smallest latency, which showed that the visual synchronization of finger and button movements is more important than visual and haptic synchronization.

References

[1] H. Benko *et al.* MirageTable: Freehand Interaction on a Projected Augmented Reality Tabletop. In *ACM CHI '12*, pages 199-208, 2012.

[2] L. Chan *et al.* Touching the Void: Direct-Touch Interaction for Intangible Displays. In *ACM CHI '10,* pages 2625-2634, 2010.

[3] O. Hilliges *et al.* HoloDesk: Direct 3D Interactions with a Situated See-Through Display. In *ACM CHI '12*, pages 2421-2430, 2012.

[4] T. Yoshida *et al.* RePro3D: Full-parallax 3D Display with Haptic Feedback using Retro-reflective Projection Technology. In *ISVRI '11*, pages 49-54, 2011.

[5] K. Yoshino and H. Shinoda. Visio-Acoustic Screen for Contactless Touch Interface with Tactile Sensation. In *IEEE HAPTICS '13*, pages 419-423, 2013.

[6] D. Valkov *et al.* 2D Touching of 3D Stereoscopic Objects. In *ACM CHI '11*, pages 1353-1362, 2011.

[7] D. Valkov *et al.* Evaluation of Depth Perception for Touch Interaction with Stereoscopic Rendered Objects. In *ACM ITS '12*, pages 21-30, 2012.

[8] M. Sinclair *et al.* TouchMover: actuated 3D touchscreen with haptic feedback. In *ACM ITS '13*, pages 287-296, 2013.

UbiBeam: An Interactive Projector-Camera System for Domestic Deployment

Jan Gugenheimer
Institute of Media Informatics
Ulm University
89069 Ulm, Germany
jan.gugenheimer@uni-ulm.de

Enrico Rukzio
Institute of Media Informatics
Ulm University
89069 Ulm, Germany
enrico.rukzio@uni-ulm.de

Pascal Knierim
Institute of Media Informatics
Ulm University
89069 Ulm, Germany
pascal.knierim@uni-ulm.de

Julian Seifert
Institute of Media Informatics
Ulm University
89069 Ulm, Germany
julian.seifert3@uni-ulm.de

ITS 2014, November 16–19, 2014, Dresden, Germany.
ACM 978-1-4503-2587-5/14/11.
http://dx.doi.org/10.1145/2669485.2669537

Abstract

Previous research on projector-camera systems has focused for a long time on interaction inside a lab environment. Currently they are no insight on how people would interact and use such a device in their everyday lives. We conducted an in-situ user study by visiting 22 households and exploring specific use cases and ideas of portable projector-camera systems in a domestic environment. Using a grounded theory approach, we identified several categories such as interaction techniques, presentation space, placement and use cases. Based on our observations, we designed and implement *UbiBeam*, a domestically deployable projector-camera system. The system comprises a projector, a depth camera and two servomotors to transform every ordinary surface into a touch-sensitive information display.

Author Keywords

Steerable projection; projector-camera system; domestic deployment; ubiquitous computing

ACM Classification Keywords

H.5.2 [Information Interfaces and Presentation (e.g. HCI)]: User Interfaces

Figure 1: The UbiBeam System a Compact and Steerable Projector-Camera System

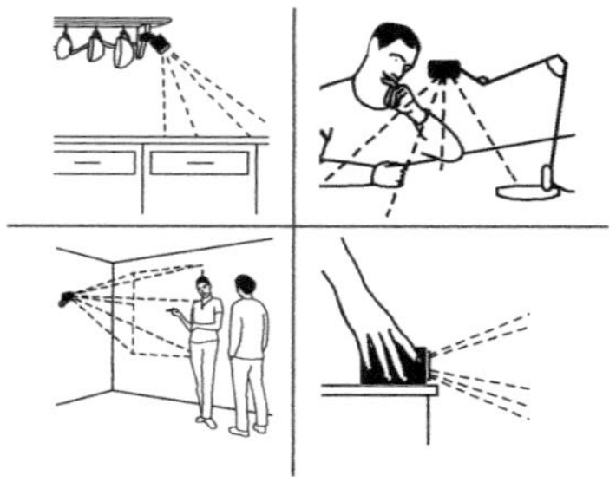

Figure 2: Possible scenarios for the usage of projector-camera systems in a domestic environment

Introduction

Public displays, smartphones, and tablets are devices that aim for constantly providing information to users in ubiquitous usage contexts. They all can be regarded as initial steps towards ubiquitous and everywhere displays as envisioned by Weiser [2]. However, such physical devices still cannot fully achieve the ubiquity and omnipresence of Weiser's vision, as they do not fully blend into the environment.

Recent research aims to achieve this ubiquity by simulating omnipresent screens with a projector-camera system (e.g. [5, 3, 1, 6, 7]). The main focus of these projects was to research the interaction with projected user interfaces. While previous work provides valuable insights into either interaction techniques or technical implementations, most of these projects focused on instrumented laboratory environments. Very little of them researched the use and interaction of projector-camera systems outside of the laboratory. Therefore, the interaction space is limited to interaction with the content and not on deployment or domestic scenarios for the user.

In this work, we introduce UbiBeam (figure 1), a small and portable projector-camera system which is designed based on an in-situ study in the homes of 22 people. We envision a future where such devices will be sold in hardware stores. They could be available in different form factors, either as a replacement for light bulbs or a simple small box which can be placed in several ways inside the users' environments (figure 2). The design of these devices will not only focus on the interaction with the content but also on aspects such as deployment and portability. This work is a first step towards developing projector-camera systems for end users as it provides system and design requirements derived from an in-situ study.

Design Process

We conducted an exploratory field study to investigate the requirements and to gain a deeper understanding of how projector-camera systems can be used in domestic environments. To collect data, we visited 22 households (10 female, 12 male) between 22 and 58 years of age (M= 29) and conducted semi-structured interviews. The participants were provided with a mock up which consisted of an APITEK Pocket Cinema V60 projector inside of a card box mounted on a Joby Gorillapod. This low-fidelity mock up was used to stimulate the creativity of the participants.

The interviews consisted of a questionnaire about the use of a projector-camera system and the creation a potential set-up using the mock up (figure 3). To analyze the data, we selected a grounded theory approach. The data gathering was conducted using semi-structured interviews, notes, pictures and video recordings of several sessions. Two of the authors coded the data using an open, axial and selective coding approach. The initial research question was: "*How would people use a small and easy deployable projector-camera system in their daily lives? When and how would they interact with such a device, and how would they integrate it into their home?*".

During the process we discovered that the four main categories the participants were focusing on when they handled the projector-camera system were:
Projector-Camera System placement: Where was the projector-camera system mounted inside the room ?
Projection surface: What projection surfaces did the participant choose ? *Interaction modalities:* What modalities were used for the input and why ? *Projected Content/Use Cases:* What content did the participant want to project for each specific room and ?

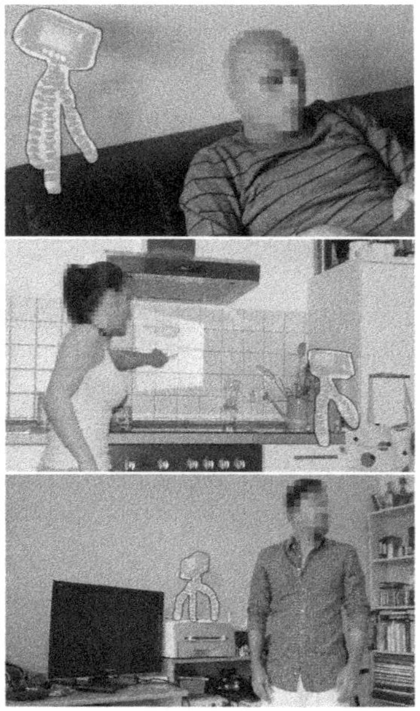

Figure 3: Users building and explaining their setups

Content and Use Cases
The exact use cases were dependent on which room the participants were referring to. However, two larger concepts could be derived from the set-ups the participants created: *information widgets* and *entertainment widgets*. We consider information widgets as use cases in which the participant almost only wants to aggregate data. The most use cases were used as an aid in finishing a specific task characteristic to the room. Entertainment use-cases were mostly created in the living room, bedroom and bathroom. Here the focus was on enhancing the free time one spends in these rooms and making the stay more enjoyable.

Placement of the Projector-Camera System
Similar to the use cases, the placement can be divided into two higher concepts: placing the devise *in reach* and *out of reach*. Participants placed the devices in the bedroom, bathroom and in the kitchen mostly within their reach. Each time the device was mounted on waist or shoulder height. In the living room, working room and corridor participants preferred a mounting above body height. These were also rooms where participants could imagine a permanent mounting. For this reason the device was placed in a way that it could project on most of the surfaces and was "*not in the way*" (P19).

Orientation and Type of Surface
For every interface participants preferred flat and planar surfaces. In the introduction to the study it was explained to each participants that it is technically possible to project onto non planar surfaces without distortion. Nevertheless, only one participant wanted to project onto a couch. All others created flat and planar interfaces: "*I prefer flat surfaces even if they are undistorted*" (P1). Therefore the only classification which could been made to the projection surfaces was if they were *horizontal*, like tables or *vertical*, like walls. Both types of surfaces were used almost evenly spread in the kitchen, bedroom, working room and living room. However in the corridor and the bathroom mostly vertical surfaces were used due to the lack of large horizontal spaces. The projection surface was mostly used to support the use-case and was influenced by the room.

Interaction Modalities
The main interaction modalities participants requested were *speech recognition*, *touch* or a *remote control*. Other techniques such as *gesture recognition*, *shadow interaction* or a *laser pointer* were mentioned rarely. The interaction modality was highly influenced by the room and the primary task in there. The location of the surface was a big influence on the interaction. If the surface was the table, touch was preferred. If the surface was a wall the remote control was used. One participant explained that his choices are mostly driven by convenience: "*You see, I am lazy and I don't want to leave my bed to interact with something*" (P22).

Derived Requirements for Prototype
After analyzing the data from the semi-structured interviews we combined the results with the questionnaires and derived several requirements for our prototype of a domestically deployed projector-camera system.

Analyzing the semi-structured interviews participants always wanted more than only one fix surface in every room. Considering the placement out of reach, we concluded that the projector-camera system must be *steerable*. Furthermore, due to the high amount of requests, the interaction with the device itself must be mediated trough a *remote control*. However the interaction with the projected interface should be

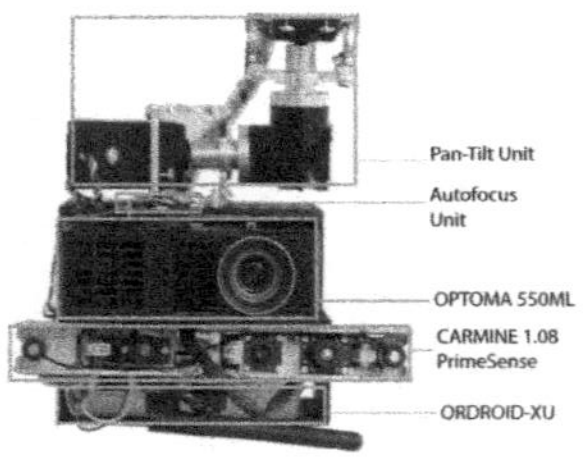

Figure 4: Implementation of the *UbiBeam*

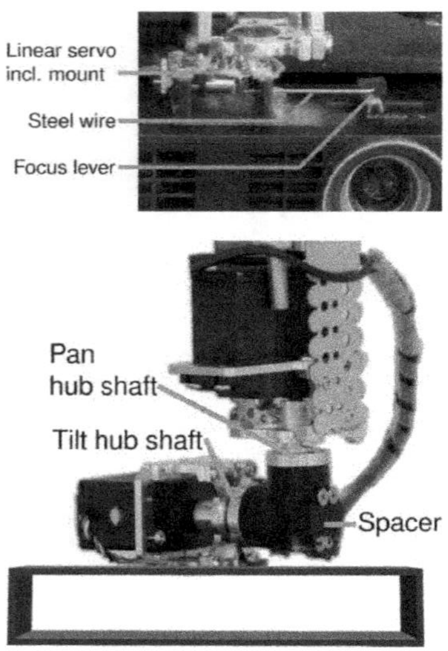

Figure 5: Hardware Construction for the Pan-Tilt Unit and the Auto Focus

implemented with *touch* to be able to create interactive tabletops. The form factor was mostly dictated by the projector used. We analyzed the set-ups of the participants and found out that the distance between the device and surface was between 40cm and 350cm (Mdn= 200cm). The projected surfaces sizes varied from the size of a cupboard door to a whole wall. Therefore, the projector used must be an *ultra-compact DLP* to have a high brightness at the required distance and still have a small form factor. Since participants wanted to carry the device into several rooms and have different use cases the mount must offer a *quick and easy deployment*. A last issue which came up several times was the focus of the projector. Participants did not want to adjust the focus every time they deploy the device in a new location. Therefore an *auto focus* must be realized.

Implementation

Hardware Architecture

UbiBeam (figure 4) uses the ORDROID-XU as the processing unit which offers a powerful eight-core system basis chip (SBC). A WiFi-Dongle and a wireless keyboard are also connected to the SBC. The Carmine 1.08 from PrimeSence is used as a depth camera. It offers a wide range advantage in comparison to smaller Time-of-Flight cameras. Moreover, it is well supported by the OpenNI framework. As for the projector we opted for the ultra-compact LED projector ML550 by OPTOMA (a 550 lumen DLP projector combined with a LED light source). It measures only 105 mm x 106 mm x 39 mm in size and weights 380 g. The projection distance is between 0.55 m and 3.23 m. For the pan and tilt of the system, two HS-785HB servo motors by HiTEC are used. These quarter scale servos offer a torque of 132 Ncm. To be able to provide an auto focus, we built similar to [6] a SPMSH2040L linear servo which is attached to the focusing unit of the projector. To control the actuators, an Arduino Pro Mini is used.

Autofocus. The focus of the Optoma 550ML is manually adjusted via a small lever. To realise automatic adjustment of the focus, the movement of the lever is controlled with a servo (SPMSH2040L). The servo is glued to the designed servo mount as shown in figure 5. To determine the required position of the servo for a given distance, a calibration task was conducted which determined a formula which calculates a PWM signal to a particular distance with a maximum error less than 40 μs.

The final hardware construction measures 10.5 cm x 12.2 cm x 22.5 cm including the pan-tilt unit and weighs 996 g. To be able to easily mount the device to a variety of surfaces we adjusted it to a Manfrotto Magic Arm. The hardware components can be bought and assembled for less than 1000 USD

Software Implementation

Building a stand-alone projector-camera system requires a lightweight and resource saving software. Therefore, we used Ubuntu 12.04 on the ODROID. For reading RGB and depth images, OpenNI version 2.2 for ARM is used. Image processing is done with OpenCV in version 2.4.6. Visualisation of widgets is accomplished with Qt (version 4.8.2), a library for UI development using C++ and QML.

Based on the results of the qualitative study, we designed the interaction with UbiBeam following a simple concept: after running our software the projection becomes a touch sensitive interaction space. The user creates widgets on this space (e.g. calender, digital image frame etc) and interacts with them via touch (figure 6). The orientation of the device itself is done with an Android application sending pan and tilt commands. After moving the device

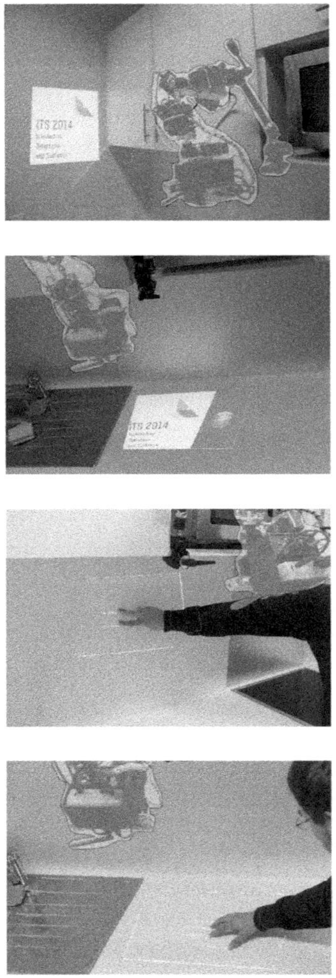

Figure 6: Deployment of UbiBeam inside a Kitchen

to a new space the auto focus and touch detection recalibrates automatically and creates a new interaction space.

Touch Algorithm. The touch detection was implemented based on an algorithm presented in [4]. A key feature is that touch is detected on any physical object without user driven calibration tasks. The developed touch detection can be separated into four parts. First the scenery is analyzed and a spatial image, the ground truth, is generated. This obtained image is filtered for noise and used to calculate a binary contact image while touch detection is running. The contact image is filtered and simple blob detection detects contact points. In a last step, contact points are tracked over time and transformed into interaction events which finally trigger events intended by the user. Detected contact points are tracked over time to classify them into different touch events (*touch down, long touch, move, touch release*). The spatial ground truth image is generated by temporal filtering of 30 single depth images.

Picture Distortion. To be able to project distortion free content onto surfaces not perpendicular to the device, a pre-warping of the projected content had to be done. First a plane detection on the depth map is executed following the concepts Yoo et al. [8]. This enabled us to find possible projection surfaces. Then four points situated on one of the detected planes, spanning a rectangle of the desired size are determined. Finally, the affine transformation which transforms the widget to the determined points is calculated and applied to render a corrected representation of the widget.

Developing Widgets. The developed framework allows a dynamic loading of widgets. All the complexity of the spatially aware projection, dynamic touch detection and movement of the projector-camera system are encapsulated and hidden from the view of the widget. This enables a straight forward widget development. Two different possibilities are supported to create a new widget. Developers are able to implement a provided interface to create a more desktop like looking widgets. Alternatively, developers can implement widgets using Qt User Interface Creation Kit (Qt Quick). It uses QML to describe modern looking, fluid UIs in a declarative manner.

Discussion and Future Work

As mentioned in the introduction we envisioned small and deployable camera-projector systems which are designed for domestic use. In current set-ups, aspects like portability, deployment or domestic use cases and projection surfaces where not taken into account. Therefore, this work provides valuable insights into the domestic use of projector-camera systems. In a next step we would like to deploy the system and collect qualitative feedback over a longer time period. The design of the system is suitable to be able to conduct a long term study. This would provide insights not only into the use of the system but also into how often it is used.

Conclusion

In this work we provided an insight into how people would use a projector-camera system inside their homes. We conducted a qualitative study using grounded theory that discovered and analyzed four important categories a domestically deployed projector-camera system must focus on (*Use Cases/Content, Placement of the Projector-Camera System, Projection Surface, Interaction Modalities*). Furthermore, the results from the qualitative study showed relationships between these categories. We showed that users differentiated between, basic information aggregation to support a specific in task in a room and entertainment to enhance free time. Based on these results, we derived requirements (*Steerable, Remote Control Interaction, Touch Input Interaction, Fast Deployment, Auto Focus*) for a first prototype, and explored different form factors. In a final step, we implemented *UbiBeam*, a steerable camera-projector system which is designed based on requirements we derived from the study.

Acknowledgments

The authors would like to thank all study participants. This work was conducted within the Transregional Collaborative Research Centre SFB/TRR 62 "Companion-Technology of Cognitive Technical Systems" funded by the German Research Foundation (DFG).

References

[1] Harrison, C., Benko, H., and Wilson, A. D. Omnitouch: Wearable multitouch interaction everywhere. In *Proceedings of the 24th Annual ACM Symposium on User Interface Software and Technology*, UIST '11, ACM (New York, NY, USA, 2011), 441–450.

[2] Weiser, M. Human-computer interaction. Morgan Kaufmann Publishers Inc., San Francisco, CA, USA, 1995, ch. The Computer for the 21st Century, 933–940.

[3] Wilson, A., Benko, H., Izadi, S., and Hilliges, O. Steerable augmented reality with the beamatron. In *Proceedings of the 25th Annual ACM Symposium on User Interface Software and Technology*, UIST '12, ACM (New York, NY, USA, 2012), 413–422.

[4] Wilson, A. D. Using a depth camera as a touch sensor. In *ACM International Conference on Interactive Tabletops and Surfaces*, ITS '10, ACM (New York, NY, USA, 2010), 69–72.

[5] Wilson, A. D., and Benko, H. Combining multiple depth cameras and projectors for interactions on, above and between surfaces. In *Proceedings of the 23Nd Annual ACM Symposium on User Interface Software and Technology*, UIST '10, ACM (New York, NY, USA, 2010), 273–282.

[6] Winkler, C., Seifert, J., Dobbelstein, D., and Rukzio, E. Pervasive information through constant personal projection: The ambient mobile pervasive display (amp-d). In *Proceedings of the 32Nd Annual ACM Conference on Human Factors in Computing Systems*, CHI '14, ACM (New York, NY, USA, 2014), 4117–4126.

[7] Xiao, R., Harrison, C., and Hudson, S. E. Worldkit: Rapid and easy creation of ad-hoc interactive applications on everyday surfaces. In *Proceedings of the SIGCHI Conference on Human Factors in Computing Systems*, CHI '13, ACM (New York, NY, USA, 2013), 879–888.

[8] Yoo, H. W., Kim, W. H., Park, J. W., Lee, W. H., and Chung, M. J. Real-time plane detection based on depth map from kinect. In *Robotics (ISR), 2013 44th International Symposium on* (Oct 2013), 1–4.

Task Assignment and Visualization on Tabletop and Smartphones

Benedikt Haas
University of Regensburg
Media Informatics Group
Regensburg, 93040 Germany
benedikt.haas@stud.uni-regensburg.de

Florian Echtler
University of Regensburg
Media Informatics Group
Regensburg, 93040 Germany
Florian.echtler@ur.de

ITS 2014, November 16–19, 2014, Dresden, Germany.
ACM 978-1-4503-2587-5/14/11.
http://dx.doi.org/10.1145/2669485.2669538

Abstract

This paper introduces a system to assign and visualize tasks of projects for tabletop computers and smartphone devices. In general, task assignment is a highly collaborative process and requires intensive discussions among project participants. Therefore, face-to-face communication is recommended for this process because it promises better results than network-based communication. It is faster in reaching a consensus, richer in terms of quality of communication and tends to be more satisfying for the group (compared to computer-mediated communication) [2]. The use of a tabletop system promises to deliver benefits of both worlds: the productivity and availability of computer-mediated systems and the social benefits of face-to-face communication. To this end, we introduce MultiTask, a digital tool to plan projects and assign related tasks. MultiTask consists of two components: a tabletop application for table discussions and an Android companion application with limited interaction possibilities in order to provide better availability while on the move. An explorative evaluation involving qualitative methodologies was conducted in order to improve the system and identify participants' preferences regarding this approach.

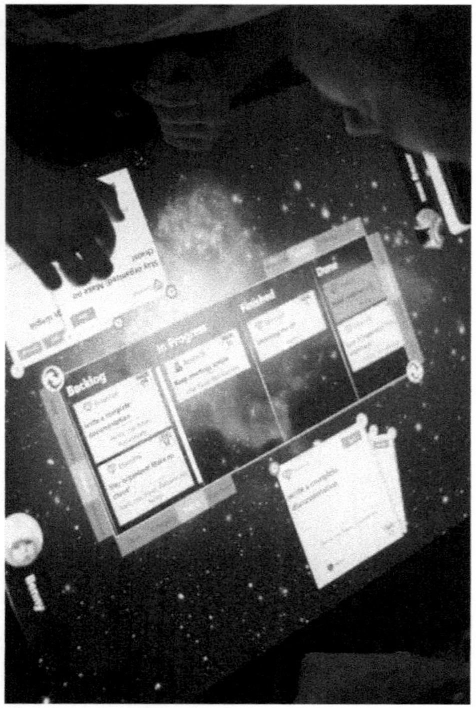

Figure 1: Exemplary use of tabletop-system MultiTask with two users

Author Keywords
Task assignment; task visualization; face-to-face collaboration; direct manipulation; tabletop (surface) computers; smartphone devices

ACM Classification Keywords

Introduction
Meetings are a group activity among participants of a project. Amongst other things, they are an important instrument to coordinate and delegate tasks. Despite this fact, meetings often have the reputation to be unproductive and inefficient. Therefore, face-to-face meetings often are avoided and the participants communicate through computer mediated systems and tools, for example e-mail or desktop applications such as Skype. Even if computer mediated systems appear to be much faster, they are worse in terms of quality and satisfaction. Moreover, face-to-face meetings are usually faster in finding a consensus [2]. To improve productivity of face-to-face meetings, certain techniques are used to structure their progress. One approach which is also used in scrum meetings – an agile method of project management – is to write index cards for gathering ideas, topics or tasks. Traditionally, the index cards are spread on a table and each participant can manipulate them. Manipulation includes editing a card, moving, rotating a card towards another person and trashing a card when it is no longer needed. [3] When a meeting is finished, one person usually gathers all index cards and keeps them until the following meeting. In the next meeting, that person has to rearrange the index cards to continue where the previous meeting has left off so that the participants can collaboratively update the status of the project.

This seems like a good practice but it has some flaws. Often the availability of the results for each team member is limited or there is a lot of effort needed to keep it up-to-date. Additionally the possibilities of index cards are limited to normally only write a short text. Therefore, we try to support and enhance this approach of face-to-face meetings with a digital system for tabletops and smartphones (but at the same time keep the core feeling of a face-to-face meeting). During development, two main pillars were kept in mind:

- Add a benefit to the traditional practice
- Keep the essential feeling of a face-to-face meeting

Related Work
There is a large number of studies which use tabletop-based applications for collaborative scenarios like meetings. However, these studies often focus on different aspects of this topic. For example, Liu and Shi [5] explored the use and benefits of oversized tabletops with 4K-Panels for big meeting scenarios. This is an interesting point of view since the supported number of participants for digital tabletop systems is often limited by the size of the tabletop. Another focus is to examine the different input modalities a tabletop can handle.

Hunter, Maes, Scott & Kaufman [4] made a complex installation including cameras alongside a tabletop system to attempt to track as much information as possible during a meeting. This includes, e.g., even handwritten information on paper which they tried to transfer automatically into the tabletop so that any information is collected in one digital system.

Ghanam, Wang and Maurer [3] focused on identifying the best modality to generate content for participants of a meeting. Their *Agile Planner for Digital Tabletops* was able to allow handwriting and speech input alongside of touch input. Their findings help to understand that touch input delivers the best and most satisfying results for participants. There was one important restriction: Since their used tabletop was only able to handle single-touch input, it was emphasized that multi-user-applications must provide multi-touch input to support its purpose properly. Nowadays this is not an obstacle since tabletops normally feature multi-touch input inherently.

Tabletop systems also deliver good results for creative group activities like mind-mapping [7] or card sorting [6]. Will, Bazo, Meier & Wolff found that tabletops and multi-device scenarios are rather successful for collaborative and creative work like building a mind-map. It was possible to interact via smartphone with the tabletop system. However, for such a system, it is important to be intuitive and error tolerant. They discovered that repeating gestures or inputs is frustrating for the user.

Tabletop systems also seem to be appropriate for task assignment. Dep [2] introduced a system that allowed project managers to assign different tasks to project members and define workloads. The system was able to deliver a Gantt Chart and display all resources. In our own work we tried to consider all their findings and concentrate on their positive aspects to deliver a user friendly system. So the system should be a combination of all successful approaches. Therefore for example our system MultiTask allows setting some parameters of a task and assigning tasks to project members.

Prototype

The developed system MultiTask consists of two components: A main application for a tabletop system and a companion application for Android devices. For the main application, a Samsung SUR40 tabletop was used. Its size is 40 inches and it runs with Microsoft PixelSense (previously called Microsoft Surface 2.0). Due to this fact MultiTask for tabletop platforms allows the user to move, rotate and scale task elements via known touch gestures. Consequently, it is easy to manipulate elements after a new project was created or an existing project was loaded.

Each task element possesses two different states: a presentation state and an edit state. In presentation state (see figure 2) set parameters are simply displayed and cannot be edited so that a user does not have to be afraid of changing tasks while moving, rotating or scaling them. In this mode the group can discuss and debate tasks. In edit mode (see figure 3) almost every parameter of a task can be changed. To this end, a virtual keyboard appears and there is additional space for manipulations. (For suitable input techniques, we used known best practices. For example, a date picker was implemented in a similar manner to existing date widgets from iOS or Android devices.)

However, there is one exception to this rule: the progress of a task can be changed in presentation mode since a progress change (backlog, in progress, finished, done) often is agreed upon in verbal discussion and it seems to be more natural to have the presentation state as a default mode. To provide better overview, tasks can be hidden and brought back when they are needed. For this purpose an organization

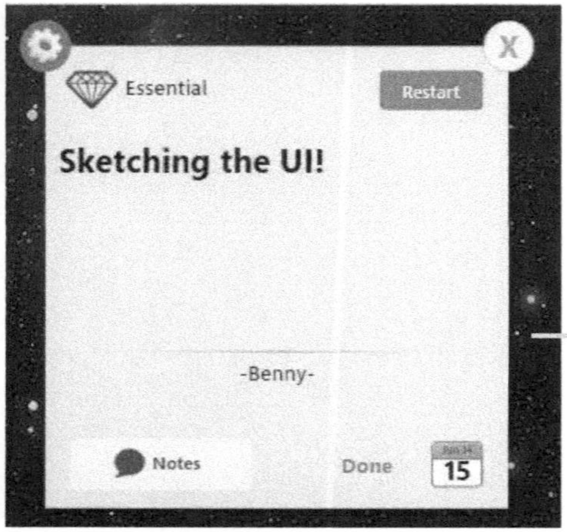

Figure 2: Presentation mode of a task

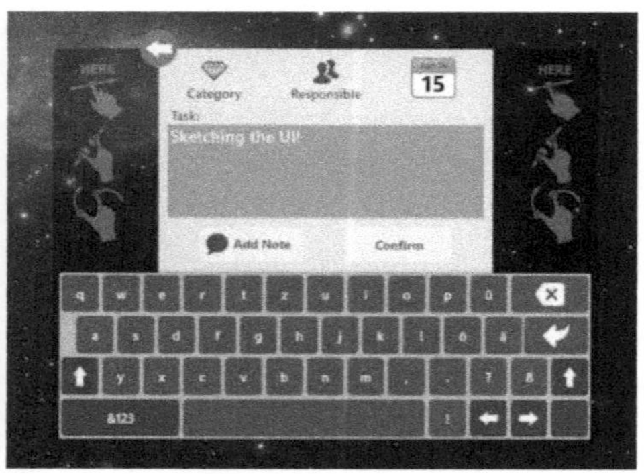

Figure 3: Editing mode of task from figure 2 with different interaction possibilities to set and change parameters

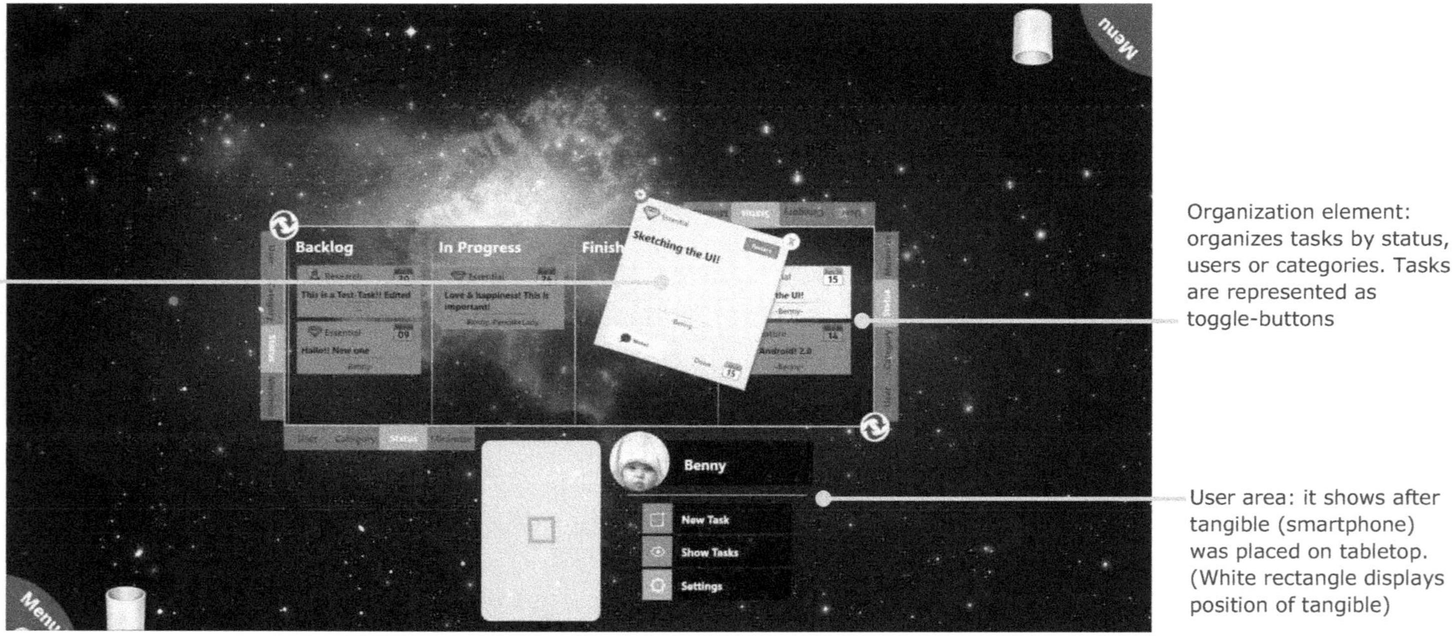

Figure 4: Tabletop application MultiTask (Screenshot from Simulator)

element (see figure 4) is located at the middle of the tabletop. It can be used to sort available tasks by users, categories and progress and gives feedback about the visibility of a specific task. This organizational element can also be minimized to offer the user the full space of the tabletop.

All the information is persistently stored in a cloud service so in theory team members can access their information on any platform. We also implemented a companion application for Android devices. Through this app, the results and changes from the tabletop application can be seen on the fly. It also gives the user some intentionally limited interaction possibilities. In the smartphone application, team members can see all the information and can change the progress of a task or write notes to a specific task. Since the app updates in real-time, it even allows team members to chat through task notes if they want to. In addition to that the user can connect the application with his existing profile or create a new one and is able to completely customize his profile with the smartphone application. However, this are the limits of the app's features because MultiTask tries to support traditional face-to-face meeting structures and tries to bring team members together to collaboratively work on refinements and changes.

Furthermore, the smartphone even can be used in parallel when using the tabletop-application. By placing a smartphone with a suitable fiducial marker on the tabletop, a user-specific area appears (see figure 4). The user can sign in and create tasks, see assigned tasks, change settings or individualize the user profile. Smartphones act as tangibles to enable each user to show, re-position and rotate the individual user area.

Evaluation
An explorative evaluation was conducted to validate the realization of our given requirements. The system should provide a tangible benefit to the user and it should provide the essential advantages of a face-to-face-meeting. Furthermore, by means of an evaluation usability issues should be identified and eliminated to improve the overall experience with MultiTask. To this end, 7 participants were involved who tested two iterations of the system. Although 7 participants are not enough to deliver a final result, they were able to identify major usability issues and give a glimpse of the system's potential. In addition, the system underwent a series of informal tests alongside the implementation until a first testable version was completed. After some major usability issues were found by the participants, a second iteration was implemented to eliminate these issues. The second testable version was also evaluated and was very positively received by users. A lot of users said that it was easy to use and appealing because of the big size of the elements and the forgiving zones for manipulation. Furthermore users mentioned positively that each element can be rotated or flipped to solve perspective problems. Furthermore the concept of having a central tabletop application for face-to-face-meetings and a companion application for mobile devices for the time between meetings was very well received and almost each participant mentioned it as a very practical and appealing combination.

We employed qualitative methodologies for the evaluation. To simulate a meeting, participants did not individually evaluate the system but were grouped into teams of 2-3 persons. They had to complete given tasks and were asked to think aloud during the evaluation. This approach was helpful to observe and identify remaining usability issues by taking notes. Afterwards, each participant was separately interviewed to determine his opinion and perception of the system. Furthermore, participants were asked to complete an AttrakDiff2 questionnaire [1] to get a first impression of the qualities of MultiTask.

Our findings showed that users have no tolerance of interaction models which are not immediately obvious. Consequently, the first testable version of the system was in some cases perceived as impractical because of one not fully intuitive function. The problem was the association of the visibility of a task and its reference-button/toggle-button (see figure 4). There were also some minor additional issues which all could be eliminated in a second iteration. Very well practical and hedonical qualities were ascribed to this second testable version of the system. According to the automated reporting of AttrakDiff2 the system MultiTask appears 'very attractive' to users. Also users are assisted by MultiTask very well and it is classified as 'desired'. However it has to be mentioned again that the number of participants weren't enough to make reliable statements. It only can be seen as a first trend.

Conclusion & Future Work
Overall the introduced system MultiTask is perceived very positively and shows a lot of potential. It delivers on the set requirements since the system adds a benefit to the traditional practice. For example, the task

data is immediately available, stored persistently and the features like settable parameters and comments enhance the experience further. It was observed that users had a certain amount of "fun" while interacting with the table and through the interviews, we discovered that users felt comfortable while using the system. This led to a comfortable atmosphere during the meetings and encouraged the discussion. Such a system could be an alternative for companies. However it also became clear that the size of the used tabletop Samsung SUR40 is not sufficient to hold a meeting with more than four persons at most. The best group size was only two persons. Furthermore, some features need to become more seamless. For example, the authentication of user profiles can be improved by connecting smartphone (acts also as tangible) and tabletop via Bluetooth and handle it automatically in the background. Also, a lot of users asked for a smart positioning of tasks so they are always visible perfectly. Moreover a live streaming service could be possible, if a participant can't make it to a meeting. Although MultiTask is not yet ready for the market, it represents a very solid basis for future systems.

References

[1] AttrakDiff http://attrakdiff.de/index-en.html.

[2] Dep, C.K. Collaborative Task Assignment on Tabletop Computer. *Proc. ITS 2013,* ACM Press (2013), 453-456.

[3] Ghanam, Y., Wang, X., Maurer, F. Utilizing Digital Tabletops in Collocated Agile Planning Meetings. *Proc. Agile 2008*, IEEE (2008), 51-62.

[4] Hunter, S., Maes, P., Scott, S., Kaufman, H. MemTable: An Integrated System for Capture and Recall of Shared Histories in Group Workspace. *Proc. CHI 2011*, ACM Press (2011), 3305-3314.

[5] Liu, J., Shi, Y. uMeeting, an Efficient Co-located Meeting System on Large-Scale Tabletop. *Human-Computer Iinteraction: Users and Applications,* Springer (2011), 368-374.

[6] Loizides, F., Vasiliou, C., Ioannou, A., Zaphiris P. Collaboratively Creating a Thematic Repository Using Interactive Table-Top Technology. *Theory and Practice of Digital Libraries*, Springer (2012), 512-516.

[7] Will, S., Bazo, A., Meier, F., Wolff, C. Multi/Touch/Device MindMapper: Digitalisierung von Kreativprozessen. Proc. ISI 2013, Fachhochschule Potsdam (2013), 105-117. opus4.kobv.de/opus4-fhpotsdam/files/401/will.pdf.

X-O Arch Menu: Combining Precise Positioning with Efficient Menu Selection on Touch Devices

Felix Thalmann
TU Dresden,
Interactive Media Lab
Nöthnitzer Straße 46
Dresden, 01062 Germany
felix.thalmann@tu-dresden.de

Marcel Heckel
Fraunhofer Institute for
Transportation and
Infrastructure Systems
IVI
Zeunerstraße 38
Dresden, 01069 Germany
marcel.heckel@ivi.fraunhofer.de

Ulrich von Zadow
TU Dresden,
Interactive Media Lab
Nöthnitzer Straße 46
Dresden, 01062 Germany
uzadow@acm.org

Raimund Dachselt
TU Dresden,
Interactive Media Lab
Nöthnitzer Straße 46
Dresden, 01062 Germany
dachselt@acm.org

Figure 1: X-O Arch Menu used in MobiKat [3], an application for disaster management

ITS 2014, November 16–19, 2014, Dresden, Germany.
ACM 978-1-4503-2587-5/14/11.
http://dx.doi.org/10.1145/2669485.2669539

Abstract
Support for precise positioning is cruical for many touch applications, and an efficient way to select the action at that point is very desirable in many cases as well. We draw upon existing work in the area of touch accuracy and touch menus to contribute the *X-O Arch Menu*. Our menu seamlessly combines precise positioning and fast, hierarcial menu selection. Furthermore, we introduce a novel optimization to pie menus that allows usage in limited screen space. The menu is fully implemented; we have created a touch-enabled version of a commercially available application using it.

Author Keywords
mobile devices; touchscreens; interaction techniques; occlusion; precise target acquisition; menu techniques

ACM Classification Keywords
H.5.2 [User Interfaces]: Input Devices and Strategies, Interaction Styles.

Introduction
Pointing at a position and then giving additional information about the object of interest is a common form of person-to-person communication. We present an innovative touch menu, the X-O Arch Menu (Figure 1), that captures this principle, seamlessly integrating positioning

and the selection of pertinent information. For instance, the technique can be used wherever precise positioning of hierarcially organized content is needed (e.g., the placement of symbols on maps).

Accurate touch positioning can always be achieved by zooming an area of interest (e.g., Bederson and Hollan's PAD++ [1]). Integrating fingerprint recognition [6] and displaying the area below the touch in an unoccluded area (Shift by Vogel and Baudisch [10]) are two further possibilities. Finally, Take-Off by Sears and Shneiderman [9] shows a crosshair at an offset to the touch position. The crosshair is shown when a touch occurs and can be dragged by moving the finger; the position is fixed when the finger is removed.

Research in the area of efficient touch menus includes Francone et al.'s Wavelet Menus [4], which expand upon the initial Marking Menus by Kurtenbach et al. [8]. Hesselmann et al. [5] provides an occclusion-aware extension for tabletops, and Kin et al. [7] adapt marking menus for two-handed use.

Drawing upon this research, we combined the Take-Off technique for precise selection with a circular menu that handles occlusion and supports arbitrary hierarchies in restricted screen space. We support the undo of intermediate steps and deliver constant feedback as well as supporting novice and expert modes. The basic steps can be seen in Figure 1: The *X-O Control* in the top image can be dragged. Upon release, a circular menu opens (middle image). Menu selection is performed either by tapping on the items (novice mode) or by performing flick gestures towards the desired items (expert mode, bottom image). In the case of hierarchial menus, all levels of the hierarchy are displayed at the same position, with feedback for previous selections provided at the crosshair position.

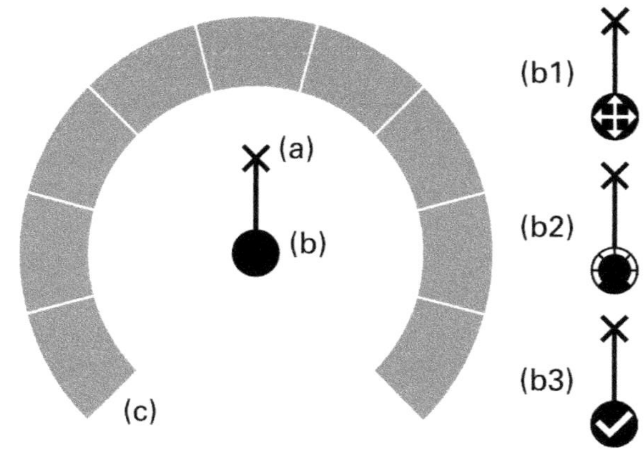

Figure 2: The elements of the X-O Arch Menu: The X-O Control consists of the (a) X Pointer and the (b) O Handle, the surrounding pie menu is the (c) Arch, (b1) Move Cross (b2) Choice Mark (b3) Check Mark.

We implemented the full X-O Arch Menu including novice and expert mode and integrated it into a preexisting application for disaster management, MobiKat [3]. Development proceeded in an iterative fashion, integrating feedback from HCI and domain experts as well as potential users.

In the remainder of the paper, we present the full menu design including static structure and possible interactions. A walkthrough of the integration into MobiKat follows. We then discuss the design decisions and alternative options we considered before closing with an outlook to future work.

Menu Design

In this section, we describe the menu design in more detail and present the structure and graphical elements

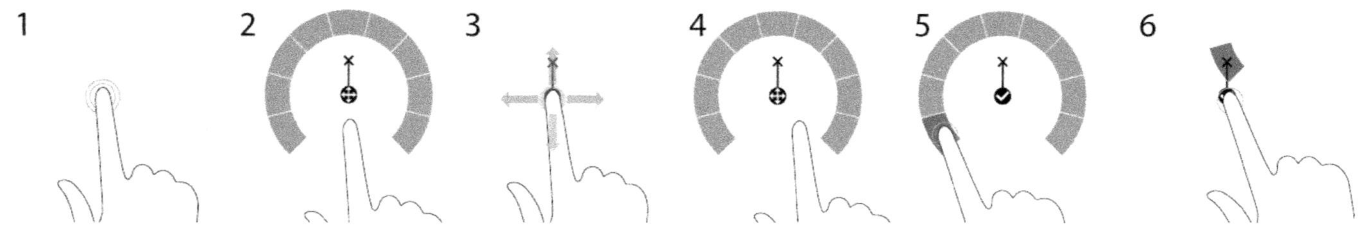

Figure 3: Novice workflow of the X-O Arch Menu: (1) doubletap to open, (2) menu is displayed, (3) precise positioning, (4) release, (5) tap on menu item to select, (6) preview on X is shown, tap on O to confirm.

used as well as the dynamics of interaction and the supported workflow.

Elements
The menu consists of two main elements (Figure 2): The central X-O Control that is used primarily for positioning and the *Arch* (c) that contains the menu items. In turn, it consists of the *O Handle* (b) for dragging and the *X Pointer* (a) that visualizes the selected position.

The O Handle This handle can be dragged around to specify the location. In addition, it functions as confirm button and displays the state of the menu. In the standard state (b1), it shows a drag icon (*Move Cross*). During stroke gestures (expert mode), it shows a *Choice Mark* (b2). Additionally, in novice mode, a *Check Mark* icon signifies the handle's function as a confirm button.

The X Pointer The pointer consists of a small semitransparent dot with an "X" symbol in its center and is used for accurate positioning. After the position has been set, the area is used to show the already selected items in the menu hierarchy and appears like a history stack (Figure 4). Tapping on the X Pointer reverts the last menu selection, while tapping on it when nothing is selected closes the menu.

The Arch This main element contains the actual menu items in an arch-like arrangement. It is visible when the position has been set; if the X-O Control is dragged, the Arch becomes semitransparent to signify that it is inactive.

Interaction and Workflow
The X-O Arch Menu supports two usage modes: novice and expert. Switching between the modes is seamless and possible at any point during the interaction.

Novice Mode In this mode, interaction with the menu consists of simple taps and drags. Figure 3 shows a prototypical interaction sequence. The menu is opened using a doubletap (1). At this point, the X-O Arch Menu is displayed. If the position is not accurate, the user can drag the O Handle to apply modifications. Following this, the user simply taps on the menu items. Each tap moves the selected item to a stack at the X Pointer position and opens a new level of hierarchy (in place of the last one) if available. At any point, a tap on the X Pointer reverses the last selection; tapping on the O Handle confirms the choice and closes the menu.

Expert Mode Expert users can use additional gestures, enabling significantly faster, more seamless interaction

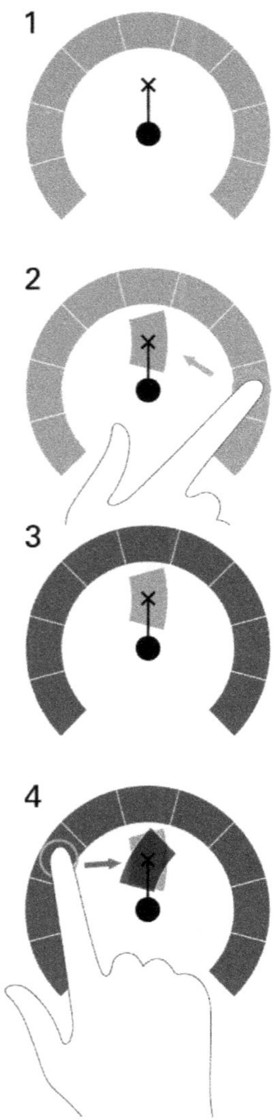

Figure 4: The history stack: As menu items are selected, the chosen items are placed at the X Pointer position.

(Figure 7 shows advanced usage in the context of the developed application). When opening the menu, the last UP of the doubletap can be omitted. The resulting *tap and a half* gesture puts the menu in positioning mode immediately, in which it can be dragged to the precise position intended. This can be followed by a *reverse tap* (UP-DOWN event) that puts the menu in a marking menu-like mode. In this mode, items are selected by swiping to the element and back. As in novice mode, selecting an item opens up a new hierarchy level in place of the last one. In this way, a series of swipes – performed without lifting the finger – can select an item deep in the hierarchy. Lifting the finger on the O Handle accepts and closes the menu, while lifting the finger at other points enables novice mode controls.

Note that expert mode swipes are enabled at any time, even after selecting one or more menu items in novice mode.

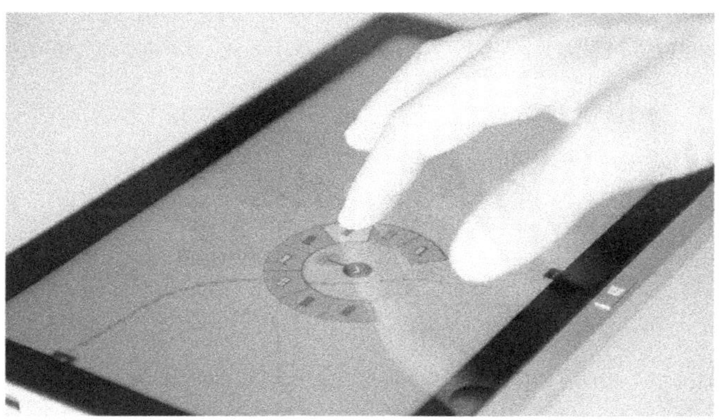

Figure 5: X-O Arch Menu in use in MobiKat.

Application Sample: Tactical Signs

We have integrated X-O Arch Menu into a mobile version of the disaster management software MobiKat [3] (Figure 5). MobiKat is used in emergency situations to coordinate relief forces, where fast and effective decisions are important. The application includes a situation map. Users can place tactical signs that denote relevant actors on this map. As can be seen in Figure 6, these signs are composed of elements that can be assembled hierarchially. An X-O Arch Menu is used to place them on the map quickly and accurately. In this case, the menu hierarchy corresponds to the hierarchy of available tactical signs, and the history stack builds to gradually show the sign the user intends.

The original MobiKat is a traditional desktop interface implemented in Java using JavaFX. The mobile version was developed in cooperation with potential users and runs on a Samsung Series 7 Slate tablet (11.6" display, 1366x768 resolution).

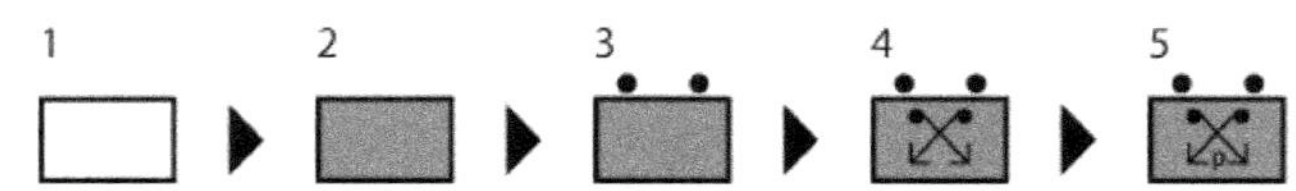

Figure 6: Tactial sign example: (1) Basis, (2) organization, (3) size, (4) mission, (5) details.

Discussion

In integrating precise positioning and complex menus, we made a series of design decisions based on feedback by novice and expert users as well as HCI professionals. We describe them here.

As mentioned in the introduction, one design goal was occlusion avoidance. At no point are menu items occluded in X-O Arch Menu. When the finger is touching

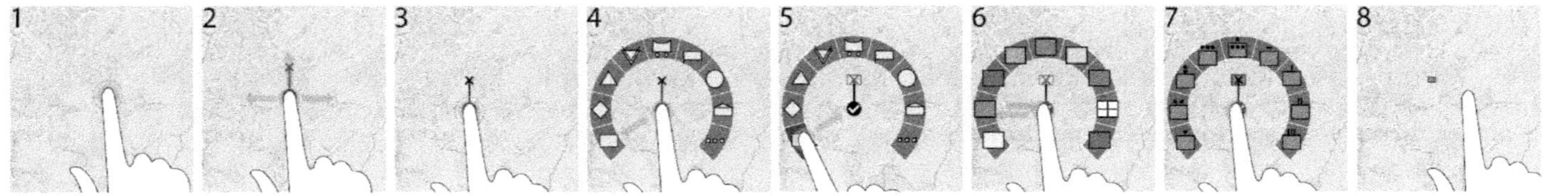

Figure 7: X-O Arch Menu when used by an expert in MobiKat: (1) Tap and a half to open X-O, (2) drag to define position, (3) reverse tap on O to open Arch, (4) swipe to item, (5) swipe from item back to O to confirm selection and go to next level (also exploring by dragging over entries is possible), (6) repeat swipes at second level, (7) display next level, (8) lift the finger on O to accept

the O, the Arch leaves room for the hand. Neither novice mode taps nor expert mode swipes cause significant occlusion. The design is similar to Brandl et al.'s occlusion-aware menus [2], with the difference that we do not distinguish between left- and right-handed users.

The choice of the appropriate technology to use for accurate touch positioning was difficult. While using fingerprint recognition [6] would have been exciting, the technology is not available on standard tablets. Also, while it allows more precise positioning, the technology does not remove occlusion. Shift [10] and Take-Off [9] both provide effective methods for accurate touch positioning. We integrated Take-Off because it is very effective, easy to learn and easy to integrate into a menu. Still, a comparison with Shift would be very interesting.

In adapting Wavelet [4] menus to a smaller screen size, we decided to only show one menu level at a time and switch to back-and-forth swipes for selection. This is a trade-off, since it does result in longer touch paths. Still, the space savings are significant, making positions closer to the screen edge are available for selection. Contrary to most menu designs, the space needed stays constant for hierarchy depths. Furthermore, occlusion is eliminated.

To provide feedback about the selected elements of the hierarchy, we use the stack (Figure 4).

We expect usage in expert mode to have similar characteristics to Wavelet menu usage. Since positions of menu items are fixed relative to the center, users should be able to leverage motor memory for fast and ultimately eyes-free operation of the menu. Compared to Wavelet menus, required paths are somewhat longer, but we expect no qualitative difference. Furthermore, the ability to switch between novice and expert mode at any time should make transition easier and provide a smooth learning curve for the menu.

Pointing close to the borders of the screen is not possible using X-O Arch Menus. This is not a restriction in the case of a pannable background such as a map, but it might be an issue in other use cases. Finally, we use a doubletap to open the menu. This is not a fixed characteristic and has no implication on menu operation. Integration into concrete applications might make other gestures (e.g., Tap, Long Tap) that are not used by the rest of the interface more appropriate.

Conclusion and Future Work

We have presented a novel touch menu technique that allows users to annotate precise positions in large information spaces. The X-O Arch Menu provides a fluid workflow for novices and advanced users. We combined existing approaches in the realms of precise touch interfaces and touch menus to adress the challenges of this area.

Furthermore, we have implemented the design and integrated the menu into an existing large application. At the current point in time, there has been no formal testing of the menu. Qualitative studies of usage in the wild as well as quantitative, comparative studies to verify efficiency are needed. Also, studies could be used to compare the different design alternatives – for instance, to test if integrating Take-Off or Shift is better in this context and to optimize menu parameters such as angles, sizes and distances.

Acknowledgements

This work was supported by the Fraunhofer Institute for Transportation and Infrastructure Systems IVI Dresden. We would like to thank them for supplying initial source code and map materials.

References

[1] Bederson, B. B., and Hollan, J. D. Pad++: A Zooming Graphical Interface for Exploring Alternate Interface Physics. In *Proc. UIST'94*, ACM (1994), 17–26.

[2] Brandl, P., Leitner, J., Seifried, T., Haller, M., Doray, B., and To, P. Occlusion-Aware Menu Design for Digital Tabletops. In *Proc. CHI'09*, ACM (2009), 3223–3228.

[3] Danowski, K. MobiKat-Integriertes System zur Unterstützung der Katastrophenbewältigung und der alltäglichen Gefahrenabwehr. *Fraunhofer-Institut fur Verkehrs-und Infrastruktursysteme IVI* (2007).

[4] Francone, J., Bailly, G., Nigay, L., and Lecolinet, E. Wavelet Menus: A Stacking Metaphor for Adapting Marking Menus to Mobile Devices. In *Proc. MobileHCI'09*, ACM (2009), 49.

[5] Hesselmann, T., Flöring, S., and Schmitt, M. Stacked Half-Pie Menus: Navigating Nested Menus on Interactive Tabletops. In *Proc. ITS'09*, ACM (2009), 173–180.

[6] Holz, C., and Baudisch, P. The Generalized Perceived Input Point Model and How to Double Touch Accuracy by Extracting Fingerprints. In *Proc. CHI'10*, ACM (2010), 581–590.

[7] Kin, K., Hartmann, B., and Agrawala, M. Two-Handed Marking Menus for Multitouch Devices. *TOCHI'11 18*, 3 (2011), 16.

[8] Kurtenbach, G., and Buxton, W. The Limits of Expert Performance Using Hierarchic Marking Menus. In *Proc. INTERACT'93 and CHI'93*, ACM (1993), 482–487.

[9] Sears, A., and Shneiderman, B. High Precision Touchscreens: Design Strategies and Comparisons with a Mouse. *Int. J. Man-Mach. Stud. 34*, 4 (Apr. 1991), 593–613.

[10] Vogel, D., and Baudisch, P. Shift: A Technique for Operating Pen-Based Interfaces using Touch. In *Proc. CHI'07*, ACM (2007), 657–666.

Second Look: Combining Interactive Surfaces with Wearable Computing to Support Creative Writing

Pedro Campos
Frederica Gonçalves
Michael Martins
Madeira-ITI
Polo Científico e Tecnológico da Madeira, floor -2
Caminho da Penteada
9020-105 Funchal, Portugal
pedro.campos@m-iti.org
frederica.goncalves@m-iti.org
michael.martins@m-iti.org

Miguel Campos
Paulo Freitas
WowSystems, LLC
R. Mary Jane Wilson, 21 G
9050-446 Funchal, Portugal
miguel.campos@wowsystems.pt
paulo.freitas@wowsystems.pt

ITS 2014, November 16–19, 2014, Dresden, Germany.
ACM 978-1-4503-2587-5/14/11.
http://dx.doi.org/10.1145/2669485.2669540

Abstract
We present "Second Look", a platform of interactive surfaces and wearable computing for helping people, in particular creative writers, to overcome writer's block. The novelty of our systems stems from the addition of wearable devices (Google Glass) and crowdsourcing to improve creative writing on tablets and phones.

A primary challenge in developing and evaluating creativity support tools is that we are not able to detect *when* a person is being creative. Our approach improves current ones by exploring the "in-the-moment" creativity and supporting it with adaptive ubiquitous technologies that try to keep people in a creative experience peak for a longer period of time.

Author Keywords
Creative writing tools; creativity support tools; interactive surfaces; wearable computing; crowdsourcing; tablets; Google Glass; glassware; augmented reality.

ACM Classification Keywords
H.5.m. Information interfaces and presentation (e.g., HCI): Miscellaneous.

Motivation and Rationale

Writing is one of the oldest human activities, dating back as far as the 3200 BCE. However, the rise of digital computing accelerated writing in all its forms, and people in today's society have even easier access to reading and writing. In this poster, we describe a platform of interactive surfaces that aims at leveraging emerging ICT technologies to design, implement and take to market a novel set of products targeted at creative writers, especially those who work at creative industries SMEs and wish to become more creative by adopting better tools for creative writing. These products are a Google Glass app and a companion iOS (iPhone and iPad) app. The Glass app's goal is to support serendipity and inspiration for writers on the move. The iOS app also supports that and allows the improvement of writing pieces as well as the evolution of creative texts, also on the move. These apps connect to a crowdsourcing engine that fosters the sharing and searching of creative bits (poetry, writing prompts, scenarios, photos, videos). In the future they will also connect to a workflow engine that will tailor the writing process to individual needs.

Our proposal is better than the current state of the art tools, because it addresses the specific challenges faced by both amateur and professional creative writers. Moreover, it embodies a platform for the creation, searching and sharing of creative bits that compose the essence of this activity. The creative writing process can be divided into six different stages: pre-writing, drafting, revising, editing, evaluating and publishing. Successful writers write regularly and develop a routine. Amateur writers struggle with this. Most of the work of successful writers (up to 90% of their work) does not make it to the final version [1,2]. However, regular writing strengthens their voice and their levels of motivation. Several take inspiration from their everyday lives and conversations. Second Look's tools are ubiquitous, which means for added support to the inspiration sources that come up everyday, anytime, anywhere. A primary challenge in developing and evaluating creativity support tools is that we are not able to detect *when* a person is being creative. Our approach improves current ones by exploring the "in-the-moment" creativity and supporting it with adaptive ubiquitous technologies that try to keep people in a creative experience peak for a longer period of time. The wearable technology Google Glass has not hit the market yet, but developers are rushing to build apps for the new device to take advantage of what they hope is the "next big thing". In this poster, we argue that interactive surfaces and wearable devices, like the Glass, may also find application as a channel for creative expression. A final aspect of innovation worth mentioning is related to the way people collect and share bits of creativity, especially writing bits. A better understanding of how creativity is spread, stored and reused is a side effect result that will arise from the data we will sample through the platform, specifically from the crowdsourcing engine, which will embody a "collective intelligence" of creative writers.

Related Work

The underlying premise of this proposal revolves around gaining insight about the creative writers' perspective on their own writing process, as a way to naturally brainstorm tools and techniques that better support that process. Surprisingly enough, there is relatively little research work performed around tools, but some researchers, e.g. Magnifico [6], have investigated how to improve the creative writing

A Second Look user – a creative writer – spots an inspirational spot for her next novel and geotags some photos with Google Glass. At the same time she also uses the mobile app to write a few lines from her "in-the-moment" creativity and geotags them along.

process. Giving students opportunities to interact with real readers of their work may not only motivate them to write, but also to take on new literacies and see themselves as writers in new ways. Advances regarding tool support have been mostly made in very specific areas. For example, Yannopoulos [4] proposed a symbolic language intended to express the content of film (motion pictures), much like notes provide a language for the writing of music, therefore bringing a new approach to the creative process of filmmaking.

Since writing is frequently a collaborative activity, some researchers such as [3] chose to study the usage of tools and resources for computer supported collaborative writing. They implemented a custom-made computer-supported environment that enables pairs of high school students to collaborate in writing an argumentative essay. They concluded that the analyzed tools reflected the writing strategies adopted by the students. Other authors focused on computer writing tools used during the production of documents in a professional setting [4]. They report on a focus group with professional writers, during which they discussed their experience using computer tools to write documents, also describing their practices, pointing out the most important problems they encounter, and analyzing their needs. Based on this work, they describe LinguisTech, a reference web site for helping language professionals. Taking into consideration that digital tools for creative writing should help users produce more, some researchers note that the productivity expectations towards writers are higher than ever [5]. Therefore, there is a need for tool support that can promote not only the writers' creativity but also productivity levels, as proposed by this project.

Usage Scenario

Figure 1 shows one possible scenario of usage. A writer – or any creative industries professional – is taking a walk through a park. He is looking for something to inspire his next novel, and wearing the Google Glass creative writing app for supporting serendipity. The Glass's GPS is connected to a crowdsourcing engine that looks up the creative writing prompts for a particular bench in that park (which were placed there previously by another Second Look user who thought the bench was a good spot). The app then displays:

TELL THIS STORY:
There's a mysterious man sitting on a park bench, reading a newspaper.

The writer finds it curious, so he scans for an augmented reality tag that triggers a series of comments other creative writers have made about stories in parks, as well as other people's photos taken during moments of inspiration.

Finally, inspiration is found everywhere, and writers tie people and places to their writings. Taking advantage of the Glass's quick picture button, the writer takes a photo of the park bench, something that he will revisit mentally when he goes back to his desktop-based creative writing app at home. The next day, another user feels in need of inspiration and opens his mobile Second Look app to check if there are any AR markers near his location. He notices that there is one active in that same park that is just across the street from his house so he goes there in order to scan the card and be able to read the original prompt and the story written by all the other users relative to that card.

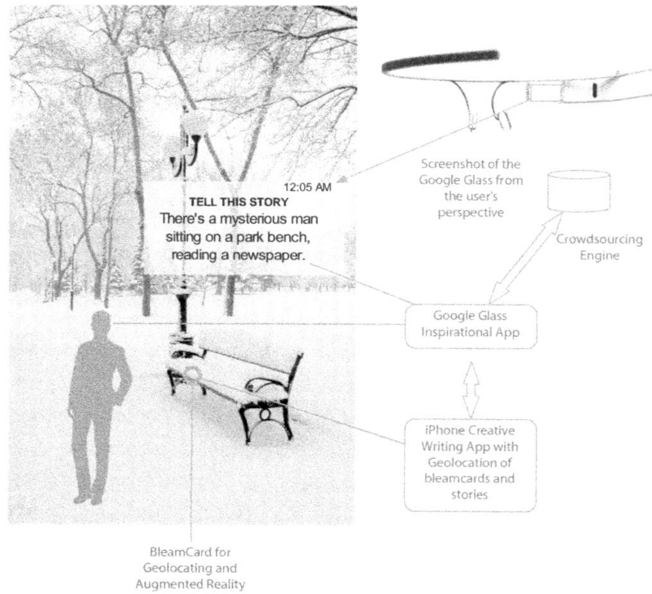

Figure 1. A possible scenario for Second Look.

Conclusions

In the near future, smartglasses will not just be a scaled down add-on to existing interactive surfaces, but also an augmentation of a user's primary sense. This will open up an entirely new market of wearable devices and their corresponding apps, synchronized with the interactive surfaces we already are familiar with. In this poster, we present a system that can integrate interactive surfaces (iPhone and iPad) in such a way they could improve the creativity and productivity of creative writers. The process for poetry generation or any other kind of creative writing is very strongly visual. A visual trigger is usually involved, and a textual leap from image or motion happens. We believe that mobile interactive surfaces coupled with Google Glass will become a natural part in that chain, and that it also will help creative writers to use their natural inventive process for writing.

Acknowledgements. This project was funded by the Portuguese Science Foundation through grant no. PEst-OE/EEI/LA0009/2013 and the Regional Funding Knowledge+, MADFDR-01-0189-FEDER-000010.

References

[1] Twyla Tharp (2006). *The Creative Habit: Learn It and Use It for Life*. Simon & Schuster.

[2] Erin A. Carroll and Celine Latulipe (2012). Triangulating the personal creative experience: self-report, external judgments, and physiology. In *Proceedings of Graphics Interface 2012* (GI '12). Canadian Information Processing Society, Toronto, Ont., Canada, Canada, 53-60.

[3] Gal Oestreicher-Singer and Lior Zalmanson. 2013. Content or community? a digital business strategy for content providers in the social age. *MIS Q.* 37, 2 (June 2013), 591-616.

[4] Angelos Yannopoulos. 2013. DirectorNotation: Artistic and technological system for professional film directing. *Journal of Computing and Cultural Heritage* 6, 1, Article 2.

[5] Khédija Nakbi. 2002. La rédactologie: domaine, méthode et compétences. *ASp*, 37-38, pages 15-26.

[6] Magnifico, A. (2010). "Getting others' perspectives": a case study of creative writing environments and mentorship. In *Proceedings of the 9th International Conference of the Learning Sciences - Volume 1* (ICLS'10), Kimberly Gomez, Leilah Lyons, and Joshua Radinsky (Eds.), Vol. 1. pp. 1151-1157.

Making Tabletop Interaction Accessible for Blind Users

Andreas Kunz
ETH Zurich
Leonhardstrasse 21
8092 Zurich, Switzerland
kunz@iwf.mavt.ethz.ch

Dirk Schnelle-Walka
TU Darmstadt
Hochschulstraβe 10
64289 Darmstadt, Germany
dirk@tk.informatik.tu-darmstadt.de

Ali Alavi
ETH Zurich
Leonhardstrasse 21
8092 Zurich, Switzerland
alavi@iwf.mavt.ethz.ch

Stephan Pölzer
Johannes Kepler-University
Altenbergerstrasse 69
4040 Linz, Austria
stephan.poelzer@jku.at

Max Mühlhäuser
TU Darmstadt
Hochschulstraβe 10
64289 Darmstadt, Germany
max@informatik.tu-darmstadt.de

Klaus Miesenberger
Johannes Kepler-University
Altenbergerstrasse 69
4040 Linz, Austria
klaus.miesenberger@jku.at

ITS '14, Nov 16-19, 2014, Dresden, Germany
ACM 978-1-4503-2587-5/14/11.
http://dx.doi.org/10.1145/2669485.2669541

Abstract
Tabletop systems and their interaction capabilities are typically a domain for sighted people only. While the content on the tabletop can already be made accessible to blind people, the interaction above the tabletop is still inaccessible. This paper describes our approach towards making the above tabletop interaction accessible to blind people by using LEAP sensors and speech recognition.

Author Keywords
Tabletop interaction; Deictic gestures; Accessibility

ACM Classification Keywords
H.5.2. Group and Organization Interfaces: Computer-supported cooperative work.

Introduction
In the recent years, interactive tabletop systems gain significant importance, since new technologies offer low-latency multi-user interaction. The latter made such systems suitable to be used in smaller team meetings for problem solving and idea generation. For such an idea generation, mind maps are one of the established ways to generate, visualize, structure and classify ideas [18] on a common workspace. Other scenarios for using interactive surfaces include teaching and learning [9]. However, they rely on visual

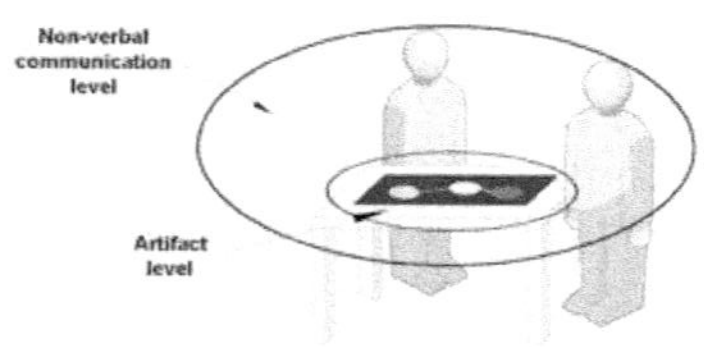

Figure 1 Brainstorming integrates non-verbal communication and artifact level elements [6], [7].

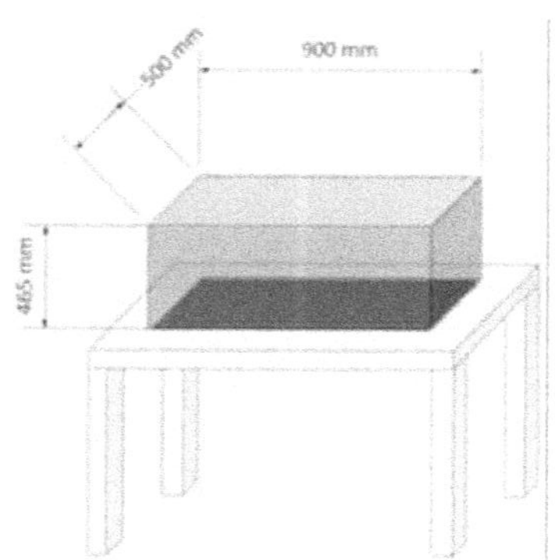

Figure 2 Sketch of the tracking above the PixelSense.

communication and visual perception of the artifacts [1], [19], excluding blind or partially sighted people or hindering their full participation in the meeting.

The use of this visual augmented communication in such settings is described by Ellis et al. [5], stating that explanatory gestures are used above the table on the non-verbal communication level (see Figure 1). Within this group of nonverbal communication elements, pointing gestures – and more specific so-called deictic gestures – are important. Deictic gestures are co-speech pointing gestures [4], which highlight a certain artifacts on the common workspace. Thus, as stated by Schnelle-Walka et al. [17], an inclusive mind map must support (i) access for the blind participants to the artifacts being displayed on the tabletop, and (ii) access to the important non-verbal communication elements.

While many digital content and interactions on the tabletop (the artifact level) can already be accessed by blind people using standard screen readers together with a Braille display and/or speech output [15], non-verbal communication elements above the tabletop are almost impossible to access, if they are not reflected by the artifacts on the tabletop. Suitable means to transfer e.g. deictic gestures in the nonverbal communication level to blind users is still an unsolved issue.

Within this paper, we describe our ongoing efforts to capture these non-verbal communication elements above the tabletop and how to reliably detect deictic gestures. Here, we introduce a first prototype for tracking deictic gestures above the tabletop and to display them together with the content on the tabletop to blind users.

Design Considerations

Our work is based on the evaluation results of a focus group with blind participants as described in [17]. This focus group was in favor of detecting deictic gestures which are known and considered to be the most relevant form of nonverbal communication elements. However, frequent use of such gestures may result in an information overload if these gestures are presented without any filtering. The participants also saw the danger of interpretation errors, distraction and information overflow [9].

Detecting Pointing Gestures

Within a preliminary study on a predefined mind map, we used a manual transcription of a videotaped session to determine the type and amount of gestures, distinguishing "specific", "area" and "coarse" gestures (see Figure 3).

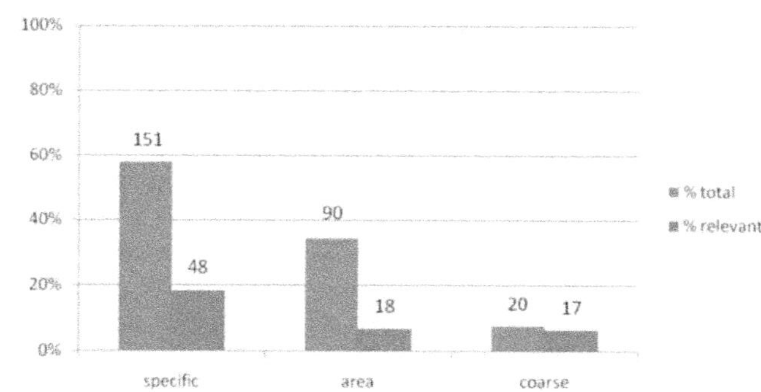

Figure 3 Comparison of relevant and irrelevant pointing gestures.

As it can be seen from Figure 3, the detection of deictic gestures becomes a delicate task, since only specific deictic gestures can be considered to be relevant for a current task.

In a first approach, we placed the MS Kinect about 820 mm above the PixelSense [11], facing downwards onto the tabletop. Since MS Kinect and MS PixelSense work on the same infrared wavelength of λ = 830 nm, their interference triggered random touches on the PixelSense.

Figure 4 Prototypical setup.

As PixelSense [11] together with MS Kinect were not capable of tracking deictic gestures above the table top, we used LEAP Motion sensors [7] to track such gestures (see Figure 5). However, the use of LEAP Motion sensors has two major drawbacks to work around. First, their limited tracking range of about 500 mm requires to equip all sides of the table (with exception of the blind user's position) with such a sensor (see Figure 4). Second, it requires the use of a dedicated computer for each LEAP. As an advantage, the observed tracking accuracy is significantly higher than alternative sensors, such as Microsoft Kinect. Given LEAP's inherent depth accuracy of +/- 0.1 mm, a finger pointing angle of 45° and a height above the tabletop of 450 mm result in a pointing accuracy of +/- 0.35% (see Figure 5).

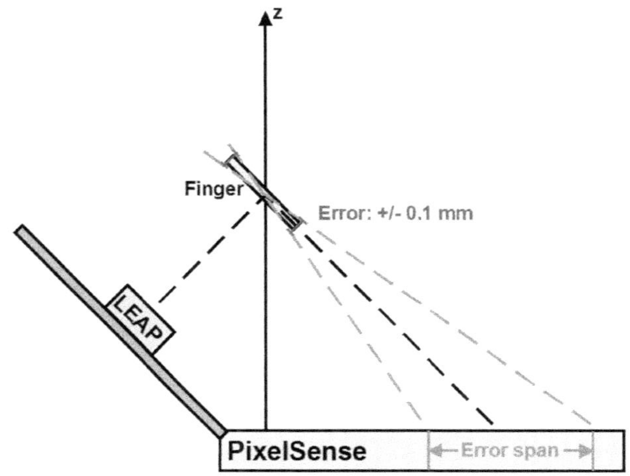

Figure 5 LEAP's measurement setup and position accuracy.

With this setup, it is possible to reliably track pointing gestures to targets on the tabletop, depending on the user's pointing accuracy. To overcome this problem, we show a visual feedback on the screen similar to the approach described by the Majewski et al. for smart homes [9], which encourages the user to align his or her pointing direction with the wanted target.

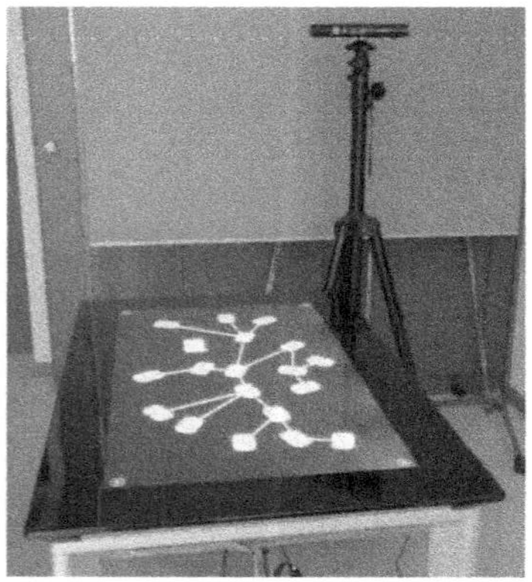

Figure 6 Kinect's microphone array is used for speech recognition.

Speech Recognition

Although pointing gestures can now be tracked with sufficient accuracy, we need to cope with relevance aspects as mentioned above, meaning to differentiate simple pointing gestures and deictic gestures. In order to avoid too many or false notifications to the blind user, it is important to filter deictic gestures only. Following Eisenstein et al. [4], deictic gestures can be understood as co-speech pointing. In a first approach we implemented word spotting for words like "this", "that", "there", etc.

In our system, we employ the Microsoft Speech Server [10] as speech recognizer. The audio is recorded by the Microsoft Kinect that is suited for distant speech recognition thanks to its microphone array, which results in a better audio selectivity in a noisy environment. We place the Kinect on a tripod at one corner of the Pixelsense directed to the opposite corner to avoid interference with the PixelSense and to exploit the capabilities of the microphone array best (Figure 6). By fusing the sensor signals from the speech recognition system and the tracking system, an efficient but simple filtering of deictic gestures is implemented, employing the melting-pot metaphor [12]. Notifications are only given to the blind user if both sensor signals appear with the same time span. Here, we follow the ideas of Nigay and Coutaz to fuse combined use of modalities [12] in the parallel case. We regard information coming from the two different modalities to be in parallel if they appear with a predefined time span. In order to define the duration of this time span, we re-used the transcription of our initial user study. Assuming that a pointing gesture takes longer than speaking to augment an utterance, we measured the duration of typical gestures (see Figure 7).

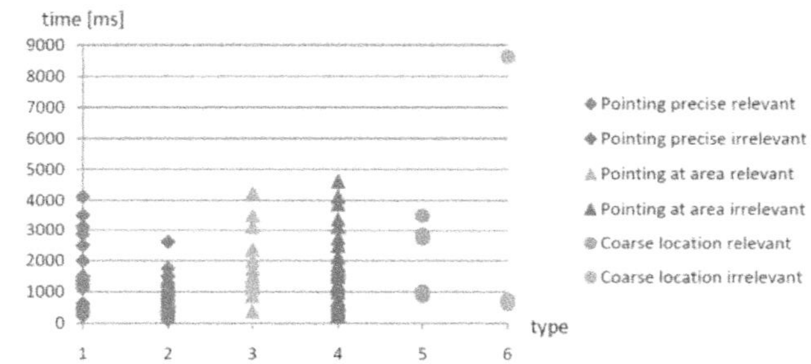

Figure 7 Duration of six different gesture types.

These different types of gestures were measured by manually transcribing a videotaped brainstorming session, in which typically a large amount of gestures occur. However, not all of them are considered to be relevant, since they were made by users without being integrated into the verbal communication flow. Moreover, gestures could be further distinguished by their precision, since users highlighted specific targets (elements of the mind map), or just regions on the table (clusters of the mind map). Also very unspecific and coarse gestures occur, referring to the complete interactive surface (the complete mind map).

For defining the duration of a pointing gesture, the movement time towards the target was not considered, but only the time the finger hovered above the target. Based on these measurements, we set the maximum duration of the observation interval to be $t = 3.5$ s. Only characteristic audio signals (words) within this time span will be further processed in order to indicate deictic gestures.

Presentation to Blind Users

Another crucial role plays the presentation technique for the blind user to make the ongoing interaction above the table-top more accessible. As stated above [9], special care has to be taken not to overload a blind user, so that he/she can still follow an ongoing discussion. Besides the alert message boxes, as they are used e.g. in [1], the blind user has now the possibility to get informed via text-to-speech messages about an occurring pointing gesture. A short beep notifies the blind user about a pointing gesture.

The text of nodes in a mind map tends to be short. An explanatory analysis by Beel and Langer [1] showed that 60% of the nodes have texts with three words at maximum. Currently, we are about to investigate if a rendering of the node contents via text to speech employing a mono-aural headset is suitable to lower distraction while still being able to follow the discussion. The early feedback from blind users for the combination of a beep and a text-to-speech message was positive. The first impression was judged as an unobtrusive possibility to present the pointing gestures to blind users. Further, it allows the blind user to get the important information of the pointing gesture in a quicker way than reading an alert message box.

For now, no empirical evaluation was conducted. However, we tested our prototype in a short brainstorming session of about 15 minutes within a mixed team of blind and sighted users, who were only partly familiar with the goals of the project. Using the serialized representation of the mind map tool[1] which is the first major research result of the project reported in [7], and displaying it on a blind user interface through a screen reader already showed an overall good behavior. The sighted and the blind user could both edit the mind map, while both representations were always consistent [15]. Integrating also the tracked and pre-selected deictic gestures above the tabletop into this presentation scheme seems to be a promising way forward to increase accessibility of non-verbal communication. Especially the synchronization of the individual presentations for the blind and the sighted user was judged to be a good achievement in enabling a visually impaired person to fully take part in a team meeting using a tabletop system. Synchronizing what is going on above the table into this evaluated and approved concept seems to be the right way forward.

[1] http://come.sourceforge.com

Conclusion and Outlook

Within this paper, we presented the procedure how gestures are detected and how they are distinguished between relevant and non-relevant using a speech analyses. This is the core part of overall system description in [7]. Within future work, the whole system will be thoroughly evaluated under various conditions. Moreover, the filtering and smoothing algorithms will be optimized to further reduce the amount of wrong notifications to the blind user.

Acknowledgements

This work has been partially supported by DFG (Germany), FWF (Austria) and SNF (Switzerland) under the project grant number CR21I2L_138601.

References

[1] Beel, J., and Langer, S. An exploratory analysis of mind maps. In: *Proceedings of the 11th ACM symposium on Document engineering*, (2011), 81-84.

[2] Budd, J.W. Mind maps as classroom exercises. In: *Journal of Economic Education*, (2004), 35(1), 35-46

[3] Chow, J., Aug, K., Lichti, D. and Teskey, W. Performance Analysis of a Low-cost Triangulation-based 3D Camera: Microsoft Kinect System. In: *International Society for Photogrammetry and Remote Sensing Congress (ISPRS)*, Vol. 39, (2012), 175-180.

[4] Eisenstein, J. and Christoudias, C.M. A Salience-based Approach to Gesture-Speech Alignment. In: *HLT-NAACL*, Vol. 4, (2004), 25-32.

[5] Ellis, C.A., Gibbs, S.J. and Rein, Groupware: Some Issues and Experiences. In: *Communications of the ACM 34.1* (1991), 39-58.

[6] Kunz, A., Alavi, A., Sinn, P. Integrating Pointing Gesture Detection for Enhancing Brainstorming Meetings Using Kinect and PixelSense. In: *8th International Conference on Digital Enterprise Technology*, (2014), 1-8.

[7] Kunz, A.; Miesenberger, K.; Mühlhäuser, M.; Alavi, A.; Pölzer, S.; Pöll, D. and Heumader, P. Accessibility of Brainstorming Sessions for Blind People. In: *14th International Conference on Computers Helping People with Special Needs*, Springer Lecture Notes in Computer Sciences 8547 (2014), 237-244.

[8] LEAP Motion: https://www.leapmotion.com (accessed 29.7.2014).

[9] Majewski, M.; Dutz, T. and Wichert, R. An Optical Guiding System for Gesture Based Interactions in Smart Environments. In: *Distributed, Ambient, and Pervasive Interactions,* (2014), 154-163.

[10] Microsoft Speech Server (accessed 26.8.2014); http://www.microsoft.com/de-ch/server-cloud/products/windows-server-2012-r2/default.aspx

[11] MS PixelSense (accessed 26.8.2014); http://www.microsoft.com/en-us/pixelsense/default.aspx

[12] Nigay, L. and Coutaz, J. A generic platform for addressing the multimodal challenge. In: *Proceedings of the SIGCHI conference on Human factors in computing systems*, (1995), 98-105.

[13] Nigay, L. and Coutaz, J. A design space for multimodal systems: concurrent processing and data fusion. In: *Proceedings of the INTERACT'93 and CHI'93 conference on Human factors in computing systems*, (1993), 172-178.

[14] Pölzer, S. and Miesenberger, K. Presenting Non-verbal Communication to Blind Users in Brainstorming Sessions. In: *14th International Conference on Computers Helping People with Special Needs*, Springer Lecture Notes in Computer Sciences 8547 (2014), 214-219.

[15] Pölzer, S.; Schnelle-Walka, D.; Pöll, D.; Heumader, P. and Miesenberger, K. Making Brainstorming Meetings Accessible for Blind Users. In: *Proceedings of the 12 European AAATE Conference*, (2013), 653–658.

[16] Roth, W.-M. Gestures: Their Role in Teaching and Learning. In: *Review of Educational Research*, Vol. 71, No. 3 (2001), 365-392.

[17] Schnelle-Walka, D., Alavi, A., Ostie, P., Mühlhäuser, M. and Kunz, A. A Mind Map for Brainstorming Sessions with Blind and Sighted Persons. In: *14th International Conference on Computers Helping People with Special Needs*, Springer Lecture Notes in Computer Sciences 8547 (2014), 214-219.

[18] Shui, W. and Le, W. Mindmap-ng: A Novel Framework for Modeling Effective Thinking. In: *3rd IEEE International Conference on Computer Science and Information Technology (ICCSIT 2010)*, Vol. 2, IEEE (2010), 480-483.

[19] Wang, H.-C., Cosley, D. and Fussell, S.R. Idea Expander: Supporting Group Brainstorming with Conversationally Triggered Visual Thinking Stimuli. In: *Proceedings of the 2010 ACN Conference on Computer Supported Cooperative Work (CSCW 2010)*, ACM Press (2010), 103-106.

Intelligent Ink Annotation Framework that uses User's Intention in Electronic Document Annotation

Hiroki Asai
Waseda University
3-4-1 Okubo,
Shinjuku-ku, Tokyo, Japan
asai@yama.info.waseda.ac.jp

Hayato Yamana
Waseda University
3-4-1 Okubo,
Shinjuku-ku, Tokyo, Japan
yamana@yama.info.waseda.ac.jp

ITS '14, Nov 16-19 2014, Dresden, Germany
ACM 978-1-4503-2587-5/14/11.
http://dx.doi.org/10.1145/2669485.2669542

Abstract
Annotating documents is one of the indispensable interaction between human and documents. The annotation system of electronic documents enables to implement effective functions, such as information retrieval and annotation-based navigation, by using the annotation information; however, traditional systems require users to perform gestures in addition to common gestures for paper-based documents. This can reduce "learnability" of the system. We propose an intelligent ink annotation framework that helps the system to increase the learnability of annotation systems by detecting recognizable intentions from natural annotation behavior on paper-based documents. Our framework recognizes "Targeting Content" and "Commenting," which are related to extraction of annotation information. We have developed a prototype annotation system using our proposed framework and conducted a user study to identify future direction.

Author Keywords
Digital Ink; Active Reading; Annotation; Handwriting

ACM Classification Keywords
H.5.2. User Interfaces: Interaction styles.

Introduction and Background

Annotation while reading a document significantly helps understand its contents and enhance accessibility [1]. Users annotate paper-based documents by highlighting content and providing comments. However, over the past several years, with the development of hardware that accepts pen and touch input, researchers have studied active reading systems that enable performing such annotation on electronic documents as well [2][3].

In comparison to paper-based annotation, softcopy annotation systems for electronic documents allow for efficient functions like information retrieval and interactive navigation [2][4]. They require users to perform gestures defined by themselves to obtain annotation information in addition to common behaviors of paper-based documents, e.g., a non-dominant-hand posture [5] and Pen + Touch interaction [6]. However, this reduces the learnability of such a system.

Thus, recognizing the need to support such systems, we developed an intelligent ink annotation framework that increases the learnability of an annotation system by detecting users' intentions from natural annotation behavior for paper-based documents. In this paper, we focus on the fundamental tasks of annotation, which are reading, targeting content and commenting.

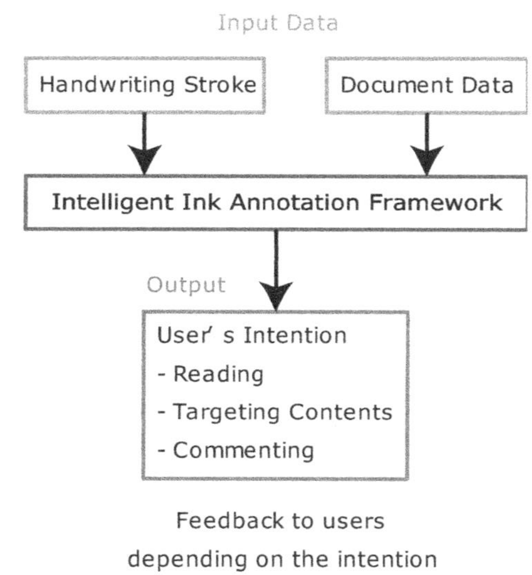

Figure 1 Intelligent ink annotation framework

In this study, we used our framework to implement a prototype annotation system. We conducted user study wherein participants annotated electronic documents using our prototype. Finally, we analyzed the results of the study to identify future direction.

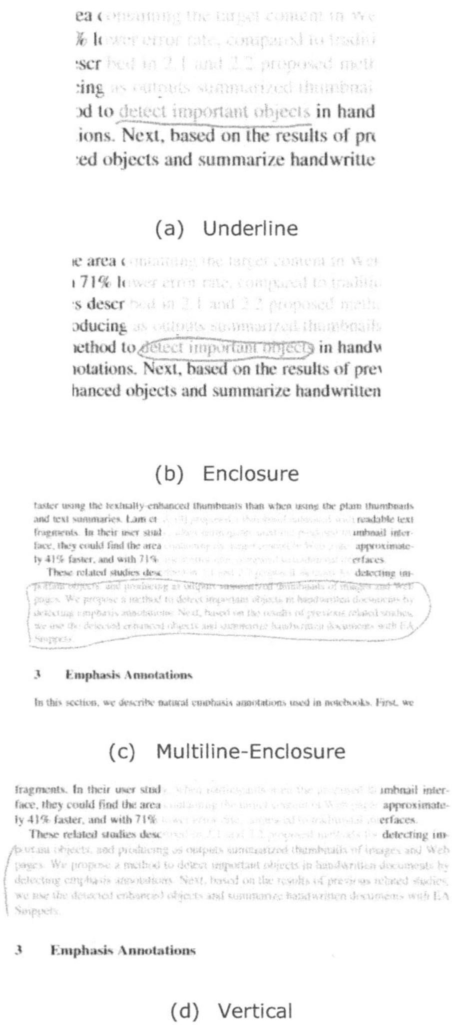

Figure 3 Targeting content annotation

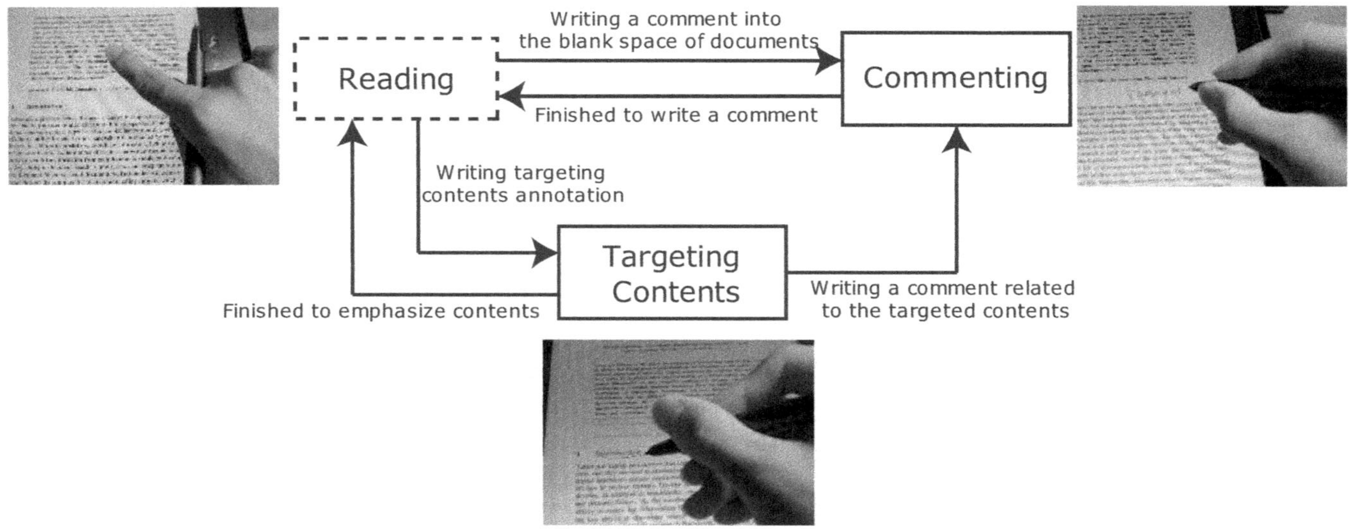

Figure 2 Annotation Lifecycle for detecting user's intentions of annotation

Intelligent Ink Annotation Framework

Figure 1 represents an overview of our proposed framework. Our framework recognizes user's intentions from natural annotation behavior. By using detected user's intention, annotation systems can support user's annotation depending on the detected intention to use the annotation information for information retrieval or annotation-based navigation.

In our framework, both an original document source and a user's handwritten stroke are required to detect user's intention of annotation. Users can get a feedback from the framework when a handwriting stroke has been finished, i.e., pen away from a display. The output of the framework is three types of user's intentions required to annotation systems.

1. Reading
   This state includes reading or navigating a document not using a pen.

2. Targeting Content
   This task includes highlighting a range of content in a document, selecting content to provide comments on specific content and extracting search terms.

3. Commenting
   This involves providing comments on specific content or in blank spaces of documents.

The input strokes are classified into four types of "Targeting Content" annotation. Then the framework

Figure 4 Prototype annotation system

determines user's current intention by analyzing positional relationship between the handwriting stroke and document content objects. In addition, the range of the targeted contents in a document is recognized when the framework detects user's intention as "Targeting Content." The detail of each function is described in the following sections.

User's Intentions based on the Annotation Lifecycle

Our framework detects user's intentions of annotation based on the Annotation Lifecycle which we define based on natural annotation behaviors on paper-based documents. Marshall investigates annotation on paper-based university-level textbooks by students [7]. He reported telegraphic annotations such as underline and explicit annotations, i.e., brief notes written between lines, were found within text field. On the other hand, brackets and extended notes were found in marginal or blank space. We classify these reported annotations into two major classes based on the aspect of user's intention required to extract annotation information. One is targeting content, and the other is commenting.

Figure 2 shows the annotation lifecycle we defined for detecting user's intentions of annotation. When users read or navigate documents, our framework recognizes the state as "Reading". When users write targeting annotation like underline in this state, the state is changed to "Targeting Content". On the other hand, the state is changed to "Commenting" when users write a comment into the blank space of documents. In "Targeting Content" state, the state is moved to "Reading" when users just select contents and write no comments, e.g. emphasizing contents. In contrast, the state is moved to "Commenting" when users intend to add a comment involved in the selected contents.

Coordinates of a handwriting stroke and bounding boxes of characters in documents are used to detect each state of the Annotation Lifecycle. Our framework recognizes the state as "Reading" when handwriting stroke is not entered. On the other hand, a handwriting stroke is assumed as "Targeting Content", and classified into the kind of targeting content annotation (Figure 3) by decision tree to use aspect ratio of the bounding box and stroke density features when handwriting stroke is entered. Then, the framework determines the assumption is correct or not, e.g. "Targeting Contents" or "Commenting", by comparing the position of handwriting stroke with the bounding boxes of characters in documents. Our collected handwriting annotation data, which we collected from several participants before implementing our system, is used for the each process.

Targeting Content Recognition

Marshall reported several types of annotations for targeting content; such as underline, circles (we call "enclosure"), brackets (we call "vertical") for the typical paper-based annotation [7]. Moreover, Golovchinsky et al. categorized such annotations into two categories: a part of the text within a line and selecting several lines [8]. According to these reports, our framework detects four types of targeting annotations (see Figure 3). Underline and enclosure are detected as "Targeting Content" which specifies the range of characters. On the other hand, multiline-enclosure and vertical are detected as "Targeting Content" which specify the range of text lines. These ranges are recognized by using coordinates of handwriting stroke, bounding boxes of characters in document and our collected annotation data set.

Figure 5 Targeting content by dragging a pen

Prototype Implementation

We have developed a prototype annotation system using our proposed framework running on Sony VAIO Duo 11. The resolution of the display is 1920*1080, and the display accepts both multi-touch input and stylus input. The software development environment is Windows store application on Windows 8.1 (see Figure 4).

The prototype system shows a single page of PDF contents on the screen. Users can change pages by swiping finger to left or right on the screen. In addition, the system accepts handwriting by stylus input. Users can annotate documents by handwriting in the following modes.

Intelligent Ink Annotation Framework Mode

The prototype system implemented two types of annotation mode. One is automatic operation mode using our proposed framework. In this mode, the selected contents are highlighted followed by opening a comment window to add comments, when the system detects "Targeting Content." When the system detects "Commenting," the system accepts writing with no other feedbacks (see Figure 4).

Manual Operation Mode

On the other hand, the system also implemented traditional manual operation mode not using proposed framework to compare with proposed framework in the user study. In this mode, users can switch between two types of functions by selecting buttons on the screen. One is selecting function which can only accept selecting range of the contents. User can select contents by dragging pen just like selecting text by mouse (see Figure 5). The other function is commenting mode which can only accepts writing comments.

User Study

We conducted user study to compare usability between proposed intelligent ink annotation framework and traditional manual operation. Four participants (A to D) who are belonging to our laboratory were invited to our user study. They are bachelor and master course students majoring in computer science.

We firstly introduced our prototype system in five minutes. After the introduction, we instructed participants to read a research paper using our proposed framework at least 10 minutes. Then participants read the paper using manual operation mode not using the framework at least 10 minutes. We recorded the annotation behavior of participants by video camera. After finishing these procedures, we discussed the prototype system with participants.

We could obtain some findings from the comments of participants and the recorded videos. Three out of four participants (B,C and D) preferred the automatic mode using our framework because the commenting and targeting functions were switched automatically. In contrast, participant A preferred the manual operation mode not using the framework because the intention recognition accuracy was too low to use. Besides the selecting contents by dragging pen was acceptable. All the participants mentioned about the recognition accuracy. Accordingly, we found the recognition accuracy of user's intention is important factor whether the system is acceptable or not. Furthermore, participant B in addition to A said selecting contents by dragging pen, which we implemented in manual operation mode, is useful. The participants also said targeting content gesture by dragging pen should be also recognized as targeting content of proposed framework.

Moreover, participants A, B and C mentioned that the no system feedbacks while in writing "Targeting Content" was uncomfortable. The prototype system displays the highlight feedback only when the handwriting stroke is finished, i.e. pen up. For this reason, it is conceivable that our framework makes user uncomfortable when recognizing "Targeting Content" followed by no feedbacks.

Conclusion and Future Direction

We proposed intelligent ink annotation framework that helps handwriting annotation on electronic documents. Our user study showed that our framework have a potential to reduce the users' burden of providing a system to annotation information. In addition, the study reveals two problems. One is our framework is required to the high-accuracy annotation recognition algorithm. Other is our framework needs to be equipped with an interactive feedback mechanism when it recognizes "targeting content."

Acknowledgements

This work was supported by JSPS KAKENHI Grant-in-Aid for Challenging Exploratory Research (25540040).

References

[1] O'Hara, K. and Sellen, A. A comparison of reading paper and on-line documents. *In Proc. CHI 1997*, ACM, 335-342.

[2] Matulic, F. and Norrie, M.C. Supporting Active Reading on Pen and Touch-Operated Tabletops. *In Proc. AVI 2012*, ACM, 612-619.

[3] Chen, N., Guimbretiere, F. and Sellen, A. Designing a Multi-slate Reading Environment to Support Active Reading Activities. *ACM Trans. CHI 2012*, vol.19, 3, A.18.

[4] Tashman, C.S. and Edwards, W.K. LiquidText: A Flexible, Multitouch Environment to Support Active Reading. *In Proc. CHI 2011*, ACM, 3285-3294.

[5] Matulic, F. and Norrie, M.C. Pen and Touch Gestural Environment for Document Editing on Interactive Tabletops. In Proc. ITS 2013, ACM, 41-50.

[6] Hinckley, K., Yatani, K., Pahud, M., Coddington, N., Rodenhouse, J., Wilson, A., Benko, H. and Buxton, B. Pen + Touch = New Tools. *In Proc. UIST 2010*, ACM, 27-36.

[7] Marshall, C.C. Annotation: From Paper Books to the Digital Library, *In Proc. DL 1997*, ACM, 131-140.

[8] Golovchinsky, G. and Denoue, L. Moving Markup: Repositioning Freeform Annotations. *In Proc. UIST 2002*, ACM, 21-30.

Studying Teacher Cognitive Load in Multi-tabletop Classrooms Using Mobile Eye-tracking

Luis P. Prieto
CHILI Lab, EPFL
RLC D1 740, Station 20
CH-1015 Lausanne
(Switzerland)
luis.prieto@epfl.ch

Yun Wen
CHILI Lab, EPFL
RLC D1 740, Station 20
CH-1015 Lausanne
(Switzerland)
yun.wen@epfl.ch

Daniela Caballero
Pontificia Universidad Católica de Chile
Av. Vicuña Mackenna 4860
Santiago (Chile)
dccaball@uc.cl

Kshitij Sharma
CHILI Lab, EPFL
RLC D1 740, Station 20
CH-1015 Lausanne
(Switzerland)
kshitij.sharma@epfl.ch

Pierre Dillenbourg
CHILI Lab, EPFL
RLC D1 740, Station 20
CH-1015 Lausanne
(Switzerland)
pierre.dillenbourg@epfl.ch

ITS '14, Nov 16-19 2014, Dresden, Germany
ACM 978-1-4503-2587-5/14/11.
http://dx.doi.org/10.1145/2669485.2669543

Abstract
Increasing affordability is making multi-tabletop spaces (e.g., in school classrooms) a real possibility, and first design guidelines for such environments are starting to appear. However, there are still very few studies into the usability of such multi-tabletop classrooms as a whole, considering well-established constructs such as cognitive load. In this poster we present an exploratory study of the usage of mobile eye-tracking techniques to follow cognitive load of a teacher during a lesson in such a multi-tabletop space. By analyzing several eye-tracking measures over three sessions of a collaborative learning lesson on fractions, we obtained insights on the user experience of the facilitator in these concrete sessions. We also show the potential of eye-tracking to identify critical episodes in the usage of a multi-tabletop space under realistic usage conditions, in a less intrusive and more objective manner.

Author Keywords
Multi-tabletop setups, classroom, cognitive load, eye-tracking, orchestration

ACM Classification Keywords
H.5.2 [Information interfaces and presentation]: User Interfaces.

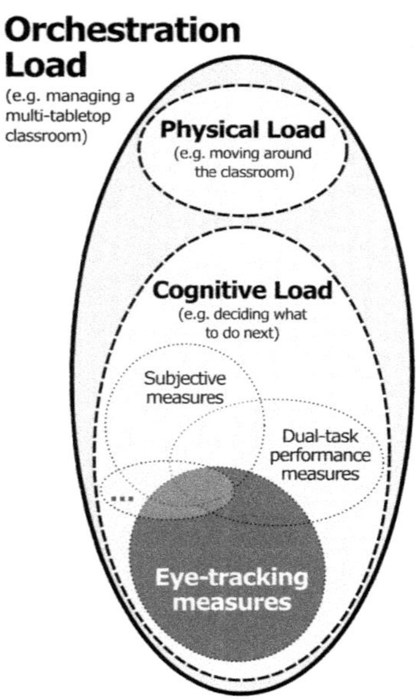

Figure 1: Representation of the relationships between orchestration load, cognitive load and the different ways to measure the latter.

Introduction
The lowering prices of tabletop technology make the possibility of having multiple tabletops in a single space a reality. One of the most common use cases for this kind of setup is the classroom, so as to enable all students to enjoy the affordances of tabletops, e.g., for small group collaboration [1, 8, 6].

However, the increased complexity of this kind of multi-device setup also poses additional usability challenges, especially for the user that most often has to deal with this multiplicity: the teacher. The specific usability challenges in the run-time management of such a complex socio-technical environments, under the multiple constraints that authentic educational settings pose, has been termed 'orchestration' [4]. Indeed, first studies have been made in the community to characterize this orchestration in multi-tabletop classrooms [8], and design guidelines for this kind of spaces are starting to appear [7].

Although studies into the usage of multi-tabletop classrooms do exist [8, 6], no effort has been made so far to measure objectively the orchestration load of the teacher while facilitating such sessions. Following cognitive load of the teacher in these classrooms can help us understand this orchestration load (see Figure 1), which in turn can help us predict whether this kind of technological setup will be adopted in the future by teachers and schools. However, existing studies dealing with orchestration load use the concept only in abstract terms, often inferring it from general observations and lessons learned from the co-design and deployment of these technologies in authentic settings [3].

In this poster, we describe the results of an exploratory study where we tried to measure, objectively and in a more fine-grained fashion, a facilitator's cognitive load during several sessions of a multi-tabletop classroom lesson, in near-authentic conditions. We used eye-tracking techniques [5] to get physiological indicators of such load, to help us detect critical classroom usability episodes.

Eye-tracking Measures and Cognitive Load
Cognitive load (CL) has been defined as a "multidimensional construct representing the load that performing a particular task imposes on the cognitive system" [9], focusing especially on attention and working memory. In general, technology designers strive to minimize extraneous cognitive load (the one that is not intrinsic to the task itself, but rather due to other elements such as unnecessarily complex user interfaces).

CL can be measured in different ways, including subjective (requiring user introspection, e.g., filling a questionnaire about perceived difficulty) as well as objective measures. Also, measures may target the CL construct directly (e.g., by brain activity measures) or indirectly (e.g., through related physiological indicators, such as heart rate) [9] (see also Figure 1). In human factors and psychology, many of these techniques have been successfully applied to measure cognitive load in relatively simple tasks (e.g., doing a web search, solving a web-based maths problem).

However, measuring cognitive load when performing a *complex* task (such as teaching in a multi-tabletop classroom) is still an open challenge for researchers. In classrooms, the mobility of the teacher and the high demands of the task in terms of attention may make dual-task performance measures (i.e. asking subjects to perform a secondary task while engaged in the task to be measured) too obtrusive [9]. The timespan of most lessons makes subjective questionnaires rely too much on the subject's memory, and makes it difficult to obtain

Figure 2: The multi-tabletop classroom setup. In the center, the main facilitator wearing a mobile eye-tracker

critical, finer-grained episodes that can be relevant to an HCI practitioner. Another feasible way of getting objective but indirect data is through physiological indicators such as heart rate monitoring (considerd unreliable by [9]) or eye-tracking measures [5, 2].

Eye-tracking is based on the fact that human vision (e.g., visual inspection of a scene) does not follow a smooth motion. Rather, eyes normally perform small pauses (of around 200ms) called *fixations*, which are followed by long jumps (termed *saccades*). These movements and other eye parameters (e.g., pupil diameter) can be recorded, thus providing a stream of fine-grained events which can be used as a proxy for human cognition and performance of tasks. More recently, off-the-shelf mobile eye-trackers have become available, enabling researchers to use these technologies out of controlled lab settings.

Research studies have found correlations between CL and several eye-tracking metrics (see [5, 2] for a selection of such studies), including mean pupil dilation or its variance (i.e., high load episodes are correlated with larger pupil diameter and higher variance). The fact that different metrics seem to correlate better with different kinds of activities indicates that researchers should probably use multiple indicators (i.e. triangulation of metrics) for ascertaining with more confidence the changes in a person's cognitive load, as done for example in [2]. This triangulation can be even more critical for very complex tasks, such as teaching (which is composed of a variety of smaller tasks of different nature).

Exploratory Study: Context and Methods

Against the aforementioned background, we can ask the following research question: *Can we use eye-tracking measures to follow a teacher's cognitive load when using a multi-tabletop classroom?* Such an objective indicator could prove invaluable to future usability studies involving tabletops, for example to choose among different design variants of multi-tabletop classroom applications. To start answering that question, we conducted an exploratory study using a mobile eye-tracker in conditions very close to those of an authentic multi-tabletop classroom.

Three sessions on comparing fractions were held at our laboratory, in the context of an "open doors" day. Each session lasted for 38-47 minutes, and 16-25 students (aged 10-12) from local primary schools (along with two of their usual teachers) attended each of the sessions. The sessions were led by a researcher playing the role of the teacher (*facilitator*, from now on, to distinguish him from the visiting school teachers), guiding the students through a series of tabletop-based group activities. This main facilitator was aided by two other researchers which helped in time management and the distribution of activity materials, while the visiting school teachers remained mostly as passive observers.

During these sessions, students used an augmented paper tabletop device, featuring manipulatives with different kinds of fraction representations, which were used to play a collaborative game involving the comparison of fractions in different forms[1]. This kind of task is in line with the students' curriculum for that age, although students showed varying levels of prior knowledge about fractions (as they came from different schools).

The sessions were recorded using SMI eye-tracking glasses with a data rate of 30 Hz. The eye-tracking glasses have a video camera (24 frames/second) that records the visual

[1]See `http://chili.epfl.ch/page-110567-en.html` for further details and a video demonstration (Last visit: 29 Aug 2014).

Table 1: Coding scheme used on the video analysis of high- and low-load episodes

Activity
Explanation
Task distribution & transition
Monitoring
Repairs & Extraneous events
Other or N/A
Social plane
Classroom
Small group
Individual
Other or N/A
Main focus
Student backs
Student faces
Teacher's desk
Tabletop computer
Paper manipulative
Fellow facilitator
Classroom whiteboard
Other or N/A
Large head movements
Yes
No

field of the participant. Additional fixed cameras were placed to record the overall classroom space (e.g., Figure 2), as well as each of the tabletop areas.

From the mobile eye-tracker, we extracted event data regarding pupil diameter, as well as eye movements (fixations and saccades). We analyzed these event data, using three of the four eye-tracking metrics for measuring cognitive load mentioned in [2][2]: pupil diameter standard deviation, mean saccade speed, and number of long ($> 500ms$) fixations. All these metrics were calculated over a sliding window of 10 seconds. By performing a median cut over each of these metrics, we obtained a 'load index' (L) ranging from 0 to 3 (e.g., $L = 3$ indicates that all three metrics were over the median), which was used to measure our confidence that a certain moment implied high cognitive load for the facilitator.

To ascertain whether these cognitive load measures provided meaningful contrast (i.e., the "high load" and "low load" episodes were clearly differentiable), we coded the video of the facilitator's visual field for the episodes with the maximum and the minimum 'load index' ($L = \{0, 3\}$), using the four-dimension scheme shown in Table 1: 1) facilitator's activity, 2) social plane at which the activity was occurring, 3) main focus of attention in that moment, and 4) whether there were large head movements (e.g., the facilitator quickly rotating his head to look at different points of the classroom). A chi-squared test was then performed to assess independence between these extreme values of L and the aforementioned four variables.

Initial Results

Figure 3 shows the evolution of the eye-tracking metrics calculated over one of the sessions, against its median value (used as the session baseline). By comparing the extreme values of the 'load index' (L) calculated from the eye-tracking measures throughout our three sessions (a total of $n = 397$ episodes, i.e., 10-second windows), with the four variables from the video coding (see Table 1), we can see that high-load and low-load episodes had distinct profiles regarding *social plane* ($p < 2.2 \times 10^{-16}$, $df = 1$ in a Pearson's chi-squared test), *main focus of attention* ($p < 2.2 \times 10^{-16}$, $df = 7$), *large head movements* ($p < 2.2 \times 10^{-16}$, $df = 1$) and facilitator activity ($p = 0.00258$, $df = 3$).

- *Low-load episodes* almost invariably happened when the facilitator was in a *small-group situation*, focusing mainly on the group's *tabletop*, *without large head movement*. Although the four kinds of activities were found, *monitoring* a group's work or providing *repair explanations* were found more often than the other kinds.
- *High-load episodes*, on the contrary, very often comprised *large head movements* of the facilitator, and implied more often a *class-wide activity*. The focus of attention in these episodes was more varied, with high occurrence of students' faces (e.g., during a class-wide explanation), students' backs (while monitoring the whole classroom, see Figure 2), a group's tabletop or the facilitator's own desk (where all the –quite numerous– activity materials were laid out). The four kinds of facilitator activities were found equally often among these episodes.

[2]A preliminary analysis of the data showed that the high luminance of the tabletop surface (projected, not a screen) could have a large effect on the fourth measure, mean pupil diameter (which normally is taken in carefully-controlled lighting conditions [2]), thus making this measure a potentially unreliable indicator of cognitive load.

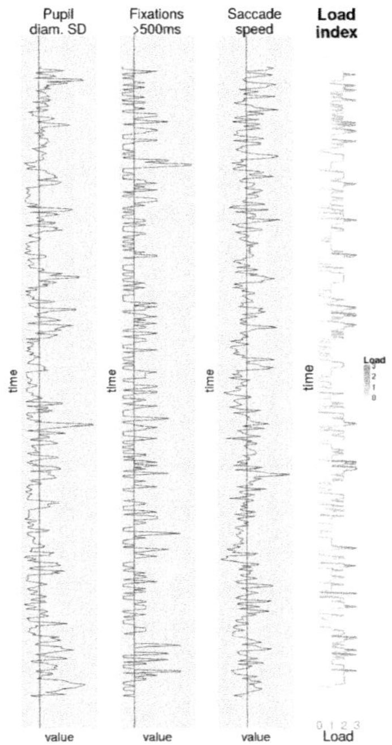

Figure 3: Graphs representing the eye-tracking metrics used to estimate the facilitator's cognitive load during one session. The last graph (right) indicates the 'load index' (confidence that this is a moment of high load) calculated on the basis of the other three.

Discussion and Future Work

Although our study cannot be said to feature an authentic classroom or school teacher, our quantitative data, along with qualitative observations of the videos taken from the facilitator's viewpoint, provide insights into the user experience of managing a multi-tabletop classroom, which may be very useful for the technology designer:

- Class-wide activities in a multi-tabletop classroom pose a higher cognitive load than small-group ones: monitoring the whole classroom, leading a task transition across multiple groups of students, etc. is much harder than just explaining an activity in front of a group of four students. Although this is something that any teacher can assert informally, our evidence backs it up empirically, and highlights the need of more research regarding the specific usability challenges of managing this kind of multi-device setting *at the classroom plane* (while most of the research so far centers on the usability challenges of using a single tabletop individually or in small group).
- As an example of such specific challenges, monitoring the progress of multiple group activities taking place in different tabletops seems like a clear place for improvement for this kind of setups: some of the high-load episodes in our study showed the facilitator's eye cursor traversing the backs of different groups of students without clearly knowing which group needed more help. This lack in the class-wide awareness of tabletops could be ameliorated with some kind of class-wide visualization, either projected in a shared display, or in a mobile device carried by the teacher.
- Another challenge, in this case specific to the tangible paper-based tabletop interface used in our study, is the risk of clutter when using this kind of user interface. This is supported by the fact that many of the high-load episodes featured the facilitator focusing on the desk where the paper manipulatives were laid out (e.g., trying to find the right paper element to provide to students), or task transitions where new paper elements were to be handed to students. This kind of difficulties may partly explain why such tangible interfaces have not yet been adopted in education on a large scale.

Furthermore, our study also demonstrates the feasibility of using eye-tracking techniques with actual teachers and school classrooms. We have also demonstrated how these techniques can serve to focus the analysis of the HCI practitioner into a more manageable set of moments, which could also be used to support other common usability practices (e.g., use the critical episode videos in interviews with the users/teachers). The eye-tracking techniques could also be complemented with other kinds of measures of cognitive load (e.g., questionnaires), to give a more comprehensive view of the user experience when using such multi-tabletop settings.

This method, however, has limitations: the cost of the mobile eye-tracker might make this technique unfeasible for some lower-budget endeavors, and teachers might be reluctant to wear the eye-tracking device (even if its calibration takes a few seconds, it might be uncomfortable to wear for long periods of time). Thus, this kind of technique can be suited researcher-led for studies in authentic settings, but probably not for longitudinal in-the-wild studies without researcher intervention.

In this poster, we have explored a relatively unobstrusive and objective method for measuring cognitive load of a teacher engaged in a complex activity using a multi-tabletop setup, with encouraging results. Eye-tracking measures can help us better understand the orchestration load of teachers managing this kind of setup, and hence deepen our knowledge about the adoption of such technologies. Our future work includes the use the techniques presented here actual primary school teachers and classrooms, complementing them with other subjective measures of cognitive load. We also plan to use these methods to inform our design decisions for classroom tabletop systems (e.g., to decide whether a shared display or a mobile device visualization is more convenient for the teacher).

Acknowledgements

The work presented here has been partially funded by the Marie Curie Fellowship MIOCTI (FP7-PEOPLE-2012-IEF project no. 327384). Daniela Caballero was a Swiss Government Excellence Scholarship holder for the academic year(s) 2013-2014 (ESKAS No. 2013.0293).

References

[1] AlAgha, I., Hatch, A., Ma, L., and Burd, L. Towards a teacher-centric approach for multi-touch surfaces in classrooms. In *ACM International Conference on Interactive Tabletops and Surfaces*, ITS '10, ACM (New York, NY, USA, 2010), 187–196.

[2] Buettner, R. Cognitive workload of humans using artificial intelligence systems: Towards objective measurement applying eye-tracking technology. In *KI 2013: Advances in Artificial Intelligence*, I. Timm and M. Thimm, Eds., vol. 8077 of *Lecture Notes in Computer Science*. Springer Berlin Heidelberg, 2013, 37–48.

[3] Cuendet, S., Bonnard, Q., Do-Lenh, S., and Dillenbourg, P. Designing augmented reality for the classroom. *Comput. Educ. 68* (Oct. 2013), 557–569.

[4] Dillenbourg, P., Zufferey, G., Alavi, H. S., Jermann, P., Do, L. H. S., Bonnard, Q., Cuendet, S., and Kaplan, F. Classroom orchestration: The third circle of usability. In *CSCL2011 Conference Proceedings*, vol. 1, International Society of the Learning Sciences (2011), 510–517.

[5] Holmqvist, K., Nyström, M., Andersson, R., Dewhurst, R., Jarodzka, H., and van de Weijer, J. *Eye Tracking: A comprehensive guide to methods and measures*. OUP Oxford, 2011.

[6] Kharrufa, A., Balaam, M., Heslop, P., Leat, D., Dolan, P., and Olivier, P. Tables in the wild: Lessons learned from a large-scale multi-tabletop deployment. In *Proceedings of the SIGCHI Conference on Human Factors in Computing Systems*, CHI '13, ACM (New York, NY, USA, 2013), 1021–1030.

[7] Kharrufa, A., Martinez-Maldonado, R., Kay, J., and Olivier, P. Extending tabletop application design to the classroom. In *Proceedings of the 2013 ACM International Conference on Interactive Tabletops and Surfaces*, ITS '13, ACM (New York, NY, USA, 2013), 115–124.

[8] Martinez Maldonado, R., Dimitriadis, Y., Kay, J., Yacef, K., and Edbauer, M.-T. Orchestrating a multi-tabletop classroom: From activity design to enactment and reflection. In *Proceedings of the 2012 ACM International Conference on Interactive Tabletops and Surfaces*, ITS '12, ACM (New York, NY, USA, 2012), 119–128.

[9] Paas, F., Tuovinen, J. E., Tabbers, H., and Van Gerven, P. W. M. Cognitive load measurement as a means to advance cognitive load theory. *Educational Psychologist 38*, 1 (2003), 63–71.

Combining Timeline and Graph Visualization

Robert Morawa
Interactive Media Lab
Technische Universität Dresden
Dresden, Germany
robert.morawa@tu-dresden.de

Annett Mitschick
Interactive Media Lab
Technische Universität Dresden
Dresden, Germany
annett.mitschick@tu-dresden.de

Tom Horak
Interactive Media Lab
Technische Universität Dresden
Dresden, Germany
tom.horak@tu-dresden.de

Raimund Dachselt
Interactive Media Lab
Technische Universität Dresden
Dresden, Germany
dachselt@acm.org

Ulrike Kister
Interactive Media Lab
Technische Universität Dresden
Dresden, Germany
ukister@acm.org

ITS 2014, November 16–19, 2014, Dresden, Germany.
ACM 978-1-4503-2587-5/14/11.
http://dx.doi.org/10.1145/2669485.2669544

Abstract
Timelines are as important for presenting temporal data as node-link diagrams are relevant for displaying graphs and relations in general. Yet, both are rarely combined. We present *Time Shadows* to precisely indicate a node's place in time, revealing associated temporal data and relations. We also introduce *Time Beads*. Created as a focus and context interaction technique for time-based graphs, Time Beads allow to continuously or discretely change the level of detail and to set multiple arbitrary focus regions if needed. We implemented both techniques in a prototype and conducted an initial user study.

Author Keywords
Time-visualization; Information Visualization; Semantic Data.

ACM Classification Keywords
H.5.2. [Information Interfaces and Presentation (e.g. HCI)]: User Interfaces.

Introduction
Understanding temporal data and phenomena is key to long-term planning, as well as decision- and sensemaking. This applies to stock prices, chemical reactions, historical events and many other domains.

Figure 1: *Time Shadow*: The transparent layer around the node indicates its duration.

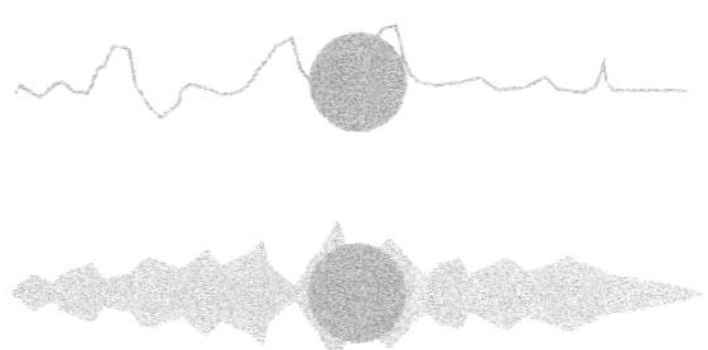

Figure 2: *Time Shadow* with sparklines or polygons can display quantitative data.

There are two main goals for analyzing temporal data; to get a sense of the past development and to detect trends and patterns for the future. This calls for dedicated interactive features like the ability to browse, to compare different regions in time and to choose hierarchical layers such as decades, years or months [1]. To achieve this, dedicated temporal visualizations tend to provide the user with overview and detail views [2], focus and context tools like vertical zoom lenses [4], or multiple timeline views [6].

Temporal data may contain multiple types of relations. The relation in time is the most important and relevant, often mapped to the spatial position as dominant visual variable [3], the elements displayed as bars or dots. Commonly, visualizations show similarity via facets [7] or color-coding [5]. More complex relations require different means. The tool *Continuum* uses mainly frames, indented lists and bars to visualize hierarchies and quantitative data [2], while Jensen uses edges and different kinds of arrows to map different relations [6].

However, complex networks like semantic data tend to be visualized as node-link diagrams. Already the creation of a meaningful, readable graph layout proves to be very challenging. A spatial timeline imposes a strict layouting constraint. This causes problems for drawing nodes that occupy a time interval, and for drawing edges of temporal distant nodes, especially when combined with zoomable interfaces.

In this paper, we propose two techniques to deal with time-based node-link diagrams. We explain the design process, including an initial study, and the concepts of *Time Shadow* and *Time Beads*. We present the prototype used in our user study, Nornir, and finally discuss the results of our work.

Design Process

The following concepts were developed using an iterative design process. The visualization of time-dependent node-link diagrams was targeted toward large multi-touch displays. Our first concepts were implemented in a proof-of-concept prototype, which featured semantic data from the DBpedia project[1].

The prototype was used for an initial study with seven participants (four male, average age: 24). We gave each user seven tasks, e.g., to read off the life span and identify relations of Albert Einstein. The interactions were video-recorded, and we took notes of the behavior and comments of the users. Each session finished with a short questionnaire.

We used the feedback to further revise the concepts and identify their strengths and weaknesses. The following sections feature the refined concepts.

Time Shadow

When displaying nodes in a spatial mapping of time, their shape has to be considered. Simple nodes can lead to confusion, especially if they represent an item with a longer duration; is the node placed at the start, the middle or the end of the interval? However, bars would cause problems when drawing edges as they occupy much more space.

Our proposal to solve this problem, the Time Shadow, is a semi-transparent layer behind an arbitrary shaped node. Using its length and spatial position, it visualizes the duration of an item as shown in Figure 1, for example the time a chemical reaction requires to finish or the lifetime of a person. Time spans may exist that are still ongoing,

[1]http://dbpedia.org

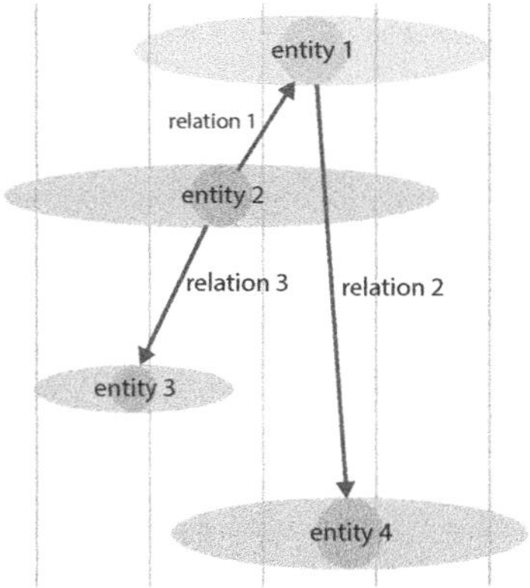

Figure 3: Time Shadows can be used easily to extend a node-link diagram.

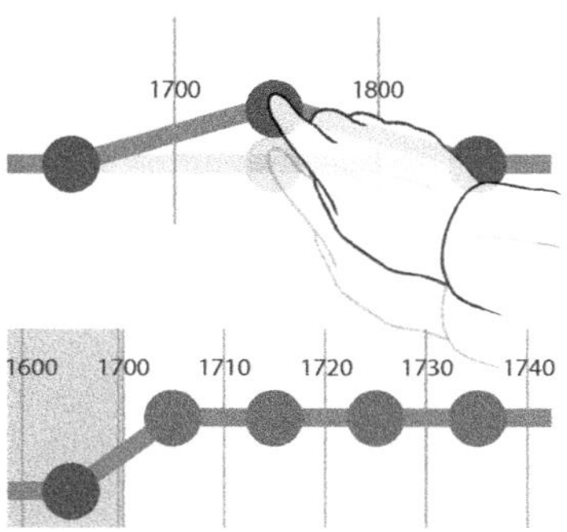

Figure 4: A Time Bead can be popped by tapping or dragging it upwards.

e.g., if the person is still alive. In this case, Time Shadows can be blurred out instead of ending on a specific point.

Time Shadow can have various shapes which can be used to visualize different classes of durations. Most remarkable, sparklines or irregular polygons can be used to display associated quantitative data, as visualized in Figure 2, their amplitudes indicating published works of an artist or the stock prices of a company.

For our study, we used ellipse shaped Time Shadows. Users required some time to identify the Time Shadow as the duration of an item, but then heavily relied on it while reading the graph. Often they were used to better grasp semantic relations that featured a time-based constraint. For example, someone whose Time Shadow started after Albert Einsteins ended, could not have influenced him in any way. Also, the task to read off the date of birth and death of Albert Einstein was the best rated of our study.

Time Shadows offer many advantages for layouting and sensemaking. They exactly define start and end of a time interval, something that is not possible with common circular nodes. This supports the understanding of temporal relations in general. Edges may cross the shadow without being associated with the node, as shown in Figure 3, in contrast to bar-shaped nodes. Nodes can have different shapes, and even vary their position within their Time Shadow, if it benefits the overall layout without changing the meaning. The Time Shadow's size makes their associated nodes easier to touch and harder to occlude either with a finger or other nodes.

However, the increased size can also lead to a cluttered visualization, when too many shadows overlap and reduces the amount of nodes that can be drawn on the canvas. This increases the importance of a meaningful and readable layout. Surveying the results of our initial study, Time Shadows are a promising approach to visualize the time aspect of entities.

Time Beads

Zoom-based overview and detail interaction is common within time visualization, but faces problems when displaying node-link diagrams. A node may have connections to nodes that are well outside the zooming level, since the time variable heavily constraints the layout. Edges would link to the edge of the screen or to an off-screen visualization, which omits the temporal context the linked nodes are placed in.

Time Beads are a visualization a focus and context interaction technique, and are inspired by TimeZoom [4]. Time Beads utilizes graph nodes to represent time intervals, potentially ranging from millenia to milliseconds. They chained at the lower edge of the screen as a timeline, the boudaries separated by thin lines. Time is hereby understood as a tree, where a millenium has its centuries as children, each century its decades and so on.

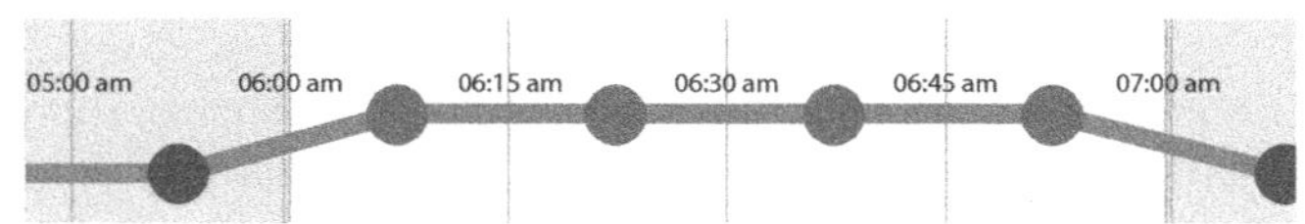

Figure 5: *Time Beads* display time intervals of different hierarchical layers.

Interaction is based on this underlying structure. With a simple tap or drag to the top, a Bead can be *popped*, disappearing and revealing its children, as visible in Figure 4. Since all Time Beads have the same default weight and distribute equally onscreen, the user stretches a focus region while the other regions compress.

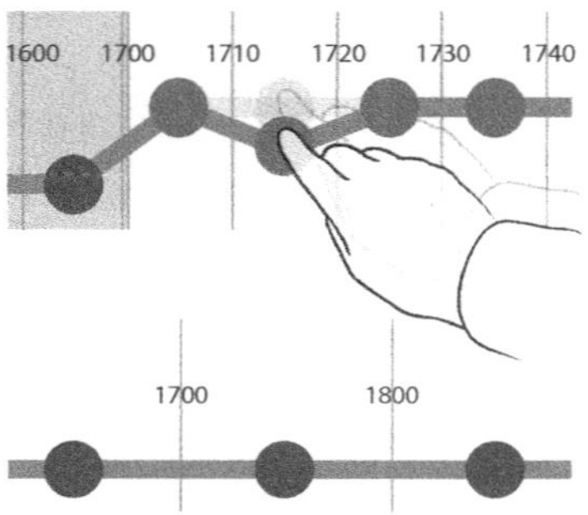

Figure 6: When pulling down a Bead, its hierarchical layer collapses.

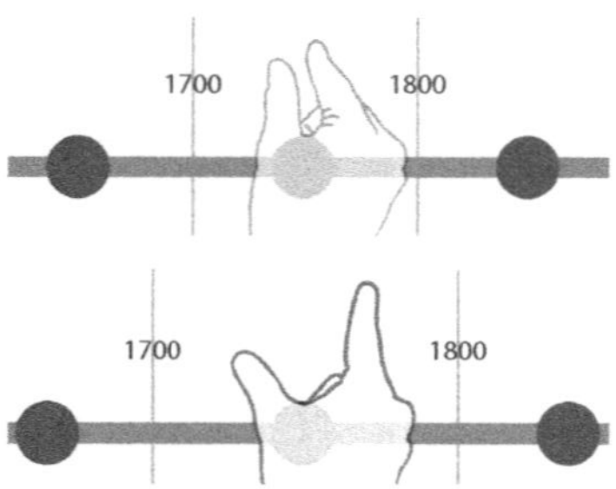

Figure 8: A spread gesture on an interval expands it.

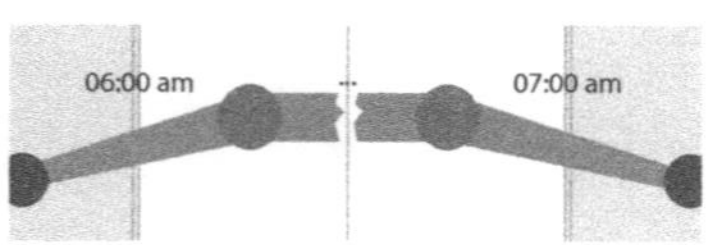

Figure 9: A 2.5D projection emphasizes the transition between layers.

If the user chooses to expand one of the children further, this Bead pops and its right and left siblings *stack*. A stack represents the time interval of all stacked Beads and can be popped to distribute them again. Beads can be stacked manually by dragging one Bead over another, as shown in Figure 7. Every Bead between them will be added to the stack. Beads can also be stacked at the edge of the screen by dragging them there, which essentially stretches the entire remaining timeline.

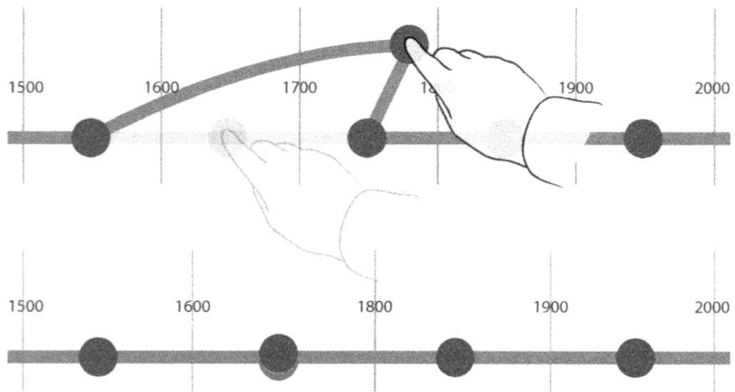

Figure 7: Multiple Time Beads can be stacked manually by dragging one Bead over another.

The user can pull down a Bead to *collapse* it, all its siblings and their children. They will be replaced by the single parent node, as visualized in Figure 6. These three techniques allow a discrete navigation along the timeline. Since Time Beads are only loosely chained, the user can open multiple focus regions to compare data at different points in time without additional tools like fisheye lenses.

To clearly distinguish different hierarchical layers, we use different visualization techniques. Beads and their interval receive a greyscale coloration, where parents are colored darker than children. Also parent Beads are closer to the bottom of the screen than their children.

While the mapping proved to be beneficial in our initial study, the interaction style was not deemed intuitive. In fact, most users at first tried to pinch-to-zoom or tap on the background of the node-link diagram. When users were browsing the graph, they generally did not interact with the Time Beads, instead they primarily used them to solve time-related tasks. Also, some users did not recognize the transition between the heterogeneous layers.

To improve Time Beads and the overall interaction, we concluded to further regard multi-touch interactions on the whitespace of the graph, but still the goal was to keep the gesture set as simple as possible. The basic concepts for discrete navigation are maintained and the basic gestures for popping, collapsing and stacking also work on the whitespace, targeting the underlying Time Bead.

The user can use the spread to zoom gesture to increase the weight of the Time Bead, as shown in Figure 8. After exceeding a certain threshold, the Bead pops, distributing its weight evenly among its children. In return, pinching decreases the weight of a Bead. The same gesture can be used bimanually. The user selects the boundaries of a time interval and scales it according to her needs, stretching or compressing the Time Beads. This enables the user to precisely focus and scale a region of interest. A double tap with the whole hand or five fingers evenly distributes weight of the Beads again, which can be necessary after several spreading gestures.

To emphasize the transition between hierarchical layers, we propose two techniques. First, we double the boundary line between these transitions. Second, we map the whole visualization to a 2.5 D projection to put an emphasis on

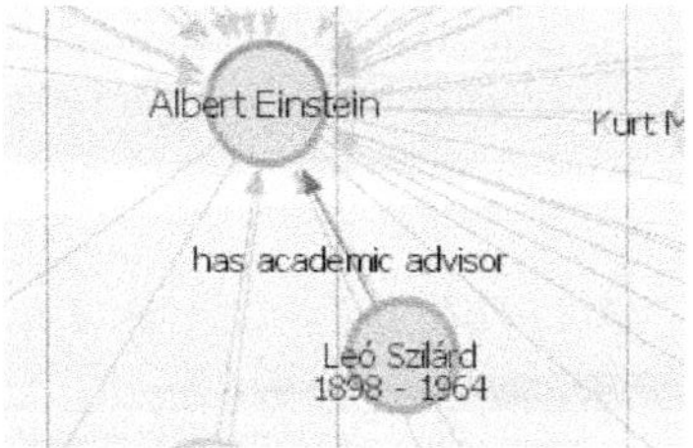

Figure 10: The prototype shows the relations of one pivotal node, here Albert Einstein.

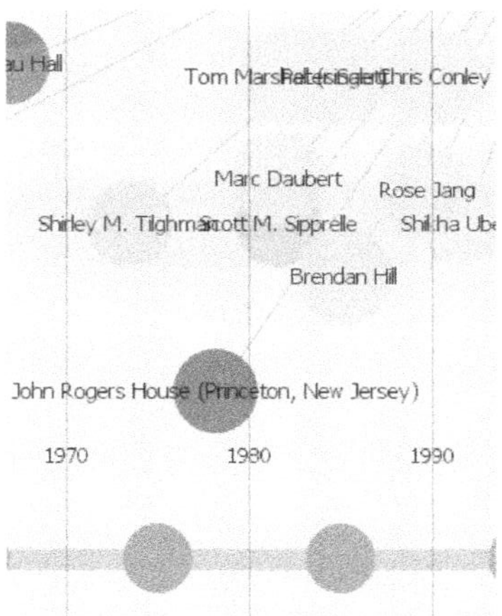

Figure 11: A snapshot of DBpedia was used, in which the user were able to explore.

the distortion effect, indicated in Figure 9. Smaller time intervals are displayed closer to the user and greater intervals, including stacked Beads, farther away. A smooth transition between the layers causes the Time Shadows, nodes and edges to skew. Since most focus regions are evenly distributed, the distortion should not dampen the readability.

Time Beads offer many advantages. The technique allows to navigate in a discrete as well as in a continuous fashion. Time Beads enable the user to directly compare multiple time intervals without additional gestures or tools. This serves the two main goals for analyzing time-related data, to compare and to find patterns. All nodes and edges are visible onscreen, reducing the need to browse.

Still, this inherently limits the amount of data shown simultaneously on screen and may lead to a cluttered visualization. Additionally, multiple sequential interactions can lead to a very heterogeneous timeline, which is harder to read than a linear one because the user has to be aware of the transitions between focus levels. Visual feedback as suggested above can counteract this effect.

Prototype: Nornir

We implemented this concept in a prototype called Nornir, again using semantic data of the DBpedia project. We used the Java-based prefuse[2] framework to display the visualization and the Apache Jena framework to query against a local Fuseki server, which held an image of the semantic graph. Mostly, Nornir ran on a Samsung SUR40 tabletop. In a later exhibition, we used a 27" Perceptive Pixel display, for its resolution and precise touch recognition. Nornir received favorable feedback from visitors, some of them addressing specifically its educational potential.

[2] http://prefuse.org/

Nornir displays only the network of a single, pivotal node at a time, the starting point in our implementation being Albert Einstein. The user can pop a node to view its network and navigate through the graph. The layout algorithm positions the pivotal node in the vertical center, sorts linked nodes vertically according to their semantic relation and places them with minimal overlap. Node size depends on the total number of nodes and the node's outgoing connections. Other methods like a history, filters, selecting items and class-dependent color coding are basic visualization techniques that were also included.

Discussion

Combining timeline and node-link visualizations creates exiting opportunities. Node-link diagrams are a well-researched mean for visualizing complex explicit relations. An interactive timeline serves as a strict data-based constraint and emphasizes the implicit temporal relations. This provides an additional context for understanding the data, and can help to understand a relation without actually reading edge labels, since it may feature inherent temporal constraints. For example, persons may only influence others who lived after their date of birth.

Especially the Time Beads concept offers room for extension. Since all Beads are nodes, they can visualize more information. The size of a Bead could encode the amount of nodes the interval contains, or the strength of directed edges could indicate the amount of connections between the intervals like in PivotGraph [8].

One participant of the initial study inspired the idea to safe nodes by dragging them below the Time Beads, dividing the visualization in a space for browsing and an analytic space where all nodes of interest can be stored. The positioning of Time Beads is very flexible and can be used to separate space in regions with different meanings.

Conclusion

There are few approaches for combining time-based visualizations with node-link diagrams. We introduce *Time Shadow* and *Time Beads* as two techniques supporting visualization of time-based node-link diagrams. Using semantic data provided by the DBpedia project, both concepts were tested in an initial study.

It confirmed that Time Shadows provide a temporal context for graph nodes which is used to better understand time-based and semantic relations. They are simple, do not interfere with edge-drawing and can be used for displaying associated quantitative data.

Time Beads offer a solution to problems that zoom-based interaction techniques face when displaying node-link diagrams that are mapped to a timeline. They allow to stretch the timeline in discrete steps or to continuously enlarge a region of interest. Additionally, the user can magnify multiple regions.

For future work, a larger user study should be designed, to clearly evaluate the trade-offs of the Time Shadow an Time Beads techniques. While the pivotal navigation proves to be sufficient for browsing data, other means to interact with the node-link diagram should be considered that support more analytic approaches. Furthermore, it should be investigated, how both concepts fare on other screen sizes such as interactive walls or smartphones.

Acknowledgements

This work was partially funded by the German Research Foundation (DFG) through the project GEMS (DA 1319/3-1).

References

[1] Aigner, W., Miksch, S., Müller, W., Schumann, H., and Tominski, C. Visualizing time-oriented data — a systematic view. *Computers & Graphics 31*, 3 (2007), 401–409.

[2] André, P., Wilson, M. L., Russell, A., Smith, D. A., Owens, A., and Schraefel, M. Continuum: designing timelines for hierarchies, relationships and scale. In *Proc. UIST*, ACM (2007), 101–110.

[3] Carpendale, M. Considering visual variables as a basis for information visualisation. *Computer Science TR #2001-693-16 16* (2003).

[4] Dachselt, R., and Weiland, M. TimeZoom: a flexible detail and context timeline. In *CHI EA*, ACM (2006), 682–687.

[5] Dörk, M., Carpendale, S., and Williamson, C. Visualizing explicit and implicit relations of complex information spaces. *Information Visualization 11*, 1 (Jan. 2012), 5–21.

[6] Jensen, M. Visualizing complex semantic timelines. *NewsBlip Technical Report NBTR2003-001, http://newsblip.com* (2003).

[7] Plaisant, C., Mushlin, R., Snyder, A., Li, J., Heller, D., and Shneiderman, B. LifeLines: using visualization to enhance navigation and analysis of patient records. In *Proc. AMIA Symposium*, American Medical Informatics Association (1998), 76.

[8] Wattenberg, M. Visual exploration of multivariate graphs. In *Proc. CHI*, ACM (2006), 811–819.

Single Locus of Control in a Tangible Paper-based Tabletop Application: An Exploratory Study

Daniela Caballero
P. Universidad Católica de Chile
Av. Vicuña Mackenna 4860
Santiago (Chile)
dccaball@uc.cl

Luis P. Prieto
CHILI Lab, EPFL
RLC D1 740, Station 20
CH-1015 Lausanne
(Switzerland)
luis.prieto@epfl.ch

Yun Wen
CHILI Lab, EPFL
RLC D1 740, Station 20
CH-1015 Lausanne
(Switzerland)
yun.wen@epfl.ch

Pierre Dillenbourg
CHILI Lab, EPFL
RLC D1 740, Station 20
CH-1015 Lausanne
(Switzerland)
pierre.dillenbourg@epfl.ch

ITS '14, Nov 16-19 2014, Dresden, Germany
ACM 978-1-4503-2587-5/14/11.
http://dx.doi.org/10.1145/2669485.2669545

Abstract
Multiple loci of control is one of the main affordances of tangible tabletop UIs due to their capability for simultaneous manipulation. However, there is a tension between the efficiency given by simultaneous manipulation and the need to coordinate and reflect in group activity. We implemented a central point of control to synchronize the group work and afford opportunities for equal participation in a tabletop application. In this study, we analyzed log and video data of seven groups of primary school students using a tabletop application. The results show that log data about this central control's position and rotation can be a predictor of equal participation, also helping interpret group performance. Finally, we discuss the implications of such findings, e.g., to provide teachers with useful information about group collaborative processes.

Author Keywords
Tabletop, collaboration, central control

ACM Classification Keywords
H.5.2 [Information interfaces and presentation]: User Interfaces.

Introduction
Unlike most educational technology, tabletops allow multiple users to interact simultaneously [12]. Multiple loci of control is one of the main affordances of Tangible UIs (TUIs) due to simultaneous manipulation. However, in education there is often a need for group activity coordination and reflection. Coordination is especially important when working with children, since they appear to be less aware of others' interactions when working on multi-touch table activities [11].

This study is concerned with whether and how a tangible central control affects equal participation. We implemented a central point of control in a tabletop collaborative learning application (based on the TinkerLamp system, see [1]), to synchronize group work and afford opportunities for reflection, thus avoiding unequal participation. Considering group dynamics, we investigate how primary school students working in small groups use this single central control to complete their group tasks, by examining its position and rotation.

Background
Tabletops have been studied in an isolated manner from the perspective of collaboration [2]. An assumption often made is that multi-touch tabletops provide higher opportunities for equal participation. When students participate equally in group work, each group member has the opportunity to contribute, manipulate materials, ask questions or provide explanations, and thus improve their knowledge and skills. One approach to avoid unequal participation is to encourage positive interdependence. Positive interdependence exists when group members realize that they need to work together in order to make a decision and to achieve a common goal [5].

Within the shared tabletop workspace, [13] identified three different territories: personal, group and storage, and provided empirical evidence on how collaborators use these three types of territories to help coordinate their interaction. Findings from [11] showed that, while participating in tabletop-based activities, children took more responsibility for the objects closer to their relative position. Besides the position, the orientation of objects also affects participants' interaction (e.g., [6, 13]). Subtle changes in position or rotation of an object can indicate a user's intention to share information, to indicate territoriality, or to invite participation [4]. Furthermore, [6] proposed that the orientation of the objects has three roles during collaboration: comprehension, coordination and communication.

We would like to support the collaboration process from a technology designer perspective. As [9] suggested, one coordination policy to avoid conflicts in a global way is to provide privileged objects, which initiate a change of state and are not available for all the participants. Moreover, in a multi-touch tabletop environment, embedding a central control element can help synchronize the group work and afford opportunities for reflection [3].

A System for Augmented-Paper Fraction Learning
Interactive tabletops have been applied successfully in geometry learning in primary schools [1]. Using the same technology, we developed a system for learning about fractions, using paper-based manipulatives. Manipulatives are concrete objects used to help students understand abstract concepts, providing students with the opportunity to explore concepts visually and tactilely [10]. We implemented multiple different fraction manipulatives, as students provided with multiple representations are more

likely to perform at higher levels [8]. [7] also evidenced the importance of manipulatives and multiple representations to facilitate fraction learning. Thus, the main aim of our system is to help students to compare fractions in a game-based form (see Figure 1). To do so, students have to move a ladybug to its home by offering her different amounts (fractions) of food from four directions.

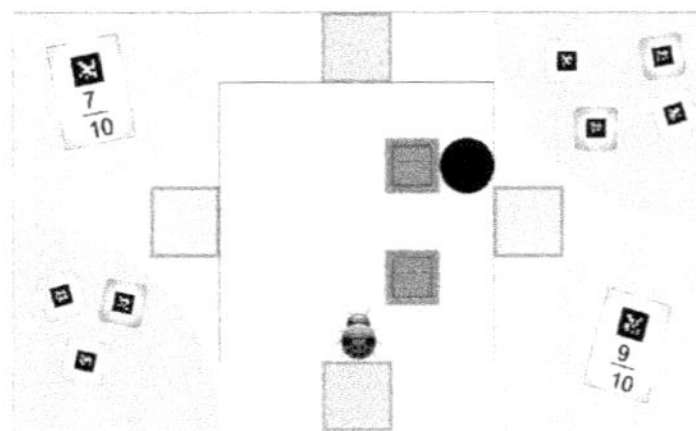

Figure 1: Game interface. Each corner has one fraction manipulative.

The system is composed of (1) an interactive lamp that projects a map wherein the ladybug moves, (2) paper-based fraction manipulatives (Figure 2), (3) hint cards, and (4) a central control (GO card with timer) (Figure 3). In terms of territoriality, each corner was defined as private space (where students can work with their manipulatives), while the map area provides group space. As shown in Figure 1, the four students (one for each corner) put a manipulative in their respective corner to express a fraction. For each map axis (X and Y) the fractions will be compared to determine the movement of the ladybug along each axis. For example, if the top fraction is greater than the bottom one and the left fraction is greater than the right one, the ladybug will move up and left. To support coordination and equal participation, the group has only *one* GO card to move the ladybug, thus encouraging children to make a group-level decision.

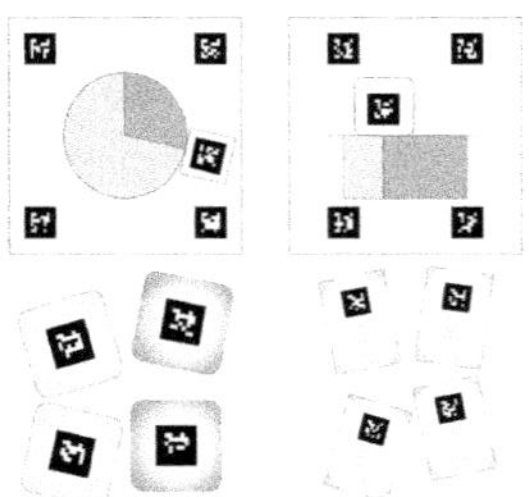

Figure 2: Paper-based fraction manipulatives. Continuous circular and rectangular (top), discrete (bottom left) and abstract (bottom right)

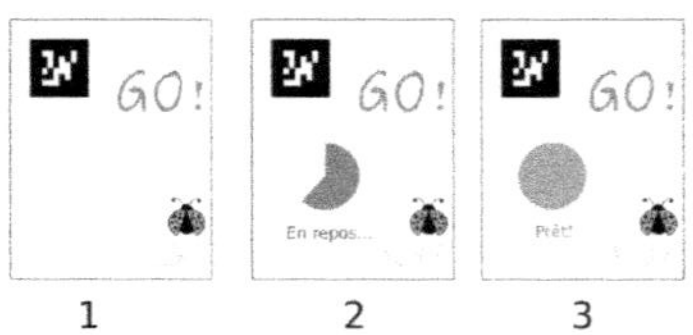

Figure 3: GO card states. (1) Static paper card, (2) Timer to let the students reflect after each move, (3) The card can be flipped to signal the next move

Exploratory User Study

We conducted an exploratory user study during an open doors event in our lab. A total of 6 classes of 14-25 students from different local primary schools (10-12 years old) participated. In each session, one class was split into groups of 4-6 students to work for 25 minutes on a tabletop, to complete the fraction game. First, students practiced how to make movements using whole numbers, then they gradually used the different kinds of fraction manipulatives.

We gathered data from each tabletop's logs (i.e., position and rotation of each paper element over time), and a camera recorded each group's tabletop workspace from the top. At the end of the session, each group was asked to answer a simple survey in which they had to write down the strategy they used during the game.

To analyze the position of the GO card, we divided the working area into 4 quadrants (upper right, upper left, bottom right, bottom left). Regarding the rotation, we divided the working area into 8 directions (4 for each corner and 4 for each side of the table). We first computed the proportion of log events where the GO card was in each quadrant and inside the map. Secondly, we calculated the rotation of the GO card for each position. Video data helped to verify whether the group work was predominated by one student, through coding the frequency of touching and pointing manipulatives. Finally, the group performance was assessed based on whether students were able to correctly elaborate their strategy in the survey (e.g., answers referring to fraction comparison), and the video-based observation regarding students' discussion and the movement of the ladybug (e.g. whether students made a consensus before making a movement).

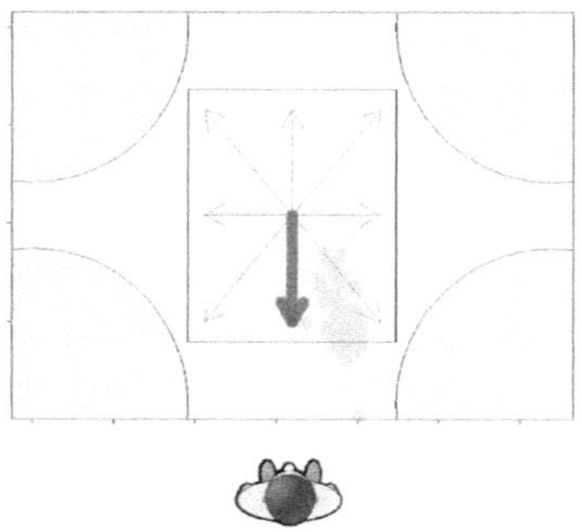

Figure 4: Distribution of the GO card condensed in one point in groups dominated by one student

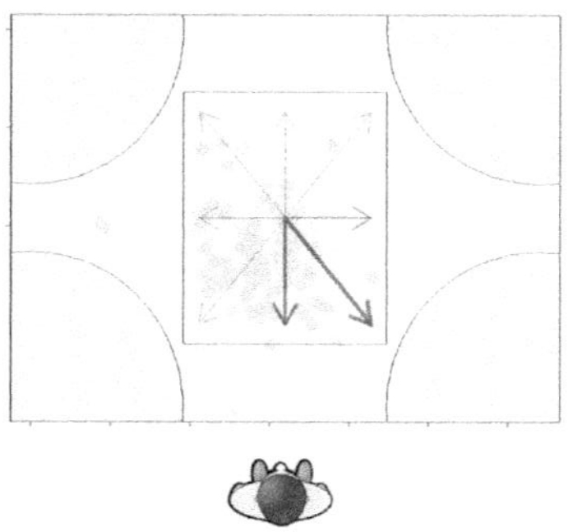

Figure 5: Distribution of the GO card dispersed in several points in groups dominated by one student

Results

We expected that the design of the single central control would help stimulate equal participation. However, preliminary analysis of video and observations in situ showed that such equal participation didn't happen in all the groups. In order to explore this fact, we selected the seven groups which went through all the proposed tasks without too much intervention of the researchers (e.g., manipulation of the fractions and GO card by the researchers). The log data showed that all the groups used the GO card inside the map area. Further video analysis highlighted that a dominant student could be observed in 3 out of 7 groups. Supplementary qualitative data helped gain insights related to group performance.

Groups with a dominant student

Based on all seven groups' log data, we found that there were three groups with the GO card placed mostly inside a single quadrant (58.8%, 99.9% and 67.7% of the time), oriented mainly towards one or two of the eight defined directions. Later video-based analysis also revealed that these three groups were in fact the groups with a dominant student. The dominant student of a group was the one who frequently flipped the GO card and tried to handle the manipulatives placed in other students' space (quadrants). In some groups, it was also observed that the student spoke aloud his/her own ideas about the ladybug movement, pointing to the materials on the tabletop. Thus, our empirical data supported that a group's central control remaining in one quadrant (more than 58.8% of the time) was a good indicator that the group had a dominant student. Two examples are provided in Figure 4 and Figure 5, along with the location of the dominant student as taken from the video analysis.

As it can be seen in the figures, the difference between the GO card position distributions of these two groups is salient as well: the distribution was highly condensed in Figure 4, while it was quite dispersed in Figure 5. According to the post-activity survey data and our video-based observation, it was found that the group shown in Figure 4 had a good performance in the activity (e.g., they made explicit how to construct fractions to move the ladybug correctly in the survey). Although the GO card was mainly kept in one point, it was observed that students took turns to flip the card. Moreover, the group discussed extensively before handling the manipulatives and flipping the GO card. On the contrary, in the group shown in Figure 5, although it was observed that the dominant student tried to explain how to move the ladybug, it seemed that not all the group members understood how to use the manipulatives. Sometimes, they tried to move the ladybug through flipping the GO card by themselves without making a consensus with one another. Furthermore, their feedback in the post survey indicated that the group did not get a clear idea about how to move the ladybug. Thus, we can see how unequal participation does not necessarily imply bad group performance.

Groups without a dominant student

In groups without a dominant student, the GO card positions were dispersed across two or more quadrants. Unlike the groups with a dominant student, it was difficult to find a clear preferred rotation to manipulate the GO card (out of eight directions, the groups had two, three, four and four preferred rotations, respectively. This finding was also triangulated with the analysis of the video data. We can further separate the GO card distributions of groups without a dominant student into two categories, depending on whether actions with this paper element

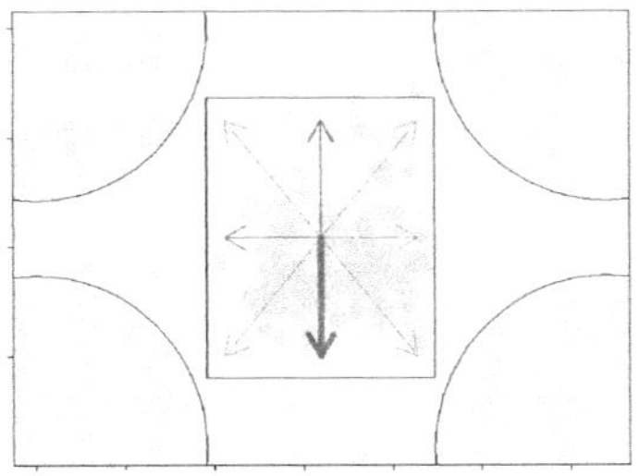

Figure 6: Distribution of the GO card spreading in private spaces in groups without dominant student

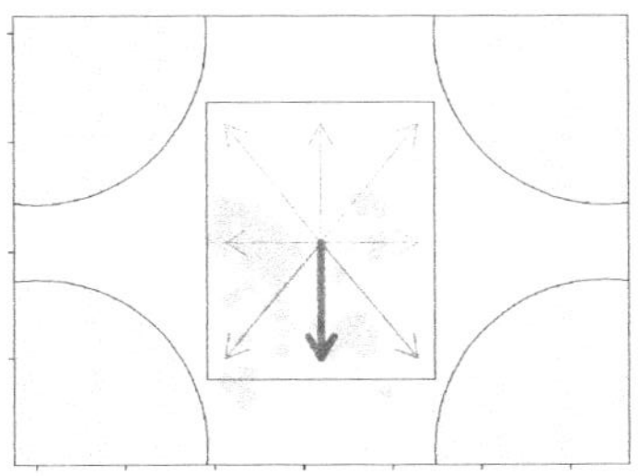

Figure 7: Distribution of the GO card without spreading in private spaces in groups without dominant student

took place in the private space or not (Figure 6 and Figure 7).

We can see in Figure 6 that the GO card was manipulated mainly in two quadrants, but at certain moments, it was manipulated inside the private space of two of the students (upper and bottom left). Also, it was rotated mainly towards three different directions. In the qualitative video analysis, group misbehaviors could be observed (e.g., one student kept flipping the GO card around his/her own private space while some other students were still manipulating other materials – marking poor group-level coordination). The group shown in Figure 7, however, mainly manipulated the GO card in the group working area, with the card rotated towards one side of the table. In the video data it was observed that, similar to the group shown in Figure 4 (in which students discussed first), this group used the manipulatives together, and took turns to manipulate the GO card. Again, these two examples illustrate that there is not necessarily a direct connection between equal participation and good group performance.

Discussion and Conclusion

In general, the initial empirical data of this study showed that embedding a central point of control in tabletop systems can enable children to coordinate and reflect in their group activity, but cannot guarantee it. Even under similar instruction, group dynamics influences greatly the way the tool is brought into use.

With the triangulation of both log data and qualitative video data, this study showed that measuring the position and rotation of the central control object can be a predictor of whether a group has a dominant student (i.e., unequal participation) or not. The dominance observed, however, doesn't mean poor group performance: we observed groups where the dominant student helped explain the concepts to others, and each group member still had opportunities to be engaged in the activity (leading to good group performance); conversely, other groups with no dominant student showed a much less organized group work.

Through examining the position distribution of the central control object and the groups' performance, this exploratory study also provided us with insights to interpret the visualized log data. For example, if the position and rotation of the control object was too widely distributed, it may indicate that the group work proceeded without good coordination; if the control object was positioned in individual private space frequently, it might indicate that the group students did not have enough awareness of each others' work.

The findings of this study can help researchers to interpret information about group work progress. However, the visualization of on-going collaboration amongst students can also be used to provide a cockpit's view *for teachers* to better orchestrate classroom activities. Since classroom time is limited, such monitoring support can help teachers identify which group needs his/her intervention most (e.g., the group with a too widely-distributed control object). In other words, it has potential for providing teachers with useful information to arrange time and adjust instructions to meet their concrete needs.

In our future work we would like to develop and test such visualizations in real classrooms, to examine whether it helps teachers to facilitate group work in a better way. Besides, we would like to explore the design space of the GO card regarding content oritentation (i.e., the fact that the current card can be understood even upside-down, due to the little textual content printed or projected on it) [6]. We would like to study how changing the GO card (to show more strongly-oriented content), affects the consistency of our findings.

Acknowledgments

The work presented here has been partially funded by the Marie Curie Fellowship MIOCTI (FP7-PEOPLE-2012-IEF project no. 327384). Daniela Caballero was a Swiss Government Excellence Scholarship holder for the academic year(s) 2013-2014 (ESKAS No. 2013.0293).

References

[1] Bonnard, Q., Verma, H., Kaplan, F., and Dillenbourg, P. Paper interfaces for learning geometry. In *21st Century Learning for 21st Century Skills*. Springer, 2012, 37–50.

[2] Dillenbourg, P., and Evans, M. Interactive tabletops in education. *International Journal of Computer-Supported Collaborative Learning 6*, 4 (2011), 491–514.

[3] Do-Lenh, S. Supporting reflection and classroom orchestration with tangible tabletops. *École Polytechnique Federale De Laussane* (2012).

[4] Hancock, M. S., Vernier, F. D., Wigdor, D., Carpendale, S., and Shen, C. Rotation and translation mechanisms for tabletop interaction. In *Horizontal Interactive Human-Computer Systems, 2006. TableTop 2006. First IEEE International Workshop on*, IEEE (2006), 79–88.

[5] Janssen, J., Erkens, G., Kanselaar, G., and Jaspers, J. Visualization of participation: Does it contribute to successful computer-supported collaborative learning? *Computers & Education 49*, 4 (2007), 1037–1065.

[6] Kruger, R., Carpendale, S., Scott, S. D., and Greenberg, S. Roles of orientation in tabletop collaboration: Comprehension, coordination and communication. *Computer Supported Cooperative Work (CSCW) 13*, 5-6 (2004), 501–537.

[7] Martin, T., and Schwartz, D. L. Physically distributed learning: Adapting and reinterpreting physical environments in the development of fraction concepts. *Cognitive Science 29*, 4 (2005), 587–625.

[8] McNeil, N., and Jarvin, L. When theories don't add up: disentangling the manipulatives debate. *Theory into Practice 46*, 4 (2007), 309–316.

[9] Morris, M. R., Ryall, K., Shen, C., Forlines, C., and Vernier, F. Beyond social protocols: Multi-user coordination policies for co-located groupware. In *Proceedings of the 2004 ACM conference on Computer supported cooperative work*, ACM (2004), 262–265.

[10] Ojose, B., and Sexton, L. The effect of manipulative materials on mathematics achievement of first grade students. *The Mathematics Educator 12*, 1 (2009), 3–14.

[11] Rick, J., Harris, A., Marshall, P., Fleck, R., Yuill, N., and Rogers, Y. Children designing together on a multi-touch tabletop: an analysis of spatial orientation and user interactions. In *Proceedings of the 8th International Conference on Interaction Design and Children*, ACM (2009), 106–114.

[12] Rick, J., Marshall, P., and Yuill, N. Beyond one-size-fits-all: How interactive tabletops support collaborative learning. In *Proceedings of the 10th International Conference on Interaction Design and Children*, ACM (2011), 109–117.

[13] Scott, S. D., Carpendale, M. S. T., and Inkpen, K. M. Territoriality in collaborative tabletop workspaces. In *Proceedings of the 2004 ACM conference on Computer supported cooperative work*, ACM (2004), 294–303.

Interact! : An Evidence-Based Framework for Digitally Supported School Field Trips

Alexandra Tanner [1]
alexandra.tanner@fhnw.ch

Beat Vollenwyder [1]
beat.vollenwyder@fhnw.ch

Ulrike Schock [1]
ulrike.schock@fhnw.ch

Michael Kalt [2]
michael.kalt@fhnw.ch

Magdalena Mateescu [1]
magdalena.mateescu@fhnw.ch

Doris Agotai [2]
Doris.agotai@fhnw.ch

Peter Gros [2]
Peter.gros@fhnw.ch

Manfred Vogel [2]
Manfred.vogel@fhnw.ch

Carmen Zahn [1]
carmen.zahn@fhnw.ch

[1] School of Applied Psychology
University of Applied Sciences and Arts Northwestern Switzerland
FHNW, Olten Switzerland

[2] School of Engineering
University of Applied Sciences and Arts Northwestern Switzerland
FHNW, Brugg Switzerland

ITS 2014, November 16–19, 2014, Dresden, Germany.
ACM 978-1-4503-2587-5/14/11.
http://dx.doi.org/10.1145/2669485.2669546

Abstract
Interact! is an evidence-based framework for the support of school class visits to science exhibitions featuring a large vertical multi-touch surface and a set of tablet computers. The overall framework is designed to foster interest in computer sciences and collaborative learning of selected topics by drawing upon subject areas of personal importance and encouraging small group knowledge processes. Interact! was implemented as a prototype and tested in a field experiment with 53 pupils.

Author Keywords
Learning in museums; School field trips; Collaborative learning; Multi-touch media; User-centered design

ACM Classification Keywords
K.3.1 [Computer Uses in Education]: Collaborative learning.

Introduction
Informal learning in museums and exhibitions is characterized as object oriented, dynamic, self-paced and including important social aspects [1]. These characterizations largely comply with requirements for collaborative learning, which is understood as active, problem-oriented, based on authentic learning experiences, mutual influence, and equity of

participation among learners [2]. It is well known that both informal and collaborative learning have potential for fostering important knowledge processes [3,4]. Likewise, it is widely acknowledged that new media and interactive surfaces provide new ways to enable and enhance such ways of learning [5]. Moreover, the Swiss curriculum for students requires that pupils till about the age of 16 years build basic knowledge and skills, enabling them to competent, appropriate, and the socially responsible use of ICT and media [6]. In our research presented here, we investigate how large interactive surfaces and tablets can be used to support informal collaborative learning during school class visits in science exhibitions. School classes are an important visitor group in most museums, especially science museums. For instance, in Switzerland, where this study was conducted, 25 percent of all visitors were pupils under the age of 16 years [7]. The research resulted in an evidence-based framework for school class visits (named Interact!) and in a prototype featuring a large, mobile, vertical multi-touch surface (interactive wall) and portable computing devices (tablets).

Following a human centered design approach, we conducted a qualitative interview study with teachers (N = 8) and museum experts (N = 5). Key findings from both perspectives show, that teachers prepare the field trip with online material but they have little time to prepare it with the pupils. Museums are reported to be suitable for constructivist learning approaches whereas passive learning strategies are barely used. Various digital media are desired; currently pupils work usually with paper and pen. For the post processing plenary discussions in classrooms, listing on website and take home material are provided and appreciated.

Based on these results, teachers' goals of school class visits and collaborative learning strategies for small groups, a framework named Interact! was developed. Then we implemented a prototype and conducted a field experiment placed in a touring exhibition called "Achtung Technik Los!" ("Ready, techy, go!") which aims at promoting interest in computer science in schools [8]. The main goals of the field experiment were, on the one hand, a proof of concept to verify our theoretical ideas and on the other hand, to investigate how the framework raises interest and supports knowledge construction in comparison to more traditional pen and paper methods.

Presentation of the framework

Interact! is built upon three basic assumptions that were derived from our interview data: Firstly, the assumption that personal interest facilitates the access of a learner to a specific science subject. Secondly, that collaborative learning in a small group is desirable and essential for students' understanding and can be applied to school class museum visits. Thirdly, that a museum field trip with a school class cannot be viewed isolated from pre- and post-visit activities [9]. These premises resulted in a framework with nine steps, which can be seen in an overview in Figure 1. Step 1: The first step takes into account that the interviewed teachers named 'convenience' as an important factor for field trips and follows didactical recommendations concerning the preparation of the students beforehand [10]. Hence, in the first step, teachers can access a web-application that provides detailed insight into the field trip program with possibilities to customize the visit, ready-to-use class material for download as well as information like opening hours and facilities. Step 2: After the teachers confirm the arrival, the class gets a first impression of the exhibition by walking through it. This addresses reported benefits for learning after novelty reducing activities [11]. Steps 3 and 4: A welcome game introduces the interactive wall. Parallel to this game, students receive a near field communication (NFC) tag that allows an individual registration for the field trip.

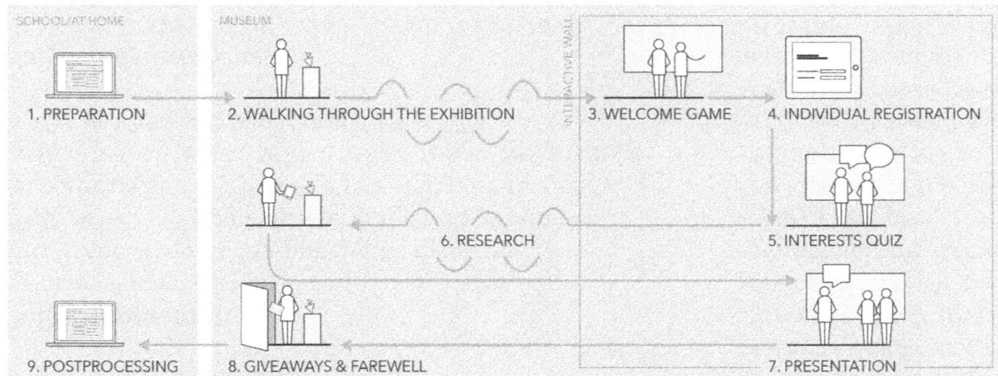

Figure 1. Overview of the nine steps of Interact! The steps marked in blue were part of the prototype.

Step 5: This step draws upon subject areas of personal importance: Ten every day questions like "I never leave my home without..." are displayed. With the help of their NFC tags, pupils can pick one out of three possible answers. The purpose of this fun process is the creation of interest groups. All answers are connected with a broader topic - in our prototype these topics were music, sports and games - and an algorithm assigns the students according to their personal preferences. Step 6: Each interest group receives a tablet computer with several research questions, putting their personal interest field in connection with a computer science topic. After the pupils familiarize themselves with these questions, they are free to find answers in the exhibition. During their search, the tablet offers the possibility to scan quick response (QR) codes attached to the exhibits in order to collect additional information and to take pictures and short video clips. The structure of this search task is built upon study results concerning learning under different levels of choice [12]. Step 7: This step contains the preparation of a presentation with the collected items on the interactive wall. The pupils then present the results to their peers. They can display the collected texts, pictures and video clips in their own pace and consolidate their knowledge by verbalizing it [13]. Steps 8 and 9: These steps consider the importance of follow-up activities for enduring learning results [14]. The students can keep and reuse their NFC tag and have the possibility to access all results via the web-application described in step one.

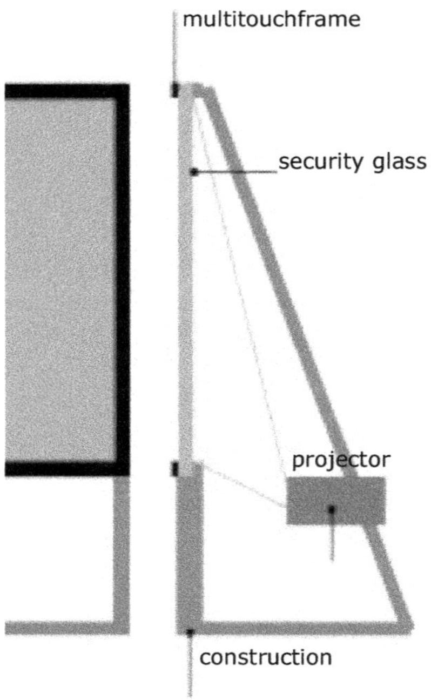

Figure 2. Scheme of the interactive wall construction.

Construction of the prototype

The construction of the prototype focused on the steps situated inside the exhibition – these parts are highlighted in Figure 1. The main technical challenge was the construction of a large interactive wall that would be still easy to transport and affordable for

Figure 3. Impression of the field experiment.

museums. As shown in Figure 2, we decided to use back projection with ultra-short throw projectors upon coated security glass with an infrared frame to track the touch interaction of more than 32 touch points. Our interactive wall offers 4 to 1.25 meters touch surface, which allows eight to twelve pupils to work simultaneously. Apart from the touch interaction, teachers can control the workshops by using special NFC tags. We decided to use windows 8.1 tablets as the server application is also programmed on the .NET framework. The tablets are configured in kiosk mode to prevent pupils from switching to other apps. The centerpiece of our application is the interactive wall server, which contains the business logic and provides a REST API for the communication between the tablets and the wall application.

Field experiment

Participants and design

Fifty-three students (31 female, 22 male, age M = 13.9, SD = 0.77) participated in the field experiment. All participants took part in a pre- and post-test and were randomly assigned to a media supported group (N = 28) or a pen and paper group (N = 27).

Materials and procedure

Upon arrival, the pupils were asked to complete a questionnaire differentiating between cognitive and affective aspects of interest. This questionnaire was constructed based on similar previous work [15]. The questionnaire further covers preferences for school subjects, mental representations of computer science, different components of interest and knowledge questions concerning specific topics of the exhibition. Upon completion of the questionnaire, students were randomly assigned to one of two groups. The media supported group had access to the full range of digital media (interactive wall and tablets), while the paper and pen group relied on more traditional materials (worksheets and notepads). Besides the media use, the program was kept as similar as possible. All pupils received the same instructions, assistance, amount of time and covered the same questions. Before leaving, the pupils were asked to complete a second questionnaire identical to the first one, except for an additional part to rate the program.

Results

The two groups (media supported vs. pen and paper) were tested on a wide range of differences in their composition - such as previous experience with touch devices or preferences in school subjects. No statistical significant differences were found (all $p > .10$). Then a 2 (pre, post) x 2 (media, paper) within subject ANOVA was conduced. For both groups, the increase in general interest in computer science from pre- to post-test was highly significant ($F(1,50) = 35.64$, $p < .01$) as well as the increase in the cognitive component of interest ($F(1,50) = 29.51$, $p < .01$). Results for self-assessed knowledge showed a similar pattern: Students rated their own knowledge about computer science topics related to music ($F(1,40) = 29.09$, $p < .01$), sports ($F(1,40) = 330.26$, $p < .01$) and games ($F(1,40) = 46,75$, $p < .01$) significantly better after participation in Interact!. This result is backed by the knowledge questions related to music ($F(1,51) = 21.66$, $p < .01$), sports ($F(1,51) = 139.21$, $p < .01$) and games ($F(1,51) = 54.03$, $p < .01$). All other results including the comparisons between groups (media vs. paper) did not yield significance.

	M	*SD*
How did you like Interact!	4.91	.84
Would you recommend Interact! to your friends?	4.49	.97
Interact! was personally relevant to me	4.02	1.03
Interact! did encourage discussion	3.72	1.32
Interact! was new to me	4.77	1.17
Interact! did encourage involvement with the topics	3.98	1.29

Table 1. Means and Standard Deviations from evaluation feedbacks to the prototype. Both groups (media and paper) are included. The highest possible rating was 6 points.

The reactions on Interact! were all in all positive - Table 1 contains some selected ratings. Also, the additional remarks contained mostly positive feedbacks. The interest quiz at the beginning was especially highlighted as was the work on the interactive wall, which was appraised as impressive and fun to use. Negative feedback included criticism about occasional technical problems with the touch functionality, slight ambiguities in the interface design and the dull questionnaires. It was observable that the media group read the information less exactly than the paper and pen group. However, pupils of the media group were already anticipating the content of their presentation (e. g. with video take up), while some of the paper and pen group just reproduced the original information word by word. An impression of the field experiment is shown in Figure 3. In sum, the results proved that our framework significantly raises students' interest in computer science and sustains knowledge construction for related topics.

Discussion

In this paper, we presented a framework for computer supported collaborative learning in a museum setting. The framework named Interact! was investigated in a field experiment. The results are showing that the prototype of Interact! enabled interest driven learning during school class museums visits: the self-assesed as well as the tested knowledge increased significantly with participation. The pupils' feedback was generally positive and the interactive wall was evaluated as impressive and fun to use. It can further be stated that tablets are suitable aids to fulfill research tasks in a collaborative learning session and that the interactive wall showed great potential creating presentations consisting of collected videos and photos. In other words: The concept Interact! proved to be successful in these respects. However, not all results met our expectations: Firstly, the affective component of interest was not raised significantly and secondly, the interactive wall with tablets group did not significantly outperform the paper and pencil group. Some experimental limitations can account for these nonsignificant results. The touch functionality of the prototype did have occasional problems and slight ambiguities in the interface design were mentioned. These issues might have reduced potential positive effects and should be adressed in further development by improving the construction and conduting additional usability studies. The observation of the pupils in both groups revealed the tendency that our participants were more acustomed doing collaborative tasks with pen and paper than working with tablets and a multi-touch surface. It is conceivable that with pupils who are more familiar with computer-supported learning as implemented in our study, the results would differ.

To conclude, the results are encouraging to advance the technology in use, including improving technical and usability aspects that could facilitate the process flow. Future implementations should take special consideration of familiarity and affect so that the positive influences on collaborative learning can be effective. Future research adresses the questions: How can we specifically address the affective component of interest? How can improved technology affordances support knowledge construction? We consider it very likely that the improvements would lead to significant differences and contend that especially the aesthetics of the interface design could influence the affective component. Further studies will address this topic.

Acknowledgements

Research reported in this publication was supported by the Gerbert Rüf Foundation research grant GRS-024/12: Digital media for school class museum visits.

References

[1] Zahn, C. Forschung zur Rolle neuer Medien im Museum - psychologische Perspektiven und Methoden am IWM. In S. Schwan, H. Trischler and M. Prenzel (Eds.), *Die Rolle von Medien für die Resituierung von Exponaten: Mitteilungen und Bericht*, Bd. 38 (2006), 9-14.

[2] Damon, W. and Phelps, E. Critical distinctions among three approaches to peer education. *International Journal of Educational Research*, 13, 1 (1989), 9-19.

[3] Jacobsen, J., Wisne, J., MacGillivray, S. and West, R.W. A New, Additional format for Changing Visitor Experiences. *Informal Learning Review, 125* (2014), 13–16.

[4] Johnson, D., Maruyama, G., Johnson, R., Nelson, D. and Skon, L. Effects of cooperative, competitive and individualistic goal structures on achievement: A meta-analysis. *Psychological Bulletin, 89* (1981), 47-62.

[5] Borchers, M., Mock, P., Zahn, C., Edelmann, J. and Hesse, F. W. Supporting School Class Visits to Fine Arts Museums in the 21st Century: A CSCL Approach for a Multitouch Table Based Video Tool. In N. Rummel, M. Kapur, M. Nathan and S. Puntambekar (Eds.), *To See the World and a Grain of Sand: Learning across Levels of Space, Time, and Scale: CSCL 2013, Volume 1 —* (2013), 57-64.

[6] Schweizerischer Lehrplan- Technik http://konsultation.lehrplan.ch/index.php?nav=10|10&code=t|102

[7] Museum visits in Switzerland – Statistical Report

[8] Achtung Technik Los! http://www.achtungtechniklos.ch

[9] Falk, J. H. and Dierking, L. D. *Learning from museums: visitor experiences and the making of meaning*. Walnut Creek, CA: AltaMira Press (2000).

[10] DeWitt, J. and Storksdieck, M. A Short Review of School Field Trips: Key Findings from the Past and Implications for the Future. *Visitor Studies*, 11, 2 (2008), 181–197.

[11] Anderson, D. and Lucas, K. B. The effectiveness of orienting students to the physical features of a science museum prior to visitation. *Research in Science Education*, 27, 4 (1997), 485–495.

[12] Bamberger, Y. and Tal, T. Learning in a personal context: Levels of choice in a free choice learning environment in science and natural history museums. *Science Education, 91*, 1 (2007), 75–95.

[13] Knipfer, K., Mayr, E., Zahn, C., Schwan, S. and Hesse, F. W. Computer support for knowledge communication in science exhibitions: Novel perspectives from research on collaborative learning. *Educational Research Review*, 4, 3 (2009), 196–209.

[14] Anderson, D., Lucas, K. B., Ginns, I. S. and Dierking, L. D. Development of knowledge about electricity and magnetism during a visit to a science museum and related post-visit activities. *Science Education*, 84, 5 (2000), 658–679.

[15] Wessel, D. Supporting interest and Knowledge exchange through Mobile devices and bookmarking in science and technology museums. Eberhard-Karls-Universität, Tübingen (2010).

Using Scalable, Interactive Floor Projection for Production Planning Scenario

Otto, Michael
Daimler AG
Wilhelm-Runge-Str. 11
D-89013 Ulm
michael.m.otto@daimler.com

Prieur, Michael
Daimler AG
Wilhelm-Runge-Str. 11
D-89013 Ulm
michael.prieur@daimler.com

Enrico Rukzio
Institute of Media Informatics
Ulm University
James-Franck-Ring
D-89081 Ulm
enrico.rukzio@uni-ulm.de

ITS 2014, November 16–19, 2014, Dresden, Germany.
ACM 978-1-4503-2587-5/14/11.
http://dx.doi.org/10.1145/2669485.2669547

Abstract
This paper introduces a novel system for interactive evaluation and verification of manual assembly processes. The approach utilizes a scalable, interactive augmented floor surface in combination with a tangible tabletop hardware and a material zone planning software. The floor projection hardware is used for true to scale assembly station layout visualizations. The advantages and drawbacks of a low-cost, true to scale visualization will be discussed. A preliminary evaluation of the proposed system during a production planning workshop has shown that the low-cost implementation is suitable for reaching the production planning goals. Additionally true to scale visualizations support users to estimate distances, speeds and spatial relationships within the digital layout. In future work, motion capture and tracking systems will be integrated and registered to the augmented floor surface area, the projection area will be extended and efficiency improvements will be showed up.

Author Keywords
manual assembly; true to scale; interactive augmented floor surface; shop-floor; floor projection

ACM Classification Keywords
H.5.m. Information interfaces and presentation

Figure 1: Hardware setup consisting of SUR40 tangible tabletop display and augmented floor surface

Introduction

Original equipment manufacturers in automotive industry work hard to acquire key market shares and intensify customer dedication via customization and a bigger model variety. This leads to higher requirements on production preparation in final assembly stage and lower set-up times during model change. Virtual technologies like virtual reality and augmented surfaces will help handling the raised complexity during production planning, ramp-up and production phase. Physical prototypes serve as an opportunity to evaluate, verify and optimize the planned manual assembly processes. Since prototype building is a major cost driver in vehicle development there is the tendency to build less prototypes or completely abolish them. Additionally physical prototypes are now being built later during production planning phase. The reduced number of physical prototypes must be compensated by new technologies and tools. Virtual technologies and the increasing quality of digital models are potential solutions to fill this gap.

Current Situation in Production Planning

The overall goal for production planners of the end assembly is ensuring a punctual, smooth and efficient series production. Traditionally the process of planning and validating is based on hardware prototypes and done under conditions close to productive ones. The whole process for production planning is changing towards the use of virtual models. The evaluation and verification goals must be achieved without the presence of physical prototypes. Roughly summarized, there are several planning phases: During product verification phase, changes in the product design are still possible, due to the relative long lead time to start of production. During the phase of planning and validation of manual assembly processes, the definition of assembly sequence, the specification of the assembly work tasks, the assignment of assembly tasks to physical stations of an assembly line and the configuration of the assembly station will take place. Based on this information the station layout will be developed. Yet production engineers still prefer to work with physical methods and are fond of the proximity to real production environment.

Advantages of Virtual Production Planning

Despite many production planners would like to use physical prototypes, there are several advantages by using virtual technologies:

- Complete simulation of processes in a factory
- Easy optimization in virtual models and instantaneous simulation
- No hardware setup times
- Automatic deduction of various parameters: duration, efficiency, ergonomics, cost, use of resources, logistic, production forecast
- Finding the optimal solution between various conflicting parameters
- optimal line balancing for model-mix production
- No limitation of combinations between products, configurations and factories

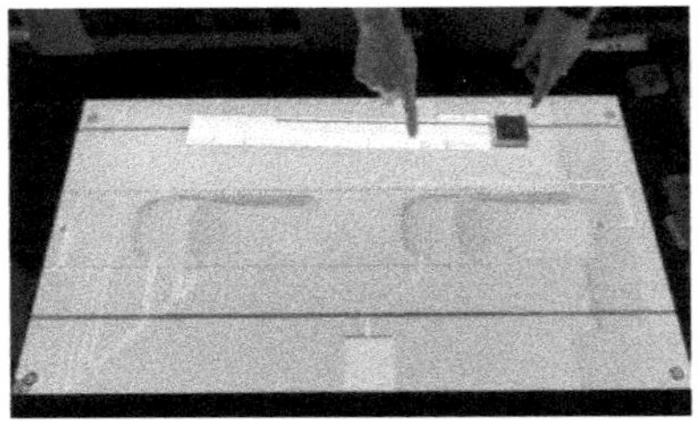

Figure 2: Interactive 2D tabletop material zone planning software with phicons

Figure 3: Production planner in front of virtual box carrier and virtual walking paths

Interaction Concept for Interdisciplinary Production Planning Workshops

We present a novel system and interaction concept for interdisciplinary production planning workshops. The system consists of a tabletop hardware with tangibles, a material zone layout planning software and the visualization hardware for a true to scale, bird's eye view visualization.

For material zone planning, a special system has been developed employing an interactive tabletop hardware with tangibles as user interfaces and specialized software, which offers a strong perceptual coupling between the tangibles and visual representations of the station layout. The user interface was designed as intuitive as possible, supporting the collaboration between the workshop participants and engaging all participants to interact with the virtual model. Each participant should have the possibility to visualize his idea of an improved station layout and to manipulate it on his own. The presented interactive tangible tabletop system is the essential interface and serves as the visualization system for the augmented floor surface. Workshop participants are encouraged to interact with the digital models without using traditional interfaces on a desktop PC like mouse and keyboard. Instead they are doing spatial planning tasks with touch inputs, gestures and phicons. No static menus are visible throughout regular use. As depicted in Figure 2 all menu items are accessible by using the haptic phicons, like "menu, process, objects, properties, etc."

The mentioned true to scale visualization offers new possibilities in workshop situations. The realization of the floor surface can be seen in Figure 3. There are two main advantages of using a huge augmented floor surface: Human beings are able to estimate lengths, spatial relations and speeds in reality linearly and precisely. True to scale visualizations support the planners to verify their digital model very intuitively. Additionally passive workshop participants will be engaged to play a more active role. The degree of activation of passive workshop participants is hard to measure, but first pilot use-cases have shown an increase of discussions on the solutions. Starting the simulation, the participant can easily step into the augmented workspace and verify the planned assembly process steps in regard to planned times, position, dependencies, effective work time and the ergonomic aspects of the assembly station.

"Interactive surfaces are another promising approach to support collaborative design and simulation that has been explored by many researchers in the past years to support a variety of spatial applications" [1].

The floor projection system does not display tracked single user's perspectives in order to support multi user collaboration. Due to the isometric bird's eye-view camera, objects with height, like carriers and products, are displayed as flat 2D objects on the floor (see Figure 3). Since the floor plane does not display depth information and has no stereoscopic view, all workshop participants see a realistic true to scale information. Therefore mutual awareness in co-located collaborative workshops is an important aspect. Single-user tracked bird's eye view in workshop situations will be evaluated in future work.

Typical use-cases for this interaction and visualization system are to define ideal position of carriers, reduce walking paths, unnecessary work tasks, dependencies

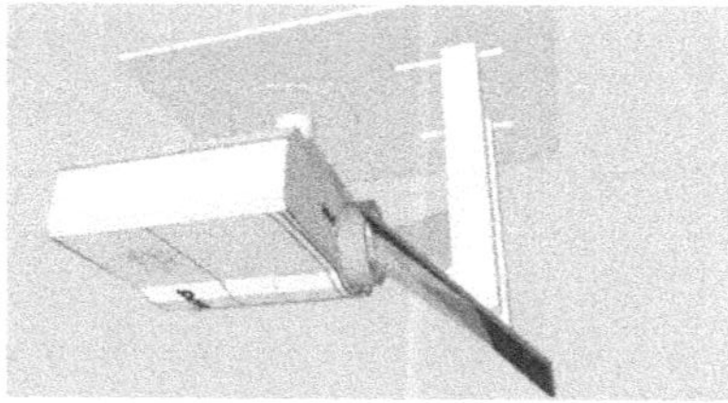

Figure 4: Rendering of a single projector mount with front surface mirror

Figure 5: Projector mounts with true to scale floor visualization

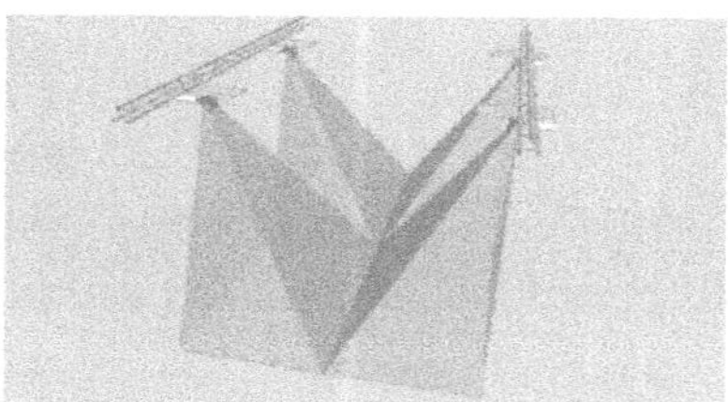

Figure 6: Rendering of projection cones for 2x2 projector arrangement

between workers and process steps and to assess the vagueness in planning quality [2]. Similar questions are often assessed during continuous improvement process workshops, which take place after start of production and take advantage of similar methods. Unwanted downtimes can be avoided by using virtual technologies in advance to direct physical changes at the assembly line. Aurich et al. also presented a virtual reality based system for CIP workshops [3].

Hardware Implementation of Floor Projection

Hardware implementations of floor projection systems have been described in literature several times [4],[5]. The system is composed of at least four overhead short-throw DLP projectors, four mirrors, a video wall controller and several pieces of event trussing and profiles. The system can be massively scaled up to 32 projectors without altering the hardware setup (see Figure 5).

The projectors used in this setup are off-the-shelf, semi-professional projectors, which offer a good price per lumen ratio. Each overhead projector is combined with front surface mirrors in order to be able to mount the projector horizontally and redirect the beam to the floor. These projectors are not mountable in each possible orientation, because the air flow for transporting hot air out of the package is designed only for upside-down ceiling mount and up-right mounting. If mounted vertically, the projector would be damaged quickly. Each projector has a short throw lens with a variable throw ratio from 0.72 to 0.87. The luminous flux of each projector is specified to 2500 lumens have been integrated to redirect the picture to the floor. Since the optically effective coating of the mirror is located directly on top of the surface of a glass, a good imaging quality can be achieved with this mirror. Regular back surface coated mirrors would have created ghost imaging. The minimum size of each mirror depends on the throw ratio, optical offset, distance of the projector to the mirror, the elevation angle of the mirror and the projector.

A multi display signal controller for four outputs is used, which can be driven as DVI display and can represent an arbitrary crop region of the original input signal. Input images can be croped, scaled, mirrored and bezel corrected. Input signals are accepted up to 4k x 4k resolution via Dual Link DVI signal.

The hardware setup consists of a 4x1 or a 2x2 (see Figure 6) configuration. Each single picture has a size of 3m x 1.68m and the resulting augmented floor area has a size of 6.75m x 3.00m or 6m x 3.36m respectively. This is sufficient for a true to scale visualization of a station on one working side. The stiffness and tolerances of the ball joint mountings could still be improved. The adjusted picture offered edges, which differed less than 10mm.

Preliminary Evaluation

The evaluation is an ongoing process, whether the depicted system reduces planning time and improves the quality. The following results do not claim statistical significance due to the low number of participants. Thirteen production planning engineers have taken part in this expert survey, which took place during an interdisciplinary production planning workshop. The overhead projector system was created under several constraints, like low-cost, portability and limited ceiling heights. Therefore some trade-offs had to be made.

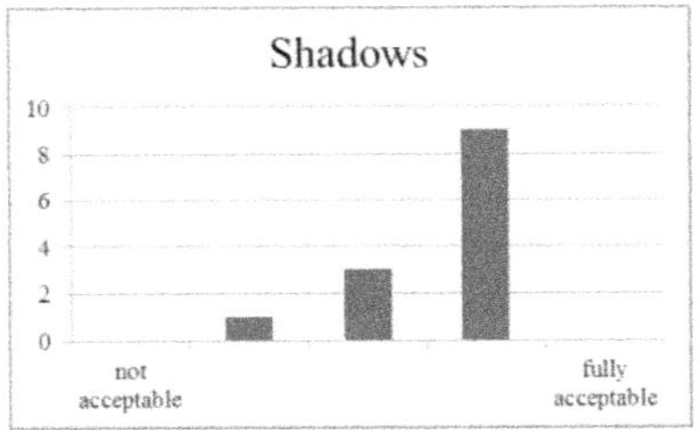

Figure 7: Survey results on: shadowing effects of human bodies

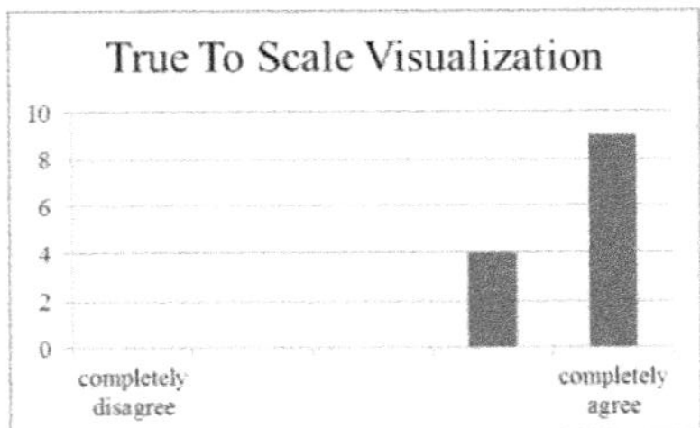

Figure 8: Survey results on: true to scale visualization

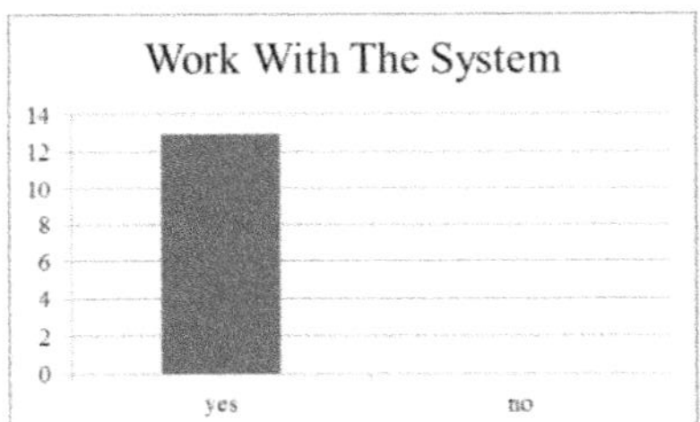

Figure 9: Survey results on: Whether the experts would like to work with the system or not

In order to understand the importance of these factors, several potential drawbacks have been discussed. By tendency, the thirteen asked production planning engineers agreed, that the height of the projectors at 2,5m is absolutely sufficient. All engineers rated the color differences as fully acceptable, because they are not crucial for reaching their goals and they are hardly recognizable. The same holds for the resolution of the augmented floor surface image. The hard-edging property of the system has been rated more diversely but by tendency still positive. Discussions with experts pointed out that a small gap between the projections areas can be accepted more easily than a small overlap with double the brightness. More expensive projectors offer soft-edging ability natively. Since each projector only offers 2500 ANSI lumen per image, the results on the brightness issue are surprising. The experts rated the brightness all in all as sufficient. Since the brightness of projection systems can easily be raised, the only limiting factor is the available budget. Interestingly, some people feel dazzled with light, when walking through the projection cone. By tendency the majority of people can cope with this property.

The most diverse results and most discussions of the experts were related to shadowing effects. By tendency, the people still found it "neutral to acceptable" for their purpose (see Figure 7), but this is the biggest drawback of the hardware implementation. There are several solutions to eliminate shadowing effects using LED or LCD floors or rear projection systems[4], but the investment costs of these systems are the limiting factor as-well. To put it in a nutshell, the experts were satisfied with the hardware implementation with some potential for improvements.

An unambiguous result of the survey is that the true to scale visualization helps the experts in spatial tasks like material zone planning. All engineers supported the statement by tendency (Figure 8). It is better suitable for estimating lengths, spatial relations and speeds than using common desktop displays or a power wall. Asking about possible efficiency improvements and the possibility to reduce the number of physical prototypes by using true to scale visualization in contrast to common desktop systems or a power wall, the results are diverse. By tendency, the engineers see this fact given for assessing walking. The given answers on the efficiency improvements and the possibility to substitute physical prototypes highly depend on the existing software. More specific experiments will be carried out in order to better understand and distinguish between the performance of the visualization software and the abilities of an augmented floor surface.

The experts were asked in a final, overall question whether they would like to use the system in general (see Figure 9). 13 out of 13 answered the question with "yes" and therefore would like to use the system operatively. This fact has proven the big potential of the system.

Conclusion and future work

We presented a scalable augmented floor surface in combination with true to scale visualization for final assembly line station layout use cases. The proposed hardware setup is movable, easy to use and scalable. The introduced hardware setup offers a station-sized visualization area realized with low-cost hardware. The system was installed, introduced and piloted during on-site production planning workshops for a mid-size premium car. A preliminary evaluation with thirteen participating production engineers found that, by tendency, true to scale visualization using the interactive augmented floor surface supports the workshop participants to better estimate sizes, speeds and spatial relationships than on traditional desktop displays. The tangible user interface on the tabletop system in combination with the augmented floor surface offers a new interaction possibility for intuitively interacting with the virtual models within production planner use-cases. In general all survey participants wanted to use the system for their work.

By improving the accessibility and making virtual environments look closer to real world situations, the acceptance of production planners for virtual methods will increase. A closer look will be taken at, whether the workshop participants reach their verification goals faster at a higher quality level or not.

Future development will head to fully augmented workshop situations. The projection cascade will be enlarged for showing multiple station layouts in true to scale visualization at the same time. Additionally a tracked virtual arena will be built on the basis of the true to scale augmented floor surface. The augmented interactive floor will cover the whole room, powerwalls will display the assembly status. In order to interact with the digital model and automatically adapt the simulation, the augmented floor surface will be registered to a motion capture tracking system. Other display technologies will be registered to the augmented floor surface as well, so that the workers can align themselves via the floor projection and assess and train the station's tasks.

Acknowledgements

We thank the University of Ulm and the Daimler AG for their support.

References

[1] H. Ishii, „Tangible bits: beyond pixels", in *Proceedings of the 2nd international conference on Tangible and embedded interaction*, 2008, S. xv–xxv.

[2] M. Manns und N. A. A. Martin, „A Vagueness Measure for Concurrent Engineering of Manual Assembly Lines", in *Enabling Manufacturing Competitiveness and Economic Sustainability*, M. F. Zaeh, Hrsg. Springer International Publishing, 2014, S. 131–135.

[3] J. C. Aurich, D. Ostermayer, und C. H. Wagenknecht, „Improvement of manufacturing processes with virtual reality-based CIP workshops", *Int. J. Prod. Res.*, Bd. 47, Nr. 19, S. 5297–5309, 2009.

[4] T. Augsten, K. Kaefer, R. Meusel, C. Fetzer, D. Kanitz, T. Stoff, T. Becker, C. Holz, und P. Baudisch, „Multitoe: high-precision interaction with back-projected floors based on high-resolution multi-touch input", in *Proceedings of the 23nd annual ACM symposium on User interface software and technology*, 2010, S. 209–218.

[5] C. Pinhanez, „The everywhere displays projector: A device to create ubiquitous graphical interfaces", in *Ubicomp 2001: Ubiquitous Computing*, 2001, S. 315–331.

Interactive Surface Composition Based on Arduino in Multi-Display Environments

Lili Tong
INSA-Lyon, LIRIS, CNRS UMR5205
F-69621, Lyon, France
lili.tong@insa-lyon.fr

Aurelien Tabard
University Lyon 1, LIRIS, CNRS UMR5205
F-69621, Lyon, France
aurelien.tabard@univ-lyon1.fr

Audrey Serna
INSA-Lyon, LIRIS, CNRS UMR5205
F-69621, Lyon, France
audrey.serna@insa-lyon.fr

Gilles Brochet
University of Lyon, LIRIS, CNRS UMR5205
F-69621, Lyon, France
gilles.brochet@insa-lyon.fr

Sebastien George
LUNAM University
University of Maine, EA 4023, LIUM
72085 Le Mans, France
sebastien.george@univ-lemans.fr

ITS'14, Nov 16-19 2014, Dresden, Germany.
ACM 978-1-4503-2587-5/14/11.
http://dx.doi.org/10.1145/2669485.2669548

Abstract
Multi-display environments (MDEs) are becoming increasingly common. They combine numerous displays in a variety of physical arrangements to support a wide range of tasks and interactions. In this context, we are investigating how to support the dynamic reconfiguration of devices by users. For instance how users can seamlessly add new displays in the environment and how the overall interaction space can be adapted accordingly. We present an architecture based on a Web server and websockets that enables rapid pairing of devices (local or remote), and simple magnetic switches to provide location awareness of devices relative to each others. We apply this concept to a simple game, whose world can be extended by holding devices next to each other.

Author Keywords
Multi-display environment; interactive tabletops; tablets; magnetic switches; Arduino board

ACM Classification Keywords
H.5.2 [Information interfaces and presentation]: User Interface; Interaction styles.

Introduction
Tabletop displays are considered beneficial to co-located collaboration due to three main characteristics: a large,

shared physical display which facilitate information sharing, a multi-touch interactive interface that allows several users to interact simultaneously, and a horizontal display that benefits more roles switches and greater awareness of others actions. But the size and weight of these devices also limits their use: they are hardly mobile. They provide little to no support for micro-mobility, like raising, tilting or bending a paper document above normal desk. And their furniture aspect makes it harder to have them evolve.

Multi-display environment [6] can mitigate some of the limitation of tabletops while retaining their benefits. These environments not only support co-located collaboration but spaces that can be re-configured. For instance to enable personal work and group work by grouping devices together, or simply to adjust the display size to the ongoing activity and number of participants.

However discovery and pairing of devices is often complex, either requiring all the devices to be connected to the same local network or involving technologies such as NFC, Bluetooth, or other ad-hoc solution working across limited distances, and still requiring manual pairing. We are interested in providing generic and low cost solutions for the dynamic management of MDEs. In this paper, we focus especially on how can we bring multiple devices into a workspace to compose a personal interactive surface in a way that involves minimal set-up? Secondly how to support exchange of information among these devices?

When pairing devices, the first problems are often at the infrastructure level. A number of frameworks have been proposed to facilitate device discovery, Zeroconf and Universal Plug and Play are two examples of existing technologies making device discovery and pairing easier. However practical networking and security constrains often hinder the wide use of these technology.

Besides connecting devices at the infrastructure level, MDE often involves the creation of a wide interactive space, in which the relative position and roles of displays in respect to each other is important. These positions, and the orientation of the devices can be detected automatically, for instance by using built-in camera to track visual patterns [1], by combining vision-based handshaking with Bluetooth to track mobile devices on a shared surface [10], or by combining vision from a surface with acceleration features of a mobile device [7]. These vision-based techniques need complex algorithms to detect devices and require one or more cameras in the environment. An alternative consists in using external sensors such as RFID or NFC [2, 8, 9]. But this often requires extra equipment not integrated in all devices.

Another approach to bind to devices to each other relies on explicit interaction from users. These techniques are based on shared sensors patterns occurring at the same time, or in a specific sequence in time. For instance using accelerometers and letting users shake devices together [5], bumping devices to each other [3] or stitching [4], i.e. a gesture moving continuously from one device to another to connect them. But these techniques can not be applied on larger devices, and have a scalability problem as they do not work for more than two devices.

In this article, we propose to use an infrastructure based on an Web server (nodejs), and websockets to develop applications for MDE. We tested this approach with rolling standing desks and tables that can be recombined at will. In order to handle spatial relationships, we used a simple solution based on magnetic sensing. Users can extend and create their own interactive surface dynamically during the task by bringing their personal devices close to any side of interactive tabletop. The manipulation of objects in and cross displays is based on drag and drops.

In the following section, we introduce a first prototype applying this concept to a simple game. We firstly present the game scenario and then explain the technical details from both the hardware and software perspective. We conclude the paper by discussing the possible avenues for future research.

Prototype

Game principle

In this prototype, we designed a simple collaborative web-based game on a multi-touch device (tabletop or tablet) where users can control the sprite, letting it jump, run to collect starts. Figure 1 shows the screen-shots of the initial game world. This world has brick walls on its both left and right side and will be extended when users bring other devices close to it. According to the position of the added device, the brick wall on the corresponding side will be killed and the corresponding scene appears on the device. Figure 2 shows a game world that is extended on three sides (left, right and up side).

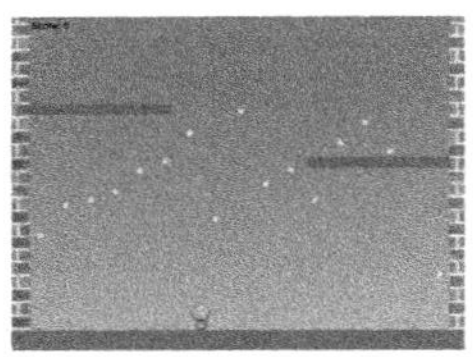

Figure 1: Inital game word

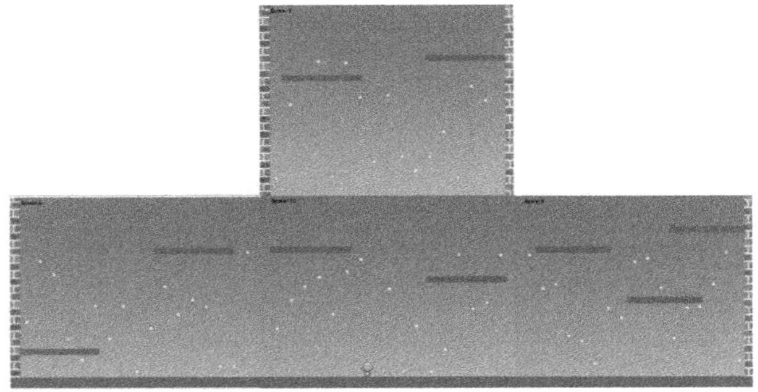

Figure 2: Game word extended on three sides

We present now a scenario that highlights the dynamic construction of the game world by connecting different devices during the game.

Scenario of interactive surface composition

In the beginning of the game, only one tabletop is active (Figure 3, tabletop A). Tabletop B (on the left side) is placed next to tabletop A. In order to bring tabletop B into the game, users simply need to push it and align it with tabletop A. When tabletop B is connected (Figure 4), the left side brick wall of the initial game world disappears. The world is extended on the two tabletops. Users can pass the little sprite to tabletop B just by making it run across the left border. When it reaches tabletop B, it keeps the same velocity and relative Y position. User B can also pass the sprite back to tabletop A in the same way.

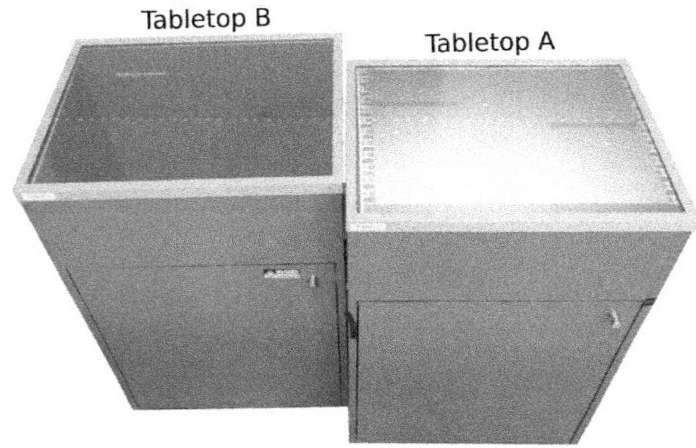

Figure 3: Before connecting

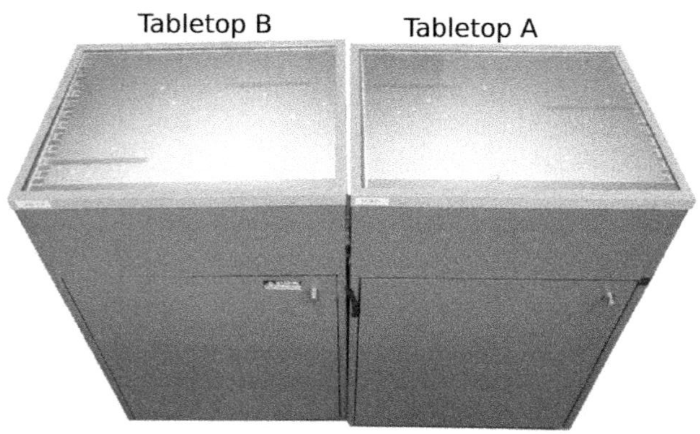

Figure 4: Add tabletop B into game

Now, another user who holds a tablet also wants to join in the game. Here are two options for him. Firstly, he could place tablet on the right side of tabletop A, by which means the game world would be extended to right side. He could also put tablet on the top side of tabletops A and make the up side world extended (Figure 5). After the tablet joins in the game, users could control the sprite to jump and run through these three displays.

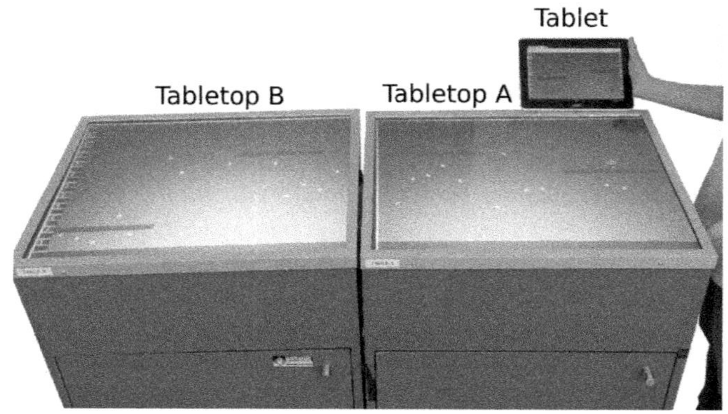

Figure 5: Add tablet into game

Technical Aspects
Our http server is based on nodejs, any device willing to become part of the MDE has to connect to a given IP address via a Web browser. The devices can thus be connected to any network Wi-Fi, wired or 3G. The server is set to listen to connection and information exchange messages, and sends feedback according to the message it receives. The physical detection in this prototype is based magnetic switches and an arduino board programmed with noduino for maintaining javascript as the unique programming language of our environment.

To detect devices relative to each other, we arranged three magnetic switches on the edges of left, right and top side of tabletop A (Figure 6). These switches are parts of the circuit of Arduino board which is also connected to the server. Magnets are attached to the edges of tabletop B, tabletop C and a tablet. When they are brought close to tabletop A, they will turn on the nearest magnet switch. The circuit board will pass the connection message to the server including the ID of switch. As soon as the server gets the message, it obtains the position of the nearby display and sends a command to the display to let it join in the game and spontaneously makes the corresponding scene appear on the screen. Meanwhile, tabletop A also receives the command. It destroys the brick wall on the corresponding side to enable the sprite to go out of the world.

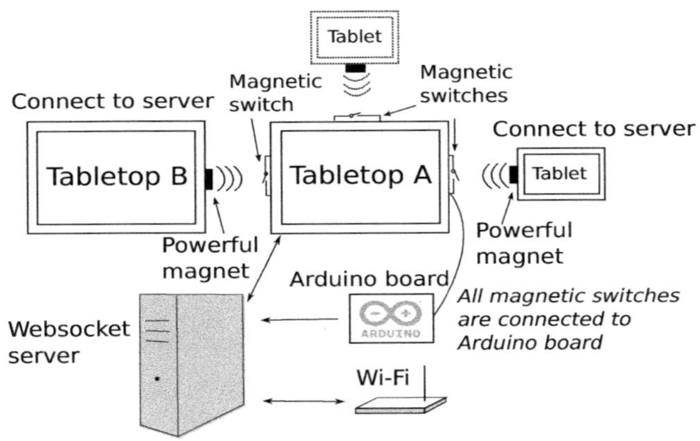

Figure 6: Layout of devices

For example, when user C wants to play game on the right side of tabletop A. He brings the tablet next to tabletop A, the magnetic switch on the right side is connected. The circuit board passes the connection message to the server. The server knows that the right side switch is connected, it sends message through Wi-Fi to make the tablet show the right side extended world. At the same time, tabletop A also receives the message, it kills the right side brick wall. Now the game world is extended on tablet, sprite can go to tablet through the right border of tabletop A. It can also return to tabletop A through the left border of tablet.

The information exchange part is also based on the Web server and websockets. If we control the sprite to go from tabletop A to tabletop B, the server records the attributes of the sprite when it reaches the border of tabletop A and sends this information to tabletop B. Then the sprite appears on the right side of tabletop B with all its former attributes.

This new method embodies spatial relationship in devices' connection which makes the interaction easy to learn. Users can clearly know which part of the game world they hold based on their spatial position. For information exchange, users just need to pass digital objects over the border to the target world. There is no need to have physical contact for each exchange. The transfer is via Wi-Fi which enables its fast speed and provides the potentiality to transform high resolution images. The pair of magnetic switch is cheap (less than 1 euro/pair) and reusable. Each switch's installation on circuit board and programming only cost several minutes. The switches can be equipped on the side of tabletop display, which do not interfere on-going task and others' views when the connection happens. The amounts and positions of switches can be rearranged based on different tasks' requirements.

The software architecture of this work is mainly written on JavaScript. We used CCV (Community Core Vision) to track touch events, and TUIO protocol to collect these events. The communication between different displays is done via web sockets. We used Phaser as the framework of the game.

Conclusion

In this paper, we presented an infrastructure that allows dynamic reconfiguration of the interactive space by grouping different devices together. The architecture is based on a Web server and websockets that enables rapid pairing of devices, and simple magnetic switches to provide location awareness of devices relative to each others. We implemented a first prototype of dynamic assembly of devices on a simple star collecting game. We are currently working on the specification of a unified environment allowing more generic aspects for composition of interactive spaces. The environment should provide a support for automatic or manual connection of different types of devices and a normalized description of the devices spatial configuration. On a more long-term perspective, we would like to integrate in this environment some interaction techniques or meta-UI to let the user control the configuration of the devices and the distribution of the UI among the available resources.

References

[1] Cuypers, T., Francken, Y., Vanaken, C., Reeth, F. V., and Bekaert, P. Smartphone localization on interactive surfaces using the built-in camera. In *Proc. Procams*, vol. 2 (2009), 3–4.

[2] Fei, S., Webb, A., Kerne, A., Qu, Y., and Jain, A. Peripheral array of tangible NFC tags: positioning portals for embodied trans-surface interaction. In *Proc. ITS* (2013), 33–36.

[3] Hinckley, K. Synchronous gestures for multiple persons and computers. In *Proc. UIST*, vol. 5 (2003), 149–158.

[4] Hinckley, K., and Ramos, G. Stitching: pen gestures that span multiple displays. In *Proc. AVI* (2004), 1–9.

[5] Holmquist, L., Mattern, F., Schiele, B., Alahuhta, P., Beigl, M., and Gellersen, H.-W. Smart-its friends: A technique for users to easily establish connections between smart artefacts. In *Proc. Ubicomp* (2001).

[6] Nacenta, M., Gutwin, C., Aliakseyeu, D., and Subramanian, S. There and Back Again: Cross-Display Object Movement in Multi-Display Environments. *Human-Computer Interaction 24*, 1 (Jan. 2009), 170–229.

[7] Schmidt, D., and Chehimi, F. PhoneTouch: a technique for direct phone interaction on surfaces. In *Proc. UIST* (2010), 13–16.

[8] Seifert, J., Simeone, A. L., Schmidt, D., Reinartz, C., Holleis, P., Wagner, M., Gellersen, H., and Rukzio, E. MobiSurf: improving co-located collaboration through integrating mobile devices and interactive surfaces. In *Proc. ITS* (2012), 51–60.

[9] Sugimoto, M., Hosoi, K., and Hashizume, H. Caretta : A System for Supporting Face-to-Face Collaboration by Integrating Personal and Shared Spaces. In *Proc. CHI*, vol. 6 (2004), 41–48.

[10] Wilson, A. D., and Sarin, R. BlueTable: connecting wireless mobile devices on interactive surfaces using vision-based handshaking. In *Proc. GI* (2007), 119–125.

Overcoming Interaction Barriers in Large Public Displays Using Personal Devices

Victor Cheung
victor.cheung@uwaterloo.ca
Systems Design Engineering
University of Waterloo
Waterloo, Ontario, Canada

Mark Hancock
mark.hancock@uwaterloo.ca
Management Sciences
University of Waterloo
Waterloo, Ontario, Canada

Diane Watson
diane.watson@uwaterloo.ca
Computer Science
University of Waterloo
Waterloo, ON, Canada

Stacey D. Scott
stacey.scott@uwaterloo.ca
Systems Design Engineering
University of Waterloo
Waterloo, Ontario, Canada

Jo Vermeulen
jo.vermeulen@hasselt.be
Hasselt University – tUL – iMinds
Expertise Centre for Digital Media
Diepenbeek, Belgium

ITS 2014, November 16–19, 2014, Dresden, Germany.
ACM 978-1-4503-2587-5/14/11.
http://dx.doi.org/10.1145/2669485.2669549

Abstract
This work presents a design space in which personal devices are used as a means to facilitate "socially safe", ad-hoc interaction with large public displays. Unlike most existing work that focuses on facilitating content placement and transfer, this approach aims at minimizing the effort required to initiate, sustain, and withdraw from interaction with a large public display, and to communicate these capabilities to passersby. We identify barriers hindering this process, and offer advice on overcoming them based on existing work and our own experiences with these displays. We illustrate how this design concept can be applied, and motivate applications in other domains.

Introduction
Large interactive displays are often installed in public spaces (e.g., museums, airports, storefronts) to provide a more engaging experience. However, studies have shown that they are highly underutilized, largely due to social inhibition (e.g., fear of looking foolish) [4,21] and uncertainty of possible interactions [12,18]. Similar to gestural interfaces, interaction with large public displays typically suffers from a lack of visibility ("what functionality is supported?") and affordances ("what actions are possible?") [17]. Moreover, due to constraints such as cost, lighting, and space, common interaction mechanisms such as touch, sound, and body

movements might be inhibited or only available to a small audience. Meanwhile, personal devices, such as smartphones and tablets, have become a widespread means for interacting with digital content. Besides being technologically capable of supporting various forms of interaction (e.g., touching, tilting, or shaking), these devices are familiar and allow personalization, and thus enjoy higher adoption [7].

In this paper, we explore a design space where personal devices are used as an alternative entry point to initiate and sustain interaction with large public displays. By taking advantage of people's familiarity and lower social inhibition with their own personal devices, and by improving the public display's ease of use and intelligibility [2], this form of interaction may instill confidence in passersby. It may also allow for a broader range of audience by, for example, helping museum patrons store information for later use, enabling pedestrians to overcome social inhibition with storefront displays, or assisting people with physical disabilities to engage with large displays.

Existing multi-surface research involving large and small displays largely focuses on content placement and transfer between devices. Instead, we focus on exploring the use of personal devices to encourage large public display use, thereby benefiting a broader audience. Our three main contributions are: 1) synthesizing design challenges of large public display use as a set of usage barriers, 2) offering design advice to overcome these barriers, and 3) describing a representative application for further development.

Classifying Existing Cross Device Work

While touch devices are often praised for supporting direct interaction—when the control and display space are super-imposed—prior research has explored using one device to indirectly control another [4-6,8,11], for example, to facilitate content transfer between large displays and personal devices [8,13,15]. We extend the idea of direct vs. indirect interaction by situating existing work in a *cross-device control-display space*:

Personal Device (PD) \ Large Display (LD)	I/O	I	O
I/O	Both devices act as control and display and provide in/direct interaction [9,14,18,20]	Indirect control of PD, which still allows direct interaction	Indirect control of LD, with feedback and/or direct interaction on PD [4-6,8,11,13,15]
I	Indirect control of LD, which still allows direct interaction [22]	No output	Indirect control of LD, neither allow direct interaction [3]
O	Direct interaction on LD, PD controlled indirectly	Indirect control of PD, no direct interaction	No input

Table 1. Cross-device control display space. Both the large display (LD) and the personal device (PD) can be used as input only (I), output only (O), or as both input and output (I/O).

Research thus far has focused on using large displays for output (column 3), with personal devices used as input, either with (row 1) or without (row 2) feedback on the devices. The large display is also sometimes interactive (column 1). However, much of this research space remains unexplored, such as the use of personal devices as passive displays (row 3, column 1) or the use of large displays to indirectly control personal devices (column 2), e.g., to activate private information.

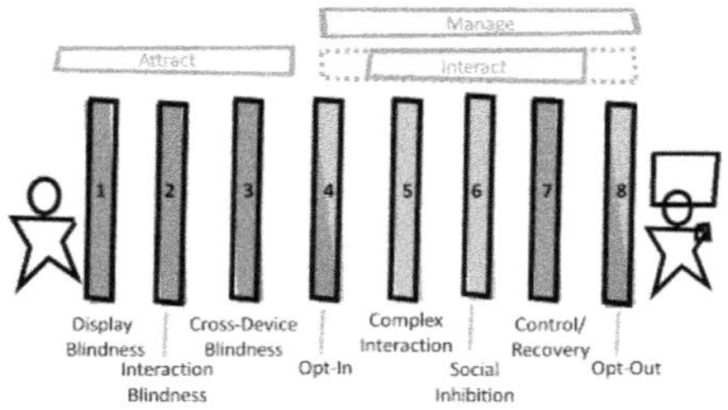

Figure 1. Partial ordering of cross-device barriers.

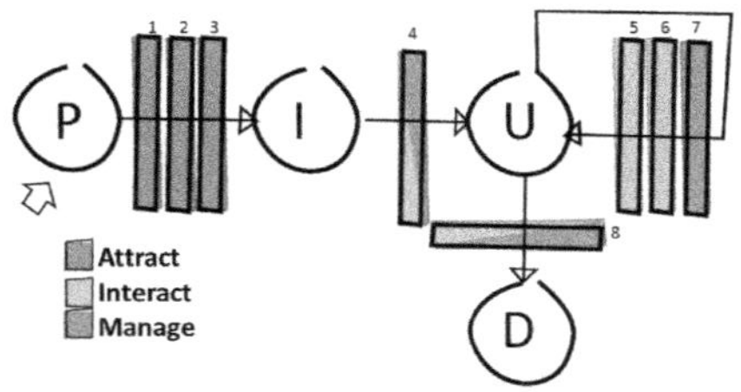

Figure 2. Diagram showing various states of interaction and barriers encountered. (P:Passing, I:Interested, U:Using, D:Done)

In this work, we consider the large display as a potential attractor (columns 1 & 3), and use the familiarity of input on personal devices (row 1 & 2) to promote engagement. Yet, many barriers remain to entice a seamless transition from single device use to cross-device interaction.

Cross-device Barriers in Public Spaces

Even with a similar hardware setup, the interaction style between large displays and personal devices in a public setting differs from those in non-public settings like classrooms and workspaces. We build upon Echtler et al.'s [9] notion of "casual interaction", where the joining step is kept minimal and no modification of the personal devices is required, and highlight the requirements of approach-and-use and graceful withdrawal [4]. The interaction process is comprised of personal devices (capturing unique traits such as privacy and novel interaction mechanisms [1]), and a large display (which is used as a shared display, and a direct input alternative, if supported).

This style of interaction poses several usage barriers for engaging passersby. We list these barriers in Figure 1 in partial order of their appearance and cluster them conceptually into *attract, interact,* and *manage.*

Attract: Before any interaction, the large display must first attract passersby's attention and interest. They first must notice the display (hindered by *display blindness*), be aware that one can interact with it (hindered by *interaction blindness*) and recognize they can use their personal device as a means of interaction (hindered by *cross-device blindness*).

Interact: During interaction, it must be easy to understand and make use of the large display and personal device (hindered by *complex interaction*). Users must also feel comfortable with the interaction (hindered by *social inhibition*). This stage may also involve *opt-in* and *opt-out* mechanisms for users to engage in or withdraw from using the system [10].

Manage: The connection between the large display and personal device must be maintained and communicated. Opting-in (connection), opting-out (explicit disconnection), or leaving the vicinity (implicit disconnection), must be handled appropriately, and interruptions (e.g., phone call) must be recovered from. It may be frustrating if these *control/recovery* actions are confusing or non-existent.

The interaction process can be modelled as a series of states (Figure 2) and ideally, a passerby will proceed through each state and engage with the system. One starts by passing (P) the display, and if attracted, they will become interested/observe the display (I). If desired, they will opt-in, then use the system (U). Finally, they will opt-out and be done (D). At any transition, they may encounter a barrier and become disinterested or leave. Figure 2 details movement from state to state and when the barriers in *attract, interact,* and *manage* may be encountered. Next, we offer design advice to overcome these barriers.

Overcoming Attract Barriers

React to Presence (A1): A way to overcome display blindness is to react subtly to the presence of passersby. If tracking capabilities are available, the display can react based on presence or movements in front of the display, e.g., by dynamically changing the content to increase audience attention towards the large display [16,23].

Provide Instructions (A2): Providing signs or instruction labels near the large display [12] can indicate that the display is interactive. Next to static instructions, the display can show animations or videos illustrating how it can be used (e.g., a self-revealing help system [24]). Based on the purpose of the context (e.g., one-time or frequent use), a combination of static instructions and animated demonstration can be included in the interface to promote learning and recall [19].

Provide Signifiers (A3): Exposing technology (e.g., sensors) is another way to convey that the display is interactive. Other recognizable technology can be used with the display. For example, a QR code can by itself be an affordance that informs those who have encountered these codes before about the potential for action [14] (although it does not describe what can be done). Once someone begins interacting with the display, the *honeypot effect* [4] can draw others in.

Overcoming Interact Barriers

Support Immediate Interaction (I1): Connections should be possible with minimal interaction (e.g., taking a photo instead of installing an app, a shorter URL link). Redundant means of connection can be used to reach more users with different devices [8]. Also, the system should not require extensive training for use.

Convey Possible Input Modalities (I2): Personal devices typically provide several input modalities, such as touch, text and accelerometer data [1], and may come in different sizes and shapes. The large display itself may also support touch, full body gestures, or the ability to locate people. Care should be taken to clearly convey the action possibilities, and how people can interact with the system. Similar to connecting to the display, we argue for a graceful degradation approach, where multiple ways of interacting are possible (e.g., use of touch buttons or gestures when accelerometer data is unavailable on the personal device).

Provide Appropriate Feedback (I3): It is essential to provide feedback during display interaction, device connection, or connection failures. We see feedback as a key strategy to overcome social inhibition, as confusion over system state or what interaction is possible is a common cause of social embarrassment. Reducing the fear of failure can reduce social inhibition.

Offer Hints/Exploration (I4): One way to convey how to interact with the system is to provide time to explore the interaction mechanisms. For example, Google's Super Sports Sync game (http://g.co/super) allows people to try out the interaction after they are connected but before the game starts. This teaches people the impact of their actions. Synchronized feedback between the large display and personal device can also be used to make the connection more visible.

Overcoming Manage Barriers

Minimize Necessary Bandwidth (M1): To support multiple devices connecting to the same display, care should be taken to reduce messages sent between each device and the display. For example, device orientation information can be sent at a reasonable interval and interpolated in-between.

Conduct Opt-In/Opt-Out (M2): Opting in to using a personal device should always be explicit. The system should not start a download or automatically open an app as this can break trust [10]. If personal data will be exposed (e.g., social networking data), it should be very clear when the system is using or purging the data (such as when someone leaves).

Figure 3. Multiplayer Breakout. Each player controls a paddle via their mobile device connected to the large display.

Figure 4. Simple signage to be posted near the public display.

Supporting an opt-in approach can also address issues of accidental interaction by passive observers. For instance, a problem of ubiquitous systems in public spaces is that they often utilize implicit input, where someone walking by may inadvertently trigger the display [2]. The personal device could provide explicit opt-in by, for instance, outputting a code or sequence of flashing lights (detected by the large display's sensors) for authentication. Then, the large display would only accept input from those who have opted-in.

Support Recovery & Control (M3): Some people may not follow "proper" disconnection procedures when leaving the display. The system should allow graceful disconnection after a period of inactivity or distance from the display. Reconnection should also be possible if failure or interruption (e.g., a phone call) occurs. Sensible defaults should exist for both the large display and personal devices.

Illustrative Prototype

To illustrate how the above design advice can be applied, we are developing a prototype where a large public display is used as the main attractor to a multiplayer version of the classic arcade game, *Breakout*. Each player controls a paddle that moves left and right to intercept the ball via their personal device. Points are earned when the ball hits a brick, and lost when the ball is not intercepted and goes off-screen.

To overcome *Attract Barriers*, simple signage (A2), as shown in Figure 4, is used to notify users that interaction is possible. Connection tokens such as QR code and URL link are used due to their familiarity to mobile users (A3). These tokens can be animated when a passerby is in proximity to draw their attention (A1).

To overcome *Interact Barriers*, upon taking a picture of the QR code, or entering the URL link into their web browser, players are immediately connected to the game, without any extra download or installation (I1). Players are randomly assigned a paddle color, which is displayed on their personal device (I3). Control mechanisms (e.g. tilt, touch-buttons) are displayed according to the device capabilities and appropriately mapped to paddle's movements (I2). Information about the player's connection status (error, connected, or disconnected) pops up on the personal device upon changes (I3). The game provides a countdown when the first person connects before starting the game to enable exploration of the interaction mechanism (I4).

To overcome *Manage Barriers*, interruptions (e.g., the phone goes to sleep, incoming calls) are handled by freezing the paddle in place on the large display until the player returns to the web browser on their personal device (M3). Players can leave or enter the game at any point; the game pauses when there is no player (M3). Inactive players will eventually timeout and be removed from play (M2). Device orientation messages are only sent at short intervals (100ms) to reduce the required bandwidth (M1).

We are planning to incorporate more interactive game elements into both the large display and mobile device, and investigate how users are enticed to interact with large public displays using this cross-device interaction.

Conclusion and Future Work

In this paper, we classify existing literature using our cross-device control-display space. We then describe a design framework that identifies barriers to cross-device interaction, and suggest methods of addressing these barriers. We demonstrate our design framework through an example of the multiplayer Breakout game on a public wall display. In the future, we intend to evaluate different techniques for overcoming each barrier to interaction, and explore the use of this framework in other settings.

References

[1] Ballagas, R., Borchers, J. et al. (2006). The smart phone: a ubiquitous input device. IEEE Pervasive Computing 5(1), 70-77.

[2] Bellotti, V. and Edwards, K. (2001). Intelligibility and accountability: human considerations in context-aware systems. Hum.-Comput. Interact. 16(2), 193-212.

[3] Boring, S., Jurmu, M., & Butz, A. Scroll, tilt or move it: using mobile phones to continuously control pointers on large public displays. Proc. OZCHI '09, 161-168.

[4] Brignull, H. and Rogers, Y. (2003) Enticing people to interact with large public displays in public spaces. INTERACT, 17-24.

[5] Cao, X., Massimi, M. and Balakrishnan, R. (2008). Flashlight jigsaw: an exploratory study of an ad-hoc multi-player game on public displays. CSCW '08, 77-86.

[6] Carter, S., Churchill, E. et al. (2004). Digital graffiti: public annotation of multimedia content. Ext. Abs. CHI '04, 1207-1210.

[7] Clinch, S. (2013). Smartphones and pervasive public displays. IEEE Pervasive Computing, 12(1), 92-95.

[8] Dearman, D. & Truong, K.N. (2009). BlueTone: a framework for interacting with public displays using dual-tone multi-frequency through bluetooth. Ubicomp '09, 97-100.

[9] Echtler, F, Nestler, S. et al. (2009). Supporting casual interactions between board games on public tabletop displays and mobile devices. Personal Ubiquitous Computing, 13(8), 609-617.

[10] Greenberg, S., Boring, S. et al. (2014). Dark patterns in proxemic interactions: a critical perspective. DIS '14, 523-532.

[11] Izadi, S., Brignull, H. et al. (2003). Dynamo: a public interactive surface supporting the cooperative sharing and exchange of media. UIST '03, 159-168.

[12] Ju, W. and Sirkin, D. (2010). Animated objects: how physical motion encourage public interaction. Persuasive Technology, Springer-Verlag: 40-51.

[13] Kaviani, N., Finke, M. et al. (2009).What goes where?: designing interactive large public display applications for mobile device interaction. ICIMCS '09, 129-138.

[14] Luojus, P., Koskela, J. et al. (2013). Wordster: collaborative versus competitive gaming using interactive public displays and mobile phones. PerDis '13, 109-114.

[15] Müller, J., Jentsch, M. et al. (2008). Exploring factors that influence the combined use of mobile devices and public displays for pedestrian navigation. NordiCHI '08, 308-317.

[16] Müller, J., Wilmsmann, D. et al. (2009). Display blindness: the effect of expectations on attention towards digital signage. Pervasive Computing, Springer-Verlag:1-8.

[17] Norman, D.A. (2002). The Design of Everyday Things. Basic Books, Inc.

[18] Ojala, T., Kostakos, V. et al. (2012). Multipurpose interactive public displays in the wild: three years later. Computer, 45(5), 42-49.

[19] Palmiter, S.L., Elkerton, J. and Baggett, P. (1991). Animated demonstrations vs written instructions for learning procedural tasks: a preliminary investigation. Int'l. Journal of Man-Machine Studies, 34(5), 687-701.

[20] Peltonen, P., Salovaara, A. et al. (2007). Extending large-scale event participation with user-created mobile media on a public display. MUM '07, 131-138.

[21] Reeves, S., Benford, S. et al. (2005). Designing the spectator experience. CHI '05, 741-750.

[22] Song, P., Goh, W.B. et al. (2011). WYSIWYF: exploring and annotating volume data with a tangible handheld device. Proc. CHI '11, 1333-1342.

[23] Wang, M., Boring, S. & Greenberg, S. (2012). Proxemic peddler: a public advertising display that captures & preserves the attention of a passerby. PerDis '12, (3)1-6.

[24] Vogel, D. and Balakrishnan, R. (2004). Interactive public ambient displays: Transitioning from implicit to explicit, public to personal, interaction with multiple users. UIST '04, 137-146.

Interactive Tactile Maps for Blind People using Smartphones' Integrated Cameras

Timo Götzelmann
Department of Computer Science
Nuremberg Institute of Technology
Kesslerplatz 12, D-90489 Nuremberg, Germany
Timo.Goetzelmann@ohm-university.eu

ITS 2014, November 16-19, 2014, Dresden, Germany.
ACM 978-1-4503-2587-5/14/11.
http://dx.doi.org/10.1145/2669485.2669550

Abstract
Tactile maps may support blind persons in orientation and understanding geographical relations, but their availability is still very limited. However, recent technologies such as 3D printers allow to autonomously print individual tactile maps which can be linked with interactive applications. Besides geographical depictions, textual annotation of maps is crucial. However, this often adds much complexity to tactile maps. To limit tactile complexity, interactive approaches may help to complement maps by the auditive modality. The presented approach integrates barcodes into tactile maps to allow their detection by standard smartphones' cameras. Automatically, more detailed map data is obtained to auditively support the exploration of the tactile map. Our experimental implementation shows the principal feasibility and provides the basis of ongoing comprehensive user studies.

Author Keywords
Tactile Graphics; Accessibility; Blind; Interactive Maps; Smartphone; 3D Printer; Annotation; Barcodes

ACM Classification Keywords
H.5.2. [User Interfaces – Haptic I/O, Voice I/O]: Information Interfaces and Presentation; K.4.2. [Social Issues – Assistive technologies for persons with disabilities]: Computers and Society

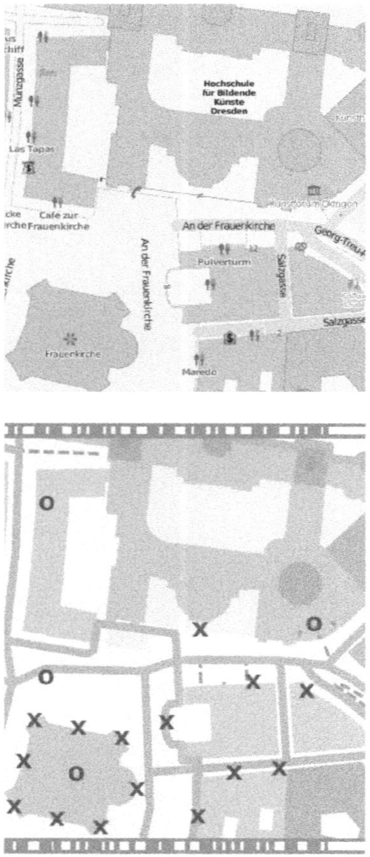

Figure 1. Top: Exemplary original map for sighted people (Source: OpenStreetMap). Bottom: Depth map of generated tactile map integrating barcodes.

Introduction

The usage of maps is common for sighted people. Map visualizations either on mobile devices or as printed version can be carried around and may support the users' orientation and understanding of geographical relations on the way. Analogously, blind people may use tactile maps, which are helping to compensate the human vision by the tactile modality. However, tactile maps have to be drastically limited in their complexity, i.e., map features have to be simplified or even to be removed. Textual annotations by Braille letters are important means to communicate verbal entities. However, due to size constraints their range of use is very limited. Additionally, their usage may negatively influence the legibility of geographic map features (e.g., [2]).

In this approach initially handy tactile maps are automatically generated by rendering simplified map data completely without textual descriptions. These maps integrate barcodes which can be recognized by standard smartphones using their integrated camera. Our concept considers the user holding a smartphone in one hand, directing the smartphone's camera towards the tactile map. After detection of the map the user may explore the tactile map by his or her other hand. By tapping on the smartphone's touch surface the user can request more detailed auditive information of the map features on the specific map position she or he is pointing at.

Related Work

In the last years several approaches for the generation and interaction with tactile maps have been presented. Some approaches generate tactile maps which exclusively support the tactile sense (e.g., [6]). Other approaches assist the tactile exploration by acoustic signals (e.g., [5]) using specialized hardware. An approach based on character recognition [8, 9] used a prototypical tablet device and utilized a popular web service for obtaining route directions and map images to be explored. Another approach [7] allowed blind users to place embossed maps on touch screens, register them manually and to obtain verbal explanations of selected map locations. Finally, there are approaches based on special matrix of pins (e.g., [10]) which allowed to adapt the displayed tactile graphic by a connected computer. In conclusion, there are different interactive approaches addressing the issues of audio/tactile exploration of maps for blind people. However, none of the existing approaches automatically recognized individual tactile maps and detected the user interaction by a standard smartphone's camera.

Our Approach

Generation of Tactile Maps

This approach is based on tactile maps which can be explored by blind people. In order to limit the complexity of the tactile map and to support their legibility these maps are generated completely without labels and keys. In order to allow to link the physical maps with off-the-shelf smartphones, printable visual markers are used which can be read by their integrated camera. These barcodes encode geographical meta-data of the map segment (e.g., longitude, latitude) which is used to obtain detailed map data from a free, worldwide map database [4]. Hence, individual maps have not to be registered with specific mobile devices.

Process of Positioning Smartphone

The initial process of reading the map's integrated

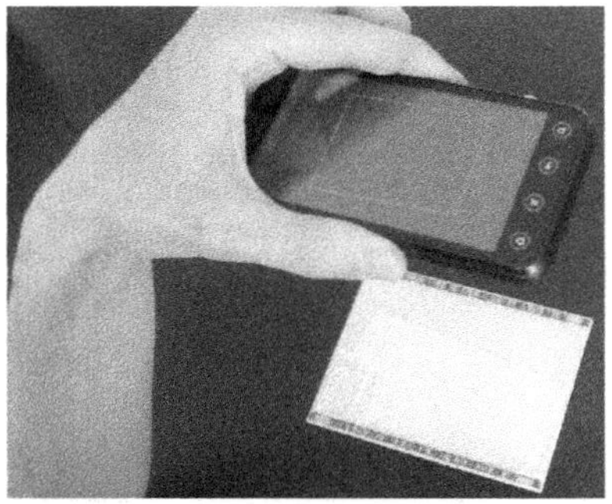

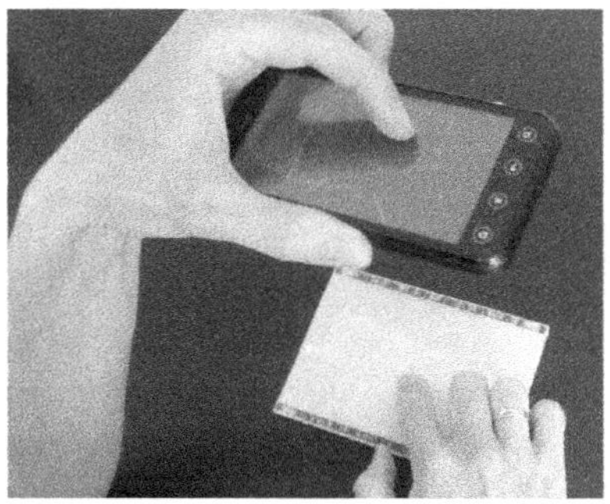

Figure 2. Top: User positioning smart smartphone's camera towards map by one hand. Bottom: While exploring the tactile map the user is pointing at map feature by other hand and obtains more detailed information by touch gesture.

barcodes requires to orient the smartphone's camera towards the tactile map (see Fig. 2-top). The mobile application detects the map's frame and decodes the barcodes attached to the tactile map. The positioning process is supported by verbal advices through a text to speech (*TTS*) interface. During the initialization the mobile application detects whether the smartphone is in a valid position by continuously analyzing the captured frames of the built-in camera. Too small map frames (less than 2/3 of the captured image) and too big frames (frame borders identical with borders of captured frame) as well as partially visible maps (frame borders partially equal borders of captured frame) are acknowledged by auditive instructions.

Map Exploration

Initially, detailed map descriptions are downloaded from OpenStreetMap using the decoded geographic coordinates. In the following, this map data is used to support the map exploration task of blind users. The current smartphone's position is kept by the user by one hand, whilst he or she uses the other hand to explore the tactile map. During map exploration the map frame detection is not carried out unless the smartphone's sensors detect a significant change in its attitude. In contrast, the user's fingertip is detected in order to determine the relative coordinates regarding the map's frame.

When a blind user is interested in more detailed information of specific map features she or he points at it and touches the smartphone's surface with the other hand (see Fig. 2-bottom). By taking the pointing finger position into account the corresponding geographic coordinate of the desired map position can be determined.

Subsequently, this coordinate is used to query the downloaded map data for more detailed information which is then verbalized by the TTS. Multiple touch gestures can be mapped to different actions (e.g., telling map a feature's name or type).

Implementation

As initial step several tactile maps had to be generated which can be automatically detected by a mobile application. In the following, an interactive application had to be developed which is able to recognize visually encoded data of the tactile map and to obtain more detailed map data by a web-interface. Finally, this application had to detect the user's finger to support the exploration of the map by more detailed (name and type of map features) auditive information corresponding the finger position on the map.

Map creation

For the generation of tactile maps a recent approach [3] has been adapted allowing to automatically generate maps which can be printed by consumer 3D printers or alternatively, on microcapsular paper. This approach abstracts OSM map data according to necessities of blind people and generates a height-map which can be printed either on microcapsular paper (only one height level) or be extruded to a 3D model (multiple height levels) of the common Stereo Lithography Format (*STL*) which can be printed by consumer 3D printers (see Fig. 3). To encode geographic information such as longitude and latitude we chose to use two 1D-Barcodes (*ITF-14*) attached on the top and the bottom of the height image. In the case of a 3D printed tactile map cavities of the printed barcode form dark regions which can be detected by the smartphone's camera.

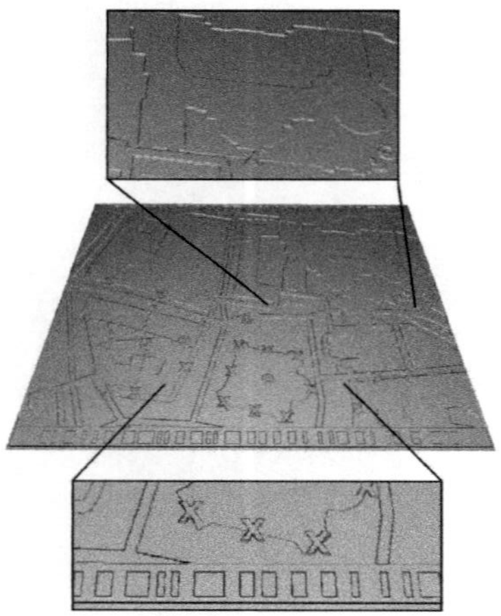

Figure 3. Exemplary STL 3D model for 3D printing containing barcodes.

During the map production process we faced several problems printing barcodes by consumer 3D printers as well as by printing them on microcapsular paper. We used a consumer 3D printer *Ultimaker 2* and experimented with different 3D print materials (*filament*) and settings (printing speed, nozzle temperature). For time-efficient printing of tactile maps on consumer 3D printers, adaptive printing settings had to be implemented, i.e., barcodes and map content can be printed in one single step, but are ideally generated by different printing settings. For several experiments we generated multiple tactile maps by 3D printing and, comparatively, on microcapsular paper each of about 15 by 10 cm physical size.

Interactive application

A prototype application has been implemented for Android smartphones using an image processing library *OpenCV* [1]. When a map's frame was detected, its corners were extracted in order to determine the current perspective distortion. Using the distortion parameters the map's frame was retransformed to rectangular dimensions. Subsequently, the geographic map coordinates were decoded from the barcodes and used to query a common OpenStreetMap web interface called OSM Extended API *XAPI* to obtain detailed map data.

For the fingertip detection we identified the user's fingers contours by color segmentation. Next, the extracted contour was simplified in order to evaluate its convex hull. The fingertip position was determined by the distances of convex hull point set to the camera frames' borders. Using the parameters of the perspective correction we determined the corresponding geographic coordinates of the fingertip position. Finally, the minimum distances between this coordinate and map features were evaluated. Hence, when the user tapped the smartphone's touch surface our implementation auditively provided more detailed information about the map feature with the smallest distance to his or her finger. The experimental application showed the principal feasibility of our approach. It has been successfully tested with several combinations of tactile maps and standard smartphones.

Conclusion

We presented a novel technique to complement tactile maps by auditive explanations through an interactive mobile application to be used on standard smartphones. Using visual markers allows to establish the link between the physical map and detailed digital map data visually. The smartphone application automatically obtains all necessary map information by a free worldwide available map database. In our approach there is no need for prior registration of tactile maps with mobile devices. By using finger detection algorithms the blind user's map exploration can be supported by auditive explanations of the map features initiated by tapping on the smartphone's touch surface. Our solution is handy enough to be carried in blind users' pockets which allows to consult the tactile map on the way. In our opinion the potential of linking tactile maps with a mobile application can be leveraged by incorporating multiple sensors and actuators built in today's smartphones. We tested the feasibility of our approach with multiple generated tactile maps and a smartphone application implementing the detection of maps and the proposed interaction. In our ongoing work a user study is being carried out to evaluate multiple interaction design alternatives.

The limited space requirements of our approach has advantages for mobility. However, this approach is designed to complement existing techniques which support larger maps, e.g., for obtaining a map overview at a larger scale.

References

[1] Bradski, G. The OpenCV Library. Dr. Dobb's Journal of Software Tools (2000).

[2] Edman, P. K. Tactile Graphics. AFB Press, New York, 1992.

[3] Götzelmann, T., and Pavkovic, A. Towards automatically generated tactile detail maps by 3d printers for blind persons. In Proc. ICCHP 2014, vol. Part II, Springer (2014), 1-7.

[4] Haklay, M., and Weber, P. Openstreetmap: User-generated street maps. Pervasive Computing, IEEE 7, 4 (Oct 2008), 12-18.

[5] Miele, J. A., Landau, S., and Gilden, D. Talking TMAP: Automated generation of audio-tactile maps using smith-kettlewell's TMAP software. British Journal of Visual Impairment 24, 2 (2006), 93-100.

[6] Minatani, K., Watanabe, T., Yamaguchi, T., Watanabe, K., Akiyama, J., Miyagi, M., and Oouchi, S. Tactile map automated creation system to enhance the mobility of blind persons: Its design concept and evaluation through experiment. In Proc. ICCHP 2012, Springer (2010), 534-540.

[7] Senette, C., Buzzi, M. C., Buzzi, M., Leporini, B., and Martusciello, L. Enriching graphic maps to enable multimodal interaction by blind people. In Universal Access in Human-Computer Interaction. Springer, 2013, 576-583.

[8] Wang, Z., Li, B., Hedgpeth, T., and Haven, T. Instant tactile-audio map: Enabling access to digital maps for people with visual impairment. In Proceedings of the 11th international ACM SIGACCESS conference on Computers and accessibility, ACM (2009), 43-50.

[9] Wang, Z., Li, N., and Li, B. Fast and independent access to map directions for people who are blind. Interacting with Computers 24, 2 (2012), 91-106.

[10] Zeng, L., and Weber, G. ATMap: Annotated tactile maps for the visually impaired. In Cognitive Behavioural Systems. Springer, 2012, 290-298.

A Cooperative Multitouch Scrum Task Board for Synchronous Face-to-Face Collaboration

Jessica Rubart
University for Applied Sciences
Ostwestfalen-Lippe
An der Wilhelmshöhe 44
37671 Höxter, Germany
jessica.rubart@hs-owl.de

ITS 2014, November 16–19, 2014, Dresden, Germany.
ACM 978-1-4503-2587-5/14/11.
http://dx.doi.org/10.1145/2669485.2669551

Abstract
The Scrum planning approach to software development is a widespread agile methodology. In a setting, which is ideal for Scrum, the team is collocated. Daily Scrum meetings support the team in organizing itself. Team members meet in front of a task board and update their status of work, originally based on paper-based notes. In this poster, we present a Multitouch Scrum Task Board, which is designed for being used by a team synchronously during face-to-face collaboration. Tasks can be created, explored, sorted, resized, and visually arranged in parallel simultaneously by multiple users on a multitouch display. We present our first experiences using the cooperative Scrum Task Board on a multitouch table.

Author Keywords
Scrum; multitouch; CSCW; Scrum Task Board; agile planning; interactive tabletops; multitouch table

ACM Classification Keywords
H.5.2. [**Information interfaces and presentation**]: User Interfaces—*Interaction Styles*. H.5.3 [**Information Interfaces and Presentation**]: Group and Organization Interfaces—*Computer-supported cooperative work.*

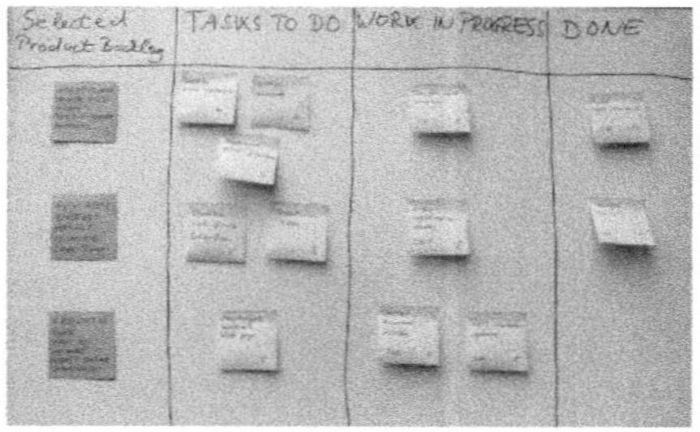

Figure 1: A Scrum Task Board with Paper-based Backlog Items and Tasks

Introduction

The Scrum planning approach to software development [13] is according to a recent survey the most often used approach among software development teams utilizing an agile methodology [14]. In this recent large-scale survey 3501 responses from a multitude of channels in the software development community have been analyzed. 73% of all responses use Scrum or a Scrum variant. In addition, Begel and Nagappan reported already 2007 that a survey of 10% of all engineers at Microsoft® indicated that more than 60% of the engineers use Scrum [2].

Scrum

Scrum is an iterative and incremental project and change management approach, which focuses on close interactions and strong communication between developers, business stakeholders, and customers [13]. Scrum uses short iterations, i.e. sprints, during which the team develops an increment of functionality. The development team works self-organized, and for each sprint it reviews, discusses, selects, and commits the functionality the team thinks it can deliver after the respective sprint. The functionality is managed with a product backlog. It contains a list of prioritized product backlog items describing the required functionality for a system. The team estimates the effort for each backlog item. A selected product backlog is addressed in a sprint. The product owner is responsible for the vision, the budget, and prioritizing the product backlog items. He is working closely together with the team. The Scrum master is not part of the team, but supporting the team achieving its goals and eliminating impediments. She makes sure that the Scrum approach is practiced correctly. After each sprint the team, the scrum master, and optionally the product owner are participating in a retrospective to reflect on and learn from the last sprint. The team aims at optimizing their working processes. They can add impediments related to the work environment to the impediment backlog and add new product backlog items, which deem important to the team, such as specific refactorings, to the product backlog.

Daily Scrum meetings, so-called Daily Standups, support the team in organizing itself. They take place once per day during a sprint, at the same time, and they are time-boxed to 15 minutes. Team members meet in front of a task board and update their status of work. The task board captures what is called the sprint backlog (cf. Figure 1). Each task belongs to one backlog item. A task is a small unit of work that has been identified and estimated by the team. A task should not take longer than 8 hours. In a daily Scrum meeting tasks are moved between the status columns and taken by team members. In addition, new tasks can be identified or an existing task can be split or removed. The team also talks about impediments because of which tasks cannot be completed and updates the impediment backlog. Finally, the team updates the so-called sprint burn down chart to visualize whether the work gets done in the necessary time. Thus, sprint burn down charts are a way of reporting the status of work.

Problem Analysis

Nearly all respondents of the survey in [14] use bug trackers and traditional task boards as agile tool support. Daily Scrum meetings play an important role for a team in organizing itself. On the one hand, using tools to enhance the effectiveness of such meetings without affecting the agile practices and keeping with the agile manifesto [1] is a challenging task. On the other hand, a common problem with Scrum sprints is that at their end not all tasks are completely done. In Scrum, credit is "all or nothing" [15]. If a task is 90% done, it still does have the status "not done". Therefore, tool support can help to identify the reasons for this problem in a daily Scrum meeting or in a Scrum retrospective, e. g. it can answer the question how often did the team split a task? Therefore, it is valuable to integrate special reporting and analysis functionality in tool support for daily Scrum meetings.

In [5] experiences are reported regarding the usage of existing tools designed for supporting distributed agile planning settings for supporting collocated settings. It is pointed out that existing tools supporting agile planning meetings in distributed settings broke the natural interactions of the agile planning team in collocated settings. E. g. creating and manipulating story cards with mouse and keyboard became a bottleneck. In collocated daily Scrum meetings participants are used to stay together in front of a task board. Therefore, tool support for collocated daily Scrum meetings needs to support the agile practices and needs to add a benefit to the traditional practice.

To address a computerized Scrum Task Board, which supports special reporting and includes analysis functionality for collocated team members, we propose a cooperative multitouch Scrum Task Board, which can run on big multitouch displays. In this way we do not break the agile practices, but keep with the agile manifesto.

Related Work

There are approaches available supporting communication and cooperation in general and some supporting the Scrum planning. In [6] and [14] different tools used by Scrum teams are reported, e. g. ScrumWorks, MS Excel, MS Project, Lotus Notes, Skype. However, big multitouch displays have not been considered explicitly as a means to support cooperative activities.

Touch and tabletop technology has been widely applied to education, e. g. [4], computer games, e. g. [9], and art design [10, 11]. Compared to traditional user interfaces richer user experience is pointed out. Another trend is to use surface technologies for analysis work [3]. Visualization techniques and exploring huge amounts of data are in the focus.

In [5] digital tabletop technology is applied to collocated agile software planning meetings. The Agile Planner for Digital Tabletops is proposed. It was developed for large horizontal, touch sensitive displays. It focuses on single touch displays and on story cards rather than on multitouch displays and Scrum. Multiple users are considered, but they cannot interact with the system at the same time. The usability evaluation focusses on single user interactions and gestures to interact with story cards and discuss them in a collocated group setting. In [10] cooperative gestures for single display groupware have been implemented and evaluated in the context of an art application. Our approach uses gestures that can be executed individually or in cooperation and applies multitouch single display groupware to the Scrum planning approach.

Figure 2: A Cooperative Multitouch Scrum Task Board

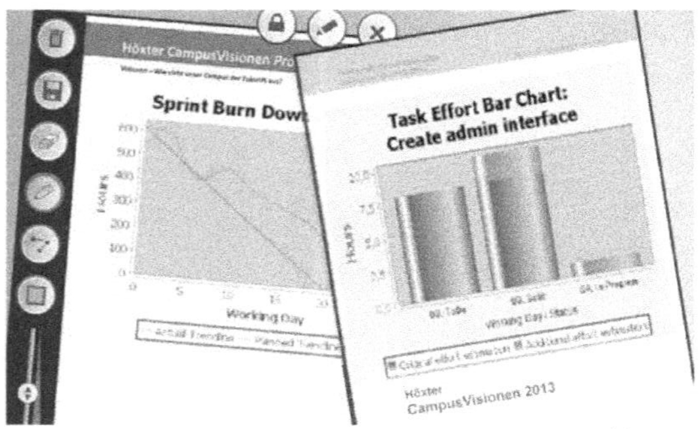

Figure 3. Presenting Reports as Multitouch Documents

A Cooperative Multitouch Scrum Task Board

Displaying visualizations on multitouch surfaces that can be manipulated cooperatively allows analysts and planners a new level of interaction [3]. Data can be explored in parallel simultaneously by multiple users. Data objects can be moved, sorted, resized, rotated, and visually arranged using natural gestures like those that would be used in exploring real-world objects. Figure 2 shows a first version of our cooperative multitouch Scrum Task Board. It runs on a MS Windows 8-based multitouch table. The display can also be used as a vertical board.

Concepts

The Scrum Task Board is targeting large displays. The board needs to show the columns *Selected Product backlog*, *Tasks to do*, *Tasks in progress*, and *Tasks done*. The backlog items are not allowed to be moved to one of the tasks' columns. The tasks are movable between their different columns to represent their status of work respectively. All interaction results need to be saved automatically. We use widespread gestures known from smartphones and tablets. These are applied to moving, resizing, and rotating an artifact, and can also be executed by multiple users, e. g. enlarging a task. A double touch event in a task column creates a new task in that column. A touch event on a task presents a menu that offers the possibilities to delete the task, to split it, or to open the task's keyboard on the display. Keyboards and tasks, which belong together, are marked with rectangles in the same color. Keyboards can be moved like tasks. This represents a kind of floor control for the respective task and supports coordination. Several keyboards for different tasks can be used simultaneously.

At any time the team can switch to the reporting view. It shows the current sprint burn down chart of Scrum to visualize whether the work gets done in the necessary time. It is generated based on the current sprint backlog. In addition to the typical Scrum reports we provide special views, such as the split task view. It shows how often a task has been split and how the effort estimation developed in total. This supports Scrum retrospectives and the evaluation of the life cycle of tasks, e.g. whether they have been split or blocked by an impediment. In this way improving estimations and learning from sprints is supported. Figure 3 shows an example piece of the reporting view. The reports are shown as documents, which can be moved, resized, rotated, and visually arranged using multitouch gestures individually or in cooperation. In addition, they can be annotated. In this way, a group discussion of the analysis results is supported.

Implementation

We are currently using the software library GestureWorks Core[1] in combination with Java and Java2D. GestureWorks Core is a software library for handling multitouch events and gestures. It addresses the hardware abstraction and the creation of suitable multitouch events. Based on this we have developed a multitouch widget library, which supports Java-based multitouch on-screen keyboards, panels, labels, buttons, menu bars, and tasks.

Evaluation

We have conducted a first study to evaluate the usability of our approach. For this we have used a lecture on IT project management. In the context of a

[1] http://gestureworks.com/core

project example four different student groups with seven students each have been asked to use the cooperative multitouch Scrum Task Board to plan sprints. We could not apply the famous "thinking aloud" method, originally reported in [8], or one of its variants as cheap evaluation method because group members thinking aloud already influence the quality of cooperation. As proposed in [6] for usability evaluation regarding shared workspaces we have focused on the low level activities that need to be carried out in order to do the planning. The following table shows our first evaluation results, which we have got through observations and interviews. Most notably, the big on-screen keyboards caused usability problems. Therefore, dictionary support or smart mechanisms for folding out the keyboards might be useful. Alternatively, handwriting support can be considered.

Activity	Results
Create a task	Tasks have been created easily by double touching on the surface. However, the group needed to agree upon who is taking care of which tasks.
Move an artifact	Moving tasks, backlog items, or reports was considered easy. The students also sometimes moved an artifact jointly.
Split a task / Remove a task	Splitting tasks did not cause any problems. After a touch on a task the task menu was shown and the first student touching the split icon executed the activity. Removing a task was similar to splitting a task. The step through the menu ensured that no task was deleted by mistake.
Resize an artifact	Resizing tasks, backlog items, or reports was considered easy. Similar to moving items this activity was done through a gesture well-known from smartphones. The students also sometimes resized an artifact jointly.
Rotate an artifact	Rotating tasks, backlog items, or reports was used to discuss the artifacts with team members on the other side of the table. The gesture was well-known and did not cause any problems.
Edit a task	Editing tasks was considered difficult and slow. Though the students have been used to on-screen keyboards from smartphones big keyboards did cause usability problems. But controlling the editing of a task by moving on-screen keyboards was considered helpful.
Switch view / close board	The students switched to the reporting view by touching on a specific button. This was considered easy, but required coordination. Similar to switching views the board was closed by touching a button.
Annotate a report	Annotating a report with virtual pens did not cause any problems, but required coordination.

Table 1: First Evaluation Results

Conclusions and Future Work

We propose a cooperative multitouch Scrum Task Board, which can run on big multitouch displays. In this way we do not break the agile practices, but keep with the agile manifesto. Our current work has two main contributions for the ITS community:

- Applying interactive tabletops and surfaces to Scrum task boards for supporting daily Scrum meetings and Scrum retrospectives, and

- Applying and evaluating gestures known from smartphones for big tabletops and group settings.

In a setting, which is ideal for Scrum, the team is collocated. However, this is not always possible. Scrum in a distributed setting is often a mixture of distributed and collocated teams. Therefore, we are working on a distributed Scrum environment, which integrates previous work, such as supporting daily Scrum meetings for distributed teams [e. g. 12] with support for collocated teams, such as presented in this poster.

Acknowledgments. I would like to thank our university for funding this project and Benjamin Lietzau for taking the main part of software development.

REFERENCES

1. Agile Manifesto: http://agilemanifesto.org/ (2001)
2. Begel, A. and Nagappan, N.: Usage and Perceptions of Agile Software Development in an Industrial Context: An Exploratory Study. In *First Int. Symposium on Empirical Software Engineering and Metrics*, IEEE Computer Society (2007)
3. Brown, J., Wilson, J., Gossage, S., Hack, C., and Biddle, R. *Surface Computing and Collaborative Analysis Work*. Morgan & Claypool Publishers (2013)
4. Döring, T., and Beckhaus, S. The card box at hand: exploring the potentials of a paper-based tangible interface for education and research in art history, *Proc. of the 1st int. conference on Tangible and embedded interaction*, 87-90 (2007)
5. Ghanam, Y., Wang, X., and Maurer, F. Utilizing Digital Tabletops in Collocated Agile Planning Meetings. In *Proc. of the int. conference Agile* 2008, 51-62 (2008)
6. Gutwin, C., and Greenberg, S. The Mechanics of Collaboration: Developing Low Cost Usability Evaluation Methods for Shared Workspaces. In *Proc. of the 9th IEEE Int. Workshops on Enabling Technologies: Infrastructure for Collaborative Enterprises* (2000)
7. Hossain, E., Bannerman, P. L., and Jeffery, R. Towards an understanding of tailoring scrum in global software development: a multi-case study. In *Proc. of the Int. Conference on Software and Systems Process*, ICSSP'11, ACM Press (2011)
8. Lewis, C. H. (1982). *Using the "Thinking Aloud" Method In Cognitive Interface Design* (Technical report). IBM. RC-9265.
9. Magerkurth, C., Memisoglu, M., Engelke, T., and Streitz, N. Towards the next generation of tabletop gaming experiences, *Proc. of Graphics Interface*, 73-80 (2004)
10. Morris, M.R., Huang, A., Paepcke, A. and Winograd, T. Cooperative Gestures: Multi-User Gestural Interactions and Co-located Groupware, *Proc. of CHI '06*, ACM, pp. 1201-1210 (2006)
11. Patten, J., Recht, B., and Ishii, H.: Interaction techniques for musical performance with tabletop tangible interfaces, *Proc. of the 2006 ACM int. conference on Advances in computer entertainment technology*, 2006, Article No. 27. (2006)
12. Rubart, J. and Freykamp, F. Supporting Daily Scrum Meetings with Change Structure. In *Proc. of the 20th Int. ACM Conference on Hypertext and Hypermedia*, HT'09, ACM Press (2009)
13. Schwaber, K. *Agile Project Management with Scrum*. Microsoft Press, 2004, ISBN 0-735-61993-X.
14. VersionOne *8th Annual State of Agile™ Survey*, versionone.com (2014)
15. Williams, L., Brown, G., Meltzer, A., and Nagappan, N. Scrum + Engineering Practices: Experiences of Three Microsoft Teams. In *Proc. of the Int. Symposium on Empirical Software Engineering and Measurement,* IEEE Computer Society (2011)

Exploring Multi-Surface Interactions in Retail Environments

Sydney Pratte
Department of Computer Science
University of Calgary
Calgary, AB, Canada
sapratte@ucalgary.ca

Teddy Seyed
Department of Computer Science
University of Calgary
Calgary, AB, Canada
teddy.seyed@ucalgary.ca

Frank Maurer
Department of Computer Science
University of Calgary
Calgary, AB, Canada
frank.maurer@ucalgary.ca

ITS '14, Nov 16-19, 2014, Dresden, Germany
ACM 978-1-4503-2587-5/14/11.
http://dx.doi.org/10.1145/2669485.2669552

ABSTRACT
Over the past several years, physical retail outlets have seen a noticeable decline in shoppers, as digital shopping has provided a newer and less costly shopping alternative for consumers. Online digital shopping provides immediate product information but lacks the experience of a physical product. Newer immersive digital shopping environments bring together digital product information with physical products. In this paper we present our early work in exploring the applicability and interaction space of spatially aware multi-surface environments in a retail space. We give an overview on our prototype designed with an industry partner, followed by early feedback on the role of multi-surface environments and interactions in the retail space.

Author Keywords
Retail; Multi-surface environments; Device Interaction;

ACM Classification Keywords
H.5.2 User Interfaces— Input Devices and Strategies; Interaction Styles

Introduction
As a whole, retail is heavily focused on providing goods and services to a customer, while a retail environment is focused on the overall experience a retailer provides

to the customer during the process of purchasing goods and services. The retail environment is extremely competitive and has seen increasing competition in several markets, resulting in a large focus on customer experience and engagement instead of past approaches that were more product focused [11]. One approach in enhancing the retail environment is to provide interactive devices to aid customers and enhance their shopping experience, e.g. touch screen information kiosks.

Currently, the biggest threat to the retail environment is online shopping, where information is typically consolidated in a manner that allows consumers to make more informed decisions quickly. Despite the lack of a physical product in online shopping, online shopping is extremely popular and has resulted in retail stores facing "showrooming" challenges, where consumers merely physically browse products and make purchases online.

Research has been exploring interactive devices and technologies as solutions for minimizing "showrooming" [3] by enhancing the retail experience from a customer perspective,e.g. engaging customers with attractive content on displays, in addition to more competitive pricing. Two of the biggest identified technologies for minimizing "showrooming" are based on location and mobile payment [3]. Location is used to allow stores to push promotions to customers when they are near or at a store, while mobile payment allows for significantly less friction when purchasing a product. More recently, retailers have created highly specialized store locations to test new technologies [1]. One example of this type of store is the digital 'lab' store concept launched by Sport Chek[1].

Given that it is already common for customers to enter stores with interactive devices (e.g. phones and tablets), our goal was to utilize these devices to explore interactions in a spatially aware retail environment. We investigated the role of multi-surface environments in tasks that are common for a typical customer, e.g. browsing for product information, requesting product information, product purchasing. In this work, we present a yearlong collaboration with a retail design partner to explore a multi-surface prototype to create immersive retail environments.

Related Work

With the surge in popularity of online shopping, retail stores are searching for new and innovative ways to increase the customer's in-store experiences. One approach to improving the retail shopping experience is to integrate physical products and digital environments. To accomplish this integration, various technologies have been introduced to designing retail environments.

An early approach to this problem was a prototype of an interactive system for a retail environment developed by Sukaviriya et al. [11]. The prototype used a steerable projector and user tracking to display product information and track customer interactions. They developed product directories (on a table surface and on a wall), interactive clothing shelves and a mixed media product table. Sukaviriya et al. focused their research on the interactions a user would have while

[1] http://www.theglobeandmail.com/technology/tech-news/sport-chek-sprints-into-digital/article12098883/

moving around a retail space without relying on any other devices [11]. Meschtscherjakov et al. investigated the use of a dynamic map in a retail store [4]. The enhanced store map displayed metric information such as customer "hotspots" and sales ranks and it displayed customer information such as product location and promotions. They discovered that customers respond well to technologies that aid them in familiar tasks such as searching for a specific item and view promotions.

Researchers have also explored the use of mobile device applications with a relationship to a physical space. For example, Newcomb et al. created a mobile application to aid in grocery shopping [5]. They examined how location based information, such as alerts in a specific section, could increase sales. The majority of the research in the retail space, particularly with digital devices, has focused on improving the retail shopping experience by integrating digital information in the physical store, and less on digital devices interacting with each other. A user is interacting with one type of device at a time in much of the research literature presented earlier. Our approach is to bridge the gap between the technologies by introducing a spatially-aware multi-surface environment to the retail space.

Multi-surface Environments (MSE) allow information to be shared among various devices such as tabletops, wall displays, mobile phones and tablets. Spatially aware MSEs use knowledge about location and orientation of devices and people in the space to enhance interactivity. Research in MSEs has been applied and analyzed in different fields. A significant amount of research explores different interactions that can take place in a MSE [8][2][6]. A majority of the research involves supporting collaborative workspaces. An early example is the i-LAND environment [10], which includes an interactive wall display and tabletop and specialized networked chairs. These components come together and allow users to share content across the different devices.

In prior research, we have applied MSEs to the oil and gas domain [9] and in emergency response [7]. The application of MSEs to these very different domains has shown value in multi-device collaboration and data sharing, both of which are very important in the design of our early prototype retail system. For the most part, however, MSEs have been explored in research environments and not in real-world settings.

Designing for the Retail Environment

To explore the retail environment and build a multi-surface environment, we collaborated with an industry design partner in the retail domain, The Brigade Creative Corp., located in Calgary, Canada. From our yearlong collaboration, we created a prototype multi-surface solution for the retail environment, with the goal of allowing different retail stakeholders (e.g. customers and employees) to interact with information across multiple devices. The prototype was designed to be scalable and applied to many different retail environments, from smaller shops to larger chain stores. The prototype is intended to aid stakeholders in the traditional retail space and not replace all previous methods. For the design of this prototype, we used a local sports equipment retailer as the initial exploration case.

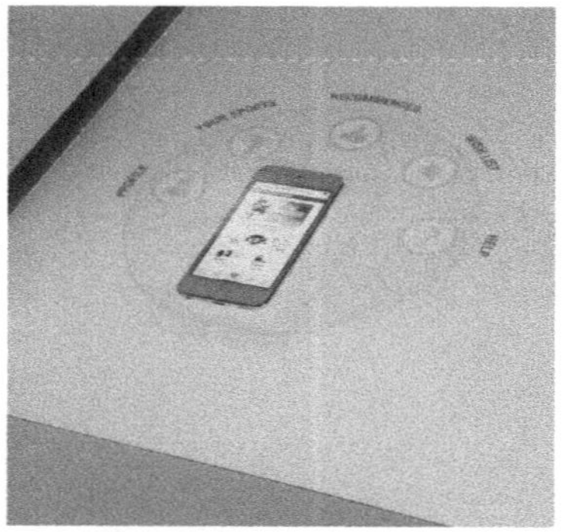

Figure 1. Personalized phone menu that appears when a smart phone device is placed on the tabletop.

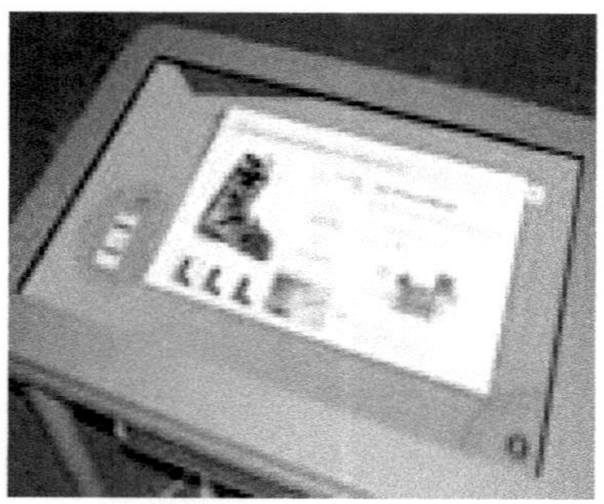

Figure 2. A customer's smart phone receiving product location information.

A RETAIL DESIGN SCENARIO

In order to illustrate how a retail environment could be supported by multi-surface environments in our prototype, we first describe the design and interaction scenario, as well as personas used with our industry partner (as shown in Figure 3).

STEP 1: A CUSTOMER ENTERS THE STORE

A customer enters the store with the intention of purchasing a ski boot. As they enter the store, their mobile phone (through a mobile application) notifies them of a type of boot that they might be interested in and directs them to a digital tabletop for more information.

STEP 2: A CUSTOMER USES A TABLETOP

The customer approaches the tabletop and places their mobile phone on the tabletop and personalized content appears on the tabletop. The customer then views product information, recommendations, ratings and store location, before eventually finding a pair of ski boots. The customer would like a video of the boot being used, and using the tabletop, a "flick" gesture is performed on the tabletop towards a large high-resolution wall display, where the video of the boot, as well as other information will be displayed and interacted with.

STEP 3: INTERACTING WITH A WALL DISPLAY

The customer can interact with a 3D image of the boot using gestures in front of the display. Sweeping either arm (left or right) to virtually rotate the boot provides a more complete aesthetic view digitally. The customer then selects the "find in store" option on the wall display by performing a closed fist gesture, causing a map to appear on their smart phone showing the store location of the boot.

STEP 4: MARKETING CONTENT

After locating the boot, the customer heads towards a checkout counter and passes by an advertising display showing new and promotional products. At the same time, a store employee is using a tablet to add a new ad to the displays carousel. The employee "flicks" an ad towards the adverting display, sending it to the display. The customer sees that the ad is a coupon for the ski boots and approaches the display in order to receive it. The customer performs a "flick down" gesture on their smart phone and the ad is now saved to their personal account for checkout.

THE PROTOTYPE

Based on the previously described scenario, we designed our prototype system with interactions from prior research into multi-surface interactions and gestures [8]. The system consists of several different components: (1) High-resolution wall displays which are used to visually compare products and to display new promotions, (2) A digital tabletop that allows users to search for specific information, (3) Personal devices

Figure 3. Overview of typical design scenario

Figure 4. Interacting with a high-resolution display through gestures to find a product in a store.

such as smart phones and tablets that can interact with the environment. The devices and the environment were built using the MSE-API framework[2].

As described in Step 2, at a digital tabletop, a customer can access product information from an interactive touch wheel menu. This menu contains information based on product categories and featured items. At the tabletop, a user can also access a menu with personal information from their smart phone devices when the phone is physically placed on the tabletop (Figure 1). Additional information also can be sent to a customer's smart phone from the tabletop, for example, a map of the store with a products location (Figure 2). The map is sent to the phone either through the interface or by performing a closed fist gesture in front of the wall display. Through the interface and a "flick towards" gesture, the tabletop also sends product information to the wall display, providing a larger view and interaction space. Once the product information is on the wall display, users can see a 360-degree view of a 3D image of the product by rotating the image with either arm (Figure 4).

For employees of the store in this environment, they are able to manipulate different advertising and promotional materials on the different displays by "flicking" towards (to add material) or away from a display (to remove material). Later, a customer can then save displayed material by performing a downward "flick" on their mobile device, as described in the earlier design scenario.

Initial Feedback from Industry Partner

For the duration of the design and implementation process of the prototype, we received continual feedback and valuable domain information and insight from our industry partner. This continual feedback helped us create this initial work that will serve as a discussion point for further deployment. Below, we briefly summarize early feedback from initial interviews received through our industry partner.

INITIAL IMPRESSIONS

When presented with the final prototype for this stage, our industry partner highlighted the result has increased "*the possibilities in the retail space*", noting that the potential impact on the shopping experience may be greater than initially believed. Feedback from retailers thus far has also mirrored this. We have also observed through feedback, that providing such an environment can also create smarter environments with additional work, such as applying analytics on the location of users in the environment, as well as the type of content they frequently consume with interactions. Overall, we see this as initial evidence that

[2] MSE-API - https://github.com/ase-lab/MSEAPI-CS

spatially-aware MSEs have potential for enriching retail experiences for both consumers and retailers.

FOCUSING ON THE CUSTOMER

From the onset of the project the prototype was to be considered a proof of concept and therefore a lot of functionality was still to be built. This was reflected in feedback, however, nearly all this feedback highlighted the need for even more interactions between customer devices and the environment. This highlights the need for even more focus on customers in designing retail multi-surface environments.

Conclusion and Future Work

In this paper, we present our initial work on a multi-surface prototype designed specifically for the retail domain. The interactions implemented were based upon prior research, as well as experience in several other domain areas. As we have shown in this initial work, there is interest and value for the retail domain with multi-surface environments and interactions.

The next step in our research is to deploy the prototype in a retail environment and conduct user studies to evaluate the impact on customers (e.g. user engagement, satisfaction) as well as retailers (e.g. reduced showrooming, impact on sales). It is our hope that this initial work will create a greater interest in adapting a multi-surface environment in the retail domain and create richer and more engaging retail experiences.

References

[1] Burke, Raymond R. Virtual Shopping: Breakthrough in Marketing Research, Harvard Business Review (1996).

[2] Dachselt, R., and Buchholz, R. Natural throw and tilt interaction between mobile phones and distant displays. *Ext. Abstracts CHI 2009,* Boston, MA, USA (2009), 3253-3258.

[3] iQmetrix. "In-Store Technology: Delivering the Shopping Experience Customers Want." http://www.iqmetrix.com/documents/XQ/Customer-Experience_Whitepaper.pdf

[4] Meschtscherjakov, A., Reitberger, W., Lankes, M., and Tscheligi, M. In *Proc. UbiComp 2008*, ACM Press (2008), 336-339.

[5] Newcomb, E., Pashley, T., and Stasko, J. Mobile computing in the retail arena. In *Proc. CHI 2003,* ACM Press (2003), 337-344.

[6] Rekimoto, J. Pick-and-drop: a direct manipulation technique for multiple computer environments. In *Proc. UIST 1997*, Banff, Alberta, Canada (1997), 31-39.

[7] Rodrigues, F. M., Seyed, T., Chokshi, A., and Maurer, F. Gesture Design and Feasibility in Emergency Response Environments. In *Proc. CHI 2014,* Toronto, Canada (2014).

[8] Seyed, T., Burns, C., Costs Sousa, M., Maurer, F., and Tang, A. Eliciting usable gestures for multi-display environments. In *Proc. ITS 2012*, ACM Press (2012), 41-50.

[9] Seyed, T., Costs Sousa, M., Maurer, F., and Tang, A. SkyHunter: a Multi-Surface Environment for Supporting Oil and Gas Exploration. In *Proc. ITS 2013,* ACM Press (2013), 15-22.

[10] Streitz, N., Geibler, J., Holmer, T., Konomi, S., Muller-Tomfelde, C., Reischi, W., Rexroth, P., Seitz, P., and Steinmetz, R. i-LAND: an interactive landscape for creative innovation. In *Proc. CHI 1999,* ACM Press (1999), 120-127.

[11] Sukaviriya, N., Podlaseck, M., Kjeldsen, R., Levas, A., Pingali, G., and Pinhanez, C. Augmenting a Retail Environment Using Steerable Interactive Displays. *Ext. Abstracts CHI 2003*, ACM Press (2003), 978-979.

A Multi-Display System for Deploying and Controlling Home Automation

Yucheng Jin
fortiss GmbH
Guerickestr. 25
Muenchen, 80805 Germany
jin@fortiss.org

Christian Prehofer
fortiss GmbH
Guerickestr. 25
Muenchen, 80805 Germany
prehofer@fortiss.org

Chi Tai Dang
Augsburg University
Universitaetsstr. 6a
Augsburg, 86159 Germany
dang@informatik.uni-augsburg.de

Elisabeth André
Augsburg University
Universitaetsstr. 6a
Augsburg, 86159 Germany
dang@informatik.uni-augsburg.de

ITS 2014, November 16–19, 2014, Dresden, Germany.
ACM 978-1-4503-2587-5/14/11.
http://dx.doi.org/10.1145/2669485.2669553

Abstract
In this paper, we present a concept of using a home devices mashup tool to wire home devices on a tabletop display in combination with web based UIs on mobile devices to control home devices. This concept is realized by a multi-display system supported by the open-source framework *Environs*. The mashup tool on the tabletop enables multiple people to deploy home networked devices co-located collaboratively with a more natural and intuitive interface. Moreover, web based UIs on mobile devices enable individuals to control home devices universally with high accessibility and mobility.

Author Keywords
Internet of Things; Networked devices; Multi-display environment; Tabletop; Mobile devices

ACM Classification Keywords
H.5.2 [User Interfaces]: User interface management systems (UIMS).

Introduction
Home automation is featured by connected home appliances and automatic awareness of the surrounding environment employing the Internet of Things (IoT) technology. Within recent years, the IoT technology has increased the available networked and intelligent devices

for such home appliances, such as Nest Learning Thermostat [1], Philips Hue Connected Bulb [2], or Smart TVs. However, due to heterogeneity of platforms and diversity of home device controllers, deploying and controlling home networked devices is still cumbersome. The emergence of IoT mashup tools, such as ClickScript [3], or WotKit [4], enable people to connect devices and compose services to create IoT applications by means of a web based graphical editor. However, these tools are designed for PCs which do not offer the advantages of horizontal tabletop displays, such as co-located collaborative or natural interaction, or a large design space. Therefore, we intend to combine a visual mashup tool with a tabletop display to wire home devices. Thereby, enable people to deploy home networked devices collaboratively with less effort. Furthermore, current home appliances require people to use different controllers to interact with home devices. Our concept replaces those controllers with familiar and personal mobile devices, such as smartphones or tablets, which play as universal controllers for the home networked devices.

This paper describes a concept build on top of a multi-display system consisting of a tabletop display and mobile devices. The tabletop shows a visual mashup tool for deploying home networked devices whereas the mobile devices make use of web based UIs for controlling a particular home device. The system aims to assist end users to create personalized home automation easily and to control home devices universally using their mobile device.

Related Works

In the light of this paper's aim, several researchers investigated the idea of using mobile devices to control home appliances. Suo et al. [11] showed the system House Genie to control and monitor home networked devices on smartphones universally. Nichols et al. [8] presented Huddle which can generate task-based UIs on handheld devices for controlling multiple connected home appliances. Pan et al. [9] demonstrated a handheld device called GeeAirfor which can control home appliances remotely through multimodal interaction using gestures, physical buttons, speech, and light. However, the usability of these existing works is restricted by limited design space of mobile devices, especially when people wire devices to deploy home automation. Moreover, they do not support multiple people to work collaboratively.

In fact, several research projects have investigated the usage of visual tools for end users to deploy and control home automation. The interactive home network management system *Eden* [12] helps people understand how a home network works and configure network and networked devices intuitively. The application OSCAR [7] supports end users to monitor and manipulate connected devices, wherein people can save reusable configurations for frequent activities. Despite the benefits of these tools for home automation, so far there is still no one proper platform to support multiple people to wire home devices conveniently and collaboratively, i.e. on a tabletop surface. Kim et al. [6] presented an *Ambient Wall* interface to monitor and control surrounding home devices by simple gestures, but the workload of building such a system is not trivial.

Seifried et al. [10] showed the system CRISTAL which uses a tabletop display to enable gestural interaction on video images of the surrounding environment. It supports multiple people to control home devices and media universally. However, controlling home devices only on a tabletop display may be restricted by its limited mobility.

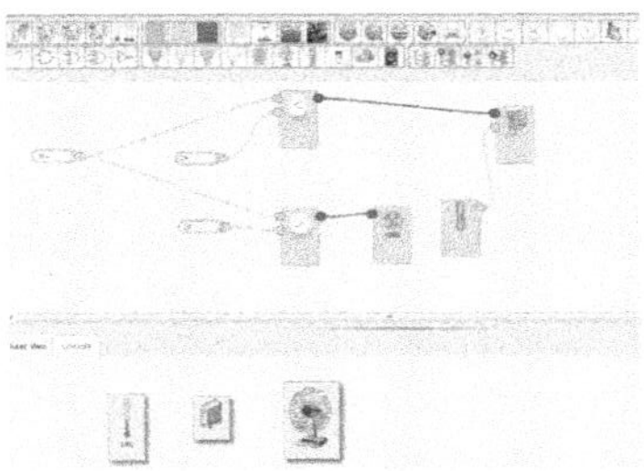

Figure 1: An example of a home heating system in ClickScript.

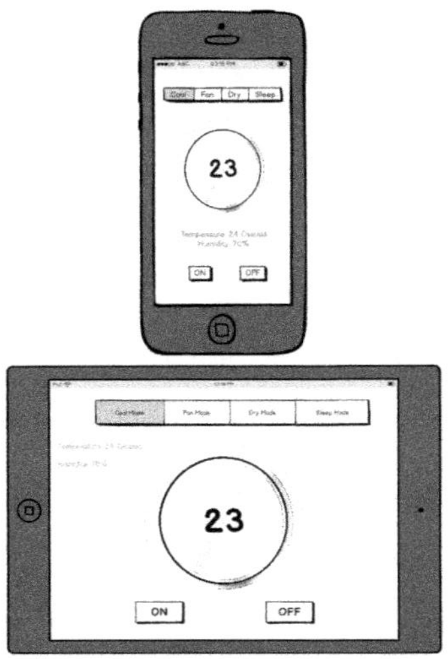

Figure 2: UIs of home devices on mobile devices.

The Concept of our System

Our system enables multiple people to manage and control home networked devices in a multi-display environment comprised of mobile devices and a tabletop display. To be specific, this system provides the following features:

- It enables multiple people to deploy home networked devices collaboratively on a tabletop display.
- It allows people to interact with a particular home device through their mobile devices.
- It supports people to interact with home devices via more natural and intuitive touch-enabled user interfaces.
- It is based on a multi-display environment with high responsiveness through low latency communication between the components.

System Architecture

The tabletop display shows a visual mashup tool for managing networked devices, whereas mobile devices present web based user interfaces for controlling home devices as sketched in Figure 3.

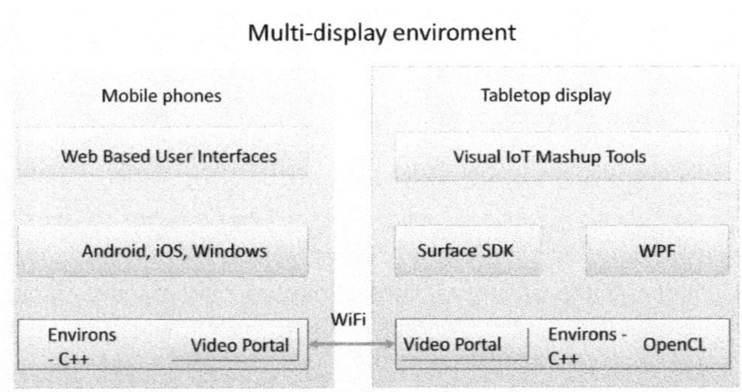

Figure 3: Multi-display system architecture.

In order to achieve low latency communication and a responsive system, our system makes use of the open-source framework *Environs* [5], which is a multi-platform software framework that enables spanning of heterogeneous multi-display environments. We use this framework to span an application environment that includes the tabletop and mobile devices in order to extend the possibilities of the tabletop application and co-located interactions with mobile devices. All participating devices in the environment are automatically identified and managed by the framework which enables mobile devices to participate in an ad-hoc way.

Furthermore, the framework enables interactive video portals between devices where touch-input on the mobile device is put through to the tabletop application and happens there in realtime. By this way, users are able to manipulate the mashup tool on the tabletop using their mobile devices. Our system thereby allows managing and controlling of the home networked devices through mobile devices and the tabletop application at the same time.

Tasks of Deployment and Control

Our concept focuses on two tasks that occur in deploying of home automation. One of the tasks is to manage connections between physical devices through visual mashup tools as exemplarily depicted in Figure 1 for ClickScript. In our system, such an application runs on the tabletop display allowing people to plan and connect home devices together by means of prevalent and familiar direct touch manipulations.

The other task is to control a particular device via its user interface which is realized in our system by providing web-based UIs of the home devices on users' mobile devices, for example as sketched in Figure 2.

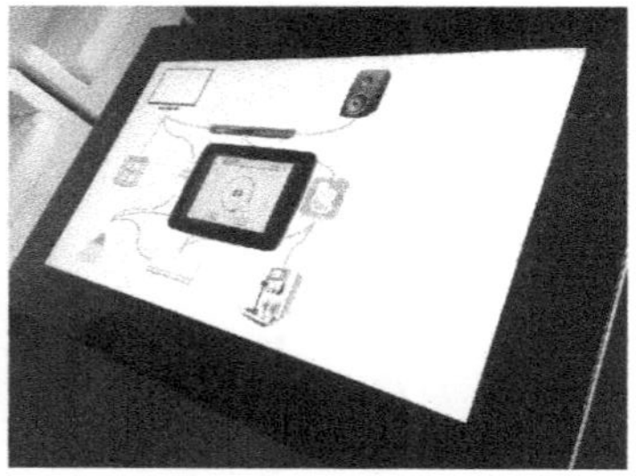

Figure 4: A mobile tablet placed on the air conditioner icon, whereupon the UI of the air conditioner is shown on the mobile tablet.

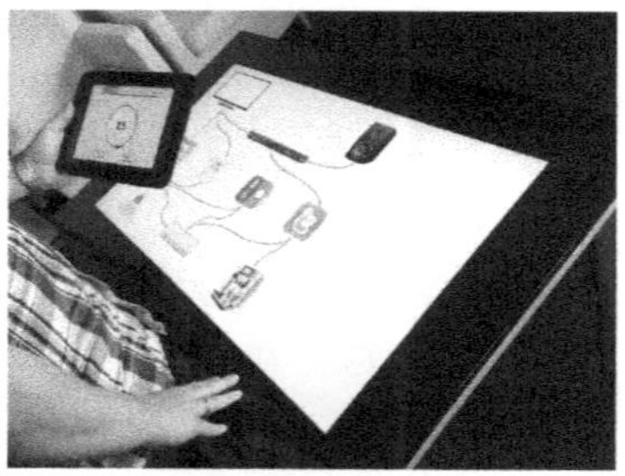

Figure 5: The user controls the air conditioner by means of the mobile tablet.

Users who want to control a specific home device either select the particular device on the mobile device or put the mobile on or near to the particular device's icon in the visual mashup tool on the tabletop display, see Figure 4.

In our setup, each mobile device has a visual marker mounted at the bottom-side which enables the tabletop to detect and identify the mobile device on the tabletop surface. Upon placement of the mobile device, the tabletop creates an interactive video portal to the mobile device in order to visually replicate the tabletop area covered by the mobile device. This video portal allows users to open the user interface of a home networked device on their mobile device by touching on the particular icon. Afterwards, the mobile device keeps showing the user interface even if it is lift off from the tabletop display, thus people can control the home devices from mobile devices anywhere, see Figure 5.

Conclusion
In this paper, we presented a concept of a system to control home networked devices in a multi-display environment. Tabletop displays and mobile devices are used to manage and control home networked devices collaboratively and conveniently. Future works include the design and implementation of a visual mashup tool for the tabletop display and web-based UIs for home networked devices in order to conduct research regarding useable UI designs or guidelines for tabletop mashup tools, or appropriate interaction techniques for collaborative or synchronized manipulations.

Acknowledgments
The work described in this paper is co-funded by OC-Trust (FOR 1085) of the DFG.

References
[1] https://nest.com/.
[2] http://www2.meethue.com/.
[3] http://clickscript.ch/.
[4] Blackstock, M., and Lea, R. Wotkit: a lightweight toolkit for the web of things. In *Proc. of WoT*,
[5] Dang, C. T., and André, E. A framework for the development of multi-display environment applications supporting interactive real-time portals. In *Proc. of EICS*, ACM Press (2014), 45–54.
[6] Kim, H., Jeong, K., Kim, S., and Han, T. Ambient wall: Smart wall display interface which can be controlled by simple gesture for smart home. In *Proc. of SIGGRAPH Asia*,
[7] Newman, M. W., Elliott, A., and Smith, T. F. Providing an integrated user experience of networked media, devices, and services through end-user composition. In *Pervasive Computing*. Springer.
[8] Nichols, J., Rothrock, B., Chau, D. H., and Myers, B. A. Huddle: automatically generating interfaces for systems of multiple connected appliances. In *Proc. of UIST*,
[9] Pan, G., Wu, J., Zhang, D., Wu, Z., Yang, Y., and Li, S. Geeair: a universal multimodal remote control device for home appliances. *Pers Ubiquit Comput.*
[10] Seifried, T., Haller, M., Scott, S. D., Perteneder, F., Rendl, C., Sakamoto, D., and Inami, M. Cristal: a collaborative home media and device controller based on a multi-touch display. In *Proc. of ITS*,
[11] Suo, Y., Wu, C., Qin, Y., Yu, C., Zhong, Y., and Shi, Y. Housegenie: Universal monitor and controller of networked devices on touchscreen phone in smart home. In *Proc. of UIC-ATC*,
[12] Yang, J., Edwards, W. K., and Haslem, D. Eden: supporting home network management through interactive visual tools. In *Proc. of UIST*,

ThumbCam: Returning to single touch interactions to explore 3D virtual environments

Daniel Mendes
INESC-ID / IST / University of Lisbon
danielmendes@ist.utl.pt

Maurício Sousa
INESC-ID / IST / University of Lisbon
antonio.sousa@ist.utl.pt

Alfredo Ferreira
INESC-ID / IST / University of Lisbon
alfredo.ferreira@ist.utl.pt

Joaquim Jorge
INESC-ID / IST / University of Lisbon
jaj@inesc-id.pt

ITS 2014, November 16–19, 2014, Dresden, Germany.
ACM 978-1-4503-2587-5/14/11.
http://dx.doi.org/10.1145/2669485.2669554

Abstract
Three-dimensional virtual environments are present in many different applications, being used even in small handheld devices. To navigate in these environments using such devices, most of current solutions rely on multi-touch interactions. However, previous works have already stated that multi-touch gestures on smartphones are not always feasible. In this work we present ThumbCam, a novel single-touch technique for camera manipulation on 3D virtual environments. With our solution, the user is able to move and look around and circle points of interest, while interacting using only his thumb. We compare ThumbCam with other state-of-the-art techniques, showing that it can offer more operations with a single touch. A qualitative user evaluation revealed that users found our solution appealing.

Author Keywords
Touch; Camera Manipulation; 3D Virtual Environments

ACM Classification Keywords
H.5.2 [User Interfaces]: Interaction styles.

Introduction
Camera manipulation is a very important task within 3D virtual environments (VE). Whether it is a design review task, a virtual tour, or even a game, it is often necessary

to explore both the virtual scene in general and have a detailed look on specific objects. On the other hand, small interactive devices, such as tablets and smartphones, are getting ever more computational power, starting to rival traditional computers in some tasks, such as design and review of 3D engineering models [2]. Today's common solutions for interacting with VE with touch enabled devices mainly rely on multi-touch gestures or buttons to apply different camera transformations. It has already been shown that multi-touch gestures can surpass button based interactions [4]. When considering smartphones, multi-touch gestures imply that the user needs to hold the device with both hands, which can be tiresome and not always possible [1]. Also, smartphones' small screens offer little space for multi-touch gestures, which may occlude a significant part of the imagery displayed. Moreover, studies [6] have shown that users tend to interact with their smartphones using a single finger, being the thumb the more often used finger.

We present ThumbCam, a camera manipulation solution that allows users to move, look and circle around within a virtual environment using only one thumb. In this paper, we show a comparison with other state-of-the-art techniques, as well as a preliminary qualitative user evaluation.

Related Work

Aware of the limitation of using both hands while interacting with smartphones, Boring et al. [1] proposed the FatThumb technique, which allows users to interact with a 2D map using the thumb's contact size.

Considering 3D Virtual Environments, Hatchet et al. [5] introduced Navidget for camera placement, that uses sketched circles to obtain the point of interest (POI) representing the end point of the desired camera's trajectory and position. ScrutiCam [3] implements a manipulation technique to move the camera around objects by moving an area of interest to the center of the screen, using a single touch. In Drag'n Go [9] the user controls the camera progression in the VE by combining target acquisition with touch input gestures.

Move&Look [8] extends the Drag'n Go method in the sense that it uses single-touch interactions to move around the VE and multi-touch to manage the camera's orientation. Jankowski et al. [7] compared several techniques and concluded that a stroke-based method can achieve better results for street level navigation tasks.

In this document, we will follow the concepts of move around, look around and circle around, as described by Marchal et al. [8]. We also resort to the notations used by the same authors for camera translations (Tx, Ty, Tz), look around rotations (Rx, Ry) and circle around transformations (Ox, Oy).

ThumbCam

Aiming for a touch solution that could enable users to manipulate the camera in 3D VE using a single contact point, we developed ThumbCam. With our solution, it is possible to look and move freely in the virtual scene and to circle around specific points of interest, without occluding too much of handheld devices' small screen. To support these different types of interaction with only one touch, we resorted to a state machine (Figure 1) to decide which behaviour should be followed at any given moment.

We have three states that modify the current view: Rotate, Drag and Move, which are described below.

These states are selected depending on user's inputs: tap (a very brief touch without any significant movement - we consider less than 0.3 seconds between touch begin and end); touch begin (longer than a tap); touch move; and touch holding (we consider a touch in the same place for longer than 0.5 seconds).

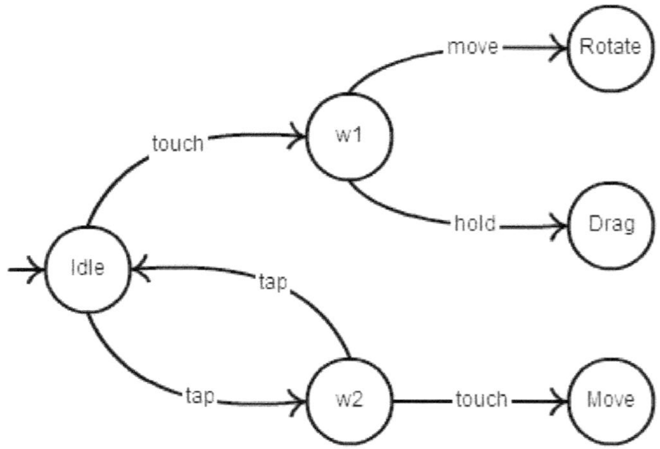

Figure 1: Simplified view of our state machine. States w1 and w2 are waiting for another input to decide which transition to make (they do not modify the current view).

Rotate

When the user starts an interaction by placing and moving a touch, we enter the Rotate state. We support two modes of camera rotation: look around (Figure 2) and circle around (Figure 3). Two sequential taps while in the Idle state toggle between these two modes. When transitioning from the look around to circle around mode, a ray from the second tap is casted into the scene, and the intersection with the nearest object defines the POI and the orbit's center. In circle around mode, a target is shown to indicate the POI being orbited. Horizontal movements of the user's touch will then rotate the camera around a vertical axis (*Ry* in look around mode or *Oy* in circle around mode). Likewise, vertical movements of the touch will rotate the camera around a horizontal axis (*Rx* in look around mode or *Ox* in circle around mode).

Figure 2: Looking around in the VE (*Rx* and *Ry* simultaneously).

Figure 3: Circling around a POI in the VE (*Ox* and *Oy* simultaneously). The red target indicates the orbit's center.

Drag
Touching and holding the screen will enter the Drag state, showing two vertical arrows to inform the user (Figure 4 left), which disappear as the user moves the finger. The behaviour of this state follows the Drag'n Go technique [9]. The intersection of the ray casted from the touch start position with the scene will define the target of the movement. Dragging the touch downwards translates the camera towards said target along the path defined by the ray casted (Figure 4), while upward movements of the touch will translate backwards along the same path (Tz). The distance between the start position of the touch and the bottom of the screen is mapped to cover the entire length of the path from the camera's start position and the target. While traversing the path, horizontal movements rotate the camera sideways (Ry). These horizontal movements do neither affect the camera position nor the previously defined path.

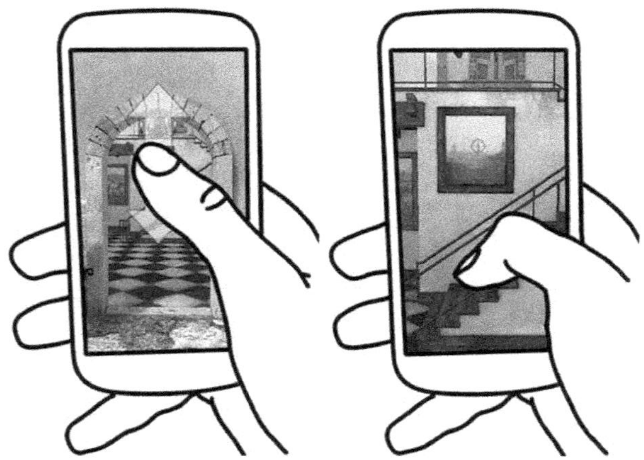

Figure 4: Moving towards a POI (indicated by the red target) using the Drag'n Go technique (Tz).

Move
The Move state can be achieved by tapping and immediately touching the screen, i.e. a quick sequence of touch begin, touch end and another touch begin actions. In this state, users can translate the camera sideways (Tx) with horizontal movements, and upwards and downwards (Ty) using vertical movements of the touch (Figure 5). In a similar fashion to the Drag state, four arrows are displayed on the screen upon entering the Move state (Figure 5 left), to inform the user of the action he is now performing.

Figure 5: Moving around in the VE (Tx and Ty simultaneously).

Comparison with Other Techniques
In Table 1 we show how ThumbCam compares to the most relevant state-of-the-art techniques for camera manipulation. Navidget offers only POI based navigation, being not possible to look around. Scruticam focus solely on object visualization, offering no actual scene exploration. Drag'n Go, although making move around

Technique	Move Around	Look Around	Circle Around	# Contact Points
Navidget [5]	Tx, Ty, Tz	-	Ox, Oy	1
ScrutiCam [3]	Tx, Ty	-	Ox, Oy	1
Drag'n Go [9]	Tz, Ry	Ry	-	1
Move&Look [8]	Tz, Ry	Rx, Ry	Oy	2
ThumbCam	Tx, Ty, Tz, Ry	Rx, Ry	Ox, Oy	1

Table 1: Comparison of the most relevant techniques and our ThumbCam.

interactions possible, neither allows looking up and down nor circle around points of interest. Move&Look is a more complete solution than the previous, but lacks *Tx* and *Ty* transformations and resorts to two touches interactions, which have been shown being not always possible. Our proposed technique, ThumbCam, offers more camera transformation than the remainder, and all actions can be done within reach of the user's thumb.

Moreover, the hand grip on a smartphone, although not being static, renders impossible the thumb to reach all screen real state, which hinders targets' acquisition. ThumbCam was designed in a way that all targets can be acquired by the user's thumb when in range, and the rotation gesture is available to relocate the target on the screen, when it is out of reach.

Qualitative Evaluation

We conducted a small user experiment to assess whether our technique was appealing to users. For this experiment, five participants were asked to explore a virtual environment and report their feedback. The ThumbCam prototype's virtual scenario was built using the cross-platform Unity3D engine.

Through this qualitative user evaluation, we found out that our method requires a small period of habituation (around 5 minutes), which when exceeded, users could fulfill the desired camera transformations without difficulty. Also, they stated that our technique was enjoyable to use, mainly due to the relaxed way of grasping of the device and interacting with only the thumb.

Conclusions and Future Work

In this work we present ThumbCam, a novel single-touch technique for camera manipulation on 3D virtual environments that builds up from the limitations of multi-touch gestures on smartphones. We described the designed interactions for move, look and circle around transformations, and also the technique's on-screen feedback system. Regarding the compared techniques, our solution is able to apply more camera transformations while using only a single touch. Although test subjects demonstrated a positive opinion, we intend to carry out a more extensive user evaluation to assess how our method performs against other techniques. Since our solution only applies one contact point, ThumbCam can be used in a multitude of devices, ranging from smartphones, tablets and tabletops to mouse-based desktop computers. In addition, we believe that ThumbCam might be suitable to remotely interact with virtual environments on large screen displays, and we would like to study its feasibility.

Acknowledgements

The work presented in this paper was partially supported by the Portuguese Foundation for Science and Technology (FCT) through projects CEDAR (PTDC/EIA-EIA/116070/2009), TECTON-3D (PTDC/EEI-SII/3154/2012) and Pest-OE/EEI/LA0021/2013, and through doctoral grant SFRH/BD/91372/2012.

References

[1] Boring, S., Ledo, D., Chen, X. A., Marquardt, N., Tang, A., and Greenberg, S. The fat thumb: Using the thumb's contact size for single-handed mobile interaction. In *Proceedings of the 14th International Conference on Human-computer Interaction with Mobile Devices and Services*, MobileHCI '12, ACM (New York, NY, USA, 2012), 39–48.

[2] Campos, P., and Noronha, H. On the usage of different work analysis methods for collaborative review of large scale 3d cad models. In *Human Work Interaction Design. Work Analysis and HCI*, vol. 407 of *IFIP Advances in Information and Communication Technology*. Springer Berlin Heidelberg, 2013, 12–21.

[3] Declec, F., Hachet, M., and Guitton, P. Tech-note: Scruticam: Camera manipulation technique for 3d objects inspection. In *3D User Interfaces, 2009. 3DUI 2009. IEEE Symposium on* (March 2009), 19–22.

[4] Fiorella, D., Sanna, A., and Lamberti, F. Multi-touch user interface evaluation for 3d object manipulation on mobile devices. *Journal on Multimodal User Interfaces 4*, 1 (2010), 3–10.

[5] Hachet, M., Declec, F., Knodel, S., and Guitton, P. Navidget for easy 3d camera positioning from 2d inputs. In *3D User Interfaces, 2008. 3DUI 2008. IEEE Symposium on* (March 2008), 83–89.

[6] Hoober, S. How do users really hold mobile devices?, February 2013. Online: http://www.uxmatters.com/mt/archives/2013/02/how-do-users-really-hold-mobile-devices.php, accessed 28-August-2014.

[7] Jankowski, J., Hulin, T., and Hachet, M. A study of street-level navigation techniques in 3d digital cities on mobile touch devices. In *3D User Interfaces (3DUI), 2014 IEEE Symposium on* (March 2014), 35–38.

[8] Marchal, D., Moerman, C., Casiez, G., and Roussel, N. Designing intuitive multi-touch 3d navigation techniques. In *Human-Computer Interaction INTERACT 2013*, P. Kotz, G. Marsden, G. Lindgaard, J. Wesson, and M. Winckler, Eds., vol. 8117 of *Lecture Notes in Computer Science*. Springer Berlin Heidelberg, 2013, 19–36.

[9] Moerman, C., Marchal, D., and Grisoni, L. Drag'n go: Simple and fast navigation in virtual environment. In *3D User Interfaces (3DUI), 2012 IEEE Symposium on* (March 2012), 15–18.

Bancada: Using Mobile Zoomable Lenses for Geospatial Exploration

Francisco Marinho Rodrigues
University of Calgary
2500 University Dr NW
Calgary, AB T2N 1N4, Canada
fm.rodrigues@ucalgary.ca

Sheelagh Carpendale
University of Calgary
2500 University Dr NW
Calgary, AB T2N 1N4, Canada
sheelagh@ucalgary.ca

Teddy Seyed
University of Calgary
2500 University Dr NW
Calgary, AB T2N 1N4, Canada
teddy.seyed@ucalgary.ca

Frank Maurer
University of Calgary
2500 University Dr NW
Calgary, AB T2N 1N4, Canada
frank.maurer@ucalgary.ca

ITS 2014, November 16–19, 2014, Dresden, Germany.
ACM 978-1-4503-2587-5/14/11.
http://dx.doi.org/10.1145/2669485.2669555

Abstract
Nowadays, looking at the path between two points on a city map has become a simple task using any modern tablet, smartphone or laptop. However, when exploring maps with different information across multiple layers and scales, users experience information discontinuity. Bancada is a multi-display system developed to investigate the exploration of geospatial information using multiple mobile devices in a multi-display environment. In Bancada, tablets are Zoomable Magic Lenses that augment, through specific geospatial layers, an overview map displayed on a tabletop or on a wall display. Users interact with lenses using touch gestures to pan and zoom; and multi-layer maps can be built by overlapping different lenses. Currently, Bancada is being used to research user interfaces separated across multiple devices and interactions with high-resolution mobile devices. Future work with Bancada includes (i) evaluating the user performance when using one tablet or multiple tablets to control all lenses; (ii) exploring what and how interactions can be performed on an overview map; and (iii) exploring how lenses can be changed.

Author Keywords
Bancada; Overview+Detail; Zoomable User Interface; Multi-Display Environment; Geospatial Information; Magic Lens

ACM Classification Keywords
H.5.2. User Interfaces: Graphical user interfaces (GUI); Input devices and strategies; Interaction styles.

Introduction
With the explosion of touch-based devices and technologies, touch interactions are now commonplace for a wide variety of devices, tasks and domains. Exploring payroll spreadsheets on laptops or navigating online maps using smartphones and tablets are two such examples of users manipulating information using touch gestures.

Typically, in situations where large amounts of information are presented, users experience information discontinuity. This means that users are often required to have keep a mental overview of the information while also interacting only with portions of the information [6].

Prior research has shown that factors such as screen size and the quantity of screens can have a direct impact on user performance when exploring large information spaces [9]. More recently, smaller devices such as smartphones and tablets have experienced an explosion in the pixel density, but the physical interaction limits of the screens have not kept pace. This highlights the *presentation* problem in information visualization [4].

Two major approaches in the research literature are common for visualizing large information sets or spaces: Overview + Detail interfaces (O+D), which separate information according to space, displaying contextual and detailed information simultaneously; and Zoomable User Interfaces (ZUI), which organize information in space and scale. In ZUI, an information space is generally manipulated through pan and zoom interactions [7]. A combination of both approaches, results in Zoomable User Interfaces with Overview (ZUIO), where users benefit from having an overview while also simultaneously exploring an information space through pan and zoom-based interactions.

According to Seyed et al., "a multi-display environment (MDE) is a system where interaction is divided over several displays, such as digital tabletops, wall displays and personal devices like tablets or mobile phones. MDEs often include heterogeneous displays to take advantage of different capabilities such as their size, position, resolution or mobility to support the task at hand" [11]. For large information spaces within MDEs, the availability of devices presents an opportunity for exploring how interaction can be divided amongst the different displays. For example, interaction could be spread across different tablets to accomplish a single goal (e.g. finding a location on different types of maps) or interaction could be limited to one tablet and a digital tabletop to accomplish the same goal.

Integrating concepts from ZUIO, Magic Lens [2], and multi-display environments, this paper presents Bancada, a system developed to study interactions in large information spaces within a multi-display environments. It focuses on geospatial information spaces, as maps are now commonplace and present a wide variety of tasks that are common for ZUIO [7]. With Bancada, a user can explore geospatial information spaces by building custom layered maps. Interaction can be performed with multiple tablets, where each tablet provides a specific lens (a specific geospatial layer), or by interacting with a single tablet containing all lenses. While a user interacts with the tablet, the tabletop (or a wall display) provides an overview map showing the respective position and content of all lenses, as seen in Figure 1.

Figure 1. User exploring geospatial information space using Bancada with overview map displayed on tabletop highlighted. Tablets are colored according to the lens they display.

The remainder of this paper consists of related work presented in the next section, followed by a description of the Bancada system and finally, the conclusion and future work.

Related Work

O+D interfaces have been extensively researched under several different conditions, such as separating the interface across multiple displays [10][14], as well as comparisons of different interfaces with distortion [1]. With the conflicting results from much of the prior research, it is not possible to generalize conclusions [4]. Despite users performing tasks faster using different approaches, they still prefer when overviews are available [8].

ZuiScat [5] provided an initial ZUI concept for the exploration of scatterplots in PDAs. Users interact by pressing buttons for zooming and dragging a stylus for panning. Results from a usability study demonstrated that pen gestures provide a "valuable alternative to space-consuming visual controls such as buttons". Burigat et al. [3] compared ZUIOs against ZUIs for navigation of large information spaces on mobile devices. They considered map navigation tasks in PDAs and the results suggested that overviews provide higher value when highlighting relevant semantic information and the information space does not provide orientation cues.

PaperLens [13] uses Tangible Magic Lenses to explore multi-layered information spaces. Interaction is provided by positioning a handheld above a tabletop and based on distance to the tabletop, a user is able to see a corresponding layer projected. However, the combination of multiple lenses, such as different overlapping lenses presented in our work, is not explored.

Bancada

Building upon prior work, Bancada was developed to investigate the use of multiple mobile devices versus a single mobile device during map-based exploration activities in a multi-display environment. Interactions with the system are made through touch gestures performed on tablets, avoiding buttons for panning or zooming the map, as recommended by [5].

Bancada can be deployed on any device running Microsoft Windows 7 or above. To perform communication between devices, the Multi-Surface

Figure 2. Overlapping lenses: Electoral Districts lens on top of Population Density lens, running in Multiple Lenses Mode.

Figure 3. Tablet in single lens mode displaying the Streets lens.

Environment framework SoD[1] was used. The geospatial information in the system is a mixture of custom data as well as information provided by the ESRI Canada Community Map Program[2].

The system provides three modes of execution: Overview, Single Lens and Multiple Lenses. Lenses, interactions and the three modes are described below.

Lenses

A lens is a porthole used to augment the base map and it is identified by a particular color in the overview. Figure 3 illustrates the example when the user activates the street lens: he can observe, on his tablet, a map containing streets and highways. The overview map presents that specific area inside a red rectangle. Currently, there are five lenses, as seen in Figure 4:

- Streets (Red), shows streets and highways.
- Population density (Yellow), shows the population density heat map according to the Canadian 2006 census.
- Cities (Blue), shows labels for cities, lakes, rivers, provinces.
- Satellite (Green), displays satellite imagery.
- Electoral districts (Black), shows the boundaries of all Canadian electoral districts.

Users can interact with lenses through touch gestures and menus available according to the mode the system is running, as detailed below.

[1] http://ase.cpsc.ucalgary.ca/index.php?page=sod---main

[2] http://maps.esri.ca/

INTERACTIONS: PINCH-AND-ZOOM AND PANNING

Users of modern mobile devices are familiar with the gestures used to interact with the lenses: dragging the finger on the screen pans the lens; and to increase/decrease the zoom level, the user performs a pinch gesture.

LENS SELECTION

A menu with colored buttons is available to choose which lens the tablet will display. The color-lens association helps the user to identify the position of each lens on the overview. During the design, using buttons was considered the simplest approach to accomplish the task, although further research is required to evaluate its impact on the interface.

ACTIVATING AND DEACTIVATING LENSES

It's possible to deactivate and activate a lens by pressing the button on top left corner. When deactivated, the lens is removed from the screen in all devices. When the user activates a lens, it is added on top of all lenses.

This feature allows lenses to be stacked, so that a user can have different combinations of layers in different regions of the overview map. This stack is determined by the order lenses are activated. For example, if a user activates the Satellite lens, and then Cities, he can see the names of the cities on top of satellite images. However, if one lens is panned, the overlapping area will be seen only where the lenses intersect, as illustrated in Figure 2.

Overview Mode

The overview mode is responsible for displaying the context in the system. As seen in Figure 1, this mode

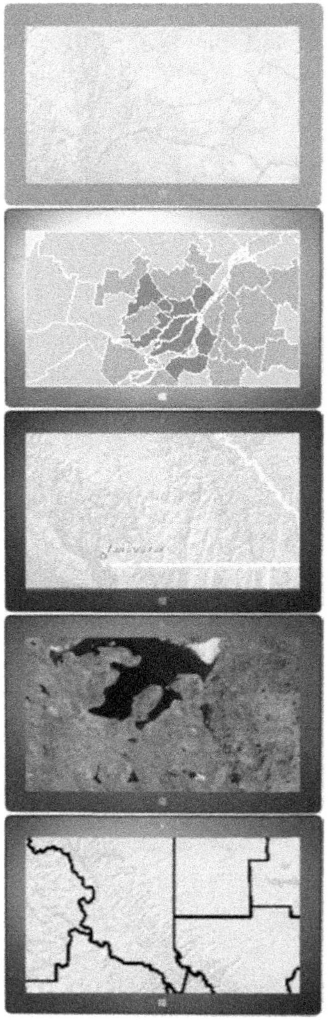

Figure 4. Available lenses.

shows a base map and all active lenses, with respect to their position in space and size. It is important to highlight that scale and extent of the base map will not change. This prevents interactions with the maps or lenses in the overview mode. This design decision was made due to the following scenario: if a user is exploring a city with the Electoral Districts lens, the zoom level might be so high that in the overview this user will only see a small rectangle showing that lens position and no other information can be extracted without adding some distortion to the overview (e.g. fisheye), which is beyond the current scope of Bancada.

Single Lens Mode
When in Single Lens mode, the system allows the user to choose one lens and that lens is the only one available for use on that particular device. It is only possible to activate and deactivate the specific lens. This mode is used when there are multiple tablets and each tablet will be used for only one specific lens.

Multiple Lenses Mode
When in Multiple Lens mode, the system allows the user to swap lenses at any moment through the lens selection menu, as seen in Figure 2. When changing lenses, for instance, from Satellite to Streets, the system will save the state of Satellite and, if Streets has been activated before, it will restore its previous state, i.e. where the user left. If Streets is being used for the first time, the system will initialize the lens according to the overview extent, respecting the visual information-seeking mantra "Overview first, zoom and filter, then details-on-demand" [12].

Limitations
Although any mode can be executed in any compatible device, e.g. Single Lens running on a wall display while Overview is running on a tablet, the Overview mode does not allow any interaction with the map or lenses. It contradicts suggestions from [6], however, for Bancada's current purpose, this aspect does not bring any impact. Also, it is considered future work to explore different possibilities to provide Overview interaction and make comparisons between lens' configurations.

We are aware that the current process of choosing a lens (i.e. pressing a button) in Multiple Lenses Mode can impact users' performance and preference between one or multiple tablets when exploring multi-layer geospatial space. A study comparing buttons, gestures, and a device's physical position and orientation provides context for future work.

Conclusion and Future Work

This paper presented Bancada, a system developed to investigate the use of multiple mobile devices in a multi-display environment when users are exploring geospatial information. In such environments, tablets are Zoomable Magic Lenses that augment an overview map displayed on a tabletop or a wall display. Also, through touch gestures, it is possible to overlap different lenses and build a custom multi-layer map.

Future work with Bancada includes:

- An exploratory study on what configuration (single or multiple tablets) users prefer and which one they perform best when executing navigational and exploratory tasks in the geospatial information space.

- An exploration on how users may interact with lenses from the Overview mode. A possibility would be to examine distortion techniques, e.g. fisheye, after zooming to a certain scale;
- To explore different approaches in how a user can change layers when using a tablet in Multiple Lenses Mode. Changes according to a device's position and orientation in the environment is one of the possibilities we will investigate.

Acknowledgements

We would like to thank Apoorve Chokshi for reviewing this paper. This research was funded by NSERC (NETGP 370791-08) and NSERC SurfNet Research Network.

References

[1] Baudisch, P. and Good, N. Keeping things in context: a comparative evaluation of focus plus context screens, overviews, and zooming. In *Proc. of ACM CHI '02*, 4 (2002), 259–266.

[2] Bier, E.A., Stone, M.C., Pier, K., Buxton, W., and Derose, T.D. Toolglass and Magic Lenses: The See-Through Interface. In *Proc. of ACM SIGGRAPH '93*, (1993), 73–80.

[3] Burigat, S. and Chittaro, L. Map, Diagram, and Web Page Navigation on Mobile Devices: the Effectiveness of Zoomable User Interfaces with Overviews. In *Proc. of the 10th Int. Conf. on Human Computer Interaction with Mobile Devices & Services* (MobileHCI '08), (2008), 147–156.

[4] Burigat, S. and Chittaro, L. On the effectiveness of Overview+Detail visualization on mobile devices. In *Pers. and Ubiquitous Computing 17*, 2 (2013), 371–385.

[5] Büring, T. and Reiterer, H. Zuiscat: querying and visualizing information spaces on personal digital assistants. In *Proc. of the 7th Int. Conf. on Human Computer Interaction with Mobile Devices & Services (MobileHCI '05)*, (2005), 129–136.

[6] Cockburn, A., Karlson, A., and Bederson, B. A review of overview+detail, zooming, and focus+context interfaces. In *ACM Computing Surveys*, (2008), 1–42.

[7] Hornbæk, K., Bederson, B.B., and Plaisant, C. Navigation patterns and usability of zoomable user interfaces with and without an overview. In *ACM Transactions on Computer-Human Interaction*, 4 (2002), 362–389.

[8] Hornbæk, K. and Frøkjær, E. Reading of Electronic Documents: The Usability of Linear, Fisheye, and Overview+Detail Interfaces. In *Proc. of ACM CHI '01*. (2001), 293–300.

[9] Jakobsen, M.R. and Hornbæk, K. Sizing Up Visualizations: Effects of Display Size in Focus+Context, Overview+Detail, and Zooming Interfaces. In *Proc. of ACM CHI '11* (2011), 1451-1460.

[10] Rashid, U., Nacenta, M., and Quigley, A. The cost of display switching: a comparison of mobile, large display and hybrid UI configurations. In *Proc. of the ACM AVI '12*, (2012), 99–106.

[11] Seyed, T., Burns, C., King, P., Rodrigues, F. M., Sousa, M., and Maurer, F. MRI Table Kinect: A multi-surface application for exploring volumetric medical imagery. In *Proc. of the Workshop on Safer Interaction in Medical Devices (MediCHI'13)*, (2013).

[12] Shneiderman, B. The Eyes Have It: A Task by Data Type Taxonomy. In *Proc. of the 1996 IEEE Symposium on Visual Languages (VL '96)*, (1996).

[13] Spindler, M. and Dachselt, R. PaperLens: advanced magic lens interaction above the tabletop. In *Proc. of the ACM ITS '09*, (2009), 69–76.

[14] Tan, D.S. and Czerwinski, M. Effects of Visual Separation and Physical Discontinuities when Distributing Information across Multiple Displays. In *Proc. of INTERACT 2003*, (2003).

ClothLens Demo: Simultaneous Multi-user Interaction with Shared Content on a Tabletop

Christian Lander
DFKI GmbH
Saarbrücken, Germany
christian.lander@dfki.de

Sven Gehring
DFKI GmbH
Saarbrücken, Germany
sven.gehring@dfki.de

Author Keywords
Surface, multitouch, multi user, cloth, magic lens, focus, context

ACM Classification Keywords
H.5.m. Information interfaces and presentation (e.g., HCI): Miscellaneous.

ITS 2014, November 16–19, 2014, Dresden, Germany.
ACM 978-1-4503-2587-5/14/11.
http://dx.doi.org/10.1145/2669485.2669524

Abstract
We present *ClothLens,* a prototype that allows simultaneous interaction of multiple users with a digital map shown on a tabletop display. With our prototype interaction with the content by panning or zooming reduces the conflicts due to interferences. *ClothLens* utilizes the Focus+Context pattern enabling users to create personal lenses on top of the map. The actual content is organized as a physical cloth object that is bend or stretched according to the interactions.

Introduction
Digital surfaces can usually be categorized by their deployment location, their dimension and resolution as well as their support for user interaction.

A common approach to make such shared digital surfaces interactive while allowing for multiple users is to offer the possibility of input by direct touch. This can be usually done in different ways. In order to interact with a touch enabled shared surface, users are usually required to be within arms reach of the surface. A common application scenario for such screens is the display of interactive information content, such as public transport timetables or maps. For situated public displays [1], the number of simultaneous users is usually limited by the number of people fitting the space *in front* of the display while still being able to

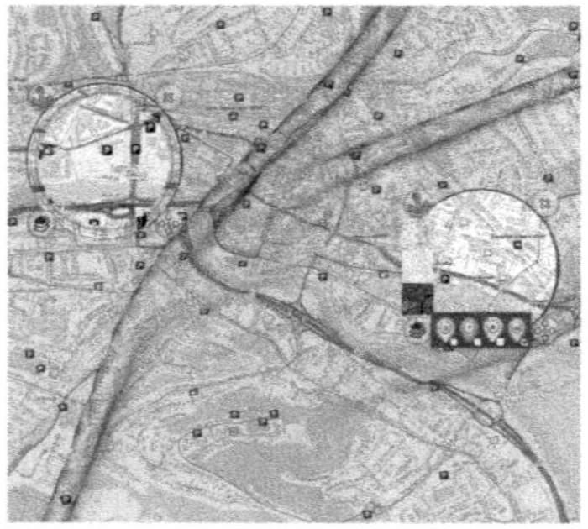

Figure 1. *ClothLens* enables simultaneous multi user interaction on a multitouch surface with big-sized content like a map. Users are able to create their own workbenches (*Focus Area*). Interactions with the *Context Area*, e.g. moving the map, does not interfere other users. Furthermore additional information can be overlaid above the map showing locations of interest.

touch the screen. In this case, all users have roughly the same orientation towards the displayed content. For tabletops, there is an additional difficulty: the number of people fitting the space around the tabletop usually limits the number of potential users. In this case, different users can have different orientations towards the content, resulting some users seeing the content rotated. If a user now tries to rotate the content to match her orientation towards the tabletop, interactions of all users with a different orientation will be interrupted and the content will no longer be displayed to them in the right orientation. The same holds when a user tries to pan or zoom the shared content (independent of the orientation). There are approaches addressing this problem, e.g. by replication of the content for each user or dividing the screen area into static regions with which one person can interact [2]. However these approaches realize static multi user interaction, so that the users have to interact consecutively [3,1] or with constant regions.

We present *ClothLens,* a technique to allow for simultaneous interaction of multiple users with a shared content on a tabletop display. For the design of *ClothLens*, we applied the *Focus+Context* [4] approach to our interface technique. We are using a natural visualization metaphor, which guarantees for keeping the point of interest (POI) usually called *Focus Area.* Additionally, the users won't lose the visual connection to the adjacent content, the *Context Area*, located around the point of interest, as can be seen in Figure 1.

Our working prototype, running on a *Microsoft Surface Pixelsense*[1] table, allows for simultaneous interaction of multiple users with a shared static map. We particularly chose this use case since it nicely illustrates the possible interferences of multi user interaction on a shared display, in particular when panning, zooming or rotating the content. Our approach is based on Bier at. al.'s Magic Lens [5], satisfying the *Focus+Context* interface pattern.

Related Work

ClothLens comprises techniques and approaches from different domains. For reasons of brevity, we only discuss directly related work. We also submitted a full paper where we discuss the complete related work.

Numerous approaches exist to address *the screen real estate problem*[2], defining the issue of having limited space on a display to visualize content and present interactive controls in a proper way. The Magic Lens metaphor proposed by Bier et. al. [5] serves as a base for most of the interface techniques.

Zooming interfaces [4] are used to separate content temporally. A person is able to directly interact with displayed information using a geometrical scaling to enlarge or shrink it. People interacting simultaneously might get into trouble, since usually the complete content is modified. Overview+Detail (o+d) interfaces [4] go one step further by combining a zoomed (detailed window) and a non zoomed (overview window) version showing the actual content in separate views. This may cause cognitive effort to link both views.

[1] http://www.microsoft.com/en-us/pixelsense/default.aspx

[2] http://goo.gl/1Vt3eP

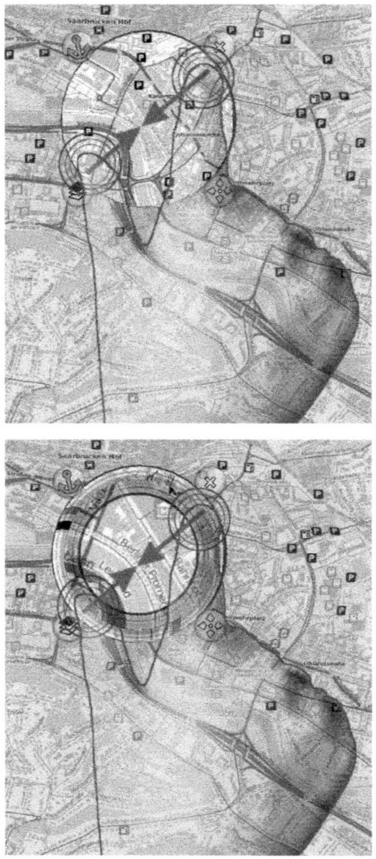

Figure 2. Two figures showing the workbench and zooming by stretching the map.

Focus+Context (f+c) [4] interfaces combine the aforementioned visualization techniques in one single view. With this method a so-called *Focus Area* is used to visualize content on a smaller part of the screen in detail and can include additional information. Simultaneously, the surrounding *Context Area* is used to keep track of the content as a whole. Both views are integrated continuously in one screen. Usual f+c interfaces are not suitable for multi user interaction, since the *Focus Area* will be modified when interaction with the *Context Area* takes place.

Sarkar et. al. [7] break out a new direction with their method. Stretching the content like a rubber sheet does zooming. Another approach is to add a third dimension to simulate a close distance to the focus area realizing the zooming functionality [8,9,10]. These methods break out the usually used magic lens metaphor for Focus+Context visualizations. However none of these techniques was tested in a multi user scenario.

Cloth Lens

ClothLens is a multi-user interaction technique utilizing the Focus+Context pattern as well as a metaphor to seamlessly integrate both areas to visualize the relation between them.

The *Context Area* is used to present the whole content in a more generally view as usual. By expanding to the third dimension the content is modeled as a physical cloth object lying on a table, as in [6]. It is provided with all properties of a cloth, like bending and stretching. The *Focus Area* is used to visualize the user's point of interest. Therefore we enable the user to create her workbench area equipped with different buttons serving as a Magic Lens with Toolglass [5]. The transparent lens is lying on top of the cloth object, the properties of the cloth object within the *Focus Area* remain the same, i.e. users zoom by stretching the map, figure 2. Additionally the lens is provided with some mass value causing the surrounding content to bunch up at the borders. Four surrounded buttons can control every workbench. Two are used to reset the mass value and activate the move functionality. One is used like a toolglass to change the visualization. So many persons are able to interact simultaneously by creating a workbench or simply moving the content around without interfering each other, figure 3.

Demo Application

We will demonstrate our prototype in the following way. Using a Microsoft Pixelsense system, we are showing a map. Passers-by are able to directly interact with the map by touching the surface. The map can be dragged around to visualize to effects of the cloth metaphor. To explore the map in more detail, people are able to create workbenches at the same time. With them they have the possibility to zoom the map, to add information about the part of the map (special locations, like restaurants) and to change the visualization type.

Conclusion

ClothLens can be used in various application scenarios. We see high potential in public information spaces like a tourist information center. There a multitouch table can easily be deployed running *ClothLens* to explore the map of the visiting city. Since a tourist information center is usually frequently attended we will have a multiuser scenario in which many persons want to

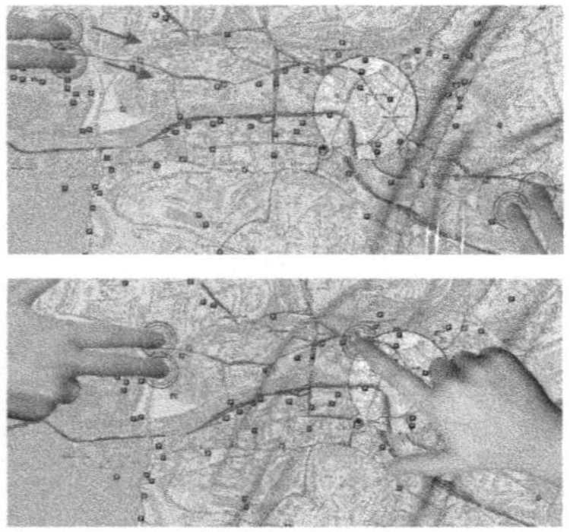

Figure 3. Two figures showing the bunching of the map at the *Focus Area.*

explore the map. ClothLens will enable them to do so in parallel without interfering each other.

By demonstrating our prototype to the ITS community, we expect discussions about improvements as well as further use cases and adaptions.

References

[1] O'Hara, K., Perry, M., Churchill, E., and Russel, D. Public Situated Displays: Social and Interactional Aspects of Shared Display Technologies, 2003.

[2] Scott, S.D., Grant, K.D, and Mandryk, R.L. System guidelines for collocated, collaborative work on a tabletop display. Proc. ECSCW 2003, 159-178.

[3] Boring, S. Gehring, S., Wiethoff, A., Blöckner, M., Schöning, J., and Butz, A. Multi-user interaction on media façades through live video on mobile devices. Proc. CHI 2011, 2721-2724.

[4] Cockburn, A., Karlson, A., and Bederson, B.B. A review of overview+detail, zooming, and focus+context interfaces. ACM Computational Sruvey 41, 2008, 1-31.

[5] Bier, E.A., Stone, M.C., Pier, K., Buxton, W., and DeRose, T.D. Toolglass and magic lenses: The see-through interface. Proc. SIGGRAPH 1993, 73-80.

[6] Mikulecky, K., Hancock, M., Brosz, J., and Carpendale, M.S.T. Exploring physical information cloth on a multitouch table. Proc. ITS 2011, 119-122

[7] Sarkar, M., Snibbe, S., Tversky, O.J., and Reiss, S.P. Stretching the rubber sheet: A metaphor for viewing large layouts on small screens. Proc. UIST 1993.

[8] Carpendale, M.S.T., and Motagnese, C. A framework for unifying presentation space. Proc UIST 2001, 61-70.

[9] Carpendale, M.S.T. 3-dimensional pliable surfaces: For the effective presentation of visual information. Proc. UIST 1995, 217-226.

[10] Ware, C., and Lewis, M. The dragmag image magnifier. Proc CHI 1995, 407-408.

The Interactive Dining Table, or: Pass the Weather Widget, Please

Florian Echtler
University of Regensburg
Media Informatics Group
florian.echtler@ur.de

Raphael Wimmer
University of Regensburg
Media Informatics Group
raphael.wimmer@ur.de

Figure 1: Augmented meal on an interactive dining table

ITS 2014, November 16–19, 2014, Dresden, Germany.
ACM 978-1-4503-2587-5/14/11.
http://dx.doi.org/10.1145/2669485.2669525

Abstract
Large-scale interactive surfaces are nearly ubiquitous in research labs and showrooms around the world today. However, unlike other recent interactive technologies such as smartphones, they have not yet found their way into people's everyday lives. Possible reasons include high cost as well as a lack of suitable applications. In this paper, we present our prototypical implementation of a low-cost, unobtrusive interactive surface, integrated with the dining table in a real-world living room. To motivate our approach, we explore three scenarios highlighting potential applications for our system and present their prototypical implementations. In the first scenario, we extend regular board games with interactive components without sacrificing their unique haptic experience. In the second scenario, we investigate ambient notifications which provide a method for delivering information to the users subconsciously. Finally, we explore the concept of *augmented dining* in which the appearance of food placed on the table is augmented or modified by the system.

Author Keywords
augmented reality; gaming; real-world setting; Kinect sensor; interactive surface; living room; dining table; board games; eating; food; ambient interface

ACM Classification Keywords
H.5.m [Information interfaces and presentation (e.g., HCI)]: Miscellaneous.

Figure 2: Interactive dining table with augmented board game, integrated into real-world living room

Introduction

Large-scale interactive surfaces, such as interactive tables or whiteboards, are now a regular sight in research labs, showrooms or education-related settings. However, unlike other recent interactive technologies such as smartphones, they are still a long way from becoming a part of people's everyday lives.

This lack of adoption has several potential reasons. As an example, we will consider the widely used Microsoft PixelSense. First, the price of such a system is still prohibitively high - the 40" PixelSense display costs approximately US$ 9000, while a similarly sized regular flatscreen display costs less than 10% of that amount. Second, it is reasonable to expect that people do not want a dedicated interactive table in their homes, but would rather have the interactive features integrated into an existing table such as the dining table. Moreover, furniture are long-lived items which are replaced far less frequently than entertainment devices and which have to cope with frequent accidents such as fluid spills or dropped glassware.

In this paper, we present and discuss an unobtrusive and low-cost system which is designed to address these issues. Our approach is to integrate the interactive components with the dining table in a real-world living room (see Figure 2). The system prototype is composed of a Kinect depth camera integrated into the table lamp for sensing interaction (based on the approach shown in [11]) and a small LED-based projector mounted on the ceiling for displaying information on the table. The total cost of the system is approximately US$ 500 (excluding computer), placing it in the same price category as game consoles or similar types of consumer electronics.

Of course, this leads to the question why people would actually be interested in having such a setup in their own living room. To motivate our creation of this system, we describe three scenarios which explore potential application areas. First, we present our concept of augmented board games which merge the unique properties of physical game pieces with the computing capabilities provided by our system. We also present a concept of ambient notifications which can be used to convey everyday information, such as weather forecasts, to the users without requiring conscious attention. Finally, we introduce the concept of *augmented dining* in which the users' efforts to make more conscious and informed decisions about their food consumption are supported by the system through various visual augmentations.

Related Work

There seems to be little related work which attempts to merge large-scale interactive surfaces into people's everyday lives. Preliminary research in this direction has recently been conducted by Kirk et al. [3], in which the authors have placed several dedicated photo browsing tables in participants' homes. Seifried et al. introduce an interactive couch table [6] which aims to replace the multitude of remote controls in modern living rooms. However, most current research still focuses on creating interactive experiences in public spaces. A defining criteria of this research is that it is geared towards brief interactions from people who are not assumed to be familiar with the system, as opposed to people interacting with appliances in their own homes.

With respect to board games, most related work focuses on adapting existing board games to interactive surfaces, not the other way round. For example, the *Settlers of Catan* [8] game we focus on has been implemented for the original Microsoft Surface [9] as a predominantly digital game. Chaboissier et al. [1] describe *RealTimeChess*, a game for digital tabletops that started as a straightforward implementation of regular chess and evolved into a touch-based four-player game that has little in common with its original inspiration. Beamatron [10] by Wilson et

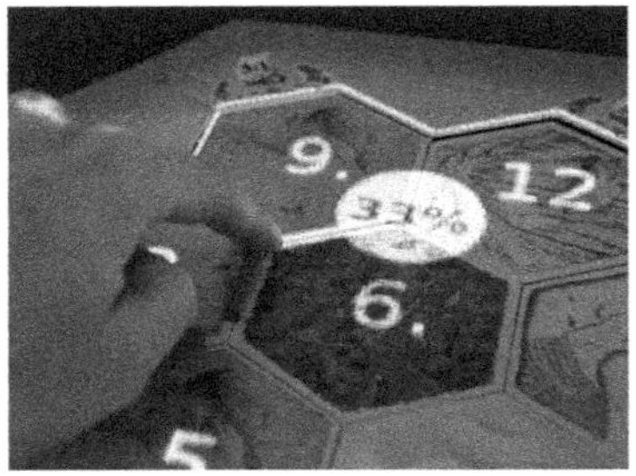

Figure 3: Augmented *Settlers of Catan* board game. A player checks the success chances of a potential location for a game piece.

Figure 4: Ambient weather notifications

al. uses a steerable Kinect-projector combination to enable augmented gaming on arbitrary surfaces, e.g. by using physical objects as an obstacle course for a virtual buggy. Rooke and Vertegaal present a concept [5] to use blank cardboard tiles as projection surfaces to turn them into dynamic board game components.

Augmented Board Games

As the first usage scenario for our setup, we have chosen *augmented board games*. An example of such a board game, the popular *Settlers of Catan* [8], is shown in Figure 2. In general, players of a board game can be expected to have little interest in an augmented version, since they are familiar with the rules and might also want to focus on a non-digital experience. However, there are some aspects where an augmented game can offer tangible benefits compared to an unaugmented variant.

In the *Settlers* game shown above, players roll two dice and receive resources from the game tiles labeled with the corresponding number if one of their game pieces has been placed on an adjacent intersection. In our setup, we have replaced the numbers indicating the required dice roll with projected labels. In the original game, these numbers are simple cardboard markers which do not offer any additional game value and have to be distributed manually before the game can start. Consequently, replacing them with virtual markers shortens the setup time required prior to playing without changing the game experience. Other side tasks such as tracking scores could also be automated, thereby lowering the players' cognitive load.

Many board games such as *Settlers* are designed to be "easy to learn, hard to master" - they are based on simple rules, which form complex relations over the course of the game. For example, it is difficult for novice players to estimate the success chances provided by a potential settlement location. Consequently, our augmentation aims to support inexperienced players in their decisions by displaying the total success chance of a particular location as a percentage when the location is touched (see also Figure 3).

Ambient Notifications

Users can be expected to spend at least some time at the dining table every day, usually at predictable times (e.g. for breakfast). Consequently, suitable information for the situation, such as weather forecasts or traffic information, could be displayed directly on the table without requiring any interaction from the users. By automatically showing a small set of relevant data in an unobtrusive manner, users can absorb this information without the need for conscious attention. As an example, a possible implementation for ambient weather notifications is shown in Figure 4. The icon and text rotate slowly to enable persons at all sides of the table to easily access the displayed information without conscious effort.

Augmented Dining

As our final scenario, we introduce the concept of *augmented dining*[1]. More and more people try to make conscious decisions about their food consumption by keeping informed about ingredients, calorie content and similar facts. Our interactive dining table is capable of supporting these goals by augmenting dishes placed on the table with projected information. Dishes can be tracked using the Kinect camera, keeping the augmentations spatially aligned with the dish they refer to. An example of such an augmented meal is shown in Figure 1.

A different variant of augmented dining might also be called *augmented dieting*, comparable to previous work by Narumi et al. [4]. As shown in numerous studies such as [7], food color can influence the taste perception and

[1] A related variant which projects *virtual* food onto the plates before the real food is served and might consequently be called *augmented ordering* is used in the inamo restaurant in London (`http://www.inamo-restaurant.com/pc/`)

consequently the amount of food consumed during a meal. Blue color in particular has been shown to markedly reduce food consumption. However, using blue lighting for the whole room may have unwanted side effects, such as influencing people's mood. We can use our augmented dining table to simply project a spot of blue light onto the dish, thereby subtly tricking people's perception of the food and lowering their food consumption without resorting to large-scale changes to the room's lighting.

Conclusion & Outlook

We have presented our concept of an interactive dining table which can be integrated with existing dining tables at reasonable cost. We have explored several variants of interactive augmentations which can be applied to tasks regularly carried out at such a table, e.g. board gaming or simply eating dinner. We plan to prototype and evaluate other types of augmented board games such as chess, look at additional classes of ambient information which could be displayed on an interactive dining table, e.g. train schedules, and conduct user studies regarding our newly introduced concept of *augmented dining*. Moreover, we plan to install this setup in other homes, thereby enabling us to receive additional feedback on our concept "from the wild".

Acknowledgements

We thank the lead author's family for graciously accepting the modifications to their living room. This demo is based on a prior submission to the CHI 2013 workshop on "Blended Interaction" [2].

References

[1] J. Chaboissier, T. Isenberg, and F. Vernier. RealTimeChess: lessons from a participatory design process for a collaborative multi-touch, multi-user game. In Proc. ITS '11, pages 97–106, New York, NY, USA, 2011. ACM.

[2] F. Echtler and R. Wimmer. The Interactive Dining Table. In Proc. Blend '13, Paris, France, Apr. 2013.

[3] D. Kirk, S. Izadi, O. Hilliges, R. Banks, S. Taylor, and A. Sellen. At home with surface computing? In Proc. CHI '12, pages 159–168, New York, NY, USA, 2012. ACM.

[4] T. Narumi, Y. Ban, T. Kajinami, T. Tanikawa, and M. Hirose. Augmented perception of satiety: controlling food consumption by changing apparent size of food with augmented reality. In Proc. CHI '12, pages 109–118, New York, NY, USA, 2012. ACM.

[5] M. Rooke and R. Vertegaal. Physics on Display: Tangible Graphics on Hexagonal Bezel-less Screens. In Proc. TEI '10, pages 233–236, New York, NY, USA, 2010. ACM.

[6] T. Seifried, M. Haller, S. D. Scott, F. Perteneder, C. Rendl, D. Sakamoto, and M. Inami. CRISTAL: a collaborative home media and device controller based on a multi-touch display. In Proc. ITS '09, pages 33–40, New York, NY, USA, 2009. ACM.

[7] C. Spence, C. A. Levitan, M. U. Shankar, and M. Zampini. Does Food Color Influence Taste and Flavor Perception in Humans? *Chemosensory Perception*, 3(1):68–84, Mar. 2010.

[8] K. Teuber. Settlers of Catan. http://www.catan.com/, 1995. accessed 2014/09/07.

[9] Vectorform. Vectorform to launch "Catan" for the Microsoft Surface. http://blog.vectorform.com/2010/06/21/the-settlers-of-catan/, 2010. accessed 2014/09/07.

[10] A. Wilson, H. Benko, S. Izadi, and O. Hilliges. Steerable Augmented Reality with the Beamatron. In Proc. UIST '12, pages 413–422, New York, NY, USA, 2012. ACM.

[11] A. D. Wilson. Using a depth camera as a touch sensor. In Proc. ITS '10, pages 69–72, New York, NY, USA, 2010. ACM.

CubeQuery: Tangible Interface for Creating and Manipulating Database Queries

Ricardo Langner
Interactive Media Lab
Technische Universität Dresden
Dresden, Germany
langner@acm.org

Anton Augsburg
Interactive Media Lab
Technische Universität Dresden
Dresden, Germany

Raimund Dachselt
Interactive Media Lab
Technische Universität Dresden
Dresden, Germany
dachselt@acm.org

Figure 1: Small tangibles allow users to create and manipulate search parameters of a database query. (↑ top) Initially every token is unbound, i.e., without a selected facet. (↓ bottom) Token with selected facet (i.e., *year*) and values.

ITS 2014, November 16–19, 2014, Dresden, Germany.
ACM 978-1-4503-2587-5/14/11.
http://dx.doi.org/10.1145/2669485.2669526

Abstract
We demonstrate *CubeQuery*, a tangible user interface providing a physical way to both create and manipulate basic database queries. This interactive installation is designed for individual faceted browsing and allows users to explore contents of a database, i.e., a music library. While each tangible represents an individual search parameter of a search request, the physical arrangement of multiple tangibles permits the combination of search parameters by utilizing basic logical operators. Goal of this research is to explore the practicality of spatial arrangement of tangibles to ease the process of faceted browsing.

Author Keywords
Tangible UIs; Faceted Browsing & Search; Database Queries; Sifteo Cubes; Microsoft Surface

ACM Classification Keywords
H.5.2 [Information Interfaces and Presentation: User Interfaces].

Introduction
Using a tangible query interface to physically create and manipulate search requests has been investigated in several research projects [1, 2, 6]. However, using active

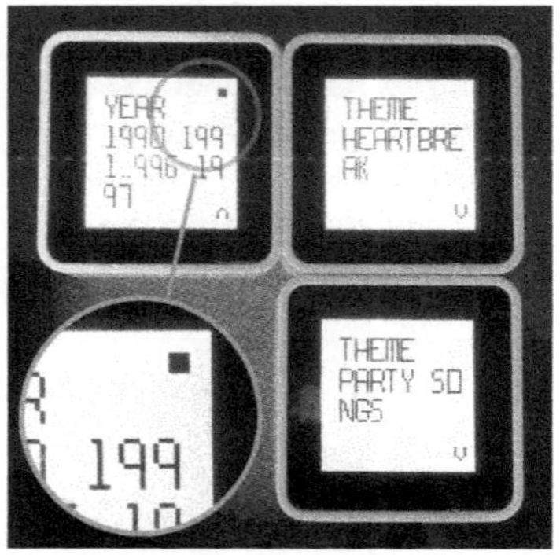

Figure 2: Spatial arrangement: tokens can be placed side by side to create combined queries. (close-up) An icon highlights the main token and active query.

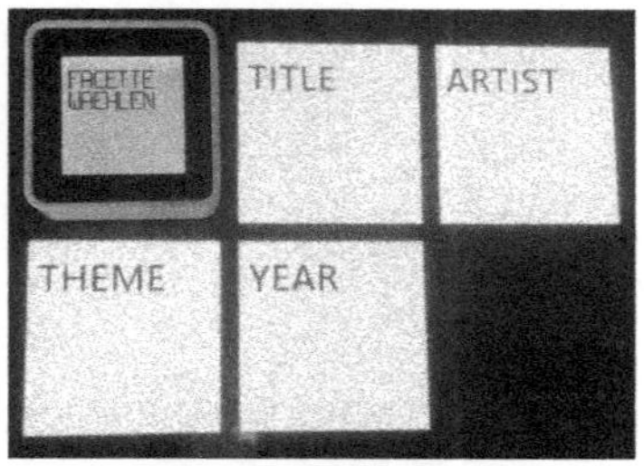

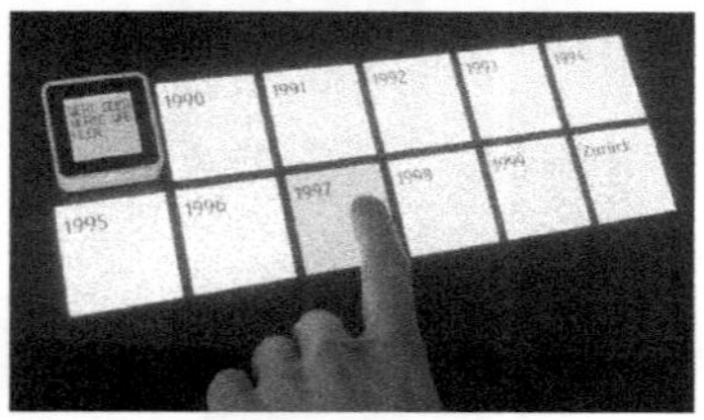

Figure 3: Available values. (↑ top) Users can selects facets, such as *title*, *artist*, *theme*, or *year*. (↓ bottom) Selection of facet-specific values.

tangibles – tangibles equipped with, e.g., a display, a number of sensors, or wireless communication – for such search tasks had previously received more attention [7]. Therefore, our *CubeQuery* concept uses Sifteo cubes [3, 4], a commercially available interactive game system that provides a SDK to create custom applications. Our interactive demonstration allows users to explore a dataset (i.e., music library) by spatially arranging tangibles on an interactive surface.

The general idea is to provide users with a set of tokens (cf. [2]), i.e., tangibles representing individual search parameters. A search parameter is defined as a facet (e.g., categorical, numeric) and one or more facet-specific values. In contrast to *Stackables* [2], where tangibles are vertically stacked, *CubeQuery* explores the spatial alignment (side by side) of tokens.

CubeQueries: Design and Concept

The *CubeQuery* concept utilizes various features of a rich interaction space. Based on the capabilities of the deployed hardware, these features can be classified into two categories: output attributes and input attributes.

Output Attributes. Output is provided both on the interactive surface as well as on the tokens. While the surface features visual and audio feedback, tokens use visual output only. In terms of an application state, tokens supply local (personalized) feedback, whereas surface feedback represents both local and global.

Input Attributes. The interaction vocabulary develops from the use of the interactive surface, tokens, and the combination of the devices. The surface provides direct touch input only, allowing users to tap, drag, or swipe visuals. Since *CubeQuery* makes use of the full functionality provided by the Sifteo cubes, features of tokens directly correspond to the hardware capabilities. Unique identifiers allow tokens to be distinguished. Tokens can be tilted, flipped, and shaken by making use of the build-in motion sensor. They also allow users to press the display. Furthermore, tokens can be positioned on the surface. This results in a token-specific location, i.e., a 2D position and orientation. Finally, tokens can be placed side by side relating to each of the four sides of a tangible (see Figure 2). Considering the interactive surface, this placement can be performed either off-screen or on-screen.

To explore a dataset, users can define search parameters and logically combine them in queries, i.e., search requests. A typical work flow of binding a search parameter involves (1) assigning a facet to a token, (2) selecting facet-specific values, (3) optionally combining parameters by using logical operators, and (4) optionally putting a request by activating the query. In this context, *CubeQuery* enables users to perform various operations.

Facet selection. An individual search parameter related to a specific facet can be bound to a specific token. Initially, a token is unbound, i.e., neither a value nor a facet is set up. If an unbound token is placed down on the surface, the application shows available facets. Users can select (bind) a facet by tapping it (see Figure 3 top). The application shows corresponding facet values immediately after a the selection of a facet (cf. value selection). To unbind a token again, i.e., clear both the values and the facet users simply grab and shake the tangible.

Value selection. Depending on the data type and value range of a selected facet, users can choose single or multiple values. Available values are shown right beside (or around) the corresponding token (see Figure 3 bottom). Exactly like the facet selection, a *single-value selection* requires the user to tap the specific value.

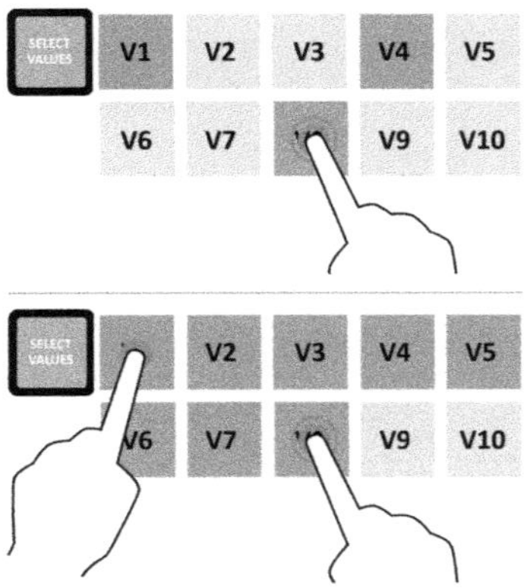

Figure 4: Multi-value selection. (↑ top) Selection of individual values separated from each other. (↓ bottom) Selection of a continuous value range.

Figure 5: (↑ top) Negation of a search parameter.
(↓ bottom) Horizontal alignment represents AND operator.

Tapping a value again allows users to undo the selection (toggle behavior). Selecting several values in sequence results in a *multi-value selection*. Such a selection can represent both individual values separated from each other as well as continuous value ranges (see Figure 4). The selection of a continuous value range can be achieved in various ways. *CubeQuery* allows a successive selection of values step by step. Although this might be obvious, it is not effective. Hence, our design considers the following alternative methods: Either touching and swiping values (uni-manual) or touching and holding the first value with one finger and tapping the last value with another finger (bi-manual), see Figure 4 bottom. Besides a common value selection, users might want to exclude specific values without selecting every other value. In contrast to value selections involving touch input, a negation of previously selected values can be achieved by physically flipping a token back and forth. To both provide adequate feedback and help users to identify such negated tokens, the visual output is inverted, i.e., white text on dark background (see Figure 5).

Activation. As the interactive surfaces shows the results of one main search request (cf. visualization of query results), one main token has to be declared. Only if a main token is present a search query will be processed. The main token can be set by pressing the display of the token. A small icon visually highlights the main token (see Figure 2 close-up).

Combining parameters. Multiple tokens can be combined to formulate more complex queries. By placing tokens side by side, users can combine search parameters using simple boolean AND or OR operators. Here, the alignment affects the boolean operator. Tokens need to be combined horizontally to apply an AND operator (see Figure 5 bottom). A vertical alignment results in a logical OR combination. The order of execution of a combined query is time-dependent, i.e., corresponds to the chronological order of the token combinations. Again, icons visualize the logical combination and indicate the type of operator.

Visualization of Query Results
The result of a query is shown on the display of the interactive surface. Similar to common media library applications, the visualization is presented as a grid view containing result elements (see Figure 1, 6). If the sample space contains more elements than the grid view can display, users can pan or swipe the grid view horizontally to scroll. The grid visualization immediately responds to query changes, e.g., adding or removing a token. This way users can dynamically modify a query and explore a dataset in an interactive way.

Figure 6: A grid view shows the result of a query. The visualization immediately responds to query changes.

Implementation
CubeQuery makes use of the first version of the Sifteo cubes [4] and a Microsoft Surface SUR40, a touch-sensitive interactive tabletop. The cubes

communicate wirelessly via a proprietary 2.4GHz protocol with the surface (host PC). To receive the location of a token, each cube is tagged with a fiducial marker, i.e., a 4x4 cm infrared reflective marker with a unique 8-bit identification pattern. The prototype consists of two components. The first component, written in C# and using the official Sifteo SDK, provides application logic and a communication interface to the Sifteo cubes. The second component, written in C# and using WPF, features the grid visualization and handles touch and marker input. Both components run on the host PC (i.e., Microsoft Surface SUR40) and communicate through a TCP socket connection. The *CubeQuery* prototype enables users to explore a musical dataset of approx. 600 songs [5] where users can select various facets, such as theme, title, artist, and year.

Conclusion

We developed *CubeQuery*, a tangible user interface providing a physical way to both create and manipulate basic database queries. We wanted to ease the process of faceted browsing and make information seeking more effective. Unlike the majority of previous work, we utilized active tangibles. With our *CubeQuery* prototype we explore the practicality of creating simple boolean query constructions by aligning these devices side by side.

Acknowledgements

We thank Mathias Frisch, Ulrike Kister, André Viergutz, and Wolfgang Büschel for productive discussions and their valuable feedback.

References

[1] Jetter, H.-C., Gerken, J., Zöllner, M., Reiterer, H., and Milic-Frayling, N. Materializing the query with facet-streams: A hybrid surface for collaborative search on tabletops. In *Proceedings of the SIGCHI Conference on Human Factors in Computing Systems*, CHI '11, ACM (New York, NY, USA, 2011), 3013–3022.

[2] Klum, S., Isenberg, P., Langner, R., Fekete, J.-D., and Dachselt, R. Stackables: Combining tangibles for faceted browsing. In *Proceedings of the International Working Conference on Advanced Visual Interfaces*, AVI '12, ACM (New York, NY, USA, 2012), 241–248.

[3] Merrill, D., Sun, E., and Kalanithi, J. Sifteo cubes. In *Proceedings of the 2012 ACM annual conference extended abstracts on Human Factors in Computing Systems Extended Abstracts*, CHI EA '12, ACM (New York, NY, USA, 2012), 1015–1018.

[4] Sifteo, Inc. Sifteo cubes. `https://www.sifteo.com/cubes`.

[5] The Guardian. The 1000 best songs ever. `https://opendata.socrata.com/dataset/1000-Songs/y5f9-excn`.

[6] Ullmer, B., Ishii, H., and Jacob, R. J. Tangible query interfaces: Physically constrained tokens for manipulating database queries. In *Proceedings of the INTERACT '03*, vol. 2003 (2003), 279–286.

[7] Valdes, C., Eastman, D., Grote, C., Thatte, S., Shaer, O., Mazalek, A., Ullmer, B., and Konkel, M. K. Exploring the design space of gestural interaction with active tokens through user-defined gestures. In *Proceedings of the SIGCHI Conference on Human Factors in Computing Systems*, CHI '14, ACM (New York, NY, USA, 2014), 4107–4116.

Fusion of Mixed Reality Tabletop and Location-Based Applications for Pervasive Games

Chris Zimmerer
University of Wuerzburg
chris.zimmerer@stud-mail.uni-wuerzburg.de

Martin Fischbach
University of Wuerzburg
martin.fischbach@uni-wuerzburg.de

Marc Erich Latoschik
University of Wuerzburg
marc.latoschik@uni-wuerzburg.de

ITS 2014, November 16–19, 2014, Dresden, Germany.
ACM 978-1-4503-2587-5/14/11.
http://dx.doi.org/10.1145/2669485.2669527

Abstract
Quest - UbiquX fuses a multimodal mixed reality implementation of a traditional tabletop role-play game with a location-based mobile aspect to provide a novel Ubiquitous gaming eXperience (UbiquX). Mobile devices are used to progress the game in a single-player adventure phase based on the players location in the real world. In addition, they support the interaction with an interactive tabletop surface in a collaborative skirmish phase.

Author Keywords
Pervasive Game; Mixed Reality; Tabletop; Multimodal; Localisation

ACM Classification Keywords
H.5.2 [Information interfaces and presentation (e.g., HCI)]: User Interfaces.

Introduction
The underlying principles of non-digital games require players to learn and apply a wide variety of skills and interactions in order to be victorious. This variety ranges from navigation, orientation and strong motor function skills in outdoor games to fine-grained motor functions, as well as strong multimodal communicational skills in social interactions in tabletop games where strategy and collaboration are of a major focus. Despite this diversity,

computer games have replaced traditional games as a leisure activity during the last decades [1]. Although classical computer games have a positive impact on the players' skills [1], they are still considered to be weak substitutions for their non-digital counterpart. *Pervasive games* integrate real world and virtual aspects into a combined experience that potentially unifies the benefits of both traditional as well as computer games [7]. They can be subdivided into several categories, particularly including location-based and mixed reality games. The benefits and opportunities of both subcategories have been researched individually in projects like [5] or [6]. Moreover, the augmentation of traditional gaming concepts with multimedia content has become more and more popular, as demonstrated by the development and success of commercial titles: *Scotland Yard - Master*, *tiptoi*, or *SmartPLAY* by Ravensburger and *The Eye of Judgment* by Sony Computer Entertainment provide hybrid gaming concepts based on a mix of real and virtual game elements.

Quest - UbiquX combines a mixed reality interactive tabletop scenario and a location-based mobile application within a single novel gaming experience. We are using a game context to evaluate the general feasibility of the approach and to develop generalized concepts and reusable technical components for other application areas (similar to [8]). The developed feature set included in the demonstration is applicable to use-cases that require (1) tasks that are carried out alone at specific locations in the environment using a private mobile device (e.g., data acquisition) and (2) tasks that have to be solved collaboratively during a face-to-face meeting using a shared interactive tabletop surface (e.g., strategic planning). In addition, (3) the mobile device is utilized to extend the interaction possibilities with an interactive tabletop surface during the collaborative phase. *Quest - UbiquX* provides a ubiquitous and pervasive gaming experience. It is an extension of the *Quest - XRoads* demonstration [3], developed within the eponymous project *XRoads* (Cross Reality On A Digital Surface).

Demonstration

The demo illustrates the porting of the traditional tabletop role-play game *Quest: Zeit der Helden* into a pervasive game. The original game is divided into two phases: The *adventure* phase, where the players follow a non-linear story line by visiting various locations to acquire rewards and information, and the *skirmish* phase, were strategic planning and collaboration is required to defeat enemies in a turn-based battle. These two phases are directly linked to the location-based and mixed reality application aspects (1) and (2). Moreover, the mobile devices of the players are used to edit secret information, extend the display surface, and access additional sensor data for interactions during the skirmish phase (3). Figure 1 depicts these three aspects by three examples.

Initially players choose characters to play in the fictive world using the mobile device. By visiting specific locations in the real world (with the mobile device), events can be triggered in the adventure phase of the game. These events can advance characters by progressing the story line and by rewarding the player with items or permanent improvements. In addition, special items allow players to mark new locations, that can then trigger events for other players. This feature enables both players to potentially change a given story line and authors to conveniently create new game content.

Figure 1: Aspects of *Quest - UbiquX*: a) Picture-based location identification during the adventure phase, b) collaborative strategic planning during the skirmish phase, and c) inspection of character properties using a mobile device.

In the skirmish phase a group of characters has to encounter evil villains in a strategic battle carried out on an interactive tabletop surface. The players have to cleverly choose their characters' specific capabilities to be victorious. Both, design and game mechanics are adapted from the original board game, where the outcome of a fight is depending on the combination of a roll of a dice and the character's attribute points. To increase the overall satisfaction while playing, the system relieves the players from inconvenient game mechanics, such as the measurement of distances, whereas typical table top elements like cards and figures are kept as tangible objects. Additional auxiliary, visual and auditive feedback supports the immersion of the players.

During the skirmish game phase players can access their characters using their mobile device. Afterwards the mobile device can be used to inspect character properties, perform a roll of a dice, or secretly lay out traps, that are triggered if a figure moves onto the corresponding location on the tabletop surface.

Multimodal Interaction

Touch, tangible, gesture and speech interfaces are utilized to foster the user experience and satisfaction of both game phases. Classic interaction with a touch interface, like one-finger tapping or dragging is supported by the direct manipulation of tangible objects. This provides traditional gameplay concepts like moving a pawn or playing a card. As an alternative to touch selections, various speech commands can be used to control the tabletop application. Moreover, an additional "throw a dice" gesture can be applied to activate a roll of a dice, either by performing a specific gesture with an empty hand above the interactive table or by shaking the mobile device.

Technical Details

The software components running on mobile devices are implemented for the *Android* operating system and utilize the *ZXing* QR decoder library and a picture-based approach [2] for location identification. A central server stores all game related information and provides access via *HTML* and *SQL* using *MySQL* and the *Play Framework*. Samsung's multitouch table *SUR40* serves as an interactive surface. The integrated software *PixelSense* from Microsoft provides tracking of position and orientation of fiducial markers ($1.9 \times 1.9\ cm$) as well as the detection of multitouch events. A leap motion sensor and a Sennheiser *EW 100 G3* microphone capture the data used for gesture and speech recognition. Speech recognition is performed by the *Dragon NaturallySpeaking* software. The software components running on the interactive table are implemented using *Simulator X* [4], a research software platform for realtime interactive systems. To compensate the limited internal hardware of the SUR40, the speech and gesture recognition are executed on an external computer by utilizing the distribution capabilities of Simulator X.

Future Work

Future efforts target three main aspects of the presented demonstration: (1) The exploration of game mechanics that are not feasible within a non-digital game scenario, e.g. highly dynamic environments or artificial players. (2) The enhancement of user experience and satisfaction by the incorporation of novel interaction techniques as well as by the evaluation of already implemented techniques. This includes the extension of the existing speech commands to a multimodal-speech and gesture-interface. (3) The technical realisation of the interactive tabletop scenario with alternative, affordable consumer-grade hardware.

Acknowledgements

The authors wish to thank Marvin Thäns, Sascha Link, and Pegasus Spiele for supporting the XRoads project.

References

[1] Connolly, T. M., Boyle, E. A., MacArthur, E., Hainey, T., and Boyle, J. M. A systematic literature review of empirical evidence on computer games and serious games. *Computers & Education 59* (2012), 661 – 686.

[2] Fischbach, M., Lugrin, J.-L., Latoschik, M. E., and Fendt, M. Picture-based localisation for pervasive gaming. In *Virtuelle und Erweiterte Realität, 11. Workshop der GI-Fachgruppe VR/AR* (2014).

[3] Fischbach, M., Zimmerer, C., Giebler-Schubert, A., and Latoschik, M. E. [DEMO] Exploring multimodal interaction techniques for a mixed reality digital surface. In *IEEE International Symposium on Mixed and Augmented Reality ISMAR* (2014).

[4] Latoschik, M., and Tramberend, H. Simulator X: A scalable and concurrent architecture for intelligent realtime interactive systems. In *Proceedings of the IEEE Virtual Reality Conference* (2011), 171–174.

[5] Leitner, J., Haller, M., Yun, K., Woo, W., Sugimoto, M., and Inami, M. Incretable, a mixed reality tabletop game experience. In *Proceedings of the 2008 International Conference on Advances in Computer Entertainment Technology*, ACM (2008), 9–16.

[6] Linaza, M., Gutierrez, A., and García, A. Pervasive augmented reality games to experience tourism destinations. In *Information and Communication Technologies in Tourism 2014*. Springer International Publishing, 2013, 497–509.

[7] Magerkurth, C., Cheok, A. D., Mandryk, R. L., and Nilsen, T. Pervasive games: bringing computer entertainment back to the real world. *Computers in Entertainment (CIE) 3*, 3 (2005), 4–4.

[8] Seifert, J., Simeone, A., Schmidt, D., Holleis, P., Reinartz, C., Wagner, M., Gellersen, H., and Rukzio, E. Mobisurf: Improving co-located collaboration through integrating mobile devices and interactive surfaces. In *Proceedings of the 2012 ACM International Conference on Interactive Tabletops and Surfaces*, ACM (2012), 51–60.

Multi-Touch Manipulation of Magic Lenses for Information Visualization

Ulrike Kister
Interactive Media Lab
Technische Universität Dresden
Dresden, Germany
ukister@acm.org

Patrick Reipschläger
Interactive Media Lab
Technische Universität Dresden
Dresden, Germany
patrick.reipschlaeger@
tu-dresden.de

Raimund Dachselt
Interactive Media Lab
Technische Universität Dresden
Dresden, Germany
dachselt@acm.org

Figure 1: Multiple lenses can be applied to explore the data set.

ITS 2014, November 16–19, 2014, Dresden, Germany.
ACM 978-1-4503-2587-5/14/11.
http://dx.doi.org/10.1145/2669485.2669528

Abstract
We introduce touch-enabled magic lenses that can be manipulated and parametrized through fluent interactions. Interaction with lenses for information visualization and data exploration has mostly been limited to single-user, single-function lenses. In this work, we present our prototype on lenses where lens function, parameters and combination of functions can be manipulated using fluent touch interaction. To achieve this, our tool consists of a widget-based approach for novice users as well as a set of continuous gestures for expert users. Additionally, we support the combination of lenses and thereby create a multi-purpose lens tool.

Author Keywords
Magic lenses; graph lenses; multi-touch interaction; information visualization.

ACM Classification Keywords
H.5.2 [Information interfaces and presentation (e.g., HCI)]: User Interfaces.

Introduction
Magic lenses [1] are focus and context tools that change the visual representation of the data in a region of interest within the visualization. Recently, Tominski et al. [8] presented a state-of-the-art report on interactive lenses in

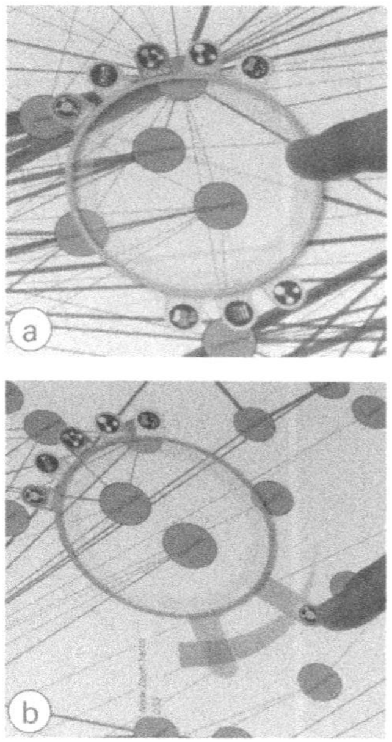

Figure 2: a) The radial touch menu presents different lens filters and their parameters.
b) Parameters can be adjusted using a slider which always snaps back to its original position.

visualization showing a multitude of application cases and data types where lenses can be helpful tools for exploration.

In previous work, lenses have mostly been discussed in terms of their individual lens filter. Few researchers have explored interaction with lenses, with mouse interaction being the prevalent technique for placing and adjusting magic lenses. However, as interactive surfaces become more common, we focus on using the potential of these devices for interactive lens manipulations.

This is not the first paper addressing lenses on interactive surfaces. However, they have mainly been applied to improve touch selection by magnifying a region of interest. One example of this is the FingerGlass approach by Käser et al. [3] who address target selection by presenting fluent bimanual interactions for lens creation and repositioning. For information visualization, lens manipulation has been applied recently to scatterplot exploration on tablets [5]. Here, a magnification lens is created and the magnification factor is set by dragging an element at the border of the lens.

Various lens filters have been proposed in research (e.g. [1, 6, 7]), magnification being only one of them. Often lens filters are specifically designed to give insight into a selected data type [8]. Each lens filter can have different filter-dependent parameters whose manipulation enhances the outcome of the filter. Additionally, the combination of different lens filters can yield better exploration tools [7]. To our knowledge, no work exists that discusses interaction for lens parameter adjustment and lens combination.

With this work, we contribute 1) fluent interaction with lenses, focusing on both novice and expert users,
2) touch-based techniques for lens adjustment, where we focus on the lens filter as a changeable attribute that can be switched and adjusted in place on the lens, and
3) the combination of different lens filters to form one coherent lens exploration tool.

Touch-enabled Magic Lenses

For the design of our lenses, we concentrated on creating consistent gestures and support fluent interaction for both novice and expert users alike. We developed each lens as an individual tool without global menus to support multiple active lenses and multi-user scenarios (Figure 1).

The interactive lenses presented in this work are circular or elliptical shaped tools. They are visually represented by a very thin visual border as to not occlude the data presented underneath. The border color encodes the currently selected lens filters (see Figure 3). The border is transparently enlarged to allow basic touch manipulations, such as drag for repositioning, pinch for scaling and two finger rotation.

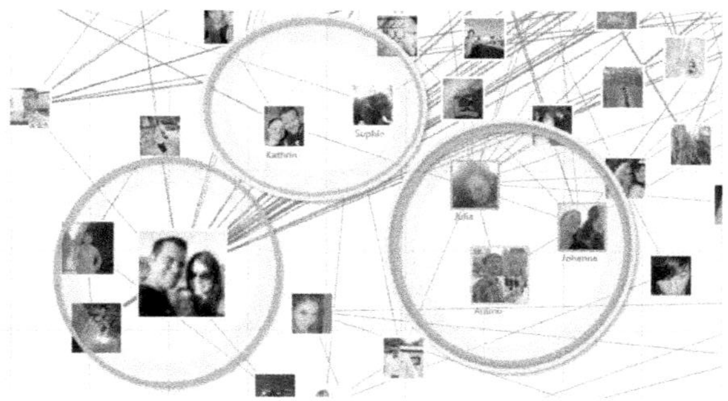

Figure 3: Lenses are shapes with a thin colored border. The color of the border describes the currently active lens filter. Lenses can have one single or multiple lens filters.

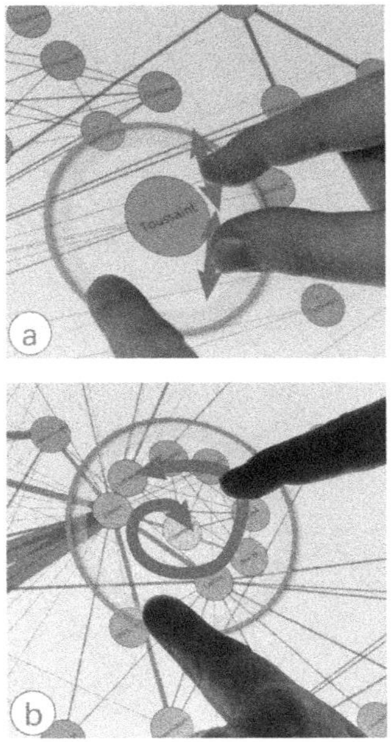

Figure 4: Two example gestures (symbolized by red arrows) who trigger a new lens function and adjust the main parameter.

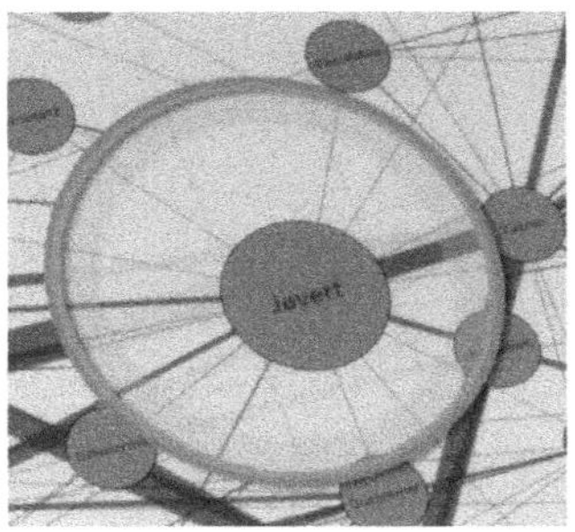

Figure 5: Lenses can be dragged on top of each other to combine their filters and create one unified lens.

Radial Touch Menu
We developed an approach of externalizing the lens filters and their parameters to the border of the lens. This way all parameters of the lens are visible to novice users. The radial touch menu is separated into a top part and a section at the bottom of the lens (see Figure 2a). In the upper menu, lens filters can be selected using a tap or drag the handle out from the lens. Different colors and icons support the recognition of the available lens filters.

In the bottom menu the parameters of the active filters are represented by their individual icon and a less saturated version of their filter color. These handles can be dragged out further and transform into be a slider thumb. They can be rotated around the border of the lens to adjust the individual filter parameter (see Figure 2b). When lifting the finger, the handle automatically snaps back to its original position. On renewed pull-out the slider has automatically adjusted, so that relative positioning is possible again.

Continuous Gestures
For efficient expert use, we also designed a gesture set where each gesture triggers a new lens filter. We focused on creating efficient and fluent interactions that can be grouped together to form a phrase [2]. Hence, we selected continuous gestures whose continuation immediately adjusts the main parameter of the activated filter. We present only two of the possible gestures in this work, to illustrate this principle. To activate a Fisheye magnification, we selected a simple pinch-gesture (see Figure 4a) where the relative distance between the two touch points adjusts the amount of distortion. A Bring Neighbors [7] filter can be triggered by dragging in a spiral movement (see Figure 4b), similar to the gesture in CycloZoom+ [4]. It symbolizes the pulling in of adjacent nodes, neighbors, for graph nodes. How much neighbors are drawn in is adjusted by the distance of the touch point to the center of the lens.

Combining Lenses
Due to insight from user tests, Tominski et al. [7] presented a *Composite Lens* which incorporates three fixed lens filters into one lens. We designed our touch-enabled magic lenses to allow flexible combination of lens filters. Lenses of about the same size can be dragged on top of each other and then snap together to form one multi-filter lens. Additionally, it is possible to simply add a filter to an existing lens using the previously described gesture set. We use a second finger on the border of the lens to distinguish the addition of filters from the simple replacement of the current lens filter. Figure 5 shows the combination of Fisheye [6] and Local Edge [7] filter for graph exploration, enlarging the node in focus and removing edge clutter simultaneously within one lens.

Implementation
To enable users to explore graph data and test our fluent interaction principle, we implemented our touch-enabled magic lens concept as a C#/WPF application running on a 27" Perceptive Pixel[1] display. We used graph exploration as an application case and implemented the graph visualization using QuickGraph[2] as graph toolkit and Graph#[3] for layouting purposes. Possible data sets are basic example graphs in graphML format, e.g., showing co-occurring diseases, or social networks in JSON format generated by the Facebook Graph API Explorer[4].

[1]http://www.perceptivepixel.com/
[2]http://quickgraph.codeplex.com/
[3]http://graphsharp.codeplex.com/
[4]http://developers.facebook.com/tools/explorer

Both the radial touch menu as well as the continuous gestures are implemented with currently five filters related to graph exploration. The radial menu and the continuous gesture set form one coherent concept where switching between gestures and menu-based manipulation is possible at any moment of interaction.

Conclusion

We present a graph exploration prototype demonstrating our concepts of fluent interaction with magic lenses. Unlike previous work, we focus on adjustment of the lens filter and its filter-dependent parameters. We present a widget-based approach that externalizes all possible filters and parameters to the border of the lens. This specifically supports novice users as all parameters are visible. We consciously refrain from using global menus to account for multi-user scenarios and large display setups. Additionally, we focused on a set of continuous gestures for expert users. These gestures allow activation of other filters, either by adding to or replacing the current filters. Allowing continuation after recognition, these gestures also adjust the main parameter of each lens filter. While our prototype is geared to graph exploration, the principles show great potential to be applied to other application areas.

Acknowledgements

This work was funded by the German Research Foundation (DFG) through the project GEMS - Graph Exploration and Manipulation on interactive Surfaces (DA 1319/3-1).

References

[1] Bier, E. A., Stone, M. C., Pier, K., Buxton, W., and DeRose, T. D. Toolglass and magic lenses: the see-through interface. In *Proc.*, SIGGRAPH '93, ACM (1993), 73–80.

[2] Buxton, W. Chunking and phrasing and the design of human-computer dialogues. In *Proc. IFIP World Computer Congress*, North Holland Publishers (1986), 475–480.

[3] Käser, D. P., Agrawala, M., and Pauly, M. Fingerglass: efficient multiscale interaction on multitouch screens. In *Proc.*, CHI '11, ACM (2011), 1601–1610.

[4] Malacria, S., Lecolinet, E., and Guiard, Y. Clutch-free panning and integrated pan-zoom control on touch-sensitive surfaces: the cyclostar approach. In *Proc.*, CHI '10, ACM (2010), 2615–2624.

[5] Sadana, R., and Stasko, J. Designing and implementing an interactive scatterplot visualization for a tablet computer. In *Proc.*, AVI '14, ACM (2014), 265–272.

[6] Sarkar, M., and Brown, M. H. Graphical fisheye views of graphs. In *Proc.*, CHI '92, ACM (1992), 83–91.

[7] Tominski, C., Abello, J., van Ham, F., and Schumann, H. Fisheye tree views and lenses for graph visualization. In *Proc.*, IV '06, IEEE Computer Society (Washington, DC, USA, 2006), 17–24.

[8] Tominski, C., Gladisch, S., Kister, U., Dachselt, R., and Schumann, H. A survey on interactive lenses in visualization. In *EuroVis State-of-the-Art Reports* (2014).

Demonstrating HuddleLamp: Spatially-Aware Mobile Displays for Ad-hoc Around-the-Table Collaboration

Roman Rädle
HCI Group
University of Konstanz
Roman.Raedle@uni-konstanz.de

Harald Reiterer
HCI Group
University of Konstanz
Harald.Reiterer@uni-konstanz.de

Hans-Christian Jetter
ICRI Cities
University College London
h.jetter@ucl.ac.uk

Yvonne Rogers
UCL Interaction Centre
University College London
y.rogers@ucl.ac.uk

Nicolai Marquardt
UCL Interaction Centre
University College London
n.marquardt@ucl.ac.uk

ITS '14, Nov 16-19 2014, Dresden, Germany
ACM 978-1-4503-2587-5/14/11.
http://dx.doi.org/10.1145/2669485.2669500

Abstract
We present HuddleLamp, a desk lamp with an integrated RGB-D camera that precisely tracks the movements and positions of mobile displays and hands on a table. This enables a new breed of spatially-aware multi-user and multi-device applications for around-the-table collaboration without an interactive tabletop. At any time users can add or remove displays and reconfigure them in space in an ad-hoc manner without the need of installing any software or attaching markers. Additionally, hands are tracked to detect interactions above and between displays, enabling fluent cross-device interactions. The demo consists of the technical implementation of HuddleLamp's hybrid sensing and a Web-based architecture for installation-free ad-hoc collaboration. We demonstrate our implementation by showing a variety of possible interaction techniques.

Author Keywords
Mobile devices; cross-device interactions; depth camera; ad hoc collaboration; society of devices; ubicomp ecologies.

ACM Classification Keywords
H.5.2 [Information Interfaces and Presentation]: Input

Introduction
We are witnessing an explosive growth of the number and density of powerful mobile devices around us. However, their great majority are still blind to the presence of other devices and performing tasks among them is usually tedious [1] and lacks recognizable guiding principles [7]. We envision a future in which mobile devices can contribute their interaction resources (e.g., their multi-touch displays) to a community of devices in their proximity that then serves as one seamless multi-device user interface (UI). At any time, users can dynamically compose and reconfigure this UI according to their current needs and the task at hand.

In this vision, users can seamlessly add or remove devices from the community in an ad-hoc fashion without explicit setup or pairing. Instead this happens implicitly as a by-product of natural use in space, for example, by bringing multiple devices to the same room, placing them side-by-side on a table or desk, and moving them around as needed. Ideally users will experience these co-located cooperating devices and reconfigurable displays as one seamless and natural UI for ad-hoc co-located collaboration.

As the first incarnation of this vision, we present HuddleLamp, a modified desk lamp with an integrated low-cost RGB-D camera that detects and identifies multiple mobile displays (e.g., smartphones or tablets) on desks or meeting tables and precisely tracks their spatial configuration and movements over time. Thereby users can add or remove off-the-shelf web-enabled devices of many different sizes in an ad-hoc fashion without prior installation of custom hardware (e.g., radio modules, IR markers) or any additional software. Due to the fully web- based architecture, no complex device pairing procedures are necessary; all a person needs to do to add a new device is opening the URL of the HuddleLamp on their device and putting it on the table so that it becomes visible to the lamp's camera. Additionally, HuddleLamp tracks users' hand positions above the surface to enable interactions between and above devices such as 'pick, drag, and drop'.

This enables a new kind of computer-supported around-the-table collaboration without interactive tabletops. Users can still sit around ordinary tables that can remain cluttered with non-digital objects (e.g., printouts, maps, notebooks) while their digital collaborations happen using spatially-aware mobile screens that blend into existing spatial and social practices. Unlike traditional interactive tabletops, HuddleLamp is portable and low-cost, so it can be used in improvised settings or where the costs for hardware and administration typically prohibit the use of large interactive tabletops, e.g., public libraries, schools, community centres.

Related Work
In order to enable cross-device interactions with co-located devices [5], the system first needs knowledge about the presence and position of other devices around it. Previous research has explored various techniques for establishing connections between co-located devices. Some techniques initiate a connection between devices after the user performs action sensed by the system [3]. Another approach is to use custom sensing hardware, for example infrared-, hall-, or radio-based position sensing [4,6]. More recently, researchers explored using the devices' built-in

Figure 1. HuddleLamp supports a device ecology of heterogeneous form factors and display sizes for ad-hoc around-the-table collaboration.

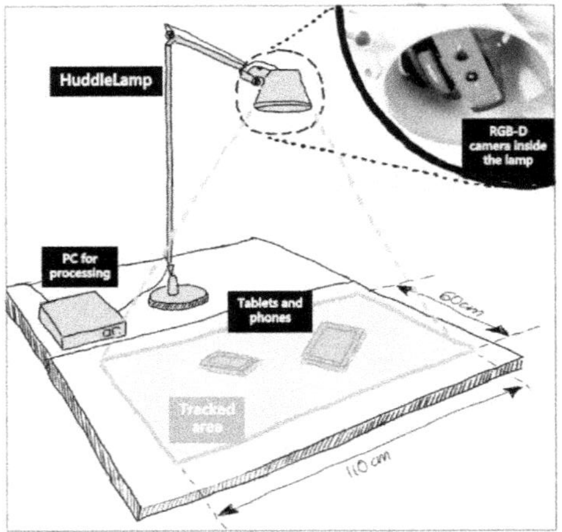

Figure 2. HuddleLamp setup with the modified desk lamp, the integrated RGB-D camera, and the PC for processing.

cameras to infer location information [9]. Alternatively, cameras positioned above a table can track the spatial layout of devices placed on the table below [8].

A special case of co-located mobile devices are (re)configurable tiled displays. For expressive interaction with digital content, the interaction space with digital surfaces can be extended beyond pure multi-touch interaction to include the space above the surface or around surfaces [2].

In HuddleLamp, we support a device ecology of heterogeneous form factors and display sizes that can be used in an ad-hoc fashion – all without requiring custom software as our platform uses entirely web-based standards. One important design goal of the HuddleLamp system is to enable similar cross-device interactions, around the ad-hoc assemblages of phones and tablets on a table (Figure 1).

HuddleLamp's Architecture

During the development of HuddleLamp, we generally used off-the-shelf hardware and free or open source software that can be easily acquired by other researchers for deployments outside our lab. In the following, we describe our technical setup and the essential architecture.

Hardware Components

The HuddleLamp uses a low-cost short range time-of-flight RGB-D camera which delivers a 1280x720 RGB colour image and a 320x240 depth image at 25 or 30 fps. It shares its technical specifications with a Creative Senz3D or SoftKinetic DepthSense 325. The camera is fixed to an Artemide Tolomeo Tavolo desk lamp (Figure 2) in which it replaces the light bulb (top right corner of Figure 2). Using the lamp, users can conveniently move the camera into its downward-facing operating position that lies 80cm above the horizontal surface to track. This results in a rectangular tracking region of approximately 110x60cm from which the camera receives sufficient RGB and depth information to track mobile devices, their spatial configurations, and users' hands and to distinguish them from non-interactive objects.

The camera was chosen for its small form factor (11x3x2.5cm) and the low noise in its depth data. Future versions of HuddleLamp could use next generation high-resolution and wide-angle depth cameras such as Kinect v2 to increase the size of the tracked area. However, we recommend time-of-flight rather than structured-light depth cameras. An advantage of the particular camera and its Perceptual SDK by Intel is that its RGB and depth images can be aligned without further calibration. Therefore it is easy to retrieve RGB values from the colour image for each pixel in the depth image and vice versa. This greatly facilitates realizing our hybrid sensing approach.

For vision processing and for hosting a web server for communication with the mobile devices, HuddleLamp uses a Windows multicore desktop PC or laptop (Figure 2, left). We have considered using small single-board computers that can be integrated directly into the lamp (e.g. Raspberry Pi) to make HuddleLamp truly portable. However, at this stage, the necessary vision processing and algorithms are too computationally expensive for achieving our targeted tracking rate of 25-30 fps with single-board PCs.

The software for the processing of the RGB and depth camera data was implemented with Microsoft .NET Framework 4.5.1 (C#/WPF) and the Emgu CV wrapper for accessing OpenCV with C#. For finding and decoding fiducial markers in the RGB stream we use the glyph decoder of the AForge.NET library[1].

System Architecture

The camera data is processed by the vision processing and the locations of all devices and hands are streamed to the connected mobile client devices using JSON and a web socket server. The clients access this stream using JavaScript from state-of-the-art browsers on mobile devices like Safari Mobile, Chrome, and Internet Explorer. Therefore an installation of native software on the devices is not required, which is of great importance for enabling ad-hoc scenarios.

For the collaborative applications, a shared data model implemented with the Meteor web framework[2] was used to synchronize application data across multiple devices. Meteor's data-driven protocol compensates for latency to achieve a reactive user interface.

Conclusion

We have described HuddleLamp, a sensing system in the form of a desk lamp with an integrated RGB-D camera that tracks the movements of multiple mobile displays on a table for around-the-table collaboration. Our implementation based on a hybrid sensing approach detects mobile screens by exploiting their optical properties in the IR range and tracks fiducial markers to distinguish them from other objects or users' hands. We also introduced HuddleLamp's web-based architecture for ad-hoc collaboration that enables users to add or remove displays and reconfigure them in space at any time without installing any software or attaching markers.

[1] http://www.aforgenet.com - AForge.NET library

[2] http://www.meteor.com - Open Source Web Platform

References

[1] Greenberg, S., Marquardt, N., Ballendat, T., Diaz-Marino, R., and Wang, M. Proxemic Interactions: The New Ubicomp? *interactions 18*, January (2011), 42–50.

[2] Hilliges, O., Izadi, S., Wilson, A.D., Hodges, S., Garcia-Mendoza, A., and Butz, A. Interactions in the air: adding further depth to interactive tabletops. *In Proc. of UIST '09*, ACM Press (2009), 139–148.

[3] Hinckley, K., Ramos, G., Guimbretiere, F., Baudisch, P., and Smith, M. Stitching: pen gestures that span multiple displays. *In Proc. of AVI '04*, ACM Press (2004), 23.

[4] Lucero, A., Holopainen, J., and Jokela, T. Pass-them-around: collaborative use of mobile phones for photo sharing. *In Proc of CHI '11*, ACM Press (2011), 1787–1796.

[5] Lucero, A., Jones, M., Jokela, T., and Robinson, S. Mobile Collocated Interactions: Taking an Offline Break Together. *interactions 20*, 2 (2013), 26.

[6] Merrill, D., Kalanithi, J., and Maes, P. Siftables: towards sensor network user interfaces. *In Proc. of TEI '07*, ACM Press (2007), 75.

[7] Oulasvirta, A. When users "do" the Ubicomp. *interactions 15*, 2 (2008), 6.

[8] Piazza, T., Zhao, S., Ramos, G., Yantaç, A.E., and Fjeld, M. Dynamic duo: phone-tablet interaction on tabletops. *In Proc. of CHI EA '13*, ACM Press (2013), 2803–2804.

[9] Schmitz, A., Li, M., Schönefeld, V., and Kobbelt, L. Ad-Hoc Multi-Displays for Mobile Interactive Applications. *The Eurographics Association*, (2010), 45–52.

FlexiWall: Exploring Layered Data with Elastic Displays

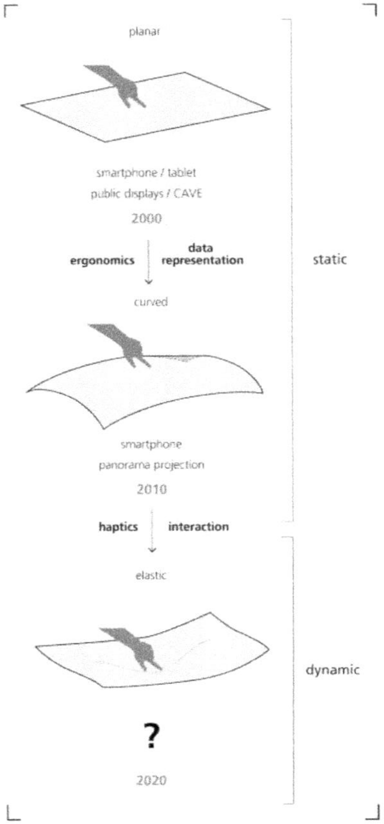

Figure 1. Evolution of interactive surfaces: From planar touch screens to elastic displays.

Mathias Müller
Technische Universität Dresden
Chair of Media Design
01062 Dresden
mathias.mueller@tu-dresden.de

Ingmar S. Franke
Technische Universität Dresden
Chair of Media Design
01062 Dresden
ingmar.franke@tu-dresden.de

Anja Knöfel
Technische Universität Dresden
Chair of Media Design
01062 Dresden
anja.knoefel@tu-dresden.de

Rainer Groh
Technische Universität Dresden
Chair of Media Design
01062 Dresden
rainer.groh@tu-dresden.de

Thomas Gründer
Technische Universität Dresden
Chair of Media Design
01062 Dresden
thomas.gruender@tu-dresden.de

ITS 2014, November 16–19, 2014, Dresden, Germany.
ACM 978-1-4503-2587-5/14/11.
http://dx.doi.org/10.1145/2669485.2669529

Abstract
By their deformable screen-materials elastic displays and projection screens provide physical three-dimensional interaction modalities like push, pull or bend. Compared with conventional Multi-Touch displays they offer an additional interaction dimension which can be used to explore data. In this article we describe the *FlexiWall*, a large elastic display, and several example applications using layered data sets. The exploration of several layers and correlations between these is not common to traditional user interfaces, where the interaction is often constrained to two dimensions. Therefore, new forms of interaction are introduced. We furthermore propose additional techniques and tools to explore layered data sets, e.g. utilizing transparent objects when interacting with elastic displays.

Author Keywords
Elastic Displays; Tangible User Interfaces; Layered Data; Visualization; Interaction

ACM Classification Keywords
H.5.m. Information interfaces and presentation (e.g., HCI): Miscellaneous.

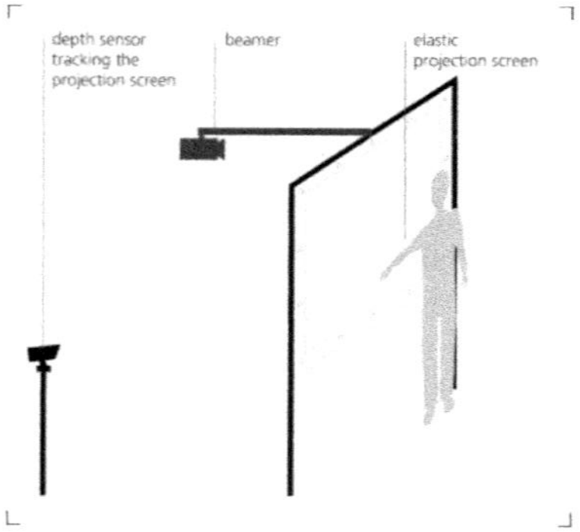

Figure 2. System setup. A Depth camera tracks the deformation of a elastic projection screen and applies this to the image on per pixel basis.

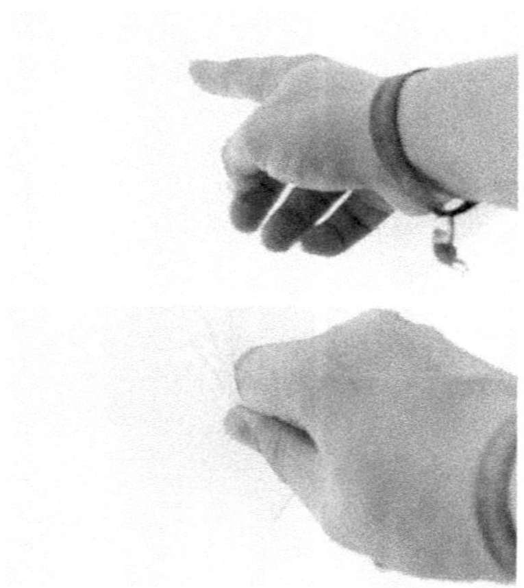

Figure 3. Interacting with the surface using push and pull gestures.

Introduction

Within the last decade, Multi-Touch devices have evolved from a research topic to consumer hardware. Nowadays, this technology and corresponding interaction techniques have been widely adopted, being used not only for smartphones and tablets but also for large public displays. In parallel, the technological development seeks for new designs and shapes for these devices to improve ergonomics and information representation [1]. Interactively deformable displays represent a further advancement in this direction which is widely discussed in research [2,3,4,5] (cf. **Figure 1**).

By their material, these types of displays offer additional ways to interact. Whereas touch addresses the two-dimensional navigation and manipulation of data, the interactive deformation of the display surface increases the expressiveness of gestures and adds additional interaction dimensions. Deformable displays offer the opportunity to explore complex datasets and provide haptic feedback about actions and the structure of the data. They can be classified into *flexible* and *elastic* displays [6]. Devices of the first category maintain their shape when the user does not interact. In contrast, the deformation of elastic displays is ephemeral so that they always return in their initial state when not being touched.

In this paper we present an implementation of an elastic display wall and propose the use of transparent objects as additional tools to improve the control of the surface deformation.

System Description

The presented system, *FlexiWall*, originates from the concept of the *DepthTouch* [7]. It consists of a large vertical fabric surface as back projection screen. The size of the projected image is about 2.25m x 1.25m. The deformation of the fabric is tracked by a Microsoft™ Kinect® which is positioned next to the projector (**Figure 2**). The imagery used in the prototype consists of multiple layers which are blended into each other on a per pixel basis according to the measured depth from the Kinect®. This enables multiple users to dig locally through the different layers by pushing or pulling the surface independently.(**Figure 3**).

Layered Data

The use of layered data sets on elastic displays offers users a variety of possible applications, such as the exploration of MRT images [4], the manipulation of time-based data [2] or map exploration [8]. Further data types include zoomable data or the interaction with 3D objects and spaces [9]. In this paper we focus on the interaction with different data layers. The *FlexiWall* system demonstrates exploration of layered data with several example use cases.

One example is a historic map where each layer contains the political situation at a certain time (**Figure 4**). The locally constrained deformation allows exploring the historical development of an area. At the same time, the overall context is preserved, so that the user can compare the state of an area with other regions at different time layers. A related use case is the exploration of geological data or layered maps by deforming the surface. As the surface is softly deformed, the area around the finger reveals a profile of the layers nearby.

Figure 4. Historical map of Central Europe (1500, 1812, and 1993) [14]. An elastic displays offers the opportunity to explore the different time layers by deforming the surface.

Figure 5. Different versions of a painting by Vermeer [15].

Another example resides in the context of arts. The different layers visualize the genesis of a painting (**Figure 5**). The user can interactively explore the different versions of a painting by deforming the surface.

The third use case originates from photography and image manipulation. The layers contain images with variable focal length, similar to focus stacking techniques [10] or light field photography [11]. The user can interactively adjust the focal plane of the image or even specify different focal areas (**Figure 6**). The underlying concepts could be transferred to other tasks related to image editing such as image composition or definition of image masks.

Interaction techniques

In the recent past we have seen several approaches of deformable displays and different discussions regarding the possible fields of application (e.g. [2,5]). One example of an empirical study using elastic displays was conducted by Troiano et al. [12]. They explored the different gestures used to interact with deformable displays. Several tasks in 2D and 3D space were used to determine different gesture sets. The majority of tasks in this study were manipulation tasks on a particular object.

When implementing the use cases discussed before, we noted that user's often used our prototype I a slightly different way. In our examples the dominant task is to 'poke' the virtual space, which can represent a real (scaled) physical space (e.g. volumetric data), time layers or a semantic mapping of depth to specific image parameters (e.g. focal length or mask intensity). Our informal observations reveal that mostly five gestures for exploration task with flexible displays are used: push with the flat hand, push with the index finger, pull with two fingers, form a straight line or expand an area with both hands. This corresponds with the findings of the mentioned study. However, additional to these gestures most users try to enlarge and stabilize the area of the deformation. By using the sides of the hands or the upper arms it is possible to span a planar region on the surface and to move it through the space. Especially when using the arms to define a larger area, the users are very close to the screen and therefore lose track of the overall image context. Additionally, the surface tension of the fabric prevents to form a real planar area. These observations led to the concept to use transparent objects as additional interaction element.

Use of Tangibles for exploration

We created different forms of flat transparent objects which are fixed on the projection screen using small magnets on each side of the surface. By pushing the transparent object into the surface the user can form complex reliefs. The transparent object can be used like a lens (e.g. [13]), specifying intersection planes between different layers or just to explore a larger region of one specific layer. This way, the user can control the deformation of the surface more precisely without losing the direct haptic feedback from the surface. Additionally, the occlusion by the hands is minimized. When interacting on different points of the surface, the use of ridged objects simplifies the control of the deformation. One major drawback is that the magnets we use on the tangibles are too weak for pulling the surface towards the user due to the large surface tension. Furthermore, due to the stretch capabilities of the fabric, the deformation is not constrained to the area of the tangible, but also affects regions nearby.

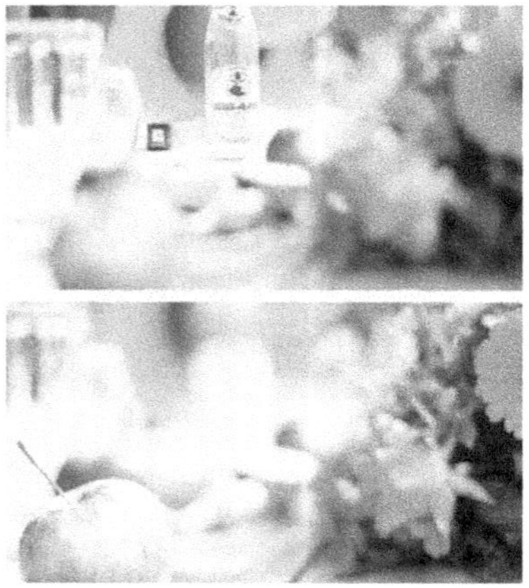

Figure 6. Example images of a scene with different focal lengths. The FlexiWall allows to adjust the focus based on several images like these.

Further research directions

Based on informal observations of several test users, we will investigate further how users perceive the system and how they interact with different types of data in more detail. There are several additional concepts which address some of the problems mentioned in the article. One idea is to span a grid of cords behind the fabric to create a grid which constrains the deformation of the fabric to the affected cell. We also want to experiment with different fabric, to find the best compromise between elasticity and precision of interaction and regarding tracking capabilities. Furthermore, we always look for additional use cases which may transport the concept of the elastic display in a context of productive use.

Acknowledgements

This work has been supported by the European Social Fund and the Free State of Saxony (Junior Research Group *CogITo – Cognitive Interface Technologies*, project no. 100076040).

References

[1] Roudaut, A., Pohl, H., and Baudisch, P., 2011. Touch Input on Curved Surfaces. In *Proc. CHI 2011*, ACM, New York.

[2] Cassinelli, A. and Ishikawa, M., 2005. Khronos Projector. In *ACM SIGGRAPH '05. Emerging Technologies.*, ACM, New York.

[3] Lee, S.-S., Kim, S., Jin, B., Choi, E., Kim, B., Jia, X., Kim, D., and Lee, K.-p., 2010. How Users Manipulate Deformable Displays as Input Devices. In *Proc. CHI '10*, ACM, New York, 1647–1656.

[4] Lepinski, J. and Vertegaal, R., 2011. Cloth Displays: Interacting with Drapable Textile Screens. In *Proc. TEI '11*, ACM, New York, 285–288.

[5] Yun, K., Song, J., Youn, K., Cho, S., and Bang, H., 2013. ElaScreen: Exploring Multi-Dimensional Data using Elastic Screen. In *CHI'13 Extended Abstracts*, ACM, New York, 1311–1316.

[6] Gründer, Kammer, Brade and Groh, 2013. Towards a Design Space for Elastic Displays. In *CHI 2013 Workshop: Displays Take New Shape*, ACM, New York.

[7] Peschke, J., Göbel, F., Gründer, T., Keck, M., Kammer, D., and Groh, R., 2012. DepthTouch: An Elastic Surface for Tangible Computing. In *Proc. AVI 2012*, ACM, New York, 770–771.

[8] Stevenson, A., Perez, C., and Vertegaal, R., 2011. An Inflatable Hemispherical Multi-touch Display. In *Proc. TEI '11*, ACM, New York, 289–292.

[9] Franke, I. S., Müller, M., Gründer, T., and Groh, R. FlexiWall: Interaction in-between 2D and 3D Interfaces. In *Proc. HCII 2014*, Springer, Berlin, 415-420.

[10] Qian, Q., Gunturk, B. K., and Batur, A. U., 2013. Joint Focus Stacking and High Dynamic Range Imaging. In *IS&T/SPIE Electronic Imaging*. SPIE Proceedings.

[11] Ng, R., 2006. *Digital Light Field Photography*. Dissertation, Stanford University.

[12] Troiano, G. M., Pedersen, E. W., and Hornbæk, K., 2014. User-Defined Gestures for Elastic, Deformable Displays. In *Proc. AVI '14*, ACM, New York, 1–8.

[13] Spindler, M., Stellmach, S., and Dachselt, R. PaperLens: Advanced magic lens interaction above the tabletop. In *Proc. ITS 2009*, ACM, New York, 69-76.

[14] IEG-MAPS · Server for digital historical maps http://www.ieg-maps.uni-mainz.de/enter.htm

[15] Sleczek, E. 2010. Johannes Vermeer. Brieflesendes Mädchen am offenen Fenster. Staatliche Kunstsammlungen Dresden, Gemäldegalerie Alte Meister, Galerie-Nr. 1335. Computergestützte Simulation einzelner Stadien der Bildentstehung. In Neidhardt, U. (Ed.): *Der frühe Vermeer. Exhibition Catalogue*, Staatliche Kunstsammlungen Dresden, Dresden, 92-93.

Demonstration and Applications of Fiberio: A Touchscreen That Senses Fingerprints

Sven Köhler
Hasso Plattner Institute
Potsdam, Germany
sven.koehler@hpi.de

Christian Holz
Yahoo Labs
Sunnyvale CA
christianh@yahoo-inc.com

Patrick Baudisch
Hasso Plattner Institute
Potsdam, Germany
patrick.baudisch@hpi.de

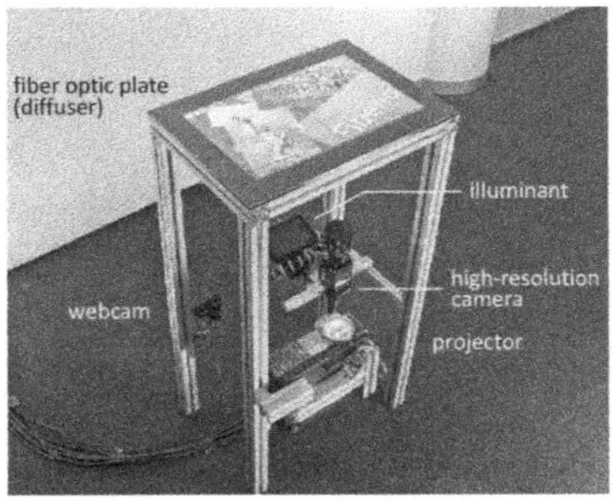

Figure 1: Fiberio is a rear-projected tabletop system that identifies users based on their fingerprints during each interaction. The key that allows Fiberio to display an image *and at the same time* sense fingerprints is its screen material: a fiber optic plate. The setup we use is a standard diffuse illumination setup, except for the diffuser.

ITS 2014, November 16–19, 2014, Dresden, Germany.
ACM 978-1-4503-2587-5/14/11.
http://dx.doi.org/10.1145/2669485.2669530

Abstract
We present a demonstration and applications of Fiberio, a rear-projected multitouch table that identifies users biometrically based on their fingerprints *during* each touch interaction. Fiberio accomplishes this using a new type of screen material: a large fiber optic plate. The plate *diffuses* light on transmission, thereby allowing it to act as projection surface. At the same time, the plate *reflects* light specularly, which produces the contrast required for fingerprint sensing. Fiberio additionally offers all the functionality known from diffused illumination systems and is the first interactive tabletop that authenticates users during touch interaction without the need for any identification tokens.

Author Keywords
Touchscreens; multitouch; user identification; fingerprints.

ACM Classification Keywords
H5.2 [Information interfaces and presentation]: User Interfaces. Input devices & strategies.

Introduction
Several researchers have proposed techniques that allow interactive tabletop systems to distinguish users during interaction. A number of existing approaches address this challenge: they either require users to carry identification tokens [7,9] or they can only distinguish among a small group of users [1,8].

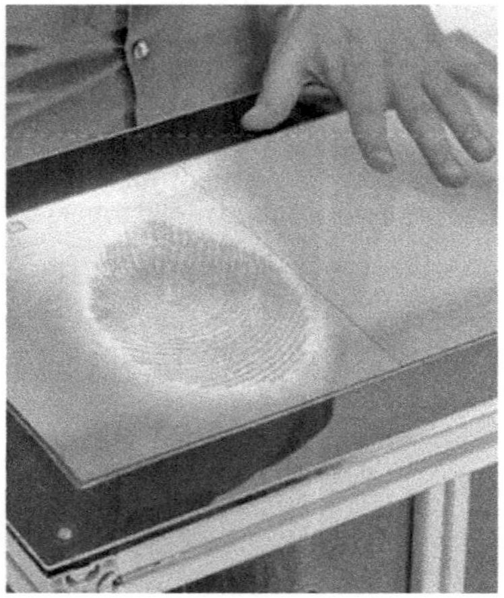

Figure 2: Fiberio is displaying a region of its high-resolution raw input image, which reveals the user's fingerprint.

Figure 3: A fiber optic plate diffuses incoming light into a ring, here from a laser pointer. A fiber plate with very small-diameter fibers (6μm) blurs ring diffusion. This scatters the light into all directions, which makes for good light diffusion and produces an image on the screen that is even visible from extreme angles.

Researchers have pointed to fingerprint recognition as a possible solution to the problem. Prototypes of such interaction include a fingerprint scanner placed *next* to the touchscreen [10] and an interactive fingerprint scanner without a screen [3].

Scanning fingerprints on a surface that *simultaneously* produces visual output needs to solve two contradicting requirements: 1) The screen has to reveal fingerprints, which requires a *specular* surface. 2) To be used as a display, the screen needs to produce an image from the rear-projection, which requires a *diffuse* surface.

In this demo, we show Fiberio [2], a multitouch table that recognizes fingerprints during touch interaction.

Fiberio

Fiberio's hardware configuration is essentially a *diffused illumination* [6] setup: a 19" screen ("diffuser"), a projector that rear-projects onto the screen, an infrared illuminant that illuminates the screen from behind, and cameras that observe touch input on the screen.

Fiberio's key difference from a regular diffused illumination setup is the nature of the diffuser: a 3mm thick, 4233dpi fiber optic plate. Its 40 million optical fibers run perpendicular to the surface and transmit light between the top and the bottom of the screen.

This fiber optic plate resolves the contradiction mentioned above. The fiber optic plate (1) diffuses light on transmission. This causes the light coming from the projector located below the screen to scatter, allowing users to see the image on the surface from all locations around the table. (2) The fiber optic plate creates a specific type of specular reflection: *frustrated Fresnel reflection*, which is different from the type of reflection used in FTIR-based tabletop systems. This setup causes the infrared light that illuminates the plate from below to produce a visible contrast between fingerprint ridges and valleys, which allows the high-resolution infrared camera below the table to capture fingerprints (Figure 2). Because of the fiber optic plate, Fiberio is capable of *simultaneously* displaying images and capturing fingerprints.

Working Principle

As explained above, the key innovation behind Fiberio is that the fiber optic plate allows the screen to serve as a *diffuse* surface for projection and simultaneously act as a *reflective* surface for fingerprint scanning. We now describe the details of the optical path that enables this. Please find additional details in our paper [2].

Producing output using diffuse transmission
The diffusion of projected images inside Fiberio's fiber optic plate is the result of two independent effects:

Ring diffusion: As shown in Figure 3, light rays that enter a fiber optic bundle form a cone on exit. This cone manifests itself as a *ring* on a projection surface, here a table surface 5cm below the fiber optic bundle.

Microstructural effects inside fibers: A fiber optic plate made from small-diameter fibers produces a highly diffuse light scattering (Figure 3), which makes Fiberio's projected image visible from all sides. At 6μm, each fiber is only an order of magnitude larger than the wavelength of the guided light, causing transmitted rays to scatter due to diffraction effects.

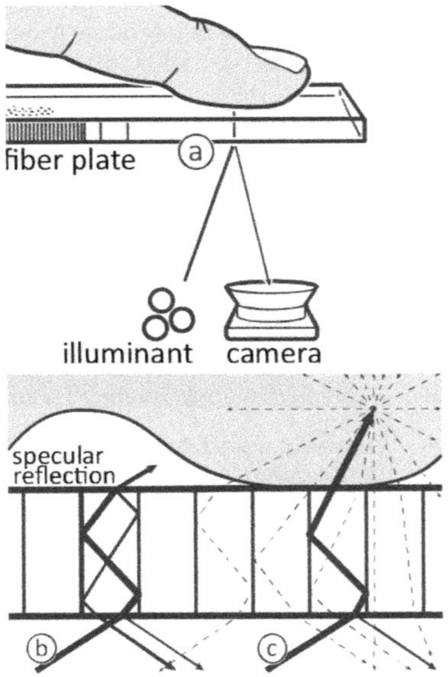

Figure 4: (a) The illuminant shines light onto the fiber optic plate. (b) A portion of the incoming light is reflected at the top of the fiber, traveling back down the fiber, where the camera observes it. (c) A fingerprint ridge touching the fiber, in contrast, frustrates the reflection at the top end of the fiber, so that only little light travels back down the fiber, causing this spot to appear dark to the camera.

Sensing fingerprints using frustrated reflections
The specular reflection of light at the *top* surface of the fiber optic plate is what allows Fiberio to capture fingerprints. These reflections when light *exits* fibers.

Fiberio shines infrared light onto the fiber optic plate from below (Figure 4a). Some light is reflected at the bottom surface, but most light enters and travels up the fibers (Figure 4b). A large portion of the light exits the fibers, but the remaining portion is reflected at the top surface, travels back down inside the fibers and exits at the bottom, where Fiberio's camera observes it. Due to the reflection at the top surface, locations of fingerprint valleys and areas around the finger appear "brighter" in the resulting image.

If a fingerprint ridge makes contact with the top end of the fiber (Figure 4c), the reflection at the top surface is frustrated and *almost all* light exits the glass fibers. Only a negligible fraction of light travels back down the fiber, so that this point appears "dark" to the camera.

Details on Hardware Setup

As shown in Figure 1, Fiberio offers a 16"×10" screen surface (19" diagonal), which consists of two tiled fiber optic plates (Incom B7D59-6). The BenQ short-throw projector pointed at the screen offers a resolution of 1024×768px. A hot mirror in front of the projector prevents interference with the cameras.

We use a high-resolution camera (Teledyne Falcon2, 4000×3000px, 60fps) to observe a sub-region of the surface (20cm×15cm). We supplement this approach with a web camera to enable touch interaction across the entire surface (Sony PS3, 640×480px, 75fps).

Image processing

Fiberio locates and tracks all touches based on the low-resolution camera, implementing a typical diffused illumination processing pipeline [6]. When touches enter the region observed by the high-resolution camera, Fiberio locates fingerprints, extracts them along with their features, and matches features against the records stored in its fingerprint database.

Fingerprint processing pipeline
To extract the locations and directions of fingerprint features, i.e., ridge endings and bifurcations (so-called *minutiae*), which allow identifying users, we implemented the algorithms commonly used to process fingerprints [5]. Figure 5 illustrates our pipeline. Our paper contains additional details [2].

Fiberio runs touch recognition, fingerprint extraction, matching, and graphics using parallel threads, allowing it to stays responsive to user input at all times. Since processing fingerprints is computationally expensive, we implemented our pipeline in CUDA 4.2 to run on the GPU (NVidia GTX 680), which allows our system to run at interactive rates.

Demo Applications

Based on the system described above, we have implemented the following applications, which we intend to show at the conference:

Regular multitouch interaction: We have a touch-based menu system and a photo sorting application, which demonstrates traditional multitouch interaction.

Raw image viewer: This is the fundament of the software part of the system: the raw image, which reveals the contrast we obtain between fingerprint ridges and valleys while projecting onto the surface of the table.

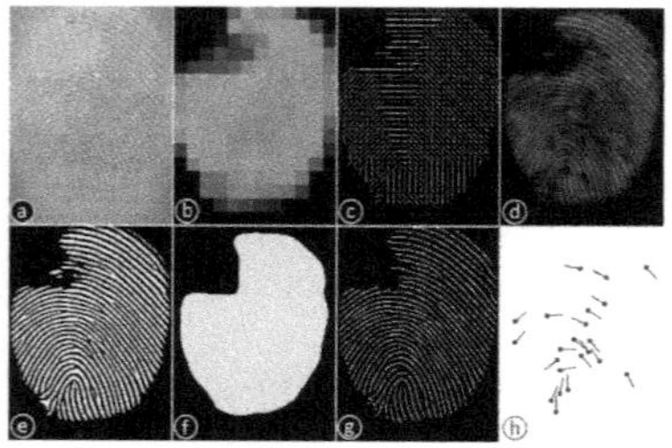

Figure 5: Fingerprint processing pipeline (images are cropped). (a) Raw image we obtain from the camera, (b) areas of high standard deviation determine the location of fingerprints, (c) flow field indicate the directions of ridges, (d) a Gabor filter enhances the contrast, (e) binarized fingerprint, (f) mask, (g) thinned ridges to (h) extract the locations and orientations of all fingerprint features, which we compare against a database of records using Bozorth matching.

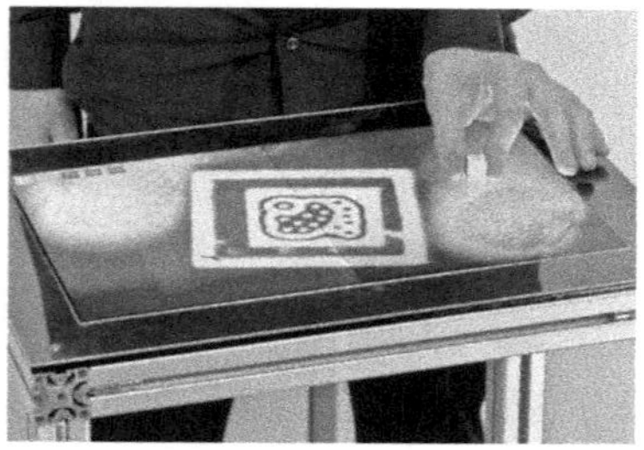

Figure 6: Fiberio recognizes touch, but also hovering objects (here fingers) as well as fiducial markers. The fiducial marker on this tangible object measures only 3mm×3mm.

This view also demonstrates Fiberio's suitability for any application that uses fiduciary markers.

Guardian fingerprint scanner: This application is modeled after the use of fingerprint scanners at airports. While this process is typically aided by an agent, our demo guides the user with visual feedback as they use it.

iPhone user interface: This application allows applications with personal data (e.g., Mail), only to be opened by the owner, while denying a touch from other users.

Conclusions

We presented a demonstration of Fiberio [2], a touchscreen that senses fingerprints. The key to making this possible is the fiber optic plate, which offers both specular reflection and diffuse transmission.

Fiberio's key contribution is a touchscreen that performs user identification and secure authentication during interaction. At the same time, Fiberio implements a standard diffused illumination table. This results in additional desirable properties, such as the ability to recognize fiducial markers and detect objects that hover above the surface, such as the user's fingers and hands as shown in Figure 6.

In summary, Fiberio opens up a lot of new possibilities for interactive systems. For fifteen years, researchers have hypothesized the existence of a touchscreen with biometric authentication, be it for activity logging [1], high degree-of-freedom touch input [10], and high-precision touch input [3, 4]. These are all possible based on the principles of Fiberio.

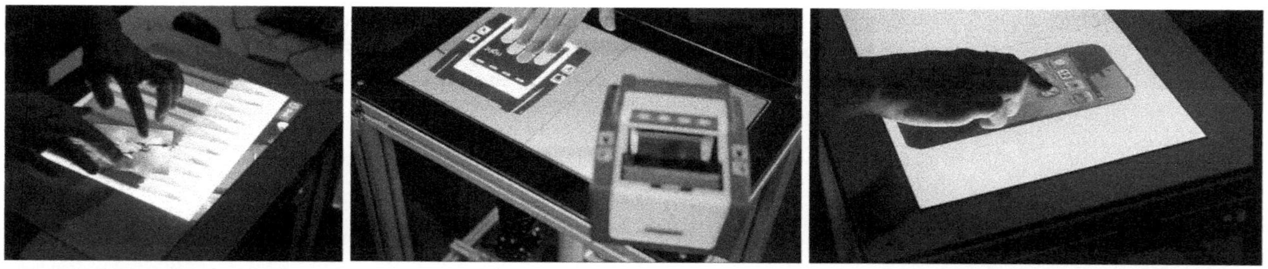

References

1. Dietz, P. and Leigh, D. DiamondTouch: a Multi-User Touch Technology. *Proc. UIST '01*, 219–226.
2. Holz, C. and Baudisch, P. Fiberio: A Touchscreen That Senses Fingerprints. *Proc. UIST '13*, 41–50.
3. Holz, C. and Baudisch, P. The Generalized Perceived Input Point Model and How to Double Touch Accuracy by Extracting Fingerprints. *Proc. CHI '10*, 581–590.
4. Holz, C. and Baudisch, P. Understanding Touch. *Proc. CHI '11*, 2501–2510
5. Maltoni, D., Maio, D., Jain, A., Prabhakar, S. Handbook of Fingerprint Recognition. *Springer*, 2009.
6. Matsushita, N. and Rekimoto, J. HoloWall: Designing a Finger, Hand, Body, Object Sensitive Wall. *Proc. UIST '97*, 209–210.
7. Olwal, A. and Wilson, A.D. SurfaceFusion: Unobtrusive Tracking of Everyday Objects in Tangible User Interfaces. *Proc. GI '08*, 235–242.
8. Richter, S., Holz, C. and Baudisch, P. Bootstrapper: Recognizing Tabletop Users by their Shoes. *Proc. CHI '12*, 1249–1252.
9. Roth, V., Schmidt, P. and Güldenring, B. The IR Ring: Authenticating Users' Touches on a Multi-touch Display. *Proc. UIST '10*, 259–262.
10. Sugiura, A. and Koseki, Y. A User Interface Using Fingerprint Recognition: Holding Commands and Data Objects on Fingers. *Proc. UIST '98*, 71–79.

ComforTable - A Tabletop for Relaxed and Playful Interactions in Museums

Michael Storz[1]
storz@informatik.tu-chemnitz.de

Kalja Kanellopoulos[2]
kalk@phil.tu-chemnitz.de

Claudia Fraas[2]
fraas@phil.tu-chemnitz.de

Maximilian Eibl[1]
eibl@informatik.tu-chemnitz.de

[1]Media Informatics
Technische Universiät Chemnitz
Chemnitz, Germany

[2]Media Communication
Technische Universiät Chemnitz
Chemnitz, Germany

ITS 2014, November 16–19, 2014, Dresden, Germany.
ACM 978-1-4503-2587-5/14/11.
http://dx.doi.org/10.1145/2669485.2669531

Abstract
We present the *ComforTable* - an all-in-one interactive tabletop system with integrated seats and a camera based user tracking system. The seats allow groups of users relaxed interactions with the interface. The system and its applications are made for and tested in museums and exhibitions. A card game and a pong game support up to six players playing competitively together. The tracking system recognizes persons approaching the table. This information is used to blend in helpful instructions and interaction options next to the users's position.

Author Keywords
Multi-touch tabletops; interactive surfaces; museums; games; user-tracking

ACM Classification Keywords
H.5.2 [Information Interfaces and Presentation:]: User Interfaces - Interaction Styles.

Introduction
In public spaces like museums visitors often come in couples or groups like families and school classes. Not only do they want to share their experience of the exhibition with one another but organize their actions and activities in relation to others.[8] Since interactive tabletops and surfaces (ITS) can allow simultaneous

Figure 1: Sitting Persons. *Natural History Museum Berlin*

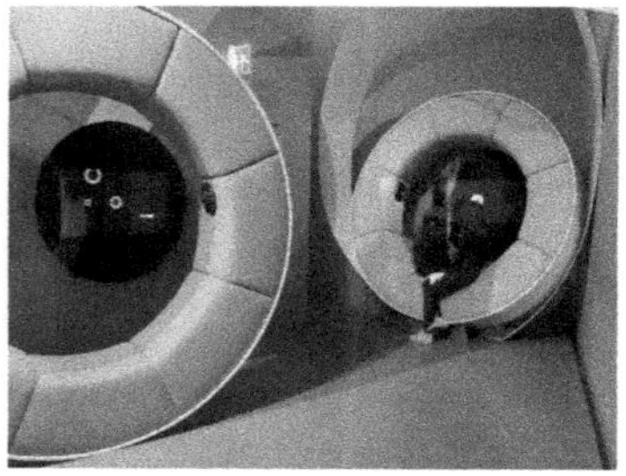

Figure 2: Combined with an interface, seating furniture can facilitate the interaction as well as attract people to use the system. *Jewish Museum Berlin*

interaction of several users, museums are an ideal application area for this kind of devices. But in the wild usage of ITS in exhibitions comes with many challenges. The diversity of users ranges from children to elderly or disabled persons, therefore heterogeneous requirements have to be fulfilled in terms of accessibility. Besides accessibility the robustness of the physical setup and the applications are very important. Complex setups of sensors augmenting ITS are usually hard to integrate in such environments. The proposed system *ComforTable* [5] faces these challenges as described in the following:

1. It supplies a robust physical setup with an arrangement of integrated elements for seating and standing as well as free spaces allowing a heterogeneity of users comfortable access to the system (including wheelchair users).
2. It includes a camera based user tracking system supplying the applications with positions of users and potential users in proximity to the table.
3. *ComforTable* includes two applications that allow simultaneous and playful interaction for up to six players.
4. The system was tested and refined in several empirical studies, conducted in controlled settings as well as in the wild by means of ethnography. The studies proved the system's physical robustness, unravelled usability issues and helped evolve its applications.

The *ComforTable* is a joint product of a interdisciplinary cooperation between social scientists and computer scientists.

Related Work

A growing number of museums is using ITS systems in their exhibitions. Companies like *ideum* in the US and Canada or *Lightwell* in Australia are supplying many museums with custom ITS installations. Most of these installations like the *Electromagnetic Spectrum*[1] or *Yiwara Kuju*[2] require people to stand or even move around the surface to explore the full content. For collaborative or competitive games in such contexts as in [4], this interaction style might eventually be tiring for the users, so that seating furniture can aid and lengthen the interactions with a system. Figure 1 shows that seating furnitures in museums are well attended places. Combined with an interface, as shown in Figure 2, they can facilitate the interaction as well as attract people to use the system.

The integration of additional sensors into ITS systems holds great promise, since sensed properties can as in [7] be integrated into a variety of new interaction styles. However these developments often do not transfer easily from a lab setting into a public space e.g. the mounting of sensors can be difficult or even impossible. Several approaches therefore try to integrate sensors into the installations. In the case of [6] and [3] an array of integrated IR-sensors is used to detect users of the system and to augment applications with this type of information.

ComforTable

The *ComforTable* (see Figure 4 and Figure 3) consists of an 82 cm high interactive surface integrated into a robust framing made of medium density fiberboard (MDF). Four legs hold this framing, serving as connection points to the seating elements and housing the PC driving the system. The connected elements have three different heights of 60, 45, and 20 cm and have different materials on top

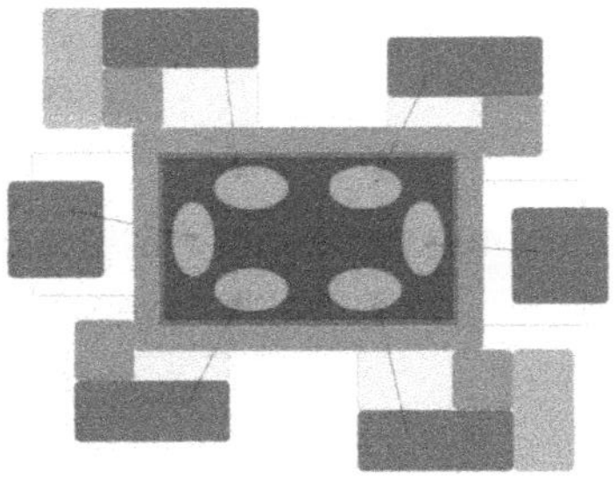

Figure 3: Schematic top-view of comfortable.

Figure 5: a/b Users choose between different standing and seating combinations.

according to their purpose of use. The 60 cm high elements have cushions on top and are intended for sitting.

The 45 cm elements have a carpet-like surface and are meant for sitting and kneeling. The 20 cm elements have a brushed steel surface and serve smaller children as a step to reach the surface. The overall setup facilitates a variety of different sitting positions but is not limit users that prefer to stand. Two flexible solitary stools of 45 cm on the short sides can be pushed away to enable access for wheel chair users.

Figure 4: *ComforTable* has seating and standing elements of different sizes. ©*Ilja Hendel/Wissenschaft im Dialog*

Figure 5a and Figure 5b show that users choose between different standing and seating combinations. Due to people sitting also bystanders in the back can get a good view of the surface.

The interactive surface consists of a 55" display with a resolution of 3840 x 2160 pixels and a multitouch IR-overlay on top.

Tracking System

The integrated user tracking system is based on four wide-angle cameras situated in the corners of the table surface. Every camera monitors its two opposing sides as depicted in Figure 6. Every side is thereby monitored by two cameras. The system is using a standard background subtraction algorithm to detect changes in the video footage. When larger changes in the camera images happen, e.g. when new users arrive at the table, the direction in respect to the table is calculated and a ray is cast from the camera into the calculated direction. Intersection points of rays cast from different cameras outside the interactive surface may indicate a current or potential user of the system.

This assumption is monitored and a certainty measure is derived from the presence or absence of camera ray intersections over time.

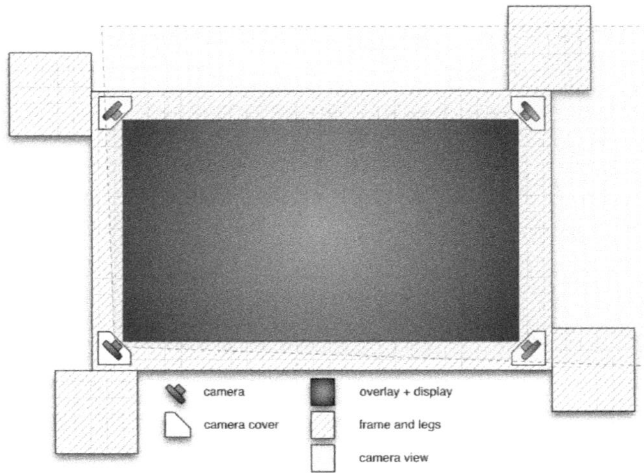

Figure 6: User tracking system is based on four cameras monitoring two sides each.

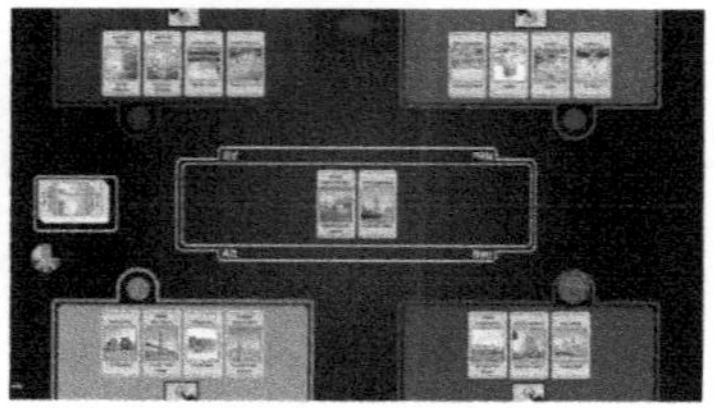

Figure 7: Turn-taking card game for up to four players. Players have to sort cards one by one from their stack into the center.

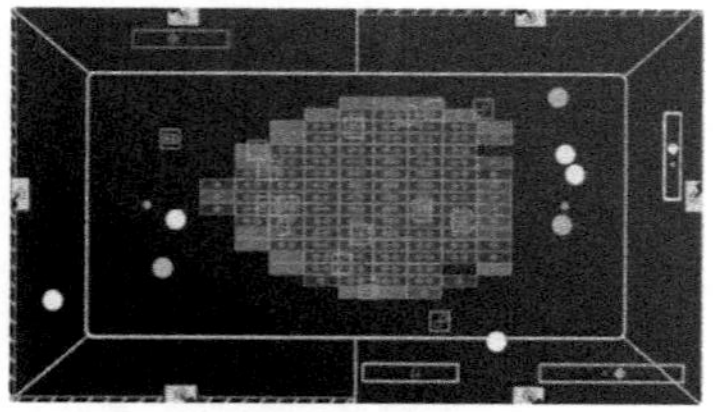

Figure 8: Pong game for up to six players. Players have paddels to deflect balls and need to break blocks in order to score points.

During the usage of the applications the position of users supplied by the user tracking system is used to show a dialog, which enables him/her to login. Afterwards it offers a simple description of the currently running application. The users presence and interaction is monitored through the applications and the tracking system. Lodged in users that left the table are automatically purged from the applications.

Applications
ComforTable offers two competitive games (see Figure 7 and Figure 8), one turn-taking card game for up to four players and a pong game for up to six players. The content of the games can easily be adjusted and two versions of both games can be played. Both card game and pong game have been evaluated in several user studies partly lasting longer than one month and refined afterwards.

Conclusion

In this paper we presented *ComforTable*, a tabletop for relaxed playful interactions in museums. *ComforTable* offers a robust setup with seating and standing elements allowing a group of users to share the interface in a comfortable way. The system recognizes the position of its users through a camera based tracking system. The integrated applications are two competitive games that can be played by up to six players.

Acknowledgements

We thank the German Science Foundation (DFG) for funding this work under grant number GRK 1780/1: Research Training Group "Connecting Virtual and Real Social Worlds" (www.crossworlds.info). Furthermore we want to thank Ana Curin, Adela Tetean, Julia Franke and Tom Schilling as well as our students for their share in this project.

References

[1] Electromagnetic spectrum. http://ideum.com/interactive-exhibits/custom-100-multitouch-table/. [Online; accessed 17-July-2014].

[2] Yiwarra kuju. http://lightwell.com.au/projects/yiwarra-kuju/. [Online; accessed 17-July-2014].

[3] Annett, M., Grossman, T., Wigdor, D., and Fitzmaurice, G. Medusa: a proximity-aware multi-touch tabletop. In *Proc. UIST*, ACM (2011), 337–346.

[4] Horn, M., Atrash Leong, Z., Block, F., Diamond, J., Evans, E. M., Phillips, B., and Shen, C. Of bats and apes: an interactive tabletop game for natural history museums. In *Proc. CHI*, ACM (2012), 2059–2068.

[5] Kanellopoulos, K., and Storz, M. Design eines Multitouch-Tisches für den musealen Kontext. In *Mensch & Computer 2013 - Workshopband*, S. Boll, S. Maaß, and R. Malaka, Eds., Oldenbourg Verlag (2013), 287–296.

[6] Klinkhammer, D., Nitsche, M., Specht, M., and Reiterer, H. Adaptive personal territories for co-located tabletop interaction in a museum setting. In *Proc. ITS*, ACM (2011), 107–110.

[7] Marquardt, N., Diaz-Marino, R., Boring, S., and Greenberg, S. The proximity toolkit: prototyping proxemic interactions in ubiquitous computing ecologies. In *Proc. UIST*, ACM (2011), 315–326.

[8] Vom Lehn, D., Heath, C., and Hindmarsh, J. Exhibiting interaction: Conduct and collaboration in museums and galleries. *Symbolic interaction 24*, 2 (2001), 189–216.

NEMOSHELL Demo: Windowing System for Concurrent Applications on Multi-user Interactive Surfaces

Junghan Kim
College of Information and
Communication Engineering
Sungkyungkwan University
Suwon, Korea
junghan@skku.edu

Taehyoung Kim
College of Information and
Communication Engineering
Sungkyungkwan University
Suwon, Korea
kim15m@skku.edu

Inhyeok Kim
College of Information and
Communication Engineering
Sungkyungkwan University
Suwon, Korea
kkojiband@skku.edu

Young Ik Eom
College of Information and
Communication Engineering
Sungkyungkwan University
Suwon, Korea
yieom@skku.edu

ITS 2014, November 16–19, 2014, Dresden, Germany.
ACM 978-1-4503-2587-5/14/11.
http://dx.doi.org/10.1145/2669485.2669532

Figure 1. Overview of NEMOSHELL. Each user can utilize multiple applications simultaneously, including legacy applications.

Abstract
Recently, the prevalence of large interactive surfaces renewed interests in windowing systems because of the advantages of enabling concurrent applications. We present the NEMOSHELL windowing system for multi-user interactive surfaces. We developed the system based on the Wayland system, a replacement for the Linux X. NEMOSHELL is designed to support multiple simultaneous applications, legacy input devices, legacy applications, and dynamic user interfaces. Finally, our demonstrations illustrate the potential of our system design.

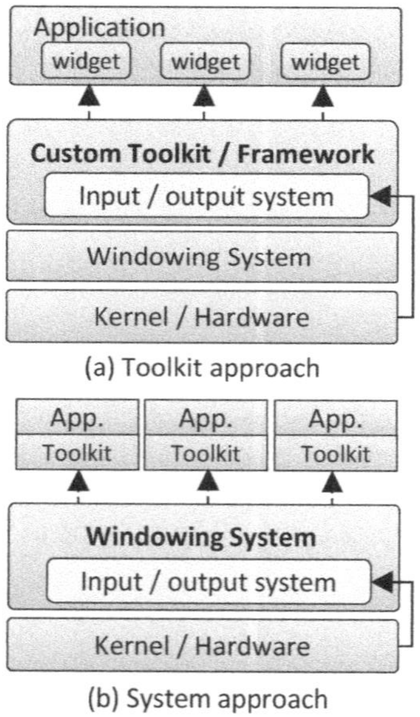

Figure 2. Differences between the architectures of the toolkit and system approaches.

Author Keywords
Interactive surface; multi-user; user interface; windowing system

ACM Classification Keywords
H.5.2 **[Information Interfaces and Presentation]**: User Interfaces - Windowing systems

Introduction
Most interactive systems have been designed with only a single application based on the custom toolkits. Recently, the use of large interactive surfaces has increased and the windowing systems have focused on the advantages of enabling concurrent applications [3, 7]. However, most studies still have several limitations, where desktop windowing systems are designed for single-user system.

We present the NEMOSHELL windowing system for concurrent applications on multi-user interactive surfaces. All the features are developed based on the Linux desktop system using the Wayland system, a replacement for the classical Linux X system, to fulfill the requirements of multi-user and legacy support.

To achieve this, we took our novel system designs: (1) Many-touch support, supporting a separate touch input to multiple simultaneous applications for multiple users, (2) Window group support, which provides a grouping mechanism for a user's group of applications, (3) Legacy support, which provides a compatibility with keyboards, mice, and preexisting applications, (4) Dynamic user interface, reinforcing the touchable animated interface (see Figure 1). Moreover, our demonstrations illustrate the windowing system features and various interactive features.

Related Work
To develop a novel windowing system for interactive surfaces, we classified the research area into two categories: the toolkit approach and system approach.

Toolkit approach
The toolkit approach is a top-down approach, where all the features of interactive systems are included in a single application based on custom toolkits or frameworks without changing the architecture of the windowing system (see Figure 2a). As the interactive toolkit field has matured, windowing systems have focused on the advantages of concurrent applications. Wu et al. [7] proposed a customizable windowing system to support multiple individuals and group work applications concurrently. Nonetheless, the actual implementation sits on top of Windows Presentation Foundation (WPF) framework. Recently, Hamdan et al. [3] proposed a conceptual framework to analyze simultaneous applications and its interface design.

System approach
The system approach is a bottom-up approach that replaces existing desktop systems (e.g., Microsoft Windows, Apple OSX, and Linux X) to resolve the system restrictions and usability challenges on interactive surfaces [4, 6]. Figure 2b shows the system approach, where all the input and output directly communicate with the windowing system at a time and multiple applications control their own toolkit subsystems. Previous researches [2, 5] developed multiple input features in the Linux X. However, classical desktop systems are limited to single-user and not available for multi-user interactive surfaces.

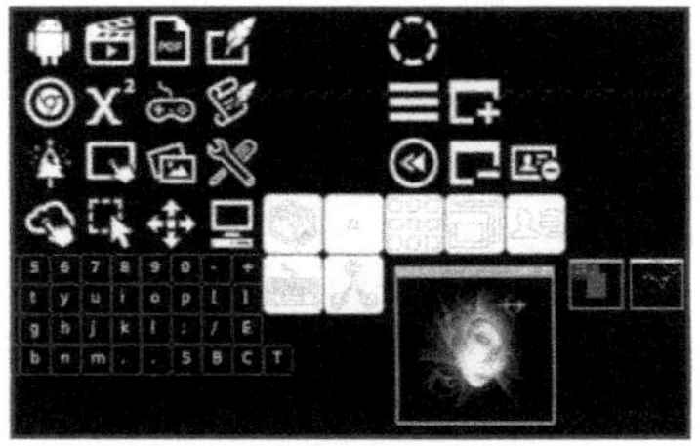

Figure 3. Group activator including app., virtual keyboard, controller, and showcase actors (from left to right).

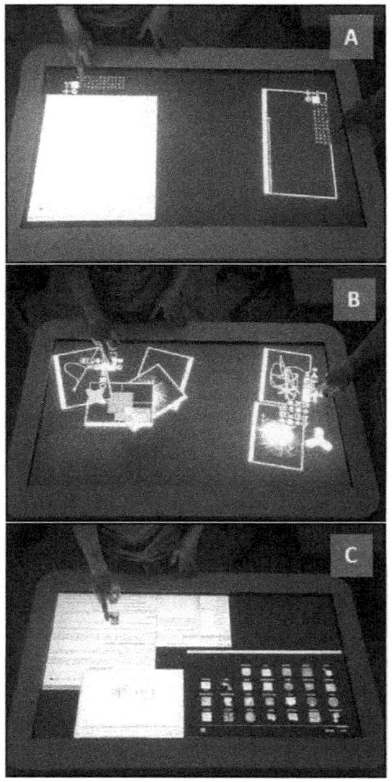

Figure 4. Three key demos of the system features.

NEMOSHELL System Design

We developed NEMOSHELL based on the Linux desktop system using the Wayland[1] windowing system, which has two advantages: openness and flexibility. Linux is a major open source project where anyone can modify its features, whereas other desktop systems (e.g., Microsoft Windows and Apple OSX) are closed source. In terms of flexibility, Linux has undergone a major change in its windowing system. The traditional X is a stable project, but this architecture is too old to apply new features. In contrast, Wayland was designed as a replacement for X, and it has a lightweight architecture that can be adapted easily to newer system requirements and it is also possible to use legacy applications because of its backward compatibility.

Many-touch support

Classical desktop systems have limitations on multi-touch input, where a single application can only receive touch inputs at a time owing to the restrictive system design. We define the term 'many-touch' to provide seamless input connections among multiple applications by unifying the TUIO[2] events into the common input handler in the windowing system.

Window group support

Co-located user scenarios are prevalent, but most studies provide the widget groups in a single application on a large surface. We propose the concept of window group, where multiple applications effectively coexist in the surfaces. We also design the group activator, where the group user manages all the application features (see Figure 3).

1 http://wayland.freedesktop.org

2 http://www.tuio.org

Legacy support

To facilitate significant improvements in the usability of interactive surfaces, previous studies [1, 6] focused on supporting legacy applications on interactive systems. Thus, we support the X and Wayland protocols, which have many backend toolkits such as GTK and QT, based on the X clients under Wayland (Xwayland) interfaces. We also provide pointer emulation to ensure compatibility with legacy input devices, such as keyboards and mice.

Dynamic user interface

Providing visual feedback of touch events is more important to augment natural interactions on large surfaces than on existing desktop systems. Thus, we developed the Scalable Vector Graphics (SVG) engine for giving the dynamic animation feature available for the basic user interfaces and physics engine for the reachability issues [6]. Moreover, we added the gesture interfaces into our many-touch input system with unimanual and bimanual actions [8].

Demonstration

In order to verify our windowing system, we illustrate demonstrations in 47-inch tabletops with the PQLabs[3] G3 multi-touch screen (32 touch points).

System features

These demonstrations indicate our fundamental windowing system features in the following ways:

- Multiple Virtual Keyboards – verify our input system and window group features for seamless connections with applications (see Figure 4a).

3 http://multitouch.com

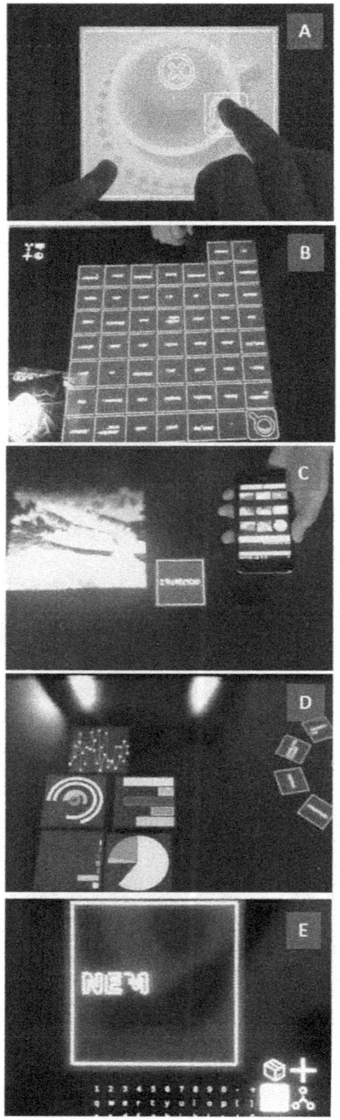

Figure 5. More complex applications.

- Group Interfaces – support the group coordinations such as show & hide and magnet & stack interfaces (see Figure 4b) [4].
- Legacy Applications – support the X applications such as the chromium, QT and GTK applications, and Android platform (see Figure 4c).

More complex applications
We will be able to demonstrate additional application features in the following ways:

- Flickr Image Search – show the connectivity with the web service and bimanual overlay user interface (see Figure 5a).
- TRON-style File Browser – present fully animated multiple layout file browser (see Figure 5b).
- Photoshare with Andriod – support the Alljoyn[4] common Internet of Things (IoT) framework (see Figure 5c).
- CPU, MEM, SYSTEM Monitor – provide the dynamic chart interfaces (see Figure 5d).
- Interactive Applications – show fully animated applications with the path animations and particle effects (see Figure 5e).

Conclusion
We have developed a novel windowing system for multi-user interactive surfaces, NEMOSHELL. We briefly describe our system design and show the potential of the system compared with existing systems. We have a plan to extend the interaction techniques and we expect that our windowing system can be available as a new Linux distribution for large surfaces.

4 https://www.alljoyn.org/

Acknowledgments
This research was supported by Basic Science Research Program through the National Research Foundation of Korea(NRF) funded by the Ministry of Education (NRF-2013R1A1A2012790).

References
[1] Besacier, G., and Vernier, F. Toward user interface virtualization: Legacy applications and innovative interaction systems. In Proc. EICS'09, 157–166.

[2] Cheng, K., Itzstein, B., Sztajer, P., and Rittenbruch, M.A unified multi-touch & multi-pointer software architecture for supporting collocated work on the desktop. Tech. Rep. ATP-2247. NICTA, 2009.

[3] Hamdan, N. A.-h., Voelker, S., and Borchers, J. O. Conceptual framework for surface manager on interactive tabletops. In Proc. CHIEA'13, 1527–1532.

[4] Hofmeester, K., and Wixon, D. Using metaphors to create a natural user interface for microsoft surface. In Proc. CHIEA'10, 4629–4644.

[5] Hutterer, P., and Thomas, B. H. Groupware support in the windowing system. In Proc. AUIC'07, 39–46.

[6] Shen, C., Ryall, K., Forlines, C., Esenther, A., Vernier, F., Everitt, K., Wu, M., Wigdor, D., Morris, M., Hancock, M., and Tse, E. Informing the design of direct-touch tabletops. IEEE CG&A 26,5 (2006), 36–46.

[7] Wu, C., Suo, Y., Yu, C., Shi, Y., and Qin, Y. uPlatform: a customizable multi-user windowing system for interactive tabletop. Vol. 6761. Springer Berlin Heidelberg, 2011, 507–516.

[8] Wu, M., and Balakrishnan, R. Multi-finger and whole hand gestural interaction techniques for multi-user tabletop displays. In Proc. UIST'03, 193–202.

Explicit & Implicit Interaction Design for Multi-Focus Visualizations

Simon Butscher
HCI Group, University of Konstanz
Universitätsstraße 10
Konstanz, 78457, Germany
Simon.Butscher@uni-konstanz.de

Abstract
Many tasks that have to be performed to analyze data in large visual information spaces require the user to have several foci. This is for example the case for comparing or organizing digital artefacts. In my research, I explore alternative interaction concepts for multi-focus visualizations in the context of single and multi-user scenarios. Alongside explicit interaction for navigating within multi-focus visualizations I investigate implicit interaction for making the visualization react on the social and spatial context. To evaluate different designs, measures like task completion time, spatial memory and subjective preferences are examined.

ITS '14, Nov 16-19, 2014, Dresden, Germany
ACM 978-1-4503-2587-5/14/11.
http://dx.doi.org/10.1145/2669485.2669487

Author Keywords
Multi-Focus+context; implicit interaction; explicit interaction; touch interaction; proxemic interactions

ACM Classification Keywords
H.5.2. Information interfaces and presentation (e.g., HCI): User Interfaces – Interaction styles

Research Background
I received a degree (german Diplom) in Business Information Systems at the University of Cooperative Education in Ravensburg, Germany. For my thesis I designed and implemented a solution for effective data analysis within a business intelligence application for companies in the healthcare sector. In addition I hold a master's degree in Information Engineering from the University of Konstanz, Germany. For my master's thesis I designed, implemented, and evaluated a focus+context visualization and remote interaction concept for the analysis of the traffic situation on a road network [13]. With this project, I gained valuable expertise and insights into the combination of focus+context visualizations with suitable input modalities for their control. Since the project's completion, I have been interested in the interplay between visualization techniques and input modalities and especially in the combination of multi-focus

visualizations with alternative input modalities to facilitate data analysis tasks in visual information spaces.

Since the beginning of my Ph.D. I have been affiliated with different projects ranging from designing future control rooms,[1] blending the physical and digital space in public[2] or academic[3] libraries and analyzing mobile health care data. One of the main tasks to be supported within all of these projects is data analysis. For my future research I will focus on two application scenarios: the analysis of traffic situation in traffic control rooms and the analysis of health data collected with mobile devices. My supervisor is Harald Reiterer from the University of Konstanz.

Motivation

Many tasks that have to be performed in multiscale visual information spaces require several foci. This is also true for data analysis tasks in which digital artifacts have to be compared or organized. Whereas virtually all interfaces allow the user to change between foci over time (e.g., by navigating a map with pan/zoom gestures), fewer interfaces allow the simultaneous presentation of multiple foci. Examples of such multi-focus visualization techniques include multi-window systems, split-screen interfaces, and a variety of research prototypes (e.g. [5,6,11]).

Figure 1. The social and spatial context within a future control room. Relationships of people to each other and to the displays can be used for an implicit interaction with visualizations.

Multi-focus visualization techniques are a well-studied field in HCI (for an overview of research about multi-focus visualizations see [4]). Yet, research on how alternative input modalities can facilitate the interaction with these visualizations is limited. Novel input modalities offer great potential to design interaction concepts which suit multi-focus visualizations better than state-of-the art approaches. For example, in contrast to many other input devices, multi-touch surfaces seem to naturally enable multi-focus interaction, e.g., by using one hand per focus point. Furthermore and with respect to multi-user scenarios, many alternative input modalities (e.g. touch or gestural input) facilitate a democratized form of collaboration, which mouse input, by contrast, does not.

However explicit interaction to navigate within a multi-focus visualization is only one part of the possible design space. The interpretation of the social and spatial context (see Figure 1) can be another part and is especially promising for an implicit interaction to automatically adapt the appearance of the visualization (e.g. placing information on a display depending on the position of a user in front of it).

Consequently, I intend to support the different activities of data analyst, such as navigating in large information spaces or comparing digital artifacts by using multi-focus visualization techniques that exploit alternative input modalities and combine explicit and implicit interaction styles.

Background and Related Work

Although multi-focus visualization techniques are a well-studied research topic, an unanswered question is how these visualization techniques can benefit from alternative input modalities. Most research has concentrated on the presentation, not on the interaction (e.g. [5]). Only some research has emphasized the interaction with the visualization and

[1] http://hci.uni-konstanz.de/HolisticWorkspace

[2] http://hci.uni-konstanz.de/Libros

[3] http://hci.uni-konstanz.de/BlendedLibrary

Figure 2. The five dimensions of proxemics [7].

makes use of input modalities like touch to facilitate the definition of areas of interest within a visual information space (e.g. [8,11]). However, they fail to exploit the additional possibilities provided by alternative input modalities in all facets.

Most research in the field of multi-focus visualizations is limited to explicit interaction and ignores the possibilities of adapting the visualizations to the implicit input of the user. Implicit interaction can be realized by analyzing and interpreting the spatial and social context. Some research areas other than multi-focus visualizations have implemented systems that provide a mixture of explicit interaction and implicit interaction. An interactive public display installation for example interprets the spatial context (position of the user in front of a display) and thus shows customized information to the user [14]. Another system designed for multi-display environments uses the users head position as implicit input to correct the perspective distortion of the elements visualized on the screens [12].

Proxemic Interactions [7], provide a general perspective on the spatial and social context in terms of relationships between persons and objects (e.g. displays) but also between persons to each other. To describe these relationships five dimensions of proximity are proposed: distance, orientation, movement, identity, and location (see Figure 2). These proxemic dimensions offer a design space for adaptive visualizations which react on the spatial and social environment.

Research Approach

I make use of a taxonomy to describe the design space for investigating data analysis tasks. This taxonomy is built on the task to perform and the number of parallel users:

Tasks: In my research I focus on data analysis in visual information spaces in the sense of exploring the space, searching for objects, comparing objects and organizing them. Depending on the task, different requirements are relevant, like orientation within the information space, spatial memory to remember object locations or multiple foci to compare or move digital artefacts to other location in the visual space.

Number of parallel users: Data analysis can be an individual but also a collaborative activity, e.g., within a control room. For collaborative scenarios I have to deal with additional requirements like a democratized from of collaboration or an enhanced situational awareness (awareness of ongoing activities, and awareness of who is in control of shared artefacts [9]).

To investigate how multi-focus techniques can facilitate data analysis tasks different combinations of the two dimensions of this taxonomy have to be explored. Depending on the task and the number of parallel users, either single-focus or multi-focus solutions may be appropriate. Whereas the visualization has to support multiple foci for multiple users regardless of the task at hand, in single user scenarios only the compare task requires multiple foci. The combination of the task and the number of parallel users also influences the choice of the input modality.

Proxemic dimensions can help to capture the spatial and social context and enable an automatic reaction (e.g. if two persons move closer to each other the focus

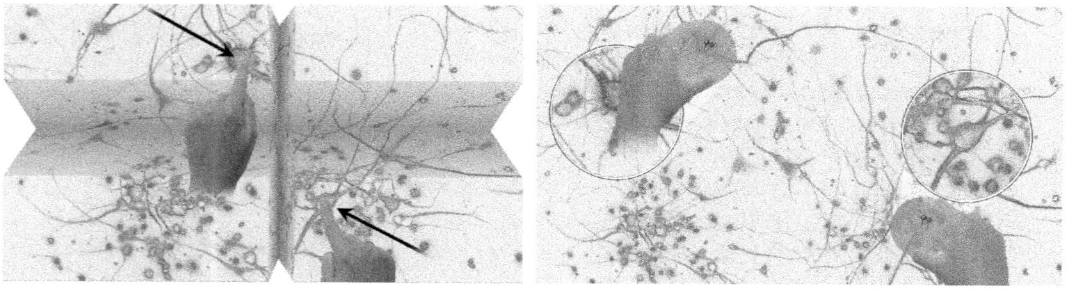

Figure 3. Supporting single users comparing human neural stem cells: (left) SpaceFold – Fold the visual space like a sheet of paper to bring two areas of interest closer to each other; (right) PhysicLenses – Create multiple magnification lenses to see detailed views of areas of interest.

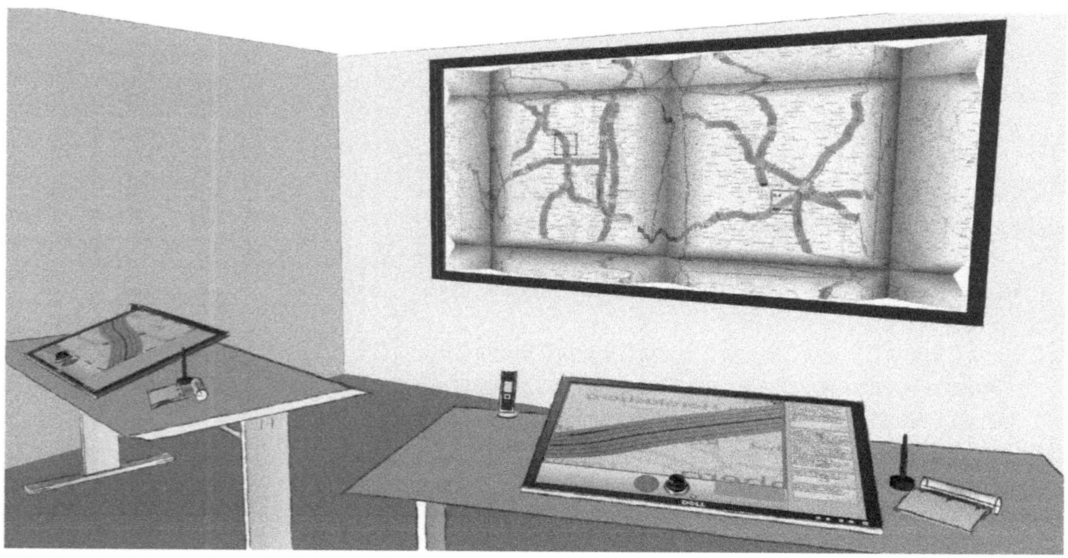

Figure 4. Supporting multiple users analyzing the traffic situation: A multi-focus visualization on a large wall-sized display can be controlled remotely by the operators through self-centering devices.

of both users could be merged in order to facilitate discussions about digital artefacts). Thus in multi-user ecosystems proxemic dimensions plays a key role in analyzing the social context, and can be used to consider social conventions. Whereas I already investigated some combinations of the taxonomy other combinations are still to be explored.

Completed Work

For the dimension of single-user interaction to perform compare and organize (drag & drop) tasks we conducted a controlled experiment to compare different solutions [1]. We introduced two novel navigation techniques that combine multiple foci and bimanual touch, and thus enable the isochronic definition of areas of interest, leading to simultaneous multifocus navigation. *SpaceFold* folds the visual space in the third dimension, allowing users to bring objects closer to each other (see Figure 3, left). Our technique enables a direct, bimanual manipulation of a folded space and is highly flexible. *PhysicLenses* uses multiple magnification lenses to compare objects (see Figure 3, right). Using a physics model, *PhysicLenses* introduces a general solution for the arrangement of multiple lenses within the viewport. We conducted a controlled experiment with 24 participants to compare the techniques with split screen. The results show that *SpaceFold* significantly outperformed all other techniques, whereas *PhysicLenses* was just as fast as split screen.

For the multi-user scenario within a traffic control room we investigated solutions for collaboratively analyzing the traffic situation [2]. First, to gain an understanding of relevant tasks and the social environment that shape the work of operators, a context-of-use analysis in two

Figure 5. Supporting multiple users to analyze a visual information space: A combination of an explicit interaction for the selection of areas of interest and an implicit interaction for the tailored positioning of the information. The position of the user in front of the display is mapped to the position were detailed information are shown. The aim is to enable seamless switching between tightly-coupled collaboration and loosely-coupled parallel work.

Figure 6. Multi-display environment equipped with OptiTrack tracking system to capture the spatial and social context.

freeway traffic monitoring control rooms was conducted. Based on the analysis we created a multi-focus visualization for large wall-sized displays, which makes it possible to examine local details without losing contextual information (see Figure 4). We combined a visualization based on the SpaceFolding technique by Elmqvist et al. [5] with our content-aware navigation technique [13]. To evaluate the applicability of the concept, a study with eleven participants from the domain of traffic control rooms was conducted. The results show that the multi-focus visualization facilitated the awareness on ongoing activities. It enabled an implicit communication, which helps the operators to coordinate themselves.

Future Work

My future research will focus on data analysis in multi-user environments. Proxemic Interactions are used to analyze and interpret the spatial and social context. I am especially interested not only in considering the distance and orientation of people to a display but also to each other. Furthermore the movement of people can give insight to the actual situation. Possible interpretations of these metrics could be that if people move closer to the display they want to see the information space in greater detail, or that if people move closer to each other they want to discuss about a shared artifact. As users switch between individual tasks and collaborative tasks, switching between several independent foci on the information space and shared foci is an issue which needs to be investigated.

Proxemic measures can either be used as explicit input (e.g. defining a focus region of a multi-focus visualization according to a user's location and orientation in physical space [3]) or as implicit input modality to adapt visualizations. Figure 5 shows a concept in which we combine explicit and implicit input for the manipulation of a multi-focus visualization. The explicit input modality in form of a smartphone used as touchpad is used to define the position of a focus region. The location of the user as an implicit input modality is used to place the enlarged view of the selected focus region directly in front of the user.

In order to implement prototypes and evaluate them to show the feasibility of multi-focus visualizations using proxemic dimensions I make use of a laboratory equipped with an OptiTrack[4] tracking system (see Figure 6). The tracking systems consists of 24 infrared camera which are connected to the Proximity Toolkit [10]. This toolkit offers great support in capturing the proximic dimensions.

Statement of Thesis and Goals

In my dissertation I address the research question of how to use combinations of explicit and implicit interaction to control multi-focus visualizations for large visual information spaces. My contributions are:

1.) Explore alternative input modalities and interaction concepts for navigating multi-focus visualizations of visual information spaces to support data analysis tasks like searching, comparing or organizing digital artefacts.

2.) Design and implement prototypes that employ proxemic dimensions as an implicit input modality for adapting multi-focus visualizations depending on the spatial and social context.

[4] https://www.naturalpoint.com/optitrack/

3.) Evaluate the developed concepts and prototypes within controlled experiments. Depending on the task metrics like task completion time, mental workload, spatial memory or subjective preferences are investigated.

Expected Contributions

Through my research, I aim to develop interaction concepts to support data analysis tasks through multi-focus visualization techniques and combine them with alternative input modalities to support explicit and implicit interaction. To show the feasibility of the concepts for real world problems I will apply the concepts to single-user and multi-user scenarios from two different domains.

References

[1] Butscher, S., Hornbæk, K., and Reiterer, H. SpaceFold and PhysicLenses : Simultaneous Multifocus Navigation on Touch Surfaces. *In Proc. AVI 2014*, ACM Press (2014), 209–216.

[2] Butscher, S., Müller, J., Schwarz, T., and Reiterer, H. Blended Interaction as an Approach for Holistic Control Room Design. *CHI 2013 Workshop on Blended Interaction*, (2013).

[3] Butscher, S., Müller, J., Weiler, A., Rädle, R., Reiterer, H., and Scholl, M. Multi-user Twitter Analysis for Crisis Room Environments. *Collaborative Human-Computer-Interaction with Big Wall Displays BigWallHCI 2013, 3rd JRC ECML Crisis Management Technology Workshop*, Publications Office of the European Union (2013), 28–34.

[4] Cockburn, A., Karlson, A., and Bederson, B.B. A Review of Overview+Detail, Zooming, and Focus+Context Interfaces. *ACM Computing Surveys (CSUR) 41*, 1 (2008).

[5] Elmqvist, N., Henry, N., Riche, Y., and Fekete, J.-D. Mélange: Space Folding for Multi-Focus Interaction. *In Proc. CHI 2008*, ACM Press (2008), 1333–1342.

[6] Forlines, C. and Shen, C. DTLens: Multi-user Tabletop Spatial Data Exploration. *In Proc. UIST 2005*, ACM Press (2005), 119–122.

[7] Greenberg, S., Marquardt, N., Ballendat, T., Diaz-Marino, R., and Wang, M. Proxemic Interactions : The New Ubicomp ? *interactions 18*, January (2011), 42–50.

[8] Käser, D., Agrawala, M., and Pauly, M. FingerGlass: Efficient Multiscale Interaction on Multitouch Screens. *In Proc. CHI 2011*, ACM Press (2011), 1601–1610.

[9] Kulyk, O., van der Veer, G., and van Dijk, B. Situational awareness support to enhance teamwork in collaborative environments. *In Proc. ECCE 2008*, ACM Press (2008), 18–22.

[10] Marquardt, N., Diaz-Marino, R., Boring, S., and Greenberg, S. The Proximity Toolkit: Prototyping Proxemic Interactions in Ubiquitous Computing Ecologies. *In Proc. UIST 2011*, ACM Press (2011), 315–325.

[11] Mikulecky, K., Hancock, M., Brosz, J., and Carpendale, S. Exploring Physical Information Cloth on a Multitouch Table. *In Proc. ITS 2011*, ACM Press (2011), 140–149.

[12] Nacenta, M.A., Sakurai, S., Yamaguchi, T., et al. E-conic: a Perspective-Aware Interface for Multi-Display Environments. *In Proc. UIST 2007*, ACM Press (2007), 279–288.

[13] Schwarz, T., Butscher, S., Müller, J., and Reiterer, H. Content-aware navigation for large displays in context of traffic control rooms. *In Proc. AVI 2012*, ACM Press (2012), 249–252.

[14] Vogel, D. and Balakrishnan, R. Interactive Public Ambient Displays: Transitioning from Implicit to Explicit, Public to Personal, Interaction with Multiple Users. *In Proc. UIST 14*, ACM Press (2004), 137–146.

Towards an Interaction Model for Multi-Surface Personal Computing Spaces

Henri Palleis
University of Munich (LMU)
Amalienstraße 17
80333 Munich
Henri.palleis@ifi.lmu.de

Author Keywords
Curved Display;Interaction Model

ACM Classification Keywords
H.5.m Information interfaces and presentation (e.g., HCI): Miscellaneous.

ITS '14, Nov 16-19, 2014, Dresden, Germany
ACM 978-1-4503-2587-5/14/11.
http://dx.doi.org/10.1145/2669485.2669488

Abstract
The prototype *Curve* was developed at our lab and its basic effects on touch interaction as well as elementary applications were explored in the recent dissertation of Hennecke [3]. My work is concerned with the concretion of his initial findings. In particular I am interested in (1) contextualizing the device by exploring specific application scenarios and (2) finding adequate interaction models that allow people using the display's input and output capabilities effectively and conveniently. In my thesis I want to provide guidelines that help user interface designers to develop interaction techniques for multi-surface personal computing spaces that comprise both horizontal and vertical touchscreens and show potential benefits of a seamless connection between them (e.g. a curved display segment).

Multi-Surface Personal Computing Spaces
I use this term to refer to computer workstations that are primarily intended for personal use. As such, it includes public terminals (e.g. in libraries, museums etc.), general-purpose personal computers (i.e. today's PC) as well as expert workspaces (e.g. in architecture offices or control rooms). Although intended for single user operation, they might be co-operated temporarily.

The integration of interactive surfaces into personal computing spaces (e.g. interactive tabletop with desktop computer) brings together WIMP and NUI interaction styles. On the one hand, this results in the coexistence of different interaction techniques. On the other hand, a combination of differently oriented interactive surfaces may help to retain an ergonomic workspace by enabling a better structuring of touch input (horizontal surface) and visual output (vertical surface). Further, a connection between these surfaces may allow for context-dependent transitions of digital content according to particular needs. To enable people to conveniently engage with digital content across differently oriented interactive surfaces, it is important to find a suitable interaction model.

Background

Several research and design prototypes propose to rethink personal computing spaces. In many cases these prototypes include large interactive surfaces. The envisioned properties of such "workspaces of the future" evolve around the broader context they emerge from.

Efforts from the NUI community mainly focus on exploiting the interaction capabilities of new hardware (e.g. interactive table-top computers). For instance, Matulic explores how to support productivity document tasks using pen and touch gestures on interactive table-top computers [7].

A different approach is illustrated by the Magic Desk [2] project (figure 1) from AutoDesk or the design concept iDesk. In these cases, WIMP and NUI interaction techniques complement one another: rich touch input can be used to enhance WIMP tasks (indirect pointing, window management, augmented mouse) and windows are used to display content on the desk. In this example, the multi-touch surface plays a subordinate role, since the use of a conventional personal computer is assumed and the prevailing interaction style (WIMP) is not in question.

Prototypes like *Curve* [15] or *BendDesk* [14] merge properties of both worlds: On the one hand, the large multi-touch surface (and the software framework used to build applications) relates it to the NUI community. On the other hand, the display's form factor picks up the idea of vertical displays known from standard computers and can easily contain all its components (dual use of the horizontal surface). Apart from ergonomic considerations ("gorilla arms", "stiff neck"), little is known about how these spheres might relate in the context of personal computing spaces.

A special property of such prototypes – the curved display segment – may help to think about possible relations between elements from NUIs and WIMP interfaces. First, it physically highlights that both spheres are connected and functionally equal. This might help to explore the interaction from a less predetermined point of view. Second, it presents a previously unallocated display space that can take on meaning.

Further combinations of vertical and horizontal interactive surfaces include for example SpaceTop [5] or MisTable [10]. These prototypes are based on the idea of an interactive see-trough (in case of MisTable even reach-through) vertical screen that also establishes a relationship with interactive surfaces or spaces behind it.

Figure 1 Magic Desk [2]

Approach
My approach is based on experimenting with different application areas, building interactive prototypes and extracting specific questions regarding the interaction model. I write multi-touch applications for the curved display using the MT4J-Framework. These applications occupy different dimensions of the above-mentioned term *Personal Computing Spaces*, such as applications for the public or expert workspaces. Specific and generalizable research questions concerning the interaction model evolve during the development of the prototypes. The goal is to identify (a) usage scenarios that involve the horizontal, the vertical and the curved part of the display and (b) to explore touch interaction techniques for these scenarios. Eventually, I hope to produce a set of guidelines that can inform the design of user interfaces for display setups with similar form factors.

Prototypes
Several interactive prototypes have been developed so far: (1) a quiz game featuring an interactive world map on one part of the display and pictures of famous places on the other part of the display (see figure 2a) [9]. The task is to answer the question "*Where is the place in the picture located*" by dragging the picture across the curve onto the corresponding location on the world map. I publicly exposed the game at our annual open lab day and observed how people approached the game. My key interest was if people without previous knowledge would recognize the possibility to drag pictures across the curve. (2) A music application (see figure 2b) allowing the composition of sound collages and rhythmic patterns. It features several components known from digital audio workstations and integrates a physical pad controller. Here, the idea was to explore how the form factor of the display can inform the design of an expert workplace. (3) A collaborative photo book layout application (see figure 2c) allowed two people to select pictures and arrange them with templates in a virtual photo book. The main focus was on the mutual awareness of two equal collaborators. (4) The latest project is an application to view and transform 3D content (see figure 2d) and is based on the visualization technique *Perspective+Detail* [11]. Here, the goal is to explore alternative ways to interact with 3D content by mapping the different orientations of the input surfaces to different.

By building and evolving these prototypes, I identified two main areas of interest, which I want to explore in my dissertation. The first *is (cross-display) object movement* and the second is *direct + indirect touch interaction*. Both topics are important for many computer-based tasks.

(Cross-Display) Object Movement
Object movement is of central importance in direct manipulation: within the borders of our monitors, we move windows, files and folders and the constant visual feedback helps us to continuously validate our actions.

Also, it helps us to structure the virtual space as well as our minds.

Figure 2 Prototypes: a) Quiz game, b) music application, c) photo book layout application, d) 3D manipulation.

I argue that independent from the underlying interaction style, extending the borders of the available display and input space requires also extending the ability to conveniently move digital objects across the whole display space. For example, it should be easily possible to comfortably arrange several text documents across both the vertical and the horizontal display without switching between mouse and touch input. In the context of *Curve* and *BendDesk*, dragging and flicking interaction techniques have been explored. While dragging across the curve is easily understandable and fun [9], it is not suited for prolonged usage due to physical demands. Flicking is an interaction technique that enables to move objects to distant places with sliding gestures. It is an open loop technique and its accuracy and error rate on a non-flat display arrangement depend on several factors (e.g. start location, direction etc.) [12]. Therefore, it is important to explore further interaction techniques that a) are accurate, b) efficient and c) comfortable. A starting point for my exploration is the work of Nacenta [8], who proposed a model for cross-display object movement and an extensive taxonomy of interaction techniques.

Direct + Indirect Touch

A second area of interest is the relation between direct and indirect touch input. Voelker has explored several state-switching techniques for indirect touch input to implement a three-state model of graphical input in Buxton's sense [12]. He used two identical touch displays with a clear separation between input (horizontal) and output (vertical) and a 1:1 spatial mapping. I am interested in how direct touch (and pen) interaction on the horizontal part of the display can be combined with the benefits of indirect touch interaction used to manipulate content on the vertical display (precision, gain, no occlusion). I think it is important to consider indirect touch not only in terms of pointing with a cursor, but as a context-dependent interaction technique that can have varying designs. Potential approaches range from a) dedicated virtual touchpads (as in Magic Table) to b) more implicit mappings that use unallocated display space on the horizontal display as input space and c) an approach where digital objects on the horizontal area allow both direct (i.e. dragging, rotation etc.) and indirect (manipulation of associated object on the vertical) touch interaction. An example for b) is illustrated in figure 3, where the gray space around the images can be used to pan and zoom the world map.

Figure 3 Indirect and direct touch

Current Projects

The Curve as File Browser

In order to improve my understanding of the interaction with the Curve, I built a simple musical application that allows the composition of sound collages. The main components of the app (sound editor, physical controller, sequencer) where distributed across the horizontal and the vertical display. One interesting outcome was the use of a horizontal file browser located in the curved area of the display. Through the use of the curved display space, the file browser may optimize cross-display interaction techniques, since a) it reduces distances and b) it might reduce errors due to the curved connection (e.g. aiming errors when flicking across the curve [13]).

Object Movement

Currently I am analyzing different contexts and interaction techniques for cross-display object movement. At the moment, I am focusing on techniques, that allow users to move objects from the horizontal to the vertical part of the display, as previous results indicate that dragging in this direction is less comfortable that dragging objects from the vertical display through the curve down onto the horizontal surface.

Virtual Mouse

For tasks that require high precision (e.g.) and for established software based on WIMP, it might be necessary to provide an adequate pointing device. In a current project I evaluate different versions of virtual mice that have been proposed for interactive surfaces. [1][6].

Indirect Touch 3D

The last current project is based on the visualization technique described in *Perspective+Detail* [11] and *Perspective Table* [4]. Here the goal is to find suitable ways to manipulate 3D objects located on the virtual part of the table by means of touch gestures on the physical part of the table. The form factor of the display allows exploring indirect touch input techniques that map the spatial arrangement of the display (i.e. horizontal layer (XZ-layer) and vertical layer (XY-layer)) to the transformation of 3D objects.

Next Steps

In the remaining time of my research I want to focus on the combination of direct and indirect touch input using the example of the 3D environment described above. Here, I want to investigate different input techniques for a set of basic tasks (e.g. selection, navigation, transformation). These input techniques can be classified along different dimensions: direct/indirect, horizontal/vertical display, graphical user interface/gesture set, touch/tangible.

Further, I am interested in how findings from the work with the Curve may be generalized to similar setups. Therefore, I currently use a combination of two conventional 23 inch touch screens as an alternative test bed. The form factor of this setup is similar to the curve, but it is smaller and the curved connection is missing.

Eventually, I want to provide design guidelines for the development of interaction techniques for multi-surface personal computing spaces that comprise both horizontal and vertical touchscreens and show potential benefits of a seamless connection between them.

References

[1] Bartindale, T., Harrison, C., Olivier, P., Hudson, S.E. SurfaceMouse: supplementing multi-touch interaction with a virtual mouse. In *Proc. TEI 2011*. ACM Press (2011), 293-296.

[2] Bi, X., Grossman, T., Matejka, J., Fitzmaurice, G. Magic desk: bringing multi-touch surfaces into desktop work. In *Proc. CHI 2011*. ACM Press (2011), 2511-2520.

[3] Hennecke, F. Effekte und Potenziale eines gebogenen interaktiven Displays. Dissertation at Ludwig-Maximilians-Universität (2014).

[4] Hennecke, F., Voelker, S., Schenk, M., Schaper, H., Borchers, J., Butz, A. Simplifying Remote Collaboration Through Spatial Mirroring. In *Proc. INTERACT 2013*. Springer (2013), 624-631.

[5] Lee, J., Olwal, A., Ishii, H., Boulanger, C. SpaceTop: integrating 2D and spatial 3D interactions in a see-through desktop environment. In *Proc. CHI 2013*. ACM Press (2013), 189-192.

[6] Matejka, J., Grossman, T., Lo, J., Fitzmaurice, G. The design and evaluation of multi-finger mouse emulation techniques. In *Proc. CHI 2009*. ACM Press (2009), 1073-1082.

[7] Matulic, F., Norrie, M.C. Pen and touch gestural environment for document editing on interactive tabletops. In *Proc. ITS 2013*. ACM Press (2013), 41-50.

[8] Nacenta, M., Gutwin, C., Aliakseyeu, D., Subramanian, S. There and back again: cross-display object movement in multi-display environments. In Human-Computer Interaction 24 1/2 2009. 170-229.

[9] Palleis, H., Hussmann, H. Towards understanding spontaneous interaction on curved displays. *In Proc. CHI 2014 Extended Abstracts*, ACM Press (2014), 2065-2070.

[10] Plasencia, D. M., Joyce, E., Subramanian, S. MisTable: reach-through personal screens for tabletops. In *Proc. CHI 2014,* ACM Press (2014), 3493-3502.

[11] Schwarz, T., Hennecke, F., Lauber, F. and Reiterer, H. Perspective+detail: a visualization technique for vertically curved displays. In *Proc. AVI 2012*. ACM Press (2012), 485-488.

[12] Voelker, S., Wacharamanotham, C., Borchers, J. An Evaluation of State Switching Methods for Indirect Touch Systems. In *Proc. CHI 2013*, ACM Press (2013), 745-754.

[13] Voelker, S., Sutter, C., Wang, L., Borchers, J. Understanding flicking on curved surfaces. In *Proc. CHI 2012*, ACM Press (2012), 189-198.

[14] Weiss, M., Voelker, S., Sutter, C., Borchers, J. BendDesk: Dragging Across the Curve. In *Proc. ITS 2010*, ACM Press (2010), 1-10.

[15] Wimmer, R., Hennecke, F., Schulz, F., Boring, S., Butz, A. and Hußmann, H. Curve: revisiting the digital desk. In *Proc. NordiCHI 2010*. ACM Press (2010), 561-570.

Improving Interaction Discoverability in Large Public Interactive Displays

Victor Cheung
Systems Design Engineering
University of Waterloo
200 University Ave. W.
Waterloo, ON, Canada, N2L 3G1
victor.cheung@uwaterloo.ca

ITS '14, Nov 16-19 2014, Dresden, Germany
ACM 978-1-4503-2587-5/14/11.
http://dx.doi.org/10.1145/2669485.2669489

Abstract
There is increasing interest in utilizing large, interactive displays in public spaces such as museums, retail stores, information centres, etc. in order to provide a more engaging user experience. Yet, prior studies have consistently reported that these systems are underutilized and, thus, not providing the desired user experience. My thesis aims to model the underlying interaction process with public interactive displays. A descriptive model of this interaction process will allow researchers and practitioners to better understand the unique design issues of these systems. It will also help specify existing and potential design advice, in order to better understand which stages of the process this design advice addresses, and which stages need more attention. My thesis also aims to develop a laboratory-based experimental methodology that enables more rapid and controlled evaluation of potential interaction design strategies for public interactive displays. My research is expected to provide insights for readers to design and build better and more usable large interactive systems for public settings.

Author Keywords
Interactive displays; interaction design; discoverability

ACM Classification Keywords
H.5. Information interfaces and presentation (e.g., HCI)

Introduction

Large interactive displays such as interactive walls and digital tabletops are gaining popularity in a variety of public settings such as museums, galleries, retail stores, and tourist information centres. Yet, studies consistently show that deployed systems are underutilized and have key usability issues that limit their effectiveness in practice [1,5,8]. These studies reveal that potential users are often oblivious to the display, or reluctant to approach and interact with the system, often due to confusion over the system's purpose, and what actions are possible or desirable. Such issues are often referred to as participation thresholds [1] or interaction blindness [8], which have to be "overcome" through good understanding of the interaction process and informed design decisions of the interface.

My thesis aims at providing a systematic approach to model and analyze the underlying interaction process, and to devise an experimental methodology that allows researchers to focus particularly on the earlier stages of display interaction. Within this work, I refer to the process through which a user transitions from being unaware of the system to interacting with it to, eventually, effectively using the system as the "discoverability" process, which is named after classic usability literature [7].

Existing Research and Opportunities

To understand the issues involved in the discoverability process, researchers have developed models and frameworks that represent a continuum of phases throughout the interaction process between users and the display [1,5,9,10]. It is generally agreed that these phases can be arranged and mapped as increasing levels of engagement towards effective use of the display. A wide range of design recommendations are given by this prior work, primarily aimed at smoothly transitioning users through various phases of the process.

Many of these models, however, were developed based on field observations of or design for specific contexts, and thus may not be generally applicable. For example, the *Interaction Zones* (ambient, notification, and interaction) in Streitz et al.'s GossipWall [9] gauged a user's desire to engage based on their distance from the display. This may not be an accurate measure due to environmental constraints, such as busy traffic or tight space. Also, a compatible personal device, which was required in the interaction, might not be available in other contexts. Similarly, the *Audience Funnel* in Michelis and Müller's Magical Mirrors [5] modeled the interaction based on user's behavior in response to their own virtual reflection on the display. While useful for understanding how interactivity was communicated, this model did not consider and address possible user's frustration towards the interface, which are likely to happen when the system is designed to provide content beyond simple visual effects.

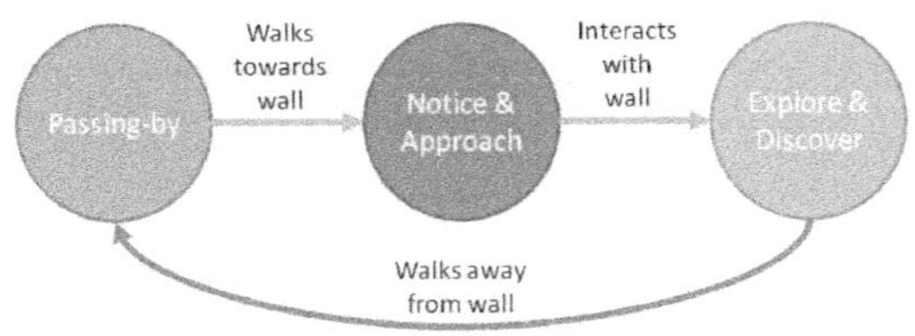

Figure 1. DISCOVER model adapted for evaluating a proposed interactive notice board application in a vertical wall setup [2].

Moreover, design recommendations derived from observations or classic usability advice may not be properly validated to be generalizable and precise [4] in the context of public settings. For example, the "honey-pot effect"[1] was observed frequently (e.g. [1,5]), and is therefore recommended to be exploited in several transitions. Yet, it is unclear if there is an optimal number of people, how much associated space is required, or how it compares with other techniques. Also, due to considerations such as space, cost, and safety, a fully functional installation might not always be available for evaluation. There is a need for a more rigorous experimental methodology that enables researchers to evaluate individual factors in any particular part of the discoverability process, and to evaluate aspects of a system before a fully functional application is installed.

My dissertation is expected to 1) offer an interaction model that unifies existing theories and models, and suggests potential research directions, and 2) devise a laboratory-based experimental methodology that allows validation of potential systems designs aimed to address specific aspects of the interaction process.

[1] Coined by Brignull and Rogers as "the progressive increase in the number of people in the vicinity of the [system]" [1, p.20]

An Interaction Model

Based on prior research and personal experience in developing large interactive displays for public settings, an interaction model called DISCOVER was developed. The DISCOVER model describes the overall interaction process with public displays using a number of transitions and user states, and focuses on the discoverability aspect of these types of systems. It is largely inspired by the *Ambient Display Framework* (ADF) by Vogel and Balakrishnan [10], where the progression of engagement is represented as transition events and system states. The DISCOVER model distinguishes itself from ADF by representing the interaction process from the user-centred discoverability perspective. It differs from other models by inclusion of unfavorable user states and transitions, such as user frustration and insufficient incentive for interaction.

In its entirety, the model can be used as a lens for synthesizing existing work on public displays, and as a summarizing framework of existing design advice. In parts, it can be used to represent different application categories. Two typical categories are 1) opportunistic applications (e.g., interactive storefront) where a user has no prior knowledge of the display, and 2) task-oriented applications (e.g., mall directory) where a user is aware of the display, but needs to discover how to interact with it.

The model can also be adapted/simplified by selecting and combining several user states to serve as an evaluation tool for proposed public interactive display systems. Figure 1 shows an example of such adaption in evaluating a proposed interactive notice board application [2].

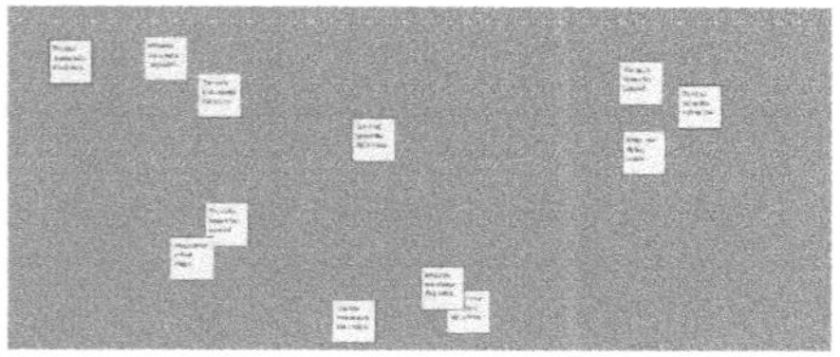

Figure 2. The interface prototype deployed on the large wall display (2560x800 screensize) in the exploratory study. Moving yellow rectangles resembling Post-it notes containing quotes and idioms were used as display content.

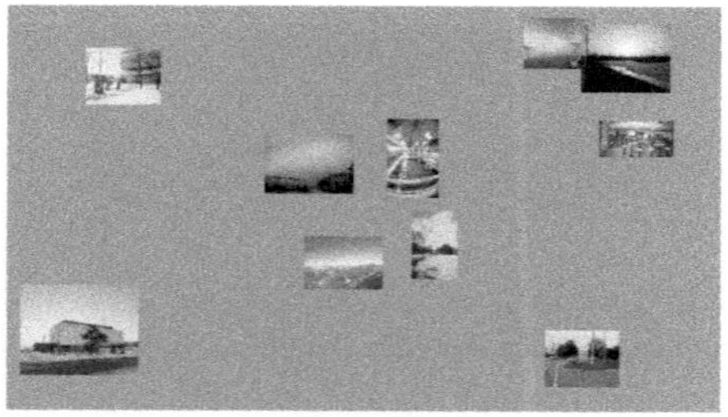

Figure 3. A control display (1280x800 screensize) in the exploratory study. Moving photos of the local university were used as the main content.

An Experimental Methodology

As mentioned, one use of the DISCOVER model is to evaluate proposed public interactive display systems. Researchers are free to select and/or combine user states to focus on any particular stage of the discoverability process. This in turn allows them to evaluate the effectiveness of a certain design technique towards the stage in question. For example, one can investigate whether animating the displayed content can better communicate interactivity to the users.

There has been a growing trend of "in-the-wild" studies, where the display is installed in a public space and its usage is observed and reported (e.g. [1,3,5]). This approach possesses a higher degree of realism, but lacks generalizability (the populations to which the results can be applied) and precision (control over extraneous variables that are not being studied) [4]. Also, the benefit of exploring a certain design technique may not outweigh the time and effort required to deploy a sufficiently robust interactive system in public, for example, a reasonably complete application in an adequately secure setup.

Thus, the second goal of my thesis is to devise a laboratory-based study methodology, which accomplishes two objectives:

- To allow for greater control of the environment and more precise measurement of user behavior, hence complementing the realism provided by the existing "in-the-wild" study methodology.
- To provide an alternative to installing a sufficiently complete interactive system, so that individual design techniques can be evaluated towards selected phases of the discoverability process.

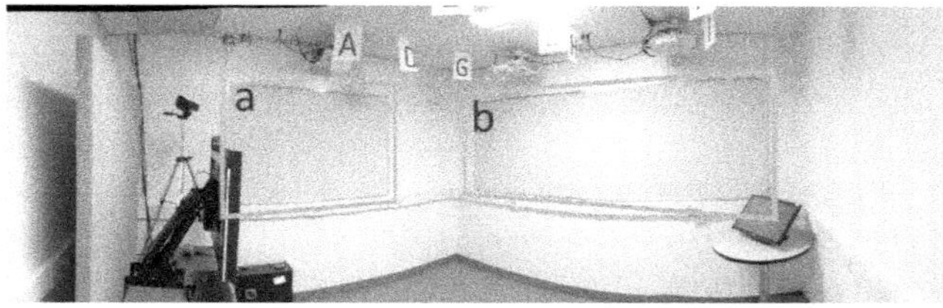

Figure 4. Experimental setup for the prototype. Display 'a' was projected from a single 1280x800 projector, display 'b' was projected from two adjacent projectors forming a 2560x800 screensize. Labels (A-I) were attached to the ceiling for participants to walk between in the deception navigation task.

The next section describes my initial efforts in developing and applying this methodology.

Prior and On-going Studies

Thus far I have conducted an exploratory study to investigate the effectiveness of variations in the display content's saliency (motion and contrast) [11] in response to user's proximity to the display, in capturing attention and communicating interactivity (i.e. the earliest stages of the discoverability process). A simple interface prototype was deployed on a large wall display powered by a Windows 7 PC and two Hitachi ultra-short-throw projectors (Figure 4b). The display content included moving yellow rectangles resembling Post-it notes containing quotes and idioms (Figure 2).

An interesting complication for the laboratory-based study was that recruited participants could not be informed of the actual purpose of the study, i.e., that the study was about capturing their attention to the wall display, as knowing this would render the results inconclusive. Therefore, a deception task was created where participants were asked to complete a navigation-related mobile phone task that involved walking between labels attached to the ceiling, while performing certain actions on their mobile phone, Meanwhile, various animation attributes were being manipulated on the nearby display (Table 1) to attempt to capture their attention during their deception task. When the deception task was completed participants were brought to another room and interviewed regarding their impression on the surroundings based on their memory (including the display), then told about the real purpose of the study, and interviewed again for further subjective feedback.

	Content speed adapting to user proximity	**Content speed constant**
Content contrast adapting to user proximity	Condition 1	Condition 2
Content contrast constant	Condition 3	Condition 4 (Baseline)

Table 1. Two factors for the exploratory study: adaptive speed and adaptive contrast (against background). A between-subject format was used where each participant was assigned with one condition only, as having multiple conditions is likely to confuse participant's impression and takes too much time.

Some key findings from the exploratory study included:

- None of the participants were offended by or upset about the deception involved after learning about the motivation behind.
- Participants were able to recall the setup, elaborate their answers, and provide further suggestions.
- Though recognized, the Post-it notes had little attractive power, especially when compared to a nearby control display with photos of the local university as the main content (Figure 3).
- The changes in content motion (slowing down when the user was close) and contrast (higher contrast when the user was close) were generally too subtle to notice and, thus, did not evoke a feeling of interactivity in participants.

Following on these findings, the methodology and prototype are currently being updated as follows, in preparation for a larger, more formal follow-on study:

- Investigate participants' impression of content interactivity with a more concise questionnaire.
- Increase relevance and interest of content to participants by replacing Post-it notes with photos of the university, similar to the control display.
- Make content's motion less subtle by introducing trajectory change and whimsical animation when the user is close by.
- Introduce a silhouette of the user, which is similar to the technique used by Müller et al. in Communiplay [6], but extended to have adaptive contrast based on user's proximity, and validate as an attention capturing mechanism in a laboratory setting.

The experimental methodology allowed us to quickly prototype an interface, and conduct a more rigorous laboratory study. It in turn allowed us to validate individual factors in a specific aspect of the interaction process, and elicit useful feedback from participants.

Figure 5. A complete interactive display with multi-touch interactivity. Currently set up inside a laboratory.

Future Plan

We are currently prototyping our modified interface for the next laboratory study. It is not intended that this methodology replaces "in-the-wild" field studies, but rather to offer a complementary methodology that enables rapid prototyping and testing in a controlled environment, yet still emulates the important factors of a public setting. To validate this methodology, its result will first be compared with findings from existing "in-the-wide" studies. Then, together with the in-depth subjective feedback, a complete interactive display (see Figure 5) will be installed in a university public foyer for a field study. However, as pointed out earlier, such installation entails considerations beyond the technology and interface design, such as security and safety, and requires more time than a laboratory setup.

Expected Contributions

My research is expected to contribute a deeper understanding of the interaction mechanisms between users and interactive public displays. Moreover, it will allow researchers and practitioners to make more informed design decisions, validate potential techniques, and ultimately building more usable interactive systems for public settings.

Acknowledgements

This work was funded in part by the Natural Science and Engineering Research Council of Canada (NSERC) and the NSERC Digital Surface Software Application Network (SurfNet). I would like to thank my co-supervisors, Drs. Stacey Scott and Edward Lank. I would also like to thank Joanne Leong, Frank Cento, Shrey Khosla, and others in the Collaborative Systems Laboratory and TouchLab for guidance and help in various stages of this work.

References

[1] Brignull, H. and Rogers, Y. Enticing people to interact with large public displays in public spaces. *INTERACT*, IOS Press (2003), 17–24.

[2] Cheung, V. and Scott, S.D. Investigating attraction and engagement of animation on large interactive walls in public settings. *ITS*, ACM Press (2013), 381–384.

[3] Hornecker, E. "I don't understand it either, but it is cool" - Visitor interactions with a multi-touch table in a museum. *TABLETOP*, IEEE (2008), 113–120.

[4] McGrath, J.E. *Groups: interaction and performance*. Prentice Hall, 1984.

[5] Michelis, D. and Müller, J. The audience funnel: observations of gesture based interaction with multiple large displays in a city center. *International Journal of Human-Computer Interaction 27*, 6 (2011), 562–579.

[6] Müller, J., Eberle, D., and Tollmar, K. Communiplay: a field study of a public display mediaspace. *CHI*, ACM Press (2014), 1415–1424.

[7] Norman, D. *The design of everyday things: revised and expanded edition*. Basic Books, Inc., New York, 2013.

[8] Ojala, T., Kostakos, V., Kukka, H., et al. Multipurpose interactive public displays in the wild: three years later. *Computer 45*, 5 (2012), 42–49.

[9] Streitz, N., Prante, T., Röcker, C., et al. Ambient displays and mobile devices for the creation of social architectural spaces. In *Public and Situated Displays*. Springer, 2003, 387–409.

[10] Vogel, D. and Balakrishnan, R. Interactive public ambient displays: transitioning from implicit to explicit, public to personal, interaction with multiple users. *UIST*, ACM Press (2004), 137–146.

[11] Yantis, S. How visual salience wins the battle for awareness. *Nature Neuroscience 8*, 8 (2005), 975–977.

Touching the Third Dimension

Paul Lubos
Human-Computer Interaction
Department of Informatics
University of Hamburg
paul.lubos@uni-hamburg.de

ITS 2014, November 16–19, 2014, Dresden, Germany.
ACM 978-1-4503-2587-5/14/11.
http://dx.doi.org/10.1145/2669485.2669490

Abstract
Natural interaction offers the user a great immersive experience and research has shown that especially multi-touch is easier to learn and utilize than classic human-computer interfaces, such as the keyboard and the mouse. However, creating 3D user interfaces (3D UIs) is a difficult endeavor, especially in fully immersive virtual environments (IVEs), such as head-mounted displays, because problems like distance underestimation and the lack of haptic feedback complicate the design and require new innovative solutions. Our research aims to identify the problems during the design of 3D UIs and the interaction with virtual objects in 3D space, and find ways to solve or avoid those problems, both for fully immersive environments and stereoscopic multi-touch displays. Furthermore, we aim to investigate new ways to utilize 3D UIs and improve on the available input devices.

Author Keywords
Spatial user interfaces, head-mounted displays, 3D interaction

ACM Classification Keywords
H.5.2 [Information Interfaces and Presentation]: User Interfaces – Input Devices and Strategies, Evaluation / Methodology..

Introduction

Currently, with the increasing popularity of 3D capable displays and the advent of low-cost head-mounted displays (HMDs), interaction with three dimensional content earned increasing interest. Also, the ability to directly touch virtual objects without using inconvenient input devices has been shown to be a very appealing experience for novice as well as expert users [20, 21]. In particular, passive haptic feedback provided by touch devices and multi-touch capabilities have considerable potential to improve the joy of use of such systems and new hardware solutions allow the tracking of user's postures and gestures in mid-air (e. g., Leap Motion, Kinect). The combination thereof provides a potential plethora of new interaction concepts in the area of multi-touch enabled stereoscopic surfaces and fully immersive HMDs. So far, only the first steps towards the wide understanding and utilization of those new technologies have been taken, due to various reasons [19]. The key challenges in the design of stereoscopic muli-touch enabled displays are, for example, missing haptic feedback, as well as well-known perceptual problems.

Also, in fully immersive environments, the lack of occlusion poses another problem. Since a lack of a real body is often unsettling, a virtual representation of the user's body or a part thereof has to be properly mapped to the virtual environment. Needless to say, the usage of a virtual body offers additional possibilities for user interfaces, since the virtual representation can be manipulated and differ from the user's actual body, which offers additional interesting challenges for the interface design. Over the course of this project a couple steps will be taken. First of all, the perceptual factors will be analyzed to determine which part of the perception plays a major role during multi-touch and mid-air interaction. Using the results, new and optimized interaction techniques will be developed to avoid and solve the perceptual problems and allow for more efficient interaction. Finally, widgets and applications will be devised which effectively utilize the combination of stereoscopic 3D and multi-touch or mid-air interaction.

Related Work

3D interaction in IVEs has been in the focus of many research groups over the last decades [1]. According to Mine et al. [16], direct interaction leads to significantly higher performance than manipulation of objects at a distance from the user's hand. Most results from similar studies agree on the point that optimal performance may be achieved when visual and motor spaces are superimposed or coupled closely [6, 11, 22]. Furthermore, a large body of literature has shown the benefits for bimanual interaction and several promising two-handed interaction techniques have been described, in particular in the area of 3D selection [9], symmetric interaction tasks [2], mobile devices [17] as well as touch interaction [18].

However, the influence of the position of virtual target objects located within arm's reach on interaction performance [10] is still an open research question. Direct interaction is subject to perceptual limitations, e. g., the vergence-accommodation mismatch, ghosting or double vision, which can result in strong misperception effects [3, 4, 5]. In particular, contributing factors may include interaction duration, hand and arm postures, frequency of movements, and comfort [1].

The main performance metric we utilized so far is Fitts' Law, which describes the tradeoff between speed and accuracy in selection tasks [8].

Results from studies of several research groups imply that Fitts' Law is indeed valid for the kinematics of arm movements in a 3D interaction space [7, 15].

Work Completed

We conducted various studies on direct selection in IVEs. First of all, we analyzed the direct selection and the effects the various perceptual problems have on selection within virtual environments.

Analysis of Direct Selection in Head-Mounted Display Environments

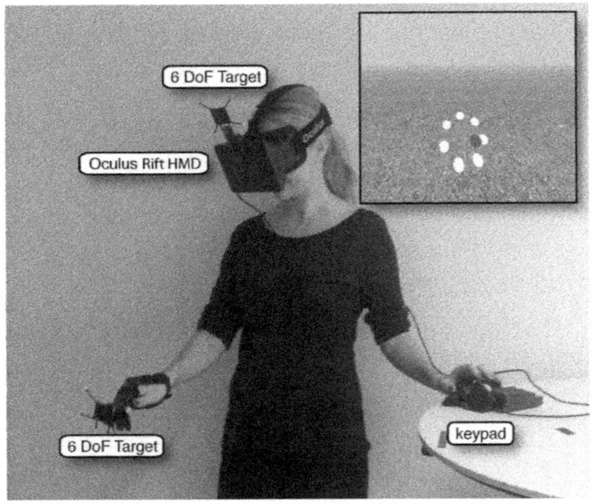

Figure 1: User during our first study. The inset shows the user's view to the VE with the white and blue target spheres as well as the yellow sphere that visually represents the virtual finger tip.

We conducted a Fitts' Law experiment, as shown in Figure 1, with 27 participants [12]. Our results show that the main factor causing errors in 3D selection is the visual perception and not, as presumed, the motor movement direction during selections. We found significantly more errors along the viewing axis than along the orthogonal axes. With these results, we suggest increased tolerance along the viewing axis, and proposed an ellipsoid cursor.

Moreover, our results indicate that the bottom regions, which are farther away along the viewing axis, are worse for precise tasks, despite the fact that they have a similar index of difficulty compared to visually close regions [15].

We propose the following guidelines for immersive HMD environments:

G1: 3D selection tasks, which require high precision, should be restricted to a level close to the eyes despite more comfortable interaction in the lower regions.

G2: For accurate selections of spherical targets, such as points, we suggest inflating the selection space using an ellipsoid cursor as illustrated in Figure 2.

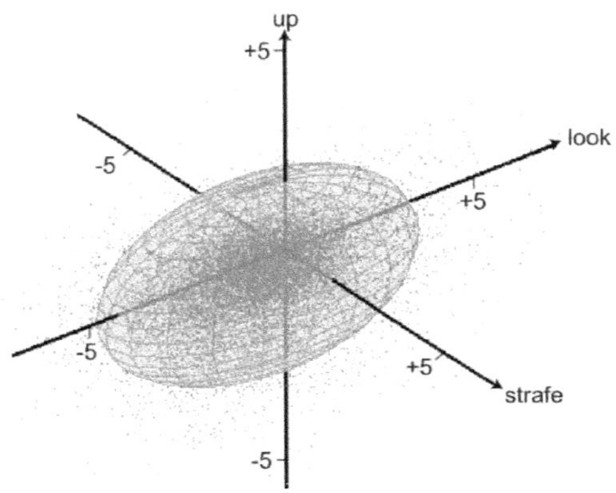

Figure 2: 95% confidence ellipsoid encompassing the hit points of the experiment around the center of the targets.

Influence of Comfort on 3D Selection Task Performance in Immersive Desktop Setups
Taking into account our results from the first study, we investigated the importance of comfort for the performance in 3D user interfaces [13]. We first conducted a pilot study to determine which regions are considered comfortable when interacting in mid-air while standing. Based on the results, we decided to analyze more comfortable body poses for the interaction. While many Science Fiction movies and novels envision a plethora of vivid virtual systems which demand that the user stands within them to navigate and control the system while moving utilizing their whole arms, prolonged use of such systems turns out to be immensely tasking for the user. Hence, we evaluated possibilities to increase the comfort. One such choice would be to allow users to rest their arm and to seat them in something similar to traditional desktop workspaces. For many application scenarios, for instance, when navigation is not required, this pose has the potential to be beneficial. The conducted Fitts' Law experiment yielded interesting results for such immersive desktop setups. To our knowledge, our experiment is one of the first studies which showed that comfort has a significant effect on effective throughput according to Fitts' Law in IVEs. Despite the high immersion of modern HMDs, it is necessary to carefully design the real environment to the user's comfort. These results offer interesting guidelines for future 3D UIs in immersive desktop setups:

G1: When the user has no possibility to rest their arm, the pose is uncomfortable and thus results in lower performance.

G2: For tasks allowing free placement of the 3D UI, the elements should be reachable without the necessity to move the arm from an armrest, e. g., along a partial sphere centered around the elbow rest.

The Interactive Spatial Surface (iSPACE)
The most recent project, mainly for further investigations regarding stereoscopic visualizations, we developed the iSPACE, as illustrated in Figure 3. The iSPACE is a setup of out-of-the-box components, which provides a shared space for collaborative interactions, e. g., point-cloud exploration and annotation. We combined a high resolution (4K) stereoscopic display with head-tracking for better depth perception, a multi-touch frame and a depth sensor for mid-air interaction [14], all of which are on a mobile stand capable of electronically adjusting the height and tilting of the screen.

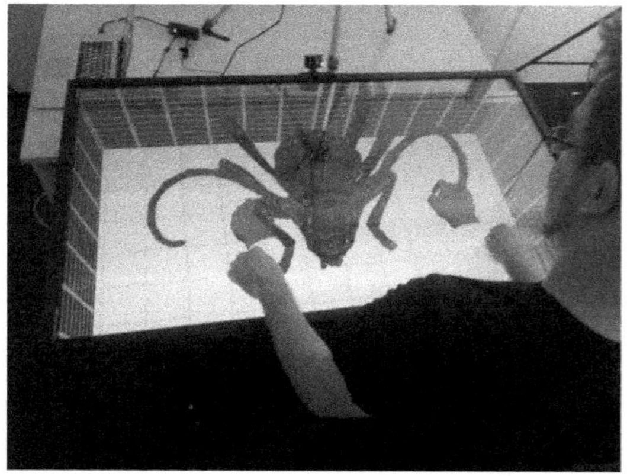

Figure 3: User exploring a point cloud data set on the iSPACE.

Future
Our research provided various possibilities for future work, for instance it is necessary to investigate the optimal size of the ellipsoid cursor and evaluate the performance gains provided. A quantitative study comparing the user's selection performance considering different ellipsoid sizes

might provide valuable insights. Additionally, our second study suggest the development of novel haptic feedback devices for immersive desktop setups. We aim to develop portable, comfortable armrests and utilize electrostimulation or vibration to provide users with simulated haptics, similar to the vibration on keypress employed by smart phones.

So far, the main research focus was on fully immersive HMD environments. In future studies we aim to focus on the challenges posed by stereoscopically displayed content on tangible displays, such as the iSPACE. As the setup offers high resolution, we hope to gain new insights on perceptual problems and provide solutions. The insights gathered during the HMD research have to be evaluated for surface research. To be precise, the suggested arm rests might increase the performance in certain tabletop setups, as well. The insights from the mid-air interaction in HMD environments could be used to provide users with natural ways of hovering. Currently, we are investigating the areas above a surface users prefer to explore spatial content.

Another project aims to determine the utility of a tiltable, mobile setup and whether this possibility can be used for collaborative, immersive exploration of 3D content. For example, a vertical screen setup offers users the possibility to use the iSPACE to directly interact with objects from a natural point of view, while the horizontal setup provides an aerial view. The transition between those setups could also be used for new interaction concepts.

References

[1] Argelaguet, F., and Andujar, C. A survey of 3D object selection techniques for virtual environments. *Computers & Graphics 37*, 3 (2013), 121–136.

[2] Balakrishnan, R., and Hinckley, K. Symmetric bimanual interaction. In *Proceedings of the SIGCHI conference on Human Factors in Computing Systems*, ACM (2000), 33–40.

[3] Bruder, G., Steinicke, F., and Stuerzlinger, W. Effects of visual conflicts on 3D selection task performance in stereoscopic display environments. In *Proc. of ACM 3DUI* (2013), 115–118.

[4] Bruder, G., Steinicke, F., and Stuerzlinger, W. Touching the Void Revisited: Analyses of Touch Behavior On and Above Tabletop Surfaces. *Lecture Notes in Computer Science: Human-Computer Interaction - INTERACT 2013 8117* (2013), 278–296.

[5] Chan, L.-W., Kao, H.-S., Chen, M. Y., Lee, M.-S., Hsu, J., and Hung, Y.-P. Touching the void: Direct-touch interaction for intangible displays. In *Proc. of ACM CHI* (2010), 2625–2634.

[6] Djajadiningrat, J. P. Cubby: what you see is where you act. interlacing the display and manipulation spaces.

[7] Dvorkin, A. Y., Kenyon, R. V., and Keshner, E. A. Reaching within a dynamic virtual environment. *J. NeuroEng. Rehabil. 4*, 23 (2007).

[8] Fitts, P. The Information Capacity of the Human Motor System in Controlling the Amplitude of Movement. *Journal of Experimental Psychology 47*, 6 (1954), 381–391.

[9] Grossman, T., and Balakrishnan, R. The design and evaluation of selection techniques for 3D volumetric displays. In *Proceedings of the 19th annual ACM symposium on User interface software and technology*, ACM (2006), 3–12.

[10] Hofmann, M., Brger, R., Frost, N., Karremann, J., Keller-Bacher, J., Kraft, S., Bruder, G., and Steinicke, F. Comparing 3D interaction performance in comfortable and uncomfortable regions. In *Proceedings of the GI-Workshop VR/AR, 3-14* (2013).

[11] Lemmerman, D. K., and LaViola, J. J. Effects of interaction-display offset on user performance in surround screen virtual environments. In *Virtual Reality Conference, 2007. VR'07. IEEE*, IEEE (2007), 303–304.

[12] Lubos, P., Bruder, G., and Steinicke, F. Analysis of Direct Selection in Head-Mounted Display Environments. In *IEEE Symposium on 3D User Interfaces (3DUI)*, IEEE (2014), 11–18.

[13] Lubos, P., Bruder, G., and Steinicke, F. Influence of Comfort on 3D Selection Task Performance in Immersive Desktop Setups. *JVRB* (2014), Accepted as Article.

[14] Lubos, P., Garber, C., Hoffert, A., Reis, I., and Steinicke, F. The Interactive Spatial Surface - Blended Interaction on a Stereoscopic Multi-Touch Surface. In *Workshop Blended Interaction, Proceedings of Mensch und Computer 2014*, Oldenbourg Publishing, München (2014), Accepted for publication.

[15] MacKenzie, I. S., and Isokoski, P. Fitts' throughput and the speed-accuracy tradeoff. In *Proc. of ACM CHI* (2008), 1633–1636.

[16] Mine, M. R., Brooks Jr, F. P., and Sequin, C. H. Moving objects in space: exploiting proprioception in virtual-environment interaction. In *Proceedings of the 24th annual conference on Computer graphics and interactive techniques*, ACM Press/Addison-Wesley Publishing Co. (1997), 19–26.

[17] Ng, A., Brewster, S. A., and Williamson, J. H. Investigating the effects of encumbrance on one-and two-handed interactions with mobile devices. In *Proceedings of the 32nd annual ACM conference on Human factors in computing systems*, ACM (2014), 1981–1990.

[18] Ohnishi, T., Lindeman, R., and Kiyokawa, K. Multiple Multi-touch Touchpads for 3D Selection. In *3D User Interfaces (3DUI), 2011 IEEE Symposium on*, IEEE (2011), 115–116.

[19] Steinicke, F., Benko, H., Daiber, F., Keefe, D., and de la Rivière, J.-B. Touching the 3rd dimension (t3d). In *CHI '11 Extended Abstracts on Human Factors in Computing Systems*, CHI EA '11, ACM (New York, NY, USA, 2011), 161–164.

[20] Steinicke, F., Benko, H., Krüger, A., Keefe, D., de la Riviére, J.-B., Anderson, K., Häkkilä, J., Arhippainen, L., and Pakanen, M. The 3rd dimension of chi (3dchi): Touching and designing 3d user interfaces. In *CHI '12 Extended Abstracts on Human Factors in Computing Systems*, CHI EA '12, ACM (New York, NY, USA, 2012), 2695–2698.

[21] Valkov, D., Steinicke, F., Bruder, G., Hinrichs, K., Schöning, J., Daiber, F., and Krüger, A. Touching floating objects in projection-based virtual reality environments. In *Proceedings of Joint Virtual Reality Conference (JVRC)* (2010), 17–24.

[22] Wang, Y., and MacKenzie, C. L. Effects of orientation disparity between haptic and graphic displays of objects in virtual environments. In *INTERACT*, vol. 99 (1999), 391–398.

Supporting Everyday Thinking Practices in Information Visualization Interfaces

Jagoda Walny
Innovis Group, Interactions Lab
University of Calgary
Calgary, AB, Canada
jkwalny@ucalgary.ca

Figure 1: Changing a bar chart into a line chart using the prototype created for our Wizard of Oz study [19] for understanding how people would approach interactively sketching visualizations.

ITS 2014, November 16–19, 2014, Dresden, Germany.
ACM 978-1-4503-2587-5/14/11.
http://dx.doi.org/10.1145/2669485.2669491

Abstract
People commonly sketch externalizations on paper and whiteboards as part of their everyday thinking processes. While common, this practice is little understood, particularly as it may relate to digital visual representation (such as information visualization) and sketch-based interaction. My research aims to better understand these thinking sketches from the perspective of information visualization and pen-and-touch interaction and to apply this understanding to the design of interfaces that can better support complex and freeform everyday thinking practices.

Author Keywords
information visualization; pen-and-touch interaction; sketched externalizations; qualitative evaluation

ACM Classification Keywords
H.5.2 [Information interfaces and presentation (e.g., HCI)]: User Interfaces.

Introduction
When visiting the offices of knowledge workers, it is not uncommon to see diagrams, mind maps, and scraps of information scribbled on whiteboards alongside notebooks filled with ideas and sketches for problem solving. These visual artifacts are residue of the process of *externalization*

- the reification of internal thought to support cognition. Externalizations support cognition in a variety of ways, including providing a way to offload memory or to solve problems more efficiently [8]. They are often ad-hoc, created on the fly to suit a given context. This spontaneous practice becomes more difficult when the objects of thought are dynamic representations of digital data that would be tedious to reproduce manually but whose manipulation is restricted by the design of the interface containing it. The availability of pen and touch hardware provides an opportunity to better support such thinking practices with digital information.

The goal of my research is to further our understanding of how to better support externalization for digital information. The information visualization community has tackled its goal of aiding cognition of digital information [5] by shaping data into more manageable and interactive representations. The approaches to this have been mainly data-centric [14] (shaped by the data) or task-centric [1] (shaped by the tasks to be accomplished with the data). However, while these approaches make the information - or select aspects of the information - easier to understand, this still leaves room for a complementary *human-centric* approach, in which people's common thinking processes are supported.

My broad approach to this research consists of two phases:

- 1. Exploration: Deepen our understanding of externalization from an information visualization perspective by performing qualitative exploratory studies. In particular, I look at *sketched* externalizations.
- 2. Application: Apply this deepened understanding to the design of interfaces and/or interaction techniques that support externalization, with a particular focus on using interactive pen- and touch-enabled surfaces.

In my research, I aim to leverage the similarity of pen and touch surfaces to conventional whiteboards to support thinking with digital information. As such, I build on prior work on pen and touch interfaces as well as work done on supporting paper- or whiteboard-based practices digitally. Sketch-based interfaces date back to Sutherland's Sketchpad [15], and have been used, among others, for modeling 3D objects [12], for interactive mathematical sketching [2, 9, 10], for creating visual queries of data [20, 13], and creating information visualizations [6, 4]. Typically, in these systems, sketches are interpreted as commands or inputs to the system. In contrast, my research is concerned with creating interfaces that support freeform sketched externalizations, which may not always have a pre-defined or expected form that can be interpreted. Pen and touch interfaces provide a richer potential set of tools [7], and recent work suggests that bimanual pen and touch interactions can be effective [3].

Prior research into supporting knowledge workers' thinking practices in general has resulted in systems that emulate and extend conventional whiteboards with the advantages of the digital environment [11]. My focus is not on creating digital whiteboards, but on supporting the kinds of behaviours one finds on conventional whiteboards for those working with digital information. One approach that allows for some externalization practices when working with digital information has involved integrating digital and analog technologies. For example, Brandl et al. created NiCEBook [3], a paper notebook that synchronizes with its digital representation. This approach has the advantage of preserving the affordances of paper, but may not be sufficient when working with dynamic visualizations of data.

Exploratory Studies

I have completed three qualitative exploratory studies of externalization through sketching, summarized here.

Visualizations on Whiteboards

To arrive at a better understanding of the nature of visuals created spontaneously during everyday thinking tasks, we studied a collection of 82 snapshots of 69 knowledge workers' whiteboards collected at a large research institution [17]. As these whiteboards were in individuals' offices, they contained the residue of various kinds of thought, from small pieces of information to remember, to sketches used to work out problems, to those used in small-group discussions. We analyzed these qualitatively from an information visualization perspective, examining the types of visual constructs used (both recognizable and novel) as well as the relationship between words and diagrammatic constructs. Follow-up interviews with a subset of the participants validated our categorization of constructs and gave us valuable insight into the nature of the visuals.

This study resulted in a taxonomy of the kinds of constructs and visual strategies people use to express their thoughts, including communicative symbols, layering, spatial organization, and information visualization constructs. It also demonstrated the *words-to-diagrams spectrum*, which describes the variable nature of how words are used in relation to diagrammatic constructs. This highlighted the restrictive nature of software that, when providing support for making diagrams or visualizations, considers words only in the role of labels.

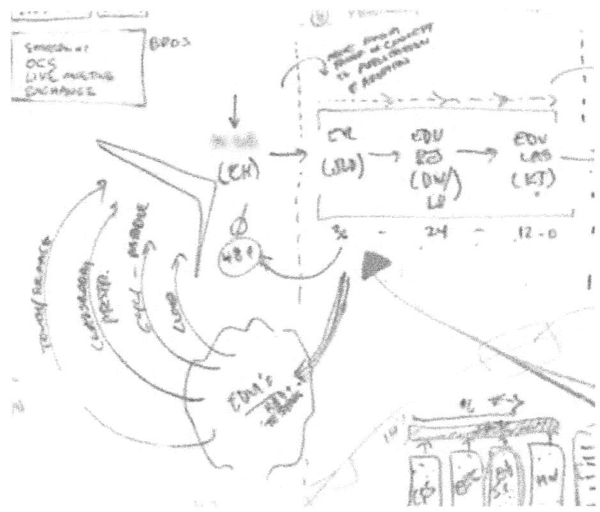

Figure 2: An example of a complex, freeform externalization on a whiteboard. ©2011 IEEE. Reprinted, with permission, from [17].

Sketching Data

Sketching concepts and ideas on whiteboards may not be entirely analogous to sketching data. We asked people to use colored pencils to sketch a small, relatable, and easily understandable dataset in whatever way they chose and to report on what they learned about the data [16]. Our analysis has focused on qualitatively classifying the wide variety of representations collected and relating the types of representations to the types of insights gained.

Lifecycles of Diagrams and Sketches

We have also examined the context of externalization practices on a broader level by interviewing computer scientists about sketches and diagrams that were important to a recent project [18]. From these interviews, we reconstructed the lifecycles of these sketches in terms of the context (personal, group, or public), the medium used (e.g. paper, tablet, whiteboard), and the transitions that a sketch underwent (e.g. creation, refinement, sharing). See Figure 3 for a sample. This study highlighted the variety of habits and strategies used by people in their thinking processes, suggesting that a one-size-fits-all interface for supporting thinking may not be feasible.

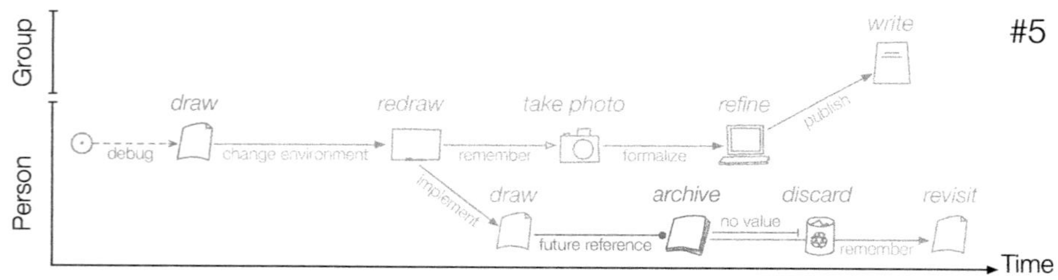

Figure 3: A lifecycle from of a single sketch significant to a computer scientist's project. ©2011 IEEE. Reprinted, with permission, from [18].

Studying Application Challenges

This phase of my research involves discovering how the insights gained in the exploratory studies can be applied to information visualization tools that support externalization. The purpose of this is to highlight the challenges inherent in the design of such tools and to suggest some design strategies moving forward. As such, my plan is to use as a basis standard interactive visualizations typical of what is commonly seen on the web, such as interactive bar charts and graph visualizations. I am focused in particular on the context of pen-and-touch surfaces due to their being the closest in nature to an analog whiteboard or piece of paper. To date, we have completed one study; the next steps are described in the following section.

Understanding Pen and Touch Interaction for Data Exploration

Our first foray into designing an interactive system that supports thinking practices was to design a system for creating simple visualizations based on real data just by sketching them [19]. We ran a Wizard of Oz study based on our design in order to see how people would approach interactively sketching a simple information visualization. During the study, we asked participants to figure out how to use the system on their own in order to see what types of interactions they tended towards naturally.

Our system, shown in Figure 1, was designed to keep the interface out of the way as much as possible by supporting specification of what one wants to see by simply drawing it, supporting manipulation of objects that is as direct as possible, minimizing explicit mode-switching, and providing good default behaviours.

Our study results indicated that participants drew on knowledge from both the physical world and from what they had already learned about the system in order to infer how to perform new tasks. Our participants had a clear idea of when to use pen and when to use multitouch interactions, which was drawn from their experience in the physical world; they also used a variety of postures when holding the pen and performing combined pen and touch interactions. They used multiple interaction paths for the same task and also tended to perform integrated interactions, where interaction with the data and other elements on the screen occurs in proximity to the objects being acted upon.

The Next Steps

My initial inquiry into applying the results of the above studies to information visualization software has highlighted some of the particular challenges of designing thinking interfaces. The design of these interfaces goes beyond usability and learnability into supporting complex and often freeform and rapid thinking practices. One challenge is in knowing how to create interfaces that do not interfere with thought processes. Another challenge is in supporting externalization practices for *dynamic* representations of information. My current project, following from our study of whiteboards [17], explores the space where words and diagrammatic elements are tightly intermingled in a single thinking diagram. This poses several interesting design challenges such as knowing when to distinguish between words and drawn elements.

The exploratory portion of my research is largely complete, and my aim is to use the remainder of my PhD to apply the understanding I have gained through these studies to the creation of software, particularly as mentioned above, making use of the words-to-diagrams spectrum. However, I believe that an important part of my PhD contribution will remain the new understanding of how people use sketched visuals as externalizations during their thinking processes.

Acknowledgements

I would like to thank my supervisor, Sheelagh Carpendale, and my collaborators and colleagues in both the Interactions Lab and Microsoft Research for their support. This research was supported in part by Microsoft Research, NSERC, SMART Technologies, Alberta Innovates Technology Futures, SurfNet, and GRAND.

References

[1] Amar, R., and Stasko, J. A knowledge task-based framework for design and evaluation of information visualizations. In *Information Visualization, IEEE Symposium on* (2004), 143–150.

[2] Bott, J. N., and LaViola, Jr., J. J. A pen-based tool for visualizing vector mathematics. In *Proceedings of the Seventh Sketch-Based Interfaces and Modeling Symposium*, SBIM '10, Eurographics Association (Aire-la-Ville, Switzerland, Switzerland, 2010), 103–110.

[3] Brandl, P., Forlines, C., Wigdor, D., Haller, M., and Shen, C. Combining and measuring the benefits of bimanual pen and direct-touch interaction on horizontal interfaces. In *Proceedings of the Working Conference on Advanced Visual Interfaces*, AVI '08, ACM (New York, NY, USA, 2008), 154–161.

[4] Browne, J., Lee, B., Carpendale, S., Riche, N., and Sherwood, T. Data analysis on interactive whiteboards through sketch-based interaction. In *Proceedings of the ACM International Conference on Interactive Tabletops and Surfaces*, ITS '11, ACM (New York, NY, USA, 2011), 154–157.

[5] Card, S. K., Mackinlay, J. D., and Shneiderman, B. *Readings in information visualization: Using vision to think*. Morgan Kaufmann, 1999.

[6] Chao, W. O., Munzner, T., and van de Panne, M. Poster: Rapid pen-centric authoring of improvisational visualizations with NapkinVis. *Posters Compendium InfoVis* (2010).

[7] Hinckley, K., Yatani, K., Pahud, M., Coddington, N., Rodenhouse, J., Wilson, A., Benko, H., and Buxton, B. Pen + touch = new tools. In *Proceedings of the 23rd Annual ACM Symposium on User Interface Software and Technology*, UIST '10, ACM (New York, NY, USA, 2010), 27–36.

[8] Kirsh, D. Thinking with external representations. *AI Society 25*, 4 (2010), 441–454.

[9] LaViola, Jr., J. J., and Zeleznik, R. C. Mathpad2: A system for the creation and exploration of mathematical sketches. In *ACM SIGGRAPH 2007 Courses*, SIGGRAPH '07, ACM (New York, NY, USA, 2007).

[10] Leitner, J., Rendl, C., Perteneder, F., Gokcezade, A., Seifried, T., Haller, M., Zeleznik, R., and Bragdon, A. NiCE formula editor. In *ACM SIGGRAPH 2010 Talks*, SIGGRAPH '10, ACM (New York, NY, USA, 2010), 55:1–55:1.

[11] Mynatt, E., Huang, E., Voida, S., and MacIntyre, B. Large displays for knowledge work. In *Public and Situated Displays*, K. OHara, M. Perry, E. Churchill, and D. Russell, Eds., vol. 2 of *The Kluwer International series on Computer Supported Cooperative Work*. Springer Netherlands, 2003, 80–102.

[12] Olsen, L., Samavati, F. F., Sousa, M. C., and Jorge, J. A. Sketch-based modeling: A survey. *Computers & Graphics 33*, 1 (2009), 85–103.

[13] Ryall, K., Lesh, N., Lanning, T., Leigh, D., Miyashita, H., and Makino, S. Querylines: Approximate query for visual browsing. In *CHI '05 Extended Abstracts on Human Factors in Computing Systems*, CHI EA '05, ACM (New York, NY, USA, 2005), 1765–1768.

[14] Shneiderman, B. The eyes have it: A task by data type taxonomy for information visualizations. In *Visual Languages, IEEE Symposium on* (1996), 336–343.

[15] Sutherland, I. E. Sketch pad: A man-machine graphical communication system. In *Proceedings of the SHARE Design Automation Workshop*, DAC '64, ACM (New York, NY, USA, 1964), 6.329–6.346.

[16] Walny, J., and Carpendale, S. Data sketches: An exploratory study. *InfoVis 2014 Posters Compendium* (to appear).

[17] Walny, J., Carpendale, S., Riche, N., Venolia, G., and Fawcett, P. Visual thinking in action: Visualizations as used on whiteboards. *Visualization and Computer Graphics, IEEE Transactions on 17*, 12 (Dec 2011), 2508–2517.

[18] Walny, J., Haber, J., Dork, M., Sillito, J., and Carpendale, S. Follow that sketch: Lifecycles of diagrams and sketches in software development. In *Visualizing Software for Understanding and Analysis (VISSOFT), 2011 6th IEEE International Workshop on* (Sept 2011), 1–8.

[19] Walny, J., Lee, B., Johns, P., Riche, N., and Carpendale, S. Understanding pen and touch interaction for data exploration on interactive whiteboards. *Visualization and Computer Graphics, IEEE Transactions on 18*, 12 (Dec 2012), 2779–2788.

[20] Wattenberg, M. Sketching a graph to query a time-series database. In *CHI '01 Extended Abstracts on Human Factors in Computing Systems*, CHI EA '01, ACM (New York, NY, USA, 2001), 381–382.

Exploiting Spatial Memory and Navigation Performance in Dynamic Peephole Environments

Jens Müller
HCI Group, University of Konstanz
Universitätsstraße 10
Konstanz, 78457, Germany
Jens.Mueller@uni-konstanz.de

Abstract

One way to handle the representation of (and the navigation in) datasets that exceed the available display space is by provisioning movable viewports which display a subset of the entire space. Unlike static viewports, where the information space is moved (e.g. by panning), dynamic viewports – so-called dynamic peepholes – allow the user to move the viewport in physical space and thereby enable egocentric navigation in digital information spaces.

ITS 2014, November 16–19, 2014, Dresden, Germany.
ACM 978-1-4503-2587-5/14/11.
http://dx.doi.org/10.1145/2669485.2669492

In my research I investigate how information spaces and the navigation with peepholes need to be designed in order to exploit spatial memory and navigation performance. In particular I focus on the interplay between the physical and the digital aspects and how they affect user performance. For study purposes I use a tablet as a dynamic peephole. I will conduct controlled studies in our research lab, which is equipped with 24 infrared cameras and enable a precise tracking of the lab environment.

Author Keywords

Information spaces; Dynamic Peephole Navigation; Egocentric Navigation; Spatial Memory; Navigation Performance; Mobile computing

ACM Classification Keywords

H.5.2. User Interfaces: Interaction styles. Input devices and strategies. Evaluation/methodology.

Research Situation

I hold a Bachelor's degree in Computer Science in Media (Furtwangen University) and a Master's degree in Information Engineering (University of Konstanz). As part of a research project on the design of control rooms (see e.g. [1][10][14][15]) my master thesis

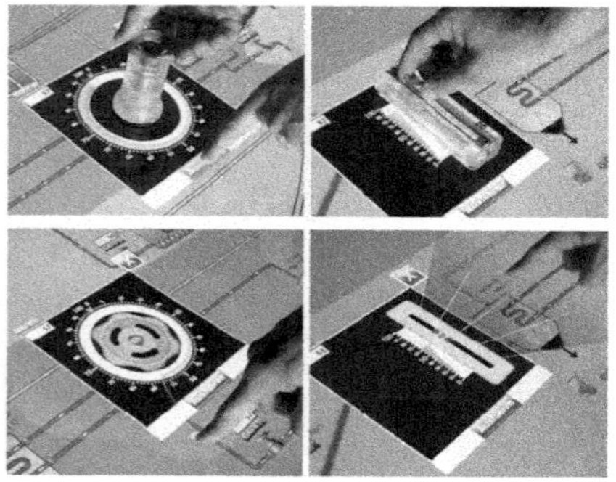

Figure 1. Two tangible concepts (top) and two touch concepts to control numeric process values [10].

Figure 2. Interactive display installation in the public library of Cologne. See [9] for the basic concept.

deals with the design of operator workplaces. For my thesis I designed and implemented several touch- and tangible concepts to manipulate numeric process values (see Figure 1) and compared them with traditional mouse- and keyboard input styles [10]. The design process was based on the Reality-Based Interaction (RBI) [5] framework. In the interim, two claims of RBI have influenced my way of thinking about interface design: First, exploit humans' preexisting skills and abilities to make interaction as natural as possible, and second, balance the interaction qualities of the analog world with the potentials of the digital world.

Since the beginning of my first year I have been affiliated with a public library project which is funded by the Ministry for Family, Youth, Culture and Sports of the Federal German State of North Rhine-Westphalia. The project investigates how new information technologies can contribute to providing appropriate access to both traditional analogue media and the expanding range of digital information and services. (See Figure 2 for the prototype in situ). I'm now in the middle of my second year.

Context and Motivation

My motivation for this proposal originates from the library project and evolved from three major observations that I made in a six-day contextual inquiry: *First*, library visitors, in particular knowledge workers, have to handle an expanding body of information – in constant physical space! *Second*, most visitors prefer seeking information by navigating in physical space (i.e. they browse the shelves) rather than using the online library catalog. And *thirdly*, the current search interface, the desktop-based online catalog, represents an isolated application which is experienced as an alternative to the physical browsing and searching process rather than complementing it.

At the same time I became familiar with *dynamic peephole navigation* [8] and learned about the potentials that spatially-aware mobile devices provide. Dynamic peephole navigation allows users to explore information spaces in an egocentric way, where the screen of a handheld device, such as a smartphone or a tablet, acts as a viewport on an information space. Instead of panning the screen content (e.g. a map), users can physically move to off-screen content (e.g. cities outside the viewport) as if it were situated in physical space. In a controlled lab experiment we [12] investigated the effect of three peephole sizes on users' navigation behavior, navigation performance, and task load (Figure 3).

Figure 3. Map navigation using a (simulated) tablet sized peephole [12].

Figure 4. The Chameleon prototype by Fitzmaurice [2]. A spatially-aware palmtop serves as a viewport on a situated information space.

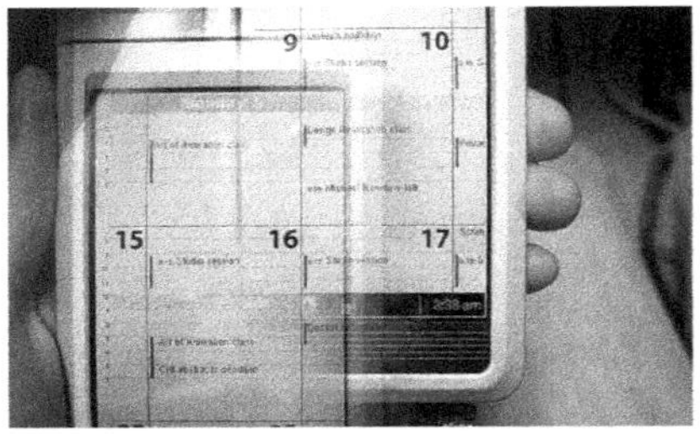

Figure 5. Yee's [17] Doodle Pad, a continuation of the Chameleon Prototype [2].

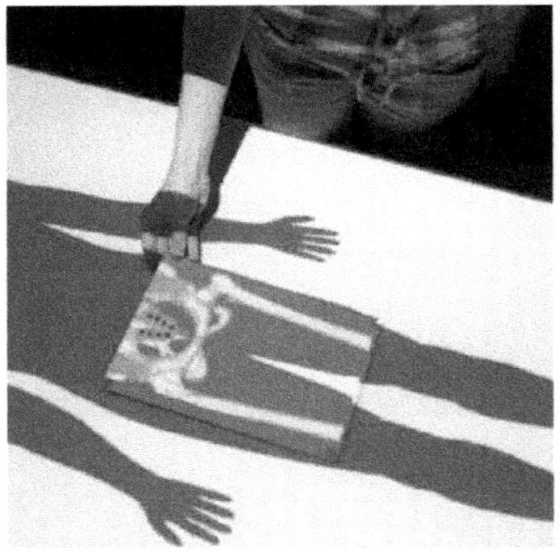

Figure 6. The PaperLens prototype [16] showing the skeleton layer above the tabletop.

My contact with dynamic peepholes as viewports on information spaces together with my prior observations in the library domain resulted in the following question:

"How can we use our physical environment (and our pre-existing knowledge and skills that refer to our environment) to create information spaces in which we can seamlessly navigate and interact with digital and physical content in a natural way?"

Referring to the RBI design trade-offs [5], I am particularly interested in the question which physical aspects of interaction should be preserved in such spaces and which aspects should be extended or even replaced by digital functionality.

Background and Related Work

This section provides an overview of both related interfaces and research on the cognitive aspects of egocentric navigation with peepholes.

Peephole Navigation Applications

In 1993 Fitzmaurice [2] presented the concept of situated information spaces – physical spaces which are semantically augmented with digital information. Spatially aware handheld devices, such as his Chameleon prototype, act as a viewport and can be used to access and navigate these spaces (Figure 4). He considered computer-augmented libraries and offices to be future application areas for situated information spaces.

In 2003 Yee [17] presented the Doodle Pad (Figure 5), a peephole prototype to create and manipulate objects that are larger than the display. He considered his work a direct descendant of Fitzmaurice's Chameleon [2].

Furthermore, he contributed a working implementation of multiple applications, arranged around the user in a personal information space. A usability test showed that the "peephole technique can be more effective than current methods for navigating information on handheld computers" [17]. He finally points out, however, that "the tracking hardware has a long way to go before it is truly robust" [17].

2009 Spindler et al. [16] presented PaperLens, a peephole prototype to navigate a virtual information space spanned above the tabletop (Figure 6) and contributed a classification of 3D spaces. Compared to the first peephole prototypes, which were based on digital displays, the image of the PaperLens [16] is generated via projection on a paper.

For a long time, study around dynamic peephole navigation has been subject to technological limitations. We now have the technology (for instance camera-based tracking systems and a variety of sensors inside our mobile devices) to design and evaluate information spaces that are accessible in an egocentric manner.

Research on Cognitive Aspects

In addition to the changes in technology, recent cognitive theories give special consideration to humans' structured environment. Distributed cognition [4] for instance assumes that our physical environment is an essential element in the cognitive system – externalizing information can, for instance, reduce memory load. Recent theories in this research area may serve as both a starting point for the design of digitally augmented environments (e.g. as in [3]) and also as a reference to explain observed effects.

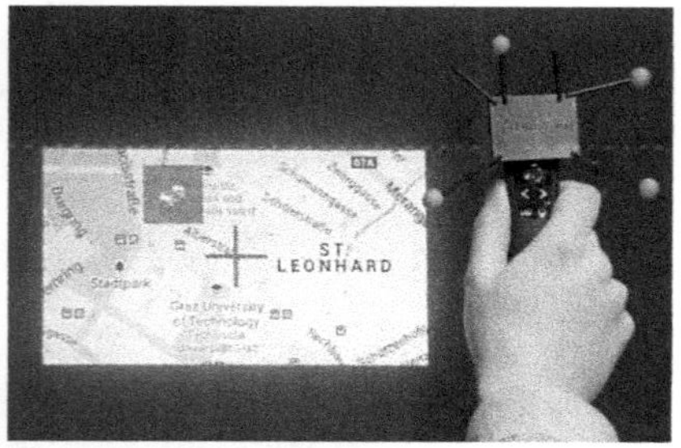

Figure 7. Tabled-sized peephole within a controlled lab study on the impact of peephole size on navigation performance, spatial memory, and subjective workload [12].

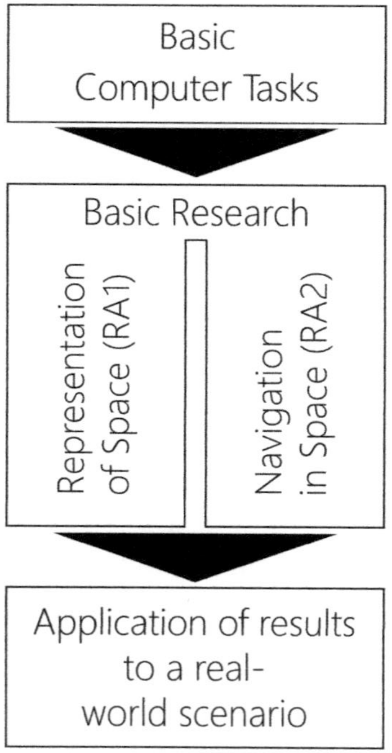

Figure 8. Anticipated research plan.

In several studies the cognitive benefits of egocentric peephole navigation has been proved, when compared to traditional interaction styles. In 2006 Mehra et al. [8] compared static peepholes (static viewport and pannable landscape) with dynamic peepholes (fixed landscape and movable viewport) and investigated the perception of line lengths on an information landscape. The study showed that dynamic peephole navigation results in a significantly better line length discrimination.

In 2012 Rädle et al. [11] compared egocentric navigation with traditional touch navigation in terms of navigation performance, spatial memory, and subjective workload. Their study revealed an effect on navigation performance and long term spatial memory in favor of egocentric navigation. For subjective workload, participants reported a significantly higher physical and a lower mental demand in the egocentric condition.

Kaufmann and Ahlström [6] investigated the impact of peephole size (projector phone vs. smartphone) on spatial memory and navigation performance. While there were no significant differences in navigation performance they showed that spatial memory performance was significantly better when participants navigated with the projector phone.

Similarly, Rädle et al. [12] investigated the effect of the peephole size on users' map navigation behavior, navigation performance, and task load. They simulated 4 peephole sizes: smartphone (4"), tablet (10.1"), projector phone (54.7"), and control condition (120", peephoe size equaled the size of the entire landscape). They identified the tablet condition as "sweet spot" in terms of peephole size and both user navigation performance and user task load.

A general overview on spatial memory in user interfaces is provided by Scarr et al. [13], who discuss the crucial role of the two spatial reference systems *landmarks* and *frame of reference*.

Thesis scope

In my research I focus on basic tasks such as navigating in digital information and organizing digital content, tools and associated activities. I assign the aspects that are relevant to these tasks to the two research areas *Representation of Space* and *Navigation in Space* (Figure 8). In the first part of my research I will do basic research in both areas in a controlled lab environment. In the second part I will apply the results of the basic research to a real-world scenario, e.g. such as the augmented library. Based on our prior study results ([12]) I will use a tablet computer as viewport.

- In the research area *Representation of Space* (RA1) I investigate the perceivable (i.e. the physical and virtual) properties of information spaces to support spatial memory and navigation performance. Critical parameters in this area refer to the effect of spatial reference systems such as *landmarks* and *frames of reference* [13] and whether their representation (e.g. virtual on screen vs. in the physical environment vs. hybrid as room-wide projection) has an impact on user performance, e.g. on spatial memory. Another aspect in this area refers to the layout of information spaces. Except for small-scale, table-based application such as the PaperLens prototype [16], research on dynamic peephole navigation refers to information spaces in

Figure 9. Sketch of a study to investigate the effects of two different orientations of the information space. (The colored rectangles are virtual, and thus can only be seen through the tablet.)

which information is laid out vertically, i.e. navigation is performed parallel to walls or large wall displays (see e.g. [6][11][12]). Little, however, is known on how well egocentric navigation works in larger, horizontally laid-out information spaces such as floors (see Figure 9). Considering our natural skills, it can be hypothesized that peephole navigation may be experienced even more natural if the information space is laid out horizontally. Additionally, this orientation provides more space accessible by the user, with which to lay out digital information. Finally, and referring to the classification of space by Spindler et al. [16], I will address the question how constant and limited physical space can be best used to layout arbitrarily large sets of data.

- In the research area *Navigation in Space* (RA2) I investigate the effects of different navigation properties and features such as modified control-display gain or (egocentric and non-egocentric) zooming on users' spatial memory and navigation performance. I will focus on the question whether yielding better results for navigation performance (e.g. by bypassing the naïve physics [5] through an increased control-display gain) are at the expense of spatial memory. Furthermore, I will design and evaluate navigation concepts that address the problem of limited physical space for the navigation of an arbitrarily large amount of digital information.

Accordingly, I will conduct studies under controlled conditions in our lab (Figure 10). For the study infrastructure I will use 24 infrared cameras and the proximity toolkit [7], a framework which provides proxemic relations, such as distance and orientation between the objects (persons, devices, and interior) within the lab infrastructure.

Dissertation Status

My current work focusses on the establishment of the study environment. The environment includes a 3D model of our lab and provides the opportunity to set up the studies for basic research associated with RA1 and RA2. The first study aims at investigating the layout of planar information spaces (Figure 9). In this study I will compare both layouts in terms of an egocentric study task, in which participants will need to navigate to virtual symbols on the information landscapes and reconstruct their position afterwards. Data referring to navigation performance and subjective workload will also be gathered.

Figure 10. Study lab equipped with 24 optitrack cameras connected to the proximity toolkit [7]. The setting allows for precise tracking and controlled lab studies.

Expected contributions

With my research I will contribute to a better understanding on how to use our physical environment and exploit the associated motor and spatial memory skills for dynamic peephole navigation. The findings of my research can then be applied to real-world problems to generate scenarios such as the digitally augmented library and the surrogate office envisioned by Fitzmaurice [2].

References

[1] Butscher, S., Müller, J., Schwarz, T., and Reiterer, H. Blended Interaction as an Approach for Holistic Control Room Design. *Workshop on Blended Interaction: Envisioning Future Collaborative Interactive Spaces (In conjunction with the CHI 2013 Conference).*

[2] Fitzmaurice, G.W. Situated information spaces and spatially aware palmtop computers. *Communications of the ACM*, 1993, 39–49.

[3] Hollan, J.D. and Hutchins, E.L. Designing User Friendly Augmented Work Environments. In S. Lahlou, ed., Springer London, London, 2010, 237–259.

[4] Hutchins, E. *Cognition in the wild*. MIT Press, 1995.

[5] Jacob, R.J.K., Girouard, A., Horn, M.S., and Zigelbaum, J. Reality-Based Interaction: A Framework for Post-WIMP Interfaces. In *Proc. CHI'08*, 201-210.

[6] Kaufmann, B. and Ahlström, D. Studying Spatial Memory and Map Navigation Performance on Projector Phones with Peephole Interaction. In *Proc. CHI'13*, 3173–3176.

[7] Marquardt, N. The Proximity Toolkit: Prototyping Proxemic Interactions in Ubiquitous Computing Ecologies. In *Proc. UIST '11*, 315–325.

[8] Mehra, S., Werkhoven, P., and Worring, M. Navigating on Handheld Displays: Dynamic versus Static Peephole Navigation. In *Proc. TOCHI'06*, 448–457.

[9] Müller, J., Butscher, S., and Reiterer, H. ADAPTIKs: Adaptive Information Keyholes for Public Libraries. *Workshop on Visual Adaptation of Interfaces (In conjunction with the ITS 2013 Conference).*

[10] Müller, J., Schwarz, T., Butscher, S., and Reiterer, H. Back to Tangibility: A Post-WIMP Perspective on Control Room Design. In *Proc. AVI'14*, 57–64.

[11] Rädle, R., Jetter, H., Butscher, S., and Reiterer, H. The Effect of Egocentric Body Movements on Users ' Navigation Performance and Spatial Memory in Zoomable User Interfaces. In *Proc. IST'13*, 23–32.

[12] Rädle, R., Jetter, H., Müller, J., and Reiterer, H. Bigger is not always better: Display Size , Performance, and Task Load during Peephole Map Navigation. In *Proc. CHI'14*, 4127–1436.

[13] Scarr, J., Cockburn, A., and Gutwin, C. Supporting and Exploiting Spatial Memory in User Interfaces. *Foundations and Trends® in Human–Computer Interaction 6*, 1 (2012), 1–84.

[14] Schwarz, T., Butscher, S., Müller, J., and Reiterer, H. Content-aware navigation for large displays in context of traffic control rooms. In *Proc. AVI'12*, 49–252.

[15] Schwarz, T., Butscher, S., Müller, J., and Reiterer, H. Blended Interaction - Neue Wege zur Vermischung realer und digitaler Interaktionskonzepte im Kontext von Leitwarten. *at – Automatisierungstechnik 61*, (2013), 749–759.

[16] Spindler, M., Stellmach, S., and Dachselt, R. PaperLens: Advanced Magic Lens Interaction Above the Tabletop. In *Proc. IST'09*, 69–76.

[17] Yee, K. Peephole Displays: Pen Interaction on Spatially Aware Handheld Computers. In *Proc. CHI'03*, 1–8.

Tactile/Haptic User Interfaces for Tabletops and Tablets

Limin Zeng
HCI Group, TU Dresden
Nöthnitzer Str. 46,
Dresden, 01187, Germany
Limin.zeng@tu-dresden.de

Gerhard Weber
HCI Group, TU Dresden
Nöthnitzer Str. 46,
Dresden, 01187, Germany
Gerhard.weber@tu-dresden.de

Abstract
Tactile/haptic user interfaces have been becoming one of the important approaches to improve user experiences on various tabletops and tablets. This workshop proposes to bring researchers who are working or interested in the field together, and share their research experiences. In addition to tactile displays and tablets, the workshop focuses on haptic tangible user interfaces, fusion of visual and tactile/haptic feedback, and accessibility studies via tactile/haptic user interfaces. Through this workshop we plan to establish a working group for possible collaboration.

ITS 2014, November 16–19, 2014, Dresden, Germany.
ACM 978-1-4503-2587-5/14/11.
http://dx.doi.org/10.1145/2669485.2669636

Author Keywords
Tactile/Haptic user interface; haptic-visual collaboration; tangible; accessibility

ACM Classification Keywords
H.5.2 [User Interfaces]: Haptic I/O

INTRODUCTION
Tactile/Haptic interaction are employed across a wide range of applications on tabletops and tablets, from controlling virtual objects locally or remotely to interaction with physical tangible widgets. By taking advantages of the sense of touch, tactile/haptic feedback provides different user experiences to visual and audible feedback. For example, in recent years many studies for touchscreen displays indicate that haptic feedback enhances user experience, while combing with visual output [1] [2]. It is an interesting topic to study the fusion of visual and tactile/haptic feedback for interactive tabletops and tablets.

Tangible user interfaces link the physical objects with virtual objects, and the sense of touch extends the tangible interaction from 2D images on a screen to 3D space [3]. Various tangible widgets and tools bridge the gap between virtual and physical controls on tabletops and surfaces [4] [5], while several commercial products are available, like the reactable tabletop[1] and Adobe's digital ruler. However, only few studies are focusing on haptic feedback by these tangibles.

Besides, tactile displays enhance touch interfaces with tactile sensations. Tactile/haptic overlay based technologies, like [6] [7] [8], allow users not only multi-touch interaction, but also explore tabletops and tablets haptically. As a new type of tactile devices, refreshable pin-matrix displays improve accessibility of graphics-based information for visually impaired people [9].

Therefore, this workshop lets the participants pay closer attention to the tactile/haptic user interfaces for tabletops and tablets, in order to provide users' a better user experiences and accessibility features.

Topic of the Workshop

Visual displays combined with tactile feedback and haptic/tactile displays combined with visual output have created new opportunities for manipulation of user interface elements. This workshop focuses on discussing various tactile/haptic user interfaces for mainstream and emerging tabletops and tablets, fusion of tactile/haptic and visual feedback and accessibility studies.

In this workshop, the following topics are covered:

- Tactile/haptic surfaces and displays
- Haptic feedback by tangibles
- Tactile user interface
- Fusion of tactile/haptic and visual feedback
- Haptic-visual collaboration (e.g., education settings)
- Accessibility of tactile displays & tangible interaction
- Related application & user studies

[1] http://www.reactable.com/

Program Committee Members

Gerhard Weber, TU Dresden, Germany

Ulrike Lucke, Universität Potsdam, Germany

Qin Zhuo, Tsinghua University, China

Makoto Kobayashi, Tsukuba University of Technology, Japan

Luca Brayda, IIT, Italy

Limin Zeng, TU Dresden, Germany

Nature of the Workshop

Workshop Aims: one of the primary aims of the workshop is to share experiences on designing tactile/haptic user interfaces on tabletops and displays, and enhancing accessibility through tactile/haptic feedback. We also aim at establishing an active community in this field, for further discussion and future collaboration.

Workshop Procedure: we will announce the call for papers to the related communities, once the workshop proposal is approved. The program committee makes final acceptance decisions, after reviewing by 2-3 reviewers. For each accepted submission, the authors need to represent for about 20-30 minutes. Additionally, after the workshop all of the accepted papers will be considered to be published, and their authors will retain the copyright of their paper.

Room Requirements

We are planning to set up several working groups depended on their research background when the number of the attendees is over 20. Therefore, we would need a room having 20-30 seats. In addition to the devices for presentation (e.g., a video-projector, cables), a whiteboard is needed for discussion.

Requested Length

We propose a half-day workshop (4 hours).

Open/Closed Workshop

The workshop proposed is open to the public.

References

[1] Pitts, M.J., Burnett, G., Skrypchuk, L., Wellings, T., Attridge, A., Williams, M.A. Visual-haptic feedback interaction in automotive touchscreens. *Displays* 22 (2012), 7-16.

[2] Blattner, A., Bengler, K., Hamberger, W., Schnieder, S. Comparison of in-car touchpads with adaptive haptic feedback. In *Proc. of IEEE HAVE 2012*, Munich, Germany, 62-65.

[3] Shaer, O., Hornecker, E. Tangible user interface: past, present, and future directions. *Foundations and Trends in Human-Computer Interaction*, 3 (1-2), 1-137.

[4] Weiss, M., Wagner, J., Jansen, Y., Jennings, R., Khosbabeh, R., Hollan, J.D., Borchers, J. SLAP widgets: bridging the gap between virtual and physcial controls on tabletops. In *Proc. of CHI 2009*, Boston, MA, USA, 481-490.

[5] Khalibeigi, M., Steimle, J., Riemann, J., Dezfuli, N., Mühlhäuser, M., Hollan, J.D. ObjecTop: occlusion awareness of physcial objects on interactive tabletops. In *Proc. of ITS 2013*, St. Andrews, UK, 255-264.

[6] Jansen, Y., Karrer, T., Borchers, J. MudPad:tactile feedback and haptic texture overlay for touch surfaces. In *Proc. of ITS 2010*, Saarbrücken, Germany, 11-14.

[7] Bau, O., Poupyrev, I., Israr, A., Harrison, C. TeslaTouch: electrovibration for touch surfaces. In *Proc. of UIST 2010*, New York, USA, 283-292.

[8] Wijekoon, D., Cecchinato, M.E., Hoggan, E., Linjama, J. Electrostatic modulated friction as tactile feedback: intensity perception. In *Proc. of EuroHaptics 2012*, Part I, LNCS 7282, 613-624.

[9] Zeng, L., Miao, M., Weber, G. Interactive audio-haptic explorers on a tactile display. *Interacting with Computers*, doi: 10.1093/iwc/iwu006, 2014.

Collaboration Meets Interactive Surfaces: Walls, Tables, Tablets, and Phones (CMIS)

Craig Anslow
Department of Computer Science
University of Calgary
Calgary, Canada
craig.anslow@ucalgary.ca

Pedro Campos
Madeira Interactive Technologies Institute
University of Madeira
Madeira, Portugal
pcampos@uma.pt

Alfredo Ferreira
INESC-ID Lisboa / Instituto Superior Tecnico
Universidade de Lisboa
Lisboa, Portugal
alfredo.ferreira@tecnico.ulisboa.pt

ITS 2014, November 16–19, 2014, Dresden, Germany.
ACM 978-1-4503-2587-5/14/11.
http://dx.doi.org/10.1145/2669485.2669635

Abstract
This workshop proposes to bring together researchers who are interested in improving collaborative experiences through the combination of multiple interaction surfaces with diverse sizes and formats, ranging from large-scale walls, to tables, tablets and phones. The opportunities for innovation exist, but the ITS, CSCW, and HCI communities have not yet thoroughly addressed the problem of bringing effective collaboration activities together using multiple interactive surfaces, especially in complex work domains. Of particular interest is the potential synergy that one can obtain by effectively combining different-sized surfaces.

Author Keywords
Collaboration, interactive surfaces, interactive walls, interactive tabletops, mobile, multi-touch interaction.

ACM Classification Keywords
H.5.m [Information interfaces and presentation (HCI)]: Miscellaneous.

General Terms
Design; Human Factors

Introduction
Large scale displays and interactive surfaces offer a unique visualization environment favorable to both individual and collaborative design tasks [?, ?]. During the last decade these devices have become both affordable and easier to setup, providing highly interactive environments with high resolution and support for stereoscopic images. Combined with emerging input devices, these provide new ways to interact with content as well as enabling new applications to support collaborative engineering tasks as well as many other activities, which involve communication, coordination, and cooperation [?].

Additionally, new devices have become available to enhance these interactions, including multi-touch tablets combining several sensors [?], non-intrusive tracking solutions based on depth cameras and other equipment. Despite this rapid technological advance, however, it still remains an unsolved problem how to bring effective collaboration capabilities to this myriad of heterogeneous interactive surfaces. This workshop aims at bringing together the most advanced techniques, user interfaces, and technological issues that are crucial in fostering co-located collaboration and remote communication between users across different facilities simultaneously [?].

Following the success of the workshop on Collaboration meets Interactive Surfaces (CMIS) co-located at ITS 2013 [?], we will host another workshop at ITS 2014 in Dresden, Germany. In the 2013 edition of the workshop, a total of 27 participants attended. Participants exchanged experiences regarding collaborative user interface design and evaluation techniques involving interactive surfaces, either remote or co-located.

Relevance to ITS Community
The vast screen real estate, which is provided in large-scale interaction environments presents novel ways to visualize and interact with data-rich models. In parallel to this technological revolution, interactive surfaces have also become widespread in different sizes and devices, from large-scale walls to small tablets. Indeed, the ITS and HCI communities witnessed, in recent years, an increased usage of large display walls, interactive tabletops, tablet-sized surfaces, and mobile phones [?].

Topics of Workshop
Topics of the workshop to be covered include, but are not limited to:

- Design and evaluation of collaborative environments with interactive surfaces, either remotely or co-located;
- Collaborative applications on interactive surfaces for different domains (e.g. 3D visualization, mechanical engineering, medical visualizations, emergency response scenarios, meeting rooms);
- Communication, cooperation and coordination as well as social protocols;
- Interactive surfaces to enhance spatial perception of content and/or support navigation during collaboration activities;
- Issues when moving from desktop-based collaboration to large-scale walls, tabletops and touch-based mobile devices;
- Integration of different devices and surfaces for collaboration;

- Physical navigation between different devices;
- Collaboration paradigms and user interface designs that address enhancement of collaborative activities using interactive surfaces and tabletops;
- Collaborative sense making and visual analytics with different interactive surfaces and devices.

Organizing Committee

The following people form the organizing committee of the workshop.

- **Craig Anslow** is a Postdoctoral Research Fellow at the University of Calgary, Canada. His research interests include multi-surface environments, emergency operations centres, and engineering novel visual analytics applications.
- **Pedro Campos** is an Assistant Professor at the University of Madeira, Portugal. His research interests include interaction design, augmented reality, natural interaction for modelling, and museums and cultural heritage.
- **Alfredo Ferreira** is an Assistant Professor at the Instituto Superior Tecnico, Universidade de Lisboa, Portugal. His research interests include 3D shape analysis and retrieval, multimedia information retrieval, natural user interfaces, augmented reality, and immersive environments.

Program Committee

The Program Committee (PC) for the workshop will review papers and help promote the workshop in the ITS, CSCW, and HCI communities. The following people have agreed to serve on the PC:

- Scott Bateman - University of Prince Edward Island, Canada
- Rachel Blagojevic, Massey University, New Zealand
- Robert Biddle, Carleton University, Canada
- Sebastian Boring, University of Copenhagen, Denmark
- Nick Graham, Queens University, Canada
- Uta Hinrichs, University of St.Andrews, UK
- Petra Isenberg, INRIA, France
- Joaquim Jorge, Technical University of Lisboa, Portugal
- Judy Kay, University of Sydney, Australia
- Harald Reiterer - University of Konstanz, Germany
- Markus Rittenbruch, Queensland University of Technology, Australia
- Johannes Schoening, Hasselt University, Belgium
- Stacey Scott, University of Waterloo, Canada
- Tony Tang, University of Calgary, Canada

Activities and Format

Table 1 outlines the activities of the one-day workshop. In the first session will have welcome and introductions by all attendees, followed by an invited talk by Sheelagh Carpendale from the University of Calgary. After the morning break the second session will have include talks of workshop papers from attendees. Lunch will follow to allow attendees to meet and mingle. In the third session more workshops papers will be presented then attendees will split into groups based on themes related to the goals of the workshop. Once the groups have been formed discussions will happen amongst attendees. The fourth session will have groups report back about their discussions and closing remarks from the organizing committee as well as feedback from attendees.

Time	Activity
0900–0930	Welcome and Introductions
0930–1030	Invited Talk by Sheelagh Carpendale (University of Calgary)
1030–1100	Morning Break
1100–1200	Presentation of Workshop Papers
1200–1330	Lunch Break
1330–1500	Presentation of Workshop Papers Group Exercise, split into groups based on themes from the workshop
1500–1530	Afternoon Break
1530–1700	Discuss Themes in Groups - Reports from Groups - Closing remarks from organizing committee

Table 1: Workshop Activities

Tutorial: Hot Topics in Personal Fabrication Research

Stefanie Mueller
Hasso Plattner Institute
Potsdam, Germany
stefanie.mueller@hpi.uni-potsdam.de

Alexandra Ion
Hasso Plattner Institute
Potsdam, Germany
alexandra.ion@hpi.uni-potsdam.de

Patrick Baudisch
Hasso Plattner Institute
Potsdam, Germany
patrick.baudisch@hpi.uni-potsdam.de

ITS 2014, November 16–19, 2014, Dresden, Germany.
ACM 978-1-4503-2587-5/14/11.
http://dx.doi.org/10.1145/2669485.2669485.2669633

Abstract
In this tutorial, we survey novel ways for interacting with personal fabrication machines, such as laser cutters, milling machines, and 3D printers. The goal is to provide attendees with an overview of recent HCI research in personal fabrication and together with attendees build a roadmap for future research directions. Towards this goal, the tutorial will provide background knowledge in how personal fabrication machines work, which types of objects they can fabricate, and how they are currently being operated.

Author Keywords
personal fabrication; rapid prototyping; 3D printing; laser cutting; milling machines.

ACM Classification Keywords
H.5.2

Overview
The recent price drop in personal fabrication tools, such as 3D printers, makes them available to a broader audience [1]. However, the way we are currently interacting with personal fabrication devices still requires a lot of expert knowledge – making it difficult for novice users to use these tools. In this tutorial, we provide an overview of current HCI research that looks into how to facilitate interacting with personal fabrication devices and how to allow for a new range of applications.

Tutorial structure

The tutorial is divided into the following three units:

(1) We start with a short introduction to personal fabrication to provide a shared understanding of what personal fabrication machines are, how they are currently being operated, and what they can fabricate. To make this part of the tutorial also interesting for attendees that are more experienced users of personal fabrication machines, we will add a section on custom 3D printed mechanics and special laser cut joints.

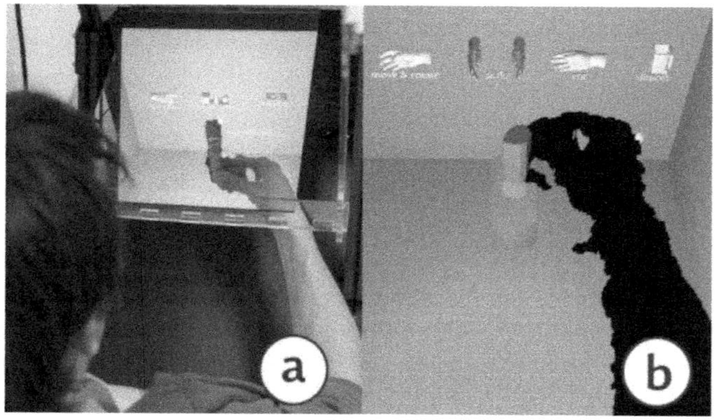

Figure 1. MixFab: mixed-reality editing that allows integrating physical objects into the digital design process.

(2) Based on that shared understanding, we will provide an overview of recent HCI research in personal fabrication. We will first survey the development of moving from solely digital editing (e.g., *SketchChair* [4]), towards mixed-reality environments (e.g., *MixFab* [6]), towards interactive fabrication in which all user input is done on the physical work-piece followed by immediate fabrication [7].

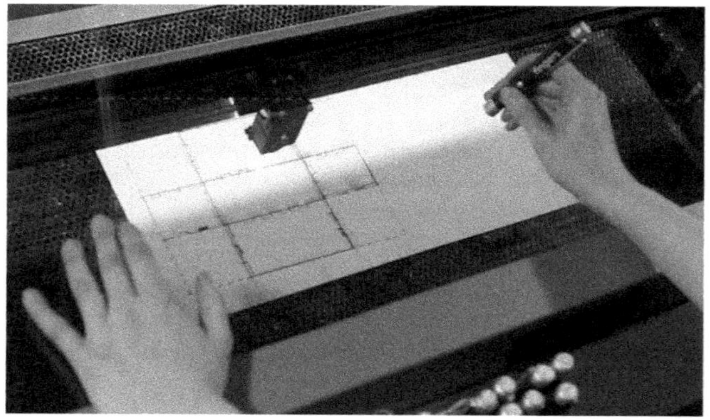

Figure 2. constructable: interactive laser-cutting by drawing directly on the work-piece using hand-held laser-pointers.

We will look into how interactive fabrication can be realized by either using constrained tools (e.g., *constructable* [2]) or by guiding the user based on a pre-selected digital model (e.g., *FreeD* [8]).

Figure 3. FreeD is a hand-held mill that guides the user through fabrication based on a pre-selected digital model.

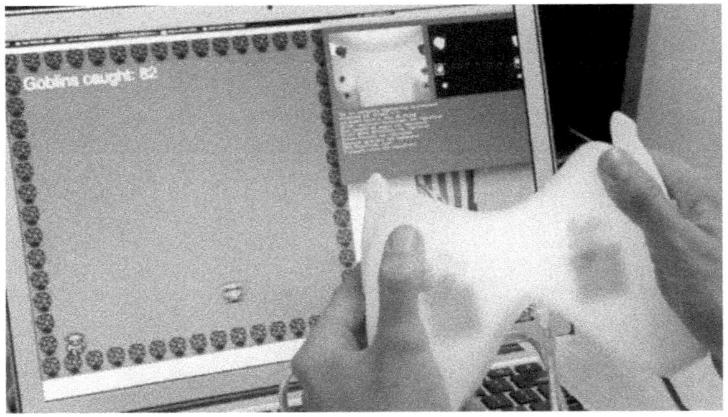

Figure 4. Low-fi prototyping: Sauron uses a single camera to detect user input on a 3D printed object.

Next, we will look at projects that allow for faster design iteration with personal fabrication machines, either by using low-fi prototyping methods in which the prototype itself is low-fidelity (e.g., *Sauron* [5]) or by using the recently introduced concept of low-fi fabrication, in which the 3D model is high-fidelity but fabricated as low-fidelity (e.g., *faBrickation* [2]).

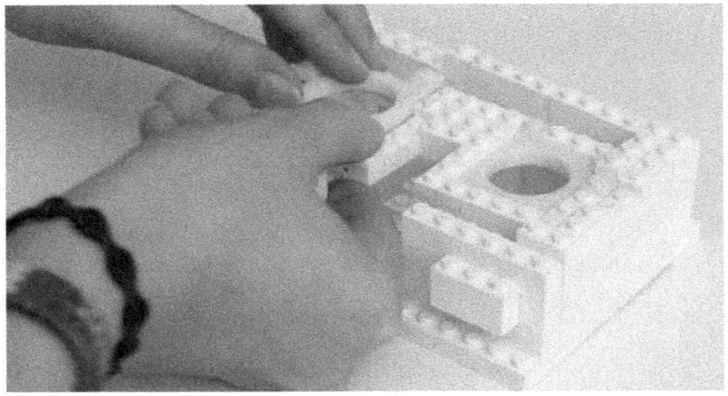

Figure 5. Low-fi fabrication: faBrickator is a system that uses 3D printing for high-detail regions and bricks everywhere else.

Finally, we will look at how personal fabrication allows for the replication of physical objects and how that affects the value of the objects.

(3) In the last part, we will share our thoughts on a future road map for personal fabrication and will open the discussion for possible novel research directions.

Short biography

Stefanie Mueller is a PhD student working with Prof. Patrick Baudisch in the Human Computer Interaction Lab at Hasso Plattner Institute. In her research she develops new types of interfaces for personal fabrication machines that allow for a fast alternation between user input and physical fabrication.

Alexandra Ion is a PhD student working with Prof. Patrick Baudisch in the Human Computer Interaction Lab at Hasso Plattner Institute. Her current research focuses on building wearable devices for haptic feedback and fabricating mechanical appliances.

Patrick Baudisch is a professor in Computer Science at Hasso Plattner Institute at Potsdam University and chair of the Human Computer Interaction Lab. His research focuses on natural user interfaces and interactive devices, including miniature mobile devices, touch input, interactive floors and rooms, and most recently interactive fabrication.

Acknowledgements

We thank the authors of the related work for providing their images for this tutorial submission.

References

[1] Gershenfeld, N. Fab: The Coming Revolution on Your Desktop. Basic Books, '07.

[2] Mueller, S., Lopes, P., Baudisch, P. Interactive Construction: Interactive Fabrication of Functional Mechanical Devices. *Proc. UIST '12,* 599-606.

[3] Mueller, S., Mohr, T., Guenther, K., Frohnhofen, J., Baudisch, P. faBrickation: Fast 3D Printing of Functioning Objects by Integrating Construction Kit Building Blocks. *Proc. CHI'14,* 3827-3834.

[4] Saul, G., Lau, M., Mitani, J., Igarashi, T. SketchChair: an all-in-one chair design system for end users. *Proc. TEI '11,* 73-80.

[5] Savage, V., Chang, C., Hartmann, B. Sauron: Embedded Single-Camera Sensing of Printed Physical User Interfaces. *Proc. UIST'13,* 447-456.

[6] Weichel, M., Lau, M., Kim, D., Villar, N., Gellersen, H.W. MixFab: a Mixed-Reality Environment for Personal Fabrication. *Proc. CHI'14,* 3855-3864.

[7] Willis, K.D.D., Xu, C., Wu, J.K., Levin, G., Gross, M.D. Interactive fabrication: new interfaces for digital fabrication. *Proc. TEI '11,* 69-72.

[8] Zoran, A., Paradiso, J.A. FreeD: a freehand digital sculpting tool. *Proc. CHI'13,* 2613-2616.

Additional information

Type: tutorial Length: 4 hours

Physical Requirements: We can bring our own projector and loud speakers for giving the slide deck. We only need a room with one white wall to project on.

Cost of Materials for Participants: We will bring all materials. No extra costs for participants.

TUIO Hackathon

Martin Kaltenbrunner
University of Art and Design Linz
4020 Linz, Austria
martin.kaltenbrunner@ufg.at

Florian Echtler
Bauhaus-University Weimar
99423 Weimar, Germany
florian.echtler@uni-weimar.de

ITS 2014, November 16–19, 2014, Dresden, Germany.
ACM 978-1-4503-2587-5/14/11.
http://dx.doi.org/10.1145/2669485.2669631

Abstract

TUIO is an open framework that defines a common protocol and API for tangible- and multitouch-surfaces. The protocol is based on Open Sound Control and allows the platform-independent encoding and transmission of an abstract description of interactive surfaces, including touch events and tangible object states. While the original TUIO specification [1] has been implemented for various hardware and software environments, there are not as many feature complete reference implementations of the next TUIO generation, although its specification [2] has been finalized and partially implemented by community members. The TUIO Hackathon at the International Conference for Interactive Tabletops and Surfaces is addressing expert users and developers of hardware and software environments for surface-based tangible user interfaces that are interested in experimenting with this new framework, with the goal of initiating the development and integration of new TUIO implementations.

Author Keywords

Tangible User Interfaces, Multitouch Surfaces, Abstraction Model, Protocols and APIS

ACM Classification Keywords

H.5.2. User Interfaces: Input devices and strategies; D.2.2. Design Tools and Techniques:User interfaces; D.2.12 Interoperability: Interface definition languages

The TUIO Protocol

Originally developed in the context of the Reactable [4] instrument, the TUIO framework focused since its very beginning on the abstraction of tangible interactive surfaces, including descriptors for marked and unmarked tangible objects as well as multi-touch interaction. The main motivation behind the creation of the protocol was the robust transmission of an elementary interface abstraction within distributed architectures and networked environments. Initial TUIO client implementations had been provided for the most common programming languages and multimedia environments in order to facilitate the creation of alternative applications for the Reactable platform within our teaching activities.

With the growing popularity of multi-touch interfaces the protocol had been since widely adopted by an open source community due to its simple and platform-independent API for the rapid realization of tangible multitouch applications. Until today this community has been also providing a large variety of TUIO implementations for countless software and hardware environments in addition to the original reference implementations. Furthermore its interface abstraction layer has been also implemented in various higher-level programming environments such as gesture toolkits.

While the pronounced simplicity of the original TUIO protocol and its implementations may have been sufficient for the realization of basic multi-touch experiences, it is not reflecting the capabilities of contemporary touch interfaces, while many current implementations also neglect the initial focus on the actual tangible interface elements.

TUIO 2.0 architecture

The tangible abstraction model behind the next generation TUIO framework therefore not only reflects the feature set of state-of-the-art touch surfaces, but also emphasizes the role of tangible interface elements. Moreover, the 2nd TUIO generation also allows to model a wider variety of hardware platforms, input devices and even body parts and is consequently able to represent a more unified framework to various kinds of multimodal surfaces and devices.

The new protocol version introduced many additional features compared to the TUIO 1.1 specification. It allows the encoding and transmission of a tangible interface component abstraction, by defining tokens (tagged objects), pointers (e.g. touch) and geometries (for untagged generic objects) as well as additional symbols and controls in the context of an interactive surface. It also includes timing information, several additional component attributes such as finger pressure, and code descriptors for symbol types such as data matrix labels or RFID tags. TUIO 2.0 also encodes the precise object geometry with general bounds, contour and skeleton descriptors that can be used to describe untagged tangible objects or retrieve additional geometry information for tokens or pointers.

TUIO 2.0 also uses a unified profile for all previously separated tangible object types, such as tokens, pointers and geometries. The state model in the form of ALIVE and FSEQ messages of the original TUIO specification was generally maintained, while the SET messages of the previous 2Dobj, 2Dcur and 2Dblb profiles, were mapped to individual messages within a flat /tuio2/* name space.

Hackathon Objectives

This workshop primarily targets software- and hardware developers that are planning to integrate the TUIO framework into their existing tangible interaction platforms and applications. After an initial overview to the general architecture of the TUIO protocol, it will introduce the extended feature set of the 2.0 specification compared to the present generation and its implementations. The goal of this hackathon is to initiate a wider adoption of the next generation TUIO framework by producing a core set of software implementations and hardware integrations, and also updating the most significant components of the present ecosystem. Finally the workshop will provide a forum to discuss possible design improvements as well as an outlook into a future organization of the TUIO community.

Biographies

Martin Kaltenbrunner is professor at the Interface Culture Lab at the University of Art and Design in Linz. As co-founder of Reactable Systems he had been mainly working on the interaction design of the Reactable - an electronic musical instrument with a tangible user interface. He is author of the open source tangible interaction framework reacTIVision and the related TUIO protocol, which are widely employed for the realization of tangible tabletop applications.

Florian Echtler is a junior professor at the Faculty of Media at the Bauhaus-University Weimar. His research interests focus on formal languages for gesture descriptions and design of multimodal development frameworks. Additional topics covered by his research include computer vision for HCI applications, sensor technology and rapid prototyping.

Hackathon Schedule

10:00 - 11:00 Introduction to TUIO 2.0
11:00 - 13:00 Hackathon Part 1
13:00 - 14:00 Lunch
14:00 - 16:00 Hackathon Part 2
16:00 - 17:00 Discussion & wrap-up

References

[1] http://www.tuio.org/?specification

[2] http://www.tuio.org/?tuio20

[3] Kaltenbrunner, M. & Bovermann, T. & Bencina, R. & Costanza, E. "TUIO - A Protocol for Table-Top Tangible User Interfaces", Proceedings of the 6th International Workshop on Gesture in Human-Computer Interaction and Simulation (GW 2005), Vannes (France)

[4] Jordà, S. & Geiger, G. & Alonso, A. & Kaltenbrunner, M. "*The reacTable: Exploring the Synergy between Live Music Performance and Tabletop Tangible Interfaces*", Proceedings of the first international conference on "Tangible and Embedded Interaction (TEI07). Baton Rouge, Louisiana

Author Index

www.ingramcontent.com/pod-product-compliance
Ingram Content Group UK Ltd.
Pitfield, Milton Keynes, MK11 3LW, UK
UKHW051415290926
15471UKWH00009B/1620